Chicano Periodical Index (ChPI)
A Comprehensive Subject, Author and Title Index
for 1987

Chicano Periodical Index (ChPI)
A Comprehensive Subject, Author and Title Index
for 1987

Edited by

Lillian Castillo-Speed
University of California at Berkeley

Richard Chabrán
University of California at Los Angeles

Chicano Studies Library Publications Unit
University of California at Berkeley
1988

The Chicano Periodical Indexing Project is directed by Lillian Castillo-Speed
at the Chicano Studies Library, University of California at Berkeley,
headquarters of the Chicano Database which produced this volume.

ACKNOWLEDGMENTS

Lillian Castillo-Speed: I wish to thank the Chicano Studies Library staff
for their dedication to ChPI and their enthusiasm for our work: Carolyn Soto,
Lisa Hernandez, Lisa Foley, Liudmila Carranza, Margita Thompson, Suzette Leyba,
Socorro Gonzalez, and Orlinda Ornelas. I also wish to thank Lupe Gallegos-Diaz,
Helen Lara-Cea, Michael Gonzalez, and Rudy Busto for always being ready to
help out.

Richard Chabrán: I wish to acknowledge Francisco García-Ayvens for the
major contribution that he has made and continues to make to the Chicano
Periodical Indexing Project.

Chicano Studies Library Publications Unit
3404 Dwinelle Hall
University of California at Berkeley
Berkeley, CA 94720

The Chicano Periodical Index (ChPI) is endorsed by the National Association
for Chicano Studies and the Chicano Information Management Consortium of
California (CIMCC).

ISBN 0-918520-16-9
ISSN 0891-6985

This publication is printed on permanent/durable acid-free paper.
MANUFACTURED IN THE UNITED STATES OF AMERICA

IN MEMORIAM

William (Willie) Velásquez

1944-1988

Founder and Director
Southwest Voter Registration and Education Project

A true Chicano visionary with a simple idea
for gaining and retaining power:

Raza, register and vote!
Raza, ¡regístresen y voten!

PANEL OF INDEXERS

Sandra Balderrama-Escobar
Berkeley Public Library, South Branch
Berkeley, California

Maria Olga Camarillo
Library Periodicals Department
California State University, Stanislaus
Turlock, California

Lillian Castillo-Speed
Chicano Studies Library
University of California at Berkeley
Berkeley, California

Richard Chabrán
Chicano Studies Research Center
University of California
Los Angeles, California

Linda Chavez
Los Angeles County Public Library
Downey, California

Norma Corral
Library Reference Department
University of California
Los Angeles, California

Karin Duran
Oviatt Library, Reference Department
California State University
Northridge, California

Francisco García-Ayvens
Chicano Resource Center
California State University
Fullerton, California

Salvador Güereña
Colección Tloque Nahuaque
University Library
University of California
Santa Barbara, California

Susan C. Luevano
Santa Ana College Library
Santa Ana, California

Sheila Milam
Original Cataloging Department
Hayden Library
Arizona State University
Tempe, Arizona

Mary Helen Moreno
Shields Library
University of California
Davis, California

Teresa M. Portilla
College Library
University of California
Los Angeles, California

Carolyn Soto
Silver Skates Publishing
Albany, California

Rina Tamayo
Villaseñor Library
San Bernardino, California

CONTENTS

KEY TO PERIODICALS INDEXED COMPLETELY

Indexing covers years indicated in italics.

For more information about the availability of Chicano periodicals,
consult "Directory of Chicano Periodicals" in the fourth volume of
The Chicano Periodical Index.

AMERICAS 2001
Los Angeles, CA
1987

THE AMERICAS REVIEW
University of Houston
Houston, TX
1987

AZTLAN
Chicano Studies Center, UCLA
Los Angeles, CA
1986 (Vol. 17, no. 1)

BILINGUAL REVIEW
Hispanic Research Center
Arizona State University
Tempe, AZ
1984 (Vol. 11, no. 3) to 1985 (Vol. 12, no. 3)

CHIRICU
Chicano-Riquena Studies
Indiana University
Bloomington, IN
1976-1987 (through Vol. 5, no. 1)

LA COMUNIDAD
Supplement to La Opinion
Los Angeles, CA
1985-1987

CONFLUENCIA
Department of Hispanic Studies
University of Northern Colorado
Greeley, CO
1985-1987

EL CUADERNO
La Academia de la Nueva Raza
Dixon, NM
1971-1976 (Vol. 4, no. 1)

**EPOCA: NATIONAL CONCILIO FOR
CHICANO STUDIES JOURNAL**
National Center for Chicano Studies
Washington, DC
1971 (Vol. 1, no. 2)

ETHNIC AFFAIRS
Center for Mexican American Studies
University of Texas at Austin
Austin, TX
1987

HISPANIC BUSINESS
Hispanic Business, Inc.
Santa Barbara, CA
1987

HISPANIC ENGINEER
Los Angeles, CA
1987

**HISPANIC JOURNAL OF BEHAVIORAL
SCIENCES**
Spanish Speaking Mental Health
Research Center
University of California at Los Angeles
Los Angeles, CA
1987

HISPANIC TIMES
Westlake Village, CA
1987 (Vol. 8, nos. 1,3,5)
(nos. 2 and 4 unavailable from the publisher)

INTERCAMBIOS FEMENILES
National Network of Hispanic Women
Los Angeles, CA
1987 (Vol. 2, no. 6)

INTERNATIONAL MIGRATION REVIEW
Staten Island, NY
1987 (Vol. 21, nos. 1-2)

JOURNAL OF AMERICAN ETHNIC HISTORY
Transaction Periodical Consortium
Rutgers University
New Brunswick, NJ
1986 (Vol. 6, no. 1) to 1987 (Vol. 7, no. 1)

JOURNAL OF ETHNIC STUDIES
Western Washington University
Bellingham, WA
1987

LATIN QUARTER
Latin Quarter Magazine
Los Angeles, CA
1974 (Vol. 1, no. 1) to 1975 (Vol. 2, no. 4)

LECTOR
Floricanto Press
Encino, CA
1986-1987

LLUEVE TLALOC
Pima Community College
Pima, AZ
1975-1987

MIGRATION WORLD
Staten Island, NY
1986 (Vol. 14, no. 5) to 1987 (Vol. 15, no.5)

NEW MEXICO HISTORICAL REVIEW
University of New Mexico
Albuquerque, NM
1987 (Vol. 62, nos. 1-4)

NOTEBOOK: A LITTLE MAGAZINE
Esoterica Press
Barstow, CA
1985 to 1987 (Vol. 3, no. 1)

NUESTRO
Washington, DC
1987 (Vol. 11, nos. 1-4)

PUERTO DEL SOL
New Mexico State University
Las Cruces, NM
1987 (Vol. 23, no. 1)

LA RED/THE NET
Tomas Rivera Center
Claremont CA
1977 to 1987 (no. 105)

**RENATO ROSALDO LECTURE SERIES
MONOGRAPH**
Mexican American Studies Research Center
University of Arizona
Tucson, AZ
1985-1986

REVISTA MUJERES
Benjamin F. Porter College
University of California at Santa Cruz
Santa Cruz, CA
1984 to 1987 (Vol. 4, no. 1)

SAGUARO
Mexican American Studies
University of Arizona
Tucson, AZ
1984-1987

TINTA
Department of Spanish and Portuguese
University of California at Santa Barbara
Santa Barbara, CA
1981 to 1987 (no. 5)

TRABAJOS MONOGRAFICOS
Chicano Studies Program
University of California at Davis
Davis, CA
1987 (Vol. 3, no. 1)

VISTA
Vista Magazine
Coral Gables, FL
1985-1987

KEY TO PERIODICALS INDEXED SELECTIVELY

Indexing covers 1987.

ABA BANKING JOURNAL
  ABA Banking Journal, Bristol, CT
ACTION IN TEACHER EDUCATION
  Association of Teacher Educators
  Washington, DC
ADVANCES IN CONSUMER RESEARCH
  Association for Consumer Research
  Urbana, IL
ADVERTISING AGE MAGAZINE
  Crain Communications, Inc., Chicago, IL
  Washington, DC
ADVERTISING WORLD
  Directories International, New York, NY
ADWEEK
  A/S/M Communications, Los Angeles, CA
AGAINST THE CURRENT
  Against the Current, New York, NY
AGRICULTURAL HISTORY
  The Agriculture History Society
  University of California Press, Berkeley, CA
AKWESASNE NOTES
  American Studies of the State
  University of New York, Buffalo, NY
AMERICAN ANTHROPOLOGIST
  American Anthropological Association
  Washington, DC
AMERICAN BEHAVIOR SCIENTISTS
  Sage Publications, Beverly Hills, CA
AMERICAN BOOK REVIEW
  American Book Review, Cooper Station
  New York, NY
AMERICAN DEMOGRAPHICS
  American Demographics, Syracuse, NY
AMERICAN EDUCATION
  American Federation of Teachers, AFL-CIO
  Washington, DC
AMERICAN HISTORICAL REVIEW
  American Historical Association, Washington, DC
AMERICAN JOURNAL OF EDUCATION
  University of Chicago Press, Chicago, IL
AMERICAN JOURNAL OF LEGAL HISTORY
  Temple University, School of Law
  Philadelphia, PA
AMERICAN JOURNAL OF MENTAL DEFICIENCY
  American Association on Mental Deficiency
  Albany, NY
AMERICAN JOURNAL OF PHYSICAL
ANTHROPOLOGY
  Alan R. Liss, Inc.
  New York, NY
AMERICAN JOURNAL OF PUBLIC HEALTH
  American Public Health Assn.
  New York, NY
AMERICAN JOURNAL OF SOCIOLOGY
  University of Chicago Press, Chicago, IL
AMERICAN LIBRARIES
  American Library Association
  Chicago, IL
AMERICAN LITERATURE
  Duke University Press, Durham, NY

AMERICAN MEDICAL NEWS
  American Medical Association, Chicago, IL
THE AMERICAN MERCURY
  Hartford, CO
AMERICAN POLITICAL SCIENCE REVIEW
  American Political Science Association
  Washington, DC
AMERICAN REFERENCE BOOKS ANNUAL
  Libraries Unlimited, Littleton, CO
AMERICAN SCHOLAR
  Phi Beta Kappa, Washington, DC
AMERICAN SPECTATOR
  Saturday Evening Club, Bloomington, IN
AMERICAN THEATRE
  Theatre Communications Group
  New York, NY
AMERICAS
  Americas, Farmingdale, NY
ANTHROPOLOGY UCLA
  University of California, Department of
  Anthropology, Los Angeles, CA
APPLIED RESEARCH IN MENTAL RETARDATION
  Pergamon Press, New York, NY
AREITO
  Ediciones Vitral, New York, NY
ARIZONA AND THE WEST
  University of Arizona Press, Tucson, AZ
ARIZONA HIGHWAYS
  Arizona Department of Transportation
  Phoenix, AZ
ARIZONA QUARTERLY
  University of Arizona, Tucson, AZ
ARMED FORCES AND SOCIETY
  Inter-University Seminar on Armed Forces
  and Society, University of Chicago
  Chicago, IL
ART IN AMERICA
  F.F. Sherman, New York, NY
ARTSPACE
  Artspace, Inc., Albuquerque, NM
ARTWEEK
  Oakland, CA
ASDC JOURNAL OF DENTISTRY FOR CHILDREN
  American Society of Dentistry for Children
  Chicago, IL
BEVERAGE INDUSTRY
  Magazine for Industry, New York, NY
THE BLOOMSBURY REVIEW
  Owaissa Publishing, Denver, CO
BOOKLIST
  American Library Association, Chicago, IL
BRITISH BOOK NEWS
  British Council, London
BROADCASTING
  Broadcasting Publications, Inc.,
  Washington, DC
CALIFORNIA HISTORY
  California Historical Society
  San Francisco, CA

CALIFORNIA MAGAZINE
New West Communications
Beverly Hills, CA
CANADIAN MODERN LANGUAGE REVIEW
Ontario Modern Language Teachers' Association
Toronto
CAPITAL AND CLASS
Conference of Socialist Economists
London
CHAIN STORE AGE SUPERMARKET
Lebhar-Friedman, New York, NY
CHILDREN AND YOUTH SERVICES REVIEW
Pergamon Press, New York, NY
CHOICE
Choice, Middletown, CN
CHRISTIANITY AND CRISIS
Christianity and Crisis, New York, NY
CHRISTIANITY TODAY
Christianity Today, Dover, NJ
CINEASTE
Cineaste, New York, NY
CLEFT PALATE JOURNAL
Baltimore, MD
COLUMBIA LAW REVIEW
New York, NY
COMMENTARY
New York, NY
COMMONGROUND MAGAZINE
Women's Center, Glendale, CA
COMMUNITY/JUNIOR COLLEGE QUARTERLY OF RESEARCH
AND PRACTICE
Hemisphere Publishing, Washington, DC
CONTEMPORARY POLICY ISSUES
Western Economic Association International
California State University, Long Beach, CA
CONTEMPORARY PSYCHOLOGY
American Psychological Association
Washington, DC
CONTEMPORARY SOCIOLOGY: A JOURNAL OF REVIEWS
American Sociological Association,
Washington, DC
Tampere, Finland
CORRECTIVE AND SOCIAL PSYCHIATRY
AND JOURNAL OF BEHAVIOR TECHNOLOGY
METHODS AND THERAPY
Technology Methods and Therapy
Kansas City, MO
CRIME AND SOCIAL JUSTICE
Synthesis Publications, San Francisco, CA
CRIMINAL LAW REPORTER
Bureau of National Affairs, Inc.
Washington, DC
CRIMINOLOGY: AN INTERDISCIPLINARY JOURNAL
American Society of Criminology
Beverly Hills, CA
CRITICA HISPANICA
East Tennessee State University
Johnson City, TN
CURRENTS
Council for Advancement and Support of
Education, Washington, DC
CURRICULUM REVIEW
Curriculum Advisory Service
Chicago, IL

DAEDALUS
American Academy of Arts and Sciences
Cambridge, MA
DEMOGRAPHY
Population Association of America,
Washington, DC
DOLLARS AND SENSE
Economic Affairs Bureau, Inc.
Somerville, MA
DRUG AND ALCOHOL DEPENDENCE
Elsevier Scientific Publishers Ireland Ltd.
Limerick, Ireland
DUN'S BUSINESS MONTH
Dun & Bradstreet, New York, NY
EARS AND HEARING
Williams & Wilkins, Baltimore, MD
ECOLOGY OF FOOD AND NUTRITION
Gordon and Breach, New York, NY
ECONOMIC BOOKS
Clifton, NY
ECONOMIC REVIEW
Federal Reserve Bank of Dallas
Dallas, TX
ECONOMIST
Economist Newsletter, Ltd., London, England
EDITOR & PUBLISHER: THE FOURTH ESTATE
Editor & Publisher Co., Inc., New York, NY
EDUCATION
State of Rhode Island, Department of Education
Providence, RI
EDUCATION AND URBAN SOCIETY
Sage Publications, Beverly Hills, CA
EDUCATIONAL LEADERSHIP
Association for Supervision and Curriculum
Development, Alexandria, VA
EDUCATIONAL RECORD
British and Foreign School Society
London, England
THE ELEMENTARY SCHOOL JOURNAL
University of Chicago Press, Chicago, IL
EMERGENCY LIBRARIAN
Winnipeg
ETHICS
University of Chicago Press, Chicago, IL
ETHNIC AND RACIAL STUDIES
Routledge Journals, Boston, MA
ETHNOMUSICOLOGY
Society for Ethnomusicology, Inc.
Ann Arbor, MI
THE FAMILY LAW REPORTER: COURT OPINIONS
Bureau of National Affairs
Washington, DC
FEM
Difusion Cultural Feminista, A.C., Mexico D.F.
FEMINIST STUDIES
Women's Studies, University of Maryland
FILM COMMENT
Film Society of Lincoln Center
New York, NY
FILM QUARTERLY
University of California, Berkeley, CA
FOCUS ON LEARNING
Indiana University of Pennsylvania
Indiana, PA

FOREIGN AFFAIRS
    Council on Foreign Relations, New York, NY
GEOGRAPHICAL REVIEW
    American Geographical Society
    New York, NY
GUARDIAN
    New York, NY
GUILD NOTES
    National Office of the National Lawyers Guild
    New York, NY
GUITAR PLAYER
    GPI Publications, Cupertino, CA
HISPANIA
    Wichita, KS
HISPANIC AMERICAN HISTORICAL REVIEW
    Duke University Press, Durham, NC
HISTORIA MEXICANA
    Colegio de Mexico, AC, Mexico, DF, Mexico
HISTORY - REVIEWS OF NEW BOOKS
    Reid Foundation, Washington, DC
HORIZONS: A MAGAZINE OF THE ARTS
    American Horizons, New York, NY
HOSPITAL AND COMMUNITY PSYCHIATRY
    American Psychiatric Association
    Washington, DC
THE HUMANIST
    Amherst, NY
HUMBOLDT JOURNAL OF SOCIAL RELATIONS
    Humboldt State University, Arcata, CA
INDUSTRIAL AND LABOR RELATIONS REVIEW
    Cornell University, Ithaca, NY
INSULA: REVISTA BIBLIOGRAFICA DE LETRAS
    Y CIENCIAS HUMANAS
    Colegio de Mexico, Mexico D.F.
INTERCIENCIA
    Asociacion Interciencia
    Caracas, Venezuela
INTERNATIONAL JOURNAL OF AGING AND HUMAN
    DEVELOPMENT
    Baywood Publishing Co., Farmingdale, NY
INTERNATIONAL JOURNAL OF INTERCULTURAL
    RELATIONS
    New Brunswick, NJ
INTERNATIONAL JOURNAL OF URBAN AND
    REGIONAL RESEARCH
    E. Arnold, London
INTERNATIONAL MIGRATION
    Netherlands
INTERNATIONAL REVIEW FOR THE SOCIOLOGY OF SPORT
    R. Oldenbourg, Verlag, Munich
INTERRACIAL BOOKS FOR CHILDREN
    Council on Interracial Books for Children
    New York, NY
IN THESE TIMES
    Institute for Public Affairs
    Chicago, IL
JOURNAL
    Smithsonian, Washington, DC
JOURNAL FOR THE SCIENTIFIC STUDY OF RELIGION
    Society for the Scientific Study of Religion
    Storrs, CT
JOURNALISM QUARTERLY
    Association for Education in Journalism
    Minneapolis, MN

JOURNAL OF AMERICAN ETHNIC HISTORY
    Transaction Periodicals Consortium
    New Brunswick, NJ
JOURNAL OF AMERICAN FOLKLORE
    American Folklore Society, Washington, DC
JOURNAL OF AMERICAN HISTORY
    Organization of American Historians
    Bloomington, IN
JOURNAL OF ANTHROPOLOGICAL RESEARCH
    University of New Mexico
    Albuquerque, NM
JOURNAL OF ARIZONA HISTORY
    Tucson Arizona Pioneers' Historical
    Society, Tucson, AZ
JOURNAL OF CLINICAL PSYCHOLOGY
    Clinical Psychology Publishing Co., Inc.
    Brandon, VT
JOURNAL OF CLINICAL PSYCHOPHARMACOLOGY
    Williams & Wilkins, Baltimore, MD
JOURNAL OF COLLEGE STUDENT PERSONNEL
    American Association for Counseling and
    Development, Alexandria, VA
JOURNAL OF CRIMINAL JUSTICE
    Pergamon Press, New York, NY
JOURNAL OF CROSS-CULTURAL PSYCHOLOGY
    Center for Cross-Cultural Research
    Department of Psychology
    Western Washington State College
    Bellingham, WA
JOURNAL OF CULTURAL GEOGRAPHY
    Bowling Green State University
    The Popular Culture Association
    The American Culture Association
    Bowling Green, OH
JOURNAL OF ECONOMIC HISTORY
    Graduate School of Business Administration
    New York University, New York, NY
JOURNAL OF EDUCATIONAL MEASUREMENT
    National Council on Measurement in Education
    East Lansing, MI
JOURNAL OF GERONTOLOGY
    Gerontological Society, Washington, DC
JOURNAL OF HIGHER EDUCATION
    Ohio State University Press
    Columbus, Ohio
JOURNAL OF HISTORICAL GEOGRAPHY
    Academic Press, London
JOURNAL OF LATIN AMERICAN STUDIES
    Cambridge University Press, London, NY
JOURNAL OF MULTICULTURAL COUNSELING
    AND DEVELOPMENT
    Association for Multicultural
    Counseling and Development
    Alexandria, VA
JOURNAL OF MULTILINGUAL AND
    MULTICULTURAL DEVELOPMENT
    Tieto, Ltd., Clevedon, England
JOURNAL OF NERVOUS AND MENTAL DISEASE
    Williams & Wilkins, Baltimore, MD
JOURNAL OF NON-WHITE CONCERNS IN PERSONNEL
    AND GUIDANCE
    American Association for Counseling and
    Development, Alexandria, VA

JOURNAL OF OFFENDER COUNSELING, SERVICES &
   REHABILITATION
   Haworth Press, New York, NY

JOURNAL OF PERSONALITY AND
SOCIAL PSYCHOLOGY
   American Psychological Assn.
   Washington, DC

JOURNAL OF POPULAR CULTURE
   Bowling Green, Ohio

JOURNAL OF POPULAR FILM AND TELEVISION
   Heldref Publications, Washington, DC

JOURNAL OF PSYCHOLOGY
   Journal Press, Provincetown, MA

JOURNAL OF PSYCHOSOCIAL NURSING AND MENTAL
   HEALTH SERVICES
   C.B. Slack, Thorofare, NJ

JOURNAL OF READING
   International Reading Association
   Newark, Delaware

JOURNAL OF RHEUMATOLOGY
   Journal of Rheumatology Publishing Co.
   Toronto, Canada

JOURNAL OF SOCIAL POLITICAL AND
   ECONOMIC STUDIES
   Council for Social and Economic
   Studies, Washington, DC

JOURNAL OF SOUTHERN HISTORY
   Southern Historical Association, History Department
   Tulane University, New Orleans, LA

JOURNAL OF SPORT HISTORY
   North American Society for Sport History
   Pennsylvania State University,
   University Park, PA

JOURNAL OF TEACHER EDUCATION
   Journal of Teacher Education, AACTE
   Washington, DC

JOURNAL OF THE ASSOCIATION OF MEXICAN AMERICAN
   EDUCATORS
   Institute for Personal Effectiveness in
   Children, San Diego, CA

JOURNAL OF THE NATIONAL CANCER INSTITUTE
   US Government Print Office, Bethesda, MD

JOURNAL OF THE WEST
   Manhattan, KS

JOURNAL OF VOCATIONAL BEHAVIOR
   Academic Press, Inc., New York, NY

JUMP CUT
   Jump Cut Associates, Berkeley, CA

KENTUCKY ROMANCE QUARTERLY
   University Press of Kentucky
   Lexington, KY

LABOR HISTORY
   Tamiment Institute, New York University,
   New York, NY

LANGUAGE
   Linguistic Society of America, Baltimore, MD

LANGUAGE IN SOCIETY
   B. Blackwell, Oxford, England

LATIN AMERICAN MUSIC REVIEW
   University of Texas Press
   Austin, TX

LATIN AMERICAN PERSPECTIVES
   Sage Publications, Beverly Hills, CA

LATIN AMERICAN RESEARCH REVIEW
   Latin American Studies Association
   Austin, TX

LATIN AMERICAN THEATRE REVIEW
   Lawrence, KS

LEARNING DISABILITY QUARTERLY
   Division for Children with Learning Disabilities
   Council for Exceptional Children, Reston, VA

LIBRARY JOURNAL
   R.R. Bowker Co., Riverton, NJ

LIFE
   Time Inc., Chicago, IL

LINGUA
   North-Holland Publishing
   Amsterdam, Holland

LITERARY ONOMASTICS STUDIES
   State University College
   Brockport, NY

LOS ANGELES TIMES BOOK REVIEW
   Los Angeles, CA

MARKETING COMMUNICATIONS
   United Business Publications
   New York, NY

MARYLAND HISTORIAN
   College Park, MD

MEDIA REPORT TO WOMEN
   Women's Institute for Freedom to the Press
   Washington, DC

MEDICAL ANTHROPOLOGY
   Redgrave Publishing
   Pleasantville, NY

MIGRATION WORLD MAGAZINE
   Staten Island, NY

MINNESOTA REVIEW
   Minneapolis, Minnesota

MODERN FICTION STUDIES
   Purdue University
   West Lafayette, IN

MODERN LANGUAGE JOURNAL
   University of Wisconsin Press,
   Madison, WI

MODERN LANGUAGE REVIEW
   Cambridge University Press
   Cambridge, England

MOMENTUM
   National Catholic Education Association,
   Washington, DC

MONTHLY LABOR REVIEW
   US Government Printing Office,
   Washington, DC

MOTHER JONES
   Foundation for National Progress
   San Francisco, CA

MS MAGAZINE
   MS Magazine Corp., New York, NY

NATION
   Nation, Marion, OH

NATIONAL MEDICAL ASSOCIATION JOURNAL
   Appleton-Century-Crofts
   Norwalk, CT

NEW CATHOLIC WORLD
   Paulist Press, Parmus, NJ

NEW DIRECTIONS FOR CONTINUING EDUCATION
   Jossey-Bass, Inc., Publishers
   San Francisco, CA

NEW DIRECTIONS FOR TEACHING AND LEARNING
   Jossey-Bass, Inc., Publishers
   San Francisco, CA

NEW MEXICO HISTORICAL REVIEW
  University of New Mexico,
  Albuquerque, NM
NEW MEXICO MAGAZINE
  Santa Fe, NM
NEW REPUBLIC
  New Republic, Farmingdale, NY
NEWSWEEK
  Newsweek, Livingston, NJ
NEW YORK FOLKLORE QUARTERLY
  Cornell University Press
  Ithaca, NY
NEW YORKER
  New Yorker Magazine, New York, NY
NORTHWESTERN JOURNAL OF INTERNATIONAL
  LAW AND BUSINESS
  Northwestern University School of Law
  Chicago, IL
OEIL-REVUE D'ART MENSUELLE
  Paris, France
OXFORD REVIEW OF EDUCATION
  Carfax Publishing Co., Oxford
PACIFIC HISTORICAL REVIEW
  University of California Press,
  Berkeley, CA
PACIFIC NORTHWEST QUARTERLY
  University of Washington
  Seattle, WA
PALACIO
  Museum of New Mexico
  Santa Fe, NM
PEDIATRIC RESEARCH
  Williams & Wilkins Co.
  Baltimore, MD
PEOPLE WEEKLY
  Time, Inc., Chicago, IL
PERSPECTIVES
  US Commission on Civil Rights
  Washington, DC
PLURAL SOCIETIES
  The Hague, Foundation for the Study
  of Plural Societies
POLICE CHIEFS
  International Association of Chiefs
  of Police, Gaithersburg, MD
POLITICAL AFFAIRS
  Political Affairs Publishing
  New York, NY
POLITICAL SCIENCE QUARTERLY
  Academy of Poltical Science
  New York, NY
POPULATION RESEARCH AND POLICY REVIEW
  Elsevier Scientific Publishing Co.
  Amsterdam, Holland
THE PRISON JOURNAL
  Pennsylvania Prison Society,
  Philadelphia, PA
PROGRESS IN CLINICAL AND BIOLOGICAL RESEARCH
  Liss, New York, NY
THE PROGRESSIVE
  The Progressive, Madison, WI
PROGRESSIVE GROCER
  Butterick, New York, NY
PROSPECTS: QUARTERLY REVIEW OF EDUCATION
  Burt Franklin, New York, NY

P.S. [AMERICAN POLITICAL SCIENCE ASSOCIATION]
  American Political Science Association
  Washington, DC
PSYCHOLOGICAL REPORTS
  Psychological Reports, Missoula, MT
PSYCHOLOGY: A QUARTERLY JOURNAL OF
  HUMAN BEHAVIOR
  Savannah, GA
PUBLIC HEALTH NURSING
  Blackwell Scientific Publications
  Boston, MA
PUBLIC MANAGEMENT
  International City Management Association
  Washington, DC
PUBLIC OPINION QUARTERLY
  Elsevier North-Holland
  New York, NY
PUBLISHER'S WEEKLY
  R.R. Bowker Co., New York, NY
QUALITATIVE SOCIOLOGY
  Human Sciences Press
  New York, NY
RACE AND CLASS
  Institute of Race Relations, London
READER'S DIGEST
  The Reader's Digest Association
  Pleasantville, NY
REFERENCE SERVICES REVIEW
  Pierian Press, Ann Arbor, MI
RELIGIOUS STUDIES REVIEW
  Council on the Study of Religion
RENATO ROSALDO LECTURE SERIES
  MONOGRAPH
  Mexican American Studies and
  Research Center, University of
  Arizona, Tucson, AZ
RESEARCH IN COMMUNITY AND MENTAL HEALTH
  JAI Press, Greenwich, CT
RESTAURANT BUSINESS
  Restaurant Business, New York, NY
REVIEW OF PUBLIC DATA USE
  Clearinghouse and Laboratory for Census Data
  Arlington, VA
REVISTA DE CRITICA LITERARIA LATINOAMERICANA
  Inti-Sol, Lima, Peru
REVISTA DE ESTUDIOS HISPANICOS
  Universidad de Puerto Rico
  Rio Piedras, Puerto Rico
ROCKY MOUNTAIN REVIEW OF
LANGUAGE AND LITERATURE
  Rocky Mountain Modern Language
  Association
  Salt Lake City, UT
ROLLING STONE
  Straight Arrow Publishers
  San Francisco, CA
RQ- REFERENCE AND ADULT SERVICES DIVISION
  American Library Association
  Chicago, IL
S & MM [SALES & MARKETING MANAGEMENT]
  Bill Communications, New York, NY
SAN FRANCISCO
  San Francisco Magazine, Inc.
  San Francisco, CA

SAN FRANCISCO REVIEW OF BOOKS
San Francisco, CA

SOCIAL FORCES
University of North Carolina Press,
Chapel Hill, NC

SOCIAL SCIENCE AND MEDICINE
Pergamon Press, Inc.,
Elmsford, NY

SOCIAL SCIENCE JOURNAL
Colorado State University,
Fort Collins, CO

SOCIAL SCIENCE QUARTERLY
University of Texas Press,
Austin, TX

SOCIAL STUDIES REVIEW
California Council for the Social Studies
Sacramento, CA

SOCIAL WORK
Social Work, Silver Spring, MD

SOCIAL WORK WITH GROUPS
Haworth Press, New York, NY

SOCIETY
Society, New Brunswick, NJ

SOUTHERN CALIFORNIA QUARTERLY
Historical Society, Los Angeles, CA

SOUTHWEST ART
Art Magazine Publishers
Houston, TX

SOUTHWESTERN HISTORICAL QUARTERLY
Texas State Historical Association,
Austin, TX

STRATEGIC REVIEW
United States Strategic Institute
Cambridge, MA

STUDIES IN LATIN AMERICAN POPULAR
CULTURE
Las Cruces, NM

SUPERMARKET NEWS
Fairchild Publications
New York, NY

TELEVISION/RADIO AGE
Television Editorial Corporation,
Baltimore, MD

TEXAS OBSERVOR
Austin, TX

TEXAS TECH JOURNAL OF EDUCATION
School of Law, Texas Tech University
Lubbock, TX

THEATRE JOURNAL
American Theatre Association
Washington, DC

THEATRE SURVEY
American Society for Theatre Research
Pittsburgh, PA

TIME
Time, Chicago, IL

THE TIMES LITERARY SUPPLEMENT
Times Newspapers Limited, London, England

TOP OF THE NEWS
Association for Library Services to
Children and the Young Adult Services
Division of the American Library Association
Chicago, IL

TRANSACTIONS OF THE ASSOCIATION OF LIFE
INSURANCE MEDICAL DIRECTORS
Association of Life Insurance Medical
Directors, Hartford, CT

TRIAL
Association of Trial Lawyers of America
Washington, DC

URBAN AFFAIRS QUARTERLY
Sage Publications, Inc.
Beverly Hills, CA

THE URBAN REVIEW
APS Publications, New York, NY

U.S. NEWS & WORLD REPORT
US News & World Report, Boulder, CO

VIRGINIA LAW REVIEW
Virginia Law Review Association
Charlottesville, VA

VITAL AND HEALTH STATISTICS. SERIES 1
National Center for Health Statistics
Rockville, MD

VITAL AND HEALTH STATISTICS. SERIES 10
National Center for Health Statistics
Rockville, MD

VOICE OF YOUTH ADVOCATES ASSOCIATION YEARBOOK
Ossining, NY

WESTERN AMERICAN LITERATURE
Western Literature Association
Logan, UT

WESTERN FOLKLORE
University of California Press
Berkeley & Los Angeles, CA

WESTERN HISTORICAL QUARTERLY
Utah State University, Logan, UT

WEST TEXAS HISTORICAL ASSOCIATION YEARBOOK
Abilene, TX

WLW JOURNAL
Women Library Workers
Women's Resource Center Library
University of California
Berkeley, CA

WOMEN & POLITICS
Haworth Press, New York, NY

WOMEN'S STUDIES QUARTERLY
Feminist Press, Old Westbury, NY

WORLD LITERATURE TODAY
University of Oklahoma Press
Norman, OK

THE YEAR LEFT
Verso, London, England

ARRANGEMENT OF THE INDEX

SUBJECT INDEX

This is the main section of *ChPI*. Here are listed over 4,500 citations arranged under appropriate descriptor (subject) terms. On average, each of the citations is indexed under three distinct descriptor terms, i.e. each of the citations is repeated in its entirety in three different locations. Each citation listing is numbered sequentially with the citation number serving as reference point for the supplementary author and title indexes.

Each of the numbered citation entries provides the unique index number, full bibliographic description, and additional descriptor terms under which that particular citation is also indexed. *The Chicano Periodical Index* uses subject headings from the fourth edition of *The Chicano Thesaurus* (published in the fourth volume of *ChPI*, 1987). USE references from variant terms to the authorized form used in *The Chicano Thesaurus* are provided.

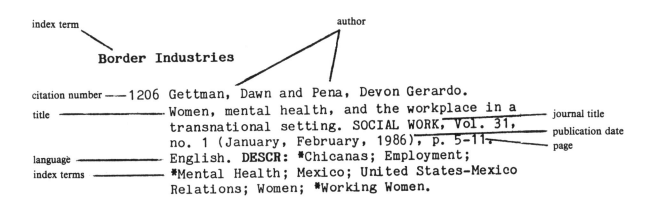

AUTHOR AND TITLE INDEXES

The second major section comprises separate AUTHOR and TITLE indexes. All articles cited in this volume of *ChPI* are listed according to the author's name, when known. In the case of multiple authors, the citation is listed under each author up to a maximum of three. In the author index, entries are grouped alphabetically by author, list the full titles, and provide the citation numbers in the subject index where full citations may be located. Name USE references from variants to the authorized form used in *ChPI* are also provided here.

author ——— **Pena, Devon Gerardo**
           Book review of: THE NEW NOMADS: FROM IMMIGRANT
              LABOR TO TRANSNATIONAL WORKING CLASS, 1104.
   title ——— **Women, mental health, and the workplace in a**
              transnational setting, 1206. ——————— citation number

1

Specific article titles may be located in the alphabetic title listing that follows the author index. A title entry includes the full text of an individual title and the citation number in the subject index where a full citation may be located.

title ——— **Women, mental health, and the workplace in a transnational setting, 1206**———— citation number

SUBJECT INDEX

1984 Republican Convention (Dallas, TX)

1 Cornell, Nancy. Forging links between societies. VISTA, Vol. 3, no. 3 (November 8, 1987), p. 24. English. **DESCR:** *Chicanas; *Olind, Rebecca Nieto; Working Women.

THE $25,000 PINATA [television show]

2 Catalano, Julia. Pinata. VISTA, Vol. 2, no. 10 (June 7, 1987), p. 14. English. **DESCR:** *Children's Television; Fiestas; History.

Abalos, David T.

3 Gonzales, Phillip B. Book review of: LATINOS IN THE UNITED STATES: THE SACRED AND THE POLITICAL. NEW MEXICO HISTORICAL REVIEW, Vol. 62, no. 4 (October 1987), p. 409-11. English. **DESCR:** Book Reviews; *LATINOS IN THE UNITED STATES: THE SACRED AND THE POLITICAL; Politics; Religion.

Abortion

4 Ramirez, Alma Beatrice. La suerte del que no nacio. REVISTA MUJERES, Vol. 2, no. 2 (June 1985), p. 35-36. Spanish. **DESCR:** *Biography.

Abrahams, Roger D.

5 Herrera-Sobek, Maria. Book review of: AND OTHER NEIGHBORLY NAMES: SOCIAL PROCESS AND CULTURAL IMAGE IN TEXAS FOLKLORE. LA RED/THE NET, no. 47 (October 1981), p. 3-4. English. **DESCR:** Bauman, Richard; Book Reviews; *Folklore; *Texas.

Academia Asociados, NM

6 Atencio, Tomas. La resolana [editorial]. EL CUADERNO, Vol. 4, no. 1 (Summer 1976), p. 2-4. English. **DESCR:** Academia Educational Model; *Chicano Studies; Culture; EL CUADERNO; ENTRE VERDE Y SECO; *La Academia de la Nueva Raza, Dixon, NM; LA MADRUGADA; Publishing Industry.

La Academia de la Nueva Raza, Dixon, NM

7 Atencio, Tomas. La Academia de la Nueva Raza: su historia. EL CUADERNO, Vol. 1, no. 1 (1971), p. 4-9. English. **DESCR:** Alternative Education; Chicano Studies; Cultural Organizations; *Educational Organizations; Oro del Barrio.

8 Atencio, Tomas. La Academia de la Nueva Raza. EL CUADERNO, Vol. 2, no. 1 (1972), p. 6-13. English. **DESCR:** *Alternative Education; Chicano Studies; Cultural Characteristics; *Cultural Organizations; Education; *Educational Organizations; Oro del Barrio; Philosophy; Values.

9 Atencio, Tomas. La Academia de la Nueva Raza: El Oro del Barrio. EL CUADERNO, Vol. 3, no. 1 (Winter 1973), p. 4-15. English. **DESCR:** Alternative Education; Chicano Studies; *Cultural Organizations; *Educational Organizations; Oro del Barrio.

10 Atencio, Tomas. No estan todos los que son, no son todos los que estan. EL CUADERNO, Vol. 4, no. 1 (Summer 1976), p. 51-61. Spanish. **DESCR:** Arellano, Estevan; *Identity; Lovato, Alberto; Martinez, Vicente; Roybal, Luis.

11 Atencio, Tomas. La resolana [editorial]. EL CUADERNO, Vol. 4, no. 1 (Summer 1976), p. 2-4. English. **DESCR:** Academia Asociados, NM; Academia Educational Model; *Chicano

Studies; Culture; EL CUADERNO; ENTRE VERDE Y SECO; LA MADRUGADA; Publishing Industry.

Academia Educational Model

12 Atencio, Tomas. La resolana [editorial]. EL CUADERNO, Vol. 4, no. 1 (Summer 1976), p. 2-4. English. **DESCR:** Academia Asociados, NM; *Chicano Studies; Culture; EL CUADERNO; ENTRE VERDE Y SECO; *La Academia de la Nueva Raza, Dixon, NM; LA MADRUGADA; Publishing Industry.

Academia Norteamericana de la Lengua

13 Joe, Barbara E. Safeguarding Spanish. NUESTRO, Vol. 11, no. 2 (March 1987), p. 32. English. **DESCR:** *Spanish Language.

Academic Achievement

14 Carpenter, Thomas P., et al. Achievement in mathematics: results from the National Assessment. THE ELEMENTARY SCHOOL JOURNAL, Vol. 84, no. 5 (May 1984), p. 485-495. English. **DESCR:** *Educational Tests and Measurements; *Mathematics; *National Assessment of Educational Progress.

15 de los Santos, Alfredo G., Jr.; Montemayor, Joaquin; and Solis, Enrique, Jr. Chicano students in higher education: access, attrition and achievement. LA RED/THE NET, no. 41 (April 1981), p. 2-3. English. **DESCR:** *California; Enrollment; *Higher Education; *Texas.

16 Duda, Joan L. Goals and achievement orientations of Anglo and Mexican-American adolescents in sport and the classroom. INTERNATIONAL REVIEW OF SPORT SOCIOLOGY, Vol. 18, no. 4 (1983), p. 63-80. English. **DESCR:** Cultural Characteristics; New Mexico; Sports; *Youth.

17 From dropout to educator. VISTA, Vol. 2, no. 1 (September 7, 1986), p. 13. English. **DESCR:** Discrimination in Education; Education; *Intelligence Tests; *Quintanilla, Guadalupe.

18 Garcia, Herman S.; Stile, Stephen W.; and Carillo, Fred M. Ethnic minority students, admissions policies, and academic support programs in institutions of higher education. TEXAS TECH JOURNAL OF EDUCATION, Vol. 11, no. 1 (Winter 1984), p. 77-89. English. **DESCR:** *Colleges and Universities; Ethnic Groups.

19 LeAna, Thomas. Dorella Martinez. VISTA, Vol. 2, no. 1 (September 7, 1986), p. 14. English. **DESCR:** *Education; *Martinez, Dorella.

20 Mortensen, Eileen. Reading achievement of native Spanish-speaking elementary students in bilingual vs. monolingual programs. BILINGUAL REVIEW, Vol. 11, no. 3 (September, December, 1984), p. 31-36. English. **DESCR:** *Bilingual Bicultural Education; Language Usage; Primary School Education; *Reading.

21 Ortiz, Vilma. Educational attainment among Hispanic youth and non-Hispanic white youth. LA RED/THE NET, no. 67 (April 1983), p. 2-4. English. **DESCR:** Educational Statistics; *Youth.

Academic Achievement (cont.)

22 Powers, Stephen and Rossman, Mark H.
Attributions for success and failure among
Anglo, Black, Hispanic, and Native-American
community-college students. JOURNAL OF
PSYCHOLOGY, Vol. 117, no. 1 (May 1984), p.
27-31. English. **DESCR:** Anglo Americans;
Blacks; Community Colleges; *Locus of
Control; Native Americans; Students.

23 Rendon, Laura Ignacia. Chicano student and
institution related determinants of
educational outcomes in south Texas
community colleges. LA RED/THE NET, no. 73
(October 1983), p. 2-6. English. **DESCR:**
Community Colleges; *South Texas; Surveys.

Academic Libraries

24 Chabran, Richard. Latino reference arrives.
AMERICAN LIBRARIES, Vol. 18, no. 5 (May
1987), p. 384-388. English. **DESCR:**
*Bibliography; *Library Collections; Library
Instruction; *Reference Works.

Academic Performance
USE: Academic Achievement

Accentedness

25 Korzenny, Felipe and Schiff, Elizabeth.
Hispanic perceptions of communication
discrimination. HISPANIC JOURNAL OF
BEHAVIORAL SCIENCES, Vol. 9, no. 1 (March,
1987), p. 33-48. English. **DESCR:**
*Discrimination; *Intercultural
Communication; Skin Color.

26 Paynter, Earlene Tash. Articulation skills
of Spanish-speaking Mexican-American
children: normative data. CLEFT PALATE
JOURNAL, Vol. 21, no. 4 (October 1984), p.
313-316. English.

Accounting

27 Aguilar, Ricardo and Elizondo, Sergio D. La
frontera. LA COMUNIDAD, No. 305 (May 25,
1986), p. 2-3+. Spanish. **DESCR:** Border
Region; Culture.

Acculturation

28 Broderick, Stephanie H., et al. Ethnicity,
acculturation, and health beliefs among
diabetes patients. MIGRATION WORLD MAGAZINE,
Vol. 15, no. 2 (1987), p. 30-32. English.
DESCR: Attitudes; Culture; *Diabetes;
*Identity; *Public Health.

29 Burnham, M. Audrey, et al. Measurement of
acculturation in a community population of
Mexican Americans. HISPANIC JOURNAL OF
BEHAVIORAL SCIENCES, Vol. 9, no. 2 (June
1987), p. 105-130. English. **DESCR:** Age
Groups; Biculturalism; Research Methodology;
Sex Roles.

30 Domino, George and Acosta, Alexandria. The
relation of acculturation and values in
Mexican Americans. HISPANIC JOURNAL OF
BEHAVIORAL SCIENCES, Vol. 9, no. 2 (June
1987), p. 131-150. English. **DESCR:** *Values.

31 Garcia, Philip. Book review of:
ACCULTURATION: THEORY, MODELS, AND SOME NEW
FINDINGS. LA RED/THE NET, no. 41 (April
1981), p. 4-5. English. **DESCR:**
*ACCULTURATION: THEORY, MODELS, AND SOME NEW
FINDINGS; Book Reviews; *Padilla, Amado M.

32 Gilbert, M. Jean. Alcohol consumption
patterns in immigrant and later generation

Mexican American women. HISPANIC JOURNAL OF
BEHAVIORAL SCIENCES, Vol. 9, no. 3
(September 1987), p. 299-313. English.
DESCR: *Alcoholism; *Attitudes; *Chicanas;
Cultural Characteristics; *Immigrants;
Mexico.

33 Jimenez, Ricardo. Understanding the culture
and learning styles of Hispanic students.
MOMENTUM, Vol. 14, no. 1 (February 1983), p.
15-18. English. **DESCR:** Religious Education;
Socialization; Students.

34 Jorgensen, Stephen R. and Adams, Russell P.
Family planning needs and behavior of
Mexican American women: a study of health
care professionals and their clientele.
HISPANIC JOURNAL OF BEHAVIORAL SCIENCES,
Vol. 9, no. 3 (September 1987), p. 265-286.
English. **DESCR:** *Attitudes; Birth Control;
*Chicanas; *Cultural Characteristics;
*Family Planning; Fertility; Public Health;
Stereotypes; Sterilization.

35 Marin, Gerardo, et al. Development of a
short acculturation scale for Hispanics.
HISPANIC JOURNAL OF BEHAVIORAL SCIENCES,
Vol. 9, no. 2 (June 1987), p. 183-205.
English. **DESCR:** *Psychological Testing.

36 Mena, Francisco; Padilla, Amado M.; and
Maldonado, Margarita. Acculturative stress
and specific coping stategies among
immigrant and later generation college
students. HISPANIC JOURNAL OF BEHAVIORAL
SCIENCES, Vol. 9, no. 2 (June 1987), p.
207-225. English. **DESCR:** Age Groups;
Colleges and Universities; Identity;
Immigrants; Stress; Students.

37 Mujica, Barbara. What's in a name? VISTA,
Vol. 1, no. 1 (September 8, 1985), p. 18.
English. **DESCR:** *Personal Names.

38 Neff, James Alan; Hoppe, Sue K.; and Perea,
Patricia. Acculturation and alcohol use:
drinking patterns and problems among Anglo
and Mexican American male drinkers. HISPANIC
JOURNAL OF BEHAVIORAL SCIENCES, Vol. 9, no.
2 (June 1987), p. 151-181. English. **DESCR:**
Age Groups; *Alcoholism; Anglo Americans;
*Males; Stress.

39 Perez, Renato E. As American as babalu.
VISTA, Vol. 2, no. 6 (February 8, 1987), p.
22. English. **DESCR:** *Arnaz, Desi; Essays; I
LOVE LUCY; Television.

40 Sabogal, Fabio, et al. Hispanic familism and
acculturation: what changes and what
doesn't? HISPANIC JOURNAL OF BEHAVIORAL
SCIENCES, Vol. 9, no. 4 (December 1987), p.
397-412. English. **DESCR:** Attitudes; Cultural
Characteristics; Ethnic Groups; Extended
Family; *Family; Natural Support Systems;
Values.

41 Salgado de Snyder, Nelly. The role of ethnic
loyalty among Mexican immigrant women.
HISPANIC JOURNAL OF BEHAVIORAL SCIENCES,
Vol. 9, no. 3 (September 1987), p. 287-298.
English. **DESCR:** Chicanas; *Culture;
*Identity; Immigrants; Mental Health;
*Mexico; *Women.

42 Shoemaker, Pamela J.; Reese, Stephen D.; and
Danielson, Wayne A. Spanish-language print
media use as an indicator of acculturation.
JOURNALISM QUARTERLY, Vol. 62, no. 4 (Winter
1985), p. 734-740. English. **DESCR:**
Magazines; Newspapers; *Print Media;
*Spanish Language.

--   --

**ACCULTURATION: THEORY, MODELS, AND SOME NEW
    FINDINGS**

43 Garcia, Philip. Book review of:
   ACCULTURATION: THEORY, MODELS, AND SOME NEW
   FINDINGS. LA RED/THE NET, no. 41 (April
   1981), p. 4-5. English. **DESCR:**
   *Acculturation; Book Reviews; *Padilla,
   Amado M.

Acosta, Oscar Zeta

44 Bruce-Novoa, Juan. Homosexuality and the
   Chicano novel. CONFLUENCIA, Vol. 2, no. 1
   (Fall 1986), p. 69-77. English. **DESCR:** CITY
   OF NIGHT; FAULTLINE [novel]; *Homosexuality;
   Islas, Arturo; *Literary Criticism;
   Machismo; *Novel; Ortiz Taylor, Sheila;
   POCHO; Rechy, John; Salas, Floyd; SPRING
   FORWARD/FALL BACK; TATOO THE WICKED CROSS;
   THE AUTOBIOGRAPHY OF A BROWN BUFFALO; THE
   RAIN GOD: A DESERT TALE; THE REVOLT OF THE
   COCKROACH PEOPLE; Villarreal, Jose Antonio.

45 Bruce-Novoa, Juan. Mexico en la literatura
   chicana (II). LA COMUNIDAD, No. 268
   (September 8, 1985), p. 14-15. Spanish.
   DESCR: Identity; *Literary Criticism; THE
   AUTOBIOGRAPHY OF A BROWN BUFFALO.

46 Padilla, Genaro Miguel. The anti-romantic
   city in Chicano fiction. PUERTO DEL SOL,
   Vol. 23, no. 1 (1987), p. 159-169. English.
   DESCR: Anaya, Rudolfo A.; *Fiction; Lattin,
   Vernon E.; *Literary Criticism; Morales,
   Alejandro; *Urban Communities.

Acquired Immune Deficiency Syndrome (AIDS)

47 Koop, C. Everett. Plain talk on AIDS for
   Hispanic Americans. VISTA, Vol. 3, no. 1
   (September 6, 1987), p. 13. English. **DESCR:**
   *Health Education.

48 Remas, Theodora A. The threat of AIDS.
   VISTA, Vol. 2, no. 10 (June 7, 1987), p.
   17-18, 25. English. **DESCR:** Directories;
   Health Education; *Medical Care;
   Preventative Medicine.

49 Sosa, Lionel. The human face of AIDS. VISTA,
   Vol. 3, no. 4 (December 6, 1987), p. 15, 36.
   English. **DESCR:** Biography; *Diseases.

**ACROSS THE BORDER: RURAL DEVELOPMENT IN MEXICO AND
RECENT MIGRATION**

50 de la Garza, Rodolfo O. Book review of:
   ACROSS THE BORDER: RURAL DEVELOPMENT IN
   MEXICO AND RECENT MIGRATION TO THE UNITED
   STATES. LA RED/THE NET, no. 69 (June 1983),
   p. 5-7. English. **DESCR:** Book Reviews; Border
   Industries; Cross, Harry E.; Sandos, James.

Actors and Actresses

51 Chavez, Lorenzo A. La Bamba. VISTA, Vol. 2,
   no. 11 (July 5, 1987), p. 12-13. English.
   DESCR: Biography; De Soto, Rosana; Films; LA
   BAMBA [film]; *Morales, Esai; Pena,
   Elizabeth; Phillips, Lou Diamond.

52 Guerrero, Dan. FALCON CREST: showcase for
   Hispanic talent. VISTA, Vol. 2, no. 2
   (October 4, 1986), p. 12-15. English.
   DESCR: *Ana-Alicia; FALCON CREST [television
   show]; Lamas, Lorenzo; Romero, Cesar;
   Television.

53 Guerrero, Dan. Tanya Sandoval: death-defying
   stunts are all in her day's work. VISTA,
   Vol. 2, no. 6 (February 8, 1987), p. 21.
   English. **DESCR:** Films; *Sandoval, Tanya.

54 Guevara, Ruben. Richard "Cheech" Marin.
   AMERICAS 2001, Vol. 1, no. 1 (June, July,
   1987), p. 18-21. Bilingual. **DESCR:** *BORN IN
   EAST L.A. [film]; Films; Immigration;
   *Marin, Richard "Cheech"; Undocumented
   Workers.

55 Gutierrez, Silvio G. The odd couple. VISTA,
   Vol. 3, no. 1 (September 6, 1987), p. 12-13.
   English. **DESCR:** *Humor; O'Brien, Jim;
   *Valdez, Alex.

56 Jimenez, Luis. En busca del talento latino.
   LA COMUNIDAD, No. 235 (January 20, 1985), p.
   14-15. Spanish. **DESCR:** *Biography; Mass
   Media; *Morones, Bob.

57 Kwain, Constance. Searching for Hispanic
   talent. VISTA, Vol. 2, no. 6 (February 8,
   1987), p. 6-7. English. **DESCR:** American
   Federation of Television & Radio Artists
   (AFTRA); *Business Enterprises; Films; Myrna
   Salazar and Associates, Inc.; Navas, Trina;
   Salazar, Myrna; Screen Actors Guild;
   Television.

58 Lomeli, Maria Magdalena S. "LATC" un espacio
   para el teatro politico. LA COMUNIDAD, No.
   333 (December 7, 1986), p. 10-11. Spanish.
   DESCR: *Los Angeles Theatre Center (LATC);
   Morales, Esai; *Teatro.

59 Medina, David. America's Hispanic Theater
   Olympics. VISTA, Vol. 1, no. 12 (August 2,
   1986), p. 12-14. English. **DESCR:** Dance;
   *Festival Latino; *Teatro.

60 Montane, Diane. Edward James Olmos: the man
   behind the tough film facade. VISTA, Vol. 1,
   no. 1 (September 8, 1985), p. 8-12. English.
   DESCR: BALLAD OF GREGORIO CORTEZ [film];
   Biography; *Olmos, Edward James; WOLFEN
   [film]; ZOOT SUIT [film].

61 Rodriguez Flores, Juan. Andy Garcia: un
   "Intocable" orgulloso de ser latino. LA
   COMUNIDAD, No. 362 (June 28, 1987), p. 8-11.
   Spanish. **DESCR:** *Biography; *Garcia, Andy.

62 Rodriguez Flores, Juan. Esai Morales: un
   joven de origen hispano con oficio de actor
   (1). LA COMUNIDAD, No. 335 (December 21,
   1986), p. 8-9. Spanish. **DESCR:** *Biography;
   *Morales, Esai.

63 Rodriguez Flores, Juan. Esai Morales y la
   pasion por el arte escenico (II). LA
   COMUNIDAD, No. 336 (December 28, 1986), p.
   2-3. Spanish. **DESCR:** *Biography; Films; LA
   BAMBA [film]; *Morales, Esai; Valdez, Luis.

64 Rodriguez Flores, Juan. Robert Redford y THE
   MILAGRO BEANFIELD WAR. LA COMUNIDAD, No. 328
   (November 2, 1986), p. 8-11+. Spanish.
   DESCR: *Films; *Redford, Robert; THE MILAGRO
   BEANFIELD WAR [film].

65 Rodriguez Flores, Juan. Ruben Blades:
   siempre he apostado a la sensibilidad del
   publico. LA COMUNIDAD, No. 330 (November 16,
   1986), p. 8-11. Spanish. **DESCR:** *Biography;
   *Blades, Ruben; Films; Music; THE MILAGRO
   BEANFIELD WAR [film].

66 Thomson, David. The Texas that got away.
   FILM COMMENT, Vol. 21, no. 3 (June 1985), p.
   32-35. English. **DESCR:** *Films; Stereotypes.

67 WISDOM: a showcase for the many talents of
   Emilio Estevez. NUESTRO, Vol. 11, no. 3
   (April 1987), p. 25. English. **DESCR:**
   *Estevez, Emilio; WISDOM [film].

ACTOS

68 Pena, Luis H. Praxis dramatica, praxis politica: los actos de Luis Valdez. REVISTA DE CRITICA LITERARIA LATINOAMERICANA, Vol. 10, no. 19 (1984), p. 161-166. Spanish. **DESCR**: Actos; El Teatro Campesino; *Teatro; *Valdez, Luis.

Actos

69 Avendano, Fausto. Fragmento dramatico. SAGUARO, Vol. 1, no. 1 (1984), p. 79-84. Spanish.

70 Beauford, Olivia. A tiempo. SAGUARO, Vol. 1, no. 1 (1984), p. 75-77. Spanish.

71 Gaxiola, Blanca. Vamonos a ver al padre Antonio. SAGUARO, Vol. 1, no. 1 (1984), p. 72-74. Spanish.

72 Jones, Maria. Las comadres. LLUEVE TLALOC, no. 5 (1978), p. 11-12. Spanish.

73 Madson, J. Diego. Demonio en el matrimonio. LLUEVE TLALOC, no. 13 (1986), p. 8. Spanish.

74 Martinez, Jose. Please disregard this notice if full payment has been made. CHIRICU, Vol. 3, no. 2 (1983), p. 47-54. Spanish. **DESCR**: Spanish Language.

75 Pena, Luis H. Praxis dramatica, praxis politica: los actos de Luis Valdez. REVISTA DE CRITICA LITERARIA LATINOAMERICANA, Vol. 10, no. 19 (1984), p. 161-166. Spanish. **DESCR**: ACTOS; El Teatro Campesino; *Teatro; *Valdez, Luis.

76 Rodriguez Flores, Juan. Mike Gomez, otro rostro hispano en Hollywood. LA COMUNIDAD, No. 339 (January 18, 1987), p. 8-9. Spanish. **DESCR**: *Biography; *Gomez, Mike.

77 Van Olphen, Yone. Llanto de lluvia. LLUEVE TLALOC, no. 1 (1974), p. 25-26. Spanish.

78 Vasquez, Ruben. Welcome back vato. CHIRICU, Vol. 3, no. 2 (1983), p. 67-71. English.

Acuna, Rudolfo

79 Garcia, Mario T. Book review of: A COMMUNITY UNDER SIEGE. LA RED/THE NET, no. 94 (March 1986), p. 5-6. English. **DESCR**: *A COMMUNITY UNDER SIEGE: A CHRONICLE OF CHICANOS EAST OF THE LOS ANGELES RIVER, 1945-1975; Book Reviews; Los Angeles, CA.

80 Garcia, Mario T. Book review of: A COMMUNITY UNDER SIEGE. PACIFIC HISTORICAL REVIEW, Vol. 55, no. 4 (1986), p. 636-638. English. **DESCR**: *A COMMUNITY UNDER SIEGE: A CHRONICLE OF CHICANOS EAST OF THE LOS ANGELES RIVER, 1945-1975; Book Reviews; East Los Angeles, CA.

81 Gutierrez, Jose Angel. Chicanos and Mexicans: under surveillance: 1940 to 1980. RENATO ROSALDO LECTURE SERIES MONOGRAPH, Vol. 2, (Spring 1986), p. [29]-58. English. **DESCR**: Border Coverage Program (BOCOV); *Civil Rights; COINTELPRO; *Federal Bureau of Investigation (FBI); *Federal Government; History; League of United Latin American Citizens (LULAC); Mexico; Political Parties and Organizations; *Political Repression.

82 Hoffman, Abraham. Book review of: A COMMUNITY UNDER SIEGE. JOURNAL OF AMERICAN HISTORY, Vol. 72, no. 2 (September 1985), p. 459. English. **DESCR**: *A COMMUNITY UNDER SIEGE: A CHRONICLE OF CHICANOS EAST OF THE LOS ANGELES RIVER, 1945-1975; Book Reviews.

83 Romo, Ricardo. Book review of: OCCUPIED AMERICA. LA RED/THE NET, no. 39 (February 1981), p. 3. English. **DESCR**: Book Reviews; History; *OCCUPIED AMERICA; *Social History and Conditions.

Adler, Mortimer

84 Rips, Geoffrey. Puritanism, pluralism, and Perot. TEXAS OBSERVOR, Vol. 75, no. 17 (September 2, 1983), p. 3-4. English. **DESCR**: *Bilingual Bicultural Education; Educational Theory and Practice; Perot, Ross.

Administration of Justice

85 McKanna, Clare V. The San Quentin prison pardon papers: a look at file no. 1808, the case of Francisco Javier Bonilla. SOUTHERN CALIFORNIA QUARTERLY, Vol. 67, no. 2 (Summer 1985), p. 187-196. English. **DESCR**: Archives; *Bonilla, Francisco Javier; *Criminal Justice System; History; *Prisoners; *San Quentin Prison.

Adolescents
USE: Youth

Adolph Coors Co.

86 Beale, Stephen. Friendly persuasion: pacts and covenants. HISPANIC BUSINESS, Vol. 9, no. 9 (September 1987), p. 20-26. English. **DESCR**: *Business; Community Organizations; Coors/HACER Agreement, 1984; *Corporations; *Hispanic Association on Corporate Responsibility (HACER); Organizations; Pacific Bell; Southland Corporation.

87 Beale, Stephen. Striking a deal with big business. HISPANIC BUSINESS, Vol. 9, no. 2 (February 1987), p. 26-33. English. **DESCR**: American G.I. Forum; Boycotts; Corporations; Cuban National Planning Council, Inc. Washington, D.C.; Employment; *Hispanic Association on Corporate Responsibility (HACER); League of United Latin American Citizens (LULAC); National Council of La Raza (NCLR); National IMAGE; National Puerto Rican Coalition; *Organizations; U.S. Hispanic Chamber of Commerce.

88 Hispanic marketing. ADVERTISING AGE MAGAZINE, Vol. 57, no. 16 (February 27, 1986), p. 11-51. English. **DESCR**: Advertising; Allstate Insurance Co.; American Greetings; Anheuser-Busch, Inc.; Business Enterprises; Coca-Cola Company; Consumers; Ford Motor Company; Hallmark Cards; *Marketing; Mass Media; McDonald's Corporation; Metropolitan Life Insurance Corporation; Pepsi-Cola Bottling Group; Prudential; Spanish International Network (SIN); State Farm Mutual Insurance; Tylenol; United Insurance Co. of America.

89 Perez, Renato E. The business of Hispanics. VISTA, Vol. 2, no. 1 (September 7, 1986), p. 10. English. **DESCR**: American G.I. Forum; Apodaca, Jerry [Gov. of New Mexico]; Business; *Collective Bargaining; Corporations; Cuban National Planning Council, Inc. Washington, D.C.; *Hispanic Association on Corporate Responsibility (HACER); League of United Latin American Citizens (LULAC); National Council of La Raza (NCLR); National IMAGE; U.S. Hispanic Chamber of Commerce.

Adolph Coors Co. (cont.)

90 Sellers, Jeff M. Golden opportunity. HISPANIC BUSINESS, Vol. 9, no. 9 (September 1987), p. 14-18, 79. English. **DESCR:** Business Enterprises; *Coors/HACER Agreement, 1984; *Corporations; Employment; Hispanic Association on Corporate Responsibility (HACER); Organizations.

Adult Education

91 Heaney, Thomas W. "Hanging on" or "gaining ground": educating marginal adults. NEW DIRECTIONS FOR CONTINUING EDUCATION, Vol. 20, (December 1983), p. 53-63. English. **DESCR:** *Adult Education Center of Lakeview; Chicago, IL; Community School Relationships; Education.

Adult Education Center of Lakeview

92 Heaney, Thomas W. "Hanging on" or "gaining ground": educating marginal adults. NEW DIRECTIONS FOR CONTINUING EDUCATION, Vol. 20, (December 1983), p. 53-63. English. **DESCR:** *Adult Education; Chicago, IL; Community School Relationships; Education.

Advanced Sciences Inc., Albuquerque, NM

93 Sellers, Jeff M. Strategic defenses: new niches for small firms. HISPANIC BUSINESS, Vol. 9, no. 10 (October 1987), p. 13-17. English. **DESCR:** Business Enterprises; Electronics Industry; *Government Contracts; *Military; *Orion International Technologies, Inc.; Rios, Miguel, Jr.; Romero, Ed.

Advertising

94 Balkan, D. Carlos. The Hispanic market's leading indicators. HISPANIC BUSINESS, Vol. 9, no. 12 (December 1987), p. 16-17. English. **DESCR:** *Marketing; Population; Statistics.

95 Beale, Stephen. The Maxwell House that Marlboro bought. HISPANIC BUSINESS, Vol. 9, no. 2 (February 1987), p. 20-21, 60. English. **DESCR:** Business Enterprises; Corporations; *Marketing; *Philip Morris, Inc.

96 Cecere, Linda. Newspapers attract attention in some categories. ADVERTISING AGE MAGAZINE, Vol. 57, no. 43 (August 11, 1986), p. S9-S10. English. **DESCR:** DIARIO DE LAS AMERICAS; EL MIAMI HERALD; LA OPINION, Los Angeles, CA; *Newspapers; NOTICIAS DEL MUNDO; Spanish Language.

97 DelPriore, Lisa. Tapping into the Hispanic market. MARKETING COMMUNICATIONS, Vol. 11, no. 6 (June 1986), p. 57-62. English. **DESCR:** *Consumers; *Marketing; *Mass Media.

98 Fever, Jack. ADWEEK's honor roll: women to watch: Dolores Valdes Zacky. ADWEEK, Vol. 36, (July 7, 1986), p. W16. English. **DESCR:** Advertising Agencies; *Zacky, Dolores Valdes.

99 Fitch, Ed. Buying power bursts poverty-stricken image. ADVERTISING AGE MAGAZINE, Vol. 58, no. 6 (February 9, 1987), p. S1-S2, S8. English. **DESCR:** Consumers; *Marketing.

100 Fitch, Ed. Paving way for national ad sales. ADVERTISING AGE MAGAZINE, Vol. 57, no. 16 (February 27, 1986), p. 50-51. English. **DESCR:** Marketing; Newspapers.

101 Fitch, Ed. Prime space available at low rates. ADVERTISING AGE MAGAZINE, Vol. 57, no. 16 (February 27, 1986), p. 11-12. English. **DESCR:** Consumers; General Foods; *Marketing.

102 Guedella, Juan. Hispanic media--Caballero style. HISPANIC BUSINESS, Vol. 9, no. 2 (February 1987), p. 17-18. English. **DESCR:** Biography; *Caballero, Eduardo; *Caballero Spanish Media (CSM); Cubanos; Marketing.

103 Hispanic marketing. ADVERTISING AGE MAGAZINE, Vol. 57, no. 16 (February 27, 1986), p. 11-51. English. **DESCR:** Adolph Coors Co.; Allstate Insurance Co.; American Greetings; Anheuser-Busch, Inc.; Business Enterprises; Coca-Cola Company; Consumers; Ford Motor Company; Hallmark Cards; *Marketing; Mass Media; McDonald's Corporation; Metropolitan Life Insurance Corporation; Pepsi-Cola Bottling Group; Prudential; Spanish International Network (SIN); State Farm Mutual Insurance; Tylenol; United Insurance Co. of America.

104 Hispanic media awards. TELEVISION/RADIO AGE, Vol. 31, (January 23, 1984), p. 17-18. English. **DESCR:** Awards; *El Cervantes Media Awards.

105 Jacobson, Harold. Upward trend in expenditures continues. HISPANIC BUSINESS, Vol. 9, no. 12 (December 1987), p. 19-20. English. **DESCR:** Consumers; Income; *Marketing; Mass Media.

106 Kane, Michael G. "Touching" minorities. EDITOR & PUBLISHER: THE FOURTH ESTATE, Vol. 119, no. 38 (September 20, 1986), p. 20-21. English. **DESCR:** Consumers; Ethnic Groups; Marketing; *Newspapers.

107 Kesler, Lori. A-B benefits from regional approach. ADVERTISING AGE MAGAZINE, Vol. 57, no. 16 (February 27, 1986), p. 48-49. English. **DESCR:** Anheuser-Busch, Inc.; Consumers; *Marketing.

108 Lawrence, Jennifer. TV signal expected to boost Houston market. ADVERTISING AGE MAGAZINE, Vol. 57, no. 43 (August 11, 1986), p. S24-S25. English. **DESCR:** Houston, TX; *KXLN, Houston, TX [television station]; Marketing; Pueblo Broadcasting Corp.; Spanish Language; Television.

109 Levin, Gary. Publisher seeks to improve "image". ADVERTISING AGE MAGAZINE, Vol. 57, no. 43 (August 11, 1986), p. S25-S27. English. **DESCR:** Asencio, John; English Language; *HISPANIC IMAGE; Magazines; Spanish Language.

110 Macias, Reynaldo Flores and Cabello-Argandona, Roberto. Media research and the Chicano. LATIN QUARTER, Vol. 1, no. 2 (October 1974), p. 14-16,18. English. **DESCR:** Consumers; Marketing; *Mass Media; Population.

111 La Mafia signs Pepsi contract. NUESTRO, Vol. 11, no. 4 (May 1987), p. 8-9. English. **DESCR:** *La Mafia [musical group]; Musicians; Pepsi-Cola Bottling Group; Rock Music.

Advertising (cont.)

112 Marketing to Hispanics. ADVERTISING AGE MAGAZINE, Vol. 57, no. 43 (August 11, 1986), p. 51-528. English. DESCR: Broadcast Media; De Armas Publications; Kinney Shoe Corp.; *Marketing; Pepsi-Cola Bottling Group; Print Media; Spanish International Network (SIN); U.S. Bureau of the Census.

113 Marketing to Hispanics. ADVERTISING AGE MAGAZINE, Vol. 58, no. 6 (February 9, 1987), p. S1-S23. English. DESCR: Consumers; Immigrants; *Marketing; Mass Media; Politics; Undocumented Workers.

114 Norris, Eileen. Print suffers in tale of two languages. ADVERTISING AGE MAGAZINE, Vol. 57, no. 16 (February 27, 1986), p. 49-51. English. DESCR: Chavarria, Jesus; English Language; HISPANIC BUSINESS; LATINA [magazine]; *Magazines; Soto, Grace; Spanish Language; Villar, Arturo; VISTA [magazine].

115 Poole, Claire. Viewers looking for the U.S. look. HISPANIC BUSINESS, Vol. 9, no. 12 (December 1987), p. 26-28. English. DESCR: Advertising Agencies; Marketing; Telemundo Television Group; *Television.

116 Rubin, Marcy Gray. Advertiser apathy hampers TV growth. ADVERTISING AGE MAGAZINE, Vol. 57, no. 43 (August 11, 1986), p. S22-S23. English. DESCR: Arbitron; Spanish International Network (SIN); Spanish Language; Strategy Research Corp.; Television.

117 Sellers, Jeff M. Good hands grasp a growing market. HISPANIC BUSINESS, Vol. 9, no. 9 (September 1987), p. 8-11. English. DESCR: *Allstate Insurance Co.; *Insurance; *Marketing.

118 Sellers, Jeff M. Market growth boosts ad rates. HISPANIC BUSINESS, Vol. 9, no. 12 (December 1987), p. 41-42, 63+. English. DESCR: *Marketing; *Spanish Language; *Television.

119 Sellers, Jeff M. Metropolitan Life continues to lead. HISPANIC BUSINESS, Vol. 9, no. 5 (May 1987), p. 12-14. English. DESCR: Corporations; *Insurance; *Marketing; *Metropolitan Life Insurance Corporation; U.S. Hispanic Chamber of Commerce.

120 Trager, Cara S. Manhattan executive forum. HISPANIC BUSINESS, Vol. 9, no. 4 (April 1987), p. 10-13. English. DESCR: *Corporations; Marketing; *National Hispanic Corporate Council (NHCC); *Organizations.

121 Valencia, Humberto. Sales pitch to Hispanics must strike right chord. VISTA, Vol. 1, no. 12 (August 2, 1986), p. 3. English. DESCR: Bilingualism; Language Usage.

Advertising Agencies

122 Banks, Marissa Elena. Army maneuvers. HISPANIC BUSINESS, Vol. 9, no. 12 (December 1987), p. 37-39. English. DESCR: Government Contracts; *Military; *Sosa & Associates; U.S. Department of Defense (DOD).

123 Fever, Jack. ADWEEK's honor roll: women to watch: Dolores Valdes Zacky. ADWEEK, Vol. 36, (July 7, 1986), p. W16. English. DESCR: *Advertising; *Zacky, Dolores Valdes.

124 Poole, Claire. Viewers looking for the U.S. look. HISPANIC BUSINESS, Vol. 9, no. 12 (December 1987), p. 26-28. English. DESCR:

*Advertising; Marketing; Telemundo Television Group; *Television.

Affirmative Action

125 High court upholds quotas. DUNS'S BUSINESS MONTH, Vol. 128, no. 2 (August 1986), p. 22. English. DESCR: Discrimination in Employment; Reagan Administration; Sexism; U.S. Supreme Court.

126 Labor department official challenges Hispanic program manager to maintain commitment, perseverance. HISPANIC TIMES, Vol. 8, no. 5 (October, November, 1987), p. 41. English. DESCR: *Harris, William J.; Office of Civil Rights, Labor Department, Washington, D.C.

127 Leon, David Jess and McNeill, Daniel. The fifth class: a 19th century forerunner of affirmative action. CALIFORNIA HISTORY, Vol. 64, no. 1 (Winter 1985), p. 52-57. English. DESCR: Colleges and Universities; Discrimination in Education; *Enrollment; *Higher Education; History; Students; *University of California.

128 Zucca, Gary J. and Gorman, Benjamin. Affirmative action: Blacks and Hispanics in United States Navy occupational specialties. ARMED FORCES AND SOCIETY, Vol. 12, no. 4 (Summer 1986), p. 513-524. English. DESCR: *Blacks; *Discrimination in Employment; *Military.

Affirmative Action Programs

129 Madrid, Vicente and Yepes, Maria Elena. National Latino Media Coalition. LATIN QUARTER, Vol. 1, no. 4 (July, August, 1975), p. 4-7. English. DESCR: Bilingual/Bicultural Coalition on Mass Media; *Broadcast Media; California Association of Latins in Broadcasting; Conferences and Meetings; Federal Communications Commission (FCC); *National Latino Media Coalition (NLMC); Puerto Rican Media Action and Educational Council.

Afro-Americans
USE: Blacks

Age Groups

130 Burnham, M. Audrey, et al. Measurement of acculturation in a community population of Mexican Americans. HISPANIC JOURNAL OF BEHAVIORAL SCIENCES, Vol. 9, no. 2 (June 1987), p. 105-130. English. DESCR: *Acculturation; Biculturalism; Research Methodology; Sex Roles.

131 Mena, Francisco; Padilla, Amado M.; and Maldonado, Margarita. Acculturative stress and specific coping stategies among immigrant and later generation college students. HISPANIC JOURNAL OF BEHAVIORAL SCIENCES, Vol. 9, no. 2 (June 1987), p. 207-225. English. DESCR: *Acculturation; Colleges and Universities; Identity; Immigrants; Stress; Students.

132 Neff, James Alan; Hoppe, Sue K.; and Perea, Patricia. Acculturation and alcohol use: drinking patterns and problems among Anglo and Mexican American male drinkers. HISPANIC JOURNAL OF BEHAVIORAL SCIENCES, Vol. 9, no. 2 (June 1987), p. 151-181. English. DESCR: *Acculturation; *Alcoholism; Anglo Americans; *Males; Stress.

Age Groups (cont.)

133 Padilla, Eligio R. and O'Grady, Kevin E. Sexuality among Mexican Americans: a case of sexual stereotyping. JOURNAL OF PERSONALITY AND SOCIAL PSYCHOLOGY, Vol. 52, no. 1 (1987), p. 5-10. English. **DESCR:** Anglo Americans; Attitudes; Religion; *Sex Roles; *Stereotypes.

134 Snipp, C. Matthew and Tienda, Marta. Intergenerational occupational mobility of Chicanos. LA RED/THE NET, no. 42 (May 1981), p. 2. English. **DESCR:** *Income; *National Chicano Survey (NCS).

135 Torres-Gil, Fernando. The Latinization of a multigenerational population: Hispanics in an aging society. DAEDALUS, Vol. 115, no. 1 (Winter 1986), p. 325-348. English. **DESCR:** Cultural Pluralism; Population; *Public Policy; Social Classes; Socioeconomic Factors.

Aged

USE: Ancianos

Agosin, Marjorie

136 Alarcon, Norma. Book Review of: BRUJAS Y ALGO MAS/WITCHES AND OTHER THINGS. CHIRICU, Vol. 4, no. 1 (1985), p. 9-12. English. **DESCR:** Book Reviews; *BRUJAS Y ALGO MAS=WITCHES AND OTHER THINGS.

Agribusiness

137 Faxon, R. Paul. Employer sanctions for hiring illegal aliens: a simplistic solution to a complex problem. NORTHWESTERN JOURNAL OF INTERNATIONAL LAW AND BUSINESS, Vol. 6, (Spring 1984), p. 203-248. English. **DESCR:** Immigration Law and Legislation; National Labor Relations Board (NLRB); Simpson-Mazzoli Bill; *Undocumented Workers.

Agricultural Extension Service

138 Jensen, Joan M. Crossing ethnic barriers in the Southwest: women's agricultural extension education, 1914-1940. AGRICULTURAL HISTORY, Vol. 60, no. 2 (Spring 1986), p. 169-181. English. **DESCR:** Agriculture; Cabeza de Baca, Fabiola; Chicanas; History; New Mexico; *Rural Education.

Agricultural Labor Unions

139 Barger, W.K. California public endorses the United Farm Workers. LA RED/THE NET, No. 105 (February 1987), p. 4-6. English. **DESCR:** California; *Farm Workers; *Public Opinion; *United Farmworkers of America (UFW).

140 Barger, W.K. Views of California farmworkers regarding the farm labor movement. LA RED/THE NET, no. 91 (October 1985), p. 3-5. English. **DESCR:** Attitudes; California; *Farm Workers; *United Farmworkers of America (UFW).

141 Echaveste, Beatrice and Huerta, Dolores. In the shadow of the eagle: Huerta=A la sombra del aguila: Huerta. AMERICAS 2001, Vol. 1, no. 3 (November, December, 1987), p. 26-30. Bilingual. **DESCR:** Boycotts; Chicanas; *Farm Workers; *Huerta, Dolores; *United Farmworkers of America (UFW).

Agricultural Laborers

USE: Farm Workers

Agricultural Workers

USE: Farm Workers

Agriculture

142 Jensen, Joan M. Crossing ethnic barriers in the Southwest: women's agricultural extension education, 1914-1940. AGRICULTURAL HISTORY, Vol. 60, no. 2 (Spring 1986), p. 169-181. English. **DESCR:** *Agricultural Extension Service; Cabeza de Baca, Fabiola; Chicanas; History; New Mexico; *Rural Education.

Aguilar [family name]

143 Instituto Genealogico e Historico Latino-Americano. Rootsearch: Aguilar: Echeverria. VISTA, Vol. 1, no. 11 (July 6, 1986), p. 22. English. **DESCR:** Echeverria [family name]; Genealogy; History; *Personal Names.

Aguilar, Gregorio

144 Families of the year. VISTA, Vol. 2, no. 2 (October 4, 1986), p. 16-18. English. **DESCR:** Aguilar, Guadalupe; Aranda, Benjamin; Aranda, Emma; *Awards; de la Rocha, Beatriz; de la Rocha, Castulo; Family; Guzman, Ofelia; Guzman, Roberto; *Hispanic Family of the Year Award.

Aguilar, Guadalupe

145 Families of the year. VISTA, Vol. 2, no. 2 (October 4, 1986), p. 16-18. English. **DESCR:** Aguilar, Gregorio; Aranda, Benjamin; Aranda, Emma; *Awards; de la Rocha, Beatriz; de la Rocha, Castulo; Family; Guzman, Ofelia; Guzman, Roberto; *Hispanic Family of the Year Award.

Aguilar, Laura

146 Rosas, Alejandro. Siete fotografos latinos en Los Angeles. LA COMUNIDAD, No. 241 (March 3, 1985), p. 4-5. Spanish. **DESCR:** Art; Avila, Adam; Callwood, Dennis O.; Carlos, Jesus; Exhibits; Miranda, Judy; *Photography; Self-Help Graphics, Los Angeles, CA; *SEVEN LATINO PHOTOGRAPHERS=SIETE FOTOGRAFOS LATINOS; Thewlis, Alan; Valverde, Richard.

Aguilar, Ricardo

147 Garcia, Nasario. El cuento chicano visto por dentro y por fuera. BILINGUAL REVIEW, Vol. 12, no. 3 (September, December, 1985), p. 262-265. Spanish. **DESCR:** Armengol, Armando; Book Reviews; *PALABRA NUEVA: CUENTOS CHICANOS; Somoza, Oscar U.

148 Valdes Medellin, Gonzalo; Elizondo, Sergio D.; and Aguilar, Ricardo. Hacia un tercer lenguaje. LA COMUNIDAD, No. 240 (February 24, 1985), p. 2-3. Spanish. **DESCR:** Elizondo, Sergio; *Literary Criticism.

Aguirre Architects, Dallas, TX

149 Garcia, Art. Financing the corporate take-off. HISPANIC BUSINESS, Vol. 9, no. 5 (May 1987), p. 22-27. English. **DESCR:** Aguirre, Pedro; Banking Industry; *Business Enterprises; Businesspeople; *Corporations; *Investments; Minority Enterprise Small Business Investment Corporation (MESBIC); Morales, Ramon; Protocom Devices, New York, NY; Villamil, Antonio.

---   --

Aguirre, Martin

   150 Hoffman, Abraham. The controversial career
      of Martin Aguirre; the rise and fall of a
      Chicano lawman. CALIFORNIA HISTORY, Vol. 63,
      no. 4 (Fall 1984), p. 295-341. English.
      DESCR: *Biography; History; Los Angeles
      County, CA; Prisoners; San Quentin Prison.

Aguirre, Pedro

   151 Garcia, Art. Financing the corporate
      take-off. HISPANIC BUSINESS, Vol. 9, no. 5
      (May 1987), p. 22-27. English. **DESCR:**
      Aguirre Architects, Dallas, TX; Banking
      Industry; *Business Enterprises;
      Businesspeople; *Corporations; *Investments;
      Minority Enterprise Small Business
      Investment Corporation (MESBIC); Morales,
      Ramon; Protocom Devices, New York, NY;
      Villamil, Antonio.

AL NORTE DEL RIO BRAVO (PASADO LEJANO, 1600-1930)

   152 Griswold del Castillo, Richard. New
      perspectives on the Mexican and American
      borderlands. LATIN AMERICAN RESEARCH REVIEW,
      Vol. 19, no. 1 (1984), p. 199-209. English.
      DESCR: AL NORTE DEL RIO BRAVO (PASADO
      INMEDIATO, 1930-1981); *Book Reviews;
      *Border Region; Gomez-Quinones, Juan;
      Maciel, David; MEXICANO RESISTANCE IN THE
      SOUTHWEST: "THE SACRED RIGHT OF
      SELF-PRESERVATION"; Rosenbaum, Robert J.;
      THE MEXICAN FRONTIER, 1821-1846: THE
      AMERICAN SOUTHWEST UNDER MEXICO; THE TEJANO
      COMMUNITY, 1836-1900; Weber, David J.

**AL NORTE DEL RIO BRAVO (PASADO INMEDIATO,
1930-1981)**

   153 Griswold del Castillo, Richard. New
      perspectives on the Mexican and American
      borderlands. LATIN AMERICAN RESEARCH REVIEW,
      Vol. 19, no. 1 (1984), p. 199-209. English.
      DESCR: AL NORTE DEL RIO BRAVO (PASADO
      LEJANO, 1600-1930); *Book Reviews; *Border
      Region; Gomez-Quinones, Juan; Maciel, David;
      MEXICANO RESISTANCE IN THE SOUTHWEST: "THE
      SACRED RIGHT OF SELF-PRESERVATION";
      Rosenbaum, Robert J.; THE MEXICAN FRONTIER,
      1821-1846: THE AMERICAN SOUTHWEST UNDER
      MEXICO; THE TEJANO COMMUNITY, 1836-1900;
      Weber, David J.

Alambristas
     USE: Undocumented Workers

Alamo Technology Inc., San Antonio, TX

   154 Seven profiles of courage. HISPANIC
      BUSINESS, Vol. 9, no. 6 (June 1987), p.
      57-70. English. **DESCR:** *Business
      Enterprises; *Businesspeople; Carrillo,
      Rosario C.; O'Campo Corporation, Walnut, CA;
      O'Campo, Peter; Rivas, Robert; TexPar Energy
      Inc., Milwaukee, WI; THE HISPANIC BUSINESS
      500.

THE ALAMO TREE [novel]

   155 Bruce-Novoa, Juan. Ernest Brawley: un
      escritor chicano desconocido. LA COMUNIDAD,
      No. 277 (November 10, 1985), p. 6-7.
      Spanish. **DESCR:** Authors; *Biography;
      *Brawley, Ernest; Literary Criticism; Novel;
      SELENA [novel]; THE RAP [novel].

   156 Bruce-Novoa, Juan. Nuevo representantes de
      la novela chicana. LA COMUNIDAD, No. 310
      (June 29, 1986), p. 6-7+. Spanish. **DESCR:**
      Brawley, Ernest; EL VAGO [novel]; FAULTLINE
      [novel]; Gonzales, Laurence; *Literary
      Criticism; Novel; Ortiz Taylor, Sheila.

Alarcon [family name]

   157 Instituto Genealogico e Historico
      Latino-Americano. Rootsearch: Alarcon:
      Saavedra. VISTA, Vol. 1, no. 8 (April 6,
      1986), p. 22. English. **DESCR:** Genealogy;
      History; *Personal Names; Saavedra [family
      name].

Alarcon, Justo S.

   158 Alarcon, Justo S. Book review of: CHULIFEAS
      FRONTERAS. CHIRICU, Vol. 3, no. 1 (1982), p.
      101-103. Spanish. **DESCR:** Book Reviews;
      *CHULIFEAS FRONTERAS.

   159 Cota-Cardenas, Margarita. La
      creacion-protesta en CRISOL: (TRILOGIA).
      CONFLUENCIA, Vol. 1, no. 2 (Spring 1986), p.
      66-72. Spanish. **DESCR:** *CRISOL; *Literary
      Criticism; Novel.

Alarcon, Norma

   160 Agosin, Marjorie. Norma Alarcon. CHIRICU,
      Vol. 2, no. 1 (Spring 1980), p. 9. Spanish.
      DESCR: Poems.

   161 Quintana, Alvina. O mama, with what's inside
      of me. REVISTA MUJERES, Vol. 3, no. 1
      (January 1986), p. 38-40. English. **DESCR:**
      *Chicanas; Feminism; *Literary Criticism;
      Poetry; *"What Kind of Lover Have You Made
      Me, Mother?: Towards a Theory of Chicanas'
      Feminism and Cultural Identity Through
      Poetry" [article].

Alatorre, Richard

   162 Los Angeles: brown versus yellow. ECONOMIST
      (London), Vol. 300, no. 7456 (July 26,
      1986), p. 21-22. English. **DESCR:** Bradley,
      Tom; Ethnic Groups; *Los Angeles, CA;
      Political Representation; Politics;
      Reapportionment; Voter Turnout; Woo,
      Michael.

Alba, Richard D.

   163 Rubin, J.H. Book review of: ETHNICITY AND
      RACE IN THE U.S.A.: TOWARD THE TWENTY-FIRST
      CENTURY. CHOICE, Vol. 23, no. 7 (March
      1986), p. 1130. English. **DESCR:** Book
      Reviews; *ETHNICITY AND RACE IN THE U.S.A.:
      TOWARD THE TWENTY-FIRST CENTURY.

Albertson, Jack

   164 Aceves Madrid, Vicente. Controversy
      surrounding NBC's CHICO AND THE MAN. LATIN
      QUARTER, Vol. 1, no. 2 (October 1974), p.
      5-7. English. **DESCR:** Artists; *CHICO AND THE
      MAN [television show]; Komack, James;
      Prinze, Freddie; Stereotypes; Teatros
      Unidos; *Television.

   165 Vasquez, Victor. More on CHICO AND THE MAN.
      LATIN QUARTER, Vol. 1, no. 3 (January,
      February, 1975), p. 13-15. English. **DESCR:**
      Andrade, Ray; Artists; Boycotts; *CHICO AND
      THE MAN [television show]; Discrimination;
      Prinze, Freddie; Stereotypes; *Television.

Albuquerque International Balloon Fiesta

   166 Holmes, John J. Up and away: ballooning
      fever grips America and Latinos have caught
      the bug. VISTA, Vol. 3, no. 2 (October 3,
      1987), p. 16-18. English. **DESCR:** *Festivals;
      Sports.

Albuquerque, NM

167 Armstrong, Ruth W. Christmas in Albuquerque. VISTA, Vol. 1, no. 4 (December 7, 1985), p. 18-20. English. DESCR: *Cultural Customs; Holidays.

168 Luckingham, Bradford. The American Southwest: an urban view. WESTERN HISTORICAL QUARTERLY, Vol. 15, no. 3 (July 1984), p. 261-280. English. DESCR: El Paso, TX; Phoenix, AZ; Social History and Conditions; *Southwestern United States; Tucson, AZ; *Urban Communities; Urban Economics.

Alcoholism

169 Costello, Raymond M. Hispanic alcoholic treatment considerations. HISPANIC JOURNAL OF BEHAVIORAL SCIENCES, Vol. 9, no. 1 (March 1987), p. 83-89. English. DESCR: Anglo Americans; Mental Health Clinics.

170 Gilbert, M. Jean. Alcohol consumption patterns in immigrant and later generation Mexican American women. HISPANIC JOURNAL OF BEHAVIORAL SCIENCES, Vol. 9, no. 3 (September 1987), p. 299-313. English. DESCR: Acculturation; *Attitudes; *Chicanas; Cultural Characteristics; *Immigrants; Mexico.

171 Mendes de Leon, Carlos F., et al. Alcohol consumption and physical symptoms in a Mexican American population. DRUG AND ALCOHOL DEPENDENCE, Vol. 16, no. 4 (February 1986), p. 369-379. English.

172 Neff, James Alan; Hoppe, Sue K.; and Perea, Patricia. Acculturation and alcohol use: drinking patterns and problems among Anglo and Mexican American male drinkers. HISPANIC JOURNAL OF BEHAVIORAL SCIENCES, Vol. 9, no. 2 (June 1987), p. 151-181. English. DESCR: *Acculturation; Age Groups; Anglo Americans; *Males; Stress.

173 New Latino group to combat problem. NUESTRO, Vol. 11, no. 2 (March 1987), p. 8. English. DESCR: *Drug Use; *National Hispanic Family Against Drug Abuse (NHFADA).

Alfaro, Henry

174 Ayala, Ernie. Henry Alfaro, ABC's Eyewitness News reporter. LATIN QUARTER, Vol. 1, no. 1 (July 1974), p. 13-15. English. DESCR: California Chicano News Media Association (CCNMA); Golden Mike Award; Journalists; *Television.

Alfaro, Victor Clark

175 Cisneros, Henry. Mexico's poorest are heading North. AKWESASNE NOTES, Vol. 18, no. 4 (Summer 1986), p. 7. English. DESCR: Centro de Promocion Popular Urbana, Tijuana, Baja California, Mexico; Farm Workers; Kearney, Michael; Mexico; Mixtec Indians; *Undocumented Workers.

Alfonso's Restaurant, San Antonio, TX

176 Bain, Laurie. Alfonso's heats up San Antonio. RESTAURANT BUSINESS, Vol. 86, (January 20, 1987), p. 120-122. English. DESCR: Burke, John; *Restaurants.

Alicia, Juana

177 Castano, Wilfredo Q. For the roses=Pa' las rosas. REVISTA MUJERES, Vol. 3, no. 2 (June 1986), p. 73. DESCR: *Mural Art; *Photography.

Alienation

178 Galindo-Ramirez, Tina. Educacion monolingue: opresion o liberacion? REVISTA MUJERES, Vol. 1, no. 1 (January 1984), p. 8-9. Spanish. DESCR: Assertiveness; Biography; *Education; English Language; *Identity.

179 Loo, Chalsa M. and Rolison, Garry. Alienation of ethnic minority students at a predominantly white university. JOURNAL OF HIGHER EDUCATION, Vol. 57, no. 1 (January, February, 1986), p. 58-77. English. DESCR: Attitudes; Discrimination in Education; *Students; Surveys; Teacher-pupil Interaction.

Allegre, Raul

180 Viuker, Steve. Man with the golden toe. VISTA, Vol. 3, no. 2 (October 3, 1987), p. 6, 24. English. DESCR: Athletes; *Football.

Allen Parish, LA

181 Kahn, Robert. Oakdale prison: documenting the abuses. IN THESE TIMES, Vol. 10, no. 35 (September 17, 1986), p. 8, 22. English. DESCR: Legal Representation; *Oakdale, LA; Oakdale Legal Assistance (OLA); Political Refugees; Prisons; Undocumented Workers; U.S. Bureau of Prisons (BOP).

Allstate Insurance Co.

182 Hispanic marketing. ADVERTISING AGE MAGAZINE, Vol. 57, no. 16 (February 27, 1986), p. 11-51. English. DESCR: Adolph Coors Co.; Advertising; American Greetings; Anheuser-Busch, Inc.; Business Enterprises; Coca-Cola Company; Consumers; Ford Motor Company; Hallmark Cards; *Marketing; Mass Media; McDonald's Corporation; Metropolitan Life Insurance Corporation; Pepsi-Cola Bottling Group; Prudential; Spanish International Network (SIN); State Farm Mutual Insurance; Tylenol; United Insurance Co. of America.

183 Sellers, Jeff M. Good hands grasp a growing market. HISPANIC BUSINESS, Vol. 9, no. 9 (September 1987), p. 8-11. English. DESCR: Advertising; *Insurance; *Marketing.

Allsup, Carl

184 Sierra, Christine Marie. Book review of: THE G.I. FORUM: ORIGINS AND EVOLUTION. LA RED/THE NET, no. 73 (October 1983), p. 12-16. English. DESCR: Book Reviews; *THE AMERICAN G.I. FORUM: ORIGINS AND EVOLUTION.

Almaguer, Tomas

185 Garcia, Mario T. Book review of: THE STATE OF CHICANO RESEARCH ON FAMILY, LABOR, AND MIGRATION: PROCEEDINGS OF THE FIRST STANFORD SYMPOSIUM ON CHICANO RESEARCH AND PUBLIC POLICY. CALIFORNIA HISTORY, Vol. 63, no. 3 (Summer 1984), p. 261-262. English. DESCR: Book Reviews; Camarillo, Alberto; Chicano Studies; *THE STATE OF CHICANO RESEARCH IN FAMILY, LABOR AND MIGRATION STUDIES; Valdez, Armando.

Almaguer, Tomas (cont.)

186 Griswold del Castillo, Richard. Book review of: THE STATE OF CHICANO RESEARCH ON FAMILY, LABOR, AND MIGRATION: PROCEEDINGS OF THE FIRST STANFORD SYMPOSIUM ON CHICANO RESEARCH AND PUBLIC POLICY. PACIFIC HISTORICAL REVIEW, Vol. 54, no. 3 (August 1985), p. 381-382. English. **DESCR:** Book Reviews; Camarillo, Alberto; Chicano Studies; *THE STATE OF CHICANO RESEARCH IN FAMILY, LABOR AND MIGRATION STUDIES; Valdez, Armando.

Almanacs

187 Book review of: THE HISPANIC ALMANAC. BOOKLIST, Vol. 82, (May 1, 1986), p. 1296. English. **DESCR:** Book Reviews; *HISPANIC ALMANAC; Hispanic Policy Development Project (HPDP).

Almanza, John

188 Winston, Bonnie. INROADS: internships that work. HISPANIC ENGINEER, Vol. 3, no. 5 (Winter 1987), p. 38-42. English. **DESCR:** Alvarez, Maria; Carr, Frank; *Educational Organizations; Educational Statistics; Garcia, Juan; Gonzales, Ana; *INROADS; Pereira, Eduardo; Raimundo, Antonio; Reza, Priscilla.

Almaraz, Carlos

189 Barragan, Ma. Antonieta. Carlos Almaraz: "El arte contemporaneo no tiene mucha emocion, es estatico...". LA COMUNIDAD, No. 324 (October 5, 1986), p. 10-11. Spanish. **DESCR:** *Art; Biography.

ALONG THE RIO GRANDE: A PASTORAL VISIT TO SOUTHWEST NEW MEXICO IN 1902

190 Foley, Patrick. Book review of: ALONG THE RIO GRANDE: PASTORAL VISIT TO SOUTHWEST NEW MEXICO IN 1902. NEW MEXICO HISTORICAL REVIEW, Vol. 62, no. 4 (October 1987), p. 405-6. English. **DESCR:** Book Reviews; *Granjon, Henry; *New Mexico.

Altars

191 Chavez, Denise. NOVENA NARRATIVAS y OFRENDAS NUEVOMEXICANAS. THE AMERICAS REVIEW, Vol. 15, no. 3-4 (Fall, Winter, 1987), p. 85-100. English. **DESCR:** *Teatro.

192 Dia de los difuntos ofrenda. THE AMERICAS REVIEW, Vol. 15, no. 3-4 (Fall, Winter, 1987), p. [84]. **DESCR:** Photography.

Alternative Education

193 Atencio, Tomas. La Academia de la Nueva Raza: su historia. EL CUADERNO, Vol. 1, no. 1 (1971), p. 4-9. English. **DESCR:** Chicano Studies; Cultural Organizations; *Educational Organizations; *La Academia de la Nueva Raza, Dixon, NM; Oro del Barrio.

194 Atencio, Tomas. La Academia de la Nueva Raza. EL CUADERNO, Vol. 2, no. 1 (1972), p. 6-13. English. **DESCR:** Chicano Studies; Cultural Characteristics; *Cultural Organizations; Education; *Educational Organizations; *La Academia de la Nueva Raza, Dixon, NM; Oro del Barrio; Philosophy; Values.

195 Atencio, Tomas. La Academia de la Nueva Raza: El Oro del Barrio. EL CUADERNO, Vol. 3, no. 1 (Winter 1973), p. 4-15. English. **DESCR:** Chicano Studies; *Cultural Organizations; *Educational Organizations; *La Academia de la Nueva Raza, Dixon, NM; Oro del Barrio.

Alurista

196 Jacob, John. Book review of: SOUTHWEST TALES: A CONTEMPORY COLLECTION. BOOKLIST, Vol. 82, no. 17 (May 1, 1986), p. 1284. English. **DESCR:** Book Reviews; Rojas-Urista, Xelina; *SOUTHWEST TALES: A CONTEMPORARY COLLECTION.

197 Klor de Alva, J. Jorge. California Chicano literature and pre-Columbian motifs: foil and fetish. CONFLUENCIA, Vol. 1, no. 2 (Spring 1986), p. 18-26. English. **DESCR:** Aztecs; Aztlan; *California; EL PLAN ESPIRITUAL DE AZTLAN; *Literature; *Precolumbian Images; *Precolumbian Philosophy; Symbolism.

198 Lomeli, Francisco A. El concepto del barrio en tres poetas chicanos. LA COMUNIDAD, No. 316 (August 10, 1986), p. 4-5+. Spanish. **DESCR:** Barrios; Delgado, Abelardo "Lalo"; *Literary Criticism; Poetry; Sanchez, Ricardo.

199 Vallejos, Tomas. Book review of: SOUTHWEST TALES: A CONTEMPORY COLLECTION. THE AMERICAS REVIEW, Vol. 15, no. 2 (Summer 1987), p. 111-113. English. **DESCR:** Book Reviews; Rojas-Urista, Xelina; *SOUTHWEST TALES: A CONTEMPORARY COLLECTION.

Alvarez [family name]

200 Instituto Genealogico e Historico Latino-Americano. Rootsearch: Alvarez: Covarrubias. VISTA, Vol. 1, no. 6 (February 2, 1986), p. 22. English. **DESCR:** *Covarrubias [family name]; Genealogy; History; *Personal Names.

Alvarez, Linda

201 Olivera, Mercedes. The new Hispanic women. VISTA, Vol. 2, no. 11 (July 5, 1987), p. 6-8. English. **DESCR:** *Chicanas; Esquiroz, Margarita; Garcia, Juliet; *Hernandez, Antonia A.; Mohr, Nicolasa; Molina, Gloria; Pabon, Maria; Working Women.

Alvarez, Maria

202 Winston, Bonnie. INROADS: internships that work. HISPANIC ENGINEER, Vol. 3, no. 5 (Winter 1987), p. 38-42. English. **DESCR:** Almanza, John; Carr, Frank; *Educational Organizations; Educational Statistics; Garcia, Juan; Gonzales, Ana; *INROADS; Pereira, Eduardo; Raimundo, Antonio; Reza, Priscilla.

Alvarez, Roberto

203 Beale, Stephen. CEOs. HISPANIC BUSINESS, Vol. 9, no. 4 (April 1987), p. 20-37, 52. English. **DESCR:** Batarse, Anthony A.; Biography; Business Enterprises; *Businesspeople; Carlo, Nelson; Estrada, Anthony; Flores, Frank; Fullana, Jaime, Jr.; Hernandez, George; *Management; Ortega, James; Quirch, Guillermo; Ruiz, Roberto; Santa Maria, Yvonne Z.; Sugranes, Rosa; Tamaya, Carlos; Young, Paul H., Jr.

Alvarez, Rodolfo

204 Meier, Matt S. Book review of: THE MEXICAN
AMERICAN EXPERIENCE: AN INTERDISCIPLINARY
ANTHOLOGY. HISPANIC AMERICAN HISTORICAL
REVIEW, Vol. 66, no. 3 (August 1986), p.
629-630. English. DESCR: Bean, Frank D.;
Bonjean, Charles M.; Book Reviews; de la
Garza, Rodolfo O.; Romo, Ricardo; *THE
MEXICAN AMERICAN EXPERIENCE: AN
INTERDISCIPLINARY ANTHOLOGY.

205 Ruiz, Vicki Lynn. Book review of: THE
MEXICAN AMERICAN EXPERIENCE: AN
INTERDISCIPLINARY ANTHOLOGY. SOUTHWESTERN
HISTORICAL QUARTERLY, Vol. 90, no. 2 (1986),
p. 205-206. English. DESCR: Bean, Frank D.;
Bonjean, Charles M.; Book Reviews; de la
Garza, Rodolfo O.; Romo, Ricardo; *THE
MEXICAN AMERICAN EXPERIENCE: AN
INTERDISCIPLINARY ANTHOLOGY.

206 Salmon, Roberto Mario. Book review of: THE
MEXICAN AMERICAN EXPERIENCE: AN
INTERDISCIPLINARY ANTHOLOGY. LA RED/THE NET,
no. 93 (January, February, 1986), p. 12-14.
English. DESCR: Bean, Frank D.; Bonjean,
Charles M.; Book Reviews; de la Garza,
Rodolfo O.; Romo, Ricardo; *THE MEXICAN
AMERICAN EXPERIENCE: AN INTERDISCIPLINARY
ANTHOLOGY.

Amado [family name]

207 Instituto Genealogico e Historico
Latino-Americano. Rootsearch: Villalobos:
Amador (Amado): Ibarra. VISTA, Vol. 3, no. 4
(December 6, 1987), p. 36. English. DESCR:
*Amador [family name]; Genealogy; History;
*Ibarra [family name]; Personal Names;
*Villalobos [family name].

Amador [family name]

208 Instituto Genealogico e Historico
Latino-Americano. Rootsearch: Villalobos:
Amador (Amado): Ibarra. VISTA, Vol. 3, no. 4
(December 6, 1987), p. 36. English. DESCR:
*Amado [family name]; Genealogy; History;
*Ibarra [family name]; Personal Names;
*Villalobos [family name].

Amastae, Jon

209 Nuessel, Frank H., Jr. Book review of:
SPANISH IN THE UNITED STATES:
SOCIOLINGUISTIC ASPECTS. LINGUA, Vol. 62,
no. 3 (1984), p. 247-255. English. DESCR:
Book Reviews; Elias-Olivares, Lucia;
Sociolinguistics; *SPANISH IN THE UNITED
STATES: SOCIOLINGUISTIC ASPECTS.

210 Penalosa, Fernando. Book review of: SPANISH
IN THE UNITED STATES: SOCIOLINGUISTIC
ASPECTS. LANGUAGE, Vol. 60, no. 1 (March
1984), p. 152-159. English. DESCR: Book
Reviews; Elias-Olivares, Lucia;
Sociolinguistics; *SPANISH IN THE UNITED
STATES: SOCIOLINGUISTIC ASPECTS.

211 Powers, Michael D. Spanish in contact with
other languages: lexical or profound
structural influence? BILINGUAL REVIEW, Vol.
12, no. 3 (September, December, 1985), p.
254-257. English. DESCR: Elias-Olivares,
Lucia; Language Usage; Literature Reviews;
*SPANISH IN THE UNITED STATES:
SOCIOLINGUISTIC ASPECTS; *SPANISH IN THE
WESTERN HEMISPHERE IN CONTACT WITH ENGLISH,
PORTUGUESE, AND THE AMERINDIAN LANGUAGES;
*Spanish Language; Zaragoza, Jorge.

Ambassadors

USE: Appointed Officials

Ambert, Alba N.

212 Gonzales-Berry, Erlinda. Book review of:
BILINGUAL EDUCATION: A SOURCEBOOK. MODERN
LANGUAGE JOURNAL, Vol. 69, no. 3 (Fall
1985), p. 299. English. DESCR: *BILINGUAL
EDUCATION: A SOURCEBOOK; Book Reviews;
Melendez, Sarah E.

213 Nieto, Sonia. Book review of: BILINGUAL
EDUCATION: A SOURCEBOOK. INTERRACIAL BOOKS
FOR CHILDREN, Vol. 17, no. 3-4 (1986), p.
29. English. DESCR: *BILINGUAL EDUCATION: A
SOURCEBOOK; Book Reviews; Melendez, Sarah
E.

214 Soudek, Lev I. Book review of: BILINGUAL
EDUCATION: A SOURCEBOOK. AMERICAN REFERENCE
BOOKS ANNUAL, Vol. 17, (1986), p. 132.
English. DESCR: *BILINGUAL EDUCATION: A
SOURCEBOOK; Book Reviews; Melendez, Sarah
E.

AMERICA WITHOUT ETHNICITY

215 Garcia, John A. Book review of: AMERICA
WITHOUT ETHNICITY. LA RED/THE NET, no. 78
(March 1984), p. 8-9. English. DESCR: Book
Reviews; Morgan, Gordon D.

American Association for Higher Education Hispanic Caucus

216 Magallan, Rafael J. Hispanic organizations
concerned with higher education. LA RED/THE
NET, no. 91 (October 1985), p. 2-3. English.
DESCR: *Educational Organizations; Higher
Education.

American Bicentennial

217 Bi-centennial [editorial]. LATIN QUARTER,
Vol. 1, no. 3 (February 1975), p. 2.
English. DESCR: *Bicentennial Commission;
Montoya, Dennis.

American Chemical Society

218 American Chemical Society honors Dr. Mario
J. Molina. HISPANIC ENGINEER, Vol. 3, no. 2
(Summer 1987), p. 12. English. DESCR:
*Awards; *Molina, Mario J.

American Education Research Association (AERA), San Francisco, April 16-20, 1988

219 Solorzano, Daniel. Impressions from the 1986
American Education Research Association
(AERA), held in San Francisco, April 16-20.
LA RED/THE NET, no. 96 (May 1986), p. 9-11.
English. DESCR: *Conferences and Meetings.

American Family Society

220 Lit, Ed. Recognition for Hispanic families.
VISTA, Vol. 1, no. 5 (January 5, 1986), p.
18-20. English. DESCR: *Awards; *Hispanic
Family of the Year Award; Moraga, Peter and
family (Los Angeles, CA); Pineda, Charles
and family (Los Angeles, CA); Private
Funding Sources.

American Federation of Television & Radio Artists (AFTRA)

221 Kwain, Constance. Searching for Hispanic
talent. VISTA, Vol. 2, no. 6 (February 8,
1987), p. 6-7. English. DESCR: *Actors and
Actresses; *Business Enterprises; Films;
Myrna Salazar and Associates, Inc.; Navas,
Trina; Salazar, Myrna; Screen Actors Guild;
Television.

American G.I. Forum

222 Beale, Stephen. Striking a deal with big
business. HISPANIC BUSINESS, Vol. 9, no. 2
(February 1987), p. 26-33. English. DESCR:
*Adolph Coors Co.; Boycotts; Corporations;
Cuban National Planning Council, Inc.
Washington, D.C.; Employment; *Hispanic
Association on Corporate Responsibility
(HACER); League of United Latin American
Citizens (LULAC); National Council of La
Raza (NCLR); National IMAGE; National Puerto
Rican Coalition; *Organizations; U.S.
Hispanic Chamber of Commerce.

223 Bueno, Patricia E. Los Chicanos y la
politica II. LA COMUNIDAD, No. 268
(September 8, 1985), p. 2-3. Spanish.
DESCR: Chicano Movement; History;
Leadership; Mexican American Political
Association (MAPA); Nationalism; Political
Association of Spanish-Speaking
Organizations (PASO); *Political Parties and
Organizations.

224 Perez, Renato E. The business of Hispanics.
VISTA, Vol. 2, no. 1 (September 7, 1986), p.
10. English. DESCR: Adolph Coors Co.;
Apodaca, Jerry [Gov. of New Mexico];
Business; *Collective Bargaining;
Corporations; Cuban National Planning
Council, Inc. Washington, D.C.; *Hispanic
Association on Corporate Responsibility
(HACER); League of United Latin American
Citizens (LULAC); National Council of La
Raza (NCLR); National IMAGE; U.S. Hispanic
Chamber of Commerce.

THE AMERICAN G.I. FORUM: ORIGINS AND EVOLUTION

225 Sierra, Christine Marie. Book review of: THE
G.I. FORUM: ORIGINS AND EVOLUTION. LA
RED/THE NET, no. 73 (October 1983), p.
12-16. English. DESCR: Allsup, Carl; Book
Reviews.

American Greetings

226 Hispanic marketing. ADVERTISING AGE
MAGAZINE, Vol. 57, no. 16 (February 27,
1986), p. 11-51. English. DESCR: Adolph
Coors Co.; Advertising; Allstate Insurance
Co.; Anheuser-Busch, Inc.; Business
Enterprises; Coca-Cola Company; Consumers;
Ford Motor Company; Hallmark Cards;
*Marketing; Mass Media; McDonald's
Corporation; Metropolitan Life Insurance
Corporation; Pepsi-Cola Bottling Group;
Prudential; Spanish International Network
(SIN); State Farm Mutual Insurance; Tylenol;
United Insurance Co. of America.

American Indians
USE: Native Americans

AMERICAN LABOR IN THE SOUTHWEST: THE FIRST ONE HUNDRED YEARS

227 Hall, Linda B. The United States-Mexican
borders: historical, political, and cultural
perspectives. LATIN AMERICAN RESEARCH
REVIEW, Vol. 20, no. 2 (1985), p. 223-229.
English. DESCR: *Book Reviews; *Border

Region; BOSS RULE IN SOUTH TEXAS: THE
PROGRESSIVE ERA; CHICANO INTERMARRIAGE: A
THEORETICAL AND EMPIRICAL STUDY; HISPANIC
CULTURE IN THE SOUTHWEST; IN DEFENSE OF LA
RAZA: THE LOS ANGELES MEXICAN CONSULATE AND
THE MEXICAN COMMUNITY; Literature Reviews;
RACE AND CLASS IN THE SOUTHWEST: A THEORY OF
RACIAL INEQUALITY; SOUTHWESTERN AGRICULTURE:
PRE-COLUMBIAN TO MODERN; THE MEXICANS IN
OKLAHOMA; THE POLITICS OF SAN ANTONIO.

228 Reisler, Mark. Book review of: AMERICAN
LABOR IN THE SOUTHWEST: THE 1ST 100 YEARS.
PACIFIC HISTORICAL REVIEW, Vol. 53, no. 2
(1984), p. 246-247. English. DESCR: Book
Reviews; Foster, James C.

American Society of Civil Engineers (ASCE)

229 El Camino Real named national historic
engineering landmark. HISPANIC ENGINEER,
Vol. 3, no. 1 (Spring 1987), p. 23. English.
DESCR: *Awards; *El Camino Real.

American Society of Civil Engineers (ASCE) Moisseif Award

230 Vitelmo V. Bertero wins ASCE's Moisseiff
Award. HISPANIC ENGINEER, Vol. 3, no. 5
(Winter 1987), p. 14. English. DESCR:
*Awards; *Bertero, Vitelmo V.; University of
California, Berkeley.

Americanization
USE: Assimilation

AMERICA'S ETHNIC POLITICS

231 Garcia, John A. Book review of: AMERICA'S
ETHNIC POLITICS. LA RED/THE NET, no. 67
(April 1983), p. 7-8. English. DESCR: Book
Reviews; Eisenberg, Bernard; Politics;
Roucek, Joseph S.

Amnesty (Immigration)
USE: Immigration Law and Legislation

Ana-Alicia

232 Guerrero, Dan. FALCON CREST: showcase for
Hispanic talent. VISTA, Vol. 2, no. 2
(October 4, 1986), p. 12-15. English.
DESCR: *Actors and Actresses; FALCON CREST
[television show]; Lamas, Lorenzo; Romero,
Cesar; Television.

Anarquismo y Comunismo: Mexican Radicalism and the Communist Party in Los Angeles in the 1930s

233 Garcia, Mario T. Chicano historiography: a
critique. LA RED/THE NET, no. 80 (May 1984),
p. 2-8. English. DESCR: Historiography;
*Monroy, Douglas.

234 Garcia, Mario T. [Letter to the editor about
Mexicans, radicals and communists in the
United States]. LABOR HISTORY, Vol. 25, no.
1 (Winter 1984), p. 152-154. English.
DESCR: *Communism; History; *Labor Unions;
Los Angeles, CA; *Monroy, Douglas.

Anaya, Rudolfo A.

235 Anaya, Rudolfo A. A Chicano in China. VISTA,
Vol. 2, no. 1 (September 7, 1986), p. 19-21.
English. DESCR: *A CHICANO IN CHINA; China;
*Culture; Philosophy; *Tourism.

Anaya, Rudolfo A. (cont.)

236 Anderson, Robert K. Marez y Luna and the masculine-feminine dialectic. CRITICA HISPANICA, Vol. 6, no. 2 (1984), p. 97-105. English. **DESCR:** *BLESS ME, ULTIMA; Literary Criticism; Novel; *Women Men Relations.

237 Bruce-Novoa, Juan. Meet the writers of the 80s. VISTA, Vol. 1, no. 11 (July 6, 1986), p. 15-16. English. **DESCR:** Arte Publico Press; *Authors; Bilingual Review Press; Cisneros, Sandra; Hinojosa-Smith, Rolando R.; Keller, Gary D.; *Literature; Pineda, Cecile; Quinto Sol Publishing, Inc.; Rivera, Tomas; Soto, Gary.

238 Chavez, Noe M. Culminacion de una busqueda de identidad. LA COMUNIDAD, No. 252 (May 19, 1985), p. 4-6. Spanish. **DESCR:** *BLESS ME, ULTIMA; Identity; *Literary Criticism; Novel.

239 Gonzalez, LaVerne. Book review of: THE SILENCE OF THE LLANO. THE AMERICAS REVIEW, Vol. 15, no. 2 (Summer 1987), p. 109-111. English. **DESCR:** Book Reviews; *THE SILENCE OF THE LLANO.

240 Leal, Luis. Book review of: THE LEGEND OF LA LLORONA. LECTOR, Vol. 4, no. 1-3 (1986), p. [59]. English. **DESCR:** Book Reviews; *THE LEGEND OF LA LLORONA.

241 Lewis, Marvin A.; Striano, Ron; and Hiura, Barbara L. Chicano ethnicity and aging [and critiques]. EXPLORATIONS IN ETHNIC STUDIES, Vol. 8, no. 2 (July 1985), p. 35-45. English. **DESCR:** *Ancianos; BLESS ME, ULTIMA; Curanderas; FAMOUS ALL OVER TOWN; Identity; James, Dan; Literary Criticism; Literature.

242 Lomeli, Francisco A. En torno a la literatura...convergencia o divergencia? LA COMUNIDAD, No. 274 (October 20, 1985), p. 8-11. Spanish. **DESCR:** Aztlan; Border Region; HEART OF AZTLAN; *Literary Criticism; Mendez M., Miguel; PEREGRINOS DE AZTLAN; *Primer Festival de Literatura Fronteriza Mexico-Estados Unidos.

243 Ortiz, Francisco. La cultura chicana, la cultura amenazada. LA COMUNIDAD, No. 305 (May 25, 1986), p. 10-11. Spanish. **DESCR:** *BLESS ME, ULTIMA; Bloomfield, NM; *Censorship; Literary Criticism; New Mexico; Textbooks.

244 Padilla, Genaro Miguel. The anti-romantic city in Chicano fiction. PUERTO DEL SOL, Vol. 23, no. 1 (1987), p. 159-169. English. **DESCR:** Acosta, Oscar Zeta; *Fiction; Lattin, Vernon E.; *Literary Criticism; Morales, Alejandro; *Urban Communities.

245 Paredes, Raymund A. Book review of: CUENTOS CHICANOS: A SHORT STORY ANTHOLOGY. WESTERN AMERICAN LITERATURE, Vol. 21, no. 3 (1986), p. 270. English. **DESCR:** Book Reviews; *CUENTOS CHICANOS: A SHORT STORY ANTHOLOGY; Marquez, Antonio.

246 Ramirez, Arthur. Book review of: CUENTOS CHICANOS: A SHORT STORY ANTHOLOGY. SAN FRANCISCO REVIEW OF BOOKS, Vol. 11, (1986), p. 11,23. English. **DESCR:** Book Reviews; *CUENTOS CHICANOS: A SHORT STORY ANTHOLOGY; Marquez, Antonio; Short Story.

247 Torres, Lourdes. Book review of: A CHICANO IN CHINA. WESTERN AMERICAN LITERATURE, Vol. 22, (Spring 1987), p. 66. English. **DESCR:** *A CHICANO IN CHINA; Book Reviews.

Anaya, Toney, Governor of New Mexico

248 Beale, Stephen. MALDEF weathers a storm. HISPANIC BUSINESS, Vol. 9, no. 5 (May 1987), p. 10-11. English. **DESCR:** Civil Rights; Hernandez, Antonia A.; *Mexican American Legal Defense and Educational Fund (MALDEF); Organizations; Serna, Eric P.

249 Guerrero, Martha and Anaya, Toney. Toney Anaya: a man with convictions=Toney Anaya: un hombre de conviccion. AMERICAS 2001, Premiere Issue, 1987, p. 20-23, 44. Bilingual. **DESCR:** Biography; Elected Officials; New Mexico; Politics.

250 Hernandez prevails in fight over job. NUESTRO, Vol. 11, no. 2 (March 1987), p. 6. English. **DESCR:** *Hernandez, Antonia A.; *Mexican American Legal Defense and Educational Fund (MALDEF); Organizations.

Ancianos

251 Bastida, Elena B. Book review of: THE HISPANIC ELDERLY. CONTEMPORARY SOCIOLOGY: A JOURNAL OF REVIEWS, Vol. 14, no. 1 (January 1985), p. 41-42. English. **DESCR:** Becerra, Rosina; Book Reviews; Shaw, David; *THE HISPANIC ELDERLY: A RESEARCH REFERENCE GUIDE.

252 Canive, Jose. Book review of: MENTAL HEALTH AND HISPANIC AMERICANS: CLINICAL PERSPECTIVES. JOURNAL OF NERVOUS AND MENTAL DISEASE, Vol. 172, no. 9 (September 1984), p. 559-561. English. **DESCR:** Becerra, Rosina; Book Reviews; Escobar, Javier I.; Karno, Marvin; *MENTAL HEALTH AND HISPANIC AMERICANS: CLINICAL PERSPECTIVES.

253 Cardenas, Gilbert. Book review of: OLDER MEXICAN AMERICANS: A STUDY IN AN URBAN BARRIO. CONTEMPORARY SOCIOLOGY: A JOURNAL OF REVIEWS, Vol. 14, no. 2 (March 1985), p. 243-244. English. **DESCR:** Book Reviews; Gomez, Ernesto; Markides, Kyriakos S.; Martin, Harry; *OLDER MEXICAN AMERICANS: A STUDY IN AN URBAN BARRIO.

254 Catalano, Julia. Raul Jimenez. VISTA, Vol. 2, no. 3 (November 2, 1986), p. 6. English. **DESCR:** Holidays; Jimenez Food Products, Inc.; *Jimenez, Raul.

255 Cuellar, Jose and Weeks, John R. Hispanic elders' needs, problems and access to public benefits and services. LA RED/THE NET, no. 36 (November 1980), p. 2,16. English. **DESCR:** *San Diego, CA; Social Services.

256 Delgado, Melvin. Book review of: THE HISPANIC ELDERLY. SOCIAL WORK, Vol. 31, no. 2 (March, April, 1986), p. 153. English. **DESCR:** Becerra, Rosina; Book Reviews; Shaw, David; *THE HISPANIC ELDERLY: A RESEARCH REFERENCE GUIDE.

257 Domino, George. Sleep habits in the elderly: a study of three Hispanic cultures. JOURNAL OF CROSS-CULTURAL PSYCHOLOGY, Vol. 17, no. 1 (March 1986), p. 109-120. English. **DESCR:** *Comparative Psychology; Cultural Characteristics; Ethnic Groups.

Ancianos (cont.)

258 Kastenbaum, Robert. Book review of: OLDER MEXICAN AMERICANS: A STUDY IN AN URBAN BARRIO. INTERNATIONAL JOURNAL OF AGING & HUMAN DEVELOPMENT, Vol. 19, no. 1 (1984), p. 75-76. English. **DESCR:** Book Reviews; Markides, Kyriakos S.; Martin, Harry; *OLDER MEXICAN AMERICANS: A STUDY IN AN URBAN BARRIO.

259 Lacayo, Carmela G. Triple jeopardy among Hispanic elderly: results from first national needs assessment of older Hispanics. LA RED/THE NET, no. 56 (July 1982), p. 2-3. English. **DESCR:** Asociacion Nacional Pro Personas Mayores; *National Study to Assess the Service Needs of the Hispanic Elderly; Research Methodology; *Social Services; Surveys.

260 Lecca, Pedro J. and McNeil, John S. Cultural factors affecting the compliance of older Mexican-Americans with hypertension regimens. LA RED/THE NET, no. 74 (November 1983), p. 7-10. English. **DESCR:** *Dallas, TX; Medical Care.

261 Lewis, Marvin A.; Striano, Ron; and Hiura, Barbara L. Chicano ethnicity and aging [and critiques]. EXPLORATIONS IN ETHNIC STUDIES, Vol. 8, no. 2 (July 1985), p. 35-45. English. **DESCR:** Anaya, Rudolfo A.; BLESS ME, ULTIMA; Curanderas; FAMOUS ALL OVER TOWN; Identity; James, Dan; Literary Criticism; Literature.

262 Luevano, Richard. Attitudes of elderly Mexican Americans towards nursing homes in Stanislaus county. LA RED/THE NET, no. 45 (August 1981), p. 2. English. **DESCR:** Nursing Homes; *Stanislaus County, CA.

263 Manuel, Ron C. Book review of: OLDER MEXICAN AMERICANS: A STUDY IN AN URBAN BARRIO. JOURNAL OF GERONTOLOGY, Vol. 39, no. 4 (July 1984), p. 506-507. English. **DESCR:** Book Reviews; Markides, Kyriakos S.; Martin, Harry; *OLDER MEXICAN AMERICANS: A STUDY IN AN URBAN BARRIO.

264 Newquist, Deborah. The health care barrier model: toward analyzing the underutilization of health care by older Mexican-Americans. ANTHROPOLOGY UCLA, Vol. 14, (1985), p. 1-12. English. **DESCR:** *Cultural Characteristics; Discrimination; Folk Medicine; *Medical Care; Medical Clinics; *Public Health.

265 Quintana, Leroy V. [Cuando l'abuelita murio...]. EL CUADERNO, Vol. 4, no. 1 (Summer 1976), p. 20. Spanish. **DESCR:** *Poems.

AND THE EARTH DID NOT PART
USE: Y NO SE LO TRAGO LA TIERRA/AND THE EARTH DID NOT PART

Andrade, Ray

266 Vasquez, Victor. More on CHICO AND THE MAN. LATIN QUARTER, Vol. 1, no. 3 (January, February, 1975), p. 13-15. English. **DESCR:** Albertson, Jack; Artists; Boycotts; *CHICO AND THE MAN [television show]; Discrimination; Prinze, Freddie; Stereotypes; *Television.

Andrade, Sally

267 Urdaneta, Maria Luisa. Book review of: LATINO FAMILIES IN THE UNITED STATES. LA RED/THE NET, no. 78 (March 1984), p. 9-10. English. **DESCR:** Book Reviews; *LATINO FAMILIES IN THE UNITED STATES: A RESOURCE BOOK FOR FAMILY LIFE EDUCATION.

Andrews, Lynn V.

268 Castillo-Speed, Lillian. Chicana/Latina literature and criticism: reviews of recent books. WLW JOURNAL, Vol. 11, no. 3 (September 1987), p. 1-4. English. **DESCR:** *Book Reviews; BORDERS; Chavez, Denise; *Chicanas; CONTEMPORARY CHICANA POETRY: A CRITICAL APPROACH TO AN EMERGING LITERATURE; Flores, Angel; Flores, Kate; JAGUAR WOMAN; Mora, Pat; Sanchez, Marta Ester; Tafolla, Carmen; THE DEFIANT MUSE: HISPANIC FEMINIST POEMS FROM THE MIDDLE AGES TO THE PRESENT; THE LAST OF THE MENU GIRLS; TO SPLIT A HUMAN: MITOS, MACHOS Y LA MUJER CHICANA; Vigil-Pinon, Evangelina; WOMAN OF HER WORD: HISPANIC WOMEN WRITE.

Angel Flight

269 Gutierrez, Silvio G. On wings of mercy. VISTA, Vol. 2, no. 3 (November 2, 1986), p. 17-18. English. **DESCR:** *Emergency Services; Malibu, CA; Medical Care; *Torres, Averi; Torres, Dennis; Transportation.

Anglo Americans

270 Acosta, Frank X., et al. Preparing low-income Hispanic, Black, and white patients for psychotherapy: evaluation of a new orientation program. JOURNAL OF CLINICAL PSYCHOLOGY, Vol. 39, no. 6 (November 1983), p. 872-877. English. **DESCR:** Blacks; *Comparative Psychology; Mental Health; *Psychotherapy.

271 Baker, George A. and Rocha, Pedro, Jr. Critical incident competencies of Mexican American and Anglo American administrators. COMMUNITY/JUNIOR COLLEGE QUARTERLY OF RESEARCH AND PRACTICE, Vol. 7, no. 4 (July, September, 1983), p. 319-332. English. **DESCR:** *Community Colleges; Comparative Psychology; Cultural Characteristics; Educational Administration; Management; Public Policy.

272 Costello, Raymond M. Hispanic alcoholic treatment considerations. HISPANIC JOURNAL OF BEHAVIORAL SCIENCES, Vol. 9, no. 1 (March 1987), p. 83-89. English. **DESCR:** *Alcoholism; Mental Health Clinics.

273 Duncan, Marilyn H., et al. Childhood cancer epidemiology in New Mexico's American Indians, Hispanic whites, and non-Hispanic whites, 1970-82. JOURNAL OF THE NATIONAL CANCER INSTITUTE, Vol. 76, no. 6 (June 1986), p. 1013-1018. English. **DESCR:** *Cancer; *Children; Diseases; Native Americans.

274 Gaviria, Moises; Gil, Ana A.; and Javaid, Javaid I. Nortriptyline kinetics in Hispanic and Anglo subjects. JOURNAL OF CLINICAL PSYCHOPHARMACOLOGY, Vol. 6, no. 4 (1986), p. 227-231. English. **DESCR:** *Comparative Psychology; *Drug Use; Genetics; Public Health.

275 Gottdiener, M. Group differentiation in a metropolitan high school: the influence of race, class, gender and culture. QUALITATIVE SOCIOLOGY, Vol. 8, no. 1 (Spring 1985), p. 29-41. English. **DESCR:** Blacks; Identity; *Secondary School Education.

Anglo Americans (cont.)

276 Gynan, Shaw Nicholas. The influence of language background on attitudes toward native and nonnative Spanish. BILINGUAL REVIEW, Vol. 12, no. 1-2 (January, August, 1985), p. 33-42. English. **DESCR:** *Attitudes; *Foreign Language Instruction; Language Proficiency; *Language Usage; Spanish Language.

277 Molina, Robert M.; Brown, Kathryn H.; and Zavaleta, Antonio N. Relative lower extremity length in Mexican American and in American Black and white youth. AMERICAN JOURNAL OF PHYSICAL ANTHROPOLOGY, Vol. 72, (1987), p. 89-94. English. **DESCR:** *Anthropometry; Blacks; *Body Mass Index (BMI); U.S. Health Examination Survey (HES); Youth.

278 Neff, James Alan; Hoppe, Sue K.; and Perea, Patricia. Acculturation and alcohol use: drinking patterns and problems among Anglo and Mexican American male drinkers. HISPANIC JOURNAL OF BEHAVIORAL SCIENCES, Vol. 9, no. 2 (June 1987), p. 151-181. English. **DESCR:** *Acculturation; Age Groups; *Alcoholism; *Males; Stress.

279 Padilla, Eligio R. and O'Grady, Kevin E. Sexuality among Mexican Americans: a case of sexual stereotyping. JOURNAL OF PERSONALITY AND SOCIAL PSYCHOLOGY, Vol. 52, no. 1 (1987), p. 5-10. English. **DESCR:** Age Groups; Attitudes; Religion; *Sex Roles; *Stereotypes.

280 Powers, Stephen and Rossman, Mark H. Attributions for success and failure among Anglo, Black, Hispanic, and Native-American community-college students. JOURNAL OF PSYCHOLOGY, Vol. 117, no. 1 (May 1984), p. 27-31. English. **DESCR:** *Academic Achievement; Blacks; Community Colleges; *Locus of Control; Native Americans; Students.

281 Roberts, Robert E. and Vernon, Sally W. Minority status and psychological distress reexamined: the case of Mexican Americans. RESEARCH IN COMMUNITY AND MENTAL HEALTH, Vol. 4, (1984), p. 131-164. English. **DESCR:** Blacks; *Mental Illness.

282 Stern, Michael P. Epidemiology of diabetes and coronary heart disease among Mexican-Americans. TRANSACTIONS OF THE ASSOC. OF LIFE INSURANCE MEDICAL DIRECTORS, Vol. 67, (1983), p. 79-90. English. **DESCR:** *Diabetes; Heart Disease; *San Antonio, TX.

283 Tienda, Marta and Glass, Jennifer. Household structure and labor-force participation of Black, Hispanic, and white mothers. DEMOGRAPHY, Vol. 22, no. 3 (August 1985), p. 381-394. English. **DESCR:** Blacks; Chicanas; *Extended Family; *Family; *Sex Roles; *Working Women.

284 Trevino, Fernando M. Health indicators for Hispanic, Black and white Americans. VITAL AND HEALTH STATISTICS. SERIES 10, (September 1984), p. 1-88. English. **DESCR:** Blacks; *Medical Care; Statistics.

285 Verdugo, Naomi and Verdugo, Richard. Income differentials between Chicano and white male workers. LA RED/THE NET, no. 57 (August 1982), p. 2-3. English. **DESCR:** Employment; *Income; Laboring Classes; *Males.

286 Zippin, David H. and Hough, Richard L. Perceived self-other differences in life

events and mental health among Mexicans and Americans. JOURNAL OF PSYCHOLOGY, Vol. 119, no. 2 (March 1985), p. 143-155. English. **DESCR:** *Comparative Psychology; *Locus of Control; *Mental Health; Mexico; Psychiatry; *Stress.

Anheuser-Busch, Inc.

287 Hispanic marketing. ADVERTISING AGE MAGAZINE, Vol. 57, no. 16 (February 27, 1986), p. 11-51. English. **DESCR:** Adolph Coors Co.; Advertising; Allstate Insurance Co.; American Greetings; Business Enterprises; Coca-Cola Company; Consumers; Ford Motor Company; Hallmark Cards; *Marketing; Mass Media; McDonald's Corporation; Metropolitan Life Insurance Corporation; Pepsi-Cola Bottling Group; Prudential; Spanish International Network (SIN); State Farm Mutual Insurance; Tylenol; United Insurance Co. of America.

288 Kesler, Lori. A-B benefits from regional approach. ADVERTISING AGE MAGAZINE, Vol. 57, no. 16 (February 27, 1986), p. 48-49. English. **DESCR:** Advertising; Consumers; *Marketing.

Anselmo, Rene

289 Mass media bureau settlement would allow SICC to sell its stations. BROADCASTING, Vol. 110, no. 26 (June 30, 1986), p. 45. English. **DESCR:** Azcarraga Family; Federal Communications Commission (FCC); KDTV, San Francisco, CA [television station]; KFTV, Fresno, CA [television station]; KMEX, Los Angeles, CA [television station]; KTVW, Phoeniz, AZ [television station]; KWEX, San Antonio, TX [television station]; Legal Cases; *Spanish International Communications Corp. (SICC); Spanish International Network (SIN); Spanish Language; Television; WLTV, Miami, FL [television station]; WXTV, Paterson, NJ [television station].

290 SICC to sell off stations. BROADCASTING, Vol. 110, no. 20 (May 19, 1986), p. 79-80. English. **DESCR:** Federal Communications Commission (FCC); Fouce, Frank; KFTV, Fresno, CA [television station]; KMEX, Los Angeles, CA [television station]; KWEX, San Antonio, TX [television station]; Legal Cases; *Spanish International Communications Corp. (SICC); Spanish International Network (SIN); Spanish Language; Television; WLTV, Miami, FL [television station]; WXTV, Paterson, NJ [television station].

Anthony Quinn Library, East Los Angeles, CA

291 Gaspar, Tomas. Anthony Quinn Library receives collection=La Biblioteca Anthony Quinn recibe coleccion. AMERICAS 2001, Premiere Issue, 1987, p. 12-14. Bilingual. **DESCR:** *Library Collections; *Quinn, Anthony.

Anthropology

292 Braun, Barbara. The Aztecs: art and sacrifice. ART IN AMERICA, Vol. 72, no. 4 (April 1984), p. 126-139. English. **DESCR:** *Aztecs; Exhibits; Gods and Dieties; *Precolumbian Images; *Precolumbian Society; Templo Mayor, Tenochtitlan.

Anthropology (cont.)

293 Rosaldo, Renato. When natives talk back:
Chicano anthropology since the late 60s.
RENATO ROSALDO LECTURE SERIES MONOGRAPH,
Vol. 2, (Spring 1986), p. [3]-20. English.
DESCR: Culture; EL GRITO; *Identity;
Paredes, Americo; *Political Ideology;
*Research Methodology; Romano-V., Octavio
Ignacio; Valdez, Facundo.

Anthropometry

294 Molina, Robert M.; Brown, Kathryn H.; and
Zavaleta, Antonio N. Relative lower
extremity length in Mexican American and in
American Black and white youth. AMERICAN
JOURNAL OF PHYSICAL ANTHROPOLOGY, Vol. 72,
(1987), p. 89-94. English. DESCR: Anglo
Americans; Blacks; *Body Mass Index (BMI);
U.S. Health Examination Survey (HES); Youth.

Apodaca, Jeff

295 Sanchez, Tom. Jeff Apodaca. VISTA, Vol. 1,
no. 8 (April 6, 1986), p. 21. English.
DESCR: *Athletes; Diseases; Sports.

Apodaca, Jerry [Gov. of New Mexico]

296 Perez, Renato E. The business of Hispanics.
VISTA, Vol. 2, no. 1 (September 7, 1986), p.
10. English. DESCR: Adolph Coors Co.;
American G.I. Forum; Business; *Collective
Bargaining; Corporations; Cuban National
Planning Council, Inc. Washington, D.C.;
*Hispanic Association on Corporate
Responsibility (HACER); League of United
Latin American Citizens (LULAC); National
Council of La Raza (NCLR); National IMAGE;
U.S. Hispanic Chamber of Commerce.

Apodaca, Roseanne

297 Reyes, Sonia. Hispanic models pursue high
stakes fashion. VISTA, Vol. 1, no. 2
(October 5, 1985), p. 6-9. English. DESCR:
Careers; Dominguez, Peter; *Fashion; Jerez,
Alicia; Soto, Talisa.

Appointed Officials

298 de la Garza, Rodolfo O. On the question of
Chicano ambassadors. LA RED/THE NET, no. 66
(March 1983), p. 15-16. English. DESCR:
*United States-Mexico Relations.

299 Herb Fernandez to serve on presidential task
force. HISPANIC ENGINEER, Vol. 3, no. 5
(Winter 1987), p. 15. English. DESCR:
*Fernandez, Herb; U.S. Task Force on Women,
Minorities & the Handicapped in Science and
Technology.

300 Interview: Rita Ricardo-Campbell.
INTERCAMBIOS FEMENILES, Vol. 2, no. 6
(Spring 1987), p. 10-11. English. DESCR:
Chicanas; Economics; Leadership;
*Ricardo-Campbell, Rita.

301 Kilgore, Julia. A risk taker. HISPANIC
BUSINESS, Vol. 9, no. 12 (December 1987), p.
44-47. English. DESCR: Biography; Careers;
*Chicanas; *Diaz Dennis, Patricia; Federal
Communications Commission (FCC).

302 MAES chairman appointed to DEOMI board of
visitors. HISPANIC TIMES, Vol. 8, no. 3
(May, June, 1987), p. 42. English. DESCR:
*Cano, Oscar; Department of Defense Equal
Opportunities Management Institute (DEOMI);
Mexican American Engineering Society (MAES).

303 Palomo, Juan R. Ernest Garcia. VISTA, Vol.
1, no. 3 (November 3, 1985), p. 10. English.
DESCR: *Garcia, Ernest.

304 Patricia Diaz Dennis. INTERCAMBIOS
FEMENILES, Vol. 2, no. 6 (Spring 1987), p.
8-9. English. DESCR: Chicanas; *Diaz Dennis,
Patricia; Federal Communications Commission
(FCC); Leadership; Legal Profession.

Apportionment
USE: Reapportionment

Aragon [family name]

305 Instituto Genealogico e Historico
Latino-Americano. Rootsearch: Aragon:
Trujillo: Ruelas. VISTA, Vol. 2, no. 8
(April 4, 1987), p. 24. English. DESCR:
Genealogy; History; *Personal Names; *Ruelas
[family name]; *Trujillo [family name].

Aragones, Sergio

306 Padilla, Steve. The mad mad world of Sergio
Aragones. VISTA, Vol. 2, no. 5 (January 4,
1987), p. 6-8. English. DESCR: Artists;
Drawings; *Humor; *MAD Magazine.

Aranda, Benjamin

307 Families of the year. VISTA, Vol. 2, no. 2
(October 4, 1986), p. 16-18. English.
DESCR: Aguilar, Gregorio; Aguilar,
Guadalupe; *Aranda, Emma; *Awards; de la
Rocha, Beatriz; de la Rocha, Castulo;
Family; Guzman, Ofelia; Guzman, Roberto;
*Hispanic Family of the Year Award.

Aranda, Emma

308 Families of the year. VISTA, Vol. 2, no. 2
(October 4, 1986), p. 16-18. English.
DESCR: Aguilar, Gregorio; Aguilar,
Guadalupe; Aranda, Benjamin; *Awards; de la
Rocha, Beatriz; de la Rocha, Castulo;
Family; Guzman, Ofelia; Guzman, Roberto;
*Hispanic Family of the Year Award.

Arbitron

309 Berling-Manuel, Lynn. Expanding radio market
battles research static. ADVERTISING AGE
MAGAZINE, Vol. 57, no. 43 (August 11, 1986),
p. S12-S16. English. DESCR: Marketing;
*Radio; Spanish Language; WADO-AM, New York,
NY [radio station]; WAQI-AM, Miami, FL
[radio station]; WOJO-FM, Chicago, IL [radio
station].

310 Rubin, Marcy Gray. Advertiser apathy hampers
TV growth. ADVERTISING AGE MAGAZINE, Vol.
57, no. 43 (August 11, 1986), p. S22-S23.
English. DESCR: *Advertising; Spanish
International Network (SIN); Spanish
Language; Strategy Research Corp.;
Television.

Architecture

311 Arreola, Daniel D. Mexican restaurants in
Tucson. JOURNAL OF CULTURAL GEOGRAPHY, Vol.
3, no. 2 (Spring, Summer, 1983), p. 108-114.
English. DESCR: Landscape Architecture;
*Restaurants; Tucson, AZ.

312 Betsky, Aaron. The Spanish influence:
architecture in America. HORIZON: A MAGAZINE
OF THE ARTS, Vol. 28, no. 10 (December
1985), p. 53-68. English. DESCR:
Photography; Spanish Influence.

Archives

313 Chabran, Richard. Book review of: MEXICAN AMERICAN ARCHIVES AT THE BENSON COLLECTION: A GUIDE FOR USERS. LA RED/THE NET, no. 52 (March 1982), p. 6-7. English. **DESCR:** Book Reviews; Flores, Maria; *Gutierrez-Witt, Laura; *MEXICAN AMERICAN ARCHIVES AT THE BENSON COLLECTION.

314 McKanna, Clare V. The San Quentin prison pardon papers: a look at file no. 1808, the case of Francisco Javier Bonilla. SOUTHERN CALIFORNIA QUARTERLY, Vol. 67, no. 2 (Summer 1985), p. 187-196. English. **DESCR:** Administration of Justice; *Bonilla, Francisco Javier; *Criminal Justice System; History; *Prisoners; *San Quentin Prison.

Archuleta, Eppie

315 Middleman, Irene. Eppie Archuleta. VISTA, Vol. 1, no. 7 (March 2, 1986), p. 14. English. **DESCR:** *Artists; Arts and Crafts; National Heritage Fellowship.

Arciniega, Miguel

316 Luzod, Jimmy. Book review of: PARENTING MODELS AND MEXICAN AMERICANS: A PROCESS ANALYSIS. LA RED/THE NET, no. 71 (August 1983), p. 8-11. English. **DESCR:** Book Reviews; Casaus, Luis; Castillo, Max; *PARENTING MODELS AND MEXICAN AMERICANS: A PROCESS ANALYSIS (2nd ed.).

Arellano, Estevan

317 Atencio, Tomas. No estan todos los que son, no son todos los que estan. EL CUADERNO, Vol. 4, no. 1 (Summer 1976), p. 51-61. Spanish. **DESCR:** *Identity; *La Academia de la Nueva Raza, Dixon, NM; Lovato, Alberto; Martinez, Vicente; Roybal, Luis.

Arguelles-Vasquez v. INS

318 Canby, J. Immigration board can't use evidence from stop based only on Hispanic appearance. CRIMINAL LAW REPORTER, Vol. 39, no. 5 (April 30, 1986), p. 2076. English. **DESCR:** *Search and Seizure; U.S. v. Brignoni-Ponce.

Arias, Ron

319 Bartlett, Catherine Vallejos. Magical realism: the Latin American influence on modern Chicano writers. CONFLUENCIA, Vol. 1, no. 2 (Spring 1986), p. 27-37. English. **DESCR:** Authors; Garcia Marquez, Gabriel; Latin America; *Literary Criticism; *Literary Influence; *Literature; Magical realism; ONE HUNDRED YEARS OF SOLITUDE; Rivera, Tomas; THE ROAD TO TAMAZUNCHALE; Y NO SE LO TRAGO LA TIERRA/AND THE EARTH DID NOT PART.

Arizona

320 Coerver, Don and Hall, Linda B. The Arizona-Sonora border and the Mexican revolution, 1910-1920. JOURNAL OF THE WEST, Vol. 24, no. 2 (1985), p. 75-87. English. **DESCR:** Arizona Rangers; *History; Sonora, Mexico; *Villa, Pancho.

321 Padilla, Raymond V. and Montiel, Miguel. A general framework for action in Chicano higher education. LA RED/THE NET, no. 81 (June 1964), p. 2-6. English. **DESCR:** Evaluation (Educational); *Higher Education.

Arizona Association of Chicanos for Higher Education (AACHE)

322 Perez, Emma. Higher education organizations. LA RED/THE NET, no. 97 (June 1986), p. 4-5. English. **DESCR:** *Educational Organizations; *Higher Education.

Arizona Bank, Phoenix, AZ

323 Arizona Bank targets Hispanic market. ABA BANKING JOURNAL, Vol. 77, no. 4 (April 1985), p. 30, 32. English. **DESCR:** *Banking Industry; Marketing.

Arizona Rangers

324 Coerver, Don and Hall, Linda B. The Arizona-Sonora border and the Mexican revolution, 1910-1920. JOURNAL OF THE WEST, Vol. 24, no. 2 (1985), p. 75-87. English. **DESCR:** Arizona; *History; Sonora, Mexico; *Villa, Pancho.

Armengol, Armando

325 Garcia, Nasario. El cuento chicano visto por dentro y por fuera. BILINGUAL REVIEW, Vol. 12, no. 3 (September, December, 1985), p. 262-265. Spanish. **DESCR:** Aguilar, Ricardo; Book Reviews; *PALABRA NUEVA: CUENTOS CHICANOS; Somoza, Oscar U.

Arnaz, Desi

326 Perez, Renato E. As American as babalu. VISTA, Vol. 2, no. 6 (February 8, 1987), p. 22. English. **DESCR:** *Acculturation; Essays; I LOVE LUCY; Television.

Arora, Shirley L.

327 Duran, Richard P. Article review of: "Proverbs in Mexican-American Tradition". LA RED/THE NET, no. 56 (July 1982), p. 6-7. English. **DESCR:** *Dichos; *"Proverbs in Mexican-American Tradition".

Arreguin, Alfredo

328 Cox, Charlene B. Motivos artisticos. AMERICAS, Vol. 37, no. 1 (January, February, 1985), p. 2-5, 64. Spanish. **DESCR:** *Artists; Folk Art; *Mexican Art; Paintings.

Art

329 Barragan, Ma. Antonieta. Carlos Almaraz: "El arte contemporaneo no tiene mucha emocion, es estatico...". LA COMUNIDAD, No. 324 (October 5, 1986), p. 10-11. Spanish. **DESCR:** *Almaraz, Carlos; Biography.

330 Bell, David. Report from Sante Fe: figuration and fantasy. ART IN AMERICA, Vol. 72, no. 1 (January 1984), p. 31-35. English. **DESCR:** Exhibits; *Santa Fe Festival of the Arts.

331 Chavez, Lorenzo A. The eyes of Texas are upon them. VISTA, Vol. 2, no. 2 (October 4, 1986), p. 20. English. **DESCR:** Cardenas, David; *Chulas Fronteras [art exhibit]; Espada, Ibsen; Gonzalez, Patricia; Hernandez, John; Huerta, Benito; Martinez, Cesar Augusto.

332 Chavez, Lorenzo A. Images of ethnic pride. VISTA, Vol. 3, no. 2 (October 3, 1987), p. 20-21. English. **DESCR:** Children's Art; *McDonald's Corporation.

Art (cont.)

333 Gamboa, Harry, Jr. El artista chicano dentro
    y fuera de la "corriente" artistica. LA
    COMUNIDAD, No. 351 (April 12, 1987), 2-5+.
    Spanish. **DESCR:** Artists; Carrasco, Barbara;
    Gamboa, Diane; Gronk (Pseud.); Martinez,
    Daniel J.; Valadez, John; Valdez, Patssi.

334 Gambrell, Jamey. Texas: state of the art.
    ART IN AMERICA, Vol. 75, no. 3 (March 1987),
    p. 114-131+. English. **DESCR:** Art Galleries;
    Art Organizations and Groups; *Artists; Dia
    de los Muertos; Folk Art; Mexican Art;
    Texas.

335 Goldman, Shifra. Arte chicano: iconografia
    de la autodeterminacion. LA COMUNIDAD, No.
    336 (December 28, 1986), p. 12-14+. Spanish.
    DESCR: Discrimination; EL PLAN ESPIRITUAL DE
    AZTLAN; History; Identity; Nationalism;
    Pachucos; Social Classes; *Symbolism.

336 Goldman, Shifra. El arte hispano en Houston.
    LA COMUNIDAD, No. 361 (June 21, 1987), p.
    6-7+. Spanish. **DESCR:** Exhibits; *HISPANIC
    ART IN THE UNITED STATES: THIRTY
    CONTEMPORARY PAINTERS & SCULPTORS
    [exhibition]; Houston, TX.

337 Goldman, Shifra. En medio de la tormenta de
    "Gronk". LA COMUNIDAD, No. 313 (July 20,
    1986), p. 8-9. Spanish. **DESCR:** Artists;
    Biography; *Gronk (Pseud.)

338 Goldman, Shifra. Escena de San Diego: texto
    y contexto. LA COMUNIDAD, No. 239 (February
    17, 1985), p. 6-7. Spanish. **DESCR:** Avalos,
    David; Chicano Park, San Diego, CA;
    Exhibits; *NUEVE ARTISTAS CHICANOS
    [exhibit]; San Diego, CA; Torres, Salvador
    Roberto; Ulloa, Domingo.

339 Goldman, Shifra. Hecho en Aztlan. LA
    COMUNIDAD, No. 278 (November 17, 1985), p.
    8-9. Spanish. **DESCR:** Centro Cultural de la
    Raza, San Diego, CA; Exhibits; *HECHO EN
    AZTLAN [exhibit].

340 Goldman, Shifra. Zarco Guerrero: tradicion y
    transformacion. LA COMUNIDAD, No. 249 (April
    28, 1985), p. 2-3. Spanish. **DESCR:**
    Biography; *Guerrero, Adolfo "El Zarco";
    Masks; Sculpture.

341 Gomez Pena, Guillermo. Dialogos fronterizos.
    LA COMUNIDAD, No. 263 (August 4, 1985), p.
    2-3. Spanish. **DESCR:** Avalos, David; Border
    Region; DIALOGOS FRONTERIZOS [radio
    program]; Osorio, Armando.

342 Gomez Pena, Guillermo. Nuevo continente
    artistico. LA COMUNIDAD, No. 275 (October
    27, 1985), p. 8-10. Spanish. **DESCR:** Artists;
    Border Region; Chicano Movement; DIALOGOS DE
    LAS AMERICAS; Indigenismo; International
    Relations; Mexico; United States-Mexico
    Relations.

343 A grand Hispanic art show. VISTA, Vol. 2,
    no. 8 (April 4, 1987), p. 20-21. English.
    DESCR: Art Galleries; *HISPANIC ART IN THE
    UNITED STATES: THIRTY CONTEMPORARY PAINTERS
    & SCULPTORS [exhibition].

344 Major exhibition planned by UCLA. NUESTRO,
    Vol. 11, no. 1-2 (1987), p. 6-7. English.
    DESCR: *Exhibits; *Wight Art Gallery,
    University of California, Los Angeles.

345 Olivares, Julian. Hispanic art in the United
    States: thirty contemporary painters &
    sculptors. THE AMERICAS REVIEW, Vol. 15, no.
    2 (Summer 1987), p. 7-10. English. **DESCR:**
    *Exhibits; *HISPANIC ART IN THE UNITED
    STATES: THIRTY CONTEMPORARY PAINTERS &
    SCULPTORS [exhibition].

346 Rosas, Alejandro. Proyecto de arte latino en
    Los Angeles. LA COMUNIDAD, No. 251 (May 12,
    1985), p. 4-5. Spanish. **DESCR:** Art
    Galleries; *Galeria Ocaso, Los Angeles, CA;
    Gamboa, Manazar; Gronk (Pseud.)

347 Rosas, Alejandro. Siete fotografos latinos
    en Los Angeles. LA COMUNIDAD, No. 241 (March
    3, 1985), p. 4-5. Spanish. **DESCR:** Aguilar,
    Laura; Avila, Adam; Callwood, Dennis O.;
    Carlos, Jesus; Exhibits; Miranda, Judy;
    *Photography; Self-Help Graphics, Los
    Angeles, CA; *SEVEN LATINO
    PHOTOGRAPHERS=SIETE FOTOGRAFOS LATINOS;
    Thewlis, Alan; Valverde, Richard.

348 Schon, Elizabeth. Introducing pre-Columbian
    and Hispanic art and artists to young adults
    through recent books. JOURNAL OF READING,
    Vol. 27, no. 3 (December 1983), p. 248-251.
    English. **DESCR:** Artists; *Bibliography;
    Precolumbian Images.

349 Shaw, Katherine. Mira! a look at America's
    Hispanic artists. VISTA, Vol. 1, no. 5
    (January 5, 1986), p. 6-8. English. **DESCR:**
    Artists; Canadian Club Hispanic Art Tour;
    Delgadillo, Ramon; Gamboa, Diane; Gonzalez,
    Nivia; *Trevino, Jesus (Jesse).

Art Galleries

350 Gambrell, Jamey. Texas: state of the art.
    ART IN AMERICA, Vol. 75, no. 3 (March 1987),
    p. 114-131+. English. **DESCR:** *Art; Art
    Organizations and Groups; *Artists; Dia de
    los Muertos; Folk Art; Mexican Art; Texas.

351 A grand Hispanic art show. VISTA, Vol. 2,
    no. 8 (April 4, 1987), p. 20-21. English.
    DESCR: *Art; *HISPANIC ART IN THE UNITED
    STATES: THIRTY CONTEMPORARY PAINTERS &
    SCULPTORS [exhibition].

352 Rosas, Alejandro. Proyecto de arte latino en
    Los Angeles. LA COMUNIDAD, No. 251 (May 12,
    1985), p. 4-5. Spanish. **DESCR:** *Art;
    *Galeria Ocaso, Los Angeles, CA; Gamboa,
    Manazar; Gronk (Pseud.)

Art History

353 Adams, Clinton. Book review of: ART IN NEW
    MEXICO, 1900-1945: PATHS TO TAOS AND SANTA
    FE. ARTSPACE, Vol. 10, (Fall 1986), p.
    34-36. English. **DESCR:** *ART IN NEW MEXICO,
    1900-1945: PATHS TO TAOS AND SANTA FE; Book
    Reviews; Eldredge, Charles; Exhibits;
    Schimmel, Julie; Truettner, William H.

354 Prehispanic America: a revelation. VISTA,
    Vol. 2, no. 6 (February 8, 1987), p. 18-20.
    English. **DESCR:** *Bowers Museum, Santa Ana,
    CA; *Precolumbian Society.

ART IN NEW MEXICO, 1900-1945: PATHS TO TAOS AND SANTA FE

355 Adams, Clinton. Book review of: ART IN NEW
    MEXICO, 1900-1945: PATHS TO TAOS AND SANTA
    FE. ARTSPACE, Vol. 10, (Fall 1986), p.
    34-36. English. **DESCR:** *Art History; Book
    Reviews; Eldredge, Charles; Exhibits;
    Schimmel, Julie; Truettner, William H.

Art Organizations and Groups

356 Gambrell, Jamey. Texas: state of the art. ART IN AMERICA, Vol. 75, no. 3 (March 1987), p. 114-131+. English. **DESCR:** *Art; Art Galleries; *Artists; Dia de los Muertos; Folk Art; Mexican Art; Texas.

Artco Contracting, Inc., Auburn Hills, MI

357 The top 100--profiles. HISPANIC BUSINESS, Vol. 9, no. 11 (November 1987), p. 31-50. English. **DESCR:** *Business Enterprises; Computer Trade Development Corp, Birmingham, MI; Corella Electric Inc., Phoenix, AZ; GSE Construction Co., Inc., Livermore, CA; National Systems & Research Co.; Unique Construction Co., Hillside, IL.

ARTE CHICANO

358 Castillo-Speed, Lillian. Annotated bibliography. LA RED/THE NET, no. 93 (January, February, 1986), p. 14-17. English. **DESCR:** A BIBLIOGRAPHY OF MEXICAN AMERICAN HISTORY; Book Reviews; Caballero, Cesar; CHICANO LITERATURE: A REFERENCE GUIDE; CHICANO ORGANIZATIONS DIRECTORY; CHICANO PERIODICAL INDEX; Goldman, Shifra M.; HISPANIC ALMANAC; HISPANIC MENTAL HEALTH RESEARCH: A REFERENCE GUIDE; Lomeli, Francisco A.; Martinez, Julio A.; Meier, Matt S.; Newton, Frank; *Reference Works; Ybarra-Frausto, Tomas.

Arte Publico Press

359 Bruce-Novoa, Juan. Meet the writers of the 80s. VISTA, Vol. 1, no. 11 (July 6, 1986), p. 15-16. English. **DESCR:** Anaya, Rudolfo A.; *Authors; Bilingual Review Press; Cisneros, Sandra; Hinojosa-Smith, Rolando R.; Keller, Gary D.; *Literature; Pineda, Cecile; Quinto Sol Publishing, Inc.; Rivera, Tomas; Soto, Gary.

Arthritis

360 Lorig, Kate R., et al. Converging and diverging beliefs about arthritis: Caucasian patients, Spanish speaking patients, and physicians. JOURNAL OF RHEUMATOLOGY, Vol. 11, no. 1 (February 1984), p. 76-79. English. **DESCR:** *Health Education.

Artists

361 Aceves Madrid, Vicente. Controversy surrounding NBC's CHICO AND THE MAN. LATIN QUARTER, Vol. 1, no. 2 (October 1974), p. 5-7. English. **DESCR:** Albertson, Jack; *CHICO AND THE MAN [television show]; Komack, James; Prinze, Freddie; Stereotypes; Teatros Unidos; *Television.

362 Blanco, Gilbert M. A vehicle for positive change. LATIN QUARTER, Vol. 1, no. 2 (October 1974), p. 27-30. English. **DESCR:** East Los Angeles, CA; *Estrada Courts, Los Angeles, CA; *Mural Art.

363 Cardinal, Roger. El mensaje de Martin Ramirez. LA COMUNIDAD, No. 361 (June 21, 1987), p. 2-3+. Spanish. **DESCR:** Biography; *Ramirez, Martin (1885-1960).

364 Cerda, Gabriela. Hidden jewel: the Frida Kahlo house of Coyoacan. NOTEBOOK: A LITTLE MAGAZINE, Vol. 1, no. 1 (1985), p. 2-7. English. **DESCR:** Biography; *Kahlo, Frida.

365 Cespedes, Marisa. "Que viva la vida" biografia de Frida Kahlo. LA COMUNIDAD, No. 345 (March 1, 1987), p. 12-13. Spanish.

366 Cox, Charlene B. Motivos artisticos. AMERICAS, Vol. 37, no. 1 (January, February, 1985), p. 2-5, 64. Spanish. **DESCR:** *Arreguin, Alfredo; Folk Art; *Mexican Art; Paintings.

367 Galeria 2001. AMERICAS 2001, Vol. 1, no. 3 (November, December, 1987), p. [8-9]. Bilingual. **DESCR:** Biographical Notes; *Gamboa, Harry, Jr.; Photography.

368 Gamboa, Harry, Jr. El artista chicano dentro y fuera de la "corriente" artistica. LA COMUNIDAD, No. 351 (April 12, 1987), 2-5+. Spanish. **DESCR:** *Art; Carrasco, Barbara; Gamboa, Diane; Gronk (Pseud.); Martinez, Daniel J.; Valadez, John; Valdez, Patssi.

369 Gambrell, Jamey. Texas: state of the art. ART IN AMERICA, Vol. 75, no. 3 (March 1987), p. 114-131+. English. **DESCR:** *Art; Art Galleries; Art Organizations and Groups; Dia de los Muertos; Folk Art; Mexican Art; Texas.

370 Goldman, Shifra. El arte social de Domingo Ulloa. LA COMUNIDAD, No. 277 (November 10, 1985), p. 8-9. Spanish. **DESCR:** Biography; *Ulloa, Domingo.

371 Goldman, Shifra. En medio de la tormenta de "Gronk". LA COMUNIDAD, No. 313 (July 20, 1986), p. 8-9. Spanish. **DESCR:** *Art; Biography; *Gronk (Pseud.)

372 Gomez Pena, Guillermo. Nuevo continente artistico. LA COMUNIDAD, No. 275 (October 27, 1985), p. 8-10. Spanish. **DESCR:** *Art; Border Region; Chicano Movement; DIALOGOS DE LAS AMERICAS; Indigenismo; International Relations; Mexico; United States-Mexico Relations.

373 Gonzalez, Miguel. Frida Kahlo entre la vida y la pasion artistica. LA COMUNIDAD, No. 345 (March 1, 1987), p. 8-10. Spanish. **DESCR:** *Biography; *Kahlo, Frida.

374 Haley, Lindsey. Gronk y su inquietante concepto del arte. LA COMUNIDAD, No. 252 (May 19, 1985), p. 2-3. Spanish. **DESCR:** ASCO [art group], Los Angeles, CA; Biography; Exhibits; *Gronk (Pseud.); OFF THE STREETS [exhibit].

375 The institute, the artist, the art. NUESTRO, Vol. 11, no. 4 (May 1987), p. 15-17. English. **DESCR:** *Gonzales, Edward; Mural Art; *Technical-Vocational Institute (T-V), Albuquerque, NM.

376 Malaspina, Ann. The city is my canvas. VISTA, Vol. 2, no. 3 (November 2, 1986), p. 14-15. English. **DESCR:** *Galvez, Daniel; Hispanic Murals Project (Cambridge, MA); *Mural Art; Oakland, CA.

377 Middleman, Irene. Eppie Archuleta. VISTA, Vol. 1, no. 7 (March 2, 1986), p. 14. English. **DESCR:** *Archuleta, Eppie; Arts and Crafts; National Heritage Fellowship.

378 Padilla, Steve. The mad mad world of Sergio Aragones. VISTA, Vol. 2, no. 5 (January 4, 1987), p. 6-8. English. **DESCR:** Aragones, Sergio; Drawings; *Humor; *MAD Magazine.

379 Pena, Margarita. Apuntes para un retrato chicano (I). LA COMUNIDAD, No. 270 (September 22, 1985), p. 12-14. Spanish. **DESCR:** *Biography; *Garza, Jose.

Artists (cont.)

380 Pena, Margarita. Apuntes para un retrato chicano (II). LA COMUNIDAD, No. 271 (September 29, 1985), p. 15. Spanish. **DESCR:** *Biography; *Garza, Jose.

381 Rivera, Diego. Frida Kahlo y el arte mexicano. LA COMUNIDAD, No. 345 (March 1, 1987), p. 6-7+. Spanish. **DESCR:** *Biography; *Kahlo, Frida.

382 Saul Solache: contemporary Chicano artist. LATIN QUARTER, Vol. 1, no. 3 (January, February, 1975), p. 24-26. English. **DESCR:** Exhibits; Mural Art; Paintings; *Solache, Saul.

383 Schon, Elizabeth. Introducing pre-Columbian and Hispanic art and artists to young adults through recent books. JOURNAL OF READING, Vol. 27, no. 3 (December 1983), p. 248-251. English. **DESCR:** Art; *Bibliography; Precolumbian Images.

384 Shaw, Katherine. Mira! a look at America's Hispanic artists. VISTA, Vol. 1, no. 5 (January 5, 1986), p. 6-8. English. **DESCR:** *Art; Canadian Club Hispanic Art Tour; Delgadillo, Ramon; Gamboa, Diane; Gonzalez, Nivia; *Trevino, Jesus (Jesse).

385 Sykes, Maltby. Diego Rivera and the Hotel Reforma murals. ARCHIVES OF AMERICAN ART JOURNAL, Vol. 25, no. 1-2 (1985), p. 29-40. English. **DESCR:** Hotel Reforma, Mexico City; Marxism; Mexico City; Mural Art; *Rivera, Diego.

386 Vasquez, Victor. More on CHICO AND THE MAN. LATIN QUARTER, Vol. 1, no. 3 (January, February, 1975), p. 13-15. English. **DESCR:** Albertson, Jack; Andrade, Ray; Boycotts; *CHICO AND THE MAN [television show]; Discrimination; Prinze, Freddie; Stereotypes; *Television.

387 Zesch, Lindy. Visa issue heats up: PEN hopes for "group waiver" of denials. AMERICAN THEATRE, Vol. 2, no. 8 (November 1985), p. 24. English. **DESCR:** Authors; Book Reviews; GETTING IN: A GUIDE TO OVERCOMING THE POLITICAL DENIAL OF NON-IMMIGRANT VISAS; National Lawyer's Guild; Politics; *Visas.

Arts and Crafts

388 Chavanell, Joe. Folk art's gift of Christmas joy. VISTA, Vol. 3, no. 4 (December 6, 1987), p. 8, 16. English. **DESCR:** Mexican Art.

389 Middleman, Irene. Eppie Archuleta. VISTA, Vol. 1, no. 7 (March 2, 1986), p. 14. English. **DESCR:** *Archuleta, Eppie; *Artists; National Heritage Fellowship.

390 Wroth, William. New hope in hard times: Hispanic crafts are revived during troubled years. PALACIO, Vol. 89, no. 2 (1983), p. 22-31. English. **DESCR:** *Las Lunas Vocational Training School; New Mexico; Spanish Colonial Arts Society; Taos Vocational School; Works Progress Administration (WPA).

ASCO [art group], Los Angeles, CA

391 Haley, Lindsey. Gronk y su inquietante concepto del arte. LA COMUNIDAD, No. 252 (May 19, 1985), p. 2-3. Spanish. **DESCR:** *Artists; Biography; Exhibits; *Gronk (Pseud.); OFF THE STREETS [exhibit].

Asencio, John

392 Levin, Gary. Publisher seeks to improve "image". ADVERTISING AGE MAGAZINE, Vol. 57, no. 43 (August 11, 1986), p. S25-S27. English. **DESCR:** Advertising; English Language; *HISPANIC IMAGE; Magazines; Spanish Language.

La Asociacion Hispano-Americana de Madres y Esposas, Tucson, AZ

393 Marin, Christine. La Asociacion Hispano-Americana de Madres y Esposas: Tucson's Mexican American women in World War II. RENATO ROSALDO LECTURE SERIES MONOGRAPH, Vol. 1, (Summer 1985), p. [5]-18. English. **DESCR:** *Chicanas; Cultural Organizations; History; Organizations; *Tucson, AZ; World War II.

Asociacion Nacional Pro Personas Mayores

394 Lacayo, Carmela G. Triple jeopardy among Hispanic elderly: results from first national needs assessment of older Hispanics. LA RED/THE NET, no. 56 (July 1982), p. 2-3. English. **DESCR:** *Ancianos; *National Study to Assess the Service Needs of the Hispanic Elderly; Research Methodology; *Social Services; Surveys.

ASPECTS OF AMERICAN HISPANIC AND INDIAN INVOLVEMENT IN BIOMEDICAL RESEARCH

395 Luzod, Jimmy. Book review of: ASPECTS OF AMERICAN HISPANIC AND INDIAN INVOLVEMENT IN BIOMEDICAL RESEARCH. LA RED/THE NET, no. 79 (April 1984), p. 9-13. English. **DESCR:** Book Reviews; Martinez, Diana I.; Martinez, J.V.; Science.

Assertiveness

396 Galindo-Ramirez, Tina. Educacion monolingue: opresion o liberacion? REVISTA MUJERES, Vol. 1, no. 1 (January 1984), p. 8-9. Spanish. **DESCR:** Alienation; Biography; *Education; English Language; *Identity.

Assimilation

397 Fernandez, Edward and Cresce, Arthur R. The Hispanic foreign-born and the assimilation experience. MIGRATION WORLD MAGAZINE, Vol. 14, no. 5 (1986), p. 7-11. English. **DESCR:** *Immigrants; Naturalization; *Socioeconomic Factors; Undocumented Workers.

398 Massey, Douglas S. and Mullan, Brendan P. Processes of Hispanic and Black spatial assimilation. AMERICAN JOURNAL OF SOCIOLOGY, Vol. 89, no. 4 (January 1984), p. 836-873. English. **DESCR:** Blacks; Census; *Ethnic Stratification; *Residential Segregation; *Social Mobility.

399 Panas, Katia. Postsecondary retention and graduation: strategies for change. REVISTA MUJERES, Vol. 4, no. 1 (January 1987), p. 66-72. English. **DESCR:** Discrimination in Education; *Education; Higher Education.

400 Reilly, Michael D. and Wallendorf, Melanie. A longitudinal study of Mexican-American assimilation. ADVANCES IN CONSUMER RESEARCH, Vol. 11, (1984), p. 735-740. English. **DESCR:** *Consumers; Culture; Food Practices; *Marketing.

Association of Minority Engineers (AME)

401 Gonzalez, Lawrence F. The University of
    Illinois, Chicago. HISPANIC ENGINEER, Vol.
    3, no. 3 (1987), p. 34-36. English. DESCR:
    Colleges and Universities; Society of
    Hispanic Professional Engineers (SHPE);
    *University of Illinois, Chicago, IL.

Astin, Alexander W.

402 Manning, Winston, et al. Book review of:
    MINORITIES IN AMERICAN HIGHER EDUCATION:
    RECENT TRENDS, CURRENT PROSPECTS AND
    RECOMMENDATIONS. LA RED/THE NET, no. 60
    (Fall 1982), p. 1-22. English. DESCR: Book
    Reviews; Ethnic Groups; *MINORITIES IN
    AMERICAN HIGHER EDUCATION: RECENT TRENDS,
    CURRENT PROSPECTS AND RECOMMENDATIONS.

Astronauts

403 Pinon, Fernando. Conquistadors of space.
    VISTA, Vol. 1, no. 4 (December 7, 1985), p.
    6-9. English. DESCR: Biography; *Chang-Diaz,
    Franklin; *Gutierrez, Sidney.

Athletes

404 Allsup, Dan. Run Reuben run. VISTA, Vol. 1,
    no. 12 (August 2, 1986), p. 18. English.
    DESCR: *Reina, Reuben; San Antonio, TX;
    Sports.

405 Barnes, Jill. The Latin pitch. VISTA, Vol.
    2, no. 9 (May 3, 1987), p. 6-8. English.
    DESCR: *Baseball.

406 Barnes, Jill. The winning formula of Nancy
    Lopez. VISTA, Vol. 2, no. 12 (August 1,
    1987), p. 6-9. English. DESCR: Biography;
    *Lopez, Nancy.

407 Chavez, Lorenzo A. Pancho Gonzales:
    pioneering champion. VISTA, Vol. 1, no. 8
    (April 6, 1986), p. 16. English. DESCR:
    *Gonzales, Richard "Pancho".

408 Chavez, Lorenzo A. Tennis superstars. VISTA,
    Vol. 1, no. 8 (April 6, 1986), p. 14-16.
    English. DESCR: Chicanas; Fernandez, Gigi;
    Fernandez, Mary Joe; *Sabatini, Gabriela;
    Sports; Torres, Michele; Women.

409 Johnson, Richard. The California housewife
    who succeeds as brave bullfighter. VISTA,
    Vol. 1, no. 5 (January 5, 1986), p. 12-15.
    English. DESCR: Chicanas; *Martinez, Raquel;
    Montes, Miguel; Munoz, Jesus.

410 Lit, Ed. Paul Gonzalez [sic]. VISTA, Vol. 1,
    no. 5 (January 5, 1986), p. 10. English.
    DESCR: *Boxing; East Los Angeles, CA;
    *Gonzales, Paul [Olympic boxer].

411 Quintana, Al. Gaining yardage in football.
    VISTA, Vol. 1, no. 2 (October 5, 1985), p.
    10-11. English. DESCR: Casillas, Tony;
    *Flores, Tom; Sports.

412 Sanchez, Tom. Jeff Apodaca. VISTA, Vol. 1,
    no. 8 (April 6, 1986), p. 21. English.
    DESCR: *Apodaca, Jeff; Diseases; Sports.

413 Viuker, Steve. Man with the golden toe.
    VISTA, Vol. 3, no. 2 (October 3, 1987), p.
    6, 24. English. DESCR: *Allegre, Raul;
    *Football.

Attitudes

414 Aboud, Frances E. and Skerry, Shelagh A. The
    development of ethnic attitudes: a critical
    review. JOURNAL OF CROSS-CULTURAL

PSYCHOLOGY, Vol. 15, no. 1 (March 1984), p.
3-34. English. DESCR: Cognition; *Identity.

415 Attitudes are changing while women go to
    work. HISPANIC TIMES, Vol. 8, no. 3 (May,
    June, 1987), p. 14. English. DESCR: *Sex
    Roles; *Working Women.

416 Barger, W.K. Public attitudes towards
    Mexican-American farmworkers in the Midwest.
    LA RED/THE NET, no. 63 (January 1983), p.
    2-4. English. DESCR: *Farm Workers;
    *Midwestern States; *Public Opinion.

417 Barger, W.K. Views of California farmworkers
    regarding the farm labor movement. LA
    RED/THE NET, no. 91 (October 1985), p. 3-5.
    English. DESCR: Agricultural Labor Unions;
    California; *Farm Workers; *United
    Farmworkers of America (UFW).

418 Berger, Peggy S. Differences in importance
    of and satisfaction from job characteristics
    by sex and occupational type among
    Mexican-American employees. JOURNAL OF
    VOCATIONAL BEHAVIOR, Vol. 28, no. 3 (June
    1986), p. 203-213. English. DESCR:
    *Employment; *Sex Roles.

419 Broderick, Stephanie H., et al. Ethnicity,
    acculturation, and health beliefs among
    diabetes patients. MIGRATION WORLD MAGAZINE,
    Vol. 15, no. 2 (1987), p. 30-32. English.
    DESCR: Acculturation; Culture; *Diabetes;
    *Identity; *Public Health.

420 Engle, Patricia L.; Scrimshaw, Susan C.M.;
    and Smidt, Robert. Sex differences in
    attitudes towards newborn infants among
    women of Mexican origin. MEDICAL
    ANTHROPOLOGY, Vol. 8, no. 2 (Spring 1984),
    p. 133-144. English. DESCR: Chicanas;
    Cultural Characteristics; *Machismo;
    *Maternal and Child Welfare; *Parent and
    Child Relationships; Sex Roles.

421 Gilbert, M. Jean. Alcohol consumption
    patterns in immigrant and later generation
    Mexican American women. HISPANIC JOURNAL OF
    BEHAVIORAL SCIENCES, Vol. 9, no. 3
    (September 1987), p. 299-313. English.
    DESCR: Acculturation; *Alcoholism;
    *Chicanas; Cultural Characteristics;
    *Immigrants; Mexico.

422 Graham, Joe S. Folk medicine and
    intra-cultural diversity among West Texas
    Americans. WESTERN FOLKLORE, Vol. 44, no. 3
    (July 1985), p. 168-193. English. DESCR:
    *Folk Medicine; *West Texas.

423 Gynan, Shaw Nicholas. The influence of
    language background on attitudes toward
    native and nonnative Spanish. BILINGUAL
    REVIEW, Vol. 12, no. 1-2 (January, August,
    1985), p. 33-42. English. DESCR: Anglo
    Americans; *Foreign Language Instruction;
    Language Proficiency; *Language Usage;
    Spanish Language.

424 Howell-Martinez, Vicky. The influence of
    gender roles on political socialization: an
    experimental study of Mexican-American
    children. WOMEN & POLITICS, Vol. 2, (Fall
    1982), p. 33-46. English. DESCR: Child
    Study; Children; Political Socialization;
    Sex Roles; *Sex Stereotypes.

Attitudes (cont.)

425 Hurtado, Aida and Gurin, Patricia. Ethnic identity and bilingualism attitudes. HISPANIC JOURNAL OF BEHAVIORAL SCIENCES, Vol. 9, no. 1 (March 1987), p. 1-18. English. DESCR: *Bilingualism; *Identity; Political Socialization.

426 Jorgensen, Stephen R. and Adams, Russell P. Family planning needs and behavior of Mexican American women: a study of health care professionals and their clientele. HISPANIC JOURNAL OF BEHAVIORAL SCIENCES, Vol. 9, no. 3 (September 1987), p. 265-286. English. DESCR: Acculturation; Birth Control; *Chicanas; *Cultural Characteristics; *Family Planning; Fertility; Public Health; Stereotypes; Sterilization.

427 Loo, Chalsa M. and Rolison, Garry. Alienation of ethnic minority students at a predominantly white university. JOURNAL OF HIGHER EDUCATION, Vol. 57, no. 1 (January, February, 1986), p. 58-77. English. DESCR: *Alienation; Discrimination in Education; *Students; Surveys; Teacher-pupil Interaction.

428 Ornelas, Yolanda. Determined to be acknowledged. REVISTA MUJERES, Vol. 4, no. 1 (January 1987), p. 14-15. English. DESCR: *Biography; *Chicanas; Cultural Characteristics.

429 Padilla, Eligio R. and O'Grady, Kevin E. Sexuality among Mexican Americans: a case of sexual stereotyping. JOURNAL OF PERSONALITY AND SOCIAL PSYCHOLOGY, Vol. 52, no. 1 (1987), p. 5-10. English. DESCR: Age Groups; Anglo Americans; Religion; *Sex Roles; *Stereotypes.

430 Ruelas, J. Oshi. Moments of change. REVISTA MUJERES, Vol. 4, no. 1 (January 1987), p. 23-33. English. DESCR: *Biography; *Chicanas.

431 Sabogal, Fabio, et al. Hispanic familism and acculturation: what changes and what doesn't? HISPANIC JOURNAL OF BEHAVIORAL SCIENCES, Vol. 9, no. 4 (December 1987), p. 397-412. English. DESCR: *Acculturation; Cultural Characteristics; Ethnic Groups; Extended Family; *Family; Natural Support Systems; Values.

432 What are your views on the new English-Only initiative?=Que piensas sobre la nueva ley, "English-Only". AMERICAS 2001, Vol. 1, no. 1 (June, July, 1987), p. 12-14. Bilingual. DESCR: *English-Only Movement; *Proposition 63 (English as the Official Language of California); Public Opinion.

Austin, TX

433 Douglas, Mark. Austin: growing fast, start-ups tough. HISPANIC BUSINESS, Vol. 9, no. 6 (June 1987), p. 19, 22. English. DESCR: *Business Enterprises; *Investments.

434 Douthat, Bill. Mariachi magic. VISTA, Vol. 2, no. 4 (December 7, 1986), p. 18. English. DESCR: *Castro, Zeke; Mariachi Rebeldes del Sur; *Mariachis; Music; Secondary School Education.

435 McNeely, Dave. Hispanic power at the polls. VISTA, Vol. 2, no. 3 (November 2, 1986), p. 8-12. English. DESCR: *Barrera, Roy, Jr.; Chavez, Linda; Elected Officials; Gonzalez, Raul; Martinez, Bob; Maryland; Political System; San Antonio, TX; Statistics; Tampa, FL; *Voter Turnout.

Authors

436 Bartlett, Catherine Vallejos. Magical realism: the Latin American influence on modern Chicano writers. CONFLUENCIA, Vol. 1, no. 2 (Spring 1986), p. 27-37. English. DESCR: Arias, Ron; Garcia Marquez, Gabriel; Latin America; *Literary Criticism; *Literary Influence; *Literature; Magical realism; ONE HUNDRED YEARS OF SOLITUDE; Rivera, Tomas; THE ROAD TO TAMAZUNCHALE; Y NO SE LO TRAGO LA TIERRA/AND THE EARTH DID NOT PART.

437 Benson, Douglas K. and Quintana, Leroy V. A conversation with Leroy V. Quintana. BILINGUAL REVIEW, Vol. 12, no. 3 (September, December, 1985), p. 218-229. English. DESCR: Biography; HIJO DEL PUEBLO; Poetry; *Quintana, Leroy V.; SANGRE.

438 Benson, Douglas K. Intuitions of a world in transition: the New Mexican poetry of Leroy V. Quintana. BILINGUAL REVIEW, Vol. 12, no. 1-2 (January, August, 1985), p. 62-80. English. DESCR: HIJO DEL PUEBLO; *Literary Criticism; New Mexico; Poetry; *Quintana, Leroy V.; SANGRE.

439 Bruce-Novoa, Juan. La critica chicana de Luis Leal (I). LA COMUNIDAD, No. 280 (December 1, 1985), p. 2-5. Spanish. DESCR: Biography; *Leal, Luis; *Literary Criticism.

440 Bruce-Novoa, Juan. La critica chicana de Luis Leal (II). LA COMUNIDAD, No. 281 (December 8, 1985), p. 14-15. Spanish. DESCR: Biography; *Leal, Luis; *Literary Criticism.

441 Bruce-Novoa, Juan. Ernest Brawley: un escritor chicano desconocido. LA COMUNIDAD, No. 277 (November 10, 1985), p. 6-7. Spanish. DESCR: *Biography; *Brawley, Ernest; Literary Criticism; Novel; SELENA [novel]; THE ALAMO TREE [novel]; THE RAP [novel].

442 Bruce-Novoa, Juan. Meet the writers of the 80s. VISTA, Vol. 1, no. 11 (July 6, 1986), p. 15-16. English. DESCR: Anaya, Rudolfo A.; Arte Publico Press; Bilingual Review Press; Cisneros, Sandra; Hinojosa-Smith, Rolando R.; Keller, Gary D.; *Literature; Pineda, Cecile; Quinto Sol Publishing, Inc.; Rivera, Tomas; Soto, Gary.

443 Bruce-Novoa, Juan. Poesia de Gary Soto: una autobiografia a plazos. LA COMUNIDAD, No. 270 (September 22, 1985), p. 8-10. Spanish. DESCR: *Literary Criticism; Poetry; *Soto, Gary; TALE OF SUNLIGHT; THE ELEMENTS OF SAN JOAQUIN; WHERE SPARROWS WORK HARD.

444 Chavez, Denise. Words of wisdom. NEW MEXICO MAGAZINE, Vol. 65, no. 12 (December 1987), p. 72-78. English. DESCR: *Literary History; Literature; *New Mexico.

445 Cisneros, Sandra. Do you know me?: I wrote THE HOUSE ON MANGO STREET. THE AMERICAS REVIEW, Vol. 15, no. 1 (Spring 1987), p. 77-79. English. DESCR: Autobiography; Chicanas; *Cisneros, Sandra; *Prose; *THE HOUSE ON MANGO STREET.

Authors (cont.)

446 Cisneros, Sandra. Ghosts and voices: writing from obsession. THE AMERICAS REVIEW, Vol. 15, no. 1 (Spring 1987), p. 69-73. English. **DESCR:** Autobiography; Chicanas; *Cisneros, Sandra; *Prose.

447 Cisneros, Sandra. Living as a writer: choice and circumstance. REVISTA MUJERES, Vol. 3, no. 2 (June 1986), p. 68-72. English. **DESCR:** Autobiography; Chicanas; *Cisneros, Sandra.

448 Cisneros, Sandra. Notes to a young(er) writer. THE AMERICAS REVIEW, Vol. 15, no. 1 (Spring 1987), p. 74-76. English. **DESCR:** Autobiography; Chicanas; *Cisneros, Sandra; *Prose.

449 Elias, Edward F. A meeting of poets from east and west: Lorna Dee Cervantes, Gary Soto, Tato Laviera. BILINGUAL REVIEW, Vol. 12, no. 1-2 (January, August, 1985), p. 150-155. English. **DESCR:** Cervantes, Lorna Dee; *EMPLUMADA; *ENCLAVE; Laviera, Tato; Literary Criticism; Literature Reviews; Poetry; Soto, Gary; *WHERE SPARROWS WORK HARD.

450 Espada, Martin and Perez-Erdelyi, Mireya. With Martin Espada. THE AMERICAS REVIEW, Vol. 15, no. 2 (Summer 1987), p. 77-85. English. **DESCR:** *Espada, Martin; Language Usage; Poetry; Puerto Ricans.

451 Hinojosa-Smith, Rolando R. Tomas Rivera: remembrances of an educator and a poet. CONFLUENCIA, Vol. 1, no. 1 (Fall 1985), p. 90-93. English. **DESCR:** Biography; *Rivera, Tomas.

452 Leal, Luis. Literary criticism and minority literatures: the case of the Chicano writer. CONFLUENCIA, Vol. 1, no. 2 (Spring 1986), p. 4-9. English. **DESCR:** Ethnic Groups; *Literary Criticism; Literary Influence; *Literature; *Third World Literature (U.S.)

453 Lomeli, Francisco A. Luis Leal y la vocacion por la literatura latinoamericana. LA COMUNIDAD, No. 279 (November 24, 1985), 6-7+. Spanish. **DESCR:** Biography; *Leal, Luis; *Literary Criticism; Literature.

454 Mohr, Nicholasa. Puerto Rican writers in the United States, Puerto Rican writers in Puerto Rico: a separation beyond language. THE AMERICAS REVIEW, Vol. 15, no. 2 (Summer 1987), p. 87-92. English. **DESCR:** Autobiography; Identity; Immigrants; *Language Usage; *Literature; *Mohr, Nicholasa; *Puerto Ricans; Spanish Language.

455 Mora, Pat and Alarcon, Norma. A poet analyzes her craft. NUESTRO, Vol. 11, no. 2 (March 1987), p. 25-27. English. **DESCR:** BORDERS; CHANTS; *Chicanas; *Mora, Pat; *Poetry.

456 A road fraught with challenge leads to view from the top. HISPANIC TIMES, Vol. 8, no. 3 (May, June, 1987), p. 28. English. **DESCR:** Biography; *Chicanas; Leadership; National Network of Hispanic Women; Torres, Celia Gonzales.

457 Wreford, Mary. Book review of: CHICANO AUTHORS: INQUIRY BY INTERVIEW. LA RED/THE NET, no. 38 (January 1981), p. 3-4. English. **DESCR:** Book Reviews; *Bruce-Novoa, Juan; *CHICANO AUTHORS: INQUIRY BY INTERVIEW.

458 Zesch, Lindy. Visa issue heats up: PEN hopes for "group waiver" of denials. AMERICAN THEATRE, Vol. 2, no. 8 (November 1985), p. 24. English. **DESCR:** Artists; Book Reviews; GETTING IN: A GUIDE TO OVERCOMING THE POLITICAL DENIAL OF NON-IMMIGRANT VISAS; National Lawyer's Guild; Politics; *Visas.

Autobiography

459 Barrera, Nancy. Mi sueno. REVISTA MUJERES, Vol. 1, no. 2 (June 1984), p. 13-14. Spanish. **DESCR:** Essays.

460 Cisneros, Sandra. Do you know me?: I wrote THE HOUSE ON MANGO STREET. THE AMERICAS REVIEW, Vol. 15, no. 1 (Spring 1987), p. 77-79. English. **DESCR:** Authors; Chicanas; *Cisneros, Sandra; *Prose; *THE HOUSE ON MANGO STREET.

461 Cisneros, Sandra. Ghosts and voices: writing from obsession. THE AMERICAS REVIEW, Vol. 15, no. 1 (Spring 1987), p. 69-73. English. **DESCR:** *Authors; Chicanas; *Cisneros, Sandra; *Prose.

462 Cisneros, Sandra. Living as a writer: choice and circumstance. REVISTA MUJERES, Vol. 3, no. 2 (June 1986), p. 68-72. English. **DESCR:** *Authors; Chicanas; *Cisneros, Sandra.

463 Cisneros, Sandra. Notes to a young(er) writer. THE AMERICAS REVIEW, Vol. 15, no. 1 (Spring 1987), p. 74-76. English. **DESCR:** *Authors; Chicanas; *Cisneros, Sandra; *Prose.

464 Marquez, Antonio. Richard Rodriguez's HUNGER OF MEMORY and the poetics of experience. ARIZONA QUARTERLY, Vol. 40, no. 2 (Summer 1984), p. 130-141. English. **DESCR:** Book Reviews; *HUNGER OF MEMORY: THE EDUCATION OF RICHARD RODRIGUEZ; Literary Criticism; Rodriguez, Richard.

465 Mendoza, Lupe. Porque lo podemos hacer--a poco no? REVISTA MUJERES, Vol. 1, no. 2 (June 1984), p. 33-37. Spanish. **DESCR:** Chicanas; Higher Education; *Mendoza, Lupe.

466 Mohr, Nicholasa. Puerto Rican writers in the United States, Puerto Rican writers in Puerto Rico: a separation beyond language. THE AMERICAS REVIEW, Vol. 15, no. 2 (Summer 1987), p. 87-92. English. **DESCR:** Authors; Identity; Immigrants; *Language Usage; *Literature; *Mohr, Nicholasa; *Puerto Ricans; Spanish Language.

467 Soriano, Diane H. and Mejia, Gabriella S. "Ni he tenido tiempo para mi:" entrevista con Gabriella S. Mejia. REVISTA MUJERES, Vol. 1, no. 2 (June 1984), p. 38-41. Spanish. **DESCR:** *Chicanas; Higher Education; *Mejia, Gabriella S.

THE AUTOBIOGRAPHY OF A BROWN BUFFALO

468 Bruce-Novoa, Juan. Homosexuality and the Chicano novel. CONFLUENCIA, Vol. 2, no. 1 (Fall 1986), p. 69-77. English. **DESCR:** Acosta, Oscar Zeta; CITY OF NIGHT; FAULTLINE [novel]; *Homosexuality; Islas, Arturo; *Literary Criticism; Machismo; *Novel; Ortiz Taylor, Sheila; POCHO; Rechy, John; Salas, Floyd; SPRING FORWARD/FALL BACK; TATOO THE WICKED CROSS; THE RAIN GOD: A DESERT TALE; THE REVOLT OF THE COCKROACH PEOPLE; Villarreal, Jose Antonio.

THE AUTOBIOGRAPHY OF A BROWN BUFFALO (cont.)

469 Bruce-Novoa, Juan. Mexico en la literatura chicana (II). LA COMUNIDAD, No. 268 (September 8, 1985), p. 14-15. Spanish. **DESCR:** Acosta, Oscar Zeta; Identity; *Literary Criticism.

Automobile Industry

470 Beale, Stephen. Moving trucks in New Mexico. HISPANIC BUSINESS, Vol. 9, no. 8 (August 1987), p. 34-37. English. **DESCR:** Baca Pontiac-Buick-GMC, Belen, NM; *Baca, Ruben; Biography; Businesspeople.

471 Dempsey, Mary. Latinas in the driver's seat. VISTA, Vol. 2, no. 5 (January 4, 1987), p. 12-15. English. **DESCR:** *Consumers.

472 Drive away with $5.2 billion. HISPANIC BUSINESS, Vol. 9, no. 9 (September 1987), p. 71. English. **DESCR:** *Consumers; *Marketing.

473 Minority programs need tune-up. HISPANIC BUSINESS, Vol. 9, no. 6 (June 1987), p. 84-90. English. **DESCR:** Business; Business Enterprises; National Association for Minority Automotive Dealers (NAMAD); *Organizations.

Avalos, David

474 Goldman, Shifra. Escena de San Diego: texto y contexto. LA COMUNIDAD, No. 239 (February 17, 1985), p. 6-7. Spanish. **DESCR:** *Art; Chicano Park, San Diego, CA; Exhibits; *NUEVE ARTISTAS CHICANOS [exhibit]; San Diego, CA; Torres, Salvador Roberto; Ulloa, Domingo.

475 Gomez Pena, Guillermo. Dialogos fronterizos. LA COMUNIDAD, No. 263 (August 4, 1985), p. 2-3. Spanish. **DESCR:** *Art; Border Region; DIALOGOS FRONTERIZOS [radio program]; Osorio, Armando.

Avila, Adam

476 Rosas, Alejandro. Siete fotografos latinos en Los Angeles. LA COMUNIDAD, No. 241 (March 3, 1985), p. 4-5. Spanish. **DESCR:** Aguilar, Laura; Art; Callwood, Dennis O.; Carlos, Jesus; Exhibits; Miranda, Judy; *Photography; Self-Help Graphics, Los Angeles, CA, *SEVEN LATINO PHOTOGRAFOS=SIETE FOTOGRAFOS LATINOS; Thewlis, Alan; Valverde, Richard.

Awards

477 American Chemical Society honors Dr. Mario J. Molina. HISPANIC ENGINEER, Vol. 3, no. 2 (Summer 1987), p. 12. English. **DESCR:** American Chemical Society; *Molina, Mario J.

478 Community and professional organizations honor Rockwell's Al Mejia at retirement dinner. HISPANIC ENGINEER, Vol. 3, no. 1 (Spring 1987), p. 22. English. **DESCR:** *Mejia, Al; Rockwell International, Thousand Oaks, CA.

479 El Camino Real named national historic engineering landmark. HISPANIC ENGINEER, Vol. 3, no. 1 (Spring 1987), p. 23. English. **DESCR:** American Society of Civil Engineers (ASCE); *El Camino Real.

480 Evans, James. From chaos to quality education. VISTA, Vol. 3, no. 4 (December 6, 1987), p. 18, 35. English. **DESCR:** *Chacon Soto, Mario; *Educational Administration;

Educational Theory and Practice; Horace Mann Middle School, Mission District, San Francisco, CA.

481 Families of the year. VISTA, Vol. 2, no. 2 (October 4, 1986), p. 16-18. English. **DESCR:** Aguilar, Gregorio; Aguilar, Guadalupe; Aranda, Benjamin; Aranda, Emma; de la Rocha, Beatriz; de la Rocha, Castulo; Family; Guzman, Ofelia; Guzman, Roberto; *Hispanic Family of the Year Award.

482 Gutierrez, Daniel M. MAES Houston chapter sponsors 3rd annual scholarship banquet. HISPANIC TIMES, Vol. 8, no. 3 (May, June, 1987), p. 42. English. **DESCR:** Financial Aid; *Mexican American Engineering Society (MAES).

483 Haley, Lindsey. Una premiacion controvertida. LA COMUNIDAD, No. 246 (April 7, 1985), p. 5-6. Spanish. **DESCR:** Discrimination; *Grammy Awards; Guevara, Ruben; *Recording Industry; Zanya Records Co., Los Angeles, CA.

484 Hispanic media awards. TELEVISION/RADIO AGE, Vol. 31, (January 23, 1984), p. 17-18. English. **DESCR:** *Advertising; *El Cervantes Media Awards.

485 Kendall, Robert. Electric excitement at the 17th Annual Golden Eagle Awards ceremony sponsored by Nosotros at the Beverly Hilton Hotel. HISPANIC TIMES, Vol. 8, no. 5 (October, November, 1987), p. 32. English. **DESCR:** Films; *Nosotros Golden Eagle Awards; Television.

486 Krampner, John. Raul Rodriguez. VISTA, Vol. 2, no. 5 (January 4, 1987), p. 21. English. **DESCR:** *Design; *Rodriguez, Raul; Rose Parade (Pasadena, CA).

487 Lit, Ed. Recognition for Hispanic families. VISTA, Vol. 1, no. 5 (January 5, 1986), p. 18-20. English. **DESCR:** American Family Society; *Hispanic Family of the Year Award; Moraga, Peter and family (Los Angeles, CA); Pineda, Charles and family (Los Angeles, CA); Private Funding Sources.

488 Lopez-Knox wins fellowship award. HISPANIC TIMES, Vol. 8, no. 1 (December, January, 1987), p. 21. English. **DESCR:** Biographical Notes; Chicanas; *Lopez-Knox, Joanne; Science.

489 Our 1986 Latino awards: triunfos, fiascos, winners and losers. NUESTRO, Vol. 11, no. 1-2 (1987), p. 9-25. English. **DESCR:** Biographical Notes.

490 Pacific Telesis senior fellows. HISPANIC ENGINEER, Vol. 3, no. 2 (Summer 1987), p. 10-11. English. **DESCR:** Castaneda, Jesus; Cruz, Jacqueline; Education; Pacific Telesis; Rodriguez, Jose; Sanchez, Alex.

491 Recipients of Ford Foundation postdoctoral fellowships for minorities have been announced. LA RED/THE NET, no. 99 (August 1986), p. 10. English. **DESCR:** *Financial Aid; *Ford Foundation Postdoctoral Fellowships for Minorities Program; Higher Education.

492 Reyes, Sonia. America's Hispanic sweethearts. VISTA, Vol. 1, no. 6 (February 2, 1986), p. 6-7. English. **DESCR:** Carthy-Deu, Deborah [Miss Universe]; *Martinez-Herring, Laura [Miss USA]; *Women.

Awards (cont.)

493 A salute to Hispanic excellence in America.
HISPANIC BUSINESS, Vol. 9, no. 6 (June
1987), p. 7-9. English. **DESCR:**
*Businesspeople; *Latin Business Association
(LBA), Los Angeles, CA; Organizations.

494 SHPE holds first ever East coast conference
for Hispanic engineers. HISPANIC ENGINEER,
Vol. 3, no. 5 (Winter 1987), p. 12-14.
English. **DESCR:** Barrios, Eugene; Chang-Diaz,
Franklin; *Conferences and Meetings; Cuevas,
Brian L.; Garay, Charles J.; Garcia, Ray;
Marrero, Charles; Martinez, Lisa;
Monteverde, Edwin; Plumey, Raymond;
Reyes-Guerra, David; Rivera, Angel; Society
of Hispanic Professional Engineers (SHPE);
Soto, Giovanni.

495 SHPE news. HISPANIC ENGINEER, Vol. 3, no. 3
(1987), p. 10-13. English. **DESCR:** Castillo,
Hector; Colmenarez, Margarita; Garcia, Raul;
Herrera, Jess; Lopez-Martin, Minnie;
Mondragon, Ricardo; Reyes-Guerra, David;
Silva, Juan; Society of Hispanic
Professional Engineers (SHPE); Vargas,
Jesus; Villanueva, Bernadette.

496 Vitelmo V. Bertero wins ASCE's Moisseiff
Award. HISPANIC ENGINEER, Vol. 3, no. 5
(Winter 1987), p. 14. English. **DESCR:**
American Society of Civil Engineers (ASCE)
Moisseif Award; *Bertero, Vitelmo V.;
University of California, Berkeley.

Azcarraga, Emilio

497 SICC sale opposed. BROADCASTING, Vol. 111,
no. 7 (August 18, 1986), p. 46-52. English.
DESCR: Federal Communications Commission
(FCC); First Chicago Venture Capital;
Hallmark Cards; KFTV, Fresno, CA [television
station]; KMEX, Los Angeles, CA [television
station]; KWEX, San Antonio, TX [television
station]; Legal Cases; *Spanish
International Communications Corp. (SICC);
Spanish Language; Tapia, Raul R.;
Television; TVL Corp.; WLTV, Miami, FL
[television station]; WXTV, Paterson, NJ
[television station].

498 SICC sells TVs for $301.5 million.
BROADCASTING, Vol. 111, no. 4 (July 28,
1986), p. 91-92. English. **DESCR:** First
Chicago Venture Capital; Hallmark Cards;
KFTV, Fresno, CA [television station]; KMEX,
Los Angeles, CA [television station]; KWEX,
San Antonio, TX [television station]; Legal
Cases; *Spanish International Communications
Corp. (SICC); Spanish International Network
(SIN); Spanish Language; Television;
Villanueva, Daniel; WLTV, Miami, FL
[television station]; WXTV, Paterson, NJ
[television station].

Azcarraga Family

499 Mass media bureau settlement would allow
SICC to sell its stations. BROADCASTING,
Vol. 110, no. 26 (June 30, 1986), p. 45.
English. **DESCR:** Anselmo, Rene; Federal
Communications Commission (FCC); KDTV, San
Francisco, CA [television station]; KFTV,
Fresno, CA [television station]; KMEX, Los
Angeles, CA [television station]; KTVW,
Phoeniz, AZ [television station]; KWEX, San
Antonio, TX [television station]; Legal
Cases; *Spanish International Communications
Corp. (SICC); Spanish International Network
(SIN); Spanish Language; Television; WLTV,
Miami, FL [television station]; WXTV,
Paterson, NJ [television station].

Aztecs

500 Book review of: LE MEXIQUE, DES ORIGINES AUX
AZTEQUES. OEIL-REVUE D'ART MENSUELLE,
(December 1986), p. 75. Other. **DESCR:** Bernal
y Garcia Pimentel, Ignacio; Book Reviews;
*LE MEXIQUE, DES ORIGENES AUX AZTEQUES;
Simoni-Abbat, Mireille.

501 Braun, Barbara. The Aztecs: art and
sacrifice. ART IN AMERICA, Vol. 72, no. 4
(April 1984), p. 126-139. English. **DESCR:**
Anthropology; Exhibits; Gods and Dieties;
*Precolumbian Images; *Precolumbian Society;
Templo Mayor, Tenochtitlan.

502 Klor de Alva, J. Jorge. California Chicano
literature and pre-Columbian motifs: foil
and fetish. CONFLUENCIA, Vol. 1, no. 2
(Spring 1986), p. 18-26. English. **DESCR:**
Alurista; Aztlan; *California; EL PLAN
ESPIRITUAL DE AZTLAN; *Literature;
*Precolumbian Images; *Precolumbian
Philosophy; Symbolism.

503 Pinon, Fernando. A dance of worship. VISTA,
Vol. 1, no. 3 (November 3, 1985), p. 16.
English. **DESCR:** *Dance; St. Luke's Catholic
Church, San Antonio, TX.

Aztlan

504 Flores, Arturo C. La literatura de Aztlan y
su reconocimiento. TINTA, Vol. 1, no. 3
(December 1983), p. 9-10. Spanish. **DESCR:**
Literary History; Literature.

505 Klor de Alva, J. Jorge. California Chicano
literature and pre-Columbian motifs: foil
and fetish. CONFLUENCIA, Vol. 1, no. 2
(Spring 1986), p. 18-26. English. **DESCR:**
Alurista; Aztecs; *California; EL PLAN
ESPIRITUAL DE AZTLAN; *Literature;
*Precolumbian Images; *Precolumbian
Philosophy; Symbolism.

506 Lomeli, Francisco A. En torno a la
literatura...convergencia o divergencia? LA
COMUNIDAD, No. 274 (October 20, 1985), p.
8-11. Spanish. **DESCR:** Anaya, Rudolfo A.;
Border Region; HEART OF AZTLAN; *Literary
Criticism; Mendez M., Miguel; PEREGRINOS DE
AZTLAN; *Primer Festival de Literatura
Fronteriza Mexico-Estados Unidos.

507 Mares, E.A. The fiesta of life: impression
of Paulo Friere. EL CUADERNO, Vol. 3, no. 2
(Spring 1974), p. 5-16. English. **DESCR:**
Cultural Characteristics; *Essays; *Freire,
Paulo; *Philosophy.

508 Mares, E.A. Myth and reality: observations
on American myths and the myth of Aztlan. EL
CUADERNO, Vol. 3, no. 1 (Winter 1973), p.
35-50. English. **DESCR:** *Stereotypes.

Baca Pontiac-Buick-GMC, Belen, NM

509 Beale, Stephen. Moving trucks in New Mexico.
HISPANIC BUSINESS, Vol. 9, no. 8 (August
1987), p. 34-37. English. **DESCR:** *Automobile
Industry; *Baca, Ruben; Biography;
Businesspeople.

Baca, Ruben

510 Beale, Stephen. Moving trucks in New Mexico.
HISPANIC BUSINESS, Vol. 9, no. 8 (August
1987), p. 34-37. English. **DESCR:** *Automobile
Industry; Baca Pontiac-Buick-GMC, Belen, NM;
Biography; Businesspeople.

Bach, Robert L.

511 Cobas, Jose A. Book review of: LATIN JOURNEY. INTERNATIONAL MIGRATION REVIEW, Vol. 21, no. 2 (Summer 1987), p. 434-435. English. DESCR: Book Reviews; *LATIN JOURNEY: CUBAN AND MEXICAN IMMIGRANTS IN THE UNITED STATES; Portes, Alejandro.

512 Madrid, Arturo. Book reviews of: CLAMOR AT THE GATES and LATIN JOURNEY. LA RED/THE NET, no. 89 (August 1985), p. 7-10. English. DESCR: Book Reviews; *CLAMOR AT THE GATES: THE NEW AMERICAN IMMIGRATION; Glazer, Nathan; Immigration; *LATIN JOURNEY: CUBAN AND MEXICAN IMMIGRANTS IN THE UNITED STATES; Portes, Alejandro.

Baja California, Mexico

513 Sandos, James A. Northern separatism during the Mexican revolution--an inquiry into the role of drug trafficking, 1910-1920. AMERICAS, Vol. 41, no. 2 (October 1984), p. 191-214. English. DESCR: Border Region; Cantu Jimenez, Esteban; Drug Addicts; Drug Laws; *Drug Traffic; *Drug Use; Medical Care; Mexican Revolution - 1910-1920; Revolutions.

Baker, Houston A., Jr.

514 Belkind, A. Book review of: THREE AMERICAN LITERATURES. WORLD LITERATURE TODAY, Vol. 57, no. 4 (Fall 1983), p. 643. English. DESCR: Book Reviews; *THREE AMERICAN LITERATURES: ESSAYS IN CHICANO, NATIVE AMERICAN, AND ASIAN-AMERICAN LITERATURE FOR TEACHERS OF AMERICAN LITERATURE.

Balboa Park, San Diego, CA

515 Ruiz, Ruben. El parque Balboa. LLUEVE TLALOC, no. 5 (1978), p. 28. Spanish. DESCR: *Prose.

Balderrama, Francisco E.

516 Cardenas, Gilbert. Book review of: IN DEFENSE OF LA RAZA. LA RED/THE NET, no. 85 (October 1984), p. 2-5. English. DESCR: Book Reviews; Crewdson, John; *IN DEFENSE OF LA RAZA: THE LOS ANGELES MEXICAN CONSULATE AND THE MEXICAN COMMUNITY; *THE TARNISHED DOOR.

517 Dagodag, William Tim. Book review of: IN DEFENSE OF LA RAZA. JOURNAL OF HISTORICAL GEOGRAPHY, Vol. 10, no. 1 (January 1984), p. 92. English. DESCR: Book Reviews; *IN DEFENSE OF LA RAZA: THE LOS ANGELES MEXICAN CONSULATE AND THE MEXICAN COMMUNITY.

518 McIlroy, Christopher. Book review of: IN DEFENSE OF LA RAZA. JOURNAL OF THE WEST, Vol. 22, (October 1983), p. 87-88. English. DESCR: Book Reviews; *IN DEFENSE OF LA RAZA: THE LOS ANGELES MEXICAN CONSULATE AND THE MEXICAN COMMUNITY.

519 Meier, Matt S. Book review of: IN DEFENSE OF LA RAZA. ARIZONA AND THE WEST, Vol. 25, no. 4 (Winter 1983), p. 356-357. English. DESCR: Book Reviews; *IN DEFENSE OF LA RAZA: THE LOS ANGELES MEXICAN CONSULATE AND THE MEXICAN COMMUNITY.

520 Monroy, Douglas. Book review of: IN DEFENSE OF LA RAZA. WESTERN HISTORICAL QUARTERLY, Vol. 15, no. 3 (July 1984), p. 331-332. English. DESCR: Book Reviews; IN DEFENSE OF LA RAZA: THE LOS ANGELES MEXICAN CONSULATE AND THE MEXICAN COMMUNITY; Los Angeles, CA.

521 Rutter, Larry G. Book review of: IN DEFENSE OF LA RAZA. JOURNAL OF THE WEST, Vol. 22, (July 1983), p. 100-101. English. DESCR: Book Reviews; *IN DEFENSE OF LA RAZA: THE LOS ANGELES MEXICAN CONSULATE AND THE MEXICAN COMMUNITY.

Ballad
USE: Corridos

BALLAD OF GREGORIO CORTEZ [film]

522 Mindiola, Tatcho, Jr. Film review of: THE BALLAD OF GREGORIO CORTEZ. LA RED/THE NET, no. 80 (May 1984), p. 11-17. English. DESCR: *Film Reviews; SEGUIN [movie]; ZOOT SUIT [film].

523 Montane, Diane. Edward James Olmos: the man behind the tough film facade. VISTA, Vol. 1, no. 1 (September 8, 1985), p. 8-12. English. DESCR: *Actors and Actresses; Biography; *Olmos, Edward James; WOLFEN [film]; ZOOT SUIT [film].

524 Trevino, Jesus Salvador. Chicano cinema overview. AREITO, Vol. 10, no. 37 (1984), p. 40-43. English. DESCR: Discrimination in Employment; *Films; Television.

Ballesteros, Octavio A.

525 Gonzalez, Gustavo. Book review of: BILINGUAL-BICULTURAL EDUCATION: AN ANNOTATED BIBLIOGRAPHY, 1936-1982. MODERN LANGUAGE JOURNAL, Vol. 69, no. 3 (Fall 1985), p. 299-300. English. DESCR: Bibliography; Bilingual Bicultural Education; *BILINGUAL-BICULTURAL EDUCATION: AN ANNOTATED BIBLIOGRAPHY; Book Reviews.

526 Nieto, Sonia. Book review of: BILINGUAL-BICULTURAL EDUCATION: AN ANNOTATED BIBLIOGRAPHY, 1936-1982. INTERRACIAL BOOKS FOR CHILDREN, Vol. 17, no. 3-4 (1986), p. 29. English. DESCR: *BILINGUAL-BICULTURAL EDUCATION: AN ANNOTATED BIBLIOGRAPHY; Book Reviews.

LA BAMBA [film]

527 Beale, Stephen and Valdez, Luis. Connecting with the American experience: an interview with Luis Valdez. HISPANIC BUSINESS, Vol. 9, no. 7 (July 1987), p. 10-13. English. DESCR: Biography; Films; Stereotypes; Teatro; *Valdez, Luis.

528 Beale, Stephen. A turning point in Hollywood. HISPANIC BUSINESS, Vol. 9, no. 7 (July 1987), p. 20-24, 36. English. DESCR: *Films; *Marketing; Spanish Language; Stereotypes; THE MILAGRO BEANFIELD WAR [film].

529 Chavez, Lorenzo A. La Bamba. VISTA, Vol. 2, no. 11 (July 5, 1987), p. 12-13. English. DESCR: *Actors and Actresses; Biography; De Soto, Rosana; Films; *Morales, Esai; Pena, Elizabeth; Phillips, Lou Diamond.

530 Kael, Pauline. The current cinema: siblings and cyborgs. NEW YORKER, (August 10, 1987), p. 70-73. English. DESCR: Film Reviews; Valens, Ritchie [stage name for Richard Valenzuela].

531 Preciado, Consuelo. LA BAMBA triumphs=LA BAMBA triunfa. AMERICAS 2001, Vol. 1, no. 2 (September, October, 1987), p. 7. Bilingual. DESCR: *Films; Valdez, Luis; Valens, Ritchie [stage name for Richard Valenzuela].

LA BAMBA [film] (cont.)

532 Rodriguez Flores, Juan. Esai Morales y la pasion por el arte escenico (II). LA COMUNIDAD, No. 336 (December 28, 1986), p. 2-3. Spanish. **DESCR**: Actors and Actresses; *Biography; Films; *Morales, Esai; Valdez, Luis.

Bandidos

533 Rodriguez, Richard. The head of Joaquin Murrieta. CALIFORNIA MAGAZINE, Vol. 10, no. 7 (July 1985), p. 55-62, 89. English. **DESCR**: Leyendas; *Murrieta, Joaquin.

Banking Industry

534 Arizona Bank targets Hispanic market. ABA BANKING JOURNAL, Vol. 77, no. 4 (April 1985), p. 30, 32. English. **DESCR**: *Arizona Bank, Phoenix, AZ; Marketing.

535 Clair, Robert T. A comparative analysis of mature Hispanic-owned banks. ECONOMIC REVIEW (FEDERAL RESERVE BANK OF DALLAS), (March 1985), p. 1-11. English. **DESCR**: Finance.

536 Garcia, Art. Financing the corporate take-off. HISPANIC BUSINESS, Vol. 9, no. 5 (May 1987), p. 22-27. English. **DESCR**: Aguirre Architects, Dallas, TX; Aguirre, Pedro; *Business Enterprises; Businesspeople; *Corporations; *Investments; Minority Enterprise Small Business Investment Corporation (MESBIC); Morales, Ramon; Protocom Devices, New York, NY; Villamil, Antonio.

Barkin, Florence

537 Penalosa, Fernando. Book review of: BILINGUALISM AND LANGUAGE CONTACT: SPANISH, ENGLISH AND NATIVE AMERICAN LANGUAGES. LA RED/THE NET, no. 66 (March 1983), p. 5-8. English. **DESCR**: *BILINGUALISM AND LANGUAGE CONTACT: SPANISH, ENGLISH, AND NATIVE AMERICAN LANGUAGES; Book Reviews; Brandt, Elizabeth H.; Ornstein-Galicia, Jacob.

Barnett-Mizrahi, Carol

538 Nieto, Sonia. Book review of: BILINGUAL MULTICULTURAL EDUCATION AND THE PROFESSIONAL: FROM THEORY TO PRACTICE. INTERRACIAL BOOKS FOR CHILDREN, Vol. 17, no. 3-4 (1986), p. 30. English. **DESCR**: *BILINGUAL MULTICULTURAL EDUCATION AND THE PROFESSIONAL; Book Reviews; Trueba, Henry T.

Baron, Augustine Jr.

539 Bernal, Martha E. Book review of: EXPLORATIONS IN CHICANO PSYCHOLOGY. LA RED/THE NET, no. 55 (June 1982), p. 5-6. English. **DESCR**: Book Reviews; *EXPLORATIONS IN CHICANO PSYCHOLOGY; *Psychology.

Barrera, Mario

540 Garcia, John A. Book review of: RACE AND CLASS IN THE SOUTHWEST: A THEORY OF INEQUALITY. LA RED/THE NET, no. 31 (June 1980), p. 4. English. **DESCR**: Book Reviews; *Discrimination; *Economics; RACE AND CLASS IN THE SOUTHWEST: A THEORY OF RACIAL INEQUALITY; *Southwestern United States.

541 Hurtado, Aida. Book review of: WORK, FAMILY, SEX ROLES, LANGUAGE. LA RED/THE NET, no. 40 (March 1981), p. 3. English. **DESCR**: Book Reviews; Camarillo, Alberto; Hernandez, Francisco; Social History and Conditions; *WORK, FAMILY, SEX ROLES, LANGUAGE: SELECTED PAPERS OF THE NATIONAL ASSOCIATION FOR CHICANO STUDIES CONFERENCE, 1979.

Barrera, Roy, Jr.

542 McNeely, Dave. Hispanic power at the polls. VISTA, Vol. 2, no. 3 (November 2, 1986), p. 8-12. English. **DESCR**: Austin, TX; Chavez, Linda; Elected Officials; Gonzalez, Raul; Martinez, Bob; Maryland; Political System; San Antonio, TX; Statistics; Tampa, FL; *Voter Turnout.

Barrio, Raymond

543 Rodriguez, Ronald. Book review of: THE PLUM PLUM PICKERS. LECTOR, Vol. 4, no. 4-6 (1987), p. 70. English. **DESCR**: Book Reviews; *THE PLUM PLUM PICKERS.

Barrios

544 Lomeli, Francisco A. El concepto del barrio en tres poetas chicanos. LA COMUNIDAD, No. 316 (August 10, 1986), p. 4-5+. Spanish. **DESCR**: Alurista; Delgado, Abelardo "Lalo"; *Literary Criticism; Poetry; Sanchez, Ricardo.

Barrios, Eugene

545 SHPE holds first ever East coast conference for Hispanic engineers. HISPANIC ENGINEER, Vol. 3, no. 5 (Winter 1987), p. 12-14. English. **DESCR**: Awards; Chang-Diaz, Franklin; *Conferences and Meetings; Cuevas, Brian L.; Garay, Charles J.; Garcia, Ray; Marrero, Charles; Martinez, Lisa; Monteverde, Edwin; Plumey, Raymond; Reyes-Guerra, David; Rivera, Angel; Society of Hispanic Professional Engineers (SHPE); Soto, Giovanni.

Baseball

546 Banks, Leo W. The Latinization of U.S. baseball. VISTA, Vol. 1, no. 7 (March 2, 1986), p. 15-16. English.

547 Barnes, Jill. The Latin pitch. VISTA, Vol. 2, no. 9 (May 3, 1987), p. 6-8. English. **DESCR**: Athletes.

548 Guppy, N. Positional centrality and racial segregation in professional baseball. INTERNATIONAL REVIEW OF SPORT SOCIOLOGY, Vol. 18, no. 4 (1983), p. 95-109. English. **DESCR**: Discrimination; Ethnic Groups; Segregation and Desegregation.

Bataan, Joe

549 Duarte, Mario. SalSoul Joe Bataan. LATIN QUARTER, Vol. 1, no. 1 (July 1974), p. 23. English. **DESCR**: SAL SOUL [record album]; *Salsa.

Batarse, Anthony A.

550 Beale, Stephen. CEOs. HISPANIC BUSINESS, Vol. 9, no. 4 (April 1987), p. 20-37, 52. English. **DESCR**: Alvarez, Roberto; Biography; Business Enterprises; *Businesspeople; Carlo, Nelson; Estrada, Anthony; Flores, Frank; Fullana, Jaime, Jr.; Hernandez, George; *Management; Ortega, James; Quirch, Guillermo; Ruiz, Roberto; Santa Maria, Yvonne Z.; Sugranes, Rosa; Tamaya, Carlos; Young, Paul H., Jr.

Batos Locos
USE: Pachucos

Battle of Valverde

551 Meketa, Charles and Meketa, Jacqueline. Heroes or cowards? A new look at the role of native New Mexicans at the Battle of Valverde. NEW MEXICO HISTORICAL REVIEW, Vol. 62, no. 1 (January 1987), p. 33-46. English. **DESCR:** *Canby, Edward; History; *New Mexico.

Bauman, Richard

552 Herrera-Sobek, Maria. Book review of: AND OTHER NEIGHBORLY NAMES: SOCIAL PROCESS AND CULTURAL IMAGE IN TEXAS FOLKLORE. LA RED/THE NET, no. 47 (October 1981), p. 3-4. English. **DESCR:** Abrahams, Roger D.; Book Reviews; *Folklore; *Texas.

Bean, Frank D.

553 Hastings, D.W. Book review of: MEXICAN AMERICAN FERTILITY PATTERNS. CHOICE, Vol. 23, no. 11-12 (July, August, 1986), p. 1738. English. **DESCR:** Book Reviews; *MEXICAN AMERICAN FERTILITY PATTERNS; Swicegood, Gray.

554 Meier, Matt S. Book review of: THE MEXICAN AMERICAN EXPERIENCE: AN INTERDISCIPLINARY ANTHOLOGY. HISPANIC AMERICAN HISTORICAL REVIEW, Vol. 66, no. 3 (August 1986), p. 629-630. English. **DESCR:** Alvarez, Rodolfo; Bonjean, Charles M.; Book Reviews; de la Garza, Rodolfo O.; Romo, Ricardo; *THE MEXICAN AMERICAN EXPERIENCE: AN INTERDISCIPLINARY ANTHOLOGY.

555 Ruiz, Vicki Lynn. Book review of: THE MEXICAN AMERICAN EXPERIENCE: AN INTERDISCIPLINARY ANTHOLOGY. SOUTHWESTERN HISTORICAL QUARTERLY, Vol. 90, no. 2 (1986), p. 205-206. English. **DESCR:** Alvarez, Rodolfo; Bonjean, Charles M.; Book Reviews; de la Garza, Rodolfo O.; Romo, Ricardo; *THE MEXICAN AMERICAN EXPERIENCE: AN INTERDISCIPLINARY ANTHOLOGY.

556 Salmon, Roberto Mario. Book review of: THE MEXICAN AMERICAN EXPERIENCE: AN INTERDISCIPLINARY ANTHOLOGY. LA RED/THE NET, no. 93 (January, February, 1986), p. 12-14. English. **DESCR:** Alvarez, Rodolfo; Bonjean, Charles M.; Book Reviews; de la Garza, Rodolfo O.; Romo, Ricardo; *THE MEXICAN AMERICAN EXPERIENCE: AN INTERDISCIPLINARY ANTHOLOGY.

BEARING WITNESS/SOBREVIVIENDO

557 Eidelberg, Nora. Book review of: BEARING WITNESS/SOBREVIVIENDO. LECTOR, Vol. 4, no. 1-3 (1986), p. [59-60]. English. **DESCR:** Book Reviews; CALYX: A JOURNAL OF ART AND LITERATURE BY WOMEN.

Becerra, Rosina

558 Bastida, Elena B. Book review of: THE HISPANIC ELDERLY. CONTEMPORARY SOCIOLOGY: A JOURNAL OF REVIEWS, Vol. 14, no. 1 (January 1985), p. 41-42. English. **DESCR:** Ancianos; Book Reviews; Shaw, David; *THE HISPANIC ELDERLY: A RESEARCH REFERENCE GUIDE.

559 Canive, Jose. Book review of: MENTAL HEALTH AND HISPANIC AMERICANS: CLINICAL PERSPECTIVES. JOURNAL OF NERVOUS AND MENTAL DISEASE, Vol. 172, no. 9 (September 1984), p. 559-561. English. **DESCR:** Ancianos; Book Reviews; Escobar, Javier I.; Karno, Marvin; *MENTAL HEALTH AND HISPANIC AMERICANS: CLINICAL PERSPECTIVES.

560 Delgado, Melvin. Book review of: THE HISPANIC ELDERLY. SOCIAL WORK, Vol. 31, no. 2 (March, April, 1986), p. 153. English. **DESCR:** Ancianos; Book Reviews; Shaw, David; *THE HISPANIC ELDERLY: A RESEARCH REFERENCE GUIDE.

561 Gibson, Guadalupe. Book review of: MENTAL HEALTH AND HISPANIC AMERICANS: CLINICAL PERSPECTIVES. SOCIAL WORK, Vol. 29, no. 1 (January, February, 1984), p. 81. English. **DESCR:** Book Reviews; Escobar, Javier I.; Karno, Marvin; *MENTAL HEALTH AND HISPANIC AMERICANS: CLINICAL PERSPECTIVES.

Behavior Modification

562 Hunsaker, Alan C. and Vicario, Tony D. A behavioral/ecological model of intervention alternatives with Chicano gang delinquents. LA RED/THE NET, no. 43 (June 1981), p. 2-3. English. **DESCR:** *Delinquency; *Gangs; Youth.

Bello [family name]

563 Instituto Genealogico e Historico Latino-Americano. Rootsearch: Bello: Ramirez: Lopez. VISTA, Vol. 3, no. 2 (October 3, 1987), p. 37. English. **DESCR:** Genealogy; History; *Lopez [family name]; *Personal Names; *Ramirez [family name].

Beltran [family name]

564 Instituto Genealogico e Historico Latino-Americano. Rootsearch: Beltran: Flores: Gomez. VISTA, Vol. 2, no. 11 (May 7, 1987), p. 22. English. **DESCR:** *Flores [family name]; Genealogy; *Gomez [family name]; History; *Personal Names.

Benavidez, Roy

565 Allsup, Dan. The private war of Roy Benavidez. VISTA, Vol. 2, no. 5 (January 4, 1987), p. 19-20. English. **DESCR:** Medal of Honor; Nationalism; *Veterans.

566 Benavidez, Roy. An embattled Chicano. VISTA, Vol. 2, no. 5 (January 4, 1987), p. 20. English. **DESCR:** *Books; Green Berets; Griffin, Oscar; *THE THREE WARS OF ROY BENAVIDEZ; Vietnam War.

Bergin-Nader, Barbara

567 Grayson, June. Sports medics. VISTA, Vol. 2, no. 9 (May 3, 1987), p. 17-18. English. **DESCR:** Cuadros, Hugo; Doctor Patient Relations; *Dominguez, Richard; *Medical Personnel; Prietto, Carlos Alfredo; *Sports.

Berkeley, CA

568 Gomez Pena, Guillermo and Erana, Maria. Sobre el arte, la rebeldia y las fronteras. LA COMUNIDAD, No. 312 (July 13, 1986), p. 6-7+. Spanish. **DESCR:** *BORDER-X-FRONTERA [radio program]; Gomez Pena, Guillermo; *Radio; Schein, David; Teatro.

Bernal y Garcia Pimentel, Ignacio

569 Book review of: LE MEXIQUE, DES ORIGINES AUX AZTEQUES. OEIL-REVUE D'ART MENSUELLE, (December 1986), p. 75. Other. **DESCR:** Aztecs; Book Reviews; *LE MEXIQUE, DES ORIGENES AUX AZTEQUES; Simoni-Abbat, Mireille.

Bertero, Vitelmo V.

570 Vitelmo V. Bertero wins ASCE's Moisseiff
Award. HISPANIC ENGINEER, Vol. 3, no. 5
(Winter 1987), p. 14. English. **DESCR:**
American Society of Civil Engineers (ASCE)
Moisseif Award; *Awards; University of
California. Berkeley.

Los Bexarenos, San Antonio, TX

571 Chavez, Lorenzo A. The quest for Hispanic
roots. VISTA, Vol. 2, no. 7 (March 8, 1987),
p. 5-6, 24. English. **DESCR:** Church of Jesus
Christ of Latter-Day Saints (Mormons);
Directories; *Garcia, Clotilde; *Genealogy;
Hispanic American Genealogical Associates,
Washington, DC; Las Porciones Genealogical
Society, Edinburg, TX; Los Californianos
[genealogical society], San Jose, CA; Pan
American University, Edinburg, TX; Texas
Southmost College.

Bibliography

572 Baezconde-Garbanati, Lourdes and Salgado de
Snyder, Nelly. Mexican immigrant women: a
selected bibliography. HISPANIC JOURNAL OF
BEHAVIORAL SCIENCES, Vol. 9, no. 3
(September 1987), p. 331-358. English.
DESCR: *Chicanas; *Immigrants; *Women.

573 Bibliography. THE AMERICAS REVIEW, Vol. 15,
no. 3-4 (Fall, Winter, 1987), p. 182-188.
English. **DESCR:** *Chicanas; *Literary
Criticism; Literature.

574 Chabran, Richard and Garcia-Ayvens,
Francisco. Book review of: THE MEXICAN
AMERICAN: A CRITICAL GUIDE TO RESEARCH AIDS.
LA RED/THE NET, no. 37 (December 1980), p.
4-5. English. **DESCR:** Book Reviews;
*Reference Works; *Robinson, Barbara J.;
*Robinson, J. Cordell; *THE MEXICAN
AMERICAN: A CRITICAL GUIDE TO RESEARCH AIDS.

575 Chabran, Richard. Latino reference arrives.
AMERICAN LIBRARIES, Vol. 18, no. 5 (May
1987), p. 384-388. English. **DESCR:** *Academic
Libraries; *Library Collections; Library
Instruction; *Reference Works.

576 Gonzalez, Gustavo. Book review of:
BILINGUAL-BICULTURAL EDUCATION: AN ANNOTATED
BIBLIOGRAPHY, 1936-1982. MODERN LANGUAGE
JOURNAL, Vol. 69, no. 3 (Fall 1985), p.
299-300. English. **DESCR:** Ballesteros,
Octavio A.; Bilingual Bicultural Education;
*BILINGUAL-BICULTURAL EDUCATION: AN
ANNOTATED BIBLIOGRAPHY; Book Reviews.

577 Ramirez, Olga Najera. Greater Mexican
folklore in the United States: an annotated
bibliography. ETHNIC AFFAIRS, no. 1 (Fall
1987), p. [64]-115. English. **DESCR:**
*Folklore.

578 Schon, Elizabeth. Introducing pre-Columbian
and Hispanic art and artists to young adults
through recent books. JOURNAL OF READING,
Vol. 27, no. 3 (December 1983), p. 248-251.
English. **DESCR:** Art; Artists; Precolumbian
Images.

579 Whatley, Patricia L. Book review of:
SPANISH-LANGUAGE BOOKS FOR PUBLIC LIBRARIES.
AMERICAN REFERENCE BOOKS ANNUAL, Vol. 18,
(1987), p. 241. English. **DESCR:** Book
Reviews; Lestrepo, Fabio; *SPANISH-LANGUAGE
BOOKS FOR PUBLIC LIBRARIES.

A BIBLIOGRAPHY OF MEXICAN AMERICAN HISTORY

580 Balderrama, Francisco E. Book review of: A

BIBLIOGRAPHY OF MEXICAN-AMERICAN HISTORY.
PACIFIC HISTORICAL REVIEW, Vol. 55, no. 1
(1986), p. 106-107. English. **DESCR:** Book
Reviews; History; Meier, Matt S.

581 Castillo-Speed, Lillian. Annotated
bibliography. LA RED/THE NET, no. 93
(January, February, 1986), p. 14-17.
English. **DESCR:** ARTE CHICANO; Book Reviews;
Caballero, Cesar; CHICANO LITERATURE: A
REFERENCE GUIDE; CHICANO ORGANIZATIONS
DIRECTORY; CHICANO PERIODICAL INDEX;
Goldman, Shifra M.; HISPANIC ALMANAC;
HISPANIC MENTAL HEALTH RESEARCH: A REFERENCE
GUIDE; Lomeli, Francisco A.; Martinez, Julio
A.; Meier, Matt S.; Newton, Frank;
*Reference Works; Ybarra-Frausto, Tomas.

582 Machado, Manuel A., Jr. Book review of: A
BIBLIOGRAPHY OF MEXICAN-AMERICAN HISTORY.
JOURNAL OF AMERICAN ETHNIC HISTORY, Vol. 5,
no. 2 (Spring 1986), p. 80. English. **DESCR:**
Book Reviews; Meier, Matt S.

Bicentennial Commission

583 Bi-centennial [editorial]. LATIN QUARTER,
Vol. 1, no. 3 (February 1975), p. 2.
English. **DESCR:** *American Bicentennial;
Montoya, Dennis.

Bicultural Education
USE: Bilingual Bicultural Education

Biculturalism

584 Burnham, M. Audrey, et al. Measurement of
acculturation in a community population of
Mexican Americans. HISPANIC JOURNAL OF
BEHAVIORAL SCIENCES, Vol. 9, no. 2 (June
1987), p. 105-130. English. **DESCR:**
*Acculturation; Age Groups; Research
Methodology; Sex Roles.

585 Mares, Antonio. El coyote: between two
cultures. EL CUADERNO, Vol. 2, no. 1 (1972),
p. 20-23. English. **DESCR:** Cultural
Pluralism; *Intermarriage.

BILINDEX: A BILINGUAL SPANISH-ENGLISH SUBJECT HEADING LIST

586 Chabran, Richard. Book review of: BILINDEX.
LA RED/THE NET, no. 87 (July 1985), p. 6-8.
English. **DESCR:** Book Reviews; HISPANEX
(Oakland, CA); Subject Headings.

BILINGUAL AND ESL CLASSROOMS: TEACHING IN MULTICULTURAL CONTEXTS

587 Hopkins, Thomas. Book review of: BILINGUAL
AND ESL CLASSROOMS: TEACHING IN
MULTICULTURAL CONTEXTS. EDUCATIONAL
LEADERSHIP, Vol. 43, no. 6 (March 1986), p.
82. English. **DESCR:** Book Reviews; Collier,
Virginia P.; Ovando, Carlos J.

588 Nieto, Sonia. Book review of: BILINGUAL AND
ESL CLASSROOMS: TEACHING IN MULTICULTURAL
CONTEXTS. INTERRACIAL BOOKS FOR CHILDREN,
Vol. 17, no. 3-4 (1986), p. 30. English.
DESCR: Book Reviews; Collier, Virginia P.;
Ovando, Carlos J.

Bilingual Ballots
USE: Voting Rights

Bilingual Bicultural Education

589 Allen, David. Bilingual education: door to
the society of the future. LLUEVE TLALOC,
no. 1 (1974), p. 22. English. **DESCR:**
*Essays.

Bilingual Bicultural Education (cont.)

590 Allen, David. Educacion bilingue: puerta a la sociedad del futuro. LLUEVE TLALOC, no. 1 (1974), p. 21. Spanish. **DESCR:** *Essays.

591 Arenas, Soledad and Trujillo, Lorenzo A. The evaluation of four Head Start bilingual multicultural curriculum models. LA RED/THE NET, no. 66 (March 1983), p. 2-5. English. **DESCR:** *Cultural Pluralism; Evaluation (Educational); *Head Start.

592 Baker, Keith and de Kanter, Adriana. An answer from research on bilingual education. AMERICAN EDUCATION, Vol. 19, no. 6, p. 40-48. English. **DESCR:** Language Assessment; Language Development; Research Methodology.

593 Bernal, Ernesto. The fate of bilingual education during an era of school reform. JOURNAL OF THE ASSOCIATION OF MEXICAN AMERICAN EDUCATORS, (1986, 1987), p. 29-36. English.

594 Bixler-Marquez, Dennis J. The introduction of bilingual education programs--a collaborative approach. EDUCATION, Vol. 105, no. 4 (Summer 1985), p. 443-448. English. **DESCR:** Educational Theory and Practice; Federal Government.

595 Cervantes, Robert A. Ethnocentric pedagogy and minority student growth: implications for the common school. EDUCATION AND URBAN SOCIETY, Vol. 16, no. 3 (May 1984), p. 274-293. English. **DESCR:** California; Discrimination in Education; *Education.

596 Chesterfield, Ray A. and Chesterfield, Kathleen Barrows. "Hojas with the H": spontaneous peer teaching in bilingual classrooms. BILINGUAL REVIEW, Vol. 12, no. 3 (September, December, 1985), p. 198-208. English. **DESCR:** Bilingualism; Education; *Teacher-pupil Interaction.

597 Cohen, Gaynor. The politics of bilingual education. OXFORD REVIEW OF EDUCATION, Vol. 10, no. 2 (1984), p. 225-241. English. **DESCR:** Educational Law and Legislation; Public Policy.

598 Eddy, John P. and Martin, William. Application of competency-based criteria to bilingual-bicultural education. FOCUS ON LEARNING, Vol. 11, no. 1 (Spring 1985), p. 13-16. English. **DESCR:** Teacher Training.

599 Elford, George. Catholic schools and bilingual education. MOMENTUM, Vol. 14, no. 1 (February 1983), p. 35-37. English. **DESCR:** *Catholic Church; Religious Education.

600 Fishman, Joshua A. Minority mother tongues in education. PROSPECTS: QUARTERLY REVIEW OF EDUCATION, Vol. 14, no. 1 (1984), p. 51-61. English. **DESCR:** *Bilingualism; Ethnic Groups.

601 Gonzalez, Gustavo. Book review of: BILINGUAL-BICULTURAL EDUCATION: AN ANNOTATED BIBLIOGRAPHY, 1936-1982. MODERN LANGUAGE JOURNAL, Vol. 69, no. 3 (Fall 1985), p. 299-300. English. **DESCR:** Ballesteros, Octavio A.; Bibliography; *BILINGUAL-BICULTURAL EDUCATION: AN ANNOTATED BIBLIOGRAPHY; Book Reviews.

602 Henkin, Alan B.; Singleton, Carole A.; and Nguyen, Liem T. Seeking goodness of fit: measuring the readability of bilingual learning materials. BILINGUAL REVIEW, Vol. 11, no. 3 (September, December, 1984), p. 9-24. English. **DESCR:** *Curriculum Materials; Reading.

603 Holt, Patricia. Richard Rodriguez. PUBLISHER'S WEEKLY, Vol. 221, (March 26, 1982), p. 6-8. English. **DESCR:** *HUNGER OF MEMORY: THE EDUCATION OF RICHARD RODRIGUEZ; *Rodriguez, Richard.

604 Magallan, Rafael J. 1983-84 NAEP data raises questions regarding the school experiences of language minority children. LA RED/THE NET, no. 92 (November, December, 1985), p. 9-11. English. **DESCR:** Bilingualism; Dropouts; English as a Second Language; *National Assessment of Educational Progress; Surveys.

605 Morales, Carlos. The controversy over bilingual education. VISTA, Vol. 1, no. 6 (February 2, 1986), p. 8-10. English. **DESCR:** *Bilingual Education Act of 1968; Educational Tests and Measurements; Educational Theory and Practice; Federal Aid.

606 Mortensen, Eileen. Reading achievement of native Spanish-speaking elementary students in bilingual vs. monolingual programs. BILINGUAL REVIEW, Vol. 11, no. 3 (September, December, 1984), p. 31-36. English. **DESCR:** *Academic Achievement; Language Usage; Primary School Education; *Reading.

607 Nelson, F. Howard. Issues in state funding for bilingual education. THE URBAN REVIEW, Vol. 16, no. 4 (1984), p. 195-208. English.

608 Nieto, Sonia. Past accomplishments, current needs: la lucha continua. INTERRACIAL BOOKS FOR CHILDREN, Vol. 17, no. 2 (1986), p. 6-8. English. **DESCR:** *Children's Literature; Council on Interracial Books for Children; Poverty; Stereotypes.

609 Nieto, Sonia. Who's afraid of bilingual parents? BILINGUAL REVIEW, Vol. 12, no. 3 (September, December, 1985), p. 179-189. English. **DESCR:** *Community School Relationships; *Family; *Parent and Child Relationships; Teacher Training.

610 Olmedo Williams, Irma. Functions of code-switching as a communicative strategy in a Spanish-English bilingual classroom. LA RED/THE NET, no. 40 (March 1981), p. 6. English. **DESCR:** Bilingualism; *Language Usage.

611 Ornstein-Galicia, Jacob. Bilingualism, bilingual education, and language contact: the agony, the rewards--or how to unravel Babel. BILINGUAL REVIEW, Vol. 11, no. 3 (September, December, 1984), p. 72-82. English. **DESCR:** Bilingualism; Book Reviews; *LANGUAGES IN CONFLICT: LINGUISTIC ACCULTURATION IN THE GREAT PLAINS; Ridge, Martin; Schach, Paul; *THE NEW BILINGUALISM: AN AMERICAN DILEMMA.

612 Oxford-Carpenter, R., et al. Projections of number of limited English proficient (LEP) persons to the year 2000. LA RED/THE NET, no. 50 (January 1982), p. 2-3. English. **DESCR:** Limited English Proficient (LEP).

613 Proefriedt, William A. Equality of opportunity and bilingual education. BILINGUAL REVIEW, Vol. 11, no. 3 (September, December, 1984), p. 3-8. English. **DESCR:** *Discrimination in Education.

Bilingual Bicultural Education (cont.)

614 Rips, Geoffrey. Puritanism, pluralism, and Perot. TEXAS OBSERVOR, Vol. 75, no. 17 (September 2, 1983), p. 3-4. English. **DESCR**: Adler, Mortimer; Educational Theory and Practice; Perot, Ross.

615 Rotberg, Iris C. Bilingual education policy in the United States. PROSPECTS: QUARTERLY REVIEW OF EDUCATION, Vol. 14, no. 1 (1984), p. 133-147. English. **DESCR**: Federal Government; *Public Policy.

616 Taking bilingualism to task. TIME, Vol. 119, (April 19, 1982), p. 68. English. **DESCR**: *Bilingualism; *Rodriguez, Richard.

617 Williams, Dennis A. Spanish as a learning tongue. NEWSWEEK, Vol. 104, (December 3, 1984), p. 92. English. **DESCR**: Language Arts.

618 Yzaguirre critical of committee action. NUESTRO, Vol. 11, no. 4 (May 1987), p. 8. English. **DESCR**: English-Only Movement; National Council of La Raza (NCLR); Yzaguirre, Raul.

BILINGUAL BOOKS IN SPANISH AND ENGLISH FOR CHILDREN

619 Bennett, Priscilla. Book review of: BILINGUAL BOOKS IN SPANISH AND ENGLISH FOR CHILDREN. EMERGENCY LIBRARIAN, Vol. 13, no. 1 (September, October, 1985), p. 31-32. English. **DESCR**: Book Reviews; Dale, Doris Cruger.

620 Martinez, Julio A. Book review of: BILINGUAL BOOKS IN SPANISH AND ENGLISH FOR CHILDREN. RQ - REFERENCE AND ADULT SERVICES DIVISION, Vol. 25, (Spring 1986), p. 387. English. **DESCR**: Book Reviews; Dale, Doris Cruger.

621 Rockman, Ilene F. Book review of: BILINGUAL BOOKS IN SPANISH AND ENGLISH FOR CHILDREN. AMERICAN REFERENCE BOOKS ANNUAL, Vol. 17, (1986), p. 431. English. **DESCR**: Book Reviews; Dale, Doris Cruger.

622 Whatley, Patricia L. Book review of: BILINGUAL BOOKS IN SPANISH AND ENGLISH FOR CHILDREN. TOP OF THE NEWS, Vol. 43, (Fall 1986), p. 120. English. **DESCR**: Book Reviews; Dale, Doris Cruger.

Bilingual Children's Television, Inc.

623 Lopez, Jose Y. A visit to VILLA ALEGRE. LATIN QUARTER, Vol. 1, no. 3 (January, February, 1975), p. 8-12. English. **DESCR**: *Children's Television; Cultural Pluralism; Public Television; *VILLA ALEGRE [television program].

Bilingual Education Act of 1968

624 Morales, Carlos. The controversy over bilingual education. VISTA, Vol. 1, no. 6 (February 2, 1986), p. 8-10. English. **DESCR**: *Bilingual Bicultural Education; Educational Tests and Measurements; Educational Theory and Practice; Federal Aid.

BILINGUAL EDUCATION FOR HISPANIC STUDENTS IN THE UNITED STATES

625 Nieto, Sonia. Book review of: BILINGUAL EDUCATION FOR HISPANIC STUDENTS IN THE UNITED STATES. INTERRACIAL BOOKS FOR CHILDREN, Vol. 17, no. 3-4 (1986), p. 29-30. English. **DESCR**: Book Reviews; Fishman, Joshua A.; Keller, Gary D.

BILINGUAL EDUCATION: EVALUATION, ASSESSMENT AND METHODOLOGY

626 Aitchison, Jean. Book review of: BILINGUAL EDUCATION: EVALUATION, ASSESSMENT AND METHODOLOGY. BRITISH BOOK NEWS, (January 1986), p. 32-33. English. **DESCR**: Book Reviews; Dodson, C.J.

BILINGUAL EDUCATION: A SOURCEBOOK

627 Gonzales-Berry, Erlinda. Book review of: BILINGUAL EDUCATION: A SOURCEBOOK. MODERN LANGUAGE JOURNAL, Vol. 69, no. 3 (Fall 1985), p. 299. English. **DESCR**: Ambert, Alba N.; Book Reviews; Melendez, Sarah E.

628 Nieto, Sonia. Book review of: BILINGUAL EDUCATION: A SOURCEBOOK. INTERRACIAL BOOKS FOR CHILDREN, Vol. 17, no. 3-4 (1986), p. 29. English. **DESCR**: Ambert, Alba N.; Book Reviews; Melendez, Sarah E.

629 Soudek, Lev I. Book review of: BILINGUAL EDUCATION: A SOURCEBOOK. AMERICAN REFERENCE BOOKS ANNUAL, Vol. 17, (1986), p. 132. English. **DESCR**: Ambert, Alba N.; Book Reviews; Melendez, Sarah E.

BILINGUAL MULTICULTURAL EDUCATION AND THE PROFESSIONAL

630 Nieto, Sonia. Book review of: BILINGUAL MULTICULTURAL EDUCATION AND THE PROFESSIONAL: FROM THEORY TO PRACTICE. INTERRACIAL BOOKS FOR CHILDREN, Vol. 17, no. 3-4 (1986), p. 30. English. **DESCR**: Barnett-Mizrahi, Carol; Book Reviews; Trueba, Henry T.

Bilingual Review Press

631 Bruce-Novoa, Juan. Meet the writers of the 80s. VISTA, Vol. 1, no. 11 (July 6, 1986), p. 15-16. English. **DESCR**: Anaya, Rudolfo A.; Arte Publico Press; *Authors; Cisneros, Sandra; Hinojosa-Smith, Rolando R.; Keller, Gary D.; *Literature; Pineda, Cecile; Quinto Sol Publishing, Inc.; Rivera, Tomas; Soto, Gary.

Bilingual/Bicultural Coalition on Mass Media

632 Madrid, Vicente and Yepes, Maria Elena. National Latino Media Coalition. LATIN QUARTER, Vol. 1, no. 4 (July, August, 1975), p. 4-7. English. **DESCR**: Affirmative Action Programs; *Broadcast Media; California Association of Latins in Broadcasting; Conferences and Meetings; Federal Communications Commission (FCC); *National Latino Media Coalition (NLMC); Puerto Rican Media Action and Educational Council.

BILINGUAL-BICULTURAL EDUCATION: AN ANNOTATED BIBLIOGRAPHY

633 Gonzalez, Gustavo. Book review of: BILINGUAL-BICULTURAL EDUCATION: AN ANNOTATED BIBLIOGRAPHY, 1936-1982. MODERN LANGUAGE JOURNAL, Vol. 69, no. 3 (Fall 1985), p. 299-300. English. **DESCR**: Ballesteros, Octavio A.; Bibliography; Bilingual Bicultural Education; Book Reviews.

634 Nieto, Sonia. Book review of: BILINGUAL-BICULTURAL EDUCATION: AN ANNOTATED BIBLIOGRAPHY, 1936-1982. INTERRACIAL BOOKS FOR CHILDREN, Vol. 17, no. 3-4 (1986), p. 29. English. **DESCR**: Ballesteros, Octavio A.; Book Reviews.

Bilingualism

635 Bohn, Martin J. and Traub, Gary S. Alienation of monolingual Hispanics in a federal correctional institution. PSYCHOLOGICAL REPORTS, Vol. 59, no. 2 (October 1986), p. 560-562. English. DESCR: *Minnesota Multiphasic Personality Inventory (MMPI); *Prisoners; *Psychological Testing.

636 Chesterfield, Ray A. and Chesterfield, Kathleen Barrows. "Hojas with the H": spontaneous peer teaching in bilingual classrooms. BILINGUAL REVIEW, Vol. 12, no. 3 (September, December, 1985), p. 198-208. English. DESCR: *Bilingual Bicultural Education; Education; *Teacher-pupil Interaction.

637 Dodson, C.J. Living with two languages. JOURNAL OF MULTILINGUAL AND MULTICULTURAL DEVELOPMENT, Vol. 4, no. 6 (1983), p. 401-414. English.

638 Duran, Richard P. Book review of: CULTURE AND THE BILINGUAL CLASSROOM. LA RED/THE NET, no. 44 (July 1981), p. 4-5. English. DESCR: Book Reviews; *CULTURE AND THE BILINGUAL CLASSROOM: STUDIES IN CLASSROOM ETHNOLOGY; Guthrie, Grace Pung; Hu-Pei Au, Kathryn; Trueba, Henry T.

639 Duran, Richard P. and Guerra, Elsa. Evidence for scripts governing bilingual children's oral reading behavior. LA RED/THE NET, no. 43 (June 1981), p. 6. English. DESCR: Children; *Reading.

640 Fishman, Joshua A. Minority mother tongues in education. PROSPECTS: QUARTERLY REVIEW OF EDUCATION, Vol. 14, no. 1 (1984), p. 51-61. English. DESCR: Bilingual Bicultural Education; Ethnic Groups.

641 Grenier, Gilles. An economic perspective on learning a second language. JOURNAL OF MULTILINGUAL AND MULTICULTURAL DEVELOPMENT, Vol. 4, no. 6 (1983), p. 471-483. English. DESCR: Canada; Economics; *Language Usage.

642 Hidalgo, Margarita. On the question of "standard" versus "dialect": implications for teaching Hispanic college students. HISPANIC JOURNAL OF BEHAVIORAL SCIENCES, Vol. 9, no. 4 (December 1987), p. 375-395. English. DESCR: Chicano Dialects; *Foreign Language Instruction; Language Usage; Puerto Ricans; Sociolinguistics; Spanish for Native Speakers; *Spanish Language.

643 Hurtado, Aida and Gurin, Patricia. Ethnic identity and bilingualism attitudes. HISPANIC JOURNAL OF BEHAVIORAL SCIENCES, Vol. 9, no. 1 (March 1987), p. 1-18. English. DESCR: *Attitudes; *Identity; Political Socialization.

644 Koike, Dale April. Theoretical linguistics: code-switching in the bilingual Chicano narrative. THE AMERICAN MERCURY, Vol. 70, no. 1 (March 1987), p. 148-154. English. DESCR: Language Usage; *Linguistic Theory; *Sociolinguistics.

645 Macias, Reynaldo Flores. Book review of: THE NEW BILINGUALISM: AN AMERICAN DILEMMA. LA RED/THE NET, no. 61 (November 1982), p. 7-9. English. DESCR: Book Reviews; Public Policy; Ridge, Martin; *THE NEW BILINGUALISM: AN AMERICAN DILEMMA.

646 Magallan, Rafael J. 1983-84 NAEP data raises questions regarding the school experiences of language minority children. LA RED/THE NET, no. 92 (November, December, 1985), p. 9-11. English. DESCR: *Bilingual Bicultural Education; Dropouts; English as a Second Language; *National Assessment of Educational Progress; Surveys.

647 McMenamin, Jerry. Language deficits in a bilingual child with cerebral cysticercosis. BILINGUAL REVIEW, Vol. 11, no. 3 (September, December, 1984), p. 25-30. English. DESCR: *Cerebral Cysticercosis; Diseases; Handicapped; *Language Development.

648 Mixed messages sent to June graduates. HISPANIC TIMES, Vol. 8, no. 3 (May, June, 1987), p. 18. English. DESCR: *Careers; *College Graduates.

649 Mujica, Barbara. Creative code switching. VISTA, Vol. 1, no. 5 (January 5, 1986), p. 22. English. DESCR: *Cognition; Language Usage; *Zentella, Ana Celia.

650 Olmedo Williams, Irma. Functions of code-switching as a communicative strategy in a Spanish-English bilingual classroom. LA RED/THE NET, no. 40 (March 1981), p. 6. English. DESCR: Bilingual Bicultural Education; *Language Usage.

651 Ornstein-Galicia, Jacob. Bilingualism, bilingual education, and language contact: the agony, the rewards--or how to unravel Babel. BILINGUAL REVIEW, Vol. 11, no. 3 (September, December, 1984), p. 72-82. English. DESCR: Bilingual Bicultural Education; Book Reviews; *LANGUAGES IN CONFLICT: LINGUISTIC ACCULTURATION IN THE GREAT PLAINS; Ridge, Martin; Schach, Paul; *THE NEW BILINGUALISM: AN AMERICAN DILEMMA.

652 Otheguy, Ricardo. Book review of: BILINGUALISM THROUGH SCHOOLING. MODERN LANGUAGE JOURNAL, Vol. 69, no. 3 (Fall 1985), p. 300-301. English. DESCR: *BILINGUALISM THROUGH SCHOOLING: CROSS-CULTURAL EDUCATION FOR MINORITY AND MAJORITY STUDENTS; Book Reviews; Ramirez, Arnulfo G.

653 Rodriguez, Salvador. El idioma de Aztlan: una lengua que surge. LA COMUNIDAD, No. 266 (August 25, 1985), p. 6-7. Spanish. DESCR: *Chicano Dialects; Language Interference; Pachucos; Sociolinguistics; Spanish Language.

654 Ryan, Ellen Bouchard. An interdisciplinary perspective on the bilingual experience. BILINGUAL REVIEW, Vol. 11, no. 3 (September, December, 1984), p. 69-71. English. DESCR: Book Reviews; Grosjean, Francois; *LIFE WITH TWO LANGUAGES: AN INTRODUCTION TO BILINGUALISM.

655 Sanchez, Nicholas. Bilingualism creates more problems than solutions. VISTA, Vol. 3, no. 3 (November 8, 1987), p. 38. English. DESCR: English Language.

656 Silva-Corvalan, Carmen. Bilingualism and language change: the extension of estar in Los Angeles Spanish. LANGUAGE, Vol. 62, no. 3 (September 1986), p. 587-608. English. DESCR: Language Interference; *Language Usage; *Linguistics; *Los Angeles, CA.

657 So, Alvin Yiu-cheong. The analysis of language minority issues in national data sets. LA RED/THE NET, no. 71 (August 1983), p. 3-5. English. DESCR: Databases; *Language Usage; *National Center for Bilingual Research; Surveys.

Bilingualism (cont.)

658 Taking bilingualism to task. TIME, Vol. 119, (April 19, 1982), p. 68. English. **DESCR:** *Bilingual Bicultural Education; *Rodriguez, Richard.

659 Taylor, Maria T. Mucho Spanglish brews unsavory linguistic stew. VISTA, Vol. 1, no. 10 (June 8, 1986), p. 3. English. **DESCR:** *Essays; Language Proficiency; Language Usage.

660 Trueba, Henry T. Book review of: BILINGUALISM THROUGH SCHOOLING. LA RED/THE NET, no. 92 (November, December, 1985), p. 18-20. English. **DESCR:** *BILINGUALISM THROUGH SCHOOLING: CROSS-CULTURAL EDUCATION FOR MINORITY AND MAJORITY STUDENTS; Book Reviews; Ramirez, Arnulfo G.

661 Valencia, Humberto. Sales pitch to Hispanics must strike right chord. VISTA, Vol. 1, no. 12 (August 2, 1986), p. 3. English. **DESCR:** *Advertising; Language Usage.

662 Wolfe, David E. Book review of: BILINGUALISM AND SPECIAL EDUCATION: ISSUES IN ASSESSMENT AND PEDAGOGY. MODERN LANGUAGE JOURNAL, Vol. 71, (Spring 1987), p. 81. English. **DESCR:** *BILINGUALISM AND SPECIAL EDUCATION; Book Reviews; Cummins, Jim; Special Education.

BILINGUALISM AND LANGUAGE CONTACT: SPANISH, ENGLISH, AND NATIVE AMERICAN LANGUAGES

663 Penalosa, Fernando. Book review of: BILINGUALISM AND LANGUAGE CONTACT: SPANISH, ENGLISH AND NATIVE AMERICAN LANGUAGES. LA RED/THE NET, no. 66 (March 1983), p. 5-8. English. **DESCR:** Barkin, Florence; Book Reviews; Brandt, Elizabeth H.; Ornstein-Galicia, Jacob.

BILINGUALISM AND MINORITY-LANGUAGE CHILDREN

664 Nieto, Sonia. Book review of: BILINGUALISM AND MINORITY-LANGUAGE CHILDREN. INTERRACIAL BOOKS FOR CHILDREN, Vol. 17, no. 3-4 (1986), p. 29. English. **DESCR:** Book Reviews; Cummins, Jim.

BILINGUALISM AND SPECIAL EDUCATION

665 Wolfe, David E. Book review of: BILINGUALISM AND SPECIAL EDUCATION: ISSUES IN ASSESSMENT AND PEDAGOGY. MODERN LANGUAGE JOURNAL, Vol. 71, (Spring 1987), p. 81. English. **DESCR:** Bilingualism; Book Reviews; Cummins, Jim; Special Education.

BILINGUALISM: SOCIAL ISSUES AND POLICY IMPLICATIONS

666 Lopez, David E. Book review of: BILINGUALISM: SOCIAL ISSUES AND POLICY IMPLICATIONS. CONTEMPORARY SOCIOLOGY: A JOURNAL OF REVIEWS, Vol. 15, no. 3 (May 1986), p. 391-392. English. **DESCR:** Book Reviews; Miracle, Andrew W.

BILINGUALISM THROUGH SCHOOLING: CROSS-CULTURAL EDUCATION FOR MINORITY AND MAJORITY STUDENTS

667 La Salle, Robin Avelar. Book review of: BILINGUALISM THROUGH SCHOOLING. HISPANIC JOURNAL OF BEHAVIORAL SCIENCES, Vol. 9, no. 2 (June 1987), p. 237-240. English. **DESCR:** Book Reviews; Ramirez, Arnulfo G.

668 Nieto, Sonia. Book review of: BILINGUALISM THROUGH SCHOOLING. INTERRACIAL BOOKS FOR CHILDREN, Vol. 17, no. 3-4 (1986), p. 30. English. **DESCR:** Book Reviews; Ramirez,

Arnulfo G.

669 Otheguy, Ricardo. Book review of: BILINGUALISM THROUGH SCHOOLING. MODERN LANGUAGE JOURNAL, Vol. 69, no. 3 (Fall 1985), p. 300-301. English. **DESCR:** Bilingualism; Book Reviews; Ramirez, Arnulfo G.

670 Swing, E. S. Book review of: BILINGUALISM THROUGH SCHOOLING. CHOICE, Vol. 23, no. 2 (October 1985), p. 340. English. **DESCR:** Book Reviews; Ramirez, Arnulfo G.

671 Trueba, Henry T. Book review of: BILINGUALISM THROUGH SCHOOLING. LA RED/THE NET, no. 92 (November, December, 1985), p. 18-20. English. **DESCR:** Bilingualism; Book Reviews; Ramirez, Arnulfo G.

Biographical Notes

672 Beale, Stephen. 100 influentials and their assessment of the critical issues. HISPANIC BUSINESS, Vol. 9, no. 8 (August 1987), p. 20-32. English. **DESCR:** *Leadership; Public Policy.

673 Estrada, William. The life and legend of Ernesto Galarza=La vida y legado de Ernesto Galarza. AMERICAS 2001, Premiere Issue, 1987, p. 26-27. Bilingual. **DESCR:** *Galarza, Ernesto.

674 Galeria 2001. AMERICAS 2001, Vol. 1, no. 3 (November, December, 1987), p. [8-9]. Bilingual. **DESCR:** Artists; *Gamboa, Harry, Jr.; Photography.

675 Lopez-Knox wins fellowship award. HISPANIC TIMES, Vol. 8, no. 1 (December, January, 1987), p. 21. English. **DESCR:** Awards; Chicanas; *Lopez-Knox, Joanne; Science.

676 Our 1986 Latino awards: triunfos, fiascos, winners and losers. NUESTRO, Vol. 11, no. 1-2 (1987), p. 9-25. English. **DESCR:** *Awards.

677 Rifkin, Jane M. New avenues for women in technology. HISPANIC TIMES, Vol. 8, no. 3 (May, June, 1987), p. 41. English. **DESCR:** *Chicanas; Engineering as a Profession; *Ponce, Alice.

678 Susana Rendon. AMERICAS 2001, Vol. 1, no. 1 (June, July, 1987), p. [31]. Bilingual. **DESCR:** Businesspeople; Chicanas; *Rendon, Susana.

Biography

679 Alonso, Miguel Angel. El significado de cruzar la frontera. LA COMUNIDAD, No. 355 (May 10, 1987), p. 10-11. Spanish. **DESCR:** *Blades, Ruben; *Music.

680 Barnes, Jill. The winning formula of Nancy Lopez. VISTA, Vol. 2, no. 12 (August 1, 1987), p. 6-9. English. **DESCR:** *Athletes; *Lopez, Nancy.

681 Barragan, Ma. Antonieta. Carlos Almaraz: "El arte contemporaneo no tiene mucha emocion, es estatico...". LA COMUNIDAD, No. 324 (October 5, 1986), p. 10-11. Spanish. **DESCR:** *Almaraz, Carlos; *Art.

682 Barrios, Greg. Efrain Gutierrez y el nuevo cine chicano. LA COMUNIDAD, No. 265 (August 18, 1985), p. 3. Spanish. **DESCR:** *Films; *Gutierrez, Efrain; PLEASE DON'T BURY ME ALIVE [film].

Biography (cont.)

683 Beale, Stephen. CEOs. HISPANIC BUSINESS,
Vol. 9, no. 4 (April 1987), p. 20-37, 52.
English. **DESCR:** Alvarez, Roberto; Batarse,
Anthony A.; Business Enterprises;
*Businesspeople; Carlo, Nelson; Estrada,
Anthony; Flores, Frank; Fullana, Jaime, Jr.;
Hernandez, George; *Management; Ortega,
James; Quirch, Guillermo; Ruiz, Roberto;
Santa Maria, Yvonne Z.; Sugranes, Rosa;
Tamaya, Carlos; Young, Paul H., Jr.

684 Beale, Stephen and Valdez, Luis. Connecting
with the American experience: an interview
with Luis Valdez. HISPANIC BUSINESS, Vol. 9,
no. 7 (July 1987), p. 10-13. English.
DESCR: Films; LA BAMBA [film]; Stereotypes;
Teatro; *Valdez, Luis.

685 Beale, Stephen. Moving trucks in New Mexico.
HISPANIC BUSINESS, Vol. 9, no. 8 (August
1987), p. 34-37. English. **DESCR:** *Automobile
Industry; Baca Pontiac-Buick-GMC, Belen, NM;
*Baca, Ruben; Businesspeople.

686 Benson, Douglas K. and Quintana, Leroy V. A
conversation with Leroy V. Quintana.
BILINGUAL REVIEW, Vol. 12, no. 3 (September,
December. 1985), p. 218-229. English.
DESCR: Authors; HIJO DEL PUEBLO; Poetry;
*Quintana, Leroy V.; SANGRE.

687 Bernal, Esmeralda. ...And she became a
proletarian. REVISTA MUJERES, Vol. 2, no. 2
(June 1985), p. 38-42. English. **DESCR:** *Farm
Workers.

688 Bradby, Marie. Solomon Trujillo of US West.
HISPANIC ENGINEER, Vol. 3, no. 5 (Winter
1987), p. 26-30. English. **DESCR:** Engineering
as a Profession; *Trujillo, Solomon; US West
[telecommunications company].

689 Bruce-Novoa, Juan. La critica chicana de
Luis Leal (I). LA COMUNIDAD, No. 280
(December 1, 1985), p. 2-5. Spanish. **DESCR:**
Authors; *Leal, Luis; *Literary Criticism.

690 Bruce-Novoa, Juan. La critica chicana de
Luis Leal (II). LA COMUNIDAD, No. 281
(December 8, 1985), p. 14-15. Spanish.
DESCR: Authors; *Leal, Luis; *Literary
Criticism.

691 Bruce-Novoa, Juan. Ernest Brawley: un
escritor chicano desconocido. LA COMUNIDAD,
No. 277 (November 10, 1985), p. 6-7.
Spanish. **DESCR:** Authors; *Brawley, Ernest;
Literary Criticism; Novel; SELENA [novel];
THE ALAMO TREE [novel]; THE RAP [novel].

692 Bruce-Novoa, Juan. Nash Candelaria:
novelista (I). LA COMUNIDAD, No. 245 (March
31, 1985), p. 6-7. Spanish. **DESCR:**
*Candelaria, Nash; *Literary Criticism;
MEMORIES OF THE ALHAMBRA; NOT BY THE SWORD;
Novel.

693 Bruce-Novoa, Juan. Nash Candelaria:
novelista (II). LA COMUNIDAD, No. 246 (April
7, 1985), p. 10-11. Spanish. **DESCR:**
*Candelaria, Nash; *Literary Criticism;
MEMORIES OF THE ALHAMBRA; NOT BY THE SWORD;
Novel.

694 Burciaga, Jose Antonio and Ronstadt, Linda.
Linda Ronstadt: my Mexican soul. VISTA, Vol.
2, no. 10 (June 7, 1987), p. 6-8. English.
DESCR: CORRIDOS [film]; *Musicians;
*Ronstadt, Linda.

695 Cano, Oscar. Profiles in engineering.
HISPANIC TIMES, Vol. 8, no. 3 (May, June,
1987), p. 43. English. **DESCR:** *Engineering
as a Profession; *Valenzuela, Ralph.

696 Cardinal, Roger. El mensaje de Martin
Ramirez. LA COMUNIDAD, No. 361 (June 21,
1987), p. 2-3+. Spanish. **DESCR:** *Artists;
*Ramirez, Martin (1885-1960).

697 Castellanos, Teresa and Lopez, Margarita. La
huelga nos ha ensenado a hablar. REVISTA
MUJERES, Vol. 3, no. 2 (June 1986), p.
22-28. Spanish. **DESCR:** Canneries; *Chicanas;
Strikes and Lockouts.

698 Castellanos, Teresa. I never lose a dream:
an interview with Yvette Galindo. REVISTA
MUJERES, Vol. 2, no. 1 (January 1985), p.
7-10. English. **DESCR:** *Galindo, Yvette.

699 Cerda, Gabriela. Hidden jewel: the Frida
Kahlo house of Coyoacan. NOTEBOOK: A LITTLE
MAGAZINE, Vol. 1, no. 1 (1985), p. 2-7.
English. **DESCR:** Artists; *Kahlo, Frida.

700 Cespedes, Marisa. "Que viva la vida"
biografia de Frida Kahlo. LA COMUNIDAD, No.
345 (March 1, 1987), p. 12-13. Spanish.
DESCR: Artists; *Kahlo, Frida.

701 Chavez, Lorenzo A. La Bamba. VISTA, Vol. 2,
no. 11 (July 5, 1987), p. 12-13. English.
DESCR: *Actors and Actresses; De Soto,
Rosana; Films; LA BAMBA [film]; *Morales,
Esai; Pena, Elizabeth; Phillips, Lou
Diamond.

702 Chavez, Lorenzo A. Ramon Duarte. VISTA, Vol.
1, no. 9 (May 3, 1986), p. 20. English.
DESCR: *Duarte, Ramon; *Medical Personnel.

703 Cortes, Ernesto, Jr. Changing the locus of
political decision making. CHRISTIANITY AND
CRISIS, Vol. 47, no. 1 (February 2, 1987),
p. 18-22. English. **DESCR:** *Communities
Organized for Public Service (COPS);
*Cortes, Ernesto, Jr.; *Political Parties
and Organizations; San Antonio, TX.

704 Davila, Elisa. Conozcamos: de charla con Pat
Zavella. REVISTA MUJERES, Vol. 1, no. 1
(January 1984), p. 10-11. Spanish. **DESCR:**
*Zavella, Pat.

705 Dempsey, Mary. John Roy Castillo. VISTA,
Vol. 1, no. 11 (July 6, 1986), p. 20.
English. **DESCR:** *Castillo, John Ray; Civil
Rights; Michigan Civil Rights Department.

706 Forte, Dan. Los Lobos: Tex-Mex rock from
East L.A. GUITAR PLAYER, Vol. 21, no. 2
(February 1987), p. 68-94. English. **DESCR:**
Discography; Hidalgo, David (Los Lobos);
*Los Lobos del Este de Los Angeles (musical
group); Lozano, Conrad (Los Lobos);
*Musicians; Perez, Louie (Los Lobos);
Recording Industry; *Rock Music; Rosas,
Cesar (Los Lobos).

707 Galindo, Luis Alberto. El dios de la
lluvia=RAIN GOD. LA COMUNIDAD, No. 241
(March 3, 1985), p. 12-13. Spanish. **DESCR:**
Islas, Arturo; *Literary Criticism; Novel;
*THE RAIN GOD: A DESERT TALE.

708 Galindo-Ramirez, Tina. Educacion monolingue:
opresion o liberacion? REVISTA MUJERES, Vol.
1, no. 1 (January 1984), p. 8-9. Spanish.
DESCR: Alienation; Assertiveness;
*Education; English Language; *Identity.

Biography (cont.)

709 Getting to the top against all odds.
HISPANIC TIMES, Vol. 8, no. 5 (October,
November, 1987), p. 26. English. **DESCR:**
*Boxing; *Olivo, Joey.

710 Goldman, Shifra. El arte social de Domingo
Ulloa. LA COMUNIDAD, No. 277 (November 10,
1985), p. 8-9. Spanish. **DESCR:** *Artists;
*Ulloa, Domingo.

711 Goldman, Shifra. En medio de la tormenta de
"Gronk". LA COMUNIDAD, No. 313 (July 20,
1986), p. 8-9. Spanish. **DESCR:** *Art;
Artists; *Gronk (Pseud.)

712 Goldman, Shifra. Zarco Guerrero: tradicion y
transformacion. LA COMUNIDAD, No. 249 (April
28, 1985), p. 2-3. Spanish. **DESCR:** *Art;
*Guerrero, Adolfo "El Zarco"; Masks;
Sculpture.

713 Gonzalez, Elma. Origins: El Baluarte.
REVISTA MUJERES, Vol. 2, no. 1 (January
1985), p. 37-39. English.

714 Gonzalez, Miguel. Frida Kahlo entre la vida
y la pasion artistica. LA COMUNIDAD, No. 345
(March 1, 1987), p. 8-10. Spanish. **DESCR:**
Artists; *Kahlo, Frida.

715 Grajeda Higley, Leilani. Irma Castro. VISTA,
Vol. 2, no. 10 (June 7, 1987), p. 20.
English. **DESCR:** *Castro, Irma; Chicanas;
*Chicano Federation of San Diego Co., Inc.;
Civil Rights; Discrimination.

716 Guedella, Juan. Hispanic media--Caballero
style. HISPANIC BUSINESS, Vol. 9, no. 2
(February 1987), p. 17-18. English. **DESCR:**
Advertising; *Caballero, Eduardo; *Caballero
Spanish Media (CSM); Cubanos; Marketing.

717 Guerrero, Martha and Anaya, Toney. Toney
Anaya: a man with convictions=Toney Anaya:
un hombre de conviccion. AMERICAS 2001,
Premiere Issue, 1987, p. 20-23, 44.
Bilingual. **DESCR:** *Anaya, Toney, Governor of
New Mexico; Elected Officials; New Mexico;
Politics.

718 Guevara, Ruben and Blades, Ruben. Ruben
Blades: music, love and revolution=Ruben
Blades: musica, amor y revolucion. AMERICAS
2001, Vol. 1, no. 2 (September, October,
1987), p. 26-29,31. Bilingual. **DESCR:**
*Blades, Ruben; Films; *Musicians; Recording
Industry.

719 Gutierrez, Felix. Ralph Guzman remembered.
LA RED/THE NET, no. 91 (October 1985), p.
1-2. English. **DESCR:** *Guzman, Ralph;
Teaching Profession.

720 Haley, Lindsey. Gronk y su inquietante
concepto del arte. LA COMUNIDAD, No. 252
(May 19, 1985), p. 2-3. Spanish. **DESCR:**
*Artists; ASCO [art group], Los Angeles, CA;
Exhibits; *Gronk (Pseud.); OFF THE STREETS
[exhibit].

721 Hernandez, Roger E. Why is everyone picking
on Geraldo Rivera? VISTA, Vol. 2, no. 8
(April 4, 1987), p. 8-10. English. **DESCR:**
*Broadcast Media; *Rivera, Geraldo.

722 Herrera Duran, Patricia and Mares, Renee.
Ernest Duran: la ultima despedida. LATIN
QUARTER, Vol. 1, no. 3 (January, February,
1975), p. 34-36. English. **DESCR:** Drug Abuse
Programs; *Duran, Ernesto; Joint Efforts
[prison organization]; Prisons.

723 Hinojosa-Smith, Rolando R. La realidad
chicana se forjo con dos culturas. LA
COMUNIDAD, No. 313 (July 20, 1986), p. 6-7.
Spanish. **DESCR:** *Hinojosa-Smith, Rolando R.;
Literary Criticism; Novel.

724 Hinojosa-Smith, Rolando R. Tomas Rivera:
remembrances of an educator and a poet.
CONFLUENCIA, Vol. 1, no. 1 (Fall 1985), p.
90-93. English. **DESCR:** Authors; *Rivera,
Tomas.

725 Hoffman, Abraham. The controversial career
of Martin Aguirre; the rise and fall of a
Chicano lawman. CALIFORNIA HISTORY, Vol. 63,
no. 4 (Fall 1984), p. 295-341. English.
DESCR: *Aguirre, Martin; History; Los
Angeles County, CA; Prisoners; San Quentin
Prison.

726 Jimenez, Luis. En busca del talento latino.
LA COMUNIDAD, No. 235 (January 20, 1985), p.
14-15. Spanish. **DESCR:** Actors and Actresses;
Mass Media; *Morones, Bob.

727 Kane, George D. The entrepreneurial
professional. HISPANIC BUSINESS, Vol. 9, no.
9 (September 1987), p. 34-37, 80. English.
DESCR: Bonilla, Tony; *Businesspeople;
Cardenas, Ruben R.; Gomez, Rudy.

728 Kilgore, Julia. A risk taker. HISPANIC
BUSINESS, Vol. 9, no. 12 (December 1987), p.
44-47. English. **DESCR:** *Appointed Officials;
Careers; *Chicanas; *Diaz Dennis, Patricia;
Federal Communications Commission (FCC).

729 Lomeli, Francisco A. Entrevista con Rolando
Hinojosa (I). LA COMUNIDAD, No. 295 (March
16, 1986), p. 2-3+. Spanish. **DESCR:**
*Hinojosa-Smith, Rolando R.; Literary
Criticism; Novel; Short Story.

730 Lomeli, Francisco A. Entrevista con Rolando
Hinojosa (II). LA COMUNIDAD, No. 296 (March
23, 1986), p. 15. Spanish. **DESCR:**
*Hinojosa-Smith, Rolando R.; Literary
Criticism.

731 Lomeli, Francisco A. Luis Leal y la vocacion
por la literatura latinoamericana. LA
COMUNIDAD, No. 279 (November 24, 1985),
6-7+. Spanish. **DESCR:** Authors; *Leal, Luis;
*Literary Criticism; Literature.

732 Mazon, Mauricio. Report to the Network. LA
RED/THE NET, no. 95 (April 1986), p. 1-2.
English. **DESCR:** *Cervantes, Frederick A.

733 Melendez, Pablo. Happy Thanksgiving.
CALIFORNIA MAGAZINE, Vol. 11, no. 11
(November 1986), p. 136. English. **DESCR:**
*Essays; *Immigrants; *Melendez, Pablo;
Youth.

734 Mellado, Carmela. Dr. George Castro:
research scientist with IBM, San Jose.
HISPANIC ENGINEER, Vol. 3, no. 3 (1987), p.
22-24, 44. English. **DESCR:** *Castro, George;
International Business Machines (IBM).

735 Mellado, Carmela. Mitch Maidique. HISPANIC
ENGINEER, Vol. 3, no. 5 (Winter 1987), p.
34-36. English. **DESCR:** Educational
Administration; Florida International
University; *Maidique, Mitch.

736 Mellado, Carmela. SHPE co-founder Rodrigo T.
Garcia. HISPANIC ENGINEER, Vol. 3, no. 2
(Summer), p. 22-25. English. **DESCR:**
*Garcia, Rodrigo T.

Biography (cont.)

737 Mills, Kay. Gloria Molina. MS. MAGAZINE,
Vol. 13, (January 1985), p. 80-81+.
English. **DESCR:** Chicanas; Elected Officials;
*Molina, Gloria.

738 Montane, Diane. Edward James Olmos: the man
behind the tough film facade. VISTA, Vol. 1,
no. 1 (September 8, 1985), p. 8-12. English.
DESCR: *Actors and Actresses; BALLAD OF
GREGORIO CORTEZ [film]; *Olmos, Edward
James; WOLFEN [film]; ZOOT SUIT [film].

739 Ornelas, Yolanda. Determined to be
acknowledged. REVISTA MUJERES, Vol. 4, no. 1
(January 1987), p. 14-15. English. **DESCR:**
Attitudes; *Chicanas; Cultural
Characteristics.

740 Orozco, Aurora E. Un dia en la pisca de
algodon. REVISTA MUJERES, Vol. 3, no. 2
(June 1986), p. 30. Spanish. **DESCR:**
*Chicanas; Farm Workers.

741 Pena, Margarita. Apuntes para un retrato
chicano (I). LA COMUNIDAD, No. 270
(September 22, 1985), p. 12-14. Spanish.
DESCR: Artists; *Garza, Jose.

742 Pena, Margarita. Apuntes para un retrato
chicano (II). LA COMUNIDAD, No. 271
(September 29, 1985), p. 15. Spanish.
DESCR: Artists; *Garza, Jose.

743 Perez, Renato E. A governor named Martinez.
VISTA, Vol. 2, no. 5 (January 4, 1987), p.
10-11. English. **DESCR:** *Elected Officials;
Florida; *Martinez, Bob.

744 Pinon, Fernando. Conquistadors of space.
VISTA, Vol. 1, no. 4 (December 7, 1985), p.
6-9. English. **DESCR:** *Astronauts;
*Chang-Diaz, Franklin; *Gutierrez, Sidney.

745 Ramirez, Alma Beatrice. La suerte del que no
nacio. REVISTA MUJERES, Vol. 2, no. 2 (June
1985), p. 35-36. Spanish. **DESCR:** *Abortion.

746 Reyes outstanding Hispanic at Kennedy Space
Center. HISPANIC TIMES, Vol. 8, no. 5
(October, November, 1987), p. 60. English.
DESCR: *Engineering as a Profession; John F.
Kennedy Space Center, NASA, FL; *Reyes, Raul
E. (Ernie).

747 Ricardo Salazar. HISPANIC ENGINEER, Vol. 3,
no. 2 (Summer), p. 14-18. English. **DESCR:**
Magic of Science and Engineering Program;
Professional Organizations; *Salazar,
Ricardo; Society of Hispanic Professional
Engineers Northern California Chapter.

748 Riding the range at Golden West. NUESTRO,
Vol. 11, no. 3 (April 1987), p. 7-8.
English. **DESCR:** Colleges and Universities;
Educational Administration; *Garcia, Fred;
Golden West College, Huntington Beach, CA.

749 Rifkin, Jane M. Manuel Castro--founder of
MAES: a compassionate commitment. HISPANIC
TIMES, Vol. 8, no. 5 (October, November,
1987), p. 44. English. **DESCR:** *Castro,
Manuel; Engineering as a Profession; Mexican
American Engineering Society (MAES).

750 Rifkin, Jane M. Ralph de la Parra travels
the MAES "bridge to the future". HISPANIC
TIMES, Vol. 8, no. 1 (December, January,
1987), p. 30. English. **DESCR:** *De la Parra,
Ralph; *Engineering as a Profession; Mexican
American Engineering Society (MAES);
Southern California Edison Co.

751 Rifkin, Jane M. Up from the barrio...to
fittest woman cop in the U.S.A. HISPANIC
TIMES, Vol. 8, no. 1 (December, January,
1987), p. 38. English. **DESCR:** Careers;
*Chicanas; *Lopez, Theresa (Terry); *Police.

752 Rivera, Diego. Frida Kahlo y el arte
mexicano. LA COMUNIDAD, No. 345 (March 1,
1987), p. 6-7+. Spanish. **DESCR:** Artists;
*Kahlo, Frida.

753 A road fraught with challenge leads to view
from the top. HISPANIC TIMES, Vol. 8, no. 3
(May, June, 1987), p. 28. English. **DESCR:**
Authors; *Chicanas; Leadership; National
Network of Hispanic Women; Torres, Celia
Gonzales.

754 Rodriguez Flores, Juan. Andy Garcia: un
"Intocable" orgulloso de ser latino. LA
COMUNIDAD, No. 362 (June 28, 1987), p. 8-11.
Spanish. **DESCR:** Actors and Actresses;
*Garcia, Andy.

755 Rodriguez Flores, Juan. Esai Morales: un
joven de origen hispano con oficio de actor
(1). LA COMUNIDAD, No. 335 (December 21,
1986), p. 8-9. Spanish. **DESCR:** Actors and
Actresses; *Morales, Esai.

756 Rodriguez Flores, Juan. Esai Morales y la
pasion por el arte escenico (II). LA
COMUNIDAD, No. 336 (December 28, 1986), p.
2-3. Spanish. **DESCR:** Actors and Actresses;
Films; LA BAMBA [film]; *Morales, Esai;
Valdez, Luis.

757 Rodriguez Flores, Juan. Mike Gomez, otro
rostro hispano en Hollywood. LA COMUNIDAD,
No. 339 (January 18, 1987), p. 8-9. Spanish.
DESCR: Actos; *Gomez, Mike.

758 Rodriguez Flores, Juan. Ruben Blades en
busca de una nueva realidad musical (II). LA
COMUNIDAD, no. 33 (November 23, 1986), p.
2-5. Spanish. **DESCR:** *Blades, Ruben; Films;
Music.

759 Rodriguez Flores, Juan. Ruben Blades:
siempre he apostado a la sensibilidad del
publico. LA COMUNIDAD, No. 330 (November 16,
1986), p. 8-11. Spanish. **DESCR:** Actors and
Actresses; *Blades, Ruben; Films; Music; THE
MILAGRO BEANFIELD WAR [film].

760 Ross, I. Mayor Cisneros of San Antonio.
READER'S DIGEST, Vol. 125, (December 1984),
p. 193-194+. English. **DESCR:** *Cisneros,
Henry, Mayor of San Antonio, TX; *Elected
Officials; Local Government; San Antonio,
TX.

761 Ruelas, J. Oshi. Moments of change. REVISTA
MUJERES, Vol. 4, no. 1 (January 1987), p.
23-33. English. **DESCR:** Attitudes; *Chicanas.

762 Shaw, Katherine. Antonia Hernandez. VISTA,
Vol. 1, no. 2 (October 5, 1985), p. 16.
English. **DESCR:** Chicanas; *Hernandez,
Antonia A.; Mexican American Legal Defense
and Educational Fund (MALDEF).

763 Silva, Sojeila Maria. Mary Corralejo:
"...there next to you.". REVISTA MUJERES,
Vol. 1, no. 1 (January 1984), p. 12-13.
English. **DESCR:** *Corralejo, Mary.

764 Soriano, Diane H. The struggle continues: an
interview with Irene Serna. REVISTA MUJERES,
Vol. 2, no. 1 (January 1985), p. 40-42.
English. **DESCR:** *Serna, Irene.

Biography (cont.)

765 Sosa, Lionel. The human face of AIDS. VISTA, Vol. 3, no. 4 (December 6, 1987), p. 15, 36. English. **DESCR**: *Acquired Immune Deficiency Syndrome (AIDS); *Diseases.

766 Stone, Eric. The daring designs of Elena Valencia. VISTA, Vol. 1, no. 9 (May 3, 1986), p. 6-8. English. **DESCR**: Chicanas; *Fashion; La Blanca [fashion label]; *Valencia, Elena.

767 Tibol, Raquel. La biografa se espanto de una vida abierta. LA COMUNIDAD, No. 302 (May 4, 1986), p. 12-13. Spanish. **DESCR**: Book Reviews; FRIDA: A BIOGRAPHY OF FRIDA KAHLO; Herrera, Hayden; *Kahlo, Frida.

768 Trager, Cara S. Carving out a niche in politics. HISPANIC BUSINESS, Vol. 9, no. 10 (October 1987), p. 29-31. English. **DESCR**: *Chicanas; *Elected Officials; *Guerrero, Lena; Texas.

769 Trager, Cara S. Women of the year. HISPANIC BUSINESS, Vol. 9, no. 6 (June 1987), p. 78-82. English. **DESCR**: *Businesspeople; *Chicanas; Rivera, Betty.

Birth Control

770 Andrade, Sally J. Chicana adolescents and contraception issues. LA RED/THE NET, no. 35 (October 1980), p. 2,14. English. **DESCR**: *Chicanas; *Southwestern United States; *Youth.

771 Jorgensen, Stephen R. and Adams, Russell P. Family planning needs and behavior of Mexican American women: a study of health care professionals and their clientele. HISPANIC JOURNAL OF BEHAVIORAL SCIENCES, Vol. 9, no. 3 (September 1987), p. 265-286. English. **DESCR**: Acculturation; *Attitudes; *Chicanas; *Cultural Characteristics; *Family Planning; Fertility; Public Health; Stereotypes; Sterilization.

BLACK HAIR

772 Espada, Martin. Book review of: BLACK HAIR. LECTOR, Vol. 4, no. 4-6 (1987), p. 77. English. **DESCR**: Book Reviews; Soto, Gary.

Blackie's House of Beef v. Castillo

773 Aguilar, J. Federal court halts workplace searches based on broad inspection warrants. CRIMINAL LAW REPORTER, Vol. 38, no. 8 (November 20, 1985), p. 2150-2151. English. **DESCR**: *INS v. Delgado; *Search and Seizure.

Blacks

774 Acosta, Frank X., et al. Preparing low-income Hispanic, Black, and white patients for psychotherapy: evaluation of a new orientation program. JOURNAL OF CLINICAL PSYCHOLOGY, Vol. 39, no. 6 (November 1983), p. 872-877. English. **DESCR**: Anglo Americans; *Comparative Psychology; Mental Health; *Psychotherapy.

775 Browning, Rufus P. and Marshall, Dale Rogers. Black and Hispanic power in city politics: a forum. P.S. [AMERICAN POLITICAL SCIENCE ASSOCIATION], Vol. 19, no. 3 (Summer 1986), p. 573-639. English. **DESCR**: Browning, Rufus P.; Marshall, Dale Rogers; *Politics; *PROTEST IS NOT ENOUGH: THE STRUGGLE OF BLACKS AND HISPANICS FOR EQUALITY IN URBAN POLITICS; Tabb, David H.; Urban Communities.

776 Browning, Rufus P.; Marshall, Dale Rogers; and Tabb, David H. Protest is not enough: a theory of political incorporation. P.S. [AMERICAN POLITICAL SCIENCE ASSOCIATION], Vol. 19, no. 3 (Summer 1986), p. 576-581. English. **DESCR**: Browning, Rufus P.; Marshall, Dale Rogers; Political Representation; Politics; *PROTEST IS NOT ENOUGH: THE STRUGGLE OF BLACKS AND HISPANICS FOR EQUALITY IN URBAN POLITICS; Tabb, David H.; Urban Communities.

777 Gottdiener, M. Group differentiation in a metropolitan high school: the influence of race, class, gender and culture. QUALITATIVE SOCIOLOGY, Vol. 8, no. 1 (Spring 1985), p. 29-41. English. **DESCR**: Anglo Americans; Identity; *Secondary School Education.

778 Krivo, Lauren J. and Mutchler, Jan E. Housing constraint and household complexity in metropolitan America: Black and Spanish-origin minorities. URBAN AFFAIRS QUARTERLY, Vol. 21, no. 3 (March 1986), p. 389-409. English. **DESCR**: *Housing; Residential Segregation.

779 Massey, Douglas S. and Mullan, Brendan P. Processes of Hispanic and Black spatial assimilation. AMERICAN JOURNAL OF SOCIOLOGY, Vol. 89, no. 4 (January 1984), p. 836-873. English. **DESCR**: Assimilation; Census; *Ethnic Stratification; *Residential Segregation; *Social Mobility.

780 Molina, Robert M.; Brown, Kathryn H.; and Zavaleta, Antonio N. Relative lower extremity length in Mexican American and in American Black and white youth. AMERICAN JOURNAL OF PHYSICAL ANTHROPOLOGY, Vol. 72, (1987), p. 89-94. English. **DESCR**: Anglo Americans; *Anthropometry; *Body Mass Index (BMI); U.S. Health Examination Survey (HES); Youth.

781 Munoz, Carlos, Jr. and Henry, Charles. Rainbow coalitions in four big cities: San Antonio, Denver, Chicago and Philadelphia. P.S. [AMERICAN POLITICAL SCIENCE ASSOCIATION], Vol. 19, no. 3 (Summer 1986), p. 598-609. English. **DESCR**: Chicago, IL; Cisneros, Henry, Mayor of San Antonio, TX; Denver, CO; Elected Officials; Ethnic Groups; Intergroup Relations; Pena, Federico; Philadelphia, PA; Political Parties and Organizations; Political Representation; *Politics; San Antonio, TX; Urban Communities.

782 Powers, Stephen and Rossman, Mark H. Attributions for success and failure among Anglo, Black, Hispanic, and Native-American community-college students. JOURNAL OF PSYCHOLOGY, Vol. 117, no. 1 (May 1984), p. 27-31. English. **DESCR**: *Academic Achievement; Anglo Americans; Community Colleges; *Locus of Control; Native Americans; Students.

783 Roberts, Robert E. and Vernon, Sally W. Minority status and psychological distress reexamined: the case of Mexican Americans. RESEARCH IN COMMUNITY AND MENTAL HEALTH, Vol. 4, (1984), p. 131-164. English. **DESCR**: Anglo Americans; *Mental Illness.

---   ---

Blacks (cont.)

784 Sonenshein, Raphe. Biracial coalition
politics in Los Angeles. P.S. [AMERICAN
POLITICAL SCIENCE ASSOCIATION], Vol. 19, no.
3 (Summer 1986), p. 582-590. English.
DESCR: Bradley, Tom; Browning, Rufus P.;
*Ethnic Groups; *Intergroup Relations; *Los
Angeles, CA; Marshall, Dale Rogers;
Political Parties and Organizations;
*Politics; PROTEST IS NOT ENOUGH: THE
STRUGGLE OF BLACKS AND HISPANICS FOR
EQUALITY IN URBAN POLITICS; Tabb, David H.

785 Tienda, Marta and Glass, Jennifer. Household
structure and labor-force participation of
Black, Hispanic, and white mothers.
DEMOGRAPHY, Vol. 22, no. 3 (August 1985), p.
381-394. English. **DESCR:** Anglo Americans;
Chicanas; *Extended Family; *Family; *Sex
Roles; *Working Women.

786 Trevino, Fernando M. Health indicators for
Hispanic, Black and white Americans. VITAL
AND HEALTH STATISTICS. SERIES 10,
(September 1984), p. 1-88. English. **DESCR:**
Anglo Americans; *Medical Care; Statistics.

787 Zucca, Gary J. and Gorman, Benjamin.
Affirmative action: Blacks and Hispanics in
United States Navy occupational specialties.
ARMED FORCES AND SOCIETY, Vol. 12, no. 4
(Summer 1986), p. 513-524. English. **DESCR:**
*Affirmative Action; *Discrimination in
Employment; *Military.

Blackwelder, Julia Kirk

788 Ruiz, Vicki Lynn. Book review of: WOMEN OF
THE DEPRESSION. SOUTHWESTERN HISTORICAL
QUARTERLY, Vol. 88, no. 3 (1985), p.
337-338. English. **DESCR:** Book Reviews;
*WOMEN OF THE DEPRESSION: CASTE AND CULTURE
IN SAN ANTONIO, 1929-1939.

Blades, Ruben

789 Alonso, Miguel Angel. El significado de
cruzar la frontera. LA COMUNIDAD, No. 355
(May 10, 1987), p. 10-11. Spanish. **DESCR:**
Biography; *Music.

790 Gordon, Polita C. Living the crossover
dream. VISTA, Vol. 1, no. 8 (April 6, 1986),
p. 6-9. English. **DESCR:** Colon, Willie; Los
Lobos del Este de Los Angeles (musical
group); Miami Sound Machine; *Musicians.

791 Guevara, Ruben and Blades, Ruben. Ruben
Blades: music, love and revolution=Ruben
Blades: musica, amor y revolucion. AMERICAS
2001, Vol. 1, no. 2 (September, October,
1987), p. 26-29,31. Bilingual. **DESCR:**
Biography; Films; *Musicians; Recording
Industry.

792 Rodriguez Flores, Juan. Ruben Blades en
busca de una nueva realidad musical (II). LA
COMUNIDAD, no. 33 (November 23, 1986), p.
2-5. Spanish. **DESCR:** *Biography; Films;
Music.

793 Rodriguez Flores, Juan. Ruben Blades:
siempre he apostado a la sensibilidad del
publico. LA COMUNIDAD, No. 330 (November 16,
1986), p. 8-11. Spanish. **DESCR:** Actors and
Actresses; *Biography; Films; Music; THE
MILAGRO BEANFIELD WAR [film].

La Blanca [fashion label]

794 Stone, Eric. The daring designs of Elena
Valencia. VISTA, Vol. 1, no. 9 (May 3,
1986), p. 6-8. English. **DESCR:** Biography;

Chicanas; *Fashion; *Valencia, Elena.

BLESS ME, ULTIMA

795 Anderson, Robert K. Marez y Luna and the
masculine-feminine dialectic. CRITICA
HISPANICA, Vol. 6, no. 2 (1984), p. 97-105.
English. **DESCR:** Anaya, Rudolfo A.; Literary
Criticism; Novel; *Women Men Relations.

796 Chavez, Noe M. Culminacion de una busqueda
de identidad. LA COMUNIDAD, No. 252 (May 19,
1985), p. 4-6. Spanish. **DESCR:** Anaya,
Rudolfo A.; Identity; *Literary Criticism;
Novel.

797 Lewis, Marvin A.; Striano, Ron; and Hiura,
Barbara L. Chicano ethnicity and aging [and
critiques]. EXPLORATIONS IN ETHNIC STUDIES,
Vol. 8, no. 2 (July 1985), p. 35-45.
English. **DESCR:** Anaya, Rudolfo A.;
*Ancianos; Curanderas; FAMOUS ALL OVER TOWN;
Identity; James, Dan; Literary Criticism;
Literature.

798 Ortiz, Francisco. La cultura chicana, la
cultura amenazada. LA COMUNIDAD, No. 305
(May 25, 1986), p. 10-11. Spanish. **DESCR:**
Anaya, Rudolfo A.; Bloomfield, NM;
*Censorship; Literary Criticism; New Mexico;
Textbooks.

Bleznick, Donald W.

799 Andrachuk, Gregory Peter. Book review of: A
SOURCEBOOK FOR HISPANIC LITERATURE AND
LANGUAGE. CANADIAN MODERN LANGUAGE REVIEW,
Vol. 43, no. 1 (October 1986), p. 168-169.
English. **DESCR:** *A SOURCEBOOK FOR HISPANIC
LITERATURE AND LANGUAGE; Book Reviews;
Reference Works.

800 Chatham, James R. Book review of: A
SOURCEBOOK FOR HISPANIC LITERATURE AND
LANGUAGE. REVISTA DE ESTUDIOS HISPANICOS,
Vol. 18, no. 3 (October 1984), p. 457-458.
English. **DESCR:** *A SOURCEBOOK FOR HISPANIC
LITERATURE AND LANGUAGE; Book Reviews;
Reference Works.

Bloomfield, NM

801 Ortiz, Francisco. La cultura chicana, la
cultura amenazada. LA COMUNIDAD, No. 305
(May 25, 1986), p. 10-11. Spanish. **DESCR:**
Anaya, Rudolfo A.; *BLESS ME, ULTIMA;
*Censorship; Literary Criticism; New Mexico;
Textbooks.

Los Blue Diamonds [musical group]

802 Alonso, Miguel Angel. El largo camino al
estrellato. LA COMUNIDAD, No. 276 (November
3, 1985), p. 12-13+. Spanish. **DESCR:** *Music.

Bodnar, John

803 Engerman, Stanley L. Book review of: THE
TRANSPLANTED. JOURNAL OF ECONOMIC HISTORY,
Vol. 46, no. 2 (June 1986), p. 552-553.
English. **DESCR:** Book Reviews; Immigrants;
*THE TRANSPLANTED: A HISTORY OF IMMIGRANTS
IN URBAN AMERICA.

804 Stolarik, M. Mark. Book review of: THE
TRANSPLANTED. JOURNAL OF AMERICAN ETHNIC
HISTORY, Vol. 6, no. 2 (Spring 1987), p.
66-68. English. **DESCR:** Book Reviews;
Immigrants; *THE TRANSPLANTED: A HISTORY OF
IMMIGRANTS IN URBAN AMERICA.

Body Mass Index (BMI)

805 Molina, Robert M.; Brown, Kathryn H.; and Zavaleta, Antonio N. Relative lower extremity length in Mexican American and in American Black and white youth. AMERICAN JOURNAL OF PHYSICAL ANTHROPOLOGY, Vol. 72, (1987), p. 89-94. English. **DESCR:** Anglo Americans; *Anthropometry; Blacks; U.S. Health Examination Survey (HES); Youth.

Body Measurements
USE: Anthropometry

Bonilla, Francisco Javier

806 McKanna, Clare V. The San Quentin prison pardon papers: a look at file no. 1808, the case of Francisco Javier Bonilla. SOUTHERN CALIFORNIA QUARTERLY, Vol. 67, no. 2 (Summer 1985), p. 187-196. English. **DESCR:** Administration of Justice; Archives; *Criminal Justice System; History; *Prisoners; *San Quentin Prison.

Bonilla, Tony

807 Kane, George D. The entrepreneurial professional. HISPANIC BUSINESS, Vol. 9, no. 9 (September 1987), p. 34-37, 80. English. **DESCR:** *Biography; *Businesspeople; Cardenas, Ruben R.; Gomez, Rudy.

Bonjean, Charles M.

808 Meier, Matt S. Book review of: THE MEXICAN AMERICAN EXPERIENCE: AN INTERDISCIPLINARY ANTHOLOGY. HISPANIC AMERICAN HISTORICAL REVIEW, Vol. 66, no. 3 (August 1986), p. 629-630. English. **DESCR:** Alvarez, Rodolfo; Bean, Frank D.; Book Reviews; de la Garza, Rodolfo O.; Romo, Ricardo; *THE MEXICAN AMERICAN EXPERIENCE: AN INTERDISCIPLINARY ANTHOLOGY.

809 Ruiz, Vicki Lynn. Book review of: THE MEXICAN AMERICAN EXPERIENCE: AN INTERDISCIPLINARY ANTHOLOGY. SOUTHWESTERN HISTORICAL QUARTERLY, Vol. 90, no. 2 (1986), p. 205-206. English. **DESCR:** Alvarez, Rodolfo; Bean, Frank D.; Book Reviews; de la Garza, Rodolfo O.; Romo, Ricardo; *THE MEXICAN AMERICAN EXPERIENCE: AN INTERDISCIPLINARY ANTHOLOGY.

810 Salmon, Roberto Mario. Book review of: THE MEXICAN AMERICAN EXPERIENCE: AN INTERDISCIPLINARY ANTHOLOGY. LA RED/THE NET, no. 93 (January, February, 1986), p. 12-14. English. **DESCR:** Alvarez, Rodolfo; Bean, Frank D.; Book Reviews; de la Garza, Rodolfo O.; Romo, Ricardo; *THE MEXICAN AMERICAN EXPERIENCE: AN INTERDISCIPLINARY ANTHOLOGY.

Book Industry
USE: Publishing Industry

Book Reviews

811 Abalos, David. Book review of: GALILEAN JOURNEY. NEW CATHOLIC WORLD, Vol. 226, (July, August, 1983), p. 190-191. English. **DESCR:** Elizondo, Virgilio; *GALILEAN JOURNEY.

812 Abney, Armando. Chicano intermarriage: a theoretical and empirical study. LA RED/THE NET, no. 59 (October 1982), p. 4-6. English. **DESCR:** *CHICANO INTERMARRIAGE: A THEORETICAL AND EMPIRICAL STUDY; *Intermarriage; *Murguia, Edward.

813 Acuna, Rodolfo. Book review of: DICTIONARY OF MEXICAN AMERICAN HISTORY. LA RED/THE NET, no. 57 (August 1982), p. 4-5. English. **DESCR:** *DICTIONARY OF MEXICAN AMERICAN HISTORY; History; Meier, Matt S.; Rivera, Feliciano.

814 Adams, Clinton. Book review of: ART IN NEW MEXICO, 1900-1945: PATHS TO TAOS AND SANTA FE. ARTSPACE, Vol. 10, (Fall 1986), p. 34-36. English. **DESCR:** *Art History; *ART IN NEW MEXICO, 1900-1945: PATHS TO TAOS AND SANTA FE; Eldredge, Charles; Exhibits; Schimmel, Julie; Truettner, William H.

815 Aguilu de Murphy, Raquel. Book review of: GIVING UP THE GHOST. THE AMERICAS REVIEW, Vol. 15, no. 2 (Summer 1987), p. 105-107. Spanish. **DESCR:** *GIVING UP THE GHOST; Moraga, Cherrie; Teatro.

816 Aguirre, Adalberto, Jr. Book review of: CHICANO SOCIOLINGUISTICS. LA RED/THE NET, no. 51 (February 1982), p. 3-4. English. **DESCR:** Chicano Dialects; *CHICANO SOCIOLINGUISTICS; *Language Usage; *Penalosa, Fernando; *Sociolinguistics.

817 Aguirre, Adalberto, Jr. Book review of: THE YALE MURDER: THE FATAL ROMANCE OF BONNIE GARLAND AND RICHARD HERRIN. LA RED/THE NET, no. 71 (August 1983), p. 5-7. English. **DESCR:** Meyer, Peter; *THE YALE MURDER: THE FATAL ROMANCE OF BONNIE GARLAND AND RICHARD HERRIN.

818 Aitchison, Jean. Book review of: BILINGUAL EDUCATION: EVALUATION, ASSESSMENT AND METHODOLOGY. BRITISH BOOK NEWS, (January 1986), p. 32-33. English. **DESCR:** *BILINGUAL EDUCATION: EVALUATION, ASSESSMENT AND METHODOLOGY; Dodson, C.J.

819 Alarcon, Justo S. Book review of: CHULIFEAS FRONTERAS. CHIRICU, Vol. 3, no. 1 (1982), p. 101-103. Spanish. **DESCR:** Alarcon, Justo S.; *CHULIFEAS FRONTERAS.

820 Alarcon, Norma. Book Review of: BRUJAS Y ALGO MAS/WITCHES AND OTHER THINGS. CHIRICU, Vol. 4, no. 1 (1985), p. 9-12. English. **DESCR:** Agosin, Marjorie; *BRUJAS Y ALGO MAS=WITCHES AND OTHER THINGS.

821 Albert, Bill. Book review of: MAN, LAND, AND WATER: MEXICO'S FARMLAND IRRIGATION POLICIES, 1885-1911. HISTORY - REVIEWS OF NEW BOOKS, Vol. 71, (October 1986), p. 482-483. English. **DESCR:** Kroeber, Clifton R.; *MAN, LAND, AND WATER: MEXICO'S FARMLAND IRRIGATION POLICIES, 1885-1911.

822 Alberts, Don E. Book review of: LEGACY OF HONOR: THE LIFE OF RAFAEL CHACON, A NINETEENTH-CENTURY NEW MEXICAN. NEW MEXICO HISTORICAL REVIEW, Vol. 62, no. 4 (October 1987), p. 403-5. English. **DESCR:** *Chacon, Rafael; *LEGACY OF HONOR: THE LIFE OF RAFAEL CHACON, A NINETEENTH CENTURY NEW MEXICAN; *Meketa, Jacqueline Dorgan.

823 Alexander, Charles C. Book review of: WAR, REVOLUTION, AND THE KU KLUX KLAN: A STUDY OF INTOLERANCE IN A BORDER CITY. NEW MEXICO HISTORICAL REVIEW, Vol. 62, no. 1 (January 1987), p. 110-111. English. **DESCR:** *Lay, Shawn; *WAR, REVOLUTION, AND THE KU KLUX KLAN: A STUDY OF INTOLERANCE IN A BORDER CITY.

Book Reviews (cont.)

824 Alexander, June Granatir. Book review of:
    URBAN ETHNICITY IN THE UNITED STATES.
    JOURNAL OF AMERICAN ETHNIC HISTORY, Vol. 7,
    no. 1 (Fall 1987), p. 95-97. English.
    DESCR: Immigrants; Maldonado, Lionel; Moore,
    Joan W.; *URBAN ETHNICITY IN THE UNITED
    STATES: NEW IMMIGRANTS AND OLD MINORITIES.

825 Almaraz, Felix D., Jr. Book review of: THE
    LOST LAND. ARIZONA AND THE WEST, Vol. 28,
    no. 1 (Spring 1986), p. 81-82. English.
    DESCR: Chavez, John R.; *THE LOST LAND: THE
    CHICANO IMAGE OF THE SOUTHWEST.

826 Alvirez, David. Book review of: THE CHANGING
    DEMOGRAPHY OF SPANISH AMERICANS. LA RED/THE
    NET, no. 48 (November 1981), p. 4. English.
    DESCR: Boswell, Thomas D.; Cullen, Ruth M.;
    Jaffee, A.J.; Population; *THE CHANGING
    DEMOGRAPHY OF SPANISH-AMERICANS.

827 Anaya, Rudolfo A. Book review of: THE
    FOLKLORE OF SPAIN IN THE AMERICAN SOUTHWEST.
    NEW MEXICO HISTORICAL REVIEW, Vol. 62, no. 3
    (July 1987), p. 313-314. English. **DESCR**:
    Espinosa, Aurelio M.; Folklore; *THE
    FOLKLORE OF SPAIN IN THE AMERICAN SOUTHWEST:
    TRADITIONAL SPANISH FOLK LITERATURE IN
    NORTHERN NEW MEXICO AND SOUTHERN COLORADO.

828 Anaya, Rudolfo A. Book review of: THE LAST
    OF THE MENU GIRLS. VISTA, Vol. 1, no. 11
    (July 6, 1986), p. 16. English. **DESCR**:
    Chavez, Denise; *THE LAST OF THE MENU GIRLS.

829 Anderson de Barret, Judit. Book review of:
    POLITICS AND CHICANO CULTURE. LECTOR, Vol.
    4, no. 4-6 (1987), p. 56. English. **DESCR**:
    *POLITICS & CHICANO CULTURE: A PERSPECTIVE
    ON EL TEATRO CAMPESINO; Teatro; Xavier, Roy
    Eric.

830 Anderson, Karen. Book review of: NEW MEXICO
    WOMEN: INTERCULTURAL PERSPECTIVES. NEW
    MEXICO HISTORICAL REVIEW, Vol. 62, no. 4
    (October 1987), p. 401-2. English. **DESCR**:
    *Jensen, Joan M.; *Miller, Darlis A.; *New
    Mexico; *NEW MEXICO WOMEN: INTERCULTURAL
    PERSPECTIVES; Women.

831 Andrachuk, Gregory Peter. Book review of: A
    SOURCEBOOK FOR HISPANIC LITERATURE AND
    LANGUAGE. CANADIAN MODERN LANGUAGE REVIEW,
    Vol. 43, no. 1 (October 1986), p. 168-169.
    English. **DESCR**: *A SOURCEBOOK FOR HISPANIC
    LITERATURE AND LANGUAGE; Bleznick, Donald
    W.; Reference Works.

832 Arce, Carlos H. Book review of: CHICANOS IN
    A CHANGING SOCIETY. LA RED/THE NET, no. 30
    (May 1980), p. 8. English. **DESCR**: Camarillo,
    Alberto; CHICANOS IN A CHANGING SOCIETY;
    History; *Santa Barbara, CA; *Social History
    and Conditions; *Southern California.

833 Arce, Carlos H. and Carlson, David. Book
    review of: HISPANIC MENTAL HEALTH RESEARCH:
    A REFERENCE GUIDE. LA RED/THE NET, no. 57
    (August 1982), p. 5-7. English. **DESCR**:
    *HISPANIC MENTAL HEALTH RESEARCH: A
    REFERENCE GUIDE; Mental Health; Newton,
    Frank; Olmedo, Esteban L.; Padilla, Amado
    M.; Reference Works.

834 Arreola, Daniel D. Book review of: CITY
    BOUND. GEOGRAPHICAL REVIEW, Vol. 77, (April
    1987), p. 240-242. English. **DESCR**: *CITY
    BOUND: URBAN LIFE AND POLITICAL ATTITUDES
    AMONG CHICANO YOUTH; Jankowski, Martin
    Sanchez.

835 Arroyo, Luis Leobardo. Book review of:

DESERT IMMIGRANTS. LA RED/THE NET, no. 43
(June 1981), p. 3-4. English. **DESCR**: *DESERT
IMMIGRANTS: THE MEXICANS OF EL PASO
1880-1920; Garcia, Mario T.; Immigrants.

836 Autry, Brick. Book review of: LATINO
    FAMILIES IN THE UNITED STATES. LECTOR, Vol.
    4, no. 1-3 (1986), p. [63]. English. **DESCR**:
    *LATINO FAMILIES IN THE UNITED STATES: A
    RESOURCE BOOK FOR FAMILY LIFE EDUCATION.

837 Avalos, Francisco. Book review of: SMALL
    BONES, LITTLE EYES. LECTOR, Vol. 4, no. 1-3
    (1986), p. [60]. English. **DESCR**: NorthSun,
    Nila; Sagel, Jim; *SMALL BONES, LITTLE EYES.

838 Baca Zinn, Maxine. Book review of: LA
    CHICANA: MEXICAN AMERICAN WOMEN. LA RED/THE
    NET, no. 28 (March 1980), p. 10. English.
    DESCR: Chicanas; Enriquez, Evangelina; LA
    CHICANA: THE MEXICAN AMERICAN WOMAN;
    *Mirande, Alfredo.

839 Baca Zinn, Maxine. Book review of: TWICE A
    MINORITY: MEXICAN-AMERICAN WOMEN. LA RED/THE
    NET, no. 32 (July 1980), p. 3-4. English.
    DESCR: *Chicanas; Melville, Margarita B.;
    *TWICE A MINORITY: MEXICAN-AMERICAN WOMEN.

840 Balderrama, Francisco E. Book review of: A
    BIBLIOGRAPHY OF MEXICAN-AMERICAN HISTORY.
    PACIFIC HISTORICAL REVIEW, Vol. 55, no. 1
    (1986), p. 106-107. English. **DESCR**: *A
    BIBLIOGRAPHY OF MEXICAN AMERICAN HISTORY;
    History; Meier, Matt S.

841 Barona, Andres and Santos de Barona,
    Maryann. Chicano psychology: a new field?
    CONTEMPORARY PSYCHOLOGY, Vol. 31, no. 2
    (February 1986), p. 106-107. English.
    DESCR: *CHICANO PSYCHOLOGY; Martinez, Joe
    L., Jr.; Mendoza, Richard H.

842 Bastida, Elena B. Book review of: THE
    HISPANIC ELDERLY. CONTEMPORARY SOCIOLOGY: A
    JOURNAL OF REVIEWS, Vol. 14, no. 1 (January
    1985), p. 41-42. English. **DESCR**: Ancianos;
    Becerra, Rosina; Shaw, David; *THE HISPANIC
    ELDERLY: A RESEARCH REFERENCE GUIDE.

843 Bayard, C.J. Book review of: LABOR IN NEW
    MEXICO: UNIONS, STRIKES AND SOCIAL HISTORY
    SINCE 1881. WESTERN HISTORICAL QUARTERLY,
    Vol. 15, no. 4 (October 1984), p. 468-469.
    English. **DESCR**: *Kern, Robert; Labor; LABOR
    IN NEW MEXICO: UNIONS, STRIKES, AND SOCIAL
    HISTORY SINCE 1881.

844 Belkind, A. Book review of: THREE AMERICAN
    LITERATURES. WORLD LITERATURE TODAY, Vol.
    57, no. 4 (Fall 1983), p. 643. English.
    DESCR: Baker, Houston A., Jr.; *THREE
    AMERICAN LITERATURES: ESSAYS IN CHICANO,
    NATIVE AMERICAN, AND ASIAN-AMERICAN
    LITERATURE FOR TEACHERS OF AMERICAN
    LITERATURE.

845 Bennett, Priscilla. Book review of:
    BILINGUAL BOOKS IN SPANISH AND ENGLISH FOR
    CHILDREN. EMERGENCY LIBRARIAN, Vol. 13, no.
    1 (September, October, 1985), p. 31-32.
    English. **DESCR**: *BILINGUAL BOOKS IN SPANISH
    AND ENGLISH FOR CHILDREN; Dale, Doris
    Cruger.

846 Bernal, Martha E. Book review of:
    EXPLORATIONS IN CHICANO PSYCHOLOGY. LA
    RED/THE NET, no. 55 (June 1982), p. 5-6.
    English. **DESCR**: *Baron, Augustine Jr.;
    *EXPLORATIONS IN CHICANO PSYCHOLOGY;
    *Psychology.

Book Reviews (cont.)

847 Bieder. Maryellen. Book review of: WOMEN IN HISPANIC LITERATURE. MODERN FICTION STUDIES, Vol. 30, no. 4 (Winter 1984), p. 738-740. English. **DESCR**: Miller, Beth; Women; *WOMEN IN HISPANIC LITERATURE: ICONS AND FALLEN IDOLS.

848 Blanco, George M. Book review of: FORM AND FUNCTION IN CHICANO ENGLISH. MODERN LANGUAGE JOURNAL, Vol. 69, no. 3 (Fall 1985), p. 328. English. **DESCR**: *FORM AND FUNCTION IN CHICANO ENGLISH; Ornstein-Galicia, Jacob.

849 Blea. Irene I. Book review of: CURANDERISMO. LA RED/THE NET, no. 55 (June 1982), p. 3-4. English. **DESCR**: Chavira, Juan Antonio; Curanderismo; *Trotter, Robert.

850 Body-Gendrot, Sophie. Book review of: PROTEST IS NOT ENOUGH. INTERNATIONAL JOURNAL OF URBAN AND REGIONAL RESEARCH, Vol. 9, no. 4 (1985), p. 576-577. English. **DESCR**: Browning, Rufus P.; Marshall, Dale Rogers; *PROTEST IS NOT ENOUGH: THE STRUGGLE OF BLACKS AND HISPANICS FOR EQUALITY IN URBAN POLITICS; Tabb, David H.

851 Book review of: BOOKS IN SPANISH FOR CHILDREN AND YOUNG ADULTS. BOOKLIST, Vol. 82, (July 1986), p. 1620. English. **DESCR**: *BOOKS IN SPANISH FOR CHILDREN AND YOUNG ADULTS: AN ANNOTATED GUIDE; Children's Literature; Reference Works; Schon, Isabel.

852 Book review of: CHICANO POETRY: A CRITICAL INTRODUCTION. AMERICAN LITERATURE, Vol. 58, no. 3 (October 1986), p. 481-482. English. **DESCR**: Candelaria, Cordelia; *CHICANO POETRY: A CRITICAL INTRODUCTION.

853 Book review of: CHICANO LITERATURE: A REFERENCE GUIDE. BOOKLIST, Vol. 82, no. 9 (January 1, 1986), p. 667-668. English. **DESCR**: *CHICANO LITERATURE: A REFERENCE GUIDE; Lomeli, Francisco A.; Martinez, Julio A.; Reference Works.

854 Book review of: CHICANO CINEMA. FILM QUARTERLY, Vol. 40, no. 1 (Fall 1986), p. 39. English. **DESCR**: *CHICANO CINEMA: RESEARCH, REVIEWS AND RESOURCES; Keller, Gary D.

855 Book review of: FREE TRADE BETWEEN MEXICO AND THE UNITED STATES? FOREIGN AFFAIRS, Vol. 63, no. 1 (Fall 1984), p. 196. English. **DESCR**: *FREE TRADE BETWEEN MEXICO AND THE UNITED STATES?; Weintraub, Sidney.

856 Book review of: HISPANIC AMERICAN VOLUNTARY ORGANIZATIONS. BOOKLIST. Vol. 82, no. 11 (February 1, 1986), p. 798, 800. English. **DESCR**: Gonzales, Sylvia Alicia; *HISPANIC AMERICAN VOLUNTARY ORGANIZATIONS.

857 Book review of: IMMIGRATION POLICY AND THE AMERICAN LABOR FORCE. ECONOMIC BOOKS, Vol. 12, no. 3 (September 1985), p. 67-68. English. **DESCR**: Briggs, Vernon M., Jr.; *IMMIGRATION POLICY AND THE AMERICAN LABOR FORCE.

858 Book review of: LE MEXIQUE, DES ORIGINES AUX AZTEQUES. OEIL-REVUE D'ART MENSUELLE, (December 1986), p. 75. Other. **DESCR**: Aztecs; Bernal y Garcia Pimentel, Ignacio; *LE MEXIQUE, DES ORIGENES AUX AZTEQUES; Simoni-Abbat. Mireille.

859 Book review of: SPANISH-LANGUAGE BOOKS FOR PUBLIC LIBRARIES. BOOKLIST. Vol. 83, no. 9 (January 1, 1987), p. 700-701. English.

DESCR: Reference Works; Restrepo, Fabio; *SPANISH-LANGUAGE BOOKS FOR PUBLIC LIBRARIES.

860 Book review of: THE CHICANO WAR. PUBLISHER'S WEEKLY, Vol. 229, (February 21, 1986), p. 157. English. **DESCR**: Gault, William Campbell; *THE CHICANO WAR.

861 Book review of: THE HISPANIC ALMANAC. BOOKLIST, Vol. 82, (May 1, 1986), p. 1296. English. **DESCR**: Almanacs; *HISPANIC ALMANAC; Hispanic Policy Development Project (HPDP).

862 Book review of: THE IMMIGRANT WOMAN IN NORTH AMERICA. BOOKLIST, Vol. 82, no. 12 (February 15, 1986), p. 855-856. English. **DESCR**: Cordasco, Francesco; Reference Works; *THE IMMIGRANT WOMAN IN NORTH AMERICA: AN ANNOTATED BIBLIOGRAPHY OF SELECTED REFERENCES.

863 Brown, D.R. Book review of: CHICANO LITERATURE: A REFERENCE GUIDE. CHOICE, Vol. 23, no. 4 (December 1985), p. 578. English. **DESCR**: *CHICANO LITERATURE: A REFERENCE GUIDE; Lomeli, Francisco A.; Martinez, Julio A.; Reference Works.

864 Bruce-Novoa, Juan. Book review of: FACE. VISTA, Vol. 1, no. 11 (July 6, 1986), p. 16. English. **DESCR**: *FACE; Pineda, Cecile.

865 Burnett, G. Wesley. Book review of: BORDERLANDS SOURCEBOOK. GEOGRAPHICAL REVIEW, Vol. 74, no. 1 (January 1984), p. 123-124. English. **DESCR**: *BORDERLANDS SOURCEBOOK; Nostrand, Richard L.; Stoddard, Ellwyn R.; West, Jonathan P.

866 Burnham-Kidwell, Debbie. Book review of: THE EDUCATION OF POOR AND MINORITY CHILDREN: A WORLD BIBLIOGRAPHY: SUPPLEMENT, 1979-1985. AMERICAN REFERENCE BOOKS ANNUAL, Vol. 18, (1987), p. 134. English. **DESCR**: *THE EDUCATION OF POOR AND MINORITY CHILDREN: A WORLD BIBLIOGRAPHY: SUPPLEMENT 1979-01985; Weinberg, Meyer.

867 Burns, Jeffrey M. Book review of: THE CHICANO EXPERIENCE. RELIGIOUS STUDIES REVIEW, Vol. 11, (October 1985), p. 418. English. **DESCR**: Mirande, Alfredo; *THE CHICANO EXPERIENCE: AN ALTERNATIVE PERSPECTIVE.

868 Butler, Anne M. Book review of: THE GENTLEMEN'S CLUB: THE STORY OF PROSTITUTION IN EL PASO, TEXAS. ARIZONA AND THE WEST, Vol. 26, no. 4 (1984), p. 365-366. English. **DESCR**: Criminal Acts; El Paso, TX; *Frost, H. Gordon; THE GENTLEMEN'S CLUB: THE STORY OF PROSTITUTION IN EL PASO, TEXAS.

869 Butler, Anne M. Book review of: THEY CALLED THEM GREASERS. MARYLAND HISTORIAN, Vol. 15, no. 2 (Fall, Winter, 1984), p. 50-51. English. **DESCR**: de Leon, Arnoldo; History; *THEY CALLED THEM GREASERS: ANGLO ATTITUDES TOWARD MEXICANS IN TEXAS, 1821-1900.

870 Candelaria, Cordelia. Book review of: FIESTA IN AZTLAN: ANTHOLOGY OF CHICANO POETRY and FLOR Y CANTO IV AND V. LA RED/THE NET, no. 62 (December 1982), p. 6-9. English. **DESCR**: Empringham, Toni; *FIESTA IN AZTLAN: AN ANTHOLOGY OF CHICANO POETRY; *FLOR Y CANTO IV AND V: AN ANTHOLOGY OF CHICANO LITERATURE FROM THE FESTIVALS HELD IN ALBUQUERQUE, NEW MEXICO; Poetry.

Book Reviews (cont.)

871 Canive, Jose. Book review of: MENTAL HEALTH AND HISPANIC AMERICANS: CLINICAL PERSPECTIVES. JOURNAL OF NERVOUS AND MENTAL DISEASE, Vol. 172, no. 9 (September 1984), p. 559-561. English. **DESCR:** Ancianos; Becerra, Rosina; Escobar, Javier I.; Karno, Marvin; *MENTAL HEALTH AND HISPANIC AMERICANS: CLINICAL PERSPECTIVES.

872 Cantu, Norma. Book review of: CUENTOS: STORIES BY LATINAS. LA RED/THE NET, no. 83 (August 1984), p. 2-3. English. **DESCR:** *CUENTOS: STORIES BY LATINAS; Gomez, Alma; Moraga, Cherrie; Romo-Carmona, Mariana.

873 Cantu, Norma. Book review of: WOMAN OF HER WORD: HISPANIC WOMEN WRITE. LA RED/THE NET, no. 83 (August 1984), p. 4. English. **DESCR:** Vigil-Pinon, Evangelina; *WOMAN OF HER WORD: HISPANIC WOMEN WRITE.

874 Cardenas, Gilbert. Book review of: IN DEFENSE OF LA RAZA. LA RED/THE NET, no. 85 (October 1984), p. 2-5. English. **DESCR:** Balderrama, Francisco E.; Crewdson, John; *IN DEFENSE OF LA RAZA: THE LOS ANGELES MEXICAN CONSULATE AND THE MEXICAN COMMUNITY; *THE TARNISHED DOOR.

875 Cardenas, Gilbert. Book review of: OLDER MEXICAN AMERICANS: A STUDY IN AN URBAN BARRIO. CONTEMPORARY SOCIOLOGY: A JOURNAL OF REVIEWS, Vol. 14, no. 2 (March 1985), p. 243-244. English. **DESCR:** Ancianos; Gomez, Ernesto; Markides, Kyriakos S.; Martin, Harry; *OLDER MEXICAN AMERICANS: A STUDY IN AN URBAN BARRIO.

876 Cardenas, Gilbert. Book review of: "TEMPORARY" ALIEN WORKERS IN THE UNITED STATES. LA RED/THE NET, no. 63 (January 1983), p. 9-10. English. **DESCR:** Ross, Stanley R.; *"TEMPORARY" ALIEN WORKERS IN THE UNITED STATES: DESIGNING POLICY FROM FACT AND OPINION; Undocumented Workers; Weintraub, Sidney.

877 Cardenas, Jose A. Book review of: EDUCATION, POLITICS, AND BILINGUAL EDUCATION IN TEXAS. LA RED/THE NET, no. 75 (December 1983), p. 5-8. English. **DESCR:** *EDUCATION, POLITICS, AND BILINGUAL EDUCATION IN TEXAS; Vega, Jose E.

878 Cardoso, Lawrence A. Book review of: THEY CALLED THEM GREASERS. WESTERN HISTORICAL QUARTERLY, Vol. 15, no. 4 (October 1984), p. 452-453. English. **DESCR:** *de Leon, Arnoldo; Texas; THEY CALLED THEM GREASERS: ANGLO ATTITUDES TOWARD MEXICANS IN TEXAS, 1821-1900.

879 Carranza, Miguel A. Book review of: LATINO LANGUAGE AND COMMUNICATIVE BEHAVIOR. LA RED/THE NET, no. 54 (May 1982), p. 10-11. English. **DESCR:** *Duran, Richard P.; Language Usage; *LATINO LANGUAGE AND COMMUNICATIVE BEHAVIOR.

880 Castillo-Speed, Lillian. Annotated bibliography. LA RED/THE NET, no. 93 (January, February, 1986), p. 14-17. English. **DESCR:** A BIBLIOGRAPHY OF MEXICAN AMERICAN HISTORY; ARTE CHICANO; Caballero, Cesar; CHICANO LITERATURE: A REFERENCE GUIDE; CHICANO ORGANIZATIONS DIRECTORY; CHICANO PERIODICAL INDEX; Goldman, Shifra M.; HISPANIC ALMANAC; HISPANIC MENTAL HEALTH RESEARCH: A REFERENCE GUIDE; Lomeli, Francisco A.; Martinez, Julio A.; Meier, Matt S.; Newton, Frank; *Reference Works; Ybarra-Frausto, Tomas.

881 Castillo-Speed, Lillian. Chicana/Latina literature and criticism: reviews of recent books. WLW JOURNAL, Vol. 11, no. 3 (September 1987), p. 1-4. English. **DESCR:** Andrews, Lynn V.; BORDERS; Chavez, Denise; *Chicanas; CONTEMPORARY CHICANA POETRY: A CRITICAL APPROACH TO AN EMERGING LITERATURE; Flores, Angel; Flores, Kate; JAGUAR WOMAN; Mora, Pat; Sanchez, Marta Ester; Tafolla, Carmen; THE DEFIANT MUSE: HISPANIC FEMINIST POEMS FROM THE MIDDLE AGES TO THE PRESENT; THE LAST OF THE MENU GIRLS; TO SPLIT A HUMAN: MITOS, MACHOS Y LA MUJER CHICANA; Vigil-Pinon, Evangelina; WOMAN OF HER WORD: HISPANIC WOMEN WRITE.

882 Chabran, Richard. Book review of: BILINDEX. LA RED/THE NET, no. 87 (July 1985), p. 6-8. English. **DESCR:** *BILINDEX: A BILINGUAL SPANISH-ENGLISH SUBJECT HEADING LIST; HISPANEX (Oakland, CA); Subject Headings.

883 Chabran, Richard. Book review of: MEXICAN AMERICAN ARCHIVES AT THE BENSON COLLECTION: A GUIDE FOR USERS. LA RED/THE NET, no. 52 (March 1982), p. 6-7. English. **DESCR:** Archives; Flores, Maria; *Gutierrez-Witt, Laura; *MEXICAN AMERICAN ARCHIVES AT THE BENSON COLLECTION.

884 Chabran, Richard and Garcia-Ayvens, Francisco. Book review of: THE MEXICAN AMERICAN: A CRITICAL GUIDE TO RESEARCH AIDS. LA RED/THE NET, no. 37 (December 1980), p. 4-5. English. **DESCR:** Bibliography; *Reference Works; *Robinson, Barbara J.; *Robinson, J. Cordell; *THE MEXICAN AMERICAN: A CRITICAL GUIDE TO RESEARCH AIDS.

885 Chatham, James R. Book review of: A SOURCEBOOK FOR HISPANIC LITERATURE AND LANGUAGE. REVISTA DE ESTUDIOS HISPANICOS, Vol. 18, no. 3 (October 1984), p. 457-458. English. **DESCR:** *A SOURCEBOOK FOR HISPANIC LITERATURE AND LANGUAGE; Bleznick, Donald W.; Reference Works.

886 Chavaria, Elvira. Book review of: THE STATE OF HISPANIC AMERICA, VOL. II and LA CHICANA: BUILDING FOR THE FUTURE. LA RED/THE NET, no. 68 (May 1983), p. 10-12. English. **DESCR:** *LA CHICANA: BUILDING FOR THE FUTURE; National Hispanic Center for Advanced Studies and Policy Analysis (NHCAS); *THE STATE OF HISPANIC AMERICA.

887 Chavez, Gene T. Book review of: MIRROR OF LANGUAGE: THE DEBATE ON BILINGUALISM. JOURNAL OF THE ASSOCIATION OF MEXICAN AMERICAN EDUCATORS, (1986, 1987), p. 52-53. English. **DESCR:** Hakuta, Kenji; *MIRROR OF LANGUAGE: THE DEBATE ON BILINGUALISM.

888 Chernick, Marc W. Book review of: THE BORDER THAT JOINS: MEXICAN MIGRANTS AND U.S. RESPONSIBILITY. POLITICAL SCIENCE QUARTERLY, Vol. 99, (Spring 1984), p. 133. English. **DESCR:** Brown, Peter G.; Shue, Henry; *THE BORDER THAT JOINS: MEXICAN MIGRANTS AND U.S. RESPONSIBILITY.

889 Chiswick, Barry R. Book review of: POLITICAL AND ECONOMIC MIGRANTS IN AMERICA. JOURNAL OF AMERICAN ETHNIC HISTORY, Vol. 7, no. 1 (Fall 1987), p. 105-106. English. **DESCR:** Immigrants; Pedraza-Bailey, Silvia; *POLITICAL AND ECONOMIC MIGRANTS IN AMERICA.

Book Reviews (cont.)

890 Christian, Garna L. Book review of: THE TEXAS-MEXICAN CONJUNTO. JOURNAL OF SOUTHERN HISTORY, Vol. 52, (May 1986), p. 325. English. **DESCR:** Pena, Manuel; *THE TEXAS-MEXICAN CONJUNTO: HISTORY OF A WORKING-CLASS MUSIC.

891 Cobas, Jose A. Book review of: LATIN JOURNEY. INTERNATIONAL MIGRATION REVIEW, Vol. 21, no. 2 (Summer 1987), p. 434-435. English. **DESCR:** Bach, Robert L.; *LATIN JOURNEY: CUBAN AND MEXICAN IMMIGRANTS IN THE UNITED STATES; Portes, Alejandro.

892 Cohen, Albert K. Book review of: HONOR AND THE AMERICAN DREAM. AMERICAN JOURNAL OF SOCIOLOGY, Vol. 90, no. 5 (March 1985), p. 1146-1147. English. **DESCR:** Culture; *HONOR AND THE AMERICAN DREAM: CULTURE AND IDENTITY IN A CHICANO COMMUNITY; Horowitz, Ruth.

893 Colecchia, F. Book review of: THE DEFIANT MUSE: HISPANIC FEMINIST POEMS FROM THE MIDDLE AGES TO THE PRESENT. CHOICE, Vol. 24, no. 2 (October 1986), p. 314. English. **DESCR:** Flores, Angel; Flores, Kate; *THE DEFIANT MUSE: HISPANIC FEMINIST POEMS FROM THE MIDDLE AGES TO THE PRESENT.

894 Compean, Mario. Book review of: PERSPECTIVES ON IMMIGRATION AND MINORITY EDUCATION. LA RED/THE NET, no. 86 (November 1984), p. 3-7. English. **DESCR:** *PERSPECTIVES ON IMMIGRANT AND MINORITY EDUCATION; Samuda, Ronald J.; Woods, Sandra L.

895 Conde, Hilda Rosina. Book review of: LIFE SPAN. LECTOR, Vol. 4, no. 4-6 (1987), p. 77-78. English. **DESCR:** *LIFE SPAN; Villanueva, Alma.

896 Cooke, John Byrne. Book review of: SOUTH BY SOUTHWEST: 24 STORIES FROM MODERN TEXAS. NEW MEXICO HISTORICAL REVIEW, Vol. 62, no. 2 (April 1987), p. 217-218. English. **DESCR:** *Graham, Don; *SOUTH BY SOUTHWEST: THE MEXICAN-AMERICAN AND HIS HERITAGE.

897 Cordasco, Francesco. Book review of: HISPANICS IN THE UNITED STATES: A NEW SOCIAL AGENDA. CHOICE, Vol. 23, no. 6 (February 1986), p. 928. English. **DESCR:** *HISPANICS IN THE UNITED STATES: A NEW SOCIAL AGENDA; McCready, William C.; San Juan Cafferty, Pastora.

898 Cortes, Carlos E. Book review of: THE ZOOT-SUIT RIOTS. PACIFIC HISTORICAL REVIEW, Vol. 55, no. 3 (1986), p. 498-499. English. **DESCR:** Mazon, Mauricio; *THE ZOOT-SUIT RIOTS: THE PSYCHOLOGY OF SYMBOLIC ANNIHILATION; Zoot Suit Riots, Los Angeles, CA, 1943.

899 Cortina, Rodolfo J. Book review of: KLAIL CITY. VISTA, Vol. 3, no. 4 (December 6, 1987), p. 26. English. **DESCR:** Hinojosa-Smith, Rolando R.; *KLAIL CITY Y SUS ALREDEDORES.

900 Cosgrove, Stuart. Book review of: THE ZOOT-SUIT RIOTS. THE TIMES LITERARY SUPPLEMENT, (July 12, 1985), p. 782. English. **DESCR:** Mazon, Mauricio; *THE ZOOT-SUIT RIOTS: THE PSYCHOLOGY OF SYMBOLIC ANNIHILATION.

901 Crisp, James E. Book review of: LOS TUCSONENSES: THE MEXICAN COMMUNITY IN TUCSON 1854-1941. JOURNAL OF ECONOMIC HISTORY, Vol. 47, (January 1987), p. 577-578. English. **DESCR:** *LOS TUCSONENSES: THE MEXICAN

COMMUNITY IN TUCSON, 1854-1941; Sheridan, Thomas E.; Tucson, AZ.

902 Crisp, James E. Book review of: THE LOST LAND. JOURNAL OF SOUTHERN HISTORY, Vol. 51, no. 4 (November 1985), p. 660-661. English. **DESCR:** Chavez, John R.; *THE LOST LAND: THE CHICANO IMAGE OF THE SOUTHWEST.

903 Crisp, James E. Book review of: THEY CALLED THEM GREASERS. JOURNAL OF SOUTHERN HISTORY, Vol. 50, no. 2 (1984), p. 313-314. English. **DESCR:** de Leon, Arnoldo; *THEY CALLED THEM GREASERS: ANGLO ATTITUDES TOWARD MEXICANS IN TEXAS, 1821-1900.

904 Dagodag, William Tim. Book review of: IN DEFENSE OF LA RAZA. JOURNAL OF HISTORICAL GEOGRAPHY, Vol. 10, no. 1 (January 1984), p. 92. English. **DESCR:** Balderrama, Francisco E.; *IN DEFENSE OF LA RAZA: THE LOS ANGELES MEXICAN CONSULATE AND THE MEXICAN COMMUNITY.

905 Daydi-Tolson, Santiago. Book review of: FROM A COP'S JOURNAL & OTHER POEMS. THE AMERICAS REVIEW, Vol. 15, no. 1 (Spring 1987), p. 102-105. English. **DESCR:** *FROM A COP'S JOURNAL & OTHER POEMS; Munoz, Arthur.

906 de Baca, Vincent C. Book review of: INDEX TO SPANISH AMERICAN COLLECTIVE BIOGRAPHY, vol. 2: MEXICO and THE MEXICAN REVOLUTION: AN ANNOTATED GUIDE TO RECENT SCHOLARSHIP. LA RED/THE NET, no. 72 (September 1983), p. 19-21. English. **DESCR:** de Mundo Lo, Sara; *INDEX TO SPANISH AMERICAN COLLECTIVE BIOGRAPHY, vol. 2: MEXICO; Raat, W. Dirk; Reference Works; THE MEXICAN REVOLUTION: AN ANNOTATED GUIDE TO RECENT SCHOLARSHIP.

907 de la Cancela, Victor. Book review of: GREEN MEDICINE. LECTOR, Vol. 4, no. 1-3 (1986), p. [64]. English. **DESCR:** *GREEN MEDICINE: TRADITIONAL MEXICAN-AMERICAN HERBAL REMEDIES; Torres, Eliseo.

908 de la Garza, Rodolfo O. Book review of: A WAR OF WORDS. JOURNAL OF AMERICAN ETHNIC HISTORY, Vol. 6, no. 2 (Spring 1987), p. 97-98. English. **DESCR:** *A WAR OF WORDS: CHICANO PROTEST IN THE 1960S AND 1970S; Gutierrez, Jose Angel; Hammerback, John C.; Jensen, Richard J.; Rhetoric.

909 de la Garza, Rodolfo O. Book review of: ACROSS THE BORDER: RURAL DEVELOPMENT IN MEXICO AND RECENT MIGRATION TO THE UNITED STATES. LA RED/THE NET, no. 69 (June 1983), p. 5-7. English. **DESCR:** *ACROSS THE BORDER: RURAL DEVELOPMENT IN MEXICO AND RECENT MIGRATION; Border Industries; Cross, Harry E.; Sandos, James.

910 de la Garza, Rodolfo O. Book review of: MEXICO'S POLITICAL ECONOMY: CHALLENGES AT HOME AND ABROAD. LA RED/THE NET, no. 69 (June 1983), p. 5-7. English. **DESCR:** Dominguez, Jorge; Mexico; *MEXICO'S POLITICAL ECONOMY: CHALLENGES AT HOME AND ABROAD.

911 de la Torre, Adela. Book review of: THE STRUGGLE FOR RURAL MEXICO. LA RED/THE NET, no. 85 (October 1984), p. 5-6. English. **DESCR:** Esteva, Gustavo; *THE STRUGGLE FOR RURAL MEXICO.

912 de Leon, Arnoldo. Book review of: CHICANO: THE EVOLUTION OF A PEOPLE. SOUTHWESTERN HISTORICAL QUARTERLY, Vol. 87, no. 3 (1984), p. 343-344. English. **DESCR:** Calvert, Robert; *CHICANO: THE EVOLUTION OF A PEOPLE; Rosaldo, Renato; Seligmann, Gustav L.

Book Reviews (cont.)

913 de Leon, Arnoldo. Book review of: LA FAMILIA. SOUTHWESTERN HISTORICAL QUARTERLY, Vol. 89, no. 4 (1986), p. 564-565. English. **DESCR:** Griswold del Castillo, Richard; *LA FAMILIA: CHICANO FAMILIES IN THE URBAN SOUTHWEST, 1848 TO THE PRESENT.

914 de Leon, Arnoldo. Book review of: LOS TUCSONENSES: THE MEXICAN COMMUNITY IN TUCSON 1854-1941. NEW MEXICO HISTORICAL REVIEW, Vol. 62, no. 4 (October 1987), p. 411-12. English. **DESCR:** *LOS TUCSONENSES: THE MEXICAN COMMUNITY IN TUCSON, 1854-1941; *Sheridan, Thomas E.; *Tucson, AZ.

915 de Leon, Arnoldo. Book review of: THE LOS ANGELES BARRIO 1850-1890: A SOCIAL HISTORY. LA RED/THE NET, no. 64 (February 1983), p. 4-5. English. **DESCR:** Griswold del Castillo, Richard; *THE LOS ANGELES BARRIO 1850-1890: A SOCIAL HISTORY.

916 de Leon, Arnoldo. Book review of: THE LOST LAND. SOUTHWESTERN HISTORICAL QUARTERLY, Vol. 89, no. 1 (1985), p. 96-98. English. **DESCR:** Chavez, John R.; *THE LOST LAND: THE CHICANO IMAGE OF THE SOUTHWEST.

917 de Ortego y Gasca, Felipe. El crepusculo y la bandera. CHIRICU, Vol. 2, no. 2 (1981), p. 65-68. Spanish. **DESCR:** *HAY PLESHA LICHENS TU DI FLAC; Sanchez, Saul.

918 Delgado, Melvin. Book review of: MEXICAN-AMERICANS AND THE MASS-MEDIA. HISPANIC JOURNAL OF BEHAVIORAL SCIENCES, Vol. 9, no. 4 (December 1987), p. 461-463. English. **DESCR:** Greenberg, Bradley S.; Mass Media; *MEXICAN AMERICANS AND THE MASS MEDIA.

919 Delgado, Melvin. Book review of: THE HISPANIC ELDERLY. SOCIAL WORK, Vol. 31, no. 2 (March, April, 1986), p. 153. English. **DESCR:** Ancianos; Becerra, Rosina; Shaw, David; *THE HISPANIC ELDERLY: A RESEARCH REFERENCE GUIDE.

920 Dennedy-Frank, David P. Book review of: CROSSING CULTURES IN THERAPY. LA RED/THE NET, no. 41 (April 1981), p. 5-6. English. **DESCR:** Counseling (Psychological); *CROSSING CULTURES IN THERAPY: PLURALISTIC COUNSELING FOR THE HISPANIC; Levine, Elaine S.; *Mental Health; Padilla, Amado M.

921 Dorn, Georgette Magassy. Book review of: MEXICAN-AMERICANS IN COMPARATIVE PERSPECTIVES. AMERICAS, Vol. 43, no. 1 (July 1986), p. 110. English. **DESCR:** Connor, Walker; *MEXICAN AMERICANS IN COMPARATIVE PERSPECTIVE.

922 Driscoll, Barbara A. Book review of: LA FAMILIA. JOURNAL OF AMERICAN ETHNIC HISTORY, Vol. 7, no. 1 (Fall 1987), p. 107-109. English. **DESCR:** Family; Griswold del Castillo, Richard; *LA FAMILIA: CHICANO FAMILIES IN THE URBAN SOUTHWEST, 1848 TO THE PRESENT.

923 Dubois, Betty Lou. Book review of: CHICANO ENGLISH: AN ETHNIC CONTACT DIALECT. CHOICE, Vol. 24, no. 1 (September 1986), p. 114. English. **DESCR:** *CHICANO ENGLISH: AN ETHNIC CONTACT DIALECT; Ornstein-Galicia, Jacob; Penfield, Joyce.

924 Dunn, Ed. Book review of: THE BORDER ECONOMY: REGIONAL DEVELOPMENT IN THE SOUTHWEST. LA RED/THE NET, no. 50 (January 1982), p. 9-10. English. **DESCR:** *Border Region; Border Studies; *Hansen, Niles; *THE BORDER ECONOMY: REGIONAL DEVELOPMENT IN THE SOUTHWEST.

925 Dunn, Geoffrey. Book review of: LIVING UP THE STREET. SAN FRANCISCO REVIEW OF BOOKS, Vol. 11, (Summer 1986), p. 11. English. **DESCR:** *LIVING UP THE STREET; Soto, Gary.

926 Duran, Richard P. Book review of: CHICANO SOCIOLINGUISTICS. LA RED/THE NET, no. 35 (October 1980), p. 3. English. **DESCR:** Chicano Dialects; CHICANO SOCIOLINGUISTICS; *Language Usage; *Penalosa, Fernando; *Sociolinguistics.

927 Duran, Richard P. Book review of: CULTURE AND THE BILINGUAL CLASSROOM. LA RED/THE NET, no. 44 (July 1981), p. 4-5. English. **DESCR:** Bilingualism; *CULTURE AND THE BILINGUAL CLASSROOM: STUDIES IN CLASSROOM ETHNOLOGY; Guthrie, Grace Pung; Hu-Pei Au, Kathryn; Trueba, Henry T.

928 Duran, Richard P. Book review of: TESTING LANGUAGE ABILITY IN THE CLASSROOM. LA RED/THE NET, no. 45 (August 1981), p. 5. English. **DESCR:** Cohen, Andrew D.; Language Proficiency; *TESTING LANGUAGE ABILITY IN THE CLASSROOM.

929 Duran, Richard P. Book reviews of: DISCOURSE STRATEGIES and LANGUAGE AND SOCIAL IDENTITY. LA RED/THE NET, no. 77 (February 1984), p. 13-14. English. **DESCR:** *DISCOURSE STRATEGIES; Gumperz, John J.; *LANGUAGE AND SOCIAL IDENTITY.

930 Dysart, Jane E. Book review of: THE IMPACT OF INTIMACY: MEXICAN-ANGLO INTERMARRIAGE IN NEW MEXICO, 1821-1846. PACIFIC HISTORICAL REVIEW, Vol. 53, no. 1 (1984), p. 82-83. English. **DESCR:** Craver, Rebecca McDowell; Intermarriage; *THE IMPACT OF INTIMACY: MEXICAN-ANGLO INTERMARRIAGE IN NEW MEXICO, 1821-1846.

931 Eidelberg, Nora. Book review of: BEARING WITNESS/SOBREVIVIENDO. LECTOR, Vol. 4, no. 1-3 (1986), p. [59-60]. English. **DESCR:** *BEARING WITNESS/SOBREVIVIENDO; CALYX: A JOURNAL OF ART AND LITERATURE BY WOMEN.

932 Elias, Edward F. Book review of: A DECADE OF HISPANIC LITERATURE. LA RED/THE NET, no. 68 (May 1983), p. 9-10. English. **DESCR:** *DECADE OF HISPANIC LITERATURE: AN ANNIVERSARY ANTHOLOGY; Literature; REVISTA CHICANO-RIQUENA.

933 Engerman, Stanley L. Book review of: THE TRANSPLANTED. JOURNAL OF ECONOMIC HISTORY, Vol. 46, no. 2 (June 1986), p. 552-553. English. **DESCR:** *Bodnar, John; Immigrants; *THE TRANSPLANTED: A HISTORY OF IMMIGRANTS IN URBAN AMERICA.

934 Espada, Martin. Book review of: BLACK HAIR. LECTOR, Vol. 4, no. 4-6 (1987), p. 77. English. **DESCR:** *BLACK HAIR; Soto, Gary.

935 Everett, D.E. Book review of: LA FAMILIA. CHOICE, Vol. 22, no. 10 (June 1985), p. 1574. English. **DESCR:** Griswold del Castillo, Richard; *LA FAMILIA: CHICANO FAMILIES IN THE URBAN SOUTHWEST, 1848 TO THE PRESENT.

936 Eysturoy, Annie O. EL DIABLO EN TEXAS: una historia popular a traves de arquetipos y simbolos. LA COMUNIDAD, No. 364 (July 12, 1987), p. 6-7. Spanish. **DESCR:** Brito, Aristeo; *EL DIABLO EN TEXAS; Literary Criticism.

Book Reviews (cont.)

937 Farley, J.E. Book review of: THE CHICANO EXPERIENCE. CHOICE, Vol. 23, no. 3 (November 1985), p. [483]. English. **DESCR:** Mirande, Alfredo; *THE CHICANO EXPERIENCE: AN ALTERNATIVE PERSPECTIVE.

938 Farley, J.E. Book review of: THE ZOOT-SUIT RIOTS. CHOICE, Vol. 22, no. 11-12 (July, August, 1985), p. 1691-1692. English. **DESCR:** Mazon, Mauricio; *THE ZOOT-SUIT RIOTS: THE PSYCHOLOGY OF SYMBOLIC ANNIHILATION.

939 Fernandez, Celestino. Book review of: LA CLASE OBRERA EN LA HISTORIA DE MEXICO: AL NORTE DEL RIO BRAVO (PASADO INMEDIATO, 1930-1981). NEW MEXICO HISTORICAL REVIEW, Vol. 59, no. 2 (April 1984), p. 214-215. English. **DESCR:** *LA CLASE OBRERA EN LA HISTORIA DE MEXICO: AL NORTE DEL RIO BRAVO (PASADO INMEDIATO, 1930-1981); Laboring Classes; Maciel, David.

940 Fields, Alicia. Small but telling moments. THE BLOOMSBURY REVIEW, no. 1-2 (1987), p. 10. English. **DESCR:** *SMALL FACES; Soto, Gary.

941 Finch, Mark S. Book review of: CHICANO AUTHORS: INQUIRY BY INTERVIEW. KENTUCKY ROMANCE QUARTERLY, Vol. 32, no. 4 (1985), p. 435. English. **DESCR:** Bruce-Novoa, Juan; *CHICANO AUTHORS: INQUIRY BY INTERVIEW.

942 Fireman, Janet R. Book review of: WATER IN THE HISPANIC SOUTHWEST. SOUTHWESTERN HISTORICAL QUARTERLY, Vol. 88, no. 4 (1985), p. 430-431. English. **DESCR:** Meyer, Michael C.; *WATER IN THE HISPANIC SOUTHWEST: A SOCIAL AND LEGAL HISTORY, 1550-1850.

943 Flores, Estevan T. Book review of: ILLEGAL ALIENS IN THE WESTERN HEMISPHERE. LA RED/THE NET, no. 56 (July 1982), p. 7-9. English. **DESCR:** *ILLEGAL ALIENS IN THE WESTERN HEMISPHERE: POLITICAL AND ECONOMIC FACTORS; Johnson, Kenneth F.; Undocumented Workers; Williams, Miles W.

944 Flores, Lauro. Book review of: EL PUEBLO: THE GALLEGOS FAMILY'S JOURNEY 1503-1980. MINNESOTA REVIEW, no. 22 (1984), p. 145-148. English. **DESCR:** Bruce-Novoa, Juan; *CHICANO POETRY: A RESPONSE TO CHAOS; *EL PUEBLO: THE GALLEGOS FAMILY'S AMERICAN JOURNEY 1503-1980; *FAMOUS ALL OVER TOWN; James, Dan; Johansen, Bruce; Maestas, Roberto.

945 Floyd, Mary Beth. Language use and communicative behavior: Hispanic bilinguals in the United States. BILINGUAL REVIEW, Vol. 12, no. 1-2 (January, August, 1985), p. 120-133. English. **DESCR:** Duran, Richard P.; Language Usage; *LATINO LANGUAGE AND COMMUNICATIVE BEHAVIOR.

946 Foley, Patrick. Book review of: ALONG THE RIO GRANDE: PASTORAL VISIT TO SOUTHWEST NEW MEXICO IN 1902. NEW MEXICO HISTORICAL REVIEW, Vol. 62, no. 4 (October 1987), p. 405-6. English. **DESCR:** *ALONG THE RIO GRANDE: A PASTORAL VISIT TO SOUTHWEST NEW MEXICO IN 1902; *Granjon, Henry; *New Mexico.

947 Foote, Cheryl. Book review of: IMAGES AND CONVERSATIONS. JOURNAL OF THE WEST, Vol. 24, no. 3 (July 1985), p. 121. English. **DESCR:** Chicanas; IMAGES AND CONVERSATIONS: MEXICAN AMERICANS RECALL A SOUTHWESTERN PAST; *Martin, Patricia Preciado; Oral History.

948 Foster, James C. Book review of: LABOR IN NEW MEXICO: UNIONS, STRIKES AND SOCIAL HISTORY SINCE 1881. NEW MEXICO HISTORICAL REVIEW, Vol. 59, no. 3 (July 1984), p. 324-326. English. **DESCR:** Kern, Robert; Labor; *LABOR IN NEW MEXICO: UNIONS, STRIKES, AND SOCIAL HISTORY SINCE 1881.

949 Freiband, Susan J. Book review of: THE IMMIGRANT WOMAN IN NORTH AMERICA. AMERICAN REFERENCE BOOKS ANNUAL, Vol. 17, (1986), p. 178. English. **DESCR:** Cordasco, Francesco; *THE IMMIGRANT WOMAN IN NORTH AMERICA: AN ANNOTATED BIBLIOGRAPHY OF SELECTED REFERENCES.

950 Ganster, Paul. Book review of: ECOLOGY AND DEVELOPMENT OF THE BORDER REGION. PACIFIC HISTORICAL REVIEW, Vol. 55, no. 2 (1986), p. 318-320. English. **DESCR:** Border Region; *ECOLOGY AND DEVELOPMENT OF THE BORDER REGION: SECOND SYMPOSIUM; Ross, Stanley R.

951 Garcia, Alma. Journal review of: CRITICA: A JOURNAL OF CRITICAL ESSAYS. LECTOR, Vol. 4, no. 4-6 (1987), p. 68. English. **DESCR:** *CRITICA: A JOURNAL OF CRITICAL ESSAYS; Journals.

952 Garcia, Chris. Book review of: MUTUAL AID FOR SURVIVAL. HISPANIC AMERICAN HISTORICAL REVIEW, Vol. 64, no. 1 (February 1984), p. 205. English. **DESCR:** Hernandez, Jose Amaro; *MUTUAL AID FOR SURVIVAL: THE CASE OF THE MEXICAN AMERICAN.

953 Garcia, Ed. On red-haired girls and the greaser in me. TEXAS OBSERVOR, Vol. 75, (October 28, 1983), p. 24-25. English. **DESCR:** de Leon, Arnoldo; Essays; Identity; *Stereotypes; Texas; *THEY CALLED THEM GREASERS: ANGLO ATTITUDES TOWARD MEXICANS IN TEXAS, 1821-1900.

954 Garcia, John A. Book review of: AMERICA'S ETHNIC POLITICS. LA RED/THE NET, no. 67 (April 1983), p. 7-8. English. **DESCR:** *AMERICA'S ETHNIC POLITICS; Eisenberg, Bernard; Politics; Roucek, Joseph S.

955 Garcia, John A. Book review of: AMERICA WITHOUT ETHNICITY. LA RED/THE NET, no. 78 (March 1984), p. 8-9. English. **DESCR:** *AMERICA WITHOUT ETHNICITY; Morgan, Gordon D.

956 Garcia, John A. Book review of: RACE AND CLASS IN THE SOUTHWEST: A THEORY OF INEQUALITY. LA RED/THE NET, no. 31 (June 1980), p. 4. English. **DESCR:** Barrera, Mario; *Discrimination; *Economics; RACE AND CLASS IN THE SOUTHWEST: A THEORY OF RACIAL INEQUALITY; *Southwestern United States.

957 Garcia, John R. Book reviews of: EL PUEBLO MEXICANO EN DETROIT Y MICHIGAN and MATERIALS ON THE HISTORY OF LATINOS IN MICHIGAN AND THE MIDWEST. LA RED/THE NET, no. 67 (April 1983), p. 13-14. English. **DESCR:** *EL PUEBLO MEXICANO EN DETROIT Y MICHIGAN: A SOCIAL HISTORY; *MATERIALS ON THE HISTORY OF LATINOS IN MICHIGAN AND THE MIDWEST; Midwestern States; Valdes, Dennis N.

958 Garcia, Mario T. Book review of: A COMMUNITY UNDER SIEGE. LA RED/THE NET, no. 94 (March 1986), p. 5-6. English. **DESCR:** *A COMMUNITY UNDER SIEGE: A CHRONICLE OF CHICANOS EAST OF THE LOS ANGELES RIVER, 1945-1975; Acuna, Rudolfo; Los Angeles, CA.

--   --

Book Reviews (cont.)

959 Garcia, Mario T. Book review of: A COMMUNITY
    UNDER SIEGE. PACIFIC HISTORICAL REVIEW, Vol.
    55, no. 4 (1986), p. 636-638. English.
    DESCR: *A COMMUNITY UNDER SIEGE: A CHRONICLE
    OF CHICANOS EAST OF THE LOS ANGELES RIVER,
    1945-1975; Acuna, Rudolfo; East Los Angeles,
    CA.

960 Garcia, Mario T. Book review of: DEVELOPMENT
    OF THE MEXICAN WORKING CLASS NORTH OF THE
    RIO BRAVO: WORK AND CULTURE AMONG LABORERS
    AND ARTISANS, 1600-1900. PACIFIC HISTORICAL
    REVIEW, Vol. 53, no. 4 (November 1984), p.
    525-527. English. **DESCR:** *DEVELOPMENT OF THE
    MEXICAN WORKING CLASS NORTH OF THE RIO
    BRAVO: WORK AND CULTURE AMONG LABORERS AND
    ARTISANS, 1600-1900; Gomez-Quinones, Juan;
    Laboring Classes.

961 Garcia, Mario T. Book review of: FRAGMENTS
    OF THE MEXICAN REVOLUTION. HISPANIC AMERICAN
    HISTORICAL REVIEW, Vol. 65, no. 1 (February
    1985), p. 150-151. English. **DESCR:**
    *FRAGMENTS OF THE MEXICAN REVOLUTION:
    PERSONAL ACCOUNTS FROM THE BORDER; Martinez,
    Oscar J.; Mexican Revolution - 1910-1920.

962 Garcia, Mario T. Book review of: LA FAMILIA.
    LA RED/THE NET, no. 99 (August 1986), p.
    4-5. English. **DESCR:** Family; Griswold del
    Castillo, Richard; *LA FAMILIA: CHICANO
    FAMILIES IN THE URBAN SOUTHWEST, 1848 TO THE
    PRESENT.

963 Garcia, Mario T. Book review of: POLITICAL
    AND ECONOMIC MIGRANTS IN AMERICA. LA RED/THE
    NET, no. 96 (May 1986), p. 11-12. English.
    DESCR: Immigration; Pedraza-Bailey, Silvia;
    *POLITICAL AND ECONOMIC MIGRANTS IN AMERICA.

964 Garcia, Mario T. Book review of: POLITICAL
    AND ECONOMIC MIGRANTS IN AMERICA. AMERICAN
    HISTORICAL REVIEW, Vol. 91, no. 4 (October
    1986), p. 1023-1024. English. **DESCR:**
    Immigrants; Immigration; Pedraza-Bailey,
    Silvia; *POLITICAL AND ECONOMIC MIGRANTS IN
    AMERICA.

965 Garcia, Mario T. Book review of: THE STATE
    OF CHICANO RESEARCH ON FAMILY, LABOR, AND
    MIGRATION: PROCEEDINGS OF THE FIRST STANFORD
    SYMPOSIUM ON CHICANO RESEARCH AND PUBLIC
    POLICY. CALIFORNIA HISTORY, Vol. 63, no. 3
    (Summer 1984), p. 261-262. English. **DESCR:**
    Almaguer, Tomas; Camarillo, Alberto; Chicano
    Studies; *THE STATE OF CHICANO RESEARCH IN
    FAMILY, LABOR AND MIGRATION STUDIES; Valdez,
    Armando.

966 Garcia, Mario T. Book review of: THEY CALLED
    THEM GREASERS. HISPANIC AMERICAN HISTORICAL
    REVIEW, Vol. 64, no. 2 (May 1984), p.
    405-406. English. **DESCR:** de Leon, Arnoldo;
    *THEY CALLED THEM GREASERS: ANGLO ATTITUDES
    TOWARD MEXICANS IN TEXAS, 1821-1900.

967 Garcia, Nasario. El cuento chicano visto por
    dentro y por fuera. BILINGUAL REVIEW, Vol.
    12, no. 3 (September, December, 1985), p.
    262-265. Spanish. **DESCR:** Aguilar, Ricardo;
    Armengol, Armando; *PALABRA NUEVA: CUENTOS
    CHICANOS; Somoza, Oscar U.

968 Garcia, Philip. Book review of:
    ACCULTURATION: THEORY, MODELS, AND SOME NEW
    FINDINGS. LA RED/THE NET, no. 41 (April
    1981), p. 4-5. English. **DESCR:**
    *Acculturation; *ACCULTURATION: THEORY,
    MODELS, AND SOME NEW FINDINGS; *Padilla,
    Amado M.

969 Garcia, Philip. Book review of: CHICANO

CINEMA. LA RED/THE NET, no. 91 (October
1985), p. 13-14. English. **DESCR:** *CHICANO
CINEMA: RESEARCH, REVIEWS AND RESOURCES;
Films; Keller, Gary D.

970 Garcia, Philip. Book review of: CHICANOS,
    CATHOLICISM, AND POLITICAL IDEOLOGY.
    AMERICAN POLITICAL SCIENCE REVIEW, Vol. 81,
    (January 1987), p. 642-643. English.
    DESCR: Catholic Church; *CHICANOS,
    CATHOLICISM, AND POLITICAL IDEOLOGY;
    Mosqueda, Lawrence J.

971 Garcia, Philip. Book review of: EAST LOS
    ANGELES. LA RED/THE NET, no. 86 (November
    1984), p. 2-3. English. **DESCR:** *EAST LOS
    ANGELES: HISTORY OF A BARRIO; Romo, Ricardo.

972 Garcia, Philip. Book review of: MEXICAN
    AMERICANS IN SCHOOL: A DECADE OF CHANGE. LA
    RED/THE NET, no. 33 (August 1980), p. 4.
    English. **DESCR:** Carter, Thomas P.;
    *Education; *MEXICAN AMERICANS IN SCHOOL: A
    DECADE OF CHANGE; Segura, Roberto D.

973 Gardiol, Rita. Book review of: CELSO.
    LECTOR, Vol. 4, no. 4-6 (1987), p. 76-77.
    English. **DESCR:** *CELSO; Romero, Leo.

974 Gibson, Guadalupe. Book review of: MENTAL
    HEALTH AND HISPANIC AMERICANS: CLINICAL
    PERSPECTIVES. SOCIAL WORK, Vol. 29, no. 1
    (January, February, 1984), p. 81. English.
    DESCR: Becerra, Rosina; Escobar, Javier I.;
    Karno, Marvin; *MENTAL HEALTH AND HISPANIC
    AMERICANS: CLINICAL PERSPECTIVES.

975 Gonzales, Juan L., Jr. Book review of: FARM
    WORKERS, AGRIBUSINESS, AND THE STATE. LABOR
    HISTORY, Vol. 27, no. 4 (Fall 1986), p.
    587-588. English. **DESCR:** Farm Workers;
    *FARMWORKERS, AGRIBUSINESS, AND THE STATE;
    Majka, Linda C.; Majka, Theo J.

976 Gonzales, Phillip B. Book review of: LATINOS
    IN THE UNITED STATES: THE SACRED AND THE
    POLITICAL. NEW MEXICO HISTORICAL REVIEW,
    Vol. 62, no. 4 (October 1987), p. 409-11.
    English. **DESCR:** *Abalos, David T.; *LATINOS
    IN THE UNITED STATES: THE SACRED AND THE
    POLITICAL; Politics; Religion.

977 Gonzales-Berry, Erlinda. Book review of:
    BILINGUAL EDUCATION: A SOURCEBOOK. MODERN
    LANGUAGE JOURNAL, Vol. 69, no. 3 (Fall
    1985), p. 299. English. **DESCR:** Ambert, Alba
    N.; *BILINGUAL EDUCATION: A SOURCEBOOK;
    Melendez, Sarah E.

978 Gonzales-Berry, Erlinda. Book review of:
    FACE. THE AMERICAS REVIEW, Vol. 15, no. 2
    (Summer 1987), p. 107-109. English. **DESCR:**
    *FACE; Pineda, Cecile.

979 Gonzales-Berry, Erlinda. Sensuality,
    repression, and death in Arturo Isla's THE
    RAIN GOD. BILINGUAL REVIEW, Vol. 12, no. 3
    (September, December, 1985), p. 258-261.
    English. **DESCR:** Islas, Arturo; *THE RAIN
    GOD: A DESERT TALE.

980 Gonzalez, Gustavo. Book review of:
    BILINGUAL-BICULTURAL EDUCATION: AN ANNOTATED
    BIBLIOGRAPHY, 1936-1982. MODERN LANGUAGE
    JOURNAL, Vol. 69, no. 3 (Fall 1985), p.
    299-300. English. **DESCR:** Ballesteros,
    Octavio A.; Bibliography; Bilingual
    Bicultural Education; *BILINGUAL-BICULTURAL
    EDUCATION: AN ANNOTATED BIBLIOGRAPHY.

Book Reviews (cont.)

981 Gonzalez, Hector Hugo. Book review of: LA
FAMILIA. LECTOR, Vol. 4, no. 4-6 (1987), p.
54. English. **DESCR**: Family; Griswold del
Castillo, Richard; *LA FAMILIA: CHICANO
FAMILIES IN THE URBAN SOUTHWEST, 1848 TO THE
PRESENT.

982 Gonzalez, LaVerne. Book review of: THE
SILENCE OF THE LLANO. THE AMERICAS REVIEW,
Vol. 15, no. 2 (Summer 1987), p. 109-111.
English. **DESCR**: Anaya, Rudolfo A.; *THE
SILENCE OF THE LLANO.

983 Grabo, Norman S. Book review of:
CONTEMPORARY CHICANA POETRY. AMERICAN
LITERATURE, Vol. 58, no. 3 (October 1986),
p. 473-475. English. **DESCR**: *CONTEMPORARY
CHICANA POETRY: A CRITICAL APPROACH TO AN
EMERGING LITERATURE; Poetry; Sanchez, Marta
Ester.

984 Griffith, James S. Book review of: HISPANIC
ARTS AND ETHNOHISTORY IN THE SOUTHWEST: NEW
PAPERS INSPIRED BY THE WORKS OF E. BOYD.
ARIZONA AND THE WEST, Vol. 26, no. 2 (Summer
1984), p. 188-189. English. **DESCR**: *HISPANIC
ARTS AND ETHNOHISTORY IN THE SOUTHWEST: NEW
PAPERS INSPIRED BY THE WORKS OF E. BOYD;
Weigle, Marta.

985 Griffith, James S. Book review of: THE
TEXAS-MEXICAN CONJUNTO. AMERICAN
ANTHROPOLOGIST, Vol. 88, no. 3 (September
1986), p. 733-734. English. **DESCR**: Pena,
Manuel; *THE TEXAS-MEXICAN CONJUNTO: HISTORY
OF A WORKING-CLASS MUSIC.

986 Griswold del Castillo, Richard. Book review
of: A BORDERLANDS TOWN IN TRANSITION:
LAREDO, 1755-1870. PACIFIC HISTORICAL
REVIEW, Vol. 54, no. 2 (May 1985), p.
223-224. English. **DESCR**: *A BORDERLANDS TOWN
IN TRANSITION: LAREDO, 1755-1870; Hinojosa,
Gilbert Miguel; Laredo, TX.

987 Griswold del Castillo, Richard. Book review
of: CHICANOS IN CALIFORNIA. PACIFIC
HISTORICAL REVIEW, Vol. 54, no. 2 (February
1985), p. 211-212. English. **DESCR**:
California; Camarillo, Alberto; *CHICANOS IN
CALIFORNIA.

988 Griswold del Castillo, Richard. Book review
of: EAST LOS ANGELES. PACIFIC HISTORICAL
REVIEW, Vol. 53, no. 4 (November 1984), p.
528-529. English. **DESCR**: East Los Angeles,
CA; Los Angeles, CA; *Romo, Ricardo.

989 Griswold del Castillo, Richard. Book review
of: ESTADOS UNIDOS HOY. PACIFIC HISTORICAL
REVIEW, Vol. 54, no. 4 (1985), p. 542-544.
English. **DESCR**: *ESTADOS UNIDOS, HOY;
Gonzalez, Casanova.

990 Griswold del Castillo, Richard. Book review
of: HISPANICS IN THE UNITED STATES: A NEW
SOCIAL AGENDA. JOURNAL OF AMERICAN ETHNIC
HISTORY, Vol. 6, no. 1 (Fall 1986), p.
112-114. English. **DESCR**: *HISPANICS IN THE
UNITED STATES: A NEW SOCIAL AGENDA;
McCready, William C.; San Juan Cafferty,
Pastora; Social History and Conditions.

991 Griswold del Castillo, Richard. Book review
of: HISPANICS IN THE UNITED STATES: A NEW
SOCIAL AGENDA. HISPANIC AMERICAN HISTORICAL
REVIEW, Vol. 66, no. 3 (August 1986), p.
627-629. English. **DESCR**: *HISPANICS IN THE
UNITED STATES: A NEW SOCIAL AGENDA;
McCready, William C.; San Juan Cafferty,
Pastora.

992 Griswold del Castillo, Richard. Book review
of: MUTUAL AID FOR SURVIVAL. SOUTHWESTERN
HISTORICAL QUARTERLY, Vol. 88, no. 3 (1985),
p. 330-332. English. **DESCR**: Hernandez, Jose
Amaro; *MUTUAL AID FOR SURVIVAL: THE CASE OF
THE MEXICAN AMERICAN; Mutualistas.

993 Griswold del Castillo, Richard. Book review
of: ROOTS OF RESISTANCE: LAND TENURE IN NEW
MEXICO, 1680-1980. LA RED/THE NET, no. 42
(May 1981), p. 10. English. **DESCR**: Dunbar
Ortiz, Roxanne; Land Tenure; *ROOTS OF
RESISTANCE: LAND TENURE IN NEW MEXICO,
1680-1980.

994 Griswold del Castillo, Richard. Book review
of: THE STATE OF CHICANO RESEARCH ON FAMILY,
LABOR, AND MIGRATION: PROCEEDINGS OF THE
FIRST STANFORD SYMPOSIUM ON CHICANO RESEARCH
AND PUBLIC POLICY. PACIFIC HISTORICAL
REVIEW, Vol. 54, no. 3 (August 1985), p.
381-382. English. **DESCR**: Almaguer, Tomas;
Camarillo, Alberto; Chicano Studies; *THE
STATE OF CHICANO RESEARCH IN FAMILY, LABOR
AND MIGRATION STUDIES; Valdez, Armando.

995 Griswold del Castillo, Richard. New
perspectives on the Mexican and American
borderlands. LATIN AMERICAN RESEARCH REVIEW,
Vol. 19, no. 1 (1984), p. 199-209. English.
DESCR: AL NORTE DEL RIO BRAVO (PASADO
INMEDIATO, 1930-1981); AL NORTE DEL RIO
BRAVO (PASADO LEJANO, 1600-1930); *Border
Region; Gomez-Quinones, Juan; Maciel, David;
MEXICANO RESISTANCE IN THE SOUTHWEST: "THE
SACRED RIGHT OF SELF-PRESERVATION";
Rosenbaum, Robert J.; THE MEXICAN FRONTIER,
1821-1846: THE AMERICAN SOUTHWEST UNDER
MEXICO; THE TEJANO COMMUNITY, 1836-1900;
Weber, David J.

996 Gutierrez, Armando. Book reviews of:
MEXICO-UNITED STATES RELATIONS and UNITED
STATES RELATIONS WITH MEXICO: CONTEXT AND
CONTENT. LA RED/THE NET, no. 62 (December
1982), p. 4-6. English. **DESCR**: Erb, Richard
D.; Kaufman, Purcell; *MEXICO-UNITED STATES
RELATIONS; Ross, Stanley R.; *UNITED STATES
RELATIONS WITH MEXICO: CONTEXT AND CONTENT.

997 Gutierrez, Ramon A. Book review of: THE
CHICANO EXPERIENCE. AMERICAS, Vol. 43, no. 1
(July 1986), p. 134-136. English. **DESCR**:
Mirande, Alfredo; *THE CHICANO EXPERIENCE:
AN ALTERNATIVE PERSPECTIVE.

998 Gutierrez, Ramon A. Book review of: THE
FOLKLORE OF SPAIN IN THE AMERICAN SOUTHWEST.
HISPANIC AMERICAN HISTORICAL REVIEW, Vol.
67, no. 1 (February 1987), p. 149-150.
English. **DESCR**: Espinosa, Aurelio M.;
Espinosa, J. Manuel; *THE FOLKLORE OF SPAIN
IN THE AMERICAN SOUTHWEST: TRADITIONAL
SPANISH FOLK LITERATURE IN NORTHERN NEW
MEXICO AND SOUTHERN COLORADO.

999 Hagle, C. Book review of: THE IMMIGRANT
WOMAN IN NORTH AMERICA. CHOICE, Vol. 23, no.
8 (April 1986), p. 1191. English. **DESCR**:
Cordasco, Francesco; Reference Works; *THE
IMMIGRANT WOMAN IN NORTH AMERICA: AN
ANNOTATED BIBLIOGRAPHY OF SELECTED
REFERENCES.

1000 Haines, Michael R. Book review of:
IMMIGRATION POLICY AND THE AMERICAN LABOR
FORCE. JOURNAL OF ECONOMIC HISTORY, Vol. 45,
no. 3 (September 1985), p. 742-744. English.
DESCR: Briggs, Vernon M., Jr.; Immigration
Law and Legislation; *IMMIGRATION POLICY AND
THE AMERICAN LABOR FORCE.

Book Reviews (cont.)

1001 Hall, Linda B. The United States-Mexican borders: historical, political, and cultural perspectives. LATIN AMERICAN RESEARCH REVIEW, Vol. 20, no. 2 (1985), p. 223-229. English. **DESCR**: AMERICAN LABOR IN THE SOUTHWEST: THE FIRST ONE HUNDRED YEARS; *Border Region; BOSS RULE IN SOUTH TEXAS: THE PROGRESSIVE ERA; CHICANO INTERMARRIAGE: A THEORETICAL AND EMPIRICAL STUDY; HISPANIC CULTURE IN THE SOUTHWEST; IN DEFENSE OF LA RAZA: THE LOS ANGELES MEXICAN CONSULATE AND THE MEXICAN COMMUNITY; Literature Reviews; RACE AND CLASS IN THE SOUTHWEST: A THEORY OF RACIAL INEQUALITY; SOUTHWESTERN AGRICULTURE: PRE-COLUMBIAN TO MODERN; THE MEXICANS IN OKLAHOMA; THE POLITICS OF SAN ANTONIO.

1002 Haro, Robert P. Book review of: CHICANO LITERATURE: A REFERENCE GUIDE. AMERICAN REFERENCE BOOKS ANNUAL, Vol. 17, (1986), p. 440. English. **DESCR**: *CHICANO LITERATURE: A REFERENCE GUIDE; Lomeli, Francisco A.; Martinez, Julio A.; Reference Works.

1003 Haro, Robert P. Book review of: CHICANO ORGANIZATIONS DIRECTORY. AMERICAN REFERENCE BOOKS ANNUAL, Vol. 17, (1986), p. 145. English. **DESCR**: Caballero, Cesar; *CHICANO ORGANIZATIONS DIRECTORY; Reference Works.

1004 Haro, Robert P. Book review of: HISPANIC AMERICAN VOLUNTARY ORGANIZATIONS. AMERICAN REFERENCE BOOKS ANNUAL, Vol. 17, (1986), p. 146. English. **DESCR**: Gonzales, Sylvia Alicia; *HISPANIC AMERICAN VOLUNTARY ORGANIZATIONS; Reference Works.

1005 Harrington, James C. GREASERS chronicles Texas racism, past and present. TEXAS OBSERVOR, Vol. 75, (October 28, 1983), p. 23-25. English. **DESCR**: de Leon, Arnoldo; *THEY CALLED THEM GREASERS: ANGLO ATTITUDES TOWARD MEXICANS IN TEXAS, 1821-1900.

1006 Hart, John M. Book review of: TEXAS AND THE MEXICAN REVOLUTION. PACIFIC HISTORICAL REVIEW, Vol. 55, no. 2 (1986), p. 324-325. English. **DESCR**: Coerver, Don M.; Hall, Linda B.; *TEXAS AND THE MEXICAN REVOLUTION: A STUDY IN STATE AND NATIONAL BORDER POLICY.

1007 Hastings, D.W. Book review of: MEXICAN AMERICAN FERTILITY PATTERNS. CHOICE, Vol. 23, no. 11-12 (July, August, 1986), p. 1738. English. **DESCR**: Bean, Frank D.; *MEXICAN AMERICAN FERTILITY PATTERNS; Swicegood, Gray.

1008 Hastings, D.W. Book review of: MEXICAN IMMIGRANTS AND MEXICAN AMERICANS: AN EVOLVING RELATION. CHOICE, Vol. 24, no. 3 (November 1986), p. 516. English. **DESCR**: Browning, Harley L.; de la Garza, Rodolfo O.; *MEXICAN IMMIGRANTS AND MEXICAN AMERICANS: AN EVOLVING RELATION.

1009 Hayes-Bautista, David Emmett. Book review of: THE HEALTH REVOLUTION IN CUBA. LA RED/THE NET, no. 11 (November 1983), p. 10-12. English. **DESCR**: Diaz-Briquets, Sergio; *THE HEALTH REVOLUTION IN CUBA.

1010 Hendershott, C. Book review of: IMMIGRANTS AND THEIR CHILDREN IN THE UNITED STATES: A BIBLIOGRAPHY OF DOCTORAL DISSERTATIONS, 1885-1982. CHOICE, Vol. 23, no. 11-12 (July, August, 1986), p. 1656. English. **DESCR**: Hoglund, A. William; *IMMIGRANTS AND THEIR CHILDREN IN THE UNITED STATES: A BIBLIOGRAPHY OF DOCTORAL DISSERTATIONS, 1885-1982.

1011 Herrera-Sobek, Maria. Book review of: AND OTHER NEIGHBORLY NAMES: SOCIAL PROCESS AND CULTURAL IMAGE IN TEXAS FOLKLORE. LA RED/THE NET, no. 47 (October 1981), p. 3-4. English. **DESCR**: Abrahams, Roger D.; Bauman, Richard; *Folklore; *Texas.

1012 Herrera-Sobek, Maria. Book review of: CUBAN AMERICANS: MASTERS OF SURVIVAL. LA RED/THE NET, no. 67 (April 1983), p. 10-12. English. **DESCR**: *CUBAN AMERICANS: MASTERS OF SURVIVAL; Cubanos; Llanes, Jose.

1013 Herrera-Sobek, Maria. Literatura y sociedad: la problematica del Chicano/Mexicano en los Estados Unidos a traves de la obra literaria. BILINGUAL REVIEW, Vol. 11, no. 3 (September, December, 1984), p. 83-87. Spanish. **DESCR**: Literary Criticism; Literature; *REQUISA TREINTA Y DOS; Sanchez, Rosaura.

1014 Herrick, R.L. Book review of: CHICANOS, CATHOLICISM, AND POLITICAL IDEOLOGY. CHOICE, Vol. 24, no. 3 (November 1986), p. 498. English. **DESCR**: *CHICANOS, CATHOLICISM, AND POLITICAL IDEOLOGY; Mosqueda, Lawrence J.

1015 Hewlett-Gomez, Michele. Book review of: THE ENGLISH-SPANISH CONNECTION. LA RED/THE NET, no. 84 (September 1984), p. 2. English. **DESCR**: *THE ENGLISH-SPANISH CONNECTION; Thonis, Elenor.

1016 Hill, Larry D. Book review of: TEXAS AND THE MEXICAN REVOLUTION. JOURNAL OF SOUTHERN HISTORY, Vol. 52, no. 4 (November 1986), p. 651-652. English. **DESCR**: Coerver, Don M.; Hall, Linda B.; *TEXAS AND THE MEXICAN REVOLUTION: A STUDY IN STATE AND NATIONAL BORDER POLICY.

1017 Hoffman, Abraham. Book review of: A COMMUNITY UNDER SIEGE. JOURNAL OF AMERICAN HISTORY, Vol. 72, no. 2 (September 1985), p. 459. English. **DESCR**: *A COMMUNITY UNDER SIEGE: A CHRONICLE OF CHICANOS EAST OF THE LOS ANGELES RIVER, 1945-1975; Acuna, Rudolfo.

1018 Hoffman, Abraham. Book review of: AN ILLUSTRATED HISTORY OF MEXICAN LOS ANGELES: 1781-1985. NEW MEXICO HISTORICAL REVIEW, Vol. 62, no. 4 (October 1987), p. 412-13. English. **DESCR**: *AN ILLUSTRATED HISTORY OF MEXICAN LOS ANGELES: 1781-1985; *Castillo, Pedro; *Los Angeles, CA; *Rios-Bustamante, Antonio.

1019 Hopkins, Thomas. Book review of: BILINGUAL AND ESL CLASSROOMS: TEACHING IN MULTICULTURAL CONTEXTS. EDUCATIONAL LEADERSHIP, Vol. 43, no. 6 (March 1986), p. 82. English. **DESCR**: *BILINGUAL AND ESL CLASSROOMS: TEACHING IN MULTICULTURAL CONTEXTS; Collier, Virginia P.; Ovando, Carlos J.

1020 Huerta, Jorge. Book review of: GIVING UP THE GHOST. THE AMERICAS REVIEW, Vol. 15, no. 2 (Summer 1987), p. 104-105. English. **DESCR**: *GIVING UP THE GHOST; Moraga, Cherrie; Teatro.

1021 Hunsaker, Alan C. Mexican immigration patterns. LA RED/THE NET, no. 93 (January, February, 1986), p. 17-19. English. **DESCR**: Immigration; *Jones, Richard C.; *Migration Patterns; PATTERNS OF UNDOCUMENTED MIGRATION: MEXICO AND THE U.S.

Book Reviews (cont.)

1022 Hurtado, Aida. Book review of: WORK, FAMILY, SEX ROLES, LANGUAGE. LA RED/THE NET, no. 40 (March 1981), p. 3. English. **DESCR:** Barrera, Mario; Camarillo, Alberto; Hernandez, Francisco; Social History and Conditions; *WORK, FAMILY, SEX ROLES, LANGUAGE: SELECTED PAPERS OF THE NATIONAL ASSOCIATION FOR CHICANO STUDIES CONFERENCE, 1979.

1023 Isaacs, D.S. Book review of: CONTEMPORARY CHICANA POETRY. CHOICE, Vol. 23, no. 8 (April 1986), p. 1217. English. **DESCR:** *CONTEMPORARY CHICANA POETRY: A CRITICAL APPROACH TO AN EMERGING LITERATURE; Sanchez, Marta Ester.

1024 Jackson, James S. Book review of: UNDERSTANDING MINORITY AGING: PERSPECTIVES AND SOURCES. LA RED/THE NET, no. 68 (May 1983), p. 12-13. English. **DESCR:** Cuellar, Jose B.; Miller-Soule, Danielle I.; Stanford, E.P. Percil; *UNDERSTANDING MINORITY AGING: PERSPECTIVES AND SOURCES.

1025 Jacob, John. Book review of: SOUTHWEST TALES: A CONTEMPORY COLLECTION. BOOKLIST, Vol. 82, no. 17 (May 1, 1986), p. 1284. English. **DESCR:** Alurista; Rojas-Urista, Xelina; *SOUTHWEST TALES: A CONTEMPORARY COLLECTION.

1026 Jimenez, Francisco. Book review of: CHICANO DISCOURSE. LECTOR, Vol. 4, no. 4-6 (1987), p. 55. English. **DESCR:** *CHICANO DISCOURSE: SOCIOHISTORIC PERSPECTIVE; Sanchez, Rosaura; Sociolinguistics.

1027 Kanellos, Nicolas. Book review of: HISPANICS IN THE UNITED STATES: AN ANTHOLOGY OF CREATIVE WRITING. LA RED/THE NET, no. 71 (August 1983), p. 12-13. English. **DESCR:** *HISPANICS IN THE UNITED STATES: AN ANTHOLOGY OF CREATIVE WRITING; Jimenez, Francisco; Keller, Gary D.

1028 Kastenbaum, Robert. Book review of: OLDER MEXICAN AMERICANS: A STUDY IN AN URBAN BARRIO. INTERNATIONAL JOURNAL OF AGING & HUMAN DEVELOPMENT, Vol. 19, no. 1 (1984), p. 75-76. English. **DESCR:** Ancianos; Markides, Kyriakos S.; Martin, Harry; *OLDER MEXICAN AMERICANS: A STUDY IN AN URBAN BARRIO.

1029 Kerr, Louise A. Book review of: THE LOS ANGELES BARRIO 1850-1890: A SOCIAL HISTORY. JOURNAL OF AMERICAN HISTORY, Vol. 70, no. 4 (March 1984), p. 894-895. English. **DESCR:** Griswold del Castillo, Richard; *THE LOS ANGELES BARRIO 1850-1890: A SOCIAL HISTORY.

1030 Kivisto, Peter. Book review of: ETHNICITY AND THE WORK FORCE. JOURNAL OF AMERICAN ETHNIC HISTORY, Vol. 6, no. 2 (Spring 1987), p. 68-69. English. **DESCR:** *ETHNICITY AND THE WORK FORCE; Laboring Classes; Van Horne, Winston A.

1031 Kraly, Ellen Percy. Book review of: CLAMOR AT THE GATES. JOURNAL OF AMERICAN ETHNIC HISTORY, Vol. 7, no. 1 (Fall 1987), p. 93-95. English. **DESCR:** *CLAMOR AT THE GATES: THE NEW AMERICAN IMMIGRATION; Glazer, Nathan; Immigration.

1032 Krauth, Leland. Book review of: CHICANO POETRY: A CRITICAL INTRODUCTION. LIBRARY JOURNAL, Vol. 111, (April 15, 1986), p. 82. English. **DESCR:** Candelaria, Cordelia; *CHICANO POETRY: A CRITICAL INTRODUCTION; Poetry.

1033 La Salle, Robin Avelar. Book review of:

1034 Laguna Diaz, Elpidio. Book review of: SMALL FACES. VISTA, Vol. 1, no. 11 (July 6, 1986), p. 16. English. **DESCR:** *SMALL FACES; Soto, Gary.

1035 Langum, David J. Book review of: WATER IN THE HISPANIC SOUTHWEST. AMERICAN JOURNAL OF LEGAL HISTORY, Vol. 30, no. 3 (July 1986), p. 273-276. English. **DESCR:** Meyer, Michael C.; *WATER IN THE HISPANIC SOUTHWEST: A SOCIAL AND LEGAL HISTORY, 1550-1850.

1036 Leal, Luis. Book review of: THE LEGEND OF LA LLORONA. LECTOR, Vol. 4, no. 1-3 (1986), p. [59]. English. **DESCR:** Anaya, Rudolfo A.; *THE LEGEND OF LA LLORONA.

1037 Lewis, Tom J. Book review of: CONTEMPORARY CHICANA POETRY. WORLD LITERATURE TODAY, Vol. 60, (Summer 1986), p. 453. English. **DESCR:** Chicanas; *CONTEMPORARY CHICANA POETRY: A CRITICAL APPROACH TO AN EMERGING LITERATURE; Poetry; Sanchez, Marta Ester.

1038 Lint, Robert G. Book review of: CHICANO POETRY: A CRITICAL INTRODUCTION. WESTERN AMERICAN LITERATURE, Vol. 21, no. 4 (1987), p. 380. English. **DESCR:** Candelaria, Cordelia; *CHICANO POETRY: A CRITICAL INTRODUCTION.

1039 Loaeza, Soledad. Alan Riding: la fuerza del prejuicio. LA COMUNIDAD, No. 255 (June 9, 1985), p. 2-5. Spanish. **DESCR:** *DISTANT NEIGHBORS: A PORTRAIT OF THE MEXICANS; Mexico; Riding, Alan.

1040 Lomeli, Francisco A. En la voragine del destino [book review of: THE FIFTH HORSEMAN]. LA COMUNIDAD, No. 258 (June 30, 1985), p. 12-13. Spanish. **DESCR:** *Literary Criticism; *THE FIFTH HORSEMAN; Villarreal, Jose Antonio.

1041 Lopez, David E. Book review of: BILINGUALISM: SOCIAL ISSUES AND POLICY IMPLICATIONS. CONTEMPORARY SOCIOLOGY: A JOURNAL OF REVIEWS, Vol. 15, no. 3 (May 1986), p. 391-392. English. **DESCR:** *BILINGUALISM: SOCIAL ISSUES AND POLICY IMPLICATIONS; Miracle, Andrew W.

1042 Lopez, Steven. Book review of: IMAGES AND CONVERSATIONS. LA RED/THE NET, no. 77 (February 1984), p. 5-7. Magazine. **DESCR:** *IMAGES AND CONVERSATIONS: MEXICAN AMERICANS RECALL A SOUTHWESTERN PAST; Preciado Martin, Patricia.

1043 Lopez-Garza, Marta. Book review of: OPERATION WETBACK. LA RED/THE NET, no. 50 (January 1982), p. 7-9. English. **DESCR:** *Deportation; *Garcia, Juan Ramon; Immigration; *OPERATION WETBACK: THE MASS DEPORTATION OF MEXICAN UNDOCUMENTED WORKERS IN 1954.

1044 Lovato, Alberto. La burra no era arisca, cabrones, los chingazos la hicieron asi... EL CUADERNO, Vol. 2, no. 1 (1972), p. 36-39. English. **DESCR:** *CANTO Y GRITO MI LIBERACION; Sanchez, Ricardo.

BILINGUALISM THROUGH SCHOOLING. HISPANIC JOURNAL OF BEHAVIORAL SCIENCES, Vol. 9, no. 2 (June 1987), p. 237-240. English. **DESCR:** *BILINGUALISM THROUGH SCHOOLING: CROSS-CULTURAL EDUCATION FOR MINORITY AND MAJORITY STUDENTS; Ramirez, Arnulfo G.

Book Reviews (cont.)

1045 Luna-Lawhn, Juanita. Book review of: CHICANO POETRY: A CRITICAL INTRODUCTION. CHOICE, Vol. 23, no. 11-12 (July, August, 1986), p. 1672. English. **DESCR:** Candelaria, Cordelia; *CHICANO POETRY: A CRITICAL INTRODUCTION.

1046 Luzod, Jimmy. Book review of: ASPECTS OF AMERICAN HISPANIC AND INDIAN INVOLVEMENT IN BIOMEDICAL RESEARCH. LA RED/THE NET, no. 79 (April 1984), p. 9-13. English. **DESCR:** *ASPECTS OF AMERICAN HISPANIC AND INDIAN INVOLVEMENT IN BIOMEDICAL RESEARCH; Martinez, Diana I.; Martinez, J.V.; Science.

1047 Luzod, Jimmy. Book review of: PARENTING MODELS AND MEXICAN AMERICANS: A PROCESS ANALYSIS. LA RED/THE NET, no. 71 (August 1983), p. 8-11. English. **DESCR:** Arciniega, Miguel; Casaus, Luis; Castillo, Max; *PARENTING MODELS AND MEXICAN AMERICANS: A PROCESS ANALYSIS (2nd ed.).

1048 Machado, Manuel A., Jr. Book review of: A BIBLIOGRAPHY OF MEXICAN-AMERICAN HISTORY. JOURNAL OF AMERICAN ETHNIC HISTORY, Vol. 5, no. 2 (Spring 1986), p. 80. English. **DESCR:** *A BIBLIOGRAPHY OF MEXICAN AMERICAN HISTORY; Meier, Matt S.

1049 Macias, Reynaldo Flores. Book review of: THE NEW BILINGUALISM: AN AMERICAN DILEMMA. LA RED/THE NET, no. 61 (November 1982), p. 7-9. English. **DESCR:** *Bilingualism; Public Policy; Ridge, Martin; *THE NEW BILINGUALISM: AN AMERICAN DILEMMA.

1050 Macias, Reynaldo Flores. Disambiguating the Veltman trilogy. BILINGUAL REVIEW, Vol. 12, no. 1-2 (January, August, 1985), p. 140-143. English. **DESCR:** *CONTRACTOR REPORT: RELATIVE EDUCATIONAL ATTAINMENT OF MINORITY LANGUAGE CHILDREN, 1976: A COMPARISON TO BLACK AND WHITE ENGLISH LANGUAGE CHILDREN; *CONTRACTOR REPORT: THE ROLE OF LANGUAGE CHARACTERISTICS IN THE SOCIOECONOMIC PROCESS OF HISPANIC ORIGIN MEN AND WOMEN; Language Usage; *THE RETENTION OF MINORITY LANGUAGES IN THE UNITED STATES: A SEMINAR ON THE ANALYTIC WORK OF CALVIN VELTMAN; Veltman, Calvin.

1051 Maciel, David R. Book review of: MEXICO AND THE UNITED STATES. LA RED/THE NET, no. 68 (May 1983), p. 8-9. English. **DESCR:** Laboring Classes; McBride, Robert H.; *MEXICO AND THE UNITED STATES: INTERNATIONAL RELATIONS IN THE HUMANITIES.

1052 Madrid, Arturo. Book review of: HUNGER OF MEMORY. LA RED/THE NET, no. 53 (April 1982), p. 6-9. English. **DESCR:** *HUNGER OF MEMORY: THE EDUCATION OF RICHARD RODRIGUEZ; *Rodriguez, Richard.

1053 Madrid, Arturo. Book review of: THE IMMIGRATION TIME BOMB. LA RED/THE NET, no. 97 (June 1986), p. 9-12. English. **DESCR:** Imhoff, Gary; Immigration; Lamm, Richard; *THE IMMIGRATION TIME BOMB: THE FRAGMENTING OF AMERICA.

1054 Madrid, Arturo. Book reviews of: A DICTIONARY OF NEW MEXICO AND SOUTHERN COLORADO SPANISH and TUNOMAS HONEY. LA RED/THE NET, no. 77 (February 1984), p. 8-10. English. **DESCR:** *A DICTIONARY OF NEW MEXICO AND SOUTHERN COLORADO SPANISH; Cobos, Ruben; Sagel, Jim; *TUNOMAS HONEY.

1055 Madrid, Arturo. Book reviews of: CLAMOR AT THE GATES and LATIN JOURNEY. LA RED/THE NET, no. 89 (August 1985), p. 7-10. English. **DESCR:** Bach, Robert L.; *CLAMOR AT THE GATES: THE NEW AMERICAN IMMIGRATION; Glazer, Nathan; Immigration; *LATIN JOURNEY: CUBAN AND MEXICAN IMMIGRANTS IN THE UNITED STATES; Portes, Alejandro.

1056 Maldonado, Lionel A. Book review of: BORDER PERSPECTIVES: ON THE US/MEXICO RELATIONSHIP. JOURNAL OF AMERICAN ETHNIC HISTORY, Vol. 7, no. 1 (Fall 1987), p. 106-107. English. **DESCR:** *BORDER PERSPECTIVES: ON THE US/MEXICO RELATIONSHIP; Border Region; Nalven, Joseph.

1057 Manning, Winston, et al. Book review of: MINORITIES IN AMERICAN HIGHER EDUCATION: RECENT TRENDS, CURRENT PROSPECTS AND RECOMMENDATIONS. LA RED/THE NET, no. 60 (Fall 1982), p. 1-22. English. **DESCR:** *Astin, Alexander W.; Ethnic Groups; *MINORITIES IN AMERICAN HIGHER EDUCATION: RECENT TRENDS, CURRENT PROSPECTS AND RECOMMENDATIONS.

1058 Manuel, Ron C. Book review of: OLDER MEXICAN AMERICANS: A STUDY IN AN URBAN BARRIO. JOURNAL OF GERONTOLOGY, Vol. 39, no. 4 (July 1984), p. 506-507. English. **DESCR:** Ancianos; Markides, Kyriakos S.; Martin, Harry; *OLDER MEXICAN AMERICANS: A STUDY IN AN URBAN BARRIO.

1059 Marcos, Luis R. Book review of: MENTAL HEALTH AND HISPANIC AMERICANS: CLINICAL PERSPECTIVES. AMERICAN JOURNAL OF PSYCHOTHERAPY, Vol. 38, no. 1 (January 1984), p. 155-156. English. **DESCR:** Escobar, Javier I.; Karno, Marvin; Mental Health; *MENTAL HEALTH AND HISPANIC AMERICANS: CLINICAL PERSPECTIVES.

1060 Marin, Christine. Book review of: OJO DE LA CUEVA. LECTOR, Vol. 4, no. 4-6 (1987), p. 75. English. **DESCR:** Candelaria, Cordelia; *OJO DE LA CUEVA: CAVE SPRINGS.

1061 Marin, Christine. Book review of: WHERE SPARROWS WORK HARD. LECTOR, Vol. 4, no. 4-6 (1987), p. 77. English. **DESCR:** Soto, Gary; *WHERE SPARROWS WORK HARD.

1062 Marquez, Antonio. Richard Rodriguez's HUNGER OF MEMORY and the poetics of experience. ARIZONA QUARTERLY, Vol. 40, no. 2 (Summer 1984), p. 130-141. English. **DESCR:** *Autobiography; *HUNGER OF MEMORY: THE EDUCATION OF RICHARD RODRIGUEZ; Literary Criticism; Rodriguez, Richard.

1063 Martinez, Alejandro M. Book review of: HISPANIC NATURAL SUPPORT SYSTEMS: MENTAL HEALTH PROMOTIONS PERSPECTIVES. LA RED/THE NET, no. 73 (October 1983), p. 7-12. English. **DESCR:** *HISPANIC NATIONAL SUPPORT SYSTEMS: MENTAL HEALTH PROMOTIONS PERSPECTIVES; Valle, Ramon; Vega, William A.

1064 Martinez, Beverly Ann. Book review of: THE MOTHS AND OTHER STORIES. VISTA, Vol. 1, no. 11 (July 6, 1986), p. 16. English. **DESCR:** *THE MOTHS AND OTHER STORIES; Viramontes, Helen.

1065 Martinez, Eliud. Book review of: HISTORY, CULTURE, AND SOCIETY. MODERN LANGUAGE JOURNAL, Vol. 69, no. 4 (Winter 1985), p. 436-437. English. **DESCR:** Chicano Studies; Garcia, Mario T.; *HISTORY, CULTURE, AND SOCIETY: CHICANO STUDIES IN THE 1980s; National Association for Chicano Studies (NACS).

Book Reviews (cont.)

1066 Martinez, Julio A. Book review of: BILINGUAL
BOOKS IN SPANISH AND ENGLISH FOR CHILDREN.
RQ - REFERENCE AND ADULT SERVICES DIVISION,
Vol. 25, (Spring 1986), p. 387. English.
DESCR: *BILINGUAL BOOKS IN SPANISH AND
ENGLISH FOR CHILDREN; Dale, Doris Cruger.

1067 Matta, Benjamin. Book review of: HISPANICS
IN THE U.S. ECONOMY. INDUSTRIAL AND LABOR
RELATIONS REVIEW, Vol. 40, no. 2 (January
1987), p. 299-300. English. **DESCR:** Borjas,
George J.; *HISPANICS IN THE U.S. ECONOMY;
Tienda, Marta.

1068 McBride, P.W. Book review of: IMMIGRANT
WOMEN IN THE LAND OF DOLLARS. CHOICE, Vol.
23, no. 9 (May 1986), p. 1448. English.
DESCR: Ewen, Elizabeth; *IMMIGRANT WOMEN IN
THE LAND OF DOLLARS: LIFE AND CULTURE ON THE
LOWER EAST SIDE, 1890-1925.

1069 McCracken, Ellen. Book review of: CHICANO
THEATER: THEMES AND FORMS. HISPANIA, Vol.
66, no. 4 (1983), p. 645. English. **DESCR:**
*CHICANO THEATER: THEMES AND FORMS; Huerta,
Jorge A.

1070 McDermott, Douglas. Book review of: CHICANO
THEATER: THEMES AND FORMS. THEATRE SURVEY,
Vol. 25, no. 1 (May 1984), p. 124-125.
English. **DESCR:** *CHICANO THEATER: THEMES AND
FORMS; Huerta, Jorge A.

1071 McIlroy, Christopher. Book review of: IN
DEFENSE OF LA RAZA. JOURNAL OF THE WEST,
Vol. 22, (October 1983), p. 87-88. English.
DESCR: Balderrama, Francisco E.; *IN DEFENSE
OF LA RAZA: THE LOS ANGELES MEXICAN
CONSULATE AND THE MEXICAN COMMUNITY.

1072 Meier, Matt S. Book review of: IN DEFENSE OF
LA RAZA. ARIZONA AND THE WEST, Vol. 25, no.
4 (Winter 1983), p. 356-357. English.
DESCR: Balderrama, Francisco E.; *IN DEFENSE
OF LA RAZA: THE LOS ANGELES MEXICAN
CONSULATE AND THE MEXICAN COMMUNITY.

1073 Meier, Matt S. Book review of: THE MEXICAN
AMERICAN EXPERIENCE: AN INTERDISCIPLINARY
ANTHOLOGY. HISPANIC AMERICAN HISTORICAL
REVIEW, Vol. 66, no. 3 (August 1986), p.
629-630. English. **DESCR:** Alvarez, Rodolfo;
Bean, Frank D.; Bonjean, Charles M.; de la
Garza, Rodolfo O.; Romo, Ricardo; *THE
MEXICAN AMERICAN EXPERIENCE: AN
INTERDISCIPLINARY ANTHOLOGY.

1074 Melson, Robert. Book review of: ETHNIC
GROUPS AND THE STATE. AMERICAN POLITICAL
SCIENCE REVIEW, Vol. 79, no. 4 (December
1985), p. 1208-1209. English. **DESCR:** Brass,
Paul R.; *ETHNIC GROUPS AND THE STATE.

1075 Melville, Margarita B. Book review of: FROM
INDIANS TO CHICANOS. LA RED/THE NET, no. 45
(August 1981), p. 3. English. **DESCR:** *FROM
INDIANS TO CHICANOS: A SOCIOCULTURAL
HISTORY; Social History and Conditions;
Vigil, James Diego.

1076 Miller, Beth. Book review of: WOMAN OF HER
WORD: HISPANIC WOMEN WRITE. HISPANIA, Vol.
68, no. 2 (May 1985), p. 326-327. English.
DESCR: Vigil-Pinon, Evangelina; *WOMAN OF
HER WORD: HISPANIC WOMEN WRITE.

1077 Miller, Robert Ryal. Book review of: THE
MEXICAN FRONTIER 1821-1846. CALIFORNIA
HISTORY, Vol. 63, no. 3 (Summer 1984), p.
260-261. English. **DESCR:** *THE MEXICAN
FRONTIER, 1821-1846: THE AMERICAN SOUTHWEST
UNDER MEXICO; Weber, David J.

1078 Milner, Clyde A. Book review of: BORDER
HEALING WOMAN: THE STORY OF JEWEL BABB.
JOURNAL OF THE WEST, Vol. 22, (January
1983), p. 95. English. **DESCR:** *BORDER
HEALING WOMAN: THE STORY OF JEWEL BABB;
Taylor, Pat Ellis.

1079 Milo, Albert J. Book review of: HISTORY,
CULTURE, AND SOCIETY. LECTOR, Vol. 4, no.
4-6 (1987), p. 55. English. **DESCR:** *HISTORY,
CULTURE, AND SOCIETY: CHICANO STUDIES IN THE
1980s; National Association for Chicano
Studies (NACS); Social History and
Conditions.

1080 Miranda, Gloria E. Book review of: CHICANOS
IN CALIFORNIA. SOUTHERN CALIFORNIA
QUARTERLY, Vol. 67, no. 4 (Winter 1985), p.
474-476. English. **DESCR:** Camarillo, Alberto;
*CHICANOS IN CALIFORNIA; Social History and
Conditions.

1081 Molina, Ida. Book review of: SMALL FACES.
CHOICE, Vol. 24, no. 2 (October 1986), p.
310-311. English. **DESCR:** *SMALL FACES; Soto,
Gary.

1082 Monroy, Douglas. Book review of: EAST LOS
ANGELES. WESTERN HISTORICAL QUARTERLY, Vol.
15, no. 4 (October 1984), p. 453. English.
DESCR: East Los Angeles, CA; *EAST LOS
ANGELES: HISTORY OF A BARRIO; Romo, Ricardo.

1083 Monroy, Douglas. Book review of: IN DEFENSE
OF LA RAZA. WESTERN HISTORICAL QUARTERLY,
Vol. 15, no. 3 (July 1984), p. 331-332.
English. **DESCR:** *Balderrama, Francisco E.;
IN DEFENSE OF LA RAZA: THE LOS ANGELES
MEXICAN CONSULATE AND THE MEXICAN COMMUNITY;
Los Angeles, CA.

1084 Montejano, David. Book review of:
IMMIGRANTS--AND IMMIGRANTS. LA RED/THE NET,
no. 43 (June 1981), p. 4. English. **DESCR:**
Corwin, Arthur F.; Immigrants;
*IMMIGRANTS---AND IMMIGRANTS: PERSPECTIVES
ON MEXICAN LABOR MIGRATION TO THE UNITED
STATES.

1085 Montejano, David. Book review of: THE TEJANO
COMMUNITY, 1836-1900. LA RED/THE NET, no. 64
(February 1983), p. 5-6. English. **DESCR:** de
Leon, Arnoldo; *THE TEJANO COMMUNITY,
1836-1900.

1086 Mosqueda, Lawrence Joseph. Mexican labor: a
most precious commodity on both sides of the
border. GUARDIAN, Vol. 39, no. 2 (October 8,
1986), p. 20. English. **DESCR:** Cockcroft,
James D.; *OUTLAWS IN THE PROMISED LAND:
MEXICAN IMMIGRANT WORKERS AND AMERICA'S
FUTURE.

1087 Nieto, Sonia. Book review of: BILINGUAL
EDUCATION: A SOURCEBOOK. INTERRACIAL BOOKS
FOR CHILDREN, Vol. 17, no. 3-4 (1986), p.
29. English. **DESCR:** Ambert, Alba N.;
*BILINGUAL EDUCATION: A SOURCEBOOK;
Melendez, Sarah E.

1088 Nieto, Sonia. Book review of:
BILINGUAL-BICULTURAL EDUCATION: AN ANNOTATED
BIBLIOGRAPHY, 1936-1982. INTERRACIAL BOOKS
FOR CHILDREN, Vol. 17, no. 3-4 (1986), p.
29. English. **DESCR:** Ballesteros, Octavio A.;
*BILINGUAL-BICULTURAL EDUCATION: AN
ANNOTATED BIBLIOGRAPHY.

Book Reviews (cont.)

1089 Nieto, Sonia. Book review of: BILINGUALISM
AND MINORITY-LANGUAGE CHILDREN. INTERRACIAL
BOOKS FOR CHILDREN, Vol. 17, no. 3-4 (1986),
p. 29. English. **DESCR:** *BILINGUALISM AND
MINORITY-LANGUAGE CHILDREN; Cummins, Jim.

1090 Nieto, Sonia. Book review of: BILINGUAL
EDUCATION FOR HISPANIC STUDENTS IN THE
UNITED STATES. INTERRACIAL BOOKS FOR
CHILDREN, Vol. 17, no. 3-4 (1986), p. 29-30.
English. **DESCR:** *BILINGUAL EDUCATION FOR
HISPANIC STUDENTS IN THE UNITED STATES;
Fishman, Joshua A.; Keller, Gary D.

1091 Nieto, Sonia. Book review of: BILINGUAL AND
ESL CLASSROOMS: TEACHING IN MULTICULTURAL
CONTEXTS. INTERRACIAL BOOKS FOR CHILDREN,
Vol. 17, no. 3-4 (1986), p. 30. English.
DESCR: *BILINGUAL AND ESL CLASSROOMS:
TEACHING IN MULTICULTURAL CONTEXTS; Collier,
Virginia P.; Ovando, Carlos J.

1092 Nieto, Sonia. Book review of: BILINGUALISM
THROUGH SCHOOLING. INTERRACIAL BOOKS FOR
CHILDREN, Vol. 17, no. 3-4 (1986), p. 30.
English. **DESCR:** *BILINGUALISM THROUGH
SCHOOLING: CROSS-CULTURAL EDUCATION FOR
MINORITY AND MAJORITY STUDENTS; Ramirez,
Arnulfo G.

1093 Nieto, Sonia. Book review of: BILINGUAL
MULTICULTURAL EDUCATION AND THE
PROFESSIONAL: FROM THEORY TO PRACTICE.
INTERRACIAL BOOKS FOR CHILDREN, Vol. 17, no.
3-4 (1986), p. 30. English. **DESCR:**
Barnett-Mizrahi, Carol; *BILINGUAL
MULTICULTURAL EDUCATION AND THE
PROFESSIONAL; Trueba, Henry T.

1094 Nuessel, Frank H., Jr. Book review of:
SPANISH IN THE UNITED STATES:
SOCIOLINGUISTIC ASPECTS. LINGUA, Vol. 62,
no. 3 (1984), p. 247-255. English. **DESCR:**
Amastae, Jon; Elias-Olivares, Lucia;
Sociolinguistics; *SPANISH IN THE UNITED
STATES: SOCIOLINGUISTIC ASPECTS.

1095 Ockerman, Janet D. Book review of:
MEXICAN-AMERICANS AND THE MASS-MEDIA. PUBLIC
OPINION QUARTERLY, Vol. 49, no. 1 (Spring
1985), p. 138-139. English. **DESCR:**
Greenberg, Bradley S.; *MEXICAN AMERICANS
AND THE MASS MEDIA.

1096 Ornstein-Galicia, Jacob. Bilingualism,
bilingual education, and language contact:
the agony, the rewards--or how to unravel
Babel. BILINGUAL REVIEW, Vol. 11, no. 3
(September, December, 1984), p. 72-82.
English. **DESCR:** Bilingual Bicultural
Education; Bilingualism; *LANGUAGES IN
CONFLICT: LINGUISTIC ACCULTURATION IN THE
GREAT PLAINS; Ridge, Martin; Schach, Paul;
*THE NEW BILINGUALISM: AN AMERICAN DILEMMA.

1097 Ortiz, Vilma. Book review of: FAMILY
INSTALLMENTS: MEMORIES OF GROWING UP
HISPANIC. LA RED/THE NET, no. 76 (January
1984), p. 7-9. English. **DESCR:** *FAMILY
INSTALLMENTS: MEMORIES OF GROWING UP
HISPANIC; *Rivera, Edward.

1098 Otheguy, Ricardo. Book review of:
BILINGUALISM THROUGH SCHOOLING. MODERN
LANGUAGE JOURNAL, Vol. 69, no. 3 (Fall
1985), p. 300-301. English. **DESCR:**
Bilingualism; *BILINGUALISM THROUGH
SCHOOLING: CROSS-CULTURAL EDUCATION FOR
MINORITY AND MAJORITY STUDENTS; Ramirez,
Arnulfo G.

1099 Papademetriou, Demetrios G. Book review of:
IMMIGRATION POLICY AND THE AMERICAN LABOR
FORCE. AMERICAN POLITICAL SCIENCE REVIEW,
Vol. 79, no. 4 (December 1985), p. 1182.
English. **DESCR:** Briggs, Vernon M., Jr.;
*IMMIGRATION POLICY AND THE AMERICAN LABOR
FORCE.

1100 Paredes, Raymund A. Book review of: CUENTOS
CHICANOS: A SHORT STORY ANTHOLOGY. WESTERN
AMERICAN LITERATURE, Vol. 21, no. 3 (1986),
p. 270. English. **DESCR:** Anaya, Rudolfo A.;
*CUENTOS CHICANOS: A SHORT STORY ANTHOLOGY;
Marquez, Antonio.

1101 Paredes, Raymund A. Book review of: THE LOST
LAND. WESTERN AMERICAN LITERATURE, Vol. 21,
no. 2 (1986), p. 135. English. **DESCR:**
Chavez, John R.; *THE LOST LAND: THE CHICANO
IMAGE OF THE SOUTHWEST.

1102 Paredes, Raymund A. Book review of: THEY
CALLED THEM GREASERS. PACIFIC HISTORICAL
REVIEW, Vol. 53, no. 3 (1984), p. 390-391.
English. **DESCR:** de Leon, Arnoldo; *THEY
CALLED THEM GREASERS: ANGLO ATTITUDES TOWARD
MEXICANS IN TEXAS, 1821-1900.

1103 Paredes, Raymund A. Book review of: TO THE
HALLS OF THE MONTEZUMAS. PACIFIC HISTORICAL
REVIEW, Vol. 56, no. 1 (February 1987), p.
123-124. English. **DESCR:** Johannsen, Robert
W.; Mexican American War, 1846-1848; *TO THE
HALLS OF THE MONTEZUMAS: THE MEXICAN WAR IN
THE AMERICAN IMAGINATION.

1104 Pena, Devon Gerardo. Book review of: THE NEW
NOMADS: FROM IMMIGRANT LABOR TO
TRANSNATIONAL WORKING CLASS. LA RED/THE NET,
no. 67 (April 1983), p. 8-10. English.
DESCR: Dixon, Marlene; Jonas, Susanne;
Labor; *THE NEW NOMADS: FROM IMMIGRANT LABOR
TO TRANSNATIONAL WORKING CLASS.

1105 Penalosa, Fernando. Book review of:
BILINGUALISM AND LANGUAGE CONTACT: SPANISH,
ENGLISH AND NATIVE AMERICAN LANGUAGES. LA
RED/THE NET, no. 66 (March 1983), p. 5-8.
English. **DESCR:** Barkin, Florence;
*BILINGUALISM AND LANGUAGE CONTACT: SPANISH,
ENGLISH, AND NATIVE AMERICAN LANGUAGES;
Brandt, Elizabeth H.; Ornstein-Galicia,
Jacob.

1106 Penalosa, Fernando. Book review of: SPANISH
IN THE UNITED STATES: SOCIOLINGUISTIC
ASPECTS. LANGUAGE, Vol. 60, no. 1 (March
1984), p. 152-159. English. **DESCR:** Amastae,
Jon; Elias-Olivares, Lucia;
Sociolinguistics; *SPANISH IN THE UNITED
STATES: SOCIOLINGUISTIC ASPECTS.

1107 Perez, Renato E. Book review of:
GENEALOGICAL RECORDS IN TEXAS. VISTA, Vol.
3, no. 2 (October 3, 1987), p. 37. English.
DESCR: *GENEALOGICAL RECORDS IN TEXAS;
Kennedy, Imogene; Kennedy, Leon.

1108 Perez, Renato E. Book review of: LA
FRONTERA: THE U.S. BORDER WITH MEXICO.
VISTA, Vol. 2, no. 10 (June 7, 1987), p. 24.
English. **DESCR:** Dusard, Jay; *LA FRONTERA:
THE U.S. BORDER WITH MEXICO; Weisman, Alan.

1109 Perry, Charles E. Book review of: CHICANO
LITERATURE: A REFERENCE GUIDE. LIBRARY
JOURNAL, Vol. 110, no. 5 (March 15, 1985),
p. 53. English. **DESCR:** *CHICANO LITERATURE:
A REFERENCE GUIDE; Literature; Lomeli,
Francisco A.; Martinez, Julio A.; Reference
Works.

Book Reviews (cont.)

1110 Powell, Carolyn L. Book review of: CHICANO ORGANIZATIONS DIRECTORY. VOICE OF YOUTH ADVOCATES, Vol. 8, no. 6 (February 1986), p. 408. English. **DESCR:** Caballero, Cesar; *CHICANO ORGANIZATIONS DIRECTORY; Directories.

1111 Quinn, Mary Ellen. Book review of: SMALL FACES. BOOKLIST, Vol. 82, no. 21 (July 1986), p. 1582. English. **DESCR:** *SMALL FACES; Soto, Gary.

1112 Raat, W. Dirk. Book review of: TEXAS AND THE MEXICAN REVOLUTION. WESTERN HISTORICAL QUARTERLY, Vol. 17, no. 1 (January 1986), p. 91-92. English. **DESCR:** Border Region; Coerver, Don M.; Hall, Linda B.; *TEXAS AND THE MEXICAN REVOLUTION: A STUDY IN STATE AND NATIONAL BORDER POLICY.

1113 Raferty, Judith R. Book review of: LATINO ETHNIC CONSCIOUSNESS. WESTERN HISTORICAL QUARTERLY, Vol. 17, no. 4 (October 1986), p. 490. English. **DESCR:** Identity; *LATINO ETHNIC CONSCIOUSNESS; Padilla, Felix M.

1114 Raksin, Alex. Book review of: LA FAMILIA. LOS ANGELES TIMES BOOK REVIEW, (April 13, 1986), p. 10. English. **DESCR:** Family; Griswold del Castillo, Richard; *LA FAMILIA: CHICANO FAMILIES IN THE URBAN SOUTHWEST, 1848 TO THE PRESENT.

1115 Ramirez, Arthur. Book review of: CUENTOS CHICANOS: A SHORT STORY ANTHOLOGY. SAN FRANCISCO REVIEW OF BOOKS, Vol. 11, (1986), p. 11,23. English. **DESCR:** Anaya, Rudolfo A.; *CUENTOS CHICANOS: A SHORT STORY ANTHOLOGY; Marquez, Antonio; Short Story.

1116 Ramirez, Daniel Moriel. Book review of: CHICANO INTERMARRIAGE: A THEORETICAL AND EMPIRICAL STUDY. SOCIAL FORCES, Vol. 62, no. 3 (March 1984), p. 833-835. English. **DESCR:** *CHICANO INTERMARRIAGE: A THEORETICAL AND EMPIRICAL STUDY; Intermarriage; Murguia, Edward.

1117 Ramirez, Genevieve M. Book review of: CHICANA VOICES. THE AMERICAS REVIEW, Vol. 15, no. 1 (Spring 1987), p. 101-102. English. **DESCR:** *CHICANA VOICES: INTERSECTIONS OF CLASS, RACE AND GENDER; Chicanas; National Association for Chicano Studies (NACS).

1118 Ramirez, Oscar. Book review of: ETHNICITY AND FAMILY THERAPY. LA RED/THE NET, no. 66 (March 1983), p. 28-30. English. **DESCR:** *ETHNICITY AND FAMILY THERAPY; Giordano, Joseph; McGoldrick, Monica; Pearce, John K.

1119 Ramirez, Oscar. Book review of: HUMAN SERVICES FOR MEXICAN-AMERICAN CHILDREN. LA RED/THE NET, no. 55 (June 1982), p. 7-8. English. **DESCR:** *Children; Social Services; *Tijerina, Andres A.

1120 Reder, Melvin W. Book review of: IMMIGRATION POLICY AND THE AMERICAN LABOR FORCE. INDUSTRIAL AND LABOR RELATIONS REVIEW, Vol. 40, no. 1 (October 1986), p. 139-140. English. **DESCR:** Briggs, Vernon M., Jr.; *IMMIGRATION POLICY AND THE AMERICAN LABOR FORCE.

1121 Reese, Stephen D. Book review of: MEXICAN-AMERICANS AND THE MASS-MEDIA. JOURNALISM QUARTERLY, Vol. 61, no. 3 (Fall 1984), p. 705-706. English. **DESCR:** Greenberg, Bradley S.; Mass Media; *MEXICAN AMERICANS AND THE MASS MEDIA.

1122 Reisler, Mark. Book review of: AMERICAN LABOR IN THE SOUTHWEST: THE 1ST 100 YEARS. PACIFIC HISTORICAL REVIEW, Vol. 53, no. 2 (1984), p. 246-247. English. **DESCR:** *AMERICAN LABOR IN THE SOUTHWEST: THE FIRST ONE HUNDRED YEARS; Foster, James C.

1123 Reisler, Mark. Book review of: FARM WORKERS, AGRIBUSINESS, AND THE STATE. PACIFIC HISTORICAL REVIEW, Vol. 53, no. 3 (1984), p. 405-407. English. **DESCR:** *FARMWORKERS, AGRIBUSINESS, AND THE STATE; Majka, Linda C.; Majka, Theo J.

1124 Reisler, Mark. Book review of: MEXICAN AND MEXICAN AMERICAN FARM WORKERS. PACIFIC HISTORICAL REVIEW, Vol. 55, (August 1986), p. 494. English. **DESCR:** Gonzales, Juan L., Jr.; *MEXICAN AND MEXICAN AMERICAN FARM WORKERS: THE CALIFORNIA AGRICULTURAL INDUSTRY.

1125 Reyes, Felix Ojeda. Book review of: HISTORY OF THE PUERTO RICAN INDEPENDENCE MOVEMENT. LA RED/THE NET, no. 76 (January 1984), p. 4-7. Spanish. **DESCR:** *HISTORY OF THE PUERTO RICAN INDEPENDENCE MOVEMENT; Lidin, Harold J.; Puerto Ricans.

1126 Reyna, Jose R. Book review of: MERIENDA TEJANA. LECTOR, Vol. 4, no. 4-6 (1987), p. 76. English. **DESCR:** Galindo, Mary Sue; *MERIENDA TEJANA.

1127 Riley, James D. Book review of: THE MEXICAN FRONTIER 1821-1846. AMERICAS, Vol. 40, no. 4 (April 1984), p. 592-593. English. **DESCR:** *THE MEXICAN FRONTIER, 1821-1846: THE AMERICAN SOUTHWEST UNDER MEXICO; Weber, David J.

1128 Rockman, Ilene F. Book review of: BILINGUAL BOOKS IN SPANISH AND ENGLISH FOR CHILDREN. AMERICAN REFERENCE BOOKS ANNUAL, Vol. 17, (1986), p. 431. English. **DESCR:** *BILINGUAL BOOKS IN SPANISH AND ENGLISH FOR CHILDREN; Dale, Doris Cruger.

1129 Rockman, Ilene F. Book review of: HISPANIC AMERICAN VOLUNTARY ORGANIZATIONS. CHOICE, Vol. 23, no. 7 (March 1986), p. 1038. English. **DESCR:** Gonzales, Sylvia Alicia; *HISPANIC AMERICAN VOLUNTARY ORGANIZATIONS.

1130 Rodriguez, Ana Maria and Calderon, Margarita. Book review of: SCHOOLING AND LANGUAGE MINORITY STUDENTS: A THEORETICAL FRAMEWORK. LA RED/THE NET, no. 66 (March 1983), p. 8-10. English. **DESCR:** Office of Bilingual Education, California State Department of Education; *SCHOOLING AND LANGUAGE MINORITY STUDENTS: A THEORETICAL FRAMEWORK.

1131 Rodriguez del Pino, Salvador. Book review of: CHICANO THEATER: THEMES AND FORMS. AMERICAN BOOK REVIEW, Vol. 5, no. 6 (September, October, 1983), p. 18. English. **DESCR:** *CHICANO THEATER: THEMES AND FORMS; Huerta, Jorge A.

1132 Rodriguez, Ronald. Book review of: THE PLUM PLUM PICKERS. LECTOR, Vol. 4, no. 4-6 (1987), p. 70. English. **DESCR:** Barrio, Raymond; *THE PLUM PLUM PICKERS.

1133 Romero, Mary. Book review of: CRITICAL TEACHING AND EVERYDAY LIFE. LA RED/THE NET, no. 69 (June 1983), p. 3-5. English. **DESCR:** *CRITICAL TEACHING AND EVERYDAY LIFE; Shor, Ira.

Book Reviews (cont.)

1134 Romo, Ricardo. Book review of: OCCUPIED AMERICA. LA RED/THE NET, no. 39 (February 1981), p. 3. English. **DESCR:** *Acuna, Rudolfo; History; *OCCUPIED AMERICA; *Social History and Conditions.

1135 Rubin, J.H. Book review of: ETHNICITY AND RACE IN THE U.S.A.: TOWARD THE TWENTY-FIRST CENTURY. CHOICE, Vol. 23, no. 7 (March 1986), p. 1130. English. **DESCR:** Alba, Richard D.; *ETHNICITY AND RACE IN THE U.S.A.: TOWARD THE TWENTY-FIRST CENTURY.

1136 Ruiz, Ivette M. Resena testimonial. REVISTA MUJERES, Vol. 1, no. 2 (June 1984), p. 7-10. English. **DESCR:** Chicanas; Elsasser, Nan; *LAS MUJERES: CONVERSATIONS FROM A HISPANIC COMMUNITY; MacKenzie, Kyle; Tixier y Vigil, Yvonne.

1137 Ruiz, Ramon Eduardo. Book review of: EVOLUCION DE LA FRONTERA NORTE. PACIFIC HISTORICAL REVIEW, Vol. 53, no. 3 (1984), p. 394-395. English. **DESCR:** *EVOLUCION DE LA FRONTERA NORTE; Flores Caballero, Romeo R.

1138 Ruiz, Vicki Lynn. Book review of: THE MEXICAN AMERICAN EXPERIENCE: AN INTERDISCIPLINARY ANTHOLOGY. SOUTHWESTERN HISTORICAL QUARTERLY, Vol. 90, no. 2 (1986), p. 205-206. English. **DESCR:** Alvarez, Rodolfo; Bean, Frank D.; Bonjean, Charles M.; de la Garza, Rodolfo O.; Romo, Ricardo; *THE MEXICAN AMERICAN EXPERIENCE: AN INTERDISCIPLINARY ANTHOLOGY.

1139 Ruiz, Vicki Lynn. Book review of: WOMEN OF THE DEPRESSION. SOUTHWESTERN HISTORICAL QUARTERLY, Vol. 88, no. 3 (1985), p. 337-338. English. **DESCR:** Blackwelder, Julia Kirk; *WOMEN OF THE DEPRESSION: CASTE AND CULTURE IN SAN ANTONIO, 1929-1939.

1140 Rutter, Larry G. Book review of: IN DEFENSE OF LA RAZA. JOURNAL OF THE WEST, Vol. 22, (July 1983), p. 100-101. English. **DESCR:** Balderrama, Francisco E.; *IN DEFENSE OF LA RAZA: THE LOS ANGELES MEXICAN CONSULATE AND THE MEXICAN COMMUNITY.

1141 Ryan, Ellen Bouchard. An interdisciplinary perspective on the bilingual experience. BILINGUAL REVIEW, Vol. 11, no. 3 (September, December, 1984), p. 69-71. English. **DESCR:** Bilingualism; Grosjean, Francois; *LIFE WITH TWO LANGUAGES: AN INTRODUCTION TO BILINGUALISM.

1142 Salmon, Roberto Mario. Book review of: MEXICANO RESISTANCE IN THE SOUTHWEST. LA RED/THE NET, no. 44 (July 1981), p. 6-7. English. **DESCR:** *MEXICANO RESISTANCE IN THE SOUTHWEST: "THE SACRED RIGHT OF SELF-PRESERVATION"; New Mexico; Rosenbaum, Robert J.

1143 Salmon, Roberto Mario. Book review of: THE MEXICAN AMERICAN EXPERIENCE: AN INTERDISCIPLINARY ANTHOLOGY. LA RED/THE NET, no. 93 (January, February, 1986), p. 12-14. English. **DESCR:** Alvarez, Rodolfo; Bean, Frank D.; Bonjean, Charles M.; de la Garza, Rodolfo O.; Romo, Ricardo; *THE MEXICAN AMERICAN EXPERIENCE: AN INTERDISCIPLINARY ANTHOLOGY.

1144 Salmon, Roberto Mario. Book review of: THEY CALLED THEM GREASERS. LA RED/THE NET, no. 75 (December 1983), p. 8-9. English. **DESCR:** de Leon, Arnoldo; *THEY CALLED THEM GREASERS: ANGLO ATTITUDES TOWARD MEXICANS IN TEXAS, 1821-1900.

1145 San Miguel, Guadalupe. Book review of: MUTUAL AID FOR SURVIVAL. LECTOR, Vol. 4, no. 4-6 (1987), p. 54-55. English. **DESCR:** Hernandez, Jose Amaro; *MUTUAL AID FOR SURVIVAL: THE CASE OF THE MEXICAN AMERICAN; Mutualistas.

1146 Sanchez, Saul. Book review of: THE VALLEY. LA RED/THE NET, no. 81 (June 1984), p. 7. Spanish. **DESCR:** Hinojosa-Smith, Rolando R.; *THE VALLEY.

1147 Saragoza, Alex M. Book review of: THEY CALLED THEM GREASERS. SOUTHWESTERN HISTORICAL QUARTERLY, Vol. 88, (1985), p. 334-336. English. **DESCR:** de Leon, Arnoldo; *THEY CALLED THEM GREASERS: ANGLO ATTITUDES TOWARD MEXICANS IN TEXAS, 1821-1900.

1148 Scanlon, Geraldine M. Book review of: WOMEN IN HISPANIC LITERATURE. MODERN LANGUAGE REVIEW, Vol. 81, (October 1986), p. 1017. English. **DESCR:** Miller, Beth; *WOMEN IN HISPANIC LITERATURE: ICONS AND FALLEN IDOLS.

1149 Schmidt, Henry C. Book review of: THE TEXAS-MEXICAN CONJUNTO. AMERICAN HISTORICAL REVIEW, Vol. 91, no. 2 (April 1986), p. 488-489. English. **DESCR:** Pena, Manuel; *THE TEXAS-MEXICAN CONJUNTO: HISTORY OF A WORKING-CLASS MUSIC.

1150 Schmitt, Jack. Book review of: CONTEMPORARY CHICANA POETRY. LOS ANGELES TIMES BOOK REVIEW, (December 29, 1985), p. 8. English. **DESCR:** Chicanas; *CONTEMPORARY CHICANA POETRY: A CRITICAL APPROACH TO AN EMERGING LITERATURE; Poetry; Sanchez, Marta Ester.

1151 Segura, Roberto D. Book review of: HISPANICS' EDUCATION AND BACKGROUND: PREDICTORS OF COLLEGE ACHIEVEMENT. LA RED/THE NET, no. 81 (June 1984), p. 6-7. English. **DESCR:** Duran, Richard P.; *HISPANICS' EDUCATION AND BACKGROUND: PREDICTORS OF COLLEGE ACHIEVEMENT.

1152 Sierra, Christine Marie. Book review of: THE G.I. FORUM: ORIGINS AND EVOLUTION. LA RED/THE NET, no. 73 (October 1983), p. 12-16. English. **DESCR:** Allsup, Carl; *THE AMERICAN G.I. FORUM: ORIGINS AND EVOLUTION.

1153 Somoza, Oscar U. Book review of: MEXICAN AMERICAN THEATRE: THEN AND NOW. LATIN AMERICAN THEATRE REVIEW, Vol. 17, no. 2 (Spring 1984), p. 105-106. Spanish. **DESCR:** Kanellos, Nicolas; *MEXICAN AMERICAN THEATRE: THEN AND NOW.

1154 Soto, Shirlene. Book review of: MEXICAN WOMEN IN THE UNITED STATES: STRUGGLES PAST AND PRESENT. LA RED/THE NET, no. 35 (October 1980), p. 4. English. **DESCR:** *Chicanas; Del Castillo, Adelaida R.; *MEXICAN WOMEN IN THE UNITED STATES: STRUGGLES PAST AND PRESENT; *Mora, Magdalena.

1155 Soudek, Lev I. Book review of: BILINGUAL EDUCATION: A SOURCEBOOK. AMERICAN REFERENCE BOOKS ANNUAL, Vol. 17, (1986), p. 132. English. **DESCR:** Ambert, Alba N.; *BILINGUAL EDUCATION: A SOURCEBOOK; Melendez, Sarah E.

1156 Stolarik, M. Mark. Book review of: THE TRANSPLANTED. JOURNAL OF AMERICAN ETHNIC HISTORY, Vol. 6, no. 2 (Spring 1987), p. 66-68. English. **DESCR:** Bodnar, John; Immigrants; *THE TRANSPLANTED: A HISTORY OF IMMIGRANTS IN URBAN AMERICA.

Book Reviews (cont.)

1157 Subervi-Velez, Federico. Book review of:
MEXICAN-AMERICANS AND THE MASS-MEDIA.
INTERNATIONAL JOURNAL OF INTERCULTURAL
RELATIONS, Vol. 8, no. 3 (1984), p. 340-342.
English. **DESCR:** Greenberg, Bradley S.; Mass
Media; *MEXICAN AMERICANS AND THE MASS
MEDIA.

1158 Suggs, George G. Book review of: LABOR IN
NEW MEXICO: UNIONS, STRIKES AND SOCIAL
HISTORY SINCE 1881. ARIZONA AND THE WEST,
Vol. 26. no. 2 (Summer 1984), p. 174-175.
English. **DESCR:** Kern, Robert; *LABOR IN NEW
MEXICO: UNIONS, STRIKES, AND SOCIAL HISTORY
SINCE 1881.

1159 Swing, E. S. Book review of: BILINGUALISM
THROUGH SCHOOLING. CHOICE, Vol. 23, no. 2
(October 1985), p. 340. English. **DESCR:**
*BILINGUALISM THROUGH SCHOOLING:
CROSS-CULTURAL EDUCATION FOR MINORITY AND
MAJORITY STUDENTS; Ramirez, Arnulfo G.

1160 Tafolla, Carmen. Book review of: THE SECOND
ST. POEMS. LA RED/THE NET, no. 83 (August
1984), p. 4-6. English. **DESCR:** Silva,
Beverly; *THE SECOND ST. POEMS.

1161 Tatum, Charles. Book review of: LA NOVELA
CHICANA ESCRITA EN ESPANOL. WORLD LITERATURE
TODAY. Vol. 57, no. 4 (Fall 1983), p.
613-614. English. **DESCR:** *LA NOVELA CHICANA
ESCRITA EN ESPANOL; Literary Criticism;
Rodriguez del Pino, Salvador.

1162 Tatum, Charles. Chicano literary criticism
comes of age. BILINGUAL REVIEW, Vol. 12, no.
1-2 (January, August, 1985), p. 144-149.
English. **DESCR:** *CHICANO THEATER: THEMES AND
FORMS; Huerta, Jorge A.; *LA NOVELA CHICANA
ESCRITA EN ESPANOL; Literary Criticism;
Rodriguez del Pino. Salvador.

1163 Thiederman, Sondra Barrett. Book review of:
CURANDERISMO. WESTERN FOLKLORE, Vol. 42, no.
4 (October 1983), p. 317-318. English.
DESCR: Chavira. Juan Antonio; *CURANDERISMO,
MEXICAN-AMERICAN FOLK HEALING; Trotter,
Robert.

1164 Thomas, Robert J. Book review of: MEXICAN
AND MEXICAN AMERICAN FARM WORKERS.
CONTEMPORARY SOCIOLOGY: A JOURNAL OF
REVIEWS, Vol. 16, no. 1 (January 1987), p.
106-107. English. **DESCR:** Gonzales, Juan L.,
Jr.; *MEXICAN AND MEXICAN AMERICAN FARM
WORKERS: THE CALIFORNIA AGRICULTURAL
INDUSTRY.

1165 Tibol, Raquel. La biografa se espanto de una
vida abierta. LA COMUNIDAD, No. 302 (May 4,
1986), p. 12-13. Spanish. **DESCR:** *Biography;
FRIDA: A BIOGRAPHY OF FRIDA KAHLO; Herrera,
Hayden; *Kahlo, Frida.

1166 Tijerina. Andres A. Book review of: SAN
ANGELENOS: MEXICAN AMERICANS IN SAN ANGELO,
TEXAS. SOUTHWESTERN HISTORICAL QUARTERLY,
Vol. 89, no. 4 (1986), p. 569-570. English.
DESCR: de Leon, Arnoldo; *SAN ANGELENOS;
MEXICAN AMERICANS IN SAN ANGELO, TEXAS.

1167 Torres, Lourdes. Book review of: A CHICANO
IN CHINA. WESTERN AMERICAN LITERATURE, Vol.
22, (Spring 1987), p. 66. English. **DESCR:**
*A CHICANO IN CHINA; Anaya, Rudolfo A.

1168 Torres, Lourdes. Book review of:
CONTEMPORARY CHICANA POETRY. WESTERN
AMERICAN LITERATURE, Vol. 21, no. 4 (1987),
p. 378-379. English. **DESCR:** *CONTEMPORARY
CHICANA POETRY: A CRITICAL APPROACH TO AN

EMERGING LITERATURE; Sanchez, Marta Ester.

1169 Trueba, Henry T. Book review of:
BILINGUALISM THROUGH SCHOOLING. LA RED/THE
NET, no. 92 (November, December, 1985), p.
18-20. English. **DESCR:** Bilingualism;
*BILINGUALISM THROUGH SCHOOLING:
CROSS-CULTURAL EDUCATION FOR MINORITY AND
MAJORITY STUDENTS; Ramirez, Arnulfo G.

1170 Trueba, Henry T. and Delgado-Gaitan, Concha.
Book review of: CHICANO DISCOURSE. LANGUAGE
IN SOCIETY, Vol. 14, no. 2 (June 1985), p.
257-259. English. **DESCR:** *CHICANO DISCOURSE:
SOCIOHISTORIC PERSPECTIVE; Sanchez, Rosaura.

1171 Trueba, Henry T. Book review of: FORM AND
FUNCTION IN CHICANO ENGLISH. LANGUAGE IN
SOCIETY, Vol. 14, no. 2 (June 1985), p.
255-257. English. **DESCR:** *FORM AND FUNCTION
IN CHICANO ENGLISH; Ornstein-Galicia, Jacob.

1172 Tryon, Roy H. Book review of: THE CHICANO
EXPERIENCE. LIBRARY JOURNAL, Vol. 110,
(August 1985), p. 109. English. **DESCR:**
Mirande, Alfredo; *THE CHICANO EXPERIENCE:
AN ALTERNATIVE PERSPECTIVE.

1173 Tryon, Roy H. Book review of: THE HISPANICS
IN THE UNITED STATES: A HISTORY. LIBRARY
JOURNAL, Vol. 111, no. 18 (November 1,
1986), p. 107. English. **DESCR:** Duignan,
Peter J.; Gann, L.H.; *HISPANICS IN THE
UNITED STATES: A HISTORY; Social History and
Conditions.

1174 Turner, Kay F. Book review of: CHRISTIAN
IMAGES IN HISPANIC NEW MEXICO. JOURNAL OF
AMERICAN FOLKLORE, Vol. 97, no. 385 (1984),
p. 361-363. English. **DESCR:** *CHRISTIAN
IMAGES IN HISPANIC NEW MEXICO; Wroth,
William.

1175 Tutino, John. Book review of: WATER IN THE
HISPANIC SOUTHWEST. AMERICAS, Vol. 42, no. 3
(January 1986), p. 355-356. English. **DESCR:**
Meyer, Michael C.; *WATER IN THE HISPANIC
SOUTHWEST: A SOCIAL AND LEGAL HISTORY,
1550-1850.

1176 Urdaneta, Maria Luisa. Book review of:
LATINO FAMILIES IN THE UNITED STATES. LA
RED/THE NET, no. 78 (March 1984), p. 9-10.
English. **DESCR:** Andrade, Sally; *LATINO
FAMILIES IN THE UNITED STATES: A RESOURCE
BOOK FOR FAMILY LIFE EDUCATION.

1177 Valdes, Dennis. Book review of: THE LOS
ANGELES BARRIO 1850-1890: A SOCIAL HISTORY.
LA RED/THE NET, no. 36 (November 1980), p.
5. English. **DESCR:** Griswold del Castillo,
Richard; History; *Los Angeles, CA; *Social
History and Conditions; *THE LOS ANGELES
BARRIO 1850-1890: A SOCIAL HISTORY.

1178 Valdez, Avelardo. Book review of: THE
CHICANO EXPERIENCE. JOURNAL OF AMERICAN
ETHNIC HISTORY, Vol. 6, no. 2 (Spring 1987),
p. 98-101. English. **DESCR:** Mirande, Alfredo;
Social History and Conditions; *THE CHICANO
EXPERIENCE: AN ALTERNATIVE PERSPECTIVE.

1179 Vallejos, Tomas. Book review of: SOUTHWEST
TALES: A CONTEMPORY COLLECTION. THE AMERICAS
REVIEW, Vol. 15, no. 2 (Summer 1987), p.
111-113. English. **DESCR:** Alurista;
Rojas-Urista, Xelina; *SOUTHWEST TALES: A
CONTEMPORARY COLLECTION.

Book Reviews (cont.)

1180 Vigelis, Adeline R. Book review of: HISPANIC FIRST NAMES. LECTOR, Vol. 4, no. 4-6 (1987), p. 55-56. English. **DESCR:** *HISPANIC FIRST NAMES: A COMPREHENSIVE DICTIONARY OF 250 YEARS OF MEXICAN-AMERICAN USAGE; Personal Names; Reference Works; Woods, Richard D.

1181 Vigil, James Diego. Book review of: DICTIONARY OF MEXICAN AMERICAN HISTORY. PACIFIC HISTORICAL REVIEW, Vol. 53, no. 2 (1984), p. 241-242. English. **DESCR:** *DICTIONARY OF MEXICAN AMERICAN HISTORY; Meier, Matt S.; Reference Works; Rivera, Feliciano.

1182 Walker, Constance L. Book review of: HISPANIC AMERICA: FREEING THE FREE, HONORING HEROES. LECTOR, Vol. 4, no. 4-6 (1987), p. 55. English. **DESCR:** *HISPANIC AMERICA: FREEING THE FREE, HONORING HEROES.

1183 Watts, Jake. Book review of: THE FOLK HEALER. LECTOR, Vol. 4, no. 1-3 (1986), p. [63-64]. English. **DESCR:** *THE FOLK HEALER: THE MEXICAN-AMERICAN TRADITION OF CURANDERISMO; Torres, Eliseo.

1184 Weas, Andrea T. Book review of: THE CHICANO STRUGGLE. LECTOR, Vol. 4, no. 4-6 (1987), p. 54. English. **DESCR:** National Association for Chicano Studies (NACS); Social History and Conditions; *THE CHICANO STRUGGLE: ANALYSES OF PAST AND PRESENT EFFORTS.

1185 Weber, David J. Book review of: MERCEDES REALES: HISPANIC LAND GRANTS OF THE UPPER RIO GRANDE REGION. AMERICAN HISTORICAL REVIEW, Vol. 89, no. 4 (October 1984), p. 1156-1157. English. **DESCR:** *MERCEDES REALES: HISPANIC LAND GRANTS OF THE UPPER RIO GRANDE REGION; Westphall, Victor.

1186 West, Dennis. Book review of: CHICANO CINEMA. CINEASTE, Vol. 15, no. 1 (1986), p. 55. English. **DESCR:** *CHICANO CINEMA: RESEARCH, REVIEWS AND RESOURCES; Keller, Gary D.

1187 Whatley, Patricia L. Book review of: BILINGUAL BOOKS IN SPANISH AND ENGLISH FOR CHILDREN. TOP OF THE NEWS, Vol. 43, (Fall 1986), p. 120. English. **DESCR:** *BILINGUAL BOOKS IN SPANISH AND ENGLISH FOR CHILDREN; Dale, Doris Cruger.

1188 Whatley, Patricia L. Book review of: SPANISH-LANGUAGE BOOKS FOR PUBLIC LIBRARIES. AMERICAN REFERENCE BOOKS ANNUAL, Vol. 18, (1987), p. 241. English. **DESCR:** Bibliography; Lestrepo, Fabio; *SPANISH-LANGUAGE BOOKS FOR PUBLIC LIBRARIES.

1189 Wolfe, David E. Book review of: BILINGUALISM AND SPECIAL EDUCATION: ISSUES IN ASSESSMENT AND PEDAGOGY. MODERN LANGUAGE JOURNAL, Vol. 71, (Spring 1987), p. 81. English. **DESCR:** Bilingualism; *BILINGUALISM AND SPECIAL EDUCATION; Cummins, Jim; Special Education.

1190 Woods, Richard D. Book review of: CHICANO PERIODICAL INDEX: A CUMULATIVE INDEX TO SELECTED CHICANO PERIODICALS BETWEEN 1967 AND 1978. LA RED/THE NET, no. 52 (March 1982), p. 5-6. English. **DESCR:** *Chabran, Richard; *CHICANO PERIODICAL INDEX; *Garcia-Ayvens, Francisco; Periodical Indexes.

1191 Woods, Richard D. Book review of: MEXICO-ESTADOS UNIDOS: BIBLIOGRAFIA GENERAL SOBRE ESTUDIOS FRONTERIZOS. LA RED/THE NET, no. 49 (December 1981), p. 4-5. English. **DESCR:** Border Studies; *Bustamante, Jorge A.; Malagamba, Francisco; *MEXICO-ESTADOS UNIDOS: BIBLIOGRAFIA GENERAL SOBRE ESTUDIOS FRONTERIZOS; Reference Works.

1192 Wreford, Mary. Book review of: CHICANO AUTHORS: INQUIRY BY INTERVIEW. LA RED/THE NET, no. 38 (January 1981), p. 3-4. English. **DESCR:** Authors; *Bruce-Novoa, Juan; *CHICANO AUTHORS: INQUIRY BY INTERVIEW.

1193 Wreford, Mary. Book review of: THE BRACERO EXPERIENCE: ELITELORE VERSUS FOLKLORE. LA RED/THE NET, no. 29 (April 1980), p. 10. English. **DESCR:** *Braceros; *Herrera-Sobek, Maria; Immigrants; THE BRACERO EXPERIENCE: ELITELORE VERSUS FOLKLORE.

1194 Ybarra, Lea. Book review of: LAS MUJERES: CONVERSATIONS FROM A HISPANIC COMMUNITY. LA RED/THE NET, no. 58 (September 1982), p. 5-6. English. **DESCR:** *Chicanas; *Elasser, Nan; *LAS MUJERES: CONVERSATIONS FROM A HISPANIC COMMUNITY; MacKenzie, Kyle; New Mexico; Tixier y Vigil, Yvonne.

1195 Zamora, Emilio. Book review of: LA CLASE OBRERA EN LA HISTORIA DE MEXICO: AL NORTE DEL RIO BRAVO (PASADO INMEDIATO, 1930-1981). LA RED/THE NET, no. 70 (July 1983), p. 13-17. English. **DESCR:** *LA CLASE OBRERA EN LA HISTORIA DE MEXICO: AL NORTE DEL RIO BRAVO (PASADO INMEDIATO, 1930-1981); Maciel, David.

1196 Zesch, Lindy. Visa issue heats up: PEN hopes for "group waiver" of denials. AMERICAN THEATRE, Vol. 2, no. 8 (November 1985), p. 24. English. **DESCR:** Artists; Authors; GETTING IN: A GUIDE TO OVERCOMING THE POLITICAL DENIAL OF NON-IMMIGRANT VISAS; National Lawyer's Guild; Politics; *Visas.

1197 Zolberg, A.R. Book review of: THE BORDER THAT JOINS: MEXICAN MIGRANTS AND U.S. RESPONSIBILITY. ETHICS, Vol. 94, no. 3 (April 1984), p. 568. English. **DESCR:** Brown, Peter G.; Shue, Henry; *THE BORDER THAT JOINS: MEXICAN MIGRANTS AND U.S. RESPONSIBILITY.

Book Sellers and Distributors
USE: Publishing Industry

Bookkeeping
USE: Accounting

Books

1198 13-part series focuses on Hispanics in America. EDITOR & PUBLISHER: THE FOURTH ESTATE, Vol. 115, no. 14 (April 3, 1982), p. 37. English. **DESCR:** Cultural Characteristics; DALLAS MORNING NEWS; Garcia, Juan; Gonzalez, John; Goodwin, Jay; Grothe, Randy Eli; Hamilton, John; Hille, Ed; LA VIDA AMERICANA; *LA VIDA AMERICANA/HISPANICS IN AMERICA; Langer, Ralph; McLemore, David; Osburne, Burl; Parks, Scott; Pusey, Allen; Sonnemair, Jan.

1199 Benavidez, Roy. An embattled Chicano. VISTA, Vol. 2, no. 5 (January 4, 1987), p. 20. English. **DESCR:** Benavidez, Roy; Green Berets; Griffin, Oscar; *THE THREE WARS OF ROY BENAVIDEZ; Vietnam War.

Books and Reading for Children
USE: Children's Literature

BOOKS IN SPANISH FOR CHILDREN AND YOUNG ADULTS: AN ANNOTATED GUIDE

1200 Book review of: BOOKS IN SPANISH FOR CHILDREN AND YOUNG ADULTS. BOOKLIST, Vol. 82, (July 1986), p. 1620. English. DESCR: Book Reviews; Children's Literature; Reference Works; Schon, Isabel.

Border Coverage Program (BOCOV)

1201 Gutierrez, Jose Angel. Chicanos and Mexicans: under surveillance: 1940 to 1980. RENATO ROSALDO LECTURE SERIES MONOGRAPH, Vol. 2, (Spring 1986), p. [29]-58. English. DESCR: Acuna, Rudolfo; *Civil Rights; COINTELPRO; *Federal Bureau of Investigation (FBI); *Federal Government; History; League of United Latin American Citizens (LULAC); Mexico; Political Parties and Organizations; *Political Repression.

THE BORDER ECONOMY: REGIONAL DEVELOPMENT IN THE SOUTHWEST

1202 Dunn, Ed. Book review of: THE BORDER ECONOMY: REGIONAL DEVELOPMENT IN THE SOUTHWEST. LA RED/THE NET, no. 50 (January 1982), p. 9-10. English. DESCR: Book Reviews; *Border Region; Border Studies; *Hansen, Niles.

THE BORDER [film]

1203 Martin, Laura. Language form and language function in ZOOT SUIT and THE BORDER: a contribution to the analysis of the role of foreign language in film. STUDIES IN LATIN AMERICAN POPULAR CULTURE, Vol. 3, (1984), p. 57-69. English. DESCR: *Films; Language Usage; Spanish Language; *ZOOT SUIT [film].

BORDER HEALING WOMAN: THE STORY OF JEWEL BABB

1204 Milner, Clyde A. Book review of: BORDER HEALING WOMAN: THE STORY OF JEWEL BABB. JOURNAL OF THE WEST, Vol. 22, (January 1983), p. 95. English. DESCR: Book Reviews; Taylor, Pat Ellis.

Border Industries

1205 de la Garza, Rodolfo O. Book review of: ACROSS THE BORDER: RURAL DEVELOPMENT IN MEXICO AND RECENT MIGRATION TO THE UNITED STATES. LA RED/THE NET, no. 69 (June 1983), p. 5-7. English. DESCR: *ACROSS THE BORDER: RURAL DEVELOPMENT IN MEXICO AND RECENT MIGRATION; Book Reviews; Cross, Harry E.; Sandos, James.

1206 Gettman, Dawn and Pena, Devon Gerardo. Women, mental health, and the workplace in a transnational setting. SOCIAL WORK, Vol. 31, no. 1 (January, February, 1986), p. 5-11. English. DESCR: *Chicanas; Employment; *Mental Health; Mexico; United States-Mexico Relations; Women; *Working Women.

1207 Harrell, Louis and Fischer, Dale. The 1982 Mexican peso devaluation and border area employment. MONTHLY LABOR REVIEW, Vol. 108, no. 10 (October 1985), p. 25-32. English. DESCR: *Border Region; *Currency; *International Economic Relations; Mexican Maquiladora Program; *Mexico.

1208 Kramer, Mark. U.S.-Mexican border: life on the line. THE AMERICAN MERCURY, Vol. 167, (June 1985), p. 720-749. English. DESCR: Border Patrol; *Border Region; Border Studies; Drug Traffic; Undocumented Workers.

1209 Sellers, Jeff M. Missed opportunities.

HISPANIC BUSINESS, Vol. 9, no. 4 (April 1987), p. 14-15. English. DESCR: *Intergroup Relations; Language Usage; *Management; Mexico.

1210 Third world women in multinational corporations--the Mexican American border. LA RED/THE NET, no. 25 (December 1979), p. 2. English. DESCR: Chicanas; *Ciudad Juarez, Chihuahua, Mexico; Labor Supply and Market; *Multinational Corporations; *Working Women.

Border Patrol

1211 Culp, Robert Alan. The Immigration and Naturalization Service and racially motivated questioning: does equal protection pick up where the Fourth Amendment left off? COLUMBIA LAW REVIEW, Vol. 86, no. 4 (May 1986), p. 800-822. English. DESCR: *Constitutional Amendments - Fourth; *Discrimination; *Immigration and Naturalization Service (INS); Immigration Law and Legislation; Immigration Regulation and Control; *Search and Seizure.

1212 Hawkins, Steve L. A cat-mouse game gets bloody. U.S. NEWS & WORLD REPORT, Vol. 100, (April 28, 1986), p. 30. English. DESCR: *Immigration Regulation and Control; *San Diego, CA.

1213 Kramer, Mark. U.S.-Mexican border: life on the line. THE AMERICAN MERCURY, Vol. 167, (June 1985), p. 720-749. English. DESCR: Border Industries; *Border Region; Border Studies; Drug Traffic; Undocumented Workers.

1214 Totality of circumstances justified stop of vehicle carrying Hispanics. CRIMINAL LAW REPORTER, Vol. 35, no. 11 (June 13, 1984), p. 2186-2187. English. DESCR: *Undocumented Workers; U.S. v. Brignoni-Ponce; *U.S. v. Garcia.

BORDER PERSPECTIVES: ON THE US/MEXICO RELATIONSHIP

1215 Maldonado, Lionel A. Book review of: BORDER PERSPECTIVES: ON THE US/MEXICO RELATIONSHIP. JOURNAL OF AMERICAN ETHNIC HISTORY, Vol. 7, no. 1 (Fall 1987), p. 106-107. English. DESCR: Book Reviews; Border Region; Nalven, Joseph.

Border Region

1216 Aguilar, Ricardo and Elizondo, Sergio D. La frontera. LA COMUNIDAD, No. 305 (May 25, 1986), p. 2-3+. Spanish. DESCR: *Accounting; Culture.

1217 Almaraz, Felix D., Jr. Introduction: the Mexican borderlands. JOURNAL OF THE WEST, Vol. 24, no. 2 (1985), p. 5-7. English. DESCR: Essays; History.

1218 Almaraz, Felix D., Jr. Texas as a Mexican borderland: a review and appraisal of salient events. JOURNAL OF THE WEST, Vol. 24, no. 2 (1985), p. 108-112. English. DESCR: History; *Texas.

1219 Campbell, Federico. Paralelo 32: la frontera como espacio literario. LA COMUNIDAD, No. 347 (March 15, 1987), p. 5. Spanish. DESCR: *Literary Criticism; *LOS MOTIVOS DE CAIN; Revueltas, Jose; Tijuana, Baja California, Mexico.

Border Region (cont.)

1220 Dunn, Ed. Book review of: THE BORDER
ECONOMY: REGIONAL DEVELOPMENT IN THE
SOUTHWEST. LA RED/THE NET, no. 50 (January
1982), p. 9-10. English. **DESCR**: Book
Reviews; Border Studies; *Hansen, Niles;
*THE BORDER ECONOMY: REGIONAL DEVELOPMENT IN
THE SOUTHWEST.

1221 Flynn, Ken. A triumph of diplomacy. VISTA,
Vol. 3, no. 2 (October 3, 1987), p. 22-24.
English. **DESCR**: Chamizal Memorial Federal
Park; Ciudad Juarez, Chihuahua, Mexico; *El
Chamizal [region]; El Paso, TX.

1222 Ganster, Paul. Book review of: ECOLOGY AND
DEVELOPMENT OF THE BORDER REGION. PACIFIC
HISTORICAL REVIEW, Vol. 55, no. 2 (1986), p.
318-320. English. **DESCR**: Book Reviews;
*ECOLOGY AND DEVELOPMENT OF THE BORDER
REGION: SECOND SYMPOSIUM; Ross, Stanley R.

1223 Garibay, Ricardo. Una frontera de lujo y
hambre [excerpt]. LA COMUNIDAD, No. 318
(August 24, 1986), p. 6-7. Spanish. **DESCR**:
Social History and Conditions; *Tijuana,
Baja California, Mexico.

1224 Gomez, Linda. Borderland: between Texas and
Mexico, a river and a troublesome future.
LIFE, Vol. 9, (August 1986), p. 40-50.
English. **DESCR**: *Texas.

1225 Gomez Pena, Guillermo. La cultura
fronteriza: un proceso de negociacion hacia
la utopia. LA COMUNIDAD, No. 305 (May 25,
1986), p. 14-15. Spanish. **DESCR**: *Culture.

1226 Gomez Pena, Guillermo. Dialogos fronterizos.
LA COMUNIDAD, No. 263 (August 4, 1985), p.
2-3. Spanish. **DESCR**: *Art; Avalos, David;
DIALOGOS FRONTERIZOS [radio program];
Osorio, Armando.

1227 Gomez Pena, Guillermo. Nuevo continente
artistico. LA COMUNIDAD, No. 275 (October
27, 1985), p. 8-10. Spanish. **DESCR**: *Art;
Artists; Chicano Movement; DIALOGOS DE LAS
AMERICAS; Indigenismo; International
Relations; Mexico; United States-Mexico
Relations.

1228 Gonzalez, Marco Vinicio. En el pais de la
frontera. LA COMUNIDAD, No. 291 (February
16, 1986), p. 6-7+. Spanish. **DESCR**: Conde,
Rosina; *DIALOGOS FRONTERIZOS [radio
program]; Gomez Pena, Guillermo; Medina,
Ruben; *Radio; San Diego, CA; Tijuana, Baja
California, Mexico.

1229 Griswold del Castillo, Richard. New
perspectives on the Mexican and American
borderlands. LATIN AMERICAN RESEARCH REVIEW,
Vol. 19, no. 1 (1984), p. 199-209. English.
DESCR: AL NORTE DEL RIO BRAVO (PASADO
INMEDIATO, 1930-1981); AL NORTE DEL RIO
BRAVO (PASADO LEJANO, 1600-1930); *Book
Reviews; Gomez-Quinones, Juan; Maciel,
David; MEXICANO RESISTANCE IN THE SOUTHWEST:
"THE SACRED RIGHT OF SELF-PRESERVATION";
Rosenbaum, Robert J.; THE MEXICAN FRONTIER,
1821-1846: THE AMERICAN SOUTHWEST UNDER
MEXICO; THE TEJANO COMMUNITY, 1836-1900;
Weber, David J.

1230 Hall, Linda B. The United States-Mexican
borders: historical, political, and cultural
perspectives. LATIN AMERICAN RESEARCH
REVIEW, Vol. 20, no. 2 (1985), p. 223-229.
English. **DESCR**: AMERICAN LABOR IN THE
SOUTHWEST: THE FIRST ONE HUNDRED YEARS;
*Book Reviews; BOSS RULE IN SOUTH TEXAS: THE
PROGRESSIVE ERA; CHICANO INTERMARRIAGE: A

THEORETICAL AND EMPIRICAL STUDY; HISPANIC
CULTURE IN THE SOUTHWEST; IN DEFENSE OF LA
RAZA: THE LOS ANGELES MEXICAN CONSULATE AND
THE MEXICAN COMMUNITY; Literature Reviews;
RACE AND CLASS IN THE SOUTHWEST: A THEORY OF
RACIAL INEQUALITY; SOUTHWESTERN AGRICULTURE:
PRE-COLUMBIAN TO MODERN; THE MEXICANS IN
OKLAHOMA; THE POLITICS OF SAN ANTONIO.

1231 Harrell, Louis and Fischer, Dale. The 1982
Mexican peso devaluation and border area
employment. MONTHLY LABOR REVIEW, Vol. 108,
no. 10 (October 1985), p. 25-32. English.
DESCR: Border Industries; *Currency;
*International Economic Relations; Mexican
Maquiladora Program; *Mexico.

1232 Kramer, Mark. U.S.-Mexican border: life on
the line. THE AMERICAN MERCURY, Vol. 167,
(June 1985), p. 720-749. English. **DESCR**:
Border Industries; Border Patrol; Border
Studies; Drug Traffic; Undocumented Workers.

1233 Lomeli, Francisco A. En torno a la
literatura...convergencia o divergencia? LA
COMUNIDAD, No. 274 (October 20, 1985), p.
8-11. Spanish. **DESCR**: Anaya, Rudolfo A.;
Aztlan; HEART OF AZTLAN; *Literary
Criticism; Mendez M., Miguel; PEREGRINOS DE
AZTLAN; *Primer Festival de Literatura
Fronteriza Mexico-Estados Unidos.

1234 Lomeli, Francisco A. En torno a la
literatura de la frontera (II). LA
COMUNIDAD, No. 275 (October 27, 1985), p.
2-3. Spanish. **DESCR**: Language Usage;
*Literary Criticism; MURIERON A MITAD DEL
RIO; Spota, Luis.

1235 Maldonado, Lionel A. Book review of: BORDER
PERSPECTIVES: ON THE US/MEXICO RELATIONSHIP.
JOURNAL OF AMERICAN ETHNIC HISTORY, Vol. 7,
no. 1 (Fall 1987), p. 106-107. English.
DESCR: Book Reviews; *BORDER PERSPECTIVES:
ON THE US/MEXICO RELATIONSHIP; Nalven,
Joseph.

1236 Mendez-M., Miguel. Observaciones sobre la
literatura fronteriza. RENATO ROSALDO
LECTURE SERIES MONOGRAPH, Vol. 2, (Spring
1986), p. [21]-27. Spanish. **DESCR**: *Literary
History; *Literature; *Mexican Literature.

1237 Monsivais, Carlos. Los cholos y la cultura
de la frontera. LA COMUNIDAD, No. 242 (March
10, 1985), p. 14-15. Spanish. **DESCR**:
Culture; Identity; *Pachucos; *Tijuana, Baja
California, Mexico.

1238 Monsivais, Carlos. Este es el pachuco, un
sujeto singular. LA COMUNIDAD, No. 243
(March 17, 1985), p. 4-5. Spanish. **DESCR**:
Culture; Identity; *Pachucos.

1239 Nuestra casa es su casa. HISPANIC TIMES,
Vol. 8, no. 3 (May, June, 1987), p. 39.
English. **DESCR**: *Tijuana, Baja California,
Mexico; University of California, Irvine.

1240 Ornstein-Galicia, Jacob. Chicano Calo:
description and review of a border variety.
HISPANIC JOURNAL OF BEHAVIORAL SCIENCES,
Vol. 9, no. 4 (December 1987), p. 359-373.
English. **DESCR**: *Chicano Dialects; Pachucos;
Sociolinguistics.

1241 Raat, W. Dirk. Book review of: TEXAS AND THE
MEXICAN REVOLUTION. WESTERN HISTORICAL
QUARTERLY, Vol. 17, no. 1 (January 1986), p.
91-92. English. **DESCR**: Book Reviews;
Coerver, Don M.; Hall, Linda B.; *TEXAS AND
THE MEXICAN REVOLUTION: A STUDY IN STATE AND
NATIONAL BORDER POLICY.

Border Region (cont.)

1242 Rigoni, Florenzo. Tijuana: the borders on the move. MIGRATION WORLD MAGAZINE, Vol. 15, no. 2 (1987), p. [22]-29. English. **DESCR:** Criminal Acts; Immigration; Scalabrini Center, Tijuana, Baja California, Mexico; *Tijuana, Baja California, Mexico; *Undocumented Workers.

1243 Sandos, James A. Northern separatism during the Mexican revolution--an inquiry into the role of drug trafficking, 1910-1920. AMERICAS, Vol. 41, no. 2 (October 1984), p. 191-214. English. **DESCR:** Baja California, Mexico; Cantu Jimenez, Esteban; Drug Addicts; Drug Laws; *Drug Traffic; *Drug Use; Medical Care; Mexican Revolution - 1910-1920; Revolutions.

Border Studies

1244 Dunn, Ed. Book review of: THE BORDER ECONOMY: REGIONAL DEVELOPMENT IN THE SOUTHWEST. LA RED/THE NET, no. 50 (January 1982), p. 9-10. English. **DESCR:** Book Reviews; *Border Region; *Hansen, Niles; *THE BORDER ECONOMY: REGIONAL DEVELOPMENT IN THE SOUTHWEST.

1245 Kramer, Mark. U.S.-Mexican border: life on the line. THE AMERICAN MERCURY, Vol. 167, (June 1985), p. 720-749. English. **DESCR:** Border Industries; Border Patrol; *Border Region; Drug Traffic; Undocumented Workers.

1246 Woods, Richard D. Book review of: MEXICO-ESTADOS UNIDOS: BIBLIOGRAFIA GENERAL SOBRE ESTUDIOS FRONTERIZOS. LA RED/THE NET, no. 49 (December 1981), p. 4-5. English. **DESCR:** Book Reviews; *Bustamante, Jorge A.; Malagamba, Francisco; *MEXICO-ESTADOS UNIDOS: BIBLIOGRAFIA GENERAL SOBRE ESTUDIOS FRONTERIZOS; Reference Works.

THE BORDER THAT JOINS: MEXICAN MIGRANTS AND U.S. RESPONSIBILITY

1247 Chernick, Marc W. Book review of: THE BORDER THAT JOINS: MEXICAN MIGRANTS AND U.S. RESPONSIBILITY. POLITICAL SCIENCE QUARTERLY, Vol. 99, (Spring 1984), p. 133. English. **DESCR:** Book Reviews; Brown, Peter G.; Shue, Henry.

1248 Zolberg, A.R. Book review of: THE BORDER THAT JOINS: MEXICAN MIGRANTS AND U.S. RESPONSIBILITY. ETHICS, Vol. 94, no. 3 (April 1984), p. 568. English. **DESCR:** Book Reviews; Brown, Peter G.; Shue, Henry.

BORDERLANDS SOURCEBOOK

1249 Burnett, G. Wesley. Book review of: BORDERLANDS SOURCEBOOK. GEOGRAPHICAL REVIEW, Vol. 74, no. 1 (January 1984), p. 123-124. English. **DESCR:** Book Reviews; Nostrand, Richard L.; Stoddard, Ellwyn R.; West, Jonathan P.

A BORDERLANDS TOWN IN TRANSITION: LAREDO, 1755-1870

1250 Griswold del Castillo, Richard. Book review of: A BORDERLANDS TOWN IN TRANSITION: LAREDO, 1755-1870. PACIFIC HISTORICAL REVIEW, Vol. 54, no. 2 (May 1985), p. 223-224. English. **DESCR:** Book Reviews; Hinojosa, Gilbert Miguel; Laredo, TX.

BORDERS

1251 Castillo-Speed, Lillian. Chicana/Latina literature and criticism: reviews of recent books. WLW JOURNAL, Vol. 11, no. 3 (September 1987), p. 1-4. English. **DESCR:** Andrews, Lynn V.; *Book Reviews; Chavez, Denise; *Chicanas; CONTEMPORARY CHICANA POETRY: A CRITICAL APPROACH TO AN EMERGING LITERATURE; Flores, Angel; Flores, Kate; JAGUAR WOMAN; Mora, Pat; Sanchez, Marta Ester; Tafolla, Carmen; THE DEFIANT MUSE: HISPANIC FEMINIST POEMS FROM THE MIDDLE AGES TO THE PRESENT; THE LAST OF THE MENU GIRLS; TO SPLIT A HUMAN: MITOS, MACHOS Y LA MUJER CHICANA; Vigil-Pinon, Evangelina; WOMAN OF HER WORD: HISPANIC WOMEN WRITE.

1252 Mora, Pat and Alarcon, Norma. A poet analyzes her craft. NUESTRO, Vol. 11, no. 2 (March 1987), p. 25-27. English. **DESCR:** *Authors; CHANTS; *Chicanas; *Mora, Pat; *Poetry.

BORDER-X-FRONTERA [radio program]

1253 Gomez Pena, Guillermo and Erana, Maria. Sobre el arte, la rebeldia y las fronteras. LA COMUNIDAD, No. 312 (July 13, 1986), p. 6-7+. Spanish. **DESCR:** Berkeley, CA; Gomez Pena, Guillermo; *Radio; Schein, David; Teatro.

Borjas, George J.

1254 Matta, Benjamin. Book review of: HISPANICS IN THE U.S. ECONOMY. INDUSTRIAL AND LABOR RELATIONS REVIEW, Vol. 40, no. 2 (January 1987), p. 299-300. English. **DESCR:** Book Reviews; *HISPANICS IN THE U.S. ECONOMY; Tienda, Marta.

BORN IN EAST L.A. [film]

1255 Guevara, Ruben. Richard "Cheech" Marin. AMERICAS 2001, Vol. 1, no. 1 (June, July, 1987), p. 18-21. Bilingual. **DESCR:** *Actors and Actresses; Films; Immigration; *Marin, Richard "Cheech"; Undocumented Workers.

BOSS RULE IN SOUTH TEXAS: THE PROGRESSIVE ERA

1256 Hall, Linda B. The United States-Mexican borders: historical, political, and cultural perspectives. LATIN AMERICAN RESEARCH REVIEW, Vol. 20, no. 2 (1985), p. 223-229. English. **DESCR:** AMERICAN LABOR IN THE SOUTHWEST: THE FIRST ONE HUNDRED YEARS; *Book Reviews; *Border Region; CHICANO INTERMARRIAGE: A THEORETICAL AND EMPIRICAL STUDY; HISPANIC CULTURE IN THE SOUTHWEST; IN DEFENSE OF LA RAZA: THE LOS ANGELES MEXICAN CONSULATE AND THE MEXICAN COMMUNITY; Literature Reviews; RACE AND CLASS IN THE SOUTHWEST: A THEORY OF RACIAL INEQUALITY; SOUTHWESTERN AGRICULTURE: PRE-COLUMBIAN TO MODERN; THE MEXICANS IN OKLAHOMA; THE POLITICS OF SAN ANTONIO.

Boswell, Thomas D.

1257 Alvirez, David. Book review of: THE CHANGING DEMOGRAPHY OF SPANISH AMERICANS. LA RED/THE NET, no. 48 (November 1981), p. 4. English. **DESCR:** Book Reviews; Cullen, Ruth M.; Jaffee, A.J.; Population; *THE CHANGING DEMOGRAPHY OF SPANISH-AMERICANS.

Boundaries
USE: Border Region

Bowers Museum, Santa Ana, CA

1258 Prehispanic America: a revelation. VISTA, Vol. 2, no. 6 (February 8, 1987), p. 18-20. English. **DESCR:** Art History; *Precolumbian Society.

Boxing

1259 Getting to the top against all odds.
HISPANIC TIMES, Vol. 8, no. 5 (October,
November, 1987), p. 26. English. DESCR:
Biography; *Olivo, Joey.

1260 Lit, Ed. Paul Gonzalez [sic]. VISTA, Vol. 1,
no. 5 (January 5, 1986), p. 10. English.
DESCR: Athletes; East Los Angeles, CA;
*Gonzales, Paul [Olympic boxer].

Boycotts

1261 Beale, Stephen. Striking a deal with big
business. HISPANIC BUSINESS, Vol. 9, no. 2
(February 1987), p. 26-33. English. DESCR:
*Adolph Coors Co.; American G.I. Forum;
Corporations; Cuban National Planning
Council, Inc. Washington, D.C.; Employment;
*Hispanic Association on Corporate
Responsibility (HACER); League of United
Latin American Citizens (LULAC); National
Council of La Raza (NCLR); National IMAGE;
National Puerto Rican Coalition;
*Organizations; U.S. Hispanic Chamber of
Commerce.

1262 Boycotts revisited: Campbell's concedes to
farm worker campaign. DOLLARS AND SENSE,
(July, August, 1986), p. 12-14, 18. English.
DESCR: California; Campbell Soup Co.; Farm
Labor Organizing Commmittee (FLOC); Farm
Workers; *Labor Disputes; Labor Unions;
Michigan; Ohio; Strikes and Lockouts; United
Farmworkers of America (UFW).

1263 Echaveste, Beatrice and Huerta, Dolores. In
the shadow of the eagle: Huerta=A la sombra
del aguila: Huerta. AMERICAS 2001, Vol. 1,
no. 3 (November, December, 1987), p. 26-30.
Bilingual. DESCR: Agricultural Labor Unions;
Chicanas; *Farm Workers; *Huerta, Dolores;
*United Farmworkers of America (UFW).

1264 Fraser, Laura. Old boycott, new battle. THE
PROGRESSIVE, Vol. 49, (October 1985), p.
16. English. DESCR: Labor Disputes; *United
Farmworkers of America (UFW).

1265 Sanders, Bob. Boycott Campbell's: Ohio
farmworkers take it to the top. DOLLARS AND
SENSE, no. 92 (December 1983), p. 16-18.
English. DESCR: Campbell Soup Co.; Chavez,
Cesar E.; Farm Labor Organizing Commmittee
(FLOC); Farm Workers; Guevas, Fernando;
*Labor Disputes; Labor Unions; Ohio; Strikes
and Lockouts; United Farmworkers of America
(UFW).

1266 Vasquez, Victor. More on CHICO AND THE MAN.
LATIN QUARTER, Vol. 1, no. 3 (January,
February, 1975), p. 13-15. English. DESCR:
Albertson, Jack; Andrade, Ray; Artists;
*CHICO AND THE MAN [television show];
Discrimination; Prinze, Freddie;
Stereotypes; *Television.

THE BRACERO EXPERIENCE: ELITELORE VERSUS FOLKLORE

1267 Wreford, Mary. Book review of: THE BRACERO
EXPERIENCE: ELITELORE VERSUS FOLKLORE. LA
RED/THE NET, no. 29 (April 1980), p. 10.
English. DESCR: Book Reviews; *Braceros;
*Herrera-Sobek, Maria; Immigrants.

Braceros

1268 Garcia, Mario T. Bracero poetry of the
1940s: two samples. BILINGUAL REVIEW, Vol.
11, no. 3 (September, December, 1984), p.
45-48. English. DESCR: EL ESPECTADOR,
Pomona, CA; *Poetry.

1269 Garcia R., Roberto. Oda a Cucamonga.
BILINGUAL REVIEW, Vol. 11, no. 3 (September,
December, 1984), p. 47-48. Spanish. DESCR:
Farm Workers; *Poems.

1270 Wreford, Mary. Book review of: THE BRACERO
EXPERIENCE: ELITELORE VERSUS FOLKLORE. LA
RED/THE NET, no. 29 (April 1980), p. 10.
English. DESCR: Book Reviews;
*Herrera-Sobek, Maria; Immigrants; THE
BRACERO EXPERIENCE: ELITELORE VERSUS
FOLKLORE.

Bradley, Tom

1271 Los Angeles: arriba! ECONOMIST (London),
Vol. 297, no. 7424 (December 14, 1985), p.
26. English. DESCR: *Los Angeles, CA;
Political Representation; Politics;
Reapportionment; Voter Turnout.

1272 Los Angeles: brown versus yellow. ECONOMIST
(London), Vol. 300, no. 7456 (July 26,
1986), p. 21-22. English. DESCR: Alatorre,
Richard; Ethnic Groups; *Los Angeles, CA;
Political Representation; Politics;
Reapportionment; Voter Turnout; Woo,
Michael.

1273 Sonenshein, Raphe. Biracial coalition
politics in Los Angeles. P.S. [AMERICAN
POLITICAL SCIENCE ASSOCIATION], Vol. 19, no.
3 (Summer 1986), p. 582-590. English.
DESCR: Blacks; Browning, Rufus P.; *Ethnic
Groups; *Intergroup Relations; *Los Angeles,
CA; Marshall, Dale Rogers; Political Parties
and Organizations; *Politics; PROTEST IS NOT
ENOUGH: THE STRUGGLE OF BLACKS AND HISPANICS
FOR EQUALITY IN URBAN POLITICS; Tabb, David
H.

Brandt, Elizabeth H.

1274 Penalosa, Fernando. Book review of:
BILINGUALISM AND LANGUAGE CONTACT: SPANISH,
ENGLISH AND NATIVE AMERICAN LANGUAGES. LA
RED/THE NET, no. 66 (March 1983), p. 5-8.
English. DESCR: Barkin, Florence;
*BILINGUALISM AND LANGUAGE CONTACT: SPANISH,
ENGLISH, AND NATIVE AMERICAN LANGUAGES; Book
Reviews; Ornstein-Galicia, Jacob.

Brass, Paul R.

1275 Melson, Robert. Book review of: ETHNIC
GROUPS AND THE STATE. AMERICAN POLITICAL
SCIENCE REVIEW, Vol. 79, no. 4 (December
1985), p. 1208-1209. English. DESCR: Book
Reviews; *ETHNIC GROUPS AND THE STATE.

Brawley, Ernest

1276 Bruce-Novoa, Juan. Ernest Brawley: un
escritor chicano desconocido. LA COMUNIDAD,
No. 277 (November 10, 1985), p. 6-7.
Spanish. DESCR: Authors; *Biography;
Literary Criticism; Novel; SELENA [novel];
THE ALAMO TREE [novel]; THE RAP [novel].

1277 Bruce-Novoa, Juan. Nuevo representantes de
la novela chicana. LA COMUNIDAD, No. 310
(June 29, 1986), p. 6-7+. Spanish. DESCR: EL
VAGO [novel]; FAULTLINE [novel]; Gonzales,
Laurence; *Literary Criticism; Novel; Ortiz
Taylor, Sheila; THE ALAMO TREE [novel].

Brecht, Bertolt

1278 Flores, Arturo C. El Teatro Campesino (1965-1986): algunas orientaciones teoricas. CONFLUENCIA, Vol. 2, no. 2 (Spring 1987), p. 116-121. Spanish. **DESCR:** *El Teatro Campesino; History; Moreno, Mario "Cantinflas"; *Teatro; Valdez, Luis.

Breland, Hunter M.

1279 Gonzalez, Juan C. Report to the Network. LA RED/THE NET, No. 105 (February 1987), p. 1-3. English. **DESCR:** *DEMOGRAPHICS, STANDARDS, AND EQUITY CHALLENGES IN COLLEGE ADMISSIONS: REPORT OF A SURVEY OF UNDERGRADUATE ADMISSIONS POLICIES, PRACTICES AND PROCEDURES; *Discrimination in Education; *Enrollment; *Higher Education.

Brigands and Robbers
USE: Bandidos

Briggs, Vernon M., Jr.

1280 Book review of: IMMIGRATION POLICY AND THE AMERICAN LABOR FORCE. ECONOMIC BOOKS, Vol. 12, no. 3 (September 1985), p. 67-68. English. **DESCR:** Book Reviews; *IMMIGRATION POLICY AND THE AMERICAN LABOR FORCE.

1281 Haines, Michael R. Book review of: IMMIGRATION POLICY AND THE AMERICAN LABOR FORCE. JOURNAL OF ECONOMIC HISTORY, Vol. 45, no. 3 (September 1985), p. 742-744. English. **DESCR:** Book Reviews; Immigration Law and Legislation; *IMMIGRATION POLICY AND THE AMERICAN LABOR FORCE.

1282 Papademetriou, Demetrios G. Book review of: IMMIGRATION POLICY AND THE AMERICAN LABOR FORCE. AMERICAN POLITICAL SCIENCE REVIEW, Vol. 79, no. 4 (December 1985), p. 1182. English. **DESCR:** Book Reviews; *IMMIGRATION POLICY AND THE AMERICAN LABOR FORCE.

1283 Reder, Melvin W. Book review of: IMMIGRATION POLICY AND THE AMERICAN LABOR FORCE. INDUSTRIAL AND LABOR RELATIONS REVIEW, Vol. 40, no. 1 (October 1986), p. 139-140. English. **DESCR:** Book Reviews; *IMMIGRATION POLICY AND THE AMERICAN LABOR FORCE.

BRING ME THE HEAD OF ALFREDO GARCIA

1284 Chavez, Andres. Film review of: BRING ME THE HEAD OF ALFREDO GARCIA. LATIN QUARTER, Vol. 1, no. 2 (October 1974), p. 36. English. **DESCR:** *Film Reviews; Peckinpah, Sam; Violence.

Briscoe, Dolph, Jr., Governor of Texas

1285 Rips, Geoffrey. Civil rights and wrongs. TEXAS OBSERVOR, Vol. 76, (December 14, 1984), p. 49-55. English. **DESCR:** *Civil Rights; Farm Workers; *Hidalgo County, TX; La Raza Unida Party; Miller, C.L.; Segregation and Desegregation; Texas Farmworkers' Union; Voting Rights.

Brito, Aristeo

1286 Eysturoy, Annie O. EL DIABLO EN TEXAS: una historia popular a traves de arquetipos y simbolos. LA COMUNIDAD, No. 364 (July 12, 1987), p. 6-7. Spanish. **DESCR:** *Book Reviews; *EL DIABLO EN TEXAS; Literary Criticism.

Broadcast Media

1287 Breiter, Toni. Pepe del Rio. VISTA, Vol. 1, no. 6 (February 2, 1986), p. 20. English. **DESCR:** *BUENOS DIAS, AMERICA [radio news & features program]; del Rio, Pepe; Perez del Rio, Jose; *Radio; Voice of America.

1288 Broadcasters license renewal bill [editorial]. LATIN QUARTER, Vol. 1, no. 2 (October 1974), p. 2,30. English. **DESCR:** *Federal Communications Commission (FCC).

1289 Hernandez, Roger E. Why is everyone picking on Geraldo Rivera? VISTA, Vol. 2, no. 8 (April 4, 1987), p. 8-10. English. **DESCR:** Biography; *Rivera, Geraldo.

1290 Jesse Jackson makes appearance at CBS board meeting. BROADCASTING, Vol. 110, no. 16 (April 21, 1986), p. 100. English. **DESCR:** *Columbia Broadcasting Studios (CBS); Discrimination; Discrimination in Employment; *Jackson, Jesse; People United to Serve Humanity (PUSH); Stereotypes; Taylor, Hycel; Wyman, Thomas.

1291 Madrid, Vicente and Yepes, Maria Elena. National Latino Media Coalition. LATIN QUARTER, Vol. 1, no. 4 (July, August, 1975), p. 4-7. English. **DESCR:** Affirmative Action Programs; Bilingual/Bicultural Coalition on Mass Media; California Association of Latins in Broadcasting; Conferences and Meetings; Federal Communications Commission (FCC); *National Latino Media Coalition (NLMC); Puerto Rican Media Action and Educational Council.

1292 Marketing to Hispanics. ADVERTISING AGE MAGAZINE, Vol. 57, no. 43 (August 11, 1986), p. 51-528. English. **DESCR:** Advertising; De Armas Publications; Kinney Shoe Corp.; *Marketing; Pepsi-Cola Bottling Group; Print Media; Spanish International Network (SIN); U.S. Bureau of the Census.

1293 Moraga, Pete. Response to a quake: hands across the border. VISTA, Vol. 1, no. 4 (December 7, 1985), p. 3. English. **DESCR:** Earthquakes; *KMEX, Los Angeles, CA [television station]; *Mexico.

1294 [Untitled editorial]. LATIN QUARTER, Vol. 1, no. 3 (January, February, 1975), p. 2. English. **DESCR:** *Federal Communications Commission (FCC).

Broward County, FL

1295 Perez, Renato E. Badge of Hispanic pride. VISTA, Vol. 1, no. 12 (August 2, 1986), p. 9-11. English. **DESCR:** Chicago, IL; Dallas, TX; Houston, TX; *Los Angeles, CA; New York, NY; *Police; San Antonio, TX; San Diego, CA; Tucson, AZ.

Brown, Peter G.

1296 Chernick, Marc W. Book review of: THE BORDER THAT JOINS: MEXICAN MIGRANTS AND U.S. RESPONSIBILITY. POLITICAL SCIENCE QUARTERLY, Vol. 99, (Spring 1984), p. 133. English. **DESCR:** Book Reviews; Shue, Henry; *THE BORDER THAT JOINS: MEXICAN MIGRANTS AND U.S. RESPONSIBILITY.

1297 Zolberg, A.R. Book review of: THE BORDER THAT JOINS: MEXICAN MIGRANTS AND U.S. RESPONSIBILITY. ETHICS, Vol. 94, no. 3 (April 1984), p. 568. English. **DESCR:** Book Reviews; Shue, Henry; *THE BORDER THAT JOINS: MEXICAN MIGRANTS AND U.S. RESPONSIBILITY.

Browning, Harley L.

1298 Hastings, D.W. Book review of: MEXICAN IMMIGRANTS AND MEXICAN AMERICANS: AN EVOLVING RELATION. CHOICE, Vol. 24, no. 3 (November 1986), p. 516. English. **DESCR:** Book Reviews; de la Garza, Rodolfo O.; *MEXICAN IMMIGRANTS AND MEXICAN AMERICANS: AN EVOLVING RELATION.

Browning, Rufus P.

1299 Body-Gendrot, Sophie. Book review of: PROTEST IS NOT ENOUGH. INTERNATIONAL JOURNAL OF URBAN AND REGIONAL RESEARCH, Vol. 9, no. 4 (1985), p. 576-577. English. **DESCR:** Book Reviews; Marshall, Dale Rogers; *PROTEST IS NOT ENOUGH: THE STRUGGLE OF BLACKS AND HISPANICS FOR EQUALITY IN URBAN POLITICS; Tabb, David H.

1300 Browning, Rufus P. and Marshall, Dale Rogers. Black and Hispanic power in city politics: a forum. P.S. [AMERICAN POLITICAL SCIENCE ASSOCIATION], Vol. 19, no. 3 (Summer 1986), p. 573-639. English. **DESCR:** Blacks; Marshall, Dale Rogers; *Politics; *PROTEST IS NOT ENOUGH: THE STRUGGLE OF BLACKS AND HISPANICS FOR EQUALITY IN URBAN POLITICS; Tabb, David H.; Urban Communities.

1301 Browning, Rufus P.; Marshall, Dale Rogers; and Tabb, David H. Protest is not enough: a theory of political incorporation. P.S. [AMERICAN POLITICAL SCIENCE ASSOCIATION], Vol. 19, no. 3 (Summer 1986), p. 576-581. English. **DESCR:** Blacks; Marshall, Dale Rogers; Political Representation; Politics; *PROTEST IS NOT ENOUGH: THE STRUGGLE OF BLACKS AND HISPANICS FOR EQUALITY IN URBAN POLITICS; Tabb, David H.; Urban Communities.

1302 Sonenshein, Raphe. Biracial coalition politics in Los Angeles. P.S. [AMERICAN POLITICAL SCIENCE ASSOCIATION], Vol. 19, no. 3 (Summer 1986), p. 582-590. English. **DESCR:** Blacks; Bradley, Tom; *Ethnic Groups; *Intergroup Relations; *Los Angeles, CA; Marshall, Dale Rogers; Political Parties and Organizations; *Politics; PROTEST IS NOT ENOUGH: THE STRUGGLE OF BLACKS AND HISPANICS FOR EQUALITY IN URBAN POLITICS; Tabb, David H.

Brownsville, TX

1303 LeAna, Thomas. From dropout to role model: a VISTA postscript. VISTA, Vol. 2, no. 4 (December 7, 1986), p. 25. English. **DESCR:** Gladys Porter High School; *Martinez, Dorella; Olivares, J.R.; *Rhetoric; Secondary School Education.

Bruce, Lenny

1304 Chavez, Andres. Film review of: LENNY. LATIN QUARTER, Vol. 1, no. 4 (July, August, 1975), p. 32-33. English. **DESCR:** *Film Reviews; Humor; LENNY [film].

Bruce-Novoa, Juan

1305 Finch, Mark S. Book review of: CHICANO AUTHORS: INQUIRY BY INTERVIEW. KENTUCKY ROMANCE QUARTERLY, Vol. 32, no. 4 (1985), p. 435. English. **DESCR:** Book Reviews; *CHICANO AUTHORS: INQUIRY BY INTERVIEW.

1306 Flores, Lauro. Book review of: EL PUEBLO: THE GALLEGOS FAMILY'S JOURNEY 1503-1980. MINNESOTA REVIEW, no. 22 (1984), p. 145-148. English. **DESCR:** Book Reviews; *CHICANO POETRY: A RESPONSE TO CHAOS; *EL PUEBLO: THE GALLEGOS FAMILY'S AMERICAN JOURNEY 1503-1980; *FAMOUS ALL OVER TOWN; James, Dan; Johansen, Bruce; Maestas, Roberto.

1307 Wreford, Mary. Book review of: CHICANO AUTHORS: INQUIRY BY INTERVIEW. LA RED/THE NET, no. 38 (January 1981), p. 3-4. English. **DESCR:** Authors; Book Reviews; *CHICANO AUTHORS: INQUIRY BY INTERVIEW.

BRUJAS Y ALGO MAS=WITCHES AND OTHER THINGS

1308 Alarcon, Norma. Book Review of: BRUJAS Y ALGO MAS/WITCHES AND OTHER THINGS. CHIRICU, Vol. 4, no. 1 (1985), p. 9-12. English. **DESCR:** Agosin, Marjorie; Book Reviews.

BUENOS DIAS, AMERICA [radio news & features program]

1309 Breiter, Toni. Pepe del Rio. VISTA, Vol. 1, no. 6 (February 2, 1986), p. 20. English. **DESCR:** Broadcast Media; del Rio, Pepe; Perez del Rio, Jose; *Radio; Voice of America.

Building
   USE: Architecture

Bureau of Applied Research in Anthropology (BARA), University of Arizona

1310 Perez, Emma. Research centers. LA RED/THE NET, no. 10 (November 1986), p. 6-7. English. **DESCR:** *Research Centers.

Bureau of Indian Affairs (BIA)

1311 Dinwoodie, David H. Indians, Hispanos, and land reform: a new deal struggle in New Mexico. WESTERN HISTORICAL QUARTERLY, Vol. 17, no. 3 (July 1986), p. 291-323. English. **DESCR:** History; Interdepartmental Rio Grande Board; Land Grants; Land Program of the Federal Emergency Relief Administration (FERA); *Land Reform; Native Americans; *New Mexico.

Burke, John

1312 Bain, Laurie. Alfonso's heats up San Antonio. RESTAURANT BUSINESS, Vol. 86, (January 20, 1987), p. 120-122. English. **DESCR:** *Alfonso's Restaurant, San Antonio, TX; *Restaurants.

Business

1313 Beale, Stephen. Friendly persuasion: pacts and covenants. HISPANIC BUSINESS, Vol. 9, no. 9 (September 1987), p. 20-26. English. **DESCR:** *Adolph Coors Co.; Community Organizations; Coors/HACER Agreement, 1984; *Corporations; *Hispanic Association on Corporate Responsibility (HACER); Organizations; Pacific Bell; Southland Corporation.

1314 Beale, Stephen. Networking the networks. HISPANIC BUSINESS, Vol. 9, no. 9 (September 1987), p. 38-43. English. **DESCR:** Conferences and Meetings; *U.S. Hispanic Chamber of Commerce.

1315 Minority programs need tune-up. HISPANIC BUSINESS, Vol. 9, no. 6 (June 1987), p. 84-90. English. **DESCR:** *Automobile Industry; Business Enterprises; National Association for Minority Automotive Dealers (NAMAD); *Organizations.

Business (cont.)

1316 Perez, Renato E. The business of Hispanics. VISTA, Vol. 2, no. 1 (September 7, 1986), p. 10. English. **DESCR:** Adolph Coors Co.; American G.I. Forum; Apodaca, Jerry [Gov. of New Mexico]; *Collective Bargaining; Corporations; Cuban National Planning Council, Inc. Washington, D.C.; *Hispanic Association on Corporate Responsibility (HACER); League of United Latin American Citizens (LULAC); National Council of La Raza (NCLR); National IMAGE; U.S. Hispanic Chamber of Commerce.

Business Administration

1317 Sellers, Jeff M. State of the art recruitment: competition for blue-chip Hispanic business graduates is fierce and expensive. HISPANIC BUSINESS, Vol. 9, no. 2 (February 1987), p. 22-25, 57. English. **DESCR:** *Careers; College Graduates; Colleges and Universities; Enrollment; *Management.

Business Enterprises

1318 The 500 largest Hispanic-owned companies in sales. HISPANIC BUSINESS, Vol. 9, no. 6 (June 1987), p. 30-47. English. **DESCR:** Statistics; *THE HISPANIC BUSINESS 500.

1319 Abalos, J. Victor. Paul Sandoval. VISTA, Vol. 1, no. 4 (December 7, 1985), p. 10. English. **DESCR:** Denver, CO; *Financial Aid; Mile Hi Cablevision; *Sandoval, Paul.

1320 Academics and entrepreneurs talk trade. HISPANIC BUSINESS, Vol. 9, no. 6 (June 1987), p. 96. English. **DESCR:** Conferences and Meetings; Fourth Symposium on Hispanic Business and Economy, San Juan, Puerto Rico, November 23-25, 1987; *International Economic Relations; Latin America; *National Association of Hispanic Professors of Business Administration and Economics (Los Profesores); Organizations; Teaching Profession.

1321 Allsup, Dan. The story of Stella. VISTA, Vol. 2, no. 1 (September 7, 1986), p. 16. English. **DESCR:** *Cosmetology; *Guerra, Stella; U.S. Air Force; U.S. Department of Defense (DOD).

1322 Beale, Stephen. CEOs. HISPANIC BUSINESS, Vol. 9, no. 4 (April 1987), p. 20-37, 52. English. **DESCR:** Alvarez, Roberto; Batarse, Anthony A.; Biography; *Businesspeople; Carlo, Nelson; Estrada, Anthony; Flores, Frank; Fullana, Jaime, Jr.; Hernandez, George; *Management; Ortega, James; Quirch, Guillermo; Ruiz, Roberto; Santa Maria, Yvonne Z.; Sugranes, Rosa; Tamaya, Carlos; Young, Paul H., Jr.

1323 Beale, Stephen. Defense cuts on the horizon? HISPANIC BUSINESS, Vol. 9, no. 10 (October 1987), p. 18-21. English. **DESCR:** *Government Contracts; *Military.

1324 Beale, Stephen. The Maxwell House that Marlboro bought. HISPANIC BUSINESS, Vol. 9, no. 2 (February 1987), p. 20-21, 60. English. **DESCR:** Advertising; Corporations; *Marketing; *Philip Morris, Inc.

1325 Beale, Stephen. A piece of the big picture. HISPANIC BUSINESS, Vol. 9, no. 3 (March 1987), p. 26-30. English. **DESCR:** *Businesspeople.

1326 Business and population maintain high growth rates. HISPANIC BUSINESS, Vol. 9, no. 2 (February 1987), p. 55. English. **DESCR:** *Income; *Statistics.

1327 California businesses up: federal procurement down. HISPANIC BUSINESS, Vol. 9, no. 12 (December 1987), p. 60. English. **DESCR:** California; *Government Contracts.

1328 Douglas, Mark. Austin: growing fast, start-ups tough. HISPANIC BUSINESS, Vol. 9, no. 6 (June 1987), p. 19, 22. English. **DESCR:** *Austin, TX; *Investments.

1329 Garcia, Art. Financing the corporate take-off. HISPANIC BUSINESS, Vol. 9, no. 5 (May 1987), p. 22-27. English. **DESCR:** Aguirre Architects, Dallas, TX; Aguirre, Pedro; Banking Industry; Businesspeople; *Corporations; *Investments; Minority Enterprise Small Business Investment Corporation (MESBIC); Morales, Ramon; Protocom Devices, New York, NY; Villamil, Antonio.

1330 Guedella, Juan. A new benchmark. HISPANIC BUSINESS, Vol. 9, no. 1 (January 1987), p. 12,16. English. **DESCR:** Statistics.

1331 Hispanic chamber endorses insurance marketing plan. HISPANIC TIMES, Vol. 8, no. 3 (May, June, 1987), p. 26. English. **DESCR:** Insurance; Lopez, Ruben; *Metropolitan Life Insurance Corporation; *U.S. Hispanic Chamber of Commerce.

1332 The Hispanic market: an untapped resource. CHAIN STORE AGE SUPERMARKET, Vol. 59, no. 6 (June 1983), p. 41. English. **DESCR:** Consumers; *Marketing.

1333 Hispanic marketing. ADVERTISING AGE MAGAZINE, Vol. 57, no. 16 (February 27, 1986), p. 11-51. English. **DESCR:** Adolph Coors Co.; Advertising; Allstate Insurance Co.; American Greetings; Anheuser-Busch, Inc.; Coca-Cola Company; Consumers; Ford Motor Company; Hallmark Cards; *Marketing; Mass Media; McDonald's Corporation; Metropolitan Life Insurance Corporation; Pepsi-Cola Bottling Group; Prudential; Spanish International Network (SIN); State Farm Mutual Insurance; Tylenol; United Insurance Co. of America.

1334 Kane, George D. Five blueprints for fueling growth. HISPANIC BUSINESS, Vol. 9, no. 5 (May 1987), p. 18-21, 42+. English. **DESCR:** *Businesspeople; Holguin Corporation, El Paso, TX; Investments; Latin Industries, Ontario, CA; One-Day Paint & Auto Body Centers, Los Angeles, CA; Terrinvest, Miami, FL; TRU & Associates, Orange County, CA.

1335 Kwain, Constance. Searching for Hispanic talent. VISTA, Vol. 2, no. 6 (February 8, 1987), p. 6-7. English. **DESCR:** *Actors and Actresses; American Federation of Television & Radio Artists (AFTRA); Films; Myrna Salazar and Associates, Inc.; Navas, Trina; Salazar, Myrna; Screen Actors Guild; Television.

1336 Marambio, Gonzalo. From San Antonio to Paris: Tex-Mex food conquers the French. VISTA, Vol. 1, no. 6 (February 2, 1986), p. 18-20. English. **DESCR:** Cantu, Mario, Jr.; *Food Practices; Gonzales, Teresa; *Mario's Restaurant, San Antonio, TX; Papa Maya's Restaurant, Paris, France.

Business Enterprises (cont.)

1337 Minority programs need tune-up. HISPANIC BUSINESS, Vol. 9, no. 6 (June 1987), p. 84-90. English. **DESCR:** *Automobile Industry; Business; National Association for Minority Automotive Dealers (NAMAD); *Organizations.

1338 Noeth, Louise Ann and Sellers, Jeff M. Fast food for thought. HISPANIC BUSINESS, Vol. 9, no. 3 (March 1987), p. 20-24. English. **DESCR:** Food Industry; *Restaurants.

1339 SBA procurements dropping off. HISPANIC BUSINESS, Vol. 9, no. 5 (May 1987), p. 41. English. **DESCR:** *Government Contracts; *Small Business Administration 8(a) Program.

1340 Sellers, Jeff M. Golden opportunity. HISPANIC BUSINESS, Vol. 9, no. 9 (September 1987), p. 14-18, 79. English. **DESCR:** *Adolph Coors Co.; *Coors/HACER Agreement, 1984; *Corporations; Employment; Hispanic Association on Corporate Responsibility (HACER); Organizations.

1341 Sellers, Jeff M. High tech directory. HISPANIC BUSINESS, Vol. 9, no. 10 (October 1987), p. 7-9. English. **DESCR:** Computers; *Electronics Industry; *Government Contracts; Military.

1342 Sellers, Jeff M. Out in front: the 100 fastest-growing companies. HISPANIC BUSINESS, Vol. 9, no. 11 (November 1987), p. 20-26. English. **DESCR:** Statistics.

1343 Sellers, Jeff M. Same-day service sells. HISPANIC BUSINESS, Vol. 9, no. 11 (November 1987), p. 16-19. English. **DESCR:** Cardenas, John; *Golden Gate Air Freight, Hayward, CA.

1344 Sellers, Jeff M. Strategic defenses: new niches for small firms. HISPANIC BUSINESS, Vol. 9, no. 10 (October 1987), p. 13-17. English. **DESCR:** *Advanced Sciences Inc., Albuquerque, NM; Electronics Industry; *Government Contracts; *Military; *Orion International Technologies, Inc.; Rios, Miguel, Jr.; Romero, Ed.

1345 Sellers, Jeff M. Wedtech fallout hits 8(a) program. HISPANIC BUSINESS, Vol. 9, no. 6 (June 1987), p. 12-13, 17. English. **DESCR:** Government Contracts; *Small Business Administration 8(a) Program; *Wedtech Corporation, Bronx, NY.

1346 Seven profiles of courage. HISPANIC BUSINESS, Vol. 9, no. 6 (June 1987), p. 57-70. English. **DESCR:** Alamo Technology Inc., San Antonio, TX; *Businesspeople; Carrillo, Rosario C.; O'Campo Corporation, Walnut, CA; O'Campo, Peter; Rivas, Robert; TexPar Energy Inc., Milwaukee, WI; THE HISPANIC BUSINESS 500.

1347 Shaw, Katherine. Love affair with chocolate. VISTA, Vol. 1, no. 6 (February 2, 1986), p. 15-16. English. **DESCR:** CHOCOLATE ARTISTRY; *Gonzalez, Elaine.

1348 The top 100--profiles. HISPANIC BUSINESS, Vol. 9, no. 11 (November 1987), p. 31-50. English. **DESCR:** Artco Contracting, Inc., Auburn Hills, MI; Computer Trade Development Corp, Birmingham, MI; Corella Electric Inc., Phoenix, AZ; GSE Construction Co., Inc., Livermore, CA; National Systems & Research Co.; Unique Construction Co., Hillside, IL.

Businesspeople

1349 Banks, Marissa Elena. Doing it right.

HISPANIC BUSINESS, Vol. 9, no. 11 (November 1987), p. 56-61. English. **DESCR:** *Chicanas; *Torrez, Esther A.; Torrez, Garnett & Associates, Los Angeles, CA.

1350 Beale, Stephen. CEOs. HISPANIC BUSINESS, Vol. 9, no. 4 (April 1987), p. 20-37, 52. English. **DESCR:** Alvarez, Roberto; Batarse, Anthony A.; Biography; Business Enterprises; Carlo, Nelson; Estrada, Anthony; Flores, Frank; Fullana, Jaime, Jr.; Hernandez, George; *Management; Ortega, James; Quirch, Guillermo; Ruiz, Roberto; Santa Maria, Yvonne Z.; Sugranes, Rosa; Tamaya, Carlos; Young, Paul H., Jr.

1351 Beale, Stephen. Inertia in the corporate boardroom. HISPANIC BUSINESS, Vol. 9, no. 8 (August 1987), p. 9-11. English. **DESCR:** *Corporations; *Management.

1352 Beale, Stephen. Moving trucks in New Mexico. HISPANIC BUSINESS, Vol. 9, no. 8 (August 1987), p. 34-37. English. **DESCR:** *Automobile Industry; Baca Pontiac-Buick-GMC, Belen, NM; *Baca, Ruben; Biography.

1353 Beale, Stephen. A piece of the big picture. HISPANIC BUSINESS, Vol. 9, no. 3 (March 1987), p. 26-30. English. **DESCR:** *Business Enterprises.

1354 Cruz, David V. Caucus & Co. orients the East. HISPANIC BUSINESS, Vol. 9, no. 11 (November 1987), p. 10-13, 71+. English. **DESCR:** *Congressional Hispanic Caucus; Elected Officials; *International Relations; *Japan; Latin Business Foundation, Los Angeles, CA; Nakasone, Yasuhiro [Prime Minister of Japan]; *Taiwan.

1355 Garcia, Art. Financing the corporate take-off. HISPANIC BUSINESS, Vol. 9, no. 5 (May 1987), p. 22-27. English. **DESCR:** Aguirre Architects, Dallas, TX; Aguirre, Pedro; Banking Industry; *Business Enterprises; *Corporations; *Investments; Minority Enterprise Small Business Investment Corporation (MESBIC); Morales, Ramon; Protocom Devices, New York, NY; Villamil, Antonio.

1356 Garcia, Philip J. Ready to go on board? HISPANIC BUSINESS, Vol. 9, no. 5 (May 1987), p. 17. English. **DESCR:** *Careers; *Corporations; *Management.

1357 Kane, George D. The entrepreneurial professional. HISPANIC BUSINESS, Vol. 9, no. 9 (September 1987), p. 34-37, 80. English. **DESCR:** *Biography; Bonilla, Tony; Cardenas, Ruben R.; Gomez, Rudy.

1358 Kane, George D. Five blueprints for fueling growth. HISPANIC BUSINESS, Vol. 9, no. 5 (May 1987), p. 18-21, 42+. English. **DESCR:** *Business Enterprises; Holguin Corporation, El Paso, TX; Investments; Latin Industries, Ontario, CA; One-Day Paint & Auto Body Centers, Los Angeles, CA; Terrinvest, Miami, FL; TRU & Associates, Orange County, CA.

1359 Ramos gives special enthusiasm to original Hispanic projects. HISPANIC TIMES, Vol. 8, no. 1 (December, January, 1987), p. 48. English. **DESCR:** Films; *Ramos, Mario.

1360 A salute to Hispanic excellence in America. HISPANIC BUSINESS, Vol. 9, no. 6 (June 1987), p. 7-9. English. **DESCR:** *Awards; *Latin Business Association (LBA), Los Angeles, CA; Organizations.

Businesspeople (cont.)

1361 Sellers, Jeff M. Challenging the myth of the traditional woman. HISPANIC BUSINESS, Vol. 9, no. 8 (August 1987), p. 15-16, 48. English. DESCR: *Careers; *Chicanas; *Management; National Network of Hispanic Women; Sex Roles; Torres, Celia; Women; Zambrana, Ruth.

1362 Seven profiles of courage. HISPANIC BUSINESS, Vol. 9, no. 6 (June 1987), p. 57-70. English. DESCR: Alamo Technology Inc., San Antonio, TX; *Business Enterprises; Carrillo, Rosario C.; O'Campo Corporation, Walnut, CA; O'Campo, Peter; Rivas, Robert; TexPar Energy Inc., Milwaukee, WI; THE HISPANIC BUSINESS 500.

1363 Susana Rendon. AMERICAS 2001, Vol. 1, no. 1 (June, July, 1987), p. [31]. Bilingual. DESCR: Biographical Notes; Chicanas; *Rendon, Susana.

1364 Trager, Cara S. Women of the year. HISPANIC BUSINESS, Vol. 9, no. 6 (June 1987), p. 78-82. English. DESCR: Biography; *Chicanas; Rivera, Betty.

Bustamante, Jorge A.

1365 Woods, Richard D. Book review of: MEXICO-ESTADOS UNIDOS: BIBLIOGRAFIA GENERAL SOBRE ESTUDIOS FRONTERIZOS. LA RED/THE NET, no. 49 (December 1981), p. 4-5. English. DESCR: Book Reviews; Border Studies; Malagamba, Francisco; *MEXICO-ESTADOS UNIDOS: BIBLIOGRAFIA GENERAL SOBRE ESTUDIOS FRONTERIZOS; Reference Works.

BY THE LIGHT OF THE MOON

1366 DeCurtis, Anthony. Los Lobos shake, rattle and worry. ROLLING STONE, (February 26, 1987), p. 51-53. English. DESCR: *Los Lobos del Este de Los Angeles (musical group); Recording Industry; Rock Music.

Caballero, Cesar

1367 Castillo-Speed, Lillian. Annotated bibliography. LA RED/THE NET, no. 93 (January, February, 1986), p. 14-17. English. DESCR: A BIBLIOGRAPHY OF MEXICAN AMERICAN HISTORY; ARTE CHICANO; Book Reviews; CHICANO LITERATURE: A REFERENCE GUIDE; CHICANO ORGANIZATIONS DIRECTORY; CHICANO PERIODICAL INDEX; Goldman, Shifra M.; HISPANIC ALMANAC; HISPANIC MENTAL HEALTH RESEARCH: A REFERENCE GUIDE; Lomeli, Francisco A.; Martinez, Julio A.; Meier, Matt S.; Newton, Frank; *Reference Works; Ybarra-Frausto, Tomas.

1368 Haro, Robert P. Book review of: CHICANO ORGANIZATIONS DIRECTORY. AMERICAN REFERENCE BOOKS ANNUAL, Vol. 17, (1986), p. 145. English. DESCR: Book Reviews; *CHICANO ORGANIZATIONS DIRECTORY; Reference Works.

1369 Powell, Carolyn L. Book review of: CHICANO ORGANIZATIONS DIRECTORY. VOICE OF YOUTH ADVOCATES, Vol. 8, no. 6 (February 1986), p. 408. English. DESCR: Book Reviews; *CHICANO ORGANIZATIONS DIRECTORY; Directories.

Caballero, Eduardo

1370 Guedella, Juan. Hispanic media--Caballero style. HISPANIC BUSINESS, Vol. 9, no. 2 (February 1987), p. 17-18. English. DESCR: Advertising; Biography; *Caballero Spanish Media (CSM); Cubanos; Marketing.

Caballero Spanish Media (CSM)

1371 Guedella, Juan. Hispanic media--Caballero style. HISPANIC BUSINESS, Vol. 9, no. 2 (February 1987), p. 17-18. English. DESCR: Advertising; Biography; *Caballero, Eduardo; Cubanos; Marketing.

Cabeza de Baca, Fabiola

1372 Jensen, Joan M. Crossing ethnic barriers in the Southwest: women's agricultural extension education, 1914-1940. AGRICULTURAL HISTORY, Vol. 60, no. 2 (Spring 1986), p. 169-181. English. DESCR: *Agricultural Extension Service; Agriculture; Chicanas; History; New Mexico; *Rural Education.

Calderon, Charles M.

1373 The California Museum of Latino History=El Museo de California de la Historia de los Latinos. AMERICAS 2001, Premiere Issue, 1987, p. 18-19, 39. Bilingual. DESCR: *California Museum of Latino History; History; *Museums; Rios-Bustamante, Antonio; Social History and Conditions.

Calendars

1374 Romero, Miguel. Tonalpohuali o calendario azteca. LLUEVE TLALOC, no. 2 (1975), p. [54]. Bilingual. DESCR: *Drawings.

California

1375 Barger, W.K. California public endorses the United Farm Workers. LA RED/THE NET, No. 105 (February 1987), p. 4-6. English. DESCR: *Agricultural Labor Unions; *Farm Workers; *Public Opinion; *United Farmworkers of America (UFW).

1376 Barger, W.K. Views of California farmworkers regarding the farm labor movement. LA RED/THE NET, no. 91 (October 1985), p. 3-5. English. DESCR: Agricultural Labor Unions; Attitudes; *Farm Workers; *United Farmworkers of America (UFW).

1377 Boycotts revisited: Campbell's concedes to farm worker campaign. DOLLARS AND SENSE, (July, August, 1986), p. 12-14, 18. English. DESCR: Boycotts; Campbell Soup Co.; Farm Labor Organizing Commmittee (FLOC); Farm Workers; *Labor Disputes; Labor Unions; Michigan; Ohio; Strikes and Lockouts; United Farmworkers of America (UFW).

1378 California businesses up: federal procurement down. HISPANIC BUSINESS, Vol. 9, no. 12 (December 1987), p. 60. English. DESCR: *Business Enterprises; *Government Contracts.

1379 Cervantes, Robert A. Ethnocentric pedagogy and minority student growth: implications for the common school. EDUCATION AND URBAN SOCIETY, Vol. 16, no. 3 (May 1984), p. 274-293. English. DESCR: Bilingual Bicultural Education; Discrimination in Education; *Education.

1380 de los Santos, Alfredo G., Jr.; Montemayor, Joaquin; and Solis, Enrique, Jr. Chicano students in higher education: access, attrition and achievement. LA RED/THE NET, no. 41 (April 1981), p. 2-3. English. DESCR: Academic Achievement; Enrollment; *Higher Education; *Texas.

California (cont.)

1381 Engstrand, Iris H.W. California ranchos: their Hispanic heritage. SOUTHERN CALIFORNIA QUARTERLY, Vol. 67, no. 3 (Fall 1985), p. 281-290. English. **DESCR:** *Californios; History; *Land Grants; *Spanish Influence.

1382 Griswold del Castillo, Richard. Book review of: CHICANOS IN CALIFORNIA. PACIFIC HISTORICAL REVIEW, Vol. 54, no. 2 (February 1985), p. 211-212. English. **DESCR:** Book Reviews; Camarillo, Alberto; *CHICANOS IN CALIFORNIA.

1383 Hayakawa, S.I.; Cejas, Paul; and Castro Feinberg, Rosa. The English-only debate. VISTA, Vol. 2, no. 6 (February 8, 1987), p. 11-13. English. **DESCR:** *English Language; *English-Only Movement; Law.

1384 Klor de Alva, J. Jorge. California Chicano literature and pre-Columbian motifs: foil and fetish. CONFLUENCIA, Vol. 1, no. 2 (Spring 1986), p. 18-26. English. **DESCR:** Alurista; Aztecs; Aztlan; EL PLAN ESPIRITUAL DE AZTLAN; *Literature; *Precolumbian Images; *Precolumbian Philosophy; Symbolism.

1385 Meyers, C.E.; Borthwick, S.A.; and Eyman, R.K. Place of residence by age, ethnicity, and level of retardation of the mentally retarded/developmentally disabled population of California. AMERICAN JOURNAL OF MENTAL DEFICIENCY, Vol. 90, no. 3 (November 1985), p. 266-270. English. **DESCR:** Identity; *Mentally Handicapped; Public Health.

1386 Zatz, Marjorie S. Race, ethnicity, and determinate sentencing: a new dimension to an old controversy. CRIMINOLOGY: AN INTERDISCIPLINARY JOURNAL, Vol. 22, no. 2 (May 1984), p. 147-171. English. **DESCR:** *Criminal Justice System; Criminology; Ethnic Groups.

California Association of Latins in Broadcasting

1387 Madrid, Vicente and Yepes, Maria Elena. National Latino Media Coalition. LATIN QUARTER, Vol. 1, no. 4 (July, August, 1975), p. 4-7. English. **DESCR:** Affirmative Action Programs; Bilingual/Bicultural Coalition on Mass Media; *Broadcast Media; Conferences and Meetings; Federal Communications Commission (FCC); *National Latino Media Coalition (NLMC); Puerto Rican Media Action and Educational Council.

California Chicano News Media Association (CCNMA)

1388 Ayala, Ernie. Henry Alfaro, ABC's Eyewitness News reporter. LATIN QUARTER, Vol. 1, no. 1 (July 1974), p. 13-15. English. **DESCR:** *Alfaro, Henry; Golden Mike Award; Journalists; *Television.

California Master Plan for Higher Education

1389 Magallan, Rafael J. Community college update. LA RED/THE NET, no. 98 (July 1986), p. 3-6. English. **DESCR:** *Community College Reassessment Study; Community Colleges; Enrollment; *Vera, Ron.

1390 Report to the Network. LA RED/THE NET, no. 97 (June 1986), p. 1-2. English. **DESCR:** *Colleges and Universities; *Evaluation (Educational); *Higher Education.

California Museum of Latino History

1391 The California Museum of Latino History=El Museo de California de la Historia de los Latinos. AMERICAS 2001, Premiere Issue, 1987, p. 18-19, 39. Bilingual. **DESCR:** Calderon, Charles M.; History; *Museums; Rios-Bustamante, Antonio; Social History and Conditions.

California Spanish Language Data Base (CSLDB)
USE: HISPANEX (Oakland, CA)

California State Constitution

1392 Rios-Bustamante, Antonio. California's bilingual constitution=La constitucion bilingue de California. AMERICAS 2001, Vol. 1, no. 1 (June, July, 1987), p. 15. Bilingual. **DESCR:** History; Spanish Language.

California State University, Long Beach

1393 Wilde, Richard H. The establishment of a Chicano studies program and its relation to the total curriculum of a college or university. EPOCA: NATIONAL CONCILIO FOR CHICANO STUDIES JOURNAL, Vol. 1, no. 2 (Winter 1971), p. 70-78. English. **DESCR:** *Chicano Studies; *Curriculum; *Research Methodology.

Los Californianos [genealogical society], San Jose, CA

1394 Chavez, Lorenzo A. The quest for Hispanic roots. VISTA, Vol. 2, no. 7 (March 8, 1987), p. 5-6, 24. English. **DESCR:** Church of Jesus Christ of Latter-Day Saints (Mormons); Directories; *Garcia, Clotilde; *Genealogy; Hispanic American Genealogical Associates, Washington, DC; Las Porciones Genealogical Society, Edinburg, TX; Los Bexarenos, San Antonio, TX; Pan American University, Edinburg, TX; Texas Southmost College.

Californios

1395 Engstrand, Iris H.W. California ranchos: their Hispanic heritage. SOUTHERN CALIFORNIA QUARTERLY, Vol. 67, no. 3 (Fall 1985), p. 281-290. English. **DESCR:** *California; History; *Land Grants; *Spanish Influence.

Callwood, Dennis O.

1396 Rosas, Alejandro. Siete fotografos latinos en Los Angeles. LA COMUNIDAD, No. 241 (March 3, 1985), p. 4-5. Spanish. **DESCR:** Aguilar, Laura; Art; Avila, Adam; Carlos, Jesus; Exhibits; Miranda, Judy; *Photography; Self-Help Graphics, Los Angeles, CA; *SEVEN LATINO PHOTOGRAPHERS=SIETE FOTOGRAFOS LATINOS; Thewlis, Alan; Valverde, Richard.

Calo
USE: Chicano Dialects

CALO TAPESTRY

1397 Duran, Richard P. Book review of: CALO TAPESTRY. LA RED/THE NET, no. 32 (July 1980), p. 5. English. **DESCR:** *Chicano Dialects; Language Usage; *Ortega, Adolfo.

Calvert, Robert

1398 de Leon, Arnoldo. Book review of: CHICANO: THE EVOLUTION OF A PEOPLE. SOUTHWESTERN HISTORICAL QUARTERLY, Vol. 87, no. 3 (1984), p. 343-344. English. **DESCR:** Book Reviews; *CHICANO: THE EVOLUTION OF A PEOPLE; Rosaldo, Renato; Seligmann, Gustav L.

CALYX: A JOURNAL OF ART AND LITERATURE BY WOMEN

1399 Eidelberg, Nora. Book review of: BEARING
     WITNESS/SOBREVIVIENDO. LECTOR, Vol. 4, no.
     1-3 (1986), p. [59-60]. English. **DESCR:**
     *BEARING WITNESS/SOBREVIVIENDO; Book
     Reviews.

Camacho, Eduardo

1400 Perez, Renato E. Chicago: Hispanic melting
     pot. VISTA, Vol. 1, no. 3 (November 3,
     1985), p. 20. English. **DESCR:** Casuso, Jorge;
     *Chicago, IL; Cultural Pluralism; Ethnic
     Groups; HISPANICS IN CHICAGO; *Population.

Camarillo, Alberto

1401 Arce, Carlos H. Book review of: CHICANOS IN
     A CHANGING SOCIETY. LA RED/THE NET, no. 30
     (May 1980), p. 8. English. **DESCR:** Book
     Reviews; CHICANOS IN A CHANGING SOCIETY;
     History; *Santa Barbara, CA; *Social History
     and Conditions; *Southern California.

1402 Garcia, Mario T. Book review of: THE STATE
     OF CHICANO RESEARCH ON FAMILY, LABOR, AND
     MIGRATION: PROCEEDINGS OF THE FIRST STANFORD
     SYMPOSIUM ON CHICANO RESEARCH AND PUBLIC
     POLICY. CALIFORNIA HISTORY, Vol. 63, no. 3
     (Summer 1984), p. 261-262. English. **DESCR:**
     Almaguer, Tomas; Book Reviews; Chicano
     Studies; *THE STATE OF CHICANO RESEARCH IN
     FAMILY, LABOR AND MIGRATION STUDIES; Valdez,
     Armando.

1403 Griswold del Castillo, Richard. Book review
     of: CHICANOS IN CALIFORNIA. PACIFIC
     HISTORICAL REVIEW, Vol. 54, no. 2 (February
     1985), p. 211-212. English. **DESCR:** Book
     Reviews; California; *CHICANOS IN
     CALIFORNIA.

1404 Griswold del Castillo, Richard. Book review
     of: THE STATE OF CHICANO RESEARCH ON FAMILY,
     LABOR, AND MIGRATION: PROCEEDINGS OF THE
     FIRST STANFORD SYMPOSIUM ON CHICANO RESEARCH
     AND PUBLIC POLICY. PACIFIC HISTORICAL
     REVIEW, Vol. 54, no. 3 (August 1985), p.
     381-382. English. **DESCR:** Almaguer, Tomas;
     Book Reviews; Chicano Studies; *THE STATE OF
     CHICANO RESEARCH IN FAMILY, LABOR AND
     MIGRATION STUDIES; Valdez, Armando.

1405 Hurtado, Aida. Book review of: WORK, FAMILY,
     SEX ROLES, LANGUAGE. LA RED/THE NET, no. 40
     (March 1981), p. 3. English. **DESCR:** Barrera,
     Mario; Book Reviews; Hernandez, Francisco;
     Social History and Conditions; *WORK,
     FAMILY, SEX ROLES, LANGUAGE: SELECTED PAPERS
     OF THE NATIONAL ASSOCIATION FOR CHICANO
     STUDIES CONFERENCE, 1979.

1406 Miranda, Gloria E. Book review of: CHICANOS
     IN CALIFORNIA. SOUTHERN CALIFORNIA
     QUARTERLY, Vol. 67, no. 4 (Winter 1985), p.
     474-476. English. **DESCR:** Book Reviews;
     *CHICANOS IN CALIFORNIA; Social History and
     Conditions.

Camhi, Morrie

1407 Muro, Rena. Walking on water. AMERICAS 2001,
     Vol. 1, no. 3 (November, December, 1987), p.
     12-14. Bilingual. **DESCR:** *Films; Olmos,
     Edward James; STAND AND DELIVER [film];
     *WALKING ON WATER [working title of film
     STAND AND DELIVER].

Campbell Soup Co.

1408 Boycotts revisited: Campbell's concedes to
     farm worker campaign. DOLLARS AND SENSE,
     (July, August, 1986), p. 12-14, 18. English.
     DESCR: Boycotts; California; Farm Labor
     Organizing Commmittee (FLOC); Farm Workers;
     *Labor Disputes; Labor Unions; Michigan;
     Ohio; Strikes and Lockouts; United
     Farmworkers of America (UFW).

1409 Sanders, Bob. Boycott Campbell's: Ohio
     farmworkers take it to the top. DOLLARS AND
     SENSE, no. 92 (December 1983), p. 16-18.
     English. **DESCR:** Boycotts; Chavez, Cesar E.;
     Farm Labor Organizing Commmittee (FLOC);
     Farm Workers; Guevas, Fernando; *Labor
     Disputes; Labor Unions; Ohio; Strikes and
     Lockouts; United Farmworkers of America
     (UFW).

Canada

1410 Grenier, Gilles. An economic perspective on
     learning a second language. JOURNAL OF
     MULTILINGUAL AND MULTICULTURAL DEVELOPMENT,
     Vol. 4, no. 6 (1983), p. 471-483. English.
     DESCR: Bilingualism; Economics; *Language
     Usage.

Canadian Club Hispanic Art Tour

1411 Shaw, Katherine. Mira! a look at America's
     Hispanic artists. VISTA, Vol. 1, no. 5
     (January 5, 1986), p. 6-8. English. **DESCR:**
     *Art; Artists; Delgadillo, Ramon; Gamboa,
     Diane; Gonzalez, Nivia; *Trevino, Jesus
     (Jesse).

Canby, Edward

1412 Meketa, Charles and Meketa, Jacqueline.
     Heroes or cowards? A new look at the role of
     native New Mexicans at the Battle of
     Valverde. NEW MEXICO HISTORICAL REVIEW, Vol.
     62, no. 1 (January 1987), p. 33-46. English.
     DESCR: *Battle of Valverde; History; *New
     Mexico.

Cancer

1413 Duncan, Marilyn H., et al. Childhood cancer
     epidemiology in New Mexico's American
     Indians, Hispanic whites, and non-Hispanic
     whites, 1970-82. JOURNAL OF THE NATIONAL
     CANCER INSTITUTE, Vol. 76, no. 6 (June
     1986), p. 1013-1018. English. **DESCR:** Anglo
     Americans; *Children; Diseases; Native
     Americans.

1414 Fighting cervical cancer. NUESTRO, Vol. 11,
     no. 3 (April 1987), p. 26-27. English.
     DESCR: *Chicanas; *Diseases.

1415 Martin, Jeanne and Suarez, Lucina. Cancer
     mortality among Mexican Americans and other
     whites in Texas, 1969-80. AMERICAN JOURNAL
     OF PUBLIC HEALTH, Vol. 77, no. 7 (July
     1987), p. 851-853. English. **DESCR:** Generally
     Useful Ethnic Search System (GUESS); Texas;
     Vital Statistics.

1416 Pascual, Jose Elias. A hope for Micheal
     [sic]=Una esperanza para Miguel. AMERICAS
     2001, Vol. 1, no. 3 (November, December,
     1987), p. 18-19. Bilingual. **DESCR:** *Essays.

1417 Weiss, K.M. Phenotype amplification, as
     illustrated by cancer of the gallbladder in
     New World peoples. PROGRESS IN CLINICAL AND
     BIOLOGICAL RESEARCH, Vol. 194, (1985), p.
     179-198. English. **DESCR:** *Diseases.

Candelaria, Cordelia

1418 Billings, Linda M. and Alurista. In verbal murals: a study of Chicana herstory and poetry. CONFLUENCIA, Vol. 2, no. 1 (Fall 1986), p. 60-68. English. **DESCR**: Cervantes, Lorna Dee; *Chicanas; Cisneros, Sandra; EMPLUMADA; *Feminism; History; Literary Criticism; *Poetry; Xelina.

1419 Book review of: CHICANO POETRY: A CRITICAL INTRODUCTION. AMERICAN LITERATURE, Vol. 58, no. 3 (October 1986), p. 481-482. English. **DESCR**: Book Reviews; *CHICANO POETRY: A CRITICAL INTRODUCTION.

1420 Krauth, Leland. Book review of: CHICANO POETRY: A CRITICAL INTRODUCTION. LIBRARY JOURNAL, Vol. 111, (April 15, 1986), p. 82. English. **DESCR**: Book Reviews; *CHICANO POETRY: A CRITICAL INTRODUCTION; Poetry.

1421 Lint, Robert G. Book review of: CHICANO POETRY: A CRITICAL INTRODUCTION. WESTERN AMERICAN LITERATURE, Vol. 21, no. 4 (1987), p. 380. English. **DESCR**: Book Reviews; *CHICANO POETRY: A CRITICAL INTRODUCTION.

1422 Luna-Lawhn, Juanita. Book review of: CHICANO POETRY: A CRITICAL INTRODUCTION. CHOICE, Vol. 23, no. 11-12 (July, August, 1986), p. 1672. English. **DESCR**: Book Reviews; *CHICANO POETRY: A CRITICAL INTRODUCTION.

1423 Marin, Christine. Book review of: OJO DE LA CUEVA. LECTOR, Vol. 4, no. 4-6 (1987), p. 75. English. **DESCR**: Book Reviews; *OJO DE LA CUEVA: CAVE SPRINGS.

Candelaria, Nash

1424 Bruce-Novoa, Juan. Nash Candelaria: novelista (I). LA COMUNIDAD, No. 245 (March 31, 1985), p. 6-7. Spanish. **DESCR**: Biography; *Literary Criticism; MEMORIES OF THE ALHAMBRA; NOT BY THE SWORD; Novel.

1425 Bruce-Novoa, Juan. Nash Candelaria: novelista (II). LA COMUNIDAD, No. 246 (April 7, 1985), p. 10-11. Spanish. **DESCR**: Biography; *Literary Criticism; MEMORIES OF THE ALHAMBRA; NOT BY THE SWORD; Novel.

Candelas Guitar Shop, Los Angeles, CA

1426 Murphy, Suzanne. The music makers. VISTA, Vol. 3, no. 4 (December 6, 1987), p. 28-29. English. **DESCR**: *Delgado, Porfirio; *Musical Instruments.

Canneries

1427 Castellanos, Teresa and Lopez, Margarita. La huelga nos ha ensenado a hablar. REVISTA MUJERES, Vol. 3, no. 2 (June 1986), p. 22-28. Spanish. **DESCR**: Biography; *Chicanas; Strikes and Lockouts.

1428 Romero, Bertha. The exploitation of Mexican women in the canning industry and the effects of capital accumulation on striking workers. REVISTA MUJERES, Vol. 3, no. 2 (June 1986), p. 16-20. English. **DESCR**: Capitalism; *Chicanas; Labor Unions; Strikes and Lockouts; *Watsonville Canning and Frozen Food Co.

1429 Shapiro, Peter. Watsonville shows "it can be done". GUARDIAN, Vol. 39, no. 24 (March 25, 1987), p. 1,9. English. **DESCR**: Chicanas; Labor Unions; NorCal Frozen Foods; *Strikes and Lockouts; *Watsonville Canning and Frozen Food Co.; Working Women.

1430 Zavella, Patricia. "Abnormal intimacy": the varying work networks of Chicana cannery workers. FEMINIST STUDIES, Vol. 11, no. 3 (Fall 1985), p. 541-557. English. **DESCR**: Chicanas; Discrimination in Employment; Labor Unions; *Natural Support Systems; *Working Women.

Cano, Eddie

1431 Halley, Lindsey. Pachuco boggie [sic]. LA COMUNIDAD, No. 305 (May 25, 1986), p. 8-9. Spanish. **DESCR**: Diaz, Raul; History; *Music; Ovalle, John; *PACHUCO BOOGIE; Smithsonian Institute; The Record Inn, East Los Angeles, CA; Tosti, Don.

Cano, Oscar

1432 MAES chairman appointed to DEOMI board of visitors. HISPANIC TIMES, Vol. 8, no. 3 (May, June, 1987), p. 42. English. **DESCR**: Appointed Officials; Department of Defense Equal Opportunities Management Institute (DEOMI); Mexican American Engineering Society (MAES).

Cantinflas
USE: Moreno, Mario "Cantinflas"

CANTO Y GRITO MI LIBERACION

1433 Lovato, Alberto. La burra no era arisca, cabrones, los chingazos la hicieron asi... EL CUADERNO, Vol. 2, no. 1 (1972), p. 36-39. English. **DESCR**: Book Reviews; Sanchez, Ricardo.

Cantu Jimenez, Esteban

1434 Sandos, James A. Northern separatism during the Mexican revolution--an inquiry into the role of drug trafficking, 1910-1920. AMERICAS, Vol. 41, no. 2 (October 1984), p. 191-214. English. **DESCR**: Baja California, Mexico; Border Region; Drug Addicts; Drug Laws; *Drug Traffic; *Drug Use; Medical Care; Mexican Revolution - 1910-1920; Revolutions.

Cantu, Mario, Jr.

1435 Marambio, Gonzalo. From San Antonio to Paris: Tex-Mex food conquers the French. VISTA, Vol. 1, no. 6 (February 2, 1986), p. 18-20. English. **DESCR**: Business Enterprises; *Food Practices; Gonzales, Teresa; *Mario's Restaurant, San Antonio, TX; Papa Maya's Restaurant, Paris, France.

Capitalism

1436 Barton, Amy E. Women farmworkers: their workplace and capitalist patriarchy. REVISTA MUJERES, Vol. 3, no. 2 (June 1986), p. 11-13. English. **DESCR**: *Chicanas; Discrimination; *Farm Workers; Sexism.

1437 Galarza, Ernesto. Platica con Galarza [interview]. EL CUADERNO, Vol. 4, no. 10 (Summer 1976), p. 6-19. Bilingual. **DESCR**: *Education; *Galarza, Ernesto.

1438 Romero, Bertha. The exploitation of Mexican women in the canning industry and the effects of capital accumulation on striking workers. REVISTA MUJERES, Vol. 3, no. 2 (June 1986), p. 16-20. English. **DESCR**: Canneries; *Chicanas; Labor Unions; Strikes and Lockouts; *Watsonville Canning and Frozen Food Co.

Car Clubs

1439 Rifkin, Jane M. The Lil' Scholars: responding to a tragedy in the noblest way! HISPANIC TIMES, Vol. 8, no. 5 (October, November, 1987), p. 9. English. **DESCR:** Financial Aid; *Lil' Scholars [car club], Pasadena, CA.

1440 Yepes, Maria Elena. Lady bugs. LATIN QUARTER, Vol. 1, no. 4 (July, August, 1975), p. 28-31. English. **DESCR:** Chicanas; *Lady Bugs [car club]; Los Angeles, CA.

CARAS VIEJAS Y VINO NUEVO

1441 Bustamante, Nuria. Permanencia y cambio en CARAS VIEJAS Y VINO NUEVO. CONFLUENCIA, Vol. 1, no. 2 (Spring 1986), p. 61-65. Spanish. **DESCR:** *Literary Criticism; *Morales, Alejandro; Novel.

1442 Gonzalez, Maria. CARAS VIEJAS Y VINO NUEVO: analisis tematica y estructural. TINTA, Vol. 1, no. 1 (May 1981), p. 15-18. Spanish. **DESCR:** *Literary Criticism; Morales, Alejandro; Novel.

Cardenas, David

1443 Chavez, Lorenzo A. The eyes of Texas are upon them. VISTA, Vol. 2, no. 2 (October 4, 1986), p. 20. English. **DESCR:** *Art; *Chulas Fronteras [art exhibit]; Espada, Ibsen; Gonzalez, Patricia; Hernandez, John; Huerta, Benito; Martinez, Cesar Augusto.

Cardenas, John

1444 Sellers, Jeff M. Same-day service sells. HISPANIC BUSINESS, Vol. 9, no. 11 (November 1987), p. 16-19. English. **DESCR:** *Business Enterprises; *Golden Gate Air Freight, Hayward, CA.

Cardenas, Ruben R.

1445 Kane, George D. The entrepreneurial professional. HISPANIC BUSINESS, Vol. 9, no. 9 (September 1987), p. 34-37, 80. English. **DESCR:** *Biography; Bonilla, Tony; *Businesspeople; Gomez, Rudy.

Careers

1446 Determined to advance. HISPANIC BUSINESS, Vol. 9, no. 7 (July 1987), p. 35. English. **DESCR:** *Chicanas; *Employment; *Latino Institute.

1447 Garcia, Philip J. Ready to go on board? HISPANIC BUSINESS, Vol. 9, no. 5 (May 1987), p. 17. English. **DESCR:** *Businesspeople; *Corporations; *Management.

1448 Kilgore, Julia. A risk taker. HISPANIC BUSINESS, Vol. 9, no. 12 (December 1987), p. 44-47. English. **DESCR:** *Appointed Officials; Biography; *Chicanas; *Diaz Dennis, Patricia; Federal Communications Commission (FCC).

1449 Marsh, Betsa. Diversidad de valores en Proctor & Gamble. HISPANIC TIMES, Vol. 8, no. 3 (May, June, 1987), p. 32-3. Spanish. **DESCR:** *Engineering as a Profession; *Proctor & Gamble, Cincinnati, OH.

1450 Marsh, Betsa. Proctor & Gamble values diversity. HISPANIC TIMES, Vol. 8, no. 3 (May, June, 1987), p. 10-11. English. **DESCR:** *Engineering as a Profession; *Proctor & Gamble, Cincinnati, OH.

1451 Mixed messages sent to June graduates. HISPANIC TIMES, Vol. 8, no. 3 (May, June, 1987), p. 18. English. **DESCR:** *Bilingualism; *College Graduates.

1452 National Council of La Raza (NCLR). Career information and Hispanic students. LA RED/THE NET, no. 75 (December 1983), p. 2-4. English. **DESCR:** Educational Services; *National Council of La Raza (NCLR); Secondary School Education; Survey of Career Information Systems in Secondary Schools; *Youth.

1453 Perkins, Claranne. We the minorities of CASE: a special survey of minorities working in institutional advancement. CURRENTS, Vol. 10, no. 5 (May 1984), p. 34-40. English. **DESCR:** Higher Education; Statistics.

1454 Pinkney, James W. and Ramirez, Marty. Career-planning myths of Chicano students. JOURNAL OF COLLEGE STUDENT PERSONNEL, Vol. 26, (July 1985), p. 300-305. English. **DESCR:** *Counseling (Educational); Cultural Characteristics.

1455 Reyes, Sonia. Hispanic models pursue high stakes fashion. VISTA, Vol. 1, no. 2 (October 5, 1985), p. 6-9. English. **DESCR:** Apodaca, Roseanne; Dominguez, Peter; *Fashion; Jerez, Alicia; Soto, Talisa.

1456 Rifkin, Jane M. Up from the barrio...to fittest woman cop in the U.S.A. HISPANIC TIMES, Vol. 8, no. 1 (December, January, 1987), p. 38. English. **DESCR:** Biography; *Chicanas; *Lopez, Theresa (Terry); *Police.

1457 Rivera, Alvin D. Laying a foundation for learning: student peer workshop groups. NEW DIRECTIONS FOR TEACHING AND LEARNING, no. 16 (December 1983), p. 81-86. English. **DESCR:** Counseling (Educational); *Engineering as a Profession; *Natural Support Systems; Organizations; Students.

1458 Sellers, Jeff M. Challenging the myth of the traditional woman. HISPANIC BUSINESS, Vol. 9, no. 8 (August 1987), p. 15-16, 48. English. **DESCR:** *Businesspeople; *Chicanas; *Management; National Network of Hispanic Women; Sex Roles; Torres, Celia; Women; Zambrana, Ruth.

1459 Sellers, Jeff M. State of the art recruitment: competition for blue-chip Hispanic business graduates is fierce and expensive. HISPANIC BUSINESS, Vol. 9, no. 2 (February 1987), p. 22-25, 57. English. **DESCR:** *Business Administration; College Graduates; Colleges and Universities; Enrollment; *Management.

Caricature

1460 Larrazabal, John. Captain Zoom and his canine wonder. AMERICAS 2001, Vol. 1, no. 2 (September, October, 1987), p. [44]. Bilingual. **DESCR:** Humor.

Carlo, Nelson

1461 Beale, Stephen. CEOs. HISPANIC BUSINESS, Vol. 9, no. 4 (April 1987), p. 20-37, 52. English. **DESCR:** Alvarez, Roberto; Batarse, Anthony A.; Biography; Business Enterprises; *Businesspeople; Estrada, Anthony; Flores, Frank; Fullana, Jaime, Jr.; Hernandez, George; *Management; Ortega, James; Quirch, Guillermo; Ruiz, Roberto; Santa Maria, Yvonne Z.; Sugranes, Rosa; Tamaya, Carlos; Young, Paul H., Jr.

Carlos, Jesus

1462 Rosas, Alejandro. Siete fotografos latinos en Los Angeles. LA COMUNIDAD, No. 241 (March 3, 1985), p. 4-5. Spanish. **DESCR:** Aguilar, Laura; Art; Avila, Adam; Callwood, Dennis O.; Exhibits; Miranda, Judy; *Photography; Self-Help Graphics, Los Angeles, CA; *SEVEN LATINO PHOTOGRAPHERS=SIETE FOTOGRAFOS LATINOS; Thewlis, Alan; Valverde, Richard.

Carnaval Miami

1463 Fernandez, Celia. The biggest Hispanic fiesta in the USA. VISTA, Vol. 2, no. 7 (March 8, 1987), p. 13-15. English. **DESCR:** *Festivals.

Carpentier, Alejo

1464 Barry, John M. Mito e ironia en LOS PASOS PERDIDOS. TINTA, Vol. 1, no. 4 (Summer 1984), p. 3-9. Spanish. **DESCR:** Latin American Literature; Literary Criticism; *LOS PASOS PERDIDOS; Mitos; *Novel.

1465 Toruno, Rhina. El protagonista verdadero de EL SIGLO DE LAS LUCES de Alejo Carpentier. CHIRICU, Vol. 4, no. 1 (1985), p. 19-39. Spanish. **DESCR:** *EL SIGLO DE LAS LUCES; Literary Criticism; Novel.

Carr, Frank

1466 Winston, Bonnie. INROADS: internships that work. HISPANIC ENGINEER, Vol. 3, no. 5 (Winter 1987), p. 38-42. English. **DESCR:** Almanza, John; Alvarez, Maria; *Educational Organizations; Educational Statistics; Garcia, Juan; Gonzales, Ana; *INROADS; Pereira, Eduardo; Raimundo, Antonio; Reza, Priscilla.

Carrasco, Barbara

1467 Gamboa, Harry, Jr. El artista chicano dentro y fuera de la "corriente" artistica. LA COMUNIDAD, No. 351 (April 12, 1987), 2-5+. Spanish. **DESCR:** *Art; Artists; Gamboa, Diane; Gronk (Pseud.); Martinez, Daniel J.; Valadez, John; Valdez, Patssi.

Carrero, Jaime

1468 Ugalde, Sharon E. Two visions of cultural domination: Carrero's EL HOMBRE QUE NO SUDABA and Hinojosa's MI QUERIDO RAFA. BILINGUAL REVIEW, Vol. 12, no. 1-2 (January, August, 1985), p. 159-165. English. **DESCR:** *EL HOMBRE QUE NO SUDABA; Hinojosa-Smith, Rolando R.; Literary Criticism; *MI QUERIDO RAFA.

Carrillo, Rosario C.

1469 Seven profiles of courage. HISPANIC BUSINESS, Vol. 9, no. 6 (June 1987), p. 57-70. English. **DESCR:** Alamo Technology Inc., San Antonio, TX; *Business Enterprises; *Businesspeople; O'Campo Corporation, Walnut, CA; O'Campo, Peter; Rivas, Robert; TexPar Energy Inc., Milwaukee, WI; THE HISPANIC BUSINESS 500.

Carter, Thomas P.

1470 Garcia, Philip. Book review of: MEXICAN AMERICANS IN SCHOOL: A DECADE OF CHANGE. LA RED/THE NET, no. 33 (August 1980), p. 4. English. **DESCR:** Book Reviews; *Education; *MEXICAN AMERICANS IN SCHOOL: A DECADE OF CHANGE; Segura, Roberto D.

Carthy-Deu, Deborah [Miss Universe]

1471 Reyes, Sonia. America's Hispanic sweethearts. VISTA, Vol. 1, no. 6 (February 2, 1986), p. 6-7. English. **DESCR:** Awards; *Martinez-Herring, Laura [Miss USA]; *Women.

Casaus, Luis

1472 Luzod, Jimmy. Book review of: PARENTING MODELS AND MEXICAN AMERICANS: A PROCESS ANALYSIS. LA RED/THE NET, no. 71 (August 1983), p. 8-11. English. **DESCR:** Arciniega, Miguel; Book Reviews; Castillo, Max; *PARENTING MODELS AND MEXICAN AMERICANS: A PROCESS ANALYSIS (2nd ed.).

Casillas, Tony

1473 Quintana, Al. Gaining yardage in football. VISTA, Vol. 1, no. 2 (October 5, 1985), p. 10-11. English. **DESCR:** *Athletes; *Flores, Tom; Sports.

Castaneda, Carlos

1474 Campbell, Federico. Carlos Castaneda: escribo como brujo, no como escritor. LA COMUNIDAD, No. 256 (June 16, 1985), p. 6-7. Spanish. **DESCR:** *Literary Criticism.

1475 Nieto, Margarita. Fronteras en la obra de Carlos Castaneda. LA COMUNIDAD, No. 325 (October 12, 1986), p. 8-10. Spanish. **DESCR:** *Literary Criticism.

Castaneda, Jesus

1476 Pacific Telesis senior fellows. HISPANIC ENGINEER, Vol. 3, no. 2 (Summer 1987), p. 10-11. English. **DESCR:** *Awards; Cruz, Jacqueline; Education; Pacific Telesis; Rodriguez, Jose; Sanchez, Alex.

Castillo, Ana

1477 Paredes, Raymund A. Review essay: recent Chicano writing. ROCKY MOUNTAIN REVIEW OF LANGUAGE AND LITERATURE, Vol. 41, (1987), p. 124-129. English. **DESCR:** Catholic Church; Chavez, Denise; Chicanas; Garcia, Lionel; GIVING UP THE GHOST; LEAVING HOME; *Literary Criticism; *Literature Reviews; Moraga, Cherrie; Poetry; Prose; Sex Roles; Silva, Beverly; SMALL FACES; Soto, Gary; THE CAT AND OTHER STORIES; THE LAST OF THE MENU GIRLS; THE MIXQUIAHUALA LETTERS.

Castillo, Hector

1478 SHPE news. HISPANIC ENGINEER, Vol. 3, no. 3 (1987), p. 10-13. English. **DESCR:** *Awards; Colmenarez, Margarita; Garcia, Raul; Herrera, Jess; Lopez-Martin, Minnie; Mondragon, Ricardo; Reyes-Guerra, David; Silva, Juan; Society of Hispanic Professional Engineers (SHPE); Vargas, Jesus; Villanueva, Bernadette.

Castillo, John Ray

1479 Dempsey, Mary. John Roy Castillo. VISTA, Vol. 1, no. 11 (July 6, 1986), p. 20. English. **DESCR:** *Biography; Civil Rights; Michigan Civil Rights Department.

Castillo, Max

1480 Luzod, Jimmy. Book review of: PARENTING
MODELS AND MEXICAN AMERICANS: A PROCESS
ANALYSIS. LA RED/THE NET, no. 71 (August
1983), p. 8-11. English. DESCR: Arciniega,
Miguel; Book Reviews; Casaus, Luis;
*PARENTING MODELS AND MEXICAN AMERICANS: A
PROCESS ANALYSIS (2nd ed.).

Castillo, Pedro

1481 Hoffman, Abraham. Book review of: AN
ILLUSTRATED HISTORY OF MEXICAN LOS ANGELES:
1781-1985. NEW MEXICO HISTORICAL REVIEW,
Vol. 62, no. 4 (October 1987), p. 412-13.
English. DESCR: *AN ILLUSTRATED HISTORY OF
MEXICAN LOS ANGELES: 1781-1985; Book
Reviews; *Los Angeles, CA; *Rios-Bustamante,
Antonio.

Castillo, Sylvia

1482 Soto, Rose Marie. National Network of
Hispanic Women. HISPANIC ENGINEER, Vol. 3,
no. 4 (Fall 1987), p. 26-28. English.
DESCR: Gonzales Torres, Celia; Gutierrez,
Nancy; *National Network of Hispanic Women;
*Professional Organizations; Women;
Zambrana, Ruth.

Castro [family name]

1483 Instituto Genealogico e Historico
Latino-Americano. Rootsearch: Castro:
Velasco. VISTA, Vol. 2, no. 2 (October 4,
1986), p. 22. English. DESCR: Genealogy;
History; *Personal Names; *Velasco [family
name].

Castro, George

1484 Mellado, Carmela. Dr. George Castro:
research scientist with IBM, San Jose.
HISPANIC ENGINEER, Vol. 3, no. 3 (1987), p.
22-24, 44. English. DESCR: *Biography;
International Business Machines (IBM).

Castro, Irma

1485 Grajeda Higley, Leilani. Irma Castro. VISTA,
Vol. 2, no. 10 (June 7, 1987), p. 20.
English. DESCR: *Biography; Chicanas;
*Chicano Federation of San Diego Co., Inc.;
Civil Rights; Discrimination.

Castro, Manuel

1486 Rifkin, Jane M. Manuel Castro--founder of
MAES: a compassionate commitment. HISPANIC
TIMES, Vol. 8, no. 5 (October, November,
1987), p. 44. English. DESCR: Biography;
Engineering as a Profession; Mexican
American Engineering Society (MAES).

Castro, Zeke

1487 Douthat, Bill. Mariachi magic. VISTA, Vol.
2, no. 4 (December 7, 1986), p. 18. English.
DESCR: Austin, TX; Mariachi Rebeldes del
Sur; *Mariachis; Music; Secondary School
Education.

Casuso, Jorge

1488 Perez, Renato E. Chicago: Hispanic melting
pot. VISTA, Vol. 1, no. 3 (November 3,
1985), p. 20. English. DESCR: Camacho,
Eduardo; *Chicago, IL; Cultural Pluralism;
Ethnic Groups; HISPANICS IN CHICAGO;
*Population.

THE CAT AND OTHER STORIES

1489 Paredes, Raymund A. Review essay: recent
Chicano writing. ROCKY MOUNTAIN REVIEW OF
LANGUAGE AND LITERATURE, Vol. 41, (1987),
p. 124-129. English. DESCR: Castillo, Ana;
Catholic Church; Chavez, Denise; Chicanas;
Garcia, Lionel; GIVING UP THE GHOST; LEAVING
HOME; *Literary Criticism; *Literature
Reviews; Moraga, Cherrie; Poetry; Prose; Sex
Roles; Silva, Beverly; SMALL FACES; Soto,
Gary; THE LAST OF THE MENU GIRLS; THE
MIXQUIAHUALA LETTERS.

Catholic Church

1490 Allsup, Dan. A Texas hello for John Paul II.
VISTA, Vol. 3, no. 1 (September 6, 1987), p.
8-9. English. DESCR: *Clergy; *Pope John
Paul II; San Antonio, TX.

1491 Burciaga, Jose Antonio. In celebration of a
man's ecumenism. VISTA, Vol. 2, no. 4
(December 7, 1986), p. 26. English. DESCR:
Congregation B'nai Zion, El Paso, TX;
Holidays; Jews; *Religion.

1492 Cutter, Donald C. With a little help from
their saints. PACIFIC HISTORICAL REVIEW,
Vol. 53, no. 2 (1984), p. 123-140. English.
DESCR: Religion; *Santos.

1493 Diekemper, Barnabas C. The Catholic Church
in the shadows: the southwestern United
States during the Mexican period. JOURNAL OF
THE WEST, Vol. 24, no. 2 (1985), p. 46-53.
English. DESCR: Missions; Religion;
*Southwestern United States.

1494 Doyle, Janet. Escoja educacion catolica!
MOMENTUM, Vol. 14, no. 1 (February 1983), p.
37-38. English. DESCR: Religious Education;
Toledo, OH.

1495 Elford, George. Catholic schools and
bilingual education. MOMENTUM, Vol. 14, no.
1 (February 1983), p. 35-37. English.
DESCR: Bilingual Bicultural Education;
Religious Education.

1496 Gann, Lewis H. and Duignan, Peter J. Latinos
& the Catholic Church in America. NUESTRO,
Vol. 11, no. 4 (May 1987), p. 10-13.
English. DESCR: Culture; Encuentro Movement
[Catholic Church]; History; Primer Encuentro
Nacional Hispano, Washington, DC, June 1972.

1497 Garcia, Philip. Book review of: CHICANOS,
CATHOLICISM, AND POLITICAL IDEOLOGY.
AMERICAN POLITICAL SCIENCE REVIEW, Vol. 81,
(January 1987), p. 642-643. English.
DESCR: Book Reviews; *CHICANOS, CATHOLICISM,
AND POLITICAL IDEOLOGY; Mosqueda, Lawrence
J.

1498 Jaramillo, Luis. A Modern Parable; Too Late
Your Tears!! EL CUADERNO, Vol. 1, no. 1
(1971), p. 15-17. English.

1499 Paredes, Raymund A. Review essay: recent
Chicano writing. ROCKY MOUNTAIN REVIEW OF
LANGUAGE AND LITERATURE, Vol. 41, (1987),
p. 124-129. English. DESCR: Castillo, Ana;
Chavez, Denise; Chicanas; Garcia, Lionel;
GIVING UP THE GHOST; LEAVING HOME; *Literary
Criticism; *Literature Reviews; Moraga,
Cherrie; Poetry; Prose; Sex Roles; Silva,
Beverly; SMALL FACES; Soto, Gary; THE CAT
AND OTHER STORIES; THE LAST OF THE MENU
GIRLS; THE MIXQUIAHUALA LETTERS.

Catholic Church (cont.)

1500 Reyes, Abraham. Autochthonous church and liberation. EL CUADERNO, Vol. 2, no. 1 (1972), p. 14-15. English. **DESCR**: Liberation Theology.

1501 Rubio Goldsmith, Raquel. Shipwrecked in the desert: a short history of the adventures and struggles for survival of the Mexican Sisters of the House of the Providence in Douglas, Arizona during their first twenty-two years of existence (1927-1949). RENATO ROSALDO LECTURE SERIES MONOGRAPH, Vol. 1, (Summer 1985), p. [39]-67. English. **DESCR**: Chicanas; Clergy; Douglas, AZ; History; *House of the Divine Providence [convent], Douglas, AZ.

1502 Stevens-Arroyo, Antonio M. Cahensly revisited?: the National Pastoral Encounter of America's Hispanic Catholics. MIGRATION WORLD MAGAZINE, Vol. 15, no. 3 (1987), p. 16-19. English. **DESCR**: Clergy; *National Hispanic Pastoral Encounter; The Lucerne Memorial.

CELSO

1503 Gardiol, Rita. Book review of: CELSO. LECTOR, Vol. 4, no. 4-6 (1987), p. 76-77. English. **DESCR**: Book Reviews; Romero, Leo.

Censorship

1504 Ortiz, Francisco. La cultura chicana, la cultura amenazada. LA COMUNIDAD, No. 305 (May 25, 1986), p. 10-11. Spanish. **DESCR**: Anaya, Rudolfo A.; *BLESS ME, ULTIMA; Bloomfield, NM; Literary Criticism; New Mexico; Textbooks.

Census

1505 Chiswick, Barry R. The labor market status of Hispanic men. JOURNAL OF AMERICAN ETHNIC HISTORY, Vol. 7, no. 1 (Fall 1987), p. 30-58. English. **DESCR**: Discrimination in Employment; *Employment; Ethnic Groups; Income; *Labor Supply and Market; Language Usage; *Males; *Undocumented Workers.

1506 Fitch, Ed. Census bureau tries to clean up its act. ADVERTISING AGE MAGAZINE, Vol. 57, no. 43 (August 11, 1986), p. S18-S20. English. **DESCR**: Marketing; *U.S. Bureau of the Census.

1507 Massey, Douglas S. and Mullan, Brendan P. Processes of Hispanic and Black spatial assimilation. AMERICAN JOURNAL OF SOCIOLOGY, Vol. 89, no. 4 (January 1984), p. 836-873. English. **DESCR**: Assimilation; Blacks; *Ethnic Stratification; *Residential Segregation; *Social Mobility.

1508 Passel, Jeffrey S. Estimating the number of undocumented aliens. MONTHLY LABOR REVIEW, Vol. 109, no. 9 (September 1986), p. 33. English. **DESCR**: *Undocumented Workers.

Center for Mexican American Studies (CMAS), University of Texas, Austin, TX

1509 Perez, Emma. Research centers. LA RED/THE NET, no. 96 (May 1986), p. 3-6. English. **DESCR**: *Research Centers.

Center for U.S.-Mexican Studies, University of California at San Diego, La Jolla, CA

1510 Hunsaker, Alan C. Institutionally-based research centers: the Center for U.S.-Mexican Studies. LA RED/THE NET, no. 92 (November, December, 1985), p. 13-15. English. **DESCR**: Del Castillo, Gustavo; Meyer, Lorenzo; *Research Centers; United States-Mexico Relations.

Central America

1511 Anaya, Toney and Lujan, Edward. Sanctuary: right or wrong? VISTA, Vol. 1, no. 11 (July 6, 1986), p. 18-19, 21. English. **DESCR**: Deportation; Political History and Conditions; *Political Refugees.

1512 Rodriguez, Nestor. Undocumented Central Americans in Houston: diverse populations. INTERNATIONAL MIGRATION REVIEW, Vol. 21, no. 1 (Spring 1987), p. 4-26. English. **DESCR**: El Salvador; Ethnic Groups; Guatemala; Honduras; *Houston, TX; Immigrants; Intergroup Relations; Latin Americans; *Political Refugees; *Undocumented Workers.

1513 Rodriguez, Roberto. Central Americans and the new immigration law=La nueva ley de inmigracion y la comunidad Centro Americana. AMERICAS 2001, Premiere Issue, 1987, p. 28,43. Bilingual. **DESCR**: *Immigration Law and Legislation; *Immigration Reform and Control Act of 1986; Latin Americans.

1514 Wald, Karen. U.S. defector "didn't want to fight in Central America". GUARDIAN, Vol. 38, no. 44 (September 10, 1986), p. 12. English. **DESCR**: *Military; *Romeu Almeida, Hugo.

1515 What is your opinion of U.S. policy towards Central America?=Cual es tu opinion sobre la politica norteamericana hacia Centro America? AMERICAS 2001, Vol. 1, no. 2 (September, October, 1987), p. 21. Bilingual. **DESCR**: International Relations; *Public Opinion; Surveys.

Centro Cultural de la Raza, San Diego, CA

1516 Goldman, Shifra. Hecho en Aztlan. LA COMUNIDAD, No. 278 (November 17, 1985), p. 8-9. Spanish. **DESCR**: *Art; Exhibits; *HECHO EN AZTLAN [exhibit].

Centro de Estudios Puertorriquenos, Hunter College of the City University of New York

1517 Perez, Emma. Research centers. LA RED/THE NET, no. 97 (June 1986), p. 6-8. English. **DESCR**: *Research Centers.

Centro de Impotencia, Coral Gables Hospital, Miami, FL

1518 Valdez, William J. Impotence: a problem with a solution. NUESTRO, Vol. 11, no. 4 (May 1987), p. 18-20. English. **DESCR**: Diseases; *Impotence; Males; Medical Clinics; *Psychotherapy.

Centro de Promocion Popular Urbana, Tijuana, Baja California, Mexico

1519 Cisneros, Henry. Mexico's poorest are heading North. AKWESASNE NOTES, Vol. 18, no. 4 (Summer 1986), p. 7. English. **DESCR**: Alfaro, Victor Clark; Farm Workers; Kearney, Michael; Mexico; Mixtec Indians; *Undocumented Workers.

Cerebral Cysticercosis

1520 McMenamin, Jerry. Language deficits in a bilingual child with cerebral cysticercosis. BILINGUAL REVIEW, Vol. 11, no. 3 (September, December, 1984), p. 25-30. English. **DESCR:** Bilingualism; Diseases; Handicapped; *Language Development.

Cervantes, Frederick A.

1521 Mazon, Mauricio. Report to the Network. LA RED/THE NET, no. 95 (April 1986), p. 1-2. English. **DESCR:** Biography.

Cervantes, Lorna Dee

1522 Billings, Linda M. and Alurista. In verbal murals: a study of Chicana herstory and poetry. CONFLUENCIA, Vol. 2, no. 1 (Fall 1986), p. 60-68. English. **DESCR:** Candelaria, Cordelia; *Chicanas; Cisneros, Sandra; EMPLUMADA; *Feminism; History; Literary Criticism; *Poetry; Xelina.

1523 Elias, Edward F. A meeting of poets from east and west: Lorna Dee Cervantes, Gary Soto, Tato Laviera. BILINGUAL REVIEW, Vol. 12, no. 1-2 (January, August, 1985), p. 150-155. English. **DESCR:** Authors; *EMPLUMADA; *ENCLAVE; Laviera, Tato; Literary Criticism; Literature Reviews; Poetry; Soto, Gary; *WHERE SPARROWS WORK HARD.

1524 Quintana, Alvina. Challenge and counter challenge: Chicana literary motifs. AGAINST THE CURRENT, Vol. 2, no. 2 (March, April, 1987), p. 25,28-32. English. **DESCR:** *Chicanas; *Feminism; *Literature; Moraga, Cherrie; THERE ARE NO MADMEN HERE; Valdes, Gina.

El Cervantes Media Awards

1525 Hispanic media awards. TELEVISION/RADIO AGE, Vol. 31, (January 23, 1984), p. 17-18. English. **DESCR:** *Advertising; Awards.

Chabran, Richard

1526 Woods, Richard D. Book review of: CHICANO PERIODICAL INDEX: A CUMULATIVE INDEX TO SELECTED CHICANO PERIODICALS BETWEEN 1967 AND 1978. LA RED/THE NET, no. 52 (March 1982), p. 5-6. English. **DESCR:** Book Reviews; *CHICANO PERIODICAL INDEX; *Garcia-Ayvens, Francisco; Periodical Indexes.

Chacon [family name]

1527 Instituto Genealogico e Historico Latino-Americano. Rootsearch: Robles: Chacon: Molina. VISTA, Vol. 3, no. 1 (September 6, 1987), p. 30. English. **DESCR:** Genealogy; History; *Molina [family name]; *Personal Names; *Robles [family name].

Chacon, Rafael

1528 Alberts, Don E. Book review of: LEGACY OF HONOR: THE LIFE OF RAFAEL CHACON, A NINETEENTH-CENTURY NEW MEXICAN. NEW MEXICO HISTORICAL REVIEW, Vol. 62, no. 4 (October 1987), p. 403-5. English. **DESCR:** Book Reviews; *LEGACY OF HONOR: THE LIFE OF RAFAEL CHACON, A NINETEENTH CENTURY NEW MEXICAN; *Meketa, Jacqueline Dorgan.

Chacon Soto, Mario

1529 Evans, James. From chaos to quality education. VISTA, Vol. 3, no. 4 (December 6, 1987), p. 18, 35. English. **DESCR:** Awards; *Educational Administration; Educational Theory and Practice; Horace Mann Middle School, Mission District, San Francisco, CA.

Chamizal Memorial Federal Park

1530 Flynn, Ken. A triumph of diplomacy. VISTA, Vol. 3, no. 2 (October 3, 1987), p. 22-24. English. **DESCR:** *Border Region; Ciudad Juarez, Chihuahua, Mexico; *El Chamizal [region]; El Paso, TX.

El Chamizal [region]

1531 Flynn, Ken. A triumph of diplomacy. VISTA, Vol. 3, no. 2 (October 3, 1987), p. 22-24. English. **DESCR:** *Border Region; Chamizal Memorial Federal Park; Ciudad Juarez, Chihuahua, Mexico; El Paso, TX.

Chang-Diaz, Franklin

1532 Pinon, Fernando. Conquistadors of space. VISTA, Vol. 1, no. 4 (December 7, 1985), p. 6-9. English. **DESCR:** *Astronauts; Biography; *Gutierrez, Sidney.

1533 SHPE holds first ever East coast conference for Hispanic engineers. HISPANIC ENGINEER, Vol. 3, no. 5 (Winter 1987), p. 12-14. English. **DESCR:** Awards; Barrios, Eugene; *Conferences and Meetings; Cuevas, Brian L.; Garay, Charles J.; Garcia, Ray; Marrero, Charles; Martinez, Lisa; Monteverde, Edwin; Plumey, Raymond; Reyes-Guerra, David; Rivera, Angel; Society of Hispanic Professional Engineers (SHPE); Soto, Giovanni.

THE CHANGING DEMOGRAPHY OF SPANISH-AMERICANS

1534 Alvirez, David. Book review of: THE CHANGING DEMOGRAPHY OF SPANISH AMERICANS. LA RED/THE NET, no. 48 (November 1981), p. 4. English. **DESCR:** Book Reviews; Boswell, Thomas D.; Cullen, Ruth M.; Jaffee, A.J.; Population.

CHANTS

1535 Mora, Pat and Alarcon, Norma. A poet analyzes her craft. NUESTRO, Vol. 11, no. 2 (March 1987), p. 25-27. English. **DESCR:** *Authors; BORDERS; *Chicanas; *Mora, Pat; *Poetry.

Charreada

1536 LeCompte, Mary Lou and Beezley, William H. Any Sunday in April: the rise of sport in San Antonio and the Hispanic borderlands. JOURNAL OF SPORT HISTORY, Vol. 13, no. 2 (Summer 1986), p. 128-146. English. **DESCR:** *Cultural Customs; History; *San Antonio, TX; *Sports.

1537 LeCompte, Mary Lou. The Hispanic influence on the history of rodeo, 1823-1922. JOURNAL OF SPORT HISTORY, Vol. 12, no. 1 (Spring 1985), p. 21-38. English. **DESCR:** *Cultural Customs; *History; *Mexico.

Chavarria, Jesus

1538 Norris, Eileen. Print suffers in tale of two languages. ADVERTISING AGE MAGAZINE, Vol. 57, no. 16 (February 27, 1986), p. 49-51. English. **DESCR:** Advertising; English Language; HISPANIC BUSINESS; LATINA [magazine]; *Magazines; Soto, Grace; Spanish Language; Villar, Arturo; VISTA [magazine].

Chaves [family name]

1539 Instituto Genealogico e Historico
Latino-Americano. Rootsearch: Garcia:
Chaves. VISTA, Vol. 1, no. 10 (June 8,
1986), p. 26. English. **DESCR**: *Garcia
[family name]; Genealogy; History; *Personal
Names.

Chaves, Tony

1540 Winston, Bonnie. High tech jobs in the
Midwest. HISPANIC ENGINEER, Vol. 3, no. 1
(Spring 1987), p. 50-53. English. **DESCR**:
*Engineering as a Profession; Mosquera,
Jaime "Jim"; Rodriguez Howell, Nilsa;
Sanchez, Francisco G.

Chavez, Andres

1541 Barro, Mary Helen. 1973 Emmy Awards. LATIN
QUARTER, Vol. 1, no. 1 (July 1974), p. 5-6.
English. **DESCR**: CINCO VIDAS; Emmy Awards;
*Esparza, Moctezuma; Identity; Quintero,
Carlos; *Recreation; REFLECCIONES;
Rodriguez, Sandra; Rodriguez, Tony; Ruiz,
Jose Luis; Stereotypes; Television.

Chavez, Cesar E.

1542 Sanders, Bob. Boycott Campbell's: Ohio
farmworkers take it to the top. DOLLARS AND
SENSE, no. 92 (December 1983), p. 16-18.
English. **DESCR**: Boycotts; Campbell Soup Co.;
Farm Labor Organizing Commmittee (FLOC);
Farm Workers; Guevas, Fernando; *Labor
Disputes; Labor Unions; Ohio; Strikes and
Lockouts; United Farmworkers of America
(UFW).

Chavez, Denise

1543 Anaya, Rudolfo A. Book review of: THE LAST
OF THE MENU GIRLS. VISTA, Vol. 1, no. 11
(July 6, 1986), p. 16. English. **DESCR**: Book
Reviews; *THE LAST OF THE MENU GIRLS.

1544 Castillo-Speed, Lillian. Chicana/Latina
literature and criticism: reviews of recent
books. WLW JOURNAL, Vol. 11, no. 3
(September 1987), p. 1-4. English. **DESCR**:
Andrews, Lynn V.; *Book Reviews; BORDERS;
*Chicanas; CONTEMPORARY CHICANA POETRY: A
CRITICAL APPROACH TO AN EMERGING LITERATURE;
Flores, Angel; Flores, Kate; JAGUAR WOMAN;
Mora, Pat; Sanchez, Marta Ester; Tafolla,
Carmen; THE DEFIANT MUSE: HISPANIC FEMINIST
POEMS FROM THE MIDDLE AGES TO THE PRESENT;
THE LAST OF THE MENU GIRLS; TO SPLIT A
HUMAN: MITOS, MACHOS Y LA MUJER CHICANA;
Vigil-Pinon, Evangelina; WOMAN OF HER WORD:
HISPANIC WOMEN WRITE.

1545 Paredes, Raymund A. Review essay: recent
Chicano writing. ROCKY MOUNTAIN REVIEW OF
LANGUAGE AND LITERATURE, Vol. 41, (1987),
p. 124-129. English. **DESCR**: Castillo, Ana;
Catholic Church; Chicanas; Garcia, Lionel;
GIVING UP THE GHOST; LEAVING HOME; *Literary
Criticism; *Literature Reviews; Moraga,
Cherrie; Poetry; Prose; Sex Roles; Silva,
Beverly; SMALL FACES; Soto, Gary; THE CAT
AND OTHER STORIES; THE LAST OF THE MENU
GIRLS; THE MIXQUIAHUALA LETTERS.

Chavez, John R.

1546 Almaraz, Felix D., Jr. Book review of: THE
LOST LAND. ARIZONA AND THE WEST, Vol. 28,
no. 1 (Spring 1986), p. 81-82. English.
DESCR: Book Reviews; *THE LOST LAND: THE
CHICANO IMAGE OF THE SOUTHWEST.

1547 Crisp, James E. Book review of: THE LOST
LAND. JOURNAL OF SOUTHERN HISTORY, Vol. 51,
no. 4 (November 1985), p. 660-661. English.
DESCR: Book Reviews; *THE LOST LAND: THE
CHICANO IMAGE OF THE SOUTHWEST.

1548 de Leon, Arnoldo. Book review of: THE LOST
LAND. SOUTHWESTERN HISTORICAL QUARTERLY,
Vol. 89, no. 1 (1985), p. 96-98. English.
DESCR: Book Reviews; *THE LOST LAND: THE
CHICANO IMAGE OF THE SOUTHWEST.

1549 Paredes, Raymund A. Book review of: THE LOST
LAND. WESTERN AMERICAN LITERATURE, Vol. 21,
no. 2 (1986), p. 135. English. **DESCR**: Book
Reviews; *THE LOST LAND: THE CHICANO IMAGE
OF THE SOUTHWEST.

Chavez, Linda

1550 Llorente, Elizabeth. Linda Chavez: thriving
on controversy. VISTA, Vol. 3, no. 3
(November 8, 1987), p. 6-9. English. **DESCR**:
*English Language; Politics; U.S. English.

1551 McNeely, Dave. Hispanic power at the polls.
VISTA, Vol. 2, no. 3 (November 2, 1986), p.
8-12. English. **DESCR**: Austin, TX; *Barrera,
Roy, Jr.; Elected Officials; Gonzalez, Raul;
Martinez, Bob; Maryland; Political System;
San Antonio, TX; Statistics; Tampa, FL;
*Voter Turnout.

Chavira, Juan Antonio

1552 Blea, Irene I. Book review of: CURANDERISMO.
LA RED/THE NET, no. 55 (June 1982), p. 3-4.
English. **DESCR**: Book Reviews; Curanderismo;
*Trotter, Robert.

1553 Thiederman, Sondra Barrett. Book review of:
CURANDERISMO. WESTERN FOLKLORE, Vol. 42, no.
4 (October 1983), p. 317-318. English.
DESCR: Book Reviews; *CURANDERISMO,
MEXICAN-AMERICAN FOLK HEALING; Trotter,
Robert.

Chicago, IL

1554 Arce, Carlos H. Chicano voting. LA RED/THE
NET, no. 53 (April 1982), p. 2-4. English.
DESCR: *Southwestern United States; *Voter
Turnout.

1555 Dunn, William. Chicago's Hispanics. AMERICAN
DEMOGRAPHICS, Vol. 9, no. 2 (February 1987),
p. 52-53. English. **DESCR**: Population;
Statistics; U.S. Bureau of the Census.

1556 Heaney, Thomas W. "Hanging on" or "gaining
ground": educating marginal adults. NEW
DIRECTIONS FOR CONTINUING EDUCATION, Vol.
20, (December 1983), p. 53-63. English.
DESCR: *Adult Education; *Adult Education
Center of Lakeview; Community School
Relationships; Education.

1557 Kuner, Charles. Peer group counseling:
applied psychology in the high school.
CURRICULUM REVIEW, Vol. 23, no. 1 (February
1984), p. 89-92. English. **DESCR**: Counseling
(Educational); *Counseling (Psychological);
Education; Farragut High School, Chicago,
IL; Students.

Chicago, IL (cont.)

1558 Munoz, Carlos, Jr. and Henry, Charles. Rainbow coalitions in four big cities: San Antonio, Denver, Chicago and Philadelphia. P.S. [AMERICAN POLITICAL SCIENCE ASSOCIATION], Vol. 19, no. 3 (Summer 1986), p. 598-609. English. **DESCR:** Blacks; Cisneros, Henry, Mayor of San Antonio, TX; Denver, CO; Elected Officials; Ethnic Groups; Intergroup Relations; Pena, Federico; Philadelphia, PA; Political Parties and Organizations; Political Representation; *Politics; San Antonio, TX; Urban Communities.

1559 Perez, Renato E. Badge of Hispanic pride. VISTA, Vol. 1, no. 12 (August 2, 1986), p. 9-11. English. **DESCR:** Broward County, FL; Dallas, TX; Houston, TX; *Los Angeles, CA; New York, NY; *Police; San Antonio, TX; San Diego, CA; Tucson, AZ.

1560 Perez, Renato E. Chicago: Hispanic melting pot. VISTA, Vol. 1, no. 3 (November 3, 1985), p. 20. English. **DESCR:** Camacho, Eduardo; Casuso, Jorge; Cultural Pluralism; Ethnic Groups; HISPANICS IN CHICAGO; *Population.

1561 Stern, Gwen. Research, action, and social betterment. AMERICAN BEHAVIOR SCIENTISTS, Vol. 29, no. 2 (November, December, 1985), p. 229-248. English. **DESCR:** *Chicanas; Medical Care; Research Methodology; The Latina Mother-Infant Project, Chicago, IL.

LA CHICANA: BUILDING FOR THE FUTURE

1562 Chavaria, Elvira. Book review of: THE STATE OF HISPANIC AMERICA, VOL. II and LA CHICANA: BUILDING FOR THE FUTURE. LA RED/THE NET, no. 68 (May 1983), p. 10-12. English. **DESCR:** Book Reviews; National Hispanic Center for Advanced Studies and Policy Analysis (NHCAS); *THE STATE OF HISPANIC AMERICA.

LA CHICANA: THE MEXICAN AMERICAN WOMAN

1563 Baca Zinn, Maxine. Book review of: LA CHICANA: MEXICAN AMERICAN WOMEN. LA RED/THE NET, no. 28 (March 1980), p. 10. English. **DESCR:** Book Reviews; Chicanas; Enriquez, Evangelina; *Mirande, Alfredo.

CHICANA VOICES: INTERSECTIONS OF CLASS, RACE AND GENDER

1564 Ramirez, Genevieve M. Book review of: CHICANA VOICES. THE AMERICAS REVIEW, Vol. 15, no. 1 (Spring 1987), p. 101-102. English. **DESCR:** Book Reviews; Chicanas; National Association for Chicano Studies (NACS).

Chicanas
SEE ALSO: Women
1565 Acuna, Rodolfo. Response to Cynthia Orozco. LA RED/THE NET, no. 79 (April 1984), p. 13-15. English. **DESCR:** *Orozco, Cynthia; Sexism.

1566 Alarcon, Norma. Making "familia" from scratch: split subjectivities in the work of Helena Maria Viramontes and Cherrie Moraga. THE AMERICAS REVIEW, Vol. 15, no. 3-4 (Fall, Winter, 1987), p. 147-159. English. **DESCR:** GIVING UP THE GHOST; *Literary Criticism; *Moraga, Cherrie; *Sex Roles; "Snapshots" [short story]; THE MOTHS AND OTHER STORIES; *Viramontes, Helen.

1567 Alvarado, Raul. Against all odds. HISPANIC ENGINEER, Vol. 3, no. 4 (Fall 1987), p. 10-11. English. **DESCR:** Education; Educational Statistics; National Merit Scholarships; Preliminary Scholastic Aptitude Test (PSAT); *Scholastic Aptitude Test (SAT); Stereotypes.

1568 Alvarez, Robert R. A profile of the citizenship process among Hispanics in the United States. INTERNATIONAL MIGRATION REVIEW, Vol. 21, no. 2 (Summer 1987), p. 327-351. English. **DESCR:** Identity; Immigration and Naturalization Service (INS); *Naturalization.

1569 Andrade, Sally J. Chicana adolescents and contraception issues. LA RED/THE NET, no. 35 (October 1980), p. 2,14. English. **DESCR:** *Birth Control; *Southwestern United States; *Youth.

1570 Baca Zinn, Maxine. Book review of: LA CHICANA: MEXICAN AMERICAN WOMEN. LA RED/THE NET, no. 28 (March 1980), p. 10. English. **DESCR:** Book Reviews; Enriquez, Evangelina; LA CHICANA: THE MEXICAN AMERICAN WOMAN; *Mirande, Alfredo.

1571 Baca Zinn, Maxine. Book review of: TWICE A MINORITY: MEXICAN-AMERICAN WOMEN. LA RED/THE NET, no. 32 (July 1980), p. 3-4. English. **DESCR:** Book Reviews; Melville, Margarita B.; *TWICE A MINORITY: MEXICAN-AMERICAN WOMEN.

1572 Baezconde-Garbanati, Lourdes and Salgado de Snyder, Nelly. Mexican immigrant women: a selected bibliography. HISPANIC JOURNAL OF BEHAVIORAL SCIENCES, Vol. 9, no. 3 (September 1987), p. 331-358. English. **DESCR:** *Bibliography; *Immigrants; *Women.

1573 Banks, Marissa Elena. Doing it right. HISPANIC BUSINESS, Vol. 9, no. 11 (November 1987), p. 56-61. English. **DESCR:** *Businesspeople; *Torrez, Esther A.; Torrez, Garnett & Associates, Los Angeles, CA.

1574 Barton, Amy E. Women farmworkers: their workplace and capitalist patriarchy. REVISTA MUJERES, Vol. 3, no. 2 (June 1986), p. 11-13. English. **DESCR:** Capitalism; Discrimination; *Farm Workers; Sexism.

1575 Bibliography. THE AMERICAS REVIEW, Vol. 15, no. 3-4 (Fall, Winter, 1987), p. 182-188. English. **DESCR:** *Bibliography; *Literary Criticism; Literature.

1576 Billings, Linda M. and Alurista. In verbal murals: a study of Chicana herstory and poetry. CONFLUENCIA, Vol. 2, no. 1 (Fall 1986), p. 60-68. English. **DESCR:** Candelaria, Cordelia; Cervantes, Lorna Dee; Cisneros, Sandra; EMPLUMADA; *Feminism; History; Literary Criticism; *Poetry; Xelina.

1577 Blanco, Gilbert M. Las Adelitas del Barrio. LATIN QUARTER, Vol. 1, no. 3 (January, February, 1975), p. 30-32. English. **DESCR:** City Terrace, CA; Community Development; Gangs; *Latin Empresses; Youth.

1578 Briody, Elizabeth K. Patterns of household immigration into South Texas. INTERNATIONAL MIGRATION REVIEW, Vol. 21, no. 1 (Spring 1987), p. 27-47. English. **DESCR:** *Family; *Immigrants; Sex Roles; *Social Mobility; *South Texas.

1579 Cabeza de Vaca, Darlene. Knowing the value God places on me... REVISTA MUJERES, Vol. 2, no. 1 (January 1985), p. 26-29. English. **DESCR:** Identity.

Chicanas (cont.)

1580 Carrillo, Ana, et al. History of Las Mujeres. REVISTA MUJERES, Vol. 1, no. 1 (January 1984), p. 4-5. English. **DESCR:** *Las Mujeres, University of California, Santa Cruz; *Organizations.

1581 Castellanos, Teresa and Lopez, Margarita. La huelga nos ha ensenado a hablar. REVISTA MUJERES, Vol. 3, no. 2 (June 1986), p. 22-28. Spanish. **DESCR:** Biography; Canneries; Strikes and Lockouts.

1582 Castillo-Speed, Lillian. Chicana/Latina literature and criticism: reviews of recent books. WLW JOURNAL, Vol. 11, no. 3 (September 1987), p. 1-4. English. **DESCR:** Andrews, Lynn V.; *Book Reviews; BORDERS; Chavez, Denise; CONTEMPORARY CHICANA POETRY: A CRITICAL APPROACH TO AN EMERGING LITERATURE; Flores, Angel; Flores, Kate; JAGUAR WOMAN; Mora, Pat; Sanchez, Marta Ester; Tafolla, Carmen; THE DEFIANT MUSE: HISPANIC FEMINIST POEMS FROM THE MIDDLE AGES TO THE PRESENT; THE LAST OF THE MENU GIRLS; TO SPLIT A HUMAN: MITOS, MACHOS Y LA MUJER CHICANA; Vigil-Pinon, Evangelina; WOMAN OF HER WORD: HISPANIC WOMEN WRITE.

1583 Chacon, Maria A., et al. Chicanas in California postsecondary education. LA RED/THE NET, no. 65 (Winter 1983), p. 3-24. English. **DESCR:** Higher Education; Research Methodology.

1584 Chavez, Lorenzo A. Tennis superstars. VISTA, Vol. 1, no. 8 (April 6, 1986), p. 14-16. English. **DESCR:** *Athletes; Fernandez, Gigi; Fernandez, Mary Joe; *Sabatini, Gabriela; Sports; Torres, Michele; Women.

1585 Cisneros, Sandra. Do you know me?: I wrote THE HOUSE ON MANGO STREET. THE AMERICAS REVIEW, Vol. 15, no. 1 (Spring 1987), p. 77-79. English. **DESCR:** Authors; Autobiography; *Cisneros, Sandra; *Prose; *THE HOUSE ON MANGO STREET.

1586 Cisneros, Sandra. Ghosts and voices: writing from obsession. THE AMERICAS REVIEW, Vol. 15, no. 1 (Spring 1987), p. 69-73. English. **DESCR:** *Authors; Autobiography; *Cisneros, Sandra; *Prose.

1587 Cisneros, Sandra. Living as a writer: choice and circumstance. REVISTA MUJERES, Vol. 3, no. 2 (June 1986), p. 68-72. English. **DESCR:** *Authors; Autobiography; *Cisneros, Sandra.

1588 Cisneros, Sandra. Notes to a young(er) writer. THE AMERICAS REVIEW, Vol. 15, no. 1 (Spring 1987), p. 74-76. English. **DESCR:** *Authors; Autobiography; *Cisneros, Sandra; *Prose.

1589 Cook, Annabel Kirschner. Diversity among Northwest Hispanics. SOCIAL SCIENCE JOURNAL, Vol. 23, no. 2 (April 1986), p. 205-216. English. **DESCR:** *Northwestern United States; *Population; *Socioeconomic Factors; Working Women.

1590 Cornell, Nancy. Forging links between societies. VISTA, Vol. 3, no. 3 (November 8, 1987), p. 24. English. **DESCR:** 1984 Republican Convention (Dallas, TX); *Olind, Rebecca Nieto; Working Women.

1591 Dates, Karen E. Coast Guard ocean engineer Lisa Martinez. HISPANIC ENGINEER, Vol. 3, no. 4 (Fall 1987), p. 30-34. English. **DESCR:** Discrimination in Education; *Engineering as a Profession; *Martinez, Lisa.

1592 Determined to advance. HISPANIC BUSINESS, Vol. 9, no. 7 (July 1987), p. 35. English. **DESCR:** *Careers; *Employment; *Latino Institute.

1593 Echaveste, Beatrice and Huerta, Dolores. In the shadow of the eagle: Huerta=A la sombra del aguila: Huerta. AMERICAS 2001, Vol. 1, no. 3 (November, December, 1987), p. 26-30. Bilingual. **DESCR:** Agricultural Labor Unions; Boycotts; *Farm Workers; *Huerta, Dolores; *United Farmworkers of America (UFW).

1594 Engle, Patricia L.; Scrimshaw, Susan C.M.; and Smidt, Robert. Sex differences in attitudes towards newborn infants among women of Mexican origin. MEDICAL ANTHROPOLOGY, Vol. 8, no. 2 (Spring 1984), p. 133-144. English. **DESCR:** *Attitudes; Cultural Characteristics; *Machismo; *Maternal and Child Welfare; *Parent and Child Relationships; Sex Roles.

1595 Fighting cervical cancer. NUESTRO, Vol. 11, no. 3 (April 1987), p. 26-27. English. **DESCR:** *Cancer; *Diseases.

1596 Foote, Cheryl. Book review of: IMAGES AND CONVERSATIONS. JOURNAL OF THE WEST, Vol. 24, no. 3 (July 1985), p. 121. English. **DESCR:** Book Reviews; IMAGES AND CONVERSATIONS: MEXICAN AMERICANS RECALL A SOUTHWESTERN PAST; *Martin, Patricia Preciado; Oral History.

1597 Frances Hesselbein. INTERCAMBIOS FEMENILES, Vol. 2, no. 6 (Spring 1987), p. 23. English. **DESCR:** *Girl Scouts of the United States of America; Hesselbein, Frances; *Leadership; Organizations; Women; Youth.

1598 Frisbie, William Parker; Opitz, Wolfgang; and Kelly, William R. Marital instability trends among Mexican Americans as compared to Blacks and Anglos: new evidence. SOCIAL SCIENCE QUARTERLY, Vol. 66, no. 3 (September 1985), p. 587-601. English. **DESCR:** Divorce; Marriage.

1599 Galindo, Letticia. Perceptions of pachuquismo and use of Calo/pachuco Spanish by various Chicana women. LA RED/THE NET, no. 48 (November 1981), p. 2,10. English. **DESCR:** Chicano Dialects; *Texas.

1600 Gettman, Dawn and Pena, Devon Gerardo. Women, mental health, and the workplace in a transnational setting. SOCIAL WORK, Vol. 31, no. 1 (January, February, 1986), p. 5-11. English. **DESCR:** *Border Industries; Employment; *Mental Health; Mexico; United States-Mexico Relations; Women; *Working Women.

1601 Gilbert, M. Jean. Alcohol consumption patterns in immigrant and later generation Mexican American women. HISPANIC JOURNAL OF BEHAVIORAL SCIENCES, Vol. 9, no. 3 (September 1987), p. 299-313. English. **DESCR:** Acculturation; *Alcoholism; *Attitudes; Cultural Characteristics; *Immigrants; Mexico.

1602 Grajeda Higley, Leilani. Irma Castro. VISTA, Vol. 2, no. 10 (June 7, 1987), p. 20. English. **DESCR:** *Biography; *Castro, Irma; *Chicano Federation of San Diego Co., Inc.; Civil Rights; Discrimination.

Chicanas (cont.)

1603 Guendelman, Sylvia. The incorporation of
     Mexican women in seasonal migration: a study
     of gender differences. HISPANIC JOURNAL OF
     BEHAVIORAL SCIENCES, Vol. 9, no. 3
     (September 1987), p. 245-264. English.
     DESCR: Immigrants; Marriage; Mexico;
     *Migration Patterns; *Sex Roles; *Women;
     *Women Men Relations; Working Women.

1604 Herrera, Alexandra. Desde Los Angeles con
     amor. FEM, Vol. 11, no. 55 (July 1987), p.
     21-23. Spanish. **DESCR:** *Criminal Acts; Los
     Angeles, CA.

1605 Herrera, Yvonne R. Professional development.
     INTERCAMBIOS FEMENILES, Vol. 2, no. 6
     (Spring 1987), p. 21. English. **DESCR:**
     *Leadership; *Women.

1606 Herrera-Sobek, Maria. Introduction. THE
     AMERICAS REVIEW, Vol. 15, no. 3-4 (Fall,
     Winter, 1987), p. 9-39. English. **DESCR:**
     *Literary Criticism; *Literature.

1607 Herrera-Sobek, Maria. The politics of rape:
     sexual transgression in Chicana fiction. THE
     AMERICAS REVIEW, Vol. 15, no. 3-4 (Fall,
     Winter, 1987), p. 171-181. English. **DESCR:**
     Cisneros, Sandra; *Feminism; Fiction; GIVING
     UP THE GHOST; *Literary Criticism;
     Lizarraga, Sylvia; Moraga, Cherrie; *Rape;
     "Red Clowns" [short story]; Sex Roles;
     "Silver Lake Road" [short story].

1608 Hurtado, Aida. Midwife practices in Hildago
     County, Texas. TRABAJOS MONOGRAFICOS, Vol.
     3, no. 1 (1987), p. 1-30. English. **DESCR:**
     *Hidalgo County, TX; *Maternal and Child
     Welfare.

1609 Interview: Rita Ricardo-Campbell.
     INTERCAMBIOS FEMENILES, Vol. 2, no. 6
     (Spring 1987), p. 10-11. English. **DESCR:**
     *Appointed Officials; Economics; Leadership;
     *Ricardo-Campbell, Rita.

1610 Jensen, Joan M. Crossing ethnic barriers in
     the Southwest: women's agricultural
     extension education, 1914-1940. AGRICULTURAL
     HISTORY, Vol. 60, no. 2 (Spring 1986), p.
     169-181. English. **DESCR:** *Agricultural
     Extension Service; Agriculture; Cabeza de
     Baca, Fabiola; History; New Mexico; *Rural
     Education.

1611 Johnson, Richard. The California housewife
     who succeeds as brave bullfighter. VISTA,
     Vol. 1, no. 5 (January 5, 1986), p. 12-15.
     English. **DESCR:** *Athletes; *Martinez,
     Raquel; Montes, Miguel; Munoz, Jesus.

1612 Jorgensen, Stephen R. and Adams, Russell P.
     Family planning needs and behavior of
     Mexican American women: a study of health
     care professionals and their clientele.
     HISPANIC JOURNAL OF BEHAVIORAL SCIENCES,
     Vol. 9, no. 3 (September 1987), p. 265-286.
     English. **DESCR:** Acculturation; *Attitudes;
     Birth Control; *Cultural Characteristics;
     *Family Planning; Fertility; Public Health;
     Stereotypes; Sterilization.

1613 Karnig, Albert K.; Welch, Susan; and Eribes,
     Richard A. Employment of women by cities in
     the Southwest. SOCIAL SCIENCE JOURNAL, Vol.
     21, no. 4 (October 1984), p. 41-48. English.
     DESCR: *Employment; Local Government;
     *Southwestern United States; Women.

1614 Kilgore, Julia. A risk taker. HISPANIC
     BUSINESS, Vol. 9, no. 12 (December 1987), p.
     44-47. English. **DESCR:** *Appointed Officials;

Biography; Careers; *Diaz Dennis, Patricia;
Federal Communications Commission (FCC).

1615 Lena Guerrero. INTERCAMBIOS FEMENILES, Vol.
     2, no. 6 (Spring 1987), p. 15,26. English.
     DESCR: *Guerrero, Lena; Leadership;
     Politics.

1616 Lewis, Tom J. Book review of: CONTEMPORARY
     CHICANA POETRY. WORLD LITERATURE TODAY, Vol.
     60, (Summer 1986), p. 453. English. **DESCR:**
     Book Reviews; *CONTEMPORARY CHICANA POETRY:
     A CRITICAL APPROACH TO AN EMERGING
     LITERATURE; Poetry; Sanchez, Marta Ester.

1617 Lomas, Clara. Libertad de no procrear: la
     voz de la mujer en "A una madre de nuestro
     tiempo" de Margarita Cota-Cardenas. REVISTA
     MUJERES, Vol. 2, no. 1 (January 1985), p.
     30-35. Spanish. **DESCR:** Feminism; Literary
     Criticism; Sex Stereotypes.

1618 Longeaux y Vasquez, Enriqueta. Soy Chicana
     Primero. EL CUADERNO, Vol. 1, no. 1 (1971),
     p. 17-22. English. **DESCR:** *Chicano Movement;
     *Feminism.

1619 Lopez-Knox wins fellowship award. HISPANIC
     TIMES, Vol. 8, no. 1 (December, January,
     1987), p. 21. English. **DESCR:** Awards;
     Biographical Notes; *Lopez-Knox, Joanne;
     Science.

1620 Marin, Christine. La Asociacion
     Hispano-Americana de Madres y Esposas:
     Tucson's Mexican American women in World War
     II. RENATO ROSALDO LECTURE SERIES MONOGRAPH,
     Vol. 1, (Summer 1985), p. [5]-18. English.
     DESCR: Cultural Organizations; History; *La
     Asociacion Hispano-Americana de Madres y
     Esposas, Tucson, AZ; Organizations; *Tucson,
     AZ; World War II.

1621 Mellado, Carmela. Hispanic women as leaders:
     expanding the stereotypes that bind us.
     HISPANIC ENGINEER, Vol. 3, no. 4 (Fall
     1987), p. 6. English. **DESCR:** Engineering as
     a Profession; *National Network of Hispanic
     Women.

1622 Mendoza, Lupe. Porque lo podemos hacer--a
     poco no? REVISTA MUJERES, Vol. 1, no. 2
     (June 1984), p. 33-37. Spanish. **DESCR:**
     Autobiography; Higher Education; *Mendoza,
     Lupe.

1623 Mills, Kay. Gloria Molina. MS. MAGAZINE,
     Vol. 13, (January 1985), p. 80-81+.
     English. **DESCR:** Biography; Elected
     Officials; *Molina, Gloria.

1624 Mora, Pat and Alarcon, Norma. A poet
     analyzes her craft. NUESTRO, Vol. 11, no. 2
     (March 1987), p. 25-27. English. **DESCR:**
     *Authors; BORDERS; CHANTS; *Mora, Pat;
     *Poetry.

1625 Olivera, Mercedes. The new Hispanic women.
     VISTA, Vol. 2, no. 11 (July 5, 1987), p.
     6-8. English. **DESCR:** Alvarez, Linda;
     Esquiroz, Margarita; Garcia, Juliet;
     *Hernandez, Antonia A.; Mohr, Nicolasa;
     Molina, Gloria; Pabon, Maria; Working Women.

1626 Ornelas, Yolanda. Determined to be
     acknowledged. REVISTA MUJERES, Vol. 4, no. 1
     (January 1987), p. 14-15. English. **DESCR:**
     Attitudes; *Biography; Cultural
     Characteristics.

Chicanas (cont.)

1627 Orozco, Aurora E. Un dia en la pisca de algodon. REVISTA MUJERES, Vol. 3, no. 2 (June 1986), p. 30. Spanish. **DESCR:** Biography; Farm Workers.

1628 Orozco, Cynthia. Chicana labor history: a critique of male consciousness in historical writing. LA RED/THE NET, no. 77 (January 1984), p. 2-5. English. **DESCR:** *Historiography; *Sexism; Working Women.

1629 Out of marriage, onto welfare and into poverty. REVISTA MUJERES, Vol. 4, no. 1 (January 1987), p. 39-40. English. **DESCR:** Divorce; Education; Welfare.

1630 Paredes, Raymund A. Review essay: recent Chicano writing. ROCKY MOUNTAIN REVIEW OF LANGUAGE AND LITERATURE, Vol. 41, (1987), p. 124-129. English. **DESCR:** Castillo, Ana; Catholic Church; Chavez, Denise; Garcia, Lionel; GIVING UP THE GHOST; LEAVING HOME; *Literary Criticism; Literature Reviews; Moraga, Cherrie; Poetry; Prose; Sex Roles; Silva, Beverly; SMALL FACES; Soto, Gary; THE CAT AND OTHER STORIES; THE LAST OF THE MENU GIRLS; THE MIXQUIAHUALA LETTERS.

1631 Patricia Diaz Dennis. INTERCAMBIOS FEMENILES, Vol. 2, no. 6 (Spring 1987), p. 8-9. English. **DESCR:** Appointed Officials; *Diaz Dennis, Patricia; Federal Communications Commission (FCC); Leadership; Legal Profession.

1632 Perez, Emma. Networks. LA RED/THE NET, No. 103 (December 1986), p. 2-5. English. **DESCR:** *Educational Organizations; *Higher Education; *Mujeres Activas en Letras y Cambio Social (MALCS).

1633 Quintana, Alvina. Challenge and counter challenge: Chicana literary motifs. AGAINST THE CURRENT, Vol. 2, no. 2 (March, April, 1987), p. 25,28-32. English. **DESCR:** Cervantes, Lorna Dee; *Feminism; *Literature; Moraga, Cherrie; THERE ARE NO MADMEN HERE; Valdes, Gina.

1634 Quintana, Alvina. Expanding a feminist view: challenge and counter-challenge in the relationship between women. REVISTA MUJERES, Vol. 2, no. 1 (January 1985), p. 11-18. English. **DESCR:** *Feminism.

1635 Quintana, Alvina. Her story. REVISTA MUJERES, Vol. 4, no. 1 (January 1987), p. 44-47. English. **DESCR:** *Oral History.

1636 Quintana, Alvina. O mama, with what's inside of me. REVISTA MUJERES, Vol. 3, no. 1 (January 1986), p. 38-40. English. **DESCR:** *Alarcon, Norma; Feminism; *Literary Criticism; Poetry; *"What Kind of Lover Have You Made Me, Mother?: Towards a Theory of Chicanas' Feminism and Cultural Identity Through Poetry" [article].

1637 Ramirez, Genevieve M. Book review of: CHICANA VOICES. THE AMERICAS REVIEW, Vol. 15, no. 1 (Spring 1987), p. 101-102. English. **DESCR:** Book Reviews; *CHICANA VOICES: INTERSECTIONS OF CLASS, RACE AND GENDER; National Association for Chicano Studies (NACS).

1638 Rebolledo, Tey Diana. The politics of poetics: or, what am I, a critic, doing in this text anyhow? THE AMERICAS REVIEW, Vol. 15, no. 3-4 (Fall, Winter, 1987), p. 129-138. English. **DESCR:** *Literary Criticism; Literary History; Literature.

1639 Rifkin, Jane M. New avenues for women in technology. HISPANIC TIMES, Vol. 8, no. 3 (May, June, 1987), p. 41. English. **DESCR:** Biographical Notes; Engineering as a Profession; *Ponce, Alice.

1640 Rifkin, Jane M. Up from the barrio...to fittest woman cop in the U.S.A. HISPANIC TIMES, Vol. 8, no. 1 (December, January, 1987), p. 38. English. **DESCR:** Biography; Careers; *Lopez, Theresa (Terry); *Police.

1641 Rivera, Yvette. Hispanic women's organizations and periodicals needed to communicate new options: Yvette Rivera report. MEDIA REPORT TO WOMEN, Vol. 12, no. 5 (September, October, 1984), p. 15. English. **DESCR:** Organizations; Periodicals.

1642 A road fraught with challenge leads to view from the top. HISPANIC TIMES, Vol. 8, no. 3 (May, June, 1987), p. 28. English. **DESCR:** Authors; Biography; Leadership; National Network of Hispanic Women; Torres, Celia Gonzales.

1643 Romero, Bertha. The exploitation of Mexican women in the canning industry and the effects of capital accumulation on striking workers. REVISTA MUJERES, Vol. 3, no. 2 (June 1986), p. 16-20. English. **DESCR:** Canneries; Capitalism; Labor Unions; Strikes and Lockouts; *Watsonville Canning and Frozen Food Co.

1644 Romero, Mary. Domestic service in the transition from rural to urban life: the case of la Chicana. WOMEN'S STUDIES QUARTERLY, Vol. 13, no. 3 (1987), p. 199-222. English. **DESCR:** Working Women.

1645 Romero, Mary and Margolis, Eric. Tending the beets: campesinas and the Great Western Sugar Company. REVISTA MUJERES, Vol. 2, no. 2 (June 1985), p. 17-27. English. **DESCR:** *Farm Workers; Food Industry; *Great Western Sugar Company, Hudson, CO.

1646 Roth, George. The sky is not her limit. VISTA, Vol. 2, no. 12 (August 1, 1987), p. 24. English. **DESCR:** *Engineering as a Profession; *Jaramillo, Sylvia.

1647 Rubio Goldsmith, Raquel. Shipwrecked in the desert: a short history of the adventures and struggles for survival of the Mexican Sisters of the House of the Providence in Douglas, Arizona during their first twenty-two years of existence (1927-1949). RENATO ROSALDO LECTURE SERIES MONOGRAPH, Vol. 1, (Summer 1985), p. [39]-67. English. **DESCR:** Catholic Church; Clergy; Douglas, AZ; History; *House of the Divine Providence [convent], Douglas, AZ.

1648 Ruelas, J. Oshi. Moments of change. REVISTA MUJERES, Vol. 4, no. 1 (January 1987), p. 23-33. English. **DESCR:** Attitudes; *Biography.

1649 Ruiz, Ivette M. Resena testimonial. REVISTA MUJERES, Vol. 1, no. 2 (June 1984), p. 7-10. English. **DESCR:** Book Reviews; Elsasser, Nan; *LAS MUJERES: CONVERSATIONS FROM A HISPANIC COMMUNITY; MacKenzie, Kyle; Tixier y Vigil, Yvonne.

Chicanas (cont.)

1650 Ruiz, Vicki Lynn. Obreras y madres: labor activism among Mexican women and its impact on the family. RENATO ROSALDO LECTURE SERIES MONOGRAPH, Vol. 1, (Summer 1985), p. [19]-38. English. **DESCR:** Child Care Centers; Children; History; *Labor Unions; *Mexico; Sex Roles; Women; *Working Women.

1651 Salazar-Nobles, Mary. Latinas must chart own course in workplace. VISTA, Vol. 2, no. 3 (November 2, 1986), p. 26. English. **DESCR:** Essays; *Feminism; Working Women.

1652 Salgado de Snyder, Nelly. The role of ethnic loyalty among Mexican immigrant women. HISPANIC JOURNAL OF BEHAVIORAL SCIENCES, Vol. 9, no. 3 (September 1987), p. 287-298. English. **DESCR:** Acculturation; *Culture; *Identity; Immigrants; Mental Health; *Mexico; *Women.

1653 Schmitt, Jack. Book review of: CONTEMPORARY CHICANA POETRY. LOS ANGELES TIMES BOOK REVIEW, (December 29, 1985), p. 8. English. **DESCR:** Book Reviews; *CONTEMPORARY CHICANA POETRY: A CRITICAL APPROACH TO AN EMERGING LITERATURE; Poetry; Sanchez, Marta Ester.

1654 Sellers, Jeff M. Challenging the myth of the traditional woman. HISPANIC BUSINESS, Vol. 9, no. 8 (August 1987), p. 15-16, 48. English. **DESCR:** *Businesspeople; *Careers; *Management; National Network of Hispanic Women; Sex Roles; Torres, Celia; Women; Zambrana, Ruth.

1655 Shapiro, Peter. Watsonville shows "it can be done". GUARDIAN, Vol. 39, no. 24 (March 25, 1987), p. 1,9. English. **DESCR:** Canneries; Labor Unions; NorCal Frozen Foods; *Strikes and Lockouts; *Watsonville Canning and Frozen Food Co.; Working Women.

1656 Shaw, Katherine. Antonia Hernandez. VISTA, Vol. 1, no. 2 (October 5, 1985), p. 16. English. **DESCR:** *Biography; *Hernandez, Antonia A.; Mexican American Legal Defense and Educational Fund (MALDEF).

1657 Soriano, Diane H. and Mejia, Gabriella S. "Ni he tenido tiempo para mi:" entrevista con Gabriella S. Mejia. REVISTA MUJERES, Vol. 1, no. 2 (June 1984), p. 38-41. Spanish. **DESCR:** Autobiography; Higher Education; *Mejia, Gabriella S.

1658 Soto, Shirlene. Book review of: MEXICAN WOMEN IN THE UNITED STATES: STRUGGLES PAST AND PRESENT. LA RED/THE NET, no. 35 (October 1980), p. 4. English. **DESCR:** Book Reviews; Del Castillo, Adelaida R.; *MEXICAN WOMEN IN THE UNITED STATES: STRUGGLES PAST AND PRESENT; *Mora, Magdalena.

1659 Soto, Shirlene. La Malinche: 16th century leader. INTERCAMBIOS FEMENILES, Vol. 2, no. 6 (Spring 1987), p. 13. English. **DESCR:** Leadership; *Malinche.

1660 Stern, Gwen. Research, action, and social betterment. AMERICAN BEHAVIOR SCIENTISTS, Vol. 29, no. 2 (November, December, 1985), p. 229-248. English. **DESCR:** Chicago, IL; Medical Care; Research Methodology; The Latina Mother-Infant Project, Chicago, IL.

1661 Stone, Eric. The daring designs of Elena Valencia. VISTA, Vol. 1, no. 9 (May 3, 1986), p. 6-8. English. **DESCR:** Biography; *Fashion; La Blanca [fashion label]; *Valencia, Elena.

1662 Susana Rendon. AMERICAS 2001, Vol. 1, no. 1 (June, July, 1987), p. [31]. Bilingual. **DESCR:** Biographical Notes; Businesspeople; *Rendon, Susana.

1663 Taylor, Elena. Chicanas in science. REVISTA MUJERES, Vol. 1, no. 1 (January 1984), p. 6-7. English. **DESCR:** *Science as a Profession.

1664 Taylor, Elena. Conversations with a Chicana physician. REVISTA MUJERES, Vol. 1, no. 2 (June 1984), p. 44-46. English. **DESCR:** Medical Education; Medical Personnel; *Solinas, Lisa.

1665 Third world women in multinational corporations--the Mexican American border. LA RED/THE NET, no. 25 (December 1979), p. 2. English. **DESCR:** *Border Industries; *Ciudad Juarez, Chihuahua, Mexico; Labor Supply and Market; *Multinational Corporations; *Working Women.

1666 Tienda, Marta and Glass, Jennifer. Household structure and labor-force participation of Black, Hispanic, and white mothers. DEMOGRAPHY, Vol. 22, no. 3 (August 1985), p. 381-394. English. **DESCR:** Anglo Americans; Blacks; *Extended Family; *Family; *Sex Roles; *Working Women.

1667 Tienda, Marta and Guhlman, Pat. The occupational position of employed Hispanic females. LA RED/THE NET, no. 69 (June 1983), p. 2-3. English. **DESCR:** Employment; Ethnic Stratification; *Women.

1668 Trager, Cara S. Carving out a niche in politics. HISPANIC BUSINESS, Vol. 9, no. 10 (October 1987), p. 29-31. English. **DESCR:** Biography; *Elected Officials; *Guerrero, Lena; Texas.

1669 Trager, Cara S. Women of the year. HISPANIC BUSINESS, Vol. 9, no. 6 (June 1987), p. 78-82. English. **DESCR:** Biography; *Businesspeople; Rivera, Betty.

1670 Varela, Vivian. Hispanic women's resource guide. COMMONGROUND MAGAZINE, Vol. 1, no. 3 (May 1983), p. 14-15. English. **DESCR:** *Directories; *Organizations.

1671 Vargas-Willis, Gloria and Cervantes, Richard C. Consideration of psychosocial stress in the treatment of the Latina immigrant. HISPANIC JOURNAL OF BEHAVIORAL SCIENCES, Vol. 9, no. 3 (September 1987), p. 315-329. English. **DESCR:** Discrimination in Employment; *Immigrants; Mental Health; *Psychotherapy; *Stress.

1672 Yarbro-Bejarano, Yvonne. Chicana literature from a Chicana feminist perspective. THE AMERICAS REVIEW, Vol. 15, no. 3-4 (Fall, Winter, 1987), p. 139-145. English. **DESCR:** *Feminism; *Literary Criticism; Literature.

1673 Yarbro-Bejarano, Yvonne. The female subject in Chicano theater: sexuality, race, and class. THEATRE JOURNAL, Vol. 38, no. 4 (December 1986), p. 389-407. English. **DESCR:** El Teatro Campesino; El Teatro de la Esperanza; Feminism; *Malinche; *Sex Roles; *Teatro; Teatro Nacional de Aztlan (TENAZ); WIT (Women in Teatro).

Chicanas (cont.)

1674 Ybarra, Lea. Book review of: LAS MUJERES: CONVERSATIONS FROM A HISPANIC COMMUNITY. LA RED/THE NET, no. 58 (September 1982), p. 5-6. English. **DESCR:** Book Reviews; *Elasser, Nan; *LAS MUJERES: CONVERSATIONS FROM A HISPANIC COMMUNITY; MacKenzie, Kyle; New Mexico; Tixier y Vigil, Yvonne.

1675 Yepes, Maria Elena. Lady bugs. LATIN QUARTER, Vol. 1, no. 4 (July, August, 1975), p. 28-31. English. **DESCR:** *Car Clubs; *Lady Bugs [car club]; Los Angeles, CA.

1676 Zavella, Patricia. "Abnormal intimacy": the varying work networks of Chicana cannery workers. FEMINIST STUDIES, Vol. 11, no. 3 (Fall 1985), p. 541-557. English. **DESCR:** Canneries; Discrimination in Employment; Labor Unions; *Natural Support Systems; *Working Women.

Chicanismo

1677 Martinez, Thomas M. Chicanismo. EPOCA: NATIONAL CONCILIO FOR CHICANO STUDIES JOURNAL, Vol. 1, no. 2 (Winter 1971), p. 35-39. English. **DESCR:** *Chicano Studies; *Values.

CHICANO AUTHORS: INQUIRY BY INTERVIEW

1678 Finch, Mark S. Book review of: CHICANO AUTHORS: INQUIRY BY INTERVIEW. KENTUCKY ROMANCE QUARTERLY, Vol. 32, no. 4 (1985), p. 435. English. **DESCR:** Book Reviews; Bruce-Novoa, Juan.

1679 Wreford, Mary. Book review of: CHICANO AUTHORS: INQUIRY BY INTERVIEW. LA RED/THE NET, no. 38 (January 1981), p. 3-4. English. **DESCR:** Authors; Book Reviews; *Bruce-Novoa, Juan.

El Chicano Cinco

1680 Duarte, Mario. El Chicano 5. LATIN QUARTER, Vol. 1, no. 1 (July 1974), p. 22. English. **DESCR:** *Rock Music.

CHICANO CINEMA: RESEARCH, REVIEWS AND RESOURCES

1681 Book review of: CHICANO CINEMA. FILM QUARTERLY, Vol. 40, no. 1 (Fall 1986), p. 39. English. **DESCR:** Book Reviews; Keller, Gary D.

1682 Garcia, Philip. Book review of: CHICANO CINEMA. LA RED/THE NET, no. 91 (October 1985), p. 13-14. English. **DESCR:** Book Reviews; Films; Keller, Gary D.

1683 West, Dennis. Book review of: CHICANO CINEMA. CINEASTE, Vol. 15, no. 1 (1986), p. 55. English. **DESCR:** Book Reviews; Keller, Gary D.

Chicano Dialects

1684 Aguirre, Adalberto, Jr. Book review of: CHICANO SOCIOLINGUISTICS. LA RED/THE NET, no. 51 (February 1982), p. 3-4. English. **DESCR:** Book Reviews; *CHICANO SOCIOLINGUISTICS; *Language Usage; *Penalosa, Fernando; *Sociolinguistics.

1685 Duran, Richard P. Book review of: CALO TAPESTRY. LA RED/THE NET, no. 32 (July 1980), p. 5. English. **DESCR:** CALO TAPESTRY; Language Usage; *Ortega, Adolfo.

1686 Duran, Richard P. Book review of: CHICANO SOCIOLINGUISTICS. LA RED/THE NET, no. 35

(October 1980), p. 3. English. **DESCR:** Book Reviews; CHICANO SOCIOLINGUISTICS; *Language Usage; *Penalosa, Fernando; *Sociolinguistics.

1687 Galindo, Letticia. Perceptions of pachuquismo and use of Calo/pachuco Spanish by various Chicana women. LA RED/THE NET, no. 48 (November 1981), p. 2,10. English. **DESCR:** *Chicanas; *Texas.

1688 Hidalgo, Margarita. On the question of "standard" versus "dialect": implications for teaching Hispanic college students. HISPANIC JOURNAL OF BEHAVIORAL SCIENCES, Vol. 9, no. 4 (December 1987), p. 375-395. English. **DESCR:** Bilingualism; *Foreign Language Instruction; Language Usage; Puerto Ricans; Sociolinguistics; Spanish for Native Speakers; *Spanish Language.

1689 Hutter, Harriet S. EL MILAGRUCHO: a linguistic commentary on a pachuco text. HISPANIA, Vol. 67, no. 2 (May 1984), p. 256-261. English. **DESCR:** EL MILAGRUCHO.

1690 Mendoza, Agapito. Barrio slang has value as communications tool. VISTA, Vol. 2, no. 12 (August 1, 1987), p. 29. English. **DESCR:** Slang.

1691 Ornstein-Galicia, Jacob. Chicano Calo: description and review of a border variety. HISPANIC JOURNAL OF BEHAVIORAL SCIENCES, Vol. 9, no. 4 (December 1987), p. 359-373. English. **DESCR:** Border Region; Pachucos; Sociolinguistics.

1692 Rodriguez, Salvador. El idioma de Aztlan: una lengua que surge. LA COMUNIDAD, No. 266 (August 25, 1985), p. 6-7. Spanish. **DESCR:** Bilingualism; Language Interference; Pachucos; Sociolinguistics; Spanish Language.

1693 Sanchez, Francisca S. The Chicano English dilemma: deficit or dialect? LA RED/THE NET, no. 79 (April 1984), p. 2-8. English. **DESCR:** Language Interference; *Language Usage.

CHICANO DISCOURSE: SOCIOHISTORIC PERSPECTIVE

1694 Jimenez, Francisco. Book review of: CHICANO DISCOURSE. LECTOR, Vol. 4, no. 4-6 (1987), p. 55. English. **DESCR:** Book Reviews; Sanchez, Rosaura; Sociolinguistics.

1695 Trueba, Henry T. and Delgado-Gaitan, Concha. Book review of: CHICANO DISCOURSE. LANGUAGE IN SOCIETY, Vol. 14, no. 2 (June 1985), p. 257-259. English. **DESCR:** Book Reviews; Sanchez, Rosaura.

CHICANO ENGLISH: AN ETHNIC CONTACT DIALECT

1696 Dubois, Betty Lou. Book review of: CHICANO ENGLISH: AN ETHNIC CONTACT DIALECT. CHOICE, Vol. 24, no. 1 (September 1986), p. 114. English. **DESCR:** Book Reviews; Ornstein-Galicia, Jacob; Penfield, Joyce.

THE CHICANO EXPERIENCE: AN ALTERNATIVE PERSPECTIVE

1697 Burns, Jeffrey M. Book review of: THE CHICANO EXPERIENCE. RELIGIOUS STUDIES REVIEW, Vol. 11, (October 1985), p. 418. English. **DESCR:** Book Reviews; Mirande, Alfredo.

THE CHICANO EXPERIENCE: AN ALTERNATIVE PERSPECTIVE
(cont.)

1698 Farley, J.E. Book review of: THE CHICANO EXPERIENCE. CHOICE, Vol. 23, no. 3 (November 1985), p. [483]. English. **DESCR:** Book Reviews; Mirande, Alfredo.

1699 Gutierrez, Ramon A. Book review of: THE CHICANO EXPERIENCE. AMERICAS, Vol. 43, no. 1 (July 1986), p. 134-136. English. **DESCR:** Book Reviews; Mirande, Alfredo.

1700 Tryon, Roy H. Book review of: THE CHICANO EXPERIENCE. LIBRARY JOURNAL, Vol. 110, (August 1985), p. 109. English. **DESCR:** Book Reviews; Mirande, Alfredo.

1701 Valdez, Avelardo. Book review of: THE CHICANO EXPERIENCE. JOURNAL OF AMERICAN ETHNIC HISTORY, Vol. 6, no. 2 (Spring 1987), p. 98-101. English. **DESCR:** Book Reviews; Mirande, Alfredo; Social History and Conditions.

Chicano Federation of San Diego Co., Inc.

1702 Grajeda Higley, Leilani. Irma Castro. VISTA, Vol. 2, no. 10 (June 7, 1987), p. 20. English. **DESCR:** *Biography; *Castro, Irma; Chicanas; Civil Rights; Discrimination.

A CHICANO IN CHINA

1703 Anaya, Rudolfo A. A Chicano in China. VISTA, Vol. 2, no. 1 (September 7, 1986), p. 19-21. English. **DESCR:** Anaya, Rudolfo A.; China; *Culture; Philosophy; *Tourism.

1704 Torres, Lourdes. Book review of: A CHICANO IN CHINA. WESTERN AMERICAN LITERATURE, Vol. 22, (Spring 1987), p. 66. English. **DESCR:** Anaya, Rudolfo A.; Book Reviews.

CHICANO INTERMARRIAGE: A THEORETICAL AND EMPIRICAL STUDY

1705 Abney, Armando. Chicano intermarriage: a theoretical and empirical study. LA RED/THE NET, no. 59 (October 1982), p. 4-6. English. **DESCR:** Book Reviews; *Intermarriage; *Murguia, Edward.

1706 Hall, Linda B. The United States-Mexican borders: historical, political, and cultural perspectives. LATIN AMERICAN RESEARCH REVIEW, Vol. 20, no. 2 (1985), p. 223-229. English. **DESCR:** AMERICAN LABOR IN THE SOUTHWEST: THE FIRST ONE HUNDRED YEARS; *Book Reviews; *Border Region; BOSS RULE IN SOUTH TEXAS: THE PROGRESSIVE ERA; HISPANIC CULTURE IN THE SOUTHWEST; IN DEFENSE OF LA RAZA: THE LOS ANGELES MEXICAN CONSULATE AND THE MEXICAN COMMUNITY; Literature Reviews; RACE AND CLASS IN THE SOUTHWEST: A THEORY OF RACIAL INEQUALITY; SOUTHWESTERN AGRICULTURE: PRE-COLUMBIAN TO MODERN; THE MEXICANS IN OKLAHOMA; THE POLITICS OF SAN ANTONIO.

1707 Ramirez, Daniel Moriel. Book review of: CHICANO INTERMARRIAGE: A THEORETICAL AND EMPIRICAL STUDY. SOCIAL FORCES, Vol. 62, no. 3 (March 1984), p. 833-835. English. **DESCR:** Book Reviews; Intermarriage; Murguia, Edward.

CHICANO LITERATURE: A REFERENCE GUIDE

1708 Book review of: CHICANO LITERATURE: A REFERENCE GUIDE. BOOKLIST, Vol. 82, no. 9 (January 1, 1986), p. 667-668. English. **DESCR:** Book Reviews; Lomeli, Francisco A.; Martinez, Julio A.; Reference Works.

1709 Brown, D.R. Book review of: CHICANO LITERATURE: A REFERENCE GUIDE. CHOICE, Vol. 23, no. 4 (December 1985), p. 578. English. **DESCR:** Book Reviews; Lomeli, Francisco A.; Martinez, Julio A.; Reference Works.

1710 Castillo-Speed, Lillian. Annotated bibliography. LA RED/THE NET, no. 93 (January, February, 1986), p. 14-17. English. **DESCR:** A BIBLIOGRAPHY OF MEXICAN AMERICAN HISTORY; ARTE CHICANO; Book Reviews; Caballero, Cesar; CHICANO ORGANIZATIONS DIRECTORY; CHICANO PERIODICAL INDEX; Goldman, Shifra M.; HISPANIC ALMANAC; HISPANIC MENTAL HEALTH RESEARCH: A REFERENCE GUIDE; Lomeli, Francisco A.; Martinez, Julio A.; Meier, Matt S.; Newton, Frank; *Reference Works; Ybarra-Frausto, Tomas.

1711 Haro, Robert P. Book review of: CHICANO LITERATURE: A REFERENCE GUIDE. AMERICAN REFERENCE BOOKS ANNUAL, Vol. 17, (1986), p. 440. English. **DESCR:** Book Reviews; Lomeli, Francisco A.; Martinez, Julio A.; Reference Works.

1712 Perry, Charles E. Book review of: CHICANO LITERATURE: A REFERENCE GUIDE. LIBRARY JOURNAL, Vol. 110, no. 5 (March 15, 1985), p. 53. English. **DESCR:** Book Reviews; Literature; Lomeli, Francisco A.; Martinez, Julio A.; Reference Works.

Chicano, Meaning of

1713 Aguilar, Andy. Mexico's children. AMERICAN SCHOLAR, Vol. 56, no. 1 (1987), p. 155-156. English.

1714 Figoli, Haydee. Dos textos a proposito de la frontera. LA COMUNIDAD, No. 350 (April 5, 1987), p. 2-5. Spanish. **DESCR:** Chicano Movement; *History; Mexico.

1715 Gutierrez, Ramon A. Unraveling America's Hispanic past: internal stratification and class boundaries. AZTLAN, Vol. 17, no. 1 (Spring 1986), p. 79-101. English. **DESCR:** Culture; *Ethnic Groups; *Identity; Intergroup Relations; *Self-Referents.

Chicano Movement

1716 Bueno, Patricia E. Los Chicanos y la politica II. LA COMUNIDAD, No. 268 (September 8, 1985), p. 2-3. Spanish. **DESCR:** American G.I. Forum; History; Leadership; Mexican American Political Association (MAPA); Nationalism; Political Association of Spanish-Speaking Organizations (PASO); *Political Parties and Organizations.

1717 East coast conference on "El Movimiento Chicano". LA RED/THE NET, no. 40 (March 1981), p. 7. English. **DESCR:** *Conferences and Meetings; *El Movimiento Chicano Conference, February 13-14, 1981.

1718 Figoli, Haydee. Dos textos a proposito de la frontera. LA COMUNIDAD, No. 350 (April 5, 1987), p. 2-5. Spanish. **DESCR:** Chicano, Meaning of; *History; Mexico.

1719 Gomez Pena, Guillermo. Nuevo continente artistico. LA COMUNIDAD, No. 275 (October 27, 1985), p. 8-10. Spanish. **DESCR:** *Art; Artists; Border Region; DIALOGOS DE LAS AMERICAS; Indigenismo; International Relations; Mexico; United States-Mexico Relations.

Chicano Movement (cont.)

1720 Longeaux y Vasquez, Enriqueta. Soy Chicana Primero. EL CUADERNO, Vol. 1, no. 1 (1971), p. 17-22. English. **DESCR:** *Chicanas; *Feminism.

1721 Martinez, Elizabeth. A decade of repression: update on the "Kiko" Martinez case. CRIME AND SOCIAL JUSTICE, no. 19 (Summer 1983), p. 100. English. **DESCR:** Civil Rights; Colorado; Criminal Justice System; Discrimination; Legal Cases; *Martinez, Francisco "Kiko"; Political Repression.

1722 Munoz, Carlos, Jr. Chicano politics: the current conjuncture. THE YEAR LEFT, Vol. 2, (1987), p. 35-52. English. **DESCR:** Identity; *Intergroup Relations; *Political Parties and Organizations; *Politics; Reagan Administration; Voter Turnout.

1723 Wells, Miriam J. Power brokers and ethnicity: the rise of a Chicano movement. AZTLAN, Vol. 17, no. 1 (Spring 1986), p. 47-77. English. **DESCR:** *Identity; *Natural Support Systems; *Patron System.

CHICANO ORGANIZATIONS DIRECTORY

1724 Castillo-Speed, Lillian. Annotated bibliography. LA RED/THE NET, no. 93 (January, February, 1986), p. 14-17. English. **DESCR:** A BIBLIOGRAPHY OF MEXICAN AMERICAN HISTORY; ARTE CHICANO; Book Reviews; Caballero, Cesar; CHICANO LITERATURE: A REFERENCE GUIDE; CHICANO PERIODICAL INDEX; Goldman, Shifra M.; HISPANIC ALMANAC; HISPANIC MENTAL HEALTH RESEARCH: A REFERENCE GUIDE; Lomeli, Francisco A.; Martinez, Julio A.; Meier, Matt S.; Newton, Frank; *Reference Works; Ybarra-Frausto, Tomas.

1725 Haro, Robert P. Book review of: CHICANO ORGANIZATIONS DIRECTORY. AMERICAN REFERENCE BOOKS ANNUAL, Vol. 17, (1986), p. 145. English. **DESCR:** Book Reviews; Caballero, Cesar; Reference Works.

1726 Powell, Carolyn L. Book review of: CHICANO ORGANIZATIONS DIRECTORY. VOICE OF YOUTH ADVOCATES, Vol. 8, no. 6 (February 1986), p. 408. English. **DESCR:** Book Reviews; Caballero, Cesar; Directories.

Chicano Park, San Diego, CA

1727 Goldman, Shifra. Escena de San Diego: texto y contexto. LA COMUNIDAD, No. 239 (February 17, 1985), p. 6-7. Spanish. **DESCR:** *Art; Avalos, David; Exhibits; *NUEVE ARTISTAS CHICANOS [exhibit]; San Diego, CA; Torres, Salvador Roberto; Ulloa, Domingo.

1728 Jacobs, Carole. Bridging cultures. SOUTHWEST ART, Vol. 15, (April 1986), p. 86. English. **DESCR:** *Mural Art; Ochoa, Victor.

CHICANO PERIODICAL INDEX

1729 Castillo-Speed, Lillian. Annotated bibliography. LA RED/THE NET, no. 93 (January, February, 1986), p. 14-17. English. **DESCR:** A BIBLIOGRAPHY OF MEXICAN AMERICAN HISTORY; ARTE CHICANO; Book Reviews; Caballero, Cesar; CHICANO LITERATURE: A REFERENCE GUIDE; CHICANO ORGANIZATIONS DIRECTORY; Goldman, Shifra M.; HISPANIC ALMANAC; HISPANIC MENTAL HEALTH RESEARCH: A REFERENCE GUIDE; Lomeli, Francisco A.; Martinez, Julio A.; Meier, Matt S.; Newton, Frank; *Reference Works; Ybarra-Frausto, Tomas.

1730 Woods, Richard D. Book review of: CHICANO PERIODICAL INDEX: A CUMULATIVE INDEX TO SELECTED CHICANO PERIODICALS BETWEEN 1967 AND 1978. LA RED/THE NET, no. 52 (March 1982), p. 5-6. English. **DESCR:** Book Reviews; *Chabran, Richard; *Garcia-Ayvens, Francisco; Periodical Indexes.

CHICANO POETRY: A CRITICAL INTRODUCTION

1731 Book review of: CHICANO POETRY: A CRITICAL INTRODUCTION. AMERICAN LITERATURE, Vol. 58, no. 3 (October 1986), p. 481-482. English. **DESCR:** Book Reviews; Candelaria, Cordelia.

1732 Krauth, Leland. Book review of: CHICANO POETRY: A CRITICAL INTRODUCTION. LIBRARY JOURNAL, Vol. 111, (April 15, 1986), p. 82. English. **DESCR:** Book Reviews; Candelaria, Cordelia; Poetry.

1733 Lint, Robert G. Book review of: CHICANO POETRY: A CRITICAL INTRODUCTION. WESTERN AMERICAN LITERATURE, Vol. 21, no. 4 (1987), p. 380. English. **DESCR:** Book Reviews; Candelaria, Cordelia.

1734 Luna-Lawhn, Juanita. Book review of: CHICANO POETRY: A CRITICAL INTRODUCTION. CHOICE, Vol. 23, no. 11-12 (July, August, 1986), p. 1672. English. **DESCR:** Book Reviews; Candelaria, Cordelia.

CHICANO POETRY: A RESPONSE TO CHAOS

1735 Flores, Lauro. Book review of: EL PUEBLO: THE GALLEGOS FAMILY'S JOURNEY 1503-1980. MINNESOTA REVIEW, no. 22 (1984), p. 145-148. English. **DESCR:** Book Reviews; Bruce-Novoa, Juan; *EL PUEBLO: THE GALLEGOS FAMILY'S AMERICAN JOURNEY 1503-1980; *FAMOUS ALL OVER TOWN; James, Dan; Johansen, Bruce; Maestas, Roberto.

Chicano Project of the University of Michigan

1736 Wreford, Mary. Reactions from the Chicano Survey respondents: no mas silencio. LA RED/THE NET, no. 33 (August 1980), p. 2-3. English. **DESCR:** Midwestern States; *National Chicano Survey (NCS); *Public Opinion; Social Science; Southwestern United States; *Surveys.

CHICANO PSYCHOLOGY

1737 Barona, Andres and Santos de Barona, Maryann. Chicano psychology: a new field? CONTEMPORARY PSYCHOLOGY, Vol. 31, no. 2 (February 1986), p. 106-107. English. **DESCR:** Book Reviews; Martinez, Joe L., Jr.; Mendoza, Richard H.

Chicano Resource Center, Los Angeles County Public Library

1738 Chavez, Linda. Celebrate! The Chicano Resource Center's 10th anniversary. LECTOR, Vol. 4, no. 1-3 (1986), p. In FtCover. English. **DESCR:** Library Collections; Public Libraries.

CHICANO SOCIOLINGUISTICS

1739 Aguirre, Adalberto, Jr. Book review of: CHICANO SOCIOLINGUISTICS. LA RED/THE NET, no. 51 (February 1982), p. 3-4. English. **DESCR:** Book Reviews; Chicano Dialects; *Language Usage; *Penalosa, Fernando; *Sociolinguistics.

CHICANO SOCIOLINGUISTICS (cont.)

1740 Duran, Richard P. Book review of: CHICANO
SOCIOLINGUISTICS. LA RED/THE NET, no. 35
(October 1980), p. 3. English. **DESCR:** Book
Reviews; Chicano Dialects; *Language Usage;
*Penalosa, Fernando; *Sociolinguistics.

THE CHICANO STRUGGLE: ANALYSES OF PAST AND PRESENT EFFORTS

1741 Weas, Andrea T. Book review of: THE CHICANO
STRUGGLE. LECTOR, Vol. 4, no. 4-6 (1987), p.
54. English. **DESCR:** Book Reviews; National
Association for Chicano Studies (NACS);
Social History and Conditions.

Chicano Studies

1742 Atencio, Tomas. La Academia de la Nueva
Raza: su historia. EL CUADERNO, Vol. 1, no.
1 (1971), p. 4-9. English. **DESCR:**
Alternative Education; Cultural
Organizations; *Educational Organizations;
*La Academia de la Nueva Raza, Dixon, NM;
Oro del Barrio.

1743 Atencio, Tomas. La Academia de la Nueva
Raza. EL CUADERNO, Vol. 2, no. 1 (1972), p.
6-13. English. **DESCR:** *Alternative
Education; Cultural Characteristics;
*Cultural Organizations; Education;
*Educational Organizations; *La Academia de
la Nueva Raza, Dixon, NM; Oro del Barrio;
Philosophy; Values.

1744 Atencio, Tomas. La Academia de la Nueva
Raza: El Oro del Barrio. EL CUADERNO, Vol.
3, no. 1 (Winter 1973), p. 4-15. English.
DESCR: Alternative Education; *Cultural
Organizations; *Educational Organizations;
*La Academia de la Nueva Raza, Dixon, NM;
Oro del Barrio.

1745 Atencio, Tomas. La resolana [editorial]. EL
CUADERNO, Vol. 4, no. 1 (Summer 1976), p.
2-4. English. **DESCR:** Academia Asociados, NM;
Academia Educational Model; Culture; EL
CUADERNO; ENTRE VERDE Y SECO; *La Academia
de la Nueva Raza, Dixon, NM; LA MADRUGADA;
Publishing Industry.

1746 Elizondo, Sergio D. Critical areas of need
for research and scholastic study. EPOCA:
NATIONAL CONCILIO FOR CHICANO STUDIES
JOURNAL, Vol. 1, no. 2 (Winter 1971), p.
1-7. English. **DESCR:** *Curriculum; Research
Methodology.

1747 Garcia, Mario T. Book review of: THE STATE
OF CHICANO RESEARCH ON FAMILY, LABOR, AND
MIGRATION: PROCEEDINGS OF THE FIRST STANFORD
SYMPOSIUM ON CHICANO RESEARCH AND PUBLIC
POLICY. CALIFORNIA HISTORY, Vol. 63, no. 3
(Summer 1984), p. 261-262. English. **DESCR:**
Almaguer, Tomas; Book Reviews; Camarillo,
Alberto; *THE STATE OF CHICANO RESEARCH IN
FAMILY, LABOR AND MIGRATION STUDIES; Valdez,
Armando.

1748 Griswold del Castillo, Richard. Book review
of: THE STATE OF CHICANO RESEARCH ON FAMILY,
LABOR, AND MIGRATION: PROCEEDINGS OF THE
FIRST STANFORD SYMPOSIUM ON CHICANO RESEARCH
AND PUBLIC POLICY. PACIFIC HISTORICAL
REVIEW, Vol. 54, no. 3 (August 1985), p.
381-382. English. **DESCR:** Almaguer, Tomas;
Book Reviews; Camarillo, Alberto; *THE STATE
OF CHICANO RESEARCH IN FAMILY, LABOR AND
MIGRATION STUDIES; Valdez, Armando.

1749 Guerra, Manuel H. What are the objectives of
Chicano studies? EPOCA: NATIONAL CONCILIO
FOR CHICANO STUDIES JOURNAL, Vol. 1, no. 2

(Winter 1971), p. 8-12. English. **DESCR:**
*Curriculum; Educational Theory and
Practice.

1750 Lopez, Manuel I. The role of the Chicano
student in the Chicano Studies Program.
EPOCA: NATIONAL CONCILIO FOR CHICANO STUDIES
JOURNAL, Vol. 1, no. 2 (Winter 1971), p.
13-17. English. **DESCR:** Higher Education; La
Raza; *Student Movements; *Students.

1751 Macias, Reynaldo Flores; Gomez-Quinones,
Juan; and Castro, Raymond. Objectives of
Chicano studies. EPOCA: NATIONAL CONCILIO
FOR CHICANO STUDIES JOURNAL, Vol. 1, no. 2
(Winter 1971), p. 31-34. English. **DESCR:**
*Educational Theory and Practice.

1752 Martinez, Eliud. Book review of: HISTORY,
CULTURE, AND SOCIETY. MODERN LANGUAGE
JOURNAL, Vol. 69, no. 4 (Winter 1985), p.
436-437. English. **DESCR:** Book Reviews;
Garcia, Mario T.; *HISTORY, CULTURE, AND
SOCIETY: CHICANO STUDIES IN THE 1980s;
National Association for Chicano Studies
(NACS).

1753 Martinez, Thomas M. Chicanismo. EPOCA:
NATIONAL CONCILIO FOR CHICANO STUDIES
JOURNAL, Vol. 1, no. 2 (Winter 1971), p.
35-39. English. **DESCR:** *Chicanismo; *Values.

1754 MEChA - University of Texas at El Paso;
MAYO, University of Texas at Austin; and
PASO, Texas A and I University. Student
perspectives on Mexican/American studies.
EPOCA: NATIONAL CONCILIO FOR CHICANO STUDIES
JOURNAL, Vol. 1, no. 2 (Winter 1971), p.
87-96. English. **DESCR:** Curriculum; Mexican
American Youth Organization (MAYO);
Movimiento Estudiantil Chicano de Aztlan
(MEChA); Student Organizations; Students;
Texas.

1755 MEChA, Cal State Long Beach. The role of the
Chicano student. EPOCA: NATIONAL CONCILIO
FOR CHICANO STUDIES JOURNAL, Vol. 1, no. 2
(Winter 1971), p. 18-22. English. **DESCR:**
Higher Education; *Student Movements;
*Students.

1756 Nunez, Rene. Criteria for employment of
Chicano studies staff. EPOCA: NATIONAL
CONCILIO FOR CHICANO STUDIES JOURNAL, Vol.
1, no. 2 (Winter 1971), p. 23-30. English.
DESCR: Higher Education; Students; *Teaching
Profession.

1757 Ramirez, Salvador. The establishment and
administration of a master's program in
Chicano Studies at the University of
Colorado. EPOCA: NATIONAL CONCILIO FOR
CHICANO STUDIES JOURNAL, Vol. 1, no. 2
(Winter 1971), p. 39-50. English. **DESCR:**
*Curriculum; Discrimination in Education;
Educational Theory and Practice; Student
Organizations; *Students; United Mexican
American Students (UMAS); *University of
Colorado, Boulder; Youth.

1758 Report to the Network from NCCHE. LA RED/THE
NET, no. 87 (July 1985), p. 1-2. English.
DESCR: *Educational Organizations; LA
RED/THE NET; *National Chicano Council on
Higher Education (NCCHE); National Chicano
Research Network (NCRN); Tomas Rivera
Center, Claremont, CA.

Chicano Studies (cont.)

1759 Rivera, Julius. The implementation of Mexican-American Studies in Texas colleges and universities. EPOCA: NATIONAL CONCILIO FOR CHICANO STUDIES JOURNAL, Vol. 1, no. 2 (Winter 1971), p. 79-86. English. **DESCR:** Colleges and Universities; *Curriculum; Texas; *Textbooks.

1760 Samora, Julian and Galarza, Ernesto. Research and scholarly activity. EPOCA: NATIONAL CONCILIO FOR CHICANO STUDIES JOURNAL, Vol. 1, no. 2 (Winter 1971), p. 51-54. English. **DESCR:** *Curriculum; *Research Methodology.

1761 Sanchez, Lionel. La Raza community and Chicano Studies. EPOCA: NATIONAL CONCILIO FOR CHICANO STUDIES JOURNAL, Vol. 1, no. 2 (Winter 1971), p. 5-59. English. **DESCR:** *Education; *La Raza.

1762 Trujillo, Marcela L. Guidelines for employment in Chicano studies. EPOCA: NATIONAL CONCILIO FOR CHICANO STUDIES JOURNAL, Vol. 1, no. 2 (Winter 1971), p. 60-65. English. **DESCR:** *Teaching Profession.

1763 Wilde, Richard H. The establishment of a Chicano studies program and its relation to the total curriculum of a college or university. EPOCA: NATIONAL CONCILIO FOR CHICANO STUDIES JOURNAL, Vol. 1, no. 2 (Winter 1971), p. 70-78. English. **DESCR:** California State University, Long Beach; *Curriculum; *Research Methodology.

1764 Zamora, Alfredo. The Mexican American community and Mexican American studies. EPOCA: NATIONAL CONCILIO FOR CHICANO STUDIES JOURNAL, Vol. 1, no. 2 (Winter 1971), p. 66-70. English. **DESCR:** *Curriculum.

Chicano Studies Research Center, UCLA

1765 Perez, Emma. Research centers. LA RED/THE NET, no. 95 (April 1986), p. 5-8. English. **DESCR:** *Research Centers.

CHICANO: THE EVOLUTION OF A PEOPLE

1766 de Leon, Arnoldo. Book review of: CHICANO: THE EVOLUTION OF A PEOPLE. SOUTHWESTERN HISTORICAL QUARTERLY, Vol. 87, no. 3 (1984), p. 343-344. English. **DESCR:** Book Reviews; Calvert, Robert; Rosaldo, Renato; Seligmann, Gustav L.

CHICANO THEATER: THEMES AND FORMS

1767 McCracken, Ellen. Book review of: CHICANO THEATER: THEMES AND FORMS. HISPANIA, Vol. 66, no. 4 (1983), p. 645. English. **DESCR:** Book Reviews; Huerta, Jorge A.

1768 McDermott, Douglas. Book review of: CHICANO THEATER: THEMES AND FORMS. THEATRE SURVEY, Vol. 25, no. 1 (May 1984), p. 124-125. English. **DESCR:** Book Reviews; Huerta, Jorge A.

1769 Rodriguez del Pino, Salvador. Book review of: CHICANO THEATER: THEMES AND FORMS. AMERICAN BOOK REVIEW, Vol. 5, no. 6 (September, October, 1983), p. 18. English. **DESCR:** Book Reviews; Huerta, Jorge A.

1770 Tatum, Charles. Chicano literary criticism comes of age. BILINGUAL REVIEW, Vol. 12, no. 1-2 (January, August, 1985), p. 144-149. English. **DESCR:** Book Reviews; Huerta, Jorge A.; *LA NOVELA CHICANA ESCRITA EN ESPANOL; Literary Criticism; Rodriguez del Pino,

Salvador.

THE CHICANO WAR

1771 Book review of: THE CHICANO WAR. PUBLISHER'S WEEKLY, Vol. 229, (February 21, 1986), p. 157. English. **DESCR:** Book Reviews; Gault, William Campbell.

CHICANOS, CATHOLICISM, AND POLITICAL IDEOLOGY

1772 Garcia, Philip. Book review of: CHICANOS, CATHOLICISM, AND POLITICAL IDEOLOGY. AMERICAN POLITICAL SCIENCE REVIEW, Vol. 81, (January 1987), p. 642-643. English. **DESCR:** Book Reviews; Catholic Church; Mosqueda, Lawrence J.

1773 Herrick, R.L. Book review of: CHICANOS, CATHOLICISM, AND POLITICAL IDEOLOGY. CHOICE, Vol. 24, no. 3 (November 1986), p. 498. English. **DESCR:** Book Reviews; Mosqueda, Lawrence J.

CHICANOS IN A CHANGING SOCIETY

1774 Arce, Carlos H. Book review of: CHICANOS IN A CHANGING SOCIETY. LA RED/THE NET, no. 30 (May 1980), p. 8. English. **DESCR:** Book Reviews; Camarillo, Alberto; History; *Santa Barbara, CA; *Social History and Conditions; *Southern California.

CHICANOS IN CALIFORNIA

1775 Griswold del Castillo, Richard. Book review of: CHICANOS IN CALIFORNIA. PACIFIC HISTORICAL REVIEW, Vol. 54, no. 2 (February 1985), p. 211-212. English. **DESCR:** Book Reviews; California; Camarillo, Alberto.

1776 Miranda, Gloria E. Book review of: CHICANOS IN CALIFORNIA. SOUTHERN CALIFORNIA QUARTERLY, Vol. 67, no. 4 (Winter 1985), p. 474-476. English. **DESCR:** Book Reviews; Camarillo, Alberto; Social History and Conditions.

CHICO AND THE MAN [television show]

1777 Aceves Madrid, Vicente. Controversy surrounding NBC's CHICO AND THE MAN. LATIN QUARTER, Vol. 1, no. 2 (October 1974), p. 5-7. English. **DESCR:** Albertson, Jack; Artists; Komack, James; Prinze, Freddie; Stereotypes; Teatros Unidos; *Television.

1778 Vasquez, Victor. More on CHICO AND THE MAN. LATIN QUARTER, Vol. 1, no. 3 (January, February, 1975), p. 13-15. English. **DESCR:** Albertson, Jack; Andrade, Ray; Artists; Boycotts; Discrimination; Prinze, Freddie; Stereotypes; *Television.

Chico Sesma Radio Show

1779 Lopez, Jose Y. Chico Sesma: a man and his music. LATIN QUARTER, Vol. 1, no. 4 (July, August, 1975), p. 10-15. English. **DESCR:** Los Angeles, CA; *Radio; Salsa; *Sesma, Chico.

Child Care Centers

1780 Ruiz, Vicki Lynn. Obreras y madres: labor activism among Mexican women and its impact on the family. RENATO ROSALDO LECTURE SERIES MONOGRAPH, Vol. 1, (Summer 1985), p. [19]-38. English. **DESCR:** *Chicanas; Children; History; *Labor Unions; *Mexico; Sex Roles; Women; *Working Women.

Child Care Centers (cont.)

1781 Weinfield, J. Day care benefits ordered for child born in U.S. to illegal alien. THE FAMILY LAW REPORTER: COURT OPINIONS, Vol. 9, no. 4 (November 23, 1982), p. 2054-2056. English. **DESCR:** *Ruiz v. Blum; *Undocumented Workers.

Child Rearing
USE: Parenting

Child Study

1782 Comstock, Cathryn L. and Martin, Frederick N. A children's Spanish word discrimination test for non-Spanish-speaking children. EAR AND HEARING, Vol. 5, no. 3 (May, June, 1984), p. 166-170. English. **DESCR:** English Language; *Language Assessment; Research Methodology; Spanish Language.

1783 Howell-Martinez, Vicky. The influence of gender roles on political socialization: an experimental study of Mexican-American children. WOMEN & POLITICS, Vol. 2, (Fall 1982), p. 33-46. English. **DESCR:** Attitudes; Children; Political Socialization; Sex Roles; *Sex Stereotypes.

Children

1784 Banker, Cynthia A., et al. Primary dental arch characteristics of Mexican-American children. ASDC JOURNAL OF DENTISTRY FOR CHILDREN, Vol. 51, no. 3 (May, June, 1984), p. 200-202. English. **DESCR:** Dentistry.

1785 Duncan, Marilyn H., et al. Childhood cancer epidemiology in New Mexico's American Indians, Hispanic whites,and non-Hispanic whites, 1970-82. JOURNAL OF THE NATIONAL CANCER INSTITUTE, Vol. 76, no. 6 (June 1986), p. 1013-1018. English. **DESCR:** Anglo Americans; *Cancer; Diseases; Native Americans.

1786 Duran, Richard P. and Guerra, Elsa. Evidence for scripts governing bilingual children's oral reading behavior. LA RED/THE NET, no. 43 (June 1981), p. 6. English. **DESCR:** *Bilingualism; *Reading.

1787 Espinosa, Maria. Children. LLUEVE TLALOC, no. 3 (1976), p. 5-9. English. **DESCR:** Lopez, Enrique Hank; *Prose.

1788 Espinosa, Mary Lou. Cosas de ninos. LLUEVE TLALOC, no. 3 (1976), p. 4-8. Spanish. **DESCR:** Lopez, Enrique Hank; *Prose.

1789 Guzman, Ralph. Bi-national policy questions generated by Mexican school-age children who migrate between the United States and Mexico. LA RED/THE NET, no. 62 (December 1982), p. 2-4. English. **DESCR:** Immigrants; Migrant Children; Public Policy; *Watsonville, CA.

1790 Hernandez, Angel. [Untitled drawing]. LLUEVE TLALOC, no. 3 (1976), p. 9. **DESCR:** *Drawings.

1791 Howell-Martinez, Vicky. The influence of gender roles on political socialization: an experimental study of Mexican-American children. WOMEN & POLITICS, Vol. 2, (Fall 1982), p. 33-46. English. **DESCR:** Attitudes; Child Study; Political Socialization; Sex Roles; *Sex Stereotypes.

1792 Miranda, Gloria E. Hispano-Mexican childrearing practices in pre-American Santa Barbara. SOUTHERN CALIFORNIA QUARTERLY, Vol. 65, no. 4 (Winter 1983), p. 307-320. English. **DESCR:** Cultural Characteristics; *Family; History; *Parenting; *Santa Barbara, CA; Socialization.

1793 Obese children focus of study. NUESTRO, Vol. 11, no. 3 (April 1987), p. 9. English. **DESCR:** *Obesity; Stanford University, Stanford, CA.

1794 Poma, Pedro A. A dangerous folk therapy. NATIONAL MEDICAL ASSOCIATION JOURNAL, Vol. 76, no. 4 (April 1984), p. 387-389. English. **DESCR:** Folk Medicine; *Lead Poisoning.

1795 Ramirez, Oscar. Book review of: HUMAN SERVICES FOR MEXICAN-AMERICAN CHILDREN. LA RED/THE NET, no. 55 (June 1982), p. 7-8. English. **DESCR:** Book Reviews; Social Services; *Tijerina, Andres A.

1796 Rueda, Robert and Smith, Doug C. Interpersonal tactics and communicative strategies of Anglo-American and Mexican-American mildly mentally retarded and nonretarded students. APPLIED RESEARCH IN MENTAL RETARDATION, Vol. 4, no. 2 (1983), p. 153-161. English. **DESCR:** *Mentally Handicapped.

1797 Ruiz, Vicki Lynn. Obreras y madres: labor activism among Mexican women and its impact on the family. RENATO ROSALDO LECTURE SERIES MONOGRAPH, Vol. 1, (Summer 1985), p. [19]-38. English. **DESCR:** *Chicanas; Child Care Centers; History; *Labor Unions; *Mexico; Sex Roles; Women; *Working Women.

Children's Art

1798 Chavez, Lorenzo A. Images of ethnic pride. VISTA, Vol. 3, no. 2 (October 3, 1987), p. 20-21. English. **DESCR:** *Art; *McDonald's Corporation.

1799 Mexico as seen by her children. VISTA, Vol. 1, no. 8 (April 6, 1986), p. 12-13. English. **DESCR:** *Smithsonian Institution Traveling Exhibition Service.

Children's Literature

1800 Book review of: BOOKS IN SPANISH FOR CHILDREN AND YOUNG ADULTS. BOOKLIST, Vol. 82, (July 1986), p. 1620. English. **DESCR:** Book Reviews; *BOOKS IN SPANISH FOR CHILDREN AND YOUNG ADULTS: AN ANNOTATED GUIDE; Reference Works; Schon, Isabel.

1801 Frank, Jerome P. Problems of books en espanol. PUBLISHER'S WEEKLY, Vol. 226, (July 27, 1984), p. 89-92. English. **DESCR:** *Publishing Industry.

1802 Nieto, Sonia. Past accomplishments, current needs: la lucha continua. INTERRACIAL BOOKS FOR CHILDREN, Vol. 17, no. 2 (1986), p. 6-8. English. **DESCR:** Bilingual Bicultural Education; Council on Interracial Books for Children; Poverty; Stereotypes.

Children's Television

1803 Catalano, Julia. Pinata. VISTA, Vol. 2, no. 10 (June 7, 1987), p. 14. English. **DESCR:** Fiestas; History; THE $25,000 PINATA [television show].

Children's Television (cont.)

1804 Lopez, Jose Y. A visit to VILLA ALEGRE. LATIN QUARTER, Vol. 1, no. 3 (January, February, 1975), p. 8-12. English. **DESCR:** Bilingual Children's Television, Inc.; Cultural Pluralism; Public Television; *VILLA ALEGRE [television program].

Chili's Restaurant

1805 Raffel, Elaine. What makes Chilis hot? RESTAURANT BUSINESS, Vol. 82, (October 1, 1983), p. 147-153+. English. **DESCR:** Larine, Larry; *Restaurants.

China

1806 Anaya, Rudolfo A. A Chicano in China. VISTA, Vol. 2, no. 1 (September 7, 1986), p. 19-21. English. **DESCR:** *A CHICANO IN CHINA; Anaya, Rudolfo A.; *Culture; Philosophy; *Tourism.

CHOCOLATE ARTISTRY

1807 Shaw, Katherine. Love affair with chocolate. VISTA, Vol. 1, no. 6 (February 2, 1986), p. 15-16. English. **DESCR:** *Business Enterprises; *Gonzalez, Elaine.

Cholos
USE: Pachucos

CHRISTIAN IMAGES IN HISPANIC NEW MEXICO

1808 Turner, Kay F. Book review of: CHRISTIAN IMAGES IN HISPANIC NEW MEXICO. JOURNAL OF AMERICAN FOLKLORE, Vol. 97, no. 385 (1984), p. 361-363. English. **DESCR:** Book Reviews; Wroth, William.

Christianity
USE: Religion

Christmas

1809 Igo, John N., Jr. Los Pastores: a triple-tradition. JOURNAL OF POPULAR CULTURE, Vol. 19, no. 3 (Winter 1985), p. 131-138. English. **DESCR:** Cultural Customs; *Folk Drama; *Los Pastores [folk drama].

Chulas Fronteras [art exhibit]

1810 Chavez, Lorenzo A. The eyes of Texas are upon them. VISTA, Vol. 2, no. 2 (October 4, 1986), p. 20. English. **DESCR:** *Art; Cardenas, David; Espada, Ibsen; Gonzalez, Patricia; Hernandez, John; Huerta, Benito; Martinez, Cesar Augusto.

CHULIFEAS FRONTERAS

1811 Alarcon, Justo S. Book review of: CHULIFEAS FRONTERAS. CHIRICU, Vol. 3, no. 1 (1982), p. 101-103. Spanish. **DESCR:** Alarcon, Justo S.; Book Reviews.

Church of Jesus Christ of Latter-Day Saints (Mormons)

1812 Chavez, Lorenzo A. The quest for Hispanic roots. VISTA, Vol. 2, no. 7 (March 8, 1987), p. 5-6, 24. English. **DESCR:** Directories; *Garcia, Clotilde; *Genealogy; Hispanic American Genealogical Associates, Washington, DC; Las Porciones Genealogical Society, Edinburg, TX; Los Bexarenos, San Antonio, TX; Los Californianos [genealogical society], San Jose, CA; Pan American University, Edinburg, TX; Texas Southmost College.

Cinco de Mayo

1813 Cisneros, Henry. The meaning for Hispanics of 5 de Mayo. VISTA, Vol. 1, no. 9 (May 3, 1986), p. 12-13. English. **DESCR:** *Festivals; History.

1814 Hazen-Hammond, Susan and Fuss, Eduardo. Vivan las celebraciones. ARIZONA HIGHWAYS, Vol. 63, no. 8 (August 1987), p. 35-45. English. **DESCR:** Cultural Customs; Dia de los Muertos; Dieciseis de Septiembre; Fiestas Patrias; *Holidays; La Virgen de Guadalupe; Las Posadas.

1815 Sommers, Laurie Kay. Symbol and style in Cinco de Mayo. JOURNAL OF AMERICAN FOLKLORE, Vol. 98, (October, December, 1985), p. 476-482. English. **DESCR:** *Cultural Customs; History; *Holidays; *San Francisco, CA; Symbolism.

CINCO VIDAS

1816 Barro, Mary Helen. 1973 Emmy Awards. LATIN QUARTER, Vol. 1, no. 1 (July 1974), p. 5-6. English. **DESCR:** Chavez, Andres; Emmy Awards; *Esparza, Moctezuma; Identity; Quintero, Carlos; *Recreation; REFLECCIONES; Rodriguez, Sandra; Rodriguez, Tony; Ruiz, Jose Luis; Stereotypes; Television.

Cinema
USE: Films

Cisneros [family name]

1817 Instituto Genealogico e Historico Latino-Americano. Rootsearch: Cisneros: Perales: Zuniga. VISTA, Vol. 2, no. 10 (June 7, 1987), p. 26. English. **DESCR:** Genealogy; History; *Perales [family name]; *Personal Names; *Zuniga [family name].

Cisneros, Henry, Mayor of San Antonio, TX

1818 Cisneros encourages LULAC to take lead in Hispanic agenda. HISPANIC ENGINEER, Vol. 3, no. 3 (1987), p. 14-15. English. **DESCR:** Conferences and Meetings; *League of United Latin American Citizens (LULAC).

1819 Munoz, Carlos, Jr. and Henry, Charles. Rainbow coalitions in four big cities: San Antonio, Denver, Chicago and Philadelphia. P.S. [AMERICAN POLITICAL SCIENCE ASSOCIATION], Vol. 19, no. 3 (Summer 1986), p. 598-609. English. **DESCR:** Blacks; Chicago, IL; Denver, CO; Elected Officials; Ethnic Groups; Intergroup Relations; Pena, Federico; Philadelphia, PA; Political Parties and Organizations; Political Representation; *Politics; San Antonio, TX; Urban Communities.

1820 Ross, I. Mayor Cisneros of San Antonio. READER'S DIGEST, Vol. 125, (December 1984), p. 193-194+. English. **DESCR:** Biography; *Elected Officials; Local Government; San Antonio, TX.

Cisneros, Sandra

1821 Billings, Linda M. and Alurista. In verbal murals: a study of Chicana herstory and poetry. CONFLUENCIA, Vol. 2, no. 1 (Fall 1986), p. 60-68. English. **DESCR:** Candelaria, Cordelia; Cervantes, Lorna Dee; *Chicanas; EMPLUMADA; *Feminism; History; Literary Criticism; *Poetry; Xelina.

Cisneros, Sandra (cont.)

1822 Bruce-Novoa, Juan. Meet the writers of the
80s. VISTA, Vol. 1, no. 11 (July 6, 1986),
p. 15-16. English. **DESCR:** Anaya, Rudolfo A.;
Arte Publico Press; *Authors; Bilingual
Review Press; Hinojosa-Smith, Rolando R.;
Keller, Gary D.; *Literature; Pineda,
Cecile; Quinto Sol Publishing, Inc.; Rivera,
Tomas; Soto, Gary.

1823 Cisneros, Sandra. Do you know me?: I wrote
THE HOUSE ON MANGO STREET. THE AMERICAS
REVIEW, Vol. 15, no. 1 (Spring 1987), p.
77-79. English. **DESCR:** Authors;
Autobiography; Chicanas; *Prose; *THE HOUSE
ON MANGO STREET.

1824 Cisneros, Sandra. Ghosts and voices: writing
from obsession. THE AMERICAS REVIEW, Vol.
15, no. 1 (Spring 1987), p. 69-73. English.
DESCR: *Authors; Autobiography; Chicanas;
*Prose.

1825 Cisneros, Sandra. Living as a writer: choice
and circumstance. REVISTA MUJERES, Vol. 3,
no. 2 (June 1986), p. 68-72. English.
DESCR: *Authors; Autobiography; Chicanas.

1826 Cisneros, Sandra. Notes to a young(er)
writer. THE AMERICAS REVIEW, Vol. 15, no. 1
(Spring 1987), p. 74-76. English. **DESCR:**
*Authors; Autobiography; Chicanas; *Prose.

1827 Herrera-Sobek, Maria. The politics of rape:
sexual transgression in Chicana fiction. THE
AMERICAS REVIEW, Vol. 15, no. 3-4 (Fall,
Winter, 1987), p. 171-181. English. **DESCR:**
*Chicanas; *Feminism; Fiction; GIVING UP THE
GHOST; *Literary Criticism; Lizarraga,
Sylvia; Moraga, Cherrie; *Rape; "Red Clowns"
[short story]; Sex Roles; "Silver Lake Road"
[short story].

1828 Olivares, Julian. Sandra Cisneros' THE HOUSE
ON MANGO STREET and the poetics of space.
THE AMERICAS REVIEW, Vol. 15, no. 3-4 (Fall,
Winter, 1987), p. 160-170. English. **DESCR:**
*Literary Criticism; *THE HOUSE ON MANGO
STREET.

Cities
USE: Urban Communities

Citizenship
USE: Naturalization

**CITY BOUND: URBAN LIFE AND POLITICAL ATTITUDES
AMONG CHICANO YOUTH**

1829 Arreola, Daniel D. Book review of: CITY
BOUND. GEOGRAPHICAL REVIEW, Vol. 77, (April
1987), p. 240-242. English. **DESCR:** Book
Reviews; Jankowski, Martin Sanchez.

CITY OF NIGHT

1830 Bruce-Novoa, Juan. Homosexuality and the
Chicano novel. CONFLUENCIA, Vol. 2, no. 1
(Fall 1986), p. 69-77. English. **DESCR:**
Acosta, Oscar Zeta; FAULTLINE [novel];
*Homosexuality; Islas, Arturo; *Literary
Criticism; Machismo; *Novel; Ortiz Taylor,
Sheila; POCHO; Rechy, John; Salas, Floyd;
SPRING FORWARD/FALL BACK; TATOO THE WICKED
CROSS; THE AUTOBIOGRAPHY OF A BROWN BUFFALO;
THE RAIN GOD: A DESERT TALE; THE REVOLT OF
THE COCKROACH PEOPLE; Villarreal, Jose
Antonio.

City Terrace, CA

1831 Blanco, Gilbert M. Las Adelitas del Barrio.
LATIN QUARTER, Vol. 1, no. 3 (January,

February, 1975), p. 30-32. English. **DESCR:**
*Chicanas; Community Development; Gangs;
*Latin Empresses; Youth.

Ciudad Juarez, Chihuahua, Mexico

1832 Flynn, Ken. A triumph of diplomacy. VISTA,
Vol. 3, no. 2 (October 3, 1987), p. 22-24.
English. **DESCR:** *Border Region; Chamizal
Memorial Federal Park; *El Chamizal
[region]; El Paso, TX.

1833 Third world women in multinational
corporations--the Mexican American border.
LA RED/THE NET, no. 25 (December 1979), p.
2. English. **DESCR:** *Border Industries;
Chicanas; Labor Supply and Market;
*Multinational Corporations; *Working Women.

Civil Rights

1834 Beale, Stephen. MALDEF weathers a storm.
HISPANIC BUSINESS, Vol. 9, no. 5 (May 1987),
p. 10-11. English. **DESCR:** Anaya, Toney,
Governor of New Mexico; Hernandez, Antonia
A.; *Mexican American Legal Defense and
Educational Fund (MALDEF); Organizations;
Serna, Eric P.

1835 Dempsey, Mary. John Roy Castillo. VISTA,
Vol. 1, no. 11 (July 6, 1986), p. 20.
English. **DESCR:** *Biography; *Castillo, John
Ray; Michigan Civil Rights Department.

1836 Escobar, Edward J. Mexican revolutionaries
and the Los Angeles police: harassment of
the Partido Liberal Mexicano, 1907-1910.
AZTLAN, Vol. 17, no. 1 (Spring 1986), p.
1-46. English. **DESCR:** *Flores Magon,
Ricardo; Gutierrez de Lara, Lazaro; Los
Angeles, CA; *Los Angeles Police Department;
*Partido Liberal Mexicano (PLM); *Police;
Police Brutality; Political Repression;
Rico, Louis; Rico, Thomas; Talamantes,
Felipe; United States-Mexico Relations.

1837 Ford, Theresa Y. United States v. Hannigan:
federal statute used to prosecute torturers.
CRIMINAL JUSTICE JOURNAL, Vol. 6, no. 1
(Fall 1982), p. 79-97. English. **DESCR:** Hobbs
Act; *Undocumented Workers; *U.S. v.
Hanigan.

1838 Grajeda Higley, Leilani. Irma Castro. VISTA,
Vol. 2, no. 10 (June 7, 1987), p. 20.
English. **DESCR:** *Biography; *Castro, Irma;
Chicanas; *Chicano Federation of San Diego
Co., Inc.; Discrimination.

1839 Gutierrez, Jose Angel. Chicanos and
Mexicans: under surveillance: 1940 to 1980.
RENATO ROSALDO LECTURE SERIES MONOGRAPH,
Vol. 2, (Spring 1986), p. [29]-58. English.
DESCR: Acuna, Rudolfo; Border Coverage
Program (BOCOV); COINTELPRO; *Federal Bureau
of Investigation (FBI); *Federal Government;
History; League of United Latin American
Citizens (LULAC); Mexico; Political Parties
and Organizations; *Political Repression.

1840 Martinez, Elizabeth. A decade of repression:
update on the "Kiko" Martinez case. CRIME
AND SOCIAL JUSTICE, no. 19 (Summer 1983), p.
100. English. **DESCR:** Chicano Movement;
Colorado; Criminal Justice System;
Discrimination; Legal Cases; *Martinez,
Francisco "Kiko"; Political Repression.

Civil Rights (cont.)

1841 Munoz, Rosalio. The Simpson-Rodino immigration law: an assault on the working class. POLITICAL AFFAIRS, Vol. 66, no. 6 (June 1987), p. 12-18. English. DESCR: *Immigration Law and Legislation; *Immigration Reform and Control Act of 1986; Undocumented Workers.

1842 Rips, Geoffrey. Civil rights and wrongs. TEXAS OBSERVOR, Vol. 76, (December 14, 1984), p. 49-55. English. DESCR: Briscoe, Dolph, Jr., Governor of Texas; Farm Workers; *Hidalgo County, TX; La Raza Unida Party; Miller, C.L.; Segregation and Desegregation; Texas Farmworkers' Union; Voting Rights.

1843 Statutes and ordinances--aliens failure to carry immigration documents. CRIMINAL LAW REPORTER, Vol. 36, no. 21 (February 27, 1985), p. 2405. English. DESCR: *U.S. v. Ritter.

1844 [Untitled editorial]. LATIN QUARTER, Vol. 1, no. 2 (October 1974), p. 2. English. DESCR: *Immigration and Naturalization Service (INS); *Immigration Regulation and Control.

CLAMOR AT THE GATES: THE NEW AMERICAN IMMIGRATION

1845 Kraly, Ellen Percy. Book review of: CLAMOR AT THE GATES. JOURNAL OF AMERICAN ETHNIC HISTORY, Vol. 7, no. 1 (Fall 1987), p. 93-95. English. DESCR: Book Reviews; Glazer, Nathan; Immigration.

1846 Madrid, Arturo. Book reviews of: CLAMOR AT THE GATES and LATIN JOURNEY. LA RED/THE NET, no. 89 (August 1985), p. 7-10. English. DESCR: Bach, Robert L.; Book Reviews; Glazer, Nathan; Immigration; *LATIN JOURNEY: CUBAN AND MEXICAN IMMIGRANTS IN THE UNITED STATES; Portes, Alejandro.

LA CLASE OBRERA EN LA HISTORIA DE MEXICO: AL NORTE DEL RIO BRAVO (PASADO INMEDIATO, 1930-1981)

1847 Fernandez, Celestino. Book review of: LA CLASE OBRERA EN LA HISTORIA DE MEXICO: AL NORTE DEL RIO BRAVO (PASADO INMEDIATO, 1930-1981). NEW MEXICO HISTORICAL REVIEW, Vol. 59, no. 2 (April 1984), p. 214-215. English. DESCR: Book Reviews; Laboring Classes; Maciel, David.

1848 Zamora, Emilio. Book review of: LA CLASE OBRERA EN LA HISTORIA DE MEXICO: AL NORTE DEL RIO BRAVO (PASADO INMEDIATO, 1930-1981). LA RED/THE NET, no. 70 (July 1983), p. 13-17. English. DESCR: Book Reviews; Maciel, David.

Class Distinction
USE: Social Classes

Clergy

1849 Allsup, Dan. A Texas hello for John Paul II. VISTA, Vol. 3, no. 1 (September 6, 1987), p. 8-9. English. DESCR: Catholic Church; *Pope John Paul II; San Antonio, TX.

1850 Rubio Goldsmith, Raquel. Shipwrecked in the desert: a short history of the adventures and struggles for survival of the Mexican Sisters of the House of the Providence in Douglas, Arizona during their first twenty-two years of existence (1927-1949). RENATO ROSALDO LECTURE SERIES MONOGRAPH, Vol. 1, (Summer 1985), p. [39]-67. English. DESCR: Catholic Church; Chicanas; Douglas, AZ; History; *House of the Divine Providence [convent], Douglas, AZ.

1851 Stevens-Arroyo, Antonio M. Cahensly revisited?: the National Pastoral Encounter of America's Hispanic Catholics. MIGRATION WORLD MAGAZINE, Vol. 15. no. 3 (1987), p. 16-19. English. DESCR: *Catholic Church; *National Hispanic Pastoral Encounter; The Lucerne Memorial.

La Clinica Nueva Esperanza, Orange County, CA

1852 Reeves, Kate. Hispanic utilization of an ethnic mental health clinic. JOURNAL OF PSYCHOSOCIAL NURSING AND MENTAL HEALTH SERVICES, Vol. 24, no. 2 (February 1986), p. 23-26. English. DESCR: *Mental Health Programs.

Clinical Psychiatry
USE: Psychiatry

Clothing Trade
USE: Garment Industry

Cobos, Ruben

1853 Madrid, Arturo. Book reviews of: A DICTIONARY OF NEW MEXICO AND SOUTHERN COLORADO SPANISH and TUNOMAS HONEY. LA RED/THE NET, no. 77 (February 1984), p. 8-10. English. DESCR: *A DICTIONARY OF NEW MEXICO AND SOUTHERN COLORADO SPANISH; *Book Reviews; Sagel, Jim; *TUNOMAS HONEY.

Coca-Cola Company

1854 Hispanic marketing. ADVERTISING AGE MAGAZINE, Vol. 57, no. 16 (February 27, 1986), p. 11-51. English. DESCR: Adolph Coors Co.; Advertising; Allstate Insurance Co.; American Greetings; Anheuser-Busch, Inc.; Business Enterprises; Consumers; Ford Motor Company; Hallmark Cards; *Marketing; Mass Media; McDonald's Corporation; Metropolitan Life Insurance Corporation; Pepsi-Cola Bottling Group; Prudential; Spanish International Network (SIN); State Farm Mutual Insurance; Tylenol; United Insurance Co. of America.

Cockcroft, James D.

1855 Mosqueda, Lawrence Joseph. Mexican labor: a most precious commodity on both sides of the border. GUARDIAN, Vol. 39, no. 2 (October 8, 1986), p. 20. English. DESCR: Book Reviews; *OUTLAWS IN THE PROMISED LAND: MEXICAN IMMIGRANT WORKERS AND AMERICA'S FUTURE.

Code-switching
USE: Language Usage

Coerver, Don M.

1856 Hart, John M. Book review of: TEXAS AND THE MEXICAN REVOLUTION. PACIFIC HISTORICAL REVIEW, Vol. 55, no. 2 (1986), p. 324-325. English. DESCR: Book Reviews; Hall, Linda B.; *TEXAS AND THE MEXICAN REVOLUTION: A STUDY IN STATE AND NATIONAL BORDER POLICY.

1857 Hill, Larry D. Book review of: TEXAS AND THE MEXICAN REVOLUTION. JOURNAL OF SOUTHERN HISTORY, Vol. 52, no. 4 (November 1986), p. 651-652. English. DESCR: Book Reviews; Hall, Linda B.; *TEXAS AND THE MEXICAN REVOLUTION: A STUDY IN STATE AND NATIONAL BORDER POLICY.

Coerver, Don M. (cont.)

1858 Raat, W. Dirk. Book review of: TEXAS AND THE
MEXICAN REVOLUTION. WESTERN HISTORICAL
QUARTERLY, Vol. 17, no. 1 (January 1986), p.
91-92. English. **DESCR:** Book Reviews; Border
Region; Hall, Linda B.; *TEXAS AND THE
MEXICAN REVOLUTION: A STUDY IN STATE AND
NATIONAL BORDER POLICY.

Cognition

1859 Aboud, Frances E. and Skerry, Shelagh A. The
development of ethnic attitudes: a critical
review. JOURNAL OF CROSS-CULTURAL
PSYCHOLOGY, Vol. 15, no. 1 (March 1984), p.
3-34. English. **DESCR:** *Attitudes; *Identity.

1860 Mujica, Barbara. Creative code switching.
VISTA, Vol. 1, no. 5 (January 5, 1986), p.
22. English. **DESCR:** Bilingualism; Language
Usage; *Zentella, Ana Celia.

Cohen, Andrew D.

1861 Duran, Richard P. Book review of: TESTING
LANGUAGE ABILITY IN THE CLASSROOM. LA
RED/THE NET, no. 45 (August 1981), p. 5.
English. **DESCR:** Book Reviews; Language
Proficiency; *TESTING LANGUAGE ABILITY IN
THE CLASSROOM.

COINTELPRO

1862 Gutierrez, Jose Angel. Chicanos and
Mexicans: under surveillance: 1940 to 1980.
RENATO ROSALDO LECTURE SERIES MONOGRAPH,
Vol. 2, (Spring 1986), p. [29]-58. English.
DESCR: Acuna, Rudolfo; Border Coverage
Program (BOCOV); *Civil Rights; *Federal
Bureau of Investigation (FBI); *Federal
Government; History; League of United Latin
American Citizens (LULAC); Mexico; Political
Parties and Organizations; *Political
Repression.

Collective Bargaining

1863 Perez, Renato E. The business of Hispanics.
VISTA, Vol. 2, no. 1 (September 7, 1986), p.
10. English. **DESCR:** Adolph Coors Co.;
American G.I. Forum; Apodaca, Jerry [Gov. of
New Mexico]; Business; Corporations; Cuban
National Planning Council, Inc. Washington,
D.C.; *Hispanic Association on Corporate
Responsibility (HACER); League of United
Latin American Citizens (LULAC); National
Council of La Raza (NCLR); National IMAGE;
U.S. Hispanic Chamber of Commerce.

1864 Segal, William. New alliances in Watsonville
strike. IN THESE TIMES, Vol. 10, no. 29
(July 9, 1986), p. 5. English. **DESCR:**
Jackson, Jesse; Labor Unions; Strikes and
Lockouts; Teamsters Union; *Watsonville, CA;
Watsonville Canning and Frozen Food Co.

College Graduates

1865 Mixed messages sent to June graduates.
HISPANIC TIMES, Vol. 8, no. 3 (May, June,
1987), p. 18. English. **DESCR:** Bilingualism;
*Careers.

1866 Sellers, Jeff M. State of the art
recruitment: competition for blue-chip
Hispanic business graduates is fierce and
expensive. HISPANIC BUSINESS, Vol. 9, no. 2
(February 1987), p. 22-25, 57. English.
DESCR: *Business Administration; *Careers;
Colleges and Universities; Enrollment;
*Management.

College Preparation

1867 Leon, David Jess and McNeill, Daniel.
Hispanics, the fifth class, and the
University of California, 1870-72. LA
RED/THE NET, no. 67 (April 1983), p. 5-6.
English. **DESCR:** *Colleges and Universities;
Enrollment; Local History; *University of
California.

Colleges and Universities

1868 Chavez, Lorenzo A. Passport to success.
VISTA, Vol. 2, no. 1 (September 7, 1986), p.
6-8. English. **DESCR:** Enrollment; *Higher
Education.

1869 Garcia, Herman S.; Stile, Stephen W.; and
Carillo, Fred M. Ethnic minority students,
admissions policies, and academic support
programs in institutions of higher
education. TEXAS TECH JOURNAL OF EDUCATION,
Vol. 11, no. 1 (Winter 1984), p. 77-89.
English. **DESCR:** Academic Achievement; Ethnic
Groups.

1870 Garza, Hisauro A. The "barrioization" of
Hispanic faculty. EDUCATIONAL RECORD,
(Fall, Winter, 1987, 1988), p. 122-124.
English. **DESCR:** *Discrimination in
Education; *Discrimination in Employment;
*Higher Education; Teaching Profession.

1871 Gonzalez, Lawrence F. The University of
Illinois, Chicago. HISPANIC ENGINEER, Vol.
3, no. 3 (1987), p. 34-36. English. **DESCR:**
Association of Minority Engineers (AME);
Society of Hispanic Professional Engineers
(SHPE); *University of Illinois, Chicago,
IL.

1872 Leon, David Jess and McNeill, Daniel. The
fifth class: a 19th century forerunner of
affirmative action. CALIFORNIA HISTORY, Vol.
64, no. 1 (Winter 1985), p. 52-57. English.
DESCR: *Affirmative Action; Discrimination
in Education; *Enrollment; *Higher
Education; History; Students; *University of
California.

1873 Leon, David Jess and McNeill, Daniel.
Hispanics, the fifth class, and the
University of California, 1870-72. LA
RED/THE NET, no. 67 (April 1983), p. 5-6.
English. **DESCR:** College Preparation;
Enrollment; Local History; *University of
California.

1874 Mena, Francisco; Padilla, Amado M.; and
Maldonado, Margarita. Acculturative stress
and specific coping stategies among
immigrant and later generation college
students. HISPANIC JOURNAL OF BEHAVIORAL
SCIENCES, Vol. 9, no. 2 (June 1987), p.
207-225. English. **DESCR:** *Acculturation; Age
Groups; Identity; Immigrants; Stress;
Students.

1875 Minsky, Alyce. California State University
at Los Angeles. HISPANIC ENGINEER, Vol. 3,
(Summer, 1987), p. 30-33, 44. English.
DESCR: Educational Organizations;
*Engineering as a Profession; Mathematics,
Engineering and Science Achievement (MESA);
*Minority Engineering Program (California
State University at Los Angeles).

1876 Report to the Network. LA RED/THE NET, no.
97 (June 1986), p. 1-2. English. **DESCR:**
California Master Plan for Higher Education;
*Evaluation (Educational); *Higher
Education.

Colleges and Universities (cont.)

1877 Riding the range at Golden West. NUESTRO,
     Vol. 11, no. 3 (April 1987), p. 7-8.
     English. **DESCR:** Biography; Educational
     Administration; *Garcia, Fred; Golden West
     College, Huntington Beach, CA.

1878 Rivera, Julius. The implementation of
     Mexican-American Studies in Texas colleges
     and universities. EPOCA: NATIONAL CONCILIO
     FOR CHICANO STUDIES JOURNAL, Vol. 1, no. 2
     (Winter 1971), p. 79-86. English. **DESCR:**
     *Chicano Studies; *Curriculum; Texas;
     *Textbooks.

1879 Sellers, Jeff M. State of the art
     recruitment: competition for blue-chip
     Hispanic business graduates is fierce and
     expensive. HISPANIC BUSINESS, Vol. 9, no. 2
     (February 1987), p. 22-25, 57. English.
     DESCR: *Business Administration; *Careers;
     College Graduates; Enrollment; *Management.

Collier, Virginia P.

1880 Hopkins, Thomas. Book review of: BILINGUAL
     AND ESL CLASSROOMS: TEACHING IN
     MULTICULTURAL CONTEXTS. EDUCATIONAL
     LEADERSHIP, Vol. 43, no. 6 (March 1986), p.
     82. English. **DESCR:** *BILINGUAL AND ESL
     CLASSROOMS: TEACHING IN MULTICULTURAL
     CONTEXTS; Book Reviews; Ovando, Carlos J.

1881 Nieto, Sonia. Book review of: BILINGUAL AND
     ESL CLASSROOMS: TEACHING IN MULTICULTURAL
     CONTEXTS. INTERRACIAL BOOKS FOR CHILDREN,
     Vol. 17, no. 3-4 (1986), p. 30. English.
     DESCR: *BILINGUAL AND ESL CLASSROOMS:
     TEACHING IN MULTICULTURAL CONTEXTS; Book
     Reviews; Ovando, Carlos J.

Colmenarez, Margarita

1882 SHPE news. HISPANIC ENGINEER, Vol. 3, no. 3
     (1987), p. 10-13. English. **DESCR:** *Awards;
     Castillo, Hector; Garcia, Raul; Herrera,
     Jess; Lopez-Martin, Minnie; Mondragon,
     Ricardo; Reyes-Guerra, David; Silva, Juan;
     Society of Hispanic Professional Engineers
     (SHPE); Vargas, Jesus; Villanueva,
     Bernadette.

Colon, Willie

1883 Gordon, Polita C. Living the crossover
     dream. VISTA, Vol. 1, no. 8 (April 6, 1986),
     p. 6-9. English. **DESCR:** *Blades, Ruben; Los
     Lobos del Este de Los Angeles (musical
     group); Miami Sound Machine; *Musicians.

Colonia
     USE: Barrios

Colorado

1884 Hero, Rodney E. Mexican Americans and urban
     politics: a consideration of governmental
     structure and policy. AZTLAN, Vol. 17, no. 1
     (Spring 1986), p. 131-147. English. **DESCR:**
     *Political Representation; *Politics; Public
     Policy; *Urban Communities.

1885 Martinez, Elizabeth. A decade of repression:
     update on the "Kiko" Martinez case. CRIME
     AND SOCIAL JUSTICE, no. 19 (Summer 1983), p.
     100. English. **DESCR:** Chicano Movement; Civil
     Rights; Criminal Justice System;
     Discrimination; Legal Cases; *Martinez,
     Francisco "Kiko"; Political Repression.

**Colorado Association of Chicanos in Higher
  Education (CACHE)**

1886 Perez, Emma. Higher education organizations.
     LA RED/THE NET, no. 99 (August 1986), p.
     2-4. English. **DESCR:** *Educational
     Organizations; *Higher Education.

Columbia Broadcasting Studios (CBS)

1887 Jesse Jackson makes appearance at CBS board
     meeting. BROADCASTING, Vol. 110, no. 16
     (April 21, 1986), p. 100. English. **DESCR:**
     Broadcast Media; Discrimination;
     Discrimination in Employment; *Jackson,
     Jesse; People United to Serve Humanity
     (PUSH); Stereotypes; Taylor, Hycel; Wyman,
     Thomas.

Commerce
     USE: Business

**Committee of Mothers and Relatives of Political
  Prisoners Disappeared and Assassinated of El
  Salvador "Monsenor Oscar Arnulfo Romero"
  (Comadres, El Salvador)**

1888 Alicia de Garcia's oral history=Historia
     oral de Alicia de Garcia. REVISTA MUJERES,
     Vol. 3, no. 2 (June 1986), p. 37-49.
     Spanish. **DESCR:** Community Organizations; de
     Garcia, Alicia; *Federation of Latin
     Americans for the Association of Relatives
     of the Detained and Disappeared (FedeFam);
     *Oral History; Terrorism; Violence; *Women.

1889 Peace with justice. REVISTA MUJERES, Vol. 3,
     no. 2 (June 1986), p. 32-35. English.
     DESCR: Community Organizations; *Federation
     of Latin Americans for the Association of
     Relatives of the Detained and Disappeared
     (FedeFam); Terrorism; Violence; *Women.

**Committee on Public Policy Research on
  Contemporary Hispanic Issues**

1890 Hispanic inter-university program grants
     awarded to 17 projects. LA RED/THE NET, no.
     92 (November, December, 1985), p. 7-9.
     English. **DESCR:** *Ford Foundation; Funding
     Sources; Inter-University Program for Latino
     Research; Social Science Research Council.

Communism

1891 Garcia, Mario T. [Letter to the editor about
     Mexicans, radicals and communists in the
     United States]. LABOR HISTORY, Vol. 25, no.
     1 (Winter 1984), p. 152-154. English.
     DESCR: *"Anarquismo y Comunismo: Mexican
     Radicalism and the Communist Party in Los
     Angeles in the 1930s"; History; *Labor
     Unions; Los Angeles, CA; *Monroy, Douglas.

1892 Monroy, Douglas. [Letter responding to Mario
     Garcia's comments]. LABOR HISTORY, Vol. 25,
     no. 1 (Winter 1984), p. 155-156. English.
     DESCR: *Garcia, Mario T.; History; *Labor
     Unions; Los Angeles, CA.

Communist Party

1893 Communist Party, U.S.A. On
     Chicano/Mexican-American equality. POLITICAL
     AFFAIRS, Vol. 66, no. 4 (April 1987), p. 35.
     English. **DESCR:** *Discrimination; Political
     Ideology; *Social History and Conditions.

Communities Organized for Public Service (COPS)

1894 Cortes, Ernesto, Jr. Changing the locus of political decision making. CHRISTIANITY AND CRISIS, Vol. 47, no. 1 (February 2, 1987), p. 18-22. English. DESCR: Biography; *Cortes, Ernesto, Jr.; *Political Parties and Organizations; San Antonio, TX.

Community College Reassessment Study

1895 Magallan, Rafael J. Community college update. LA RED/THE NET, no. 98 (July 1986), p. 3-6. English. DESCR: *California Master Plan for Higher Education; Community Colleges; Enrollment; *Vera, Ron.

Community Colleges

1896 Baker, George A. and Rocha, Pedro, Jr. Critical incident competencies of Mexican American and Anglo American administrators. COMMUNITY/JUNIOR COLLEGE QUARTERLY OF RESEARCH AND PRACTICE, Vol. 7, no. 4 (July, September, 1983), p. 319-332. English. DESCR: Anglo Americans; Comparative Psychology; Cultural Characteristics; Educational Administration; Management; Public Policy.

1897 Magallan, Rafael J. Community college update. LA RED/THE NET, no. 98 (July 1986), p. 3-6. English. DESCR: *California Master Plan for Higher Education; *Community College Reassessment Study; Enrollment; *Vera, Ron.

1898 Powers, Stephen and Rossman, Mark H. Attributions for success and failure among Anglo, Black, Hispanic, and Native-American community-college students. JOURNAL OF PSYCHOLOGY, Vol. 117, no. 1 (May 1984), p. 27-31. English. DESCR: *Academic Achievement; Anglo Americans; Blacks; *Locus of Control; Native Americans; Students.

1899 Rendon, Laura Ignacia. Chicano student and institution related determinants of educational outcomes in south Texas community colleges. LA RED/THE NET, no. 73 (October 1983), p. 2-6. English. DESCR: *Academic Achievement; *South Texas; Surveys.

1900 Rendon, Laura Ignacia. Mathematics education for Hispanic students in community colleges. LA RED/THE NET, no. 76 (January 1984), p. 2-4. English. DESCR: *Mathematics; Students; Surveys.

Community Development

1901 Blanco, Gilbert M. Las Adelitas del Barrio. LATIN QUARTER, Vol. 1, no. 3 (January, February, 1975), p. 30-32. English. DESCR: *Chicanas; City Terrace, CA; Gangs; *Latin Empresses; Youth.

1902 Grant from L.A. Pepsi to benefit city program. BEVERAGE INDUSTRY, Vol. 74, no. 7 (April 8, 1983), p. 25. English. DESCR: Los Angeles, CA; *Pepsi-Cola Bottling Group; Private Funding Sources.

1903 Muro, Rena. Hispanic walk of fame=Camino hispano de la fama. AMERICAS 2001, Vol. 1, no. 2 (September, October, 1987), p. 33. Bilingual. DESCR: *Hispanic Walk of Fame; *Whittier Blvd., Los Angeles, CA.

1904 Sharpe, Maria Elena. Back to the future. VISTA, Vol. 3, no. 4 (December 6, 1987), p. 10-12, 32. English. DESCR: Las Vegas, NM; *Plaza Vieja, Las Vegas, NM; Santa Fe Trail.

1905 Yzaguirre, Raul. Task force on social services and community development. LA RED/THE NET, no. 88 (Winter 1984), p. 10-14. English. DESCR: *Public Policy; *Social Services.

Community Organizations

1906 Alicia de Garcia's oral history=Historia oral de Alicia de Garcia. REVISTA MUJERES, Vol. 3, no. 2 (June 1986), p. 37-49. Spanish. DESCR: *Committee of Mothers and Relatives of Political Prisoners Disappeared and Assassinated of El Salvador "Monsenor Oscar Arnulfo Romero" (Comadres, El Salvador); de Garcia, Alicia; *Federation of Latin Americans for the Association of Relatives of the Detained and Disappeared (FedeFam); *Oral History; Terrorism; Violence; *Women.

1907 Beale, Stephen. Friendly persuasion: pacts and covenants. HISPANIC BUSINESS, Vol. 9, no. 9 (September 1987), p. 20-26. English. DESCR: *Adolph Coors Co.; *Business; Coors/HACER Agreement, 1984; *Corporations; *Hispanic Association on Corporate Responsibility (HACER); Organizations; Pacific Bell; Southland Corporation.

1908 Hardy-Fanta, Carol. Social action in Hispanic groups. SOCIAL WORK, Vol. 31, no. 2 (March, April, 1986), p. 119-123. English. DESCR: Natural Support Systems; Psychotherapy; *Social Work.

1909 Peace with justice. REVISTA MUJERES, Vol. 3, no. 2 (June 1986), p. 32-35. English. DESCR: *Committee of Mothers and Relatives of Political Prisoners Disappeared and Assassinated of El Salvador "Monsenor Oscar Arnulfo Romero" (Comadres, El Salvador); *Federation of Latin Americans for the Association of Relatives of the Detained and Disappeared (FedeFam); Terrorism; Violence; *Women.

Community School Relationships

1910 Heaney, Thomas W. "Hanging on" or "gaining ground": educating marginal adults. NEW DIRECTIONS FOR CONTINUING EDUCATION, Vol. 20, (December 1983), p. 53-63. English. DESCR: *Adult Education; *Adult Education Center of Lakeview; Chicago, IL; Education.

1911 Nieto, Sonia. Who's afraid of bilingual parents? BILINGUAL REVIEW, Vol. 12, no. 3 (September, December, 1985), p. 179-189. English. DESCR: *Bilingual Bicultural Education; *Family; *Parent and Child Relationships; Teacher Training.

Community Service Organization, Los Angeles, (CSO)

1912 Bueno, Patricia E. Los Chicanos y la politica. LA COMUNIDAD, No. 267 (September 1, 1985), p. 6-7. Spanish. DESCR: Discrimination; History; Leadership; League of United Latin American Citizens (LULAC); Orden Hijos de America, San Antonio, TX; *Political Parties and Organizations.

A COMMUNITY UNDER SIEGE: A CHRONICLE OF CHICANOS EAST OF THE LOS ANGELES RIVER, 1945-1975

1913 Garcia, Mario T. Book review of: A COMMUNITY UNDER SIEGE. LA RED/THE NET, no. 94 (March 1986), p. 5-6. English. DESCR: Acuna, Rudolfo; Book Reviews; Los Angeles, CA.

A COMMUNITY UNDER SIEGE: A CHRONICLE OF CHICANOS EAST OF THE LOS ANGELES RIVER, 1945-1975 (cont.)

1914 Garcia. Mario T. Book review of: A COMMUNITY UNDER SIEGE. PACIFIC HISTORICAL REVIEW, Vol. 55, no. 4 (1986), p. 636-638. English. **DESCR:** Acuna, Rudolfo; Book Reviews; East Los Angeles, CA.

1915 Hoffman, Abraham. Book review of: A COMMUNITY UNDER SIEGE. JOURNAL OF AMERICAN HISTORY, Vol. 72, no. 2 (September 1985), p. 459. English. **DESCR:** Acuna, Rudolfo; Book Reviews.

Comparative Psychology

1916 Acosta, Frank X., et al. Preparing low-income Hispanic, Black, and white patients for psychotherapy: evaluation of a new orientation program. JOURNAL OF CLINICAL PSYCHOLOGY, Vol. 39, no. 6 (November 1983), p. 872-877. English. **DESCR:** Anglo Americans; Blacks; Mental Health; *Psychotherapy.

1917 Baker, George A. and Rocha, Pedro, Jr. Critical incident competencies of Mexican American and Anglo American administrators. COMMUNITY/JUNIOR COLLEGE QUARTERLY OF RESEARCH AND PRACTICE, Vol. 7, no. 4 (July, September, 1983), p. 319-332. English. **DESCR:** Anglo Americans; *Community Colleges; Cultural Characteristics; Educational Administration; Management; Public Policy.

1918 Domino, George. Sleep habits in the elderly: a study of three Hispanic cultures. JOURNAL OF CROSS-CULTURAL PSYCHOLOGY, Vol. 17, no. 1 (March 1986), p. 109-120. English. **DESCR:** *Ancianos; Cultural Characteristics; Ethnic Groups.

1919 Gaviria, Moises; Gil, Ana A.; and Javaid, Javaid I. Nortriptyline kinetics in Hispanic and Anglo subjects. JOURNAL OF CLINICAL PSYCHOPHARMACOLOGY, Vol. 6, no. 4 (1986), p. 227-231. English. **DESCR:** Anglo Americans; *Drug Use; Genetics; Public Health.

1920 Isonio, Steven A. and Garza, Raymond T. Protestant work ethic endorsement among Anglo Americans, Chicanos and Mexicans: a comparison of factor structures. HISPANIC JOURNAL OF BEHAVIORAL SCIENCES, Vol. 9, no. 4 (December 1987), p. 413-425. English. **DESCR:** *Cultural Characteristics; Ethnic Groups; *Protestant Work Ethic (PWE) Scale; *Values.

1921 Martinez, Ruben and Dukes, Richard L. Race, gender and self-esteem among youth. HISPANIC JOURNAL OF BEHAVIORAL SCIENCES, Vol. 9, no. 4 (December 1987), p. 427-443. English. **DESCR:** *Identity; *Sex Roles; *Youth.

1922 Zippin. David H. and Hough, Richard L. Perceived self-other differences in life events and mental health among Mexicans and Americans. JOURNAL OF PSYCHOLOGY, Vol. 119, no. 2 (March 1985), p. 143-155. English. **DESCR:** Anglo Americans; *Locus of Control; *Mental Health; Mexico; Psychiatry; *Stress.

Computer Trade Development Corp, Birmingham, MI

1923 The top 100--profiles. HISPANIC BUSINESS, Vol. 9, no. 11 (November 1987), p. 31-50. English. **DESCR:** Artco Contracting, Inc., Auburn Hills, MI; *Business Enterprises; Corella Electric Inc., Phoenix, AZ; GSE Construction Co., Inc., Livermore, CA; National Systems & Research Co.; Unique

Construction Co., Hillside, IL.

Computers

1924 Abalos, J. Victor. Whiz kids of the microchip melody. VISTA, Vol. 1, no. 5 (January 5, 1986), p. 9-10. English. **DESCR:** *Musical Instruments; *Romero, Eddie, Jr.

1925 Flores, Juan. Chicanos and the computer age: the best of times, the worst of times. JOURNAL OF THE ASSOCIATION OF MEXICAN AMERICAN EDUCATORS, (1986, 1987), p. 37-41. English. **DESCR:** Education.

1926 Report to the Network. LA RED/THE NET, No. 104 (January 1987), p. 1-2. English. **DESCR:** *Contreras, Reynaldo A.; *Higher Education; *Midwestern States; *Natural Support Systems; Research Methodology; Surveys.

1927 Sellers, Jeff M. High tech directory. HISPANIC BUSINESS, Vol. 9, no. 10 (October 1987), p. 7-9. English. **DESCR:** *Business Enterprises; *Electronics Industry; *Government Contracts; Military.

1928 Snyder, Patricia. A bilingual printwheel. HISPANIA, Vol. 70, no. 1 (March 1987), p. 202. English.

Concheros Xinachtli

1929 Segura, Andres. Continuidad de la tradicion filosofica Nahuatl en las danzas de concheros. EL CUADERNO, Vol. 3, no. 1 (Winter 1973), p. 16-33. Spanish. **DESCR:** *Folklore; *Precolumbian Philosophy.

Conde, Rosina

1930 Gonzalez, Marco Vinicio. En el pais de la frontera. LA COMUNIDAD, No. 291 (February 16, 1986), p. 6-7+. Spanish. **DESCR:** Border Region; *DIALOGOS FRONTERIZOS [radio program]; Gomez Pena, Guillermo; Medina, Ruben; *Radio; San Diego, CA; Tijuana, Baja California, Mexico.

Conferences and Meetings

1931 Academics and entrepreneurs talk trade. HISPANIC BUSINESS, Vol. 9, no. 6 (June 1987), p. 96. English. **DESCR:** *Business Enterprises; Fourth Symposium on Hispanic Business and Economy, San Juan, Puerto Rico, November 23-25, 1987; *International Economic Relations; Latin America; *National Association of Hispanic Professors of Business Administration and Economics (Los Profesores); Organizations; Teaching Profession.

1932 Architects of America's future. VISTA, Vol. 1, no. 11 (July 6, 1986), p. 10. English. **DESCR:** National Council of La Raza (NCLR); Social History and Conditions; *Yzaguirre, Raul.

1933 Beale, Stephen. Networking the networks. HISPANIC BUSINESS, Vol. 9, no. 9 (September 1987), p. 38-43. English. **DESCR:** Business; *U.S. Hispanic Chamber of Commerce.

1934 Cisneros encourages LULAC to take lead in Hispanic agenda. HISPANIC ENGINEER, Vol. 3, no. 3 (1987), p. 14-15. English. **DESCR:** *Cisneros, Henry, Mayor of San Antonio, TX; *League of United Latin American Citizens (LULAC).

Conferences and Meetings (cont.)

1935 East coast conference on "El Movimiento Chicano". LA RED/THE NET, no. 40 (March 1981), p. 7. English. DESCR: Chicano Movement; *El Movimiento Chicano Conference, February 13-14, 1981.

1936 Madrid, Vicente and Yepes, Maria Elena. National Latino Media Coalition. LATIN QUARTER, Vol. 1, no. 4 (July, August, 1975), p. 4-7. English. DESCR: Affirmative Action Programs; Bilingual/Bicultural Coalition on Mass Media; *Broadcast Media; California Association of Latins in Broadcasting; Federal Communications Commission (FCC); *National Latino Media Coalition (NLMC); Puerto Rican Media Action and Educational Council.

1937 Marketing to U.S. Hispanics. ADVERTISING WORLD, no. 6 (December 1983), p. 26-27. English. DESCR: *Marketing; Mass Media.

1938 Scenes from the February SHPE careers conference. HISPANIC ENGINEER, Vol. 3, no. 1 (Spring 1987), p. 14-15. English. DESCR: Guerrero, Art; *Salazar, Diane; Society of Hispanic Professional Engineers (SHPE).

1939 SHPE holds first ever East coast conference for Hispanic engineers. HISPANIC ENGINEER, Vol. 3, no. 5 (Winter 1987), p. 12-14. English. DESCR: Awards; Barrios, Eugene; Chang-Diaz, Franklin; Cuevas, Brian L.; Garay, Charles J.; Garcia, Ray; Marrero, Charles; Martinez, Lisa; Monteverde, Edwin; Plumey, Raymond; Reyes-Guerra, David; Rivera, Angel; Society of Hispanic Professional Engineers (SHPE); Soto, Giovanni.

1940 Solorzano, Daniel. Impressions from the 1986 American Education Research Association (AERA), held in San Francisco, April 16-20. LA RED/THE NET, no. 96 (May 1986), p. 9-11. English. DESCR: *American Education Research Association (AERA), San Francisco, April 16-20, 1988.

1941 Solorzano, Daniel. Reflections on the 1986 National Association for Chicano Studies (NACS) held in El Paso, Texas, April 9-12. LA RED/THE NET, no. 96 (May 1986), p. 8-9. English. DESCR: *National Association for Chicano Studies (NACS) Annual Conference, El Paso, TX, April 9-12, 1986.

1942 Texas Association of Chicanos in Higher Education (TACHE) holds annual conference. LA RED/THE NET, No. 100 (September 1986), p. 2-5. English. DESCR: *Educational Organizations; *Higher Education; *Texas Association of Chicanos in Higher Education (TACHE).

1943 USHCC to host 8th annual convention in Los Angeles. HISPANIC ENGINEER, Vol. 3, no. 3 (1987), p. 16. English. DESCR: *U.S. Hispanic Chamber of Commerce.

Congregation B'nai Zion, El Paso, TX

1944 Burciaga, Jose Antonio. In celebration of a man's ecumenism. VISTA, Vol. 2, no. 4 (December 7, 1986), p. 26. English. DESCR: *Catholic Church; Holidays; Jews; *Religion.

Congressional Hispanic Caucus

1945 Cruz, David V. Caucus & Co. orients the East. HISPANIC BUSINESS, Vol. 9, no. 11 (November 1987), p. 10-13, 71+. English. DESCR: Businesspeople; Elected Officials; *International Relations; *Japan; Latin Business Foundation, Los Angeles, CA; Nakasone, Yasuhiro [Prime Minister of Japan]; *Taiwan.

Conjuntos

1946 Arreola, Daniel D. The Mexican American cultural capital. GEOGRAPHICAL REVIEW, Vol. 77, (January 1987), p. 17-34. English. DESCR: Food Industry; History; Immigration; LA PRENSA, San Antonio, TX; La Raza Unida Party; League of United Latin American Citizens (LULAC); Lozano, Ignacio; Mexican American Youth Organization, San Antonio, TX; Music; Orden Hijos de America, San Antonio, TX; Railroads; *San Antonio, TX; *Social History and Conditions.

1947 Pena, Manuel. From ranchero to jaiton: ethnicity and class in Texas-Mexican music (two styles in the form of a pair). ETHNOMUSICOLOGY, Vol. 29, no. 1 (Winter 1985), p. 29-55. English. DESCR: *Ethnomusicology; Musical Instruments; Villa, Beto.

Connor, Walker

1948 Dorn, Georgette Magassy. Book review of: MEXICAN-AMERICANS IN COMPARATIVE PERSPECTIVES. AMERICAS, Vol. 43, no. 1 (July 1986), p. 110. English. DESCR: Book Reviews; *MEXICAN AMERICANS IN COMPARATIVE PERSPECTIVE.

Constitution of the United States

1949 Perez, Renato E. The United States Constitution: an inspiration to Latin America. VISTA, Vol. 3, no. 1 (September 6, 1987), p. 6-7, 24. English. DESCR: *History.

Constitutional Amendments - Fourth

1950 Culp, Robert Alan. The Immigration and Naturalization Service and racially motivated questioning: does equal protection pick up where the Fourth Amendment left off? COLUMBIA LAW REVIEW, Vol. 86, no. 4 (May 1986), p. 800-822. English. DESCR: Border Patrol; *Discrimination; *Immigration and Naturalization Service (INS); Immigration Law and Legislation; Immigration Regulation and Control; *Search and Seizure.

Consumers

1951 DelPriore, Lisa. Tapping into the Hispanic market. MARKETING COMMUNICATIONS, Vol. 11, no. 6 (June 1986), p. 57-62. English. DESCR: *Advertising; *Marketing; *Mass Media.

1952 Dempsey, Mary. Latinas in the driver's seat. VISTA, Vol. 2, no. 5 (January 4, 1987), p. 12-15. English. DESCR: *Automobile Industry.

1953 Drive away with $5.2 billion. HISPANIC BUSINESS, Vol. 9, no. 9 (September 1987), p. 71. English. DESCR: *Automobile Industry; *Marketing.

1954 Edmondson, Brad. Met Life mines minority market. AMERICAN DEMOGRAPHICS, Vol. 8, no. 7 (July 1986), p. 18-19. English. DESCR: Ethnic Groups; Immigrants; Insurance; Marketing; *Metropolitan Life Insurance Corporation.

Consumers (cont.)

1955 Fitch, Ed. Buying power bursts poverty-stricken image. ADVERTISING AGE MAGAZINE, Vol. 58, no. 6 (February 9, 1987), p. S1-S2, S8. English. **DESCR:** Advertising; *Marketing.

1956 Fitch, Ed. Prime space available at low rates. ADVERTISING AGE MAGAZINE, Vol. 57, no. 16 (February 27, 1986), p. 11-12. English. **DESCR:** Advertising; General Foods; *Marketing.

1957 The Hispanic market: an untapped resource. CHAIN STORE AGE SUPERMARKET, Vol. 59, no. 6 (June 1983), p. 41. English. **DESCR:** Business Enterprises; *Marketing.

1958 Hispanic marketing. ADVERTISING AGE MAGAZINE, Vol. 57, no. 16 (February 27, 1986), p. 11-51. English. **DESCR:** Adolph Coors Co.; Advertising; Allstate Insurance Co.; American Greetings; Anheuser-Busch, Inc.; Business Enterprises; Coca-Cola Company; Ford Motor Company; Hallmark Cards; *Marketing; Mass Media; McDonald's Corporation; Metropolitan Life Insurance Corporation; Pepsi-Cola Bottling Group; Prudential; Spanish International Network (SIN); State Farm Mutual Insurance; Tylenol; United Insurance Co. of America.

1959 Jacobson, Harold. Upward trend in expenditures continues. HISPANIC BUSINESS, Vol. 9, no. 12 (December 1987), p. 19-20. English. **DESCR:** *Advertising; Income; *Marketing; Mass Media.

1960 Kane, Michael G. "Touching" minorities. EDITOR & PUBLISHER: THE FOURTH ESTATE, Vol. 119, no. 38 (September 20, 1986), p. 20-21. English. **DESCR:** Advertising; Ethnic Groups; Marketing; *Newspapers.

1961 Kesler, Lori. A-B benefits from regional approach. ADVERTISING AGE MAGAZINE, Vol. 57, no. 16 (February 27, 1986), p. 48-49. English. **DESCR:** Advertising; Anheuser-Busch, Inc.; *Marketing.

1962 Macias, Reynaldo Flores and Cabello-Argandona, Roberto. Media research and the Chicano. LATIN QUARTER, Vol. 1, no. 2 (October 1974), p. 14-16,18. English. **DESCR:** Advertising; Marketing; *Mass Media; Population.

1963 Magiera, Marcy. New arrivals find warm welcome as consumers. ADVERTISING AGE MAGAZINE, Vol. 58, no. 6 (February 9, 1987), p. S14. English. **DESCR:** Immigrants; *Marketing; Undocumented Workers.

1964 Marketing to Hispanics. ADVERTISING AGE MAGAZINE, Vol. 58, no. 6 (February 9, 1987), p. S1-S23. English. **DESCR:** Advertising; Immigrants; *Marketing; Mass Media; Politics; Undocumented Workers.

1965 Moya, Steven. Foreign relations: implementing an Hispanic marketing program. S & MM [SALES & MARKETING MANAGEMENT], Vol. 135, no. 2 (July 22, 1985), p. A22+. English. **DESCR:** *Marketing; *Public Relations.

1966 Reilly, Michael D. and Wallendorf, Melanie. A longitudinal study of Mexican-American assimilation. ADVANCES IN CONSUMER RESEARCH, Vol. 11, (1984), p. 735-740. English. **DESCR:** *Assimilation; Culture; Food Practices; *Marketing.

1967 Rifkin, Jane M. Courting the Latino market. HISPANIC TIMES, Vol. 8, no. 1 (December, January, 1987), p. 49. English. **DESCR:** *Marketing.

1968 Sansolo, Michael. Merchandising to Hispanics: are you speaking their language? PROGRESSIVE GROCER, Vol. 65, no. 2 (February 1986), p. 20-22+. English. **DESCR:** *Cultural Characteristics; *Marketing.

1969 Valencia, Bert. Purchasing power rises 10 percent. HISPANIC BUSINESS, Vol. 9, no. 12 (December 1987), p. 15. English. **DESCR:** *Income; *Statistics.

CONTEMPORARY CHICANA POETRY: A CRITICAL APPROACH TO AN EMERGING LITERATURE

1970 Castillo-Speed, Lillian. Chicana/Latina literature and criticism: reviews of recent books. WLW JOURNAL, Vol. 11, no. 3 (September 1987), p. 1-4. English. **DESCR:** Andrews, Lynn V.; *Book Reviews; BORDERS; Chavez, Denise; *Chicanas; Flores, Angel; Flores, Kate; JAGUAR WOMAN; Mora, Pat; Sanchez, Marta Ester; Tafolla, Carmen; THE DEFIANT MUSE: HISPANIC FEMINIST POEMS FROM THE MIDDLE AGES TO THE PRESENT; THE LAST OF THE MENU GIRLS; TO SPLIT A HUMAN: MITOS, MACHOS Y LA MUJER CHICANA; Vigil-Pinon, Evangelina; WOMAN OF HER WORD: HISPANIC WOMEN WRITE.

1971 Grabo, Norman S. Book review of: CONTEMPORARY CHICANA POETRY. AMERICAN LITERATURE, Vol. 58, no. 3 (October 1986), p. 473-475. English. **DESCR:** Book Reviews; Poetry; Sanchez, Marta Ester.

1972 Isaacs, D.S. Book review of: CONTEMPORARY CHICANA POETRY. CHOICE, Vol. 23, no. 8 (April 1986), p. 1217. English. **DESCR:** Book Reviews; Sanchez, Marta Ester.

1973 Lewis, Tom J. Book review of: CONTEMPORARY CHICANA POETRY. WORLD LITERATURE TODAY, Vol. 60, (Summer 1986), p. 453. English. **DESCR:** Book Reviews; Chicanas; Poetry; Sanchez, Marta Ester.

1974 Schmitt, Jack. Book review of: CONTEMPORARY CHICANA POETRY. LOS ANGELES TIMES BOOK REVIEW, (December 29, 1985), p. 8. English. **DESCR:** Book Reviews; Chicanas; Poetry; Sanchez, Marta Ester.

1975 Torres, Lourdes. Book review of: CONTEMPORARY CHICANA POETRY. WESTERN AMERICAN LITERATURE, Vol. 21, no. 4 (1987), p. 378-379. English. **DESCR:** Book Reviews; Sanchez, Marta Ester.

Contraception
USE: Birth Control

CONTRACTOR REPORT: RELATIVE EDUCATIONAL ATTAINMENT OF MINORITY LANGUAGE CHILDREN, 1976: A COMPARISON TO BLACK AND WHITE ENGLISH LANGUAGE CHILDREN

1976 Macias, Reynaldo Flores. Disambiguating the Veltman trilogy. BILINGUAL REVIEW, Vol. 12, no. 1-2 (January, August, 1985), p. 140-143. English. **DESCR:** Book Reviews; *CONTRACTOR REPORT: THE ROLE OF LANGUAGE CHARACTERISTICS IN THE SOCIOECONOMIC PROCESS OF HISPANIC ORIGIN MEN AND WOMEN; Language Usage; *THE RETENTION OF MINORITY LANGUAGES IN THE UNITED STATES: A SEMINAR ON THE ANALYTIC WORK OF CALVIN VELTMAN; Veltman, Calvin.

CONTRACTOR REPORT: THE ROLE OF LANGUAGE CHARACTERISTICS IN THE SOCIOECONOMIC PROCESS OF HISPANIC ORIGIN MEN AND WOMEN

1977 Macias, Reynaldo Flores. Disambiguating the Veltman trilogy. BILINGUAL REVIEW, Vol. 12, no. 1-2 (January, August, 1985), p. 140-143. English. **DESCR**: Book Reviews; *CONTRACTOR REPORT: RELATIVE EDUCATIONAL ATTAINMENT OF MINORITY LANGUAGE CHILDREN, 1976: A COMPARISON TO BLACK AND WHITE ENGLISH LANGUAGE CHILDREN; Language Usage; *THE RETENTION OF MINORITY LANGUAGES IN THE UNITED STATES: A SEMINAR ON THE ANALYTIC WORK OF CALVIN VELTMAN; Veltman, Calvin.

Contreras, Reynaldo A.

1978 Report to the Network. LA RED/THE NET, No. 104 (January 1987), p. 1-2. English. **DESCR**: Computers; *Higher Education; *Midwestern States; *Natural Support Systems; Research Methodology; Surveys.

Cookery
USE: Recipes

Cooperative Preschool Inventory (CPI)

1979 Powers, Stephen and Medina, Marcello, Jr. Factorial validity of the Cooperative Preschool Inventory for English- and Spanish-speaking Hispanic children. JOURNAL OF PSYCHOLOGY, Vol. 119, no. 3 (May 1985), p. 277-280. English. **DESCR**: *Cooperative Preschool Inventory [Spanish edition]; *Educational Tests and Measurements; *Psychological Testing.

Cooperative Preschool Inventory [Spanish edition]

1980 Powers, Stephen and Medina, Marcello, Jr. Factorial validity of the Cooperative Preschool Inventory for English- and Spanish-speaking Hispanic children. JOURNAL OF PSYCHOLOGY, Vol. 119, no. 3 (May 1985), p. 277-280. English. **DESCR**: *Cooperative Preschool Inventory (CPI); *Educational Tests and Measurements; *Psychological Testing.

Coors/HACER Agreement, 1984

1981 Beale, Stephen. Friendly persuasion: pacts and covenants. HISPANIC BUSINESS, Vol. 9, no. 9 (September 1987), p. 20-26. English. **DESCR**: *Adolph Coors Co.; *Business; Community Organizations; *Corporations; *Hispanic Association on Corporate Responsibility (HACER); Organizations; Pacific Bell; Southland Corporation.

1982 Sellers, Jeff M. Golden opportunity. HISPANIC BUSINESS, Vol. 9, no. 9 (September 1987), p. 14-18, 79. English. **DESCR**: *Adolph Coors Co.; Business Enterprises; *Corporations; Employment; Hispanic Association on Corporate Responsibility (HACER); Organizations.

LAS COPLAS A LA MUERTE DE SU PADRE

1983 Bruce-Novoa, Juan. Elegias a la frontera hispanica. BILINGUAL REVIEW, Vol. 11, no. 3 (September, December, 1984), p. 37-44. Spanish. **DESCR**: *"El Louie" [poem]; Literary Criticism; Manrique, Jorge; Montoya, Jose E.; Poetry.

Copyright
USE: Publishing Industry

Cordasco, Francesco

1984 Book review of: THE IMMIGRANT WOMAN IN NORTH AMERICA. BOOKLIST, Vol. 82, no. 12 (February 15, 1986), p. 855-856. English. **DESCR**: Book Reviews; Reference Works; *THE IMMIGRANT WOMAN IN NORTH AMERICA: AN ANNOTATED BIBLIOGRAPHY OF SELECTED REFERENCES.

1985 Freiband, Susan J. Book review of: THE IMMIGRANT WOMAN IN NORTH AMERICA. AMERICAN REFERENCE BOOKS ANNUAL, Vol. 17, (1986), p. 178. English. **DESCR**: Book Reviews; *THE IMMIGRANT WOMAN IN NORTH AMERICA: AN ANNOTATED BIBLIOGRAPHY OF SELECTED REFERENCES.

1986 Hagle, C. Book review of: THE IMMIGRANT WOMAN IN NORTH AMERICA. CHOICE, Vol. 23, no. 8 (April 1986), p. 1191. English. **DESCR**: Book Reviews; Reference Works; *THE IMMIGRANT WOMAN IN NORTH AMERICA: AN ANNOTATED BIBLIOGRAPHY OF SELECTED REFERENCES.

Corella Electric Inc., Phoenix, AZ

1987 The top 100--profiles. HISPANIC BUSINESS, Vol. 9, no. 11 (November 1987), p. 31-50. English. **DESCR**: Artco Contracting, Inc., Auburn Hills, MI; *Business Enterprises; Computer Trade Development Corp, Birmingham, MI; GSE Construction Co., Inc., Livermore, CA; National Systems & Research Co.; Unique Construction Co., Hillside, IL.

Corporations

1988 Beale, Stephen. Friendly persuasion: pacts and covenants. HISPANIC BUSINESS, Vol. 9, no. 9 (September 1987), p. 20-26. English. **DESCR**: *Adolph Coors Co.; *Business; Community Organizations; Coors/HACER Agreement, 1984; *Hispanic Association on Corporate Responsibility (HACER); Organizations; Pacific Bell; Southland Corporation.

1989 Beale, Stephen. Inertia in the corporate boardroom. HISPANIC BUSINESS, Vol. 9, no. 8 (August 1987), p. 9-11. English. **DESCR**: *Businesspeople; *Management.

1990 Beale, Stephen. The Maxwell House that Marlboro bought. HISPANIC BUSINESS, Vol. 9, no. 2 (February 1987), p. 20-21, 60. English. **DESCR**: Advertising; Business Enterprises; *Marketing; *Philip Morris, Inc..

1991 Beale, Stephen. New blood, fresh money: Telemundo, Univision bullish on television market. HISPANIC BUSINESS, Vol. 9, no. 12 (December 1987), p. 30-36. English. **DESCR**: Hallmark Cards; LatCom; Radio; Spanish International Communications Corp. (SICC); *Spanish Language; *Telemundo Television Group; *Television; Univision.

1992 Beale, Stephen. Striking a deal with big business. HISPANIC BUSINESS, Vol. 9, no. 2 (February 1987), p. 26-33. English. **DESCR**: *Adolph Coors Co.; American G.I. Forum; Boycotts; Cuban National Planning Council, Inc. Washington, D.C.; Employment; *Hispanic Association on Corporate Responsibility (HACER); League of United Latin American Citizens (LULAC); National Council of La Raza (NCLR); National IMAGE; National Puerto Rican Coalition; *Organizations; U.S. Hispanic Chamber of Commerce.

Corporations (cont.)

1993 Garcia, Art. Financing the corporate take-off. HISPANIC BUSINESS, Vol. 9, no. 5 (May 1987), p. 22-27. English. **DESCR:** Aguirre Architects, Dallas, TX; Aguirre, Pedro; Banking Industry; *Business Enterprises; Businesspeople; *Investments; Minority Enterprise Small Business Investment Corporation (MESBIC); Morales, Ramon; Protocom Devices, New York, NY; Villamil, Antonio.

1994 Garcia, Philip J. Ready to go on board? HISPANIC BUSINESS, Vol. 9, no. 5 (May 1987), p. 17. English. **DESCR:** *Businesspeople; *Careers; *Management.

1995 Lopez, Dayne E. Job security? It could be a myth! HISPANIC TIMES, Vol. 8, no. 5 (October, November, 1987), p. 10. English. **DESCR:** *Employment.

1996 Perez, Renato E. The business of Hispanics. VISTA, Vol. 2, no. 1 (September 7, 1986), p. 10. English. **DESCR:** Adolph Coors Co.; American G.I. Forum; Apodaca, Jerry [Gov. of New Mexico]; Business; *Collective Bargaining; Cuban National Planning Council, Inc. Washington, D.C.; *Hispanic Association on Corporate Responsibility (HACER); League of United Latin American Citizens (LULAC); National Council of La Raza (NCLR); National IMAGE; U.S. Hispanic Chamber of Commerce.

1997 Sellers, Jeff M. Golden opportunity. HISPANIC BUSINESS, Vol. 9, no. 9 (September 1987), p. 14-18, 79. English. **DESCR:** *Adolph Coors Co.; Business Enterprises; *Coors/HACER Agreement, 1984; Employment; Hispanic Association on Corporate Responsibility (HACER); Organizations.

1998 Sellers, Jeff M. Metropolitan Life continues to lead. HISPANIC BUSINESS, Vol. 9, no. 5 (May 1987), p. 12-14. English. **DESCR:** Advertising; *Insurance; *Marketing; *Metropolitan Life Insurance Corporation; U.S. Hispanic Chamber of Commerce.

1999 Trager, Cara S. Manhattan executive forum. HISPANIC BUSINESS, Vol. 9, no. 4 (April 1987), p. 10-13. English. **DESCR:** Advertising; Marketing; *National Hispanic Corporate Council (NHCC); *Organizations.

Corralejo, Mary

2000 Silva, Sojeila Maria. Mary Corralejo: "...there next to you.". REVISTA MUJERES, Vol. 1, no. 1 (January 1984), p. 12-13. English. **DESCR:** *Biography.

Corridos

2001 Bensusan, Guy. A consideration of Nortena and Chicano music. STUDIES IN LATIN AMERICAN POPULAR CULTURE, Vol. 4, (1985), p. 158-169. English. **DESCR:** Music; *Nortenas.

2002 Burciaga, Jose Antonio. Corridos. VISTA, Vol. 3, no. 2 (October 3, 1987), p. 10. English. **DESCR:** *CORRIDOS [film]; Ronstadt, Linda; *Teatro; Television; Valdez, Luis.

2003 Cobos, Ruben. Cantares nuevomexicanos. EL CUADERNO, Vol. 3, no. 2 (Spring 1974), p. 41. Spanish. **DESCR:** *Folklore.

2004 Preciado, Consuelo. CORRIDOS: the movie=CORRIDOS: la pelicula. AMERICAS 2001, Vol. 1, no. 2 (September, October, 1987), p. 5-6. Bilingual. **DESCR:** *CORRIDOS [film]; El Teatro Campesino; *Films; Teatro; Valdez, Luis.

2005 Ramirez, Norma. El corrido de Jose Elisalde. LLUEVE TLALOC, no. 9 (1982), p. 1. Spanish. **DESCR:** *Elisalde, Jose; *Poems.

2006 Saldivar, Jose David. Towards a Chicano poetics: the making of the Chicano subject. CONFLUENCIA, Vol. 1, no. 2 (Spring 1986), p. 10-17. English. **DESCR:** Feminism; *Literary Criticism; "Los vatos" [poem]; Montoya, Jose E.; *Poetry; RESTLESS SERPENTS; Rios, Alberto; WHISPERING TO FOOL THE WIND; Zamora, Bernice.

CORRIDOS [film]

2007 Burciaga, Jose Antonio. Corridos. VISTA, Vol. 3, no. 2 (October 3, 1987), p. 10. English. **DESCR:** Corridos; Ronstadt, Linda; *Teatro; Television; Valdez, Luis.

2008 Burciaga, Jose Antonio and Ronstadt, Linda. Linda Ronstadt: my Mexican soul. VISTA, Vol. 2, no. 10 (June 7, 1987), p. 6-8. English. **DESCR:** Biography; *Musicians; *Ronstadt, Linda.

2009 Preciado, Consuelo. CORRIDOS: the movie=CORRIDOS: la pelicula. AMERICAS 2001, Vol. 1, no. 2 (September, October, 1987), p. 5-6. Bilingual. **DESCR:** Corridos; El Teatro Campesino; *Films; Teatro; Valdez, Luis.

CORRIDOS [play]

2010 Burciaga, Jose Antonio. A man with his teatro. VISTA, Vol. 1, no. 3 (November 3, 1985), p. 8-10. English. **DESCR:** El Teatro Campesino; *Teatro; *Valdez, Luis; ZOOT SUIT [play].

Cortes, Ernesto, Jr.

2011 Cortes, Ernesto, Jr. Changing the locus of political decision making. CHRISTIANITY AND CRISIS, Vol. 47, no. 1 (February 2, 1987), p. 18-22. English. **DESCR:** Biography; *Communities Organized for Public Service (COPS); *Political Parties and Organizations; San Antonio, TX.

Cortes [family name]

2012 Instituto Genealogico e Historico Latino-Americano. Rootsearch: Cortes: Ulibarri. VISTA, Vol. 1, no. 5 (January 5, 1986), p. 22. English. **DESCR:** Genealogy; History; *Personal Names; Ulibarri [family name].

Corwin, Arthur F.

2013 Montejano, David. Book review of: IMMIGRANTS--AND IMMIGRANTS. LA RED/THE NET, no. 43 (June 1981), p. 4. English. **DESCR:** Book Reviews; Immigrants; *IMMIGRANTS---AND IMMIGRANTS: PERSPECTIVES ON MEXICAN LABOR MIGRATION TO THE UNITED STATES.

Cosmetology

2014 Allsup, Dan. The story of Stella. VISTA, Vol. 2, no. 1 (September 7, 1986), p. 16. English. **DESCR:** Business Enterprises; *Guerra, Stella; U.S. Air Force; U.S. Department of Defense (DOD).

2015 Cordova, Gilbert Benito. Certain curious colonial Chicano cosmetological customs. EL CUADERNO, Vol. 3, no. 2 (Spring 1974), p. 19-27. English. **DESCR:** *Precolumbian Society; Women.

Cosmetology (cont.)

2016 Remas, Theodora A. The beauty in cosmetics. VISTA, Vol. 2, no. 7 (March 8, 1987), p. 8-11. English.

Council on Interracial Books for Children

2017 Nieto, Sonia. Past accomplishments, current needs: la lucha continua. INTERRACIAL BOOKS FOR CHILDREN, Vol. 17, no. 2 (1986), p. 6-8. English. **DESCR**: Bilingual Bicultural Education; *Children's Literature; Poverty; Stereotypes.

Counseling (Educational)

2018 Eisen, Marvin. Working for positive change in the barrio. LATIN QUARTER, Vol. 1, no. 1 (July 1974), p. 8-10. English. **DESCR**: *East Los Angeles Skills Center; *Gangs; Maravilla.

2019 Kuner, Charles. Peer group counseling: applied psychology in the high school. CURRICULUM REVIEW, Vol. 23, no. 1 (February 1984), p. 89-92. English. **DESCR**: Chicago, IL; *Counseling (Psychological); Education; Farragut High School, Chicago, IL; Students.

2020 Pinkney, James W. and Ramirez, Marty. Career-planning myths of Chicano students. JOURNAL OF COLLEGE STUDENT PERSONNEL, Vol. 26, (July 1985), p. 300-305. English. **DESCR**: *Careers; Cultural Characteristics.

2021 Rivera, Alvin D. Laying a foundation for learning: student peer workshop groups. NEW DIRECTIONS FOR TEACHING AND LEARNING, no. 16 (December 1983), p. 81-86. English. **DESCR**: *Careers; *Engineering as a Profession; *Natural Support Systems; Organizations; Students.

2022 Smith, Mary Perry. Early identification and support: the University of California-Berkeley's MESA program. NEW DIRECTIONS FOR TEACHING AND LEARNING, no. 24 (December 1985), p. 19-25. English. **DESCR**: *Engineering as a Profession; Enrollment; Higher Education; *Mathematics, Engineering and Science Achievement (MESA); University of California, Berkeley.

Counseling (Psychological)

2023 Anderson, John W. The effects of culture and social class on client preference for counseling methods. JOURNAL OF NON-WHITE CONCERNS IN PERSONNEL AND GUIDANCE, Vol. 11, no. 3 (April 1983), p. 84-88. English. **DESCR**: Cultural Characteristics; Ethnic Groups; Social Classes.

2024 Dennedy-Frank, David P. Book review of: CROSSING CULTURES IN THERAPY. LA RED/THE NET, no. 41 (April 1981), p. 5-6. English. **DESCR**: Book Reviews; *CROSSING CULTURES IN THERAPY: PLURALISTIC COUNSELING FOR THE HISPANIC; Levine, Elaine S.; *Mental Health; Padilla, Amado M.

2025 Kuner, Charles. Peer group counseling: applied psychology in the high school. CURRICULUM REVIEW, Vol. 23, no. 1 (February 1984), p. 89-92. English. **DESCR**: Chicago, IL; Counseling (Educational); Education; Farragut High School, Chicago, IL; Students.

2026 Remas, Theodora A. Down and blue. VISTA, Vol. 2, no. 5 (January 4, 1987), p. 16-18. English. **DESCR**: *Depression (Psychological); *National Institute of Mental Health; Social History and Conditions; Spanish Family Guidance Clinic, Miami, FL.

Court Decisions
USE: Administration of Justice

Courts of Law

2027 Evans, James. The voice in between. VISTA, Vol. 2, no. 6 (February 8, 1987), p. 9-10. English. **DESCR**: Translations.

2028 Interpreters--"borrowing" of defense interpreter by trial court. CRIMINAL LAW REPORTER, Vol. 38, no. 4 (October 23, 1985), p. 2077. English. **DESCR**: People v. Baez; *People v. Guillen; *Translations.

Covarrubias [family name]

2029 Instituto Genealogico e Historico Latino-Americano. Rootsearch: Alvarez: Covarrubias. VISTA, Vol. 1, no. 6 (February 2, 1986), p. 22. English. **DESCR**: *Alvarez [family name]; Genealogy; History; *Personal Names.

Cowboys
USE: Vaqueros

Craver, Rebecca McDowell

2030 Dysart, Jane E. Book review of: THE IMPACT OF INTIMACY: MEXICAN-ANGLO INTERMARRIAGE IN NEW MEXICO, 1821-1846. PACIFIC HISTORICAL REVIEW, Vol. 53, no. 1 (1984), p. 82-83. English. **DESCR**: Book Reviews; Intermarriage; *THE IMPACT OF INTIMACY: MEXICAN-ANGLO INTERMARRIAGE IN NEW MEXICO, 1821-1846.

Crewdson, John

2031 Cardenas, Gilbert. Book review of: IN DEFENSE OF LA RAZA. LA RED/THE NET, no. 85 (October 1984), p. 2-5. English. **DESCR**: Balderrama, Francisco E.; Book Reviews; *IN DEFENSE OF LA RAZA: THE LOS ANGELES MEXICAN CONSULATE AND THE MEXICAN COMMUNITY; *THE TARNISHED DOOR.

Crime and Corrections
USE: Criminology

Criminal Acts

2032 Butler, Anne M. Book review of: THE GENTLEMEN'S CLUB: THE STORY OF PROSTITUTION IN EL PASO, TEXAS. ARIZONA AND THE WEST, Vol. 26, no. 4 (1984), p. 365-366. English. **DESCR**: Book Reviews; El Paso, TX; *Frost, H. Gordon; THE GENTLEMEN'S CLUB: THE STORY OF PROSTITUTION IN EL PASO, TEXAS.

2033 Herrera, Alexandra. Desde Los Angeles con amor. FEM, Vol. 11, no. 55 (July 1987), p. 21-23. Spanish. **DESCR**: Chicanas; Los Angeles, CA.

2034 Rigoni, Florenzo. Tijuana: the borders on the move. MIGRATION WORLD MAGAZINE, Vol. 15, no. 2 (1987), p. [22]-29. English. **DESCR**: *Border Region; Immigration; Scalabrini Center, Tijuana, Baja California, Mexico; *Tijuana, Baja California, Mexico; *Undocumented Workers.

Criminal Justice System

2035 Carter, David L. Hispanic interaction with the criminal justice system in Texas: experiences, attitudes, and perceptions. JOURNAL OF CRIMINAL JUSTICE, Vol. 11, no. 3 (1983), p. 213-227. English. **DESCR**: Cultural Characteristics.

Criminal Justice System (cont.)

2036 Chicano activist "Kiko" Martinez convicted. GUARDIAN, Vol. 39, no. 7 (November 12, 1986), p. 4. English. **DESCR:** Legal Cases; *Martinez, Francisco "Kiko"; Militancy.

2037 Garcia, Richard. The ordeal of "Kiko" Martinez. GUARDIAN, Vol. 39, no. 3 (October 15, 1986), p. 2. English. **DESCR:** Legal Cases; *Martinez, Francisco "Kiko"; Militancy.

2038 Martinez, David A. The nightmare of Kiko Martinez. GUILD NOTES, Vol. 9, no. 2 (Spring 1985), p. 4. English. **DESCR:** Legal Cases; *Legal Profession; *Martinez, Francisco "Kiko"; Political Repression.

2039 Martinez, Elizabeth. A decade of repression: update on the "Kiko" Martinez case. CRIME AND SOCIAL JUSTICE, no. 19 (Summer 1983), p. 100. English. **DESCR:** Chicano Movement; Civil Rights; Colorado; Discrimination; Legal Cases; *Martinez, Francisco "Kiko"; Political Repression.

2040 McKanna, Clare V. The San Quentin prison pardon papers: a look at file no. 1808, the case of Francisco Javier Bonilla. SOUTHERN CALIFORNIA QUARTERLY, Vol. 67, no. 2 (Summer 1985), p. 187-196. English. **DESCR:** Administration of Justice; Archives; *Bonilla, Francisco Javier; History; *Prisoners; *San Quentin Prison.

2041 Zanger, Maggy. Trial of an activist lawyer. THE PROGRESSIVE, Vol. 50, no. 12 (December 1986), p. 16-17. English. **DESCR:** Legal Cases; *Martinez, Francisco "Kiko"; Tucson, AZ.

2042 Zatz, Marjorie S. Race, ethnicity, and determinate sentencing: a new dimension to an old controversy. CRIMINOLOGY: AN INTERDISCIPLINARY JOURNAL, Vol. 22, no. 2 (May 1984), p. 147-171. English. **DESCR:** California; Criminology; Ethnic Groups.

Criminology

2043 Zatz, Marjorie S. Race, ethnicity, and determinate sentencing: a new dimension to an old controversy. CRIMINOLOGY: AN INTERDISCIPLINARY JOURNAL, Vol. 22, no. 2 (May 1984), p. 147-171. English. **DESCR:** California; *Criminal Justice System; Ethnic Groups.

CRISOL

2044 Cota-Cardenas, Margarita. La creacion-protesta en CRISOL: (TRILOGIA). CONFLUENCIA, Vol. 1, no. 2 (Spring 1986), p. 66-72. Spanish. **DESCR:** *Alarcon, Justo S.; *Literary Criticism; Novel.

CRITICA: A JOURNAL OF CRITICAL ESSAYS

2045 Garcia, Alma. Journal review of: CRITICA: A JOURNAL OF CRITICAL ESSAYS. LECTOR, Vol. 4, no. 4-6 (1987), p. 68. English. **DESCR:** Book Reviews; Journals.

CRITICAL TEACHING AND EVERYDAY LIFE

2046 Romero, Mary. Book review of: CRITICAL TEACHING AND EVERYDAY LIFE. LA RED/THE NET, no. 69 (June 1983), p. 3-5. English. **DESCR:** Book Reviews; Shor, Ira.

Crops

2047 Chile charm. VISTA, Vol. 2, no. 7 (March 8, 1987), p. 20-22. English. **DESCR:** History; Recipes.

Cross, Harry E.

2048 de la Garza, Rodolfo O. Book review of: ACROSS THE BORDER: RURAL DEVELOPMENT IN MEXICO AND RECENT MIGRATION TO THE UNITED STATES. LA RED/THE NET, no. 69 (June 1983), p. 5-7. English. **DESCR:** *ACROSS THE BORDER: RURAL DEVELOPMENT IN MEXICO AND RECENT MIGRATION; Book Reviews; Border Industries; Sandos, James.

CROSSING CULTURES IN THERAPY: PLURALISTIC COUNSELING FOR THE HISPANIC

2049 Dennedy-Frank, David P. Book review of: CROSSING CULTURES IN THERAPY. LA RED/THE NET, no. 41 (April 1981), p. 5-6. English. **DESCR:** Book Reviews; Counseling (Psychological); Levine, Elaine S.; *Mental Health; Padilla, Amado M.

Cruz, Jacqueline

2050 Pacific Telesis senior fellows. HISPANIC ENGINEER, Vol. 3, no. 2 (Summer 1987), p. 10-11. English. **DESCR:** *Awards; Castaneda, Jesus; Education; Pacific Telesis; Rodriguez, Jose; Sanchez, Alex.

The Cruzados [musical group]

2051 Sellers, Jeff M. The sound of musica: moving into the mainstream. HISPANIC BUSINESS, Vol. 9, no. 7 (July 1987), p. 14-18. English. **DESCR:** Los Lobos del Este de Los Angeles (musical group); *Marketing; Miami Sound Machine; Music; *Musicians; Zerimar [musical group].

EL CUADERNO

2052 Atencio, Tomas. La resolana [editorial]. EL CUADERNO, Vol. 4, no. 1 (Summer 1976), p. 2-4. English. **DESCR:** Academia Asociados, NM; Academia Educational Model; *Chicano Studies; Culture; ENTRE VERDE Y SECO; *La Academia de la Nueva Raza, Dixon, NM; LA MADRUGADA; Publishing Industry.

Cuadros, Hugo

2053 Grayson, June. Sports medics. VISTA, Vol. 2, no. 9 (May 3, 1987), p. 17-18. English. **DESCR:** Bergin-Nader, Barbara; Doctor Patient Relations; *Dominguez, Richard; *Medical Personnel; Prietto, Carlos Alfredo; *Sports.

CUANDO ESTEMOS JUNTOS [phonograph record]

2054 Machado, Melinda. Saying "no" to teenage sex. VISTA, Vol. 2, no. 11 (July 5, 1987), p. 14. English. **DESCR:** DETENTE [phonograph record]; Music; *Musical Lyrics; Planned Parenthood Federation of America; Sex Education; Tatiana and Johnny.

Cuban Americans
USE: Cubanos

CUBAN AMERICANS: MASTERS OF SURVIVAL

2055 Herrera-Sobek, Maria. Book review of: CUBAN AMERICANS: MASTERS OF SURVIVAL. LA RED/THE NET, no. 67 (April 1983), p. 10-12. English. **DESCR:** Book Reviews; Cubanos; Llanes, Jose.

Cuban National Planning Council, Inc. Washington, D.C.

2056 Beale, Stephen. Striking a deal with big business. HISPANIC BUSINESS, Vol. 9, no. 2 (February 1987), p. 26-33. English. **DESCR**: *Adolph Coors Co.; American G.I. Forum; Boycotts; Corporations; Employment; *Hispanic Association on Corporate Responsibility (HACER); League of United Latin American Citizens (LULAC); National Council of La Raza (NCLR); National IMAGE; National Puerto Rican Coalition; *Organizations; U.S. Hispanic Chamber of Commerce.

2057 Perez, Renato E. The business of Hispanics. VISTA, Vol. 2, no. 1 (September 7, 1986), p. 10. English. **DESCR**: Adolph Coors Co.; American G.I. Forum; Apodaca, Jerry [Gov. of New Mexico]; Business; *Collective Bargaining; Corporations; *Hispanic Association on Corporate Responsibility (HACER); League of United Latin American Citizens (LULAC); National Council of La Raza (NCLR); National IMAGE; U.S. Hispanic Chamber of Commerce.

Cubanos

2058 Guedella, Juan. Hispanic media--Caballero style. HISPANIC BUSINESS, Vol. 9, no. 2 (February 1987), p. 17-18. English. **DESCR**: Advertising; Biography; *Caballero, Eduardo; *Caballero Spanish Media (CSM); Marketing.

2059 Herrera-Sobek, Maria. Book review of: CUBAN AMERICANS: MASTERS OF SURVIVAL. LA RED/THE NET, no. 67 (April 1983), p. 10-12. English. **DESCR**: Book Reviews; *CUBAN AMERICANS: MASTERS OF SURVIVAL; Llanes, Jose.

2060 Volsky, George. A new voting block making its mark. HISPANIC BUSINESS, Vol. 9, no. 2 (February 1987), p. 9, 11. English. **DESCR**: Democratic Party; Elections; *Political Parties and Organizations; Republican Party; *Voter Turnout.

Cuco's Restaurant

2061 Lang, Joan M. Sizzler franchisee is going Cucos! RESTAURANT BUSINESS, Vol. 83, (June 10, 1984), p. 142-152. English. **DESCR**: *Restaurants.

Cuellar, Jose B.

2062 Jackson, James S. Book review of: UNDERSTANDING MINORITY AGING: PERSPECTIVES AND SOURCES. LA RED/THE NET, no. 68 (May 1983), p. 12-13. English. **DESCR**: Book Reviews; Miller-Soule, Danielle I.; Stanford, E.P. Percil; *UNDERSTANDING MINORITY AGING: PERSPECTIVES AND SOURCES.

Cuentos

2063 Arellano, Estevan. Cuentos de cafe y tortilla. EL CUADERNO, Vol. 4, no. 1 (Summer 1976), p. 66-79. Spanish.

2064 Castillo, Victoria. Las tres naranjas. LLUEVE TLALOC, no. 12 (1985), p. 24. Spanish.

2065 Castro, Anna. La leyenda de la siquanaba y el zipitillo. LLUEVE TLALOC, no. 12 (1985), p. 9. Spanish. **DESCR**: *El Salvador.

2066 Castro, Anna. El zipitillo. LLUEVE TLALOC, no. 12 (1985), p. 13. Spanish.

2067 Cerda, Gabriela. La serpiente. NOTEBOOK: A LITTLE MAGAZINE, Vol. 2, no. 2 (1986), p. 14-26. English. **DESCR**: Leyendas; Mayas; *Mitos.

2068 Estrada, Javier. El pez espada y la langosta. LLUEVE TLALOC, no. 13 (1986), p. 20. Spanish.

2069 Huerta, Margarita A. Narraciones de dona Mariquita. LLUEVE TLALOC, no. 9 (1982), p. 20. Spanish. **DESCR**: *Prose.

2070 Martinez, Jose. Juan Ladron. EL CUADERNO, Vol. 4, no. 1 (Summer 1976), p. 80-88. Spanish.

2071 Mendez-M., Miguel. Huachusey. LLUEVE TLALOC, no. 9 (1982), p. 3-5. Bilingual. **DESCR**: *Short Story.

2072 Uribe, Ainoa. Rumbo hacia el Salto Angel (Canaima). LLUEVE TLALOC, no. 12 (1985), p. 27. Spanish.

2073 Vigil, Cleofes. El carbonero. EL CUADERNO, Vol. 1, no. 1 (1971), p. 23-27. Spanish.

2074 Villareal, Maria Antonia. El cuento del gallo pipirripin. LLUEVE TLALOC, no. 12 (1985), p. 13. Spanish.

2075 Yubeta, Alma. La Llorona. LLUEVE TLALOC, no. 13 (1986), p. 13. Spanish.

CUENTOS CHICANOS: A SHORT STORY ANTHOLOGY

2076 Paredes, Raymund A. Book review of: CUENTOS CHICANOS: A SHORT STORY ANTHOLOGY. WESTERN AMERICAN LITERATURE, Vol. 21, no. 3 (1986), p. 270. English. **DESCR**: Anaya, Rudolfo A.; Book Reviews; Marquez, Antonio.

2077 Ramirez, Arthur. Book review of: CUENTOS CHICANOS: A SHORT STORY ANTHOLOGY. SAN FRANCISCO REVIEW OF BOOKS, Vol. 11, (1986), p. 11,23. English. **DESCR**: Anaya, Rudolfo A.; Book Reviews; Marquez, Antonio; Short Story.

CUENTOS: STORIES BY LATINAS

2078 Cantu, Norma. Book review of: CUENTOS: STORIES BY LATINAS. LA RED/THE NET, no. 83 (August 1984), p. 2-3. English. **DESCR**: Book Reviews; Gomez, Alma; Moraga, Cherrie; Romo-Carmona, Mariana.

Cuevas, Brian L.

2079 SHPE holds first ever East coast conference for Hispanic engineers. HISPANIC ENGINEER, Vol. 3, no. 5 (Winter 1987), p. 12-14. English. **DESCR**: Awards; Barrios, Eugene; Chang-Diaz, Franklin; *Conferences and Meetings; Garay, Charles J.; Garcia, Ray; Marrero, Charles; Martinez, Lisa; Monteverde, Edwin; Plumey, Raymond; Reyes-Guerra, David; Rivera, Angel; Society of Hispanic Professional Engineers (SHPE); Soto, Giovanni.

Cullen, Ruth M.

2080 Alvirez, David. Book review of: THE CHANGING DEMOGRAPHY OF SPANISH AMERICANS. LA RED/THE NET, no. 48 (November 1981), p. 4. English. **DESCR**: Book Reviews; Boswell, Thomas D.; Jaffee, A.J.; Population; *THE CHANGING DEMOGRAPHY OF SPANISH-AMERICANS.

Cultural Characteristics

2081 13-part series focuses on Hispanics in America. EDITOR & PUBLISHER: THE FOURTH ESTATE, Vol. 115, no. 14 (April 3, 1982), p. 37. English. **DESCR:** Books; DALLAS MORNING NEWS; Garcia, Juan; Gonzalez, John; Goodwin, Jay; Grothe, Randy Eli; Hamilton, John; Hille, Ed; LA VIDA AMERICANA; *LA VIDA AMERICANA/HISPANICS IN AMERICA; Langer, Ralph; McLemore, David; Osburne, Burl; Parks, Scott; Pusey, Allen; Sonnemair, Jan.

2082 Anderson, John W. The effects of culture and social class on client preference for counseling methods. JOURNAL OF NON-WHITE CONCERNS IN PERSONNEL AND GUIDANCE, Vol. 11, no. 3 (April 1983), p. 84-88. English. **DESCR:** *Counseling (Psychological); Ethnic Groups; Social Classes.

2083 Arellano, Estevan. Chicanos nortenos. EL CUADERNO, Vol. 2, no. 1 (1972), p. 27-35. English. **DESCR:** *Discrimination; *Short Story.

2084 Atencio, Tomas. La Academia de la Nueva Raza. EL CUADERNO, Vol. 2, no. 1 (1972), p. 6-13. English. **DESCR:** *Alternative Education; Chicano Studies; *Cultural Organizations; Education; *Educational Organizations; *La Academia de la Nueva Raza, Dixon, NM; Oro del Barrio; Philosophy; Values.

2085 Baker, George A. and Rocha, Pedro, Jr. Critical incident competencies of Mexican American and Anglo American administrators. COMMUNITY/JUNIOR COLLEGE QUARTERLY OF RESEARCH AND PRACTICE, Vol. 7, no. 4 (July, September, 1983), p. 319-332. English. **DESCR:** Anglo Americans; *Community Colleges; Comparative Psychology; Educational Administration; Management; Public Policy.

2086 Carter, David L. Hispanic interaction with the criminal justice system in Texas: experiences, attitudes, and perceptions. JOURNAL OF CRIMINAL JUSTICE, Vol. 11, no. 3 (1983), p. 213-227. English. **DESCR:** *Criminal Justice System.

2087 Domino, George. Sleep habits in the elderly: a study of three Hispanic cultures. JOURNAL OF CROSS-CULTURAL PSYCHOLOGY, Vol. 17, no. 1 (March 1986), p. 109-120. English. **DESCR:** *Ancianos; *Comparative Psychology; Ethnic Groups.

2088 Duda, Joan L. Goals and achievement orientations of Anglo and Mexican-American adolescents in sport and the classroom. INTERNATIONAL REVIEW OF SPORT SOCIOLOGY, Vol. 18, no. 4 (1983), p. 63-80. English. **DESCR:** Academic Achievement; New Mexico; Sports; *Youth.

2089 Engle, Patricia L.; Scrimshaw, Susan C.M.; and Smidt, Robert. Sex differences in attitudes towards newborn infants among women of Mexican origin. MEDICAL ANTHROPOLOGY, Vol. 8, no. 2 (Spring 1984), p. 133-144. English. **DESCR:** *Attitudes; Chicanas; *Machismo; *Maternal and Child Welfare; *Parent and Child Relationships; Sex Roles.

2090 Gilbert, M. Jean. Alcohol consumption patterns in immigrant and later generation Mexican American women. HISPANIC JOURNAL OF BEHAVIORAL SCIENCES, Vol. 9, no. 3 (September 1987), p. 299-313. English. **DESCR:** Acculturation; *Alcoholism; *Attitudes; *Chicanas; *Immigrants; Mexico.

2091 Isonio, Steven A. and Garza, Raymond T. Protestant work ethic endorsement among Anglo Americans, Chicanos and Mexicans: a comparison of factor structures. HISPANIC JOURNAL OF BEHAVIORAL SCIENCES, Vol. 9, no. 4 (December 1987), p. 413-425. English. **DESCR:** *Comparative Psychology; Ethnic Groups; *Protestant Work Ethic (PWE) Scale; *Values.

2092 Jorgensen, Stephen R. and Adams, Russell P. Family planning needs and behavior of Mexican American women: a study of health care professionals and their clientele. HISPANIC JOURNAL OF BEHAVIORAL SCIENCES, Vol. 9, no. 3 (September 1987), p. 265-286. English. **DESCR:** Acculturation; *Attitudes; Birth Control; *Chicanas; *Family Planning; Fertility; Public Health; Stereotypes; Sterilization.

2093 Korzenny, Felipe, et al. Cultural identification as predictor of content preferences of Hispanics. JOURNALISM QUARTERLY, Vol. 60, no. 4 (Winter 1983), p. 677-685+. English. **DESCR:** English Language; Identity; *Newspapers; Spanish Language.

2094 Lefton, Doug. Culture a factor in treating Latino patients. AMERICAN MEDICAL NEWS, Vol. 25, (July 9, 1982), p. 17-19. English. **DESCR:** Doctor Patient Relations; Medical Care.

2095 Mares, E.A. The fiesta of life: impression of Paulo Friere. EL CUADERNO, Vol. 3, no. 2 (Spring 1974), p. 5-16. English. **DESCR:** *Aztlan; *Essays; *Freire, Paulo; *Philosophy.

2096 Miranda, Gloria E. Hispano-Mexican childrearing practices in pre-American Santa Barbara. SOUTHERN CALIFORNIA QUARTERLY, Vol. 65, no. 4 (Winter 1983), p. 307-320. English. **DESCR:** *Children; *Family; History; *Parenting; *Santa Barbara, CA; Socialization.

2097 Neibel, Barbara A. Health care utilization: the case of the Mexican-American. ANTHROPOLOGY UCLA, Vol. 14, (1985), p. 13-26. English. **DESCR:** *Medical Care; *Public Health; Vital Statistics.

2098 Nelson, Candace and Tienda, Marta. The structuring of Hispanic ethnicity: historical and contemporary perspectives. ETHNIC AND RACIAL STUDIES, Vol. 8, no. 1 (January 1985), p. 49-74. English. **DESCR:** Ethnic Groups; *Identity; Immigrants.

2099 Newquist, Deborah. The health care barrier model: toward analyzing the underutilization of health care by older Mexican-Americans. ANTHROPOLOGY UCLA, Vol. 14, (1985), p. 1-12. English. **DESCR:** *Ancianos; Discrimination; Folk Medicine; *Medical Care; Medical Clinics; *Public Health.

2100 Ornelas, Yolanda. Determined to be acknowledged. REVISTA MUJERES, Vol. 4, no. 1 (January 1987), p. 14-15. English. **DESCR:** Attitudes; *Biography; *Chicanas.

2101 Pinkney, James W. and Ramirez, Marty. Career-planning myths of Chicano students. JOURNAL OF COLLEGE STUDENT PERSONNEL, Vol. 26, (July 1985), p. 300-305. English. **DESCR:** *Careers; *Counseling (Educational).

Cultural Characteristics (cont.)

2102 Rodriguez-Scheel, Jaclyn and Beals, Janette. Chicano Survey report #5: group naming and cultural inclinations. LA RED/THE NET, no. 42 (May 1981), p. 3-4. English. DESCR: *National Chicano Survey (NCS); *Self-Referents.

2103 Sabogal, Fabio, et al. Hispanic familism and acculturation: what changes and what doesn't? HISPANIC JOURNAL OF BEHAVIORAL SCIENCES, Vol. 9, no. 4 (December 1987), p. 397-412. English. DESCR: *Acculturation; Attitudes; Ethnic Groups; Extended Family; *Family; Natural Support Systems; Values.

2104 Sansolo, Michael. Merchandising to Hispanics: are you speaking their language? PROGRESSIVE GROCER, Vol. 65, no. 2 (February 1986), p. 20-22+. English. DESCR: *Consumers; *Marketing.

Cultural Customs

2105 Armstrong, Ruth W. Christmas in Albuquerque. VISTA, Vol. 1, no. 4 (December 7, 1985), p. 18-20. English. DESCR: *Albuquerque, NM; Holidays.

2106 Hazen-Hammond, Susan and Fuss, Eduardo. Vivan las celebraciones. ARIZONA HIGHWAYS, Vol. 63, no. 8 (August 1987), p. 35-45. English. DESCR: Cinco de Mayo; Dia de los Muertos; Dieciseis de Septiembre; Fiestas Patrias; *Holidays; La Virgen de Guadalupe; Las Posadas.

2107 Igo, John N., Jr. Los Pastores: a triple-tradition. JOURNAL OF POPULAR CULTURE, Vol. 19, no. 3 (Winter 1985), p. 131-138. English. DESCR: Christmas; *Folk Drama; *Los Pastores [folk drama].

2108 LeCompte, Mary Lou and Beezley, William H. Any Sunday in April: the rise of sport in San Antonio and the Hispanic borderlands. JOURNAL OF SPORT HISTORY, Vol. 13, no. 2 (Summer 1986), p. 128-146. English. DESCR: *Charreada; History; *San Antonio, TX; *Sports.

2109 LeCompte, Mary Lou. The Hispanic influence on the history of rodeo, 1823-1922. JOURNAL OF SPORT HISTORY, Vol. 12, no. 1 (Spring 1985), p. 21-38. English. DESCR: *Charreada; *History; *Mexico.

2110 Morales, Cecilio. Judaism's Hispanic thread. VISTA, Vol. 2, no. 3 (November 2, 1986), p. 20-23. English. DESCR: History; *Jews; *Religion.

2111 Sommers, Laurie Kay. Symbol and style in Cinco de Mayo. JOURNAL OF AMERICAN FOLKLORE, Vol. 98, (October, December, 1985), p. 476-482. English. DESCR: *Cinco de Mayo; History; *Holidays; *San Francisco, CA; Symbolism.

Cultural Organizations

2112 Atencio, Tomas. La Academia de la Nueva Raza: su historia. EL CUADERNO, Vol. 1, no. 1 (1971), p. 4-9. English. DESCR: Alternative Education; Chicano Studies; *Educational Organizations; *La Academia de la Nueva Raza, Dixon, NM; Oro del Barrio.

2113 Atencio, Tomas. La Academia de la Nueva Raza. EL CUADERNO, Vol. 2, no. 1 (1972), p. 6-13. English. DESCR: *Alternative Education; Chicano Studies; Cultural Characteristics; Education; *Educational Organizations; *La Academia de la Nueva Raza, Dixon, NM; Oro del Barrio; Philosophy; Values.

2114 Atencio, Tomas. La Academia de la Nueva Raza: El Oro del Barrio. EL CUADERNO, Vol. 3, no. 1 (Winter 1973), p. 4-15. English. DESCR: Alternative Education; Chicano Studies; *Educational Organizations; *La Academia de la Nueva Raza, Dixon, NM; Oro del Barrio.

2115 Marin, Christine. La Asociacion Hispano-Americana de Madres y Esposas: Tucson's Mexican American women in World War II. RENATO ROSALDO LECTURE SERIES MONOGRAPH, Vol. 1, (Summer 1985), p. [5]-18. English. DESCR: *Chicanas; History; *La Asociacion Hispano-Americana de Madres y Esposas, Tucson, AZ; Organizations; *Tucson, AZ; World War II.

Cultural Pluralism

2116 Arenas, Soledad and Trujillo, Lorenzo A. The evaluation of four Head Start bilingual multicultural curriculum models. LA RED/THE NET, no. 66 (March 1983), p. 2-5. English. DESCR: *Bilingual Bicultural Education; Evaluation (Educational); *Head Start.

2117 Garcia, Jesus. Multiethnic education: past, present, and future. TEXAS TECH JOURNAL OF EDUCATION, Vol. 11, no. 1 (Winter 1984), p. 13-29. English. DESCR: *Education.

2118 Gonzalez, Alex. Classroom cooperation and ethnic balance: Chicanos and equal status. LA RED/THE NET, no. 68 (May 1983), p. 6-8. English. DESCR: Education; *Intergroup Relations.

2119 Lopez, Jose Y. A visit to VILLA ALEGRE. LATIN QUARTER, Vol. 1, no. 3 (January, February, 1975), p. 8-12. English. DESCR: Bilingual Children's Television, Inc.; *Children's Television; Public Television; *VILLA ALEGRE [television program].

2120 Mares, Antonio. El coyote: between two cultures. EL CUADERNO, Vol. 2, no. 1 (1972), p. 20-23. English. DESCR: Biculturalism; *Intermarriage.

2121 Perez, Renato E. Chicago: Hispanic melting pot. VISTA, Vol. 1, no. 3 (November 3, 1985), p. 20. English. DESCR: Camacho, Eduardo; Casuso, Jorge; *Chicago, IL; Ethnic Groups; HISPANICS IN CHICAGO; *Population.

2122 Torres-Gil, Fernando. The Latinization of a multigenerational population: Hispanics in an aging society. DAEDALUS, Vol. 115, no. 1 (Winter 1986), p. 325-348. English. DESCR: *Age Groups; Population; *Public Policy; Social Classes; Socioeconomic Factors.

Culture

2123 Aguilar, Ricardo and Elizondo, Sergio D. La frontera. LA COMUNIDAD, No. 305 (May 25, 1986), p. 2-3+. Spanish. DESCR: *Accounting; Border Region.

2124 Anaya, Rudolfo A. A Chicano in China. VISTA, Vol. 2, no. 1 (September 7, 1986), p. 19-21. English. DESCR: *A CHICANO IN CHINA; Anaya, Rudolfo A.; China; Philosophy; *Tourism.

Culture (cont.)

2125 Atencio, Tomas. La resolana [editorial]. EL
CUADERNO, Vol. 4, no. 1 (Summer 1976), p.
2-4. English. **DESCR:** Academia Asociados, NM;
Academia Educational Model; *Chicano
Studies; EL CUADERNO; ENTRE VERDE Y SECO;
*La Academia de la Nueva Raza, Dixon, NM; LA
MADRUGADA; Publishing Industry.

2126 Broderick, Stephanie H., et al. Ethnicity,
acculturation, and health beliefs among
diabetes patients. MIGRATION WORLD MAGAZINE,
Vol. 15, no. 2 (1987), p. 30-32. English.
DESCR: Acculturation; Attitudes; *Diabetes;
*Identity; *Public Health.

2127 Chavez, Linda. Trivia. AMERICAS 2001,
Premiere Issue, 1987, p. 45. Bilingual.

2128 Chavez, Linda. Trivia. AMERICAS 2001, Vol.
1, no. 1 (June, July, 1987), p. 30.
Bilingual.

2129 Cohen, Albert K. Book review of: HONOR AND
THE AMERICAN DREAM. AMERICAN JOURNAL OF
SOCIOLOGY, Vol. 90, no. 5 (March 1985), p.
1146-1147. English. **DESCR:** Book Reviews;
*HONOR AND THE AMERICAN DREAM: CULTURE AND
IDENTITY IN A CHICANO COMMUNITY; Horowitz,
Ruth.

2130 Dewey, Kathryn G.; Strode, Margaret A.; and
Fitch, Yolanda Ruiz. Dietary change among
migrant and nonmigrant Mexican-American
families in northern California. ECOLOGY OF
FOOD AND NUTRITION, Vol. 14, no. 1 (1984),
p. 11-24. English. **DESCR:** *Food Practices;
*Migrant Children; Migrant Labor; Northern
California; *Nutrition.

2131 Gann, Lewis H. and Duignan, Peter J. Latinos
& the Catholic Church in America. NUESTRO,
Vol. 11, no. 4 (May 1987), p. 10-13.
English. **DESCR:** *Catholic Church; Encuentro
Movement [Catholic Church]; History; Primer
Encuentro Nacional Hispano, Washington, DC,
June 1972.

2132 Garcia, John A. The political integration of
Mexican immigrants: examining some political
orientations. INTERNATIONAL MIGRATION
REVIEW, Vol. 21, no. 2 (Summer 1987), p.
372-389. English. **DESCR:** *Immigrants;
*National Chicano Survey (NCS); Political
Ideology; *Political Socialization.

2133 Gomez Pena, Guillermo. La cultura
fronteriza: un proceso de negociacion hacia
la utopia. LA COMUNIDAD, No. 305 (May 25,
1986), p. 14-15. Spanish. **DESCR:** Border
Region.

2134 Gutierrez, Ramon A. Unraveling America's
Hispanic past: internal stratification and
class boundaries. AZTLAN, Vol. 17, no. 1
(Spring 1986), p. 79-101. English. **DESCR:**
*Chicano, Meaning of; *Ethnic Groups;
*Identity; Intergroup Relations;
*Self-Referents.

2135 Monsivais, Carlos. Los cholos y la cultura
de la frontera. LA COMUNIDAD, No. 242 (March
10, 1985), p. 14-15. Spanish. **DESCR:** Border
Region; Identity; *Pachucos; *Tijuana, Baja
California, Mexico.

2136 Monsivais, Carlos. Este es el pachuco, un
sujeto singular. LA COMUNIDAD, No. 243
(March 17, 1985), p. 4-5. Spanish. **DESCR:**
Border Region; Identity; *Pachucos.

2137 Reilly, Michael D. and Wallendorf, Melanie.
A longitudinal study of Mexican-American

assimilation. ADVANCES IN CONSUMER RESEARCH,
Vol. 11, (1984), p. 735-740. English.
DESCR: *Assimilation; *Consumers; Food
Practices; *Marketing.

2138 Rosaldo, Renato. When natives talk back:
Chicano anthropology since the late 60s.
RENATO ROSALDO LECTURE SERIES MONOGRAPH,
Vol. 2, (Spring 1986), p. [3]-20. English.
DESCR: *Anthropology; EL GRITO; *Identity;
Paredes, Americo; *Political Ideology;
*Research Methodology; Romano-V., Octavio
Ignacio; Valdez, Facundo.

2139 Salgado de Snyder, Nelly. The role of ethnic
loyalty among Mexican immigrant women.
HISPANIC JOURNAL OF BEHAVIORAL SCIENCES,
Vol. 9, no. 3 (September 1987), p. 287-298.
English. **DESCR:** Acculturation; Chicanas;
*Identity; Immigrants; Mental Health;
*Mexico; *Women.

2140 Sanchez, Rosaura. Ethnicity, ideology and
academia. THE AMERICAS REVIEW, Vol. 15, no.
1 (Spring 1987), p. 80-88. English. **DESCR:**
*Ethnic Studies; Political Ideology.

**CULTURE AND THE BILINGUAL CLASSROOM: STUDIES IN
CLASSROOM ETHNOLOGY**

2141 Duran, Richard P. Book review of: CULTURE
AND THE BILINGUAL CLASSROOM. LA RED/THE NET,
no. 44 (July 1981), p. 4-5. English. **DESCR:**
Bilingualism; Book Reviews; Guthrie, Grace
Pung; Hu-Pei Au, Kathryn; Trueba, Henry T.

Cummins, Jim

2142 Nieto, Sonia. Book review of: BILINGUALISM
AND MINORITY-LANGUAGE CHILDREN. INTERRACIAL
BOOKS FOR CHILDREN, Vol. 17, no. 3-4 (1986),
p. 29. English. **DESCR:** *BILINGUALISM AND
MINORITY-LANGUAGE CHILDREN; Book Reviews.

2143 Wolfe, David E. Book review of: BILINGUALISM
AND SPECIAL EDUCATION: ISSUES IN ASSESSMENT
AND PEDAGOGY. MODERN LANGUAGE JOURNAL, Vol.
71, (Spring 1987), p. 81. English. **DESCR:**
Bilingualism; *BILINGUALISM AND SPECIAL
EDUCATION; Book Reviews; Special Education.

Curanderas

2144 Lewis, Marvin A.; Striano, Ron; and Hiura,
Barbara L. Chicano ethnicity and aging [and
critiques]. EXPLORATIONS IN ETHNIC STUDIES,
Vol. 8, no. 2 (July 1985), p. 35-45.
English. **DESCR:** Anaya, Rudolfo A.;
*Ancianos; BLESS ME, ULTIMA; FAMOUS ALL OVER
TOWN; Identity; James, Dan; Literary
Criticism; Literature.

Curanderismo

2145 Blea, Irene I. Book review of: CURANDERISMO.
LA RED/THE NET, no. 55 (June 1982), p. 3-4.
English. **DESCR:** Book Reviews; Chavira, Juan
Antonio; *Trotter, Robert.

2146 Gomez, Efrain A. and Gomez, Gerda E. Folk
healing among Hispanic Americans. PUBLIC
HEALTH NURSING, Vol. 2, no. 4 (December
1985), p. 245-249. English. **DESCR:** *Folk
Medicine; Herbal Medicine.

2147 Lefton, Doug. Some Latinos place trust in
cures of folk healers. AMERICAN MEDICAL
NEWS, Vol. 25, (July 9, 1982), p. 17-18.
English.

2148 Lopez, Raymundo. Dona Angelita. LLUEVE
TLALOC, no. 3 (1976), p. 16. Spanish.
DESCR: *Prose.

CURANDERISMO, MEXICAN-AMERICAN FOLK HEALING

2149 Thiederman, Sondra Barrett. Book review of:
CURANDERISMO. WESTERN FOLKLORE, Vol. 42, no.
4 (October 1983), p. 317-318. English.
DESCR: Book Reviews; Chavira, Juan Antonio;
Trotter, Robert.

Currency

2150 Bustamante, Jorge A. International labor
migration and external debt. MIGRATION WORLD
MAGAZINE, Vol. 15, no. 3 (1987), p. 13-15.
English. **DESCR:** *International Economic
Relations; *Labor Supply and Market;
*Migrant Labor; *Undocumented Workers;
United States-Mexico Relations.

2151 Harrell, Louis and Fischer, Dale. The 1982
Mexican peso devaluation and border area
employment. MONTHLY LABOR REVIEW, Vol. 108,
no. 10 (October 1985), p. 25-32. English.
DESCR: Border Industries; *Border Region;
*International Economic Relations; Mexican
Maquiladora Program; *Mexico.

Curriculum

2152 Elizondo, Sergio D. Critical areas of need
for research and scholastic study. EPOCA:
NATIONAL CONCILIO FOR CHICANO STUDIES
JOURNAL, Vol. 1, no. 2 (Winter 1971), p.
1-7. English. **DESCR:** *Chicano Studies;
Research Methodology.

2153 Guerra, Manuel H. What are the objectives of
Chicano studies? EPOCA: NATIONAL CONCILIO
FOR CHICANO STUDIES JOURNAL, Vol. 1, no. 2
(Winter 1971), p. 8-12. English. **DESCR:**
*Chicano Studies; Educational Theory and
Practice.

2154 MEChA - University of Texas at El Paso;
MAYO, University of Texas at Austin; and
PASO, Texas A and I University. Student
perspectives on Mexican/American studies.
EPOCA: NATIONAL CONCILIO FOR CHICANO STUDIES
JOURNAL, Vol. 1, no. 2 (Winter 1971), p.
87-96. English. **DESCR:** *Chicano Studies;
Mexican American Youth Organization (MAYO);
Movimiento Estudiantil Chicano de Aztlan
(MEChA); Student Organizations; Students;
Texas.

2155 Ramirez, Salvador. The establishment and
administration of a master's program in
Chicano Studies at the University of
Colorado. EPOCA: NATIONAL CONCILIO FOR
CHICANO STUDIES JOURNAL, Vol. 1, no. 2
(Winter 1971), p. 39-50. English. **DESCR:**
*Chicano Studies; Discrimination in
Education; Educational Theory and Practice;
Student Organizations; *Students; United
Mexican American Students (UMAS);
*University of Colorado, Boulder; Youth.

2156 Rivera, Julius. The implementation of
Mexican-American Studies in Texas colleges
and universities. EPOCA: NATIONAL CONCILIO
FOR CHICANO STUDIES JOURNAL, Vol. 1, no. 2
(Winter 1971), p. 79-86. English. **DESCR:**
*Chicano Studies; Colleges and Universities;
Texas; *Textbooks.

2157 Samora, Julian and Galarza, Ernesto.
Research and scholarly activity. EPOCA:
NATIONAL CONCILIO FOR CHICANO STUDIES
JOURNAL, Vol. 1, no. 2 (Winter 1971), p.
51-54. English. **DESCR:** *Chicano Studies;
*Research Methodology.

2158 Wilde, Richard H. The establishment of a
Chicano studies program and its relation to
the total curriculum of a college or

university. EPOCA: NATIONAL CONCILIO FOR
CHICANO STUDIES JOURNAL, Vol. 1, no. 2
(Winter 1971), p. 70-78. English. **DESCR:**
California State University, Long Beach;
*Chicano Studies; *Research Methodology.

2159 Zamora, Alfredo. The Mexican American
community and Mexican American studies.
EPOCA: NATIONAL CONCILIO FOR CHICANO STUDIES
JOURNAL, Vol. 1, no. 2 (Winter 1971), p.
66-70. English. **DESCR:** *Chicano Studies.

Curriculum Materials

2160 Henkin, Alan B.; Singleton, Carole A.; and
Nguyen, Liem T. Seeking goodness of fit:
measuring the readability of bilingual
learning materials. BILINGUAL REVIEW, Vol.
11, no. 3 (September, December, 1984), p.
9-24. English. **DESCR:** *Bilingual Bicultural
Education; Reading.

Dale, Doris Cruger

2161 Bennett, Priscilla. Book review of:
BILINGUAL BOOKS IN SPANISH AND ENGLISH FOR
CHILDREN. EMERGENCY LIBRARIAN, Vol. 13, no.
1 (September, October, 1985), p. 31-32.
English. **DESCR:** *BILINGUAL BOOKS IN SPANISH
AND ENGLISH FOR CHILDREN; Book Reviews.

2162 Martinez, Julio A. Book review of: BILINGUAL
BOOKS IN SPANISH AND ENGLISH FOR CHILDREN.
RQ - REFERENCE AND ADULT SERVICES DIVISION,
Vol. 25, (Spring 1986), p. 387. English.
DESCR: *BILINGUAL BOOKS IN SPANISH AND
ENGLISH FOR CHILDREN; Book Reviews.

2163 Rockman, Ilene F. Book review of: BILINGUAL
BOOKS IN SPANISH AND ENGLISH FOR CHILDREN.
AMERICAN REFERENCE BOOKS ANNUAL, Vol. 17,
(1986), p. 431. English. **DESCR:** *BILINGUAL
BOOKS IN SPANISH AND ENGLISH FOR CHILDREN;
Book Reviews.

2164 Whatley, Patricia L. Book review of:
BILINGUAL BOOKS IN SPANISH AND ENGLISH FOR
CHILDREN. TOP OF THE NEWS, Vol. 43, (Fall
1986), p. 120. English. **DESCR:** *BILINGUAL
BOOKS IN SPANISH AND ENGLISH FOR CHILDREN;
Book Reviews.

DALLAS MORNING NEWS

2165 13-part series focuses on Hispanics in
America. EDITOR & PUBLISHER: THE FOURTH
ESTATE, Vol. 115, no. 14 (April 3, 1982), p.
37. English. **DESCR:** Books; Cultural
Characteristics; Garcia, Juan; Gonzalez,
John; Goodwin, Jay; Grothe, Randy Eli;
Hamilton, John; Hille, Ed; LA VIDA
AMERICANA; *LA VIDA AMERICANA/HISPANICS IN
AMERICA; Langer, Ralph; McLemore, David;
Osburne, Burl; Parks, Scott; Pusey, Allen;
Sonnemair, Jan.

Dallas, TX

2166 Lecca, Pedro J. and McNeil, John S. Cultural
factors affecting the compliance of older
Mexican-Americans with hypertension
regimens. LA RED/THE NET, no. 74 (November
1983), p. 7-10. English. **DESCR:** *Ancianos;
Medical Care.

2167 Perez, Renato E. Badge of Hispanic pride.
VISTA, Vol. 1, no. 12 (August 2, 1986), p.
9-11. English. **DESCR:** Broward County, FL;
Chicago, IL; Houston, TX; *Los Angeles, CA;
New York, NY; *Police; San Antonio, TX; San
Diego, CA; Tucson, AZ.

Dance

2168 Limon, Jose E. Texas-Mexican popular music and dancing: some notes on history and symbolic process. LATIN AMERICAN MUSIC REVIEW, Vol. 4, no. 2 (Fall, Winter, 1983), p. 229-246. English. **DESCR**: Ethnomusicology; *Music; *Texas; *Texas Mexicans.

2169 Medina, David. America's Hispanic Theater Olympics. VISTA, Vol. 1, no. 12 (August 2, 1986), p. 12-14. English. **DESCR**: Actors and Actresses; *Festival Latino; *Teatro.

2170 Pinon, Fernando. A dance of worship. VISTA, Vol. 1, no. 3 (November 3, 1985), p. 16. English. **DESCR**: *Aztecs; St. Luke's Catholic Church, San Antonio, TX.

Databases

2171 Cabello-Argandona, Roberto. Hispanex is here to stay. LECTOR, Vol. 4, no. 4-6 (1987), p. 6-8. English. **DESCR**: *HISPANEX (Oakland, CA); Library Services.

2172 So, Alvin Yiu-cheong. The analysis of language minority issues in national data sets. LA RED/THE NET, no. 71 (August 1983), p. 3-5. English. **DESCR**: Bilingualism; *Language Usage; *National Center for Bilingual Research; Surveys.

2173 Tienda, Marta. Task force on statistical policy and data needs. LA RED/THE NET, no. 88 (Winter, 1984), p. 2-6. English. **DESCR**: *Population; Public Policy; Research Methodology; *Statistics; Vital Statistics.

Davila, Robert

2174 Garcia, Philip. Robert Davila. VISTA, Vol. 2, no. 7 (March 8, 1987), p. 25. English. **DESCR**: *Deaf; Education.

Day Care Centers
USE: Child Care Centers

Day of the Dead
USE: Dia de los Muertos

De Armas Publications

2175 Marketing to Hispanics. ADVERTISING AGE MAGAZINE, Vol. 57, no. 43 (August 11, 1986), p. 51-528. English. **DESCR**: Advertising; Broadcast Media; Kinney Shoe Corp.; *Marketing; Pepsi-Cola Bottling Group; Print Media; Spanish International Network (SIN); U.S. Bureau of the Census.

de Garcia, Alicia

2176 Alicia de Garcia's oral history=Historia oral de Alicia de Garcia. REVISTA MUJERES, Vol. 3, no. 2 (June 1986), p. 37-49. Spanish. **DESCR**: *Committee of Mothers and Relatives of Political Prisoners Disappeared and Assassinated of El Salvador "Monsenor Oscar Arnulfo Romero" (Comadres, El Salvador); Community Organizations; *Federation of Latin Americans for the Association of Relatives of the Detained and Disappeared (FedeFam); *Oral History; Terrorism; Violence; *Women.

de la Garza [family name]

2177 Instituto Genealogico e Historico Latino-Americano. Rootsearch: Rodriguez: Garza (De La Garza). VISTA, Vol. 3, no. 3 (November 8, 1987), p. 37. English. **DESCR**: *Garza [family name]; Genealogy; History; *Personal Names; *Rodriguez, [family name].

de la Garza [family name]

2178 Instituto Genealogico e Historico Latino-Americano. Rootsearch: De La Garza: Pacheco. VISTA, Vol. 2, no. 6 (February 8, 1987), p. 21. English. **DESCR**: Genealogy; History; Pacheco [family name]; *Personal Names.

de la Garza, Rodolfo O.

2179 Hastings, D.W. Book review of: MEXICAN IMMIGRANTS AND MEXICAN AMERICANS: AN EVOLVING RELATION. CHOICE, Vol. 24, no. 3 (November 1986), p. 516. English. **DESCR**: Book Reviews; Browning, Harley L.; *MEXICAN IMMIGRANTS AND MEXICAN AMERICANS: AN EVOLVING RELATION.

2180 Meier, Matt S. Book review of: THE MEXICAN AMERICAN EXPERIENCE: AN INTERDISCIPLINARY ANTHOLOGY. HISPANIC AMERICAN HISTORICAL REVIEW, Vol. 66, no. 3 (August 1986), p. 629-630. English. **DESCR**: Alvarez, Rodolfo; Bean, Frank D.; Bonjean, Charles M.; Book Reviews; Romo, Ricardo; *THE MEXICAN AMERICAN EXPERIENCE: AN INTERDISCIPLINARY ANTHOLOGY.

2181 Ruiz, Vicki Lynn. Book review of: THE MEXICAN AMERICAN EXPERIENCE: AN INTERDISCIPLINARY ANTHOLOGY. SOUTHWESTERN HISTORICAL QUARTERLY, Vol. 90, no. 2 (1986), p. 205-206. English. **DESCR**: Alvarez, Rodolfo; Bean, Frank D.; Bonjean, Charles M.; Book Reviews; Romo, Ricardo; *THE MEXICAN AMERICAN EXPERIENCE: AN INTERDISCIPLINARY ANTHOLOGY.

2182 Salmon, Roberto Mario. Book review of: THE MEXICAN AMERICAN EXPERIENCE: AN INTERDISCIPLINARY ANTHOLOGY. LA RED/THE NET, no. 93 (January, February, 1986), p. 12-14. English. **DESCR**: Alvarez, Rodolfo; Bean, Frank D.; Bonjean, Charles M.; Book Reviews; Romo, Ricardo; *THE MEXICAN AMERICAN EXPERIENCE: AN INTERDISCIPLINARY ANTHOLOGY.

De la Parra, Ralph

2183 Rifkin, Jane M. Ralph de la Parra travels the MAES "bridge to the future". HISPANIC TIMES, Vol. 8, no. 1 (December, January, 1987), p. 30. English. **DESCR**: Biography; *Engineering as a Profession; Mexican American Engineering Society (MAES); Southern California Edison Co..

de la Rocha, Beatriz

2184 Families of the year. VISTA, Vol. 2, no. 2 (October 4, 1986), p. 16-18. English. **DESCR**: Aguilar, Gregorio; Aguilar, Guadalupe; Aranda, Benjamin; Aranda, Emma; *Awards; de la Rocha, Castulo; Family; Guzman, Ofelia; Guzman, Roberto; *Hispanic Family of the Year Award.

de la Rocha, Castulo

2185 Families of the year. VISTA, Vol. 2, no. 2 (October 4, 1986), p. 16-18. English. **DESCR**: Aguilar, Gregorio; Aguilar, Guadalupe; Aranda, Benjamin; Aranda, Emma; *Awards; de la Rocha, Beatriz; Family; Guzman, Ofelia; Guzman, Roberto; *Hispanic Family of the Year Award.

de Leon, Arnoldo

2186 Butler, Anne M. Book review of: THEY
     THEM GREASERS. MARYLAND HISTORIAN, Vol. 15,
     no. 2 (Fall, Winter, 1984), p. 50-51.
     English. **DESCR:** Book Reviews; History; *THEY
     CALLED THEM GREASERS: ANGLO ATTITUDES TOWARD
     MEXICANS IN TEXAS, 1821-1900.

2187 Cardoso, Lawrence A. Book review of: THEY
     CALLED THEM GREASERS. WESTERN HISTORICAL
     QUARTERLY, Vol. 15, no. 4 (October 1984), p.
     452-453. English. **DESCR:** Book Reviews;
     Texas; THEY CALLED THEM GREASERS: ANGLO
     ATTITUDES TOWARD MEXICANS IN TEXAS,
     1821-1900.

2188 Crisp, James E. Book review of: THEY CALLED
     THEM GREASERS. JOURNAL OF SOUTHERN HISTORY,
     Vol. 50, no. 2 (1984), p. 313-314. English.
     DESCR: Book Reviews; *THEY CALLED THEM
     GREASERS: ANGLO ATTITUDES TOWARD MEXICANS IN
     TEXAS, 1821-1900.

2189 Garcia, Ed. On red-haired girls and the
     greaser in me. TEXAS OBSERVOR, Vol. 75,
     (October 28, 1983), p. 24-25. English.
     DESCR: Book Reviews; Essays; Identity;
     *Stereotypes; Texas; *THEY CALLED THEM
     GREASERS: ANGLO ATTITUDES TOWARD MEXICANS IN
     TEXAS, 1821-1900.

2190 Garcia, Mario T. Book review of: THEY CALLED
     THEM GREASERS. HISPANIC AMERICAN HISTORICAL
     REVIEW, Vol. 64, no. 2 (May 1984), p.
     405-406. English. **DESCR:** Book Reviews; *THEY
     CALLED THEM GREASERS: ANGLO ATTITUDES TOWARD
     MEXICANS IN TEXAS, 1821-1900.

2191 Harrington, James C. GREASERS chronicles
     Texas racism, past and present. TEXAS
     OBSERVOR, Vol. 75, (October 28, 1983), p.
     23-25. English. **DESCR:** Book Reviews; *THEY
     CALLED THEM GREASERS: ANGLO ATTITUDES TOWARD
     MEXICANS IN TEXAS, 1821-1900.

2192 Montejano, David. Book review of: THE TEJANO
     COMMUNITY, 1836-1900. LA RED/THE NET, no. 64
     (February 1983), p. 5-6. English. **DESCR:**
     Book Reviews; *THE TEJANO COMMUNITY,
     1836-1900.

2193 Paredes, Raymund A. Book review of: THEY
     CALLED THEM GREASERS. PACIFIC HISTORICAL
     REVIEW, Vol. 53, no. 3 (1984), p. 390-391.
     English. **DESCR:** Book Reviews; *THEY CALLED
     THEM GREASERS: ANGLO ATTITUDES TOWARD
     MEXICANS IN TEXAS, 1821-1900.

2194 Salmon, Roberto Mario. Book review of: THEY
     CALLED THEM GREASERS. LA RED/THE NET, no. 75
     (December 1983), p. 8-9. English. **DESCR:**
     Book Reviews; *THEY CALLED THEM GREASERS:
     ANGLO ATTITUDES TOWARD MEXICANS IN TEXAS,
     1821-1900.

2195 Saragoza, Alex M. Book review of: THEY
     CALLED THEM GREASERS. SOUTHWESTERN
     HISTORICAL QUARTERLY, Vol. 88, (1985), p.
     334-336. English. **DESCR:** Book Reviews; *THEY
     CALLED THEM GREASERS: ANGLO ATTITUDES TOWARD
     MEXICANS IN TEXAS, 1821-1900.

2196 Tijerina, Andres A. Book review of: SAN
     ANGELENOS: MEXICAN AMERICANS IN SAN ANGELO,
     TEXAS. SOUTHWESTERN HISTORICAL QUARTERLY,
     Vol. 89, no. 4 (1986), p. 569-570. English.
     DESCR: Book Reviews; *SAN ANGELENOS; MEXICAN
     AMERICANS IN SAN ANGELO, TEXAS.

de Mundo Lo, Sara

2197 de Baca, Vincent C. Book review of: INDEX TO
     SPANISH AMERICAN COLLECTIVE BIOGRAPHY, vol.
     2: MEXICO and THE MEXICAN REVOLUTION: AN
     ANNOTATED GUIDE TO RECENT SCHOLARSHIP. LA
     RED/THE NET, no. 72 (September 1983), p.
     19-21. English. **DESCR:** Book Reviews; *INDEX
     TO SPANISH AMERICAN COLLECTIVE BIOGRAPHY,
     vol. 2: MEXICO; Raat, W. Dirk; Reference
     Works; THE MEXICAN REVOLUTION: AN ANNOTATED
     GUIDE TO RECENT SCHOLARSHIP.

De Soto, Rosana

2198 Chavez, Lorenzo A. La Bamba. VISTA, Vol. 2,
     no. 11 (July 5, 1987), p. 12-13. English.
     DESCR: *Actors and Actresses; Biography;
     Films; LA BAMBA [film]; *Morales, Esai;
     Pena, Elizabeth; Phillips, Lou Diamond.

Deaf

2199 Garcia, Philip. Robert Davila. VISTA, Vol.
     2, no. 7 (March 8, 1987), p. 25. English.
     DESCR: *Davila, Robert; Education.

Death (Concept)

2200 Randolph, Donald A. Death's aesthetic
     proliferation in works of Hinojosa.
     CONFLUENCIA, Vol. 1, no. 2 (Spring 1986), p.
     38-47. English. **DESCR:** GENERACIONES Y
     SEMBLANZAS; *Hinojosa-Smith, Rolando R.;
     KLAIL CITY Y SUS ALREDEDORES; KOREAN LOVE
     SONGS; *Literary Criticism; Novel.

THE DEATH OF ARTEMIO CRUZ

2201 Eberstadt, Fernanda. Montezuma's literary
     revenge. COMMENTARY, Vol. 81, no. 5 (May
     1986), p. 35-40. English. **DESCR:** *Fuentes,
     Carlos; GRINGO VIEJO; *Literary Criticism;
     Mexican Literature; THE GOOD CONSCIENCE;
     WHERE THE AIR IS CLEAR.

**Decays, Missing, Filed Surfaces (DMFS) [dental
   scale]**

2202 Ismail, Amid L.; Burt, Brian A.; and
     Brunelle, Janet A. Prevalence of dental
     caries and periodontal disease in Mexican
     American children aged 5 to 17 years:
     results from Southwestern HHANES, 1982-83.
     AMERICAN JOURNAL OF PUBLIC HEALTH, Vol. 77,
     no. 8 (August 1987), p. 967-970. English.
     DESCR: *Dentistry; *Hispanic Health and
     Nutrition Examination Survey (HHANES);
     Youth.

Decorative Arts
     USE: Arts and Crafts

**THE DEFIANT MUSE: HISPANIC FEMINIST POEMS FROM THE
   MIDDLE AGES TO THE PRESENT**

2203 Castillo-Speed, Lillian. Chicana/Latina
     literature and criticism: reviews of recent
     books. WLW JOURNAL, Vol. 11, no. 3
     (September 1987), p. 1-4. English. **DESCR:**
     Andrews, Lynn V.; *Book Reviews; BORDERS;
     Chavez, Denise; *Chicanas; CONTEMPORARY
     CHICANA POETRY: A CRITICAL APPROACH TO AN
     EMERGING LITERATURE; Flores, Angel; Flores,
     Kate; JAGUAR WOMAN; Mora, Pat; Sanchez,
     Marta Ester; Tafolla, Carmen; THE LAST OF
     THE MENU GIRLS; TO SPLIT A HUMAN: MITOS,
     MACHOS Y LA MUJER CHICANA; Vigil-Pinon,
     Evangelina; WOMAN OF HER WORD: HISPANIC
     WOMEN WRITE.

2204 Colecchia, F. Book review of: THE DEFIANT
     MUSE: HISPANIC FEMINIST POEMS FROM THE
     MIDDLE AGES TO THE PRESENT. CHOICE, Vol. 24,
     no. 2 (October 1986), p. 314. English.
     DESCR: Book Reviews; Flores, Angel; Flores,
     Kate.

Del Castillo, Adelaida R.

2205 Soto, Shirlene. Book review of: MEXICAN WOMEN IN THE UNITED STATES: STRUGGLES PAST AND PRESENT. LA RED/THE NET, no. 35 (October 1980), p. 4. English. DESCR: Book Reviews; *Chicanas; *MEXICAN WOMEN IN THE UNITED STATES: STRUGGLES PAST AND PRESENT; *Mora, Magdalena.

Del Castillo, Gustavo

2206 Hunsaker, Alan C. Institutionally-based research centers: the Center for U.S.-Mexican Studies. LA RED/THE NET, no. 92 (November, December, 1985), p. 13-15. English. DESCR: *Center for U.S.-Mexican Studies, University of California at San Diego, La Jolla, CA; Meyer, Lorenzo; *Research Centers; United States-Mexico Relations.

del Rio, Pepe

2207 Breiter, Toni. Pepe del Rio. VISTA, Vol. 1, no. 6 (February 2, 1986), p. 20. English. DESCR: Broadcast Media; *BUENOS DIAS, AMERICA [radio news & features program]; Perez del Rio, Jose; *Radio; Voice of America.

Del Taco Restaurants

2208 Raffio, Ralph. Del Taco targets adult audience. RESTAURANT BUSINESS, Vol. 84, (April 10, 1985), p. 260-264. English. DESCR: Marketing; *Restaurants.

Delgadillo, Ramon

2209 Shaw, Katherine. Mira! a look at America's Hispanic artists. VISTA, Vol. 1, no. 5 (January 5, 1986), p. 6-8. English. DESCR: *Art; Artists; Canadian Club Hispanic Art Tour; Gamboa, Diane; Gonzalez, Nivia; *Trevino, Jesus (Jesse).

Delgado, Abelardo "Lalo"

2210 Lomeli, Francisco A. El concepto del barrio en tres poetas chicanos. LA COMUNIDAD, No. 316 (August 10, 1986), p. 4-5+. Spanish. DESCR: Alurista; Barrios; *Literary Criticism; Poetry; Sanchez, Ricardo.

Delgado, Jane

2211 Morales, Cecilio. A question of health. VISTA, Vol. 3, no. 3 (November 8, 1987), p. 14, 19. English. DESCR: *Health Education; *National Coalition of Hispanic Mental Health and Human Services Organizations (COSSMHO); Preventative Medicine.

Delgado, Porfirio

2212 Murphy, Suzanne. The music makers. VISTA, Vol. 3, no. 4 (December 6, 1987), p. 28-29. English. DESCR: Candelas Guitar Shop, Los Angeles, CA; *Musical Instruments.

Delinquency

2213 Hunsaker, Alan C. and Vicario, Tony D. A behavioral/ecological model of intervention alternatives with Chicano gang delinquents. LA RED/THE NET, no. 43 (June 1981), p. 2-3. English. DESCR: *Behavior Modification; *Gangs; Youth.

Democratic Party

2214 Volsky, George. A new voting block making its mark. HISPANIC BUSINESS, Vol. 9, no. 2 (February 1987), p. 9, 11. English. DESCR: Cubanos; Elections; *Political Parties and Organizations; Republican Party; *Voter Turnout.

DEMOGRAPHICS, STANDARDS, AND EQUITY CHALLENGES IN COLLEGE ADMISSIONS: REPORT OF A SURVEY OF UNDERGRADUATE ADMISSIONS POLICIES, PRACTICES AND PROCEDURES

2215 Gonzalez, Juan C. Report to the Network. LA RED/THE NET, No. 105 (February 1987), p. 1-3. English. DESCR: Breland, Hunter M.; *Discrimination in Education; *Enrollment; *Higher Education.

Demography
USE: Population

Dentistry

2216 Banker, Cynthia A., et al. Primary dental arch characteristics of Mexican-American children. ASDC JOURNAL OF DENTISTRY FOR CHILDREN, Vol. 51, no. 3 (May, June, 1984), p. 200-202. English. DESCR: *Children.

2217 Ismail, Amid L.; Burt, Brian A.; and Brunelle, Janet A. Prevalence of dental caries and periodontal disease in Mexican American children aged 5 to 17 years: results from Southwestern HHANES, 1982-83. AMERICAN JOURNAL OF PUBLIC HEALTH, Vol. 77, no. 8 (August 1987), p. 967-970. English. DESCR: Decays, Missing, Filed Surfaces (DMFS) [dental scale]; *Hispanic Health and Nutrition Examination Survey (HHANES); Youth.

Denver, CO

2218 Abalos, J. Victor. Paul Sandoval. VISTA, Vol. 1, no. 4 (December 7, 1985), p. 10. English. DESCR: Business Enterprises; *Financial Aid; Mile Hi Cablevision; *Sandoval, Paul.

2219 Munoz, Carlos, Jr. and Henry, Charles. Rainbow coalitions in four big cities: San Antonio, Denver, Chicago and Philadelphia. P.S. [AMERICAN POLITICAL SCIENCE ASSOCIATION], Vol. 19, no. 3 (Summer 1986), p. 598-609. English. DESCR: Blacks; Chicago, IL; Cisneros, Henry, Mayor of San Antonio, TX; Elected Officials; Ethnic Groups; Intergroup Relations; Pena, Federico; Philadelphia, PA; Political Parties and Organizations; Political Representation; *Politics; San Antonio, TX; Urban Communities.

Department of Defense Equal Opportunities Management Institute (DEOMI)

2220 MAES chairman appointed to DEOMI board of visitors. HISPANIC TIMES, Vol. 8, no. 3 (May, June, 1987), p. 42. English. DESCR: Appointed Officials; *Cano, Oscar; Mexican American Engineering Society (MAES).

Deportation

2221 Anaya, Toney and Lujan, Edward. Sanctuary: right or wrong? VISTA, Vol. 1, no. 11 (July 6, 1986), p. 18-19, 21. English. DESCR: *Central America; Political History and Conditions; *Political Refugees.

Deportation (cont.)

2222 Gordon, Charles. The rights of aliens: an expanding role for trial lawyers. TRIAL, Vol. 19, no. 12 (December 1983), p. 54-58. English. DESCR: Immigration Law and Legislation; *Legal Profession; *Political Prisoners; *Undocumented Workers.

2223 Immigration violations--collateral attack on deportation order. CRIMINAL LAW REPORTER, Vol. 38, no. 16 (January 22, 1986), p. 2311-2312. English. DESCR: *U.S. v. Mendoza-Lopez.

2224 Lopez-Garza, Marta. Book review of: OPERATION WETBACK. LA RED/THE NET, no. 50 (January 1982), p. 7-9. English. DESCR: Book Reviews; *Garcia, Juan Ramon; Immigration; *OPERATION WETBACK: THE MASS DEPORTATION OF MEXICAN UNDOCUMENTED WORKERS IN 1954.

Depression (Psychological)

2225 Chesser, Barbara and Inguanzo-Schleff, Dania. Loneliness among Mexican migrant children. LA RED/THE NET, no. 44 (July 1981), p. 3-4. English. DESCR: Mental Health; *Migrant Children.

2226 Remas, Theodora A. Down and blue. VISTA, Vol. 2, no. 5 (January 4, 1987), p. 16-18. English. DESCR: Counseling (Psychological); *National Institute of Mental Health; Social History and Conditions; Spanish Family Guidance Clinic, Miami, FL.

Desegregation
USE: Segregation and Desegregation

DESERT IMMIGRANTS: THE MEXICANS OF EL PASO 1880-1920

2227 Arroyo, Luis Leobardo. Book review of: DESERT IMMIGRANTS. LA RED/THE NET, no. 43 (June 1981), p. 3-4. English. DESCR: Book Reviews; Garcia, Mario T.; Immigrants.

Design

2228 Krampner, John. Raul Rodriguez. VISTA, Vol. 2, no. 5 (January 4, 1987), p. 21. English. DESCR: Awards; *Rodriguez, Raul; Rose Parade (Pasadena, CA).

DETENTE [phonograph record]

2229 Machado, Melinda. Saying "no" to teenage sex. VISTA, Vol. 2, no. 11 (July 5, 1987), p. 14. English. DESCR: *CUANDO ESTEMOS JUNTOS [phonograph record]; Music; *Musical Lyrics; Planned Parenthood Federation of America; Sex Education; Tatiana and Johnny.

Detroit, MI

2230 Ramirez, Oscar. Extended family support and mental health status among Mexicans in Detroit. LA RED/THE NET, no. 28 (March 1980), p. 2. English. DESCR: *Extended Family; Mental Health.

DEVELOPMENT OF THE MEXICAN WORKING CLASS NORTH OF THE RIO BRAVO: WORK AND CULTURE AMONG LABORERS AND ARTISANS, 1600-1900

2231 Garcia, Mario T. Book review of: DEVELOPMENT OF THE MEXICAN WORKING CLASS NORTH OF THE RIO BRAVO: WORK AND CULTURE AMONG LABORERS AND ARTISANS, 1600-1900. PACIFIC HISTORICAL REVIEW, Vol. 53, no. 4 (November 1984), p. 525-527. English. DESCR: Book Reviews; Gomez-Quinones, Juan; Laboring Classes.

Dia de la Raza

2232 Mark, Samuel. Dia de la Raza deserves wide-scoped celebration. VISTA, Vol. 2, no. 2 (October 4, 1986), p. 3. English. DESCR: *Festivals.

Dia de los Muertos

2233 Gambrell, Jamey. Texas: state of the art. ART IN AMERICA, Vol. 75, no. 3 (March 1987), p. 114-131+. English. DESCR: *Art; Art Galleries; Art Organizations and Groups; *Artists; Folk Art; Mexican Art; Texas.

2234 Hazen-Hammond, Susan and Fuss, Eduardo. Vivan las celebraciones. ARIZONA HIGHWAYS, Vol. 63, no. 8 (August 1987), p. 35-45. English. DESCR: Cinco de Mayo; Cultural Customs; Dieciseis de Septiembre; Fiestas Patrias; *Holidays; La Virgen de Guadalupe; Las Posadas.

Diabetes

2235 Broderick, Stephanie H., et al. Ethnicity, acculturation, and health beliefs among diabetes patients. MIGRATION WORLD MAGAZINE, Vol. 15, no. 2 (1987), p. 30-32. English. DESCR: Acculturation; Attitudes; Culture; *Identity; *Public Health.

2236 O'Donnell, Patrick J. A preliminary report on the incidence of gestational diabetes in a Hispanic migrant population. MIGRATION WORLD MAGAZINE, Vol. 15, no. 1 (), p. 27-30. English. DESCR: Farm Workers; *Migrant Labor; *Public Health.

2237 Remas, Theodora A. The threat of diabetes. VISTA, Vol. 1, no. 2 (October 5, 1985), p. 14-16. English. DESCR: Health Education; *Mezitis, Nicholas; *Nutrition; Public Health; Rico-Perez, Manuel.

2238 Stern, Michael P. Epidemiology of diabetes and coronary heart disease among Mexican-Americans. TRANSACTIONS OF THE ASSOC. OF LIFE INSURANCE MEDICAL DIRECTORS, Vol. 67, (1983), p. 79-90. English. DESCR: Anglo Americans; Heart Disease; *San Antonio, TX.

EL DIABLO EN TEXAS

2239 Eysturoy, Annie O. EL DIABLO EN TEXAS: una historia popular a traves de arquetipos y simbolos. LA COMUNIDAD, No. 364 (July 12, 1987), p. 6-7. Spanish. DESCR: *Book Reviews; Brito, Aristeo; Literary Criticism.

DIALOGOS DE LAS AMERICAS

2240 Gomez Pena, Guillermo. Nuevo continente artistico. LA COMUNIDAD, No. 275 (October 27, 1985), p. 8-10. Spanish. DESCR: *Art; Artists; Border Region; Chicano Movement; Indigenismo; International Relations; Mexico; United States-Mexico Relations.

DIALOGOS FRONTERIZOS [radio program]

2241 Gomez Pena, Guillermo. Dialogos fronterizos. LA COMUNIDAD, No. 263 (August 4, 1985), p. 2-3. Spanish. DESCR: *Art; Avalos, David; Border Region; Osorio, Armando.

DIALOGOS FRONTERIZOS [radio program] (cont.)

2242 Gonzalez, Marco Vinicio. En el pais de la frontera. LA COMUNIDAD, No. 291 (February 16, 1986), p. 6-7+. Spanish. **DESCR:** Border Region; Conde, Rosina; Gomez Pena, Guillermo; Medina, Ruben; *Radio; San Diego, CA; Tijuana. Baja California, Mexico.

DIARIO DE LAS AMERICAS

2243 Cecere, Linda. Newspapers attract attention in some categories. ADVERTISING AGE MAGAZINE, Vol. 57, no. 43 (August 11, 1986), p. S9-S10. English. **DESCR:** Advertising; EL MIAMI HERALD; LA OPINION, Los Angeles, CA; *Newspapers; NOTICIAS DEL MUNDO; Spanish Language.

Diaz Dennis, Patricia

2244 Kilgore, Julia. A risk taker. HISPANIC BUSINESS, Vol. 9, no. 12 (December 1987), p. 44-47. English. **DESCR:** *Appointed Officials; Biography; Careers; *Chicanas; Federal Communications Commission (FCC).

2245 Patricia Diaz Dennis. INTERCAMBIOS FEMENILES, Vol. 2, no. 6 (Spring 1987), p. 8-9. English. **DESCR:** Appointed Officials; Chicanas; Federal Communications Commission (FCC); Leadership; Legal Profession.

Diaz, Porfirio

2246 Parlee, Lorena M. The impact of United States railroad unions on organized labor and government policy in Mexico (1880-1911). HISPANIC AMERICAN HISTORICAL REVIEW, Vol. 64, no. 3 (August 1984), p. 443-475. English. **DESCR:** Discrimination in Employment; History; *Labor Unions; Mexico; Partido Liberal Mexicano (PLM); Railroads; United States-Mexico Relations.

Diaz, Raul

2247 Halley, Lindsey. Pachuco boggie [sic]. LA COMUNIDAD, No. 305 (May 25, 1986), p. 8-9. Spanish. **DESCR:** Cano, Eddie; History; *Music; Ovalle, John; *PACHUCO BOOGIE; Smithsonian Institute; The Record Inn, East Los Angeles, CA; Tosti, Don.

Diaz, Ricardo

2248 Haslanger, Phil. A rival to the gangs. THE PROGRESSIVE, Vol. 50, (October 1986), p. 15. English. **DESCR:** *Gangs; Milwaukee, WI.

Diaz-Briquets, Sergio

2249 Hayes-Bautista, David Emmett. Book review of: THE HEALTH REVOLUTION IN CUBA. LA RED/THE NET, no. 11 (November 1983), p. 10-12. English. **DESCR:** Book Reviews; *THE HEALTH REVOLUTION IN CUBA.

Dichos

2250 Atencio, Tomas. La resolana. EL CUADERNO, Vol. 3, no. 2 (Spring 1974), p. 2-4. English.

2251 Atencio, Tomas. La resolana: entre el dicho y el hecho. EL CUADERNO. Vol. 2, no. 1 (1972), p. 4-5. English.

2252 Duran, Richard P. Article review of: "Proverbs in Mexican-American Tradition". LA RED/THE NET, no. 56 (July 1982), p. 6-7. English. **DESCR:** Arora, Shirley L.; *"Proverbs in Mexican-American Tradition".

DICTIONARY OF MEXICAN AMERICAN HISTORY

2253 Acuna, Rodolfo. Book review of: DICTIONARY OF MEXICAN AMERICAN HISTORY. LA RED/THE NET, no. 57 (August 1982), p. 4-5. English. **DESCR:** Book Reviews; History; Meier, Matt S.; Rivera, Feliciano.

2254 Vigil, James Diego. Book review of: DICTIONARY OF MEXICAN AMERICAN HISTORY. PACIFIC HISTORICAL REVIEW, Vol. 53, no. 2 (1984), p. 241-242. English. **DESCR:** Book Reviews; Meier, Matt S.; Reference Works; Rivera, Feliciano.

A DICTIONARY OF NEW MEXICO AND SOUTHERN COLORADO SPANISH

2255 Madrid, Arturo. Book reviews of: A DICTIONARY OF NEW MEXICO AND SOUTHERN COLORADO SPANISH and TUNOMAS HONEY. LA RED/THE NET, no. 77 (February 1984), p. 8-10. English. **DESCR:** *Book Reviews; Cobos, Ruben; Sagel, Jim; *TUNOMAS HONEY.

Dieciseis de Septiembre

2256 Gomez-Quinones, Juan. September 16th: a historical perspective. LATIN QUARTER, Vol. 1, no. 2 (October 1974), p. 8,9,11,12. English. **DESCR:** Hidalgo y Costilla, Miguel; *History; *Holidays; Los Angeles, CA.

2257 Hazen-Hammond, Susan and Fuss, Eduardo. Vivan las celebraciones. ARIZONA HIGHWAYS, Vol. 63, no. 8 (August 1987), p. 35-45. English. **DESCR:** Cinco de Mayo; Cultural Customs; Dia de los Muertos; Fiestas Patrias; *Holidays; La Virgen de Guadalupe; Las Posadas.

Dietetics

USE: Nutrition

Diplomats

2258 Breiter, Toni. Speaker for Uncle Sam. VISTA, Vol. 2, no. 8 (April 4, 1987), p. 23. English. **DESCR:** *Martinez, Peter.

Directories

2259 Chavez, Lorenzo A. A brief guide to financial aid for college-bound students. VISTA, Vol. 2, no. 1 (September 7, 1986), p. 7. English. **DESCR:** *Financial Aid; LULAC National Scholarship Fund; MALDEF Law School Fellowship; National Hispanic Scholar Awards Program; *National Hispano Scholarship Fund.

2260 Chavez, Lorenzo A. The quest for Hispanic roots. VISTA, Vol. 2, no. 7 (March 8, 1987), p. 5-6, 24. English. **DESCR:** Church of Jesus Christ of Latter-Day Saints (Mormons); *Garcia, Clotilde; *Genealogy; Hispanic American Genealogical Associates, Washington, DC; Las Porciones Genealogical Society, Edinburg, TX; Los Bexarenos, San Antonio, TX; Los Californianos [genealogical society], San Jose, CA; Pan American University, Edinburg, TX; Texas Southmost College.

2261 Holmes, John J. Zarzuela lives again. VISTA, Vol. 3, no. 3 (November 8, 1987), p. 10-12. English. **DESCR:** Festival de la Zarzuela; *La Zarzuela de Albuquerque; *Music; Musicals.

2262 Information/Informacion. AMERICAS 2001, Premiere Issue, 1987, p. 11. Bilingual. **DESCR:** *Immigration; *Organizations.

Directories (cont.)

2263 Powell, Carolyn L. Book review of: CHICANO ORGANIZATIONS DIRECTORY. VOICE OF YOUTH ADVOCATES, Vol. 8, no. 6 (February 1986), p. 408. English. DESCR: Book Reviews; Caballero, Cesar; *CHICANO ORGANIZATIONS DIRECTORY.

2264 Remas, Theodora A. The threat of AIDS. VISTA, Vol. 2, no. 10 (June 7, 1987), p. 17-18, 25. English. DESCR: *Acquired Immune Deficiency Syndrome (AIDS); Health Education; *Medical Care; Preventative Medicine.

2265 Varela, Vivian. Hispanic women's resource guide. COMMONGROUND MAGAZINE, Vol. 1, no. 3 (May 1983), p. 14-15. English. DESCR: *Chicanas; *Organizations.

Discography

2266 Forte, Dan. Los Lobos: Tex-Mex rock from East L.A. GUITAR PLAYER, Vol. 21, no. 2 (February 1987), p. 68-94. English. DESCR: Biography; Hidalgo, David (Los Lobos); *Los Lobos del Este de Los Angeles (musical group); Lozano, Conrad (Los Lobos); *Musicians; Perez, Louie (Los Lobos); Recording Industry; *Rock Music; Rosas, Cesar (Los Lobos).

2267 Holscher, Louis M. Billboard charts and Chicanos, 1955-1974. LA RED/THE NET, no. 41 (April 1981), p. 10,12. English. DESCR: *Music; *Musicians; *Recording Industry; Rock Music.

DISCOURSE STRATEGIES

2268 Duran, Richard P. Book reviews of: DISCOURSE STRATEGIES and LANGUAGE AND SOCIAL IDENTITY. LA RED/THE NET, no. 77 (February 1984), p. 13-14. English. DESCR: *Book Reviews; Gumperz, John J.; *LANGUAGE AND SOCIAL IDENTITY.

Discrimination

2269 Arce, Carlos H.; Murguia, Edward; and Frisbie, William Parker. Phenotype and life chances among Chicanos. HISPANIC JOURNAL OF BEHAVIORAL SCIENCES, Vol. 9, no. 1 (March 1987), p. 19-32. English. DESCR: National Chicano Survey (NCS); *Skin Color; Social Classes; *Socioeconomic Factors.

2270 Arellano, Estevan. Chicanos nortenos. EL CUADERNO, Vol. 2, no. 1 (1972), p. 27-35. English. DESCR: *Cultural Characteristics; *Short Story.

2271 Barton, Amy E. Women farmworkers: their workplace and capitalist patriarchy. REVISTA MUJERES, Vol. 3, no. 2 (June 1986), p. 11-13. English. DESCR: Capitalism; *Chicanas; *Farm Workers; Sexism.

2272 Bethell, Tom. Senator Simpson's reward. AMERICAN SPECTATOR, Vol. 19, no. 2 (February 1986), p. 11-13. English. DESCR: Immigration Law and Legislation; Politics; *Simpson, Alan K.; Undocumented Workers.

2273 Bueno, Patricia E. Los Chicanos y la politica. LA COMUNIDAD, No. 267 (September 1, 1985), p. 6-7. Spanish. DESCR: Community Service Organization, Los Angeles, (CSO); History; Leadership; League of United Latin American Citizens (LULAC); Orden Hijos de America, San Antonio, TX; *Political Parties and Organizations.

2274 Communist Party, U.S.A. On Chicano/Mexican-American equality. POLITICAL AFFAIRS, Vol. 66, no. 4 (April 1987), p. 35. English. DESCR: Communist Party; Political Ideology; *Social History and Conditions.

2275 Culp, Robert Alan. The Immigration and Naturalization Service and racially motivated questioning: does equal protection pick up where the Fourth Amendment left off? COLUMBIA LAW REVIEW, Vol. 86, no. 4 (May 1986), p. 800-822. English. DESCR: Border Patrol; *Constitutional Amendments - Fourth; *Immigration and Naturalization Service (INS); Immigration Law and Legislation; Immigration Regulation and Control; *Search and Seizure.

2276 English only forces promoting racist measures nationwide. GUARDIAN, Vol. 39, no. 24 (March 25, 1987), p. 7. English. DESCR: *English Language; English-Only Movement.

2277 Garcia, John A. Book review of: RACE AND CLASS IN THE SOUTHWEST: A THEORY OF INEQUALITY. LA RED/THE NET, no. 31 (June 1980), p. 4. English. DESCR: Barrera, Mario; Book Reviews; *Economics; RACE AND CLASS IN THE SOUTHWEST: A THEORY OF RACIAL INEQUALITY; *Southwestern United States.

2278 Goldman, Shifra. Arte chicano: iconografia de la autodeterminacion. LA COMUNIDAD, No. 336 (December 28, 1986), p. 12-14+. Spanish. DESCR: *Art; EL PLAN ESPIRITUAL DE AZTLAN; History; Identity; Nationalism; Pachucos; Social Classes; *Symbolism.

2279 Grajeda Higley, Leilani. Irma Castro. VISTA, Vol. 2, no. 10 (June 7, 1987), p. 20. English. DESCR: *Biography; *Castro, Irma; Chicanas; *Chicano Federation of San Diego Co., Inc.; Civil Rights.

2280 Guppy, N. Positional centrality and racial segregation in professional baseball. INTERNATIONAL REVIEW OF SPORT SOCIOLOGY, Vol. 18, no. 4 (1983), p. 95-109. English. DESCR: *Baseball; Ethnic Groups; Segregation and Desegregation.

2281 Haley, Lindsey. Una premiacion controvertida. LA COMUNIDAD, No. 246 (April 7, 1985), p. 5-6. Spanish. DESCR: Awards; *Grammy Awards; Guevara, Ruben; *Recording Industry; Zanya Records Co., Los Angeles, CA.

2282 Herrera, Irma D. The color barrier to full equality. VISTA, Vol. 1, no. 6 (February 2, 1986), p. 3. English. DESCR: *Skin Color.

2283 Jesse Jackson makes appearance at CBS board meeting. BROADCASTING, Vol. 110, no. 16 (April 21, 1986), p. 100. English. DESCR: Broadcast Media; *Columbia Broadcasting Studios (CBS); Discrimination in Employment; *Jackson, Jesse; People United to Serve Humanity (PUSH); Stereotypes; Taylor, Hycel; Wyman, Thomas.

2284 Jimenez, Luis. Cambia la imagen del latino en Hollywood. LA COMUNIDAD, No. 255 (June 9, 1985), p. 14-15. Spanish. DESCR: Employment; Films; *Hispanic Academy of Media Arts and Sciences (HAMAS); *Mass Media; Organizations; Reyna, Phil.

Discrimination (cont.)

2285 Korzenny, Felipe and Schiff, Elizabeth. Hispanic perceptions of communication discrimination. HISPANIC JOURNAL OF BEHAVIORAL SCIENCES, Vol. 9, no. 1 (March, 1987), p. 33-48. English. DESCR: Accentedness; *Intercultural Communication; Skin Color.

2286 Lucero, Rubel Jose. The enemy within. EL CUADERNO, Vol. 1, no. 1 (1971), p. 10-13. English. DESCR: *Identity; *Self-Referents.

2287 Martinez, Elizabeth. A decade of repression: update on the "Kiko" Martinez case. CRIME AND SOCIAL JUSTICE, no. 19 (Summer 1983), p. 100. English. DESCR: Chicano Movement; Civil Rights; Colorado; Criminal Justice System; Legal Cases; *Martinez, Francisco "Kiko"; Political Repression.

2288 Newquist, Deborah. The health care barrier model: toward analyzing the underutilization of health care by older Mexican-Americans. ANTHROPOLOGY UCLA, Vol. 14, (1985), p. 1-12. English. DESCR: *Ancianos; *Cultural Characteristics; Folk Medicine; *Medical Care; Medical Clinics; *Public Health.

2289 Sellers, Jeff M. Opportunity no, regulations yes. HISPANIC BUSINESS, Vol. 9, no. 2 (February 1987), p. 12-[14]. English. DESCR: Employment; *Immigration Law and Legislation; *Immigration Reform and Control Act of 1986; Undocumented Workers.

2290 Trevino, Jesus Salvador. Latino portrayals in film and television. JUMP CUT, no. 30 (March 1985), p. 14. English. DESCR: *Films; *Stereotypes.

2291 Vasquez, Victor. More on CHICO AND THE MAN. LATIN QUARTER, Vol. 1, no. 3 (January, February, 1975), p. 13-15. English. DESCR: Albertson, Jack; Andrade, Ray; Artists; Boycotts; *CHICO AND THE MAN [television show]; Prinze, Freddie; Stereotypes; *Television.

2292 Weller, David L. and Reyes, Laurie Hart. Stereotyping: impact on teachers and students. ACTION IN TEACHER EDUCATION, Vol. 5, no. 3 (Fall 1983), p. 1-7. English. DESCR: Education; Sex Stereotypes; *Stereotypes.

2293 Wreford, Mary. Chicano Survey report #2: perceptions and experience of discrimination. LA RED/THE NET, no. 39 (February 1981), p. 7,16. English. DESCR: Discrimination in Employment; Midwestern States; *National Chicano Survey (NCS); Southwestern United States; *Surveys.

Discrimination in Education

2294 Beltran, Christina. Minority access into higher education. REVISTA MUJERES, Vol. 4, no. 1 (January 1987), p. 54-55. English. DESCR: *Higher Education.

2295 Cervantes, Robert A. Ethnocentric pedagogy and minority student growth: implications for the common school. EDUCATION AND URBAN SOCIETY, Vol. 16, no. 3 (May 1984), p. 274-293. English. DESCR: Bilingual Bicultural Education; California; *Education.

2296 Dates, Karen E. Coast Guard ocean engineer Lisa Martinez. HISPANIC ENGINEER, Vol. 3, no. 4 (Fall 1987), p. 30-34. English. DESCR: Chicanas; *Engineering as a Profession; *Martinez, Lisa.

2297 Educational hierarchies and social differentiation. LA RED/THE NET, no. 37 (December 1980), p. 2-3. English. DESCR: Enrollment; *Higher Education; *Southwestern United States.

2298 From dropout to educator. VISTA, Vol. 2, no. 1 (September 7, 1986), p. 13. English. DESCR: *Academic Achievement; Education; *Intelligence Tests; *Quintanilla, Guadalupe.

2299 Garza, Hisauro A. The "barrioization" of Hispanic faculty. EDUCATIONAL RECORD, (Fall, Winter, 1987, 1988), p. 122-124. English. DESCR: *Colleges and Universities; *Discrimination in Employment; *Higher Education; Teaching Profession.

2300 Gonzalez, Gilbert G. Segregation of Mexican children in a southern California city: the legacy of expansion and the American Southwest. WESTERN HISTORICAL QUARTERLY, Vol. 16, no. 1 (January 1985), p. 55-76. English. DESCR: Education; Educational Administration; Primary School Education; *Santa Ana, CA; Segregation and Desegregation.

2301 Gonzalez, Juan C. Report to the Network. LA RED/THE NET, No. 105 (February 1987), p. 1-3. English. DESCR: Breland, Hunter M.; *DEMOGRAPHICS, STANDARDS, AND EQUITY CHALLENGES IN COLLEGE ADMISSIONS: REPORT OF A SURVEY OF UNDERGRADUATE ADMISSIONS POLICIES, PRACTICES AND PROCEDURES; *Enrollment; *Higher Education.

2302 Leon, David Jess and McNeill, Daniel. The fifth class: a 19th century forerunner of affirmative action. CALIFORNIA HISTORY, Vol. 64, no. 1 (Winter 1985), p. 52-57. English. DESCR: *Affirmative Action; Colleges and Universities; *Enrollment; *Higher Education; History; Students; *University of California.

2303 Loo, Chalsa M. and Rolison, Garry. Alienation of ethnic minority students at a predominantly white university. JOURNAL OF HIGHER EDUCATION, Vol. 57, no. 1 (January, February, 1986), p. 58-77. English. DESCR: *Alienation; Attitudes; *Students; Surveys; Teacher-pupil Interaction.

2304 Madrid, Arturo. Report to the Network. LA RED/THE NET, no. 92 (November, December, 1985), p. 1-3. English. DESCR: *Higher Education.

2305 Olivas, Michael A. The condition of Hispanic education. LA RED/THE NET, no. 56 (July 1982), p. 3-6. English. DESCR: *Education; *Segregation and Desegregation.

2306 Panas, Katia. Postsecondary retention and graduation: strategies for change. REVISTA MUJERES, Vol. 4, no. 1 (January 1987), p. 66-72. English. DESCR: Assimilation; *Education; Higher Education.

2307 Proefriedt, William A. Equality of opportunity and bilingual education. BILINGUAL REVIEW, Vol. 11, no. 3 (September, December, 1984), p. 3-8. English. DESCR: *Bilingual Bicultural Education.

Discrimination in Education (cont.)

2308 Ramirez, Salvador. The establishment and administration of a master's program in Chicano Studies at the University of Colorado. EPOCA: NATIONAL CONCILIO FOR CHICANO STUDIES JOURNAL, Vol. 1, no. 2 (Winter 1971), p. 39-50. English. DESCR: *Chicano Studies; *Curriculum; Educational Theory and Practice; Student Organizations; *Students; United Mexican American Students (UMAS); *University of Colorado, Boulder; Youth.

2309 Stewart, Kenneth L. and de Leon, Arnoldo. Education, literacy, and occupational structure in West Texas, 1860-1900. WEST TEXAS HISTORICAL ASSOCIATION YEARBOOK, Vol. 60, (1984), p. 127-143. English. DESCR: Economic Development; Education; Employment; *Labor; Literacy; *Texas.

2310 Texas' higher education "Adams" compliance report. LA RED/THE NET. No. 102 (November 1986), p. 2-5. English. DESCR: *Higher Education; Public Policy; Texas; *Texas Equal Education Opportunity Plan for Higher Education.

Discrimination in Employment

2311 Chiswick, Barry R. The labor market status of Hispanic men. JOURNAL OF AMERICAN ETHNIC HISTORY, Vol. 7, no. 1 (Fall 1987), p. 30-58. English. DESCR: Census; *Employment; Ethnic Groups; Income; *Labor Supply and Market; Language Usage; *Males; *Undocumented Workers.

2312 Ericksen, Charles. Wanted: Hispanics in the newsroom. CIVIL RIGHTS DIGEST/PERSPECTIVES, Vol. 14, no. 1 (Spring 1982), p. 40-44. English. DESCR: Journalism; *Journalists; *Print Media; *Stereotypes.

2313 Garza, Hisauro A. The "barrioization" of Hispanic faculty. EDUCATIONAL RECORD, (Fall, Winter, 1987, 1988), p. 122-124. English. DESCR: *Colleges and Universities; *Discrimination in Education; *Higher Education; Teaching Profession.

2314 High court upholds quotas. DUNS'S BUSINESS MONTH, Vol. 128, no. 2 (August 1986), p. 22. English. DESCR: *Affirmative Action; Reagan Administration; Sexism; U.S. Supreme Court.

2315 Jesse Jackson makes appearance at CBS board meeting. BROADCASTING, Vol. 110, no. 16 (April 21, 1986), p. 100. English. DESCR: Broadcast Media; *Columbia Broadcasting Studios (CBS); Discrimination; *Jackson, Jesse; People United to Serve Humanity (PUSH); Stereotypes; Taylor, Hycel; Wyman, Thomas.

2316 Parlee, Lorena M. The impact of United States railroad unions on organized labor and government policy in Mexico (1880-1911). HISPANIC AMERICAN HISTORICAL REVIEW, Vol. 64, no. 3 (August 1984), p. 443-475. English. DESCR: Diaz, Porfirio; History; *Labor Unions; Mexico; Partido Liberal Mexicano (PLM); Railroads; United States-Mexico Relations.

2317 Trevino, Jesus Salvador. Chicano cinema overview. AREITO, Vol. 10, no. 37 (1984), p. 40-43. English. DESCR: BALLAD OF GREGORIO CORTEZ [film]; *Films; Television.

2318 Vargas-Willis, Gloria and Cervantes, Richard C. Consideration of psychosocial stress in the treatment of the Latina immigrant.

HISPANIC JOURNAL OF BEHAVIORAL SCIENCES, Vol. 9, no. 3 (September 1987), p. 315-329. English. DESCR: *Chicanas; *Immigrants; Mental Health; *Psychotherapy; *Stress.

2319 Wreford, Mary. Chicano Survey report #2: perceptions and experience of discrimination. LA RED/THE NET, no. 39 (February 1981), p. 7,16. English. DESCR: *Discrimination; Midwestern States; *National Chicano Survey (NCS); Southwestern United States; *Surveys.

2320 Zavella, Patricia. "Abnormal intimacy": the varying work networks of Chicana cannery workers. FEMINIST STUDIES, Vol. 11, no. 3 (Fall 1985), p. 541-557. English. DESCR: Canneries; Chicanas; Labor Unions; *Natural Support Systems; *Working Women.

2321 Zucca, Gary J. and Gorman, Benjamin. Affirmative action: Blacks and Hispanics in United States Navy occupational specialties. ARMED FORCES AND SOCIETY, Vol. 12, no. 4 (Summer 1986), p. 513-524. English. DESCR: *Affirmative Action; *Blacks; *Military.

Discrimination in Housing
USE: Residential Segregation

Discriminatory Hiring Practices
USE: Discrimination in Employment

Disease Prevention and Control
USE: Preventative Medicine

Diseases

2322 Duncan, Marilyn H., et al. Childhood cancer epidemiology in New Mexico's American Indians, Hispanic whites, and non-Hispanic whites, 1970-82. JOURNAL OF THE NATIONAL CANCER INSTITUTE, Vol. 76, no. 6 (June 1986), p. 1013-1018. English. DESCR: Anglo Americans; *Cancer; *Children; Native Americans.

2323 Fighting cervical cancer. NUESTRO, Vol. 11, no. 3 (April 1987), p. 26-27. English. DESCR: *Cancer; *Chicanas.

2324 McMenamin, Jerry. Language deficits in a bilingual child with cerebral cysticercosis. BILINGUAL REVIEW, Vol. 11, no. 3 (September, December, 1984), p. 25-30. English. DESCR: Bilingualism; *Cerebral Cysticercosis; Handicapped; *Language Development.

2325 Remas, Theodora A. Cancer: early detection can help prevent a deadly disease. VISTA, Vol. 1, no. 8 (April 6, 1986), p. 10-11. English. DESCR: Health Education; Preventative Medicine.

2326 Sanchez, Tom. Jeff Apodaca. VISTA, Vol. 1, no. 8 (April 6, 1986), p. 21. English. DESCR: *Apodaca, Jeff; *Athletes; Sports.

2327 Sosa, Lionel. The human face of AIDS. VISTA, Vol. 3, no. 4 (December 6, 1987), p. 15, 36. English. DESCR: *Acquired Immune Deficiency Syndrome (AIDS); Biography.

2328 Valdez, William J. Impotence: a problem with a solution. NUESTRO, Vol. 11, no. 4 (May 1987), p. 18-20. English. DESCR: Centro de Impotencia, Coral Gables Hospital, Miami, FL; *Impotence; Males; Medical Clinics; *Psychotherapy.

Diseases (cont.)

2329 Weiss, K.M. Phenotype amplification, as
     illustrated by cancer of the gallbladder in
     New World peoples. PROGRESS IN CLINICAL AND
     BIOLOGICAL RESEARCH, Vol. 194, (1985), p.
     179-198. English. **DESCR**: *Cancer.

DISTANT NEIGHBORS: A PORTRAIT OF THE MEXICANS

2330 Loaeza, Soledad. Alan Riding: la fuerza del
     prejuicio. LA COMUNIDAD, No. 255 (June 9,
     1985), p. 2-5. Spanish. **DESCR**: Book Reviews;
     Mexico; Riding, Alan.

Divorce

2331 Anonymous UCSC Community Member. An extinct
     relationship. REVISTA MUJERES, Vol. 2, no. 1
     (January 1985), p. 21-22. English. **DESCR**:
     *Marriage; Women Men Relations.

2332 Frisbie, William Parker; Opitz, Wolfgang;
     and Kelly. William R. Marital instability
     trends among Mexican Americans as compared
     to Blacks and Anglos: new evidence. SOCIAL
     SCIENCE QUARTERLY, Vol. 66, no. 3 (September
     1985), p. 587-601. English. **DESCR**:
     *Chicanas; Marriage.

2333 Out of marriage, onto welfare and into
     poverty. REVISTA MUJERES, Vol. 4, no. 1
     (January 1987), p. 39-40. English. **DESCR**:
     *Chicanas; Education; Welfare.

Dixon, Marlene

2334 Pena, Devon Gerardo. Book review of: THE NEW
     NOMADS: FROM IMMIGRANT LABOR TO
     TRANSNATIONAL WORKING CLASS. LA RED/THE NET,
     no. 67 (April 1983), p. 8-10. English.
     DESCR: Book Reviews; Jonas, Susanne; Labor;
     *THE NEW NOMADS: FROM IMMIGRANT LABOR TO
     TRANSNATIONAL WORKING CLASS.

Doctor Patient Relations

2335 Grayson, June. Sports medics. VISTA, Vol. 2,
     no. 9 (May 3, 1987), p. 17-18. English.
     DESCR: Bergin-Nader, Barbara; Cuadros, Hugo;
     *Dominguez, Richard; *Medical Personnel;
     Prietto, Carlos Alfredo; *Sports.

2336 Lefton, Doug. Culture a factor in treating
     Latino patients. AMERICAN MEDICAL NEWS, Vol.
     25, (July 9, 1982), p. 17-19. English.
     DESCR: *Cultural Characteristics; Medical
     Care.

Dodson, C.J.

2337 Aitchison, Jean. Book review of: BILINGUAL
     EDUCATION: EVALUATION, ASSESSMENT AND
     METHODOLOGY. BRITISH BOOK NEWS, (January
     1986), p. 32-33. English. **DESCR**: *BILINGUAL
     EDUCATION: EVALUATION, ASSESSMENT AND
     METHODOLOGY; Book Reviews.

Dominguez, Jorge

2338 de la Garza, Rodolfo O. Book review of:
     MEXICO'S POLITICAL ECONOMY: CHALLENGES AT
     HOME AND ABROAD. LA RED/THE NET, no. 69
     (June 1983), p. 5-7. English. **DESCR**: Book
     Reviews; Mexico; *MEXICO'S POLITICAL
     ECONOMY: CHALLENGES AT HOME AND ABROAD.

Dominguez, Peter

2339 Reyes, Sonia. Hispanic models pursue high
     stakes fashion. VISTA, Vol. 1, no. 2
     (October 5, 1985), p. 6-9. English. **DESCR**:
     Apodaca, Roseanne; Careers; *Fashion; Jerez,
     Alicia; Soto, Talisa.

Dominguez, Richard

2340 Grayson, June. Sports medics. VISTA, Vol. 2,
     no. 9 (May 3, 1987), p. 17-18. English.
     DESCR: Bergin-Nader, Barbara; Cuadros, Hugo;
     Doctor Patient Relations; *Medical
     Personnel; Prietto, Carlos Alfredo; *Sports.

Douglas, AZ

2341 Rubio Goldsmith, Raquel. Shipwrecked in the
     desert: a short history of the adventures
     and struggles for survival of the Mexican
     Sisters of the House of the Providence in
     Douglas, Arizona during their first
     twenty-two years of existence (1927-1949).
     RENATO ROSALDO LECTURE SERIES MONOGRAPH,
     Vol. 1, (Summer 1985), p. [39]-67. English.
     DESCR: Catholic Church; Chicanas; Clergy;
     History; *House of the Divine Providence
     [convent], Douglas, AZ.

Draft

     USE: Military

Drawings

2342 Aguero Rojas, Pilar. [Untitled drawing].
     REVISTA MUJERES, Vol. 2, no. 1 (January
     1985), p. 19.

2343 Aguero Rojas, Pilar. [Untitled drawing].
     REVISTA MUJERES, Vol. 2, no. 2 (June 1985),
     p. 28.

2344 Aguero Rojas, Pilar. [Untitled drawing].
     REVISTA MUJERES, Vol. 3, no. 1 (January
     1986), p. 16.

2345 Aguero Rojas, Pilar. [Untitled drawing].
     REVISTA MUJERES, Vol. 3, no. 1 (January
     1986), p. 47.

2346 Aguero Rojas, Pilar. [Untitled drawing].
     REVISTA MUJERES, Vol. 3, no. 1 (January
     1986), p. 55.

2347 Aguero Rojas, Pilar. [Woman and broom
     (drawing)]. REVISTA MUJERES, Vol. 3, no. 2
     (June 1986), p. 10.

2348 Aguero Rojas, Pilar. [Woman and iron
     (drawing)]. REVISTA MUJERES, Vol. 3, no. 2
     (June 1986), p. 63.

2349 Aguiar, Antonia. [Arms]. REVISTA MUJERES,
     Vol. 4, no. 1 (January 1987), p. FT COVER.

2350 Aguiar, Antonia. [Bodies]. REVISTA MUJERES,
     Vol. 4, no. 1 (January 1987), p. 16.

2351 Aguiar, Antonia. [Untitled drawing]. REVISTA
     MUJERES, Vol. 3, no. 1 (January 1986), p. Ft
     cover.

2352 Aguiar, Antonia. [Untitled drawing]. REVISTA
     MUJERES, Vol. 3, no. 1 (January 1986), p.
     32.

2353 Aguiar, Antonia. [Untitled drawing]. REVISTA
     MUJERES, Vol. 3, no. 1 (January 1986), p.
     43.

2354 Alarcon, Norma. Honey [drawing]. CHIRICU,
     no. 2 (Spring 1977), p. 15.

2355 Borboa, Roberto. [Untitled drawing].
     SAGUARO, Vol. 1, no. 1 (1984), p. Ft cover.

2356 Borboa, Roberto. [Untitled drawing].
     SAGUARO, Vol. 1, no. 1 (1984), p. 12.

Drawings (cont.)

2357 Borboa, Roberto. [Untitled drawing].
SAGUARO, Vol. 1, no. 1 (1984), p. 21.

2358 Borboa, Roberto. [Untitled drawing].
SAGUARO, Vol. 1, no. 1 (1984), p. 33.

2359 Borboa, Roberto. [Untitled drawing].
SAGUARO, Vol. 1, no. 1 (1984), p. 40.

2360 Borboa, Roberto. [Untitled drawing].
SAGUARO, Vol. 1, no. 1 (1984), p. 52.

2361 Borboa, Roberto. [Untitled drawing].
SAGUARO, Vol. 1, no. 1 (1984), p. 66.

2362 Borboa, Roberto. [Untitled drawing].
SAGUARO, Vol. 1, no. 1 (1984), p. 78.

2363 Cabeza de Vaca, Darlene. [Campesina].
REVISTA MUJERES, Vol. 2, no. 2 (June 1985),
p. 51.

2364 Cabeza de Vaca, Darlene. Home. REVISTA
MUJERES, Vol. 2, no. 1 (January 1985), p.
25.

2365 Cabeza de Vaca, Darlene. Nursing mother.
REVISTA MUJERES, Vol. 2, no. 2 (June 1985),
p. 45.

2366 Cabeza de Vaca, Darlene. [Untitled drawing].
REVISTA MUJERES, Vol. 2, no. 2 (June 1985),
p. 6.

2367 Cabeza de Vaca, Darlene. [Woman (drawing)].
REVISTA MUJERES, Vol. 2, no. 1 (January
1985), p. Ft cover.

2368 Cabeza de Vaca, Darlene. [Woman's torso
(drawing)]. REVISTA MUJERES, Vol. 2, no. 2
(June 1985), p. FT COVER.

2369 Clair, Denise. [Working woman]. REVISTA
MUJERES, Vol. 3, no. 2 (June 1986), p. 29.

2370 Corpus, Alfonso. [Untitled drawing].
CHIRICU, no. 1 (Spring 1976), p. 15.

2371 Corpus, Alfonso. [Untitled drawing].
CHIRICU, no. 1 (Spring 1976), p. 11.

2372 Cruz, Frank. [Untitled drawing]. CHIRICU,
no. 2 (Spring 1977), p. 34.

2373 de la Riva, Lola. [Circular design]. REVISTA
MUJERES, Vol. 4, no. 1 (January 1987), p.
56.

2374 de la Riva, Lola. [Circular design]. REVISTA
MUJERES, Vol. 4, no. 1 (January 1987), p.
78.

2375 Delgado, Jorge. Las palabras [drawing].
CONFLUENCIA, Vol. 1, no. 2 (Spring 1986), p.
112.

2376 Ginghofer, R. [Mary Corralejo]. REVISTA
MUJERES, Vol. 1, no. 1 (January 1984), p.
13.

2377 Hernandez, Angel. [Untitled drawing]. LLUEVE
TLALOC, no. 1 (1974), p. Ft cover.

2378 Hernandez, Angel. [Untitled drawing]. LLUEVE
TLALOC, no. 3 (1976), p. 9. **DESCR:** Children.

2379 Hernandez, Angel. [Untitled drawing]. LLUEVE
TLALOC, no. 3 (1976), p. 32.

2380 Huaco-Nuzum, Carmen J. Half-moon bay.
REVISTA MUJERES, Vol. 4, no. 1 (January
1987), p. 19.

2381 Huaco-Nuzum, Carmen J. Kachina #2. REVISTA
MUJERES, Vol. 4, no. 1 (January 1987), p.
10.

2382 Huaco-Nuzum, Carmen J. Kachina #3. REVISTA
MUJERES, Vol. 4, no. 1 (January 1987), p.
12.

2383 Huaco-Nuzum, Carmen J. Light my bulb.
REVISTA MUJERES, Vol. 4, no. 1 (January
1987), p. 65.

2384 Huaco-Nuzum, Carmen J. Lollipop #1. REVISTA
MUJERES, Vol. 4, no. 1 (January 1987), p.
13.

2385 Huaco-Nuzum, Carmen J. [Untitled drawing].
REVISTA MUJERES, Vol. 4, no. 1 (January
1987), p. 11.

2386 Huaco-Nuzum, Carmen J. [Untitled drawing].
REVISTA MUJERES, Vol. 4, no. 1 (January
1987), p. 11.

2387 Huaco-Nuzum, Carmen J. [Untitled drawing].
REVISTA MUJERES, Vol. 4, no. 1 (January
1987), p. 12.

2388 Huaco-Nuzum, Carmen J. [Untitled drawing].
REVISTA MUJERES, Vol. 4, no. 1 (January
1987), p. 65.

2389 Juana Alicia. La mujer del Rio Sumpul.
REVISTA MUJERES, Vol. 3, no. 2 (June 1986),
p. 36.

2390 Kreisberg, Polly. [Untitled drawing].
REVISTA MUJERES, Vol. 3, no. 2 (June 1986),
p. 15.

2391 Lomas, Clara. [Untitled drawing]. REVISTA
MUJERES, Vol. 1, no. 1 (January 1984), p. Ft
cover.

2392 Martinez, Ferdinand. [This is
Debra...(drawing)]. CHIRICU, no. 1 (Spring
1976), p. 17.

2393 Martinez, Sue. [Woman (drawing)]. REVISTA
MUJERES, Vol. 3, no. 2 (June 1986), p. FT
COVER.

2394 McCoy, Michelle. [Untitled drawing]. REVISTA
MUJERES, Vol. 4, no. 1 (January 1987), p.
53.

2395 McCoy, Michelle. [Woman and man (drawing)].
REVISTA MUJERES, Vol. 3, no. 2 (June 1986),
p. 53.

2396 McCoy, Michelle. [Woman (drawing)]. REVISTA
MUJERES, Vol. 4, no. 1 (January 1987), p.
34.

2397 McKesson, Jon. El jardin [drawing]. CHIRICU,
no. 2 (Spring 1977), p. 24.

2398 McKesson, Jon. Sunday afternoons [drawing].
CHIRICU, no. 2 (Spring 1977), p. 8.

2399 McKesson, Jon. [Untitled drawing]. CHIRICU,
no. 2 (Spring 1977), p. 1.

2400 O'Hagen, Linda. [Woman]. REVISTA MUJERES,
Vol. 4, no. 1 (January 1987), p. 49.

2401 Ordaz, Carmel. [Untitled drawing]. REVISTA
MUJERES, Vol. 4, no. 1 (January 1987), p.
22.

Drawings (cont.)

2402 Ordaz, Carmel. [Untitled drawing]. REVISTA MUJERES, Vol. 4, no. 1 (January 1987), p. 38.

2403 Ordaz, Carmel. [Untitled drawing]. REVISTA MUJERES, Vol. 4, no. 1 (January 1987), p. 60.

2404 Ordaz, Carmel. [Untitled drawing]. REVISTA MUJERES, Vol. 4, no. 1 (January 1987), p. 74.

2405 Ortiz-Muraida, Thelma. [Untitled drawing]. SAGUARO, Vol. 1, no. 1 (1984), p. Ft cover.

2406 Padilla, Steve. The mad mad world of Sergio Aragones. VISTA, Vol. 2, no. 5 (January 4, 1987), p. 6-8. English. **DESCR:** Aragones, Sergio; Artists; *Humor; *MAD Magazine.

2407 Pasas. Reflexiones. LLUEVE TLALOC, no. 3 (1976), p. 51.

2408 Pasas. [Untitled drawing]. LLUEVE TLALOC, no. 3 (1976), p. 49.

2409 Pazos, Antonio. [340 W. Simpson drawing]. LLUEVE TLALOC, no. 4 (1977), p. 34.

2410 Pazos, Antonio. El cholo. LLUEVE TLALOC, no. 6 (1979), p. 15.

2411 Pazos, Antonio. [El cine plaza drawing]. LLUEVE TLALOC, no. 3 (1976), p. 43.

2412 Pazos, Antonio. [Con el poncho embravecido (drawing)]. LLUEVE TLALOC, no. 5 (1978), p. 15.

2413 Pazos, Antonio. Dos arbolitos. LLUEVE TLALOC, no. 12 (1985), p. 11.

2414 Pazos, Antonio. Dos arbolitos slate 1. LLUEVE TLALOC, no. 12 (1985), p. 40.

2415 Pazos, Antonio. [Drunken angel drawing]. LLUEVE TLALOC, no. 5 (1978), p. 25.

2416 Pazos, Antonio. [Emiliano Zapata drawing]. LLUEVE TLALOC, no. 4 (1977), p. 61.

2417 Pazos, Antonio. Hasta siempre. LLUEVE TLALOC, no. 12 (1985), p. 30.

2418 Pazos, Antonio. [Image of Mexican mysticism]. LLUEVE TLALOC, no. 11 (1984), p. Ft cover.

2419 Pazos, Antonio. Llueve tlaloc. LLUEVE TLALOC, no. 4 (1977), p. Ft cover.

2420 Pazos, Antonio. [Llueve Tlaloc drawing]. LLUEVE TLALOC, no. 6 (1979), p. Ft cover.

2421 Pazos, Antonio. [Loui Romero]. LLUEVE TLALOC, no. 6 (1979), p. 43.

2422 Pazos, Antonio. Maria salina. LLUEVE TLALOC, no. 12 (1985), p. 26.

2423 Pazos, Antonio. My Nana's rosary. LLUEVE TLALOC, no. 12 (1985), p. 17.

2424 Pazos, Antonio. Pajaro Urogue. LLUEVE TLALOC, no. 8 (1981), p. Ft cover.

2425 Pazos, Antonio. [El poeta suena...(drawing)]. LLUEVE TLALOC, no. 5 (1978), p. 6.

2426 Pazos, Antonio. [Untitled drawing]. LLUEVE TLALOC, no. 3 (1976), p. 8.

2427 Pazos, Antonio. [Untitled drawing]. LLUEVE TLALOC, no. 3 (1976), p. 14-15.

2428 Pazos, Antonio. [Untitled drawing]. LLUEVE TLALOC, no. 3 (1976), p. 17.

2429 Pazos, Antonio. [Untitled drawing]. LLUEVE TLALOC, no. 3 (1976), p. 19.

2430 Pazos, Antonio. [Untitled drawing]. LLUEVE TLALOC, no. 3 (1976), p. 25.

2431 Pazos, Antonio. [Untitled drawing]. LLUEVE TLALOC, no. 3 (1976), p. 28.

2432 Pazos, Antonio. [Untitled drawing]. LLUEVE TLALOC, no. 3 (1976), p. 33.

2433 Pazos, Antonio. [Untitled drawing]. LLUEVE TLALOC, no. 3 (1976), p. 35.

2434 Pazos, Antonio. [Untitled drawing]. LLUEVE TLALOC, no. 3 (1976), p. 37.

2435 Pazos, Antonio. [Untitled drawing]. LLUEVE TLALOC, no. 3 (1976), p. 39.

2436 Pazos, Antonio. [Untitled drawing]. LLUEVE TLALOC, no. 3 (1976), p. 45.

2437 Pazos, Antonio. [Untitled drawing]. LLUEVE TLALOC, no. 3 (1976), p. 60.

2438 Pazos, Antonio. [Untitled drawing]. LLUEVE TLALOC, no. 3 (1976), p. 62.

2439 Pazos, Antonio. [Untitled drawing]. LLUEVE TLALOC, no. 4 (1977), p. 25.

2440 Pazos, Antonio. [Untitled drawing]. LLUEVE TLALOC, no. 4 (1977), p. 45.

2441 Pazos, Antonio. [Untitled drawing]. LLUEVE TLALOC, no. 4 (1977), p. 53.

2442 Pazos, Antonio. [Untitled drawing]. LLUEVE TLALOC, no. 4 (1977), p. 55.

2443 Pazos, Antonio. [Untitled drawing]. LLUEVE TLALOC, no. 4 (1977), p. 66.

2444 Pazos, Antonio. [Untitled drawing]. LLUEVE TLALOC, no. 4 (1977), p. 71.

2445 Pazos, Antonio. [Untitled drawing]. LLUEVE TLALOC, no. 4 (1977), p. 79.

2446 Pazos, Antonio. [Untitled drawing]. LLUEVE TLALOC, no. 4 (1977), p. 82.

2447 Pazos, Antonio. [Untitled drawing]. LLUEVE TLALOC, no. 4 (1977), p. 90.

2448 Pazos, Antonio. [Untitled drawing]. LLUEVE TLALOC, no. 4 (1977), p. 95.

2449 Pazos, Antonio. [Untitled drawing]. LLUEVE TLALOC, no. 4 (1977), p. 106.

2450 Pazos, Antonio. [Untitled drawing]. LLUEVE TLALOC, no. 4 (1977), p. 108.

2451 Pazos, Antonio. [Untitled drawing]. LLUEVE TLALOC, no. 5 (1978), p. Ft cover.

2452 Pazos, Antonio. [Untitled drawing]. LLUEVE TLALOC, no. 5 (1978), p. 13.

2453 Pazos, Antonio. [Untitled drawing]. LLUEVE TLALOC, no. 5 (1978), p. 17.

Drawings (cont.)

2454 Pazos, Antonio. [Untitled drawing]. LLUEVE TLALOC, no. 5 (1978), p. 19.

2455 Pazos, Antonio. [Untitled drawing]. LLUEVE TLALOC, no. 5 (1978), p. 21.

2456 Pazos, Antonio. [Untitled drawing]. LLUEVE TLALOC, no. 5 (1978), p. 23.

2457 Pazos, Antonio. [Untitled drawing]. LLUEVE TLALOC, no. 5 (1978), p. 27.

2458 Pazos, Antonio. [Untitled drawing]. LLUEVE TLALOC, no. 5 (1978), p. 31.

2459 Pazos, Antonio. [Untitled drawing]. LLUEVE TLALOC, no. 5 (1978), p. 34.

2460 Pazos, Antonio. [Untitled drawing]. LLUEVE TLALOC, no. 5 (1978), p. 38.

2461 Pazos, Antonio. [Untitled drawing]. LLUEVE TLALOC, no. 5 (1978), p. 40.

2462 Pazos, Antonio. [Untitled drawing]. LLUEVE TLALOC, no. 6 (1979), p. 10.

2463 Pazos, Antonio. [Untitled drawing]. LLUEVE TLALOC, no. 6 (1979), p. 12.

2464 Pazos, Antonio. [Untitled drawing]. LLUEVE TLALOC, no. 6 (1979), p. 17.

2465 Pazos, Antonio. [Untitled drawing]. LLUEVE TLALOC, no. 6 (1979), p. 19.

2466 Pazos, Antonio. [Untitled drawing]. LLUEVE TLALOC, no. 6 (1979), p. 21.

2467 Pazos, Antonio. [Untitled drawing]. LLUEVE TLALOC, no. 6 (1979), p. 23.

2468 Pazos, Antonio. [Untitled drawing]. LLUEVE TLALOC, no. 6 (1979), p. 25.

2469 Pazos, Antonio. [Untitled drawing]. LLUEVE TLALOC, no. 6 (1979), p. 27.

2470 Pazos, Antonio. [Untitled drawing]. LLUEVE TLALOC, no. 6 (1979), p. 29.

2471 Pazos, Antonio. [Untitled drawing]. LLUEVE TLALOC, no. 6 (1979), p. 31.

2472 Pazos, Antonio. [Untitled drawing]. LLUEVE TLALOC, no. 6 (1979), p. 33.

2473 Pazos, Antonio. [Untitled drawing]. LLUEVE TLALOC, no. 6 (1979), p. 35.

2474 Pazos, Antonio. [Untitled drawing]. LLUEVE TLALOC, no. 6 (1979), p. 37.

2475 Pazos, Antonio. [Untitled drawing]. LLUEVE TLALOC, no. 6 (1979), p. 44.

2476 Pazos, Antonio. [Untitled drawing]. LLUEVE TLALOC, no. 7 (1980), p. Ft cover.

2477 Pazos, Antonio. [Untitled drawing]. LLUEVE TLALOC, no. 7 (1980), p. 9.

2478 Pazos, Antonio. [Untitled drawing]. LLUEVE TLALOC, no. 7 (1980), p. 11.

2479 Pazos, Antonio. [Untitled drawing]. LLUEVE TLALOC, no. 7 (1980), p. 16.

2480 Pazos, Antonio. [Untitled drawing]. LLUEVE TLALOC, no. 7 (1980), p. 18.

2481 Pazos, Antonio. [Untitled drawing]. LLUEVE TLALOC, no. 7 (1980), p. 20.

2482 Pazos, Antonio. [Untitled drawing]. LLUEVE TLALOC, no. 7 (1980), p. 22.

2483 Pazos, Antonio. [Untitled drawing]. LLUEVE TLALOC, no. 7 (1980), p. 23.

2484 Pazos, Antonio. [Untitled drawing]. LLUEVE TLALOC, no. 7 (1980), p. 26.

2485 Pazos, Antonio. [Untitled drawing]. LLUEVE TLALOC, no. 7 (1980), p. 27.

2486 Pazos, Antonio. [Untitled drawing]. LLUEVE TLALOC, no. 7 (1980), p. 30.

2487 Pazos, Antonio. [Untitled drawing]. LLUEVE TLALOC, no. 7 (1980), p. 32.

2488 Pazos, Antonio. [Untitled drawing]. LLUEVE TLALOC, no. 7 (1980), p. 33.

2489 Pazos, Antonio. [Untitled drawing]. LLUEVE TLALOC, no. 7 (1980), p. 35.

2490 Pazos, Antonio. [Untitled drawing]. LLUEVE TLALOC, no. 7 (1980), p. 36.

2491 Pazos, Antonio. [Untitled drawing]. LLUEVE TLALOC, no. 7 (1980), p. 40.

2492 Pazos, Antonio. [Untitled drawing]. LLUEVE TLALOC, no. 8 (1981), p. 5.

2493 Pazos, Antonio. [Untitled drawing]. LLUEVE TLALOC, no. 8 (1981), p. 11.

2494 Pazos, Antonio. [Untitled drawing]. LLUEVE TLALOC, no. 8 (1981), p. 17.

2495 Pazos, Antonio. [Untitled drawing]. LLUEVE TLALOC, no. 8 (1981), p. 19.

2496 Pazos, Antonio. [Untitled drawing]. LLUEVE TLALOC, no. 8 (1981), p. 23.

2497 Pazos, Antonio. [Untitled drawing]. LLUEVE TLALOC, no. 8 (1981), p. 25.

2498 Pazos, Antonio. [Untitled drawing]. LLUEVE TLALOC, no. 8 (1981), p. 27.

2499 Pazos, Antonio. [Untitled drawing]. LLUEVE TLALOC, no. 8 (1981), p. 29.

2500 Pazos, Antonio. [Untitled drawing]. LLUEVE TLALOC, no. 8 (1981), p. 33.

2501 Pazos, Antonio. [Untitled drawing]. LLUEVE TLALOC, no. 8 (1981), p. 40.

2502 Pazos, Antonio. [Untitled drawing]. LLUEVE TLALOC, no. 9 (1982), p. Ft cover.

2503 Pazos, Antonio. [Untitled drawing]. LLUEVE TLALOC, no. 9 (1982), p. 2.

2504 Pazos, Antonio. [Untitled drawing]. LLUEVE TLALOC, no. 9 (1982), p. 5.

2505 Pazos, Antonio. [Untitled drawing]. LLUEVE TLALOC, no. 9 (1982), p. 7.

2506 Pazos, Antonio. [Untitled drawing]. LLUEVE TLALOC, no. 9 (1982), p. 9.

2507 Pazos, Antonio. [Untitled drawing]. LLUEVE TLALOC, no. 9 (1982), p. 11.

2508 Pazos, Antonio. [Untitled drawing]. LLUEVE TLALOC, no. 9 (1982), p. 13.

Drawings (cont.)

2509 Pazos, Antonio. [Untitled drawing]. LLUEVE TLALOC, no. 9 (1982), p. 15.

2510 Pazos, Antonio. [Untitled drawing]. LLUEVE TLALOC, no. 9 (1982), p. 18.

2511 Pazos, Antonio. [Untitled drawing]. LLUEVE TLALOC, no. 9 (1982), p. 22.

2512 Pazos, Antonio. [Untitled drawing]. LLUEVE TLALOC, no. 9 (1982), p. 25.

2513 Pazos, Antonio. [Untitled drawing]. LLUEVE TLALOC, no. 9 (1982), p. 27.

2514 Pazos, Antonio. [Untitled drawing]. LLUEVE TLALOC, no. 9 (1982), p. 28.

2515 Pazos, Antonio. [Untitled drawing]. LLUEVE TLALOC, no. 9 (1982), p. 30.

2516 Pazos, Antonio. [Untitled drawing]. LLUEVE TLALOC, no. 9 (1982), p. 35.

2517 Pazos, Antonio. [Untitled drawing]. LLUEVE TLALOC, no. 9 (1982), p. 40.

2518 Pazos, Antonio. [Untitled drawing]. LLUEVE TLALOC, no. 10 (1983), p. 4.

2519 Pazos, Antonio. [Untitled drawing]. LLUEVE TLALOC, no. 10 (1983), p. 5.

2520 Pazos, Antonio. [Untitled drawing]. LLUEVE TLALOC, no. 10 (1983), p. 40.

2521 Pazos, Antonio. [Untitled drawing]. LLUEVE TLALOC, no. 11 (1984), p. 3.

2522 Pazos, Antonio. [Untitled drawing]. LLUEVE TLALOC, no. 11 (1984), p. 7.

2523 Pazos, Antonio. [Untitled drawing]. LLUEVE TLALOC, no. 11 (1984), p. 12.

2524 Pazos, Antonio. [Untitled drawing]. LLUEVE TLALOC, no. 11 (1984), p. 15.

2525 Pazos, Antonio. [Untitled drawing]. LLUEVE TLALOC, no. 11 (1984), p. 18.

2526 Pazos, Antonio. [Untitled drawing]. LLUEVE TLALOC, no. 11 (1984), p. 21.

2527 Pazos, Antonio. [Untitled drawing]. LLUEVE TLALOC, no. 11 (1984), p. 22.

2528 Pazos, Antonio. [Untitled drawing]. LLUEVE TLALOC, no. 11 (1984), p. 25.

2529 Pazos, Antonio. [Untitled drawing]. LLUEVE TLALOC, no. 11 (1984), p. 29.

2530 Pazos, Antonio. [Untitled drawing]. LLUEVE TLALOC, no. 11 (1984), p. 30.

2531 Pazos, Antonio. [Untitled drawing]. LLUEVE TLALOC, no. 11 (1984), p. 31.

2532 Pazos, Antonio. [Untitled drawing]. LLUEVE TLALOC, no. 11 (1984), p. 33.

2533 Pazos, Antonio. [Untitled drawing]. LLUEVE TLALOC, no. 11 (1984), p. 39.

2534 Pazos, Antonio. [Untitled drawing]. LLUEVE TLALOC, no. 12 (1985), p. 41.

2535 Pazos, Antonio. [Untitled drawing of cactus]. LLUEVE TLALOC, no. 9 (1982), p. 21.

2536 Pazos, Antonio. [Untitled drawing of cat].

LLUEVE TLALOC, no. 9 (1982), p. 38.

2537 Pazos, Antonio. [Untitled drawing of trumpet player]. LLUEVE TLALOC, no. 9 (1982), p. 39.

2538 Pazos, Antonio. [Untitled drawing of African figure]. LLUEVE TLALOC, no. 10 (1983), p. 1.

2539 Pazos, Antonio. [Untitled drawing of man with a horse]. LLUEVE TLALOC, no. 10 (1983), p. 14.

2540 Pazos, Antonio. [Untitled drawing of a snake]. LLUEVE TLALOC, no. 10 (1983), p. 17.

2541 Pazos, Antonio. [Untitled drawing of pianist]. LLUEVE TLALOC, no. 10 (1983), p. 21.

2542 Pazos, Antonio. [Untitled drawing of Chinese man]. LLUEVE TLALOC, no. 10 (1983), p. 23.

2543 Pazos, Antonio. [Untitled drawing of boy drinking from a pond]. LLUEVE TLALOC, no. 10 (1983), p. 26.

2544 Pazos, Antonio. [Untitled painting]. LLUEVE TLALOC, no. 4 (1977), p. 97.

2545 Pazos, Antonio. [Winged boxer drawing]. LLUEVE TLALOC, no. 5 (1978), p. 9.

2546 Pochio. Death. LLUEVE TLALOC, no. 7 (1980), p. 13.

2547 Quintana, Rosa Maria. [Untitled drawing]. REVISTA MUJERES, Vol. 2, no. 2 (June 1985), p. 37.

2548 Quintana, Rosa Maria. [Untitled drawing]. REVISTA MUJERES, Vol. 3, no. 1 (January 1986), p. 49.

2549 Ramirez, Martin. Untitled (tunnels and trains) [drawing]. THE AMERICAS REVIEW, Vol. 15, no. 2 (Summer 1987), p. 68.

2550 Reyes Aponte, Cynthia. [Untitled drawing]. LLUEVE TLALOC, no. 11 (1984), p. 5.

2551 Reyes Aponte, Cynthia. [Untitled drawing]. LLUEVE TLALOC, no. 11 (1984), p. 27.

2552 Reyes Aponte, Cynthia. [Untitled drawing]. LLUEVE TLALOC, no. 11 (1984), p. 32.

2553 Reyes Aponte, Cynthia. [Untitled drawing]. LLUEVE TLALOC, no. 11 (1984), p. 35.

2554 Reyes Aponte, Cynthia. [Untitled drawing]. LLUEVE TLALOC, no. 12 (1985), p. 6.

2555 Reyes Aponte, Cynthia. [Untitled drawing]. LLUEVE TLALOC, no. 12 (1985), p. 14.

2556 Reyes Aponte, Cynthia. [Untitled drawing]. LLUEVE TLALOC, no. 12 (1985), p. 23.

2557 Reyes Aponte, Cynthia. [Untitled drawing]. LLUEVE TLALOC, no. 12 (1985), p. 36.

2558 Reyes Aponte, Cynthia. [Untitled drawing]. LLUEVE TLALOC, no. 12 (1985), p. 43.

2559 Rizo-Patron, Jenny. Cycad. REVISTA MUJERES, Vol. 2, no. 1 (January 1985), p. 42.

2560 Rizo-Patron, Jenny. [Dinosaurs]. REVISTA MUJERES, Vol. 2, no. 1 (January 1985), p. 22.

Drawings (cont.)

2561 Rizo-Patron, Jenny. Magnolia bud. REVISTA MUJERES, Vol. 2, no. 1 (January 1985), p. 30.

2562 Romero, Miguel. Chalchihuitlicue. LLUEVE TLALOC, no. 3 (1976), p. Ft cover.

2563 Romero, Miguel. Tonalpohuali o calendario azteca. LLUEVE TLALOC, no. 2 (1975), p. [54]. Bilingual. **DESCR:** Calendars.

2564 Romero, Miguel. [Untitled drawing]. LLUEVE TLALOC, no. 2 (1975), p. Ft cover.

2565 Romero, Miguel. [Untitled drawing]. LLUEVE TLALOC, no. 2 (1975), p. Bk cover.

2566 Romo, Al. [Untitled drawing]. SAGUARO, Vol. 2, (1985), p. Ft cover.

2567 Tineo, David. [Untitled drawing]. LLUEVE TLALOC, no. 12 (1985), p. 39.

2568 Tineo, David. [Untitled drawing]. LLUEVE TLALOC, no. 13 (1986), p. 10.

2569 Tineo, David. [Untitled drawing]. LLUEVE TLALOC, no. 13 (1986), p. 18.

2570 Tineo, David. [Untitled drawing]. LLUEVE TLALOC, no. 13 (1986), p. 28.

2571 Tineo, David. [Untitled portfolio]. LLUEVE TLALOC, no. 13 (1986), p. 34-35. **DESCR:** Photography.

2572 [Untitled drawing]. LLUEVE TLALOC, no. 4 (1977), p. 22.

2573 [Untitled drawing]. LLUEVE TLALOC, no. 12 (1985), p. 8.

2574 [Untitled drawing]. LLUEVE TLALOC, no. 13 (1986), p. 6.

2575 [Untitled drawing]. LLUEVE TLALOC, no. 13 (1986), p. 12.

2576 [Untitled drawing of raven]. LLUEVE TLALOC, no. 11 (1984), p. 9.

2577 Vela, Esther. Estrellas. REVISTA MUJERES, Vol. 2, no. 1 (January 1985), p. 44.

2578 Yrigoyen, Edna A. [Untitled drawing]. LLUEVE TLALOC, no. 13 (1986), p. 2.

2579 Yrigoyen, Edna A. [Untitled drawing]. LLUEVE TLALOC, no. 13 (1986), p. 15.

2580 Yrigoyen, Edna A. [Untitled drawing]. LLUEVE TLALOC, no. 13 (1986), p. 23.

2581 Yrigoyen, Edna A. [Untitled drawing]. LLUEVE TLALOC, no. 13 (1986), p. 26.

2582 Yrigoyen, Edna A. [Untitled drawing]. LLUEVE TLALOC, no. 13 (1986), p. 31.

2583 Yrigoyen, Edna A. [Untitled drawing]. SAGUARO, Vol. 4, (1987), p. Ft cover.

Dropouts

2584 Magallan, Rafael J. 1983-84 NAEP data raises questions regarding the school experiences of language minority children. LA RED/THE NET, no. 92 (November, December, 1985), p. 9-11. English. **DESCR:** *Bilingual Bicultural Education; Bilingualism; English as a Second Language; *National Assessment of Educational Progress; Surveys.

2585 Quintanilla, Guadalupe. Dropping out of school. VISTA, Vol. 2, no. 1 (September 7, 1986), p. 12-14. English. **DESCR:** Educational Statistics; Language Interference; Social History and Conditions.

2586 Rodriguez, Eloy. Chicanos/Hispanics in higher education: now and beyond. HISPANIC TIMES, Vol. 8, no. 3 (May, June, 1987), p. 44-45. English. **DESCR:** *Higher Education; Statistics.

2587 Stern, Gary M. Keep the kids in school. VISTA, Vol. 3, no. 1 (September 6, 1987), p. 16-19. English. **DESCR:** Education; Educational Statistics.

Drug Abuse Programs

2588 Herrera Duran, Patricia and Mares, Renee. Ernest Duran: la ultima despedida. LATIN QUARTER, Vol. 1, no. 3 (January, February, 1975), p. 34-36. English. **DESCR:** Biography; *Duran, Ernesto; Joint Efforts [prison organization]; Prisons.

Drug Addicts

2589 Sandos, James A. Northern separatism during the Mexican revolution--an inquiry into the role of drug trafficking, 1910-1920. AMERICAS, Vol. 41, no. 2 (October 1984), p. 191-214. English. **DESCR:** Baja California, Mexico; Border Region; Cantu Jimenez, Esteban; Drug Laws; *Drug Traffic; *Drug Use; Medical Care; Mexican Revolution - 1910-1920; Revolutions.

Drug Laws

2590 Sandos, James A. Northern separatism during the Mexican revolution--an inquiry into the role of drug trafficking, 1910-1920. AMERICAS, Vol. 41, no. 2 (October 1984), p. 191-214. English. **DESCR:** Baja California, Mexico; Border Region; Cantu Jimenez, Esteban; Drug Addicts; *Drug Traffic; *Drug Use; Medical Care; Mexican Revolution - 1910-1920; Revolutions.

Drug Traffic

2591 Kramer, Mark. U.S.-Mexican border: life on the line. THE AMERICAN MERCURY, Vol. 167, (June 1985), p. 720-749. English. **DESCR:** Border Industries; Border Patrol; *Border Region; Border Studies; Undocumented Workers.

2592 Sandos, James A. Northern separatism during the Mexican revolution--an inquiry into the role of drug trafficking, 1910-1920. AMERICAS, Vol. 41, no. 2 (October 1984), p. 191-214. English. **DESCR:** Baja California, Mexico; Border Region; Cantu Jimenez, Esteban; Drug Addicts; Drug Laws; *Drug Use; Medical Care; Mexican Revolution - 1910-1920; Revolutions.

Drug Use

2593 Gaviria, Moises; Gil, Ana A.; and Javaid, Javaid I. Nortriptyline kinetics in Hispanic and Anglo subjects. JOURNAL OF CLINICAL PSYCHOPHARMACOLOGY, Vol. 6, no. 4 (1986), p. 227-231. English. **DESCR:** Anglo Americans; *Comparative Psychology; Genetics; Public Health.

Drug Use (cont.)

2594 Humm-Delgado, Denise and Delgado, Melvin. Hispanic adolescents and substance abuse: issues for the 1980s. CHILDREN AND YOUTH SERVICES REVIEW, Vol. 6, no. 1-2 (Spring, Summer, 1983), p. 71-87. English. DESCR: *Youth.

2595 New Latino group to combat problem. NUESTRO, Vol. 11, no. 2 (March 1987), p. 8. English. DESCR: *Alcoholism; *National Hispanic Family Against Drug Abuse (NHFADA).

2596 Sandos, James A. Northern separatism during the Mexican revolution--an inquiry into the role of drug trafficking, 1910-1920. AMERICAS. Vol. 41, no. 2 (October 1984), p. 191-214. English. DESCR: Baja California, Mexico; Border Region; Cantu Jimenez, Esteban; Drug Addicts; Drug Laws; *Drug Traffic; Medical Care; Mexican Revolution - 1910-1920; Revolutions.

Duarte [family name]

2597 Instituto Genealogico e Historico Latino-Americano. Rootsearch: Duarte: Sandoval. VISTA, Vol. 1, no. 9 (May 3, 1986), p. 22. English. DESCR: Genealogy; History; *Personal Names; *Sandoval [family name].

Duarte, Ramon

2598 Chavez, Lorenzo A. Ramon Duarte. VISTA, Vol. 1, no. 9 (May 3, 1986), p. 20. English. DESCR: Biography; *Medical Personnel.

Duignan, Peter J.

2599 Tryon, Roy H. Book review of: THE HISPANICS IN THE UNITED STATES: A HISTORY. LIBRARY JOURNAL, Vol. 111, no. 18 (November 1, 1986), p. 107. English. DESCR: Book Reviews; Gann, L.H.; *HISPANICS IN THE UNITED STATES: A HISTORY; Social History and Conditions.

Dunbar Ortiz, Roxanne

2600 Griswold del Castillo, Richard. Book review of: ROOTS OF RESISTANCE: LAND TENURE IN NEW MEXICO, 1680-1980. LA RED/THE NET, no. 42 (May 1981), p. 10. English. DESCR: Book Reviews; Land Tenure; *ROOTS OF RESISTANCE: LAND TENURE IN NEW MEXICO, 1680-1980.

Duran, Ernesto

2601 Herrera Duran, Patricia and Mares, Renee. Ernest Duran: la ultima despedida. LATIN QUARTER, Vol. 1, no. 3 (January, February, 1975), p. 34-36. English. DESCR: Biography; Drug Abuse Programs; Joint Efforts [prison organization]; Prisons.

Duran, Richard P.

2602 Carranza, Miguel A. Book review of: LATINO LANGUAGE AND COMMUNICATIVE BEHAVIOR. LA RED/THE NET, no. 54 (May 1982), p. 10-11. English. DESCR: Book Reviews; Language Usage; *LATINO LANGUAGE AND COMMUNICATIVE BEHAVIOR.

2603 Floyd, Mary Beth. Language use and communicative behavior: Hispanic bilinguals in the United States. BILINGUAL REVIEW, Vol. 12, no. 1-2 (January, August, 1985), p. 120-133. English. DESCR: Book Reviews; Language Usage; *LATINO LANGUAGE AND COMMUNICATIVE BEHAVIOR.

2604 Segura, Roberto D. Book review of:

HISPANICS' EDUCATION AND BACKGROUND: PREDICTORS OF COLLEGE ACHIEVEMENT. LA RED/THE NET, no. 81 (June 1984), p. 6-7. English. DESCR: Book Reviews; *HISPANICS' EDUCATION AND BACKGROUND: PREDICTORS OF COLLEGE ACHIEVEMENT.

Dusard, Jay

2605 Perez, Renato E. Book review of: LA FRONTERA: THE U.S. BORDER WITH MEXICO. VISTA, Vol. 2, no. 10 (June 7, 1987), p. 24. English. DESCR: *Book Reviews; *LA FRONTERA: THE U.S. BORDER WITH MEXICO; Weisman, Alan.

Earthquakes

2606 Cano, Oscar. MAES technical brief. HISPANIC TIMES, Vol. 8, no. 1 (December, January, 1987), p. 27. English. DESCR: Emergency Services; *Mexico City.

2607 Moraga, Pete. Response to a quake: hands across the border. VISTA, Vol. 1, no. 4 (December 7, 1985), p. 3. English. DESCR: Broadcast Media; *KMEX, Los Angeles, CA [television station]; *Mexico.

East Los Angeles, CA

2608 Blanco, Gilbert M. A vehicle for positive change. LATIN QUARTER, Vol. 1, no. 2 (October 1974), p. 27-30. English. DESCR: Artists; *Estrada Courts, Los Angeles, CA; *Mural Art.

2609 Garcia, Mario T. Book review of: A COMMUNITY UNDER SIEGE. PACIFIC HISTORICAL REVIEW, Vol. 55, no. 4 (1986), p. 636-638. English. DESCR: *A COMMUNITY UNDER SIEGE: A CHRONICLE OF CHICANOS EAST OF THE LOS ANGELES RIVER, 1945-1975; Acuna, Rudolfo; Book Reviews.

2610 Griswold del Castillo, Richard. Book review of: EAST LOS ANGELES. PACIFIC HISTORICAL REVIEW, Vol. 53, no. 4 (November 1984), p. 528-529. English. DESCR: Book Reviews; Los Angeles, CA; *Romo, Ricardo.

2611 Lit, Ed. Paul Gonzalez [sic]. VISTA, Vol. 1, no. 5 (January 5, 1986), p. 10. English. DESCR: Athletes; *Boxing; *Gonzales, Paul [Olympic boxer].

2612 Monroy, Douglas. Book review of: EAST LOS ANGELES. WESTERN HISTORICAL QUARTERLY, Vol. 15, no. 4 (October 1984), p. 453. English. DESCR: Book Reviews; *EAST LOS ANGELES: HISTORY OF A BARRIO; Romo, Ricardo.

East Los Angeles College

2613 Soto, Rose Marie. East Los Angeles College in Monterey Park. HISPANIC ENGINEER, Vol. 3, no. 3 (1987), p. 18-20, 43. English. DESCR: *Education; Educational Statistics.

EAST LOS ANGELES: HISTORY OF A BARRIO

2614 Garcia, Philip. Book review of: EAST LOS ANGELES. LA RED/THE NET, no. 86 (November 1984), p. 2-3. English. DESCR: Book Reviews; Romo, Ricardo.

2615 Monroy, Douglas. Book review of: EAST LOS ANGELES. WESTERN HISTORICAL QUARTERLY, Vol. 15, no. 4 (October 1984), p. 453. English. DESCR: Book Reviews; East Los Angeles, CA; Romo, Ricardo.

East Los Angeles Skills Center

2616 Eisen, Marvin. Working for positive change in the barrio. LATIN QUARTER, Vol. 1, no. 1 (July 1974), p. 8-10. English. **DESCR:** Counseling (Educational); *Gangs; Maravilla.

Eastman Kodak Co.

2617 NACME scholarships at Forum '87. HISPANIC ENGINEER, Vol. 3, no. 3 (1987), p. 14. English. **DESCR:** *Financial Aid; Fuentes, Theresa; Molina, Daniel.

Echeverria [family name]

2618 Instituto Genealogico e Historico Latino-Americano. Rootsearch: Aguilar: Echeverria. VISTA, Vol. 1, no. 11 (July 6, 1986), p. 22. English. **DESCR:** *Aguilar [family name]; Genealogy; History; *Personal Names.

ECOLOGY AND DEVELOPMENT OF THE BORDER REGION: SECOND SYMPOSIUM

2619 Ganster, Paul. Book review of: ECOLOGY AND DEVELOPMENT OF THE BORDER REGION. PACIFIC HISTORICAL REVIEW, Vol. 55, no. 2 (1986), p. 318-320. English. **DESCR:** Book Reviews; Border Region; Ross, Stanley R.

Economic Development

2620 Stewart, Kenneth L. and de Leon, Arnoldo. Education, literacy, and occupational structure in West Texas, 1860-1900. WEST TEXAS HISTORICAL ASSOCIATION YEARBOOK, Vol. 60, (1984), p. 127-143. English. **DESCR:** Discrimination in Education; Education; Employment; *Labor; Literacy; *Texas.

Economic History and Conditions

2621 de Leon, Arnoldo and Stewart, Kenneth L. A tale of 3 cities: a comparative analysis of the socio-economic conditions of Mexican-Americans in Los Angeles, Tucson, and San Antonio, 1850-1900. JOURNAL OF THE WEST, Vol. 24, no. 2 (1985), p. 64-74. English. **DESCR:** Employment; Griswold del Castillo, Richard; Labor; *Los Angeles, CA; San Antonio, TX; *Social History and Conditions; Tucson, AZ; Urban Communities.

2622 Griswold del Castillo, Richard. Quantitative history in the American Southwest: a survey and critique. WESTERN HISTORICAL QUARTERLY, Vol. 15, no. 4 (October 1984), p. 407-426. English. **DESCR:** Historiography; History; *Social History and Conditions; *Southwestern United States.

2623 Valdez, Lorenzo. Labor history in the villages. EL CUADERNO, Vol. 3, no. 2 (Spring 1974), p. 54-63. English. **DESCR:** *Labor; *New Mexico; *Social History and Conditions.

Economically Disadvantaged
    USE: Poverty

Economics

2624 Garcia, John A. Book review of: RACE AND CLASS IN THE SOUTHWEST: A THEORY OF INEQUALITY. LA RED/THE NET, no. 31 (June 1980), p. 4. English. **DESCR:** Barrera, Mario; Book Reviews; *Discrimination; RACE AND CLASS IN THE SOUTHWEST: A THEORY OF RACIAL INEQUALITY; *Southwestern United States.

2625 Grenier, Gilles. An economic perspective on learning a second language. JOURNAL OF

MULTILINGUAL AND MULTICULTURAL DEVELOPMENT, Vol. 4, no. 6 (1983), p. 471-483. English. **DESCR:** Bilingualism; Canada; *Language Usage.

2626 Interview: Rita Ricardo-Campbell. INTERCAMBIOS FEMENILES, Vol. 2, no. 6 (Spring 1987), p. 10-11. English. **DESCR:** *Appointed Officials; Chicanas; Leadership; *Ricardo-Campbell, Rita.

2627 Pearce, James E. and Gunther, Jeffery W. Illegal immigration from Mexico: effects on the Texas economy. ECONOMIC REVIEW (FEDERAL RESERVE BANK OF DALLAS), no. 9 (1985), p. 1-14. English. **DESCR:** *Mexico; Texas; *Undocumented Workers.

Edible Plants
    USE: Herbal Medicine

Educable Mentally Retarded (EMR)

2628 Argulewicz, Ed N. Effects of ethnic membership, socioeconomic status, and home language on LD, EMR, and EH placements. LEARNING DISABILITY QUARTERLY, Vol. 6, no. 2 (Spring 1983), p. 195-200. English. **DESCR:** Ethnic Groups; *Special Education.

Education

2629 Alvarado, Raul. Against all odds. HISPANIC ENGINEER, Vol. 3, no. 4 (Fall 1987), p. 10-11. English. **DESCR:** *Chicanas; Educational Statistics; National Merit Scholarships; Preliminary Scholastic Aptitude Test (PSAT); *Scholastic Aptitude Test (SAT); Stereotypes.

2630 Atencio, Tomas. La Academia de la Nueva Raza. EL CUADERNO, Vol. 2, no. 1 (1972), p. 6-13. English. **DESCR:** *Alternative Education; Chicano Studies; Cultural Characteristics; *Cultural Organizations; *Educational Organizations; *La Academia de la Nueva Raza, Dixon, NM; Oro del Barrio; Philosophy; Values.

2631 Bennett, Ruth. A bilingual perspective on teaching history. SOCIAL STUDIES REVIEW, Vol. 23, no. 3 (Spring 1984), p. 50-55. English. **DESCR:** *Ethnic Groups; History.

2632 Campbell, Duane. How the grinch stole the social sciences: moving teaching to the right in California. JOURNAL OF THE ASSOCIATION OF MEXICAN AMERICAN EDUCATORS, (1986, 1987), p. 43-50. English. **DESCR:** *Social Science.

2633 Cervantes, Robert A. Ethnocentric pedagogy and minority student growth: implications for the common school. EDUCATION AND URBAN SOCIETY, Vol. 16, no. 3 (May 1984), p. 274-293. English. **DESCR:** Bilingual Bicultural Education; California; Discrimination in Education.

2634 Challem, Jack. Pied piper of science. VISTA, Vol. 3, no. 2 (October 3, 1987), p. 14. English. **DESCR:** *Romero, Leo; *Science as a Profession.

2635 Chesterfield, Ray A. and Chesterfield, Kathleen Barrows. "Hojas with the H": spontaneous peer teaching in bilingual classrooms. BILINGUAL REVIEW, Vol. 12, no. 3 (September, December, 1985), p. 198-208. English. **DESCR:** *Bilingual Bicultural Education; Bilingualism; *Teacher-pupil Interaction.

Education (cont.)

2636 Flores, Juan. Chicanos and the computer age: the best of times, the worst of times. JOURNAL OF THE ASSOCIATION OF MEXICAN AMERICAN EDUCATORS, (1986, 1987), p. 37-41. English. **DESCR:** *Computers.

2637 From dropout to educator. VISTA, Vol. 2, no. 1 (September 7, 1986), p. 13. English. **DESCR:** *Academic Achievement; Discrimination in Education; *Intelligence Tests; *Quintanilla, Guadalupe.

2638 Galarza, Ernesto. Platica con Galarza [interview]. EL CUADERNO, Vol. 4, no. 10 (Summer 1976), p. 6-19. Bilingual. **DESCR:** Capitalism; *Galarza, Ernesto.

2639 Galindo-Ramirez, Tina. Educacion monolingue: opresion o liberacion? REVISTA MUJERES, Vol. 1, no. 1 (January 1984), p. 8-9. Spanish. **DESCR:** Alienation; Assertiveness; Biography; English Language; *Identity.

2640 Garcia, Jesus. Multiethnic education: past, present, and future. TEXAS TECH JOURNAL OF EDUCATION, Vol. 11, no. 1 (Winter 1984), p. 13-29. English. **DESCR:** Cultural Pluralism.

2641 Garcia, Philip. Book review of: MEXICAN AMERICANS IN SCHOOL: A DECADE OF CHANGE. LA RED/THE NET, no. 33 (August 1980), p. 4. English. **DESCR:** Book Reviews; Carter, Thomas P.; *MEXICAN AMERICANS IN SCHOOL: A DECADE OF CHANGE; Segura, Roberto D.

2642 Garcia, Philip. Robert Davila. VISTA, Vol. 2, no. 7 (March 8, 1987), p. 25. English. **DESCR:** *Davila, Robert; *Deaf.

2643 Gonzalez, Alex. Classroom cooperation and ethnic balance: Chicanos and equal status. LA RED/THE NET, no. 68 (May 1983), p. 6-8. English. **DESCR:** Cultural Pluralism; *Intergroup Relations.

2644 Gonzalez, Gilbert G. Segregation of Mexican children in a southern California city: the legacy of expansion and the American Southwest. WESTERN HISTORICAL QUARTERLY, Vol. 16, no. 1 (January 1985), p. 55-76. English. **DESCR:** *Discrimination in Education; Educational Administration; Primary School Education; *Santa Ana, CA; Segregation and Desegregation.

2645 Heaney, Thomas W. "Hanging on" or "gaining ground": educating marginal adults. NEW DIRECTIONS FOR CONTINUING EDUCATION, Vol. 20, (December 1983), p. 53-63. English. **DESCR:** *Adult Education; *Adult Education Center of Lakeview; Chicago, IL; Community School Relationships.

2646 Kuner, Charles. Peer group counseling: applied psychology in the high school. CURRICULUM REVIEW, Vol. 23, no. 1 (February 1984), p. 89-92. English. **DESCR:** Chicago, IL; Counseling (Educational); *Counseling (Psychological); Farragut High School, Chicago, IL; Students.

2647 Latino reading and ed progress. LA RED/THE NET, No. 100 (September 1986), p. 11. English. **DESCR:** *Literacy; National Assessment of Educational Progress; National Institute of Education (NIE).

2648 LeAna, Thomas. Dorella Martinez. VISTA, Vol. 2, no. 1 (September 7, 1986), p. 14. English. **DESCR:** *Academic Achievement; *Martinez, Dorella.

2649 Mendez-M., Miguel. Introduccion. LLUEVE TLALOC, no. 10 (1983), p. iv. Spanish. **DESCR:** Pima Community College, Tucson, AZ; *Spanish Language.

2650 Mendez-M., Miguel. Introduction. LLUEVE TLALOC, no. 10 (1983), p. iv. English. **DESCR:** *Pima Community College, Tucson, AZ; *Spanish Language.

2651 Montane, Diane. Learning survival Spanish. VISTA, Vol. 1, no. 5 (January 5, 1986), p. 16. English. **DESCR:** Ruiz, Vivian; *Spanish Language; *SURVIVAL SPANISH; Television.

2652 Olivas, Michael A. The condition of Hispanic education. LA RED/THE NET, no. 56 (July 1982), p. 3-6. English. **DESCR:** *Discrimination in Education; *Segregation and Desegregation.

2653 Olivas, Michael A. Task force on education. LA RED/THE NET, no. 88 (Winter 1984), p. 14-17. English. **DESCR:** *Public Policy.

2654 Out of marriage, onto welfare and into poverty. REVISTA MUJERES, Vol. 4, no. 1 (January 1987), p. 39-40. English. **DESCR:** *Chicanas; Divorce; Welfare.

2655 Pacific Telesis senior fellows. HISPANIC ENGINEER, Vol. 3, no. 2 (Summer 1987), p. 10-11. English. **DESCR:** *Awards; Castaneda, Jesus; Cruz, Jacqueline; Pacific Telesis; Rodriguez, Jose; Sanchez, Alex.

2656 Panas, Katia. Postsecondary retention and graduation: strategies for change. REVISTA MUJERES, Vol. 4, no. 1 (January 1987), p. 66-72. English. **DESCR:** Assimilation; Discrimination in Education; Higher Education.

2657 Sanchez, Lionel. La Raza community and Chicano Studies. EPOCA: NATIONAL CONCILIO FOR CHICANO STUDIES JOURNAL, Vol. 1, no. 2 (Winter 1971), p. 5-59. English. **DESCR:** *Chicano Studies; *La Raza.

2658 Smith, Chuck. Commitment to Hispanic education. HISPANIC ENGINEER, Vol. 3, no. 1 (Spring 1987), p. 16-20. English. **DESCR:** Engineering as a Profession; *Pacific Telesis.

2659 Soto, Rose Marie. East Los Angeles College in Monterey Park. HISPANIC ENGINEER, Vol. 3, no. 3 (1987), p. 18-20, 43. English. **DESCR:** *East Los Angeles College; Educational Statistics.

2660 Stern, Gary M. Keep the kids in school. VISTA, Vol. 3, no. 1 (September 6, 1987), p. 16-19. English. **DESCR:** *Dropouts; Educational Statistics.

2661 Stewart, Kenneth L. and de Leon, Arnoldo. Education, literacy, and occupational structure in West Texas, 1860-1900. WEST TEXAS HISTORICAL ASSOCIATION YEARBOOK, Vol. 60, (1984), p. 127-143. English. **DESCR:** Discrimination in Education; Economic Development; Employment; *Labor; Literacy; *Texas.

2662 Torres, Isaias D. The U.S. Supreme Court and public education for undocumented immigrants. LA RED/THE NET, no. 58 (September 1982), p. 2-4. English. **DESCR:** Educational Law and Legislation; *Undocumented Children; *U.S. Supreme Court.

Education (cont.)

2663 Weller, David L. and Reyes, Laurie Hart. Stereotyping: impact on teachers and students. ACTION IN TEACHER EDUCATION, Vol. 5, no. 3 (Fall 1983), p. 1-7. English. DESCR: Discrimination; Sex Stereotypes; *Stereotypes.

Education Equalization
USE: Discrimination in Education

THE EDUCATION OF POOR AND MINORITY CHILDREN: A WORLD BIBLIOGRAPHY: SUPPLEMENT 1979-01985

2664 Burnham-Kidwell, Debbie. Book review of: THE EDUCATION OF POOR AND MINORITY CHILDREN: A WORLD BIBLIOGRAPHY: SUPPLEMENT, 1979-1985. AMERICAN REFERENCE BOOKS ANNUAL, Vol. 18, (1987), p. 134. English. DESCR: Book Reviews; Weinberg, Meyer.

EDUCATION, POLITICS, AND BILINGUAL EDUCATION IN TEXAS

2665 Cardenas, Jose A. Book review of: EDUCATION, POLITICS, AND BILINGUAL EDUCATION IN TEXAS. LA RED/THE NET, no. 75 (December 1983), p. 5-8. English. DESCR: Book Reviews; Vega, Jose E.

Educational Administration

2666 Baker, George A. and Rocha, Pedro, Jr. Critical incident competencies of Mexican American and Anglo American administrators. COMMUNITY/JUNIOR COLLEGE QUARTERLY OF RESEARCH AND PRACTICE, Vol. 7, no. 4 (July, September, 1983), p. 319-332. English. DESCR: Anglo Americans; *Community Colleges; Comparative Psychology; Cultural Characteristics; Management; Public Policy.

2667 Evans, James. From chaos to quality education. VISTA, Vol. 3, no. 4 (December 6, 1987), p. 18, 35. English. DESCR: Awards; *Chacon Soto, Mario; Educational Theory and Practice; Horace Mann Middle School, Mission District, San Francisco, CA.

2668 Gonzalez, Gilbert G. Segregation of Mexican children in a southern California city: the legacy of expansion and the American Southwest. WESTERN HISTORICAL QUARTERLY, Vol. 16, no. 1 (January 1985), p. 55-76. English. DESCR: *Discrimination in Education; Education; Primary School Education; *Santa Ana, CA; Segregation and Desegregation.

2669 Mellado, Carmela. Mitch Maidique. HISPANIC ENGINEER, Vol. 3, no. 5 (Winter 1987), p. 34-36. English. DESCR: *Biography; Florida International University; *Maidique, Mitch.

2670 Riding the range at Golden West. NUESTRO, Vol. 11, no. 3 (April 1987), p. 7-8. English. DESCR: Biography; Colleges and Universities; *Garcia, Fred; Golden West College, Huntington Beach, CA.

Educational Law and Legislation

2671 99th Congress fails to act on literacy legislation. LA RED/THE NET, No. 102 (November 1986), p. 11. English. DESCR: *Literacy.

2672 Cohen, Gaynor. The politics of bilingual education. OXFORD REVIEW OF EDUCATION, Vol. 10, no. 2 (1984), p. 225-241. English. DESCR: *Bilingual Bicultural Education; Public Policy.

2673 Gutierrez, Felix. House approves Higher Education Act amendments. LA RED/THE NET, no. 92 (November, December, 1985), p. 3-4. English. DESCR: Educational Organizations; Financial Aid; *Higher Education; *Higher Education Amendments of 1985 (H.R. 3700); Hispanic Higher Education Coalition (HHEC).

2674 Hispanics affected by major provisions in Higher Ed Act. LA RED/THE NET, no. 92 (November, December, 1985), p. 4-7. English. DESCR: *Higher Education; *Higher Education Amendments of 1985 (H.R. 3700).

2675 Latino literacy update: literacy bill introduced in house. LA RED/THE NET, No. 100 (September 1986), p. 9. English. DESCR: *English Language; *English Proficiency Act (H.R. 5042); *Literacy.

2676 Torres, Isaias D. The U.S. Supreme Court and public education for undocumented immigrants. LA RED/THE NET, no. 58 (September 1982), p. 2-4. English. DESCR: Education; *Undocumented Children; *U.S. Supreme Court.

Educational Materials
USE: Curriculum Materials

Educational Organizations

2677 Atencio, Tomas. La Academia de la Nueva Raza: su historia. EL CUADERNO, Vol. 1, no. 1 (1971), p. 4-9. English. DESCR: Alternative Education; Chicano Studies; Cultural Organizations; *La Academia de la Nueva Raza, Dixon, NM; Oro del Barrio.

2678 Atencio, Tomas. La Academia de la Nueva Raza. EL CUADERNO, Vol. 2, no. 1 (1972), p. 6-13. English. DESCR: *Alternative Education; Chicano Studies; Cultural Characteristics; *Cultural Organizations; Education; *La Academia de la Nueva Raza, Dixon, NM; Oro del Barrio; Philosophy; Values.

2679 Atencio, Tomas. La Academia de la Nueva Raza: El Oro del Barrio. EL CUADERNO, Vol. 3, no. 1 (Winter 1973), p. 4-15. English. DESCR: Alternative Education; Chicano Studies; *Cultural Organizations; *La Academia de la Nueva Raza, Dixon, NM; Oro del Barrio.

2680 Gutierrez, Felix. House approves Higher Education Act amendments. LA RED/THE NET, no. 92 (November, December, 1985), p. 3-4. English. DESCR: Educational Law and Legislation; Financial Aid; *Higher Education; *Higher Education Amendments of 1985 (H.R. 3700); Hispanic Higher Education Coalition (HHEC).

2681 Higher education organizations. LA RED/THE NET, no. 92 (November, December, 1985), p. 11-13. English. DESCR: *Higher Education; *Texas Association of Chicanos in Higher Education (TACHE).

2682 Higher education organizations. LA RED/THE NET, no. 93 (January, February, 1986), p. 5-8. English. DESCR: *Higher Education; *Raza Advocates for California Higher Education (RACHE).

2683 Madrid, Arturo. Letter to the Network. LA RED/THE NET, no. 56 (July 1982), p. 13. English. DESCR: *National Chicano Council on Higher Education (NCCHE); *National Chicano Research Network (NCRN).

Educational Organizations (cont.)

2684 Madrid, Arturo. Report to the Network. LA RED/THE NET, No. 103 (December 1986), p. 1-2. English. **DESCR:** *Higher Education; *National Chicano Council on Higher Education (NCCHE).

2685 Magallan, Rafael J. Hispanic organizations concerned with higher education. LA RED/THE NET, no. 91 (October 1985), p. 2-3. English. **DESCR:** *American Association for Higher Education Hispanic Caucus; Higher Education.

2686 Minsky, Alyce. California State University at Los Angeles. HISPANIC ENGINEER, Vol. 3, (Summer, 1987), p. 30-33, 44. English. **DESCR:** Colleges and Universities; *Engineering as a Profession; Mathematics, Engineering and Science Achievement (MESA); *Minority Engineering Program (California State University at Los Angeles).

2687 Perez, Emma. Higher education organizations. LA RED/THE NET, no. 94 (March 1986), p. 2-4. English. **DESCR:** Higher Education; *Mexican American Studies and Research Center, University of Arizona, Tucson, AZ; *Research Centers.

2688 Perez, Emma. Higher education organizations. LA RED/THE NET, no. 96 (May 1986), p. 6-8. English. **DESCR:** *Higher Education; *Wisconsin Hispanic Council on Higher Education (WHCHE).

2689 Perez, Emma. Higher education organizations. LA RED/THE NET, no. 97 (June 1986), p. 4-5. English. **DESCR:** *Arizona Association of Chicanos for Higher Education (AACHE); *Higher Education.

2690 Perez, Emma. Higher education organizations. LA RED/THE NET, no. 99 (August 1986), p. 2-4. English. **DESCR:** *Colorado Association of Chicanos in Higher Education (CACHE); *Higher Education.

2691 Perez, Emma. Higher education organizations. LA RED/THE NET, No. 101 (October 1986), p. 6-10. English. **DESCR:** Higher Education; *Hispanic Association of Higher Education (HAHE); *Puerto Rican Council on Higher Education (PRCHE); *SUNY Hispanic Research and Information Network.

2692 Perez, Emma. Networks. LA RED/THE NET, No. 103 (December 1986), p. 2-5. English. **DESCR:** *Chicanas; *Higher Education; *Mujeres Activas en Letras y Cambio Social (MALCS).

2693 Perez, Emma. Report to the Network. LA RED/THE NET, no. 95 (April 1986), p. 3-5. English. **DESCR:** *Higher Education; *Hispanic Association of Higher Education of New Jersey (HAHE).

2694 Report to the Network from NCCHE. LA RED/THE NET, no. 87 (July 1985), p. 1-2. English. **DESCR:** Chicano Studies; LA RED/THE NET; *National Chicano Council on Higher Education (NCCHE); National Chicano Research Network (NCRN); Tomas Rivera Center, Claremont, CA.

2695 Texas Association of Chicanos in Higher Education (TACHE) holds annual conference. LA RED/THE NET, No. 100 (September 1986), p. 2-5. English. **DESCR:** *Conferences and Meetings; *Higher Education; *Texas Association of Chicanos in Higher Education (TACHE).

2696 Winston, Bonnie. INROADS: internships that work. HISPANIC ENGINEER, Vol. 3, no. 5 (Winter 1987), p. 38-42. English. **DESCR:** Almanza, John; Alvarez, Maria; Carr, Frank; Educational Statistics; Garcia, Juan; Gonzales, Ana; *INROADS; Pereira, Eduardo; Raimundo, Antonio; Reza, Priscilla.

Educational Services

2697 National Council of La Raza (NCLR). Career information and Hispanic students. LA RED/THE NET, no. 75 (December 1983), p. 2-4. English. **DESCR:** *Careers; *National Council of La Raza (NCLR); Secondary School Education; Survey of Career Information Systems in Secondary Schools; *Youth.

Educational Statistics

2698 Alvarado, Raul. Against all odds. HISPANIC ENGINEER, Vol. 3, no. 4 (Fall 1987), p. 10-11. English. **DESCR:** *Chicanas; Education; National Merit Scholarships; Preliminary Scholastic Aptitude Test (PSAT); *Scholastic Aptitude Test (SAT); Stereotypes.

2699 Ortiz, Vilma. Educational attainment among Hispanic youth and non-Hispanic white youth. LA RED/THE NET, no. 67 (April 1983), p. 2-4. English. **DESCR:** Academic Achievement; *Youth.

2700 Quintanilla, Guadalupe. Dropping out of school. VISTA, Vol. 2, no. 1 (September 7, 1986), p. 12-14. English. **DESCR:** *Dropouts; Language Interference; Social History and Conditions.

2701 Soto, Rose Marie. East Los Angeles College in Monterey Park. HISPANIC ENGINEER, Vol. 3, no. 3 (1987), p. 18-20, 43. English. **DESCR:** *East Los Angeles College; *Education.

2702 Stern, Gary M. Keep the kids in school. VISTA, Vol. 3, no. 1 (September 6, 1987), p. 16-19. English. **DESCR:** *Dropouts; Education.

2703 Winston, Bonnie. INROADS: internships that work. HISPANIC ENGINEER, Vol. 3, no. 5 (Winter 1987), p. 38-42. English. **DESCR:** Almanza, John; Alvarez, Maria; Carr, Frank; *Educational Organizations; Garcia, Juan; Gonzales, Ana; *INROADS; Pereira, Eduardo; Raimundo, Antonio; Reza, Priscilla.

Educational Tests and Measurements

2704 Carpenter, Thomas P., et al. Achievement in mathematics: results from the National Assessment. THE ELEMENTARY SCHOOL JOURNAL, Vol. 84, no. 5 (May 1984), p. 485-495. English. **DESCR:** Academic Achievement; *Mathematics; *National Assessment of Educational Progress.

2705 Lee, James F. The relationship between decoding accuracy and the reading achievement of monolingual Spanish-speaking children. BILINGUAL REVIEW, Vol. 12, no. 3 (September, December, 1985), p. 209-217. English. **DESCR:** *Language Development; *Reading; *Spanish Language.

2706 Merino, Barbara J. and Lyons, Joseph. The problem of exit criteria in second language learners: California as a case study. JOURNAL OF THE ASSOCIATION OF MEXICAN AMERICAN EDUCATORS, (1986, 1987), p. 5-28. English. **DESCR:** *Language.

Educational Tests and Measurements (cont.)

2707 Morales, Carlos. The controversy over
     bilingual education. VISTA, Vol. 1, no. 6
     (February 2, 1986), p. 8-10. English.
     DESCR: *Bilingual Bicultural Education;
     *Bilingual Education Act of 1968;
     Educational Theory and Practice; Federal
     Aid.

2708 Powers, Stephen and Medina, Marcello, Jr.
     Factorial validity of the Cooperative
     Preschool Inventory for English- and
     Spanish-speaking Hispanic children. JOURNAL
     OF PSYCHOLOGY, Vol. 119, no. 3 (May 1985),
     p. 277-280. English. **DESCR:** *Cooperative
     Preschool Inventory (CPI); *Cooperative
     Preschool Inventory [Spanish edition];
     *Psychological Testing.

2709 Report to the Network. LA RED/THE NET, no.
     96 (May 1986), p. 1-3. English. **DESCR:**
     *Joint Committee on Testing Practices
     (JCTP).

2710 Texas update. LA RED/THE NET, no. 97 (June
     1986), p. 3. English. **DESCR:** Teaching
     Profession; *Texas Examination of Current
     Administrators and Teachers (TECAT).

2711 Wainer, Howard. An exploratory analysis of
     performance on the SAT. JOURNAL OF
     EDUCATIONAL MEASUREMENT. Vol. 21, no. 2
     (Summer 1984), p. 81-91. English. **DESCR:**
     Scholastic Aptitude Test (SAT).

Educational Theory and Practice

2712 Bixler-Marquez, Dennis J. The introduction
     of bilingual education programs--a
     collaborative approach. EDUCATION, Vol. 105,
     no. 4 (Summer 1985), p. 443-448. English.
     DESCR: *Bilingual Bicultural Education;
     Federal Government.

2713 Evans, James. From chaos to quality
     education. VISTA, Vol. 3, no. 4 (December 6,
     1987), p. 18, 35. English. **DESCR:** Awards;
     *Chacon Soto, Mario; *Educational
     Administration; Horace Mann Middle School,
     Mission District, San Francisco, CA.

2714 Guerra, Manuel H. What are the objectives of
     Chicano studies? EPOCA: NATIONAL CONCILIO
     FOR CHICANO STUDIES JOURNAL, Vol. 1, no. 2
     (Winter 1971), p. 8-12. English. **DESCR:**
     *Chicano Studies; *Curriculum.

2715 Macias, Reynaldo Flores; Gomez-Quinones,
     Juan; and Castro, Raymond. Objectives of
     Chicano studies. EPOCA: NATIONAL CONCILIO
     FOR CHICANO STUDIES JOURNAL, Vol. 1, no. 2
     (Winter 1971), p. 31-34. English. **DESCR:**
     *Chicano Studies.

2716 Mendez-M., Miguel. Introduccion. LLUEVE
     TLALOC, no. 12 (1985), p. iv. Spanish.
     DESCR: Fiction; *Pima Community College,
     Tucson, AZ; Poetry.

2717 Mendez-M., Miguel. Introduction. LLUEVE
     TLALOC, no. 12 (1985), p. iv. English.
     DESCR: Fiction; *Pima Community College,
     Tucson, AZ; Poetry.

2718 Morales, Carlos. The controversy over
     bilingual education. VISTA, Vol. 1, no. 6
     (February 2, 1986), p. 8-10. English.
     DESCR: *Bilingual Bicultural Education;
     *Bilingual Education Act of 1968;
     Educational Tests and Measurements; Federal
     Aid.

2719 Ramirez, Salvador. The establishment and

administration of a master's program in
Chicano Studies at the University of
Colorado. EPOCA: NATIONAL CONCILIO FOR
CHICANO STUDIES JOURNAL, Vol. 1, no. 2
(Winter 1971), p. 39-50. English. **DESCR:**
*Chicano Studies; *Curriculum;
Discrimination in Education; Student
Organizations; *Students; United Mexican
American Students (UMAS); *University of
Colorado, Boulder; Youth.

2720 Rips, Geoffrey. Puritanism, pluralism, and
     Perot. TEXAS OBSERVOR, Vol. 75, no. 17
     (September 2, 1983), p. 3-4. English.
     DESCR: Adler, Mortimer; *Bilingual
     Bicultural Education; Perot, Ross.

**Eighteenth Street Development Corporation,
Chicago, IL**

2721 Heuer, Robert J. To save a neighborhood.
     VISTA, Vol. 3, no. 3 (November 8, 1987), p.
     32-34. English. **DESCR:** *Housing; Overa,
     Agustin; Pilsen, IL; Statistics.

Eisenberg, Bernard

2722 Garcia, John A. Book review of: AMERICA'S
     ETHNIC POLITICS. LA RED/THE NET, no. 67
     (April 1983), p. 7-8. English. **DESCR:**
     *AMERICA'S ETHNIC POLITICS; Book Reviews;
     Politics; Roucek, Joseph S.

El Camino Real

2723 El Camino Real named national historic
     engineering landmark. HISPANIC ENGINEER,
     Vol. 3, no. 1 (Spring 1987), p. 23. English.
     DESCR: American Society of Civil Engineers
     (ASCE); *Awards.

EL GRITO

2724 Rosaldo, Renato. When natives talk back:
     Chicano anthropology since the late 60s.
     RENATO ROSALDO LECTURE SERIES MONOGRAPH,
     Vol. 2, (Spring 1986), p. [3]-20. English.
     DESCR: *Anthropology; Culture; *Identity;
     Paredes, Americo; *Political Ideology;
     *Research Methodology; Romano-V., Octavio
     Ignacio; Valdez, Facundo.

El Paso, TX

2725 Butler, Anne M. Book review of: THE
     GENTLEMEN'S CLUB: THE STORY OF PROSTITUTION
     IN EL PASO, TEXAS. ARIZONA AND THE WEST,
     Vol. 26, no. 4 (1984), p. 365-366. English.
     DESCR: Book Reviews; Criminal Acts; *Frost,
     H. Gordon; THE GENTLEMEN'S CLUB: THE STORY
     OF PROSTITUTION IN EL PASO, TEXAS.

2726 Cardenas, Antonio J. and Cardenas, Cecilia.
     Traditions of Christmas. VISTA, Vol. 2, no.
     4 (December 7, 1986), p. 14-17. English.
     DESCR: Festivals; *Holidays; Miami, FL;
     *Reyes Magos Tradition.

2727 Flynn, Ken. A triumph of diplomacy. VISTA,
     Vol. 3, no. 2 (October 3, 1987), p. 22-24.
     English. **DESCR:** *Border Region; Chamizal
     Memorial Federal Park; Ciudad Juarez,
     Chihuahua, Mexico; *El Chamizal [region].

2728 Luckingham, Bradford. The American
     Southwest: an urban view. WESTERN HISTORICAL
     QUARTERLY, Vol. 15, no. 3 (July 1984), p.
     261-280. English. **DESCR:** Albuquerque, NM;
     Phoenix, AZ; Social History and Conditions;
     *Southwestern United States; Tucson, AZ;
     *Urban Communities; Urban Economics.

EL PUEBLO MEXICANO EN DETROIT Y MICHIGAN: A SOCIAL HISTORY

2729 Garcia, John R. Book reviews of: EL PUEBLO MEXICANO EN DETROIT Y MICHIGAN and MATERIALS ON THE HISTORY OF LATINOS IN MICHIGAN AND THE MIDWEST. LA RED/THE NET, no. 67 (April 1983), p. 13-14. English. DESCR: Book Reviews; *MATERIALS ON THE HISTORY OF LATINOS IN MICHIGAN AND THE MIDWEST; Midwestern States; Valdes, Dennis N.

El Salvador

2730 Aparicio, Edgar. The virgin and child in the revolution [painting]. AMERICAS 2001, Vol. 1, no. 1 (June, July, 1987), p. [16-17]. DESCR: *Paintings.

2731 Castro, Anna. La leyenda de la siquanaba y el zipitillo. LLUEVE TLALOC, no. 12 (1985), p. 9. Spanish. DESCR: *Cuentos.

2732 Martinez, Carmen. Un mensaje de El Salvador. REVISTA MUJERES, Vol. 2, no. 2 (June 1985), p. 13. Spanish. DESCR: *Poems.

2733 Rodriguez, Nestor. Undocumented Central Americans in Houston: diverse populations. INTERNATIONAL MIGRATION REVIEW, Vol. 21, no. 1 (Spring 1987), p. 4-26. English. DESCR: *Central America; Ethnic Groups; Guatemala; Honduras; *Houston, TX; Immigrants; Intergroup Relations; Latin Americans; *Political Refugees; *Undocumented Workers.

Elasser, Nan

2734 Ybarra, Lea. Book review of: LAS MUJERES: CONVERSATIONS FROM A HISPANIC COMMUNITY. LA RED/THE NET, no. 58 (September 1982), p. 5-6. English. DESCR: Book Reviews; *Chicanas; *LAS MUJERES: CONVERSATIONS FROM A HISPANIC COMMUNITY; MacKenzie, Kyle; New Mexico; Tixier y Vigil, Yvonne.

Eldredge, Charles

2735 Adams, Clinton. Book review of: ART IN NEW MEXICO. 1900-1945: PATHS TO TAOS AND SANTA FE. ARTSPACE, Vol. 10, (Fall 1986), p. 34-36. English. DESCR: *Art History; *ART IN NEW MEXICO. 1900-1945: PATHS TO TAOS AND SANTA FE; Book Reviews; Exhibits; Schimmel, Julie; Truettner, William H.

Elected Officials

2736 Avila, Joaquin; Arce, Carlos H.; and Mexican American Legal Defense and Education Fund (MALDEF). Task force on civic identity and political participation. LA RED/THE NET, no. 88 (Winter 1984), p. 17-21. English. DESCR: *Political Representation; *Public Policy.

2737 Cruz, David V. Caucus & Co. orients the East. HISPANIC BUSINESS, Vol. 9, no. 11 (November 1987), p. 10-13, 71+. English. DESCR: Businesspeople; *Congressional Hispanic Caucus; *International Relations; *Japan; Latin Business Foundation, Los Angeles, CA; Nakasone, Yasuhiro [Prime Minister of Japan]; *Taiwan.

2738 Guerrero, Martha and Anaya, Toney. Toney Anaya: a man with convictions=Toney Anaya: un hombre de conviccion. AMERICAS 2001, Premiere Issue, 1987, p. 20-23, 44. Bilingual. DESCR: *Anaya, Toney, Governor of New Mexico; Biography; New Mexico; Politics.

2739 McNeely, Dave. Hispanic power at the polls. VISTA, Vol. 2, no. 3 (November 2, 1986), p. 8-12. English. DESCR: Austin, TX; *Barrera,

Roy, Jr.; Chavez, Linda; Gonzalez, Raul; Martinez, Bob; Maryland; Political System; San Antonio, TX; Statistics; Tampa, FL; *Voter Turnout.

2740 Mills, Kay. Gloria Molina. MS. MAGAZINE, Vol. 13, (January 1985), p. 80-81+. English. DESCR: Biography; Chicanas; *Molina, Gloria.

2741 Munoz, Carlos, Jr. and Henry, Charles. Rainbow coalitions in four big cities: San Antonio, Denver, Chicago and Philadelphia. P.S. [AMERICAN POLITICAL SCIENCE ASSOCIATION], Vol. 19, no. 3 (Summer 1986), p. 598-609. English. DESCR: Blacks; Chicago, IL; Cisneros, Henry, Mayor of San Antonio, TX; Denver, CO; Ethnic Groups; Intergroup Relations; Pena, Federico; Philadelphia, PA; Political Parties and Organizations; Political Representation; *Politics; San Antonio, TX; Urban Communities.

2742 Perez, Renato E. A governor named Martinez. VISTA, Vol. 2, no. 5 (January 4, 1987), p. 10-11. English. DESCR: Biography; Florida; *Martinez, Bob.

2743 Ross, I. Mayor Cisneros of San Antonio. READER'S DIGEST, Vol. 125, (December 1984), p. 193-194+. English. DESCR: Biography; *Cisneros, Henry, Mayor of San Antonio, TX; Local Government; San Antonio, TX.

2744 Trager, Cara S. Carving out a niche in politics. HISPANIC BUSINESS, Vol. 9, no. 10 (October 1987), p. 29-31. English. DESCR: Biography; *Chicanas; *Guerrero, Lena; Texas.

Elections

2745 Volsky, George. A new voting block making its mark. HISPANIC BUSINESS, Vol. 9, no. 2 (February 1987), p. 9, 11. English. DESCR: Cubanos; Democratic Party; *Political Parties and Organizations; Republican Party; *Voter Turnout.

Electronics Industry

2746 Sellers, Jeff M. High tech directory. HISPANIC BUSINESS, Vol. 9, no. 10 (October 1987), p. 7-9. English. DESCR: *Business Enterprises; Computers; *Government Contracts; Military.

2747 Sellers, Jeff M. Strategic defenses: new niches for small firms. HISPANIC BUSINESS, Vol. 9, no. 10 (October 1987), p. 13-17. English. DESCR: *Advanced Sciences Inc., Albuquerque, NM; Business Enterprises; *Government Contracts; *Military; *Orion International Technologies, Inc.; Rios, Miguel, Jr.; Romero, Ed.

Elementary School Education
USE: Primary School Education

THE ELEMENTS OF SAN JOAQUIN

2748 Bruce-Novoa, Juan. Poesia de Gary Soto: una autobiografia a plazos. LA COMUNIDAD, No. 270 (September 22, 1985), p. 8-10. Spanish. DESCR: Authors; *Literary Criticism; Poetry; *Soto, Gary; TALE OF SUNLIGHT; WHERE SPARROWS WORK HARD.

Elias-Olivares, Lucia

2749 Nuessel, Frank H., Jr. Book review of:
SPANISH IN THE UNITED STATES:
SOCIOLINGUISTIC ASPECTS. LINGUA, Vol. 62,
no. 3 (1984), p. 247-255. English. DESCR:
Amastae, Jon; Book Reviews;
Sociolinguistics; *SPANISH IN THE UNITED
STATES: SOCIOLINGUISTIC ASPECTS.

2750 Penalosa, Fernando. Book review of: SPANISH
IN THE UNITED STATES: SOCIOLINGUISTIC
ASPECTS. LANGUAGE, Vol. 60, no. 1 (March
1984), p. 152-159. English. DESCR: Amastae,
Jon; Book Reviews; Sociolinguistics;
*SPANISH IN THE UNITED STATES:
SOCIOLINGUISTIC ASPECTS.

2751 Powers, Michael D. Spanish in contact with
other languages: lexical or profound
structural influence? BILINGUAL REVIEW, Vol.
12, no. 3 (September, December, 1985), p.
254-257. English. DESCR: Amastae, Jon;
Language Usage; Literature Reviews; *SPANISH
IN THE UNITED STATES: SOCIOLINGUISTIC
ASPECTS; *SPANISH IN THE WESTERN HEMISPHERE
IN CONTACT WITH ENGLISH, PORTUGUESE, AND THE
AMERINDIAN LANGUAGES; *Spanish Language;
Zaragoza, Jorge.

Elisalde, Jose

2752 Ramirez, Norma. El corrido de Jose Elisalde.
LLUEVE TLALOC, no. 9 (1982), p. 1. Spanish.
DESCR: Corridos; *Poems.

Elizondo, Sergio

2753 Valdes Medellin, Gonzalo; Elizondo, Sergio
D.; and Aguilar, Ricardo. Hacia un tercer
lenguaje. LA COMUNIDAD, No. 240 (February
24, 1985), p. 2-3. Spanish. DESCR: Aguilar,
Ricardo; *Literary Criticism.

Elizondo, Virgilio

2754 Abalos, David. Book review of: GALILEAN
JOURNEY. NEW CATHOLIC WORLD, Vol. 226,
(July, August, 1983), p. 190-191. English.
DESCR: Book Reviews; *GALILEAN JOURNEY.

Elsasser, Nan

2755 Ruiz, Ivette M. Resena testimonial. REVISTA
MUJERES, Vol. 1, no. 2 (June 1984), p. 7-10.
English. DESCR: Book Reviews; Chicanas; *LAS
MUJERES: CONVERSATIONS FROM A HISPANIC
COMMUNITY; MacKenzie, Kyle; Tixier y Vigil,
Yvonne.

Emergency Services

2756 Cano, Oscar. MAES technical brief. HISPANIC
TIMES, Vol. 8, no. 1 (December, January,
1987), p. 27. English. DESCR: *Earthquakes;
*Mexico City.

2757 Gutierrez, Silvio G. On wings of mercy.
VISTA, Vol. 2, no. 3 (November 2, 1986), p.
17-18. English. DESCR: Angel Flight; Malibu,
CA; Medical Care; *Torres, Averi; Torres,
Dennis; Transportation.

2758 Pena, Raymundo. Tornado disaster tests
mettle of Texas Latinos. VISTA, Vol. 3, no.
1 (September 6, 1987), p. 28. English.
DESCR: *Saragosa, TX.

Emmy Awards

2759 Barro, Mary Helen. 1973 Emmy Awards. LATIN
QUARTER, Vol. 1, no. 1 (July 1974), p. 5-6.
English. DESCR: Chavez, Andres; CINCO VIDAS;
*Esparza, Moctezuma; Identity; Quintero,

Carlos; *Recreation; REFLECCIONES;
Rodriguez, Sandra; Rodriguez, Tony; Ruiz,
Jose Luis; Stereotypes; Television.

Employment

2760 Beale, Stephen. Striking a deal with big
business. HISPANIC BUSINESS, Vol. 9, no. 2
(February 1987), p. 26-33. English. DESCR:
*Adolph Coors Co.; American G.I. Forum;
Boycotts; Corporations; Cuban National
Planning Council, Inc. Washington, D.C.;
*Hispanic Association on Corporate
Responsibility (HACER); League of United
Latin American Citizens (LULAC); National
Council of La Raza (NCLR); National IMAGE;
National Puerto Rican Coalition;
*Organizations; U.S. Hispanic Chamber of
Commerce.

2761 Berger, Peggy S. Differences in importance
of and satisfaction from job characteristics
by sex and occupational type among
Mexican-American employees. JOURNAL OF
VOCATIONAL BEHAVIOR, Vol. 28, no. 3 (June
1986), p. 203-213. English. DESCR:
*Attitudes; *Sex Roles.

2762 Chiswick, Barry R. The labor market status
of Hispanic men. JOURNAL OF AMERICAN ETHNIC
HISTORY, Vol. 7, no. 1 (Fall 1987), p.
30-58. English. DESCR: Census;
Discrimination in Employment; Ethnic Groups;
Income; *Labor Supply and Market; Language
Usage; *Males; *Undocumented Workers.

2763 de Leon, Arnoldo and Stewart, Kenneth L. A
tale of 3 cities: a comparative analysis of
the socio-economic conditions of
Mexican-Americans in Los Angeles, Tucson,
and San Antonio, 1850-1900. JOURNAL OF THE
WEST, Vol. 24, no. 2 (1985), p. 64-74.
English. DESCR: Economic History and
Conditions; Griswold del Castillo, Richard;
Labor; *Los Angeles, CA; San Antonio, TX;
*Social History and Conditions; Tucson, AZ;
Urban Communities.

2764 Determined to advance. HISPANIC BUSINESS,
Vol. 9, no. 7 (July 1987), p. 35. English.
DESCR: *Careers; *Chicanas; *Latino
Institute.

2765 Estrada, Leobardo F. Task force on
employment and economic well-being. LA
RED/THE NET, no. 88 (Winter 1984), p. 6-10.
English. DESCR: Labor Supply and Market;
*Public Policy.

2766 Facing up to new occupational challenges.
HISPANIC BUSINESS, Vol. 9, no. 6 (June
1987), p. 113. English. DESCR: *Immigration;
*Population; Rand Corporation.

2767 Garcia, John A. Chicano unemployment in the
seventies. LA RED/THE NET, no. 32 (July
1980), p. 2-3. English.

2768 Gettman, Dawn and Pena, Devon Gerardo.
Women, mental health, and the workplace in a
transnational setting. SOCIAL WORK, Vol. 31,
no. 1 (January, February, 1986), p. 5-11.
English. DESCR: *Border Industries;
*Chicanas; *Mental Health; Mexico; United
States-Mexico Relations; Women; *Working
Women.

2769 Hunsaker, Alan C. Contingency management
with Chicano adolescents in a federal
manpower program. CORRECTIVE AND SOCIAL
PSYCHIATRY, Vol. 30, no. 1 (1984), p. 10-13.
English. DESCR: *Management; *Manpower
Programs; Psychology; *Youth.

Employment (cont.)

2770 Jimenez, Luis. Cambia la imagen del latino en Hollywood. LA COMUNIDAD, No. 255 (June 9, 1985), p. 14-15. Spanish. **DESCR:** Discrimination; Films; *Hispanic Academy of Media Arts and Sciences (HAMAS); *Mass Media; Organizations; Reyna, Phil.

2771 Karnig, Albert K.; Welch, Susan; and Eribes, Richard A. Employment of women by cities in the Southwest. SOCIAL SCIENCE JOURNAL, Vol. 21, no. 4 (October 1984), p. 41-48. English. **DESCR:** Chicanas; Local Government; *Southwestern United States; Women.

2772 Lopez, Dayne E. Job security? It could be a myth! HISPANIC TIMES, Vol. 8, no. 5 (October, November, 1987), p. 10. English. **DESCR:** *Corporations.

2773 Massey, Douglas S. Do undocumented migrants earn lower wages than legal immigrants? New evidence from Mexico. INTERNATIONAL MIGRATION REVIEW, Vol. 21, no. 2 (Summer 1987), p. 236-274. English. **DESCR:** *Immigrants; *Income; *Mexico; Migration Patterns; *Undocumented Workers.

2774 National Commission for Employment Policy. Hispanics and jobs: barriers to progress. LA RED/THE NET, no. 64 (January 1983), p. 5-8. English. **DESCR:** *Labor Supply and Market.

2775 Sellers, Jeff M. Golden opportunity. HISPANIC BUSINESS, Vol. 9, no. 9 (September 1987), p. 14-18, 79. English. **DESCR:** *Adolph Coors Co.; Business Enterprises; *Coors/HACER Agreement, 1984; *Corporations; Hispanic Association on Corporate Responsibility (HACER); Organizations.

2776 Sellers, Jeff M. Opportunity no, regulations yes. HISPANIC BUSINESS, Vol. 9, no. 2 (February 1987), p. 12-[14]. English. **DESCR:** Discrimination; *Immigration Law and Legislation; *Immigration Reform and Control Act of 1986; Undocumented Workers.

2777 Stewart, Kenneth L. and de Leon, Arnoldo. Education, literacy, and occupational structure in West Texas, 1860-1900. WEST TEXAS HISTORICAL ASSOCIATION YEARBOOK, Vol. 60, (1984), p. 127-143. English. **DESCR:** Discrimination in Education; Economic Development; Education; *Labor; Literacy; *Texas.

2778 Tienda, Marta and Guhlman, Pat. The occupational position of employed Hispanic females. LA RED/THE NET, no. 69 (June 1983), p. 2-3. English. **DESCR:** *Chicanas; Ethnic Stratification; *Women.

2779 Verdugo, Naomi and Verdugo, Richard. Income differentials between Chicano and white male workers. LA RED/THE NET, no. 57 (August 1982), p. 2-3. English. **DESCR:** Anglo Americans; *Income; Laboring Classes; *Males.

EMPLUMADA

2780 Billings, Linda M. and Alurista. In verbal murals: a study of Chicana herstory and poetry. CONFLUENCIA, Vol. 2, no. 1 (Fall 1986), p. 60-68. English. **DESCR:** Candelaria, Cordelia; Cervantes, Lorna Dee; *Chicanas; Cisneros, Sandra; *Feminism; History; Literary Criticism; *Poetry; Xelina.

2781 Elias, Edward F. A meeting of poets from east and west: Lorna Dee Cervantes, Gary Soto, Tato Laviera. BILINGUAL REVIEW, Vol. 12, no. 1-2 (January, August, 1985), p. 150-155. English. **DESCR:** Authors; Cervantes, Lorna Dee; *ENCLAVE; Laviera, Tato; Literary Criticism; Literature Reviews; Poetry; Soto, Gary; *WHERE SPARROWS WORK HARD.

Empringham, Toni

2782 Candelaria, Cordelia. Book review of: FIESTA IN AZTLAN: ANTHOLOGY OF CHICANO POETRY and FLOR Y CANTO IV AND V. LA RED/THE NET, no. 62 (December 1982), p. 6-9. English. **DESCR:** Book Reviews; *FIESTA IN AZTLAN: AN ANTHOLOGY OF CHICANO POETRY; *FLOR Y CANTO IV AND V: AN ANTHOLOGY OF CHICANO LITERATURE FROM THE FESTIVALS HELD IN ALBUQUERQUE, NEW MEXICO; Poetry.

ENCLAVE

2783 Elias, Edward F. A meeting of poets from east and west: Lorna Dee Cervantes, Gary Soto, Tato Laviera. BILINGUAL REVIEW, Vol. 12, no. 1-2 (January, August, 1985), p. 150-155. English. **DESCR:** Authors; Cervantes, Lorna Dee; *EMPLUMADA; Laviera, Tato; Literary Criticism; Literature Reviews; Poetry; Soto, Gary; *WHERE SPARROWS WORK HARD.

Encomiendas
USE: Land Grants

Encuentro Movement [Catholic Church]

2784 Gann, Lewis H. and Duignan, Peter J. Latinos & the Catholic Church in America. NUESTRO, Vol. 11, no. 4 (May 1987), p. 10-13. English. **DESCR:** *Catholic Church; Culture; History; Primer Encuentro Nacional Hispano, Washington, DC, June 1972.

Engineering as a Profession

2785 Alvarado, Raul. Another "decade of the Hispanic"? HISPANIC ENGINEER, Vol. 3, no. 1 (Spring 1987), p. 10-11. English. **DESCR:** Social History and Conditions; *Society of Hispanic Professional Engineers (SHPE).

2786 Bradby, Marie. The naval research laboratory. HISPANIC ENGINEER, Vol. 3, no. 2 (Summer 1987), p. 34-38. English. **DESCR:** Military; *Naval Research Laboratory; Rojas, Richard Raimond; Urrutia, Jorge R.

2787 Bradby, Marie. Solomon Trujillo of US West. HISPANIC ENGINEER, Vol. 3, no. 5 (Winter 1987), p. 26-30. English. **DESCR:** *Biography; *Trujillo, Solomon; US West [telecommunications company].

2788 Cano, Oscar. Profiles in engineering. HISPANIC TIMES, Vol. 8, no. 3 (May, June, 1987), p. 43. English. **DESCR:** Biography; *Valenzuela, Ralph.

2789 Dates, Karen E. Coast Guard ocean engineer Lisa Martinez. HISPANIC ENGINEER, Vol. 3, no. 4 (Fall 1987), p. 30-34. English. **DESCR:** Chicanas; Discrimination in Education; *Martinez, Lisa.

2790 Keep pace with MAES: Sociedad de Ingenieria de Mexicano Americanos (Mexican American Engineering Society). HISPANIC TIMES, Vol. 8, no. 1 (December, January, 1987), p. 28. Bilingual. **DESCR:** *Mexican American Engineering Society (MAES); Organizations.

Engineering as a Profession (cont.)

2791 Maes, Jim. Latinos in high
technology=Latinos en alta tecnologia.
AMERICAS 2001, Vol. 1, no. 1 (June, July,
1987), p. 5. Bilingual.

2792 MAES now has eleven professional chapters
nationwide (and more to come). HISPANIC
TIMES, Vol. 8, no. 5 (October, November,
1987), p. 42. English. **DESCR**: *Mexican
American Engineering Society (MAES);
Organizations.

2793 MAES sets the pace. HISPANIC TIMES, Vol. 8,
no. 1 (December, January, 1987), p. 26.
English. **DESCR**: *Mexican American
Engineering Society (MAES); Organizations.

2794 Marsh, Betsa. Diversidad de valores en
Proctor & Gamble. HISPANIC TIMES, Vol. 8,
no. 3 (May, June, 1987), p. 32-3. Spanish.
DESCR: Careers; *Proctor & Gamble,
Cincinnati. OH.

2795 Marsh, Betsa. Proctor & Gamble values
diversity. HISPANIC TIMES, Vol. 8, no. 3
(May, June, 1987), p. 10-11. English.
DESCR: Careers; *Proctor & Gamble,
Cincinnati. OH.

2796 Mejias-Rivera. Ann E. Steven Perez of Xerox.
HISPANIC ENGINEER, Vol. 3, no. 1 (Spring
1987), p. 26-30. English. **DESCR**: Language
Arts; *Perez, Steven; Xerox.

2797 Mellado, Carmela. Hispanic women as leaders:
expanding the stereotypes that bind us.
HISPANIC ENGINEER, Vol. 3, no. 4 (Fall
1987), p. 6. English. **DESCR**: *Chicanas;
*National Network of Hispanic Women.

2798 Minsky, Alyce. California State University
at Los Angeles. HISPANIC ENGINEER, Vol. 3,
(Summer, 1987), p. 30-33, 44. English.
DESCR: Colleges and Universities;
Educational Organizations; Mathematics,
Engineering and Science Achievement (MESA);
*Minority Engineering Program (California
State University at Los Angeles).

2799 Reyes outstanding Hispanic at Kennedy Space
Center. HISPANIC TIMES, Vol. 8, no. 5
(October, November, 1987), p. 60. English.
DESCR: Biography; *John F. Kennedy Space
Center, NASA, FL; *Reyes, Raul E. (Ernie).

2800 Rifkin, Jane M. Manuel Castro--founder of
MAES: a compassionate commitment. HISPANIC
TIMES, Vol. 8, no. 5 (October, November,
1987), p. 44. English. **DESCR**: Biography;
*Castro, Manuel; Mexican American
Engineering Society (MAES).

2801 Rifkin, Jane M. New avenues for women in
technology. HISPANIC TIMES, Vol. 8, no. 3
(May, June, 1987), p. 41. English. **DESCR**:
Biographical Notes; *Chicanas; *Ponce,
Alice.

2802 Rifkin, Jane M. Ralph de la Parra travels
the MAES "bridge to the future". HISPANIC
TIMES, Vol. 8, no. 1 (December, January,
1987), p. 30. English. **DESCR**: Biography; *De
la Parra, Ralph; Mexican American
Engineering Society (MAES); Southern
California Edison Co..

2803 Rivera, Alvin D. Laying a foundation for
learning: student peer workshop groups. NEW
DIRECTIONS FOR TEACHING AND LEARNING, no. 16
(December 1983), p. 81-86. English. **DESCR**:
*Careers; Counseling (Educational); *Natural
Support Systems; Organizations; Students.

2804 Roth, George. The sky is not her limit.
VISTA, Vol. 2, no. 12 (August 1, 1987), p.
24. English. **DESCR**: Chicanas; *Jaramillo,
Sylvia.

2805 Smith, Chuck. Commitment to Hispanic
education. HISPANIC ENGINEER, Vol. 3, no. 1
(Spring 1987), p. 16-20. English. **DESCR**:
*Education; *Pacific Telesis.

2806 Smith, Mary Perry. Early identification and
support: the University of
California-Berkeley's MESA program. NEW
DIRECTIONS FOR TEACHING AND LEARNING, no. 24
(December 1985), p. 19-25. English. **DESCR**:
*Counseling (Educational); Enrollment;
Higher Education; *Mathematics, Engineering
and Science Achievement (MESA); University
of California, Berkeley.

2807 Taylor, Wendy. Una asociacion que trabaja.
HISPANIC TIMES, Vol. 8, no. 5 (October,
November, 1987), p. 36-38. Spanish. **DESCR**:
Mexican American Engineering Society (MAES);
*TRW Defense Systems Group.

2808 Taylor, Wendy. A working partnership.
HISPANIC TIMES, Vol. 8, no. 5 (October,
November, 1987), p. 12-13. English. **DESCR**:
*Mexican American Engineering Society
(MAES); *TRW Defense Systems Group.

2809 Winston, Bonnie. High tech jobs in the
Midwest. HISPANIC ENGINEER, Vol. 3, no. 1
(Spring 1987), p. 50-53. English. **DESCR**:
Chaves, Tony; Mosquera, Jaime "Jim";
Rodriguez Howell, Nilsa; Sanchez, Francisco
G.

English as a Second Language

2810 Magallan, Rafael J. 1983-84 NAEP data raises
questions regarding the school experiences
of language minority children. LA RED/THE
NET, no. 92 (November, December, 1985), p.
9-11. English. **DESCR**: *Bilingual Bicultural
Education; Bilingualism; Dropouts; *National
Assessment of Educational Progress; Surveys.

English Language

2811 Comstock, Cathryn L. and Martin, Frederick
N. A children's Spanish word discrimination
test for non-Spanish-speaking children. EAR
AND HEARING, Vol. 5, no. 3 (May, June,
1984), p. 166-170. English. **DESCR**: Child
Study; *Language Assessment; Research
Methodology; Spanish Language.

2812 English only forces promoting racist
measures nationwide. GUARDIAN, Vol. 39, no.
24 (March 25, 1987), p. 7. English. **DESCR**:
Discrimination; English-Only Movement.

2813 Galindo-Ramirez, Tina. Educacion monolingue:
opresion o liberacion? REVISTA MUJERES, Vol.
1, no. 1 (January 1984), p. 8-9. Spanish.
DESCR: Alienation; Assertiveness; Biography;
*Education; *Identity.

2814 Gonzales-Berry, Erlinda. Enmienda de ingles
en Nuevo Mexico. LA COMUNIDAD, No. 352
(April 19, 1987), p. 4-7. Spanish. **DESCR**:
*English-Only Movement; History;
Legislation; *New Mexico; Spanish Language.

2815 Hayakawa, S.I.; Cejas, Paul; and Castro
Feinberg, Rosa. The English-only debate.
VISTA, Vol. 2, no. 6 (February 8, 1987), p.
11-13. English. **DESCR**: California;
*English-Only Movement; Law.

English Language (cont.)

2816 Korzenny, Felipe, et al. Cultural
     identification as predictor of content
     preferences of Hispanics. JOURNALISM
     QUARTERLY, Vol. 60, no. 4 (Winter 1983), p.
     677-685+. English. **DESCR:** Cultural
     Characteristics; Identity; *Newspapers;
     Spanish Language.

2817 Latino literacy update: literacy bill
     introduced in house. LA RED/THE NET, No. 100
     (September 1986), p. 9. English. **DESCR:**
     Educational Law and Legislation; *English
     Proficiency Act (H.R. 5042); *Literacy.

2818 Levin, Gary. Publisher seeks to improve
     "image". ADVERTISING AGE MAGAZINE, Vol. 57,
     no. 43 (August 11, 1986), p. S25-S27.
     English. **DESCR:** Advertising; Asencio, John;
     *HISPANIC IMAGE; Magazines; Spanish
     Language.

2819 Llorente, Elizabeth. Linda Chavez: thriving
     on controversy. VISTA, Vol. 3, no. 3
     (November 8, 1987), p. 6-9. English. **DESCR:**
     *Chavez, Linda; Politics; U.S. English.

2820 More findings based upon the NCS. LA RED/THE
     NET, No. 102 (November 1986), p. 9-11.
     English. **DESCR:** *Literacy; *National Chicano
     Survey (NCS).

2821 Moss, Ambler H., Jr. America needs to face
     world in many languages. VISTA, Vol. 2, no.
     8 (April 4, 1987), p. 26. English.

2822 Norris, Eileen. Print suffers in tale of two
     languages. ADVERTISING AGE MAGAZINE, Vol.
     57, no. 16 (February 27, 1986), p. 49-51.
     English. **DESCR:** Advertising; Chavarria,
     Jesus; HISPANIC BUSINESS; LATINA [magazine];
     *Magazines; Soto, Grace; Spanish Language;
     Villar, Arturo; VISTA [magazine].

2823 Novick, Michael. "English only" gets
     go-ahead in California. GUARDIAN, Vol. 39,
     no. 9 (November 26, 1986), p. 5. English.
     DESCR: *English-Only Movement.

2824 Novick, Michael. English-only crusade
     threatens bilingual program. GUARDIAN, Vol.
     38, no. 44 (September 10, 1986), p. 9.
     English. **DESCR:** *English-Only Movement.

2825 Sanchez, Nicholas. Bilingualism creates more
     problems than solutions. VISTA, Vol. 3, no.
     3 (November 8, 1987), p. 38. English.
     DESCR: *Bilingualism.

English Language Proficiency Survey (ELPS)

2826 Latino literacy update: ELPS/survey updates
     illiteracy profile. LA RED/THE NET, no. 98
     (July 1986), p. 10-12. English. **DESCR:**
     *Literacy; Surveys.

2827 Latino literacy update: NCLR reports on
     illiteracy among Latinos. LA RED/THE NET,
     No. 102 (November 1986), p. 8-9. English.
     DESCR: *Literacy; National Council of La
     Raza (NCLR).

English Proficiency Act (H.R. 5042)

2828 Latino literacy update: literacy bill
     introduced in house. LA RED/THE NET, No. 100
     (September 1986), p. 9. English. **DESCR:**
     Educational Law and Legislation; *English
     Language; *Literacy.

English-Only Movement

2829 Acuna, Rodolfo and Hill, Frank. English as
     the official language?=El ingles como idioma
     oficial. AMERICAS 2001, Vol. 1, no. 1 (June,
     July, 1987), p. 6-11. Bilingual. **DESCR:**
     Language Usage; *Proposition 63 (English as
     the Official Language of California).

2830 English only forces promoting racist
     measures nationwide. GUARDIAN, Vol. 39, no.
     24 (March 25, 1987), p. 7. English. **DESCR:**
     Discrimination; *English Language.

2831 Flores, Lorenzo T. Your turn=Su turno.
     AMERICAS 2001, Vol. 1, no. 1 (June, July,
     1987), p. 26-29. Bilingual. **DESCR:** Language
     Usage; *Short Story.

2832 Gonzales-Berry, Erlinda. Enmienda de ingles
     en Nuevo Mexico. LA COMUNIDAD, No. 352
     (April 19, 1987), p. 4-7. Spanish. **DESCR:**
     English Language; History; Legislation; *New
     Mexico; Spanish Language.

2833 Hayakawa, S.I.; Cejas, Paul; and Castro
     Feinberg, Rosa. The English-only debate.
     VISTA, Vol. 2, no. 6 (February 8, 1987), p.
     11-13. English. **DESCR:** California; *English
     Language; Law.

2834 Novick, Michael. "English only" gets
     go-ahead in California. GUARDIAN, Vol. 39,
     no. 9 (November 26, 1986), p. 5. English.
     DESCR: *English Language.

2835 Novick, Michael. English-only crusade
     threatens bilingual program. GUARDIAN, Vol.
     38, no. 44 (September 10, 1986), p. 9.
     English. **DESCR:** *English Language.

2836 Report to the Network. LA RED/THE NET, No.
     101 (October 1986), p. 1-6. English.

2837 What are your views on the new English-Only
     initiative?=Que piensas sobre la nueva ley,
     "English-Only". AMERICAS 2001, Vol. 1, no. 1
     (June, July, 1987), p. 12-14. Bilingual.
     DESCR: Attitudes; *Proposition 63 (English
     as the Official Language of California);
     Public Opinion.

2838 Yzaguirre critical of committee action.
     NUESTRO, Vol. 11, no. 4 (May 1987), p. 8.
     English. **DESCR:** *Bilingual Bicultural
     Education; National Council of La Raza
     (NCLR); Yzaguirre, Raul.

THE ENGLISH-SPANISH CONNECTION

2839 Hewlett-Gomez, Michele. Book review of: THE
     ENGLISH-SPANISH CONNECTION. LA RED/THE NET,
     no. 84 (September 1984), p. 2. English.
     DESCR: Book Reviews; Thonis, Elenor.

Enriquez, Evangelina

2840 Baca Zinn, Maxine. Book review of: LA
     CHICANA: MEXICAN AMERICAN WOMEN. LA RED/THE
     NET, no. 28 (March 1980), p. 10. English.
     DESCR: Book Reviews; Chicanas; LA CHICANA:
     THE MEXICAN AMERICAN WOMAN; *Mirande,
     Alfredo.

Enrollment

2841 Chavez, Lorenzo A. Passport to success.
     VISTA, Vol. 2, no. 1 (September 7, 1986), p.
     6-8. English. **DESCR:** Colleges and
     Universities; *Higher Education.

Enrollment (cont.)

2842 de los Santos, Alfredo G., Jr.; Montemayor, Joaquin; and Solis, Enrique, Jr. Chicano students in higher education: access, attrition and achievement. LA RED/THE NET, no. 41 (April 1981), p. 2-3. English. DESCR: Academic Achievement; *California; *Higher Education; *Texas.

2843 Educational hierarchies and social differentiation. LA RED/THE NET, no. 37 (December 1980), p. 2-3. English. DESCR: Discrimination in Education; *Higher Education; *Southwestern United States.

2844 Estimating the demand for private school enrollment. AMERICAN JOURNAL OF EDUCATION, Vol. 92, no. 3 (May 1984), p. 262-279. English. DESCR: *Private Education.

2845 Gonzalez, Juan C. Report to the Network. LA RED/THE NET, No. 105 (February 1987), p. 1-3. English. DESCR: Breland, Hunter M.; *DEMOGRAPHICS, STANDARDS, AND EQUITY CHALLENGES IN COLLEGE ADMISSIONS: REPORT OF A SURVEY OF UNDERGRADUATE ADMISSIONS POLICIES, PRACTICES AND PROCEDURES; *Discrimination in Education; *Higher Education.

2846 Leon, David Jess and McNeill, Daniel. The fifth class: a 19th century forerunner of affirmative action. CALIFORNIA HISTORY, Vol. 64, no. 1 (Winter 1985), p. 52-57. English. DESCR: *Affirmative Action; Colleges and Universities; Discrimination in Education; *Higher Education; History; Students; *University of California.

2847 Leon, David Jess and McNeill, Daniel. Hispanics, the fifth class, and the University of California. 1870-72. LA RED/THE NET, no. 67 (April 1983), p. 5-6. English. DESCR: College Preparation; *Colleges and Universities; Local History; *University of California.

2848 Magallan, Rafael J. Community college update. LA RED/THE NET, no. 98 (July 1986), p. 3-6. English. DESCR: *California Master Plan for Higher Education; *Community College Reassessment Study; Community Colleges; *Vera, Ron.

2849 Report to the Network. LA RED/THE NET, no. 98 (July 1986), p. 1-2. English. DESCR: *Higher Education; Statistics.

2850 Sellers, Jeff M. State of the art recruitment: competition for blue-chip Hispanic business graduates is fierce and expensive. HISPANIC BUSINESS, Vol. 9, no. 2 (February 1987), p. 22-25, 57. English. DESCR: *Business Administration; *Careers; College Graduates; Colleges and Universities; *Management.

2851 Smith, Mary Perry. Early identification and support: the University of California-Berkeley's MESA program. NEW DIRECTIONS FOR TEACHING AND LEARNING, no. 24 (December 1985), p. 19-25. English. DESCR: *Counseling (Educational); *Engineering as a Profession; Higher Education; *Mathematics, Engineering and Science Achievement (MESA); University of California, Berkeley.

Entertainment
USE: Recreation

ENTRE VERDE Y SECO

2852 Atencio, Tomas. La resolana [editorial]. EL

CUADERNO, Vol. 4, no. 1 (Summer 1976), p. 2-4. English. DESCR: Academia Asociados, NM; Academia Educational Model; *Chicano Studies; Culture; EL CUADERNO; *La Academia de la Nueva Raza, Dixon, NM; LA MADRUGADA; Publishing Industry.

Equal Opportunity
USE: Affirmative Action

Equal Opportunity Programs
USE: Affirmative Action Programs

Equality Before the Law
USE: Civil Rights

Equality in Education
USE: Discrimination in Education

Erb, Richard D.

2853 Gutierrez, Armando. Book reviews of: MEXICO-UNITED STATES RELATIONS and UNITED STATES RELATIONS WITH MEXICO: CONTEXT AND CONTENT. LA RED/THE NET, no. 62 (December 1982), p. 4-6. English. DESCR: Book Reviews; Kaufman, Purcell; *MEXICO-UNITED STATES RELATIONS; Ross, Stanley R.; *UNITED STATES RELATIONS WITH MEXICO: CONTEXT AND CONTENT.

Escobar [family name]

2854 Instituto Genealogico e Historico Latino-Americano. Rootsearch: Patino: Herrera: Escobar. VISTA, Vol. 2, no. 9 (May 3, 1987), p. 22. English. DESCR: Genealogy; *Herrera [family name]; History; *Patino [family name]; *Personal Names.

Escobar, Javier I.

2855 Canive, Jose. Book review of: MENTAL HEALTH AND HISPANIC AMERICANS: CLINICAL PERSPECTIVES. JOURNAL OF NERVOUS AND MENTAL DISEASE, Vol. 172, no. 9 (September 1984), p. 559-561. English. DESCR: Ancianos; Becerra, Rosina; Book Reviews; Karno, Marvin; *MENTAL HEALTH AND HISPANIC AMERICANS: CLINICAL PERSPECTIVES.

2856 Gibson, Guadalupe. Book review of: MENTAL HEALTH AND HISPANIC AMERICANS: CLINICAL PERSPECTIVES. SOCIAL WORK, Vol. 29, no. 1 (January, February, 1984), p. 81. English. DESCR: Becerra, Rosina; Book Reviews; Karno, Marvin; *MENTAL HEALTH AND HISPANIC AMERICANS: CLINICAL PERSPECTIVES.

2857 Marcos, Luis R. Book review of: MENTAL HEALTH AND HISPANIC AMERICANS: CLINICAL PERSPECTIVES. AMERICAN JOURNAL OF PSYCHOTHERAPY, Vol. 38, no. 1 (January 1984), p. 155-156. English. DESCR: Book Reviews; Karno, Marvin; Mental Health; *MENTAL HEALTH AND HISPANIC AMERICANS: CLINICAL PERSPECTIVES.

ESL
USE: English as a Second Language

Espada, Ibsen

2858 Chavez, Lorenzo A. The eyes of Texas are upon them. VISTA, Vol. 2, no. 2 (October 4, 1986), p. 20. English. DESCR: *Art; Cardenas, David; *Chulas Fronteras [art exhibit]; Gonzalez, Patricia; Hernandez, John; Huerta, Benito; Martinez, Cesar Augusto.

Espada, Martin

2859 Espada, Martin and Perez-Erdelyi, Mireya. With Martin Espada. THE AMERICAS REVIEW, Vol. 15, no. 2 (Summer 1987), p. 77-85. English. **DESCR:** Authors; Language Usage; Poetry; Puerto Ricans.

Esparza, Moctezuma

2860 Barro, Mary Helen. 1973 Emmy Awards. LATIN QUARTER, Vol. 1, no. 1 (July 1974), p. 5-6. English. **DESCR:** Chavez, Andres; CINCO VIDAS; Emmy Awards; Identity; Quintero, Carlos; *Recreation; REFLECCIONES; Rodriguez, Sandra; Rodriguez, Tony; Ruiz, Jose Luis; Stereotypes; Television.

EL ESPECTADOR, Pomona, CA

2861 Garcia, Mario T. Bracero poetry of the 1940s: two samples. BILINGUAL REVIEW, Vol. 11, no. 3 (September, December, 1984), p. 45-48. English. **DESCR:** *Braceros; *Poetry.

Espinosa, Aurelio M.

2862 Anaya, Rudolfo A. Book review of: THE FOLKLORE OF SPAIN IN THE AMERICAN SOUTHWEST. NEW MEXICO HISTORICAL REVIEW, Vol. 62, no. 3 (July 1987), p. 313-314. English. **DESCR:** Book Reviews; Folklore; *THE FOLKLORE OF SPAIN IN THE AMERICAN SOUTHWEST: TRADITIONAL SPANISH FOLK LITERATURE IN NORTHERN NEW MEXICO AND SOUTHERN COLORADO.

2863 Gutierrez, Ramon A. Book review of: THE FOLKLORE OF SPAIN IN THE AMERICAN SOUTHWEST. HISPANIC AMERICAN HISTORICAL REVIEW, Vol. 67, no. 1 (February 1987), p. 149-150. English. **DESCR:** Book Reviews; Espinosa, J. Manuel; *THE FOLKLORE OF SPAIN IN THE AMERICAN SOUTHWEST: TRADITIONAL SPANISH FOLK LITERATURE IN NORTHERN NEW MEXICO AND SOUTHERN COLORADO.

Espinosa, J. Manuel

2864 Gutierrez, Ramon A. Book review of: THE FOLKLORE OF SPAIN IN THE AMERICAN SOUTHWEST. HISPANIC AMERICAN HISTORICAL REVIEW, Vol. 67, no. 1 (February 1987), p. 149-150. English. **DESCR:** Book Reviews; Espinosa, Aurelio M.; *THE FOLKLORE OF SPAIN IN THE AMERICAN SOUTHWEST: TRADITIONAL SPANISH FOLK LITERATURE IN NORTHERN NEW MEXICO AND SOUTHERN COLORADO.

Espiritismo
USE: Curanderismo

Esquiroz, Margarita

2865 Olivera, Mercedes. The new Hispanic women. VISTA, Vol. 2, no. 11 (July 5, 1987), p. 6-8. English. **DESCR:** Alvarez, Linda; *Chicanas; Garcia, Juliet; *Hernandez, Antonia A.; Mohr, Nicolasa; Molina, Gloria; Pabon, Maria; Working Women.

Essays

2866 Allen, David. Bilingual education: door to the society of the future. LLUEVE TLALOC, no. 1 (1974), p. 22. English. **DESCR:** Bilingual Bicultural Education.

2867 Allen, David. Educacion bilingue: puerta a la sociedad del futuro. LLUEVE TLALOC, no. 1 (1974), p. 21. Spanish. **DESCR:** Bilingual Bicultural Education.

2868 Almaraz, Felix D., Jr. Introduction: the Mexican borderlands. JOURNAL OF THE WEST, Vol. 24, no. 2 (1985), p. 5-7. English. **DESCR:** *Border Region; History.

2869 Barrera, Nancy. Mi sueno. REVISTA MUJERES, Vol. 1, no. 2 (June 1984), p. 13-14. Spanish. **DESCR:** *Autobiography.

2870 Castro, Richard T. A role for Hispanic Americans in foreign policy formulation. VISTA, Vol. 1, no. 9 (May 3, 1986), p. 3. English. **DESCR:** *Hispanic Caucus; International Relations; Political System.

2871 Garcia, Ed. On red-haired girls and the greaser in me. TEXAS OBSERVOR, Vol. 75, (October 28, 1983), p. 24-25. English. **DESCR:** Book Reviews; de Leon, Arnoldo; Identity; *Stereotypes; Texas; *THEY CALLED THEM GREASERS: ANGLO ATTITUDES TOWARD MEXICANS IN TEXAS, 1821-1900.

2872 Lawrence, Gene. Grampa's car: a reminiscence. VISTA, Vol. 2, no. 5 (January 4, 1987), p. 14. English.

2873 Mares, E.A. The fiesta of life: impression of Paulo Friere. EL CUADERNO, Vol. 3, no. 2 (Spring 1974), p. 5-16. English. **DESCR:** *Aztlan; Cultural Characteristics; *Freire, Paulo; *Philosophy.

2874 Melendez, Pablo. Happy Thanksgiving. CALIFORNIA MAGAZINE, Vol. 11, no. 11 (November 1986), p. 136. English. **DESCR:** *Biography; *Immigrants; *Melendez, Pablo; Youth.

2875 Padilla, Steve. Lessons to be learned from a playful hoax. VISTA, Vol. 1, no. 7 (March 2, 1986), p. 3. English. **DESCR:** Humor; Librarians; Public Opinion; Solar, Marta-Luisa; Stereotypes; *Valdez, Juan.

2876 Pascual, Jose Elias. A hope for Micheal [sic]=Una esperanza para Miguel. AMERICAS 2001, Vol. 1, no. 3 (November, December, 1987), p. 18-19. Bilingual. **DESCR:** Cancer.

2877 Perez, Renato E. As American as babalu. VISTA, Vol. 2, no. 6 (February 8, 1987), p. 22. English. **DESCR:** *Acculturation; *Arnaz, Desi; I LOVE LUCY; Television.

2878 Ruiz Garza, Pedro. Taking a fresh look at the decade of the Hispanic. VISTA, Vol. 1, no. 11 (July 6, 1986), p. 3. English. **DESCR:** *Political History and Conditions.

2879 Salazar-Nobles, Mary. Latinas must chart own course in workplace. VISTA, Vol. 2, no. 3 (November 2, 1986), p. 26. English. **DESCR:** Chicanas; *Feminism; Working Women.

2880 Taylor, Maria T. Mucho Spanglish brews unsavory linguistic stew. VISTA, Vol. 1, no. 10 (June 8, 1986), p. 3. English. **DESCR:** Bilingualism; Language Proficiency; Language Usage.

2881 Villalobos Galligan, Martha. The legacy of Mama. VISTA, Vol. 1, no. 9 (May 3, 1986), p. 18-19. English. **DESCR:** Parent and Child Relationships; Parenting.

ESTADOS UNIDOS, HOY

2882 Griswold del Castillo, Richard. Book review of: ESTADOS UNIDOS HOY. PACIFIC HISTORICAL REVIEW, Vol. 54, no. 4 (1985), p. 542-544. English. **DESCR:** Book Reviews; Gonzalez, Casanova.

Esteva, Gustavo

2883 de la Torre. Adela. Book review of: THE STRUGGLE FOR RURAL MEXICO. LA RED/THE NET, no. 85 (October 1984), p. 5-6. English. **DESCR:** Book Reviews; *THE STRUGGLE FOR RURAL MEXICO.

Estevez, Emilio

2884 WISDOM: a showcase for the many talents of Emilio Estevez. NUESTRO, Vol. 11, no. 3 (April 1987), p. 25. English. **DESCR:** *Actors and Actresses; WISDOM [film].

Estrada, Anthony

2885 Beale, Stephen. CEOs. HISPANIC BUSINESS, Vol. 9, no. 4 (April 1987), p. 20-37, 52. English. **DESCR:** Alvarez, Roberto; Batarse, Anthony A.; Biography; Business Enterprises; *Businesspeople; Carlo, Nelson; Flores, Frank; Fullana. Jaime, Jr.; Hernandez, George; *Management; Ortega, James; Quirch, Guillermo; Ruiz, Roberto; Santa Maria, Yvonne Z.; Sugranes, Rosa; Tamaya, Carlos; Young, Paul H., Jr.

Estrada Courts, Los Angeles, CA

2886 Blanco, Gilbert M. A vehicle for positive change. LATIN QUARTER, Vol. 1, no. 2 (October 1974), p. 27-30. English. **DESCR:** Artists; East Los Angeles, CA; *Mural Art.

Ethnic Groups

2887 Anderson, John W. The effects of culture and social class on client preference for counseling methods. JOURNAL OF NON-WHITE CONCERNS IN PERSONNEL AND GUIDANCE, Vol. 11, no. 3 (April 1983), p. 84-88. English. **DESCR:** *Counseling (Psychological); Cultural Characteristics; Social Classes.

2888 Argulewicz, Ed N. Effects of ethnic membership, socioeconomic status, and home language on LD, EMR, and EH placements. LEARNING DISABILITY QUARTERLY, Vol. 6, no. 2 (Spring 1983), p. 195-200. English. **DESCR:** Educable Mentally Retarded (EMR); *Special Education.

2889 Bennett, Ruth. A bilingual perspective on teaching history. SOCIAL STUDIES REVIEW, Vol. 23, no. 3 (Spring 1984), p. 50-55. English. **DESCR:** Education; History.

2890 Bransford, Luis A. The Chicano as surplus population. EL CUADERNO, Vol. 2, no. 1 (1972), p. 16-19. English. **DESCR:** Labor Supply and Market.

2891 Chiswick, Barry R. The labor market status of Hispanic men. JOURNAL OF AMERICAN ETHNIC HISTORY, Vol. 7, no. 1 (Fall 1987), p. 30-58. English. **DESCR:** Census; Discrimination in Employment; *Employment; Income; *Labor Supply and Market; Language Usage; *Males; *Undocumented Workers.

2892 Cortese. Anthony J. Ethnic ethics: subjective choice and interference in Chicano, white and Black children. LA RED/THE NET, no. 38 (January 1981), p. 2-3. English. **DESCR:** *Values.

2893 Domino, George. Sleep habits in the elderly: a study of three Hispanic cultures. JOURNAL OF CROSS-CULTURAL PSYCHOLOGY, Vol. 17, no. 1 (March 1986), p. 109-120. English. **DESCR:** *Ancianos; *Comparative Psychology; Cultural Characteristics.

2894 Edmondson, Brad. Met Life mines minority market. AMERICAN DEMOGRAPHICS, Vol. 8, no. 7 (July 1986), p. 18-19. English. **DESCR:** Consumers; Immigrants; Insurance; Marketing; *Metropolitan Life Insurance Corporation.

2895 Esman, Milton J. Two dimensions of ethnic politics: defense of homelands, immigrant rights. ETHNIC AND RACIAL STUDIES, Vol. 8, no. 3 (July 1985), p. 438-440. English. **DESCR:** *Immigrants; Politics.

2896 Fishman, Joshua A. Minority mother tongues in education. PROSPECTS: QUARTERLY REVIEW OF EDUCATION, Vol. 14, no. 1 (1984), p. 51-61. English. **DESCR:** Bilingual Bicultural Education; *Bilingualism.

2897 Garcia, Herman S.; Stile, Stephen W.; and Carillo, Fred M. Ethnic minority students, admissions policies, and academic support programs in institutions of higher education. TEXAS TECH JOURNAL OF EDUCATION, Vol. 11, no. 1 (Winter 1984), p. 77-89. English. **DESCR:** Academic Achievement; *Colleges and Universities.

2898 Guppy, N. Positional centrality and racial segregation in professional baseball. INTERNATIONAL REVIEW OF SPORT SOCIOLOGY, Vol. 18, no. 4 (1983), p. 95-109. English. **DESCR:** *Baseball; Discrimination; Segregation and Desegregation.

2899 Gutierrez, Ramon A. Unraveling America's Hispanic past: internal stratification and class boundaries. AZTLAN, Vol. 17, no. 1 (Spring 1986), p. 79-101. English. **DESCR:** *Chicano, Meaning of; Culture; *Identity; Intergroup Relations; *Self-Referents.

2900 Hayes-Bautista, David Emmett and Chapa, Jorge. Latino terminology: conceptual bases for standardized terminology. AMERICAN JOURNAL OF PUBLIC HEALTH, Vol. 77, no. 1 (January 1987), p. 61-68. English. **DESCR:** *Identity; Self-Referents.

2901 Hurtado, Aida and Arce, Carlos H. Mexicans, Chicanos, Mexican Americans, or pochos...Que somos? The impact of language and nativity on ethnic labeling. AZTLAN, Vol. 17, no. 1 (Spring 1986), p. 103-130. English. **DESCR:** *Identity; Language Usage; *Self-Referents.

2902 Isonio, Steven A. and Garza, Raymond T. Protestant work ethic endorsement among Anglo Americans, Chicanos and Mexicans: a comparison of factor structures. HISPANIC JOURNAL OF BEHAVIORAL SCIENCES, Vol. 9, no. 4 (December 1987), p. 413-425. English. **DESCR:** *Comparative Psychology; *Cultural Characteristics; *Protestant Work Ethic (PWE) Scale; *Values.

2903 Kane, Michael G. "Touching" minorities. EDITOR & PUBLISHER: THE FOURTH ESTATE, Vol. 119, no. 38 (September 20, 1986), p. 20-21. English. **DESCR:** Advertising; Consumers; Marketing; *Newspapers.

2904 Leal, Luis. Literary criticism and minority literatures: the case of the Chicano writer. CONFLUENCIA, Vol. 1, no. 2 (Spring 1986), p. 4-9. English. **DESCR:** Authors; *Literary Criticism; Literary Influence; *Literature; *Third World Literature (U.S.)

Ethnic Groups (cont.)

2905 Los Angeles: brown versus yellow. ECONOMIST (London), Vol. 300, no. 7456 (July 26, 1986), p. 21-22. English. **DESCR**: Alatorre, Richard; Bradley, Tom; *Los Angeles, CA; Political Representation; Politics; Reapportionment; Voter Turnout; Woo, Michael.

2906 Lowe, Virginia A.P. Presentation of ethnic identity in Chicano theater. CHIRICU, Vol. 2, no. 1 (Spring 1980), p. 52-58. English. **DESCR**: Folklore Institute at Indiana University; Gary, IN; Identity; *Teatro; *Teatro Desangano del Pueblo, Washington Park, East Chicago, IN.

2907 Manning, Winston, et al. Book review of: MINORITIES IN AMERICAN HIGHER EDUCATION: RECENT TRENDS, CURRENT PROSPECTS AND RECOMMENDATIONS. LA RED/THE NET, no. 60 (Fall 1982), p. 1-22. English. **DESCR**: *Astin, Alexander W.; Book Reviews; *MINORITIES IN AMERICAN HIGHER EDUCATION: RECENT TRENDS, CURRENT PROSPECTS AND RECOMMENDATIONS.

2908 Munoz, Carlos, Jr. and Henry, Charles. Rainbow coalitions in four big cities: San Antonio, Denver. Chicago and Philadelphia. P.S. [AMERICAN POLITICAL SCIENCE ASSOCIATION], Vol. 19, no. 3 (Summer 1986), p. 598-609. English. **DESCR**: Blacks; Chicago, IL; Cisneros, Henry, Mayor of San Antonio, TX; Denver, CO; Elected Officials; Intergroup Relations; Pena, Federico; Philadelphia. PA; Political Parties and Organizations; Political Representation; *Politics; San Antonio, TX; Urban Communities.

2909 Nelson, Candace and Tienda, Marta. The structuring of Hispanic ethnicity: historical and contemporary perspectives. ETHNIC AND RACIAL STUDIES, Vol. 8, no. 1 (January 1985), p. 49-74. English. **DESCR**: Cultural Characteristics; *Identity; Immigrants.

2910 Olarte, Silvia W. and Masnik, Ruth. Benefits of long-term group therapy for disadvantaged Hispanic outpatients. HOSPITAL AND COMMUNITY PSYCHIATRY, Vol. 36, no. 10 (October 1985), p. 1093-1097. English. **DESCR**: Metropolitan Hospital. New York, NY; New York, NY; Psychotherapy; Sex Roles; *Women.

2911 Perez, Renato E. Chicago: Hispanic melting pot. VISTA, Vol. 1, no. 3 (November 3, 1985), p. 20. English. **DESCR**: Camacho, Eduardo; Casuso, Jorge; *Chicago, IL; Cultural Pluralism; HISPANICS IN CHICAGO; *Population.

2912 Rodriguez, Nestor. Undocumented Central Americans in Houston: diverse populations. INTERNATIONAL MIGRATION REVIEW, Vol. 21, no. 1 (Spring 1987), p. 4-26. English. **DESCR**: *Central America; El Salvador; Guatemala; Honduras; *Houston, TX; Immigrants; Intergroup Relations; Latin Americans; *Political Refugees; *Undocumented Workers.

2913 Sabogal, Fabio, et al. Hispanic familism and acculturation: what changes and what doesn't? HISPANIC JOURNAL OF BEHAVIORAL SCIENCES, Vol. 9, no. 4 (December 1987), p. 397-412. English. **DESCR**: *Acculturation; Attitudes; Cultural Characteristics; Extended Family; *Family; Natural Support Systems; Values.

2914 Sonenshein, Raphe. Biracial coalition politics in Los Angeles. P.S. [AMERICAN POLITICAL SCIENCE ASSOCIATION], Vol. 19, no. 3 (Summer 1986), p. 582-590. English. **DESCR**: Blacks; Bradley, Tom; Browning, Rufus P.; *Intergroup Relations; *Los Angeles, CA; Marshall, Dale Rogers; Political Parties and Organizations; *Politics; PROTEST IS NOT ENOUGH: THE STRUGGLE OF BLACKS AND HISPANICS FOR EQUALITY IN URBAN POLITICS; Tabb, David H.

2915 Zatz, Marjorie S. Race, ethnicity, and determinate sentencing: a new dimension to an old controversy. CRIMINOLOGY: AN INTERDISCIPLINARY JOURNAL, Vol. 22, no. 2 (May 1984), p. 147-171. English. **DESCR**: California; *Criminal Justice System; Criminology.

ETHNIC GROUPS AND THE STATE

2916 Melson, Robert. Book review of: ETHNIC GROUPS AND THE STATE. AMERICAN POLITICAL SCIENCE REVIEW, Vol. 79, no. 4 (December 1985), p. 1208-1209. English. **DESCR**: Book Reviews; Brass, Paul R.

Ethnic Identity
USE: Identity

Ethnic Stratification

2917 Massey, Douglas S. and Mullan, Brendan P. Processes of Hispanic and Black spatial assimilation. AMERICAN JOURNAL OF SOCIOLOGY, Vol. 89, no. 4 (January 1984), p. 836-873. English. **DESCR**: Assimilation; Blacks; Census; *Residential Segregation; *Social Mobility.

2918 Tienda, Marta and Guhlman, Pat. The occupational position of employed Hispanic females. LA RED/THE NET, no. 69 (June 1983), p. 2-3. English. **DESCR**: *Chicanas; Employment; *Women.

Ethnic Studies

2919 Sanchez, Rosaura. Ethnicity, ideology and academia. THE AMERICAS REVIEW, Vol. 15, no. 1 (Spring 1987), p. 80-88. English. **DESCR**: Culture; Political Ideology.

Ethnicity
USE: Identity

ETHNICITY AND FAMILY THERAPY

2920 Ramirez, Oscar. Book review of: ETHNICITY AND FAMILY THERAPY. LA RED/THE NET, no. 66 (March 1983), p. 28-30. English. **DESCR**: Book Reviews; Giordano, Joseph; McGoldrick, Monica; Pearce, John K.

ETHNICITY AND RACE IN THE U.S.A.: TOWARD THE TWENTY-FIRST CENTURY

2921 Rubin, J.H. Book review of: ETHNICITY AND RACE IN THE U.S.A.: TOWARD THE TWENTY-FIRST CENTURY. CHOICE, Vol. 23, no. 7 (March 1986), p. 1130. English. **DESCR**: Alba, Richard D.; Book Reviews.

ETHNICITY AND THE WORK FORCE

2922 Kivisto, Peter. Book review of: ETHNICITY AND THE WORK FORCE. JOURNAL OF AMERICAN ETHNIC HISTORY, Vol. 6, no. 2 (Spring 1987), p. 68-69. English. **DESCR**: Book Reviews; Laboring Classes; Van Horne, Winston A.

Ethnobotany
USE: Herbal Medicine

Ethnology

2923 Leal, Luis. Americo Paredes and modern
      Mexican American scholarship. ETHNIC
      AFFAIRS, no. 1 (Fall 1987), p. [1]-11.
      English. **DESCR**: Folklore; History;
      Literature Reviews; *Paredes, Americo.

Ethnomusicology

2924 Limon. Jose E. Texas-Mexican popular music
      and dancing: some notes on history and
      symbolic process. LATIN AMERICAN MUSIC
      REVIEW, Vol. 4, no. 2 (Fall, Winter, 1983),
      p. 229-246. English. **DESCR**: *Dance; *Music;
      *Texas; *Texas Mexicans.

2925 Pena, Manuel. From ranchero to jaiton:
      ethnicity and class in Texas-Mexican music
      (two styles in the form of a pair).
      ETHNOMUSICOLOGY, Vol. 29, no. 1 (Winter
      1985), p. 29-55. English. **DESCR**: Conjuntos;
      Musical Instruments; Villa, Beto.

Ethnopsychology
     USE: Social Psychology

Evaluation (Educational)

2926 Arenas, Soledad and Trujillo, Lorenzo A. The
      evaluation of four Head Start bilingual
      multicultural curriculum models. LA RED/THE
      NET, no. 66 (March 1983), p. 2-5. English.
      DESCR: *Bilingual Bicultural Education;
      *Cultural Pluralism; *Head Start.

2927 Padilla, Raymond V. and Montiel, Miguel. A
      general framework for action in Chicano
      higher education. LA RED/THE NET, no. 81
      (June 1964), p. 2-6. English. **DESCR**:
      *Arizona; *Higher Education.

2928 Report to the Network. LA RED/THE NET, no.
      97 (June 1986), p. 1-2. English. **DESCR**:
      California Master Plan for Higher Education;
      *Colleges and Universities; *Higher
      Education.

EVOLUCION DE LA FRONTERA NORTE

2929 Ruiz, Ramon Eduardo. Book review of:
      EVOLUCION DE LA FRONTERA NORTE. PACIFIC
      HISTORICAL REVIEW, Vol. 53, no. 3 (1984), p.
      394-395. English. **DESCR**: Book Reviews;
      Flores Caballero. Romeo R.

Ewen, Elizabeth

2930 McBride, P.W. Book review of: IMMIGRANT
      WOMEN IN THE LAND OF DOLLARS. CHOICE, Vol.
      23, no. 9 (May 1986), p. 1448. English.
      DESCR: Book Reviews; *IMMIGRANT WOMEN IN THE
      LAND OF DOLLARS: LIFE AND CULTURE ON THE
      LOWER EAST SIDE, 1890-1925.

Excavations
     USE: Anthropology

Exhibits

2931 Adams, Clinton. Book review of: ART IN NEW
      MEXICO, 1900-1945: PATHS TO TAOS AND SANTA
      FE. ARTSPACE. Vol. 10, (Fall 1986), p.
      34-36. English. **DESCR**: *Art History; *ART IN
      NEW MEXICO. 1900-1945: PATHS TO TAOS AND
      SANTA FE; Book Reviews; Eldredge, Charles;
      Schimmel, Julie; Truettner. William H.

2932 Bell, David. Report from Sante Fe:
      figuration and fantasy. ART IN AMERICA, Vol.
      72, no. 1 (January 1984), p. 31-35. English.
      DESCR: Art; *Santa Fe Festival of the Arts.

2933 Braun, Barbara. The Aztecs: art and

sacrifice. ART IN AMERICA, Vol. 72, no. 4
(April 1984), p. 126-139. English. **DESCR**:
Anthropology; *Aztecs; Gods and Dieties;
*Precolumbian Images; *Precolumbian Society;
Templo Mayor, Tenochtitlan.

2934 Goldman, Shifra. El arte hispano en Houston.
      LA COMUNIDAD, No. 361 (June 21, 1987), p.
      6-7+. Spanish. **DESCR**: *Art; *HISPANIC ART IN
      THE UNITED STATES: THIRTY CONTEMPORARY
      PAINTERS & SCULPTORS [exhibition]; Houston,
      TX.

2935 Goldman, Shifra. Escena de San Diego: texto
      y contexto. LA COMUNIDAD, No. 239 (February
      17, 1985), p. 6-7. Spanish. **DESCR**: *Art;
      Avalos, David; Chicano Park, San Diego, CA;
      *NUEVE ARTISTAS CHICANOS [exhibit]; San
      Diego, CA; Torres, Salvador Roberto; Ulloa,
      Domingo.

2936 Goldman, Shifra. Hecho en Aztlan. LA
      COMUNIDAD, No. 278 (November 17, 1985), p.
      8-9. Spanish. **DESCR**: *Art; Centro Cultural
      de la Raza, San Diego, CA; *HECHO EN AZTLAN
      [exhibit].

2937 Haley, Lindsey. Gronk y su inquietante
      concepto del arte. LA COMUNIDAD, No. 252
      (May 19, 1985), p. 2-3. Spanish. **DESCR**:
      *Artists; ASCO [art group], Los Angeles, CA;
      Biography; *Gronk (Pseud.); OFF THE STREETS
      [exhibit].

2938 Major exhibition planned by UCLA. NUESTRO,
      Vol. 11, no. 1-2 (1987), p. 6-7. English.
      DESCR: *Art; *Wight Art Gallery, University
      of California, Los Angeles.

2939 Olivares, Julian. Hispanic art in the United
      States: thirty contemporary painters &
      sculptors. THE AMERICAS REVIEW, Vol. 15, no.
      2 (Summer 1987), p. 7-10. English. **DESCR**:
      *Art; *HISPANIC ART IN THE UNITED STATES:
      THIRTY CONTEMPORARY PAINTERS & SCULPTORS
      [exhibition].

2940 Rosas, Alejandro. Siete fotografos latinos
      en Los Angeles. LA COMUNIDAD, No. 241 (March
      3, 1985), p. 4-5. Spanish. **DESCR**: Aguilar,
      Laura; Art; Avila, Adam; Callwood, Dennis
      O.; Carlos, Jesus; Miranda, Judy;
      *Photography; Self-Help Graphics, Los
      Angeles, CA; *SEVEN LATINO
      PHOTOGRAPHERS=SIETE FOTOGRAFOS LATINOS;
      Thewlis, Alan; Valverde, Richard.

2941 Saul Solache: contemporary Chicano artist.
      LATIN QUARTER, Vol. 1, no. 3 (January,
      February, 1975), p. 24-26. English. **DESCR**:
      *Artists; Mural Art; Paintings; *Solache,
      Saul.

EXPLORATIONS IN CHICANO PSYCHOLOGY

2942 Bernal, Martha E. Book review of:
      EXPLORATIONS IN CHICANO PSYCHOLOGY. LA
      RED/THE NET, no. 55 (June 1982), p. 5-6.
      English. **DESCR**: *Baron, Augustine Jr.; Book
      Reviews; *Psychology.

Extended Family

2943 Griswold del Castillo, Richard. Familism,
      the extended family and Chicanos in the
      nineteenth century. LA RED/THE NET, no. 49
      (December 1981), p. 2. English. **DESCR**:
      *Family; Los Angeles, CA; *Nineteenth
      century; San Antonio, TX; Santa Fe, NM;
      *Social History and Conditions; Tucson, AZ.

Extended Family (cont.)

2944 Ramirez, Oscar. Extended family support and mental health status among Mexicans in Detroit. LA RED/THE NET, no. 28 (March 1980), p. 2. English. **DESCR:** *Detroit, MI; Mental Health.

2945 Sabogal, Fabio, et al. Hispanic familism and acculturation: what changes and what doesn't? HISPANIC JOURNAL OF BEHAVIORAL SCIENCES, Vol. 9, no. 4 (December 1987), p. 397-412. English. **DESCR:** *Acculturation; Attitudes; Cultural Characteristics; Ethnic Groups; *Family; Natural Support Systems; Values.

2946 Tienda, Marta and Glass, Jennifer. Household structure and labor-force participation of Black, Hispanic, and white mothers. DEMOGRAPHY, Vol. 22, no. 3 (August 1985), p. 381-394. English. **DESCR:** Anglo Americans; Blacks; Chicanas; *Family; *Sex Roles; *Working Women.

Fables
   USE: Cuentos

FACE

2947 Bruce-Novoa, Juan. Book review of: FACE. VISTA, Vol. 1, no. 11 (July 6, 1986), p. 16. English. **DESCR:** Book Reviews; Pineda, Cecile.

2948 Gonzales-Berry, Erlinda. Book review of: FACE. THE AMERICAS REVIEW, Vol. 15, no. 2 (Summer 1987), p. 107-109. English. **DESCR:** Book Reviews; Pineda, Cecile.

Fairytales
   USE: Cuentos

FALCON CREST [television show]

2949 Guerrero, Dan. FALCON CREST: showcase for Hispanic talent. VISTA, Vol. 2, no. 2 (October 4, 1986), p. 12-15. English. **DESCR:** *Actors and Actresses; *Ana-Alicia; Lamas, Lorenzo; Romero, Cesar; Television.

Familia
   USE: Family

LA FAMILIA: CHICANO FAMILIES IN THE URBAN SOUTHWEST, 1848 TO THE PRESENT

2950 de Leon, Arnoldo. Book review of: LA FAMILIA. SOUTHWESTERN HISTORICAL QUARTERLY, Vol. 89, no. 4 (1986), p. 564-565. English. **DESCR:** Book Reviews; Griswold del Castillo, Richard.

2951 Driscoll, Barbara A. Book review of: LA FAMILIA. JOURNAL OF AMERICAN ETHNIC HISTORY, Vol. 7, no. 1 (Fall 1987), p. 107-109. English. **DESCR:** Book Reviews; Family; Griswold del Castillo, Richard.

2952 Everett, D.E. Book review of: LA FAMILIA. CHOICE, Vol. 22, no. 10 (June 1985), p. 1574. English. **DESCR:** Book Reviews; Griswold del Castillo, Richard.

2953 Garcia, Mario T. Book review of: LA FAMILIA. LA RED/THE NET, no. 99 (August 1986), p. 4-5. English. **DESCR:** Book Reviews; Family; Griswold del Castillo, Richard.

2954 Gonzalez, Hector Hugo. Book review of: LA FAMILIA. LECTOR, Vol. 4, no. 4-6 (1987), p. 54. English. **DESCR:** Book Reviews; Family; Griswold del Castillo, Richard.

2955 Raksin, Alex. Book review of: LA FAMILIA. LOS ANGELES TIMES BOOK REVIEW, (April 13, 1986), p. 10. English. **DESCR:** Book Reviews; Family; Griswold del Castillo, Richard.

Family

2956 Briody, Elizabeth K. Patterns of household immigration into South Texas. INTERNATIONAL MIGRATION REVIEW, Vol. 21, no. 1 (Spring 1987), p. 27-47. English. **DESCR:** Chicanas; *Immigrants; Sex Roles; *Social Mobility; *South Texas.

2957 Driscoll, Barbara A. Book review of: LA FAMILIA. JOURNAL OF AMERICAN ETHNIC HISTORY, Vol. 7, no. 1 (Fall 1987), p. 107-109. English. **DESCR:** Book Reviews; Griswold del Castillo, Richard; *LA FAMILIA: CHICANO FAMILIES IN THE URBAN SOUTHWEST, 1848 TO THE PRESENT.

2958 Families of the year. VISTA, Vol. 2, no. 2 (October 4, 1986), p. 16-18. English. **DESCR:** Aguilar, Gregorio; Aguilar, Guadalupe; Aranda, Benjamin; Aranda, Emma; *Awards; de la Rocha, Beatriz; de la Rocha, Castulo; Guzman, Ofelia; Guzman, Roberto; *Hispanic Family of the Year Award.

2959 Garcia, Mario T. Book review of: LA FAMILIA. LA RED/THE NET, no. 99 (August 1986), p. 4-5. English. **DESCR:** Book Reviews; Griswold del Castillo, Richard; *LA FAMILIA: CHICANO FAMILIES IN THE URBAN SOUTHWEST, 1848 TO THE PRESENT.

2960 Gonzalez, Hector Hugo. Book review of: LA FAMILIA. LECTOR, Vol. 4, no. 4-6 (1987), p. 54. English. **DESCR:** Book Reviews; Griswold del Castillo, Richard; *LA FAMILIA: CHICANO FAMILIES IN THE URBAN SOUTHWEST, 1848 TO THE PRESENT.

2961 Griswold del Castillo, Richard. Familism, the extended family and Chicanos in the nineteenth century. LA RED/THE NET, no. 49 (December 1981), p. 2. English. **DESCR:** *Extended Family; Los Angeles, CA; *Nineteenth century; San Antonio, TX; Santa Fe, NM; *Social History and Conditions; Tucson, AZ.

2962 LeVine, Sarah Ethel; Correa, Clara Sunderland; and Uribe, F. Medardo Tapia. The marital morality of Mexican women--an urban study. JOURNAL OF ANTHROPOLOGICAL RESEARCH, Vol. 42, no. 2 (Summer 1986), p. 183-202. English. **DESCR:** Los Robles, Cuernavaca, Morelos, Mexico; *Machismo; Marriage; Parent and Child Relationships; *Sex Roles; *Women Men Relations.

2963 Miranda, Gloria E. Hispano-Mexican childrearing practices in pre-American Santa Barbara. SOUTHERN CALIFORNIA QUARTERLY, Vol. 65, no. 4 (Winter 1983), p. 307-320. English. **DESCR:** *Children; Cultural Characteristics; History; *Parenting; *Santa Barbara, CA; Socialization.

2964 Nieto, Sonia. Who's afraid of bilingual parents? BILINGUAL REVIEW, Vol. 12, no. 3 (September. December, 1985), p. 179-189. English. **DESCR:** *Bilingual Bicultural Education; *Community School Relationships; *Parent and Child Relationships; Teacher Training.

Family (cont.)

2965 Raksin, Alex. Book review of: LA FAMILIA. LOS ANGELES TIMES BOOK REVIEW, (April 13, 1986), p. 10. English. **DESCR:** Book Reviews; Griswold del Castillo, Richard; *LA FAMILIA: CHICANO FAMILIES IN THE URBAN SOUTHWEST, 1848 TO THE PRESENT.

2966 Sabogal, Fabio, et al. Hispanic familism and acculturation: what changes and what doesn't? HISPANIC JOURNAL OF BEHAVIORAL SCIENCES, Vol. 9, no. 4 (December 1987), p. 397-412. English. **DESCR:** *Acculturation; Attitudes; Cultural Characteristics; Ethnic Groups; Extended Family; Natural Support Systems; Values.

2967 Tienda, Marta and Glass, Jennifer. Household structure and labor-force participation of Black, Hispanic, and white mothers. DEMOGRAPHY, Vol. 22, no. 3 (August 1985), p. 381-394. English. **DESCR:** Anglo Americans; Blacks; Chicanas; *Extended Family; *Sex Roles; *Working Women.

2968 Ybarra, Lea. Empirical and theoretical developments in the study of Chicano families. LA RED/THE NET, no. 52 (March 1982), p. 7-9. English. **DESCR:** Machismo.

FAMILY INSTALLMENTS: MEMORIES OF GROWING UP HISPANIC

2969 Ortiz, Vilma. Book review of: FAMILY INSTALLMENTS: MEMORIES OF GROWING UP HISPANIC. LA RED/THE NET, no. 76 (January 1984), p. 7-9. English. **DESCR:** Book Reviews; *Rivera, Edward.

Family Planning

2970 Jorgensen, Stephen R. and Adams, Russell P. Family planning needs and behavior of Mexican American women: a study of health care professionals and their clientele. HISPANIC JOURNAL OF BEHAVIORAL SCIENCES, Vol. 9, no. 3 (September 1987), p. 265-286. English. **DESCR:** Acculturation; *Attitudes; Birth Control; *Chicanas; *Cultural Characteristics; Fertility; Public Health; Stereotypes; Sterilization.

FAMOUS ALL OVER TOWN

2971 Flores, Lauro. Book review of: EL PUEBLO: THE GALLEGOS FAMILY'S JOURNEY 1503-1980. MINNESOTA REVIEW, no. 22 (1984), p. 145-148. English. **DESCR:** Book Reviews; Bruce-Novoa, Juan; *CHICANO POETRY: A RESPONSE TO CHAOS; *EL PUEBLO: THE GALLEGOS FAMILY'S AMERICAN JOURNEY 1503-1980; James, Dan; Johansen, Bruce; Maestas, Roberto.

2972 Lewis, Marvin A.; Striano, Ron; and Hiura, Barbara L. Chicano ethnicity and aging [and critiques]. EXPLORATIONS IN ETHNIC STUDIES, Vol. 8, no. 2 (July 1985), p. 35-45. English. **DESCR:** Anaya, Rudolfo A.; *Ancianos; BLESS ME, ULTIMA; Curanderas; Identity; James, Dan; Literary Criticism; Literature.

Farm Labor Organizing Commmittee (FLOC)

2973 Boycotts revisited: Campbell's concedes to farm worker campaign. DOLLARS AND SENSE, (July, August, 1986), p. 12-14, 18. English. **DESCR:** Boycotts; California; Campbell Soup Co.; Farm Workers; *Labor Disputes; Labor Unions; Michigan; Ohio; Strikes and Lockouts; United Farmworkers of America (UFW).

2974 Sanders, Bob. Boycott Campbell's: Ohio farmworkers take it to the top. DOLLARS AND SENSE, no. 92 (December 1983), p. 16-18. English. **DESCR:** Boycotts; Campbell Soup Co.; Chavez, Cesar E.; Farm Workers; Guevas, Fernando; *Labor Disputes; Labor Unions; Ohio; Strikes and Lockouts; United Farmworkers of America (UFW).

Farm Women

USE: Working Women

Farm Workers

2975 Barger, W.K. California public endorses the United Farm Workers. LA RED/THE NET, No. 105 (February 1987), p. 4-6. English. **DESCR:** *Agricultural Labor Unions; California; *Public Opinion; *United Farmworkers of America (UFW).

2976 Barger, W.K. and Reza, Ernesto. Midwestern farmworkers and the farm labor movement. LA RED/THE NET, no. 78 (March 1984), p. 2-7. English. **DESCR:** *Midwestern States; Migrant Labor; Surveys.

2977 Barger, W.K. Public attitudes towards Mexican-American farmworkers in the Midwest. LA RED/THE NET, no. 63 (January 1983), p. 2-4. English. **DESCR:** Attitudes; *Midwestern States; *Public Opinion.

2978 Barger, W.K. Views of California farmworkers regarding the farm labor movement. LA RED/THE NET, no. 91 (October 1985), p. 3-5. English. **DESCR:** Agricultural Labor Unions; Attitudes; California; *United Farmworkers of America (UFW).

2979 Barton, Amy E. Women farmworkers: their workplace and capitalist patriarchy. REVISTA MUJERES, Vol. 3, no. 2 (June 1986), p. 11-13. English. **DESCR:** Capitalism; *Chicanas; Discrimination; Sexism.

2980 Bennett, Jonathan A. At last, farmworkers are allowed clean water. GUARDIAN, Vol. 39, no. 20 (February 18, 1987), p. 9. English. **DESCR:** Migrant Labor; *Occupational Hazards.

2981 Bernal, Esmeralda. ...And she became a proletarian. REVISTA MUJERES, Vol. 2, no. 2 (June 1985), p. 38-42. English. **DESCR:** Biography.

2982 Boycotts revisited: Campbell's concedes to farm worker campaign. DOLLARS AND SENSE, (July, August, 1986), p. 12-14, 18. English. **DESCR:** Boycotts; California; Campbell Soup Co.; Farm Labor Organizing Commmittee (FLOC); *Labor Disputes; Labor Unions; Michigan; Ohio; Strikes and Lockouts; United Farmworkers of America (UFW).

2983 Cisneros, Henry. Mexico's poorest are heading North. AKWESASNE NOTES, Vol. 18, no. 4 (Summer 1986), p. 7. English. **DESCR:** Alfaro, Victor Clark; Centro de Promocion Popular Urbana, Tijuana, Baja California, Mexico; Kearney, Michael; Mexico; Mixtec Indians; *Undocumented Workers.

2984 Echaveste, Beatrice and Huerta, Dolores. In the shadow of the eagle: Huerta=A la sombra del aguila: Huerta. AMERICAS 2001, Vol. 1, no. 3 (November, December, 1987), p. 26-30. Bilingual. **DESCR:** Agricultural Labor Unions; Boycotts; Chicanas; *Huerta, Dolores; *United Farmworkers of America (UFW).

Farm Workers (cont.)

2985 Garcia R., Roberto. Oda a Cucamonga. BILINGUAL REVIEW, Vol. 11, no. 3 (September, December. 1984), p. 47-48. Spanish. **DESCR:** Braceros; *Poems.

2986 Gonzales, Juan L., Jr. Book review of: FARM WORKERS, AGRIBUSINESS, AND THE STATE. LABOR HISTORY, Vol. 27, no. 4 (Fall 1986), p. 587-588. English. **DESCR:** Book Reviews; *FARMWORKERS, AGRIBUSINESS, AND THE STATE; Majka, Linda C.; Majka, Theo J.

2987 Lopez-Flores, Beatriz. Testimonios de las campesinas de Pantasma. REVISTA MUJERES, Vol. 2, no. 2 (June 1985), p. 7-9. Spanish. **DESCR:** *Nicaragua; *Oral History.

2988 O'Donnell. Patrick J. A preliminary report on the incidence of gestational diabetes in a Hispanic migrant population. MIGRATION WORLD MAGAZINE. Vol. 15, no. 1 (), p. 27-30. English. **DESCR:** *Diabetes; *Migrant Labor; *Public Health.

2989 Orozco, Aurora E. Un dia en la pisca de algodon. REVISTA MUJERES, Vol. 3, no. 2 (June 1986), p. 30. Spanish. **DESCR:** Biography; *Chicanas.

2990 Rips, Geoffrey. Civil rights and wrongs. TEXAS OBSERVOR. Vol. 76, (December 14, 1984), p. 49-55. English. **DESCR:** Briscoe, Dolph, Jr., Governor of Texas; *Civil Rights; *Hidalgo County, TX; La Raza Unida Party; Miller, C.L.; Segregation and Desegregation; Texas Farmworkers' Union; Voting Rights.

2991 Romero, Mary and Margolis, Eric. Tending the beets: campesinas and the Great Western Sugar Company. REVISTA MUJERES, Vol. 2, no. 2 (June 1985), p. 17-27. English. **DESCR:** *Chicanas; Food Industry; *Great Western Sugar Company, Hudson, CO.

2992 Sanders, Bob. Boycott Campbell's: Ohio farmworkers take it to the top. DOLLARS AND SENSE, no. 92 (December 1983), p. 16-18. English. **DESCR:** Boycotts; Campbell Soup Co.; Chavez, Cesar E.; Farm Labor Organizing Commmittee (FLOC); Guevas, Fernando; *Labor Disputes; Labor Unions; Ohio; Strikes and Lockouts; United Farmworkers of America (UFW).

FARMWORKERS, AGRIBUSINESS, AND THE STATE

2993 Gonzales, Juan L., Jr. Book review of: FARM WORKERS, AGRIBUSINESS, AND THE STATE. LABOR HISTORY, Vol. 27, no. 4 (Fall 1986), p. 587-588. English. **DESCR:** Book Reviews; Farm Workers; Majka, Linda C.; Majka, Theo J.

2994 Reisler. Mark. Book review of: FARM WORKERS, AGRIBUSINESS, AND THE STATE. PACIFIC HISTORICAL REVIEW, Vol. 53, no. 3 (1984), p. 405-407. English. **DESCR:** Book Reviews; Majka, Linda C.; Majka, Theo J.

Farragut High School, Chicago, IL

2995 Kuner. Charles. Peer group counseling: applied psychology in the high school. CURRICULUM REVIEW, Vol. 23, no. 1 (February 1984), p. 89-92. English. **DESCR:** Chicago, IL; Counseling (Educational); *Counseling (Psychological); Education; Students.

Fashion

2996 Remas. Theodora A. Hot weather antidote: the cool guayabera. VISTA, Vol. 1, no. 10 (June

8, 1986), p. 24-25. English.

2997 Reyes, Sonia. Hispanic models pursue high stakes fashion. VISTA, Vol. 1, no. 2 (October 5, 1985), p. 6-9. English. **DESCR:** Apodaca, Roseanne; Careers; Dominguez, Peter; Jerez, Alicia; Soto, Talisa.

2998 Stone, Eric. The daring designs of Elena Valencia. VISTA, Vol. 1, no. 9 (May 3, 1986), p. 6-8. English. **DESCR:** Biography; Chicanas; La Blanca [fashion label]; *Valencia, Elena.

Fatalism

USE: Locus of Control

FAULTLINE [novel]

2999 Bruce-Novoa, Juan. Homosexuality and the Chicano novel. CONFLUENCIA, Vol. 2, no. 1 (Fall 1986), p. 69-77. English. **DESCR:** Acosta, Oscar Zeta; CITY OF NIGHT; *Homosexuality; Islas, Arturo; *Literary Criticism; Machismo; *Novel; Ortiz Taylor, Sheila; POCHO; Rechy, John; Salas. Floyd; SPRING FORWARD/FALL BACK; TATOO THE WICKED CROSS; THE AUTOBIOGRAPHY OF A BROWN BUFFALO; THE RAIN GOD: A DESERT TALE; THE REVOLT OF THE COCKROACH PEOPLE; Villarreal, Jose Antonio.

3000 Bruce-Novoa, Juan. Nuevo representantes de la novela chicana. LA COMUNIDAD. No. 310 (June 29, 1986), p. 6-7+. Spanish. **DESCR:** Brawley, Ernest; EL VAGO [novel]; Gonzales, Laurence; *Literary Criticism; Novel; Ortiz Taylor, Sheila; THE ALAMO TREE [novel].

Febres-Cordero [family name]

3001 Instituto Genealogico e Historico Latino-Americano. Rootsearch: Gonzalez: Febres-Cordero. VISTA, Vol. 1, no. 7 (March 2, 1986), p. 22. English. **DESCR:** Genealogy; *Gonzalez [family name]; History; *Personal Names.

Federal Aid

3002 Morales, Carlos. The controversy over bilingual education. VISTA, Vol. 1, no. 6 (February 2, 1986), p. 8-10. English. **DESCR:** *Bilingual Bicultural Education; *Bilingual Education Act of 1968; Educational Tests and Measurements; Educational Theory and Practice.

3003 Morales, Cecilio. Budget cutting and Hispanics. VISTA, Vol. 1, no. 6 (February 2, 1986), p. 22. English. **DESCR:** *Gramm-Rudman Balanced Budget Amendment; National Association of Latino Elected Officials (NALEO); National Council of La Raza (NCLR).

3004 Report to the Network. LA RED/THE NET, no. 92 (January, February, 1986), p. 1-4. English. **DESCR:** Finance; *Gramm-Rudman-Hollings Deficit Control Act (PL 99-177); *Higher Education; Reagan Administration; *School Finance.

Federal Bureau of Investigation (FBI)

3005 Gutierrez, Jose Angel. Chicanos and
     Mexicans: under surveillance: 1940 to 1980.
     RENATO ROSALDO LECTURE SERIES MONOGRAPH,
     Vol. 2, (Spring 1986), p. [29]-58. English.
     DESCR: Acuna, Rudolfo; Border Coverage
     Program (BOCOV); *Civil Rights; COINTELPRO;
     *Federal Government; History; League of
     United Latin American Citizens (LULAC);
     Mexico; Political Parties and Organizations;
     *Political Repression.

Federal Communications Commission (FCC)

3006 Broadcasters license renewal bill
     [editorial]. LATIN QUARTER, Vol. 1, no. 2
     (October 1974), p. 2,30. English. DESCR:
     *Broadcast Media.

3007 Kilgore, Julia. A risk taker. HISPANIC
     BUSINESS, Vol. 9, no. 12 (December 1987), p.
     44-47. English. DESCR: *Appointed Officials;
     Biography; Careers; *Chicanas; *Diaz Dennis,
     Patricia.

3008 Madrid, Vicente and Yepes, Maria Elena.
     National Latino Media Coalition. LATIN
     QUARTER, Vol. 1, no. 4 (July, August, 1975),
     p. 4-7. English. DESCR: Affirmative Action
     Programs; Bilingual/Bicultural Coalition on
     Mass Media; *Broadcast Media; California
     Association of Latins in Broadcasting;
     Conferences and Meetings; *National Latino
     Media Coalition (NLMC); Puerto Rican Media
     Action and Educational Council.

3009 Mass media bureau settlement would allow
     SICC to sell its stations. BROADCASTING,
     Vol. 110, no. 26 (June 30, 1986), p. 45.
     English. DESCR: Anselmo, Rene; Azcarraga
     Family; KDTV, San Francisco. CA [television
     station]; KFTV, Fresno, CA [television
     station]; KMEX, Los Angeles, CA [television
     station]; KTVW, Phoenix, AZ [television
     station]; KWEX, San Antonio, TX [television
     station]; Legal Cases; *Spanish
     International Communications Corp. (SICC);
     Spanish International Network (SIN); Spanish
     Language; Television; WLTV, Miami, FL
     [television station]; WXTV, Paterson, NJ
     [television station].

3010 Patricia Diaz Dennis. INTERCAMBIOS
     FEMENILES. Vol. 2, no. 6 (Spring 1987), p.
     8-9. English. DESCR: Appointed Officials;
     Chicanas; *Diaz Dennis, Patricia;
     Leadership; Legal Profession.

3011 SICC sale opposed. BROADCASTING, Vol. 111,
     no. 7 (August 18, 1986), p. 46-52. English.
     DESCR: Azcarraga, Emilio; First Chicago
     Venture Capital; Hallmark Cards; KFTV,
     Fresno, CA [television station]; KMEX, Los
     Angeles, CA [television station]; KWEX, San
     Antonio, TX [television station]; Legal
     Cases; *Spanish International Communications
     Corp. (SICC); Spanish Language; Tapia, Raul
     R.; Television; TVL Corp.; WLTV, Miami, FL
     [television station]; WXTV, Paterson, NJ
     [television station].

3012 SICC to sell off stations. BROADCASTING,
     Vol. 110, no. 20 (May 19, 1986), p. 79-80.
     English. DESCR: Anselmo, Rene; Fouce, Frank;
     KFTV, Fresno, CA [television station]; KMEX,
     Los Angeles, CA [television station]; KWEX,
     San Antonio, TX [television station]; Legal
     Cases; *Spanish International Communications
     Corp. (SICC); Spanish International Network
     (SIN); Spanish Language; Television; WLTV,
     Miami, FL [television station]; WXTV,
     Paterson, NJ [television station].

3013 [Untitled editorial]. LATIN QUARTER, Vol. 1,
     no. 3 (January, February, 1975), p. 2.
     English. DESCR: *Broadcast Media.

Federal Government

3014 Bixler-Marquez, Dennis J. The introduction
     of bilingual education programs--a
     collaborative approach. EDUCATION, Vol. 105,
     no. 4 (Summer 1985), p. 443-448. English.
     DESCR: *Bilingual Bicultural Education;
     Educational Theory and Practice.

3015 Gutierrez, Jose Angel. Chicanos and
     Mexicans: under surveillance: 1940 to 1980.
     RENATO ROSALDO LECTURE SERIES MONOGRAPH,
     Vol. 2, (Spring 1986), p. [29]-58. English.
     DESCR: Acuna, Rudolfo; Border Coverage
     Program (BOCOV); *Civil Rights; COINTELPRO;
     *Federal Bureau of Investigation (FBI);
     History; League of United Latin American
     Citizens (LULAC); Mexico; Political Parties
     and Organizations; *Political Repression.

3016 Rotberg, Iris C. Bilingual education policy
     in the United States. PROSPECTS: QUARTERLY
     REVIEW OF EDUCATION, Vol. 14, no. 1 (1984),
     p. 133-147. English. DESCR: *Bilingual
     Bicultural Education; *Public Policy.

Federation for American Immigration Reform (FAIR)

3017 Conner, Roger and Moreno, G. Mario. The
     Immigration Reform Law: how fair to
     Hispanics? VISTA, Vol. 2, no. 8 (April 4,
     1987), p. 12, 17, 18. English. DESCR:
     *Immigration; *Immigration Reform and
     Control Act of 1986; League of United Latin
     American Citizens (LULAC); Mexican American
     Legal Defense and Educational Fund (MALDEF).

Federation of Latin Americans for the Association of Relatives of the Detained and Disappeared (FedeFam)

3018 Alicia de Garcia's oral history=Historia
     oral de Alicia de Garcia. REVISTA MUJERES,
     Vol. 3, no. 2 (June 1986), p. 37-49.
     Spanish. DESCR: *Committee of Mothers and
     Relatives of Political Prisoners Disappeared
     and Assassinated of El Salvador "Monsenor
     Oscar Arnulfo Romero" (Comadres, El
     Salvador); Community Organizations; de
     Garcia, Alicia; *Oral History; Terrorism;
     Violence; *Women.

3019 Peace with justice. REVISTA MUJERES, Vol. 3,
     no. 2 (June 1986), p. 32-35. English.
     DESCR: *Committee of Mothers and Relatives
     of Political Prisoners Disappeared and
     Assassinated of El Salvador "Monsenor Oscar
     Arnulfo Romero" (Comadres, El Salvador);
     Community Organizations; Terrorism;
     Violence; *Women.

Fellowship
     USE: Financial Aid

Females
     USE: Chicanas

Feminism

3020 Billings, Linda M. and Alurista. In verbal
     murals: a study of Chicana herstory and
     poetry. CONFLUENCIA, Vol. 2, no. 1 (Fall
     1986), p. 60-68. English. DESCR: Candelaria,
     Cordelia; Cervantes, Lorna Dee; *Chicanas;
     Cisneros, Sandra; EMPLUMADA; History;
     Literary Criticism; *Poetry; Xelina.

Feminism (cont.)

3021 Herrera-Sobek, Maria. The politics of rape: sexual transgression in Chicana fiction. THE AMERICAS REVIEW, Vol. 15, no. 3-4 (Fall, Winter. 1987), p. 171-181. English. DESCR: *Chicanas; Cisneros, Sandra; Fiction; GIVING UP THE GHOST; *Literary Criticism; Lizarraga, Sylvia; Moraga, Cherrie; *Rape; "Red Clowns" [short story]; Sex Roles; "Silver Lake Road" [short story].

3022 Limon, Jose E. La Llorona, the third legend of greater Mexico: cultural symbols, women, and the political unconscious. RENATO ROSALDO LECTURE SERIES MONOGRAPH, Vol. 2, (Spring 1986), p. [59]-93. English. DESCR: Folklore; *La Llorona; La Virgen de Guadalupe; *Leyendas; Malinche; Mexico; *Symbolism; Women.

3023 Lomas, Clara. Libertad de no procrear: la voz de la mujer en "A una madre de nuestro tiempo" de Margarita Cota-Cardenas. REVISTA MUJERES, Vol. 2, no. 1 (January 1985), p. 30-35. Spanish. DESCR: *Chicanas; Literary Criticism; Sex Stereotypes.

3024 Longeaux y Vasquez, Enriqueta. Soy Chicana Primero. EL CUADERNO, Vol. 1, no. 1 (1971), p. 17-22. English. DESCR: *Chicanas; *Chicano Movement.

3025 Quintana. Alvina. Challenge and counter challenge: Chicana literary motifs. AGAINST THE CURRENT, Vol. 2, no. 2 (March, April, 1987), p. 25,28-32. English. DESCR: Cervantes, Lorna Dee; *Chicanas; *Literature; Moraga, Cherrie; THERE ARE NO MADMEN HERE; Valdes, Gina.

3026 Quintana, Alvina. Expanding a feminist view: challenge and counter-challenge in the relationship between women. REVISTA MUJERES, Vol. 2, no. 1 (January 1985), p. 11-18. English. DESCR: *Chicanas.

3027 Quintana, Alvina. O mama, with what's inside of me. REVISTA MUJERES, Vol. 3, no. 1 (January 1986), p. 38-40. English. DESCR: *Alarcon, Norma; *Chicanas; *Literary Criticism; Poetry; *"What Kind of Lover Have You Made Me, Mother?: Towards a Theory of Chicanas' Feminism and Cultural Identity Through Poetry" [article].

3028 Salazar-Nobles, Mary. Latinas must chart own course in workplace. VISTA, Vol. 2, no. 3 (November 2, 1986), p. 26. English. DESCR: Chicanas; Essays; Working Women.

3029 Saldivar, Jose David. Towards a Chicano poetics: the making of the Chicano subject. CONFLUENCIA, Vol. 1, no. 2 (Spring 1986), p. 10-17. English. DESCR: Corridos; *Literary Criticism; "Los vatos" [poem]; Montoya, Jose E.; *Poetry; RESTLESS SERPENTS; Rios, Alberto; WHISPERING TO FOOL THE WIND; Zamora, Bernice.

3030 Yarbro-Bejarano, Yvonne. Chicana literature from a Chicana feminist perspective. THE AMERICAS REVIEW, Vol. 15, no. 3-4 (Fall, Winter. 1987), p. 139-145. English. DESCR: *Chicanas; *Literary Criticism; Literature.

3031 Yarbro-Bejarano, Yvonne. The female subject in Chicano theater: sexuality, race, and class. THEATRE JOURNAL, Vol. 38, no. 4 (December 1986), p. 389-407. English. DESCR: *Chicanas; El Teatro Campesino; El Teatro de la Esperanza; *Malinche; *Sex Roles; *Teatro; Teatro Nacional de Aztlan (TENAZ); WIT (Women in Teatro).

Fernandez, Gigi

3032 Chavez, Lorenzo A. Tennis superstars. VISTA, Vol. 1, no. 8 (April 6, 1986), p. 14-16. English. DESCR: *Athletes; Chicanas; Fernandez, Mary Joe; *Sabatini, Gabriela; Sports; Torres, Michele; Women.

Fernandez, Herb

3033 Herb Fernandez to serve on presidential task force. HISPANIC ENGINEER, Vol. 3, no. 5 (Winter 1987), p. 15. English. DESCR: *Appointed Officials; U.S. Task Force on Women, Minorities & the Handicapped in Science and Technology.

Fernandez, Mary Joe

3034 Chavez, Lorenzo A. Tennis superstars. VISTA, Vol. 1, no. 8 (April 6, 1986), p. 14-16. English. DESCR: *Athletes; Chicanas; Fernandez, Gigi; *Sabatini, Gabriela; Sports; Torres, Michele; Women.

Fernandez-Roque v. Smith

3035 Aliens: detention in prisons. CRIMINAL LAW REPORTER, Vol. 35, no. 15 (July 18, 1984), p. 2265. English. DESCR: *Prisoners; Undocumented Workers.

Fertility

3036 Jorgensen, Stephen R. and Adams, Russell P. Family planning needs and behavior of Mexican American women: a study of health care professionals and their clientele. HISPANIC JOURNAL OF BEHAVIORAL SCIENCES, Vol. 9, no. 3 (September 1987), p. 265-286. English. DESCR: Acculturation; *Attitudes; Birth Control; *Chicanas; *Cultural Characteristics; *Family Planning; Public Health; Stereotypes; Sterilization.

Festival de la Zarzuela

3037 Holmes, John J. Zarzuela lives again. VISTA, Vol. 3, no. 3 (November 8, 1987), p. 10-12. English. DESCR: Directories; *La Zarzuela de Albuquerque; *Music; Musicals.

Festival Latino

3038 Medina, David. America's Hispanic Theater Olympics. VISTA, Vol. 1, no. 12 (August 2, 1986), p. 12-14. English. DESCR: Actors and Actresses; Dance; *Teatro.

Festivals

3039 Cardenas, Antonio J. and Cardenas, Cecilia. Traditions of Christmas. VISTA, Vol. 2, no. 4 (December 7, 1986), p. 14-17. English. DESCR: El Paso, TX; *Holidays; Miami, FL; *Reyes Magos Tradition.

3040 Cisneros, Henry. The meaning for Hispanics of 5 de Mayo. VISTA, Vol. 1, no. 9 (May 3, 1986), p. 12-13. English. DESCR: Cinco de Mayo; History.

3041 Fernandez, Celia. The biggest Hispanic fiesta in the USA. VISTA, Vol. 2, no. 7 (March 8, 1987), p. 13-15. English. DESCR: *Carnaval Miami.

3042 Gonzales, Juan. Quinto Festival de los Teatros Chicanos - Primer Encuentro Latinoamericano. LATIN QUARTER, Vol. 1, no. 2 (October 1974), p. 31-33,35. English. DESCR: *Mexico; Teatro.

Festivals (cont.)

3043 Holmes, John J. Up and away: ballooning fever grips America and Latinos have caught the bug. VISTA. Vol. 3, no. 2 (October 3, 1987), p. 16-18. English. **DESCR:** *Albuquerque International Balloon Fiesta; Sports.

3044 Machado, Melinda. Happy 500th, America. VISTA. Vol. 3, no. 2 (October 3, 1987), p. 8, 34, 35. English. **DESCR:** *Spanish Influence.

3045 Mark, Samuel. Dia de la Raza deserves wide-scoped celebration. VISTA. Vol. 2, no. 2 (October 4, 1986), p. 3. English. **DESCR:** Dia de la Raza.

3046 National Hispanic Book Fair and Writers Festival [photographs]. THE AMERICAS REVIEW, Vol. 15, no. 2 (Summer 1987), p. 40-41. **DESCR:** *National Hispanic Book Fair and Writers Festival, Houston, TX, May 30-31, 1987; Publishing Industry.

3047 Santistevan, Henry. Hispanic heritage. VISTA, Vol. 1, no. 2 (October 5, 1985), p. 18-20. English.

Fiction

3048 Herrera-Sobek, Maria. The politics of rape: sexual transgression in Chicana fiction. THE AMERICAS REVIEW, Vol. 15, no. 3-4 (Fall, Winter, 1987), p. 171-181. English. **DESCR:** *Chicanas; Cisneros, Sandra; *Feminism; GIVING UP THE GHOST; *Literary Criticism; Lizarraga, Sylvia; Moraga, Cherrie; *Rape; "Red Clowns" [short story]; Sex Roles; "Silver Lake Road" [short story].

3049 Mendez-M., Miguel. Introduccion. LLUEVE TLALOC, no. 12 (1985), p. iv. Spanish. **DESCR:** *Educational Theory and Practice; *Pima Community College, Tucson, AZ; Poetry.

3050 Mendez-M., Miguel. Introduction. LLUEVE TLALOC, no. 12 (1985), p. iv. English. **DESCR:** Educational Theory and Practice; *Pima Community College, Tucson, AZ; Poetry.

3051 Padilla, Genaro Miguel. The anti-romantic city in Chicano fiction. PUERTO DEL SOL, Vol. 23, no. 1 (1987), p. 159-169. English. **DESCR:** Acosta, Oscar Zeta; Anaya, Rudolfo A.; Lattin, Vernon E.; *Literary Criticism; Morales, Alejandro; *Urban Communities.

Field Crops
USE: Crops

FIESTA IN AZTLAN: AN ANTHOLOGY OF CHICANO POETRY

3052 Candelaria, Cordelia. Book review of: FIESTA IN AZTLAN: ANTHOLOGY OF CHICANO POETRY and FLOR Y CANTO IV AND V. LA RED/THE NET, no. 62 (December 1982), p. 6-9. English. **DESCR:** Book Reviews; Empringham, Toni; *FLOR Y CANTO IV AND V: AN ANTHOLOGY OF CHICANO LITERATURE FROM THE FESTIVALS HELD IN ALBUQUERQUE, NEW MEXICO; Poetry.

Fiestas

3053 Catalano, Julia. Pinata. VISTA, Vol. 2, no. 10 (June 7, 1987), p. 14. English. **DESCR:** *Children's Television; History; THE $25,000 PINATA [television show].

Fiestas Patrias

3054 Hazen-Hammond, Susan and Fuss, Eduardo. Vivan las celebraciones. ARIZONA HIGHWAYS,

Vol. 63, no. 8 (August 1987), p. 35-45. English. **DESCR:** Cinco de Mayo; Cultural Customs; Dia de los Muertos; Dieciseis de Septiembre; *Holidays; La Virgen de Guadalupe; Las Posadas.

THE FIFTH HORSEMAN

3055 Lomeli, Francisco A. En la voragine del destino [book review of: THE FIFTH HORSEMAN]. LA COMUNIDAD, No. 258 (June 30, 1985), p. 12-13. Spanish. **DESCR:** Book Reviews; *Literary Criticism; Villarreal, Jose Antonio.

Film Reviews

3056 Aceves Madrid, Vicente. Film review of: FREEBIE AND THE BEAN. LATIN QUARTER, Vol. 1, no. 3 (January, February, 1975), p. 22-23. English. **DESCR:** FREEBIE AND THE BEAN; Stereotypes; Violence.

3057 Chavez, Andres. Film review of: BRING ME THE HEAD OF ALFREDO GARCIA. LATIN QUARTER, Vol. 1, no. 2 (October 1974), p. 36. English. **DESCR:** *BRING ME THE HEAD OF ALFREDO GARCIA; Peckinpah, Sam; Violence.

3058 Chavez, Andres. Film review of: LENNY. LATIN QUARTER, Vol. 1, no. 4 (July, August, 1975), p. 32-33. English. **DESCR:** *Bruce, Lenny; Humor; LENNY [film].

3059 Kael, Pauline. The current cinema: siblings and cyborgs. NEW YORKER, (August 10, 1987), p. 70-73. English. **DESCR:** *LA BAMBA [film]; Valens, Ritchie [stage name for Richard Valenzuela].

3060 Mindiola, Tatcho, Jr. Film review of: THE BALLAD OF GREGORIO CORTEZ. LA RED/THE NET, no. 80 (May 1984), p. 11-17. English. **DESCR:** *BALLAD OF GREGORIO CORTEZ [film]; SEGUIN [movie]; ZOOT SUIT [film].

3061 Perez, Joel Oseas. EL NORTE: imagenes peyorativas de Mexico y los Chicanos. CHIRICU, Vol. 5, no. 1 (1987), p. 13-21. Spanish. **DESCR:** *EL NORTE [film]; Nava, Greg; Thomas, Anna.

3062 Sanchez, Ricardo. FRIDA: una pelicula de imagen y poder [film review]. REVISTA MUJERES, Vol. 3, no. 2 (June 1986), p. 74-75. Spanish. **DESCR:** *FRIDA: NATURALEZA VIDA [film]; Kahlo, Frida; Leduc, Paul.

Films

3063 Barrios, Greg. Efrain Gutierrez y el nuevo cine chicano. LA COMUNIDAD, No. 265 (August 18, 1985), p. 3. Spanish. **DESCR:** Biography; *Gutierrez, Efrain; PLEASE DON'T BURY ME ALIVE [film].

3064 Beale, Stephen and Valdez, Luis. Connecting with the American experience: an interview with Luis Valdez. HISPANIC BUSINESS, Vol. 9, no. 7 (July 1987), p. 10-13. English. **DESCR:** Biography; LA BAMBA [film]; Stereotypes; Teatro; *Valdez, Luis.

3065 Beale, Stephen. A turning point in Hollywood. HISPANIC BUSINESS, Vol. 9, no. 7 (July 1987), p. 20-24, 36. English. **DESCR:** LA BAMBA [film]; *Marketing; Spanish Language; Stereotypes; THE MILAGRO BEANFIELD WAR [film].

Films (cont.)

3066 Callahan, Jaime M. LATINO: un nuevo concepto de cine. LA COMUNIDAD, No. 279 (November 24, 1985), p. 2-3. Spanish. **DESCR:** Identity; *LATINO [film]; Military; Military Service; Wexler, Haskell.

3067 Chavez, Lorenzo A. La Bamba. VISTA, Vol. 2, no. 11 (July 5, 1987), p. 12-13. English. **DESCR:** *Actors and Actresses; Biography; De Soto, Rosana; LA BAMBA [film]; *Morales, Esai; Pena. Elizabeth; Phillips, Lou Diamond.

3068 Delpar. Helen. Goodbye to the greaser: Mexico, the MPPDA, and derogatory films, 1922-1926. JOURNAL OF POPULAR FILM AND TELEVISION, no. 12 (Spring 1984), p. 34-41. English. **DESCR:** *Motion Picture Producers and Distributors of America (MPPDA); Stereotypes.

3069 Garcia, Philip. Book review of: CHICANO CINEMA. LA RED/THE NET, no. 91 (October 1985), p. 13-14. English. **DESCR:** Book Reviews; *CHICANO CINEMA: RESEARCH, REVIEWS AND RESOURCES; Keller. Gary D.

3070 Garcia, Philip. Book review of: THE LATIN IMAGE IN AMERICAN FILM. LA RED/THE NET, no. 50 (January 1982), p. 11-12. English. **DESCR:** *THE LATIN IMAGE IN AMERICAN FILM; *Woll. Allen L.

3071 Guerrero, Dan. Tanya Sandoval: death-defying stunts are all in her day's work. VISTA, Vol. 2, no. 6 (February 8, 1987), p. 21. English. **DESCR:** *Actors and Actresses; *Sandoval, Tanya.

3072 Guevara. Ruben. Richard "Cheech" Marin. AMERICAS 2001, Vol. 1, no. 1 (June, July, 1987), p. 18-21. Bilingual. **DESCR:** *Actors and Actresses; *BORN IN EAST L.A. [film]; Immigration; *Marin, Richard "Cheech"; Undocumented Workers.

3073 Guevara, Ruben and Blades, Ruben. Ruben Blades: music, love and revolution=Ruben Blades: musica, amor y revolucion. AMERICAS 2001, Vol. 1, no. 2 (September, October, 1987), p. 26-29,31. Bilingual. **DESCR:** Biography; *Blades, Ruben; *Musicians; Recording Industry.

3074 Jimenez, Luis. Cambia la imagen del latino en Hollywood. LA COMUNIDAD, No. 255 (June 9, 1985), p. 14-15. Spanish. **DESCR:** Discrimination; Employment; *Hispanic Academy of Media Arts and Sciences (HAMAS); *Mass Media; Organizations; Reyna, Phil.

3075 Kendall. Robert. Electric excitement at the 17th Annual Golden Eagle Awards ceremony sponsored by Nosotros at the Beverly Hilton Hotel. HISPANIC TIMES. Vol. 8, no. 5 (October, November, 1987), p. 32. English. **DESCR:** *Awards; *Nosotros Golden Eagle Awards; Television.

3076 Kwain, Constance. Searching for Hispanic talent. VISTA, Vol. 2, no. 6 (February 8, 1987), p. 6-7. English. **DESCR:** *Actors and Actresses; American Federation of Television & Radio Artists (AFTRA); *Business Enterprises; Myrna Salazar and Associates, Inc.; Navas, Trina; Salazar, Myrna; Screen Actors Guild; Television.

3077 Latino culture making strides in film. HISPANIC TIMES, Vol. 8, no. 3 (May, June, 1987), p. 38. English. **DESCR:** Kansas; *Ramos, Mario.

3078 Martin, Laura. Language form and language function in ZOOT SUIT and THE BORDER: a contribution to the analysis of the role of foreign language in film. STUDIES IN LATIN AMERICAN POPULAR CULTURE, Vol. 3, (1984), p. 57-69. English. **DESCR:** Language Usage; Spanish Language; THE BORDER [film]; *ZOOT SUIT [film].

3079 Muro, Rena. Walking on water. AMERICAS 2001, Vol. 1, no. 3 (November, December, 1987), p. 12-14. Bilingual. **DESCR:** Camhi, Morrie; Olmos, Edward James; STAND AND DELIVER [film]; *WALKING ON WATER [working title of film STAND AND DELIVER].

3080 Preciado, Consuelo. LA BAMBA triumphs=LA BAMBA triunfa. AMERICAS 2001, Vol. 1, no. 2 (September, October, 1987), p. 7. Bilingual. **DESCR:** *LA BAMBA [film]; Valdez, Luis; Valens, Ritchie [stage name for Richard Valenzuela].

3081 Preciado, Consuelo. CORRIDOS: the movie=CORRIDOS: la pelicula. AMERICAS 2001, Vol. 1, no. 2 (September, October, 1987), p. 5-6. Bilingual. **DESCR:** Corridos; *CORRIDOS [film]; El Teatro Campesino; Teatro; Valdez, Luis.

3082 Ramos gives special enthusiasm to original Hispanic projects. HISPANIC TIMES, Vol. 8, no. 1 (December, January, 1987), p. 48. English. **DESCR:** *Businesspeople; *Ramos, Mario.

3083 Rodriguez Flores, Juan. Esai Morales y la pasion por el arte escenico (II). LA COMUNIDAD, No. 336 (December 28, 1986), p. 2-3. Spanish. **DESCR:** Actors and Actresses; *Biography; LA BAMBA [film]; *Morales, Esai; Valdez, Luis.

3084 Rodriguez Flores, Juan. Paul Leduc, FRIDA y el otro cine que no se exhibe en Los Angeles. LA COMUNIDAD, No. 290 (February 9, 1986), p. 12-13. Spanish. **DESCR:** FRIDA: NATURALEZA VIDA [film]; History; *Kahlo, Frida; Mexico.

3085 Rodriguez Flores, Juan. Robert Redford y THE MILAGRO BEANFIELD WAR. LA COMUNIDAD. No. 328 (November 2, 1986), p. 8-11+. Spanish. **DESCR:** Actors and Actresses; *Redford, Robert; THE MILAGRO BEANFIELD WAR [film].

3086 Rodriguez Flores, Juan. Ruben Blades en busca de una nueva realidad musical (II). LA COMUNIDAD. no. 33 (November 23, 1986), p. 2-5. Spanish. **DESCR:** *Biography; *Blades, Ruben; Music.

3087 Rodriguez Flores, Juan. Ruben Blades: siempre he apostado a la sensibilidad del publico. LA COMUNIDAD, No. 330 (November 16, 1986), p. 8-11. Spanish. **DESCR:** Actors and Actresses; *Biography; *Blades, Ruben; Music; THE MILAGRO BEANFIELD WAR [film].

3088 Thomson, David. The Texas that got away. FILM COMMENT. Vol. 21, no. 3 (June 1985), p. 32-35. English. **DESCR:** Actors and Actresses; Stereotypes.

3089 Trevino, Jesus Salvador. Chicano cinema overview. AREITO, Vol. 10, no. 37 (1984), p. 40-43. English. **DESCR:** BALLAD OF GREGORIO CORTEZ [film]; Discrimination in Employment; Television.

Films (cont.)

3090 Trevino, Jesus Salvador. Latino portrayals
in film and television. JUMP CUT, no. 30
(March 1985), p. 14. English. **DESCR:**
Discrimination; *Stereotypes.

Finance

3091 Clair, Robert T. A comparative analysis of
mature Hispanic-owned banks. ECONOMIC REVIEW
(FEDERAL RESERVE BANK OF DALLAS), (March
1985), p. 1-11. English. **DESCR:** *Banking
Industry.

3092 Report to the Network. LA RED/THE NET, no.
92 (January, February, 1986), p. 1-4.
English. **DESCR:** Federal Aid;
*Gramm-Rudman-Hollings Deficit Control Act
(PL 99-177); *Higher Education; Reagan
Administration; *School Finance.

Financial Aid

3093 Abalos, J. Victor. Paul Sandoval. VISTA,
Vol. 1, no. 4 (December 7, 1985), p. 10.
English. **DESCR:** Business Enterprises;
Denver, CO; Mile Hi Cablevision; *Sandoval,
Paul.

3094 Chavez, Lorenzo A. A brief guide to
financial aid for college-bound students.
VISTA. Vol. 2, no. 1 (September 7, 1986), p.
7. English. **DESCR:** Directories; LULAC
National Scholarship Fund; MALDEF Law School
Fellowship; National Hispanic Scholar Awards
Program; *National Hispano Scholarship Fund.

3095 Gutierrez, Daniel M. MAES Houston chapter
sponsors 3rd annual scholarship banquet.
HISPANIC TIMES, Vol. 8, no. 3 (May, June,
1987), p. 42. English. **DESCR:** Awards;
*Mexican American Engineering Society
(MAES).

3096 Gutierrez, Felix. House approves Higher
Education Act amendments. LA RED/THE NET,
no. 92 (November, December, 1985), p. 3-4.
English. **DESCR:** Educational Law and
Legislation; Educational Organizations;
*Higher Education; *Higher Education
Amendments of 1985 (H.R. 3700); Hispanic
Higher Education Coalition (HHEC).

3097 NACME scholarships at Forum '87. HISPANIC
ENGINEER, Vol. 3, no. 3 (1987), p. 14.
English. **DESCR:** *Eastman Kodak Co.; Fuentes,
Theresa; Molina, Daniel.

3098 Paikoff, Mark. National Science Foundation
Programs for minority engineers, students,
and graduate students. HISPANIC ENGINEER,
Vol. 3, no. 5 (Winter 1987), p. 45. English.
DESCR: *National Science Foundation.

3099 Recipients of Ford Foundation postdoctoral
fellowships for minorities have been
announced. LA RED/THE NET, no. 99 (August
1986), p. 10. English. **DESCR:** Awards; *Ford
Foundation Postdoctoral Fellowships for
Minorities Program; Higher Education.

3100 Rifkin, Jane M. The Lil' Scholars:
responding to a tragedy in the noblest way!
HISPANIC TIMES, Vol. 8, no. 5 (October,
November, 1987), p. 9. English. **DESCR:** *Car
Clubs; *Lil' Scholars [car club], Pasadena,
CA.

3101 Student financial aid: Hispanic access and
packaging policies. LA RED/THE NET, no. 51
(February 1982), p. 2-3. English.

First Chicago Venture Capital

3102 SICC sale opposed. BROADCASTING, Vol. 111,
no. 7 (August 18, 1986), p. 46-52. English.
DESCR: Azcarraga, Emilio; Federal
Communications Commission (FCC); Hallmark
Cards; KFTV, Fresno, CA [television
station]; KMEX, Los Angeles, CA [television
station]; KWEX, San Antonio, TX [television
station]; Legal Cases; *Spanish
International Communications Corp. (SICC);
Spanish Language; Tapia, Raul R.;
Television; TVL Corp.; WLTV, Miami, FL
[television station]; WXTV, Paterson, NJ
[television station].

3103 SICC sells TVs for $301.5 million.
BROADCASTING, Vol. 111, no. 4 (July 28,
1986), p. 91-92. English. **DESCR:** Azcarraga,
Emilio; Hallmark Cards; KFTV, Fresno, CA
[television station]; KMEX, Los Angeles, CA
[television station]; KWEX, San Antonio, TX
[television station]; Legal Cases; *Spanish
International Communications Corp. (SICC);
Spanish International Network (SIN); Spanish
Language; Television; Villanueva, Daniel;
WLTV, Miami, FL [television station]; WXTV,
Paterson, NJ [television station].

Fishman, Joshua A.

3104 Nieto, Sonia. Book review of: BILINGUAL
EDUCATION FOR HISPANIC STUDENTS IN THE
UNITED STATES. INTERRACIAL BOOKS FOR
CHILDREN, Vol. 17, no. 3-4 (1986), p. 29-30.
English. **DESCR:** *BILINGUAL EDUCATION FOR
HISPANIC STUDENTS IN THE UNITED STATES; Book
Reviews; Keller, Gary D.

FLOR Y CANTO IV AND V: AN ANTHOLOGY OF CHICANO LITERATURE FROM THE FESTIVALS HELD IN ALBUQUERQUE, NEW MEXICO

3105 Candelaria, Cordelia. Book review of: FIESTA
IN AZTLAN: ANTHOLOGY OF CHICANO POETRY and
FLOR Y CANTO IV AND V. LA RED/THE NET, no.
62 (December 1982), p. 6-9. English. **DESCR:**
Book Reviews; Empringham, Toni ; *FIESTA IN
AZTLAN: AN ANTHOLOGY OF CHICANO POETRY;
Poetry.

Flores, Angel

3106 Castillo-Speed, Lillian. Chicana/Latina
literature and criticism: reviews of recent
books. WLW JOURNAL, Vol. 11, no. 3
(September 1987), p. 1-4. English. **DESCR:**
Andrews, Lynn V.; *Book Reviews; BORDERS;
Chavez, Denise; *Chicanas; CONTEMPORARY
CHICANA POETRY: A CRITICAL APPROACH TO AN
EMERGING LITERATURE; Flores, Kate; JAGUAR
WOMAN; Mora, Pat; Sanchez, Marta Ester;
Tafolla, Carmen; THE DEFIANT MUSE: HISPANIC
FEMINIST POEMS FROM THE MIDDLE AGES TO THE
PRESENT; THE LAST OF THE MENU GIRLS; TO
SPLIT A HUMAN: MITOS, MACHOS Y LA MUJER
CHICANA; Vigil-Pinon, Evangelina; WOMAN OF
HER WORD: HISPANIC WOMEN WRITE.

3107 Colecchia, F. Book review of: THE DEFIANT
MUSE: HISPANIC FEMINIST POEMS FROM THE
MIDDLE AGES TO THE PRESENT. CHOICE, Vol. 24,
no. 2 (October 1986), p. 314. English.
DESCR: Book Reviews; Flores, Kate; *THE
DEFIANT MUSE: HISPANIC FEMINIST POEMS FROM
THE MIDDLE AGES TO THE PRESENT.

Flores Caballero, Romeo R.

3108 Ruiz, Ramon Eduardo. Book review of:
EVOLUCION DE LA FRONTERA NORTE. PACIFIC
HISTORICAL REVIEW, Vol. 53, no. 3 (1984), p.
394-395. English. **DESCR:** Book Reviews;
*EVOLUCION DE LA FRONTERA NORTE.

Flores [family name]

3109 Instituto Genealogico e Historico
Latino-Americano. Rootsearch: Beltran:
Flores: Gomez. VISTA, Vol. 2, no. 11 (May 7,
1987), p. 22. English. **DESCR:** *Beltran
[family name]; Genealogy; *Gomez [family
name]; History; *Personal Names.

Flores, Frank

3110 Beale, Stephen. CEOs. HISPANIC BUSINESS,
Vol. 9, no. 4 (April 1987), p. 20-37, 52.
English. **DESCR:** Alvarez, Roberto; Batarse,
Anthony A.; Biography; Business Enterprises;
*Businesspeople; Carlo, Nelson; Estrada,
Anthony; Fullana, Jaime, Jr.; Hernandez,
George; *Management; Ortega, James; Quirch,
Guillermo; Ruiz, Roberto; Santa Maria,
Yvonne Z.; Sugranes, Rosa; Tamaya, Carlos;
Young, Paul H., Jr.

Flores, Kate

3111 Castillo-Speed, Lillian. Chicana/Latina
literature and criticism: reviews of recent
books. WLW JOURNAL, Vol. 11, no. 3
(September 1987), p. 1-4. English. **DESCR:**
Andrews, Lynn V.; *Book Reviews; BORDERS;
Chavez, Denise; *Chicanas; CONTEMPORARY
CHICANA POETRY: A CRITICAL APPROACH TO AN
EMERGING LITERATURE; Flores, Angel; JAGUAR
WOMAN; Mora, Pat; Sanchez, Marta Ester;
Tafolla, Carmen; THE DEFIANT MUSE: HISPANIC
FEMINIST POEMS FROM THE MIDDLE AGES TO THE
PRESENT; THE LAST OF THE MENU GIRLS; TO
SPLIT A HUMAN: MITOS, MACHOS Y LA MUJER
CHICANA; Vigil-Pinon, Evangelina; WOMAN OF
HER WORD: HISPANIC WOMEN WRITE.

3112 Colecchia, F. Book review of: THE DEFIANT
MUSE: HISPANIC FEMINIST POEMS FROM THE
MIDDLE AGES TO THE PRESENT. CHOICE, Vol. 24,
no. 2 (October 1986), p. 314. English.
DESCR: Book Reviews; Flores, Angel; *THE
DEFIANT MUSE: HISPANIC FEMINIST POEMS FROM
THE MIDDLE AGES TO THE PRESENT.

Flores Magon, Ricardo

3113 Escobar, Edward J. Mexican revolutionaries
and the Los Angeles police: harassment of
the Partido Liberal Mexicano, 1907-1910.
AZTLAN, Vol. 17, no. 1 (Spring 1986), p.
1-46. English. **DESCR:** Civil Rights;
Gutierrez de Lara, Lazaro; Los Angeles, CA;
*Los Angeles Police Department; *Partido
Liberal Mexicano (PLM); *Police; Police
Brutality; Political Repression; Rico,
Louis; Rico, Thomas; Talamantes, Felipe;
United States-Mexico Relations.

Flores, Maria

3114 Chabran, Richard. Book review of: MEXICAN
AMERICAN ARCHIVES AT THE BENSON COLLECTION:
A GUIDE FOR USERS. LA RED/THE NET, no. 52
(March 1982), p. 6-7. English. **DESCR:**
Archives; Book Reviews; *Gutierrez-Witt,
Laura; *MEXICAN AMERICAN ARCHIVES AT THE
BENSON COLLECTION.

Flores, Tom

3115 Quintana, Al. Gaining yardage in football.
VISTA, Vol. 1, no. 2 (October 5, 1985), p.
10-11. English. **DESCR:** *Athletes; Casillas,
Tony; Sports.

Florida

3116 Perez, Renato E. A governor named Martinez.
VISTA, Vol. 2, no. 5 (January 4, 1987), p.
10-11. English. **DESCR:** Biography; *Elected
Officials; *Martinez, Bob.

Florida International University

3117 Mellado, Carmela. Mitch Maidique. HISPANIC
ENGINEER, Vol. 3, no. 5 (Winter 1987), p.
34-36. English. **DESCR:** *Biography;
Educational Administration; *Maidique,
Mitch.

Folk Art

3118 Cox, Charlene B. Motivos artisticos.
AMERICAS, Vol. 37, no. 1 (January, February,
1985), p. 2-5, 64. Spanish. **DESCR:**
*Arreguin, Alfredo; *Artists; *Mexican Art;
Paintings.

3119 Gambrell, Jamey. Texas: state of the art.
ART IN AMERICA, Vol. 75, no. 3 (March 1987),
p. 114-131+. English. **DESCR:** *Art; Art
Galleries; Art Organizations and Groups;
*Artists; Dia de los Muertos; Mexican Art;
Texas.

3120 Griffith, James S. The Magdalena holy
picture: religious folk art in two cultures.
NEW YORK FOLKLORE QUARTERLY, Vol. 8, no. 3-4
(Winter 1982), p. 71-82. English. **DESCR:**
*Magdalena de Kino, Mexico; *Religious Art.

Folk Dancing
USE: Dance

Folk Drama

3121 Igo, John N., Jr. Los Pastores: a
triple-tradition. JOURNAL OF POPULAR
CULTURE, Vol. 19, no. 3 (Winter 1985), p.
131-138. English. **DESCR:** Christmas; Cultural
Customs; *Los Pastores [folk drama].

**THE FOLK HEALER: THE MEXICAN-AMERICAN TRADITION OF
CURANDERISMO**

3122 Watts, Jake. Book review of: THE FOLK
HEALER. LECTOR, Vol. 4, no. 1-3 (1986), p.
[63-64]. English. **DESCR:** Book Reviews;
Torres, Eliseo.

Folk Medicine

3123 Gomez, Efrain A. and Gomez, Gerda E. Folk
healing among Hispanic Americans. PUBLIC
HEALTH NURSING, Vol. 2, no. 4 (December
1985), p. 245-249. English. **DESCR:**
Curanderismo; Herbal Medicine.

3124 Graham, Joe S. Folk medicine and
intra-cultural diversity among West Texas
Americans. WESTERN FOLKLORE, Vol. 44, no. 3
(July 1985), p. 168-193. English. **DESCR:**
Attitudes; *West Texas.

3125 Newquist, Deborah. The health care barrier
model: toward analyzing the underutilization
of health care by older Mexican-Americans.
ANTHROPOLOGY UCLA, Vol. 14, (1985), p.
1-12. English. **DESCR:** *Ancianos; *Cultural
Characteristics; Discrimination; *Medical
Care; Medical Clinics; *Public Health.

Folk Medicine (cont.)

3126 Poma, Pedro A. A dangerous folk therapy.
NATIONAL MEDICAL ASSOCIATION JOURNAL, Vol.
76, no. 4 (April 1984), p. 387-389. English.
DESCR: Children; *Lead Poisoning.

Folklife
USE: Cultural Customs

Folklore

3127 Anaya, Rudolfo A. Book review of: THE
FOLKLORE OF SPAIN IN THE AMERICAN SOUTHWEST.
NEW MEXICO HISTORICAL REVIEW, Vol. 62, no. 3
(July 1987), p. 313-314. English. **DESCR:**
Book Reviews; Espinosa, Aurelio M.; *THE
FOLKLORE OF SPAIN IN THE AMERICAN SOUTHWEST:
TRADITIONAL SPANISH FOLK LITERATURE IN
NORTHERN NEW MEXICO AND SOUTHERN COLORADO.

3128 Cobos, Ruben. Cantares nuevomexicanos. EL
CUADERNO. Vol. 3, no. 2 (Spring 1974), p.
41. Spanish. **DESCR:** *Corridos.

3129 Herrera-Sobek, Maria. Book review of: AND
OTHER NEIGHBORLY NAMES: SOCIAL PROCESS AND
CULTURAL IMAGE IN TEXAS FOLKLORE. LA RED/THE
NET. no. 47 (October 1981), p. 3-4. English.
DESCR: Abrahams, Roger D.; Bauman, Richard;
Book Reviews; *Texas.

3130 Leal, Luis. Americo Paredes and modern
Mexican American scholarship. ETHNIC
AFFAIRS, no. 1 (Fall 1987), p. [1]-11.
English. **DESCR:** Ethnology; History;
Literature Reviews; *Paredes, Americo.

3131 Limon, Jose E. La Llorona, the third legend
of greater Mexico: cultural symbols, women,
and the political unconscious. RENATO
ROSALDO LECTURE SERIES MONOGRAPH, Vol. 2,
(Spring 1986), p. [59]-93. English. **DESCR:**
*Feminism; *La Llorona; La Virgen de
Guadalupe; *Leyendas; Malinche; Mexico;
*Symbolism; Women.

3132 Ramirez, Olga Najera. Greater Mexican
folklore in the United States: an annotated
bibliography. ETHNIC AFFAIRS, no. 1 (Fall
1987), p. [64]-115. English. **DESCR:**
*Bibliography.

3133 Segura, Andres. Continuidad de la tradicion
filosofica Nahuatl en las danzas de
concheros. EL CUADERNO, Vol. 3, no. 1
(Winter 1973), p. 16-33. Spanish. **DESCR:**
Concheros Xinachtli; *Precolumbian
Philosophy.

Folklore Institute at Indiana University

3134 Lowe, Virginia A.P. Presentation of ethnic
identity in Chicano theater. CHIRICU, Vol.
2, no. 1 (Spring 1980), p. 52-58. English.
DESCR: Ethnic Groups; Gary, IN; Identity;
*Teatro; *Teatro Desangano del Pueblo,
Washington Park, East Chicago, IN.

**THE FOLKLORE OF SPAIN IN THE AMERICAN SOUTHWEST:
TRADITIONAL SPANISH FOLK LITERATURE IN
NORTHERN NEW MEXICO AND SOUTHERN COLORADO**

3135 Anaya, Rudolfo A. Book review of: THE
FOLKLORE OF SPAIN IN THE AMERICAN SOUTHWEST.
NEW MEXICO HISTORICAL REVIEW, Vol. 62, no. 3
(July 1987), p. 313-314. English. **DESCR:**
Book Reviews; Espinosa, Aurelio M.;
Folklore.

3136 Gutierrez, Ramon A. Book review of: THE
FOLKLORE OF SPAIN IN THE AMERICAN SOUTHWEST.
HISPANIC AMERICAN HISTORICAL REVIEW, Vol.
67, no. 1 (February 1987), p. 149-150.

English. **DESCR:** Book Reviews; Espinosa,
Aurelio M.; Espinosa, J. Manuel.

Folktales
USE: Cuentos

Food
USE: Recipes

Food Industry

3137 Allsup, Dan. South of the brewer. VISTA,
Vol. 2, no. 10 (June 7, 1987), p. 10-12.
English. **DESCR:** History.

3138 Arreola, Daniel D. The Mexican American
cultural capital. GEOGRAPHICAL REVIEW, Vol.
77, (January 1987), p. 17-34. English.
DESCR: Conjuntos; History; Immigration; LA
PRENSA, San Antonio, TX; La Raza Unida
Party; League of United Latin American
Citizens (LULAC); Lozano, Ignacio; Mexican
American Youth Organization, San Antonio,
TX; Music; Orden Hijos de America, San
Antonio, TX; Railroads; *San Antonio, TX;
*Social History and Conditions.

3139 Catalano, Julia. Fajitas madness. VISTA,
Vol. 2, no. 4 (December 7, 1986), p. 23-24.
English. **DESCR:** *Food Practices; South
Texas.

3140 Keremitsis, Dawn. Del metate al molino: la
mujer mexicana de 1910 a 1940. HISTORIA
MEXICANA, Vol. 33, no. 2 (1983), p. 285-302.
Spanish. **DESCR:** Labor Unions; *Mexico; Sex
Roles; Strikes and Lockouts; Tortillas;
*Working Women.

3141 Noeth, Louise Ann and Sellers, Jeff M. Fast
food for thought. HISPANIC BUSINESS, Vol. 9,
no. 3 (March 1987), p. 20-24. English.
DESCR: *Business Enterprises; *Restaurants.

3142 Romero, Mary and Margolis, Eric. Tending the
beets: campesinas and the Great Western
Sugar Company. REVISTA MUJERES, Vol. 2, no.
2 (June 1985), p. 17-27. English. **DESCR:**
*Chicanas; *Farm Workers; *Great Western
Sugar Company, Hudson, CO.

Food Practices

3143 Cardenas, Antonio J. and Cardenas, Cecilia.
Asado: churrasco: piquete: barbacoa:
barbecue. VISTA, Vol. 1, no. 10 (June 8,
1986), p. 11-12. English.

3144 Catalano, Julia. Fajitas madness. VISTA,
Vol. 2, no. 4 (December 7, 1986), p. 23-24.
English. **DESCR:** Food Industry; South Texas.

3145 Dewey, Kathryn G.; Strode, Margaret A.; and
Fitch, Yolanda Ruiz. Dietary change among
migrant and nonmigrant Mexican-American
families in northern California. ECOLOGY OF
FOOD AND NUTRITION, Vol. 14, no. 1 (1984),
p. 11-24. English. **DESCR:** Culture; *Migrant
Children; Migrant Labor; Northern
California; *Nutrition.

3146 Marambio, Gonzalo. From San Antonio to
Paris: Tex-Mex food conquers the French.
VISTA, Vol. 1, no. 6 (February 2, 1986), p.
18-20. English. **DESCR:** Business Enterprises;
Cantu, Mario, Jr.; Gonzales, Teresa;
*Mario's Restaurant, San Antonio, TX; Papa
Maya's Restaurant, Paris, France.

Food Practices (cont.)

3147 Reilly, Michael D. and Wallendorf, Melanie. A longitudinal study of Mexican-American assimilation. ADVANCES IN CONSUMER RESEARCH, Vol. 11, (1984), p. 735-740. English. **DESCR**: *Assimilation; *Consumers; Culture; *Marketing.

Football

3148 Viuker, Steve. Man with the golden toe. VISTA, Vol. 3, no. 2 (October 3, 1987), p. 6, 24. English. **DESCR**: *Allegre, Raul; Athletes.

Ford Foundation

3149 Hispanic inter-university program grants awarded to 17 projects. LA RED/THE NET, no. 92 (November, December, 1985), p. 7-9. English. **DESCR**: Committee on Public Policy Research on Contemporary Hispanic Issues; Funding Sources; Inter-University Program for Latino Research; Social Science Research Council.

3150 Public policy research and the Hispanic community: recommendations from five task forces [special issue]. LA RED/THE NET, no. 88 (Winter 1984), p. 1-24. English. **DESCR**: *Ford Foundation's Hispanic Task Forces Policy Research Reports; *Public Policy.

Ford Foundation Postdoctoral Fellowships for Minorities Program

3151 Recipients of Ford Foundation postdoctoral fellowships for minorities have been announced. LA RED/THE NET, no. 99 (August 1986), p. 10. English. **DESCR**: Awards; *Financial Aid; Higher Education.

Ford Foundation's Hispanic Task Forces Policy Research Reports

3152 Public policy research and the Hispanic community: recommendations from five task forces [special issue]. LA RED/THE NET, no. 88 (Winter 1984), p. 1-24. English. **DESCR**: Ford Foundation; *Public Policy.

Ford Motor Company

3153 Hispanic marketing. ADVERTISING AGE MAGAZINE, Vol. 57, no. 16 (February 27, 1986), p. 11-51. English. **DESCR**: Adolph Coors Co.; Advertising; Allstate Insurance Co.; American Greetings; Anheuser-Busch, Inc.; Business Enterprises; Coca-Cola Company; Consumers; Hallmark Cards; *Marketing; Mass Media; McDonald's Corporation; Metropolitan Life Insurance Corporation; Pepsi-Cola Bottling Group; Prudential; Spanish International Network (SIN); State Farm Mutual Insurance; Tylenol; United Insurance Co. of America.

Foreign Language Instruction

3154 Gynan, Shaw Nicholas. The influence of language background on attitudes toward native and nonnative Spanish. BILINGUAL REVIEW, Vol. 12, no. 1-2 (January, August, 1985), p. 33-42. English. **DESCR**: Anglo Americans; *Attitudes; Language Proficiency; *Language Usage; Spanish Language.

3155 Hidalgo, Margarita. On the question of "standard" versus "dialect": implications for teaching Hispanic college students. HISPANIC JOURNAL OF BEHAVIORAL SCIENCES, Vol. 9, no. 4 (December 1987), p. 375-395. English. **DESCR**: Bilingualism; Chicano Dialects; Language Usage; Puerto Ricans; Sociolinguistics; Spanish for Native Speakers; *Spanish Language.

Foreign Policy
    USE: International Relations

"The Forgotten People" [senior thesis]

3156 Panas, Katia. The forgotten people. REVISTA MUJERES, Vol. 1, no. 2 (June 1984), p. 15. English. **DESCR**: Immigration; Nunez Wilson, Carmen.

FORM AND FUNCTION IN CHICANO ENGLISH

3157 Blanco, George M. Book review of: FORM AND FUNCTION IN CHICANO ENGLISH. MODERN LANGUAGE JOURNAL, Vol. 69, no. 3 (Fall 1985), p. 328. English. **DESCR**: Book Reviews; Ornstein-Galicia, Jacob.

3158 Trueba, Henry T. Book review of: FORM AND FUNCTION IN CHICANO ENGLISH. LANGUAGE IN SOCIETY, Vol. 14, no. 2 (June 1985), p. 255-257. English. **DESCR**: Book Reviews; Ornstein-Galicia, Jacob.

Foster, James C.

3159 Reisler, Mark. Book review of: AMERICAN LABOR IN THE SOUTHWEST: THE 1ST 100 YEARS. PACIFIC HISTORICAL REVIEW, Vol. 53, no. 2 (1984), p. 246-247. English. **DESCR**: *AMERICAN LABOR IN THE SOUTHWEST: THE FIRST ONE HUNDRED YEARS; Book Reviews.

Fouce, Frank

3160 SICC to sell off stations. BROADCASTING, Vol. 110, no. 20 (May 19, 1986), p. 79-80. English. **DESCR**: Anselmo, Rene; Federal Communications Commission (FCC); KFTV, Fresno, CA [television station]; KMEX, Los Angeles, CA [television station]; KWEX, San Antonio, TX [television station]; Legal Cases; *Spanish International Communications Corp. (SICC); Spanish International Network (SIN); Spanish Language; Television; WLTV, Miami, FL [television station]; WXTV, Paterson, NJ [television station].

Fourth Amendment
    USE: Constitutional Amendments - Fourth

Fourth Symposium on Hispanic Business and Economy, San Juan, Puerto Rico, November 23-25, 1987

3161 Academics and entrepreneurs talk trade. HISPANIC BUSINESS, Vol. 9, no. 6 (June 1987), p. 96. English. **DESCR**: *Business Enterprises; Conferences and Meetings; *International Economic Relations; Latin America; *National Association of Hispanic Professors of Business Administration and Economics (Los Profesores); Organizations; Teaching Profession.

FRAGMENTS OF THE MEXICAN REVOLUTION: PERSONAL ACCOUNTS FROM THE BORDER

3162 Garcia, Mario T. Book review of: FRAGMENTS OF THE MEXICAN REVOLUTION. HISPANIC AMERICAN HISTORICAL REVIEW, Vol. 65, no. 1 (February 1985), p. 150-151. English. **DESCR**: Book Reviews; Martinez, Oscar J.; Mexican Revolution - 1910-1920.

Fred Harvey Co.

3163 Ahlborn, Richard E. The Hispanic horseman: a sampling of horse gear from the Fred Harvey Collection. PALACIO. Vol. 89, no. 2 (1983), p. 12-21. English. **DESCR:** Museum of New Mexico; *Vaqueros.

FREE TRADE BETWEEN MEXICO AND THE UNITED STATES?

3164 Book review of: FREE TRADE BETWEEN MEXICO AND THE UNITED STATES? FOREIGN AFFAIRS, Vol. 63. no. 1 (Fall 1984), p. 196. English. **DESCR:** Book Reviews; Weintraub, Sidney.

FREEBIE AND THE BEAN

3165 Aceves Madrid, Vicente. Film review of: FREEBIE AND THE BEAN. LATIN QUARTER, Vol. 1, no. 3 (January, February, 1975), p. 22-23. English. **DESCR:** *Film Reviews; Stereotypes; Violence.

Freire, Paulo

3166 Mares, E.A. The fiesta of life: impression of Paulo Friere. EL CUADERNO. Vol. 3, no. 2 (Spring 1974), p. 5-16. English. **DESCR:** *Aztlan; Cultural Characteristics; *Essays; *Philosophy.

FRIDA: A BIOGRAPHY OF FRIDA KAHLO

3167 Tibol, Raquel. La biografa se espanto de una vida abierta. LA COMUNIDAD, No. 302 (May 4, 1986), p. 12-13. Spanish. **DESCR:** *Biography; Book Reviews; Herrera, Hayden; *Kahlo, Frida.

FRIDA: NATURALEZA VIDA [film]

3168 Rodriguez Flores, Juan. Paul Leduc, FRIDA y el otro cine que no se exhibe en Los Angeles. LA COMUNIDAD, No. 290 (February 9, 1986), p. 12-13. Spanish. **DESCR:** *Films; History; *Kahlo, Frida; Mexico.

3169 Sanchez, Ricardo. FRIDA: una pelicula de imagen y poder [film review]. REVISTA MUJERES. Vol. 3, no. 2 (June 1986), p. 74-75. Spanish. **DESCR:** Film Reviews; Kahlo, Frida; Leduc, Paul.

FROM A COP'S JOURNAL & OTHER POEMS

3170 Daydi-Tolson, Santiago. Book review of: FROM A COP'S JOURNAL & OTHER POEMS. THE AMERICAS REVIEW, Vol. 15, no. 1 (Spring 1987), p. 102-105. English. **DESCR:** Book Reviews; Munoz, Arthur.

FROM INDIANS TO CHICANOS: A SOCIOCULTURAL HISTORY

3171 Melville, Margarita B. Book review of: FROM INDIANS TO CHICANOS. LA RED/THE NET, no. 45 (August 1981), p. 3. English. **DESCR:** Book Reviews; Social History and Conditions; Vigil, James Diego.

LA FRONTERA: THE U.S. BORDER WITH MEXICO

3172 Perez, Renato E. Book review of: LA FRONTERA: THE U.S. BORDER WITH MEXICO. VISTA, Vol. 2, no. 10 (June 7, 1987), p. 24. English. **DESCR:** *Book Reviews; Dusard, Jay; Weisman, Alan.

Frost, H. Gordon

3173 Butler. Anne M. Book review of: THE GENTLEMEN'S CLUB: THE STORY OF PROSTITUTION IN EL PASO, TEXAS. ARIZONA AND THE WEST, Vol. 26, no. 4 (1984), p. 365-366. English. **DESCR:** Book Reviews; Criminal Acts; El Paso, TX; THE GENTLEMEN'S CLUB: THE STORY OF PROSTITUTION IN EL PASO, TEXAS.

Fuentes, Carlos

3174 Eberstadt, Fernanda. Montezuma's literary revenge. COMMENTARY, Vol. 81, no. 5 (May 1986), p. 35-40. English. **DESCR:** GRINGO VIEJO; *Literary Criticism; Mexican Literature; THE DEATH OF ARTEMIO CRUZ; THE GOOD CONSCIENCE; WHERE THE AIR IS CLEAR.

3175 Lower, Andrea. La unidad narrativa en LA MUERTE DE ARTEMIO CRUZ. TINTA, Vol. 1, no. 3 (December 1983), p. 19-26. Spanish. **DESCR:** *LA MUERTE DE ARTEMIO CRUZ; Literary Criticism; Mexican Literature; *Novel.

Fuentes, Theresa

3176 NACME scholarships at Forum '87. HISPANIC ENGINEER, Vol. 3, no. 3 (1987), p. 14. English. **DESCR:** *Eastman Kodak Co.; *Financial Aid; Molina, Daniel.

Fullana, Jaime, Jr.

3177 Beale, Stephen. CEOs. HISPANIC BUSINESS, Vol. 9, no. 4 (April 1987), p. 20-37, 52. English. **DESCR:** Alvarez, Roberto; Batarse, Anthony A.; Biography; Business Enterprises; *Businesspeople; Carlo, Nelson; Estrada, Anthony; Flores, Frank; Hernandez, George; *Management; Ortega, James; Quirch, Guillermo; Ruiz, Roberto; Santa Maria, Yvonne Z.; Sugranes, Rosa; Tamaya, Carlos; Young, Paul H., Jr.

Funding Sources

3178 Hispanic inter-university program grants awarded to 17 projects. LA RED/THE NET, no. 92 (November, December, 1985), p. 7-9. English. **DESCR:** Committee on Public Policy Research on Contemporary Hispanic Issues; *Ford Foundation; Inter-University Program for Latino Research; Social Science Research Council.

Gabacho
USE: Anglo Americans

Galarza, Ernesto

3179 Estrada, William. The life and legend of Ernesto Galarza=La vida y legado de Ernesto Galarza. AMERICAS 2001, Premiere Issue, 1987, p. 26-27. Bilingual. **DESCR:** Biographical Notes.

3180 Galarza, Ernesto. Platica con Galarza [interview]. EL CUADERNO, Vol. 4, no. 10 (Summer 1976), p. 6-19. Bilingual. **DESCR:** Capitalism; *Education.

Galeria Ocaso, Los Angeles, CA

3181 Rosas, Alejandro. Proyecto de arte latino en Los Angeles. LA COMUNIDAD, No. 251 (May 12, 1985), p. 4-5. Spanish. **DESCR:** *Art; Art Galleries; Gamboa, Manazar; Gronk (Pseud.).

GALILEAN JOURNEY

3182 Abalos, David. Book review of: GALILEAN JOURNEY. NEW CATHOLIC WORLD, Vol. 226, (July, August, 1983), p. 190-191. English. **DESCR:** Book Reviews; Elizondo, Virgilio.

Galindo, Mary Sue

3183 Reyna, Jose R. Book review of: MERIENDA TEJANA. LECTOR, Vol. 4, no. 4-6 (1987), p. 76. English. **DESCR:** Book Reviews; *MERIENDA TEJANA.

Galindo, P. (Pseud. for Rolando Hinojosa-Smith)
USE: Hinojosa-Smith. Rolando R.

Galindo, Yvette

3184 Castellanos, Teresa. I never lose a dream: an interview with Yvette Galindo. REVISTA MUJERES. Vol. 2, no. 1 (January 1985), p. 7-10. English. **DESCR:** *Biography.

Galvez, Daniel

3185 Malaspina, Ann. The city is my canvas. VISTA, Vol. 2, no. 3 (November 2, 1986), p. 14-15. English. **DESCR:** Artists; Hispanic Murals Project (Cambridge, MA); *Mural Art; Oakland, CA.

Galvo [family name]

3186 Instituto Genealogico e Historico Latino-Americano. Rootsearch: Montoya: Galvo. VISTA, Vol. 1, no. 4 (December 7, 1985), p. 22. English. **DESCR:** Genealogy; History; *Montoya [family name]; *Personal Names.

Gamboa, Diane

3187 Gamboa, Harry, Jr. El artista chicano dentro y fuera de la "corriente" artistica. LA COMUNIDAD, No. 351 (April 12, 1987), 2-5+. Spanish. **DESCR:** *Art; Artists; Carrasco, Barbara; Gronk (Pseud.); Martinez, Daniel J.; Valadez, John; Valdez, Patssi.

3188 Shaw, Katherine. Mira! a look at America's Hispanic artists. VISTA, Vol. 1, no. 5 (January 5, 1986), p. 6-8. English. **DESCR:** *Art; Artists; Canadian Club Hispanic Art Tour; Delgadillo, Ramon; Gonzalez, Nivia; *Trevino, Jesus (Jesse).

Gamboa, Harry, Jr.

3189 Galeria 2001. AMERICAS 2001, Vol. 1, no. 3 (November, December, 1987), p. [8-9]. Bilingual. **DESCR:** Artists; Biographical Notes; Photography.

Gamboa, Manazar

3190 Rosas, Alejandro. Proyecto de arte latino en Los Angeles. LA COMUNIDAD, No. 251 (May 12, 1985), p. 4-5. Spanish. **DESCR:** *Art; Art Galleries; *Galeria Ocaso, Los Angeles, CA; Gronk (Pseud.)

Gangs

3191 Blanco, Gilbert M. Las Adelitas del Barrio. LATIN QUARTER, Vol. 1, no. 3 (January, February, 1975), p. 30-32. English. **DESCR:** *Chicanas; City Terrace, CA; Community Development; *Latin Empresses; Youth.

3192 Eisen, Marvin. Working for positive change in the barrio. LATIN QUARTER, Vol. 1, no. 1 (July 1974), p. 8-10. English. **DESCR:** Counseling (Educational); *East Los Angeles Skills Center; Maravilla.

3193 Haslanger, Phil. A rival to the gangs. THE PROGRESSIVE, Vol. 50, (October 1986), p. 15. English. **DESCR:** Diaz, Ricardo; Milwaukee, WI.

3194 Hunsaker, Alan C. and Vicario, Tony D. A behavioral/ecological model of intervention alternatives with Chicano gang delinquents. LA RED/THE NET, no. 43 (June 1981), p. 2-3. English. **DESCR:** *Behavior Modification; *Delinquency; Youth.

Gann, L.H.

3195 Tryon, Roy H. Book review of: THE HISPANICS IN THE UNITED STATES: A HISTORY. LIBRARY JOURNAL, Vol. 111, no. 18 (November 1, 1986), p. 107. English. **DESCR:** Book Reviews; Duignan, Peter J.; *HISPANICS IN THE UNITED STATES: A HISTORY; Social History and Conditions.

Garay, Charles J.

3196 SHPE holds first ever East coast conference for Hispanic engineers. HISPANIC ENGINEER, Vol. 3, no. 5 (Winter 1987), p. 12-14. English. **DESCR:** Awards; Barrios, Eugene; Chang-Diaz, Franklin; *Conferences and Meetings; Cuevas, Brian L.; Garcia, Ray; Marrero, Charles; Martinez, Lisa; Monteverde, Edwin; Plumey, Raymond; Reyes-Guerra, David; Rivera, Angel; Society of Hispanic Professional Engineers (SHPE); Soto, Giovanni.

Garcia, Andy

3197 Rodriguez Flores, Juan. Andy Garcia: un "Intocable" orgulloso de ser latino. LA COMUNIDAD, No. 362 (June 28, 1987), p. 8-11. Spanish. **DESCR:** Actors and Actresses; *Biography.

Garcia, Clotilde

3198 Chavez, Lorenzo A. The quest for Hispanic roots. VISTA, Vol. 2, no. 7 (March 8, 1987), p. 5-6, 24. English. **DESCR:** Church of Jesus Christ of Latter-Day Saints (Mormons); Directories; *Genealogy; Hispanic American Genealogical Associates, Washington, DC; Las Porciones Genealogical Society, Edinburg, TX; Los Bexarenos, San Antonio, TX; Los Californianos [genealogical society], San Jose, CA; Pan American University, Edinburg, TX; Texas Southmost College.

Garcia, Ernest

3199 Palomo, Juan R. Ernest Garcia. VISTA, Vol. 1, no. 3 (November 3, 1985), p. 10. English. **DESCR:** *Appointed Officials.

Garcia [family name]

3200 Instituto Genealogico e Historico Latino-Americano. Rootsearch: Garcia: Chaves. VISTA, Vol. 1, no. 10 (June 8, 1986), p. 26. English. **DESCR:** *Chaves [family name]; Genealogy; History; *Personal Names.

Garcia, Frances [mayor of Hutchinson, KS]

3201 Valenzuela-Crocker, Elvira. Small town Hispanic America. VISTA, Vol. 1, no. 11 (July 6, 1986), p. 12-14. English. **DESCR:** Political History and Conditions; *Population; Spanish Speaking Affairs Council of St. Paul; *Trejo, Jose.

Garcia, Fred

3202 Riding the range at Golden West. NUESTRO,
Vol. 11. no. 3 (April 1987), p. 7-8.
English. DESCR: Biography; Colleges and
Universities; Educational Administration;
Golden West College, Huntington Beach, CA.

Garcia, Juan

3203 13-part series focuses on Hispanics in
America. EDITOR & PUBLISHER: THE FOURTH
ESTATE, Vol. 115, no. 14 (April 3, 1982), p.
37. English. DESCR: Books; Cultural
Characteristics; DALLAS MORNING NEWS;
Gonzalez, John; Goodwin, Jay; Grothe, Randy
Eli; Hamilton, John; Hille, Ed; LA VIDA
AMERICANA; *LA VIDA AMERICANA/HISPANICS IN
AMERICA; Langer, Ralph; McLemore. David;
Osburne, Burl; Parks, Scott; Pusey, Allen;
Sonnemair, Jan.

3204 Winston, Bonnie. INROADS: internships that
work. HISPANIC ENGINEER, Vol. 3, no. 5
(Winter 1987), p. 38-42. English. DESCR:
Almanza, John; Alvarez, Maria; Carr, Frank;
*Educational Organizations; Educational
Statistics; Gonzales, Ana; *INROADS;
Pereira. Eduardo; Raimundo, Antonio; Reza,
Priscilla.

Garcia, Juan Ramon

3205 Lopez-Garza, Marta. Book review of:
OPERATION WETBACK. LA RED/THE NET, no. 50
(January 1982), p. 7-9. English. DESCR: Book
Reviews; *Deportation; Immigration;
*OPERATION WETBACK: THE MASS DEPORTATION OF
MEXICAN UNDOCUMENTED WORKERS IN 1954.

Garcia, Juliet

3206 Olivera. Mercedes. The new Hispanic women.
VISTA, Vol. 2, no. 11 (July 5, 1987), p.
6-8. English. DESCR: Alvarez, Linda;
*Chicanas; Esquiroz, Margarita; *Hernandez,
Antonia A.; Mohr, Nicolasa; Molina, Gloria;
Pabon, Maria; Working Women.

Garcia, Lionel

3207 Paredes, Raymund A. Review essay: recent
Chicano writing. ROCKY MOUNTAIN REVIEW OF
LANGUAGE AND LITERATURE, Vol. 41, (1987),
p. 124-129. English. DESCR: Castillo, Ana;
Catholic Church; Chavez, Denise; Chicanas;
GIVING UP THE GHOST; LEAVING HOME; *Literary
Criticism; *Literature Reviews; Moraga,
Cherrie; Poetry; Prose; Sex Roles; Silva,
Beverly; SMALL FACES; Soto, Gary; THE CAT
AND OTHER STORIES; THE LAST OF THE MENU
GIRLS; THE MIXQUIAHUALA LETTERS.

Garcia, Mario T.

3208 Arroyo, Luis Leobardo. Book review of:
DESERT IMMIGRANTS. LA RED/THE NET. no. 43
(June 1981), p. 3-4. English. DESCR: Book
Reviews; *DESERT IMMIGRANTS: THE MEXICANS OF
EL PASO 1880-1920; Immigrants.

3209 Martinez, Eliud. Book review of: HISTORY,
CULTURE. AND SOCIETY. MODERN LANGUAGE
JOURNAL, Vol. 69, no. 4 (Winter 1985), p.
436-437. English. DESCR: Book Reviews;
Chicano Studies; *HISTORY, CULTURE, AND
SOCIETY: CHICANO STUDIES IN THE 1980s;
National Association for Chicano Studies
(NACS).

3210 Monroy, Douglas. In support of lapses into
radicalism: a response to Mario Garcia. LA
RED/THE NET, no. 80 (May 1984), p. 8-11.
English. DESCR: *Historiography.

3211 Monroy, Douglas. [Letter responding to Mario
Garcia's comments]. LABOR HISTORY, Vol. 25,
no. 1 (Winter 1984), p. 155-156. English.
DESCR: *Communism; History; *Labor Unions;
Los Angeles, CA.

Garcia Marquez, Gabriel

3212 Bartlett, Catherine Vallejos. Magical
realism: the Latin American influence on
modern Chicano writers. CONFLUENCIA, Vol. 1,
no. 2 (Spring 1986), p. 27-37. English.
DESCR: Arias, Ron; Authors; Latin America;
*Literary Criticism; *Literary Influence;
*Literature; Magical realism; ONE HUNDRED
YEARS OF SOLITUDE; Rivera, Tomas; THE ROAD
TO TAMAZUNCHALE; Y NO SE LO TRAGO LA
TIERRA/AND THE EARTH DID NOT PART.

Garcia, Raul

3213 SHPE news. HISPANIC ENGINEER, Vol. 3, no. 3
(1987), p. 10-13. English. DESCR: *Awards;
Castillo, Hector; Colmenarez, Margarita;
Herrera, Jess; Lopez-Martin, Minnie;
Mondragon, Ricardo; Reyes-Guerra, David;
Silva, Juan; Society of Hispanic
Professional Engineers (SHPE); Vargas,
Jesus; Villanueva, Bernadette.

Garcia, Ray

3214 SHPE holds first ever East coast conference
for Hispanic engineers. HISPANIC ENGINEER,
Vol. 3, no. 5 (Winter 1987), p. 12-14.
English. DESCR: Awards; Barrios, Eugene;
Chang-Diaz, Franklin; *Conferences and
Meetings; Cuevas, Brian L.; Garay, Charles
J.; Marrero, Charles; Martinez, Lisa;
Monteverde, Edwin; Plumey, Raymond;
Reyes-Guerra, David; Rivera, Angel; Society
of Hispanic Professional Engineers (SHPE);
Soto, Giovanni.

Garcia, Rodrigo T.

3215 Mellado, Carmela. SHPE co-founder Rodrigo.T.
Garcia. HISPANIC ENGINEER, Vol. 3, no. 2
(Summer), p. 22-25. English. DESCR:
*Biography.

Garcia, Ruben

3216 Corona, Al. Life in the fast lane. VISTA,
Vol. 3, no. 3 (November 8, 1987), p. 30.
English. DESCR: National Association of
Stock Car Automobile Racing (NASCAR);
*Sports.

Garcia-Ayvens, Francisco

3217 Woods, Richard D. Book review of: CHICANO
PERIODICAL INDEX: A CUMULATIVE INDEX TO
SELECTED CHICANO PERIODICALS BETWEEN 1967
AND 1978. LA RED/THE NET, no. 52 (March
1982), p. 5-6. English. DESCR: Book Reviews;
*Chabran, Richard; *CHICANO PERIODICAL
INDEX; Periodical Indexes.

Garment Industry

3218 Olivares, Yvette. The sweatshop: the garment
industry's reborn child. REVISTA MUJERES,
Vol. 3, no. 2 (June 1986), p. 55-62.
English. DESCR: Labor; Public Health; Third
World; *Undocumented Workers; *Women;
Working Women.

Gary, IN

3219 Lowe, Virginia A.P. Presentation of ethnic identity in Chicano theater. CHIRICU, Vol. 2, no. 1 (Spring 1980), p. 52-58. English. **DESCR:** Ethnic Groups; Folklore Institute at Indiana University; Identity; *Teatro; *Teatro Desangano del Pueblo, Washington Park, East Chicago, IN.

Garza [family name]

3220 Instituto Genealogico e Historico Latino-Americano. Rootsearch: Rodriguez: Garza (De La Garza). VISTA. Vol. 3, no. 3 (November 8, 1987), p. 37. English. **DESCR:** *de la Garza [family name]; Genealogy; History; *Personal Names; *Rodriguez, [family name].

Garza, Jose

3221 Pena, Margarita. Apuntes para un retrato chicano (I). LA COMUNIDAD, No. 270 (September 22, 1985), p. 12-14. Spanish. **DESCR:** Artists; *Biography.

3222 Pena, Margarita. Apuntes para un retrato chicano (II). LA COMUNIDAD, No. 271 (September 29, 1985), p. 15. Spanish. **DESCR:** Artists; *Biography.

Gault, William Campbell

3223 Book review of: THE CHICANO WAR. PUBLISHER'S WEEKLY, Vol. 229, (February 21, 1986), p. 157. English. **DESCR:** Book Reviews; *THE CHICANO WAR.

Gavin, John

3224 Gavin joins group pursuing SICC stations. BROADCASTING, Vol. 110, no. 22 (June 2, 1986), p. 68. English. **DESCR:** KFTV, Fresno, CA [television station]; KMEX, Los Angeles, CA [television station]; KWEX, San Antonio, TX [television station]; Legal Cases; Perenchio, A. Jerrold; *Spanish International Communications Corp. (SICC); Spanish International Network (SIN); Spanish Language; Television; Thompson, William; WLTV, Miami, FL [television station]; WXTV, Paterson, NJ [television station].

Gays

USE: Homosexuality

GENEALOGICAL RECORDS IN TEXAS

3225 Perez, Renato E. Book review of: GENEALOGICAL RECORDS IN TEXAS. VISTA. Vol. 3, no. 2 (October 3, 1987), p. 37. English. **DESCR:** Book Reviews; Kennedy, Imogene; Kennedy, Leon.

Genealogy

3226 Chavez, Lorenzo A. The quest for Hispanic roots. VISTA, Vol. 2, no. 7 (March 8, 1987), p. 5-6, 24. English. **DESCR:** Church of Jesus Christ of Latter-Day Saints (Mormons); Directories; *Garcia, Clotilde; Hispanic American Genealogical Associates, Washington, DC; Las Porciones Genealogical Society, Edinburg, TX; Los Bexarenos, San Antonio, TX; Los Californianos [genealogical society], San Jose, CA; Pan American University, Edinburg, TX; Texas Southmost College.

3227 Instituto Genealogico e Historico Latino-Americano. Rootsearch: Aguilar: Echeverria. VISTA, Vol. 1, no. 11 (July 6, 1986), p. 22. English. **DESCR:** *Aguilar [family name]; Echeverria [family name]; History; *Personal Names.

3228 Instituto Genealogico e Historico Latino-Americano. Rootsearch: Alarcon: Saavedra. VISTA, Vol. 1, no. 8 (April 6, 1986), p. 22. English. **DESCR:** *Alarcon [family name]; History; *Personal Names; Saavedra [family name].

3229 Instituto Genealogico e Historico Latino-Americano. Rootsearch: Alvarez: Covarrubias. VISTA, Vol. 1, no. 6 (February 2, 1986), p. 22. English. **DESCR:** *Alvarez [family name]; *Covarrubias [family name]; History; *Personal Names.

3230 Instituto Genealogico e Historico Latino-Americano. Rootsearch: Aragon: Trujillo: Ruelas. VISTA, Vol. 2, no. 8 (April 4, 1987), p. 24. English. **DESCR:** *Aragon [family name]; History; *Personal Names; *Ruelas [family name]; *Trujillo [family name].

3231 Instituto Genealogico e Historico Latino-Americano. Rootsearch: Bello: Ramirez: Lopez. VISTA, Vol. 3, no. 2 (October 3, 1987), p. 37. English. **DESCR:** *Bello [family name]; History; *Lopez [family name]; *Personal Names; *Ramirez [family name].

3232 Instituto Genealogico e Historico Latino-Americano. Rootsearch: Beltran: Flores: Gomez. VISTA, Vol. 2, no. 11 (May 7, 1987), p. 22. English. **DESCR:** *Beltran [family name]; *Flores [family name]; *Gomez [family name]; History; *Personal Names.

3233 Instituto Genealogico e Historico Latino-Americano. Rootsearch: Castro: Velasco. VISTA, Vol. 2, no. 2 (October 4, 1986), p. 22. English. **DESCR:** *Castro [family name]; History; *Personal Names; *Velasco [family name].

3234 Instituto Genealogico e Historico Latino-Americano. Rootsearch: Cisneros: Perales: Zuniga. VISTA, Vol. 2, no. 10 (June 7, 1987), p. 26. English. **DESCR:** *Cisneros [family name]; History; *Perales [family name]; *Personal Names; *Zuniga [family name].

3235 Instituto Genealogico e Historico Latino-Americano. Rootsearch: Cortes: Ulibarri. VISTA, Vol. 1, no. 5 (January 5, 1986), p. 22. English. **DESCR:** *Cortes [family name]; History; *Personal Names; Ulibarri [family name].

3236 Instituto Genealogico e Historico Latino-Americano. Rootsearch: De La Garza: Pacheco. VISTA, Vol. 2, no. 6 (February 8, 1987), p. 21. English. **DESCR:** *de la Garza [family name]; History; Pacheco [family name]; *Personal Names.

3237 Instituto Genealogico e Historico Latino-Americano. Rootsearch: Duarte: Sandoval. VISTA, Vol. 1, no. 9 (May 3, 1986), p. 22. English. **DESCR:** *Duarte [family name]; History; *Personal Names; *Sandoval [family name].

3238 Instituto Genealogico e Historico Latino-Americano. Rootsearch: Garcia: Chaves. VISTA, Vol. 1, no. 10 (June 8, 1986), p. 26. English. **DESCR:** *Chaves [family name]; *Garcia [family name]; History; *Personal Names.

Genealogy (cont.)

3239 Instituto Genealogico e Historico
Latino-Americano. Rootsearch: Gonzalez:
Febres-Cordero. VISTA, Vol. 1, no. 7 (March
2, 1986), p. 22. English. **DESCR:**
Febres-Cordero [family name]; *Gonzalez
[family name]; History; *Personal Names.

3240 Instituto Genealogico e Historico
Latino-Americano. Rootsearch: Gutierrez.
VISTA, Vol. 1, no. 2 (October 5, 1985), p.
22. English. **DESCR:** *Gutierrez [family
name]; History; *Personal Names.

3241 Instituto Genealogico e Historico
Latino-Americano. Rootsearch: Guzman:
Zamora. VISTA, Vol. 2, no. 7 (March 8,
1987), p. 25. English. **DESCR:** *Guzman
[family name]; History; *Personal Names;
*Zamora [family name].

3242 Instituto Genealogico e Historico
Latino-Americano. Rootsearch: Jimenez
(Ximenez): Olmo. VISTA, Vol. 2, no. 4
(December 7, 1986), p. 25. English. **DESCR:**
History; *Jimenez [family name]; *Olmo
[family name]; *Personal Names; *Ximenez
[family name].

3243 Instituto Genealogico e Historico
Latino-Americano. Rootsearch: Montoya:
Galvo. VISTA, Vol. 1, no. 4 (December 7,
1985), p. 22. English. **DESCR:** *Galvo [family
name]; History; *Montoya [family name];
*Personal Names.

3244 Instituto Genealogico e Historico
Latino-Americano. Rootsearch: Olivares:
Yrigoyen: Montemayor. VISTA, Vol. 2, no. 12
(August 1, 1987), p. 30. English. **DESCR:**
History; *Montemayor [family name];
*Olivares [family name]; *Personal Names;
*Yrigoyen [family name].

3245 Instituto Genealogico e Historico
Latino-Americano. Rootsearch: Padron:
Machado. VISTA, Vol. 2, no. 1 (September 7,
1986), p. 22. English. **DESCR:** History;
*Machado [family name]; *Padron [family
name]; *Personal Names.

3246 Instituto Genealogico e Historico
Latino-Americano. Rootsearch: Patino:
Herrera: Escobar. VISTA, Vol. 2, no. 9 (May
3, 1987), p. 22. English. **DESCR:** *Escobar
[family name]; *Herrera [family name];
History; *Patino [family name]; *Personal
Names.

3247 Instituto Genealogico e Historico
Latino-Americano. Rootsearch: Peraza: Yanez.
VISTA, Vol. 1, no. 12 (August 2, 1986), p.
22. English. **DESCR:** History; *Peraza [family
name]; *Personal Names; Yanez [family name].

3248 Instituto Genealogico e Historico
Latino-Americano. Rootsearch: Rivera:
Navarro: Salazar. VISTA, Vol. 2, no. 3
(November 2, 1986), p. 24. English. **DESCR:**
History; *Navarro [family name]; *Personal
Names; *Rivera [family name]; *Salazar
[family name].

3249 Instituto Genealogico e Historico
Latino-Americano. Rootsearch: Robles:
Chacon: Molina. VISTA, Vol. 3, no. 1
(September 6, 1987), p. 30. English. **DESCR:**
*Chacon [family name]; History; *Molina
[family name]; *Personal Names; *Robles
[family name].

3250 Instituto Genealogico e Historico
Latino-Americano. Rootsearch: Rodriguez:

Garza (De La Garza). VISTA, Vol. 3, no. 3
(November 8, 1987), p. 37. English. **DESCR:**
*de la Garza [family name]; *Garza [family
name]; History; *Personal Names; *Rodriguez,
[family name].

3251 Instituto Genealogico e Historico
Latino-Americano. Rootsearch: Villalobos:
Amador (Amado): Ibarra. VISTA, Vol. 3, no. 4
(December 6, 1987), p. 36. English. **DESCR:**
*Amado [family name]; *Amador [family name];
History; *Ibarra [family name]; Personal
Names; *Villalobos [family name].

GENERACIONES Y SEMBLANZAS

3252 Randolph, Donald A. Death's aesthetic
proliferation in works of Hinojosa.
CONFLUENCIA, Vol. 1, no. 2 (Spring 1986), p.
38-47. English. **DESCR:** Death (Concept);
*Hinojosa-Smith, Rolando R.; KLAIL CITY Y
SUS ALREDEDORES; KOREAN LOVE SONGS;
*Literary Criticism; Novel.

General Foods

3253 Fitch, Ed. Prime space available at low
rates. ADVERTISING AGE MAGAZINE, Vol. 57,
no. 16 (February 27, 1986), p. 11-12.
English. **DESCR:** Advertising; Consumers;
*Marketing.

Generally Useful Ethnic Search System (GUESS)

3254 Martin, Jeanne and Suarez, Lucina. Cancer
mortality among Mexican Americans and other
whites in Texas, 1969-80. AMERICAN JOURNAL
OF PUBLIC HEALTH, Vol. 77, no. 7 (July
1987), p. 851-853. English. **DESCR:** *Cancer;
Texas; Vital Statistics.

Generations
USE: Age Groups

Genetics

3255 Gaviria, Moises; Gil, Ana A.; and Javaid,
Javaid I. Nortriptyline kinetics in Hispanic
and Anglo subjects. JOURNAL OF CLINICAL
PSYCHOPHARMACOLOGY, Vol. 6, no. 4 (1986), p.
227-231. English. **DESCR:** Anglo Americans;
*Comparative Psychology; *Drug Use; Public
Health.

THE GENTLEMEN'S CLUB: THE STORY OF PROSTITUTION IN EL PASO, TEXAS

3256 Butler, Anne M. Book review of: THE
GENTLEMEN'S CLUB: THE STORY OF PROSTITUTION
IN EL PASO, TEXAS. ARIZONA AND THE WEST,
Vol. 26, no. 4 (1984), p. 365-366. English.
DESCR: Book Reviews; Criminal Acts; El Paso,
TX; *Frost, H. Gordon.

Gerrymandering
USE: Reapportionment

GETTING IN: A GUIDE TO OVERCOMING THE POLITICAL DENIAL OF NON-IMMIGRANT VISAS

3257 Zesch, Lindy. Visa issue heats up: PEN hopes
for "group waiver" of denials. AMERICAN
THEATRE, Vol. 2, no. 8 (November 1985), p.
24. English. **DESCR:** Artists; Authors; Book
Reviews; National Lawyer's Guild; Politics;
*Visas.

Ghetto
USE: Barrios

Giordano, Joseph

3258 Ramirez, Oscar. Book review of: ETHNICITY AND FAMILY THERAPY. LA RED/THE NET, no. 66 (March 1983), p. 28-30. English. DESCR: Book Reviews; *ETHNICITY AND FAMILY THERAPY; McGoldrick, Monica; Pearce, John K.

Girl Scouts of the United States of America

3259 Frances Hesselbein. INTERCAMBIOS FEMENILES, Vol. 2, no. 6 (Spring 1987), p. 23. English. DESCR: *Chicanas; Hesselbein, Frances; *Leadership; Organizations; Women; Youth.

GIVING UP THE GHOST

3260 Aguilu de Murphy, Raquel. Book review of: GIVING UP THE GHOST. THE AMERICAS REVIEW, Vol. 15, no. 2 (Summer 1987), p. 105-107. Spanish. DESCR: Book Reviews; Moraga, Cherrie; Teatro.

3261 Alarcon, Norma. Making "familia" from scratch: split subjectivities in the work of Helena Maria Viramontes and Cherrie Moraga. THE AMERICAS REVIEW, Vol. 15, no. 3-4 (Fall, Winter. 1987), p. 147-159. English. DESCR: Chicanas; *Literary Criticism; *Moraga, Cherrie; *Sex Roles; "Snapshots" [short story]; THE MOTHS AND OTHER STORIES; *Viramontes, Helen.

3262 Herrera-Sobek, Maria. The politics of rape: sexual transgression in Chicana fiction. THE AMERICAS REVIEW, Vol. 15, no. 3-4 (Fall, Winter. 1987), p. 171-181. English. DESCR: *Chicanas; Cisneros, Sandra; *Feminism; Fiction; *Literary Criticism; Lizarraga, Sylvia; Moraga, Cherrie; *Rape; "Red Clowns" [short story]; Sex Roles; "Silver Lake Road" [short story].

3263 Huerta. Jorge. Book review of: GIVING UP THE GHOST. THE AMERICAS REVIEW, Vol. 15, no. 2 (Summer 1987), p. 104-105. English. DESCR: Book Reviews; Moraga, Cherrie; Teatro.

3264 Paredes, Raymund A. Review essay: recent Chicano writing. ROCKY MOUNTAIN REVIEW OF LANGUAGE AND LITERATURE. Vol. 41, (1987), p. 124-129. English. DESCR: Castillo, Ana; Catholic Church; Chavez, Denise; Chicanas; Garcia, Lionel; LEAVING HOME, *Literary Criticism; *Literature Reviews; Moraga, Cherrie; Poetry; Prose; Sex Roles; Silva, Beverly; SMALL FACES; Soto, Gary; THE CAT AND OTHER STORIES; THE LAST OF THE MENU GIRLS; THE MIXQUIAHUALA LETTERS.

Gladys Porter High School

3265 LeAna, Thomas. From dropout to role model: a VISTA postscript. VISTA, Vol. 2, no. 4 (December 7, 1986), p. 25. English. DESCR: Brownsville, TX; *Martinez, Dorella; Olivares, J.R.; *Rhetoric; Secondary School Education.

Glazer, Nathan

3266 Kraly. Ellen Percy. Book review of: CLAMOR AT THE GATES. JOURNAL OF AMERICAN ETHNIC HISTORY, Vol. 7, no. 1 (Fall 1987), p. 93-95. English. DESCR: Book Reviews; *CLAMOR AT THE GATES: THE NEW AMERICAN IMMIGRATION; Immigration.

3267 Madrid, Arturo. Book reviews of: CLAMOR AT THE GATES and LATIN JOURNEY. LA RED/THE NET, no. 89 (August 1985), p. 7-10. English. DESCR: Bach, Robert L.; Book Reviews; *CLAMOR AT THE GATES: THE NEW AMERICAN IMMIGRATION; Immigration; *LATIN JOURNEY:

CUBAN AND MEXICAN IMMIGRANTS IN THE UNITED STATES; Portes, Alejandro.

Glue Sniffing

USE: Drug Use

Godoy, Gustavo

3268 Beale, Stephen. More changes at SIN. HISPANIC BUSINESS, Vol. 9, no. 1 (January 1987), p. 10. English. DESCR: Journalism; *Noticiero SIN; *Spanish International Network (SIN); *Television.

Gods and Dieties

3269 Braun, Barbara. The Aztecs: art and sacrifice. ART IN AMERICA, Vol. 72, no. 4 (April 1984), p. 126-139. English. DESCR: Anthropology; *Aztecs; Exhibits; *Precolumbian Images; *Precolumbian Society; Templo Mayor, Tenochtitlan.

Golden Gate Air Freight, Hayward, CA

3270 Sellers, Jeff M. Same-day service sells. HISPANIC BUSINESS, Vol. 9, no. 11 (November 1987), p. 16-19. English. DESCR: *Business Enterprises; Cardenas, John.

Golden Knights [skydiving team]

3271 Perez, Renato E. Skydiving daredevils. VISTA, Vol. 1, no. 10 (June 8, 1986), p. 14-16. English. DESCR: *Military; Minino, Virgilio; *U.S. Army.

Golden Mike Award

3272 Ayala, Ernie. Henry Alfaro, ABC's Eyewitness News reporter. LATIN QUARTER, Vol. 1, no. 1 (July 1974), p. 13-15. English. DESCR: *Alfaro, Henry; California Chicano News Media Association (CCNMA); Journalists; *Television.

3273 Gutierrez, Gloria. Chicano news-man wins award. LATIN QUARTER, Vol. 1, no. 4 (July, August, 1975), p. 17. English. DESCR: Journalists; *Radio; Southern California Radio and Television News Association; *Vasquez, Victor.

Golden West College, Huntington Beach, CA

3274 Riding the range at Golden West. NUESTRO, Vol. 11, no. 3 (April 1987), p. 7-8. English. DESCR: Biography; Colleges and Universities; Educational Administration; *Garcia, Fred.

Goldman, Shifra M.

3275 Castillo-Speed, Lillian. Annotated bibliography. LA RED/THE NET, no. 93 (January, February, 1986), p. 14-17. English. DESCR: A BIBLIOGRAPHY OF MEXICAN AMERICAN HISTORY; ARTE CHICANO; Book Reviews; Caballero, Cesar; CHICANO LITERATURE: A REFERENCE GUIDE; CHICANO ORGANIZATIONS DIRECTORY; CHICANO PERIODICAL INDEX; HISPANIC ALMANAC; HISPANIC MENTAL HEALTH RESEARCH: A REFERENCE GUIDE; Lomeli, Francisco A.; Martinez, Julio A.; Meier, Matt S.; Newton, Frank, *Reference Works; Ybarra-Frausto, Tomas.

Gomez, Alma

3276 Cantu, Norma. Book review of: CUENTOS:
STORIES BY LATINAS. LA RED/THE NET, no. 83
(August 1984), p. 2-3. English. **DESCR:** Book
Reviews; *CUENTOS: STORIES BY LATINAS;
Moraga, Cherrie; Romo-Carmona, Mariana.

Gomez, Ernesto

3277 Cardenas, Gilbert. Book review of: OLDER
MEXICAN AMERICANS: A STUDY IN AN URBAN
BARRIO. CONTEMPORARY SOCIOLOGY: A JOURNAL OF
REVIEWS, Vol. 14, no. 2 (March 1985), p.
243-244. English. **DESCR:** Ancianos; Book
Reviews; Markides, Kyriakos S.; Martin,
Harry; *OLDER MEXICAN AMERICANS: A STUDY IN
AN URBAN BARRIO.

Gomez [family name]

3278 Instituto Genealogico e Historico
Latino-Americano. Rootsearch: Beltran:
Flores: Gomez. VISTA, Vol. 2, no. 11 (May 7,
1987), p. 22. English. **DESCR:** *Beltran
[family name]; *Flores [family name];
Genealogy; History; *Personal Names.

Gomez, Mike

3279 Rodriguez Flores, Juan. Mike Gomez, otro
rostro hispano en Hollywood. LA COMUNIDAD,
No. 339 (January 18, 1987), p. 8-9. Spanish.
DESCR: Actos; *Biography.

Gomez Pena, Guillermo

3280 Gomez Pena. Guillermo and Erana, Maria.
Sobre el arte, la rebeldia y las fronteras.
LA COMUNIDAD, No. 312 (July 13, 1986), p.
6-7+. Spanish. **DESCR:** Berkeley, CA;
*BORDER-X-FRONTERA [radio program]; *Radio;
Schein, David; Teatro.

3281 Gonzalez, Marco Vinicio. En el pais de la
frontera. LA COMUNIDAD, No. 291 (February
16. 1986), p. 6-7+. Spanish. **DESCR:** Border
Region; Conde, Rosina; *DIALOGOS FRONTERIZOS
[radio program]; Medina, Ruben; *Radio; San
Diego, CA; Tijuana. Baja California. Mexico.

Gomez, Rudy

3282 Kane. George D. The entrepreneurial
professional. HISPANIC BUSINESS, Vol. 9, no.
9 (September 1987), p. 34-37, 80. English.
DESCR: *Biography; Bonilla, Tony;
*Businesspeople; Cardenas, Ruben R.

Gomez-Quinones, Juan

3283 Garcia, Mario T. Book review of: DEVELOPMENT
OF THE MEXICAN WORKING CLASS NORTH OF THE
RIO BRAVO: WORK AND CULTURE AMONG LABORERS
AND ARTISANS, 1600-1900. PACIFIC HISTORICAL
REVIEW, Vol. 53, no. 4 (November 1984), p.
525-527. English. **DESCR:** Book Reviews;
*DEVELOPMENT OF THE MEXICAN WORKING CLASS
NORTH OF THE RIO BRAVO: WORK AND CULTURE
AMONG LABORERS AND ARTISANS, 1600-1900;
Laboring Classes.

3284 Griswold del Castillo, Richard. New
perspectives on the Mexican and American
borderlands. LATIN AMERICAN RESEARCH REVIEW,
Vol. 19, no. 1 (1984), p. 199-209. English.
DESCR: AL NORTE DEL RIO BRAVO (PASADO
INMEDIATO. 1930-1981); AL NORTE DEL RIO
BRAVO (PASADO LEJANO. 1600-1930); *Book
Reviews; *Border Region; Maciel, David;
MEXICANO RESISTANCE IN THE SOUTHWEST: "THE
SACRED RIGHT OF SELF-PRESERVATION";
Rosenbaum, Robert J.; THE MEXICAN FRONTIER,

1821-1846: THE AMERICAN SOUTHWEST UNDER
MEXICO; THE TEJANO COMMUNITY, 1836-1900;
Weber, David J.

Gonzales, Ana

3285 Winston, Bonnie. INROADS: internships that
work. HISPANIC ENGINEER, Vol. 3, no. 5
(Winter 1987), p. 38-42. English. **DESCR:**
Almanza, John; Alvarez, Maria; Carr, Frank;
*Educational Organizations; Educational
Statistics; Garcia, Juan; *INROADS; Pereira,
Eduardo; Raimundo, Antonio; Reza, Priscilla.

Gonzales, Edward

3286 The institute, the artist, the art. NUESTRO,
Vol. 11, no. 4 (May 1987), p. 15-17.
English. **DESCR:** Artists; Mural Art;
*Technical-Vocational Institute (T-V),
Albuquerque, NM.

Gonzales, Juan L., Jr.

3287 Reisler, Mark. Book review of: MEXICAN AND
MEXICAN AMERICAN FARM WORKERS. PACIFIC
HISTORICAL REVIEW, Vol. 55, (August 1986),
p. 494. English. **DESCR:** Book Reviews;
*MEXICAN AND MEXICAN AMERICAN FARM WORKERS:
THE CALIFORNIA AGRICULTURAL INDUSTRY.

3288 Thomas, Robert J. Book review of: MEXICAN
AND MEXICAN AMERICAN FARM WORKERS.
CONTEMPORARY SOCIOLOGY: A JOURNAL OF
REVIEWS, Vol. 16, no. 1 (January 1987), p.
106-107. English. **DESCR:** Book Reviews;
*MEXICAN AND MEXICAN AMERICAN FARM WORKERS:
THE CALIFORNIA AGRICULTURAL INDUSTRY.

Gonzales, Laurence

3289 Bruce-Novoa, Juan. Nuevo representantes de
la novela chicana. LA COMUNIDAD, No. 310
(June 29, 1986), p. 6-7+. Spanish. **DESCR:**
Brawley, Ernest; EL VAGO [novel]; FAULTLINE
[novel]; *Literary Criticism; Novel; Ortiz
Taylor, Sheila; THE ALAMO TREE [novel].

Gonzales, Paul [Olympic boxer]

3290 Lit, Ed. Paul Gonzalez [sic]. VISTA, Vol. 1,
no. 5 (January 5, 1986), p. 10. English.
DESCR: Athletes; *Boxing; East Los Angeles,
CA.

Gonzales, Richard "Pancho"

3291 Chavez, Lorenzo A. Pancho Gonzales:
pioneering champion. VISTA, Vol. 1, no. 8
(April 6, 1986), p. 16. English. **DESCR:**
*Athletes.

Gonzales, Rodolfo (Corky)

3292 Gurza, Esperanza. I AM JOAQUIN: speech act
theory applied. CONFLUENCIA, Vol. 1, no. 2
(Spring 1986), p. 85-97. English. **DESCR:** *I
AM JOAQUIN [book]; *Poetry; Rhetoric.

Gonzales, Sylvia Alicia

3293 Book review of: HISPANIC AMERICAN VOLUNTARY
ORGANIZATIONS. BOOKLIST, Vol. 82, no. 11
(February 1, 1986), p. 798, 800. English.
DESCR: Book Reviews; *HISPANIC AMERICAN
VOLUNTARY ORGANIZATIONS.

Gonzales, Sylvia Alicia (cont.)

3294 Haro, Robert P. Book review of: HISPANIC AMERICAN VOLUNTARY ORGANIZATIONS. AMERICAN REFERENCE BOOKS ANNUAL, Vol. 17, (1986), p. 146. English. **DESCR:** Book Reviews; *HISPANIC AMERICAN VOLUNTARY ORGANIZATIONS; Reference Works.

3295 Rockman, Ilene F. Book review of: HISPANIC AMERICAN VOLUNTARY ORGANIZATIONS. CHOICE, Vol. 23, no. 7 (March 1986), p. 1038. English. **DESCR:** Book Reviews; *HISPANIC AMERICAN VOLUNTARY ORGANIZATIONS.

Gonzales, Teresa

3296 Marambio, Gonzalo. From San Antonio to Paris: Tex-Mex food conquers the French. VISTA, Vol. 1, no. 6 (February 2, 1986), p. 18-20. English. **DESCR:** Business Enterprises; Cantu, Mario, Jr.; *Food Practices; *Mario's Restaurant. San Antonio, TX; Papa Maya's Restaurant. Paris, France.

Gonzales Torres, Celia

3297 Soto, Rose Marie. National Network of Hispanic Women. HISPANIC ENGINEER, Vol. 3, no. 4 (Fall 1987), p. 26-28. English. **DESCR:** Castillo, Sylvia; Gutierrez, Nancy; *National Network of Hispanic Women; *Professional Organizations; Women; Zambrana, Ruth.

Gonzalez, Casanova

3298 Griswold del Castillo, Richard. Book review of: ESTADOS UNIDOS HOY. PACIFIC HISTORICAL REVIEW, Vol. 54, no. 4 (1985), p. 542-544. English. **DESCR:** Book Reviews; *ESTADOS UNIDOS. HOY.

Gonzalez, Elaine

3299 Shaw, Katherine. Love affair with chocolate. VISTA, Vol. 1, no. 6 (February 2, 1986), p. 15-16. English. **DESCR:** *Business Enterprises; CHOCOLATE ARTISTRY.

Gonzalez [family name]

3300 Instituto Genealogico e Historico Latino-Americano. Rootsearch: Gonzalez: Febres-Cordero. VISTA, Vol. 1, no. 7 (March 2, 1986), p. 22. English. **DESCR:** Febres-Cordero [family name]; Genealogy; History; *Personal Names.

Gonzalez, John

3301 13-part series focuses on Hispanics in America. EDITOR & PUBLISHER: THE FOURTH ESTATE, Vol. 115, no. 14 (April 3, 1982), p. 37. English. **DESCR:** Books; Cultural Characteristics; DALLAS MORNING NEWS; Garcia, Juan; Goodwin, Jay; Grothe, Randy Eli; Hamilton, John; Hille, Ed; LA VIDA AMERICANA; *LA VIDA AMERICANA/HISPANICS IN AMERICA; Langer, Ralph; McLemore, David; Osburne, Burl; Parks, Scott; Pusey, Allen; Sonnemair, Jan.

Gonzalez, Nivia

3302 Shaw, Katherine. Mira! a look at America's Hispanic artists. VISTA, Vol. 1, no. 5 (January 5, 1986), p. 6-8. English. **DESCR:** *Art; Artists; Canadian Club Hispanic Art Tour; Delgadillo, Ramon; Gamboa, Diane; *Trevino, Jesus (Jesse).

Gonzalez, Patricia

3303 Chavez, Lorenzo A. The eyes of Texas are upon them. VISTA, Vol. 2, no. 2 (October 4, 1986), p. 20. English. **DESCR:** *Art; Cardenas, David; *Chulas Fronteras [art exhibit]; Espada, Ibsen; Hernandez, John; Huerta, Benito; Martinez, Cesar Augusto.

Gonzalez, Raul

3304 McNeely, Dave. Hispanic power at the polls. VISTA, Vol. 2, no. 3 (November 2, 1986), p. 8-12. English. **DESCR:** Austin, TX; *Barrera, Roy, Jr.; Chavez, Linda; Elected Officials; Martinez, Bob; Maryland; Political System; San Antonio, TX; Statistics; Tampa, FL; *Voter Turnout.

THE GOOD CONSCIENCE

3305 Eberstadt, Fernanda. Montezuma's literary revenge. COMMENTARY, Vol. 81, no. 5 (May 1986), p. 35-40. English. **DESCR:** *Fuentes, Carlos; GRINGO VIEJO; *Literary Criticism; Mexican Literature; THE DEATH OF ARTEMIO CRUZ; WHERE THE AIR IS CLEAR.

Goodwin, Jay

3306 13-part series focuses on Hispanics in America. EDITOR & PUBLISHER: THE FOURTH ESTATE, Vol. 115, no. 14 (April 3, 1982), p. 37. English. **DESCR:** Books; Cultural Characteristics; DALLAS MORNING NEWS; Garcia, Juan; Gonzalez, John; Grothe, Randy Eli; Hamilton, John; Hille, Ed; LA VIDA AMERICANA; *LA VIDA AMERICANA/HISPANICS IN AMERICA; Langer, Ralph; McLemore, David; Osburne, Burl; Parks, Scott; Pusey, Allen; Sonnemair, Jan.

Government Contracts

3307 Banks, Marissa Elena. Army maneuvers. HISPANIC BUSINESS, Vol. 9, no. 12 (December 1987), p. 37-39. English. **DESCR:** Advertising Agencies; *Military; *Sosa & Associates; U.S. Department of Defense (DOD).

3308 Beale, Stephen. Defense cuts on the horizon? HISPANIC BUSINESS, Vol. 9, no. 10 (October 1987), p. 18-21. English. **DESCR:** *Business Enterprises; *Military.

3309 California businesses up: federal procurement down. HISPANIC BUSINESS, Vol. 9, no. 12 (December 1987), p. 60. English. **DESCR:** *Business Enterprises; California.

3310 SBA procurements dropping off. HISPANIC BUSINESS, Vol. 9, no. 5 (May 1987), p. 41. English. **DESCR:** *Business Enterprises; *Small Business Administration 8(a) Program.

3311 Sellers, Jeff M. High tech directory. HISPANIC BUSINESS, Vol. 9, no. 10 (October 1987), p. 7-9. English. **DESCR:** *Business Enterprises; Computers; *Electronics Industry; Military.

3312 Sellers, Jeff M. Strategic defenses: new niches for small firms. HISPANIC BUSINESS, Vol. 9, no. 10 (October 1987), p. 13-17. English. **DESCR:** *Advanced Sciences Inc., Albuquerque, NM; Business Enterprises; Electronics Industry; *Military; *Orion International Technologies, Inc.; Rios, Miguel, Jr.; Romero, Ed.

Government Contracts (cont.)

3313 Sellers, Jeff M. Wedtech fallout hits 8(a)
program. HISPANIC BUSINESS. Vol. 9, no. 6
(June 1987), p. 12-13, 17. English. DESCR:
*Business Enterprises; *Small Business
Administration 8(a) Program; *Wedtech
Corporation, Bronx, NY.

Graffiti

3314 Frias, Armando. [Graffiti]. CHIRICU, no. 2
(Spring 1977), p. 37-39.

Graham, Don

3315 Cooke, John Byrne. Book review of: SOUTH BY
SOUTHWEST: 24 STORIES FROM MODERN TEXAS. NEW
MEXICO HISTORICAL REVIEW, Vol. 62, no. 2
(April 1987), p. 217-218. English. DESCR:
Book Reviews; *SOUTH BY SOUTHWEST: THE
MEXICAN-AMERICAN AND HIS HERITAGE.

Gramm-Rudman Balanced Budget Amendment

3316 Morales, Cecilio. Budget cutting and
Hispanics. VISTA, Vol. 1, no. 6 (February 2,
1986), p. 22. English. DESCR: *Federal Aid;
National Association of Latino Elected
Officials (NALEO); National Council of La
Raza (NCLR).

Gramm-Rudman-Hollings Deficit Control Act (PL 99-177)

3317 Report to the Network. LA RED/THE NET, no.
92 (January, February, 1986), p. 1-4.
English. DESCR: Federal Aid; Finance;
*Higher Education; Reagan Administration;
*School Finance.

Grammy Awards

3318 Haley, Lindsey. Una premiacion
controvertida. LA COMUNIDAD, No. 246 (April
7, 1985), p. 5-6. Spanish. DESCR: Awards;
Discrimination; Guevara, Ruben; *Recording
Industry; Zanya Records Co., Los Angeles,
CA.

Granjon, Henry

3319 Foley, Patrick. Book review of: ALONG THE
RIO GRANDE: PASTORAL VISIT TO SOUTHWEST NEW
MEXICO IN 1902. NEW MEXICO HISTORICAL
REVIEW, Vol. 62, no. 4 (October 1987), p.
405-6. English. DESCR: *ALONG THE RIO
GRANDE: A PASTORAL VISIT TO SOUTHWEST NEW
MEXICO IN 1902; Book Reviews; *New Mexico.

Grants
USE: Funding Sources

Grape Boycott
USE: Boycotts

Great Western Sugar Company, Hudson, CO

3320 Romero, Mary and Margolis, Eric. Tending the
beets: campesinas and the Great Western
Sugar Company. REVISTA MUJERES, Vol. 2, no.
2 (June 1985), p. 17-27. English. DESCR:
*Chicanas; *Farm Workers; Food Industry.

Green Berets

3321 Benavidez, Roy. An embattled Chicano. VISTA,
Vol. 2, no. 5 (January 4, 1987), p. 20.
English. DESCR: Benavidez, Roy; *Books;
Griffin, Oscar; *THE THREE WARS OF ROY
BENAVIDEZ; Vietnam War.

GREEN MEDICINE: TRADITIONAL MEXICAN-AMERICAN HERBAL REMEDIES

3322 de la Cancela, Victor. Book review of: GREEN
MEDICINE. LECTOR, Vol. 4, no. 1-3 (1986), p.
[64]. English. DESCR: Book Reviews; Torres,
Eliseo.

Greenberg, Bradley S.

3323 Delgado, Melvin. Book review of:
MEXICAN-AMERICANS AND THE MASS-MEDIA.
HISPANIC JOURNAL OF BEHAVIORAL SCIENCES,
Vol. 9, no. 4 (December 1987), p. 461-463.
English. DESCR: Book Reviews; Mass Media;
*MEXICAN AMERICANS AND THE MASS MEDIA.

3324 Ockerman, Janet D. Book review of:
MEXICAN-AMERICANS AND THE MASS-MEDIA. PUBLIC
OPINION QUARTERLY, Vol. 49, no. 1 (Spring
1985), p. 138-139. English. DESCR: Book
Reviews; *MEXICAN AMERICANS AND THE MASS
MEDIA.

3325 Reese, Stephen D. Book review of:
MEXICAN-AMERICANS AND THE MASS-MEDIA.
JOURNALISM QUARTERLY, Vol. 61, no. 3 (Fall
1984), p. 705-706. English. DESCR: Book
Reviews; Mass Media; *MEXICAN AMERICANS AND
THE MASS MEDIA.

3326 Subervi-Velez, Federico. Book review of:
MEXICAN-AMERICANS AND THE MASS-MEDIA.
INTERNATIONAL JOURNAL OF INTERCULTURAL
RELATIONS, Vol. 8, no. 3 (1984), p. 340-342.
English. DESCR: Book Reviews; Mass Media;
*MEXICAN AMERICANS AND THE MASS MEDIA.

Griffin, Oscar

3327 Benavidez, Roy. An embattled Chicano. VISTA,
Vol. 2, no. 5 (January 4, 1987), p. 20.
English. DESCR: Benavidez, Roy; *Books;
Green Berets; *THE THREE WARS OF ROY
BENAVIDEZ; Vietnam War.

Gringo
USE: Anglo Americans

GRINGO VIEJO

3328 Eberstadt, Fernanda. Montezuma's literary
revenge. COMMENTARY, Vol. 81, no. 5 (May
1986), p. 35-40. English. DESCR: *Fuentes,
Carlos; *Literary Criticism; Mexican
Literature; THE DEATH OF ARTEMIO CRUZ; THE
GOOD CONSCIENCE; WHERE THE AIR IS CLEAR.

Griswold del Castillo, Richard

3329 de Leon, Arnoldo. Book review of: LA
FAMILIA. SOUTHWESTERN HISTORICAL QUARTERLY,
Vol. 89, no. 4 (1986), p. 564-565. English.
DESCR: Book Reviews; *LA FAMILIA: CHICANO
FAMILIES IN THE URBAN SOUTHWEST, 1848 TO THE
PRESENT.

3330 de Leon, Arnoldo. Book review of: THE LOS
ANGELES BARRIO 1850-1890: A SOCIAL HISTORY.
LA RED/THE NET, no. 64 (February 1983), p.
4-5. English. DESCR: Book Reviews; *THE LOS
ANGELES BARRIO 1850-1890: A SOCIAL HISTORY.

Griswold del Castillo, Richard (cont.)

3331 de Leon, Arnoldo and Stewart, Kenneth L. A tale of 3 cities: a comparative analysis of the socio-economic conditions of Mexican-Americans in Los Angeles, Tucson, and San Antonio, 1850-1900. JOURNAL OF THE WEST. Vol. 24, no. 2 (1985), p. 64-74. English. DESCR: Economic History and Conditions; Employment; Labor; *Los Angeles, CA; San Antonio, TX; *Social History and Conditions; Tucson, AZ; Urban Communities.

3332 Driscoll, Barbara A. Book review of: LA FAMILIA. JOURNAL OF AMERICAN ETHNIC HISTORY, Vol. 7, no. 1 (Fall 1987), p. 107-109. English. DESCR: Book Reviews; Family; *LA FAMILIA: CHICANO FAMILIES IN THE URBAN SOUTHWEST, 1848 TO THE PRESENT.

3333 Everett. D.E. Book review of: LA FAMILIA. CHOICE, Vol. 22, no. 10 (June 1985), p. 1574. English. DESCR: Book Reviews; *LA FAMILIA: CHICANO FAMILIES IN THE URBAN SOUTHWEST. 1848 TO THE PRESENT.

3334 Garcia, Mario T. Book review of: LA FAMILIA. LA RED/THE NET, no. 99 (August 1986), p. 4-5. English. DESCR: Book Reviews; Family; *LA FAMILIA: CHICANO FAMILIES IN THE URBAN SOUTHWEST, 1848 TO THE PRESENT.

3335 Gonzalez, Hector Hugo. Book review of: LA FAMILIA. LECTOR. Vol. 4, no. 4-6 (1987), p. 54. English. DESCR: Book Reviews; Family; *LA FAMILIA: CHICANO FAMILIES IN THE URBAN SOUTHWEST. 1848 TO THE PRESENT.

3336 Kerr. Louise A. Book review of: THE LOS ANGELES BARRIO 1850-1890: A SOCIAL HISTORY. JOURNAL OF AMERICAN HISTORY, Vol. 70, no. 4 (March 1984), p. 894-895. English. DESCR: Book Reviews; *THE LOS ANGELES BARRIO 1850-1890: A SOCIAL HISTORY.

3337 Raksin, Alex. Book review of: LA FAMILIA. LOS ANGELES TIMES BOOK REVIEW, (April 13, 1986), p. 10. English. DESCR: Book Reviews; Family; *LA FAMILIA: CHICANO FAMILIES IN THE URBAN SOUTHWEST. 1848 TO THE PRESENT.

3338 Valdes, Dennis. Book review of: THE LOS ANGELES BARRIO 1850-1890: A SOCIAL HISTORY. LA RED/THE NET, no. 36 (November 1980), p. 5. English. DESCR: Book Reviews; History; *Los Angeles, CA; *Social History and Conditions; *THE LOS ANGELES BARRIO 1850-1890: A SOCIAL HISTORY.

Gronk (Pseud.)

3339 Gamboa, Harry, Jr. El artista chicano dentro y fuera de la "corriente" artistica. LA COMUNIDAD, No. 351 (April 12, 1987), 2-5+. Spanish. DESCR: *Art; Artists; Carrasco, Barbara; Gamboa, Diane; Martinez, Daniel J.; Valadez, John; Valdez, Patssi.

3340 Goldman, Shifra. En medio de la tormenta de "Gronk". LA COMUNIDAD, No. 313 (July 20, 1986), p. 8-9. Spanish. DESCR: *Art; Artists; Biography.

3341 Haley, Lindsey. Gronk y su inquietante concepto del arte. LA COMUNIDAD, No. 252 (May 19, 1985), p. 2-3. Spanish. DESCR: *Artists; ASCO [art group], Los Angeles, CA; Biography; Exhibits; OFF THE STREETS [exhibit].

3342 Rosas, Alejandro. Proyecto de arte latino en Los Angeles. LA COMUNIDAD, No. 251 (May 12, 1985), p. 4-5. Spanish. DESCR: *Art; Art Galleries; *Galeria Ocaso, Los Angeles, CA;

Gamboa, Manazar.

Grosjean, Francois

3343 Ryan, Ellen Bouchard. An interdisciplinary perspective on the bilingual experience. BILINGUAL REVIEW, Vol. 11, no. 3 (September, December, 1984), p. 69-71. English. DESCR: Bilingualism; Book Reviews; *LIFE WITH TWO LANGUAGES: AN INTRODUCTION TO BILINGUALISM.

Grothe, Randy Eli

3344 13-part series focuses on Hispanics in America. EDITOR & PUBLISHER: THE FOURTH ESTATE, Vol. 115, no. 14 (April 3, 1982), p. 37. English. DESCR: Books; Cultural Characteristics; DALLAS MORNING NEWS; Garcia, Juan; Gonzalez, John; Goodwin, Jay; Hamilton, John; Hille, Ed; LA VIDA AMERICANA; *LA VIDA AMERICANA/HISPANICS IN AMERICA; Langer, Ralph; McLemore, David; Osburne, Burl; Parks, Scott; Pusey, Allen; Sonnemair, Jan.

GSE Construction Co., Inc., Livermore, CA

3345 The top 100--profiles. HISPANIC BUSINESS, Vol. 9, no. 11 (November 1987), p. 31-50. English. DESCR: Artco Contracting, Inc., Auburn Hills, MI; *Business Enterprises; Computer Trade Development Corp, Birmingham, MI; Corella Electric Inc., Phoenix, AZ; National Systems & Research Co.; Unique Construction Co., Hillside, IL.

Guadalupe Hidalgo, Treaty of 1848

3346 Baker, Ross K. Border follies. AMERICAN DEMOGRAPHICS, Vol. 8, no. 8 (August 1986), p. 60. English. DESCR: Immigration; Rio Grande; Texas; *Undocumented Workers.

Guatemala

3347 Rodriguez, Nestor. Undocumented Central Americans in Houston: diverse populations. INTERNATIONAL MIGRATION REVIEW, Vol. 21, no. 1 (Spring 1987), p. 4-26. English. DESCR: *Central America; El Salvador; Ethnic Groups; Honduras; *Houston, TX; Immigrants; Intergroup Relations; Latin Americans; *Political Refugees; *Undocumented Workers.

Guerra, Stella

3348 Allsup, Dan. The story of Stella. VISTA, Vol. 2, no. 1 (September 7, 1986), p. 16. English. DESCR: Business Enterprises; *Cosmetology; U.S. Air Force; U.S. Department of Defense (DOD).

Guerrero, Adolfo "El Zarco"

3349 Goldman, Shifra. Zarco Guerrero: tradicion y transformacion. LA COMUNIDAD, No. 249 (April 28, 1985), p. 2-3. Spanish. DESCR: *Art; Biography; Masks; Sculpture.

Guerrero, Art

3350 Scenes from the February SHPE careers conference. HISPANIC ENGINEER, Vol. 3, no. 1 (Spring 1987), p. 14-15. English. DESCR: *Conferences and Meetings; *Salazar, Diane; Society of Hispanic Professional Engineers (SHPE).

Guerrero, Lena

3351 Lena Guerrero. INTERCAMBIOS FEMENILES, Vol. 2, no. 6 (Spring 1987), p. 15,26. English. DESCR: Chicanas; Leadership; Politics.

Guerrero, Lena (cont.)

3352 Trager, Cara S. Carving out a niche in politics. HISPANIC BUSINESS, Vol. 9, no. 10 (October 1987), p. 29-31. English. **DESCR:** Biography; *Chicanas; *Elected Officials; Texas.

Guevara, Ruben

3353 Haley, Lindsey. Una premiacion controvertida. LA COMUNIDAD, No. 246 (April 7, 1985), p. 5-6. Spanish. **DESCR:** Awards; Discrimination; *Grammy Awards; *Recording Industry; Zanya Records Co., Los Angeles, CA.

Guevas, Fernando

3354 Sanders, Bob. Boycott Campbell's: Ohio farmworkers take it to the top. DOLLARS AND SENSE. no. 92 (December 1983), p. 16-18. English. **DESCR:** Boycotts; Campbell Soup Co.; Chavez, Cesar E.; Farm Labor Organizing Commmittee (FLOC); Farm Workers; *Labor Disputes; Labor Unions; Ohio; Strikes and Lockouts; United Farmworkers of America (UFW).

Gumperz, John J.

3355 Duran, Richard P. Book reviews of: DISCOURSE STRATEGIES and LANGUAGE AND SOCIAL IDENTITY. LA RED/THE NET, no. 77 (February 1984), p. 13-14. English. **DESCR:** *Book Reviews; *DISCOURSE STRATEGIES; *LANGUAGE AND SOCIAL IDENTITY.

Guthrie, Grace Pung

3356 Duran, Richard P. Book review of: CULTURE AND THE BILINGUAL CLASSROOM. LA RED/THE NET, no. 44 (July 1981), p. 4-5. English. **DESCR:** Bilingualism; Book Reviews; *CULTURE AND THE BILINGUAL CLASSROOM: STUDIES IN CLASSROOM ETHNOLOGY; Hu-Pei Au, Kathryn; Trueba, Henry T.

Gutierrez de Lara, Lazaro

3357 Escobar. Edward J. Mexican revolutionaries and the Los Angeles police: harassment of the Partido Liberal Mexicano, 1907-1910. AZTLAN. Vol. 17, no. 1 (Spring 1986), p. 1-46. English. **DESCR:** Civil Rights; *Flores Magon, Ricardo; Los Angeles, CA; *Los Angeles Police Department; *Partido Liberal Mexicano (PLM); *Police; Police Brutality; Political Repression; Rico, Louis; Rico, Thomas; Talamantes, Felipe; United States-Mexico Relations.

Gutierrez, Efrain

3358 Barrios, Greg. Efrain Gutierrez y el nuevo cine chicano. LA COMUNIDAD, No. 265 (August 18, 1985), p. 3. Spanish. **DESCR:** Biography; *Films; PLEASE DON'T BURY ME ALIVE [film].

Gutierrez [family name]

3359 Instituto Genealogico e Historico Latino-Americano. Rootsearch: Gutierrez. VISTA, Vol. 1, no. 2 (October 5, 1985), p. 22. English. **DESCR:** Genealogy; History; *Personal Names.

Gutierrez, Jose Angel

3360 de la Garza, Rodolfo O. Book review of: A WAR OF WORDS. JOURNAL OF AMERICAN ETHNIC HISTORY, Vol. 6, no. 2 (Spring 1987), p. 97-98. English. **DESCR:** *A WAR OF WORDS: CHICANO PROTEST IN THE 1960S AND 1970S; Book

Reviews; Hammerback, John C.; Jensen, Richard J.; Rhetoric.

Gutierrez, Nancy

3361 Soto, Rose Marie. National Network of Hispanic Women. HISPANIC ENGINEER, Vol. 3, no. 4 (Fall 1987), p. 26-28. English. **DESCR:** Castillo, Sylvia; Gonzales Torres, Celia; *National Network of Hispanic Women; *Professional Organizations; Women; Zambrana, Ruth.

Gutierrez, Sidney

3362 Pinon, Fernando. Conquistadors of space. VISTA, Vol. 1, no. 4 (December 7, 1985), p. 6-9. English. **DESCR:** *Astronauts; Biography; *Chang-Diaz, Franklin.

Gutierrez-Witt, Laura

3363 Chabran, Richard. Book review of: MEXICAN AMERICAN ARCHIVES AT THE BENSON COLLECTION: A GUIDE FOR USERS. LA RED/THE NET, no. 52 (March 1982), p. 6-7. English. **DESCR:** Archives; Book Reviews; Flores, Maria; *MEXICAN AMERICAN ARCHIVES AT THE BENSON COLLECTION.

Guzman [family name]

3364 Instituto Genealogico e Historico Latino-Americano. Rootsearch: Guzman: Zamora. VISTA, Vol. 2, no. 7 (March 8, 1987), p. 25. English. **DESCR:** Genealogy; History; *Personal Names; *Zamora [family name].

Guzman, Ofelia

3365 Families of the year. VISTA, Vol. 2, no. 2 (October 4, 1986), p. 16-18. English. **DESCR:** Aguilar, Gregorio; Aguilar, Guadalupe; Aranda, Benjamin; Aranda, Emma; *Awards; de la Rocha, Beatriz; de la Rocha, Castulo; Family; Guzman, Roberto; *Hispanic Family of the Year Award.

Guzman, Ralph

3366 Gutierrez, Felix. Ralph Guzman remembered. LA RED/THE NET, no. 91 (October 1985), p. 1-2. English. **DESCR:** Biography; Teaching Profession.

Guzman, Roberto

3367 Families of the year. VISTA, Vol. 2, no. 2 (October 4, 1986), p. 16-18. English. **DESCR:** Aguilar, Gregorio; Aguilar, Guadalupe; Aranda, Benjamin; Aranda, Emma; *Awards; de la Rocha, Beatriz; de la Rocha, Castulo; Family; Guzman, Ofelia; *Hispanic Family of the Year Award.

Hakuta, Kenji

3368 Chavez, Gene T. Book review of: MIRROR OF LANGUAGE: THE DEBATE ON BILINGUALISM. JOURNAL OF THE ASSOCIATION OF MEXICAN AMERICAN EDUCATORS, (1986, 1987), p. 52-53. English. **DESCR:** Book Reviews; *MIRROR OF LANGUAGE: THE DEBATE ON BILINGUALISM.

3369 Duran, Richard P. Article review of: "The Second Language Learner in the Context of the Study of Language Acquisition". LA RED/THE NET, no. 57 (August 1982), p. 8. English. **DESCR:** Language Development; *"The Second Language Learner in the Context of the Study of Language Acquisition".

Hall, Linda B.

3370 Hart, John M. Book review of: TEXAS AND THE MEXICAN REVOLUTION. PACIFIC HISTORICAL REVIEW, Vol. 55, no. 2 (1986), p. 324-325. English. **DESCR:** Book Reviews; Coerver, Don M.; *TEXAS AND THE MEXICAN REVOLUTION: A STUDY IN STATE AND NATIONAL BORDER POLICY.

3371 Hill, Larry D. Book review of: TEXAS AND THE MEXICAN REVOLUTION. JOURNAL OF SOUTHERN HISTORY, Vol. 52, no. 4 (November 1986), p. 651-652. English. **DESCR:** Book Reviews; Coerver. Don M.; *TEXAS AND THE MEXICAN REVOLUTION: A STUDY IN STATE AND NATIONAL BORDER POLICY.

3372 Raat, W. Dirk. Book review of: TEXAS AND THE MEXICAN REVOLUTION. WESTERN HISTORICAL QUARTERLY, Vol. 17, no. 1 (January 1986), p. 91-92. English. **DESCR:** Book Reviews; Border Region; Coerver, Don M.; *TEXAS AND THE MEXICAN REVOLUTION: A STUDY IN STATE AND NATIONAL BORDER POLICY.

Hallmark Cards

3373 Beale, Stephen. New blood, fresh money: Telemundo, Univision bullish on television market. HISPANIC BUSINESS, Vol. 9, no. 12 (December 1987), p. 30-36. English. **DESCR:** *Corporations; LatCom; Radio; Spanish International Communications Corp. (SICC); *Spanish Language; *Telemundo Television Group; *Television; Univision.

3374 Fever, Jack. Hispanic marketplace: the SICC sale: it is indeed a Hallmark. ADWEEK, Vol. 36, (July 28, 1986), p. 18. English. **DESCR:** KMEX, Los Angeles, CA [television station]; *Spanish International Communications Corp. (SICC); *Television.

3375 Hispanic marketing. ADVERTISING AGE MAGAZINE, Vol. 57, no. 16 (February 27, 1986), p. 11-51. English. **DESCR:** Adolph Coors Co.; Advertising; Allstate Insurance Co.; American Greetings; Anheuser-Busch, Inc.; Business Enterprises; Coca-Cola Company; Consumers; Ford Motor Company; *Marketing; Mass Media; McDonald's Corporation; Metropolitan Life Insurance Corporation; Pepsi-Cola Bottling Group; Prudential; Spanish International Network (SIN); State Farm Mutual Insurance; Tylenol; United Insurance Co. of America.

3376 SICC sale opposed. BROADCASTING, Vol. 111, no. 7 (August 18, 1986), p. 46-52. English. **DESCR:** Azcarraga, Emilio; Federal Communications Commission (FCC); First Chicago Venture Capital; KFTV, Fresno, CA [television station]; KMEX, Los Angeles, CA [television station]; KWEX, San Antonio, TX [television station]; Legal Cases; *Spanish International Communications Corp. (SICC); Spanish Language; Tapia, Raul R.; Television; TVL Corp.; WLTV, Miami, FL [television station]; WXTV, Paterson, NJ [television station].

3377 SICC sells TVs for $301.5 million. BROADCASTING, Vol. 111, no. 4 (July 28, 1986), p. 91-92. English. **DESCR:** Azcarraga, Emilio; First Chicago Venture Capital; KFTV, Fresno, CA [television station]; KMEX, Los Angeles, CA [television station]; KWEX, San Antonio, TX [television station]; Legal Cases; *Spanish International Communications Corp. (SICC); Spanish International Network (SIN); Spanish Language; Television; Villanueva, Daniel; WLTV, Miami, FL [television station]; WXTV, Paterson, NJ [television station].

Hamilton, John

3378 13-part series focuses on Hispanics in America. EDITOR & PUBLISHER: THE FOURTH ESTATE, Vol. 115, no. 14 (April 3, 1982), p. 37. English. **DESCR:** Books; Cultural Characteristics; DALLAS MORNING NEWS; Garcia, Juan; Gonzalez, John; Goodwin, Jay; Grothe, Randy Eli; Hille, Ed; LA VIDA AMERICANA; *LA VIDA AMERICANA/HISPANICS IN AMERICA; Langer, Ralph; McLemore, David; Osburne, Burl; Parks, Scott; Pusey, Allen; Sonnemair, Jan.

Hammerback, John C.

3379 de la Garza, Rodolfo O. Book review of: A WAR OF WORDS. JOURNAL OF AMERICAN ETHNIC HISTORY, Vol. 6, no. 2 (Spring 1987), p. 97-98. English. **DESCR:** *A WAR OF WORDS: CHICANO PROTEST IN THE 1960S AND 1970S; Book Reviews; Gutierrez, Jose Angel; Jensen, Richard J.; Rhetoric.

Handicapped

3380 McMenamin, Jerry. Language deficits in a bilingual child with cerebral cysticercosis. BILINGUAL REVIEW, Vol. 11, no. 3 (September, December, 1984), p. 25-30. English. **DESCR:** Bilingualism; *Cerebral Cysticercosis; Diseases; *Language Development.

Handicrafts
  USE: Arts and Crafts

Hansen, Niles

3381 Dunn, Ed. Book review of: THE BORDER ECONOMY: REGIONAL DEVELOPMENT IN THE SOUTHWEST. LA RED/THE NET, no. 50 (January 1982), p. 9-10. English. **DESCR:** Book Reviews; *Border Region; Border Studies; *THE BORDER ECONOMY: REGIONAL DEVELOPMENT IN THE SOUTHWEST.

Harris, William J.

3382 Labor department official challenges Hispanic program manager to maintain commitment, perseverance. HISPANIC TIMES, Vol. 8, no. 5 (October, November, 1987), p. 41. English. **DESCR:** *Affirmative Action; Office of Civil Rights, Labor Department, Washington, D.C.

HAY PLESHA LICHENS TU DI FLAC

3383 de Ortego y Gasca, Felipe. El crepusculo y la bandera. CHIRICU, Vol. 2, no. 2 (1981), p. 65-68. Spanish. **DESCR:** Book Reviews; Sanchez, Saul.

Head Start

3384 Arenas, Soledad and Trujillo, Lorenzo A. The evaluation of four Head Start bilingual multicultural curriculum models. LA RED/THE NET, no. 66 (March 1983), p. 2-5. English. **DESCR:** *Bilingual Bicultural Education; *Cultural Pluralism; Evaluation (Educational).

Health
  USE: Public Health

Health Care
  USE: Medical Care

Health Education

3385 Koop, C. Everett. Plain talk on AIDS for
     Hispanic Americans. VISTA, Vol. 3, no. 1
     (September 6, 1987), p. 13. English. DESCR:
     *Acquired Immune Deficiency Syndrome (AIDS).

3386 Lorig, Kate R., et al. Converging and
     diverging beliefs about arthritis: Caucasian
     patients, Spanish speaking patients, and
     physicians. JOURNAL OF RHEUMATOLOGY, Vol.
     11. no. 1 (February 1984), p. 76-79.
     English. DESCR: *Arthritis.

3387 Morales, Cecilio. A question of health.
     VISTA, Vol. 3, no. 3 (November 8, 1987), p.
     14, 19. English. DESCR: Delgado, Jane;
     *National Coalition of Hispanic Mental
     Health and Human Services Organizations
     (COSSMHO); Preventative Medicine.

3388 Remas, Theodora A. Cancer: early detection
     can help prevent a deadly disease. VISTA,
     Vol. 1, no. 8 (April 6, 1986), p. 10-11.
     English. DESCR: *Diseases; Preventative
     Medicine.

3389 Remas, Theodora A. The threat of AIDS.
     VISTA, Vol. 2, no. 10 (June 7, 1987), p.
     17-18, 25. English. DESCR: *Acquired Immune
     Deficiency Syndrome (AIDS); Directories;
     *Medical Care; Preventative Medicine.

3390 Remas, Theodora A. The threat of diabetes.
     VISTA, Vol. 1, no. 2 (October 5, 1985), p.
     14-16. English. DESCR: *Diabetes; *Mezitis,
     Nicholas; *Nutrition; Public Health;
     Rico-Perez, Manuel.

THE HEALTH REVOLUTION IN CUBA

3391 Hayes-Bautista, David Emmett. Book review
     of: THE HEALTH REVOLUTION IN CUBA. LA
     RED/THE NET, no. 11 (November 1983), p.
     10-12. English. DESCR: Book Reviews;
     Diaz-Briquets, Sergio.

Health Status
     USE: Public Health

Hearing Impaired
     USE: Deaf

Heart Disease

3392 Diet cited as cause of hypertension among
     Hispanics. HISPANIC TIMES, Vol. 8, no. 3
     (May, June, 1987), p. 16. English. DESCR:
     *Hypertension; *Nutrition.

3393 Stern, Michael P. Epidemiology of diabetes
     and coronary heart disease among
     Mexican-Americans. TRANSACTIONS OF THE
     ASSOC. OF LIFE INSURANCE MEDICAL DIRECTORS,
     Vol. 67, (1983), p. 79-90. English. DESCR:
     Anglo Americans; *Diabetes; *San Antonio,
     TX.

HEART OF AZTLAN

3394 Lomeli, Francisco A. En torno a la
     literatura...convergencia o divergencia? LA
     COMUNIDAD, No. 274 (October 20, 1985), p.
     8-11. Spanish. DESCR: Anaya, Rudolfo A.;
     Aztlan; Border Region; *Literary Criticism;
     Mendez M., Miguel; PEREGRINOS DE AZTLAN;
     *Primer Festival de Literatura Fronteriza
     Mexico-Estados Unidos.

HECHO EN AZTLAN [exhibit]

3395 Goldman, Shifra. Hecho en Aztlan. LA
     COMUNIDAD, No. 278 (November 17, 1985), p.
     8-9. Spanish. DESCR: *Art; Centro Cultural

de la Raza, San Diego, CA; Exhibits.

Hembrismo

3396 Rivera, Miquela. In battle of the sexes,
     time for a ceasefire. VISTA, Vol. 3, no. 2
     (October 3, 1987), p. 38. English. DESCR:
     Sex Stereotypes.

Herbal Medicine

3397 Gomez, Efrain A. and Gomez, Gerda E. Folk
     healing among Hispanic Americans. PUBLIC
     HEALTH NURSING, Vol. 2, no. 4 (December
     1985), p. 245-249. English. DESCR:
     Curanderismo; *Folk Medicine.

Hernandez, Antonia A.

3398 Beale, Stephen. MALDEF weathers a storm.
     HISPANIC BUSINESS, Vol. 9, no. 5 (May 1987),
     p. 10-11. English. DESCR: Anaya, Toney,
     Governor of New Mexico; Civil Rights;
     *Mexican American Legal Defense and
     Educational Fund (MALDEF); Organizations;
     Serna, Eric P.

3399 Hernandez prevails in fight over job.
     NUESTRO, Vol. 11, no. 2 (March 1987), p. 6.
     English. DESCR: *Anaya, Toney, Governor of
     New Mexico; *Mexican American Legal Defense
     and Educational Fund (MALDEF);
     Organizations.

3400 Olivera, Mercedes. The new Hispanic women.
     VISTA, Vol. 2, no. 11 (July 5, 1987), p.
     6-8. English. DESCR: Alvarez, Linda;
     *Chicanas; Esquiroz, Margarita; Garcia,
     Juliet; Mohr, Nicolasa; Molina, Gloria;
     Pabon, Maria; Working Women.

3401 Shaw, Katherine. Antonia Hernandez. VISTA,
     Vol. 1, no. 2 (October 5, 1985), p. 16.
     English. DESCR: *Biography; Chicanas;
     Mexican American Legal Defense and
     Educational Fund (MALDEF).

Hernandez, Francisco

3402 Hurtado, Aida. Book review of: WORK, FAMILY,
     SEX ROLES, LANGUAGE. LA RED/THE NET, no. 40
     (March 1981), p. 3. English. DESCR: Barrera,
     Mario; Book Reviews; Camarillo, Alberto;
     Social History and Conditions; *WORK,
     FAMILY, SEX ROLES, LANGUAGE: SELECTED PAPERS
     OF THE NATIONAL ASSOCIATION FOR CHICANO
     STUDIES CONFERENCE, 1979.

Hernandez, George

3403 Beale, Stephen. CEOs. HISPANIC BUSINESS,
     Vol. 9, no. 4 (April 1987), p. 20-37, 52.
     English. DESCR: Alvarez, Roberto; Batarse,
     Anthony A.; Biography; Business Enterprises;
     *Businesspeople; Carlo, Nelson; Estrada,
     Anthony; Flores, Frank; Fullana, Jaime, Jr.;
     *Management; Ortega, James; Quirch,
     Guillermo; Ruiz, Roberto; Santa Maria,
     Yvonne Z.; Sugranes, Rosa; Tamaya, Carlos;
     Young, Paul H., Jr.

Hernandez, John

3404 Chavez, Lorenzo A. The eyes of Texas are
     upon them. VISTA, Vol. 2, no. 2 (October 4,
     1986), p. 20. English. DESCR: *Art;
     Cardenas, David; *Chulas Fronteras [art
     exhibit]; Espada, Ibsen; Gonzalez, Patricia;
     Huerta, Benito; Martinez, Cesar Augusto.

Hernandez, Jose Amaro

3405 Garcia, Chris. Book review of: MUTUAL AID
     FOR SURVIVAL. HISPANIC AMERICAN HISTORICAL
     REVIEW, Vol. 64, no. 1 (February 1984), p.
     205. English. **DESCR**: Book Reviews; *MUTUAL
     AID FOR SURVIVAL: THE CASE OF THE MEXICAN
     AMERICAN.

3406 Griswold del Castillo, Richard. Book review
     of: MUTUAL AID FOR SURVIVAL. SOUTHWESTERN
     HISTORICAL QUARTERLY, Vol. 88, no. 3 (1985),
     p. 330-332. English. **DESCR**: Book Reviews;
     *MUTUAL AID FOR SURVIVAL: THE CASE OF THE
     MEXICAN AMERICAN; Mutualistas.

3407 San Miguel, Guadalupe. Book review of:
     MUTUAL AID FOR SURVIVAL. LECTOR. Vol. 4, no.
     4-6 (1987), p. 54-55. English. **DESCR**: Book
     Reviews; *MUTUAL AID FOR SURVIVAL: THE CASE
     OF THE MEXICAN AMERICAN; Mutualistas.

Herrera [family name]

3408 Instituto Genealogico e Historico
     Latino-Americano. Rootsearch: Patino:
     Herrera: Escobar. VISTA. Vol. 2, no. 9 (May
     3, 1987), p. 22. English. **DESCR**: *Escobar
     [family name]; Genealogy; History; *Patino
     [family name]; *Personal Names.

Herrera, Hayden

3409 Tibol, Raquel. La biografa se espanto de una
     vida abierta. LA COMUNIDAD, No. 302 (May 4,
     1986), p. 12-13. Spanish. **DESCR**: *Biography;
     Book Reviews; FRIDA: A BIOGRAPHY OF FRIDA
     KAHLO; *Kahlo, Frida.

Herrera, Jess

3410 SHPE news. HISPANIC ENGINEER, Vol. 3, no. 3
     (1987), p. 10-13. English. **DESCR**: *Awards;
     Castillo, Hector; Colmenarez, Margarita;
     Garcia, Raul; Lopez-Martin, Minnie;
     Mondragon, Ricardo; Reyes-Guerra, David;
     Silva, Juan; Society of Hispanic
     Professional Engineers (SHPE); Vargas,
     Jesus; Villanueva, Bernadette.

Herrera-Sobek, Maria

3411 Wreford, Mary. Book review of: THE BRACERO
     EXPERIENCE: ELITELORE VERSUS FOLKLORE. LA
     RED/THE NET, no. 29 (April 1980), p. 10.
     English. **DESCR**: Book Reviews; *Braceros;
     Immigrants; THE BRACERO EXPERIENCE:
     ELITELORE VERSUS FOLKLORE.

Hesselbein, Frances

3412 Frances Hesselbein. INTERCAMBIOS FEMENILES,
     Vol. 2, no. 6 (Spring 1987), p. 23. English.
     DESCR: *Chicanas; *Girl Scouts of the United
     States of America; *Leadership;
     Organizations; Women; Youth.

Hester v. U.S.

3413 Search and seizure. CRIMINAL LAW REPORTER,
     Vol. 35. no. 3 (April 18, 1984), p.
     3011-3027. English. **DESCR**: INS v. Delgado;
     Katz v. U.S.; Maine v. Thornton; Oliver v.
     U.S.; *Search and Seizure; *U.S. Supreme
     Court.

Hidalgo County, TX

3414 Hurtado, Aida. Midwife practices in Hildago
     County, Texas. TRABAJOS MONOGRAFICOS, Vol.
     3, no. 1 (1987), p. 1-30. English. **DESCR**:
     Chicanas; *Maternal and Child Welfare.

3415 Rips, Geoffrey. Civil rights and wrongs.

     TEXAS OBSERVOR, Vol. 76, (December 14,
     1984), p. 49-55. English. **DESCR**: Briscoe,
     Dolph, Jr., Governor of Texas; *Civil
     Rights; Farm Workers; La Raza Unida Party;
     Miller, C.L.; Segregation and Desegregation;
     Texas Farmworkers' Union; Voting Rights.

Hidalgo, David (Los Lobos)

3416 Forte, Dan. Los Lobos: Tex-Mex rock from
     East L.A. GUITAR PLAYER, Vol. 21, no. 2
     (February 1987), p. 68-94. English. **DESCR**:
     Biography; Discography; *Los Lobos del Este
     de Los Angeles (musical group); Lozano,
     Conrad (Los Lobos); *Musicians; Perez, Louie
     (Los Lobos); Recording Industry; *Rock
     Music; Rosas, Cesar (Los Lobos).

Hidalgo y Costilla, Miguel

3417 Gomez-Quinones, Juan. September 16th: a
     historical perspective. LATIN QUARTER, Vol.
     1, no. 2 (October 1974), p. 8,9,11,12.
     English. **DESCR**: *Dieciseis de Septiembre;
     *History; *Holidays; Los Angeles, CA.

High School Education
     USE: Secondary School Education

Higher Education

3418 Beltran, Christina. Minority access into
     higher education. REVISTA MUJERES, Vol. 4,
     no. 1 (January 1987), p. 54-55. English.
     DESCR: Discrimination in Education.

3419 Chacon, Maria A., et al. Chicanas in
     California postsecondary education. LA
     RED/THE NET, no. 65 (Winter 1983), p. 3-24.
     English. **DESCR**: *Chicanas; Research
     Methodology.

3420 Chavez, Lorenzo A. Passport to success.
     VISTA, Vol. 2, no. 1 (September 7, 1986), p.
     6-8. English. **DESCR**: Colleges and
     Universities; Enrollment.

3421 de los Santos, Alfredo G., Jr.; Montemayor,
     Joaquin; and Solis, Enrique, Jr. Chicano
     students in higher education: access,
     attrition and achievement. LA RED/THE NET,
     no. 41 (April 1981), p. 2-3. English.
     DESCR: Academic Achievement; *California;
     Enrollment; *Texas.

3422 Educational hierarchies and social
     differentiation. LA RED/THE NET, no. 37
     (December 1980), p. 2-3. English. **DESCR**:
     Discrimination in Education; Enrollment;
     *Southwestern United States.

3423 Garza, Hisauro A. The "barrioization" of
     Hispanic faculty. EDUCATIONAL RECORD,
     (Fall, Winter, 1987, 1988), p. 122-124.
     English. **DESCR**: *Colleges and Universities;
     *Discrimination in Education;
     *Discrimination in Employment; Teaching
     Profession.

3424 Gonzalez, Juan C. Report to the Network. LA
     RED/THE NET, No. 105 (February 1987), p.
     1-3. English. **DESCR**: Breland, Hunter M.;
     *DEMOGRAPHICS, STANDARDS, AND EQUITY
     CHALLENGES IN COLLEGE ADMISSIONS: REPORT OF
     A SURVEY OF UNDERGRADUATE ADMISSIONS
     POLICIES, PRACTICES AND PROCEDURES;
     *Discrimination in Education; *Enrollment.

Higher Education (cont.)

3425 Gutierrez, Felix. House approves Higher Education Act amendments. LA RED/THE NET, no. 92 (November, December, 1985), p. 3-4. English. **DESCR:** Educational Law and Legislation; Educational Organizations; Financial Aid; *Higher Education Amendments of 1985 (H.R. 3700); Hispanic Higher Education Coalition (HHEC).

3426 Higher education organizations. LA RED/THE NET, no. 92 (November, December, 1985), p. 11-13. English. **DESCR:** Educational Organizations; *Texas Association of Chicanos in Higher Education (TACHE).

3427 Higher education organizations. LA RED/THE NET, no. 93 (January, February, 1986), p. 5-8. English. **DESCR:** Educational Organizations; *Raza Advocates for California Higher Education (RACHE).

3428 Hispanics affected by major provisions in Higher Ed Act. LA RED/THE NET, no. 92 (November, 1985), p. 4-7. English. **DESCR:** Educational Law and Legislation; *Higher Education Amendments of 1985 (H.R. 3700).

3429 Leon, David Jess and McNeill, Daniel. The fifth class: a 19th century forerunner of affirmative action. CALIFORNIA HISTORY, Vol. 64, no. 1 (Winter 1985), p. 52-57. English. **DESCR:** *Affirmative Action; Colleges and Universities; Discrimination in Education; *Enrollment; History; Students; *University of California.

3430 Lopez, Manuel I. The role of the Chicano student in the Chicano Studies Program. EPOCA: NATIONAL CONCILIO FOR CHICANO STUDIES JOURNAL, Vol. 1, no. 2 (Winter 1971), p. 13-17. English. **DESCR:** *Chicano Studies; La Raza; *Student Movements; *Students.

3431 Madrid, Arturo. Report to the Network. LA RED/THE NET, no. 92 (November, December, 1985), p. 1-3. English. **DESCR:** Discrimination in Education.

3432 Madrid, Arturo. Report to the Network. LA RED/THE NET, No. 102 (November 1986), p. 1-2. English. **DESCR:** Literature Reviews.

3433 Madrid, Arturo. Report to the Network. LA RED/THE NET, No. 103 (December 1986), p. 1-2. English. **DESCR:** Educational Organizations; *National Chicano Council on Higher Education (NCCHE).

3434 Magallan, Rafael J. Hispanic organizations concerned with higher education. LA RED/THE NET, no. 91 (October 1985), p. 2-3. English. **DESCR:** *American Association for Higher Education Hispanic Caucus; *Educational Organizations.

3435 MEChA, Cal State Long Beach. The role of the Chicano student. EPOCA: NATIONAL CONCILIO FOR CHICANO STUDIES JOURNAL, Vol. 1, no. 2 (Winter 1971), p. 18-22. English. **DESCR:** *Chicano Studies; *Student Movements; *Students.

3436 Mendoza, Lupe. Porque lo podemos hacer--a poco no? REVISTA MUJERES, Vol. 1, no. 2 (June 1984), p. 33-37. Spanish. **DESCR:** Autobiography; Chicanas; *Mendoza, Lupe.

3437 Nunez, Rene. Criteria for employment of Chicano studies staff. EPOCA: NATIONAL CONCILIO FOR CHICANO STUDIES JOURNAL, Vol. 1, no. 2 (Winter 1971), p. 23-30. English.

DESCR: *Chicano Studies; Students; *Teaching Profession.

3438 Padilla, Raymond V. and Montiel, Miguel. A general framework for action in Chicano higher education. LA RED/THE NET, no. 81 (June 1964), p. 2-6. English. **DESCR:** *Arizona; Evaluation (Educational).

3439 Panas, Katia. Postsecondary retention and graduation: strategies for change. REVISTA MUJERES, Vol. 4, no. 1 (January 1987), p. 66-72. English. **DESCR:** Assimilation; Discrimination in Education; *Education.

3440 Perez, Emma. Higher education organizations. LA RED/THE NET, no. 94 (March 1986), p. 2-4. English. **DESCR:** Educational Organizations; *Mexican American Studies and Research Center, University of Arizona, Tucson, AZ; *Research Centers.

3441 Perez, Emma. Higher education organizations. LA RED/THE NET, no. 96 (May 1986), p. 6-8. English. **DESCR:** Educational Organizations; *Wisconsin Hispanic Council on Higher Education (WHCHE).

3442 Perez, Emma. Higher education organizations. LA RED/THE NET, no. 97 (June 1986), p. 4-5. English. **DESCR:** *Arizona Association of Chicanos for Higher Education (AACHE); *Educational Organizations.

3443 Perez, Emma. Higher education organizations. LA RED/THE NET, no. 99 (August 1986), p. 2-4. English. **DESCR:** *Colorado Association of Chicanos in Higher Education (CACHE); *Educational Organizations.

3444 Perez, Emma. Higher education organizations. LA RED/THE NET, No. 101 (October 1986), p. 6-10. English. **DESCR:** *Educational Organizations; *Hispanic Association of Higher Education (HAHE); *Puerto Rican Council on Higher Education (PRCHE); *SUNY Hispanic Research and Information Network.

3445 Perez, Emma. Networks. LA RED/THE NET, No. 103 (December 1986), p. 2-5. English. **DESCR:** *Chicanas; *Educational Organizations; *Mujeres Activas en Letras y Cambio Social (MALCS).

3446 Perez, Emma. Report to the Network. LA RED/THE NET, no. 95 (April 1986), p. 3-5. English. **DESCR:** *Educational Organizations; *Hispanic Association of Higher Education of New Jersey (HAHE).

3447 Perkins, Claranne. We the minorities of CASE: a special survey of minorities working in institutional advancement. CURRENTS, Vol. 10, no. 5 (May 1984), p. 34-40. English. **DESCR:** *Careers; Statistics.

3448 Recipients of Ford Foundation postdoctoral fellowships for minorities have been announced. LA RED/THE NET, no. 99 (August 1986), p. 10. English. **DESCR:** Awards; *Financial Aid; *Ford Foundation Postdoctoral Fellowships for Minorities Program.

3449 Report to the Network. LA RED/THE NET, no. 92 (January, February, 1986), p. 1-4. English. **DESCR:** Federal Aid; Finance; *Gramm-Rudman-Hollings Deficit Control Act (PL 99-177); Reagan Administration; *School Finance.

Higher Education (cont.)

3450 Report to the Network. LA RED/THE NET, no. 97 (June 1986), p. 1-2. English. **DESCR:** California Master Plan for Higher Education; *Colleges and Universities; *Evaluation (Educational).

3451 Report to the Network. LA RED/THE NET, no. 98 (July 1986), p. 1-2. English. **DESCR:** *Enrollment; Statistics.

3452 Report to the Network. LA RED/THE NET. No. 104 (January 1987), p. 1-2. English. **DESCR:** Computers; *Contreras, Reynaldo A.; *Midwestern States; *Natural Support Systems; Research Methodology; Surveys.

3453 Rodriguez, Eloy. Chicanos/Hispanics in higher education: now and beyond. HISPANIC TIMES. Vol. 8, no. 3 (May, June, 1987), p. 44-45. English. **DESCR:** Dropouts; Statistics.

3454 Scarpaci, Joseph L. and Fradd, Sandra. Latin Americans at the university level: implications for instruction. JOURNAL OF MULTICULTURAL COUNSELING AND DEVELOPMENT, Vol. 13, no. 4 (October 1985), p. 183-189. English. **DESCR:** Latin Americans.

3455 Smith, Mary Perry. Early identification and support: the University of California-Berkeley's MESA program. NEW DIRECTIONS FOR TEACHING AND LEARNING, no. 24 (December 1985), p. 19-25. English. **DESCR:** *Counseling (Educational); *Engineering as a Profession; Enrollment; *Mathematics, Engineering and Science Achievement (MESA); University of California, Berkeley.

3456 Soriano, Diane H. and Mejia, Gabriella S. "Ni he tenido tiempo para mi:" entrevista con Gabriella S. Mejia. REVISTA MUJERES, Vol. 1, no. 2 (June 1984), p. 38-41. Spanish. **DESCR:** Autobiography; *Chicanas; *Mejia, Gabriella S.

3457 Texas Association of Chicanos in Higher Education (TACHE) holds annual conference. LA RED/THE NET. No. 100 (September 1986), p. 2-5. English. **DESCR:** *Conferences and Meetings; *Educational Organizations; *Texas Association of Chicanos in Higher Education (TACHE).

3458 Texas' higher education "Adams" compliance report. LA RED/THE NET. No. 102 (November 1986), p. 2-5. English. **DESCR:** *Discrimination in Education; Public Policy; Texas; *Texas Equal Education Opportunity Plan for Higher Education.

Higher Education Amendments of 1985 (H.R. 3700)

3459 Gutierrez, Felix. House approves Higher Education Act amendments. LA RED/THE NET, no. 92 (November, December, 1985), p. 3-4. English. **DESCR:** Educational Law and Legislation; Educational Organizations; Financial Aid; *Higher Education; Hispanic Higher Education Coalition (HHEC).

3460 Hispanics affected by major provisions in Higher Ed Act. LA RED/THE NET, no. 92 (November, December, 1985), p. 4-7. English. **DESCR:** Educational Law and Legislation; *Higher Education.

HIJO DEL PUEBLO

3461 Benson, Douglas K. and Quintana, Leroy V. A conversation with Leroy V. Quintana. BILINGUAL REVIEW, Vol. 12, no. 3 (September, December, 1985), p. 218-229. English.

DESCR: Authors; Biography; Poetry; *Quintana, Leroy V.; SANGRE.

3462 Benson, Douglas K. Intuitions of a world in transition: the New Mexican poetry of Leroy V. Quintana. BILINGUAL REVIEW, Vol. 12, no. 1-2 (January, August, 1985), p. 62-80. English. **DESCR:** Authors; *Literary Criticism; New Mexico; Poetry; *Quintana, Leroy V.; SANGRE.

Hille, Ed

3463 13-part series focuses on Hispanics in America. EDITOR & PUBLISHER: THE FOURTH ESTATE, Vol. 115, no. 14 (April 3, 1982), p. 37. English. **DESCR:** Books; Cultural Characteristics; DALLAS MORNING NEWS; Garcia, Juan; Gonzalez, John; Goodwin, Jay; Grothe, Randy Eli; Hamilton, John; LA VIDA AMERICANA; *LA VIDA AMERICANA/HISPANICS IN AMERICA; Langer, Ralph; McLemore, David; Osburne, Burl; Parks, Scott; Pusey, Allen; Sonnemair, Jan.

Hinojosa, Gilbert Miguel

3464 Griswold del Castillo, Richard. Book review of: A BORDERLANDS TOWN IN TRANSITION: LAREDO, 1755-1870. PACIFIC HISTORICAL REVIEW, Vol. 54, no. 2 (May 1985), p. 223-224. English. **DESCR:** *A BORDERLANDS TOWN IN TRANSITION: LAREDO, 1755-1870; Book Reviews; Laredo, TX.

Hinojosa-Smith, Rolando R.

3465 Bruce-Novoa, Juan. Meet the writers of the 80s. VISTA, Vol. 1, no. 11 (July 6, 1986), p. 15-16. English. **DESCR:** Anaya, Rudolfo A.; Arte Publico Press; *Authors; Bilingual Review Press; Cisneros, Sandra; Keller, Gary D.; *Literature; Pineda, Cecile; Quinto Sol Publishing, Inc.; Rivera, Tomas; Soto, Gary.

3466 Cortina, Rodolfo J. Book review of: KLAIL CITY. VISTA, Vol. 3, no. 4 (December 6, 1987), p. 26. English. **DESCR:** Book Reviews; *KLAIL CITY Y SUS ALREDEDORES.

3467 Hinojosa-Smith, Rolando R. La realidad chicana se forjo con dos culturas. LA COMUNIDAD, No. 313 (July 20, 1986), p. 6-7. Spanish. **DESCR:** *Biography; Literary Criticism; Novel.

3468 Lomeli, Francisco A. Entrevista con Rolando Hinojosa (I). LA COMUNIDAD, No. 295 (March 16, 1986), p. 2-3+. Spanish. **DESCR:** *Biography; Literary Criticism; Novel; Short Story.

3469 Lomeli, Francisco A. Entrevista con Rolando Hinojosa (II). LA COMUNIDAD, No. 296 (March 23, 1986), p. 15. Spanish. **DESCR:** *Biography; Literary Criticism.

3470 Randolph, Donald A. Death's aesthetic proliferation in works of Hinojosa. CONFLUENCIA, Vol. 1, no. 2 (Spring 1986), p. 38-47. English. **DESCR:** Death (Concept); GENERACIONES Y SEMBLANZAS; KLAIL CITY Y SUS ALREDEDORES; KOREAN LOVE SONGS; *Literary Criticism; Novel.

3471 Sanchez, Saul. Book review of: THE VALLEY. LA RED/THE NET, no. 81 (June 1984), p. 7. Spanish. **DESCR:** Book Reviews; *THE VALLEY.

Hinojosa-Smith, Rolando R. (cont.)

3472 Seeking more readers for Hispanic literature. VISTA. Vol. 2, no. 3 (November 2, 1986), p. 25. English. DESCR: *Literature; *Miami Book Fair International; Mohr, Nicolasa; Munoz, Elias Miguel; Rodriguez, Richard.

3473 Torres, Hector. Discourse and plot in Rolando Hinojosa's THE VALLEY: narrativity and the recovery of Chicano heritage. CONFLUENCIA, Vol. 2, no. 1 (Fall 1986), p. 84-93. English. DESCR: *Literary Criticism; Novel; *THE VALLEY.

3474 Ugalde, Sharon E. Two visions of cultural domination: Carrero's EL HOMBRE QUE NO SUDABA and Hinojosa's MI QUERIDO RAFA. BILINGUAL REVIEW, Vol. 12, no. 1-2 (January, August. 1985), p. 159-165. English. DESCR: Carrero, Jaime; *EL HOMBRE QUE NO SUDABA; Literary Criticism; *MI QUERIDO RAFA.

HISPANEX (Oakland, CA)

3475 Cabello-Argandona, Roberto. Hispanex is here to stay. LECTOR, Vol. 4, no. 4-6 (1987), p. 6-8. English. DESCR: Databases; Library Services.

3476 Chabran, Richard. Book review of: BILINDEX. LA RED/THE NET. no. 87 (July 1985), p. 6-8. English. DESCR: *BILINDEX: A BILINGUAL SPANISH-ENGLISH SUBJECT HEADING LIST; Book Reviews; Subject Headings.

Hispanic Academy of Media Arts and Sciences (HAMAS)

3477 Jimenez, Luis. Cambia la imagen del latino en Hollywood. LA COMUNIDAD, No. 255 (June 9, 1985), p. 14-15. Spanish. DESCR: Discrimination; Employment; Films; *Mass Media; Organizations; Reyna, Phil.

HISPANIC ALMANAC

3478 Book review of: THE HISPANIC ALMANAC. BOOKLIST, Vol. 82. (May 1, 1986), p. 1296. English. DESCR: Almanacs; Book Reviews; Hispanic Policy Development Project (HPDP).

3479 Castillo-Speed, Lillian. Annotated bibliography. LA RED/THE NET. no. 93 (January, February, 1986), p. 14-17. English. DESCR: A BIBLIOGRAPHY OF MEXICAN AMERICAN HISTORY; ARTE CHICANO; Book Reviews; Caballero, Cesar; CHICANO LITERATURE: A REFERENCE GUIDE; CHICANO ORGANIZATIONS DIRECTORY; CHICANO PERIODICAL INDEX; Goldman, Shifra M.; HISPANIC MENTAL HEALTH RESEARCH: A REFERENCE GUIDE; Lomeli, Francisco A.; Martinez, Julio A.; Meier, Matt S.; Newton, Frank; *Reference Works; Ybarra-Frausto, Tomas.

HISPANIC AMERICA: FREEING THE FREE, HONORING HEROES

3480 Walker, Constance L. Book review of: HISPANIC AMERICA: FREEING THE FREE, HONORING HEROES. LECTOR. Vol. 4, no. 4-6 (1987), p. 55. English. DESCR: Book Reviews.

Hispanic American Genealogical Associates, Washington, DC

3481 Chavez, Lorenzo A. The quest for Hispanic roots. VISTA. Vol. 2, no. 7 (March 8, 1987), p. 5-6, 24. English. DESCR: Church of Jesus Christ of Latter-Day Saints (Mormons); Directories; *Garcia, Clotilde; *Genealogy; Las Porciones Genealogical Society,

Edinburg, TX; Los Bexarenos, San Antonio, TX; Los Californianos [genealogical society], San Jose, CA; Pan American University, Edinburg, TX; Texas Southmost College.

HISPANIC AMERICAN VOLUNTARY ORGANIZATIONS

3482 Book review of: HISPANIC AMERICAN VOLUNTARY ORGANIZATIONS. BOOKLIST, Vol. 82, no. 11 (February 1, 1986), p. 798, 800. English. DESCR: Book Reviews; Gonzales, Sylvia Alicia.

3483 Haro, Robert P. Book review of: HISPANIC AMERICAN VOLUNTARY ORGANIZATIONS. AMERICAN REFERENCE BOOKS ANNUAL, Vol. 17, (1986), p. 146. English. DESCR: Book Reviews; Gonzales, Sylvia Alicia; Reference Works.

3484 Rockman, Ilene F. Book review of: HISPANIC AMERICAN VOLUNTARY ORGANIZATIONS. CHOICE, Vol. 23, no. 7 (March 1986), p. 1038. English. DESCR: Book Reviews; Gonzales, Sylvia Alicia.

HISPANIC ART IN THE UNITED STATES: THIRTY CONTEMPORARY PAINTERS & SCULPTORS [exhibition]

3485 Goldman, Shifra. El arte hispano en Houston. LA COMUNIDAD, No. 361 (June 21, 1987), p. 6-7+. Spanish. DESCR: *Art; Exhibits; Houston, TX.

3486 A grand Hispanic art show. VISTA, Vol. 2, no. 8 (April 4, 1987), p. 20-21. English. DESCR: *Art; Art Galleries.

3487 Olivares, Julian. Hispanic art in the United States: thirty contemporary painters & sculptors. THE AMERICAS REVIEW, Vol. 15, no. 2 (Summer 1987), p. 7-10. English. DESCR: *Art; *Exhibits.

HISPANIC ARTS AND ETHNOHISTORY IN THE SOUTHWEST: NEW PAPERS INSPIRED BY THE WORKS OF E. BOYD

3488 Griffith, James S. Book review of: HISPANIC ARTS AND ETHNOHISTORY IN THE SOUTHWEST: NEW PAPERS INSPIRED BY THE WORKS OF E. BOYD. ARIZONA AND THE WEST, Vol. 26, no. 2 (Summer 1984), p. 188-189. English. DESCR: Book Reviews; Weigle, Marta.

Hispanic Association on Corporate Responsibility (HACER)

3489 Beale, Stephen. Friendly persuasion: pacts and covenants. HISPANIC BUSINESS, Vol. 9, no. 9 (September 1987), p. 20-26. English. DESCR: *Adolph Coors Co.; *Business; Community Organizations; Coors/HACER Agreement, 1984; *Corporations; Organizations; Pacific Bell; Southland Corporation.

3490 Beale, Stephen. Striking a deal with big business. HISPANIC BUSINESS, Vol. 9, no. 2 (February 1987), p. 26-33. English. DESCR: *Adolph Coors Co.; American G.I. Forum; Boycotts; Corporations; Cuban National Planning Council, Inc. Washington, D.C.; Employment; League of United Latin American Citizens (LULAC); National Council of La Raza (NCLR); National IMAGE; National Puerto Rican Coalition; *Organizations; U.S. Hispanic Chamber of Commerce.

Hispanic Association on Corporate Responsibility (HACER) (cont.)

3491 Perez, Renato E. The business of Hispanics. VISTA, Vol. 2, no. 1 (September 7, 1986), p. 10. English. **DESCR:** Adolph Coors Co.; American G.I. Forum; Apodaca, Jerry [Gov. of New Mexico]; Business; *Collective Bargaining; Corporations; Cuban National Planning Council, Inc. Washington, D.C.; League of United Latin American Citizens (LULAC); National Council of La Raza (NCLR); National IMAGE; U.S. Hispanic Chamber of Commerce.

3492 Sellers, Jeff M. Golden opportunity. HISPANIC BUSINESS, Vol. 9, no. 9 (September 1987), p. 14-18, 79. English. **DESCR:** *Adolph Coors Co.; Business Enterprises; *Coors/HACER Agreement, 1984; *Corporations; Employment; Organizations.

Hispanic Association of Higher Education of New Jersey (HAHE)

3493 Perez, Emma. Report to the Network. LA RED/THE NET, no. 95 (April 1986), p. 3-5. English. **DESCR:** *Educational Organizations; *Higher Education.

Hispanic Association of Higher Education (HAHE)

3494 Perez, Emma. Higher education organizations. LA RED/THE NET. No. 101 (October 1986), p. 6-10. English. **DESCR:** *Educational Organizations; Higher Education; *Puerto Rican Council on Higher Education (PRCHE); *SUNY Hispanic Research and Information Network.

HISPANIC BUSINESS

3495 Norris, Eileen. Print suffers in tale of two languages. ADVERTISING AGE MAGAZINE, Vol. 57, no. 16 (February 27, 1986), p. 49-51. English. **DESCR:** Advertising; Chavarria, Jesus; English Language; LATINA [magazine]; *Magazines; Soto, Grace; Spanish Language; Villar, Arturo; VISTA [magazine].

THE HISPANIC BUSINESS 500

3496 The 500 largest Hispanic-owned companies in sales. HISPANIC BUSINESS, Vol. 9, no. 6 (June 1987), p. 30-47. English. **DESCR:** *Business Enterprises; Statistics.

3497 Seven profiles of courage. HISPANIC BUSINESS, Vol. 9, no. 6 (June 1987), p. 57-70. English. **DESCR:** Alamo Technology Inc., San Antonio, TX; *Business Enterprises; *Businesspeople; Carrillo, Rosario C.; O'Campo Corporation. Walnut, CA; O'Campo, Peter; Rivas, Robert; TexPar Energy Inc., Milwaukee. WI.

Hispanic Caucus

3498 Castro, Richard T. A role for Hispanic Americans in foreign policy formulation. VISTA, Vol. 1, no. 9 (May 3, 1986), p. 3. English. **DESCR:** *Essays; International Relations; Political System.

Hispanic Congress on Evangelization (HCE)

3499 Plowman, Edward E. Hispanic Christians in the United States. CHRISTIANITY TODAY, Vol. 30. no. 1 (January 17, 1986), p. 44-45. English. **DESCR:** Los Angeles, CA; Protestant Church; Religion.

HISPANIC CULTURE IN THE SOUTHWEST

3500 Hall, Linda B. The United States-Mexican borders: historical, political, and cultural perspectives. LATIN AMERICAN RESEARCH REVIEW, Vol. 20, no. 2 (1985), p. 223-229. English. **DESCR:** AMERICAN LABOR IN THE SOUTHWEST: THE FIRST ONE HUNDRED YEARS; *Book Reviews; *Border Region; BOSS RULE IN SOUTH TEXAS: THE PROGRESSIVE ERA; CHICANO INTERMARRIAGE: A THEORETICAL AND EMPIRICAL STUDY; IN DEFENSE OF LA RAZA: THE LOS ANGELES MEXICAN CONSULATE AND THE MEXICAN COMMUNITY; Literature Reviews; RACE AND CLASS IN THE SOUTHWEST: A THEORY OF RACIAL INEQUALITY; SOUTHWESTERN AGRICULTURE: PRE-COLUMBIAN TO MODERN; THE MEXICANS IN OKLAHOMA; THE POLITICS OF SAN ANTONIO.

THE HISPANIC ELDERLY: A RESEARCH REFERENCE GUIDE

3501 Bastida, Elena B. Book review of: THE HISPANIC ELDERLY. CONTEMPORARY SOCIOLOGY: A JOURNAL OF REVIEWS, Vol. 14, no. 1 (January 1985), p. 41-42. English. **DESCR:** Ancianos; Becerra, Rosina; Book Reviews; Shaw, David.

3502 Delgado, Melvin. Book review of: THE HISPANIC ELDERLY. SOCIAL WORK, Vol. 31, no. 2 (March, April, 1986), p. 153. English. **DESCR:** Ancianos; Becerra, Rosina; Book Reviews; Shaw, David.

Hispanic Family of the Year Award

3503 Families of the year. VISTA, Vol. 2, no. 2 (October 4, 1986), p. 16-18. English. **DESCR:** Aguilar, Gregorio; Aguilar, Guadalupe; Aranda, Benjamin; Aranda, Emma; *Awards; de la Rocha, Beatriz; de la Rocha, Castulo; Family; Guzman, Ofelia; Guzman, Roberto.

3504 Lit, Ed. Recognition for Hispanic families. VISTA, Vol. 1, no. 5 (January 5, 1986), p. 18-20. English. **DESCR:** American Family Society; *Awards; Moraga, Peter and family (Los Angeles, CA); Pineda, Charles and family (Los Angeles, CA); Private Funding Sources.

HISPANIC FIRST NAMES: A COMPREHENSIVE DICTIONARY OF 250 YEARS OF MEXICAN-AMERICAN USAGE

3505 Vigelis, Adeline R. Book review of: HISPANIC FIRST NAMES. LECTOR, Vol. 4, no. 4-6 (1987), p. 55-56. English. **DESCR:** Book Reviews; Personal Names; Reference Works; Woods, Richard D.

Hispanic Health and Nutrition Examination Survey (HHANES)

3506 Ismail, Amid L.; Burt, Brian A.; and Brunelle, Janet A. Prevalence of dental caries and periodontal disease in Mexican American children aged 5 to 17 years: results from Southwestern HHANES, 1982-83. AMERICAN JOURNAL OF PUBLIC HEALTH, Vol. 77, no. 8 (August 1987), p. 967-970. English. **DESCR:** Decays, Missing, Filed Surfaces (DMFS) [dental scale]; *Dentistry; Youth.

3507 Plan and operation of the Hispanic Health and Nutrition Examination Survey 1982-84. VITAL AND HEALTH STATISTICS. SERIES 1, no. 19 (September 1985), p. 1-429. English. **DESCR:** *Nutrition; Public Health.

Hispanic Higher Education Coalition (HHEC)

3508 Gutierrez, Felix. House approves Higher Education Act amendments. LA RED/THE NET, no. 92 (November, December, 1985), p. 3-4. English. DESCR: Educational Law and Legislation; Educational Organizations; Financial Aid; *Higher Education; *Higher Education Amendments of 1985 (H.R. 3700).

HISPANIC IMAGE

3509 Levin, Gary. Publisher seeks to improve "image". ADVERTISING AGE MAGAZINE, Vol. 57, no. 43 (August 11, 1986), p. S25-S27. English. DESCR: Advertising; Asencio, John; English Language; Magazines; Spanish Language.

HISPANIC JOURNAL OF BEHAVIORAL SCIENCES

3510 Index to volume 9. HISPANIC JOURNAL OF BEHAVIORAL SCIENCES, Vol. 9, no. 4 (December 1987), p. 469-473. English. DESCR: *Indexes; Periodicals.

HISPANIC MENTAL HEALTH RESEARCH: A REFERENCE GUIDE

3511 Arce, Carlos H. and Carlson, David. Book review of: HISPANIC MENTAL HEALTH RESEARCH: A REFERENCE GUIDE. LA RED/THE NET, no. 57 (August 1982), p. 5-7. English. DESCR: Book Reviews; Mental Health; Newton, Frank; Olmedo, Esteban L.; Padilla, Amado M.; Reference Works.

3512 Castillo-Speed, Lillian. Annotated bibliography. LA RED/THE NET, no. 93 (January, February, 1986), p. 14-17. English. DESCR: A BIBLIOGRAPHY OF MEXICAN AMERICAN HISTORY; ARTE CHICANO; Book Reviews; Caballero, Cesar; CHICANO LITERATURE: A REFERENCE GUIDE; CHICANO ORGANIZATIONS DIRECTORY; CHICANO PERIODICAL INDEX; Goldman, Shifra M.; HISPANIC ALMANAC; Lomeli, Francisco A.; Martinez, Julio A.; Meier, Matt S.; Newton, Frank; *Reference Works; Ybarra-Frausto, Tomas.

Hispanic Murals Project (Cambridge, MA)

3513 Malaspina, Ann. The city is my canvas. VISTA, Vol. 2, no. 3 (November 2, 1986), p. 14-15. English. DESCR: Artists; *Galvez, Daniel; *Mural Art; Oakland, CA.

HISPANIC NATIONAL SUPPORT SYSTEMS: MENTAL HEALTH PROMOTIONS PERSPECTIVES

3514 Martinez, Alejandro M. Book review of: HISPANIC NATURAL SUPPORT SYSTEMS: MENTAL HEALTH PROMOTIONS PERSPECTIVES. LA RED/THE NET, no. 73 (October 1983), p. 7-12. English. DESCR: Book Reviews; Valle, Ramon; Vega, William A.

Hispanic Policy Development Project (HPDP)

3515 Book review of: THE HISPANIC ALMANAC. BOOKLIST, Vol. 82, (May 1, 1986), p. 1296. English. DESCR: Almanacs; Book Reviews; *HISPANIC ALMANAC.

Hispanic Research Center, Arizona State University, Tempe, AZ

3516 Perez, Emma. Research centers. LA RED/THE NET, no. 98 (July 1986), p. 6-9. English. DESCR: *Research Centers.

Hispanic Walk of Fame

3517 Muro, Rena. Hispanic walk of fame=Camino hispano de la fama. AMERICAS 2001, Vol. 1, no. 2 (September, October, 1987), p. 33. Bilingual. DESCR: Community Development; *Whittier Blvd., Los Angeles, CA.

HISPANICS' EDUCATION AND BACKGROUND: PREDICTORS OF COLLEGE ACHIEVEMENT

3518 Segura, Roberto D. Book review of: HISPANICS' EDUCATION AND BACKGROUND: PREDICTORS OF COLLEGE ACHIEVEMENT. LA RED/THE NET, no. 81 (June 1984), p. 6-7. English. DESCR: Book Reviews; Duran, Richard P.

HISPANICS IN CHICAGO

3519 Perez, Renato E. Chicago: Hispanic melting pot. VISTA, Vol. 1, no. 3 (November 3, 1985), p. 20. English. DESCR: Camacho, Eduardo; Casuso, Jorge; *Chicago, IL; Cultural Pluralism; Ethnic Groups; *Population.

HISPANICS IN THE UNITED STATES: A NEW SOCIAL AGENDA

3520 Cordasco, Francesco. Book review of: HISPANICS IN THE UNITED STATES: A NEW SOCIAL AGENDA. CHOICE, Vol. 23, no. 6 (February 1986), p. 928. English. DESCR: Book Reviews; McCready, William C.; San Juan Cafferty, Pastora.

3521 Griswold del Castillo, Richard. Book review of: HISPANICS IN THE UNITED STATES: A NEW SOCIAL AGENDA. JOURNAL OF AMERICAN ETHNIC HISTORY, Vol. 6, no. 1 (Fall 1986), p. 112-114. English. DESCR: Book Reviews; McCready, William C.; San Juan Cafferty, Pastora; Social History and Conditions.

3522 Griswold del Castillo, Richard. Book review of: HISPANICS IN THE UNITED STATES: A NEW SOCIAL AGENDA. HISPANIC AMERICAN HISTORICAL REVIEW, Vol. 66, no. 3 (August 1986), p. 627-629. English. DESCR: Book Reviews; McCready, William C.; San Juan Cafferty, Pastora.

HISPANICS IN THE UNITED STATES: AN ANTHOLOGY OF CREATIVE WRITING

3523 Kanellos, Nicolas. Book review of: HISPANICS IN THE UNITED STATES: AN ANTHOLOGY OF CREATIVE WRITING. LA RED/THE NET, no. 71 (August 1983), p. 12-13. English. DESCR: Book Reviews; Jimenez, Francisco; Keller, Gary D.

HISPANICS IN THE UNITED STATES: A HISTORY

3524 Tryon, Roy H. Book review of: THE HISPANICS IN THE UNITED STATES: A HISTORY. LIBRARY JOURNAL, Vol. 111, no. 18 (November 1, 1986), p. 107. English. DESCR: Book Reviews; Duignan, Peter J.; Gann, L.H.; Social History and Conditions.

HISPANICS IN THE U.S. ECONOMY

3525 Matta, Benjamin. Book review of: HISPANICS IN THE U.S. ECONOMY. INDUSTRIAL AND LABOR RELATIONS REVIEW, Vol. 40, no. 2 (January 1987), p. 299-300. English. DESCR: Book Reviews; Borjas, George J.; Tienda, Marta.

Historiography

3526 de Leon, Arnoldo. Tejano history scholarship: a review of the recent literature. WEST TEXAS HISTORICAL ASSOCIATION YEARBOOK, Vol. 61, (1985), p. 116-133. English. DESCR: *Literature Reviews; Political History and Conditions; Social History and Conditions; *Texas.

3527 Garcia, Mario T. Chicano historiography: a critique. LA RED/THE NET, no. 80 (May 1984), p. 2-8. English. DESCR: "Anarquismo y Comunismo: Mexican Radicalism and the Communist Party in Los Angeles in the 1930s"; *Monroy, Douglas.

3528 Griswold del Castillo, Richard. Quantitative history in the American Southwest: a survey and critique. WESTERN HISTORICAL QUARTERLY, Vol. 15, no. 4 (October 1984), p. 407-426. English. DESCR: Economic History and Conditions; History; *Social History and Conditions; *Southwestern United States.

3529 Monroy, Douglas. In support of lapses into radicalism: a response to Mario Garcia. LA RED/THE NET, no. 80 (May 1984), p. 8-11. English. DESCR: *Garcia, Mario T.

3530 Orozco, Cynthia. Chicana labor history: a critique of male consciousness in historical writing. LA RED/THE NET, no. 77 (January 1984), p. 2-5. English. DESCR: *Chicanas; *Sexism; Working Women.

3531 Saragoza, Alex M. The significance of recent Chicano-related historical writings: an appraisal. ETHNIC AFFAIRS, no. 1 (Fall 1987), p. [24]-62. English. DESCR: *History; *Literature Reviews.

History

3532 Acuna, Rodolfo. Book review of: DICTIONARY OF MEXICAN AMERICAN HISTORY. LA RED/THE NET, no. 57 (August 1982), p. 4-5. English. DESCR: Book Reviews; *DICTIONARY OF MEXICAN AMERICAN HISTORY; Meier, Matt S.; Rivera, Feliciano.

3533 Allsup, Dan. South of the brewer. VISTA, Vol. 2, no. 10 (June 7, 1987), p. 10-12. English. DESCR: *Food Industry.

3534 Almaraz, Felix D., Jr. Introduction: the Mexican borderlands. JOURNAL OF THE WEST, Vol. 24, no. 2 (1985), p. 5-7. English. DESCR: *Border Region; Essays.

3535 Almaraz, Felix D., Jr. Texas as a Mexican borderland: a review and appraisal of salient events. JOURNAL OF THE WEST, Vol. 24, no. 2 (1985), p. 108-112. English. DESCR: *Border Region; *Texas.

3536 Arce, Carlos H. Book review of: CHICANOS IN A CHANGING SOCIETY. LA RED/THE NET, no. 30 (May 1980), p. 8. English. DESCR: Book Reviews; Camarillo, Alberto; CHICANOS IN A CHANGING SOCIETY; *Santa Barbara, CA; *Social History and Conditions; *Southern California.

3537 Arreola, Daniel D. The Mexican American cultural capital. GEOGRAPHICAL REVIEW, Vol. 77, (January 1987), p. 17-34. English. DESCR: Conjuntos; Food Industry; Immigration; LA PRENSA, San Antonio, TX; La Raza Unida Party; League of United Latin American Citizens (LULAC); Lozano, Ignacio; Mexican American Youth Organization, San Antonio, TX; Music; Orden Hijos de America, San Antonio, TX; Railroads; *San Antonio, TX; *Social History and Conditions.

3538 Balderrama, Francisco E. Book review of: A BIBLIOGRAPHY OF MEXICAN-AMERICAN HISTORY. PACIFIC HISTORICAL REVIEW, Vol. 55, no. 1 (1986), p. 106-107. English. DESCR: *A BIBLIOGRAPHY OF MEXICAN AMERICAN HISTORY; Book Reviews; Meier, Matt S.

3539 Bennett, Ruth. A bilingual perspective on teaching history. SOCIAL STUDIES REVIEW, Vol. 23, no. 3 (Spring 1984), p. 50-55. English. DESCR: Education; *Ethnic Groups.

3540 Billings, Linda M. and Alurista. In verbal murals: a study of Chicana herstory and poetry. CONFLUENCIA, Vol. 2, no. 1 (Fall 1986), p. 60-68. English. DESCR: Candelaria, Cordelia; Cervantes, Lorna Dee; *Chicanas; Cisneros, Sandra; EMPLUMADA; *Feminism; Literary Criticism; *Poetry; Xelina.

3541 Bruce-Novoa, Juan. Mexico en la literatura chicana (I). LA COMUNIDAD, No. 267 (September 1, 1985), p. 12-13. Spanish. DESCR: *Literary Criticism; Mestizaje; Mexican Revolution - 1910-1920; *Mexico; Precolumbian Society.

3542 Bueno, Patricia E. Los Chicanos y la politica. LA COMUNIDAD, No. 267 (September 1, 1985), p. 6-7. Spanish. DESCR: Community Service Organization, Los Angeles, (CSO); Discrimination; Leadership; League of United Latin American Citizens (LULAC); Orden Hijos de America, San Antonio, TX; *Political Parties and Organizations.

3543 Bueno, Patricia E. Los Chicanos y la politica II. LA COMUNIDAD, No. 268 (September 8, 1985), p. 2-3. Spanish. DESCR: American G.I. Forum; Chicano Movement; Leadership; Mexican American Political Association (MAPA); Nationalism; Political Association of Spanish-Speaking Organizations (PASO); *Political Parties and Organizations.

3544 Butler, Anne M. Book review of: THEY CALLED THEM GREASERS. MARYLAND HISTORIAN, Vol. 15. no. 2 (Fall, Winter, 1984), p. 50-51. English. DESCR: Book Reviews; de Leon, Arnoldo; *THEY CALLED THEM GREASERS: ANGLO ATTITUDES TOWARD MEXICANS IN TEXAS, 1821-1900.

3545 The California Museum of Latino History=El Museo de California de la Historia de los Latinos. AMERICAS 2001, Premiere Issue, 1987, p. 18-19, 39. Bilingual. DESCR: Calderon, Charles M.; *California Museum of Latino History; *Museums; Rios-Bustamante, Antonio; Social History and Conditions.

3546 Campbell, Federico. Henry Reyna, pachuco. LA COMUNIDAD, No. 247 (April 14, 1985), p. 11. Spanish. DESCR: *Pachucos; ZOOT SUIT [play]; *Zoot Suit Riots, Los Angeles, CA, 1943.

3547 Catalano, Julia. Pinata. VISTA, Vol. 2, no. 10 (June 7, 1987), p. 14. English. DESCR: *Children's Television; Fiestas; THE $25,000 PINATA [television show].

3548 Chile charm. VISTA, Vol. 2, no. 7 (March 8, 1987), p. 20-22. English. DESCR: *Crops; Recipes.

3549 Cisneros, Henry. The meaning for Hispanics of 5 de Mayo. VISTA, Vol. 1, no. 9 (May 3, 1986), p. 12-13. English. DESCR: Cinco de Mayo; *Festivals.

History (cont.)

3550 Coerver, Don and Hall, Linda B. The
Arizona-Sonora border and the Mexican
revolution, 1910-1920. JOURNAL OF THE WEST,
Vol. 24, no. 2 (1985), p. 75-87. English.
DESCR: Arizona; Arizona Rangers; Sonora,
Mexico; *Villa, Pancho.

3551 Dinwoodie, David H. Indians, Hispanos, and
land reform: a new deal struggle in New
Mexico. WESTERN HISTORICAL QUARTERLY, Vol.
17, no. 3 (July 1986), p. 291-323. English.
DESCR: Bureau of Indian Affairs (BIA);
Interdepartmental Rio Grande Board; Land
Grants; Land Program of the Federal
Emergency Relief Administration (FERA);
*Land Reform; Native Americans; *New Mexico.

3552 Engstrand, Iris H.W. California ranchos:
their Hispanic heritage. SOUTHERN CALIFORNIA
QUARTERLY, Vol. 67, no. 3 (Fall 1985), p.
281-290. English. **DESCR:** *California;
*Californios; *Land Grants; *Spanish
Influence.

3553 Figoli, Haydee. Dos textos a proposito de la
frontera. LA COMUNIDAD, No. 350 (April 5,
1987), p. 2-5. Spanish. **DESCR:** Chicano,
Meaning of; Chicano Movement; Mexico.

3554 Flores, Arturo C. El Teatro Campesino
(1965-1986): algunas orientaciones teoricas.
CONFLUENCIA, Vol. 2, no. 2 (Spring 1987), p.
116-121. Spanish. **DESCR:** Brecht, Bertolt;
*El Teatro Campesino; Moreno, Mario
"Cantinflas"; *Teatro; Valdez, Luis.

3555 Gann, Lewis H. and Duignan, Peter J. Latinos
& the Catholic Church in America. NUESTRO,
Vol. 11, no. 4 (May 1987), p. 10-13.
English. **DESCR:** *Catholic Church; Culture;
Encuentro Movement [Catholic Church]; Primer
Encuentro Nacional Hispano, Washington, DC,
June 1972.

3556 Garcia, Mario T. [Letter to the editor about
Mexicans, radicals and communists in the
United States]. LABOR HISTORY, Vol. 25, no.
1 (Winter 1984), p. 152-154. English.
DESCR: *"Anarquismo y Comunismo: Mexican
Radicalism and the Communist Party in Los
Angeles in the 1930s"; *Communism; *Labor
Unions; Los Angeles, CA; *Monroy, Douglas.

3557 Goldman, Shifra. Arte chicano: iconografia
de la autodeterminacion. LA COMUNIDAD, No.
336 (December 28, 1986), p. 12-14+. Spanish.
DESCR: *Art; Discrimination; EL PLAN
ESPIRITUAL DE AZTLAN; Identity; Nationalism;
Pachucos; Social Classes; *Symbolism.

3558 Gomez-Quinones, Juan. September 16th: a
historical perspective. LATIN QUARTER, Vol.
1, no. 2 (October 1974), p. 8,9,11,12.
English. **DESCR:** *Dieciseis de Septiembre;
Hidalgo y Costilla, Miguel; *Holidays; Los
Angeles, CA.

3559 Gonzales-Berry, Erlinda. Enmienda de ingles
en Nuevo Mexico. LA COMUNIDAD, No. 352
(April 19, 1987), p. 4-7. Spanish. **DESCR:**
English Language; *English-Only Movement;
Legislation; *New Mexico; Spanish Language.

3560 Griswold del Castillo, Richard. Quantitative
history in the American Southwest: a survey
and critique. WESTERN HISTORICAL QUARTERLY,
Vol. 15, no. 4 (October 1984), p. 407-426.
English. **DESCR:** Economic History and
Conditions; Historiography; *Social History
and Conditions; *Southwestern United States.

3561 Gutierrez, Jose Angel. Chicanos and

Mexicans: under surveillance: 1940 to 1980.
RENATO ROSALDO LECTURE SERIES MONOGRAPH,
Vol. 2, (Spring 1986), p. [29]-58. English.
DESCR: Acuna, Rudolfo; Border Coverage
Program (BOCOV); *Civil Rights; COINTELPRO;
*Federal Bureau of Investigation (FBI);
*Federal Government; League of United Latin
American Citizens (LULAC); Mexico; Political
Parties and Organizations; *Political
Repression.

3562 Halley, Lindsey. Pachuco boogie [sic]. LA
COMUNIDAD, No. 305 (May 25, 1986), p. 8-9.
Spanish. **DESCR:** Cano, Eddie; Diaz, Raul;
*Music; Ovalle, John; *PACHUCO BOOGIE;
Smithsonian Institute; The Record Inn, East
Los Angeles, CA; Tosti, Don.

3563 Hoffman, Abraham. The controversial career
of Martin Aguirre; the rise and fall of a
Chicano lawman. CALIFORNIA HISTORY, Vol. 63,
no. 4 (Fall 1984), p. 295-341. English.
DESCR: *Aguirre, Martin; *Biography; Los
Angeles County, CA; Prisoners; San Quentin
Prison.

3564 Instituto Genealogico e Historico
Latino-Americano. Rootsearch: Aguilar:
Echeverria. VISTA, Vol. 1, no. 11 (July 6,
1986), p. 22. English. **DESCR:** *Aguilar
[family name]; Echeverria [family name];
Genealogy; *Personal Names.

3565 Instituto Genealogico e Historico
Latino-Americano. Rootsearch: Alarcon:
Saavedra. VISTA, Vol. 1, no. 8 (April 6,
1986), p. 22. English. **DESCR:** *Alarcon
[family name]; Genealogy; *Personal Names;
Saavedra [family name].

3566 Instituto Genealogico e Historico
Latino-Americano. Rootsearch: Alvarez:
Covarrubias. VISTA, Vol. 1, no. 6 (February
2, 1986), p. 22. English. **DESCR:** *Alvarez
[family name]; *Covarrubias [family name];
Genealogy; *Personal Names.

3567 Instituto Genealogico e Historico
Latino-Americano. Rootsearch: Aragon:
Trujillo: Ruelas. VISTA, Vol. 2, no. 8
(April 4, 1987), p. 24. English. **DESCR:**
*Aragon [family name]; Genealogy; *Personal
Names; *Ruelas [family name]; *Trujillo
[family name].

3568 Instituto Genealogico e Historico
Latino-Americano. Rootsearch: Bello:
Ramirez: Lopez. VISTA, Vol. 3, no. 2
(October 3, 1987), p. 37. English. **DESCR:**
*Bello [family name]; Genealogy; *Lopez
[family name]; *Personal Names; *Ramirez
[family name].

3569 Instituto Genealogico e Historico
Latino-Americano. Rootsearch: Beltran:
Flores: Gomez. VISTA, Vol. 2, no. 11 (May 7,
1987), p. 22. English. **DESCR:** *Beltran
[family name]; *Flores [family name];
Genealogy; *Gomez [family name]; *Personal
Names.

3570 Instituto Genealogico e Historico
Latino-Americano. Rootsearch: Castro:
Velasco. VISTA, Vol. 2, no. 2 (October 4,
1986), p. 22. English. **DESCR:** *Castro
[family name]; Genealogy; *Personal Names;
*Velasco [family name].

History (cont.)

3571 Instituto Genealogico e Historico
Latino-Americano. Rootsearch: Cisneros:
Perales: Zuniga. VISTA. Vol. 2, no. 10 (June
7, 1987), p. 26. English. **DESCR:** *Cisneros
[family name]; Genealogy; *Perales [family
name]; *Personal Names; *Zuniga [family
name].

3572 Instituto Genealogico e Historico
Latino-Americano. Rootsearch: Cortes:
Ulibarri. VISTA. Vol. 1, no. 5 (January 5,
1986), p. 22. English. **DESCR:** *Cortes
[family name]; Genealogy; *Personal Names;
Ulibarri [family name].

3573 Instituto Genealogico e Historico
Latino-Americano. Rootsearch: De La Garza:
Pacheco. VISTA, Vol. 2, no. 6 (February 8,
1987), p. 21. English. **DESCR:** *de la Garza
[family name]; Genealogy; Pacheco [family
name]; *Personal Names.

3574 Instituto Genealogico e Historico
Latino-Americano. Rootsearch: Duarte:
Sandoval. VISTA. Vol. 1, no. 9 (May 3,
1986), p. 22. English. **DESCR:** *Duarte
[family name]; Genealogy; *Personal Names;
*Sandoval [family name].

3575 Instituto Genealogico e Historico
Latino-Americano. Rootsearch: Garcia:
Chaves. VISTA. Vol. 1, no. 10 (June 8,
1986), p. 26. English. **DESCR:** *Chaves
[family name]; *Garcia [family name];
Genealogy; *Personal Names.

3576 Instituto Genealogico e Historico
Latino-Americano. Rootsearch: Gonzalez:
Febres-Cordero. VISTA. Vol. 1, no. 7 (March
2, 1986), p. 22. English. **DESCR:**
Febres-Cordero [family name]; Genealogy;
*Gonzalez [family name]; *Personal Names.

3577 Instituto Genealogico e Historico
Latino-Americano. Rootsearch: Gutierrez.
VISTA. Vol. 1, no. 2 (October 5, 1985), p.
22. English. **DESCR:** Genealogy; *Gutierrez
[family name]; *Personal Names.

3578 Instituto Genealogico e Historico
Latino-Americano. Rootsearch: Guzman:
Zamora. VISTA. Vol. 2, no. 7 (March 8,
1987), p. 25. English. **DESCR:** Genealogy;
*Guzman [family name]; *Personal Names;
*Zamora [family name].

3579 Instituto Genealogico e Historico
Latino-Americano. Rootsearch: Jimenez
(Ximenez): Olmo. VISTA. Vol. 2, no. 4
(December 7, 1986), p. 25. English. **DESCR:**
Genealogy; *Jimenez [family name]; *Olmo
[family name]; *Personal Names; *Ximenez
[family name].

3580 Instituto Genealogico e Historico
Latino-Americano. Rootsearch: Montoya:
Galvo. VISTA. Vol. 1, no. 4 (December 7,
1985), p. 22. English. **DESCR:** *Galvo [family
name]; Genealogy; *Montoya [family name];
*Personal Names.

3581 Instituto Genealogico e Historico
Latino-Americano. Rootsearch: Olivares:
Yrigoyen: Montemayor. VISTA. Vol. 2, no. 12
(August 1, 1987), p. 30. English. **DESCR:**
Genealogy; *Montemayor [family name];
*Olivares [family name]; *Personal Names;
*Yrigoyen [family name].

3582 Instituto Genealogico e Historico
Latino-Americano. Rootsearch: Ortega: Munoz.
VISTA. Vol. 1, no. 3 (November 3, 1985), p.
22. English. **DESCR:** *Munoz [family name];
*Ortega [family name]; *Personal Names.

3583 Instituto Genealogico e Historico
Latino-Americano. Rootsearch: Padron:
Machado. VISTA, Vol. 2, no. 1 (September 7,
1986), p. 22. English. **DESCR:** Genealogy;
*Machado [family name]; *Padron [family
name]; *Personal Names.

3584 Instituto Genealogico e Historico
Latino-Americano. Rootsearch: Patino:
Herrera: Escobar. VISTA, Vol. 2, no. 9 (May
3, 1987), p. 22. English. **DESCR:** *Escobar
[family name]; Genealogy; *Herrera [family
name]; *Patino [family name]; *Personal
Names.

3585 Instituto Genealogico e Historico
Latino-Americano. Rootsearch: Peraza: Yanez.
VISTA, Vol. 1, no. 12 (August 2, 1986), p.
22. English. **DESCR:** Genealogy; *Peraza
[family name]; *Personal Names; Yanez
[family name].

3586 Instituto Genealogico e Historico
Latino-Americano. Rootsearch: Rivera:
Navarro: Salazar. VISTA, Vol. 2, no. 3
(November 2, 1986), p. 24. English. **DESCR:**
Genealogy; *Navarro [family name]; *Personal
Names; *Rivera [family name]; *Salazar
[family name].

3587 Instituto Genealogico e Historico
Latino-Americano. Rootsearch: Robles:
Chacon: Molina. VISTA, Vol. 3, no. 1
(September 6, 1987), p. 30. English. **DESCR:**
*Chacon [family name]; Genealogy; *Molina
[family name]; *Personal Names; *Robles
[family name].

3588 Instituto Genealogico e Historico
Latino-Americano. Rootsearch: Rodriguez:
Garza (De La Garza). VISTA, Vol. 3, no. 3
(November 8, 1987), p. 37. English. **DESCR:**
*de la Garza [family name]; *Garza [family
name]; Genealogy; *Personal Names;
*Rodriguez, [family name].

3589 Instituto Genealogico e Historico
Latino-Americano. Rootsearch: Villalobos:
Amador (Amado): Ibarra. VISTA, Vol. 3, no. 4
(December 6, 1987), p. 36. English. **DESCR:**
*Amado [family name]; *Amador [family name];
Genealogy; *Ibarra [family name]; Personal
Names, *Villalobos [family name].

3590 Jenkins, Myra Ellen. Land tenure history of
New Mexico. EL CUADERNO, Vol. 4, no. 1
(Summer 1976), p. 33-46. English. **DESCR:**
Land Grants; *Land Tenure; *New Mexico;
Pueblo Indians.

3591 Jensen, Joan M. Crossing ethnic barriers in
the Southwest: women's agricultural
extension education, 1914-1940. AGRICULTURAL
HISTORY, Vol. 60, no. 2 (Spring 1986), p.
169-181. English. **DESCR:** *Agricultural
Extension Service; Agriculture; Cabeza de
Baca, Fabiola; Chicanas; New Mexico; *Rural
Education.

3592 Jensen, Leif and Tienda, Marta. The new
immigration: implications for poverty and
public assistance utilization. MIGRATION
WORLD MAGAZINE, Vol. 15. no. 5 (1987), p.
7-18. English. **DESCR:** Immigrants;
*Immigration; *Immigration and
Naturalization Act, 1965; Poverty; Public
Policy; *Welfare.

History (cont.)

3593 Leal, Luis. Americo Paredes and modern Mexican American scholarship. ETHNIC AFFAIRS, no. 1 (Fall 1987), p. [1]-11. English. **DESCR:** Ethnology; Folklore; Literature Reviews; *Paredes, Americo.

3594 LeCompte, Mary Lou and Beezley, William H. Any Sunday in April: the rise of sport in San Antonio and the Hispanic borderlands. JOURNAL OF SPORT HISTORY, Vol. 13, no. 2 (Summer 1986), p. 128-146. English. **DESCR:** *Charreada; *Cultural Customs; *San Antonio, TX; *Sports.

3595 LeCompte, Mary Lou. The Hispanic influence on the history of rodeo, 1823-1922. JOURNAL OF SPORT HISTORY, Vol. 12, no. 1 (Spring 1985), p. 21-38. English. **DESCR:** *Charreada; *Cultural Customs; *Mexico.

3596 Leon, David Jess and McNeill, Daniel. The fifth class: a 19th century forerunner of affirmative action. CALIFORNIA HISTORY, Vol. 64, no. 1 (Winter 1985), p. 52-57. English. **DESCR:** *Affirmative Action; Colleges and Universities; Discrimination in Education; *Enrollment; *Higher Education; Students; *University of California.

3597 Marin, Christine. La Asociacion Hispano-Americana de Madres y Esposas: Tucson's Mexican American women in World War II. RENATO ROSALDO LECTURE SERIES MONOGRAPH, Vol. 1, (Summer 1985), p. [5]-18. English. **DESCR:** *Chicanas; Cultural Organizations; *La Asociacion Hispano-Americana de Madres y Esposas, Tucson, AZ; Organizations; *Tucson, AZ; World War II.

3598 McKanna, Clare V. The San Quentin prison pardon papers: a look at file no. 1808, the case of Francisco Javier Bonilla. SOUTHERN CALIFORNIA QUARTERLY, Vol. 67, no. 2 (Summer 1985), p. 187-196. English. **DESCR:** Administration of Justice; Archives; *Bonilla, Francisco Javier; *Criminal Justice System; *Prisoners; *San Quentin Prison.

3599 Meketa, Charles and Meketa, Jacqueline. Heroes or cowards? A new look at the role of native New Mexicans at the Battle of Valverde. NEW MEXICO HISTORICAL REVIEW, Vol. 62, no. 1 (January 1987), p. 33-46. English. **DESCR:** *Battle of Valverde; *Canby, Edward; *New Mexico.

3600 Miller, Darlis A. Los Pinos, New Mexico: civil war post on the Rio Grande. NEW MEXICO HISTORICAL REVIEW, Vol. 62, no. 1 (January 1987), p. 1-31. English. **DESCR:** *Los Pinos, NM; *New Mexico; *Rio Grande; *Southwestern United States.

3601 Miranda, Gloria E. Hispano-Mexican childrearing practices in pre-American Santa Barbara. SOUTHERN CALIFORNIA QUARTERLY, Vol. 65, no. 4 (Winter 1983), p. 307-320. English. **DESCR:** *Children; Cultural Characteristics; *Family; *Parenting; *Santa Barbara, CA; Socialization.

3602 Monroy, Douglas. [Letter responding to Mario Garcia's comments]. LABOR HISTORY, Vol. 25, no. 1 (Winter 1984), p. 155-156. **DESCR:** *Communism; *Garcia, Mario T.; *Labor Unions; Los Angeles, CA.

3603 Morales, Cecilio. Judaism's Hispanic thread. VISTA, Vol. 2, no. 3 (November 2, 1986), p. 20-23. English. **DESCR:** Cultural Customs; *Jews; *Religion.

3604 Morales, Patricia. Indocumentados y chicanos: un intento de aproximacion. LA COMUNIDAD, No. 318 (August 24, 1986), p. 2-5. Spanish. **DESCR:** *Immigration; Labor; Undocumented Workers.

3605 Parlee, Lorena M. The impact of United States railroad unions on organized labor and government policy in Mexico (1880-1911). HISPANIC AMERICAN HISTORICAL REVIEW, Vol. 64, no. 3 (August 1984), p. 443-475. English. **DESCR:** Diaz, Porfirio; Discrimination in Employment; *Labor Unions; Mexico; Partido Liberal Mexicano (PLM); Railroads; United States-Mexico Relations.

3606 Perez, Renato E. The United States Constitution: an inspiration to Latin America. VISTA, Vol. 3, no. 1 (September 6, 1987), p. 6-7, 24. English. **DESCR:** *Constitution of the United States.

3607 Rios-Bustamante, Antonio. California's bilingual constitution=La constitucion bilingue de California. AMERICAS 2001, Vol. 1, no. 1 (June, July, 1987), p. 15. Bilingual. **DESCR:** *California State Constitution; Spanish Language.

3608 Rodriguez Flores, Juan. Paul Leduc, FRIDA y el otro cine que no se exhibe en Los Angeles. LA COMUNIDAD, No. 290 (February 9, 1986), p. 12-13. Spanish. **DESCR:** *Films; FRIDA: NATURALEZA VIDA [film]; *Kahlo, Frida; Mexico.

3609 Romo, Ricardo. Book review of: OCCUPIED AMERICA. LA RED/THE NET, no. 39 (February 1981), p. 3. English. **DESCR:** *Acuna, Rudolfo; Book Reviews; *OCCUPIED AMERICA; *Social History and Conditions.

3610 Rubio Goldsmith, Raquel. Shipwrecked in the desert: a short history of the adventures and struggles for survival of the Mexican Sisters of the House of the Providence in Douglas, Arizona during their first twenty-two years of existence (1927-1949). RENATO ROSALDO LECTURE SERIES MONOGRAPH, Vol. 1, (Summer 1985), p. [39]-67. English. **DESCR:** Catholic Church; Chicanas; Clergy; Douglas, AZ; *House of the Divine Providence [convent], Douglas, AZ.

3611 Ruiz, Vicki Lynn. Obreras y madres: labor activism among Mexican women and its impact on the family. RENATO ROSALDO LECTURE SERIES MONOGRAPH, Vol. 1, (Summer 1985), p. [19]-38. English. **DESCR:** *Chicanas; Child Care Centers; Children; *Labor Unions; *Mexico; Sex Roles; Women; *Working Women.

3612 Sagel, Jim. A question of history. CONFLUENCIA, Vol. 1, no. 1 (Fall 1985), p. 94-101. English. **DESCR:** *Land Grants; *New Mexico.

3613 Saragoza, Alex M. The significance of recent Chicano-related historical writings: an appraisal. ETHNIC AFFAIRS, no. 1 (Fall 1987), p. [24]-62. English. **DESCR:** *Historiography; *Literature Reviews.

3614 Sifuentes, Frank. Huntington Park: city on the upswing=Huntington Park: una ciudad ascendiente. AMERICAS 2001, Premiere Issue, 1987, p. 36-39. Bilingual. **DESCR:** *Huntington Park, CA; *Urban Communities.

History (cont.)

3615 Sommers, Laurie Kay. Symbol and style in Cinco de Mayo. JOURNAL OF AMERICAN FOLKLORE, Vol. 98, (October. December, 1985), p. 476-482. English. **DESCR**: *Cinco de Mayo; *Cultural Customs; *Holidays; *San Francisco, CA; Symbolism.

3616 Valdes, Dennis. Book review of: THE LOS ANGELES BARRIO 1850-1890: A SOCIAL HISTORY. LA RED/THE NET, no. 36 (November 1980), p. 5. English. **DESCR**: Book Reviews; Griswold del Castillo, Richard; *Los Angeles, CA; *Social History and Conditions; *THE LOS ANGELES BARRIO 1850-1890: A SOCIAL HISTORY.

HISTORY, CULTURE, AND SOCIETY: CHICANO STUDIES IN THE 1980s

3617 Martinez, Eliud. Book review of: HISTORY, CULTURE, AND SOCIETY. MODERN LANGUAGE JOURNAL, Vol. 69, no. 4 (Winter 1985), p. 436-437. English. **DESCR**: Book Reviews; Chicano Studies; Garcia, Mario T.; National Association for Chicano Studies (NACS).

3618 Milo, Albert J. Book review of: HISTORY, CULTURE. AND SOCIETY. LECTOR, Vol. 4, no. 4-6 (1987), p. 55. English. **DESCR**: Book Reviews; National Association for Chicano Studies (NACS); Social History and Conditions.

HISTORY OF THE PUERTO RICAN INDEPENDENCE MOVEMENT

3619 Reyes, Felix Ojeda. Book review of: HISTORY OF THE PUERTO RICAN INDEPENDENCE MOVEMENT. LA RED/THE NET, no. 76 (January 1984), p. 4-7. Spanish. **DESCR**: Book Reviews; Lidin, Harold J.; Puerto Ricans.

Hobbs Act

3620 Ford, Theresa Y. United States v. Hannigan: federal statute used to prosecute torturers. CRIMINAL JUSTICE JOURNAL, Vol. 6, no. 1 (Fall 1982), p. 79-97. English. **DESCR**: Civil Rights; *Undocumented Workers; *U.S. v. Hanigan.

Hoglund, A. William

3621 Hendershott, C. Book review of: IMMIGRANTS AND THEIR CHILDREN IN THE UNITED STATES: A BIBLIOGRAPHY OF DOCTORAL DISSERTATIONS, 1885-1982. CHOICE. Vol. 23, no. 11-12 (July, August. 1986), p. 1656. English. **DESCR**: Book Reviews; *IMMIGRANTS AND THEIR CHILDREN IN THE UNITED STATES: A BIBLIOGRAPHY OF DOCTORAL DISSERTATIONS. 1885-1982.

Holguin Corporation, El Paso, TX

3622 Kane. George D. Five blueprints for fueling growth. HISPANIC BUSINESS, Vol. 9, no. 5 (May 1987), p. 18-21. 42+. English. **DESCR**: *Business Enterprises; *Businesspeople; Investments; Latin Industries, Ontario, CA; One-Day Paint & Auto Body Centers, Los Angeles, CA; Terrinvest. Miami. FL; TRU & Associates, Orange County, CA.

Holidays

3623 Armstrong, Ruth W. Christmas in Albuquerque. VISTA, Vol. 1, no. 4 (December 7, 1985), p. 18-20. English. **DESCR**: *Albuquerque, NM; *Cultural Customs.

3624 Burciaga, Jose Antonio. In celebration of a man's ecumenism. VISTA. Vol. 2, no. 4 (December 7, 1986), p. 26. English. **DESCR**: *Catholic Church; Congregation B'nai Zion, El Paso, TX; Jews; *Religion.

3625 Cardenas, Antonio J. and Cardenas, Cecilia. Traditions of Christmas. VISTA, Vol. 2, no. 4 (December 7, 1986), p. 14-17. English. **DESCR**: El Paso, TX; Festivals; Miami, FL; *Reyes Magos Tradition.

3626 Catalano, Julia. Raul Jimenez. VISTA, Vol. 2, no. 3 (November 2, 1986), p. 6. English. **DESCR**: *Ancianos; Jimenez Food Products, Inc.; *Jimenez, Raul.

3627 Gomez-Quinones, Juan. September 16th: a historical perspective. LATIN QUARTER, Vol. 1, no. 2 (October 1974), p. 8,9,11,12. English. **DESCR**: *Dieciseis de Septiembre; Hidalgo y Costilla, Miguel; *History; Los Angeles, CA.

3628 Hazen-Hammond, Susan and Fuss, Eduardo. Vivan las celebraciones. ARIZONA HIGHWAYS, Vol. 63, no. 8 (August 1987), p. 35-45. English. **DESCR**: Cinco de Mayo; Cultural Customs; Dia de los Muertos; Dieciseis de Septiembre; Fiestas Patrias; La Virgen de Guadalupe; Las Posadas.

3629 Sommers, Laurie Kay. Symbol and style in Cinco de Mayo. JOURNAL OF AMERICAN FOLKLORE, Vol. 98, (October. December, 1985), p. 476-482. English. **DESCR**: *Cinco de Mayo; *Cultural Customs; History; *San Francisco, CA; Symbolism.

EL HOMBRE QUE NO SUDABA

3630 Ugalde, Sharon E. Two visions of cultural domination: Carrero's EL HOMBRE QUE NO SUDABA and Hinojosa's MI QUERIDO RAFA. BILINGUAL REVIEW, Vol. 12, no. 1-2 (January, August, 1985), p. 159-165. English. **DESCR**: Carrero, Jaime; Hinojosa-Smith, Rolando R.; Literary Criticism; *MI QUERIDO RAFA.

Home Altars

USE: Altars

Homosexuality

3631 Bruce-Novoa, Juan. Homosexuality and the Chicano novel. CONFLUENCIA, Vol. 2, no. 1 (Fall 1986), p. 69-77. English. **DESCR**: Acosta, Oscar Zeta; CITY OF NIGHT; FAULTLINE [novel]; Islas, Arturo; *Literary Criticism; Machismo; *Novel; Ortiz Taylor, Sheila; POCHO; Rechy, John; Salas, Floyd; SPRING FORWARD/FALL BACK; TATOO THE WICKED CROSS; THE AUTOBIOGRAPHY OF A BROWN BUFFALO; THE RAIN GOD: A DESERT TALE; THE REVOLT OF THE COCKROACH PEOPLE; Villarreal, Jose Antonio.

3632 Ruiz, Ariel. Raza, sexo y politica en SHORT EYES by Miguel Pinero. THE AMERICAS REVIEW, Vol. 15, no. 2 (Summer 1987), p. 93-102. Spanish. **DESCR**: Literary Criticism; Pinero, Miguel; Prisoners; Puerto Ricans; Sex Roles; *SHORT EYES; Teatro.

Honduras

3633 Rodriguez, Nestor. Undocumented Central Americans in Houston: diverse populations. INTERNATIONAL MIGRATION REVIEW, Vol. 21, no. 1 (Spring 1987), p. 4-26. English. **DESCR**: *Central America; El Salvador; Ethnic Groups; Guatemala; *Houston, TX; Immigrants; Intergroup Relations; Latin Americans; *Political Refugees; *Undocumented Workers.

HONOR AND THE AMERICAN DREAM: CULTURE AND IDENTITY IN A CHICANO COMMUNITY

3634 Cohen, Albert K. Book review of: HONOR AND THE AMERICAN DREAM. AMERICAN JOURNAL OF SOCIOLOGY, Vol. 90. no. 5 (March 1985), p. 1146-1147. English. DESCR: Book Reviews; Culture; Horowitz, Ruth.

Honors
USE: Awards

Horace Mann Middle School, Mission District, San Francisco, CA

3635 Evans, James. From chaos to quality education. VISTA. Vol. 3, no. 4 (December 6, 1987), p. 18, 35. English. DESCR: Awards; *Chacon Soto, Mario; *Educational Administration; Educational Theory and Practice.

Horowitz, Ruth

3636 Cohen, Albert K. Book review of: HONOR AND THE AMERICAN DREAM. AMERICAN JOURNAL OF SOCIOLOGY, Vol. 90. no. 5 (March 1985), p. 1146-1147. English. DESCR: Book Reviews; Culture; *HONOR AND THE AMERICAN DREAM: CULTURE AND IDENTITY IN A CHICANO COMMUNITY.

Hotel Reforma, Mexico City

3637 Sykes, Maltby. Diego Rivera and the Hotel Reforma murals. ARCHIVES OF AMERICAN ART JOURNAL. Vol. 25. no. 1-2 (1985), p. 29-40. English. DESCR: Artists; Marxism; Mexico City; Mural Art; *Rivera. Diego.

House of the Divine Providence [convent], Douglas, AZ

3638 Rubio Goldsmith. Raquel. Shipwrecked in the desert: a short history of the adventures and struggles for survival of the Mexican Sisters of the House of the Providence in Douglas, Arizona during their first twenty-two years of existence (1927-1949). RENATO ROSALDO LECTURE SERIES MONOGRAPH, Vol. 1, (Summer 1985), p. [39]-67. English. DESCR: Catholic Church; Chicanas; Clergy; Douglas, AZ; History.

THE HOUSE ON MANGO STREET

3639 Cisneros, Sandra. Do you know me?: I wrote THE HOUSE ON MANGO STREET. THE AMERICAS REVIEW, Vol. 15. no. 1 (Spring 1987), p. 77-79. English. DESCR: Authors; Autobiography; Chicanas; *Cisneros, Sandra; *Prose.

3640 Olivares, Julian. Sandra Cisneros' THE HOUSE ON MANGO STREET and the poetics of space. THE AMERICAS REVIEW, Vol. 15. no. 3-4 (Fall, Winter, 1987), p. 160-170. English. DESCR: *Cisneros, Sandra; *Literary Criticism.

Housing

3641 Heuer. Robert J. To save a neighborhood. VISTA, Vol. 3, no. 3 (November 8, 1987), p. 32-34. English. DESCR: *Eighteenth Street Development Corporation. Chicago, IL; Overa. Agustin; Pilsen, IL; Statistics.

3642 Krivo, Lauren J. and Mutchler. Jan E. Housing constraint and household complexity in metropolitan America: Black and Spanish-origin minorities. URBAN AFFAIRS QUARTERLY, Vol. 21. no. 3 (March 1986), p. 389-409. English. DESCR: Blacks; Residential Segregation.

Houston, TX

3643 Goldman, Shifra. El arte hispano en Houston. LA COMUNIDAD, No. 361 (June 21, 1987), p. 6-7+. Spanish. DESCR: *Art; Exhibits; *HISPANIC ART IN THE UNITED STATES: THIRTY CONTEMPORARY PAINTERS & SCULPTORS [exhibition].

3644 Lawrence, Jennifer. TV signal expected to boost Houston market. ADVERTISING AGE MAGAZINE, Vol. 57, no. 43 (August 11, 1986), p. S24-S25. English. DESCR: Advertising; *KXLN, Houston, TX [television station]; Marketing; Pueblo Broadcasting Corp.; Spanish Language; Television.

3645 Perez, Renato E. Badge of Hispanic pride. VISTA, Vol. 1, no. 12 (August 2, 1986), p. 9-11. English. DESCR: Broward County, FL; Chicago, IL; Dallas, TX; *Los Angeles, CA; New York, NY; *Police; San Antonio, TX; San Diego, CA; Tucson, AZ.

3646 Rodriguez, Nestor. Undocumented Central Americans in Houston: diverse populations. INTERNATIONAL MIGRATION REVIEW, Vol. 21, no. 1 (Spring 1987), p. 4-26. English. DESCR: *Central America; El Salvador; Ethnic Groups; Guatemala; Honduras; Immigrants; Intergroup Relations; Latin Americans; *Political Refugees; *Undocumented Workers.

La Huelga
USE: Boycotts

Huerta, Benito

3647 Chavez, Lorenzo A. The eyes of Texas are upon them. VISTA, Vol. 2, no. 2 (October 4, 1986), p. 20. English. DESCR: *Art; Cardenas, David; *Chulas Fronteras [art exhibit]; Espada, Ibsen; Gonzalez, Patricia; Hernandez, John; Martinez, Cesar Augusto.

Huerta, Dolores

3648 Echaveste, Beatrice and Huerta, Dolores. In the shadow of the eagle: Huerta=A la sombra del aguila: Huerta. AMERICAS 2001, Vol. 1, no. 3 (November, December, 1987), p. 26-30. Bilingual. DESCR: Agricultural Labor Unions; Boycotts; Chicanas; *Farm Workers; *United Farmworkers of America (UFW).

Huerta, Jorge A.

3649 McCracken, Ellen. Book review of: CHICANO THEATER: THEMES AND FORMS. HISPANIA, Vol. 66, no. 4 (1983), p. 645. English. DESCR: Book Reviews; *CHICANO THEATER: THEMES AND FORMS.

3650 McDermott, Douglas. Book review of: CHICANO THEATER: THEMES AND FORMS. THEATRE SURVEY, Vol. 25, no. 1 (May 1984), p. 124-125. English. DESCR: Book Reviews; *CHICANO THEATER: THEMES AND FORMS.

3651 Rodriguez del Pino, Salvador. Book review of: CHICANO THEATER: THEMES AND FORMS. AMERICAN BOOK REVIEW, Vol. 5, no. 6 (September, October, 1983), p. 18. English. DESCR: Book Reviews; *CHICANO THEATER: THEMES AND FORMS.

Huerta, Jorge A. (cont.)

3652 Tatum, Charles. Chicano literary criticism comes of age. BILINGUAL REVIEW, Vol. 12, no. 1-2 (January, August. 1985), p. 144-149. English. **DESCR:** Book Reviews; *CHICANO THEATER: THEMES AND FORMS; *LA NOVELA CHICANA ESCRITA EN ESPANOL; Literary Criticism; Rodriguez del Pino, Salvador.

El Huitlacoche
USE: Keller. Gary D.

Humor

3653 Chavez, Andres. Film review of: LENNY. LATIN QUARTER, Vol. 1, no. 4 (July, August. 1975), p. 32-33. English. **DESCR:** *Bruce, Lenny; *Film Reviews; LENNY [film].

3654 Gutierrez, Silvio G. The odd couple. VISTA, Vol. 3, no. 1 (September 6, 1987), p. 12-13. English. **DESCR:** Actors and Actresses; O'Brien, Jim; *Valdez, Alex.

3655 Larrazabal, John. Captain Zoom and his canine wonder. AMERICAS 2001. Vol. 1, no. 2 (September, October. 1987), p. [44]. Bilingual. **DESCR:** *Caricature.

3656 Padilla, Steve. Lessons to be learned from a playful hoax. VISTA, Vol. 1, no. 7 (March 2, 1986), p. 3. English. **DESCR:** *Essays; Librarians; Public Opinion; Solar, Marta-Luisa; Stereotypes; *Valdez, Juan.

3657 Padilla, Steve. The mad mad world of Sergio Aragones. VISTA. Vol. 2, no. 5 (January 4, 1987), p. 6-8. English. **DESCR:** Aragones, Sergio; Artists; Drawings; *MAD Magazine.

HUNGER OF MEMORY: THE EDUCATION OF RICHARD RODRIGUEZ

3658 Holt, Patricia. Richard Rodriguez. PUBLISHER'S WEEKLY, Vol. 221. (March 26, 1982), p. 6-8. English. **DESCR:** *Bilingual Bicultural Education; *Rodriguez, Richard.

3659 Madrid, Arturo. Book review of: HUNGER OF MEMORY. LA RED/THE NET, no. 53 (April 1982), p. 6-9. English. **DESCR:** Book Reviews; *Rodriguez, Richard.

3660 Marquez, Antonio. Richard Rodriguez's HUNGER OF MEMORY and the poetics of experience. ARIZONA QUARTERLY, Vol. 40, no. 2 (Summer 1984), p. 130-141. English. **DESCR:** *Autobiography; Book Reviews; Literary Criticism; Rodriguez, Richard.

Huntington Park, CA

3661 Sifuentes, Frank. Huntington Park: city on the upswing=Huntington Park: una ciudad ascendiente. AMERICAS 2001. Premiere Issue, 1987, p. 36-39. Bilingual. **DESCR:** History; *Urban Communities.

Hu-Pei Au, Kathryn

3662 Duran, Richard P. Book review of: CULTURE AND THE BILINGUAL CLASSROOM. LA RED/THE NET, no. 44 (July 1981), p. 4-5. English. **DESCR:** Bilingualism; Book Reviews; *CULTURE AND THE BILINGUAL CLASSROOM: STUDIES IN CLASSROOM ETHNOLOGY; Guthrie. Grace Pung; Trueba, Henry T.

Hypertension

3663 Diet cited as cause of hypertension among Hispanics. HISPANIC TIMES. Vol. 8, no. 3 (May, June. 1987), p. 16. English. **DESCR:** *Heart Disease; *Nutrition.

I AM JOAQUIN [book]

3664 Gurza, Esperanza. I AM JOAQUIN: speech act theory applied. CONFLUENCIA, Vol. 1, no. 2 (Spring 1986), p. 85-97. English. **DESCR:** Gonzales, Rodolfo (Corky); *Poetry; Rhetoric.

I DON'T HAVE TO SHOW YOU NO STINKING BADGES

3665 Mejias Rentas, Antonio. Luis Valdez y su Teatro Campesino de nuevo en L.A. LA COMUNIDAD, No. 294 (March 9, 1986), p. 8-9. Spanish. **DESCR:** *Teatro; Teatro Reviews; *Valdez, Luis.

I LOVE LUCY

3666 Perez, Renato E. As American as babalu. VISTA, Vol. 2, no. 6 (February 8, 1987), p. 22. English. **DESCR:** *Acculturation; *Arnaz, Desi; Essays; Television.

Ibarra [family name]

3667 Instituto Genealogico e Historico Latino-Americano. Rootsearch: Villalobos: Amador (Amado): Ibarra. VISTA, Vol. 3, no. 4 (December 6, 1987), p. 36. English. **DESCR:** *Amado [family name]; *Amador [family name]; Genealogy; History; Personal Names; *Villalobos [family name].

Iconography
USE: Symbolism

Identity

3668 Aboud, Frances E. and Skerry, Shelagh A. The development of ethnic attitudes: a critical review. JOURNAL OF CROSS-CULTURAL PSYCHOLOGY, Vol. 15, no. 1 (March 1984), p. 3-34. English. **DESCR:** *Attitudes; Cognition.

3669 Alvarez, Robert R. A profile of the citizenship process among Hispanics in the United States. INTERNATIONAL MIGRATION REVIEW, Vol. 21, no. 2 (Summer 1987), p. 327-351. English. **DESCR:** Chicanas; Immigration and Naturalization Service (INS); *Naturalization.

3670 Atencio, Tomas. No estan todos los que son, no son todos los que estan. EL CUADERNO, Vol. 4, no. 1 (Summer 1976), p. 51-61. Spanish. **DESCR:** Arellano, Estevan; *La Academia de la Nueva Raza, Dixon, NM; Lovato, Alberto; Martinez, Vicente; Roybal, Luis.

3671 Barro, Mary Helen. 1973 Emmy Awards. LATIN QUARTER, Vol. 1, no. 1 (July 1974), p. 5-6. English. **DESCR:** Chavez, Andres; CINCO VIDAS; Emmy Awards; *Esparza, Moctezuma; Quintero, Carlos; *Recreation; REFLECCIONES; Rodriguez, Sandra; Rodriguez, Tony; Ruiz, Jose Luis; Stereotypes; Television.

3672 Briceno, Carlos. Defining the difference between Carlos and Chuck. VISTA, Vol. 2, no. 9 (May 3, 1987), p. 26. English. **DESCR:** *Personal Names.

3673 Broderick, Stephanie H., et al. Ethnicity, acculturation, and health beliefs among diabetes patients. MIGRATION WORLD MAGAZINE, Vol. 15, no. 2 (1987), p. 30-32. English. **DESCR:** Acculturation; Attitudes; Culture; *Diabetes; *Public Health.

--   --

Identity (cont.)

3674 Bruce-Novoa, Juan. Mexico en la literatura chicana (II). LA COMUNIDAD, No. 268 (September 8, 1985), p. 14-15. Spanish. **DESCR**: Acosta, Oscar Zeta; *Literary Criticism; THE AUTOBIOGRAPHY OF A BROWN BUFFALO.

3675 Cabeza de Vaca, Darlene. Knowing the value God places on me... REVISTA MUJERES, Vol. 2, no. 1 (January 1985), p. 26-29. English. **DESCR**: *Chicanas.

3676 Callahan, Jaime M. LATINO: un nuevo concepto de cine. LA COMUNIDAD, No. 279 (November 24, 1985), p. 2-3. Spanish. **DESCR**: *Films; *LATINO [film]; Military; Military Service; Wexler, Haskell.

3677 Chavez, Noe M. Culminacion de una busqueda de identidad. LA COMUNIDAD, No. 252 (May 19, 1985), p. 4-6. Spanish. **DESCR**: Anaya, Rudolfo A.; *BLESS ME, ULTIMA; *Literary Criticism; Novel.

3678 Galindo-Ramirez, Tina. Educacion monolingue: opresion o liberacion? REVISTA MUJERES, Vol. 1, no. 1 (January 1984), p. 8-9. Spanish. **DESCR**: Alienation; Assertiveness; Biography; *Education; English Language.

3679 Garcia, Ed. On red-haired girls and the greaser in me. TEXAS OBSERVOR. Vol. 75, (October 28, 1983), p. 24-25. English. **DESCR**: Book Reviews; de Leon, Arnoldo; Essays; *Stereotypes; Texas; *THEY CALLED THEM GREASERS: ANGLO ATTITUDES TOWARD MEXICANS IN TEXAS, 1821-1900.

3680 Garcia, John A. Ethnic identity and background traits: explorations of Mexican-origin populations. LA RED/THE NET. no. 29 (April 1980), p. 2. English. **DESCR**: *Self-Referents; *Southwestern United States; *SURVEY OF INCOME AND EDUCATION, 1976.

3681 Goldman, Shifra. Arte chicano: iconografia de la autodeterminacion. LA COMUNIDAD, No. 336 (December 28, 1986), p. 12-14+. Spanish. **DESCR**: *Art; Discrimination; EL PLAN ESPIRITUAL DE AZTLAN; History; Nationalism; Pachucos; Social Classes; *Symbolism.

3682 Gottdiener, M. Group differentiation in a metropolitan high school: the influence of race, class, gender and culture. QUALITATIVE SOCIOLOGY, Vol. 8, no. 1 (Spring 1985), p. 29-41. English. **DESCR**: Anglo Americans; Blacks; *Secondary School Education.

3683 Gutierrez, Ramon A. Unraveling America's Hispanic past: internal stratification and class boundaries. AZTLAN, Vol. 17, no. 1 (Spring 1986), p. 79-101. English. **DESCR**: *Chicano, Meaning of; Culture; *Ethnic Groups; Intergroup Relations; *Self-Referents.

3684 Hayes-Bautista, David Emmett and Chapa, Jorge. Latino terminology: conceptual bases for standardized terminology. AMERICAN JOURNAL OF PUBLIC HEALTH. Vol. 77, no. 1 (January 1987), p. 61-68. English. **DESCR**: Ethnic Groups; Self-Referents.

3685 Hurtado, Aida and Gurin, Patricia. Ethnic identity and bilingualism attitudes. HISPANIC JOURNAL OF BEHAVIORAL SCIENCES, Vol. 9, no. 1 (March 1987), p. 1-18. English. **DESCR**: *Attitudes; *Bilingualism; Political Socialization.

3686 Hurtado, Aida and Arce, Carlos H. Mexicans, Chicanos, Mexican Americans, or pochos...Que somos? The impact of language and nativity on ethnic labeling. AZTLAN. Vol. 17, no. 1 (Spring 1986), p. 103-130. English. **DESCR**: *Ethnic Groups; Language Usage; *Self-Referents.

3687 Korzenny, Felipe, et al. Cultural identification as predictor of content preferences of Hispanics. JOURNALISM QUARTERLY, Vol. 60, no. 4 (Winter 1983), p. 677-685+. English. **DESCR**: Cultural Characteristics; English Language; *Newspapers; Spanish Language.

3688 Lawlor, William T. Ethnic identification: shades of gray in living color. VISTA, Vol. 2, no. 11 (May 7, 1987), p. 21. English. **DESCR**: Skin Color.

3689 Lewis, Marvin A.; Striano, Ron; and Hiura, Barbara L. Chicano ethnicity and aging [and critiques]. EXPLORATIONS IN ETHNIC STUDIES, Vol. 8, no. 2 (July 1985), p. 35-45. English. **DESCR**: Anaya, Rudolfo A.; *Ancianos; BLESS ME, ULTIMA; Curanderas; FAMOUS ALL OVER TOWN; James, Dan; Literary Criticism; Literature.

3690 Lowe, Virginia A.P. Presentation of ethnic identity in Chicano theater. CHIRICU, Vol. 2, no. 1 (Spring 1980), p. 52-58. English. **DESCR**: Ethnic Groups; Folklore Institute at Indiana University; Gary, IN; *Teatro; *Teatro Desangano del Pueblo, Washington Park, East Chicago, IN.

3691 Lucero, Rubel Jose. The enemy within. EL CUADERNO, Vol. 1, no. 1 (1971), p. 10-13. English. **DESCR**: *Discrimination; *Self-Referents.

3692 Martinez, Ruben and Dukes, Richard L. Race, gender and self-esteem among youth. HISPANIC JOURNAL OF BEHAVIORAL SCIENCES, Vol. 9, no. 4 (December 1987), p. 427-443. English. **DESCR**: *Comparative Psychology; *Sex Roles; *Youth.

3693 Mena, Francisco; Padilla, Amado M.; and Maldonado, Margarita. Acculturative stress and specific coping stategies among immigrant and later generation college students. HISPANIC JOURNAL OF BEHAVIORAL SCIENCES, Vol. 9, no. 2 (June 1987), p. 207-225. English. **DESCR**: *Acculturation; Age Groups; Colleges and Universities; Immigrants; Stress; Students.

3694 Meyers, C.E.; Borthwick, S.A.; and Eyman, R.K. Place of residence by age, ethnicity, and level of retardation of the mentally retarded/developmentally disabled population of California. AMERICAN JOURNAL OF MENTAL DEFICIENCY, Vol. 90, no. 3 (November 1985), p. 266-270. English. **DESCR**: California; *Mentally Handicapped; Public Health.

3695 Mohr, Nicholasa. Puerto Rican writers in the United States, Puerto Rican writers in Puerto Rico: a separation beyond language. THE AMERICAS REVIEW, Vol. 15, no. 2 (Summer 1987), p. 87-92. English. **DESCR**: Authors; Autobiography; Immigrants; *Language Usage; *Literature; *Mohr, Nicolasa; *Puerto Ricans; Spanish Language.

3696 Monsivais, Carlos. Los cholos y la cultura de la frontera. LA COMUNIDAD, No. 242 (March 10, 1985), p. 14-15. Spanish. **DESCR**: Border Region; Culture; *Pachucos; *Tijuana, Baja California, Mexico.

Identity (cont.)

3697 Monsivais, Carlos. Este es el pachuco, un sujeto singular. LA COMUNIDAD, No. 243 (March 17. 1985), p. 4-5. Spanish. **DESCR:** Border Region; Culture; *Pachucos.

3698 Munoz, Carlos, Jr. Chicano politics: the current conjuncture. THE YEAR LEFT, Vol. 2, (1987), p. 35-52. English. **DESCR:** Chicano Movement; *Intergroup Relations; *Political Parties and Organizations; *Politics; Reagan Administration; Voter Turnout.

3699 Nelson. Candace and Tienda, Marta. The structuring of Hispanic ethnicity: historical and contemporary perspectives. ETHNIC AND RACIAL STUDIES, Vol. 8, no. 1 (January 1985), p. 49-74. English. **DESCR:** Cultural Characteristics; Ethnic Groups; Immigrants.

3700 Raferty, Judith R. Book review of: LATINO ETHNIC CONSCIOUSNESS. WESTERN HISTORICAL QUARTERLY, Vol. 17, no. 4 (October 1986), p. 490. English. **DESCR:** Book Reviews; *LATINO ETHNIC CONSCIOUSNESS; Padilla, Felix M.

3701 Rosaldo, Renato. When natives talk back: Chicano anthropology since the late 60s. RENATO ROSALDO LECTURE SERIES MONOGRAPH, Vol. 2, (Spring 1986), p. [3]-20. English. **DESCR:** *Anthropology; Culture; EL GRITO; Paredes, Americo; *Political Ideology; *Research Methodology; Romano-V., Octavio Ignacio; Valdez, Facundo.

3702 Rosas, Alejandro. Teatro chicano: un teatro de la esperanza. LA COMUNIDAD, No. 247 (April 14, 1985), 2-3. Spanish. **DESCR:** El Teatro de la Esperanza; *ONCE A FAMILY [play]; *Teatro; Teatro Reviews.

3703 Salgado de Snyder. Nelly. The role of ethnic loyalty among Mexican immigrant women. HISPANIC JOURNAL OF BEHAVIORAL SCIENCES, Vol. 9, no. 3 (September 1987), p. 287-298. English. **DESCR:** Acculturation; Chicanas; *Culture; Immigrants; Mental Health; *Mexico; *Women.

3704 Wells, Miriam J. Power brokers and ethnicity: the rise of a Chicano movement. AZTLAN. Vol. 17, no. 1 (Spring 1986), p. 47-77. English. **DESCR:** *Chicano Movement; *Natural Support Systems; *Patron System.

Ideology
USE: Political Ideology

Idioms
USE: Chicano Dialects

Illegal Aliens
USE: Undocumented Workers

ILLEGAL ALIENS IN THE WESTERN HEMISPHERE: POLITICAL AND ECONOMIC FACTORS

3705 Flores, Estevan T. Book review of: ILLEGAL ALIENS IN THE WESTERN HEMISPHERE. LA RED/THE NET. no. 56 (July 1982), p. 7-9. English. **DESCR:** Book Reviews; Johnson, Kenneth F.; Undocumented Workers; Williams, Miles W.

Illiteracy
USE: Literacy

AN ILLUSTRATED HISTORY OF MEXICAN LOS ANGELES: 1781-1985

3706 Hoffman, Abraham. Book review of: AN ILLUSTRATED HISTORY OF MEXICAN LOS ANGELES: 1781-1985. NEW MEXICO HISTORICAL REVIEW,

Vol. 62, no. 4 (October 1987), p. 412-13. English. **DESCR:** Book Reviews; *Castillo, Pedro; *Los Angeles, CA; *Rios-Bustamante, Antonio.

IMAGES AND CONVERSATIONS: MEXICAN AMERICANS RECALL A SOUTHWESTERN PAST

3707 Foote, Cheryl. Book review of: IMAGES AND CONVERSATIONS. JOURNAL OF THE WEST, Vol. 24, no. 3 (July 1985), p. 121. English. **DESCR:** Book Reviews; Chicanas; *Martin, Patricia Preciado; Oral History.

3708 Lopez, Steven. Book review of: IMAGES AND CONVERSATIONS. LA RED/THE NET, no. 77 (February 1984), p. 5-7. Magazine. **DESCR:** Book Reviews; Preciado Martin, Patricia.

Imhoff, Gary

3709 Madrid, Arturo. Book review of: THE IMMIGRATION TIME BOMB. LA RED/THE NET, no. 97 (June 1986), p. 9-12. English. **DESCR:** Book Reviews; Immigration; Lamm, Richard; *THE IMMIGRATION TIME BOMB: THE FRAGMENTING OF AMERICA.

THE IMMIGRANT WOMAN IN NORTH AMERICA: AN ANNOTATED BIBLIOGRAPHY OF SELECTED REFERENCES

3710 Book review of: THE IMMIGRANT WOMAN IN NORTH AMERICA. BOOKLIST, Vol. 82, no. 12 (February 15, 1986), p. 855-856. English. **DESCR:** Book Reviews; Cordasco, Francesco; Reference Works.

3711 Freiband, Susan J. Book review of: THE IMMIGRANT WOMAN IN NORTH AMERICA. AMERICAN REFERENCE BOOKS ANNUAL, Vol. 17, (1986), p. 178. English. **DESCR:** Book Reviews; Cordasco, Francesco.

3712 Hagle, C. Book review of: THE IMMIGRANT WOMAN IN NORTH AMERICA. CHOICE, Vol. 23, no. 8 (April 1986), p. 1191. English. **DESCR:** Book Reviews; Cordasco, Francesco; Reference Works.

IMMIGRANT WOMEN IN THE LAND OF DOLLARS: LIFE AND CULTURE ON THE LOWER EAST SIDE, 1890-1925

3713 McBride, P.W. Book review of: IMMIGRANT WOMEN IN THE LAND OF DOLLARS. CHOICE, Vol. 23, no. 9 (May 1986), p. 1448. English. **DESCR:** Book Reviews; Ewen, Elizabeth.

Immigrants

3714 Alexander, June Granatir. Book review of: URBAN ETHNICITY IN THE UNITED STATES. JOURNAL OF AMERICAN ETHNIC HISTORY, Vol. 7, no. 1 (Fall 1987), p. 95-97. English. **DESCR:** Book Reviews; Maldonado, Lionel; Moore, Joan W.; *URBAN ETHNICITY IN THE UNITED STATES: NEW IMMIGRANTS AND OLD MINORITIES.

3715 Arroyo, Luis Leobardo. Book review of: DESERT IMMIGRANTS. LA RED/THE NET, no. 43 (June 1981), p. 3-4. English. **DESCR:** Book Reviews; *DESERT IMMIGRANTS: THE MEXICANS OF EL PASO 1880-1920; Garcia, Mario T..

3716 Baezconde-Garbanati, Lourdes and Salgado de Snyder, Nelly. Mexican immigrant women: a selected bibliography. HISPANIC JOURNAL OF BEHAVIORAL SCIENCES, Vol. 9, no. 3 (September 1987), p. 331-358. English. **DESCR:** *Bibliography; *Chicanas; *Women.

Immigrants (cont.)

3717 Briody, Elizabeth K. Patterns of household immigration into South Texas. INTERNATIONAL MIGRATION REVIEW, Vol. 21. no. 1 (Spring 1987), p. 27-47. English. **DESCR:** Chicanas; *Family; Sex Roles; *Social Mobility; *South Texas.

3718 Chiswick, Barry R. Book review of: POLITICAL AND ECONOMIC MIGRANTS IN AMERICA. JOURNAL OF AMERICAN ETHNIC HISTORY, Vol. 7, no. 1 (Fall 1987), p. 105-106. English. **DESCR:** Book Reviews; Pedraza-Bailey, Silvia; *POLITICAL AND ECONOMIC MIGRANTS IN AMERICA.

3719 DeSipio, Louis. Social science literature and the naturalization process. INTERNATIONAL MIGRATION REVIEW, Vol. 21. no. 2 (Summer 1987), p. 390-405. English. **DESCR:** *Naturalization; *Research Methodology; *Social Science.

3720 Edmondson, Brad. Met Life mines minority market. AMERICAN DEMOGRAPHICS, Vol. 8, no. 7 (July 1986), p. 18-19. English. **DESCR:** Consumers; Ethnic Groups; Insurance; Marketing; *Metropolitan Life Insurance Corporation.

3721 Engerman, Stanley L. Book review of: THE TRANSPLANTED. JOURNAL OF ECONOMIC HISTORY, Vol. 46. no. 2 (June 1986), p. 552-553. English. **DESCR:** *Bodnar. John; Book Reviews; *THE TRANSPLANTED: A HISTORY OF IMMIGRANTS IN URBAN AMERICA.

3722 Esman, Milton J. Two dimensions of ethnic politics: defense of homelands. immigrant rights. ETHNIC AND RACIAL STUDIES, Vol. 8, no. 3 (July 1985), p. 438-440. English. **DESCR:** Ethnic Groups; Politics.

3723 Fernandez, Edward and Cresce, Arthur R. The Hispanic foreign-born and the assimilation experience. MIGRATION WORLD MAGAZINE. Vol. 14, no. 5 (1986), p. 7-11. English. **DESCR:** *Assimilation; Naturalization; *Socioeconomic Factors; Undocumented Workers.

3724 Garcia, John A. The political integration of Mexican immigrants: examining some political orientations. INTERNATIONAL MIGRATION REVIEW, Vol. 21. no. 2 (Summer 1987), p. 372-389. English. **DESCR:** Culture; *National Chicano Survey (NCS); Political Ideology; *Political Socialization.

3725 Garcia, Mario T. Book review of: POLITICAL AND ECONOMIC MIGRANTS IN AMERICA. AMERICAN HISTORICAL REVIEW, Vol. 91. no. 4 (October 1986), p. 1023-1024. English. **DESCR:** Book Reviews; Immigration; Pedraza-Bailey, Silvia; *POLITICAL AND ECONOMIC MIGRANTS IN AMERICA.

3726 Gilbert. M. Jean. Alcohol consumption patterns in immigrant and later generation Mexican American women. HISPANIC JOURNAL OF BEHAVIORAL SCIENCES, Vol. 9, no. 3 (September 1987), p. 299-313. English. **DESCR:** Acculturation; *Alcoholism; *Attitudes; *Chicanas; Cultural Characteristics; Mexico.

3727 Guendelman, Sylvia. The incorporation of Mexican women in seasonal migration: a study of gender differences. HISPANIC JOURNAL OF BEHAVIORAL SCIENCES. Vol. 9, no. 3 (September 1987), p. 245-264. English. **DESCR:** Chicanas; Marriage; Mexico; *Migration Patterns; *Sex Roles; *Women; *Women Men Relations; Working Women.

3728 Guzman, Ralph. Bi-national policy questions generated by Mexican school-age children who migrate between the United States and Mexico. LA RED/THE NET, no. 62 (December 1982), p. 2-4. English. **DESCR:** *Children; Migrant Children; Public Policy; *Watsonville, CA.

3729 Jensen, Leif and Tienda, Marta. The new immigration: implications for poverty and public assistance utilization. MIGRATION WORLD MAGAZINE, Vol. 15, no. 5 (1987), p. 7-18. English. **DESCR:** History; *Immigration; *Immigration and Naturalization Act, 1965; Poverty; Public Policy; *Welfare.

3730 Lopez, Maria Isabel. La tia Julia. REVISTA MUJERES, Vol. 2, no. 2 (June 1985), p. 11-12. Spanish. **DESCR:** *Short Story.

3731 Magiera, Marcy. New arrivals find warm welcome as consumers. ADVERTISING AGE MAGAZINE. Vol. 58, no. 6 (February 9, 1987), p. S14. English. **DESCR:** Consumers; *Marketing; Undocumented Workers.

3732 Marketing to Hispanics. ADVERTISING AGE MAGAZINE. Vol. 58, no. 6 (February 9, 1987), p. S1-S23. English. **DESCR:** Advertising; Consumers; *Marketing; Mass Media; Politics; Undocumented Workers.

3733 Massey, Douglas S. Do undocumented migrants earn lower wages than legal immigrants? New evidence from Mexico. INTERNATIONAL MIGRATION REVIEW, Vol. 21, no. 2 (Summer 1987), p. 236-274. English. **DESCR:** Employment; *Income; *Mexico; Migration Patterns; *Undocumented Workers.

3734 Melendez, Pablo. Happy Thanksgiving. CALIFORNIA MAGAZINE, Vol. 11, no. 11 (November 1986), p. 136. English. **DESCR:** *Biography; *Essays; *Melendez, Pablo; Youth.

3735 Mena, Francisco; Padilla, Amado M.; and Maldonado, Margarita. Acculturative stress and specific coping stategies among immigrant and later generation college students. HISPANIC JOURNAL OF BEHAVIORAL SCIENCES, Vol. 9, no. 2 (June 1987), p. 207-225. English. **DESCR:** *Acculturation; Age Groups; Colleges and Universities; Identity; Stress; Students.

3736 Mohr, Nicholasa. Puerto Rican writers in the United States, Puerto Rican writers in Puerto Rico: a separation beyond language. THE AMERICAS REVIEW, Vol. 15, no. 2 (Summer 1987), p. 87-92. English. **DESCR:** Authors; Autobiography; Identity; *Language Usage; *Literature; *Mohr, Nicolasa; *Puerto Ricans; Spanish Language.

3737 Montejano, David. Book review of: IMMIGRANTS--AND IMMIGRANTS. LA RED/THE NET, no. 43 (June 1981), p. 4. English. **DESCR:** Book Reviews; Corwin, Arthur F.; *IMMIGRANTS---AND IMMIGRANTS: PERSPECTIVES ON MEXICAN LABOR MIGRATION TO THE UNITED STATES.

3738 Nelson, Candace and Tienda, Marta. The structuring of Hispanic ethnicity: historical and contemporary perspectives. ETHNIC AND RACIAL STUDIES, Vol. 8, no. 1 (January 1985), p. 49-74. English. **DESCR:** Cultural Characteristics; Ethnic Groups; *Identity.

Immigrants (cont.)

3739 Pachon, Harry. An overview of citizenship in the Hispanic community. INTERNATIONAL MIGRATION REVIEW, Vol. 21, no. 2 (Summer 1987), p. 299-310. English. **DESCR:** *Naturalization.

3740 Portes, Alejandro and Curtis, John W. Changing flags: naturalization and its determinants among Mexican immigrants. INTERNATIONAL MIGRATION REVIEW, Vol. 21, no. 2 (Summer 1987), p. 352-371. English. **DESCR:** *Naturalization.

3741 Rodriguez, Nestor. Undocumented Central Americans in Houston: diverse populations. INTERNATIONAL MIGRATION REVIEW, Vol. 21, no. 1 (Spring 1987), p. 4-26. English. **DESCR:** *Central America; El Salvador; Ethnic Groups; Guatemala; Honduras; *Houston, TX; Intergroup Relations; Latin Americans; *Political Refugees; *Undocumented Workers.

3742 Salgado de Snyder, Nelly. The role of ethnic loyalty among Mexican immigrant women. HISPANIC JOURNAL OF BEHAVIORAL SCIENCES, Vol. 9, no. 3 (September 1987), p. 287-298. English. **DESCR:** Acculturation; Chicanas; *Culture; *Identity; Mental Health; *Mexico; *Women.

3743 Stewart, Kenneth L. and de Leon, Arnoldo. Age and sex composition among inmigrantes to Texas. LA RED/THE NET, no. 64 (February 1983), p. 2-3. English. **DESCR:** Nineteenth century; *Texas.

3744 Stolarik, M. Mark. Book review of: THE TRANSPLANTED. JOURNAL OF AMERICAN ETHNIC HISTORY, Vol. 6, no. 2 (Spring 1987), p. 66-68. English. **DESCR:** Bodnar, John; Book Reviews; *THE TRANSPLANTED: A HISTORY OF IMMIGRANTS IN URBAN AMERICA.

3745 Sullivan, Teresa A. and Tienda, Marta. Integration of multiple data sources in immigrant studies. REVIEW OF PUBLIC DATA USE, Vol. 12, no. 4 (December 1984), p. 233-244. English. **DESCR:** *Immigration; *Research Methodology; *Statistics.

3746 Vargas-Willis, Gloria and Cervantes, Richard C. Consideration of psychosocial stress in the treatment of the Latina immigrant. HISPANIC JOURNAL OF BEHAVIORAL SCIENCES, Vol. 9, no. 3 (September 1987), p. 315-329. English. **DESCR:** *Chicanas; Discrimination in Employment; Mental Health; *Psychotherapy; *Stress.

3747 Wreford, Mary. Book review of: THE BRACERO EXPERIENCE: ELITELORE VERSUS FOLKLORE. LA RED/THE NET, no. 29 (April 1980), p. 10. English. **DESCR:** Book Reviews; *Braceros; *Herrera-Sobek, Maria; THE BRACERO EXPERIENCE: ELITELORE VERSUS FOLKLORE.

IMMIGRANTS AND THEIR CHILDREN IN THE UNITED STATES: A BIBLIOGRAPHY OF DOCTORAL DISSERTATIONS, 1885-1982

3748 Hendershott, C. Book review of: IMMIGRANTS AND THEIR CHILDREN IN THE UNITED STATES: A BIBLIOGRAPHY OF DOCTORAL DISSERTATIONS, 1885-1982. CHOICE, Vol. 23, no. 11-12 (July, August, 1986), p. 1656. English. **DESCR:** Book Reviews; Hoglund, A. William.

IMMIGRANTS---AND IMMIGRANTS: PERSPECTIVES ON MEXICAN LABOR MIGRATION TO THE UNITED STATES

3749 Montejano, David. Book review of: IMMIGRANTS--AND IMMIGRANTS. LA RED/THE NET, no. 43 (June 1981), p. 4. English. **DESCR:** Book Reviews; Corwin, Arthur F.; Immigrants.

Immigration

3750 Arreola, Daniel D. The Mexican American cultural capital. GEOGRAPHICAL REVIEW, Vol. 77, (January 1987), p. 17-34. English. **DESCR:** Conjuntos; Food Industry; History; LA PRENSA, San Antonio, TX; La Raza Unida Party; League of United Latin American Citizens (LULAC); Lozano, Ignacio; Mexican American Youth Organization, San Antonio, TX; Music; Orden Hijos de America, San Antonio, TX; Railroads; *San Antonio, TX; *Social History and Conditions.

3751 Baker, Ross K. Border follies. AMERICAN DEMOGRAPHICS, Vol. 8, no. 8 (August 1986), p. 60. English. **DESCR:** Guadalupe Hidalgo, Treaty of 1848; Rio Grande; Texas; *Undocumented Workers.

3752 Bracamonte, Jose A. Book review of: MEXICAN IMMIGRANT WORKERS IN THE U.S. LA RED/THE NET, no. 49 (December 1981), p. 3-4. English. **DESCR:** *MEXICAN IMMIGRANT WORKERS IN THE U.S.; *Rios-Bustamante, Antonio.

3753 Conner, Roger and Moreno, G. Mario. The Immigration Reform Law: how fair to Hispanics? VISTA, Vol. 2, no. 8 (April 4, 1987), p. 12, 17, 18. English. **DESCR:** Federation for American Immigration Reform (FAIR); *Immigration Reform and Control Act of 1986; League of United Latin American Citizens (LULAC); Mexican American Legal Defense and Educational Fund (MALDEF).

3754 Facing up to new occupational challenges. HISPANIC BUSINESS, Vol. 9, no. 6 (June 1987), p. 113. English. **DESCR:** *Employment; *Population; Rand Corporation.

3755 Garcia, Mario T. Book review of: POLITICAL AND ECONOMIC MIGRANTS IN AMERICA. LA RED/THE NET, no. 96 (May 1986), p. 11-12. English. **DESCR:** Book Reviews; Pedraza-Bailey, Silvia; *POLITICAL AND ECONOMIC MIGRANTS IN AMERICA.

3756 Garcia, Mario T. Book review of: POLITICAL AND ECONOMIC MIGRANTS IN AMERICA. AMERICAN HISTORICAL REVIEW, Vol. 91, no. 4 (October 1986), p. 1023-1024. English. **DESCR:** Book Reviews; Immigrants; Pedraza-Bailey, Silvia; *POLITICAL AND ECONOMIC MIGRANTS IN AMERICA.

3757 Greenwood, Michael J. and McDowell, John H. U.S. immigration reform: policy issues and economic analysis. CONTEMPORARY POLICY ISSUES, Vol. 3, (Spring 1985), p. 59-75. English. **DESCR:** *Immigration Reform and Control Act of 1986; Public Policy.

3758 Guevara, Ruben. Richard "Cheech" Marin. AMERICAS 2001, Vol. 1, no. 1 (June, July, 1987), p. 18-21. Bilingual. **DESCR:** *Actors and Actresses; *BORN IN EAST L.A. [film]; Films; *Marin, Richard "Cheech"; Undocumented Workers.

3759 Horta, Gerardo. Emigrante. LA COMUNIDAD, No. 347 (March 15, 1987), p. 2-3. Spanish. **DESCR:** *Short Story.

3760 Hunsaker, Alan C. Mexican immigration patterns. LA RED/THE NET, no. 93 (January, February, 1986), p. 17-19. English. **DESCR:** Book Reviews; *Jones, Richard C.; *Migration Patterns; PATTERNS OF UNDOCUMENTED MIGRATION: MEXICO AND THE U.S.

Immigration (cont.)

3761 Information/Informacion. AMERICAS 2001, Premiere Issue, 1987, p. 11. Bilingual. **DESCR:** *Directories; *Organizations.

3762 Jensen, Leif and Tienda, Marta. The new immigration: implications for poverty and public assistance utilization. MIGRATION WORLD MAGAZINE, Vol. 15, no. 5 (1987), p. 7-18. English. **DESCR:** History; Immigrants; *Immigration and Naturalization Act, 1965; Poverty; Public Policy; *Welfare.

3763 Kelly, Peter. American bosses have jobs; Mexicans need work. GUARDIAN, Vol. 39, no. 8 (November 19, 1986), p. 11. English. **DESCR:** Labor Supply and Market; *Undocumented Workers.

3764 Kraly, Ellen Percy. Book review of: CLAMOR AT THE GATES. JOURNAL OF AMERICAN ETHNIC HISTORY, Vol. 7, no. 1 (Fall 1987), p. 93-95. English. **DESCR:** Book Reviews; *CLAMOR AT THE GATES: THE NEW AMERICAN IMMIGRATION; Glazer, Nathan.

3765 Lopez-Garza, Marta. Book review of: OPERATION WETBACK. LA RED/THE NET, no. 50 (January 1982), p. 7-9. English. **DESCR:** Book Reviews; *Deportation; *Garcia, Juan Ramon; *OPERATION WETBACK: THE MASS DEPORTATION OF MEXICAN UNDOCUMENTED WORKERS IN 1954.

3766 Madrid, Arturo. Book review of: THE IMMIGRATION TIME BOMB. LA RED/THE NET, no. 97 (June 1986), p. 9-12. English. **DESCR:** Book Reviews; Imhoff, Gary; Lamm, Richard; *THE IMMIGRATION TIME BOMB: THE FRAGMENTING OF AMERICA.

3767 Madrid, Arturo. Book reviews of: CLAMOR AT THE GATES and LATIN JOURNEY. LA RED/THE NET, no. 89 (August 1985), p. 7-10. English. **DESCR:** Bach, Robert L.; Book Reviews; *CLAMOR AT THE GATES: THE NEW AMERICAN IMMIGRATION; Glazer, Nathan; *LATIN JOURNEY: CUBAN AND MEXICAN IMMIGRANTS IN THE UNITED STATES; Portes, Alejandro.

3768 Morales, Patricia. Indocumentados y chicanos: un intento de aproximacion. LA COMUNIDAD, No. 318 (August 24, 1986), p. 2-5. Spanish. **DESCR:** History; Labor; Undocumented Workers.

3769 Morris, Richard W. Psychosocial consequences of Mexican migration. LA RED/THE NET, no. 44 (July 1981), p. 2-3. English. **DESCR:** *Mental Health.

3770 Panas, Katia. The forgotten people. REVISTA MUJERES, Vol. 1, no. 2 (June 1984), p. 15. English. **DESCR:** Nunez Wilson, Carmen; *"The Forgotten People" [senior thesis].

3771 Rigoni, Florenzo. Tijuana: the borders on the move. MIGRATION WORLD MAGAZINE, Vol. 15, no. 2 (1987), p. [22]-29. English. **DESCR:** *Border Region; Criminal Acts; Scalabrini Center, Tijuana, Baja California, Mexico; *Tijuana, Baja California, Mexico; *Undocumented Workers.

3772 Rodriguez Flores, Juan. Una historia de todos los dias. LA COMUNIDAD, No. 321 (September 14, 1986), p. 12-13. Spanish. **DESCR:** Undocumented Workers.

3773 Sanders, Sol. Mexican immigration: specter of a fortress America? STRATEGIC REVIEW, Vol. 14, (Winter 1986), p. 30-38. English.

3774 Stacy, G. Palmer and Lutton, Wayne. The U.S.

immigration crisis. JOURNAL OF SOCIAL POLITICAL AND ECONOMIC STUDIES, Vol. 10, no. 3 (Fall 1985), p. 333-350. English. **DESCR:** Political Refugees; Population.

3775 Sullivan, Teresa A. and Tienda, Marta. Integration of multiple data sources in immigrant studies. REVIEW OF PUBLIC DATA USE, Vol. 12, no. 4 (December 1984), p. 233-244. English. **DESCR:** *Immigrants; *Research Methodology; *Statistics.

Immigration and Naturalization Act, 1965

3776 Jensen, Leif and Tienda, Marta. The new immigration: implications for poverty and public assistance utilization. MIGRATION WORLD MAGAZINE, Vol. 15, no. 5 (1987), p. 7-18. English. **DESCR:** History; Immigrants; *Immigration; Poverty; Public Policy; *Welfare.

Immigration and Naturalization Service (INS)

3777 Alvarez, Robert R. A profile of the citizenship process among Hispanics in the United States. INTERNATIONAL MIGRATION REVIEW, Vol. 21, no. 2 (Summer 1987), p. 327-351. English. **DESCR:** Chicanas; Identity; *Naturalization.

3778 Culp, Robert Alan. The Immigration and Naturalization Service and racially motivated questioning: does equal protection pick up where the Fourth Amendment left off? COLUMBIA LAW REVIEW, Vol. 86, no. 4 (May 1986), p. 800-822. English. **DESCR:** Border Patrol; *Constitutional Amendments - Fourth; *Discrimination; Immigration Law and Legislation; Immigration Regulation and Control; *Search and Seizure.

3779 Mosqueda, Lawrence Joseph. How to keep a bad bill from getting worse. GUARDIAN, Vol. 38, no. 46 (September 24, 1986), p. 5. English. **DESCR:** *Immigration Law and Legislation; Immigration Regulation and Control; Simpson-Rodino Bill; Undocumented Workers.

3780 [Untitled editorial]. LATIN QUARTER, Vol. 1, no. 2 (October 1974), p. 2. English. **DESCR:** Civil Rights; *Immigration Regulation and Control.

3781 Vanderpool, Tim. Immigration reform crosses an uncertain border into law. IN THESE TIMES, Vol. 11, no. 6 (December 17, 1986), p. 5, 7. English. **DESCR:** Immigration Law and Legislation; *Immigration Reform and Control Act of 1986; Simpson-Rodino Bill; Undocumented Workers.

Immigration Law and Legislation

3782 Barr, Evan T. Borderline hypocrisy. NEW REPUBLIC, Vol. 195, (July 14, 1986), p. 12-13. English.

3783 Bethell, Tom. Senator Simpson's reward. AMERICAN SPECTATOR, Vol. 19, no. 2 (February 1986), p. 11-13. English. **DESCR:** Discrimination; Politics; *Simpson, Alan K.; Undocumented Workers.

Immigration Law and Legislation (cont.)

3784 Culp, Robert Alan. The Immigration and Naturalization Service and racially motivated questioning: does equal protection pick up where the Fourth Amendment left off? COLUMBIA LAW REVIEW, Vol. 86, no. 4 (May 1986), p. 800-822. English. **DESCR:** Border Patrol; *Constitutional Amendments - Fourth; *Discrimination; *Immigration and Naturalization Service (INS); Immigration Regulation and Control; *Search and Seizure.

3785 Ezell, Howard. Why immigration reform passed=Porque fue aprobada la reforma de inmigracion. AMERICAS 2001, Premiere Issue, 1987, p. 7, 9, 40-41. Bilingual. **DESCR:** *Immigration Reform and Control Act of 1986; Undocumented Workers.

3786 Faxon, R. Paul. Employer sanctions for hiring illegal aliens: a simplistic solution to a complex problem. NORTHWESTERN JOURNAL OF INTERNATIONAL LAW AND BUSINESS, Vol. 6, (Spring 1984), p. 203-248. English. **DESCR:** Agribusiness; National Labor Relations Board (NLRB); Simpson-Mazzoli Bill; *Undocumented Workers.

3787 Flores, Estevan T. 1982 Simpson-Mazzoli immigration reform and the Hispanic community. LA RED/THE NET, no. 64 (February 1983), p. 14-16. English. **DESCR:** *Simpson-Mazzoli Bill.

3788 Gill, Eric K. Notaries: clearing the air. HISPANIC BUSINESS, Vol. 9, no. 3 (March 1987), p. 14. English. **DESCR:** *Legal Aid; *Naturalization; Undocumented Workers.

3789 Gollobin, Ira. No pasaran. NATION, Vol. 243, no. 14 (November 1, 1986), p. 429. English. **DESCR:** *Immigration Reform and Control Act of 1986; Undocumented Workers.

3790 Gordon, Charles. The rights of aliens: an expanding role for trial lawyers. TRIAL, Vol. 19, no. 12 (December 1983), p. 54-58. English. **DESCR:** Deportation; *Legal Profession; *Political Prisoners; *Undocumented Workers.

3791 Gunderson, Kay. White does about-face on Simpson-Mazzoli. TEXAS OBSERVOR, Vol. 75, (March 25, 1983), p. 4. English. **DESCR:** League of United Latin American Citizens (LULAC); *Simpson-Mazzoli Bill; Texas; White, Mark.

3792 Haines, Michael R. Book review of: IMMIGRATION POLICY AND THE AMERICAN LABOR FORCE. JOURNAL OF ECONOMIC HISTORY, Vol. 45, no. 3 (September 1985), p. 742-744. English. **DESCR:** Book Reviews; Briggs, Vernon M., Jr.; *IMMIGRATION POLICY AND THE AMERICAN LABOR FORCE.

3793 Hernandez, Antonia A. The politics of the new immigration law=La politica de la nueva ley de inmigracion. AMERICAS 2001, Premiere issue, 1987, p. 6,8,40. Bilingual. **DESCR:** *Immigration Reform and Control Act of 1986.

3794 Immigration Reform and Control Act of 1986. MIGRATION WORLD MAGAZINE, Vol. 15, no. 1 (1987), p. 31-32. English. **DESCR:** *Immigration Reform and Control Act of 1986.

3795 Isgro, Francesco. Implementation of the legalization provisions under the Immigration Reform and Control Act of 1986. MIGRATION WORLD MAGAZINE, Vol. 15, no. 3 (1987), p. 24-39. English. **DESCR:** *Immigration Reform and Control Act of 1986.

3796 Levy, Deborah M. By invitation only. THE PROGRESSIVE, Vol. 50, no. 8 (August 1986), p. 35-38. English. **DESCR:** *League of United Latin American Citizens (LULAC).

3797 Mosqueda, Lawrence Joseph. How to keep a bad bill from getting worse. GUARDIAN, Vol. 38, no. 46 (September 24, 1986), p. 5. English. **DESCR:** Immigration and Naturalization Service (INS); Immigration Regulation and Control; Simpson-Rodino Bill; Undocumented Workers.

3798 Munoz, Rosalio. The Simpson-Rodino immigration law: an assault on the working class. POLITICAL AFFAIRS, Vol. 66, no. 6 (June 1987), p. 12-18. English. **DESCR:** Civil Rights; *Immigration Reform and Control Act of 1986; Undocumented Workers.

3799 Novick, Michael. INS makes a bad Simpson-Rodino law worse. GUARDIAN, Vol. 39, no. 16 (January 21, 1987), p. 5. English. **DESCR:** *Immigration Reform and Control Act of 1986; *Simpson-Rodino Bill; Undocumented Workers.

3800 Rodriguez, Roberto. Central Americans and the new immigration law=La nueva ley de inmigracion y la comunidad Centro Americana. AMERICAS 2001, Premiere Issue, 1987, p. 28,43. Bilingual. **DESCR:** *Central America; *Immigration Reform and Control Act of 1986; Latin Americans.

3801 Roth, Michael. Panic and fear in Latino communities. GUARDIAN, Vol. 39, no. 8 (November 19, 1986), p. 10-11. English. **DESCR:** *Simpson-Rodino Bill; Undocumented Workers.

3802 Sellers, Jeff M. Opportunity no, regulations yes. HISPANIC BUSINESS, Vol. 9, no. 2 (February 1987), p. 12-[14]. English. **DESCR:** Discrimination; Employment; *Immigration Reform and Control Act of 1986; Undocumented Workers.

3803 Toney, Bill. Employment is the key. U.S. NEWS & WORLD REPORT, Vol. 101, (August 4, 1986), p. 65. English. **DESCR:** Undocumented Workers.

3804 U.S. immigration legislation and practice. MIGRATION WORLD MAGAZINE, Vol. 15, no. 4 (1987), p. 35-36. English.

3805 Vanderpool, Tim. Immigration reform crosses an uncertain border into law. IN THESE TIMES, Vol. 11, no. 6 (December 17, 1986), p. 5, 7. English. **DESCR:** Immigration and Naturalization Service (INS); *Immigration Reform and Control Act of 1986; Simpson-Rodino Bill; Undocumented Workers.

IMMIGRATION POLICY AND THE AMERICAN LABOR FORCE

3806 Book review of: IMMIGRATION POLICY AND THE AMERICAN LABOR FORCE. ECONOMIC BOOKS, Vol. 12, no. 3 (September 1985), p. 67-68. English. **DESCR:** Book Reviews; Briggs, Vernon M., Jr.

3807 Haines, Michael R. Book review of: IMMIGRATION POLICY AND THE AMERICAN LABOR FORCE. JOURNAL OF ECONOMIC HISTORY, Vol. 45, no. 3 (September 1985), p. 742-744. English. **DESCR:** Book Reviews; Briggs, Vernon M., Jr.; Immigration Law and Legislation.

IMMIGRATION POLICY AND THE AMERICAN LABOR FORCE
(cont.)

3808 Papademetriou, Demetrios G. Book review of:
IMMIGRATION POLICY AND THE AMERICAN LABOR
FORCE. AMERICAN POLITICAL SCIENCE REVIEW,
Vol. 79, no. 4 (December 1985), p. 1182.
English. **DESCR:** Book Reviews; Briggs, Vernon
M., Jr.

3809 Reder, Melvin W. Book review of: IMMIGRATION
POLICY AND THE AMERICAN LABOR FORCE.
INDUSTRIAL AND LABOR RELATIONS REVIEW, Vol.
40, no. 1 (October 1986), p. 139-140.
English. **DESCR:** Book Reviews; Briggs, Vernon
M., Jr.

Immigration Raids
USE: Immigration Regulation and Control

Immigration Reform and Control Act of 1986

3810 Conner, Roger and Moreno, G. Mario. The
Immigration Reform Law: how fair to
Hispanics? VISTA, Vol. 2, no. 8 (April 4,
1987), p. 12, 17, 18. English. **DESCR:**
Federation for American Immigration Reform
(FAIR); *Immigration; League of United Latin
American Citizens (LULAC); Mexican American
Legal Defense and Educational Fund (MALDEF).

3811 Ezell, Howard. Why immigration reform
passed=Porque fue aprobada la reforma de
inmigracion. AMERICAS 2001, Premiere Issue,
1987, p. 7, 9, 40-41. Bilingual. **DESCR:**
*Immigration Law and Legislation;
Undocumented Workers.

3812 Gollobin, Ira. No pasaran. NATION, Vol. 243,
no. 14 (November 1, 1986), p. 429. English.
DESCR: *Immigration Law and Legislation;
Undocumented Workers.

3813 Greenwood, Michael J. and McDowell, John H.
U.S. immigration reform: policy issues and
economic analysis. CONTEMPORARY POLICY
ISSUES, Vol. 3, (Spring 1985), p. 59-75.
English. **DESCR:** *Immigration; Public Policy.

3814 Hernandez, Antonia A. The politics of the
new immigration law=La politica de la nueva
ley de inmigracion. AMERICAS 2001, Premiere
issue, 1987, p. 6,8,40. Bilingual. **DESCR:**
*Immigration Law and Legislation.

3815 Immigration Reform and Control Act of 1986.
MIGRATION WORLD MAGAZINE, Vol. 15, no. 1
(1987), p. 31-32. English. **DESCR:**
*Immigration Law and Legislation.

3816 Isgro, Francesco. Implementation of the
legalization provisions under the
Immigration Reform and Control Act of 1986.
MIGRATION WORLD MAGAZINE, Vol. 15, no. 3
(1987), p. 24-39. English. **DESCR:**
*Immigration Law and Legislation.

3817 Munoz, Rosalio. The Simpson-Rodino
immigration law: an assault on the working
class. POLITICAL AFFAIRS, Vol. 66, no. 6
(June 1987), p. 12-18. English. **DESCR:** Civil
Rights; *Immigration Law and Legislation;
Undocumented Workers.

3818 Novick, Michael. INS makes a bad
Simpson-Rodino law worse. GUARDIAN, Vol. 39,
no. 16 (January 21, 1987), p. 5. English.
DESCR: *Immigration Law and Legislation;
*Simpson-Rodino Bill; Undocumented Workers.

3819 Rodriguez, Roberto. Central Americans and
the new immigration law=La nueva ley de
inmigracion y la comunidad Centro Americana.
AMERICAS 2001, Premiere Issue, 1987, p.
28,43. Bilingual. **DESCR:** *Central America;
*Immigration Law and Legislation; Latin
Americans.

3820 Sellers, Jeff M. Opportunity no, regulations
yes. HISPANIC BUSINESS, Vol. 9, no. 2
(February 1987), p. 12-[14]. English.
DESCR: Discrimination; Employment;
*Immigration Law and Legislation;
Undocumented Workers.

3821 Vanderpool, Tim. Immigration reform crosses
an uncertain border into law. IN THESE
TIMES, Vol. 11, no. 6 (December 17, 1986),
p. 5, 7. English. **DESCR:** Immigration and
Naturalization Service (INS); Immigration
Law and Legislation; Simpson-Rodino Bill;
Undocumented Workers.

Immigration Reform and Control Act of 1983
USE: Simpson-Mazzoli Bill

Immigration Regulation and Control

3822 Avina, Jeffrey. The uninvited: immigration
is a hot issue--but who's really getting
burned? SAN FRANCISCO, Vol. 26, no. 8
(August 1984), p. 58+. English. **DESCR:** San
Francisco, CA; *Undocumented Workers.

3823 Cabeza de Vaca, Darlene. Can a person be
illegal? REVISTA MUJERES, Vol. 2, no. 2
(June 1985), p. 31-33. English. **DESCR:**
Undocumented Workers.

3824 Culp, Robert Alan. The Immigration and
Naturalization Service and racially
motivated questioning: does equal protection
pick up where the Fourth Amendment left off?
COLUMBIA LAW REVIEW, Vol. 86, no. 4 (May
1986), p. 800-822. English. **DESCR:** Border
Patrol; *Constitutional Amendments - Fourth;
*Discrimination; *Immigration and
Naturalization Service (INS); Immigration
Law and Legislation; *Search and Seizure.

3825 Hawkins, Steve L. A cat-mouse game gets
bloody. U.S. NEWS & WORLD REPORT, Vol. 100,
(April 28, 1986), p. 30. English. **DESCR:**
*Border Patrol; *San Diego, CA.

3826 Hernandez, Beatriz Johnston. A dogged attack
on immigration. MOTHER JONES, Vol. 11, no. 6
(September 1986), p. 10,12. English. **DESCR:**
*National City, CA.

3827 Mosqueda, Lawrence Joseph. How to keep a bad
bill from getting worse. GUARDIAN, Vol. 38,
no. 46 (September 24, 1986), p. 5. English.
DESCR: Immigration and Naturalization
Service (INS); *Immigration Law and
Legislation; Simpson-Rodino Bill;
Undocumented Workers.

3828 [Untitled editorial]. LATIN QUARTER, Vol. 1,
no. 2 (October 1974), p. 2. English. **DESCR:**
Civil Rights; *Immigration and
Naturalization Service (INS).

THE IMMIGRATION TIME BOMB: THE FRAGMENTING OF AMERICA

3829 Madrid, Arturo. Book review of: THE
IMMIGRATION TIME BOMB. LA RED/THE NET, no.
97 (June 1986), p. 9-12. English. **DESCR:**
Book Reviews; Imhoff, Gary; Immigration;
Lamm, Richard.

Immunization
USE: Preventative Medicine

THE IMPACT OF INTIMACY: MEXICAN-ANGLO INTERMARRIAGE IN NEW MEXICO, 1821-1846

3830 Dysart, Jane E. Book review of: THE IMPACT OF INTIMACY: MEXICAN-ANGLO INTERMARRIAGE IN NEW MEXICO, 1821-1846. PACIFIC HISTORICAL REVIEW, Vol. 53, no. 1 (1984), p. 82-83. English. DESCR: Book Reviews; Craver, Rebecca McDowell; Intermarriage.

Impotence

3831 Valdez, William J. Impotence: a problem with a solution. NUESTRO, Vol. 11, no. 4 (May 1987), p. 18-20. English. DESCR: Centro de Impotencia, Coral Gables Hospital, Miami, FL; Diseases; Males; Medical Clinics; *Psychotherapy.

IN DEFENSE OF LA RAZA: THE LOS ANGELES MEXICAN CONSULATE AND THE MEXICAN COMMUNITY

3832 Cardenas, Gilbert. Book review of: IN DEFENSE OF LA RAZA. LA RED/THE NET, no. 85 (October 1984), p. 2-5. English. DESCR: Balderrama, Francisco E.; Book Reviews; Crewdson, John; *THE TARNISHED DOOR.

3833 Dagodag, William Tim. Book review of: IN DEFENSE OF LA RAZA. JOURNAL OF HISTORICAL GEOGRAPHY, Vol. 10, no. 1 (January 1984), p. 92. English. DESCR: Balderrama, Francisco E.; Book Reviews.

3834 Hall, Linda B. The United States-Mexican borders: historical, political, and cultural perspectives. LATIN AMERICAN RESEARCH REVIEW, Vol. 20, no. 2 (1985), p. 223-229. English. DESCR: AMERICAN LABOR IN THE SOUTHWEST: THE FIRST ONE HUNDRED YEARS; *Book Reviews; *Border Region; BOSS RULE IN SOUTH TEXAS: THE PROGRESSIVE ERA; CHICANO INTERMARRIAGE: A THEORETICAL AND EMPIRICAL STUDY; HISPANIC CULTURE IN THE SOUTHWEST; Literature Reviews; RACE AND CLASS IN THE SOUTHWEST: A THEORY OF RACIAL INEQUALITY; SOUTHWESTERN AGRICULTURE: PRE-COLUMBIAN TO MODERN; THE MEXICANS IN OKLAHOMA; THE POLITICS OF SAN ANTONIO.

3835 McIlroy, Christopher. Book review of: IN DEFENSE OF LA RAZA. JOURNAL OF THE WEST, Vol. 22, (October 1983), p. 87-88. English. DESCR: Balderrama, Francisco E.; Book Reviews.

3836 Meier, Matt S. Book review of: IN DEFENSE OF LA RAZA. ARIZONA AND THE WEST, Vol. 25, no. 4 (Winter 1983), p. 356-357. English. DESCR: Balderrama, Francisco E.; Book Reviews.

3837 Monroy, Douglas. Book review of: IN DEFENSE OF LA RAZA. WESTERN HISTORICAL QUARTERLY, Vol. 15, no. 3 (July 1984), p. 331-332. English. DESCR: *Balderrama, Francisco E.; Book Reviews; Los Angeles, CA.

3838 Rutter, Larry G. Book review of: IN DEFENSE OF LA RAZA. JOURNAL OF THE WEST, Vol. 22, (July 1983), p. 100-101. English. DESCR: Balderrama, Francisco E.; Book Reviews.

Income

3839 Business and population maintain high growth rates. HISPANIC BUSINESS, Vol. 9, no. 2 (February 1987), p. 55. English. DESCR: *Business Enterprises; *Statistics.

3840 Chiswick, Barry R. The labor market status of Hispanic men. JOURNAL OF AMERICAN ETHNIC HISTORY, Vol. 7, no. 1 (Fall 1987), p. 30-58. English. DESCR: Census; Discrimination in Employment; *Employment; Ethnic Groups; *Labor Supply and Market; Language Usage; *Males; *Undocumented Workers.

3841 Hayghe, Howard. Married couples: work and income patterns. MONTHLY LABOR REVIEW, Vol. 106, no. 12 (December 1983), p. 26-29. English. DESCR: *Laborers; Marriage; Women Men Relations; Working Women.

3842 Jacobson, Harold. Upward trend in expenditures continues. HISPANIC BUSINESS, Vol. 9, no. 12 (December 1987), p. 19-20. English. DESCR: *Advertising; Consumers; *Marketing; Mass Media.

3843 Massey, Douglas S. Do undocumented migrants earn lower wages than legal immigrants? New evidence from Mexico. INTERNATIONAL MIGRATION REVIEW, Vol. 21, no. 2 (Summer 1987), p. 236-274. English. DESCR: Employment; *Immigrants; *Mexico; Migration Patterns; *Undocumented Workers.

3844 Snipp, C. Matthew and Tienda, Marta. Intergenerational occupational mobility of Chicanos. LA RED/THE NET, no. 42 (May 1981), p. 2. English. DESCR: Age Groups; *National Chicano Survey (NCS).

3845 Valencia, Bert. Purchasing power rises 10 percent. HISPANIC BUSINESS, Vol. 9, no. 12 (December 1987), p. 15. English. DESCR: *Consumers; *Statistics.

3846 Verdugo, Naomi and Verdugo, Richard. Income differentials between Chicano and white male workers. LA RED/THE NET, no. 57 (August 1982), p. 2-3. English. DESCR: Anglo Americans; Employment; Laboring Classes; *Males.

INDEX TO SPANISH AMERICAN COLLECTIVE BIOGRAPHY, vol. 2: MEXICO

3847 de Baca, Vincent C. Book review of: INDEX TO SPANISH AMERICAN COLLECTIVE BIOGRAPHY, vol. 2: MEXICO and THE MEXICAN REVOLUTION: AN ANNOTATED GUIDE TO RECENT SCHOLARSHIP. LA RED/THE NET, no. 72 (September 1983), p. 19-21. English. DESCR: Book Reviews; de Mundo Lo, Sara; Raat, W. Dirk; Reference Works; THE MEXICAN REVOLUTION: AN ANNOTATED GUIDE TO RECENT SCHOLARSHIP.

Indexes

3848 Index to volume 9. HISPANIC JOURNAL OF BEHAVIORAL SCIENCES, Vol. 9, no. 4 (December 1987), p. 469-473. English. DESCR: *HISPANIC JOURNAL OF BEHAVIORAL SCIENCES; Periodicals.

Indianismo
USE: Indigenismo

Indigenismo

3849 Gomez Pena, Guillermo. Nuevo continente artistico. LA COMUNIDAD, No. 275 (October 27, 1985), p. 8-10. Spanish. DESCR: *Art; Artists; Border Region; Chicano Movement; DIALOGOS DE LAS AMERICAS; International Relations; Mexico; United States-Mexico Relations.

Industries

3850 Denyer, Tom. Obreros en la corazon del bruto. RACE AND CLASS, Vol. 27, no. 4 (Spring 1986), p. 53. English. DESCR: *Labor; Laborers.

Inner City
USE: Urban Communities

INROADS

3851 Winston, Bonnie. INROADS: internships that work. HISPANIC ENGINEER, Vol. 3, no. 5 (Winter 1987), p. 38-42. English. DESCR: Almanza, John; Alvarez, Maria; Carr, Frank; *Educational Organizations; Educational Statistics; Garcia, Juan; Gonzales, Ana; Pereira, Eduardo; Raimundo, Antonio; Reza, Priscilla.

INS v. Delgado

3852 Aguilar, J. Federal court halts workplace searches based on broad inspection warrants. CRIMINAL LAW REPORTER, Vol. 38, no. 8 (November 20, 1985), p. 2150-2151. English. DESCR: Blackie's House of Beef v. Castillo; *Search and Seizure.

3853 Ferguson, J. Warrantless INS "farm checks" at migrant camps properly enjoined. CRIMINAL LAW REPORTER, Vol. 37, no. 14 (July 3, 1985), p. 2256. English. DESCR: *La Duke v. Nelson; *Search and Seizure.

3854 Search and seizure. CRIMINAL LAW REPORTER, Vol. 35, no. 3 (April 18, 1984), p. 3011-3027. English. DESCR: Hester v. U.S.; Katz v. U.S.; Maine v. Thornton; Oliver v. U.S.; *Search and Seizure; *U.S. Supreme Court.

Instructional Materials
USE: Curriculum Materials

Insurance

3855 Edmondson, Brad. Met Life mines minority market. AMERICAN DEMOGRAPHICS, Vol. 8, no. 7 (July 1986), p. 18-19. English. DESCR: Consumers; Ethnic Groups; Immigrants; Marketing; *Metropolitan Life Insurance Corporation.

3856 Hispanic chamber endorses insurance marketing plan. HISPANIC TIMES, Vol. 8, no. 3 (May, June, 1987), p. 26. English. DESCR: Business Enterprises; Lopez, Ruben; *Metropolitan Life Insurance Corporation; *U.S. Hispanic Chamber of Commerce.

3857 Sellers, Jeff M. Good hands grasp a growing market. HISPANIC BUSINESS, Vol. 9, no. 9 (September 1987), p. 8-11. English. DESCR: Advertising; *Allstate Insurance Co.; *Marketing.

3858 Sellers, Jeff M. Metropolitan Life continues to lead. HISPANIC BUSINESS, Vol. 9, no. 5 (May 1987), p. 12-14. English. DESCR: Advertising; Corporations; *Marketing; *Metropolitan Life Insurance Corporation; U.S. Hispanic Chamber of Commerce.

Integration
USE: Segregation and Desegregation

Intelligence Levels
USE: Intelligence Tests

Intelligence Tests

3859 From dropout to educator. VISTA, Vol. 2, no. 1 (September 7, 1986), p. 13. English. DESCR: *Academic Achievement; Discrimination in Education; Education; *Quintanilla, Guadalupe.

Intercultural Communication

3860 Korzenny, Felipe and Schiff, Elizabeth. Hispanic perceptions of communication discrimination. HISPANIC JOURNAL OF BEHAVIORAL SCIENCES, Vol. 9, no. 1 (March, 1987), p. 33-48. English. DESCR: Accentedness; *Discrimination; Skin Color.

Intercultural Education
USE: Cultural Pluralism

Interdepartmental Rio Grande Board

3861 Dinwoodie, David H. Indians, Hispanos, and land reform: a new deal struggle in New Mexico. WESTERN HISTORICAL QUARTERLY, Vol. 17, no. 3 (July 1986), p. 291-323. English. DESCR: Bureau of Indian Affairs (BIA); History; Land Grants; Land Program of the Federal Emergency Relief Administration (FERA); *Land Reform; Native Americans; *New Mexico.

Interethnic Relationships
USE: Intergroup Relations

Intergroup Relations

3862 Gonzalez, Alex. Classroom cooperation and ethnic balance: Chicanos and equal status. LA RED/THE NET, no. 68 (May 1983), p. 6-8. English. DESCR: Cultural Pluralism; Education.

3863 Gutierrez, Ramon A. Unraveling America's Hispanic past: internal stratification and class boundaries. AZTLAN, Vol. 17, no. 1 (Spring 1986), p. 79-101. English. DESCR: *Chicano, Meaning of; Culture; *Ethnic Groups; *Identity; *Self-Referents.

3864 Munoz, Carlos, Jr. Chicano politics: the current conjuncture. THE YEAR LEFT, Vol. 2, (1987), p. 35-52. English. DESCR: Chicano Movement; Identity; *Political Parties and Organizations; *Politics; Reagan Administration; Voter Turnout.

3865 Munoz, Carlos, Jr. and Henry, Charles. Rainbow coalitions in four big cities: San Antonio, Denver, Chicago and Philadelphia. P.S. [AMERICAN POLITICAL SCIENCE ASSOCIATION], Vol. 19, no. 3 (Summer 1986), p. 598-609. English. DESCR: Blacks; Chicago, IL; Cisneros, Henry, Mayor of San Antonio, TX; Denver, CO; Elected Officials; Ethnic Groups; Pena, Federico; Philadelphia, PA; Political Parties and Organizations; Political Representation; *Politics; San Antonio, TX; Urban Communities.

3866 Rodriguez, Nestor. Undocumented Central Americans in Houston: diverse populations. INTERNATIONAL MIGRATION REVIEW, Vol. 21, no. 1 (Spring 1987), p. 4-26. English. DESCR: *Central America; El Salvador; Ethnic Groups; Guatemala; Honduras; *Houston, TX; Immigrants; Latin Americans; *Political Refugees; *Undocumented Workers.

3867 Sellers, Jeff M. Missed opportunities. HISPANIC BUSINESS, Vol. 9, no. 4 (April 1987), p. 14-15. English. DESCR: *Border Industries; Language Usage; *Management; Mexico.

Intergroup Relations (cont.)

3868 Sonenshein, Raphe. Biracial coalition politics in Los Angeles. P.S. [AMERICAN POLITICAL SCIENCE ASSOCIATION], Vol. 19, no. 3 (Summer 1986), p. 582-590. English. **DESCR:** Blacks; Bradley, Tom; Browning, Rufus P.; *Ethnic Groups; *Los Angeles, CA; Marshall, Dale Rogers; Political Parties and Organizations; *Politics; PROTEST IS NOT ENOUGH: THE STRUGGLE OF BLACKS AND HISPANICS FOR EQUALITY IN URBAN POLITICS; Tabb, David H.

Intermarriage

3869 Abney, Armando. Chicano intermarriage: a theoretical and empirical study. LA RED/THE NET, no. 59 (October 1982), p. 4-6. English. **DESCR:** Book Reviews; *CHICANO INTERMARRIAGE: A THEORETICAL AND EMPIRICAL STUDY; *Murguia, Edward.

3870 Arce, Carlos H. and Abney, Armando. Regional differences in Chicano intermarriage. LA RED/THE NET, no. 52 (March 1982), p. 2-3. English.

3871 Dysart, Jane E. Book review of: THE IMPACT OF INTIMACY: MEXICAN-ANGLO INTERMARRIAGE IN NEW MEXICO, 1821-1846. PACIFIC HISTORICAL REVIEW, Vol. 53, no. 1 (1984), p. 82-83. English. **DESCR:** Book Reviews; Craver, Rebecca McDowell; *THE IMPACT OF INTIMACY: MEXICAN-ANGLO INTERMARRIAGE IN NEW MEXICO, 1821-1846.

3872 Herrera, Irma D. Mixed marriages: will the happiness last? VISTA, Vol. 1, no. 10 (June 8, 1986), p. 8-10. English. **DESCR:** *Salgado de Snyder, Nelly; Spanish-Speaking Mental Health Research Center.

3873 Leonard, Karen. A note on given names and Chicano intermarriage. LA RED/THE NET, no. 52 (March 1982), p. 4-5. English. **DESCR:** Personal Names.

3874 Mares, Antonio. El coyote: between two cultures. EL CUADERNO, Vol. 2, no. 1 (1972), p. 20-23. English. **DESCR:** Biculturalism; Cultural Pluralism.

3875 Murguia, Edward. Given names and Chicano intermarriage. LA RED/THE NET, no. 40 (March 1981), p. 2. English. **DESCR:** *Personal Names.

3876 Ramirez, Daniel Moriel. Book review of: CHICANO INTERMARRIAGE: A THEORETICAL AND EMPIRICAL STUDY. SOCIAL FORCES, Vol. 62, no. 3 (March 1984), p. 833-835. English. **DESCR:** Book Reviews; *CHICANO INTERMARRIAGE: A THEORETICAL AND EMPIRICAL STUDY; Murguia, Edward.

International Business Machines (IBM)

3877 Mellado, Carmela. Dr. George Castro: research scientist with IBM, San Jose. HISPANIC ENGINEER, Vol. 3, no. 3 (1987), p. 22-24, 44. English. **DESCR:** *Biography; *Castro, George.

International Economic Relations

3878 Academics and entrepreneurs talk trade. HISPANIC BUSINESS, Vol. 9, no. 6 (June 1987), p. 96. English. **DESCR:** *Business Enterprises; Conferences and Meetings; Fourth Symposium on Hispanic Business and Economy, San Juan, Puerto Rico, November 23-25, 1987; Latin America; *National Association of Hispanic Professors of Business Administration and Economics (Los Profesores); Organizations; Teaching Profession.

3879 Bustamante, Jorge A. International labor migration and external debt. MIGRATION WORLD MAGAZINE, Vol. 15, no. 3 (1987), p. 13-15. English. **DESCR:** Currency; *Labor Supply and Market; *Migrant Labor; *Undocumented Workers; United States-Mexico Relations.

3880 Harrell, Louis and Fischer, Dale. The 1982 Mexican peso devaluation and border area employment. MONTHLY LABOR REVIEW, Vol. 108, no. 10 (October 1985), p. 25-32. English. **DESCR:** Border Industries; *Border Region; *Currency; Mexican Maquiladora Program; *Mexico.

International Relations

3881 Castro, Richard T. A role for Hispanic Americans in foreign policy formulation. VISTA, Vol. 1, no. 9 (May 3, 1986), p. 3. English. **DESCR:** *Essays; *Hispanic Caucus; Political System.

3882 Cruz, David V. Caucus & Co. orients the East. HISPANIC BUSINESS, Vol. 9, no. 11 (November 1987), p. 10-13, 71+. English. **DESCR:** Businesspeople; *Congressional Hispanic Caucus; Elected Officials; *Japan; Latin Business Foundation, Los Angeles, CA; Nakasone, Yasuhiro [Prime Minister of Japan]; *Taiwan.

3883 Gomez Pena, Guillermo. Nuevo continente artistico. LA COMUNIDAD, No. 275 (October 27, 1985), p. 8-10. Spanish. **DESCR:** *Art; Artists; Border Region; Chicano Movement; DIALOGOS DE LAS AMERICAS; Indigenismo; Mexico; United States-Mexico Relations.

3884 What is your opinion of U.S. policy towards Central America?=Cual es tu opinion sobre la politica norteamericana hacia Centro America? AMERICAS 2001, Vol. 1, no. 2 (September, October, 1987), p. 21. Bilingual. **DESCR:** *Central America; *Public Opinion; Surveys.

Inter-University Program for Latino Research

3885 Hispanic inter-university program grants awarded to 17 projects. LA RED/THE NET, no. 92 (November, December, 1985), p. 7-9. English. **DESCR:** Committee on Public Policy Research on Contemporary Hispanic Issues; *Ford Foundation; Funding Sources; Social Science Research Council.

Investments

3886 Douglas, Mark. Austin: growing fast, start-ups tough. HISPANIC BUSINESS, Vol. 9, no. 6 (June 1987), p. 19, 22. English. **DESCR:** *Austin, TX; *Business Enterprises.

3887 Garcia, Art. Financing the corporate take-off. HISPANIC BUSINESS, Vol. 9, no. 5 (May 1987), p. 22-27. English. **DESCR:** Aguirre Architects, Dallas, TX; Aguirre, Pedro; Banking Industry; *Business Enterprises; Businesspeople; *Corporations; Minority Enterprise Small Business Investment Corporation (MESBIC); Morales, Ramon; Protocom Devices, New York, NY; Villamil, Antonio.

Investments (cont.)

3888 Kane, George D. Five blueprints for fueling growth. HISPANIC BUSINESS, Vol. 9, no. 5 (May 1987), p. 18-21, 42+. English. DESCR: *Business Enterprises; *Businesspeople; Holguin Corporation, El Paso, TX; Latin Industries, Ontario, CA; One-Day Paint & Auto Body Centers, Los Angeles, CA; Terrinvest, Miami, FL; TRU & Associates, Orange County, CA.

I.Q. Testing
USE: Intelligence Tests

Islas, Arturo

3889 Bruce-Novoa, Juan. Homosexuality and the Chicano novel. CONFLUENCIA, Vol. 2, no. 1 (Fall 1986), p. 69-77. English. DESCR: Acosta, Oscar Zeta; CITY OF NIGHT; FAULTLINE [novel]; *Homosexuality; *Literary Criticism; Machismo; *Novel; Ortiz Taylor, Sheila; POCHO; Rechy, John; Salas, Floyd; SPRING FORWARD/FALL BACK; TATOO THE WICKED CROSS; THE AUTOBIOGRAPHY OF A BROWN BUFFALO; THE RAIN GOD: A DESERT TALE; THE REVOLT OF THE COCKROACH PEOPLE; Villarreal, Jose Antonio.

3890 Galindo, Luis Alberto. El dios de la lluvia=RAIN GOD. LA COMUNIDAD, No. 241 (March 3, 1985), p. 12-13. Spanish. DESCR: Biography; *Literary Criticism; Novel; *THE RAIN GOD: A DESERT TALE.

3891 Gonzales-Berry, Erlinda. Sensuality, repression, and death in Arturo Isla's THE RAIN GOD. BILINGUAL REVIEW, Vol. 12, no. 3 (September, December, 1985), p. 258-261. English. DESCR: Book Reviews; *THE RAIN GOD: A DESERT TALE.

Jackson, Jesse

3892 Jesse Jackson makes appearance at CBS board meeting. BROADCASTING, Vol. 110, no. 16 (April 21, 1986), p. 100. English. DESCR: Broadcast Media; *Columbia Broadcasting Studios (CBS); Discrimination; Discrimination in Employment; People United to Serve Humanity (PUSH); Stereotypes; Taylor, Hycel; Wyman, Thomas.

3893 Segal, William. New alliances in Watsonville strike. IN THESE TIMES, Vol. 10, no. 29 (July 9, 1986), p. 5. English. DESCR: Collective Bargaining; Labor Unions; Strikes and Lockouts; Teamsters Union; *Watsonville, CA; Watsonville Canning and Frozen Food Co..

Jaffee, A.J.

3894 Alvirez, David. Book review of: THE CHANGING DEMOGRAPHY OF SPANISH AMERICANS. LA RED/THE NET, no. 48 (November 1981), p. 4. English. DESCR: Book Reviews; Boswell, Thomas D.; Cullen, Ruth M.; Population; *THE CHANGING DEMOGRAPHY OF SPANISH-AMERICANS.

JAGUAR WOMAN

3895 Castillo-Speed, Lillian. Chicana/Latina literature and criticism: reviews of recent books. WLW JOURNAL, Vol. 11, no. 3 (September 1987), p. 1-4. English. DESCR: Andrews, Lynn V.; *Book Reviews; BORDERS; Chavez, Denise; *Chicanas; CONTEMPORARY CHICANA POETRY: A CRITICAL APPROACH TO AN EMERGING LITERATURE; Flores, Angel; Flores, Kate; Mora, Pat; Sanchez, Marta Ester; Tafolla, Carmen; THE DEFIANT MUSE: HISPANIC FEMINIST POEMS FROM THE MIDDLE AGES TO THE PRESENT; THE LAST OF THE MENU GIRLS; TO SPLIT A HUMAN: MITOS, MACHOS Y LA MUJER CHICANA; Vigil-Pinon, Evangelina; WOMAN OF HER WORD: HISPANIC WOMEN WRITE.

Jails
USE: Prisons

Jalapa, Veracruz, Mexico

3896 Hopper, Richard H. The road from Mexico's Jalapa to jalopies. VISTA, Vol. 2, no. 11 (July 5, 1987), p. 16. English. DESCR: *Slang.

James, Dan

3897 Flores, Lauro. Book review of: EL PUEBLO: THE GALLEGOS FAMILY'S JOURNEY 1503-1980. MINNESOTA REVIEW, no. 22 (1984), p. 145-148. English. DESCR: Book Reviews; Bruce-Novoa, Juan; *CHICANO POETRY: A RESPONSE TO CHAOS; *EL PUEBLO: THE GALLEGOS FAMILY'S AMERICAN JOURNEY 1503-1980; *FAMOUS ALL OVER TOWN; Johansen, Bruce; Maestas, Roberto.

3898 Lewis, Marvin A.; Striano, Ron; and Hiura, Barbara L. Chicano ethnicity and aging [and critiques]. EXPLORATIONS IN ETHNIC STUDIES, Vol. 8, no. 2 (July 1985), p. 35-45. English. DESCR: Anaya, Rudolfo A.; *Ancianos; BLESS ME, ULTIMA; Curanderas; FAMOUS ALL OVER TOWN; Identity; Literary Criticism; Literature.

Jankowski, Martin Sanchez

3899 Arreola, Daniel D. Book review of: CITY BOUND. GEOGRAPHICAL REVIEW, Vol. 77, (April 1987), p. 240-242. English. DESCR: Book Reviews; *CITY BOUND: URBAN LIFE AND POLITICAL ATTITUDES AMONG CHICANO YOUTH.

Japan

3900 Cruz, David V. Caucus & Co. orients the East. HISPANIC BUSINESS, Vol. 9, no. 11 (November 1987), p. 10-13, 71+. English. DESCR: Businesspeople; *Congressional Hispanic Caucus; Elected Officials; *International Relations; Latin Business Foundation, Los Angeles, CA; Nakasone, Yasuhiro [Prime Minister of Japan]; *Taiwan.

Jaramillo, Mari-Luci

3901 Perez, Renato E. Who are the Hispanic heroes? VISTA, Vol. 1, no. 7 (March 2, 1986), p. 12-14. English. DESCR: Leadership; *Public Opinion; University of New Mexico.

Jaramillo, Sylvia

3902 Roth, George. The sky is not her limit. VISTA, Vol. 2, no. 12 (August 1, 1987), p. 24. English. DESCR: Chicanas; *Engineering as a Profession.

Jensen, Joan M.

3903 Anderson, Karen. Book review of: NEW MEXICO WOMEN: INTERCULTURAL PERSPECTIVES. NEW MEXICO HISTORICAL REVIEW, Vol. 62, no. 4 (October 1987), p. 401-2. English. DESCR: Book Reviews; *Miller, Darlis A.; *New Mexico; *NEW MEXICO WOMEN: INTERCULTURAL PERSPECTIVES; Women.

Jensen, Richard J.

3904 de la Garza, Rodolfo O. Book review of: A WAR OF WORDS. JOURNAL OF AMERICAN ETHNIC HISTORY, Vol. 6, no. 2 (Spring 1987), p. 97-98. English. **DESCR:** *A WAR OF WORDS: CHICANO PROTEST IN THE 1960S AND 1970S; Book Reviews; Gutierrez, Jose Angel; Hammerback, John C.; Rhetoric.

Jerez, Alicia

3905 Reyes, Sonia. Hispanic models pursue high stakes fashion. VISTA, Vol. 1, no. 2 (October 5, 1985), p. 6-9. English. **DESCR:** Apodaca, Roseanne; Careers; Dominguez, Peter; *Fashion; Soto, Talisa.

Jews

3906 Burciaga, Jose Antonio. In celebration of a man's ecumenism. VISTA, Vol. 2, no. 4 (December 7, 1986), p. 26. English. **DESCR:** *Catholic Church; Congregation B'nai Zion, El Paso, TX; Holidays; *Religion.

3907 Morales, Cecilio. Judaism's Hispanic thread. VISTA, Vol. 2, no. 3 (November 2, 1986), p. 20-23. English. **DESCR:** Cultural Customs; History; *Religion.

Jimenez [family name]

3908 Instituto Genealogico e Historico Latino-Americano. Rootsearch: Jimenez (Ximenez): Olmo. VISTA, Vol. 2, no. 4 (December 7, 1986), p. 25. English. **DESCR:** Genealogy; History; *Olmo [family name]; *Personal Names; *Ximenez [family name].

Jimenez Food Products, Inc.

3909 Catalano, Julia. Raul Jimenez. VISTA, Vol. 2, no. 3 (November 2, 1986), p. 6. English. **DESCR:** *Ancianos; Holidays; *Jimenez, Raul.

Jimenez, Francisco

3910 Kanellos, Nicolas. Book review of: HISPANICS IN THE UNITED STATES: AN ANTHOLOGY OF CREATIVE WRITING. LA RED/THE NET, no. 71 (August 1983), p. 12-13. English. **DESCR:** Book Reviews; *HISPANICS IN THE UNITED STATES: AN ANTHOLOGY OF CREATIVE WRITING; Keller, Gary D.

Jimenez, Raul

3911 Catalano, Julia. Raul Jimenez. VISTA, Vol. 2, no. 3 (November 2, 1986), p. 6. English. **DESCR:** *Ancianos; Holidays; Jimenez Food Products, Inc.

Job Discrimination
    USE: Discrimination in Employment

Johannsen, Robert W.

3912 Paredes, Raymund A. Book review of: TO THE HALLS OF THE MONTEZUMAS. PACIFIC HISTORICAL REVIEW, Vol. 56, no. 1 (February 1987), p. 123-124. English. **DESCR:** Book Reviews; Mexican American War, 1846-1848; *TO THE HALLS OF THE MONTEZUMAS: THE MEXICAN WAR IN THE AMERICAN IMAGINATION.

Johansen, Bruce

3913 Flores, Lauro. Book review of: EL PUEBLO: THE GALLEGOS FAMILY'S JOURNEY 1503-1980. MINNESOTA REVIEW, no. 22 (1984), p. 145-148. English. **DESCR:** Book Reviews; Bruce-Novoa, Juan; *CHICANO POETRY: A RESPONSE TO CHAOS; *EL PUEBLO: THE GALLEGOS FAMILY'S AMERICAN JOURNEY 1503-1980; *FAMOUS ALL OVER TOWN; James, Dan; Maestas, Roberto.

John F. Kennedy Space Center, NASA, FL

3914 Reyes outstanding Hispanic at Kennedy Space Center. HISPANIC TIMES, Vol. 8, no. 5 (October, November, 1987), p. 60. English. **DESCR:** Biography; *Engineering as a Profession; *Reyes, Raul E. (Ernie).

Johnson, Kenneth F.

3915 Flores, Estevan T. Book review of: ILLEGAL ALIENS IN THE WESTERN HEMISPHERE. LA RED/THE NET, no. 56 (July 1982), p. 7-9. English. **DESCR:** Book Reviews; *ILLEGAL ALIENS IN THE WESTERN HEMISPHERE: POLITICAL AND ECONOMIC FACTORS; Undocumented Workers; Williams, Miles W.

Joint Committee on Testing Practices (JCTP)

3916 Report to the Network. LA RED/THE NET, no. 96 (May 1986), p. 1-3. English. **DESCR:** *Educational Tests and Measurements.

Joint Efforts [prison organization]

3917 Herrera Duran, Patricia and Mares, Renee. Ernest Duran: la ultima despedida. LATIN QUARTER, Vol. 1, no. 3 (January, February, 1975), p. 34-36. English. **DESCR:** Biography; Drug Abuse Programs; *Duran, Ernesto; Prisons.

Jonas, Susanne

3918 Pena, Devon Gerardo. Book review of: THE NEW NOMADS: FROM IMMIGRANT LABOR TO TRANSNATIONAL WORKING CLASS. LA RED/THE NET, no. 67 (April 1983), p. 8-10. English. **DESCR:** Book Reviews; Dixon, Marlene; Labor; *THE NEW NOMADS: FROM IMMIGRANT LABOR TO TRANSNATIONAL WORKING CLASS.

Jones, Richard C.

3919 Hunsaker, Alan C. Mexican immigration patterns. LA RED/THE NET, no. 93 (January, February, 1986), p. 17-19. English. **DESCR:** Book Reviews; Immigration; *Migration Patterns; PATTERNS OF UNDOCUMENTED MIGRATION: MEXICO AND THE U.S.

Journalism

3920 Beale, Stephen. More changes at SIN. HISPANIC BUSINESS, Vol. 9, no. 1 (January 1987), p. 10. English. **DESCR:** *Godoy, Gustavo; *Noticiero SIN; *Spanish International Network (SIN); *Television.

3921 Ericksen, Charles. Wanted: Hispanics in the newsroom. CIVIL RIGHTS DIGEST/PERSPECTIVES, Vol. 14, no. 1 (Spring 1982), p. 40-44. English. **DESCR:** *Discrimination in Employment; *Journalists; *Print Media; *Stereotypes.

3922 Greenberg, Bradley S., et al. Local newspaper coverage of Mexican Americans. JOURNALISM QUARTERLY, Vol. 60, no. 4 (Winter 1983), p. 671-676. English. **DESCR:** *Newspapers.

Journalists

3923 Ayala, Ernie. Henry Alfaro, ABC's Eyewitness News reporter. LATIN QUARTER, Vol. 1, no. 1 (July 1974), p. 13-15. English. DESCR: *Alfaro, Henry; California Chicano News Media Association (CCNMA); Golden Mike Award; *Television.

3924 Ericksen, Charles. Wanted: Hispanics in the newsroom. CIVIL RIGHTS DIGEST/PERSPECTIVES, Vol. 14, no. 1 (Spring 1982), p. 40-44. English. DESCR: *Discrimination in Employment; Journalism; *Print Media; *Stereotypes.

3925 Gutierrez, Gloria. Chicano news-man wins award. LATIN QUARTER, Vol. 1, no. 4 (July, August, 1975), p. 17. English. DESCR: Golden Mike Award; *Radio; Southern California Radio and Television News Association; *Vasquez, Victor.

Journals

3926 Garcia, Alma. Journal review of: CRITICA: A JOURNAL OF CRITICAL ESSAYS. LECTOR, Vol. 4, no. 4-6 (1987), p. 68. English. DESCR: Book Reviews; *CRITICA: A JOURNAL OF CRITICAL ESSAYS.

Juana Ines de la Cruz, Sor

3927 Wilson, Patricia. Sor Juana (Juana de Asbaje). CONFLUENCIA, Vol. 1, no. 2 (Spring 1986), p. 129. English. DESCR: *Poems.

Junior Colleges
USE: Community Colleges

Juries

3928 Grand juries: underrepresentation of Hispanics. CRIMINAL LAW REPORTER, Vol. 36, no. 2 (October 10, 1984), p. 2033-2034. English. DESCR: *State v. Castonguay.

3929 Juries--peremptory challenges--Spanish surnames. CRIMINAL LAW REPORTER, Vol. 38, no. 1 (October 2, 1985), p. 2018. English. DESCR: People v. Harris; *People v. Trevino; People v. Wheeler.

Juvenile Literature
USE: Children's Literature

Kahlo, Frida

3930 Bernal, Esmeralda. Frida Kahlo. REVISTA MUJERES, Vol. 1, no. 2 (June 1984), p. 18. Bilingual. DESCR: *Poems.

3931 Cerda, Gabriela. Hidden jewel: the Frida Kahlo house of Coyoacan. NOTEBOOK: A LITTLE MAGAZINE, Vol. 1, no. 1 (1985), p. 2-7. English. DESCR: Artists; Biography.

3932 Cespedes, Marisa. "Que viva la vida" biografia de Frida Kahlo. LA COMUNIDAD, No. 345 (March 1, 1987), p. 12-13. Spanish. DESCR: Artists; *Biography.

3933 Gonzalez, Miguel. Frida Kahlo entre la vida y la pasion artistica. LA COMUNIDAD, No. 345 (March 1, 1987), p. 8-10. Spanish. DESCR: Artists; *Biography.

3934 Rivera, Diego. Frida Kahlo y el arte mexicano. LA COMUNIDAD, No. 345 (March 1, 1987), p. 6-7+. Spanish. DESCR: Artists; *Biography.

3935 Rodriguez Flores, Juan. Paul Leduc, FRIDA y el otro cine que no se exhibe en Los Angeles. LA COMUNIDAD, No. 290 (February 9, 1986), p. 12-13. Spanish. DESCR: *Films; FRIDA: NATURALEZA VIDA [film]; History; Mexico.

3936 Sanchez, Ricardo. FRIDA: una pelicula de imagen y poder [film review]. REVISTA MUJERES, Vol. 3, no. 2 (June 1986), p. 74-75. Spanish. DESCR: Film Reviews; *FRIDA: NATURALEZA VIDA [film]; Leduc, Paul.

3937 Tibol, Raquel. La biografa se espanto de una vida abierta. LA COMUNIDAD, No. 302 (May 4, 1986), p. 12-13. Spanish. DESCR: *Biography; Book Reviews; FRIDA: A BIOGRAPHY OF FRIDA KAHLO; Herrera, Hayden.

Kanellos, Nicolas

3938 Somoza, Oscar U. Book review of: MEXICAN AMERICAN THEATRE: THEN AND NOW. LATIN AMERICAN THEATRE REVIEW, Vol. 17, no. 2 (Spring 1984), p. 105-106. Spanish. DESCR: Book Reviews; *MEXICAN AMERICAN THEATRE: THEN AND NOW.

Kansas

3939 Latino culture making strides in film. HISPANIC TIMES, Vol. 8, no. 3 (May, June, 1987), p. 38. English. DESCR: *Films; *Ramos, Mario.

Karno, Marvin

3940 Canive, Jose. Book review of: MENTAL HEALTH AND HISPANIC AMERICANS: CLINICAL PERSPECTIVES. JOURNAL OF NERVOUS AND MENTAL DISEASE, Vol. 172, no. 9 (September 1984), p. 559-561. English. DESCR: Ancianos; Becerra, Rosina; Book Reviews; Escobar, Javier I.; *MENTAL HEALTH AND HISPANIC AMERICANS: CLINICAL PERSPECTIVES.

3941 Gibson, Guadalupe. Book review of: MENTAL HEALTH AND HISPANIC AMERICANS: CLINICAL PERSPECTIVES. SOCIAL WORK, Vol. 29, no. 1 (January, February, 1984), p. 81. English. DESCR: Becerra, Rosina; Book Reviews; Escobar, Javier I.; *MENTAL HEALTH AND HISPANIC AMERICANS: CLINICAL PERSPECTIVES.

3942 Marcos, Luis R. Book review of: MENTAL HEALTH AND HISPANIC AMERICANS: CLINICAL PERSPECTIVES. AMERICAN JOURNAL OF PSYCHOTHERAPY, Vol. 38, no. 1 (January 1984), p. 155-156. English. DESCR: Book Reviews; Escobar, Javier I.; Mental Health; *MENTAL HEALTH AND HISPANIC AMERICANS: CLINICAL PERSPECTIVES.

Katz v. U.S.

3943 Search and seizure. CRIMINAL LAW REPORTER, Vol. 35, no. 3 (April 18, 1984), p. 3011-3027. English. DESCR: Hester v. U.S.; INS v. Delgado; Maine v. Thornton; Oliver v. U.S.; *Search and Seizure; *U.S. Supreme Court.

Kaufman, Purcell

3944 Gutierrez, Armando. Book reviews of: MEXICO-UNITED STATES RELATIONS and UNITED STATES RELATIONS WITH MEXICO: CONTEXT AND CONTENT. LA RED/THE NET, no. 62 (December 1982), p. 4-6. English. DESCR: Book Reviews; Erb, Richard D.; *MEXICO-UNITED STATES RELATIONS; Ross, Stanley R.; *UNITED STATES RELATIONS WITH MEXICO: CONTEXT AND CONTENT.

KDTV, San Francisco, CA [television station]

3945 Mass media bureau settlement would allow SICC to sell its stations. BROADCASTING, Vol. 110, no. 26 (June 30, 1986), p. 45. English. **DESCR:** Anselmo, Rene; Azcarraga Family; Federal Communications Commission (FCC); KFTV, Fresno, CA [television station]; KMEX, Los Angeles, CA [television station]; KTVW, Phoeniz, AZ [television station]; KWEX, San Antonio, TX [television station]; Legal Cases; *Spanish International Communications Corp. (SICC); Spanish International Network (SIN); Spanish Language; Television; WLTV, Miami, FL [television station]; WXTV, Paterson, NJ [television station].

Kearney, Michael

3946 Cisneros, Henry. Mexico's poorest are heading North. AKWESASNE NOTES, Vol. 18, no. 4 (Summer 1986), p. 7. English. **DESCR:** Alfaro, Victor Clark; Centro de Promocion Popular Urbana, Tijuana, Baja California, Mexico; Farm Workers; Mexico; Mixtec Indians; *Undocumented Workers.

Keller, Gary D.

3947 Book review of: CHICANO CINEMA. FILM QUARTERLY, Vol. 40, no. 1 (Fall 1986), p. 39. English. **DESCR:** Book Reviews; *CHICANO CINEMA: RESEARCH, REVIEWS AND RESOURCES.

3948 Bruce-Novoa, Juan. Meet the writers of the 80s. VISTA, Vol. 1, no. 11 (July 6, 1986), p. 15-16. English. **DESCR:** Anaya, Rudolfo A.; Arte Publico Press; *Authors; Bilingual Review Press; Cisneros, Sandra; Hinojosa-Smith, Rolando R.; *Literature; Pineda, Cecile; Quinto Sol Publishing, Inc.; Rivera, Tomas; Soto, Gary.

3949 Garcia, Philip. Book review of: CHICANO CINEMA. LA RED/THE NET, no. 91 (October 1985), p. 13-14. English. **DESCR:** Book Reviews; *CHICANO CINEMA: RESEARCH, REVIEWS AND RESOURCES; Films.

3950 Kanellos, Nicolas. Book review of: HISPANICS IN THE UNITED STATES: AN ANTHOLOGY OF CREATIVE WRITING. LA RED/THE NET, no. 71 (August 1983), p. 12-13. English. **DESCR:** Book Reviews; *HISPANICS IN THE UNITED STATES: AN ANTHOLOGY OF CREATIVE WRITING; Jimenez, Francisco.

3951 Nieto, Sonia. Book review of: BILINGUAL EDUCATION FOR HISPANIC STUDENTS IN THE UNITED STATES. INTERRACIAL BOOKS FOR CHILDREN, Vol. 17, no. 3-4 (1986), p. 29-30. English. **DESCR:** *BILINGUAL EDUCATION FOR HISPANIC STUDENTS IN THE UNITED STATES; Book Reviews; Fishman, Joshua A.

3952 West, Dennis. Book review of: CHICANO CINEMA. CINEASTE, Vol. 15, no. 1 (1986), p. 55. English. **DESCR:** Book Reviews; *CHICANO CINEMA: RESEARCH, REVIEWS AND RESOURCES.

Kennedy, Imogene

3953 Perez, Renato E. Book review of: GENEALOGICAL RECORDS IN TEXAS. VISTA, Vol. 3, no. 2 (October 3, 1987), p. 37. English. **DESCR:** Book Reviews; *GENEALOGICAL RECORDS IN TEXAS; Kennedy, Leon.

Kennedy, Leon

3954 Perez, Renato E. Book review of: GENEALOGICAL RECORDS IN TEXAS. VISTA, Vol. 3, no. 2 (October 3, 1987), p. 37. English. **DESCR:** Book Reviews; *GENEALOGICAL RECORDS IN TEXAS; Kennedy, Imogene.

Kern, Robert

3955 Bayard, C.J. Book review of: LABOR IN NEW MEXICO: UNIONS, STRIKES AND SOCIAL HISTORY SINCE 1881. WESTERN HISTORICAL QUARTERLY, Vol. 15, no. 4 (October 1984), p. 468-469. English. **DESCR:** Book Reviews; Labor; LABOR IN NEW MEXICO: UNIONS, STRIKES, AND SOCIAL HISTORY SINCE 1881.

3956 Foster, James C. Book review of: LABOR IN NEW MEXICO: UNIONS, STRIKES AND SOCIAL HISTORY SINCE 1881. NEW MEXICO HISTORICAL REVIEW, Vol. 59, no. 3 (July 1984), p. 324-326. English. **DESCR:** Book Reviews; Labor; *LABOR IN NEW MEXICO: UNIONS, STRIKES, AND SOCIAL HISTORY SINCE 1881.

3957 Suggs, George G. Book review of: LABOR IN NEW MEXICO: UNIONS, STRIKES AND SOCIAL HISTORY SINCE 1881. ARIZONA AND THE WEST, Vol. 26, no. 2 (Summer 1984), p. 174-175. English. **DESCR:** Book Reviews; *LABOR IN NEW MEXICO: UNIONS, STRIKES, AND SOCIAL HISTORY SINCE 1881.

KFTV, Fresno, CA [television station]

3958 Gavin joins group pursuing SICC stations. BROADCASTING, Vol. 110, no. 22 (June 2, 1986), p. 68. English. **DESCR:** Gavin, John; KMEX, Los Angeles, CA [television station]; KWEX, San Antonio, TX [television station]; Legal Cases; Perenchio, A. Jerrold; *Spanish International Communications Corp. (SICC); Spanish International Network (SIN); Spanish Language; Television; Thompson, William; WLTV, Miami, FL [television station]; WXTV, Paterson, NJ [television station].

3959 Mass media bureau settlement would allow SICC to sell its stations. BROADCASTING, Vol. 110, no. 26 (June 30, 1986), p. 45. English. **DESCR:** Anselmo, Rene; Azcarraga Family; Federal Communications Commission (FCC); KDTV, San Francisco, CA [television station]; KMEX, Los Angeles, CA [television station]; KTVW, Phoeniz, AZ [television station]; KWEX, San Antonio, TX [television station]; Legal Cases; *Spanish International Communications Corp. (SICC); Spanish International Network (SIN); Spanish Language; Television; WLTV, Miami, FL [television station]; WXTV, Paterson, NJ [television station].

3960 SICC sale opposed. BROADCASTING, Vol. 111, no. 7 (August 18, 1986), p. 46-52. English. **DESCR:** Azcarraga, Emilio; Federal Communications Commission (FCC); First Chicago Venture Capital; Hallmark Cards; KMEX, Los Angeles, CA [television station]; KWEX, San Antonio, TX [television station]; Legal Cases; *Spanish International Communications Corp. (SICC); Spanish Language; Tapia, Raul R.; Television; TVL Corp.; WLTV, Miami, FL [television station]; WXTV, Paterson, NJ [television station].

KFTV, Fresno, CA [television station] (cont.)

3961 SICC sells TVs for $301.5 million.
BROADCASTING, Vol. 111, no. 4 (July 28,
1986), p. 91-92. English. **DESCR:** Azcarraga,
Emilio; First Chicago Venture Capital;
Hallmark Cards; KMEX, Los Angeles, CA
[television station]; KWEX, San Antonio, TX
[television station]; Legal Cases; *Spanish
International Communications Corp. (SICC);
Spanish International Network (SIN); Spanish
Language; Television; Villanueva, Daniel;
WLTV, Miami, FL [television station]; WXTV,
Paterson, NJ [television station].

3962 SICC to sell off stations. BROADCASTING,
Vol. 110, no. 20 (May 19, 1986), p. 79-80.
English. **DESCR:** Anselmo, Rene; Federal
Communications Commission (FCC); Fouce,
Frank; KMEX, Los Angeles, CA [television
station]; KWEX, San Antonio, TX [television
station]; Legal Cases; *Spanish
International Communications Corp. (SICC);
Spanish International Network (SIN); Spanish
Language; Television; WLTV, Miami, FL
[television station]; WXTV, Paterson, NJ
[television station].

Kinney Shoe Corp.

3963 Marketing to Hispanics. ADVERTISING AGE
MAGAZINE, Vol. 57, no. 43 (August 11, 1986),
p. 51-528. English. **DESCR:** Advertising;
Broadcast Media; De Armas Publications;
*Marketing; Pepsi-Cola Bottling Group; Print
Media; Spanish International Network (SIN);
U.S. Bureau of the Census.

KLAIL CITY Y SUS ALREDEDORES

3964 Cortina, Rodolfo J. Book review of: KLAIL
CITY. VISTA, Vol. 3, no. 4 (December 6,
1987), p. 26. English. **DESCR:** Book Reviews;
Hinojosa-Smith, Rolando R.

3965 Randolph, Donald A. Death's aesthetic
proliferation in works of Hinojosa.
CONFLUENCIA, Vol. 1, no. 2 (Spring 1986), p.
38-47. English. **DESCR:** Death (Concept);
GENERACIONES Y SEMBLANZAS; *Hinojosa-Smith,
Rolando R.; KOREAN LOVE SONGS; *Literary
Criticism; Novel.

KMEX, Los Angeles, CA [television station]

3966 Fever, Jack. Hispanic marketplace: the SICC
sale: it is indeed a Hallmark. ADWEEK, Vol.
36, (July 28, 1986), p. 18. English.
DESCR: *Hallmark Cards; *Spanish
International Communications Corp. (SICC);
*Television.

3967 Gavin joins group pursuing SICC stations.
BROADCASTING, Vol. 110, no. 22 (June 2,
1986), p. 68. English. **DESCR:** Gavin, John;
KFTV, Fresno, CA [television station]; KWEX,
San Antonio, TX [television station]; Legal
Cases; Perenchio, A. Jerrold; *Spanish
International Communications Corp. (SICC);
Spanish International Network (SIN); Spanish
Language; Television; Thompson, William;
WLTV, Miami, FL [television station]; WXTV,
Paterson, NJ [television station].

3968 Mass media bureau settlement would allow
SICC to sell its stations. BROADCASTING,
Vol. 110, no. 26 (June 30, 1986), p. 45.
English. **DESCR:** Anselmo, Rene; Azcarraga
Family; Federal Communications Commission
(FCC); KDTV, San Francisco, CA [television
station]; KFTV, Fresno, CA [television
station]; KTVW, Phoeniz, AZ [television
station]; KWEX, San Antonio, TX [television
station]; Legal Cases; *Spanish

International Communications Corp. (SICC);
Spanish International Network (SIN); Spanish
Language; Television; WLTV, Miami, FL
[television station]; WXTV, Paterson, NJ
[television station].

3969 Moraga, Pete. Response to a quake: hands
across the border. VISTA, Vol. 1, no. 4
(December 7, 1985), p. 3. English. **DESCR:**
Broadcast Media; Earthquakes; *Mexico.

3970 SICC sale opposed. BROADCASTING, Vol. 111,
no. 7 (August 18, 1986), p. 46-52. English.
DESCR: Azcarraga, Emilio; Federal
Communications Commission (FCC); First
Chicago Venture Capital; Hallmark Cards;
KFTV, Fresno, CA [television station]; KWEX,
San Antonio, TX [television station]; Legal
Cases; *Spanish International Communications
Corp. (SICC); Spanish Language; Tapia, Raul
R.; Television; TVL Corp.; WLTV, Miami, FL
[television station]; WXTV, Paterson, NJ
[television station].

3971 SICC sells TVs for $301.5 million.
BROADCASTING, Vol. 111, no. 4 (July 28,
1986), p. 91-92. English. **DESCR:** Azcarraga,
Emilio; First Chicago Venture Capital;
Hallmark Cards; KFTV, Fresno, CA [television
station]; KWEX, San Antonio, TX [television
station]; Legal Cases; *Spanish
International Communications Corp. (SICC);
Spanish International Network (SIN); Spanish
Language; Television; Villanueva, Daniel;
WLTV, Miami, FL [television station]; WXTV,
Paterson, NJ [television station].

3972 SICC to sell off stations. BROADCASTING,
Vol. 110, no. 20 (May 19, 1986), p. 79-80.
English. **DESCR:** Anselmo, Rene; Federal
Communications Commission (FCC); Fouce,
Frank; KFTV, Fresno, CA [television
station]; KWEX, San Antonio, TX [television
station]; Legal Cases; *Spanish
International Communications Corp. (SICC);
Spanish International Network (SIN); Spanish
Language; Television; WLTV, Miami, FL
[television station]; WXTV, Paterson, NJ
[television station].

Komack, James

3973 Aceves Madrid, Vicente. Controversy
surrounding NBC's CHICO AND THE MAN. LATIN
QUARTER, Vol. 1, no. 2 (October 1974), p.
5-7. English. **DESCR:** Albertson, Jack;
Artists; *CHICO AND THE MAN [television
show]; Prinze, Freddie; Stereotypes; Teatros
Unidos; *Television.

KOREAN LOVE SONGS

3974 Randolph, Donald A. Death's aesthetic
proliferation in works of Hinojosa.
CONFLUENCIA, Vol. 1, no. 2 (Spring 1986), p.
38-47. English. **DESCR:** Death (Concept);
GENERACIONES Y SEMBLANZAS; *Hinojosa-Smith,
Rolando R.; KLAIL CITY Y SUS ALREDEDORES;
*Literary Criticism; Novel.

Kroeber, Clifton R.

3975 Albert, Bill. Book review of: MAN, LAND, AND
WATER: MEXICO'S FARMLAND IRRIGATION
POLICIES, 1885-1911. HISTORY - REVIEWS OF
NEW BOOKS, Vol. 71, (October 1986), p.
482-483. English. **DESCR:** Book Reviews; *MAN,
LAND, AND WATER: MEXICO'S FARMLAND
IRRIGATION POLICIES, 1885-1911.

KRVE, Los Gatos, CA [radio station]

3976 Aguirre, Antonio (Jake). Salsa Na Ma in San
Francisco. LATIN QUARTER, Vol. 1, no. 2
(October 1974), p. 23. English. **DESCR**: *Rock
Music; *Salsa; San Francisco, CA; *Valentin,
Ruben.

KTVW, Phoeniz, AZ [television station]

3977 Mass media bureau settlement would allow
SICC to sell its stations. BROADCASTING,
Vol. 110, no. 26 (June 30, 1986), p. 45.
English. **DESCR**: Anselmo, Rene; Azcarraga
Family; Federal Communications Commission
(FCC); KDTV, San Francisco, CA [television
station]; KFTV, Fresno, CA [television
station]; KMEX, Los Angeles, CA [television
station]; KWEX, San Antonio, TX [television
station]; Legal Cases; *Spanish
International Communications Corp. (SICC);
Spanish International Network (SIN); Spanish
Language; Television; WLTV, Miami, FL
[television station]; WXTV, Paterson, NJ
[television station].

KWEX, San Antonio, TX [television station]

3978 Gavin joins group pursuing SICC stations.
BROADCASTING, Vol. 110, no. 22 (June 2,
1986), p. 68. English. **DESCR**: Gavin, John;
KFTV, Fresno, CA [television station]; KMEX,
Los Angeles, CA [television station]; Legal
Cases; Perenchio, A. Jerrold; *Spanish
International Communications Corp. (SICC);
Spanish International Network (SIN); Spanish
Language; Television; Thompson, William;
WLTV, Miami, FL [television station]; WXTV,
Paterson, NJ [television station].

3979 Mass media bureau settlement would allow
SICC to sell its stations. BROADCASTING,
Vol. 110, no. 26 (June 30, 1986), p. 45.
English. **DESCR**: Anselmo, Rene; Azcarraga
Family; Federal Communications Commission
(FCC); KDTV, San Francisco, CA [television
station]; KFTV, Fresno, CA [television
station]; KMEX, Los Angeles, CA [television
station]; KTVW, Phoeniz, AZ [television
station]; Legal Cases; *Spanish
International Communications Corp. (SICC);
Spanish International Network (SIN); Spanish
Language; Television; WLTV, Miami, FL
[television station]; WXTV, Paterson, NJ
[television station].

3980 SICC sale opposed. BROADCASTING, Vol. 111,
no. 7 (August 18, 1986), p. 46-52. English.
DESCR: Azcarraga, Emilio; Federal
Communications Commission (FCC); First
Chicago Venture Capital; Hallmark Cards;
KFTV, Fresno, CA [television station]; KMEX,
Los Angeles, CA [television station]; Legal
Cases; *Spanish International Communications
Corp. (SICC); Spanish Language; Tapia, Raul
R.; Television; TVL Corp.; WLTV, Miami, FL
[television station]; WXTV, Paterson, NJ
[television station].

3981 SICC sells TVs for $301.5 million.
BROADCASTING, Vol. 111, no. 4 (July 28,
1986), p. 91-92. English. **DESCR**: Azcarraga,
Emilio; First Chicago Venture Capital;
Hallmark Cards; KFTV, Fresno, CA [television
station]; KMEX, Los Angeles, CA [television
station]; Legal Cases; *Spanish
International Communications Corp. (SICC);
Spanish International Network (SIN); Spanish
Language; Television; Villanueva, Daniel;
WLTV, Miami, FL [television station]; WXTV,
Paterson, NJ [television station].

3982 SICC to sell off stations. BROADCASTING,
Vol. 110, no. 20 (May 19, 1986), p. 79-80.
English. **DESCR**: Anselmo, Rene; Federal
Communications Commission (FCC); Fouce,
Frank; KFTV, Fresno, CA [television
station]; KMEX, Los Angeles, CA [television
station]; Legal Cases; *Spanish
International Communications Corp. (SICC);
Spanish International Network (SIN); Spanish
Language; Television; WLTV, Miami, FL
[television station]; WXTV, Paterson, NJ
[television station].

KXLN, Houston, TX [television station]

3983 Lawrence, Jennifer. TV signal expected to
boost Houston market. ADVERTISING AGE
MAGAZINE, Vol. 57, no. 43 (August 11, 1986),
p. S24-S25. English. **DESCR**: Advertising;
Houston, TX; Marketing; Pueblo Broadcasting
Corp.; Spanish Language; Television.

La Duke v. Nelson

3984 Ferguson, J. Warrantless INS "farm checks"
at migrant camps properly enjoined. CRIMINAL
LAW REPORTER, Vol. 37, no. 14 (July 3,
1985), p. 2256. English. **DESCR**: INS v.
Delgado; *Search and Seizure.

Labels

USE: Self-Referents

Labor

3985 Almaguer, Tomas. Urban Chicano workers in
historical perspective: a review of recent
literature. LA RED/THE NET, no. 68 (May
1983), p. 2-6. English. **DESCR**: Laborers;
*Literature Reviews; Working Women.

3986 Bayard, C.J. Book review of: LABOR IN NEW
MEXICO: UNIONS, STRIKES AND SOCIAL HISTORY
SINCE 1881. WESTERN HISTORICAL QUARTERLY,
Vol. 15, no. 4 (October 1984), p. 468-469.
English. **DESCR**: Book Reviews; *Kern, Robert;
LABOR IN NEW MEXICO: UNIONS, STRIKES, AND
SOCIAL HISTORY SINCE 1881.

3987 Chicano Survey report #1: labor force
experiences. LA RED/THE NET, no. 38 (January
1981), p. 1,12. English. **DESCR**: *Labor
Supply and Market; *National Chicano Survey
(NCS); Surveys.

3988 de Leon, Arnoldo and Stewart, Kenneth L. A
tale of 3 cities: a comparative analysis of
the socio-economic conditions of
Mexican-Americans in Los Angeles, Tucson,
and San Antonio, 1850-1900. JOURNAL OF THE
WEST, Vol. 24, no. 2 (1985), p. 64-74.
English. **DESCR**: Economic History and
Conditions; Employment; Griswold del
Castillo, Richard; *Los Angeles, CA; San
Antonio, TX; *Social History and Conditions;
Tucson, AZ; Urban Communities.

3989 Denyer, Tom. Obreros en la corazon del
bruto. RACE AND CLASS, Vol. 27, no. 4
(Spring 1986), p. 53. English. **DESCR**:
Industries; Laborers.

3990 Foster, James C. Book review of: LABOR IN
NEW MEXICO: UNIONS, STRIKES AND SOCIAL
HISTORY SINCE 1881. NEW MEXICO HISTORICAL
REVIEW, Vol. 59, no. 3 (July 1984), p.
324-326. English. **DESCR**: Book Reviews; Kern,
Robert; *LABOR IN NEW MEXICO: UNIONS,
STRIKES, AND SOCIAL HISTORY SINCE 1881.

3991 Morales, Patricia. Indocumentados y
chicanos: un intento de aproximacion. LA
COMUNIDAD, No. 318 (August 24, 1986), p.
2-5. Spanish. **DESCR**: History; *Immigration;
Undocumented Workers.

Labor (cont.)

3992 Olivares, Yvette. The sweatshop: the garment industry's reborn child. REVISTA MUJERES, Vol. 3, no. 2 (June 1986), p. 55-62. English. **DESCR:** Garment Industry; Public Health; Third World; *Undocumented Workers; *Women; Working Women.

3993 Pena, Devon Gerardo. Book review of: THE NEW NOMADS: FROM IMMIGRANT LABOR TO TRANSNATIONAL WORKING CLASS. LA RED/THE NET, no. 67 (April 1983), p. 8-10. English. **DESCR:** Book Reviews; Dixon, Marlene; Jonas, Susanne; *THE NEW NOMADS: FROM IMMIGRANT LABOR TO TRANSNATIONAL WORKING CLASS.

3994 Stewart, Kenneth L. and de Leon, Arnoldo. Education, literacy, and occupational structure in West Texas, 1860-1900. WEST TEXAS HISTORICAL ASSOCIATION YEARBOOK, Vol. 60, (1984), p. 127-143. English. **DESCR:** Discrimination in Education; Economic Development; Education; Employment; Literacy; *Texas.

3995 Valdez, Lorenzo. Labor history in the villages. EL CUADERNO, Vol. 3, no. 2 (Spring 1974), p. 54-63. English. **DESCR:** *Economic History and Conditions; *New Mexico; *Social History and Conditions.

Labor Certification
USE: Collective Bargaining

Labor Classes
USE: Laboring Classes

Labor Disputes

3996 Boycotts revisited: Campbell's concedes to farm worker campaign. DOLLARS AND SENSE, (July, August, 1986), p. 12-14, 18. English. **DESCR:** Boycotts; California; Campbell Soup Co.; Farm Labor Organizing Commmittee (FLOC); Farm Workers; Labor Unions; Michigan; Ohio; Strikes and Lockouts; United Farmworkers of America (UFW).

3997 Fraser, Laura. Old boycott, new battle. THE PROGRESSIVE, Vol. 49, (October 1985), p. 16. English. **DESCR:** *Boycotts; *United Farmworkers of America (UFW).

3998 Sanders, Bob. Boycott Campbell's: Ohio farmworkers take it to the top. DOLLARS AND SENSE, no. 92 (December 1983), p. 16-18. English. **DESCR:** Boycotts; Campbell Soup Co.; Chavez, Cesar E.; Farm Labor Organizing Commmittee (FLOC); Farm Workers; Guevas, Fernando; Labor Unions; Ohio; Strikes and Lockouts; United Farmworkers of America (UFW).

LABOR IN NEW MEXICO: UNIONS, STRIKES, AND SOCIAL HISTORY SINCE 1881

3999 Bayard, C.J. Book review of: LABOR IN NEW MEXICO: UNIONS, STRIKES AND SOCIAL HISTORY SINCE 1881. WESTERN HISTORICAL QUARTERLY, Vol. 15, no. 4 (October 1984), p. 468-469. English. **DESCR:** Book Reviews; *Kern, Robert; Labor.

4000 Foster, James C. Book review of: LABOR IN NEW MEXICO: UNIONS, STRIKES AND SOCIAL HISTORY SINCE 1881. NEW MEXICO HISTORICAL REVIEW, Vol. 59, no. 3 (July 1984), p. 324-326. English. **DESCR:** Book Reviews; Kern, Robert; Labor.

4001 Suggs, George G. Book review of: LABOR IN NEW MEXICO: UNIONS, STRIKES AND SOCIAL HISTORY SINCE 1881. ARIZONA AND THE WEST, Vol. 26, no. 2 (Summer 1984), p. 174-175. English. **DESCR:** Book Reviews; Kern, Robert.

Labor Supply and Market

4002 Bransford, Luis A. The Chicano as surplus population. EL CUADERNO, Vol. 2, no. 1 (1972), p. 16-19. English. **DESCR:** *Ethnic Groups.

4003 Bustamante, Jorge A. International labor migration and external debt. MIGRATION WORLD MAGAZINE, Vol. 15, no. 3 (1987), p. 13-15. English. **DESCR:** Currency; *International Economic Relations; *Migrant Labor; *Undocumented Workers; United States-Mexico Relations.

4004 Chicano Survey report #1: labor force experiences. LA RED/THE NET, no. 38 (January 1981), p. 1,12. English. **DESCR:** Labor; *National Chicano Survey (NCS); Surveys.

4005 Chiswick, Barry R. The labor market status of Hispanic men. JOURNAL OF AMERICAN ETHNIC HISTORY, Vol. 7, no. 1 (Fall 1987), p. 30-58. English. **DESCR:** Census; Discrimination in Employment; *Employment; Ethnic Groups; Income; Language Usage; *Males; *Undocumented Workers.

4006 Estrada, Leobardo F. Task force on employment and economic well-being. LA RED/THE NET, no. 88 (Winter 1984), p. 6-10. English. **DESCR:** *Employment; *Public Policy.

4007 Kelly, Peter. American bosses have jobs; Mexicans need work. GUARDIAN, Vol. 39, no. 8 (November 19, 1986), p. 11. English. **DESCR:** Immigration; *Undocumented Workers.

4008 National Commission for Employment Policy. Hispanics and jobs: barriers to progress. LA RED/THE NET, no. 64 (January 1983), p. 5-8. English. **DESCR:** Employment.

4009 Rochin, Refugio I. Chicanos in rural labor markets. LA RED/THE NET, no. 31 (June 1980), p. 2. English. **DESCR:** *Northern California; *Rural Population.

4010 Rochin, Refugio I. Chicanos in rural labor markets: part 2. LA RED/THE NET, no. 47 (October 1981), p. 2,10. English. **DESCR:** *Northern California; *Rural Population; SURVEY OF INCOME AND EDUCATION, 1976; *Surveys.

4011 Third world women in multinational corporations--the Mexican American border. LA RED/THE NET, no. 25 (December 1979), p. 2. English. **DESCR:** *Border Industries; Chicanas; *Ciudad Juarez, Chihuahua, Mexico; *Multinational Corporations; *Working Women.

4012 Tienda, Marta. Hispanics in the U.S. labor market: an overview of recent evidence. LA RED/THE NET, no. 50 (January 1982), p. 4-7. English. **DESCR:** Laborers; Working Women.

Labor Unions

4013 Boycotts revisited: Campbell's concedes to farm worker campaign. DOLLARS AND SENSE, (July, August, 1986), p. 12-14, 18. English. **DESCR:** Boycotts; California; Campbell Soup Co.; Farm Labor Organizing Commmittee (FLOC); Farm Workers; *Labor Disputes; Michigan; Ohio; Strikes and Lockouts; United Farmworkers of America (UFW).

Labor Unions (cont.)

4014 Garcia, Mario T. [Letter to the editor about Mexicans, radicals and communists in the United States]. LABOR HISTORY, Vol. 25, no. 1 (Winter 1984), p. 152-154. English. **DESCR:** *"Anarquismo y Comunismo: Mexican Radicalism and the Communist Party in Los Angeles in the 1930s"; *Communism; History; Los Angeles, CA; *Monroy, Douglas.

4015 Keremitsis, Dawn. Del metate al molino: la mujer mexicana de 1910 a 1940. HISTORIA MEXICANA, Vol. 33, no. 2 (1983), p. 285-302. Spanish. **DESCR:** Food Industry; *Mexico; Sex Roles; Strikes and Lockouts; Tortillas; *Working Women.

4016 Monroy, Douglas. [Letter responding to Mario Garcia's comments]. LABOR HISTORY, Vol. 25, no. 1 (Winter 1984), p. 155-156. English. **DESCR:** *Communism; *Garcia, Mario T.; History; Los Angeles, CA.

4017 Parlee, Lorena M. The impact of United States railroad unions on organized labor and government policy in Mexico (1880-1911). HISPANIC AMERICAN HISTORICAL REVIEW, Vol. 64, no. 3 (August 1984), p. 443-475. English. **DESCR:** Diaz, Porfirio; Discrimination in Employment; History; Mexico; Partido Liberal Mexicano (PLM); Railroads; United States-Mexico Relations.

4018 Ramos, Hector. Latino caucuses in U.S. labor unions. RACE AND CLASS, Vol. 27, no. 4 (Spring 1986), p. 69. English. **DESCR:** *Migrant Labor; *Undocumented Workers.

4019 Romero, Bertha. The exploitation of Mexican women in the canning industry and the effects of capital accumulation on striking workers. REVISTA MUJERES, Vol. 3, no. 2 (June 1986), p. 16-20. English. **DESCR:** Canneries; Capitalism; *Chicanas; Strikes and Lockouts; *Watsonville Canning and Frozen Food Co.

4020 Ruiz, Vicki Lynn. Obreras y madres: labor activism among Mexican women and its impact on the family. RENATO ROSALDO LECTURE SERIES MONOGRAPH, Vol. 1, (Summer 1985), p. [19]-38. English. **DESCR:** *Chicanas; Child Care Centers; Children; History; *Mexico; Sex Roles; Women; *Working Women.

4021 Sanders, Bob. Boycott Campbell's: Ohio farmworkers take it to the top. DOLLARS AND SENSE, no. 92 (December 1983), p. 16-18. English. **DESCR:** Boycotts; Campbell Soup Co.; Chavez, Cesar E.; Farm Labor Organizing Commmittee (FLOC); Farm Workers; Guevas, Fernando; *Labor Disputes; Ohio; Strikes and Lockouts; United Farmworkers of America (UFW).

4022 Segal, William. New alliances in Watsonville strike. IN THESE TIMES, Vol. 10, no. 29 (July 9, 1986), p. 5. English. **DESCR:** Collective Bargaining; Jackson, Jesse; Strikes and Lockouts; Teamsters Union; *Watsonville, CA; Watsonville Canning and Frozen Food Co.

4023 Shapiro, Peter. Watsonville shows "it can be done". GUARDIAN, Vol. 39, no. 24 (March 25, 1987), p. 1,9. English. **DESCR:** Canneries; Chicanas; NorCal Frozen Foods; *Strikes and Lockouts; *Watsonville Canning and Frozen Food Co.; Working Women.

4024 Zavella, Patricia. "Abnormal intimacy": the varying work networks of Chicana cannery workers. FEMINIST STUDIES, Vol. 11, no. 3 (Fall 1985), p. 541-557. English. **DESCR:** Canneries; Chicanas; Discrimination in Employment; *Natural Support Systems; *Working Women.

Laborers

4025 Almaguer, Tomas. Urban Chicano workers in historical perspective: a review of recent literature. LA RED/THE NET, no. 68 (May 1983), p. 2-6. English. **DESCR:** *Labor; *Literature Reviews; Working Women.

4026 Denyer, Tom. Obreros en la corazon del bruto. RACE AND CLASS, Vol. 27, no. 4 (Spring 1986), p. 53. English. **DESCR:** Industries; *Labor.

4027 Hayghe, Howard. Married couples: work and income patterns. MONTHLY LABOR REVIEW, Vol. 106, no. 12 (December 1983), p. 26-29. English. **DESCR:** Income; Marriage; Women Men Relations; Working Women.

4028 Hayghe, Howard. Working mothers reach record number in 1984. MONTHLY LABOR REVIEW, Vol. 107, no. 12 (1984), p. 31-34. English. **DESCR:** Women; *Working Women.

4029 Tienda, Marta. Hispanics in the U.S. labor market: an overview of recent evidence. LA RED/THE NET, no. 50 (January 1982), p. 4-7. English. **DESCR:** *Labor Supply and Market; Working Women.

Laboring Classes

4030 Fernandez, Celestino. Book review of: LA CLASE OBRERA EN LA HISTORIA DE MEXICO: AL NORTE DEL RIO BRAVO (PASADO INMEDIATO, 1930-1981). NEW MEXICO HISTORICAL REVIEW, Vol. 59, no. 2 (April 1984), p. 214-215. English. **DESCR:** Book Reviews; *LA CLASE OBRERA EN LA HISTORIA DE MEXICO: AL NORTE DEL RIO BRAVO (PASADO INMEDIATO, 1930-1981); Maciel, David.

4031 Garcia, Mario T. Book review of: DEVELOPMENT OF THE MEXICAN WORKING CLASS NORTH OF THE RIO BRAVO: WORK AND CULTURE AMONG LABORERS AND ARTISANS, 1600-1900. PACIFIC HISTORICAL REVIEW, Vol. 53, no. 4 (November 1984), p. 525-527. English. **DESCR:** Book Reviews; *DEVELOPMENT OF THE MEXICAN WORKING CLASS NORTH OF THE RIO BRAVO: WORK AND CULTURE AMONG LABORERS AND ARTISANS, 1600-1900; Gomez-Quinones, Juan.

4032 Kivisto, Peter. Book review of: ETHNICITY AND THE WORK FORCE. JOURNAL OF AMERICAN ETHNIC HISTORY, Vol. 6, no. 2 (Spring 1987), p. 68-69. English. **DESCR:** Book Reviews; *ETHNICITY AND THE WORK FORCE; Van Horne, Winston A.

4033 Maciel, David R. Book review of: MEXICO AND THE UNITED STATES. LA RED/THE NET, no. 68 (May 1983), p. 8-9. English. **DESCR:** Book Reviews; McBride, Robert H.; *MEXICO AND THE UNITED STATES: INTERNATIONAL RELATIONS IN THE HUMANITIES.

4034 Verdugo, Naomi and Verdugo, Richard. Income differentials between Chicano and white male workers. LA RED/THE NET, no. 57 (August 1982), p. 2-3. English. **DESCR:** Anglo Americans; Employment; *Income; *Males.

THE LABYRINTH OF SOLITUDE: LIFE AND THOUGHT IN MEXICO

4035 Sanchez Tranquilino, Marcos. Un ensayo sobre la representacion del ZOOT SUIT en la obra de Octavio Paz. LA COMUNIDAD, No. 355 (May 10, 1987), p. 4-7+. Spanish. **DESCR:** Los Angeles, CA; *Pachucos; *Paz, Octavio; Sleepy Lagoon Case; Zoot Suit Riots, Los Angeles, CA, 1943.

Lady Bugs [car club]

4036 Yepes, Maria Elena. Lady bugs. LATIN QUARTER, Vol. 1, no. 4 (July, August, 1975), p. 28-31. English. **DESCR:** *Car Clubs; Chicanas; Los Angeles, CA.

Lamas, Lorenzo

4037 Guerrero, Dan. FALCON CREST: showcase for Hispanic talent. VISTA, Vol. 2, no. 2 (October 4, 1986), p. 12-15. English. **DESCR:** *Actors and Actresses; *Ana-Alicia; FALCON CREST [television show]; Romero, Cesar; Television.

Lamm, Richard

4038 Madrid, Arturo. Book review of: THE IMMIGRATION TIME BOMB. LA RED/THE NET, no. 97 (June 1986), p. 9-12. English. **DESCR:** Book Reviews; Imhoff, Gary; Immigration; *THE IMMIGRATION TIME BOMB: THE FRAGMENTING OF AMERICA.

Land Grants

4039 Dinwoodie, David H. Indians, Hispanos, and land reform: a new deal struggle in New Mexico. WESTERN HISTORICAL QUARTERLY, Vol. 17, no. 3 (July 1986), p. 291-323. English. **DESCR:** Bureau of Indian Affairs (BIA); History; Interdepartmental Rio Grande Board; Land Program of the Federal Emergency Relief Administration (FERA); *Land Reform; Native Americans; *New Mexico.

4040 Engstrand, Iris H.W. California ranchos: their Hispanic heritage. SOUTHERN CALIFORNIA QUARTERLY, Vol. 67, no. 3 (Fall 1985), p. 281-290. English. **DESCR:** *California; *Californios; History; *Spanish Influence.

4041 Jenkins, Myra Ellen. Land tenure history of New Mexico. EL CUADERNO, Vol. 4, no. 1 (Summer 1976), p. 33-46. English. **DESCR:** History; *Land Tenure; *New Mexico; Pueblo Indians.

4042 Sagel, Jim. A question of history. CONFLUENCIA, Vol. 1, no. 1 (Fall 1985), p. 94-101. English. **DESCR:** History; *New Mexico.

Land Program of the Federal Emergency Relief Administration (FERA)

4043 Dinwoodie, David H. Indians, Hispanos, and land reform: a new deal struggle in New Mexico. WESTERN HISTORICAL QUARTERLY, Vol. 17, no. 3 (July 1986), p. 291-323. English. **DESCR:** Bureau of Indian Affairs (BIA); History; Interdepartmental Rio Grande Board; Land Grants; *Land Reform; Native Americans; *New Mexico.

Land Reform

4044 Dinwoodie, David H. Indians, Hispanos, and land reform: a new deal struggle in New Mexico. WESTERN HISTORICAL QUARTERLY, Vol. 17, no. 3 (July 1986), p. 291-323. English. **DESCR:** Bureau of Indian Affairs (BIA); History; Interdepartmental Rio Grande Board; Land Grants; Land Program of the Federal Emergency Relief Administration (FERA); Native Americans; *New Mexico.

Land Tenure

4045 Griswold del Castillo, Richard. Book review of: ROOTS OF RESISTANCE: LAND TENURE IN NEW MEXICO, 1680-1980. LA RED/THE NET, no. 42 (May 1981), p. 10. English. **DESCR:** Book Reviews; Dunbar Ortiz, Roxanne; *ROOTS OF RESISTANCE: LAND TENURE IN NEW MEXICO, 1680-1980.

4046 Jenkins, Myra Ellen. Land tenure history of New Mexico. EL CUADERNO, Vol. 4, no. 1 (Summer 1976), p. 33-46. English. **DESCR:** History; Land Grants; *New Mexico; Pueblo Indians.

Land Titles
USE: Land Grants

Landscape Architecture

4047 Arreola, Daniel D. Mexican restaurants in Tucson. JOURNAL OF CULTURAL GEOGRAPHY, Vol. 3, no. 2 (Spring, Summer, 1983), p. 108-114. English. **DESCR:** Architecture; *Restaurants; Tucson, AZ.

Langer, Ralph

4048 13-part series focuses on Hispanics in America. EDITOR & PUBLISHER: THE FOURTH ESTATE, Vol. 115, no. 14 (April 3, 1982), p. 37. English. **DESCR:** Books; Cultural Characteristics; DALLAS MORNING NEWS; Garcia, Juan; Gonzalez, John; Goodwin, Jay; Grothe, Randy Eli; Hamilton, John; Hille, Ed; LA VIDA AMERICANA; *LA VIDA AMERICANA/HISPANICS IN AMERICA; McLemore, David; Osburne, Burl; Parks, Scott; Pusey, Allen; Sonnemair, Jan.

Language

4049 Merino, Barbara J. and Lyons, Joseph. The problem of exit criteria in second language learners: California as a case study. JOURNAL OF THE ASSOCIATION OF MEXICAN AMERICAN EDUCATORS, (1986, 1987), p. 5-28. English. **DESCR:** *Educational Tests and Measurements.

LANGUAGE AND SOCIAL IDENTITY

4050 Duran, Richard P. Book reviews of: DISCOURSE STRATEGIES and LANGUAGE AND SOCIAL IDENTITY. LA RED/THE NET, no. 77 (February 1984), p. 13-14. English. **DESCR:** *Book Reviews; *DISCOURSE STRATEGIES; Gumperz, John J.

Language Arts

4051 Mejias-Rivera, Ann E. Steven Perez of Xerox. HISPANIC ENGINEER, Vol. 3, no. 1 (Spring 1987), p. 26-30. English. **DESCR:** *Engineering as a Profession; *Perez, Steven; Xerox.

4052 Williams, Dennis A. Spanish as a learning tongue. NEWSWEEK, Vol. 104, (December 3, 1984), p. 92. English. **DESCR:** *Bilingual Bicultural Education.

Language Assessment

4053 Baker, Keith and de Kanter, Adriana. An answer from research on bilingual education. AMERICAN EDUCATION, Vol. 19, no. 6, p. 40-48. English. **DESCR:** *Bilingual Bicultural Education; Language Development; Research Methodology.

4054 Comstock, Cathryn L. and Martin, Frederick N. A children's Spanish word discrimination test for non-Spanish-speaking children. EAR AND HEARING, Vol. 5, no. 3 (May, June, 1984), p. 166-170. English. **DESCR:** Child Study; English Language; Research Methodology; Spanish Language.

Language Development

4055 Baker, Keith and de Kanter, Adriana. An answer from research on bilingual education. AMERICAN EDUCATION, Vol. 19, no. 6, p. 40-48. English. **DESCR:** *Bilingual Bicultural Education; Language Assessment; Research Methodology.

4056 Duran, Richard P. Article review of: "The Second Language Learner in the Context of the Study of Language Acquisition". LA RED/THE NET, no. 57 (August 1982), p. 8. English. **DESCR:** Hakuta, Kenji; *"The Second Language Learner in the Context of the Study of Language Acquisition".

4057 Lee, James F. The relationship between decoding accuracy and the reading achievement of monolingual Spanish-speaking children. BILINGUAL REVIEW, Vol. 12, no. 3 (September, December, 1985), p. 209-217. English. **DESCR:** Educational Tests and Measurements; *Reading; *Spanish Language.

4058 McMenamin, Jerry. Language deficits in a bilingual child with cerebral cysticercosis. BILINGUAL REVIEW, Vol. 11, no. 3 (September, December, 1984), p. 25-30. English. **DESCR:** Bilingualism; *Cerebral Cysticercosis; Diseases; Handicapped.

Language Fluency
USE: Language Proficiency

Language Interference

4059 Quintanilla, Guadalupe. Dropping out of school. VISTA, Vol. 2, no. 1 (September 7, 1986), p. 12-14. English. **DESCR:** *Dropouts; Educational Statistics; Social History and Conditions.

4060 Rodriguez, Salvador. El idioma de Aztlan: una lengua que surge. LA COMUNIDAD, No. 266 (August 25, 1985), p. 6-7. Spanish. **DESCR:** Bilingualism; *Chicano Dialects; Pachucos; Sociolinguistics; Spanish Language.

4061 Sanchez, Francisca S. The Chicano English dilemma: deficit or dialect? LA RED/THE NET, no. 79 (April 1984), p. 2-8. English. **DESCR:** Chicano Dialects; *Language Usage.

4062 Silva-Corvalan, Carmen. Bilingualism and language change: the extension of estar in Los Angeles Spanish. LANGUAGE, Vol. 62, no. 3 (September 1986), p. 587-608. English. **DESCR:** Bilingualism; *Language Usage; *Linguistics; *Los Angeles, CA.

Language Proficiency

4063 Duran, Richard P. Book review of: TESTING LANGUAGE ABILITY IN THE CLASSROOM. LA RED/THE NET, no. 45 (August 1981), p. 5. English. **DESCR:** Book Reviews; Cohen, Andrew D.; *TESTING LANGUAGE ABILITY IN THE CLASSROOM.

4064 Gynan, Shaw Nicholas. The influence of language background on attitudes toward native and nonnative Spanish. BILINGUAL REVIEW, Vol. 12, no. 1-2 (January, August, 1985), p. 33-42. English. **DESCR:** Anglo Americans; *Attitudes; *Foreign Language Instruction; *Language Usage; Spanish Language.

4065 Survey report #5: language of Chicanos. LA RED/THE NET, no. 43 (June 1981), p. 7. English. **DESCR:** *Language Usage; Surveys.

4066 Taylor, Maria T. Mucho Spanglish brews unsavory linguistic stew. VISTA, Vol. 1, no. 10 (June 8, 1986), p. 3. English. **DESCR:** Bilingualism; *Essays; Language Usage.

Language Usage

4067 Acuna, Rodolfo and Hill, Frank. English as the official language?=El ingles como idioma oficial. AMERICAS 2001, Vol. 1, no. 1 (June, July, 1987), p. 6-11. Bilingual. **DESCR:** *English-Only Movement; *Proposition 63 (English as the Official Language of California).

4068 Aguirre, Adalberto, Jr. Book review of: CHICANO SOCIOLINGUISTICS. LA RED/THE NET, no. 51 (February 1982), p. 3-4. English. **DESCR:** Book Reviews; Chicano Dialects; *CHICANO SOCIOLINGUISTICS; *Penalosa, Fernando; *Sociolinguistics.

4069 Carranza, Miguel A. Book review of: LATINO LANGUAGE AND COMMUNICATIVE BEHAVIOR. LA RED/THE NET, no. 54 (May 1982), p. 10-11. English. **DESCR:** Book Reviews; *Duran, Richard P.; *LATINO LANGUAGE AND COMMUNICATIVE BEHAVIOR.

4070 Chiswick, Barry R. The labor market status of Hispanic men. JOURNAL OF AMERICAN ETHNIC HISTORY, Vol. 7, no. 1 (Fall 1987), p. 30-58. English. **DESCR:** Census; Discrimination in Employment; *Employment; Ethnic Groups; Income; *Labor Supply and Market; *Males; *Undocumented Workers.

4071 Duran, Richard P. Book review of: CALO TAPESTRY. LA RED/THE NET, no. 32 (July 1980), p. 5. English. **DESCR:** CALO TAPESTRY; *Chicano Dialects; *Ortega, Adolfo.

4072 Duran, Richard P. Book review of: CHICANO SOCIOLINGUISTICS. LA RED/THE NET, no. 35 (October 1980), p. 3. English. **DESCR:** Book Reviews; Chicano Dialects; CHICANO SOCIOLINGUISTICS; *Penalosa, Fernando; *Sociolinguistics.

4073 Espada, Martin and Perez-Erdelyi, Mireya. With Martin Espada. THE AMERICAS REVIEW, Vol. 15, no. 2 (Summer 1987), p. 77-85. English. **DESCR:** Authors; *Espada, Martin; Poetry; Puerto Ricans.

4074 Fishman, Joshua A. What is happening to Spanish on the U.S. mainland? ETHNIC AFFAIRS, no. 1 (Fall 1987), p. [12]-23. English. **DESCR:** Sociolinguistics; *Spanish Language.

4075 Flores, Lorenzo T. Your turn=Su turno. AMERICAS 2001, Vol. 1, no. 1 (June, July, 1987), p. 26-29. Bilingual. **DESCR:** English-Only Movement; *Short Story.

Language Usage (cont.)

4076 Floyd, Mary Beth. Language use and communicative behavior: Hispanic bilinguals in the United States. BILINGUAL REVIEW, Vol. 12, no. 1-2 (January, August, 1985), p. 120-133. English. DESCR: Book Reviews; Duran, Richard P.; *LATINO LANGUAGE AND COMMUNICATIVE BEHAVIOR.

4077 Garcia, Steve. Language usage and status attainment of Chicanos. LA RED/THE NET, no. 30 (May 1980), p. 2-3. English. DESCR: *Socioeconomic Factors; *SURVEY OF INCOME AND EDUCATION, 1976.

4078 Grenier, Gilles. An economic perspective on learning a second language. JOURNAL OF MULTILINGUAL AND MULTICULTURAL DEVELOPMENT, Vol. 4, no. 6 (1983), p. 471-483. English. DESCR: Bilingualism; Canada; Economics.

4079 Gynan, Shaw Nicholas. The influence of language background on attitudes toward native and nonnative Spanish. BILINGUAL REVIEW, Vol. 12, no. 1-2 (January, August, 1985), p. 33-42. English. DESCR: Anglo Americans; *Attitudes; *Foreign Language Instruction; Language Proficiency; Spanish Language.

4080 Hidalgo, Margarita. On the question of "standard" versus "dialect": implications for teaching Hispanic college students. HISPANIC JOURNAL OF BEHAVIORAL SCIENCES, Vol. 9, no. 4 (December 1987), p. 375-395. English. DESCR: Bilingualism; Chicano Dialects; *Foreign Language Instruction; Puerto Ricans; Sociolinguistics; Spanish for Native Speakers; *Spanish Language.

4081 Hurtado, Aida and Arce, Carlos H. Mexicans, Chicanos, Mexican Americans, or pochos...Que somos? The impact of language and nativity on ethnic labeling. AZTLAN, Vol. 17, no. 1 (Spring 1986), p. 103-130. English. DESCR: *Ethnic Groups; *Identity; *Self-Referents.

4082 Koike, Dale April. Theoretical linguistics: code-switching in the bilingual Chicano narrative. THE AMERICAN MERCURY, Vol. 70, no. 1 (March 1987), p. 148-154. English. DESCR: Bilingualism; *Linguistic Theory; *Sociolinguistics.

4083 Lomeli, Francisco A. En torno a la literatura de la frontera (II). LA COMUNIDAD, No. 275 (October 27, 1985), p. 2-3. Spanish. DESCR: Border Region; *Literary Criticism; MURIERON A MITAD DEL RIO; Spota, Luis.

4084 Macias, Reynaldo Flores. Disambiguating the Veltman trilogy. BILINGUAL REVIEW, Vol. 12, no. 1-2 (January, August, 1985), p. 140-143. English. DESCR: Book Reviews; *CONTRACTOR REPORT: RELATIVE EDUCATIONAL ATTAINMENT OF MINORITY LANGUAGE CHILDREN, 1976: A COMPARISON TO BLACK AND WHITE ENGLISH LANGUAGE CHILDREN; *CONTRACTOR REPORT: THE ROLE OF LANGUAGE CHARACTERISTICS IN THE SOCIOECONOMIC PROCESS OF HISPANIC ORIGIN MEN AND WOMEN; *THE RETENTION OF MINORITY LANGUAGES IN THE UNITED STATES: A SEMINAR ON THE ANALYTIC WORK OF CALVIN VELTMAN; Veltman, Calvin.

4085 Macias, Reynaldo Flores. Language studies and Chicanos. LA RED/THE NET, no. 66 (March 1983), p. 26-28. English. DESCR: Literature Reviews.

4086 Martin, Laura. Language form and language function in ZOOT SUIT and THE BORDER: a contribution to the analysis of the role of foreign language in film. STUDIES IN LATIN AMERICAN POPULAR CULTURE, Vol. 3, (1984), p. 57-69. English. DESCR: *Films; Spanish Language; THE BORDER [film]; *ZOOT SUIT [film].

4087 Mohr, Nicholasa. Puerto Rican writers in the United States, Puerto Rican writers in Puerto Rico: a separation beyond language. THE AMERICAS REVIEW, Vol. 15, no. 2 (Summer 1987), p. 87-92. English. DESCR: Authors; Autobiography; Identity; Immigrants; *Literature; *Mohr, Nicholasa; *Puerto Ricans; Spanish Language.

4088 Mortensen, Eileen. Reading achievement of native Spanish-speaking elementary students in bilingual vs. monolingual programs. BILINGUAL REVIEW, Vol. 11, no. 3 (September, December, 1984), p. 31-36. English. DESCR: *Academic Achievement; *Bilingual Bicultural Education; Primary School Education; *Reading.

4089 Mujica, Barbara. Creative code switching. VISTA, Vol. 1, no. 5 (January 5, 1986), p. 22. English. DESCR: Bilingualism; *Cognition; *Zentella, Ana Celia.

4090 Olmedo Williams, Irma. Functions of code-switching as a communicative strategy in a Spanish-English bilingual classroom. LA RED/THE NET, no. 40 (March 1981), p. 6. English. DESCR: Bilingual Bicultural Education; Bilingualism.

4091 Powers, Michael D. Spanish in contact with other languages: lexical or profound structural influence? BILINGUAL REVIEW, Vol. 12, no. 3 (September, December, 1985), p. 254-257. English. DESCR: Amastae, Jon; Elias-Olivares, Lucia; Literature Reviews; *SPANISH IN THE UNITED STATES: SOCIOLINGUISTIC ASPECTS; *SPANISH IN THE WESTERN HEMISPHERE IN CONTACT WITH ENGLISH, PORTUGUESE, AND THE AMERINDIAN LANGUAGES; *Spanish Language; Zaragoza, Jorge.

4092 Sanchez, Francisca S. The Chicano English dilemma: deficit or dialect? LA RED/THE NET, no. 79 (April 1984), p. 2-8. English. DESCR: Chicano Dialects; Language Interference.

4093 Sellers, Jeff M. Missed opportunities. HISPANIC BUSINESS, Vol. 9, no. 4 (April 1987), p. 14-15. English. DESCR: *Border Industries; *Intergroup Relations; *Management; Mexico.

4094 Silva-Corvalan, Carmen. Bilingualism and language change: the extension of estar in Los Angeles Spanish. LANGUAGE, Vol. 62, no. 3 (September 1986), p. 587-608. English. DESCR: Bilingualism; Language Interference; *Linguistics; *Los Angeles, CA.

4095 So, Alvin Yiu-cheong. The analysis of language minority issues in national data sets. LA RED/THE NET, no. 71 (August 1983), p. 3-5. English. DESCR: Bilingualism; Databases; *National Center for Bilingual Research; Surveys.

4096 Survey report #5: language of Chicanos. LA RED/THE NET, no. 43 (June 1981), p. 7. English. DESCR: Language Proficiency; Surveys.

Language Usage (cont.)

4097 Taylor, Maria T. Mucho Spanglish brews unsavory linguistic stew. VISTA, Vol. 1, no. 10 (June 8, 1986), p. 3. English. **DESCR:** Bilingualism; *Essays; Language Proficiency.

4098 Valencia, Humberto. Sales pitch to Hispanics must strike right chord. VISTA, Vol. 1, no. 12 (August 2, 1986), p. 3. English. **DESCR:** *Advertising; Bilingualism.

LANGUAGES IN CONFLICT: LINGUISTIC ACCULTURATION IN THE GREAT PLAINS

4099 Ornstein-Galicia, Jacob. Bilingualism, bilingual education, and language contact: the agony, the rewards--or how to unravel Babel. BILINGUAL REVIEW, Vol. 11, no. 3 (September, December, 1984), p. 72-82. English. **DESCR:** Bilingual Bicultural Education; Bilingualism; Book Reviews; Ridge, Martin; Schach, Paul; *THE NEW BILINGUALISM: AN AMERICAN DILEMMA.

Laredo, TX

4100 Griswold del Castillo, Richard. Book review of: A BORDERLANDS TOWN IN TRANSITION: LAREDO, 1755-1870. PACIFIC HISTORICAL REVIEW, Vol. 54, no. 2 (May 1985), p. 223-224. English. **DESCR:** *A BORDERLANDS TOWN IN TRANSITION: LAREDO, 1755-1870; Book Reviews; Hinojosa, Gilbert Miguel.

Larine, Larry

4101 Raffel, Elaine. What makes Chilis hot? RESTAURANT BUSINESS, Vol. 82, (October 1, 1983), p. 147-153+. English. **DESCR:** *Chili's Restaurant; *Restaurants.

Las Vegas, NM

4102 Sharpe, Maria Elena. Back to the future. VISTA, Vol. 3, no. 4 (December 6, 1987), p. 10-12, 32. English. **DESCR:** *Community Development; *Plaza Vieja, Las Vegas, NM; Santa Fe Trail.

THE LAST OF THE MENU GIRLS

4103 Anaya, Rudolfo A. Book review of: THE LAST OF THE MENU GIRLS. VISTA, Vol. 1, no. 11 (July 6, 1986), p. 16. English. **DESCR:** Book Reviews; Chavez, Denise.

4104 Castillo-Speed, Lillian. Chicana/Latina literature and criticism: reviews of recent books. WLW JOURNAL, Vol. 11, no. 3 (September 1987), p. 1-4. English. **DESCR:** Andrews, Lynn V.; *Book Reviews; BORDERS; Chavez, Denise; *Chicanas; CONTEMPORARY CHICANA POETRY: A CRITICAL APPROACH TO AN EMERGING LITERATURE; Flores, Angel; Flores, Kate; JAGUAR WOMAN; Mora, Pat; Sanchez, Marta Ester; Tafolla, Carmen; THE DEFIANT MUSE: HISPANIC FEMINIST POEMS FROM THE MIDDLE AGES TO THE PRESENT; TO SPLIT A HUMAN: MITOS, MACHOS Y LA MUJER CHICANA; Vigil-Pinon, Evangelina; WOMAN OF HER WORD: HISPANIC WOMEN WRITE.

4105 Paredes, Raymund A. Review essay: recent Chicano writing. ROCKY MOUNTAIN REVIEW OF LANGUAGE AND LITERATURE, Vol. 41, (1987), p. 124-129. English. **DESCR:** Castillo, Ana; Catholic Church; Chavez, Denise; Chicanas; Garcia, Lionel; GIVING UP THE GHOST; LEAVING HOME; *Literary Criticism; *Literature Reviews; Moraga, Cherrie; Poetry; Prose; Sex Roles; Silva, Beverly; SMALL FACES; Soto, Gary; THE CAT AND OTHER STORIES; THE MIXQUIAHUALA LETTERS.

LatCom

4106 Beale, Stephen. New blood, fresh money: Telemundo, Univision bullish on television market. HISPANIC BUSINESS, Vol. 9, no. 12 (December 1987), p. 30-36. English. **DESCR:** *Corporations; Hallmark Cards; Radio; Spanish International Communications Corp. (SICC); *Spanish Language; *Telemundo Television Group; *Television; Univision.

Latin America

4107 Academics and entrepreneurs talk trade. HISPANIC BUSINESS, Vol. 9, no. 6 (June 1987), p. 96. English. **DESCR:** *Business Enterprises; Conferences and Meetings; Fourth Symposium on Hispanic Business and Economy, San Juan, Puerto Rico, November 23-25, 1987; *International Economic Relations; *National Association of Hispanic Professors of Business Administration and Economics (Los Profesores); Organizations; Teaching Profession.

4108 Bartlett, Catherine Vallejos. Magical realism: the Latin American influence on modern Chicano writers. CONFLUENCIA, Vol. 1, no. 2 (Spring 1986), p. 27-37. English. **DESCR:** Arias, Ron; Authors; Garcia Marquez, Gabriel; *Literary Criticism; *Literary Influence; *Literature; Magical realism; ONE HUNDRED YEARS OF SOLITUDE; Rivera, Tomas; THE ROAD TO TAMAZUNCHALE; Y NO SE LO TRAGO LA TIERRA/AND THE EARTH DID NOT PART.

4109 Hispanic Peace Corps volunteers serve in Latin America. HISPANIC TIMES, Vol. 8, no. 5 (October, November, 1987), p. 16. English. **DESCR:** *Peace Corps.

Latin American Literature

4110 Barry, John M. Mito e ironia en LOS PASOS PERDIDOS. TINTA, Vol. 1, no. 4 (Summer 1984), p. 3-9. Spanish. **DESCR:** Carpentier, Alejo; Literary Criticism; *LOS PASOS PERDIDOS; Mitos; *Novel.

4111 Spanish/English. NEW YORKER, Vol. 61, (September 30, 1985), p. 26-27. English. **DESCR:** *Primera Feria del Libro Latinoamericano.

Latin Americans

4112 Rodriguez, Nestor. Undocumented Central Americans in Houston: diverse populations. INTERNATIONAL MIGRATION REVIEW, Vol. 21, no. 1 (Spring 1987), p. 4-26. English. **DESCR:** *Central America; El Salvador; Ethnic Groups; Guatemala; Honduras; *Houston, TX; Immigrants; Intergroup Relations; *Political Refugees; *Undocumented Workers.

4113 Rodriguez, Roberto. Central Americans and the new immigration law=La nueva ley de inmigracion y la comunidad Centro Americana. AMERICAS 2001, Premiere Issue, 1987, p. 28,43. Bilingual. **DESCR:** *Central America; *Immigration Law and Legislation; *Immigration Reform and Control Act of 1986.

4114 Scarpaci, Joseph L. and Fradd, Sandra. Latin Americans at the university level: implications for instruction. JOURNAL OF MULTICULTURAL COUNSELING AND DEVELOPMENT, Vol. 13, no. 4 (October 1985), p. 183-189. English. **DESCR:** *Higher Education.

Latin Business Association (LBA), Los Angeles, CA

4115 A salute to Hispanic excellence in America. HISPANIC BUSINESS, Vol. 9, no. 6 (June 1987), p. 7-9. English. DESCR: *Awards; *Businesspeople; Organizations.

Latin Business Foundation, Los Angeles, CA

4116 Cruz, David V. Caucus & Co. orients the East. HISPANIC BUSINESS, Vol. 9, no. 11 (November 1987), p. 10-13, 71+. English. DESCR: Businesspeople; *Congressional Hispanic Caucus; Elected Officials; *International Relations; *Japan; Nakasone, Yasuhiro [Prime Minister of Japan]; *Taiwan.

Latin Businessmen's Association (LBA),
USE: Latin Business Association (LBA), Los Angeles, CA

Latin Empresses

4117 Blanco, Gilbert M. Las Adelitas del Barrio. LATIN QUARTER, Vol. 1, no. 3 (January, February, 1975), p. 30-32. English. DESCR: *Chicanas; City Terrace, CA; Community Development; Gangs; Youth.

THE LATIN IMAGE IN AMERICAN FILM

4118 Garcia, Philip. Book review of: THE LATIN IMAGE IN AMERICAN FILM. LA RED/THE NET, no. 50 (January 1982), p. 11-12. English. DESCR: Films; *Woll, Allen L.

Latin Industries, Ontario, CA

4119 Kane, George D. Five blueprints for fueling growth. HISPANIC BUSINESS, Vol. 9, no. 5 (May 1987), p. 18-21, 42+. English. DESCR: *Business Enterprises; *Businesspeople; Holguin Corporation, El Paso, TX; Investments; One-Day Paint & Auto Body Centers, Los Angeles, CA; Terrinvest, Miami, FL; TRU & Associates, Orange County, CA.

LATIN JOURNEY: CUBAN AND MEXICAN IMMIGRANTS IN THE UNITED STATES

4120 Cobas, Jose A. Book review of: LATIN JOURNEY. INTERNATIONAL MIGRATION REVIEW, Vol. 21, no. 2 (Summer 1987), p. 434-435. English. DESCR: Bach, Robert L.; Book Reviews; Portes, Alejandro.

4121 Madrid, Arturo. Book reviews of: CLAMOR AT THE GATES and LATIN JOURNEY. LA RED/THE NET, no. 89 (August 1985), p. 7-10. English. DESCR: Bach, Robert L.; Book Reviews; *CLAMOR AT THE GATES: THE NEW AMERICAN IMMIGRATION; Glazer, Nathan; Immigration; Portes, Alejandro.

LATINA [magazine]

4122 Norris, Eileen. Print suffers in tale of two languages. ADVERTISING AGE MAGAZINE, Vol. 57, no. 16 (February 27, 1986), p. 49-51. English. DESCR: Advertising; Chavarria, Jesus; English Language; HISPANIC BUSINESS; *Magazines; Soto, Grace; Spanish Language; Villar, Arturo; VISTA [magazine].

The Latina Mother-Infant Project, Chicago, IL

4123 Stern, Gwen. Research, action, and social betterment. AMERICAN BEHAVIOR SCIENTISTS, Vol. 29, no. 2 (November, December, 1985), p. 229-248. English. DESCR: Chicago, IL; *Chicanas; Medical Care; Research Methodology.

LATINO ETHNIC CONSCIOUSNESS

4124 Raferty, Judith R. Book review of: LATINO ETHNIC CONSCIOUSNESS. WESTERN HISTORICAL QUARTERLY, Vol. 17, no. 4 (October 1986), p. 490. English. DESCR: Book Reviews; Identity; Padilla, Felix M.

LATINO FAMILIES IN THE UNITED STATES: A RESOURCE BOOK FOR FAMILY LIFE EDUCATION

4125 Autry, Brick. Book review of: LATINO FAMILIES IN THE UNITED STATES. LECTOR, Vol. 4, no. 1-3 (1986), p. [63]. English. DESCR: Book Reviews.

4126 Urdaneta, Maria Luisa. Book review of: LATINO FAMILIES IN THE UNITED STATES. LA RED/THE NET, no. 78 (March 1984), p. 9-10. English. DESCR: Andrade, Sally; Book Reviews.

LATINO [film]

4127 Callahan, Jaime M. LATINO: un nuevo concepto de cine. LA COMUNIDAD, No. 279 (November 24, 1985), p. 2-3. Spanish. DESCR: *Films; Identity; Military; Military Service; Wexler, Haskell.

Latino Institute

4128 Determined to advance. HISPANIC BUSINESS, Vol. 9, no. 7 (July 1987), p. 35. English. DESCR: *Careers; *Chicanas; *Employment.

LATINO LANGUAGE AND COMMUNICATIVE BEHAVIOR

4129 Carranza, Miguel A. Book review of: LATINO LANGUAGE AND COMMUNICATIVE BEHAVIOR. LA RED/THE NET, no. 54 (May 1982), p. 10-11. English. DESCR: Book Reviews; *Duran, Richard P.; Language Usage.

4130 Floyd, Mary Beth. Language use and communicative behavior: Hispanic bilinguals in the United States. BILINGUAL REVIEW, Vol. 12, no. 1-2 (January, August, 1985), p. 120-133. English. DESCR: Book Reviews; Duran, Richard P.; Language Usage.

Latino Literacy Project, Tomas Rivera Center, Claremont, CA

4131 Latino literacy update: Tomas Rivera Center focuses on illiteracy. LA RED/THE NET, no. 95 (April 1986), p. 10-12. English. DESCR: *Literacy; Macias, Reynaldo F.; *Tomas Rivera Center, Claremont, CA.

LATINOS IN THE UNITED STATES: THE SACRED AND THE POLITICAL

4132 Gonzales, Phillip B. Book review of: LATINOS IN THE UNITED STATES: THE SACRED AND THE POLITICAL. NEW MEXICO HISTORICAL REVIEW, Vol. 62, no. 4 (October 1987), p. 409-11. English. DESCR: *Abalos, David T.; Book Reviews; Politics; Religion.

Lattin, Vernon E.

4133 Padilla, Genaro Miguel. The anti-romantic city in Chicano fiction. PUERTO DEL SOL, Vol. 23, no. 1 (1987), p. 159-169. English. DESCR: Acosta, Oscar Zeta; Anaya, Rudolfo A.; *Fiction; *Literary Criticism; Morales, Alejandro; *Urban Communities.

Laviera, Tato

4134 Elias, Edward F. A meeting of poets from
      east and west: Lorna Dee Cervantes, Gary
      Soto, Tato Laviera. BILINGUAL REVIEW, Vol.
      12, no. 1-2 (January, August, 1985), p.
      150-155. English. DESCR: Authors; Cervantes,
      Lorna Dee; *EMPLUMADA; *ENCLAVE; Literary
      Criticism; Literature Reviews; Poetry; Soto,
      Gary; *WHERE SPARROWS WORK HARD.

Law

4135 Hayakawa, S.I.; Cejas, Paul; and Castro
      Feinberg, Rosa. The English-only debate.
      VISTA, Vol. 2, no. 6 (February 8, 1987), p.
      11-13. English. DESCR: California; *English
      Language; *English-Only Movement.

Lawyers
      USE: Legal Profession

Lay, Shawn

4136 Alexander, Charles C. Book review of: WAR,
      REVOLUTION, AND THE KU KLUX KLAN: A STUDY OF
      INTOLERANCE IN A BORDER CITY. NEW MEXICO
      HISTORICAL REVIEW, Vol. 62, no. 1 (January
      1987), p. 110-111. English. DESCR: Book
      Reviews; *WAR, REVOLUTION, AND THE KU KLUX
      KLAN: A STUDY OF INTOLERANCE IN A BORDER
      CITY.

Lead Poisoning

4137 Poma, Pedro A. A dangerous folk therapy.
      NATIONAL MEDICAL ASSOCIATION JOURNAL, Vol.
      76, no. 4 (April 1984), p. 387-389. English.
      DESCR: Children; Folk Medicine.

Leadership

4138 Beale, Stephen. 100 influentials and their
      assessment of the critical issues. HISPANIC
      BUSINESS, Vol. 9, no. 8 (August 1987), p.
      20-32. English. DESCR: Biographical Notes;
      Public Policy.

4139 Bueno, Patricia E. Los Chicanos y la
      politica. LA COMUNIDAD, No. 267 (September
      1, 1985), p. 6-7. Spanish. DESCR: Community
      Service Organization, Los Angeles, (CSO);
      Discrimination; History; League of United
      Latin American Citizens (LULAC); Orden Hijos
      de America, San Antonio, TX; *Political
      Parties and Organizations.

4140 Bueno, Patricia E. Los Chicanos y la
      politica II. LA COMUNIDAD, No. 268
      (September 8, 1985), p. 2-3. Spanish.
      DESCR: American G.I. Forum; Chicano
      Movement; History; Mexican American
      Political Association (MAPA); Nationalism;
      Political Association of Spanish-Speaking
      Organizations (PASO); *Political Parties and
      Organizations.

4141 Frances Hesselbein. INTERCAMBIOS FEMENILES,
      Vol. 2, no. 6 (Spring 1987), p. 23. English.
      DESCR: *Chicanas; *Girl Scouts of the United
      States of America; Hesselbein, Frances;
      Organizations; Women; Youth.

4142 Herrera, Yvonne R. Professional development.
      INTERCAMBIOS FEMENILES, Vol. 2, no. 6
      (Spring 1987), p. 21. English. DESCR:
      *Chicanas; *Women.

4143 Interview: Rita Ricardo-Campbell.
      INTERCAMBIOS FEMENILES, Vol. 2, no. 6
      (Spring 1987), p. 10-11. English. DESCR:
      *Appointed Officials; Chicanas; Economics;
      *Ricardo-Campbell, Rita.

4144 Lena Guerrero. INTERCAMBIOS FEMENILES, Vol.
      2, no. 6 (Spring 1987), p. 15,26. English.
      DESCR: Chicanas; *Guerrero, Lena; Politics.

4145 Patricia Diaz Dennis. INTERCAMBIOS
      FEMENILES, Vol. 2, no. 6 (Spring 1987), p.
      8-9. English. DESCR: Appointed Officials;
      Chicanas; *Diaz Dennis, Patricia; Federal
      Communications Commission (FCC); Legal
      Profession.

4146 Perez, Renato E. Who are the Hispanic
      heroes? VISTA, Vol. 1, no. 7 (March 2,
      1986), p. 12-14. English. DESCR: Jaramillo,
      Mari-Luci; *Public Opinion; University of
      New Mexico.

4147 A road fraught with challenge leads to view
      from the top. HISPANIC TIMES, Vol. 8, no. 3
      (May, June, 1987), p. 28. English. DESCR:
      Authors; Biography; *Chicanas; National
      Network of Hispanic Women; Torres, Celia
      Gonzales.

4148 Soto, Shirlene. La Malinche: 16th century
      leader. INTERCAMBIOS FEMENILES, Vol. 2, no.
      6 (Spring 1987), p. 13. English. DESCR:
      Chicanas; *Malinche.

League of United Latin American Citizens (LULAC)

4149 Arreola, Daniel D. The Mexican American
      cultural capital. GEOGRAPHICAL REVIEW, Vol.
      77, (January 1987), p. 17-34. English.
      DESCR: Conjuntos; Food Industry; History;
      Immigration; LA PRENSA, San Antonio, TX; La
      Raza Unida Party; Lozano, Ignacio; Mexican
      American Youth Organization, San Antonio,
      TX; Music; Orden Hijos de America, San
      Antonio, TX; Railroads; *San Antonio, TX;
      *Social History and Conditions.

4150 Beale, Stephen. Striking a deal with big
      business. HISPANIC BUSINESS, Vol. 9, no. 2
      (February 1987), p. 26-33. English. DESCR:
      *Adolph Coors Co.; American G.I. Forum;
      Boycotts; Corporations; Cuban National
      Planning Council, Inc. Washington, D.C.;
      Employment; *Hispanic Association on
      Corporate Responsibility (HACER); National
      Council of La Raza (NCLR); National IMAGE;
      National Puerto Rican Coalition;
      *Organizations; U.S. Hispanic Chamber of
      Commerce.

4151 Bueno, Patricia E. Los Chicanos y la
      politica. LA COMUNIDAD, No. 267 (September
      1, 1985), p. 6-7. Spanish. DESCR: Community
      Service Organization, Los Angeles, (CSO);
      Discrimination; History; Leadership; Orden
      Hijos de America, San Antonio, TX;
      *Political Parties and Organizations.

4152 Cisneros encourages LULAC to take lead in
      Hispanic agenda. HISPANIC ENGINEER, Vol. 3,
      no. 3 (1987), p. 14-15. English. DESCR:
      *Cisneros, Henry, Mayor of San Antonio, TX;
      Conferences and Meetings.

4153 Conner, Roger and Moreno, G. Mario. The
      Immigration Reform Law: how fair to
      Hispanics? VISTA, Vol. 2, no. 8 (April 4,
      1987), p. 12, 17, 18. English. DESCR:
      Federation for American Immigration Reform
      (FAIR); *Immigration; *Immigration Reform
      and Control Act of 1986; Mexican American
      Legal Defense and Educational Fund (MALDEF).

4154 Gunderson, Kay. White does about-face on
      Simpson-Mazzoli. TEXAS OBSERVOR, Vol. 75,
      (March 25, 1983), p. 4. English. DESCR:
      *Immigration Law and Legislation;
      *Simpson-Mazzoli Bill; Texas; White, Mark.

League of United Latin American Citizens (LULAC)
(cont.)

4155 Gutierrez, Jose Angel. Chicanos and Mexicans: under surveillance: 1940 to 1980. RENATO ROSALDO LECTURE SERIES MONOGRAPH, Vol. 2, (Spring 1986), p. [29]-58. English. DESCR: Acuna, Rudolfo; Border Coverage Program (BOCOV); *Civil Rights; COINTELPRO; *Federal Bureau of Investigation (FBI); *Federal Government; History; Mexico; Political Parties and Organizations; *Political Repression.

4156 Levy, Deborah M. By invitation only. THE PROGRESSIVE, Vol. 50, no. 8 (August 1986), p. 35-38. English. DESCR: *Immigration Law and Legislation.

4157 Perez, Renato E. The business of Hispanics. VISTA, Vol. 2, no. 1 (September 7, 1986), p. 10. English. DESCR: Adolph Coors Co.; American G.I. Forum; Apodaca, Jerry [Gov. of New Mexico]; Business; *Collective Bargaining; Corporations; Cuban National Planning Council, Inc. Washington, D.C.; *Hispanic Association on Corporate Responsibility (HACER); National Council of La Raza (NCLR); National IMAGE; U.S. Hispanic Chamber of Commerce.

Leal, Luis

4158 Bruce-Novoa, Juan. La critica chicana de Luis Leal (I). LA COMUNIDAD, No. 280 (December 1, 1985), p. 2-5. Spanish. DESCR: Authors; Biography; *Literary Criticism.

4159 Bruce-Novoa, Juan. La critica chicana de Luis Leal (II). LA COMUNIDAD, No. 281 (December 8, 1985), p. 14-15. Spanish. DESCR: Authors; Biography; *Literary Criticism.

4160 Lomeli, Francisco A. Luis Leal y la vocacion por la literatura latinoamericana. LA COMUNIDAD, No. 279 (November 24, 1985), 6-7+. Spanish. DESCR: Authors; Biography; *Literary Criticism; Literature.

LEAVING HOME

4161 Paredes, Raymund A. Review essay: recent Chicano writing. ROCKY MOUNTAIN REVIEW OF LANGUAGE AND LITERATURE, Vol. 41, (1987), p. 124-129. English. DESCR: Castillo, Ana; Catholic Church; Chavez, Denise; Chicanas; Garcia, Lionel; GIVING UP THE GHOST; *Literary Criticism; *Literature Reviews; Moraga, Cherrie; Poetry; Prose; Sex Roles; Silva, Beverly; SMALL FACES; Soto, Gary; THE CAT AND OTHER STORIES; THE LAST OF THE MENU GIRLS; THE MIXQUIAHUALA LETTERS.

Leduc, Paul

4162 Sanchez, Ricardo. FRIDA: una pelicula de imagen y poder [film review]. REVISTA MUJERES, Vol. 3, no. 2 (June 1986), p. 74-75. Spanish. DESCR: Film Reviews; *FRIDA: NATURALEZA VIDA [film]; Kahlo, Frida.

LEGACY OF HONOR: THE LIFE OF RAFAEL CHACON, A NINETEENTH CENTURY NEW MEXICAN

4163 Alberts, Don E. Book review of: LEGACY OF HONOR: THE LIFE OF RAFAEL CHACON, A NINETEENTH-CENTURY NEW MEXICAN. NEW MEXICO HISTORICAL REVIEW, Vol. 62, no. 4 (October 1987), p. 403-5. English. DESCR: Book Reviews; *Chacon, Rafael; *Meketa, Jacqueline Dorgan.

Legal Aid

4164 Gill, Eric K. Notaries: clearing the air. HISPANIC BUSINESS, Vol. 9, no. 3 (March 1987), p. 14. English. DESCR: *Immigration Law and Legislation; *Naturalization; Undocumented Workers.

Legal Assistance
USE: Legal Aid

Legal Cases

4165 Chicano activist "Kiko" Martinez convicted. GUARDIAN, Vol. 39, no. 7 (November 12, 1986), p. 4. English. DESCR: Criminal Justice System; *Martinez, Francisco "Kiko"; Militancy.

4166 Garcia, Richard. The ordeal of "Kiko" Martinez. GUARDIAN, Vol. 39, no. 3 (October 15, 1986), p. 2. English. DESCR: Criminal Justice System; *Martinez, Francisco "Kiko"; Militancy.

4167 Gavin joins group pursuing SICC stations. BROADCASTING, Vol. 110, no. 22 (June 2, 1986), p. 68. English. DESCR: Gavin, John; KFTV, Fresno, CA [television station]; KMEX, Los Angeles, CA [television station]; KWEX, San Antonio, TX [television station]; Perenchio, A. Jerrold; *Spanish International Communications Corp. (SICC); Spanish International Network (SIN); Spanish Language; Television; Thompson, William; WLTV, Miami, FL [television station]; WXTV, Paterson, NJ [television station].

4168 Martinez, David A. The nightmare of Kiko Martinez. GUILD NOTES, Vol. 9, no. 2 (Spring 1985), p. 4. English. DESCR: Criminal Justice System; *Legal Profession; *Martinez, Francisco "Kiko"; Political Repression.

4169 Martinez, Elizabeth. A decade of repression: update on the "Kiko" Martinez case. CRIME AND SOCIAL JUSTICE, no. 19 (Summer 1983), p. 100. English. DESCR: Chicano Movement; Civil Rights; Colorado; Criminal Justice System; Discrimination; *Martinez, Francisco "Kiko"; Political Repression.

4170 Mass media bureau settlement would allow SICC to sell its stations. BROADCASTING, Vol. 110, no. 26 (June 30, 1986), p. 45. English. DESCR: Anselmo, Rene; Azcarraga Family; Federal Communications Commission (FCC); KDTV, San Francisco, CA [television station]; KFTV, Fresno, CA [television station]; KMEX, Los Angeles, CA [television station]; KTVW, Phoeniz, AZ [television station]; KWEX, San Antonio, TX [television station]; *Spanish International Communications Corp. (SICC); Spanish International Network (SIN); Spanish Language; Television; WLTV, Miami, FL [television station]; WXTV, Paterson, NJ [television station].

Legal Cases (cont.)

4171 SICC sale opposed. BROADCASTING, Vol. 111, no. 7 (August 18, 1986), p. 46-52. English. **DESCR:** Azcarraga, Emilio; Federal Communications Commission (FCC); First Chicago Venture Capital; Hallmark Cards; KFTV, Fresno, CA [television station]; KMEX, Los Angeles, CA [television station]; KWEX, San Antonio, TX [television station]; *Spanish International Communications Corp. (SICC); Spanish Language; Tapia, Raul R.; Television; TVL Corp.; WLTV, Miami, FL [television station]; WXTV, Paterson, NJ [television station].

4172 SICC sells TVs for $301.5 million. BROADCASTING, Vol. 111, no. 4 (July 28, 1986), p. 91-92. English. **DESCR:** Azcarraga, Emilio; First Chicago Venture Capital; Hallmark Cards; KFTV, Fresno, CA [television station]; KMEX, Los Angeles, CA [television station]; KWEX, San Antonio, TX [television station]; *Spanish International Communications Corp. (SICC); Spanish International Network (SIN); Spanish Language; Television; Villanueva, Daniel; WLTV, Miami, FL [television station]; WXTV, Paterson, NJ [television station].

4173 SICC to sell off stations. BROADCASTING, Vol. 110, no. 20 (May 19, 1986), p. 79-80. English. **DESCR:** Anselmo, Rene; Federal Communications Commission (FCC); Fouce, Frank; KFTV, Fresno, CA [television station]; KMEX, Los Angeles, CA [television station]; KWEX, San Antonio, TX [television station]; *Spanish International Communications Corp. (SICC); Spanish International Network (SIN); Spanish Language; Television; WLTV, Miami, FL [television station]; WXTV, Paterson, NJ [television station].

4174 Zanger, Maggy. Trial of an activist lawyer. THE PROGRESSIVE, Vol. 50, no. 12 (December 1986), p. 16-17. English. **DESCR:** Criminal Justice System; *Martinez, Francisco "Kiko"; Tucson, AZ.

Legal Defense
USE: Legal Representation

Legal Profession

4175 Gordon, Charles. The rights of aliens: an expanding role for trial lawyers. TRIAL, Vol. 19, no. 12 (December 1983), p. 54-58. English. **DESCR:** Deportation; Immigration Law and Legislation; *Political Prisoners; *Undocumented Workers.

4176 Martinez, David A. The nightmare of Kiko Martinez. GUILD NOTES, Vol. 9, no. 2 (Spring 1985), p. 4. English. **DESCR:** Criminal Justice System; Legal Cases; *Martinez, Francisco "Kiko"; Political Repression.

4177 Patricia Diaz Dennis. INTERCAMBIOS FEMENILES, Vol. 2, no. 6 (Spring 1987), p. 8-9. English. **DESCR:** Appointed Officials; Chicanas; *Diaz Dennis, Patricia; Federal Communications Commission (FCC); Leadership.

Legal Representation

4178 Kahn, Robert. Oakdale prison: documenting the abuses. IN THESE TIMES, Vol. 10, no. 35 (September 17, 1986), p. 8, 22. English. **DESCR:** Allen Parish, LA; *Oakdale, LA; Oakdale Legal Assistance (OLA); Political Refugees; Prisons; Undocumented Workers; U.S. Bureau of Prisons (BOP).

Legal Services
USE: Legal Aid

THE LEGEND OF LA LLORONA

4179 Leal, Luis. Book review of: THE LEGEND OF LA LLORONA. LECTOR, Vol. 4, no. 1-3 (1986), p. [59]. English. **DESCR:** Anaya, Rudolfo A.; Book Reviews.

Legends
USE: Leyendas

Legislation

4180 Gonzales-Berry, Erlinda. Enmienda de ingles en Nuevo Mexico. LA COMUNIDAD, No. 352 (April 19, 1987), p. 4-7. Spanish. **DESCR:** English Language; *English-Only Movement; History; *New Mexico; Spanish Language.

Leisure
USE: Recreation

LENNY [film]

4181 Chavez, Andres. Film review of: LENNY. LATIN QUARTER, Vol. 1, no. 4 (July, August, 1975), p. 32-33. English. **DESCR:** *Bruce, Lenny; *Film Reviews; Humor.

Leon, Richard

4182 Ayala, Ernie. Richard Leon, L.A.'s leading Latin jazz D.J. LATIN QUARTER, Vol. 1, no. 1 (July 1974), p. 19-21. English. **DESCR:** Los Angeles, CA; *Salsa.

Lesbians
USE: Homosexuality

Lestrepo, Fabio

4183 Whatley, Patricia L. Book review of: SPANISH-LANGUAGE BOOKS FOR PUBLIC LIBRARIES. AMERICAN REFERENCE BOOKS ANNUAL, Vol. 18, (1987), p. 241. English. **DESCR:** Bibliography; Book Reviews; *SPANISH-LANGUAGE BOOKS FOR PUBLIC LIBRARIES.

Lettuce Boycotts
USE: Boycotts

Levine, Elaine S.

4184 Dennedy-Frank, David P. Book review of: CROSSING CULTURES IN THERAPY. LA RED/THE NET, no. 41 (April 1981), p. 5-6. English. **DESCR:** Book Reviews; Counseling (Psychological); *CROSSING CULTURES IN THERAPY: PLURALISTIC COUNSELING FOR THE HISPANIC; *Mental Health; Padilla, Amado M.

Leyendas

4185 Cerda, Gabriela. La serpiente. NOTEBOOK: A LITTLE MAGAZINE, Vol. 2, no. 2 (1986), p. 14-26. English. **DESCR:** Cuentos; Mayas; *Mitos.

4186 Glazer, Mark. Traditionalization of the contemporary legend--the Mexican-American example. FABULA, Vol. 26, no. 3-4 (1985), p. 288-297. English.

Leyendas (cont.)

4187 Limon, Jose E. La Llorona, the third legend of greater Mexico: cultural symbols, women, and the political unconscious. RENATO ROSALDO LECTURE SERIES MONOGRAPH, Vol. 2, (Spring 1986), p. [59]-93. English. **DESCR:** *Feminism; Folklore; *La Llorona; La Virgen de Guadalupe; Malinche; Mexico; *Symbolism; Women.

4188 Rodriguez, Richard. The head of Joaquin Murrieta. CALIFORNIA MAGAZINE, Vol. 10, no. 7 (July 1985), p. 55-62, 89. English. **DESCR:** Bandidos; *Murrieta, Joaquin.

Liberation Theology

4189 Reyes, Abraham. Autochthonous church and liberation. EL CUADERNO, Vol. 2, no. 1 (1972), p. 14-15. English. **DESCR:** *Catholic Church.

Librarians

4190 Padilla, Steve. Lessons to be learned from a playful hoax. VISTA, Vol. 1, no. 7 (March 2, 1986), p. 3. English. **DESCR:** *Essays; Humor; Public Opinion; Sclar, Marta-Luisa; Stereotypes; *Valdez, Juan.

Library Collections

4191 Chabran, Richard. Latino reference arrives. AMERICAN LIBRARIES, Vol. 18, no. 5 (May 1987), p. 384-388. English. **DESCR:** *Academic Libraries; *Bibliography; Library Instruction; *Reference Works.

4192 Chavez, Linda. Celebrate! The Chicano Resource Center's 10th anniversary. LECTOR, Vol. 4, no. 1-3 (1986), p. In FtCover. English. **DESCR:** *Chicano Resource Center, Los Angeles County Public Library; Public Libraries.

4193 Gaspar, Tomas. Anthony Quinn Library receives collection=La Biblioteca Anthony Quinn recibe coleccion. AMERICAS 2001, Premiere Issue, 1987, p. 12-14. Bilingual. **DESCR:** *Anthony Quinn Library, East Los Angeles, CA; *Quinn, Anthony.

4194 Tarin, Patricia and Josslin, Daniel. Books for the Spanish-speaking: si se puede. LIBRARY JOURNAL, (July 1987), p. 25-31. English. **DESCR:** Library Services; Publishing Industry; *Spanish Language.

Library Instruction

4195 Chabran, Richard. Latino reference arrives. AMERICAN LIBRARIES, Vol. 18, no. 5 (May 1987), p. 384-388. English. **DESCR:** *Academic Libraries; *Bibliography; *Library Collections; *Reference Works.

Library Services

4196 Cabello-Argandona, Roberto. Hispanex is here to stay. LECTOR, Vol. 4, no. 4-6 (1987), p. 6-8. English. **DESCR:** Databases; *HISPANEX (Oakland, CA).

4197 Tarin, Patricia and Josslin, Daniel. Books for the Spanish-speaking: si se puede. LIBRARY JOURNAL, (July 1987), p. 25-31. English. **DESCR:** *Library Collections; Publishing Industry; *Spanish Language.

Lidin, Harold J.

4198 Reyes, Felix Ojeda. Book review of: HISTORY OF THE PUERTO RICAN INDEPENDENCE MOVEMENT. LA RED/THE NET, no. 76 (January 1984), p. 4-7. Spanish. **DESCR:** Book Reviews; *HISTORY OF THE PUERTO RICAN INDEPENDENCE MOVEMENT; Puerto Ricans.

LIFE SPAN

4199 Conde, Hilda Rosina. Book review of: LIFE SPAN. LECTOR, Vol. 4, no. 4-6 (1987), p. 77-78. English. **DESCR:** Book Reviews; Villanueva, Alma.

LIFE WITH TWO LANGUAGES: AN INTRODUCTION TO BILINGUALISM

4200 Ryan, Ellen Bouchard. An interdisciplinary perspective on the bilingual experience. BILINGUAL REVIEW, Vol. 11, no. 3 (September, December, 1984), p. 69-71. English. **DESCR:** Bilingualism; Book Reviews; Grosjean, Francois.

Lil' Scholars [car club], Pasadena, CA

4201 Rifkin, Jane M. The Lil' Scholars: responding to a tragedy in the noblest way! HISPANIC TIMES, Vol. 8, no. 5 (October, November, 1987), p. 9. English. **DESCR:** *Car Clubs; Financial Aid.

Limited English Proficient (LEP)

4202 Oxford-Carpenter, R., et al. Projections of number of limited English proficient (LEP) persons to the year 2000. LA RED/THE NET, no. 50 (January 1982), p. 2-3. English. **DESCR:** *Bilingual Bicultural Education.

Linguistic Theory

4203 Koike, Dale April. Theoretical linguistics: code-switching in the bilingual Chicano narrative. THE AMERICAN MERCURY, Vol. 70, no. 1 (March 1987), p. 148-154. English. **DESCR:** Bilingualism; Language Usage; *Sociolinguistics.

Linguistics

4204 Silva-Corvalan, Carmen. Bilingualism and language change: the extension of estar in Los Angeles Spanish. LANGUAGE, Vol. 62, no. 3 (September 1986), p. 587-608. English. **DESCR:** Bilingualism; Language Interference; *Language Usage; *Los Angeles, CA.

Literacy

4205 99th Congress fails to act on literacy legislation. LA RED/THE NET, No. 102 (November 1986), p. 11. English. **DESCR:** Educational Law and Legislation.

4206 Latino literacy update: Tomas Rivera Center focuses on illiteracy. LA RED/THE NET, no. 95 (April 1986), p. 10-12. English. **DESCR:** Latino Literacy Project, Tomas Rivera Center, Claremont, CA; Macias, Reynaldo F.; *Tomas Rivera Center, Claremont, CA.

4207 Latino literacy update: ELPS/survey updates illiteracy profile. LA RED/THE NET, no. 98 (July 1986), p. 10-12. English. **DESCR:** *English Language Proficiency Survey (ELPS); Surveys.

4208 Latino literacy update: literacy bill introduced in house. LA RED/THE NET, No. 100 (September 1986), p. 9. English. **DESCR:** Educational Law and Legislation; *English Language; *English Proficiency Act (H.R. 5042).

Literacy (cont.)

4209 Latino literacy update: NCLR reports on illiteracy among Latinos. LA RED/THE NET, No. 102 (November 1986), p. 8-9. English. **DESCR:** *English Language Proficiency Survey (ELPS); National Council of La Raza (NCLR).

4210 Latino reading and ed progress. LA RED/THE NET, No. 100 (September 1986), p. 11. English. **DESCR:** Education; National Assessment of Educational Progress; National Institute of Education (NIE).

4211 More findings based upon the NCS. LA RED/THE NET, No. 102 (November 1986), p. 9-11. English. **DESCR:** English Language; *National Chicano Survey (NCS).

4212 Nat'l Chicano Survey analyzed. LA RED/THE NET, No. 100 (September 1986), p. 10. English. **DESCR:** *National Chicano Survey (NCS); Surveys.

4213 Stewart, Kenneth L. and de Leon, Arnoldo. Education, literacy, and occupational structure in West Texas, 1860-1900. WEST TEXAS HISTORICAL ASSOCIATION YEARBOOK, Vol. 60, (1984), p. 127-143. English. **DESCR:** Discrimination in Education; Economic Development; Education; Employment; *Labor; *Texas.

Literary Characters

4214 Ekstrom, Margaret V. Wanderers from an Aztec land: Chicano naming devices used by Miguel Mendez. LITERARY ONOMASTICS STUDIES, Vol. 12, (1985), p. 85-92. English. **DESCR:** *Literary Criticism; Mendez M., Miguel; Novel; *PEREGRINOS DE AZTLAN.

Literary Criticism

4215 Alarcon, Justo S. Estructuras narrativas en TATA CASEHUA de Miguel Mendez. CONFLUENCIA, Vol. 1, no. 2 (Spring 1986), p. 48-54. Spanish. **DESCR:** *Mendez M., Miguel; Short Story; *"Tata Casehua" [short story].

4216 Alarcon, Norma. Making "familia" from scratch: split subjectivities in the work of Helena Maria Viramontes and Cherrie Moraga. THE AMERICAS REVIEW, Vol. 15, no. 3-4 (Fall, Winter, 1987), p. 147-159. English. **DESCR:** Chicanas; GIVING UP THE GHOST; *Moraga, Cherrie; *Sex Roles; "Snapshots" [short story]; THE MOTHS AND OTHER STORIES; *Viramontes, Helen.

4217 Anderson, Robert K. Marez y Luna and the masculine-feminine dialectic. CRITICA HISPANICA, Vol. 6, no. 2 (1984), p. 97-105. English. **DESCR:** Anaya, Rudolfo A.; *BLESS ME, ULTIMA; Novel; *Women Men Relations.

4218 Barry, John M. Mito e ironia en LOS PASOS PERDIDOS. TINTA, Vol. 1, no. 4 (Summer 1984), p. 3-9. Spanish. **DESCR:** Carpentier, Alejo; Latin American Literature; *LOS PASOS PERDIDOS; Mitos; *Novel.

4219 Bartlett, Catherine Vallejos. Magical realism: the Latin American influence on modern Chicano writers. CONFLUENCIA, Vol. 1, no. 2 (Spring 1986), p. 27-37. English. **DESCR:** Arias, Ron; Authors; Garcia Marquez, Gabriel; Latin America; *Literary Influence; *Literature; Magical realism; ONE HUNDRED YEARS OF SOLITUDE; Rivera, Tomas; THE ROAD TO TAMAZUNCHALE; Y NO SE LO TRAGO LA TIERRA/AND THE EARTH DID NOT PART.

4220 Benson, Douglas K. Intuitions of a world in transition: the New Mexican poetry of Leroy V. Quintana. BILINGUAL REVIEW, Vol. 12, no. 1-2 (January, August, 1985), p. 62-80. English. **DESCR:** Authors; HIJO DEL PUEBLO; New Mexico; Poetry; *Quintana, Leroy V.; SANGRE.

4221 Bernal, Alejandro. La estructura tematica en Y NO SE LO TRAGO LA TIERRA de Tomas Rivera. CHIRICU, Vol. 3, no. 1 (1982), p. 83-89. Spanish. **DESCR:** Novel; Rivera, Tomas; *Y NO SE LO TRAGO LA TIERRA/AND THE EARTH DID NOT PART.

4222 Bibliography. THE AMERICAS REVIEW, Vol. 15, no. 3-4 (Fall, Winter, 1987), p. 182-188. English. **DESCR:** *Bibliography; *Chicanas; Literature.

4223 Billings, Linda M. and Alurista. In verbal murals: a study of Chicana herstory and poetry. CONFLUENCIA, Vol. 2, no. 1 (Fall 1986), p. 60-68. English. **DESCR:** Candelaria, Cordelia; Cervantes, Lorna Dee; *Chicanas; Cisneros, Sandra; EMPLUMADA; *Feminism; History; *Poetry; Xelina.

4224 Bruce-Novoa, Juan. La critica chicana de Luis Leal (I). LA COMUNIDAD, No. 280 (December 1, 1985), p. 2-5. Spanish. **DESCR:** Authors; Biography; *Leal, Luis.

4225 Bruce-Novoa, Juan. La critica chicana de Luis Leal (II). LA COMUNIDAD, No. 281 (December 8, 1985), p. 14-15. Spanish. **DESCR:** Authors; Biography; *Leal, Luis.

4226 Bruce-Novoa, Juan. Elegias a la frontera hispanica. BILINGUAL REVIEW, Vol. 11, no. 3 (September, December, 1984), p. 37-44. Spanish. **DESCR:** *"El Louie" [poem]; *LAS COPLAS A LA MUERTE DE SU PADRE; Manrique, Jorge; Montoya, Jose E.; Poetry.

4227 Bruce-Novoa, Juan. Ernest Brawley: un escritor chicano desconocido. LA COMUNIDAD, No. 277 (November 10, 1985), p. 6-7. Spanish. **DESCR:** Authors; *Biography; *Brawley, Ernest; Novel; SELENA [novel]; THE ALAMO TREE [novel]; THE RAP [novel].

4228 Bruce-Novoa, Juan. Homosexuality and the Chicano novel. CONFLUENCIA, Vol. 2, no. 1 (Fall 1986), p. 69-77. English. **DESCR:** Acosta, Oscar Zeta; CITY OF NIGHT; FAULTLINE [novel]; *Homosexuality; Islas, Arturo; Machismo; *Novel; Ortiz Taylor, Sheila; POCHO; Rechy, John; Salas, Floyd; SPRING FORWARD/FALL BACK; TATOO THE WICKED CROSS; THE AUTOBIOGRAPHY OF A BROWN BUFFALO; THE RAIN GOD: A DESERT TALE; THE REVOLT OF THE COCKROACH PEOPLE; Villarreal, Jose Antonio.

4229 Bruce-Novoa, Juan. Mexico en la literatura chicana (I). LA COMUNIDAD, No. 267 (September 1, 1985), p. 12-13. Spanish. **DESCR:** History; Mestizaje; Mexican Revolution - 1910-1920; *Mexico; Precolumbian Society.

4230 Bruce-Novoa, Juan. Mexico en la literatura chicana (II). LA COMUNIDAD, No. 268 (September 8, 1985), p. 14-15. Spanish. **DESCR:** Acosta, Oscar Zeta; Identity; THE AUTOBIOGRAPHY OF A BROWN BUFFALO.

4231 Bruce-Novoa, Juan. Nash Candelaria: novelista (I). LA COMUNIDAD, No. 245 (March 31, 1985), p. 6-7. Spanish. **DESCR:** Biography; *Candelaria, Nash; MEMORIES OF THE ALHAMBRA; NOT BY THE SWORD; Novel.

Literary Criticism (cont.)

4232 Bruce-Novoa, Juan. Nash Candelaria: novelista (II). LA COMUNIDAD, No. 246 (April 7, 1985), p. 10-11. Spanish. DESCR: Biography; *Candelaria, Nash; MEMORIES OF THE ALHAMBRA; NOT BY THE SWORD; Novel.

4233 Bruce-Novoa, Juan. Nuevo representantes de la novela chicana. LA COMUNIDAD, No. 310 (June 29, 1986), p. 6-7+. Spanish. DESCR: Brawley, Ernest; EL VAGO [novel]; FAULTLINE [novel]; Gonzales, Laurence; Novel; Ortiz Taylor, Sheila; THE ALAMO TREE [novel].

4234 Bruce-Novoa, Juan. One more rosary for Dona Marina. CONFLUENCIA, Vol. 1, no. 2 (Spring 1986), p. 73-84. English. DESCR: *A ROSARY FOR DONA MARINA; *Romano-V., Octavio Ignacio; Sex Roles; Short Story.

4235 Bruce-Novoa, Juan. Poesia de Gary Soto: una autobiografia a plazos. LA COMUNIDAD, No. 270 (September 22, 1985), p. 8-10. Spanish. DESCR: Authors; Poetry; *Soto, Gary; TALE OF SUNLIGHT; THE ELEMENTS OF SAN JOAQUIN; WHERE SPARROWS WORK HARD.

4236 Bustamante, Nuria. Permanencia y cambio en CARAS VIEJAS Y VINO NUEVO. CONFLUENCIA, Vol. 1, no. 2 (Spring 1986), p. 61-65. Spanish. DESCR: *CARAS VIEJAS Y VINO NUEVO; *Morales, Alejandro; Novel.

4237 Campbell, Federico. Carlos Castaneda: escribo como brujo, no como escritor. LA COMUNIDAD, No. 256 (June 16, 1985), p. 6-7. Spanish. DESCR: *Castaneda, Carlos.

4238 Campbell, Federico. Paralelo 32: la frontera como espacio literario. LA COMUNIDAD, No. 347 (March 15, 1987), p. 5. Spanish. DESCR: Border Region; *LOS MOTIVOS DE CAIN; Revueltas, Jose; Tijuana, Baja California, Mexico.

4239 Campos, Jorge. Noticia de la literatura chicana. INSULA: REVISTA BIBLIOGRAFICA DE LETRAS Y CIENCIAS HUMANAS, Vol. 37, no. 422 (January 1982), p. 11. Spanish. DESCR: *Literature.

4240 Chavez, Noe M. Culminacion de una busqueda de identidad. LA COMUNIDAD, No. 252 (May 19, 1985), p. 4-6. Spanish. DESCR: Anaya, Rudolfo A.; *BLESS ME, ULTIMA; Identity; Novel.

4241 Claymendez, Luis Felipe. La naturaleza en la literatura chicana y sus antecedentes prehispanicos. REVISTA DE ESTUDIOS HISPANICOS, Vol. 19, no. 2 (May 1985), p. 107-127. Spanish. DESCR: Literary History; *Literature; Precolumbian Literature.

4242 Cota-Cardenas, Margarita. La creacion-protesta en CRISOL: (TRILOGIA). CONFLUENCIA, Vol. 1, no. 2 (Spring 1986), p. 66-72. Spanish. DESCR: *Alarcon, Justo S.; *CRISOL; Novel.

4243 Eberstadt, Fernanda. Montezuma's literary revenge. COMMENTARY, Vol. 81, no. 5 (May 1986), p. 35-40. English. DESCR: *Fuentes, Carlos; GRINGO VIEJO; Mexican Literature; THE DEATH OF ARTEMIO CRUZ; THE GOOD CONSCIENCE; WHERE THE AIR IS CLEAR.

4244 Ekstrom, Margaret V. Wanderers from an Aztec land: Chicano naming devices used by Miguel Mendez. LITERARY ONOMASTICS STUDIES, Vol. 12, (1985), p. 85-92. English. DESCR: Literary Characters; Mendez M., Miguel; Novel; *PEREGRINOS DE AZTLAN.

4245 Elias, Edward F. A meeting of poets from east and west: Lorna Dee Cervantes, Gary Soto, Tato Laviera. BILINGUAL REVIEW, Vol. 12, no. 1-2 (January, August, 1985), p. 150-155. English. DESCR: Authors; Cervantes, Lorna Dee; *EMPLUMADA; *ENCLAVE; Laviera, Tato; Literature Reviews; Poetry; Soto, Gary; *WHERE SPARROWS WORK HARD.

4246 Eysturoy, Annie O. EL DIABLO EN TEXAS: una historia popular a traves de arquetipos y simbolos. LA COMUNIDAD, No. 364 (July 12, 1987), p. 6-7. Spanish. DESCR: *Book Reviews; Brito, Aristeo; *EL DIABLO EN TEXAS.

4247 Galindo, Luis Alberto. El dios de la lluvia=RAIN GOD. LA COMUNIDAD, No. 241 (March 3, 1985), p. 12-13. Spanish. DESCR: Biography; Islas, Arturo; Novel; *THE RAIN GOD: A DESERT TALE.

4248 Gonzalez, Maria. CARAS VIEJAS Y VINO NUEVO: analisis tematica y estructural. TINTA, Vol. 1, no. 1 (May 1981), p. 15-18. Spanish. DESCR: *CARAS VIEJAS Y VINO NUEVO; Morales, Alejandro; Novel.

4249 Herrera-Sobek, Maria. Introduction. THE AMERICAS REVIEW, Vol. 15, no. 3-4 (Fall, Winter, 1987), p. 9-39. English. DESCR: *Chicanas; *Literature.

4250 Herrera-Sobek, Maria. Literatura y sociedad: la problematica del Chicano/Mexicano en los Estados Unidos a traves de la obra literaria. BILINGUAL REVIEW, Vol. 11, no. 3 (September, December, 1984), p. 83-87. Spanish. DESCR: Book Reviews; Literature; *REQUISA TREINTA Y DOS; Sanchez, Rosaura.

4251 Herrera-Sobek, Maria. The politics of rape: sexual transgression in Chicana fiction. THE AMERICAS REVIEW, Vol. 15, no. 3-4 (Fall, Winter, 1987), p. 171-181. English. DESCR: *Chicanas; Cisneros, Sandra; *Feminism; Fiction; GIVING UP THE GHOST; Lizarraga, Sylvia; Moraga, Cherrie; *Rape; "Red Clowns" [short story]; Sex Roles; "Silver Lake Road" [short story].

4252 Hinojosa-Smith, Rolando R. La realidad chicana se forjo con dos culturas. LA COMUNIDAD, No. 313 (July 20, 1986), p. 6-7. Spanish. DESCR: *Biography; *Hinojosa-Smith, Rolando R.; Novel.

4253 Leal, Luis. Literary criticism and minority literatures: the case of the Chicano writer. CONFLUENCIA, Vol. 1, no. 2 (Spring 1986), p. 4-9. English. DESCR: Authors; Ethnic Groups; Literary Influence; *Literature; *Third World Literature (U.S.)

4254 Lewis, Marvin A.; Striano, Ron; and Hiura, Barbara L. Chicano ethnicity and aging [and critiques]. EXPLORATIONS IN ETHNIC STUDIES, Vol. 8, no. 2 (July 1985), p. 35-45. English. DESCR: Anaya, Rudolfo A.; *Ancianos; BLESS ME, ULTIMA; Curanderas; FAMOUS ALL OVER TOWN; Identity; James, Dan; Literature.

4255 Lomas, Clara. Libertad de no procrear: la voz de la mujer en "A una madre de nuestro tiempo" de Margarita Cota-Cardenas. REVISTA MUJERES, Vol. 2, no. 1 (January 1985), p. 30-35. Spanish. DESCR: *Chicanas; Feminism; Sex Stereotypes.

Literary Criticism (cont.)

4256 Lomeli, Francisco A. El concepto del barrio en tres poetas chicanos. LA COMUNIDAD, No. 316 (August 10, 1986), p. 4-5+. Spanish. **DESCR:** Alurista; Barrios; Delgado, Abelardo "Lalo"; Poetry; Sanchez, Ricardo.

4257 Lomeli, Francisco A. En la voragine del destino [book review of: THE FIFTH HORSEMAN]. LA COMUNIDAD, No. 258 (June 30, 1985), p. 12-13. Spanish. **DESCR:** Book Reviews; *THE FIFTH HORSEMAN; Villarreal, Jose Antonio.

4258 Lomeli, Francisco A. En torno a la literatura...convergencia o divergencia? LA COMUNIDAD, No. 274 (October 20, 1985), p. 8-11. Spanish. **DESCR:** Anaya, Rudolfo A.; Aztlan; Border Region; HEART OF AZTLAN; Mendez M., Miguel; PEREGRINOS DE AZTLAN; *Primer Festival de Literatura Fronteriza Mexico-Estados Unidos.

4259 Lomeli, Francisco A. En torno a la literatura de la frontera (II). LA COMUNIDAD, No. 275 (October 27, 1985), p. 2-3. Spanish. **DESCR:** Border Region; Language Usage; MURIERON A MITAD DEL RIO; Spota, Luis.

4260 Lomeli, Francisco A. Entrevista con Rolando Hinojosa (I). LA COMUNIDAD, No. 295 (March 16, 1986), p. 2-3+. Spanish. **DESCR:** *Biography; *Hinojosa-Smith, Rolando R.; Novel; Short Story.

4261 Lomeli, Francisco A. Entrevista con Rolando Hinojosa (II). LA COMUNIDAD, No. 296 (March 23, 1986), p. 15. Spanish. **DESCR:** *Biography; *Hinojosa-Smith, Rolando R.

4262 Lomeli, Francisco A. Luis Leal y la vocacion por la literatura latinoamericana. LA COMUNIDAD, No. 279 (November 24, 1985), 6-7+. Spanish. **DESCR:** Authors; Biography; *Leal, Luis; Literature.

4263 Lomeli, Francisco A. Novela chicana: sus variantes y contradicciones (I). LA COMUNIDAD, No. 292 (February 23, 1986), p. 12-13. Spanish. **DESCR:** Literature; Novel; Publishing Industry; Quinto Sol Publishing, Inc.

4264 Lomeli, Francisco A. Novela chicana: sus variantes y contradicciones (II). LA COMUNIDAD, No. 293 (March 2, 1986), p. 14-15. Spanish. **DESCR:** Literature Reviews; Novel.

4265 Lower, Andrea. La unidad narrativa en LA MUERTE DE ARTEMIO CRUZ. TINTA, Vol. 1, no. 3 (December 1983), p. 19-26. Spanish. **DESCR:** Fuentes, Carlos; *LA MUERTE DE ARTEMIO CRUZ; Mexican Literature; *Novel.

4266 Mariscal, George. Alejandro Morales in utopia. CONFLUENCIA, Vol. 2, no. 1 (Fall 1986), p. 78-83. English. **DESCR:** *Morales, Alejandro; Novel; *RETO EN EL PARAISO.

4267 Marquez, Antonio. Richard Rodriguez's HUNGER OF MEMORY and the poetics of experience. ARIZONA QUARTERLY, Vol. 40, no. 2 (Summer 1984), p. 130-141. English. **DESCR:** *Autobiography; Book Reviews; *HUNGER OF MEMORY: THE EDUCATION OF RICHARD RODRIGUEZ; Rodriguez, Richard.

4268 Martin-Rodriguez, Manuel M. El sentimiento de culpa en RETO EN EL PARAISO de Alejandro Morales. THE AMERICAS REVIEW, Vol. 15, no. 1 (Spring 1987), p. 89-97. Spanish. **DESCR:** *Morales, Alejandro; Novel; *RETO EN EL PARAISO.

4269 Nieto, Margarita. Fronteras en la obra de Carlos Castaneda. LA COMUNIDAD, No. 325 (October 12, 1986), p. 8-10. Spanish. **DESCR:** *Castaneda, Carlos.

4270 Olivares, Julian. Sandra Cisneros' THE HOUSE ON MANGO STREET and the poetics of space. THE AMERICAS REVIEW, Vol. 15, no. 3-4 (Fall, Winter, 1987), p. 160-170. English. **DESCR:** *Cisneros, Sandra; *THE HOUSE ON MANGO STREET.

4271 Olivares, Julian. Self and society in Tino Villanueva's SHAKING OFF THE DARK. CONFLUENCIA, Vol. 1, no. 2 (Spring 1986), p. 98-110. English. **DESCR:** *Poetry; *SHAKING OFF THE DARK; Villanueva, Tino.

4272 Ortiz, Francisco. La cultura chicana, la cultura amenazada. LA COMUNIDAD, No. 305 (May 25, 1986), p. 10-11. Spanish. **DESCR:** Anaya, Rudolfo A.; *BLESS ME, ULTIMA; Bloomfield, NM; *Censorship; New Mexico; Textbooks.

4273 Padilla, Genaro Miguel. The anti-romantic city in Chicano fiction. PUERTO DEL SOL, Vol. 23, no. 1 (1987), p. 159-169. English. **DESCR:** Acosta, Oscar Zeta; Anaya, Rudolfo A.; *Fiction; Lattin, Vernon E.; Morales, Alejandro; *Urban Communities.

4274 Paredes, Raymund A. Review essay: recent Chicano writing. ROCKY MOUNTAIN REVIEW OF LANGUAGE AND LITERATURE, Vol. 41, (1987), p. 124-129. English. **DESCR:** Castillo, Ana; Catholic Church; Chavez, Denise; Chicanas; Garcia, Lionel; GIVING UP THE GHOST; LEAVING HOME; *Literature Reviews; Moraga, Cherrie; Poetry; Prose; Sex Roles; Silva, Beverly; SMALL FACES; Soto, Gary; THE CAT AND OTHER STORIES; THE LAST OF THE MENU GIRLS; THE MIXQUIAHUALA LETTERS.

4275 Quintana, Alvina. O mama, with what's inside of me. REVISTA MUJERES, Vol. 3, no. 1 (January 1986), p. 38-40. English. **DESCR:** *Alarcon, Norma; *Chicanas; Feminism; Poetry; *"What Kind of Lover Have You Made Me, Mother?: Towards a Theory of Chicanas' Feminism and Cultural Identity Through Poetry" [article].

4276 Randolph, Donald A. Death's aesthetic proliferation in works of Hinojosa. CONFLUENCIA, Vol. 1, no. 2 (Spring 1986), p. 38-47. English. **DESCR:** Death (Concept); GENERACIONES Y SEMBLANZAS; *Hinojosa-Smith, Rolando R.; KLAIL CITY Y SUS ALREDEDORES; KOREAN LOVE SONGS; Novel.

4277 Rebolledo, Tey Diana. The politics of poetics: or, what am I, a critic, doing in this text anyhow? THE AMERICAS REVIEW, Vol. 15, no. 3-4 (Fall, Winter, 1987), p. 129-138. English. **DESCR:** *Chicanas; Literary History; Literature.

4278 Ruiz, Ariel. Raza, sexo y politica en SHORT EYES by Miguel Pinero. THE AMERICAS REVIEW, Vol. 15, no. 2 (Summer 1987), p. 93-102. Spanish. **DESCR:** Homosexuality; Pinero, Miguel; Prisoners; Puerto Ricans; Sex Roles; *SHORT EYES; Teatro.

Literary Criticism (cont.)

4279 Saldivar, Jose David. Towards a Chicano poetics: the making of the Chicano subject. CONFLUENCIA, Vol. 1, no. 2 (Spring 1986), p. 10-17. English. **DESCR:** Corridos; Feminism; "Los vatos" [poem]; Montoya, Jose E.; *Poetry; RESTLESS SERPENTS; Rios, Alberto; WHISPERING TO FOOL THE WIND; Zamora, Bernice.

4280 Tatum, Charles. Book review of: LA NOVELA CHICANA ESCRITA EN ESPANOL. WORLD LITERATURE TODAY, Vol. 57, no. 4 (Fall 1983), p. 613-614. English. **DESCR:** Book Reviews; *LA NOVELA CHICANA ESCRITA EN ESPANOL; Rodriguez del Pino, Salvador.

4281 Tatum, Charles. Chicano literary criticism comes of age. BILINGUAL REVIEW, Vol. 12, no. 1-2 (January, August, 1985), p. 144-149. English. **DESCR:** Book Reviews; *CHICANO THEATER: THEMES AND FORMS; Huerta, Jorge A.; *LA NOVELA CHICANA ESCRITA EN ESPANOL; Rodriguez del Pino, Salvador.

4282 Torres, Hector. Discourse and plot in Rolando Hinojosa's THE VALLEY: narrativity and the recovery of Chicano heritage. CONFLUENCIA, Vol. 2, no. 1 (Fall 1986), p. 84-93. English. **DESCR:** *Hinojosa-Smith, Rolando R.; Novel; *THE VALLEY.

4283 Toruno, Rhina. El protagonista verdadero de EL SIGLO DE LAS LUCES de Alejo Carpentier. CHIRICU, Vol. 4, no. 1 (1985), p. 19-39. Spanish. **DESCR:** Carpentier, Alejo; *EL SIGLO DE LAS LUCES; Novel.

4284 Ugalde, Sharon E. Two visions of cultural domination: Carrero's EL HOMBRE QUE NO SUDABA and Hinojosa's MI QUERIDO RAFA. BILINGUAL REVIEW, Vol. 12, no. 1-2 (January, August, 1985), p. 159-165. English. **DESCR:** Carrero, Jaime; *EL HOMBRE QUE NO SUDABA; Hinojosa-Smith, Rolando R.; *MI QUERIDO RAFA.

4285 Valdes Medellin, Gonzalo; Elizondo, Sergio D.; and Aguilar, Ricardo. Hacia un tercer lenguaje. LA COMUNIDAD, No. 240 (February 24, 1985), p. 2-3. Spanish. **DESCR:** Aguilar, Ricardo; Elizondo, Sergio.

4286 Vogt, Gregory M. Archetypal images of apocalypse in Miguel Mendez's TATA CASEHUA. CONFLUENCIA, Vol. 1, no. 2 (Spring 1986), p. 55-60. English. **DESCR:** *Mendez M., Miguel; Short Story; *"Tata Casehua" [short story].

4287 Yarbro-Bejarano, Yvonne. Chicana literature from a Chicana feminist perspective. THE AMERICAS REVIEW, Vol. 15, no. 3-4 (Fall, Winter, 1987), p. 139-145. English. **DESCR:** *Chicanas; *Feminism; Literature.

Literary History

4288 Chavez, Denise. Words of wisdom. NEW MEXICO MAGAZINE, Vol. 65, no. 12 (December 1987), p. 72-78. English. **DESCR:** *Authors; Literature; *New Mexico.

4289 Claymendez, Luis Felipe. La naturaleza en la literatura chicana y sus antecedentes prehispanicos. REVISTA DE ESTUDIOS HISPANICOS, Vol. 19, no. 2 (May 1985), p. 107-127. Spanish. **DESCR:** Literary Criticism; *Literature; Precolumbian Literature.

4290 Flores, Arturo C. La literatura de Aztlan y su reconocimiento. TINTA, Vol. 1, no. 3 (December 1983), p. 9-10. Spanish. **DESCR:** *Aztlan; Literature.

4291 Lomeli, Francisco A. Critica y literatura chicana: maduracion y reto. CONFLUENCIA, Vol. 1, no. 2 (Spring 1986), p. 1-3. Spanish. **DESCR:** *Literature; Literature Reviews.

4292 Mendez-M., Miguel. Observaciones sobre la literatura fronteriza. RENATO ROSALDO LECTURE SERIES MONOGRAPH, Vol. 2, (Spring 1986), p. [21]-27. Spanish. **DESCR:** *Border Region; *Literature; *Mexican Literature.

4293 Rebolledo, Tey Diana. The politics of poetics: or, what am I, a critic, doing in this text anyhow? THE AMERICAS REVIEW, Vol. 15, no. 3-4 (Fall, Winter, 1987), p. 129-138. English. **DESCR:** *Chicanas; *Literary Criticism; Literature.

Literary Influence

4294 Bartlett, Catherine Vallejos. Magical realism: the Latin American influence on modern Chicano writers. CONFLUENCIA, Vol. 1, no. 2 (Spring 1986), p. 27-37. English. **DESCR:** Arias, Ron; Authors; Garcia Marquez, Gabriel; Latin America; *Literary Criticism; *Literature; Magical realism; ONE HUNDRED YEARS OF SOLITUDE; Rivera, Tomas; THE ROAD TO TAMAZUNCHALE; Y NO SE LO TRAGO LA TIERRA/AND THE EARTH DID NOT PART.

4295 Leal, Luis. Literary criticism and minority literatures: the case of the Chicano writer. CONFLUENCIA, Vol. 1, no. 2 (Spring 1986), p. 4-9. English. **DESCR:** Authors; Ethnic Groups; *Literary Criticism; *Literature; *Third World Literature (U.S.)

Literature

4296 Bartlett, Catherine Vallejos. Magical realism: the Latin American influence on modern Chicano writers. CONFLUENCIA, Vol. 1, no. 2 (Spring 1986), p. 27-37. English. **DESCR:** Arias, Ron; Authors; Garcia Marquez, Gabriel; Latin America; *Literary Criticism; *Literary Influence; Magical realism; ONE HUNDRED YEARS OF SOLITUDE; Rivera, Tomas; THE ROAD TO TAMAZUNCHALE; Y NO SE LO TRAGO LA TIERRA/AND THE EARTH DID NOT PART.

4297 Bibliography. THE AMERICAS REVIEW, Vol. 15, no. 3-4 (Fall, Winter, 1987), p. 182-188. English. **DESCR:** *Bibliography; *Chicanas; *Literary Criticism.

4298 Bruce-Novoa, Juan. Meet the writers of the 80s. VISTA, Vol. 1, no. 11 (July 6, 1986), p. 15-16. English. **DESCR:** Anaya, Rudolfo A.; Arte Publico Press; *Authors; Bilingual Review Press; Cisneros, Sandra; Hinojosa-Smith, Rolando R.; Keller, Gary D.; Pineda, Cecile; Quinto Sol Publishing, Inc.; Rivera, Tomas; Soto, Gary.

4299 Campos, Jorge. Noticia de la literatura chicana. INSULA: REVISTA BIBLIOGRAFICA DE LETRAS Y CIENCIAS HUMANAS, Vol. 37, no. 422 (January 1982), p. 11. Spanish. **DESCR:** Literary Criticism.

4300 Chavez, Denise. Words of wisdom. NEW MEXICO MAGAZINE, Vol. 65, no. 12 (December 1987), p. 72-78. English. **DESCR:** *Authors; *Literary History; *New Mexico.

Literature (cont.)

4301 Claymendez, Luis Felipe. La naturaleza en la literatura chicana y sus antecedentes prehispanicos. REVISTA DE ESTUDIOS HISPANICOS, Vol. 19, no. 2 (May 1985), p. 107-127. Spanish. **DESCR:** Literary Criticism; Literary History; Precolumbian Literature.

4302 Elias, Edward F. Book review of: A DECADE OF HISPANIC LITERATURE. LA RED/THE NET, no. 68 (May 1983), p. 9-10. English. **DESCR:** Book Reviews; *DECADE OF HISPANIC LITERATURE: AN ANNIVERSARY ANTHOLOGY; REVISTA CHICANO-RIQUENA.

4303 Flores, Arturo C. La literatura de Aztlan y su reconocimiento. TINTA, Vol. 1, no. 3 (December 1983), p. 9-10. Spanish. **DESCR:** *Aztlan; Literary History.

4304 Herrera-Sobek, Maria. Introduction. THE AMERICAS REVIEW, Vol. 15, no. 3-4 (Fall, Winter, 1987), p. 9-39. English. **DESCR:** *Chicanas; *Literary Criticism.

4305 Herrera-Sobek, Maria. Literatura y sociedad: la problematica del Chicano/Mexicano en los Estados Unidos a traves de la obra literaria. BILINGUAL REVIEW, Vol. 11, no. 3 (September, December, 1984), p. 83-87. Spanish. **DESCR:** Book Reviews; Literary Criticism; *REQUISA TREINTA Y DOS; Sanchez, Rosaura.

4306 Klor de Alva, J. Jorge. California Chicano literature and pre-Columbian motifs: foil and fetish. CONFLUENCIA, Vol. 1, no. 2 (Spring 1986), p. 18-26. English. **DESCR:** Alurista; Aztecs; Aztlan; *California; EL PLAN ESPIRITUAL DE AZTLAN; *Precolumbian Images; *Precolumbian Philosophy; Symbolism.

4307 Leal, Luis. Literary criticism and minority literatures: the case of the Chicano writer. CONFLUENCIA, Vol. 1, no. 2 (Spring 1986), p. 4-9. English. **DESCR:** Authors; Ethnic Groups; *Literary Criticism; Literary Influence; *Third World Literature (U.S.).

4308 Lewis, Marvin A.; Striano, Ron; and Hiura, Barbara L. Chicano ethnicity and aging [and critiques]. EXPLORATIONS IN ETHNIC STUDIES, Vol. 8, no. 2 (July 1985), p. 35-45. English. **DESCR:** Anaya, Rudolfo A.; *Ancianos; BLESS ME, ULTIMA; Curanderas; FAMOUS ALL OVER TOWN; Identity; James, Dan; Literary Criticism.

4309 Lomeli, Francisco A. Critica y literatura chicana: maduracion y reto. CONFLUENCIA, Vol. 1, no. 2 (Spring 1986), p. 1-3. Spanish. **DESCR:** *Literary History; Literature Reviews.

4310 Lomeli, Francisco A. Luis Leal y la vocacion por la literatura latinoamericana. LA COMUNIDAD, No. 279 (November 24, 1985), 6-7+. Spanish. **DESCR:** Authors; Biography; *Leal, Luis; *Literary Criticism.

4311 Lomeli, Francisco A. Novela chicana: sus variantes y contradicciones (I). LA COMUNIDAD, No. 292 (February 23, 1986), p. 12-13. Spanish. **DESCR:** *Literary Criticism; Novel; Publishing Industry; Quinto Sol Publishing, Inc.

4312 Mendez-M., Miguel. Introduccion. LLUEVE TLALOC, no. 4 (1977), p. vii. Spanish. **DESCR:** Pima Community College, Tucson, AZ.

4313 Mendez-M., Miguel. Introduction. LLUEVE TLALOC, no. 4 (1977), p. viii. English.

DESCR: *Pima Community College, Tucson, AZ.

4314 Mendez-M., Miguel. Observaciones sobre la literatura fronteriza. RENATO ROSALDO LECTURE SERIES MONOGRAPH, Vol. 2, (Spring 1986), p. [21]-27. Spanish. **DESCR:** *Border Region; *Literary History; *Mexican Literature.

4315 Mohr, Nicholasa. Puerto Rican writers in the United States, Puerto Rican writers in Puerto Rico: a separation beyond language. THE AMERICAS REVIEW, Vol. 15, no. 2 (Summer 1987), p. 87-92. English. **DESCR:** Authors; Autobiography; Identity; Immigrants; *Language Usage; *Mohr, Nicolasa; *Puerto Ricans; Spanish Language.

4316 Perry, Charles E. Book review of: CHICANO LITERATURE: A REFERENCE GUIDE. LIBRARY JOURNAL, Vol. 110, no. 5 (March 15, 1985), p. 53. English. **DESCR:** Book Reviews; *CHICANO LITERATURE: A REFERENCE GUIDE; Lomeli, Francisco A.; Martinez, Julio A.; Reference Works.

4317 Quintana, Alvina. Challenge and counter challenge: Chicana literary motifs. AGAINST THE CURRENT, Vol. 2, no. 2 (March, April, 1987), p. 25,28-32. English. **DESCR:** Cervantes, Lorna Dee; *Chicanas; *Feminism; Moraga, Cherrie; THERE ARE NO MADMEN HERE; Valdes, Gina.

4318 Rebolledo, Tey Diana. The politics of poetics: or, what am I, a critic, doing in this text anyhow? THE AMERICAS REVIEW, Vol. 15, no. 3-4 (Fall, Winter, 1987), p. 129-138. English. **DESCR:** *Chicanas; *Literary Criticism; Literary History.

4319 Seeking more readers for Hispanic literature. VISTA, Vol. 2, no. 3 (November 2, 1986), p. 25. English. **DESCR:** Hinojosa-Smith, Rolando R.; *Miami Book Fair International; Mohr, Nicolasa; Munoz, Elias Miguel; Rodriguez, Richard.

4320 Yarbro-Bejarano, Yvonne. Chicana literature from a Chicana feminist perspective. THE AMERICAS REVIEW, Vol. 15, no. 3-4 (Fall, Winter, 1987), p. 139-145. English. **DESCR:** *Chicanas; *Feminism; *Literary Criticism.

Literature Reviews

4321 Almaguer, Tomas. Urban Chicano workers in historical perspective: a review of recent literature. LA RED/THE NET, no. 68 (May 1983), p. 2-6. English. **DESCR:** *Labor; Laborers; Working Women.

4322 de Leon, Arnoldo. Tejano history scholarship: a review of the recent literature. WEST TEXAS HISTORICAL ASSOCIATION YEARBOOK, Vol. 61, (1985), p. 116-133. English. **DESCR:** Historiography; Political History and Conditions; Social History and Conditions; *Texas.

4323 Delgado, Melvin and Humm-Delgado, Denise. Hispanics and group work: a review of the literature. SOCIAL WORK WITH GROUPS, Vol. 7, no. 3 (Fall 1984), p. 85-96. English. **DESCR:** *Psychotherapy; *Social Work.

Literature Reviews (cont.)

4324 Elias, Edward F. A meeting of poets from east and west: Lorna Dee Cervantes, Gary Soto, Tato Laviera. BILINGUAL REVIEW, Vol. 12, no. 1-2 (January, August, 1985), p. 150-155. English. **DESCR:** Authors; Cervantes, Lorna Dee; *EMPLUMADA; *ENCLAVE; Laviera, Tato; Literary Criticism; Poetry; Soto, Gary; *WHERE SPARROWS WORK HARD.

4325 Falcon, Angelo. Puerto Rican politics in urban America: an introduction to the literature. LA RED/THE NET, no. 70 (July 1983), p. 2-9. English. **DESCR:** Political History and Conditions; Politics; *Puerto Ricans.

4326 Hall, Linda B. The United States-Mexican borders: historical, political, and cultural perspectives. LATIN AMERICAN RESEARCH REVIEW, Vol. 20, no. 2 (1985), p. 223-229. English. **DESCR:** AMERICAN LABOR IN THE SOUTHWEST: THE FIRST ONE HUNDRED YEARS; *Book Reviews; *Border Region; BOSS RULE IN SOUTH TEXAS: THE PROGRESSIVE ERA; CHICANO INTERMARRIAGE: A THEORETICAL AND EMPIRICAL STUDY; HISPANIC CULTURE IN THE SOUTHWEST; IN DEFENSE OF LA RAZA: THE LOS ANGELES MEXICAN CONSULATE AND THE MEXICAN COMMUNITY; RACE AND CLASS IN THE SOUTHWEST: A THEORY OF RACIAL INEQUALITY; SOUTHWESTERN AGRICULTURE: PRE-COLUMBIAN TO MODERN; THE MEXICANS IN OKLAHOMA; THE POLITICS OF SAN ANTONIO.

4327 Leal, Luis. Americo Paredes and modern Mexican American scholarship. ETHNIC AFFAIRS, no. 1 (Fall 1987), p. [1]-11. English. **DESCR:** Ethnology; Folklore; History; *Paredes, Americo.

4328 Lomeli, Francisco A. Critica y literatura chicana: maduracion y reto. CONFLUENCIA, Vol. 1, no. 2 (Spring 1986), p. 1-3. Spanish. **DESCR:** *Literary History; *Literature.

4329 Lomeli, Francisco A. Novela chicana: sus variantes y contradicciones (II). LA COMUNIDAD, No. 293 (March 2, 1986), p. 14-15. Spanish. **DESCR:** *Literary Criticism; Novel.

4330 Macias, Reynaldo Flores. Language studies and Chicanos. LA RED/THE NET, no. 66 (March 1983), p. 26-28. English. **DESCR:** *Language Usage.

4331 Madrid, Arturo. Report to the Network. LA RED/THE NET, No. 102 (November 1986), p. 1-2. English. **DESCR:** *Higher Education.

4332 Paredes, Raymund A. Review essay: recent Chicano writing. ROCKY MOUNTAIN REVIEW OF LANGUAGE AND LITERATURE, Vol. 41, (1987), p. 124-129. English. **DESCR:** Castillo, Ana; Catholic Church; Chavez, Denise; Chicanas; Garcia, Lionel; GIVING UP THE GHOST; LEAVING HOME; *Literary Criticism; Moraga, Cherrie; Poetry; Prose; Sex Roles; Silva, Beverly; SMALL FACES; Soto, Gary; THE CAT AND OTHER STORIES; THE LAST OF THE MENU GIRLS; THE MIXQUIAHUALA LETTERS.

4333 Powers, Michael D. Spanish in contact with other languages: lexical or profound structural influence? BILINGUAL REVIEW, Vol. 12, no. 3 (September, December, 1985), p. 254-257. English. **DESCR:** Amastae, Jon; Elias-Olivares, Lucia; Language Usage; *SPANISH IN THE UNITED STATES: SOCIOLINGUISTIC ASPECTS; *SPANISH IN THE WESTERN HEMISPHERE IN CONTACT WITH ENGLISH, PORTUGUESE, AND THE AMERINDIAN LANGUAGES;

*Spanish Language; Zaragoza, Jorge.

4334 Saragoza, Alex M. The significance of recent Chicano-related historical writings: an appraisal. ETHNIC AFFAIRS, no. 1 (Fall 1987), p. [24]-62. English. **DESCR:** *Historiography; *History.

LIVING UP THE STREET

4335 Dunn, Geoffrey. Book review of: LIVING UP THE STREET. SAN FRANCISCO REVIEW OF BOOKS, Vol. 11, (Summer 1986), p. 11. English. **DESCR:** Book Reviews; Soto, Gary.

Lizarraga, Sylvia

4336 Herrera-Sobek, Maria. The politics of rape: sexual transgression in Chicana fiction. THE AMERICAS REVIEW, Vol. 15, no. 3-4 (Fall, Winter, 1987), p. 171-181. English. **DESCR:** *Chicanas; Cisneros, Sandra; *Feminism; Fiction; GIVING UP THE GHOST; *Literary Criticism; Moraga, Cherrie; *Rape; "Red Clowns" [short story]; Sex Roles; "Silver Lake Road" [short story].

Llanes, Jose

4337 Herrera-Sobek, Maria. Book review of: CUBAN AMERICANS: MASTERS OF SURVIVAL. LA RED/THE NET, no. 67 (April 1983), p. 10-12. English. **DESCR:** Book Reviews; *CUBAN AMERICANS: MASTERS OF SURVIVAL; Cubanos.

La Llorona

4338 Limon, Jose E. La Llorona, the third legend of greater Mexico: cultural symbols, women, and the political unconscious. RENATO ROSALDO LECTURE SERIES MONOGRAPH, Vol. 2, (Spring 1986), p. [59]-93. English. **DESCR:** *Feminism; Folklore; La Virgen de Guadalupe; *Leyendas; Malinche; Mexico; *Symbolism; Women.

4339 Valenzuela, Oscar N. One of the many stories about la Llorona. LLUEVE TLALOC, no. 2 (1975), p. 10. English. **DESCR:** *Prose.

4340 Valenzuela, Oscar N. Uno de tantos cuentos de la Llorona. LLUEVE TLALOC, no. 2 (1975), p. 9. Spanish. **DESCR:** *Prose.

LLUEVE TLALOC

4341 Brito, Aristeo. [Note]. LLUEVE TLALOC, no. 14 (1987), p. xi. English. **DESCR:** *Precolumbian Images.

Loans (Student)
USE: Financial Aid

Los Lobos del Este de Los Angeles (musical group)

4342 Alonso, Miguel Angel. Los Lobos y la importancia de la continuidad musical. LA COMUNIDAD, No. 341 (February 1, 1987), p. 12-13. Spanish. **DESCR:** *Music; Rock Music.

4343 Bellinhausen, Hermann. El lobo estepario en Olvera Street. LA COMUNIDAD, No. 267 (September 1, 1985), p. 10-11. Spanish. **DESCR:** *Rock Music; Valens, Ritchie [stage name for Richard Valenzuela].

4344 DeCurtis, Anthony. Los Lobos shake, rattle and worry. ROLLING STONE, (February 26, 1987), p. 51-53. English. **DESCR:** *BY THE LIGHT OF THE MOON; Recording Industry; Rock Music.

Los Lobos del Este de Los Angeles (musical group)
(cont.)

4345 Forte, Dan. Los Lobos: Tex-Mex rock from East L.A. GUITAR PLAYER, Vol. 21, no. 2 (February 1987), p. 68-94. English. **DESCR:** Biography; Discography; Hidalgo, David (Los Lobos); Lozano, Conrad (Los Lobos); *Musicians; Perez, Louie (Los Lobos); Recording Industry; *Rock Music; Rosas, Cesar (Los Lobos).

4346 Fricke, David. Los motivos del lobo. LA COMUNIDAD, No. 266 (August 25, 1985), p. 12. Spanish. **DESCR:** *Rock Music.

4347 Gordon, Polita C. Living the crossover dream. VISTA, Vol. 1, no. 8 (April 6, 1986), p. 6-9. English. **DESCR:** *Blades, Ruben; Colon, Willie; Miami Sound Machine; *Musicians.

4348 Sellers, Jeff M. The sound of musica: moving into the mainstream. HISPANIC BUSINESS, Vol. 9, no. 7 (July 1987), p. 14-18. English. **DESCR:** *Marketing; Miami Sound Machine; Music; *Musicians; The Cruzados [musical group]; Zerimar [musical group].

Local Government

4349 Karnig, Albert K.; Welch, Susan; and Eribes, Richard A. Employment of women by cities in the Southwest. SOCIAL SCIENCE JOURNAL, Vol. 21, no. 4 (October 1984), p. 41-48. English. **DESCR:** Chicanas; *Employment; *Southwestern United States; Women.

4350 Ross, I. Mayor Cisneros of San Antonio. READER'S DIGEST, Vol. 125, (December 1984), p. 193-194+. English. **DESCR:** Biography; *Cisneros, Henry, Mayor of San Antonio, TX; *Elected Officials; San Antonio, TX.

Local History

4351 Gonzales, Juan. San Francisco's Mission District: part I. LATIN QUARTER, Vol. 1, no. 4 (July, August, 1975), p. 21-25. English. **DESCR:** La Mision Dolores Iglesia Catolica; *Mission District, San Francisco, CA; Political Parties and Organizations; San Francisco, CA; *Urban Communities.

4352 Leon, David Jess and McNeill, Daniel. Hispanics, the fifth class, and the University of California, 1870-72. LA RED/THE NET, no. 67 (April 1983), p. 5-6. English. **DESCR:** College Preparation; *Colleges and Universities; Enrollment; *University of California.

Locus of Control

4353 Powers, Stephen and Rossman, Mark H. Attributions for success and failure among Anglo, Black, Hispanic, and Native-American community-college students. JOURNAL OF PSYCHOLOGY, Vol. 117, no. 1 (May 1984), p. 27-31. English. **DESCR:** *Academic Achievement; Anglo Americans; Blacks; Community Colleges; Native Americans; Students.

4354 Zippin, David H. and Hough, Richard L. Perceived self-other differences in life events and mental health among Mexicans and Americans. JOURNAL OF PSYCHOLOGY, Vol. 119, no. 2 (March 1985), p. 143-155. English. **DESCR:** Anglo Americans; *Comparative Psychology; *Mental Health; Mexico; Psychiatry; *Stress.

Logos
USE: Symbolism

Lomeli, Francisco A.

4355 Book review of: CHICANO LITERATURE: A REFERENCE GUIDE. BOOKLIST, Vol. 82, no. 9 (January 1, 1986), p. 667-668. English. **DESCR:** Book Reviews; *CHICANO LITERATURE: A REFERENCE GUIDE; Martinez, Julio A.; Reference Works.

4356 Brown, D.R. Book review of: CHICANO LITERATURE: A REFERENCE GUIDE. CHOICE, Vol. 23, no. 4 (December 1985), p. 578. English. **DESCR:** Book Reviews; *CHICANO LITERATURE: A REFERENCE GUIDE; Martinez, Julio A.; Reference Works.

4357 Castillo-Speed, Lillian. Annotated bibliography. LA RED/THE NET, no. 93 (January, February, 1986), p. 14-17. English. **DESCR:** A BIBLIOGRAPHY OF MEXICAN AMERICAN HISTORY; ARTE CHICANO; Book Reviews; Caballero, Cesar; CHICANO LITERATURE: A REFERENCE GUIDE; CHICANO ORGANIZATIONS DIRECTORY; CHICANO PERIODICAL INDEX; Goldman, Shifra M.; HISPANIC ALMANAC; HISPANIC MENTAL HEALTH RESEARCH: A REFERENCE GUIDE; Martinez, Julio A.; Meier, Matt S.; Newton, Frank; *Reference Works; Ybarra-Frausto, Tomas.

4358 Haro, Robert P. Book review of: CHICANO LITERATURE: A REFERENCE GUIDE. AMERICAN REFERENCE BOOKS ANNUAL, Vol. 17, (1986), p. 440. English. **DESCR:** Book Reviews; *CHICANO LITERATURE: A REFERENCE GUIDE; Martinez, Julio A.; Reference Works.

4359 Perry, Charles E. Book review of: CHICANO LITERATURE: A REFERENCE GUIDE. LIBRARY JOURNAL, Vol. 110, no. 5 (March 15, 1985), p. 53. English. **DESCR:** Book Reviews; *CHICANO LITERATURE: A REFERENCE GUIDE; Literature; Martinez, Julio A.; Reference Works.

Lopez, Enrique Hank

4360 Espinosa, Maria. Children. LLUEVE TLALOC, no. 3 (1976), p. 5-9. English. **DESCR:** Children; *Prose.

4361 Espinosa, Mary Lou. Cosas de ninos. LLUEVE TLALOC, no. 3 (1976), p. 4-8. Spanish. **DESCR:** Children; *Prose.

Lopez [family name]

4362 Instituto Genealogico e Historico Latino-Americano. Rootsearch: Bello: Ramirez: Lopez. VISTA, Vol. 3, no. 2 (October 3, 1987), p. 37. English. **DESCR:** *Bello [family name]; Genealogy; History; *Personal Names; *Ramirez [family name].

Lopez, Nancy

4363 Barnes, Jill. The winning formula of Nancy Lopez. VISTA, Vol. 2, no. 12 (August 1, 1987), p. 6-9. English. **DESCR:** *Athletes; Biography.

Lopez, Ruben

4364 Hispanic chamber endorses insurance marketing plan. HISPANIC TIMES, Vol. 8, no. 3 (May, June, 1987), p. 26. English. **DESCR:** Business Enterprises; Insurance; *Metropolitan Life Insurance Corporation; *U.S. Hispanic Chamber of Commerce.

Lopez, Theresa (Terry)

4365 Rifkin, Jane M. Up from the barrio...to fittest woman cop in the U.S.A. HISPANIC TIMES, Vol. 8, no. 1 (December, January, 1987), p. 38. English. DESCR: Biography; Careers; *Chicanas; *Police.

Lopez-Knox, Joanne

4366 Lopez-Knox wins fellowship award. HISPANIC TIMES, Vol. 8, no. 1 (December, January, 1987), p. 21. English. DESCR: Awards; Biographical Notes; Chicanas; Science.

Lopez-Martin, Minnie

4367 SHPE news. HISPANIC ENGINEER, Vol. 3, no. 3 (1987), p. 10-13. English. DESCR: *Awards; Castillo, Hector; Colmenarez, Margarita; Garcia, Raul; Herrera, Jess; Mondragon, Ricardo; Reyes-Guerra, David; Silva, Juan; Society of Hispanic Professional Engineers (SHPE); Vargas, Jesus; Villanueva, Bernadette.

THE LOS ANGELES BARRIO 1850-1890: A SOCIAL HISTORY

4368 de Leon, Arnoldo. Book review of: THE LOS ANGELES BARRIO 1850-1890: A SOCIAL HISTORY. LA RED/THE NET, no. 64 (February 1983), p. 4-5. English. DESCR: Book Reviews; Griswold del Castillo, Richard.

4369 Kerr, Louise A. Book review of: THE LOS ANGELES BARRIO 1850-1890: A SOCIAL HISTORY. JOURNAL OF AMERICAN HISTORY, Vol. 70, no. 4 (March 1984), p. 894-895. English. DESCR: Book Reviews; Griswold del Castillo, Richard.

4370 Valdes, Dennis. Book review of: THE LOS ANGELES BARRIO 1850-1890: A SOCIAL HISTORY. LA RED/THE NET, no. 36 (November 1980), p. 5. English. DESCR: Book Reviews; Griswold del Castillo, Richard; History; *Los Angeles, CA; *Social History and Conditions.

Los Angeles, CA

4371 Ayala, Ernie. Richard Leon, L.A.'s leading Latin jazz D.J. LATIN QUARTER, Vol. 1, no. 1 (July 1974), p. 19-21. English. DESCR: *Leon, Richard; *Salsa.

4372 Baca, Reynaldo and Bryan, Dexter. Citizen aspirations and residency preferences: the Mexican undocumented worker in the binational community. LA RED/THE NET, no. 34 (September 1980), p. 2. English. DESCR: Naturalization; *Undocumented Workers.

4373 Casteleiro, Gus. Hot salsa and other sounds. LATIN QUARTER, Vol. 1, no. 3 (January, February, 1975), p. 19-20. English. DESCR: Musicians; *Salsa; San Francisco, CA.

4374 de Leon, Arnoldo and Stewart, Kenneth L. A tale of 3 cities: a comparative analysis of the socio-economic conditions of Mexican-Americans in Los Angeles, Tucson, and San Antonio, 1850-1900. JOURNAL OF THE WEST, Vol. 24, no. 2 (1985), p. 64-74. English. DESCR: Economic History and Conditions; Employment; Griswold del Castillo, Richard; Labor; San Antonio, TX; *Social History and Conditions; Tucson, AZ; Urban Communities.

4375 Escobar, Edward J. Mexican revolutionaries and the Los Angeles police: harassment of the Partido Liberal Mexicano, 1907-1910. AZTLAN, Vol. 17, no. 1 (Spring 1986), p.

1-46. English. DESCR: Civil Rights; *Flores Magon, Ricardo; Gutierrez de Lara, Lazaro; *Los Angeles Police Department; *Partido Liberal Mexicano (PLM); *Police; Police Brutality; Political Repression; Rico, Louis; Rico, Thomas; Talamantes, Felipe; United States-Mexico Relations.

4376 Garcia, Mario T. Book review of: A COMMUNITY UNDER SIEGE. LA RED/THE NET, no. 94 (March 1986), p. 5-6. English. DESCR: *A COMMUNITY UNDER SIEGE: A CHRONICLE OF CHICANOS EAST OF THE LOS ANGELES RIVER, 1945-1975; Acuna, Rudolfo; Book Reviews.

4377 Garcia, Mario T. [Letter to the editor about Mexicans, radicals and communists in the United States]. LABOR HISTORY, Vol. 25, no. 1 (Winter 1984), p. 152-154. English. DESCR: *"Anarquismo y Comunismo: Mexican Radicalism and the Communist Party in Los Angeles in the 1930s"; *Communism; History; *Labor Unions; *Monroy, Douglas.

4378 Gomez-Quinones, Juan. September 16th: a historical perspective. LATIN QUARTER, Vol. 1, no. 2 (October 1974), p. 8,9,11,12. English. DESCR: *Dieciseis de Septiembre; Hidalgo y Costilla, Miguel; *History; *Holidays.

4379 Grant from L.A. Pepsi to benefit city program. BEVERAGE INDUSTRY, Vol. 74, no. 7 (April 8, 1983), p. 25. English. DESCR: Community Development; *Pepsi-Cola Bottling Group; Private Funding Sources.

4380 Griswold del Castillo, Richard. Book review of: EAST LOS ANGELES. PACIFIC HISTORICAL REVIEW, Vol. 53, no. 4 (November 1984), p. 528-529. English. DESCR: Book Reviews; East Los Angeles, CA; *Romo, Ricardo.

4381 Griswold del Castillo, Richard. Familism, the extended family and Chicanos in the nineteenth century. LA RED/THE NET, no. 49 (December 1981), p. 2. English. DESCR: *Extended Family; *Family; *Nineteenth century; San Antonio, TX; Santa Fe, NM; *Social History and Conditions; Tucson, AZ.

4382 Herrera, Alexandra. Desde Los Angeles con amor. FEM, Vol. 11, no. 55 (July 1987), p. 21-23. Spanish. DESCR: Chicanas; *Criminal Acts.

4383 Hoffman, Abraham. Book review of: AN ILLUSTRATED HISTORY OF MEXICAN LOS ANGELES: 1781-1985. NEW MEXICO HISTORICAL REVIEW, Vol. 62, no. 4 (October 1987), p. 412-13. English. DESCR: *AN ILLUSTRATED HISTORY OF MEXICAN LOS ANGELES: 1781-1985; Book Reviews; *Castillo, Pedro; *Rios-Bustamante, Antonio.

4384 Lopez, Jose Y. Chico Sesma: a man and his music. LATIN QUARTER, Vol. 1, no. 4 (July, August, 1975), p. 10-15. English. DESCR: Chico Sesma Radio Show; *Radio; Salsa; *Sesma, Chico.

4385 Los Angeles: arriba! ECONOMIST (London), Vol. 297, no. 7424 (December 14, 1985), p. 26. English. DESCR: Bradley, Tom; Political Representation; Politics; Reapportionment; Voter Turnout.

Los Angeles, CA (cont.)

4386 Los Angeles: brown versus yellow. ECONOMIST (London), Vol. 300, no. 7456 (July 26, 1986), p. 21-22. English. **DESCR:** Alatorre, Richard; Bradley, Tom; Ethnic Groups; Political Representation; Politics; Reapportionment; Voter Turnout; Woo, Michael.

4387 Monroy, Douglas. Book review of: IN DEFENSE OF LA RAZA. WESTERN HISTORICAL QUARTERLY, Vol. 15, no. 3 (July 1984), p. 331-332. English. **DESCR:** *Balderrama, Francisco E.; Book Reviews; IN DEFENSE OF LA RAZA: THE LOS ANGELES MEXICAN CONSULATE AND THE MEXICAN COMMUNITY.

4388 Monroy, Douglas. [Letter responding to Mario Garcia's comments]. LABOR HISTORY, Vol. 25, no. 1 (Winter 1984), p. 155-156. English. **DESCR:** *Communism; *Garcia, Mario T.; History; *Labor Unions.

4389 Perez, Renato E. Badge of Hispanic pride. VISTA, Vol. 1, no. 12 (August 2, 1986), p. 9-11. English. **DESCR:** Broward County, FL; Chicago, IL; Dallas, TX; Houston, TX; New York, NY; *Police; San Antonio, TX; San Diego, CA; Tucson, AZ.

4390 Plowman, Edward E. Hispanic Christians in the United States. CHRISTIANITY TODAY, Vol. 30, no. 1 (January 17, 1986), p. 44-45. English. **DESCR:** *Hispanic Congress on Evangelization (HCE); Protestant Church; Religion.

4391 Sanchez Tranquilino, Marcos. Un ensayo sobre la representacion del ZOOT SUIT en la obra de Octavio Paz. LA COMUNIDAD, No. 355 (May 10, 1987), p. 4-7+. Spanish. **DESCR:** *Pachucos; *Paz, Octavio; Sleepy Lagoon Case; THE LABYRINTH OF SOLITUDE: LIFE AND THOUGHT IN MEXICO; Zoot Suit Riots, Los Angeles, CA, 1943.

4392 Seal, Kathy. La pintura del barrio. LA COMUNIDAD, No. 266 (August 25, 1985), p. 13. Spanish. **DESCR:** *Mural Art; Pule, Benny.

4393 Silva-Corvalan, Carmen. Bilingualism and language change: the extension of estar in Los Angeles Spanish. LANGUAGE, Vol. 62, no. 3 (September 1986), p. 587-608. English. **DESCR:** Bilingualism; Language Interference; *Language Usage; *Linguistics.

4394 Sonenshein, Raphe. Biracial coalition politics in Los Angeles. P.S. [AMERICAN POLITICAL SCIENCE ASSOCIATION], Vol. 19, no. 3 (Summer 1986), p. 582-590. English. **DESCR:** Blacks; Bradley, Tom; Browning, Rufus P.; *Ethnic Groups; *Intergroup Relations; Marshall, Dale Rogers; Political Parties and Organizations; *Politics; PROTEST IS NOT ENOUGH: THE STRUGGLE OF BLACKS AND HISPANICS FOR EQUALITY IN URBAN POLITICS; Tabb, David H.

4395 Valdes, Dennis. Book review of: THE LOS ANGELES BARRIO 1850-1890: A SOCIAL HISTORY. LA RED/THE NET, no. 36 (November 1980), p. 5. English. **DESCR:** Book Reviews; Griswold del Castillo, Richard; History; *Social History and Conditions; *THE LOS ANGELES BARRIO 1850-1890: A SOCIAL HISTORY.

4396 Yepes, Maria Elena. Lady bugs. LATIN QUARTER, Vol. 1, no. 4 (July, August, 1975), p. 28-31. English. **DESCR:** *Car Clubs; Chicanas; *Lady Bugs [car club].

Los Angeles County, CA

4397 Hoffman, Abraham. The controversial career of Martin Aguirre; the rise and fall of a Chicano lawman. CALIFORNIA HISTORY, Vol. 63, no. 4 (Fall 1984), p. 295-341. English. **DESCR:** *Aguirre, Martin; *Biography; History; Prisoners; San Quentin Prison.

Los Angeles Police Department

4398 Escobar, Edward J. Mexican revolutionaries and the Los Angeles police: harassment of the Partido Liberal Mexicano, 1907-1910. AZTLAN, Vol. 17, no. 1 (Spring 1986), p. 1-46. English. **DESCR:** Civil Rights; *Flores Magon, Ricardo; Gutierrez de Lara, Lazaro; Los Angeles, CA; *Partido Liberal Mexicano (PLM); *Police; Police Brutality; Political Repression; Rico, Louis; Rico, Thomas; Talamantes, Felipe; United States-Mexico Relations.

Los Angeles Theatre Center (LATC)

4399 Lomeli, Maria Magdalena S. "LATC" un espacio para el teatro politico. LA COMUNIDAD, No. 333 (December 7, 1986), p. 10-11. Spanish. **DESCR:** Actors and Actresses; Morales, Esai; *Teatro.

Los Pinos, NM

4400 Miller, Darlis A. Los Pinos, New Mexico: civil war post on the Rio Grande. NEW MEXICO HISTORICAL REVIEW, Vol. 62, no. 1 (January 1987), p. 1-31. English. **DESCR:** History; *New Mexico; *Rio Grande; *Southwestern United States.

Los Robles, Cuernavaca, Morelos, Mexico

4401 LeVine, Sarah Ethel; Correa, Clara Sunderland; and Uribe, F. Medardo Tapia. The marital morality of Mexican women--an urban study. JOURNAL OF ANTHROPOLOGICAL RESEARCH, Vol. 42, no. 2 (Summer 1986), p. 183-202. English. **DESCR:** Family; *Machismo; Marriage; Parent and Child Relationships; *Sex Roles; *Women Men Relations.

THE LOST LAND: THE CHICANO IMAGE OF THE SOUTHWEST

4402 Almaraz, Felix D., Jr. Book review of: THE LOST LAND. ARIZONA AND THE WEST, Vol. 28, no. 1 (Spring 1986), p. 81-82. English. **DESCR:** Book Reviews; Chavez, John R.

4403 Crisp, James E. Book review of: THE LOST LAND. JOURNAL OF SOUTHERN HISTORY, Vol. 51, no. 4 (November 1985), p. 660-661. English. **DESCR:** Book Reviews; Chavez, John R.

4404 de Leon, Arnoldo. Book review of: THE LOST LAND. SOUTHWESTERN HISTORICAL QUARTERLY, Vol. 89, no. 1 (1985), p. 96-98. English. **DESCR:** Book Reviews; Chavez, John R.

4405 Paredes, Raymund A. Book review of: THE LOST LAND. WESTERN AMERICAN LITERATURE, Vol. 21, no. 2 (1986), p. 135. English. **DESCR:** Book Reviews; Chavez, John R.

"El Louie" [poem]

4406 Bruce-Novoa, Juan. Elegias a la frontera hispanica. BILINGUAL REVIEW, Vol. 11, no. 3 (September, December, 1984), p. 37-44. Spanish. **DESCR:** *LAS COPLAS A LA MUERTE DE SU PADRE; Literary Criticism; Manrique, Jorge; Montoya, Jose E.; Poetry.

Lovato, Alberto

4407 Atencio, Tomas. No estan todos los que son,
no son todos los que estan. EL CUADERNO,
Vol. 4, no. 1 (Summer 1976), p. 51-61.
Spanish. DESCR: Arellano, Estevan;
*Identity; *La Academia de la Nueva Raza,
Dixon, NM; Martinez, Vicente; Roybal, Luis.

Low Income

4408 Schreiner, Tim. West: poor Hispanics.
AMERICAN DEMOGRAPHICS, Vol. 9, no. 3 (March
1987), p. 54. English. DESCR: *Poverty.

Lower Class
USE: Social Classes

Lozano, Conrad (Los Lobos)

4409 Forte, Dan. Los Lobos: Tex-Mex rock from
East L.A. GUITAR PLAYER, Vol. 21, no. 2
(February 1987), p. 68-94. English. DESCR:
Biography; Discography; Hidalgo, David (Los
Lobos); *Los Lobos del Este de Los Angeles
(musical group); *Musicians; Perez, Louie
(Los Lobos); Recording Industry; *Rock
Music; Rosas, Cesar (Los Lobos).

Lozano, Ignacio

4410 Arreola, Daniel D. The Mexican American
cultural capital. GEOGRAPHICAL REVIEW, Vol.
77, (January 1987), p. 17-34. English.
DESCR: Conjuntos; Food Industry; History;
Immigration; LA PRENSA, San Antonio, TX; La
Raza Unida Party; League of United Latin
American Citizens (LULAC); Mexican American
Youth Organization, San Antonio, TX; Music;
Orden Hijos de America, San Antonio, TX;
Railroads; *San Antonio, TX; *Social History
and Conditions.

The Lucerne Memorial

4411 Stevens-Arroyo, Antonio M. Cahensly
revisited?: the National Pastoral Encounter
of America's Hispanic Catholics. MIGRATION
WORLD MAGAZINE, Vol. 15, no. 3 (1987), p.
16-19. English. DESCR: *Catholic Church;
Clergy; *National Hispanic Pastoral
Encounter.

LULAC National Scholarship Fund

4412 Chavez, Lorenzo A. A brief guide to
financial aid for college-bound students.
VISTA, Vol. 2, no. 1 (September 7, 1986), p.
7. English. DESCR: Directories; *Financial
Aid; MALDEF Law School Fellowship; National
Hispanic Scholar Awards Program; *National
Hispano Scholarship Fund.

Las Lunas Vocational Training School

4413 Wroth, William. New hope in hard times:
Hispanic crafts are revived during troubled
years. PALACIO, Vol. 89, no. 2 (1983), p.
22-31. English. DESCR: *Arts and Crafts; New
Mexico; Spanish Colonial Arts Society; Taos
Vocational School; Works Progress
Administration (WPA).

Machado, Antonio

4414 Mares, E.A. Homenaje a Antonio Machado. EL
CUADERNO, Vol. 4, no. 1 (Summer 1976), p.
30. Spanish. DESCR: *Poems.

Machado [family name]

4415 Instituto Genealogico e Historico
Latino-Americano. Rootsearch: Padron:
Machado. VISTA, Vol. 2, no. 1 (September 7,
1986), p. 22. English. DESCR: Genealogy;
History; *Padron [family name]; *Personal
Names.

Machismo

4416 Bruce-Novoa, Juan. Homosexuality and the
Chicano novel. CONFLUENCIA, Vol. 2, no. 1
(Fall 1986), p. 69-77. English. DESCR:
Acosta, Oscar Zeta; CITY OF NIGHT; FAULTLINE
[novel]; *Homosexuality; Islas, Arturo;
*Literary Criticism; *Novel; Ortiz Taylor,
Sheila; POCHO; Rechy, John; Salas, Floyd;
SPRING FORWARD/FALL BACK; TATOO THE WICKED
CROSS; THE AUTOBIOGRAPHY OF A BROWN BUFFALO;
THE RAIN GOD: A DESERT TALE; THE REVOLT OF
THE COCKROACH PEOPLE; Villarreal, Jose
Antonio.

4417 Engle, Patricia L.; Scrimshaw, Susan C.M.;
and Smidt, Robert. Sex differences in
attitudes towards newborn infants among
women of Mexican origin. MEDICAL
ANTHROPOLOGY, Vol. 8, no. 2 (Spring 1984),
p. 133-144. English. DESCR: *Attitudes;
Chicanas; Cultural Characteristics;
*Maternal and Child Welfare; *Parent and
Child Relationships; Sex Roles.

4418 LeVine, Sarah Ethel; Correa, Clara
Sunderland; and Uribe, F. Medardo Tapia. The
marital morality of Mexican women--an urban
study. JOURNAL OF ANTHROPOLOGICAL RESEARCH,
Vol. 42, no. 2 (Summer 1986), p. 183-202.
English. DESCR: Family; Los Robles,
Cuernavaca, Morelos, Mexico; Marriage;
Parent and Child Relationships; *Sex Roles;
*Women Men Relations.

4419 Ybarra, Lea. Empirical and theoretical
developments in the study of Chicano
families. LA RED/THE NET, no. 52 (March
1982), p. 7-9. English. DESCR: *Family.

Macias, Reynaldo F.

4420 Latino literacy update: Tomas Rivera Center
focuses on illiteracy. LA RED/THE NET, no.
95 (April 1986), p. 10-12. English. DESCR:
Latino Literacy Project, Tomas Rivera
Center, Claremont, CA; *Literacy; *Tomas
Rivera Center, Claremont, CA.

Maciel, David

4421 Fernandez, Celestino. Book review of: LA
CLASE OBRERA EN LA HISTORIA DE MEXICO: AL
NORTE DEL RIO BRAVO (PASADO INMEDIATO,
1930-1981). NEW MEXICO HISTORICAL REVIEW,
Vol. 59, no. 2 (April 1984), p. 214-215.
English. DESCR: Book Reviews; *LA CLASE
OBRERA EN LA HISTORIA DE MEXICO: AL NORTE
DEL RIO BRAVO (PASADO INMEDIATO, 1930-1981);
Laboring Classes.

4422 Griswold del Castillo, Richard. New
perspectives on the Mexican and American
borderlands. LATIN AMERICAN RESEARCH REVIEW,
Vol. 19, no. 1 (1984), p. 199-209. English.
DESCR: AL NORTE DEL RIO BRAVO (PASADO
INMEDIATO, 1930-1981); AL NORTE DEL RIO
BRAVO (PASADO LEJANO, 1600-1930); *Book
Reviews; *Border Region; Gomez-Quinones,
Juan; MEXICANO RESISTANCE IN THE SOUTHWEST:
"THE SACRED RIGHT OF SELF-PRESERVATION";
Rosenbaum, Robert J.; THE MEXICAN FRONTIER,
1821-1846: THE AMERICAN SOUTHWEST UNDER
MEXICO; THE TEJANO COMMUNITY, 1836-1900;
Weber, David J.

Maciel, David (cont.)

4423 Zamora, Emilio. Book review of: LA CLASE OBRERA EN LA HISTORIA DE MEXICO: AL NORTE DEL RIO BRAVO (PASADO INMEDIATO, 1930-1981). LA RED/THE NET, no. 70 (July 1983), p. 13-17. English. **DESCR**: Book Reviews; *LA CLASE OBRERA EN LA HISTORIA DE MEXICO: AL NORTE DEL RIO BRAVO (PASADO INMEDIATO, 1930-1981).

MacKenzie, Kyle

4424 Ruiz, Ivette M. Resena testimonial. REVISTA MUJERES, Vol. 1, no. 2 (June 1984), p. 7-10. English. **DESCR**: Book Reviews; Chicanas; Elsasser, Nan; *LAS MUJERES: CONVERSATIONS FROM A HISPANIC COMMUNITY; Tixier y Vigil, Yvonne.

4425 Ybarra, Lea. Book review of: LAS MUJERES: CONVERSATIONS FROM A HISPANIC COMMUNITY. LA RED/THE NET, no. 58 (September 1982), p. 5-6. English. **DESCR**: Book Reviews; *Chicanas; *Elsasser, Nan; *LAS MUJERES: CONVERSATIONS FROM A HISPANIC COMMUNITY; New Mexico; Tixier y Vigil, Yvonne.

MAD Magazine

4426 Padilla, Steve. The mad mad world of Sergio Aragones. VISTA, Vol. 2, no. 5 (January 4, 1987), p. 6-8. English. **DESCR**: Aragones, Sergio; Artists; Drawings; *Humor.

Madrid, Arturo

4427 Dellinger, Robert W. Hispanic think tank. VISTA, Vol. 3, no. 3 (November 8, 1987), p. 28. English. **DESCR**: *Public Policy; Research Centers; *Tomas Rivera Center, Claremont, CA.

LA MADRUGADA

4428 Atencio, Tomas. La resolana [editorial]. EL CUADERNO, Vol. 4, no. 1 (Summer 1976), p. 2-4. English. **DESCR**: Academia Asociados, NM; Academia Educational Model; *Chicano Studies; Culture; EL CUADERNO; ENTRE VERDE Y SECO; *La Academia de la Nueva Raza, Dixon, NM; Publishing Industry.

Maestas, Roberto

4429 Flores, Lauro. Book review of: EL PUEBLO: THE GALLEGOS FAMILY'S JOURNEY 1503-1980. MINNESOTA REVIEW, no. 22 (1984), p. 145-148. English. **DESCR**: Book Reviews; Bruce-Novoa, Juan; *CHICANO POETRY: A RESPONSE TO CHAOS; *EL PUEBLO: THE GALLEGOS FAMILY'S AMERICAN JOURNEY 1503-1980; *FAMOUS ALL OVER TOWN; James, Dan; Johansen, Bruce.

La Mafia [musical group]

4430 La Mafia signs Pepsi contract. NUESTRO, Vol. 11, no. 4 (May 1987), p. 8-9. English. **DESCR**: Advertising; Musicians; Pepsi-Cola Bottling Group; Rock Music.

Magazines

4431 Levin, Gary. Publisher seeks to improve "image". ADVERTISING AGE MAGAZINE, Vol. 57, no. 43 (August 11, 1986), p. S25-S27. English. **DESCR**: Advertising; Asencio, John; English Language; *HISPANIC IMAGE; Spanish Language.

4432 Norris, Eileen. Print suffers in tale of two languages. ADVERTISING AGE MAGAZINE, Vol. 57, no. 16 (February 27, 1986), p. 49-51. English. **DESCR**: Advertising; Chavarria,

Jesus; English Language; HISPANIC BUSINESS; LATINA [magazine]; Soto, Grace; Spanish Language; Villar, Arturo; VISTA [magazine].

4433 Shoemaker, Pamela J.; Reese, Stephen D.; and Danielson, Wayne A. Spanish-language print media use as an indicator of acculturation. JOURNALISM QUARTERLY, Vol. 62, no. 4 (Winter 1985), p. 734-740. English. **DESCR**: *Acculturation; Newspapers; *Print Media; *Spanish Language.

Magdalena de Kino, Mexico

4434 Griffith, James S. The Magdalena holy picture: religious folk art in two cultures. NEW YORK FOLKLORE QUARTERLY, Vol. 8, no. 3-4 (Winter 1982), p. 71-82. English. **DESCR**: Folk Art; *Religious Art.

Magic of Science and Engineering Program

4435 Ricardo Salazar. HISPANIC ENGINEER, Vol. 3, no. 2 (Summer), p. 14-18. English. **DESCR**: Biography; Professional Organizations; *Salazar, Ricardo; Society of Hispanic Professional Engineers Northern California Chapter.

Magical realism

4436 Bartlett, Catherine Vallejos. Magical realism: the Latin American influence on modern Chicano writers. CONFLUENCIA, Vol. 1, no. 2 (Spring 1986), p. 27-37. English. **DESCR**: Arias, Ron; Authors; Garcia Marquez, Gabriel; Latin America; *Literary Criticism; *Literary Influence; *Literature; ONE HUNDRED YEARS OF SOLITUDE; Rivera, Tomas; THE ROAD TO TAMAZUNCHALE; Y NO SE LO TRAGO LA TIERRA/AND THE EARTH DID NOT PART.

Maidique, Mitch

4437 Mellado, Carmela. Mitch Maidique. HISPANIC ENGINEER, Vol. 3, no. 5 (Winter 1987), p. 34-36. English. **DESCR**: *Biography; Educational Administration; Florida International University.

Maine v. Thornton

4438 Search and seizure. CRIMINAL LAW REPORTER, Vol. 35, no. 3 (April 18, 1984), p. 3011-3027. English. **DESCR**: Hester v. U.S.; INS v. Delgado; Katz v. U.S.; Oliver v. U.S.; *Search and Seizure; *U.S. Supreme Court.

Majka, Linda C.

4439 Gonzales, Juan L., Jr. Book review of: FARM WORKERS, AGRIBUSINESS, AND THE STATE. LABOR HISTORY, Vol. 27, no. 4 (Fall 1986), p. 587-588. English. **DESCR**: Book Reviews; Farm Workers; *FARMWORKERS, AGRIBUSINESS, AND THE STATE; Majka, Theo J.

4440 Reisler, Mark. Book review of: FARM WORKERS, AGRIBUSINESS, AND THE STATE. PACIFIC HISTORICAL REVIEW, Vol. 53, no. 3 (1984), p. 405-407. English. **DESCR**: Book Reviews; *FARMWORKERS, AGRIBUSINESS, AND THE STATE; Majka, Theo J.

Majka, Theo J.

4441 Gonzales, Juan L., Jr. Book review of: FARM WORKERS, AGRIBUSINESS, AND THE STATE. LABOR HISTORY, Vol. 27, no. 4 (Fall 1986), p. 587-588. English. **DESCR**: Book Reviews; Farm Workers; *FARMWORKERS, AGRIBUSINESS, AND THE STATE; Majka, Linda C.

Majka, Theo J. (cont.)

4442 Reisler, Mark. Book review of: FARM WORKERS, AGRIBUSINESS, AND THE STATE. PACIFIC HISTORICAL REVIEW, Vol. 53, no. 3 (1984), p. 405-407. English. **DESCR:** Book Reviews; *FARMWORKERS, AGRIBUSINESS, AND THE STATE; Majka, Linda C.

Make up
USE: Fashion

Malagamba, Francisco

4443 Woods, Richard D. Book review of: MEXICO-ESTADOS UNIDOS: BIBLIOGRAFIA GENERAL SOBRE ESTUDIOS FRONTERIZOS. LA RED/THE NET, no. 49 (December 1981), p. 4-5. English. **DESCR:** Book Reviews; Border Studies; *Bustamante, Jorge A.; *MEXICO-ESTADOS UNIDOS: BIBLIOGRAFIA GENERAL SOBRE ESTUDIOS FRONTERIZOS; Reference Works.

MALDEF Law School Fellowship

4444 Chavez, Lorenzo A. A brief guide to financial aid for college-bound students. VISTA, Vol. 2, no. 1 (September 7, 1986), p. 7. English. **DESCR:** Directories; *Financial Aid; LULAC National Scholarship Fund; National Hispanic Scholar Awards Program; *National Hispano Scholarship Fund.

Maldonado, Lionel

4445 Alexander, June Granatir. Book review of: URBAN ETHNICITY IN THE UNITED STATES. JOURNAL OF AMERICAN ETHNIC HISTORY, Vol. 7, no. 1 (Fall 1987), p. 95-97. English. **DESCR:** Book Reviews; Immigrants; Moore, Joan W.; *URBAN ETHNICITY IN THE UNITED STATES: NEW IMMIGRANTS AND OLD MINORITIES.

Male and Female Roles
USE: Sex Roles

Males

4446 Angel, Ronald. The economic cost of chronic health limitations for Hispanic males. LA RED/THE NET, no. 61 (November 1982), p. 2-3. English. **DESCR:** *Medical Care.

4447 Chiswick, Barry R. The labor market status of Hispanic men. JOURNAL OF AMERICAN ETHNIC HISTORY, Vol. 7, no. 1 (Fall 1987), p. 30-58. English. **DESCR:** Census; Discrimination in Employment; *Employment; Ethnic Groups; Income; *Labor Supply and Market; Language Usage; *Undocumented Workers.

4448 Neff, James Alan; Hoppe, Sue K.; and Perea, Patricia. Acculturation and alcohol use: drinking patterns and problems among Anglo and Mexican American male drinkers. HISPANIC JOURNAL OF BEHAVIORAL SCIENCES, Vol. 9, no. 2 (June 1987), p. 151-181. English. **DESCR:** *Acculturation; Age Groups; *Alcoholism; Anglo Americans; Stress.

4449 Valdez, William J. Impotence: a problem with a solution. NUESTRO, Vol. 11, no. 4 (May 1987), p. 18-20. English. **DESCR:** Centro de Impotencia, Coral Gables Hospital, Miami, FL; Diseases; *Impotence; Medical Clinics; *Psychotherapy.

4450 Verdugo, Naomi and Verdugo, Richard. Income differentials between Chicano and white male workers. LA RED/THE NET, no. 57 (August 1982), p. 2-3. English. **DESCR:** Anglo Americans; Employment; *Income; Laboring Classes.

Malibu, CA

4451 Gutierrez, Silvio G. On wings of mercy. VISTA, Vol. 2, no. 3 (November 2, 1986), p. 17-18. English. **DESCR:** Angel Flight; *Emergency Services; Medical Care; *Torres, Averi; Torres, Dennis; Transportation.

Malinche

4452 Limon, Jose E. La Llorona, the third legend of greater Mexico: cultural symbols, women, and the political unconscious. RENATO ROSALDO LECTURE SERIES MONOGRAPH, Vol. 2, (Spring 1986), p. [59]-93. English. **DESCR:** *Feminism; Folklore; *La Llorona; La Virgen de Guadalupe; *Leyendas; Mexico; *Symbolism; Women.

4453 Soto, Shirlene. La Malinche: 16th century leader. INTERCAMBIOS FEMENILES, Vol. 2, no. 6 (Spring 1987), p. 13. English. **DESCR:** Chicanas; Leadership.

4454 Yarbro-Bejarano, Yvonne. The female subject in Chicano theater: sexuality, race, and class. THEATRE JOURNAL, Vol. 38, no. 4 (December 1986), p. 389-407. English. **DESCR:** *Chicanas; El Teatro Campesino; El Teatro de la Esperanza; Feminism; *Sex Roles; *Teatro; Teatro Nacional de Aztlan (TENAZ); WIT (Women in Teatro).

Malintzin Tenepal
USE: Malinche

MAN, LAND, AND WATER: MEXICO'S FARMLAND IRRIGATION POLICIES, 1885-1911

4455 Albert, Bill. Book review of: MAN, LAND, AND WATER: MEXICO'S FARMLAND IRRIGATION POLICIES, 1885-1911. HISTORY - REVIEWS OF NEW BOOKS, Vol. 71, (October 1986), p. 482-483. English. **DESCR:** Book Reviews; Kroeber, Clifton R.

Management

4456 Baker, George A. and Rocha, Pedro, Jr. Critical incident competencies of Mexican American and Anglo American administrators. COMMUNITY/JUNIOR COLLEGE QUARTERLY OF RESEARCH AND PRACTICE, Vol. 7, no. 4 (July, September, 1983), p. 319-332. English. **DESCR:** Anglo Americans; *Community Colleges; Comparative Psychology; Cultural Characteristics; Educational Administration; Public Policy.

4457 Beale, Stephen. CEOs. HISPANIC BUSINESS, Vol. 9, no. 4 (April 1987), p. 20-37, 52. English. **DESCR:** Alvarez, Roberto; Batarse, Anthony A.; Biography; Business Enterprises; *Businesspeople; Carlo, Nelson; Estrada, Anthony; Flores, Frank; Fullana, Jaime, Jr.; Hernandez, George; Ortega, James; Quirch, Guillermo; Ruiz, Roberto; Santa Maria, Yvonne Z.; Sugranes, Rosa; Tamaya, Carlos; Young, Paul H., Jr.

4458 Beale, Stephen. Inertia in the corporate boardroom. HISPANIC BUSINESS, Vol. 9, no. 8 (August 1987), p. 9-11. English. **DESCR:** *Businesspeople; *Corporations.

4459 Garcia, Philip J. Ready to go on board? HISPANIC BUSINESS, Vol. 9, no. 5 (May 1987), p. 17. English. **DESCR:** *Businesspeople; *Careers; *Corporations.

Management (cont.)

4460 Hunsaker, Alan C. Contingency management with Chicano adolescents in a federal manpower program. CORRECTIVE AND SOCIAL PSYCHIATRY, Vol. 30, no. 1 (1984), p. 10-13. English. DESCR: *Employment; *Manpower Programs; Psychology; *Youth.

4461 Sellers, Jeff M. Challenging the myth of the traditional woman. HISPANIC BUSINESS, Vol. 9, no. 8 (August 1987), p. 15-16, 48. English. DESCR: *Businesspeople; *Careers; *Chicanas; National Network of Hispanic Women; Sex Roles; Torres, Celia; Women; Zambrana, Ruth.

4462 Sellers, Jeff M. Missed opportunities. HISPANIC BUSINESS, Vol. 9, no. 4 (April 1987), p. 14-15. English. DESCR: *Border Industries; *Intergroup Relations; Language Usage; Mexico.

4463 Sellers, Jeff M. State of the art recruitment: competition for blue-chip Hispanic business graduates is fierce and expensive. HISPANIC BUSINESS, Vol. 9, no. 2 (February 1987), p. 22-25, 57. English. DESCR: *Business Administration; *Careers; College Graduates; Colleges and Universities; Enrollment.

Manpower Programs

4464 Hunsaker, Alan C. Contingency management with Chicano adolescents in a federal manpower program. CORRECTIVE AND SOCIAL PSYCHIATRY, Vol. 30, no. 1 (1984), p. 10-13. English. DESCR: *Employment; *Management; Psychology; *Youth.

Manrique, Jorge

4465 Bruce-Novoa, Juan. Elegias a la frontera hispanica. BILINGUAL REVIEW, Vol. 11, no. 3 (September, December, 1984), p. 37-44. Spanish. DESCR: *"El Louie" [poem]; *LAS COPLAS A LA MUERTE DE SU PADRE; Literary Criticism; Montoya, Jose E.; Poetry.

Maquiladoras

USE: Border Industries

Maravilla

4466 Eisen, Marvin. Working for positive change in the barrio. LATIN QUARTER, Vol. 1, no. 1 (July 1974), p. 8-10. English. DESCR: Counseling (Educational); *East Los Angeles Skills Center; *Gangs.

Mariachi Rebeldes del Sur

4467 Douthat, Bill. Mariachi magic. VISTA, Vol. 2, no. 4 (December 7, 1986), p. 18. English. DESCR: Austin, TX; *Castro, Zeke; *Mariachis; Music; Secondary School Education.

Mariachis

4468 Douthat, Bill. Mariachi magic. VISTA, Vol. 2, no. 4 (December 7, 1986), p. 18. English. DESCR: Austin, TX; *Castro, Zeke; Mariachi Rebeldes del Sur; Music; Secondary School Education.

Marijuanos

USE: Drug Addicts

Marin, Richard "Cheech"

4469 Guevara, Ruben. Richard "Cheech" Marin. AMERICAS 2001, Vol. 1, no. 1 (June, July, 1987), p. 18-21. Bilingual. DESCR: *Actors and Actresses; *BORN IN EAST L.A. [film]; Films; Immigration; Undocumented Workers.

Mario's Restaurant, San Antonio, TX

4470 Marambio, Gonzalo. From San Antonio to Paris: Tex-Mex food conquers the French. VISTA, Vol. 1, no. 6 (February 2, 1986), p. 18-20. English. DESCR: Business Enterprises; Cantu, Mario, Jr.; *Food Practices; Gonzales, Teresa; Papa Maya's Restaurant, Paris, France.

Marketing

4471 Arizona Bank targets Hispanic market. ABA BANKING JOURNAL, Vol. 77, no. 4 (April 1985), p. 30, 32. English. DESCR: *Arizona Bank, Phoenix, AZ; *Banking Industry.

4472 Balkan, D. Carlos. The Hispanic market's leading indicators. HISPANIC BUSINESS, Vol. 9, no. 12 (December 1987), p. 16-17. English. DESCR: Advertising; Population; Statistics.

4473 Beale, Stephen. The Maxwell House that Marlboro bought. HISPANIC BUSINESS, Vol. 9, no. 2 (February 1987), p. 20-21, 60. English. DESCR: Advertising; Business Enterprises; Corporations; *Philip Morris, Inc.

4474 Beale, Stephen. A turning point in Hollywood. HISPANIC BUSINESS, Vol. 9, no. 7 (July 1987), p. 20-24, 36. English. DESCR: *Films; LA BAMBA [film]; Spanish Language; Stereotypes; THE MILAGRO BEANFIELD WAR [film].

4475 Berling-Manuel, Lynn. Expanding radio market battles research static. ADVERTISING AGE MAGAZINE, Vol. 57, no. 43 (August 11, 1986), p. S12-S16. English. DESCR: Arbitron; *Radio; Spanish Language; WADO-AM, New York, NY [radio station]; WAQI-AM, Miami, FL [radio station]; WOJO-FM, Chicago, IL [radio station].

4476 DelPriore, Lisa. Tapping into the Hispanic market. MARKETING COMMUNICATIONS, Vol. 11, no. 6 (June 1986), p. 57-62. English. DESCR: *Advertising; *Consumers; *Mass Media.

4477 Drive away with $5.2 billion. HISPANIC BUSINESS, Vol. 9, no. 9 (September 1987), p. 71. English. DESCR: *Automobile Industry; *Consumers.

4478 Edmondson, Brad. Met Life mines minority market. AMERICAN DEMOGRAPHICS, Vol. 8, no. 7 (July 1986), p. 18-19. English. DESCR: Consumers; Ethnic Groups; Immigrants; Insurance; *Metropolitan Life Insurance Corporation.

4479 Fernandez, Castor A. Differences within the Hispanic market. TELEVISION/RADIO AGE, Vol. 31, (December 19, 1983), p. 105. English.

4480 Fitch, Ed. Buying power bursts poverty-stricken image. ADVERTISING AGE MAGAZINE, Vol. 58, no. 6 (February 9, 1987), p. S1-S2, S8. English. DESCR: Advertising; Consumers.

4481 Fitch, Ed. Census bureau tries to clean up its act. ADVERTISING AGE MAGAZINE, Vol. 57, no. 43 (August 11, 1986), p. S18-S20. English. DESCR: Census; *U.S. Bureau of the Census.

Marketing (cont.)

4482 Fitch, Ed. Paving way for national ad sales. ADVERTISING AGE MAGAZINE, Vol. 57, no. 16 (February 27, 1986), p. 50-51. English. **DESCR:** *Advertising; Newspapers.

4483 Fitch, Ed. Prime space available at low rates. ADVERTISING AGE MAGAZINE, Vol. 57, no. 16 (February 27, 1986), p. 11-12. English. **DESCR:** Advertising; Consumers; General Foods.

4484 Guedella, Juan. Hispanic media--Caballero style. HISPANIC BUSINESS, Vol. 9, no. 2 (February 1987), p. 17-18. English. **DESCR:** Advertising; Biography; *Caballero, Eduardo; *Caballero Spanish Media (CSM); Cubanos.

4485 The Hispanic market: an untapped resource. CHAIN STORE AGE SUPERMARKET, Vol. 59, no. 6 (June 1983), p. 41. English. **DESCR:** Business Enterprises; Consumers.

4486 Hispanic marketing. ADVERTISING AGE MAGAZINE, Vol. 57, no. 16 (February 27, 1986), p. 11-51. English. **DESCR:** Adolph Coors Co.; Advertising; Allstate Insurance Co.; American Greetings; Anheuser-Busch, Inc.; Business Enterprises; Coca-Cola Company; Consumers; Ford Motor Company; Hallmark Cards; Mass Media; McDonald's Corporation; Metropolitan Life Insurance Corporation; Pepsi-Cola Bottling Group; Prudential; Spanish International Network (SIN); State Farm Mutual Insurance; Tylenol; United Insurance Co. of America.

4487 Jacobson, Harold. Upward trend in expenditures continues. HISPANIC BUSINESS, Vol. 9, no. 12 (December 1987), p. 19-20. English. **DESCR:** *Advertising; Consumers; Income; Mass Media.

4488 Kane, Michael G. "Touching" minorities. EDITOR & PUBLISHER: THE FOURTH ESTATE, Vol. 119, no. 38 (September 20, 1986), p. 20-21. English. **DESCR:** Advertising; Consumers; Ethnic Groups; *Newspapers.

4489 Kesler, Lori. A-B benefits from regional approach. ADVERTISING AGE MAGAZINE, Vol. 57, no. 16 (February 27, 1986), p. 48-49. English. **DESCR:** Advertising; Anheuser-Busch, Inc.; Consumers.

4490 Lawrence, Jennifer. TV signal expected to boost Houston market. ADVERTISING AGE MAGAZINE, Vol. 57, no. 43 (August 11, 1986), p. S24-S25. English. **DESCR:** Advertising; Houston, TX; *KXLN, Houston, TX [television station]; Pueblo Broadcasting Corp.; Spanish Language; Television.

4491 Macias, Reynaldo Flores and Cabello-Argandona, Roberto. Media research and the Chicano. LATIN QUARTER, Vol. 1, no. 2 (October 1974), p. 14-16,18. English. **DESCR:** Advertising; Consumers; *Mass Media; Population.

4492 Magiera, Marcy. New arrivals find warm welcome as consumers. ADVERTISING AGE MAGAZINE, Vol. 58, no. 6 (February 9, 1987), p. S14. English. **DESCR:** Consumers; Immigrants; Undocumented Workers.

4493 Marketing to Hispanics. ADVERTISING AGE MAGAZINE, Vol. 57, no. 43 (August 11, 1986), p. 51-528. English. **DESCR:** Advertising; Broadcast Media; De Armas Publications; Kinney Shoe Corp.; Pepsi-Cola Bottling Group; Print Media; Spanish International Network (SIN); U.S. Bureau of the Census.

4494 Marketing to Hispanics. ADVERTISING AGE MAGAZINE, Vol. 58, no. 6 (February 9, 1987), p. S1-S23. English. **DESCR:** Advertising; Consumers; Immigrants; Mass Media; Politics; Undocumented Workers.

4495 Marketing to U.S. Hispanics. ADVERTISING WORLD, no. 6 (December 1983), p. 26-27. English. **DESCR:** *Conferences and Meetings; Mass Media.

4496 Moya, Steven. Foreign relations: implementing an Hispanic marketing program. S & MM [SALES & MARKETING MANAGEMENT], Vol. 135, no. 2 (July 22, 1985), p. A22+. English. **DESCR:** *Consumers; *Public Relations.

4497 Poole, Claire. Viewers looking for the U.S. look. HISPANIC BUSINESS, Vol. 9, no. 12 (December 1987), p. 26-28. English. **DESCR:** *Advertising; Advertising Agencies; Telemundo Television Group; *Television.

4498 Raffio, Ralph. Del Taco targets adult audience. RESTAURANT BUSINESS, Vol. 84, (April 10, 1985), p. 260-264. English. **DESCR:** *Del Taco Restaurants; *Restaurants.

4499 Reilly, Michael D. and Wallendorf, Melanie. A longitudinal study of Mexican-American assimilation. ADVANCES IN CONSUMER RESEARCH, Vol. 11, (1984), p. 735-740. English. **DESCR:** *Assimilation; *Consumers; Culture; Food Practices.

4500 Rifkin, Jane M. Courting the Latino market. HISPANIC TIMES, Vol. 8, no. 1 (December, January, 1987), p. 49. English. **DESCR:** Consumers.

4501 Sansolo, Michael. Merchandising to Hispanics: are you speaking their language? PROGRESSIVE GROCER, Vol. 65, no. 2 (February 1986), p. 20-22+. English. **DESCR:** *Consumers; *Cultural Characteristics.

4502 Sellers, Jeff M. Good hands grasp a growing market. HISPANIC BUSINESS, Vol. 9, no. 9 (September 1987), p. 8-11. English. **DESCR:** Advertising; *Allstate Insurance Co.; *Insurance.

4503 Sellers, Jeff M. Market growth boosts ad rates. HISPANIC BUSINESS, Vol. 9, no. 12 (December 1987), p. 41-42, 63+. English. **DESCR:** *Advertising; *Spanish Language; *Television.

4504 Sellers, Jeff M. Metropolitan Life continues to lead. HISPANIC BUSINESS, Vol. 9, no. 5 (May 1987), p. 12-14. English. **DESCR:** Advertising; Corporations; *Insurance; *Metropolitan Life Insurance Corporation; U.S. Hispanic Chamber of Commerce.

4505 Sellers, Jeff M. The sound of musica: moving into the mainstream. HISPANIC BUSINESS, Vol. 9, no. 7 (July 1987), p. 14-18. English. **DESCR:** Los Lobos del Este de Los Angeles (musical group); Miami Sound Machine; Music; *Musicians; The Cruzados [musical group]; Zerimar [musical group].

4506 Spanish buying power rises to estimated $60 billion-plus as population, income keep growing. TELEVISION/RADIO AGE, Vol. 31, (December 19, 1983), p. A3-A18. English.

Marketing (cont.)

4507 Trager, Cara S. Manhattan executive forum. HISPANIC BUSINESS, Vol. 9, no. 4 (April 1987), p. 10-13. English. **DESCR:** Advertising; *Corporations; *National Hispanic Corporate Council (NHCC); *Organizations.

4508 U.S. Hispanic population: year 2080. HISPANIC BUSINESS, Vol. 9, no. 3 (March 1987), p. 50. English. **DESCR:** *Population.

4509 Zwiebach, Elliot. An important and growing consumer segment. SUPERMARKET NEWS, Vol. 34, (May 7, 1984), p. 8,10,120. English. **DESCR:** Mexican American Grocers Association (MAGA); Television.

Markides, Kyriakos S.

4510 Cardenas, Gilbert. Book review of: OLDER MEXICAN AMERICANS: A STUDY IN AN URBAN BARRIO. CONTEMPORARY SOCIOLOGY: A JOURNAL OF REVIEWS, Vol. 14, no. 2 (March 1985), p. 243-244. English. **DESCR:** Ancianos; Book Reviews; Gomez, Ernesto; Martin, Harry; *OLDER MEXICAN AMERICANS: A STUDY IN AN URBAN BARRIO.

4511 Kastenbaum, Robert. Book review of: OLDER MEXICAN AMERICANS: A STUDY IN AN URBAN BARRIO. INTERNATIONAL JOURNAL OF AGING & HUMAN DEVELOPMENT, Vol. 19, no. 1 (1984), p. 75-76. English. **DESCR:** Ancianos; Book Reviews; Martin, Harry; *OLDER MEXICAN AMERICANS: A STUDY IN AN URBAN BARRIO.

4512 Manuel, Ron C. Book review of: OLDER MEXICAN AMERICANS: A STUDY IN AN URBAN BARRIO. JOURNAL OF GERONTOLOGY, Vol. 39, no. 4 (July 1984), p. 506-507. English. **DESCR:** Ancianos; Book Reviews; Martin, Harry; *OLDER MEXICAN AMERICANS: A STUDY IN AN URBAN BARRIO.

Marquez, Antonio

4513 Paredes, Raymund A. Book review of: CUENTOS CHICANOS: A SHORT STORY ANTHOLOGY. WESTERN AMERICAN LITERATURE, Vol. 21, no. 3 (1986), p. 270. English. **DESCR:** Anaya, Rudolfo A.; Book Reviews; *CUENTOS CHICANOS: A SHORT STORY ANTHOLOGY.

4514 Ramirez, Arthur. Book review of: CUENTOS CHICANOS: A SHORT STORY ANTHOLOGY. SAN FRANCISCO REVIEW OF BOOKS, Vol. 11, (1986), p. 11,23. English. **DESCR:** Anaya, Rudolfo A.; Book Reviews; *CUENTOS CHICANOS: A SHORT STORY ANTHOLOGY; Short Story.

Marrero, Charles

4515 SHPE holds first ever East coast conference for Hispanic engineers. HISPANIC ENGINEER, Vol. 3, no. 5 (Winter 1987), p. 12-14. English. **DESCR:** Awards; Barrios, Eugene; Chang-Diaz, Franklin; *Conferences and Meetings; Cuevas, Brian L.; Garay, Charles J.; Garcia, Ray; Martinez, Lisa; Monteverde, Edwin; Plumey, Raymond; Reyes-Guerra, David; Rivera, Angel; Society of Hispanic Professional Engineers (SHPE); Soto, Giovanni.

Marriage

4516 Anonymous UCSC Community Member. An extinct relationship. REVISTA MUJERES, Vol. 2, no. 1 (January 1985), p. 21-22. English. **DESCR:** Divorce; Women Men Relations.

4517 Curtis, Theodore T. and Baca Zinn, Maxine. Marital role orientation among Chicanos: an

analysis of structural and cultural factors. LA RED/THE NET, no. 59 (October 1982), p. 2-4. English. **DESCR:** *Sex Roles.

4518 Frisbie, William Parker; Opitz, Wolfgang; and Kelly, William R. Marital instability trends among Mexican Americans as compared to Blacks and Anglos: new evidence. SOCIAL SCIENCE QUARTERLY, Vol. 66, no. 3 (September 1985), p. 587-601. English. **DESCR:** *Chicanas; Divorce.

4519 Guendelman, Sylvia. The incorporation of Mexican women in seasonal migration: a study of gender differences. HISPANIC JOURNAL OF BEHAVIORAL SCIENCES, Vol. 9, no. 3 (September 1987), p. 245-264. English. **DESCR:** Chicanas; Immigrants; Mexico; *Migration Patterns; *Sex Roles; *Women; *Women Men Relations; Working Women.

4520 Gutierrez, Ramon A. Honor ideology, marriage negotiation, and class-gender domination in New Mexico, 1690-1846. LATIN AMERICAN PERSPECTIVES, Vol. 12, no. 1 (Winter 1985), p. 81-104. English. **DESCR:** Sex Roles; *Social Classes; Social History and Conditions; *Southwestern United States; Values; Women Men Relations.

4521 Hayghe, Howard. Married couples: work and income patterns. MONTHLY LABOR REVIEW, Vol. 106, no. 12 (December 1983), p. 26-29. English. **DESCR:** Income; *Laborers; Women Men Relations; Working Women.

4522 LeVine, Sarah Ethel; Correa, Clara Sunderland; and Uribe, F. Medardo Tapia. The marital morality of Mexican women--an urban study. JOURNAL OF ANTHROPOLOGICAL RESEARCH, Vol. 42, no. 2 (Summer 1986), p. 183-202. English. **DESCR:** Family; Los Robles, Cuernavaca, Morelos, Mexico; *Machismo; Parent and Child Relationships; *Sex Roles; *Women Men Relations.

Marshall, Dale Rogers

4523 Body-Gendrot, Sophie. Book review of: PROTEST IS NOT ENOUGH. INTERNATIONAL JOURNAL OF URBAN AND REGIONAL RESEARCH, Vol. 9, no. 4 (1985), p. 576-577. English. **DESCR:** Book Reviews; Browning, Rufus P.; *PROTEST IS NOT ENOUGH: THE STRUGGLE OF BLACKS AND HISPANICS FOR EQUALITY IN URBAN POLITICS; Tabb, David H.

4524 Browning, Rufus P. and Marshall, Dale Rogers. Black and Hispanic power in city politics: a forum. P.S. [AMERICAN POLITICAL SCIENCE ASSOCIATION], Vol. 19, no. 3 (Summer 1986), p. 573-639. English. **DESCR:** Blacks; Browning, Rufus P.; *Politics; *PROTEST IS NOT ENOUGH: THE STRUGGLE OF BLACKS AND HISPANICS FOR EQUALITY IN URBAN POLITICS; Tabb, David H.; Urban Communities.

4525 Browning, Rufus P.; Marshall, Dale Rogers; and Tabb, David H. Protest is not enough: a theory of political incorporation. P.S. [AMERICAN POLITICAL SCIENCE ASSOCIATION], Vol. 19, no. 3 (Summer 1986), p. 576-581. English. **DESCR:** Blacks; Browning, Rufus P.; Political Representation; Politics; *PROTEST IS NOT ENOUGH: THE STRUGGLE OF BLACKS AND HISPANICS FOR EQUALITY IN URBAN POLITICS; Tabb, David H.; Urban Communities.

Marshall, Dale Rogers (cont.)

4526 Sonenshein, Raphe. Biracial coalition
politics in Los Angeles. P.S. [AMERICAN
POLITICAL SCIENCE ASSOCIATION], Vol. 19, no.
3 (Summer 1986), p. 582-590. English.
DESCR: Blacks; Bradley, Tom; Browning, Rufus
P.; *Ethnic Groups; *Intergroup Relations;
*Los Angeles, CA; Political Parties and
Organizations; *Politics; PROTEST IS NOT
ENOUGH: THE STRUGGLE OF BLACKS AND HISPANICS
FOR EQUALITY IN URBAN POLITICS; Tabb, David
H.

Martin, Harry

4527 Cardenas, Gilbert. Book review of: OLDER
MEXICAN AMERICANS: A STUDY IN AN URBAN
BARRIO. CONTEMPORARY SOCIOLOGY: A JOURNAL OF
REVIEWS, Vol. 14, no. 2 (March 1985), p.
243-244. English. DESCR: Ancianos; Book
Reviews; Gomez, Ernesto; Markides, Kyriakos
S.; *OLDER MEXICAN AMERICANS: A STUDY IN AN
URBAN BARRIO.

4528 Kastenbaum, Robert. Book review of: OLDER
MEXICAN AMERICANS: A STUDY IN AN URBAN
BARRIO. INTERNATIONAL JOURNAL OF AGING &
HUMAN DEVELOPMENT, Vol. 19, no. 1 (1984), p.
75-76. English. DESCR: Ancianos; Book
Reviews; Markides, Kyriakos S.; *OLDER
MEXICAN AMERICANS: A STUDY IN AN URBAN
BARRIO.

4529 Manuel, Ron C. Book review of: OLDER MEXICAN
AMERICANS: A STUDY IN AN URBAN BARRIO.
JOURNAL OF GERONTOLOGY, Vol. 39, no. 4 (July
1984), p. 506-507. English. DESCR: Ancianos;
Book Reviews; Markides, Kyriakos S.; *OLDER
MEXICAN AMERICANS: A STUDY IN AN URBAN
BARRIO.

Martin, Patricia Preciado

4530 Foote, Cheryl. Book review of: IMAGES AND
CONVERSATIONS. JOURNAL OF THE WEST, Vol. 24,
no. 3 (July 1985), p. 121. English. DESCR:
Book Reviews; Chicanas; IMAGES AND
CONVERSATIONS: MEXICAN AMERICANS RECALL A
SOUTHWESTERN PAST; Oral History.

Martinez, Bob

4531 McNeely, Dave. Hispanic power at the polls.
VISTA, Vol. 2, no. 3 (November 2, 1986), p.
8-12. English. DESCR: Austin, TX; *Barrera,
Roy, Jr.; Chavez, Linda; Elected Officials;
Gonzalez, Raul; Maryland; Political System;
San Antonio, TX; Statistics; Tampa, FL;
*Voter Turnout.

4532 Perez, Renato E. A governor named Martinez.
VISTA, Vol. 2, no. 5 (January 4, 1987), p.
10-11. English. DESCR: Biography; *Elected
Officials; Florida.

Martinez, Cesar Augusto

4533 Chavez, Lorenzo A. The eyes of Texas are
upon them. VISTA, Vol. 2, no. 2 (October 4,
1986), p. 20. English. DESCR: *Art;
Cardenas, David; *Chulas Fronteras [art
exhibit]; Espada, Ibsen; Gonzalez, Patricia;
Hernandez, John; Huerta, Benito.

Martinez, Daniel J.

4534 Gamboa, Harry, Jr. El artista chicano dentro
y fuera de la "corriente" artistica. LA
COMUNIDAD, No. 351 (April 12, 1987), 2-5+.
Spanish. DESCR: *Art; Artists; Carrasco,
Barbara; Gamboa, Diane; Gronk (Pseud.);
Valadez, John; Valdez, Patssi.

Martinez, Diana I.

4535 Luzod, Jimmy. Book review of: ASPECTS OF
AMERICAN HISPANIC AND INDIAN INVOLVEMENT IN
BIOMEDICAL RESEARCH. LA RED/THE NET, no. 79
(April 1984), p. 9-13. English. DESCR:
*ASPECTS OF AMERICAN HISPANIC AND INDIAN
INVOLVEMENT IN BIOMEDICAL RESEARCH; Book
Reviews; Martinez, J.V.; Science.

Martinez, Dorella

4536 LeAna, Thomas. Dorella Martinez. VISTA, Vol.
2, no. 1 (September 7, 1986), p. 14.
English. DESCR: *Academic Achievement;
*Education.

4537 LeAna, Thomas. From dropout to role model: a
VISTA postscript. VISTA, Vol. 2, no. 4
(December 7, 1986), p. 25. English. DESCR:
Brownsville, TX; Gladys Porter High School;
Olivares, J.R.; *Rhetoric; Secondary School
Education.

Martinez, Francisco "Kiko"

4538 Chicano activist "Kiko" Martinez convicted.
GUARDIAN, Vol. 39, no. 7 (November 12,
1986), p. 4. English. DESCR: Criminal
Justice System; Legal Cases; Militancy.

4539 Garcia, Richard. The ordeal of "Kiko"
Martinez. GUARDIAN, Vol. 39, no. 3 (October
15, 1986), p. 2. English. DESCR: Criminal
Justice System; Legal Cases; Militancy.

4540 Martinez, David A. The nightmare of Kiko
Martinez. GUILD NOTES, Vol. 9, no. 2 (Spring
1985), p. 4. English. DESCR: Criminal
Justice System; Legal Cases; *Legal
Profession; Political Repression.

4541 Martinez, Elizabeth. A decade of repression:
update on the "Kiko" Martinez case. CRIME
AND SOCIAL JUSTICE, no. 19 (Summer 1983), p.
100. English. DESCR: Chicano Movement; Civil
Rights; Colorado; Criminal Justice System;
Discrimination; Legal Cases; Political
Repression.

4542 Zanger, Maggy. Trial of an activist lawyer.
THE PROGRESSIVE, Vol. 50, no. 12 (December
1986), p. 16-17. English. DESCR: Criminal
Justice System; Legal Cases; Tucson, AZ.

Martinez, Joe L., Jr.

4543 Barona, Andres and Santos de Barona,
Maryann. Chicano psychology: a new field?
CONTEMPORARY PSYCHOLOGY, Vol. 31, no. 2
(February 1986), p. 106-107. English.
DESCR: Book Reviews; *CHICANO PSYCHOLOGY;
Mendoza, Richard H.

Martinez, Julio A.

4544 Book review of: CHICANO LITERATURE: A
REFERENCE GUIDE. BOOKLIST, Vol. 82, no. 9
(January 1, 1986), p. 667-668. English.
DESCR: Book Reviews; *CHICANO LITERATURE: A
REFERENCE GUIDE; Lomeli, Francisco A.;
Reference Works.

4545 Brown, D.R. Book review of: CHICANO
LITERATURE: A REFERENCE GUIDE. CHOICE, Vol.
23, no. 4 (December 1985), p. 578. English.
DESCR: Book Reviews; *CHICANO LITERATURE: A
REFERENCE GUIDE; Lomeli, Francisco A.;
Reference Works.

Martinez, Julio A. (cont.)

4546 Castillo-Speed, Lillian. Annotated bibliography. LA RED/THE NET, no. 93 (January, February, 1986), p. 14-17. English. **DESCR:** A BIBLIOGRAPHY OF MEXICAN AMERICAN HISTORY; ARTE CHICANO; Book Reviews; Caballero, Cesar; CHICANO LITERATURE: A REFERENCE GUIDE; CHICANO ORGANIZATIONS DIRECTORY; CHICANO PERIODICAL INDEX; Goldman, Shifra M.; HISPANIC ALMANAC; HISPANIC MENTAL HEALTH RESEARCH: A REFERENCE GUIDE; Lomeli, Francisco A.; Meier, Matt S.; Newton, Frank; *Reference Works; Ybarra-Frausto, Tomas.

4547 Haro, Robert P. Book review of: CHICANO LITERATURE: A REFERENCE GUIDE. AMERICAN REFERENCE BOOKS ANNUAL, Vol. 17, (1986), p. 440. English. **DESCR:** Book Reviews; *CHICANO LITERATURE: A REFERENCE GUIDE; Lomeli, Francisco A.; Reference Works.

4548 Perry, Charles E. Book review of: CHICANO LITERATURE: A REFERENCE GUIDE. LIBRARY JOURNAL, Vol. 110, no. 5 (March 15, 1985), p. 53. English. **DESCR:** Book Reviews; *CHICANO LITERATURE: A REFERENCE GUIDE; Literature; Lomeli, Francisco A.; Reference Works.

Martinez, J.V.

4549 Luzod, Jimmy. Book review of: ASPECTS OF AMERICAN HISPANIC AND INDIAN INVOLVEMENT IN BIOMEDICAL RESEARCH. LA RED/THE NET, no. 79 (April 1984), p. 9-13. English. **DESCR:** *ASPECTS OF AMERICAN HISPANIC AND INDIAN INVOLVEMENT IN BIOMEDICAL RESEARCH; Book Reviews; Martinez, Diana I.; Science.

Martinez, Lisa

4550 Dates, Karen E. Coast Guard ocean engineer Lisa Martinez. HISPANIC ENGINEER, Vol. 3, no. 4 (Fall 1987), p. 30-34. English. **DESCR:** Chicanas; Discrimination in Education; *Engineering as a Profession.

4551 SHPE holds first ever East coast conference for Hispanic engineers. HISPANIC ENGINEER, Vol. 3, no. 5 (Winter 1987), p. 12-14. English. **DESCR:** Awards; Barrios, Eugene; Chang-Diaz, Franklin; *Conferences and Meetings; Cuevas, Brian L.; Garay, Charles J.; Garcia, Ray; Marrero, Charles; Monteverde, Edwin; Plumey, Raymond; Reyes-Guerra, David; Rivera, Angel; Society of Hispanic Professional Engineers (SHPE); Soto, Giovanni.

Martinez, Oscar J.

4552 Garcia, Mario T. Book review of: FRAGMENTS OF THE MEXICAN REVOLUTION. HISPANIC AMERICAN HISTORICAL REVIEW, Vol. 65, no. 1 (February 1985), p. 150-151. English. **DESCR:** Book Reviews; *FRAGMENTS OF THE MEXICAN REVOLUTION: PERSONAL ACCOUNTS FROM THE BORDER; Mexican Revolution - 1910-1920.

Martinez, Peter

4553 Breiter, Toni. Speaker for Uncle Sam. VISTA, Vol. 2, no. 8 (April 4, 1987), p. 23. English. **DESCR:** *Diplomats.

Martinez, Raquel

4554 Johnson, Richard. The California housewife who succeeds as brave bullfighter. VISTA, Vol. 1, no. 5 (January 5, 1986), p. 12-15. English. **DESCR:** *Athletes; Chicanas; Montes, Miguel; Munoz, Jesus.

Martinez, Vicente

4555 Atencio, Tomas. No estan todos los que son, no son todos los que estan. EL CUADERNO, Vol. 4, no. 1 (Summer 1976), p. 51-61. Spanish. **DESCR:** Arellano, Estevan; *Identity; *La Academia de la Nueva Raza, Dixon, NM; Lovato, Alberto; Roybal, Luis.

Martinez-Herring, Laura [Miss USA]

4556 Reyes, Sonia. America's Hispanic sweethearts. VISTA, Vol. 1, no. 6 (February 2, 1986), p. 6-7. English. **DESCR:** Awards; Carthy-Deu, Deborah [Miss Universe]; *Women.

Marxism

4557 Sykes, Maltby. Diego Rivera and the Hotel Reforma murals. ARCHIVES OF AMERICAN ART JOURNAL, Vol. 25, no. 1-2 (1985), p. 29-40. English. **DESCR:** Artists; Hotel Reforma, Mexico City; Mexico City; Mural Art; *Rivera, Diego.

Maryland

4558 McNeely, Dave. Hispanic power at the polls. VISTA, Vol. 2, no. 3 (November 2, 1986), p. 8-12. English. **DESCR:** Austin, TX; *Barrera, Roy, Jr.; Chavez, Linda; Elected Officials; Gonzalez, Raul; Martinez, Bob; Political System; San Antonio, TX; Statistics; Tampa, FL; *Voter Turnout.

Masks

4559 Goldman, Shifra. Zarco Guerrero: tradicion y transformacion. LA COMUNIDAD, No. 249 (April 28, 1985), p. 2-3. Spanish. **DESCR:** *Art; Biography; *Guerrero, Adolfo "El Zarco"; Sculpture.

Mass Media

4560 Delgado, Melvin. Book review of: MEXICAN-AMERICANS AND THE MASS-MEDIA. HISPANIC JOURNAL OF BEHAVIORAL SCIENCES, Vol. 9, no. 4 (December 1987), p. 461-463. English. **DESCR:** Book Reviews; Greenberg, Bradley S.; *MEXICAN AMERICANS AND THE MASS MEDIA.

4561 DelPriore, Lisa. Tapping into the Hispanic market. MARKETING COMMUNICATIONS, Vol. 11, no. 6 (June 1986), p. 57-62. English. **DESCR:** *Advertising; *Consumers; *Marketing.

4562 Hispanic marketing. ADVERTISING AGE MAGAZINE, Vol. 57, no. 16 (February 27, 1986), p. 11-51. English. **DESCR:** Adolph Coors Co.; Advertising; Allstate Insurance Co.; American Greetings; Anheuser-Busch, Inc.; Business Enterprises; Coca-Cola Company; Consumers; Ford Motor Company; Hallmark Cards; *Marketing; McDonald's Corporation; Metropolitan Life Insurance Corporation; Pepsi-Cola Bottling Group; Prudential; Spanish International Network (SIN); State Farm Mutual Insurance; Tylenol; United Insurance Co. of America.

4563 Jacobson, Harold. Upward trend in expenditures continues. HISPANIC BUSINESS, Vol. 9, no. 12 (December 1987), p. 19-20. English. **DESCR:** *Advertising; Consumers; Income; *Marketing.

Mass Media (cont.)

4564 Jimenez, Luis. Cambia la imagen del latino en Hollywood. LA COMUNIDAD, No. 255 (June 9, 1985), p. 14-15. Spanish. **DESCR:** Discrimination; Employment; Films; *Hispanic Academy of Media Arts and Sciences (HAMAS); Organizations; Reyna, Phil.

4565 Jimenez, Luis. En busca del talento latino. LA COMUNIDAD, No. 235 (January 20, 1985), p. 14-15. Spanish. **DESCR:** Actors and Actresses; *Biography; *Morones, Bob.

4566 Macias, Reynaldo Flores and Cabello-Argandona, Roberto. Media research and the Chicano. LATIN QUARTER, Vol. 1, no. 2 (October 1974), p. 14-16,18. English. **DESCR:** Advertising; Consumers; Marketing; Population.

4567 Marketing to Hispanics. ADVERTISING AGE MAGAZINE, Vol. 58, no. 6 (February 9, 1987), p. S1-S23. English. **DESCR:** Advertising; Consumers; Immigrants; *Marketing; Politics; Undocumented Workers.

4568 Marketing to U.S. Hispanics. ADVERTISING WORLD, no. 6 (December 1983), p. 26-27. English. **DESCR:** *Conferences and Meetings; *Marketing.

4569 Reese, Stephen D. Book review of: MEXICAN-AMERICANS AND THE MASS-MEDIA. JOURNALISM QUARTERLY, Vol. 61, no. 3 (Fall 1984), p. 705-706. English. **DESCR:** Book Reviews; Greenberg, Bradley S.; *MEXICAN AMERICANS AND THE MASS MEDIA.

4570 Subervi-Velez, Federico. Book review of: MEXICAN-AMERICANS AND THE MASS-MEDIA. INTERNATIONAL JOURNAL OF INTERCULTURAL RELATIONS, Vol. 8, no. 3 (1984), p. 340-342. English. **DESCR:** Book Reviews; Greenberg, Bradley S.; *MEXICAN AMERICANS AND THE MASS MEDIA.

MATERIALS ON THE HISTORY OF LATINOS IN MICHIGAN AND THE MIDWEST

4571 Garcia, John R. Book reviews of: EL PUEBLO MEXICANO EN DETROIT Y MICHIGAN and MATERIALS ON THE HISTORY OF LATINOS IN MICHIGAN AND THE MIDWEST. LA RED/THE NET, no. 67 (April 1983), p. 13-14. English. **DESCR:** Book Reviews; *EL PUEBLO MEXICANO EN DETROIT Y MICHIGAN: A SOCIAL HISTORY; Midwestern States; Valdes, Dennis N.

Maternal and Child Welfare

4572 Engle, Patricia L.; Scrimshaw, Susan C.M.; and Smidt, Robert. Sex differences in attitudes towards newborn infants among women of Mexican origin. MEDICAL ANTHROPOLOGY, Vol. 8, no. 2 (Spring 1984), p. 133-144. English. **DESCR:** *Attitudes; Chicanas; Cultural Characteristics; *Machismo; *Parent and Child Relationships; Sex Roles.

4573 Hurtado, Aida. Midwife practices in Hildago County, Texas. TRABAJOS MONOGRAFICOS, Vol. 3, no. 1 (1987), p. 1-30. English. **DESCR:** Chicanas; *Hidalgo County, TX.

Mathematics

4574 Carpenter, Thomas P., et al. Achievement in mathematics: results from the National Assessment. THE ELEMENTARY SCHOOL JOURNAL, Vol. 84, no. 5 (May 1984), p. 485-495. English. **DESCR:** Academic Achievement; *Educational Tests and Measurements; *National Assessment of Educational Progress.

4575 Rendon, Laura Ignacia. Mathematics education for Hispanic students in community colleges. LA RED/THE NET, no. 76 (January 1984), p. 2-4. English. **DESCR:** Community Colleges; Students; Surveys.

Mathematics, Engineering and Science Achievement (MESA)

4576 Minsky, Alyce. California State University at Los Angeles. HISPANIC ENGINEER, Vol. 3, (Summer, 1987), p. 30-33, 44. English. **DESCR:** Colleges and Universities; Educational Organizations; *Engineering as a Profession; *Minority Engineering Program (California State University at Los Angeles).

4577 Smith, Mary Perry. Early identification and support: the University of California-Berkeley's MESA program. NEW DIRECTIONS FOR TEACHING AND LEARNING, no. 24 (December 1985), p. 19-25. English. **DESCR:** *Counseling (Educational); *Engineering as a Profession; Enrollment; Higher Education; University of California, Berkeley.

Maxims
   USE: Dichos

Mayas

4578 Cerda, Gabriela. La serpiente. NOTEBOOK: A LITTLE MAGAZINE, Vol. 2, no. 2 (1986), p. 14-26. English. **DESCR:** Cuentos; Leyendas; *Mitos.

Mazon, Mauricio

4579 Cortes, Carlos E. Book review of: THE ZOOT-SUIT RIOTS. PACIFIC HISTORICAL REVIEW, Vol. 55, no. 3 (1986), p. 498-499. English. **DESCR:** Book Reviews; *THE ZOOT-SUIT RIOTS: THE PSYCHOLOGY OF SYMBOLIC ANNIHILATION; Zoot Suit Riots, Los Angeles, CA, 1943.

4580 Cosgrove, Stuart. Book review of: THE ZOOT-SUIT RIOTS. THE TIMES LITERARY SUPPLEMENT, (July 12, 1985), p. 782. English. **DESCR:** Book Reviews; *THE ZOOT-SUIT RIOTS: THE PSYCHOLOGY OF SYMBOLIC ANNIHILATION.

4581 Farley, J.E. Book review of: THE ZOOT-SUIT RIOTS. CHOICE, Vol. 22, no. 11-12 (July, August, 1985), p. 1691-1692. English. **DESCR:** Book Reviews; *THE ZOOT-SUIT RIOTS: THE PSYCHOLOGY OF SYMBOLIC ANNIHILATION.

McBride, Robert H.

4582 Maciel, David R. Book review of: MEXICO AND THE UNITED STATES. LA RED/THE NET, no. 68 (May 1983), p. 8-9. English. **DESCR:** Book Reviews; Laboring Classes; *MEXICO AND THE UNITED STATES: INTERNATIONAL RELATIONS IN THE HUMANITIES.

McCready, William C.

4583 Cordasco, Francesco. Book review of: HISPANICS IN THE UNITED STATES: A NEW SOCIAL AGENDA. CHOICE, Vol. 23, no. 6 (February 1986), p. 928. English. **DESCR:** Book Reviews; *HISPANICS IN THE UNITED STATES: A NEW SOCIAL AGENDA; San Juan Cafferty, Pastora.

McCready, William C. (cont.)

4584 Griswold del Castillo, Richard. Book review of: HISPANICS IN THE UNITED STATES: A NEW SOCIAL AGENDA. JOURNAL OF AMERICAN ETHNIC HISTORY, Vol. 6, no. 1 (Fall 1986), p. 112-114. English. **DESCR:** Book Reviews; *HISPANICS IN THE UNITED STATES: A NEW SOCIAL AGENDA; San Juan Cafferty, Pastora; Social History and Conditions.

4585 Griswold del Castillo, Richard. Book review of: HISPANICS IN THE UNITED STATES: A NEW SOCIAL AGENDA. HISPANIC AMERICAN HISTORICAL REVIEW, Vol. 66, no. 3 (August 1986), p. 627-629. English. **DESCR:** Book Reviews; *HISPANICS IN THE UNITED STATES: A NEW SOCIAL AGENDA; San Juan Cafferty, Pastora.

McDonald's Corporation

4586 Chavez, Lorenzo A. Images of ethnic pride. VISTA, Vol. 3, no. 2 (October 3, 1987), p. 20-21. English. **DESCR:** *Art; Children's Art.

4587 Hispanic marketing. ADVERTISING AGE MAGAZINE, Vol. 57, no. 16 (February 27, 1986), p. 11-51. English. **DESCR:** Adolph Coors Co.; Advertising; Allstate Insurance Co.; American Greetings; Anheuser-Busch, Inc.; Business Enterprises; Coca-Cola Company; Consumers; Ford Motor Company; Hallmark Cards; *Marketing; Mass Media; Metropolitan Life Insurance Corporation; Pepsi-Cola Bottling Group; Prudential; Spanish International Network (SIN); State Farm Mutual Insurance; Tylenol; United Insurance Co. of America.

McGoldrick, Monica

4588 Ramirez, Oscar. Book review of: ETHNICITY AND FAMILY THERAPY. LA RED/THE NET, no. 66 (March 1983), p. 28-30. English. **DESCR:** Book Reviews; *ETHNICITY AND FAMILY THERAPY; Giordano, Joseph; Pearce, John K.

McLemore, David

4589 13-part series focuses on Hispanics in America. EDITOR & PUBLISHER: THE FOURTH ESTATE, Vol. 115, no. 14 (April 3, 1982), p. 37. English. **DESCR:** Books; Cultural Characteristics; DALLAS MORNING NEWS; Garcia, Juan; Gonzalez, John; Goodwin, Jay; Grothe, Randy Eli; Hamilton, John; Hille, Ed; LA VIDA AMERICANA; *LA VIDA AMERICANA/HISPANICS IN AMERICA; Langer, Ralph; Osburne, Burl; Parks, Scott; Pusey, Allen; Sonnemair, Jan.

MEChA
USE: Movimiento Estudiantil Chicano de Aztlan (MEChA)

Medal of Honor

4590 Allsup, Dan. The private war of Roy Benavidez. VISTA, Vol. 2, no. 5 (January 4, 1987), p. 19-20. English. **DESCR:** *Benavidez, Roy; Nationalism; *Veterans.

Media
USE: Mass Media

Medical Botany
USE: Herbal Medicine

Medical Care

4591 Angel, Ronald. The economic cost of chronic health limitations for Hispanic males. LA RED/THE NET, no. 61 (November 1982), p. 2-3. English. **DESCR:** *Males.

4592 Angel, Ronald. Problems in studying the impact of social structure and culture on the health and medical care utilization of Chicanos. LA RED/THE NET, no. 55 (June 1982), p. 2-3. English. **DESCR:** *Public Health.

4593 Angel, Ronald. The study of the health of Chicanos: some recent findings. LA RED/THE NET, no. 74 (November 1983), p. 2-7. English. **DESCR:** *Public Health; Research Methodology.

4594 Fitzpatrick, Sherahe B., et al. Do health care needs of Mexican-American and Caucasian teens differ? PEDIATRIC RESEARCH, Vol. 20, no. 4 (1986), p. A153. English. **DESCR:** *Youth.

4595 Gutierrez, Silvio G. On wings of mercy. VISTA, Vol. 2, no. 3 (November 2, 1986), p. 17-18. English. **DESCR:** Angel Flight; *Emergency Services; Malibu, CA; *Torres, Averi; Torres, Dennis; Transportation.

4596 Lecca, Pedro J. and McNeil, John S. Cultural factors affecting the compliance of older Mexican-Americans with hypertension regimens. LA RED/THE NET, no. 74 (November 1983), p. 7-10. English. **DESCR:** *Ancianos; *Dallas, TX.

4597 Lefton, Doug. Culture a factor in treating Latino patients. AMERICAN MEDICAL NEWS, Vol. 25, (July 9, 1982), p. 17-19. English. **DESCR:** *Cultural Characteristics; Doctor Patient Relations.

4598 Neibel, Barbara A. Health care utilization: the case of the Mexican-American. ANTHROPOLOGY UCLA, Vol. 14, (1985), p. 13-26. English. **DESCR:** Cultural Characteristics; *Public Health; Vital Statistics.

4599 Newquist, Deborah. The health care barrier model: toward analyzing the underutilization of health care by older Mexican-Americans. ANTHROPOLOGY UCLA, Vol. 14, (1985), p. 1-12. English. **DESCR:** *Ancianos; *Cultural Characteristics; Discrimination; Folk Medicine; Medical Clinics; *Public Health.

4600 Remas, Theodora A. The threat of AIDS. VISTA, Vol. 2, no. 10 (June 7, 1987), p. 17-18, 25. English. **DESCR:** *Acquired Immune Deficiency Syndrome (AIDS); Directories; Health Education; Preventative Medicine.

4601 Sandos, James A. Northern separatism during the Mexican revolution--an inquiry into the role of drug trafficking, 1910-1920. AMERICAS, Vol. 41, no. 2 (October 1984), p. 191-214. English. **DESCR:** Baja California, Mexico; Border Region; Cantu Jimenez, Esteban; Drug Addicts; Drug Laws; *Drug Traffic; *Drug Use; Mexican Revolution - 1910-1920; Revolutions.

4602 Stern, Gwen. Research, action, and social betterment. AMERICAN BEHAVIOR SCIENTISTS, Vol. 29, no. 2 (November, December, 1985), p. 229-248. English. **DESCR:** Chicago, IL; *Chicanas; Research Methodology; The Latina Mother-Infant Project, Chicago, IL.

4603 Trevino, Fernando M. Health indicators for Hispanic, Black and white Americans. VITAL AND HEALTH STATISTICS. SERIES 10, (September 1984), p. 1-88. English. **DESCR:** Anglo Americans; Blacks; Statistics.

Medical Clinics

4604 Newquist, Deborah. The health care barrier model: toward analyzing the underutilization of health care by older Mexican-Americans. ANTHROPOLOGY UCLA, Vol. 14, (1985), p. 1-12. English. **DESCR**: *Ancianos; *Cultural Characteristics; Discrimination; Folk Medicine; *Medical Care; *Public Health.

4605 Valdez, William J. Impotence: a problem with a solution. NUESTRO, Vol. 11, no. 4 (May 1987), p. 18-20. English. **DESCR**: Centro de Impotencia, Coral Gables Hospital, Miami, FL; Diseases; *Impotence; Males; *Psychotherapy.

Medical Education

4606 Looking for a few good MDs. HISPANIC BUSINESS, Vol. 9, no. 4 (April 1987), p. 16. English. **DESCR**: Students; *Texas Association of Mexican-American Medical Students (TAMAMS).

4607 Taylor, Elena. Conversations with a Chicana physician. REVISTA MUJERES, Vol. 1, no. 2 (June 1984), p. 44-46. English. **DESCR**: *Chicanas; Medical Personnel; *Solinas, Lisa.

Medical Personnel

4608 Chavez, Lorenzo A. Ramon Duarte. VISTA, Vol. 1, no. 9 (May 3, 1986), p. 20. English. **DESCR**: Biography; *Duarte, Ramon.

4609 Grayson, June. Sports medics. VISTA, Vol. 2, no. 9 (May 3, 1987), p. 17-18. English. **DESCR**: Bergin-Nader, Barbara; Cuadros, Hugo; Doctor Patient Relations; *Dominguez, Richard; Prietto, Carlos Alfredo; *Sports.

4610 Taylor, Elena. Conversations with a Chicana physician. REVISTA MUJERES, Vol. 1, no. 2 (June 1984), p. 44-46. English. **DESCR**: *Chicanas; Medical Education; *Solinas, Lisa.

Medical Services
USE: Medical Care

Medicine
USE: Medical Care

Medina, Ruben

4611 Gonzalez, Marco Vinicio. En el pais de la frontera. LA COMUNIDAD, No. 291 (February 16, 1986), p. 6-7+. Spanish. **DESCR**: Border Region; Conde, Rosina; *DIALOGOS FRONTERIZOS [radio program]; Gomez Pena, Guillermo; *Radio; San Diego, CA; Tijuana, Baja California, Mexico.

MEGATRENDS

4612 Morales, Cecilio. Upbeat future for Hispanics. VISTA, Vol. 1, no. 1 (September 8, 1985), p. 6-7. English. **DESCR**: Naisbitt Group; Naisbitt, John; *Population.

Meier, Matt S.

4613 Acuna, Rodolfo. Book review of: DICTIONARY OF MEXICAN AMERICAN HISTORY. LA RED/THE NET, no. 57 (August 1982), p. 4-5. English. **DESCR**: Book Reviews; *DICTIONARY OF MEXICAN AMERICAN HISTORY; History; Rivera, Feliciano.

4614 Balderrama, Francisco E. Book review of: A BIBLIOGRAPHY OF MEXICAN-AMERICAN HISTORY. PACIFIC HISTORICAL REVIEW, Vol. 55, no. 1 (1986), p. 106-107. English. **DESCR**: *A BIBLIOGRAPHY OF MEXICAN AMERICAN HISTORY; Book Reviews; History.

4615 Castillo-Speed, Lillian. Annotated bibliography. LA RED/THE NET, no. 93 (January, February, 1986), p. 14-17. English. **DESCR**: A BIBLIOGRAPHY OF MEXICAN AMERICAN HISTORY; ARTE CHICANO; Book Reviews; Caballero, Cesar; CHICANO LITERATURE: A REFERENCE GUIDE; CHICANO ORGANIZATIONS DIRECTORY; CHICANO PERIODICAL INDEX; Goldman, Shifra M.; HISPANIC ALMANAC; HISPANIC MENTAL HEALTH RESEARCH: A REFERENCE GUIDE; Lomeli, Francisco A.; Martinez, Julio A.; Newton, Frank; *Reference Works; Ybarra-Frausto, Tomas.

4616 Machado, Manuel A., Jr. Book review of: A BIBLIOGRAPHY OF MEXICAN-AMERICAN HISTORY. JOURNAL OF AMERICAN ETHNIC HISTORY, Vol. 5, no. 2 (Spring 1986), p. 80. English. **DESCR**: *A BIBLIOGRAPHY OF MEXICAN AMERICAN HISTORY; Book Reviews.

4617 Vigil, James Diego. Book review of: DICTIONARY OF MEXICAN AMERICAN HISTORY. PACIFIC HISTORICAL REVIEW, Vol. 53, no. 2 (1984), p. 241-242. English. **DESCR**: Book Reviews; *DICTIONARY OF MEXICAN AMERICAN HISTORY; Reference Works; Rivera, Feliciano.

Mejia, Al

4618 Community and professional organizations honor Rockwell's Al Mejia at retirement dinner. HISPANIC ENGINEER, Vol. 3, no. 1 (Spring 1987), p. 22. English. **DESCR**: *Awards; Rockwell International, Thousand Oaks, CA.

Mejia, Gabriella S.

4619 Soriano, Diane H. and Mejia, Gabriella S. "Ni he tenido tiempo para mi:" entrevista con Gabriella S. Mejia. REVISTA MUJERES, Vol. 1, no. 2 (June 1984), p. 38-41. Spanish. **DESCR**: Autobiography; *Chicanas; Higher Education.

Meketa, Jacqueline Dorgan

4620 Alberts, Don E. Book review of: LEGACY OF HONOR: THE LIFE OF RAFAEL CHACON, A NINETEENTH-CENTURY NEW MEXICAN. NEW MEXICO HISTORICAL REVIEW, Vol. 62, no. 4 (October 1987), p. 403-5. English. **DESCR**: Book Reviews; *Chacon, Rafael; *LEGACY OF HONOR: THE LIFE OF RAFAEL CHACON, A NINETEENTH CENTURY NEW MEXICAN.

Melendez, Pablo

4621 Melendez, Pablo. Happy Thanksgiving. CALIFORNIA MAGAZINE, Vol. 11, no. 11 (November 1986), p. 136. English. **DESCR**: *Biography; *Essays; *Immigrants; Youth.

Melendez, Sarah E.

4622 Gonzales-Berry, Erlinda. Book review of: BILINGUAL EDUCATION: A SOURCEBOOK. MODERN LANGUAGE JOURNAL, Vol. 69, no. 3 (Fall 1985), p. 299. English. **DESCR**: Ambert, Alba N.; *BILINGUAL EDUCATION: A SOURCEBOOK; Book Reviews.

Melendez, Sarah E. (cont.)

4623 Nieto, Sonia. Book review of: BILINGUAL EDUCATION: A SOURCEBOOK. INTERRACIAL BOOKS FOR CHILDREN, Vol. 17, no. 3-4 (1986), p. 29. English. DESCR: Ambert, Alba N.; *BILINGUAL EDUCATION: A SOURCEBOOK; Book Reviews.

4624 Soudek, Lev I. Book review of: BILINGUAL EDUCATION: A SOURCEBOOK. AMERICAN REFERENCE BOOKS ANNUAL, Vol. 17, (1986), p. 132. English. DESCR: Ambert, Alba N.; *BILINGUAL EDUCATION: A SOURCEBOOK; Book Reviews.

Melville, Margarita B.

4625 Baca Zinn, Maxine. Book review of: TWICE A MINORITY: MEXICAN-AMERICAN WOMEN. LA RED/THE NET, no. 32 (July 1980), p. 3-4. English. DESCR: Book Reviews; *Chicanas; *TWICE A MINORITY: MEXICAN-AMERICAN WOMEN.

MEMORIES OF THE ALHAMBRA

4626 Bruce-Novoa, Juan. Nash Candelaria: novelista (I). LA COMUNIDAD, No. 245 (March 31, 1985), p. 6-7. Spanish. DESCR: Biography; *Candelaria, Nash; *Literary Criticism; NOT BY THE SWORD; Novel.

4627 Bruce-Novoa, Juan. Nash Candelaria: novelista (II). LA COMUNIDAD, No. 246 (April 7, 1985), p. 10-11. Spanish. DESCR: Biography; *Candelaria, Nash; *Literary Criticism; NOT BY THE SWORD; Novel.

Mendez M., Miguel

4628 Alarcon, Justo S. Estructuras narrativas en TATA CASEHUA de Miguel Mendez. CONFLUENCIA, Vol. 1, no. 2 (Spring 1986), p. 48-54. Spanish. DESCR: *Literary Criticism; Short Story; *"Tata Casehua" [short story].

4629 Bernal, Louis Carlos. Miguel M. Mendez [photograph]. LLUEVE TLALOC, no. 12 (1985), p. iv. DESCR: *Photography.

4630 Ekstrom, Margaret V. Wanderers from an Aztec land: Chicano naming devices used by Miguel Mendez. LITERARY ONOMASTICS STUDIES, Vol. 12, (1985), p. 85-92. English. DESCR: Literary Characters; *Literary Criticism; Novel; *PEREGRINOS DE AZTLAN.

4631 Lomeli, Francisco A. En torno a la literatura...convergencia o divergencia? LA COMUNIDAD, No. 274 (October 20, 1985), p. 8-11. Spanish. DESCR: Anaya, Rudolfo A.; Aztlan; Border Region; HEART OF AZTLAN; *Literary Criticism; PEREGRINOS DE AZTLAN; *Primer Festival de Literatura Fronteriza Mexico-Estados Unidos.

4632 Vogt, Gregory M. Archetypal images of apocalypse in Miguel Mendez's TATA CASEHUA. CONFLUENCIA, Vol. 1, no. 2 (Spring 1986), p. 55-60. English. DESCR: *Literary Criticism; Short Story; *"Tata Casehua" [short story].

Mendoza, Lupe

4633 Mendoza, Lupe. Porque lo podemos hacer--a poco no? REVISTA MUJERES, Vol. 1, no. 2 (June 1984), p. 33-37. Spanish. DESCR: Autobiography; Chicanas; Higher Education.

Mendoza, Richard H.

4634 Barona, Andres and Santos de Barona, Maryann. Chicano psychology: a new field? CONTEMPORARY PSYCHOLOGY, Vol. 31, no. 2 (February 1986), p. 106-107. English. DESCR: Book Reviews; *CHICANO PSYCHOLOGY; Martinez, Joe L., Jr.

Mental Health

4635 Acosta, Frank X., et al. Preparing low-income Hispanic, Black, and white patients for psychotherapy: evaluation of a new orientation program. JOURNAL OF CLINICAL PSYCHOLOGY, Vol. 39, no. 6 (November 1983), p. 872-877. English. DESCR: Anglo Americans; Blacks; *Comparative Psychology; *Psychotherapy.

4636 Arce, Carlos H. and Carlson, David. Book review of: HISPANIC MENTAL HEALTH RESEARCH: A REFERENCE GUIDE. LA RED/THE NET, no. 57 (August 1982), p. 5-7. English. DESCR: Book Reviews; *HISPANIC MENTAL HEALTH RESEARCH: A REFERENCE GUIDE; Newton, Frank; Olmedo, Esteban L.; Padilla, Amado M.; Reference Works.

4637 Chesser, Barbara and Inguanzo-Schleff, Dania. Loneliness among Mexican migrant children. LA RED/THE NET, no. 44 (July 1981), p. 3-4. English. DESCR: Depression (Psychological); *Migrant Children.

4638 Dennedy-Frank, David P. Book review of: CROSSING CULTURES IN THERAPY. LA RED/THE NET, no. 41 (April 1981), p. 5-6. English. DESCR: Book Reviews; Counseling (Psychological); *CROSSING CULTURES IN THERAPY: PLURALISTIC COUNSELING FOR THE HISPANIC; Levine, Elaine S.; Padilla, Amado M.

4639 Gettman, Dawn and Pena, Devon Gerardo. Women, mental health, and the workplace in a transnational setting. SOCIAL WORK, Vol. 31, no. 1 (January, February, 1986), p. 5-11. English. DESCR: *Border Industries; *Chicanas; Employment; Mexico; United States-Mexico Relations; Women; *Working Women.

4640 Marcos, Luis R. Book review of: MENTAL HEALTH AND HISPANIC AMERICANS: CLINICAL PERSPECTIVES. AMERICAN JOURNAL OF PSYCHOTHERAPY, Vol. 38, no. 1 (January 1984), p. 155-156. English. DESCR: Book Reviews; Escobar, Javier I.; Karno, Marvin; *MENTAL HEALTH AND HISPANIC AMERICANS: CLINICAL PERSPECTIVES.

4641 Morris, Richard W. Psychosocial consequences of Mexican migration. LA RED/THE NET, no. 44 (July 1981), p. 2-3. English. DESCR: *Immigration.

4642 Ramirez, Oscar. Extended family support and mental health status among Mexicans in Detroit. LA RED/THE NET, no. 28 (March 1980), p. 2. English. DESCR: *Detroit, MI; *Extended Family.

4643 Ruiz, Rene A. Mental health, Hispanics and service. LA RED/THE NET, no. 61 (November 1982), p. 3-7. English. DESCR: Mental Health Personnel; Mental Health Programs.

4644 Salgado de Snyder, Nelly. The role of ethnic loyalty among Mexican immigrant women. HISPANIC JOURNAL OF BEHAVIORAL SCIENCES, Vol. 9, no. 3 (September 1987), p. 287-298. English. DESCR: Acculturation; Chicanas; *Culture; *Identity; Immigrants; *Mexico; *Women.

Mental Health (cont.)

4645 Vargas-Willis, Gloria and Cervantes, Richard C. Consideration of psychosocial stress in the treatment of the Latina immigrant. HISPANIC JOURNAL OF BEHAVIORAL SCIENCES, Vol. 9, no. 3 (September 1987), p. 315-329. English. **DESCR:** *Chicanas; Discrimination in Employment; *Immigrants; *Psychotherapy; *Stress.

4646 Zippin, David H. and Hough, Richard L. Perceived self-other differences in life events and mental health among Mexicans and Americans. JOURNAL OF PSYCHOLOGY, Vol. 119, no. 2 (March 1985), p. 143-155. English. **DESCR:** Anglo Americans; *Comparative Psychology; *Locus of Control; Mexico; Psychiatry; *Stress.

MENTAL HEALTH AND HISPANIC AMERICANS: CLINICAL PERSPECTIVES

4647 Canive, Jose. Book review of: MENTAL HEALTH AND HISPANIC AMERICANS: CLINICAL PERSPECTIVES. JOURNAL OF NERVOUS AND MENTAL DISEASE, Vol. 172, no. 9 (September 1984), p. 559-561. English. **DESCR:** Ancianos; Becerra, Rosina; Book Reviews; Escobar, Javier I.; Karno, Marvin.

4648 Gibson, Guadalupe. Book review of: MENTAL HEALTH AND HISPANIC AMERICANS: CLINICAL PERSPECTIVES. SOCIAL WORK, Vol. 29, no. 1 (January, February, 1984), p. 81. English. **DESCR:** Becerra, Rosina; Book Reviews; Escobar, Javier I.; Karno, Marvin.

4649 Marcos, Luis R. Book review of: MENTAL HEALTH AND HISPANIC AMERICANS: CLINICAL PERSPECTIVES. AMERICAN JOURNAL OF PSYCHOTHERAPY, Vol. 38, no. 1 (January 1984), p. 155-156. English. **DESCR:** Book Reviews; Escobar, Javier I.; Karno, Marvin; Mental Health.

Mental Health Clinics

4650 Costello, Raymond M. Hispanic alcoholic treatment considerations. HISPANIC JOURNAL OF BEHAVIORAL SCIENCES, Vol. 9, no. 1 (March 1987), p. 83-89. English. **DESCR:** *Alcoholism; Anglo Americans.

Mental Health Personnel

4651 Evans, Leonard A., et al. Orienting psychotherapists to better serve low income and minority patients. JOURNAL OF CLINICAL PSYCHOLOGY, Vol. 40, no. 1 (January 1984), p. 90-96. English. **DESCR:** Psychiatry; *Psychotherapy.

4652 Ruiz, Rene A. Mental health, Hispanics and service. LA RED/THE NET, no. 61 (November 1982), p. 3-7. English. **DESCR:** *Mental Health; Mental Health Programs.

Mental Health Programs

4653 Reeves, Kate. Hispanic utilization of an ethnic mental health clinic. JOURNAL OF PSYCHOSOCIAL NURSING AND MENTAL HEALTH SERVICES, Vol. 24, no. 2 (February 1986), p. 23-26. English. **DESCR:** La Clinica Nueva Esperanza, Orange County, CA.

4654 Ruiz, Rene A. Mental health, Hispanics and service. LA RED/THE NET, no. 61 (November 1982), p. 3-7. English. **DESCR:** *Mental Health; Mental Health Personnel.

Mental Hygiene
USE: Mental Health

Mental Illness

4655 Roberts, Robert E. and Vernon, Sally W. Minority status and psychological distress reexamined: the case of Mexican Americans. RESEARCH IN COMMUNITY AND MENTAL HEALTH, Vol. 4, (1984), p. 131-164. English. **DESCR:** Anglo Americans; Blacks.

Mentally Handicapped

4656 Meyers, C.E.; Borthwick, S.A.; and Eyman, R.K. Place of residence by age, ethnicity, and level of retardation of the mentally retarded/developmentally disabled population of California. AMERICAN JOURNAL OF MENTAL DEFICIENCY, Vol. 90, no. 3 (November 1985), p. 266-270. English. **DESCR:** California; Identity; Public Health.

4657 Rueda, Robert and Smith, Doug C. Interpersonal tactics and communicative strategies of Anglo-American and Mexican-American mildly mentally retarded and nonretarded students. APPLIED RESEARCH IN MENTAL RETARDATION, Vol. 4, no. 2 (1983), p. 153-161. English. **DESCR:** Children.

MERCEDES REALES: HISPANIC LAND GRANTS OF THE UPPER RIO GRANDE REGION

4658 Weber, David J. Book review of: MERCEDES REALES: HISPANIC LAND GRANTS OF THE UPPER RIO GRANDE REGION. AMERICAN HISTORICAL REVIEW, Vol. 89, no. 4 (October 1984), p. 1156-1157. English. **DESCR:** Book Reviews; Westphall, Victor.

MERIENDA TEJANA

4659 Reyna, Jose R. Book review of: MERIENDA TEJANA. LECTOR, Vol. 4, no. 4-6 (1987), p. 76. English. **DESCR:** Book Reviews; Galindo, Mary Sue.

Mestizaje

4660 Bruce-Novoa, Juan. Mexico en la literatura chicana (I). LA COMUNIDAD, No. 267 (September 1, 1985), p. 12-13. Spanish. **DESCR:** History; *Literary Criticism; Mexican Revolution - 1910-1920; *Mexico; Precolumbian Society.

Methodology
USE: Research Methodology

Metropolitan Hospital, New York, NY

4661 Olarte, Silvia W. and Masnik, Ruth. Benefits of long-term group therapy for disadvantaged Hispanic outpatients. HOSPITAL AND COMMUNITY PSYCHIATRY, Vol. 36, no. 10 (October 1985), p. 1093-1097. English. **DESCR:** Ethnic Groups; New York, NY; Psychotherapy; Sex Roles; *Women.

Metropolitan Life Insurance Corporation

4662 Edmondson, Brad. Met Life mines minority market. AMERICAN DEMOGRAPHICS, Vol. 8, no. 7 (July 1986), p. 18-19. English. **DESCR:** Consumers; Ethnic Groups; Immigrants; Insurance; Marketing.

Metropolitan Life Insurance Corporation (cont.)

4663 Hispanic chamber endorses insurance
     marketing plan. HISPANIC TIMES, Vol. 8, no.
     3 (May, June, 1987), p. 26. English. **DESCR:**
     Business Enterprises; Insurance; Lopez,
     Ruben; *U.S. Hispanic Chamber of Commerce.

4664 Hispanic marketing. ADVERTISING AGE
     MAGAZINE, Vol. 57, no. 16 (February 27,
     1986), p. 11-51. English. **DESCR:** Adolph
     Coors Co.; Advertising; Allstate Insurance
     Co.; American Greetings; Anheuser-Busch,
     Inc.; Business Enterprises; Coca-Cola
     Company; Consumers; Ford Motor Company;
     Hallmark Cards; *Marketing; Mass Media;
     McDonald's Corporation; Pepsi-Cola Bottling
     Group; Prudential; Spanish International
     Network (SIN); State Farm Mutual Insurance;
     Tylenol; United Insurance Co. of America.

4665 Sellers, Jeff M. Metropolitan Life continues
     to lead. HISPANIC BUSINESS, Vol. 9, no. 5
     (May 1987), p. 12-14. English. **DESCR:**
     Advertising; Corporations; *Insurance;
     *Marketing; U.S. Hispanic Chamber of
     Commerce.

THE MEXICAN AMERICAN: A CRITICAL GUIDE TO RESEARCH AIDS

4666 Chabran, Richard and Garcia-Ayvens,
     Francisco. Book review of: THE MEXICAN
     AMERICAN: A CRITICAL GUIDE TO RESEARCH AIDS.
     LA RED/THE NET, no. 37 (December 1980), p.
     4-5. English. **DESCR:** Bibliography; Book
     Reviews; *Reference Works; *Robinson,
     Barbara J.; *Robinson, J. Cordell.

MEXICAN AMERICAN ARCHIVES AT THE BENSON COLLECTION

4667 Chabran, Richard. Book review of: MEXICAN
     AMERICAN ARCHIVES AT THE BENSON COLLECTION:
     A GUIDE FOR USERS. LA RED/THE NET, no. 52
     (March 1982), p. 6-7. English. **DESCR:**
     Archives; Book Reviews; Flores, Maria;
     *Gutierrez-Witt, Laura.

Mexican American Engineering Society (MAES)

4668 Gutierrez, Daniel M. MAES Houston chapter
     sponsors 3rd annual scholarship banquet.
     HISPANIC TIMES, Vol. 8, no. 3 (May, June,
     1987), p. 42. English. **DESCR:** Awards;
     Financial Aid.

4669 Keep pace with MAES: Sociedad de Ingenieria
     de Mexicano Americanos (Mexican American
     Engineering Society). HISPANIC TIMES, Vol.
     8, no. 1 (December, January, 1987), p. 28.
     Bilingual. **DESCR:** Engineering as a
     Profession; Organizations.

4670 MAES chairman appointed to DEOMI board of
     visitors. HISPANIC TIMES, Vol. 8, no. 3
     (May, June, 1987), p. 42. English. **DESCR:**
     Appointed Officials; *Cano, Oscar;
     Department of Defense Equal Opportunities
     Management Institute (DEOMI).

4671 MAES now has eleven professional chapters
     nationwide (and more to come). HISPANIC
     TIMES, Vol. 8, no. 5 (October, November,
     1987), p. 42. English. **DESCR:** *Engineering
     as a Profession; Organizations.

4672 MAES sets the pace. HISPANIC TIMES, Vol. 8,
     no. 1 (December, January, 1987), p. 26.
     English. **DESCR:** Engineering as a Profession;
     Organizations.

4673 Rifkin, Jane M. Manuel Castro--founder of
     MAES: a compassionate commitment. HISPANIC
     TIMES, Vol. 8, no. 5 (October, November,

1987), p. 44. English. **DESCR:** Biography;
     *Castro, Manuel; Engineering as a
     Profession.

4674 Rifkin, Jane M. Ralph de la Parra travels
     the MAES "bridge to the future". HISPANIC
     TIMES, Vol. 8, no. 1 (December, January,
     1987), p. 30. English. **DESCR:** Biography; *De
     la Parra, Ralph; *Engineering as a
     Profession; Southern California Edison Co.

4675 Taylor, Wendy. Una asociacion que trabaja.
     HISPANIC TIMES, Vol. 8, no. 5 (October,
     November, 1987), p. 36-38. Spanish. **DESCR:**
     *Engineering as a Profession; *TRW Defense
     Systems Group.

4676 Taylor, Wendy. A working partnership.
     HISPANIC TIMES, Vol. 8, no. 5 (October,
     November, 1987), p. 12-13. English. **DESCR:**
     *Engineering as a Profession; *TRW Defense
     Systems Group.

THE MEXICAN AMERICAN EXPERIENCE: AN INTERDISCIPLINARY ANTHOLOGY

4677 Meier, Matt S. Book review of: THE MEXICAN
     AMERICAN EXPERIENCE: AN INTERDISCIPLINARY
     ANTHOLOGY. HISPANIC AMERICAN HISTORICAL
     REVIEW, Vol. 66, no. 3 (August 1986), p.
     629-630. English. **DESCR:** Alvarez, Rodolfo;
     Bean, Frank D.; Bonjean, Charles M.; Book
     Reviews; de la Garza, Rodolfo O.; Romo,
     Ricardo.

4678 Ruiz, Vicki Lynn. Book review of: THE
     MEXICAN AMERICAN EXPERIENCE: AN
     INTERDISCIPLINARY ANTHOLOGY. SOUTHWESTERN
     HISTORICAL QUARTERLY, Vol. 90, no. 2 (1986),
     p. 205-206. English. **DESCR:** Alvarez,
     Rodolfo; Bean, Frank D.; Bonjean, Charles
     M.; Book Reviews; de la Garza, Rodolfo O.;
     Romo, Ricardo.

4679 Salmon, Roberto Mario. Book review of: THE
     MEXICAN AMERICAN EXPERIENCE: AN
     INTERDISCIPLINARY ANTHOLOGY. LA RED/THE NET,
     no. 93 (January, February, 1986), p. 12-14.
     English. **DESCR:** Alvarez, Rodolfo; Bean,
     Frank D.; Bonjean, Charles M.; Book Reviews;
     de la Garza, Rodolfo O.; Romo, Ricardo.

MEXICAN AMERICAN FERTILITY PATTERNS

4680 Hastings, D.W. Book review of: MEXICAN
     AMERICAN FERTILITY PATTERNS. CHOICE, Vol.
     23, no. 11-12 (July, August, 1986), p. 1738.
     English. **DESCR:** Bean, Frank D.; Book
     Reviews; Swicegood, Gray.

Mexican American Grocers Association (MAGA)

4681 Zwiebach, Elliot. An important and growing
     consumer segment. SUPERMARKET NEWS, Vol. 34,
     (May 7, 1984), p. 8,10,120. English.
     DESCR: *Marketing; Television.

Mexican American Legal Defense and Educational Fund (MALDEF)

4682 Beale, Stephen. MALDEF weathers a storm.
     HISPANIC BUSINESS, Vol. 9, no. 5 (May 1987),
     p. 10-11. English. **DESCR:** Anaya, Toney,
     Governor of New Mexico; Civil Rights;
     Hernandez, Antonia A.; Organizations; Serna,
     Eric P.

Mexican American Legal Defense and Educational Fund (MALDEF) (cont.)

4683 Conner, Roger and Moreno, G. Mario. The Immigration Reform Law: how fair to Hispanics? VISTA, Vol. 2, no. 8 (April 4, 1987), p. 12, 17, 18. English. **DESCR:** Federation for American Immigration Reform (FAIR); *Immigration; *Immigration Reform and Control Act of 1986; League of United Latin American Citizens (LULAC).

4684 Hernandez prevails in fight over job. NUESTRO, Vol. 11, no. 2 (March 1987), p. 6. English. **DESCR:** *Anaya, Toney, Governor of New Mexico; *Hernandez, Antonia A.; Organizations.

4685 Shaw, Katherine. Antonia Hernandez. VISTA, Vol. 1, no. 2 (October 5, 1985), p. 16. English. **DESCR:** *Biography; Chicanas; *Hernandez, Antonia A.

Mexican American Political Association (MAPA)

4686 Bueno, Patricia E. Los Chicanos y la politica II. LA COMUNIDAD, No. 268 (September 8, 1985), p. 2-3. Spanish. **DESCR:** American G.I. Forum; Chicano Movement; History; Leadership; Nationalism; Political Association of Spanish-Speaking Organizations (PASO); *Political Parties and Organizations.

Mexican American Studies and Research Center, University of Arizona, Tucson, AZ

4687 Perez, Emma. Higher education organizations. LA RED/THE NET, no. 94 (March 1986), p. 2-4. English. **DESCR:** Educational Organizations; Higher Education; *Research Centers.

MEXICAN AMERICAN THEATRE: THEN AND NOW

4688 Somoza, Oscar U. Book review of: MEXICAN AMERICAN THEATRE: THEN AND NOW. LATIN AMERICAN THEATRE REVIEW, Vol. 17, no. 2 (Spring 1984), p. 105-106. Spanish. **DESCR:** Book Reviews; Kanellos, Nicolas.

Mexican American War, 1846-1848

4689 Paredes, Raymund A. Book review of: TO THE HALLS OF THE MONTEZUMAS. PACIFIC HISTORICAL REVIEW, Vol. 56, no. 1 (February 1987), p. 123-124. English. **DESCR:** Book Reviews; Johannsen, Robert W.; *TO THE HALLS OF THE MONTEZUMAS: THE MEXICAN WAR IN THE AMERICAN IMAGINATION.

Mexican American Youth Organization (MAYO)

4690 MEChA - University of Texas at El Paso; MAYO, University of Texas at Austin; and PASO, Texas A and I University. Student perspectives on Mexican/American studies. EPOCA: NATIONAL CONCILIO FOR CHICANO STUDIES JOURNAL, Vol. 1, no. 2 (Winter 1971), p. 87-96. English. **DESCR:** *Chicano Studies; Curriculum; Movimiento Estudiantil Chicano de Aztlan (MEChA); Student Organizations; Students; Texas.

Mexican American Youth Organization, San Antonio, TX

4691 Arreola, Daniel D. The Mexican American cultural capital. GEOGRAPHICAL REVIEW, Vol. 77, (January 1987), p. 17-34. English. **DESCR:** Conjuntos; Food Industry; History; Immigration; LA PRENSA, San Antonio, TX; La Raza Unida Party; League of United Latin American Citizens (LULAC); Lozano, Ignacio; Music; Orden Hijos de America, San Antonio,

TX; Railroads; *San Antonio, TX; *Social History and Conditions.

MEXICAN AMERICANS AND THE MASS MEDIA

4692 Delgado, Melvin. Book review of: MEXICAN-AMERICANS AND THE MASS-MEDIA. HISPANIC JOURNAL OF BEHAVIORAL SCIENCES, Vol. 9, no. 4 (December 1987), p. 461-463. English. **DESCR:** Book Reviews; Greenberg, Bradley S.; Mass Media.

4693 Ockerman, Janet D. Book review of: MEXICAN-AMERICANS AND THE MASS-MEDIA. PUBLIC OPINION QUARTERLY, Vol. 49, no. 1 (Spring 1985), p. 138-139. English. **DESCR:** Book Reviews; Greenberg, Bradley S.

4694 Reese, Stephen D. Book review of: MEXICAN-AMERICANS AND THE MASS-MEDIA. JOURNALISM QUARTERLY, Vol. 61, no. 3 (Fall 1984), p. 705-706. English. **DESCR:** Book Reviews; Greenberg, Bradley S.; Mass Media.

4695 Subervi-Velez, Federico. Book review of: MEXICAN-AMERICANS AND THE MASS-MEDIA. INTERNATIONAL JOURNAL OF INTERCULTURAL RELATIONS, Vol. 8, no. 3 (1984), p. 340-342. English. **DESCR:** Book Reviews; Greenberg, Bradley S.; Mass Media.

MEXICAN AMERICANS IN SCHOOL: A DECADE OF CHANGE

4696 Garcia, Philip. Book review of: MEXICAN AMERICANS IN SCHOOL: A DECADE OF CHANGE. LA RED/THE NET, no. 33 (August 1980), p. 4. English. **DESCR:** Book Reviews; Carter, Thomas P.; *Education; Segura, Roberto D.

MEXICAN AMERICANS IN COMPARATIVE PERSPECTIVE

4697 Dorn, Georgette Magassy. Book review of: MEXICAN-AMERICANS IN COMPARATIVE PERSPECTIVES. AMERICAS, Vol. 43, no. 1 (July 1986), p. 110. English. **DESCR:** Book Reviews; Connor, Walker.

MEXICAN AND MEXICAN AMERICAN FARM WORKERS: THE CALIFORNIA AGRICULTURAL INDUSTRY

4698 Reisler, Mark. Book review of: MEXICAN AND MEXICAN AMERICAN FARM WORKERS. PACIFIC HISTORICAL REVIEW, Vol. 55, (August 1986), p. 494. English. **DESCR:** Book Reviews; Gonzales, Juan L., Jr.

4699 Thomas, Robert J. Book review of: MEXICAN AND MEXICAN AMERICAN FARM WORKERS. CONTEMPORARY SOCIOLOGY: A JOURNAL OF REVIEWS, Vol. 16, no. 1 (January 1987), p. 106-107. English. **DESCR:** Book Reviews; Gonzales, Juan L., Jr.

Mexican Art

4700 Chavanell, Joe. Folk art's gift of Christmas joy. VISTA, Vol. 3, no. 4 (December 6, 1987), p. 8, 16. English. **DESCR:** *Arts and Crafts.

4701 Cox, Charlene B. Motivos artisticos. AMERICAS, Vol. 37, no. 1 (January, February, 1985), p. 2-5, 64. Spanish. **DESCR:** *Arreguin, Alfredo; *Artists; Folk Art; Paintings.

4702 Gambrell, Jamey. Texas: state of the art. ART IN AMERICA, Vol. 75, no. 3 (March 1987), p. 114-131+. English. **DESCR:** *Art; Art Galleries; Art Organizations and Groups; *Artists; Dia de los Muertos; Folk Art; Texas.

THE MEXICAN FRONTIER, 1821-1846: THE AMERICAN SOUTHWEST UNDER MEXICO

4703 Griswold del Castillo, Richard. New perspectives on the Mexican and American borderlands. LATIN AMERICAN RESEARCH REVIEW, Vol. 19, no. 1 (1984), p. 199-209. English. DESCR: AL NORTE DEL RIO BRAVO (PASADO INMEDIATO, 1930-1981); AL NORTE DEL RIO BRAVO (PASADO LEJANO, 1600-1930); *Book Reviews; *Border Region; Gomez-Quinones, Juan; Maciel, David; MEXICANO RESISTANCE IN THE SOUTHWEST: "THE SACRED RIGHT OF SELF-PRESERVATION"; Rosenbaum, Robert J.; THE TEJANO COMMUNITY, 1836-1900; Weber, David J.

4704 Miller, Robert Ryal. Book review of: THE MEXICAN FRONTIER 1821-1846. CALIFORNIA HISTORY, Vol. 63, no. 3 (Summer 1984), p. 260-261. English. DESCR: Book Reviews; Weber, David J.

4705 Riley, James D. Book review of: THE MEXICAN FRONTIER 1821-1846. AMERICAS, Vol. 40, no. 4 (April 1984), p. 592-593. English. DESCR: Book Reviews; Weber, David J.

MEXICAN IMMIGRANT WORKERS IN THE U.S.

4706 Bracamonte, Jose A. Book review of: MEXICAN IMMIGRANT WORKERS IN THE U.S. LA RED/THE NET, no. 49 (December 1981), p. 3-4. English. DESCR: Immigration; *Rios-Bustamante, Antonio.

MEXICAN IMMIGRANTS AND MEXICAN AMERICANS: AN EVOLVING RELATION

4707 Hastings, D.W. Book review of: MEXICAN IMMIGRANTS AND MEXICAN AMERICANS: AN EVOLVING RELATION. CHOICE, Vol. 24, no. 3 (November 1986), p. 516. English. DESCR: Book Reviews; Browning, Harley L.; de la Garza, Rodolfo O.

Mexican Literature

4708 Eberstadt, Fernanda. Montezuma's literary revenge. COMMENTARY, Vol. 81, no. 5 (May 1986), p. 35-40. English. DESCR: *Fuentes, Carlos; GRINGO VIEJO; *Literary Criticism; THE DEATH OF ARTEMIO CRUZ; THE GOOD CONSCIENCE; WHERE THE AIR IS CLEAR.

4709 Lower, Andrea. La unidad narrativa en LA MUERTE DE ARTEMIO CRUZ. TINTA, Vol. 1, no. 3 (December 1983), p. 19-26. Spanish. DESCR: Fuentes, Carlos; *LA MUERTE DE ARTEMIO CRUZ; Literary Criticism; *Novel.

4710 Mendez-M., Miguel. Observaciones sobre la literatura fronteriza. RENATO ROSALDO LECTURE SERIES MONOGRAPH, Vol. 2, (Spring 1986), p. [21]-27. Spanish. DESCR: *Border Region; *Literary History; *Literature.

Mexican Maquiladora Program

4711 Harrell, Louis and Fischer, Dale. The 1982 Mexican peso devaluation and border area employment. MONTHLY LABOR REVIEW, Vol. 108, no. 10 (October 1985), p. 25-32. English. DESCR: Border Industries; *Border Region; *Currency; *International Economic Relations; *Mexico.

Mexican Revolution - 1910-1920

4712 Bruce-Novoa, Juan. Mexico en la literatura chicana (I). LA COMUNIDAD, No. 267 (September 1, 1985), p. 12-13. Spanish. DESCR: History; *Literary Criticism; Mestizaje; *Mexico; Precolumbian Society.

4713 Garcia, Mario T. Book review of: FRAGMENTS OF THE MEXICAN REVOLUTION. HISPANIC AMERICAN HISTORICAL REVIEW, Vol. 65, no. 1 (February 1985), p. 150-151. English. DESCR: Book Reviews; *FRAGMENTS OF THE MEXICAN REVOLUTION: PERSONAL ACCOUNTS FROM THE BORDER; Martinez, Oscar J.

4714 Sandos, James A. Northern separatism during the Mexican revolution--an inquiry into the role of drug trafficking, 1910-1920. AMERICAS, Vol. 41, no. 2 (October 1984), p. 191-214. English. DESCR: Baja California, Mexico; Border Region; Cantu Jimenez, Esteban; Drug Addicts; Drug Laws; *Drug Traffic; *Drug Use; Medical Care; Revolutions.

THE MEXICAN REVOLUTION: AN ANNOTATED GUIDE TO RECENT SCHOLARSHIP

4715 de Baca, Vincent C. Book review of: INDEX TO SPANISH AMERICAN COLLECTIVE BIOGRAPHY, vol. 2: MEXICO and THE MEXICAN REVOLUTION: AN ANNOTATED GUIDE TO RECENT SCHOLARSHIP. LA RED/THE NET, no. 72 (September 1983), p. 19-21. English. DESCR: Book Reviews; de Mundo Lo, Sara; *INDEX TO SPANISH AMERICAN COLLECTIVE BIOGRAPHY, vol. 2: MEXICO; Raat, W. Dirk; Reference Works.

MEXICAN WOMEN IN THE UNITED STATES: STRUGGLES PAST AND PRESENT

4716 Soto, Shirlene. Book review of: MEXICAN WOMEN IN THE UNITED STATES: STRUGGLES PAST AND PRESENT. LA RED/THE NET, no. 35 (October 1980), p. 4. English. DESCR: Book Reviews; *Chicanas; Del Castillo, Adelaida R.; *Mora, Magdalena.

Mexicanism
USE: Nationalism

MEXICANO RESISTANCE IN THE SOUTHWEST: "THE SACRED RIGHT OF SELF-PRESERVATION"

4717 Griswold del Castillo, Richard. New perspectives on the Mexican and American borderlands. LATIN AMERICAN RESEARCH REVIEW, Vol. 19, no. 1 (1984), p. 199-209. English. DESCR: AL NORTE DEL RIO BRAVO (PASADO INMEDIATO, 1930-1981); AL NORTE DEL RIO BRAVO (PASADO LEJANO, 1600-1930); *Book Reviews; *Border Region; Gomez-Quinones, Juan; Maciel, David; Rosenbaum, Robert J.; THE MEXICAN FRONTIER, 1821-1846: THE AMERICAN SOUTHWEST UNDER MEXICO; THE TEJANO COMMUNITY, 1836-1900; Weber, David J.

4718 Salmon, Roberto Mario. Book review of: MEXICANO RESISTANCE IN THE SOUTHWEST. LA RED/THE NET, no. 44 (July 1981), p. 6-7. English. DESCR: Book Reviews; New Mexico; Rosenbaum, Robert J.

THE MEXICANS IN OKLAHOMA

4719 Hall, Linda B. The United States-Mexican borders: historical, political, and cultural perspectives. LATIN AMERICAN RESEARCH REVIEW, Vol. 20, no. 2 (1985), p. 223-229. English. DESCR: AMERICAN LABOR IN THE SOUTHWEST: THE FIRST ONE HUNDRED YEARS; *Book Reviews; *Border Region; BOSS RULE IN SOUTH TEXAS: THE PROGRESSIVE ERA; CHICANO INTERMARRIAGE: A THEORETICAL AND EMPIRICAL STUDY; HISPANIC CULTURE IN THE SOUTHWEST; IN DEFENSE OF LA RAZA: THE LOS ANGELES MEXICAN CONSULATE AND THE MEXICAN COMMUNITY; Literature Reviews; RACE AND CLASS IN THE SOUTHWEST: A THEORY OF RACIAL INEQUALITY; SOUTHWESTERN AGRICULTURE: PRE-COLUMBIAN TO MODERN; THE POLITICS OF SAN ANTONIO.

Mexico

4720 Bruce-Novoa, Juan. Mexico en la literatura chicana (I). LA COMUNIDAD, No. 267 (September 1, 1985), p. 12-13. Spanish. DESCR: History; *Literary Criticism; Mestizaje; Mexican Revolution - 1910-1920; Precolumbian Society.

4721 Cisneros, Henry. Mexico's poorest are heading North. AKWESASNE NOTES, Vol. 18, no. 4 (Summer 1986), p. 7. English. DESCR: Alfaro, Victor Clark; Centro de Promocion Popular Urbana, Tijuana, Baja California, Mexico; Farm Workers; Kearney, Michael; Mixtec Indians; *Undocumented Workers.

4722 de la Garza, Rodolfo O. Book review of: MEXICO'S POLITICAL ECONOMY: CHALLENGES AT HOME AND ABROAD. LA RED/THE NET, no. 69 (June 1983), p. 5-7. English. DESCR: Book Reviews; Dominguez, Jorge; *MEXICO'S POLITICAL ECONOMY: CHALLENGES AT HOME AND ABROAD.

4723 Figoli, Haydee. Dos textos a proposito de la frontera. LA COMUNIDAD, No. 350 (April 5, 1987), p. 2-5. Spanish. DESCR: Chicano, Meaning of; Chicano Movement; *History.

4724 Gettman, Dawn and Pena, Devon Gerardo. Women, mental health, and the workplace in a transnational setting. SOCIAL WORK, Vol. 31, no. 1 (January, February, 1986), p. 5-11. English. DESCR: *Border Industries; *Chicanas; Employment; *Mental Health; United States-Mexico Relations; Women; *Working Women.

4725 Gilbert, M. Jean. Alcohol consumption patterns in immigrant and later generation Mexican American women. HISPANIC JOURNAL OF BEHAVIORAL SCIENCES, Vol. 9, no. 3 (September 1987), p. 299-313. English. DESCR: Acculturation; *Alcoholism; *Attitudes; *Chicanas; Cultural Characteristics; *Immigrants.

4726 Gomez Pena, Guillermo. Nuevo continente artistico. LA COMUNIDAD, No. 275 (October 27, 1985), p. 8-10. Spanish. DESCR: *Art; Artists; Border Region; Chicano Movement; DIALOGOS DE LAS AMERICAS; Indigenismo; International Relations; United States-Mexico Relations.

4727 Gonzales, Juan. Quinto Festival de los Teatros Chicanos - Primer Encuentro Latinoamericano. LATIN QUARTER, Vol. 1, no. 2 (October 1974), p. 31-33,35. English. DESCR: *Festivals; Teatro.

4728 Guendelman, Sylvia. The incorporation of Mexican women in seasonal migration: a study of gender differences. HISPANIC JOURNAL OF BEHAVIORAL SCIENCES, Vol. 9, no. 3 (September 1987), p. 245-264. English. DESCR: Chicanas; Immigrants; Marriage; *Migration Patterns; *Sex Roles; *Women; *Women Men Relations; Working Women.

4729 Gutierrez, Jose Angel. Chicanos and Mexicans: under surveillance: 1940 to 1980. RENATO ROSALDO LECTURE SERIES MONOGRAPH, Vol. 2, (Spring 1986), p. [29]-58. English. DESCR: Acuna, Rudolfo; Border Coverage Program (BOCOV); *Civil Rights; COINTELPRO; *Federal Bureau of Investigation (FBI); *Federal Government; History; League of United Latin American Citizens (LULAC); Political Parties and Organizations; *Political Repression.

4730 Harrell, Louis and Fischer, Dale. The 1982 Mexican peso devaluation and border area employment. MONTHLY LABOR REVIEW, Vol. 108, no. 10 (October 1985), p. 25-32. English. DESCR: Border Industries; *Border Region; *Currency; *International Economic Relations; Mexican Maquiladora Program.

4731 Keremitsis, Dawn. Del metate al molino: la mujer mexicana de 1910 a 1940. HISTORIA MEXICANA, Vol. 33, no. 2 (1983), p. 285-302. Spanish. DESCR: Food Industry; Labor Unions; Sex Roles; Strikes and Lockouts; Tortillas; *Working Women.

4732 LeCompte, Mary Lou. The Hispanic influence on the history of rodeo, 1823-1922. JOURNAL OF SPORT HISTORY, Vol. 12, no. 1 (Spring 1985), p. 21-38. English. DESCR: *Charreada; *Cultural Customs; *History.

4733 Limon, Jose E. La Llorona, the third legend of greater Mexico: cultural symbols, women, and the political unconscious. RENATO ROSALDO LECTURE SERIES MONOGRAPH, Vol. 2, (Spring 1986), p. [59]-93. English. DESCR: *Feminism; Folklore; *La Llorona; La Virgen de Guadalupe; *Leyendas; Malinche; *Symbolism; Women.

4734 Loaeza, Soledad. Alan Riding: la fuerza del prejuicio. LA COMUNIDAD, No. 255 (June 9, 1985), p. 2-5. Spanish. DESCR: Book Reviews; *DISTANT NEIGHBORS: A PORTRAIT OF THE MEXICANS; Riding, Alan.

4735 Massey, Douglas S. Do undocumented migrants earn lower wages than legal immigrants? New evidence from Mexico. INTERNATIONAL MIGRATION REVIEW, Vol. 21, no. 2 (Summer 1987), p. 236-274. English. DESCR: Employment; *Immigrants; *Income; Migration Patterns; *Undocumented Workers.

4736 Moraga, Pete. Response to a quake: hands across the border. VISTA, Vol. 1, no. 4 (December 7, 1985), p. 3. English. DESCR: Broadcast Media; Earthquakes; *KMEX, Los Angeles, CA [television station].

4737 Parlee, Lorena M. The impact of United States railroad unions on organized labor and government policy in Mexico (1880-1911). HISPANIC AMERICAN HISTORICAL REVIEW, Vol. 64, no. 3 (August 1984), p. 443-475. English. DESCR: Diaz, Porfirio; Discrimination in Employment; History; *Labor Unions; Partido Liberal Mexicano (PLM); Railroads; United States-Mexico Relations.

Mexico (cont.)

4738 Pearce, James E. and Gunther, Jeffery W. Illegal immigration from Mexico: effects on the Texas economy. ECONOMIC REVIEW (FEDERAL RESERVE BANK OF DALLAS), no. 9 (1985), p. 1-14. English. **DESCR:** Economics; Texas; *Undocumented Workers.

4739 Rodriguez Flores, Juan. Paul Leduc, FRIDA y el otro cine que no se exhibe en Los Angeles. LA COMUNIDAD, No. 290 (February 9, 1986), p. 12-13. Spanish. **DESCR:** *Films; FRIDA: NATURALEZA VIDA [film]; History; *Kahlo, Frida.

4740 Ruiz, Vicki Lynn. Obreras y madres: labor activism among Mexican women and its impact on the family. RENATO ROSALDO LECTURE SERIES MONOGRAPH, Vol. 1, (Summer 1985), p. [19]-38. English. **DESCR:** *Chicanas; Child Care Centers; Children; History; *Labor Unions; Sex Roles; Women; *Working Women.

4741 Salgado de Snyder, Nelly. The role of ethnic loyalty among Mexican immigrant women. HISPANIC JOURNAL OF BEHAVIORAL SCIENCES, Vol. 9, no. 3 (September 1987), p. 287-298. English. **DESCR:** Acculturation; Chicanas; *Culture; *Identity; Immigrants; Mental Health; *Women.

4742 Sellers, Jeff M. Missed opportunities. HISPANIC BUSINESS, Vol. 9, no. 4 (April 1987), p. 14-15. English. **DESCR:** *Border Industries; *Intergroup Relations; Language Usage; *Management.

4743 Zippin, David H. and Hough, Richard L. Perceived self-other differences in life events and mental health among Mexicans and Americans. JOURNAL OF PSYCHOLOGY, Vol. 119, no. 2 (March 1985), p. 143-155. English. **DESCR:** Anglo Americans; *Comparative Psychology; *Locus of Control; *Mental Health; Psychiatry; *Stress.

MEXICO AND THE UNITED STATES: INTERNATIONAL RELATIONS IN THE HUMANITIES

4744 Maciel, David R. Book review of: MEXICO AND THE UNITED STATES. LA RED/THE NET, no. 68 (May 1983), p. 8-9. English. **DESCR:** Book Reviews; Laboring Classes; McBride, Robert H.

Mexico City

4745 Cano, Oscar. MAES technical brief. HISPANIC TIMES, Vol. 8, no. 1 (December, January, 1987), p. 27. English. **DESCR:** *Earthquakes; Emergency Services.

4746 Sykes, Maltby. Diego Rivera and the Hotel Reforma murals. ARCHIVES OF AMERICAN ART JOURNAL, Vol. 25, no. 1-2 (1985), p. 29-40. English. **DESCR:** Artists; Hotel Reforma, Mexico City; Marxism; Mural Art; *Rivera, Diego.

MEXICO-ESTADOS UNIDOS: BIBLIOGRAFIA GENERAL SOBRE ESTUDIOS FRONTERIZOS

4747 Woods, Richard D. Book review of: MEXICO-ESTADOS UNIDOS: BIBLIOGRAFIA GENERAL SOBRE ESTUDIOS FRONTERIZOS. LA RED/THE NET, no. 49 (December 1981), p. 4-5. English. **DESCR:** Book Reviews; Border Studies; *Bustamante, Jorge A.; Malagamba, Francisco; Reference Works.

MEXICO'S POLITICAL ECONOMY: CHALLENGES AT HOME AND ABROAD

4748 de la Garza, Rodolfo O. Book review of: MEXICO'S POLITICAL ECONOMY: CHALLENGES AT HOME AND ABROAD. LA RED/THE NET, no. 69 (June 1983), p. 5-7. English. **DESCR:** Book Reviews; Dominguez, Jorge; Mexico.

MEXICO-UNITED STATES RELATIONS

4749 Gutierrez, Armando. Book reviews of: MEXICO-UNITED STATES RELATIONS and UNITED STATES RELATIONS WITH MEXICO: CONTEXT AND CONTENT. LA RED/THE NET, no. 62 (December 1982), p. 4-6. English. **DESCR:** Book Reviews; Erb, Richard D.; Kaufman, Purcell; Ross, Stanley R.; *UNITED STATES RELATIONS WITH MEXICO: CONTEXT AND CONTENT.

LE MEXIQUE, DES ORIGENES AUX AZTEQUES

4750 Book review of: LE MEXIQUE, DES ORIGINES AUX AZTEQUES. OEIL-REVUE D'ART MENSUELLE, (December 1986), p. 75. Other. **DESCR:** Aztecs; Bernal y Garcia Pimentel, Ignacio; Book Reviews; Simoni-Abbat, Mireille.

Meyer, Lorenzo

4751 Hunsaker, Alan C. Institutionally-based research centers: the Center for U.S.-Mexican Studies. LA RED/THE NET, no. 92 (November, December, 1985), p. 13-15. English. **DESCR:** *Center for U.S.-Mexican Studies, University of California at San Diego, La Jolla, CA; Del Castillo, Gustavo; *Research Centers; United States-Mexico Relations.

Meyer, Michael C.

4752 Fireman, Janet R. Book review of: WATER IN THE HISPANIC SOUTHWEST. SOUTHWESTERN HISTORICAL QUARTERLY, Vol. 88, no. 4 (1985), p. 430-431. English. **DESCR:** Book Reviews; *WATER IN THE HISPANIC SOUTHWEST: A SOCIAL AND LEGAL HISTORY, 1550-1850.

4753 Langum, David J. Book review of: WATER IN THE HISPANIC SOUTHWEST. AMERICAN JOURNAL OF LEGAL HISTORY, Vol. 30, no. 3 (July 1986), p. 273-276. English. **DESCR:** Book Reviews; *WATER IN THE HISPANIC SOUTHWEST: A SOCIAL AND LEGAL HISTORY, 1550-1850.

4754 Tutino, John. Book review of: WATER IN THE HISPANIC SOUTHWEST. AMERICAS, Vol. 42, no. 3 (January 1986), p. 355-356. English. **DESCR:** Book Reviews; *WATER IN THE HISPANIC SOUTHWEST: A SOCIAL AND LEGAL HISTORY, 1550-1850.

Meyer, Peter

4755 Aguirre, Adalberto, Jr. Book review of: THE YALE MURDER: THE FATAL ROMANCE OF BONNIE GARLAND AND RICHARD HERRIN. LA RED/THE NET, no. 71 (August 1983), p. 5-7. English. **DESCR:** Book Reviews; *THE YALE MURDER: THE FATAL ROMANCE OF BONNIE GARLAND AND RICHARD HERRIN.

Mezitis, Nicholas

4756 Remas, Theodora A. The threat of diabetes. VISTA, Vol. 1, no. 2 (October 5, 1985), p. 14-16. English. **DESCR:** *Diabetes; Health Education; *Nutrition; Public Health; Rico-Perez, Manuel.

MI QUERIDO RAFA

4757 Ugalde, Sharon E. Two visions of cultural domination: Carrero's EL HOMBRE QUE NO SUDABA and Hinojosa's MI QUERIDO RAFA. BILINGUAL REVIEW, Vol. 12, no. 1-2 (January, August, 1985), p. 159-165. English. DESCR: Carrero, Jaime; *EL HOMBRE QUE NO SUDABA; Hinojosa-Smith, Rolando R.; Literary Criticism.

Miami Book Fair International

4758 Seeking more readers for Hispanic literature. VISTA, Vol. 2, no. 3 (November 2, 1986), p. 25. English. DESCR: Hinojosa-Smith, Rolando R.; *Literature; Mohr, Nicolasa; Munoz, Elias Miguel; Rodriguez, Richard.

Miami, FL

4759 Cardenas, Antonio J. and Cardenas, Cecilia. Traditions of Christmas. VISTA, Vol. 2, no. 4 (December 7, 1986), p. 14-17. English. DESCR: El Paso, TX; Festivals; *Holidays; *Reyes Magos Tradition.

EL MIAMI HERALD

4760 Cecere, Linda. Newspapers attract attention in some categories. ADVERTISING AGE MAGAZINE, Vol. 57, no. 43 (August 11, 1986), p. S9-S10. English. DESCR: Advertising; DIARIO DE LAS AMERICAS; LA OPINION, Los Angeles, CA; *Newspapers; NOTICIAS DEL MUNDO; Spanish Language.

Miami Sound Machine

4761 Gordon, Polita C. Living the crossover dream. VISTA, Vol. 1, no. 8 (April 6, 1986), p. 6-9. English. DESCR: *Blades, Ruben; Colon, Willie; Los Lobos del Este de Los Angeles (musical group); *Musicians.

4762 Sellers, Jeff M. The sound of musica: moving into the mainstream. HISPANIC BUSINESS, Vol. 9, no. 7 (July 1987), p. 14-18. English. DESCR: Los Lobos del Este de Los Angeles (musical group); *Marketing; Music; *Musicians; The Cruzados [musical group]; Zerimar [musical group].

Michigan

4763 Boycotts revisited: Campbell's concedes to farm worker campaign. DOLLARS AND SENSE, (July, August, 1986), p. 12-14, 18. English. DESCR: Boycotts; California; Campbell Soup Co.; Farm Labor Organizing Commmittee (FLOC); Farm Workers; *Labor Disputes; Labor Unions; Ohio; Strikes and Lockouts; United Farmworkers of America (UFW).

Michigan Civil Rights Department

4764 Dempsey, Mary. John Roy Castillo. VISTA, Vol. 1, no. 11 (July 6, 1986), p. 20. English. DESCR: *Biography; *Castillo, John Ray; Civil Rights.

Middle Class
USE: Social Classes

Midwestern States

4765 Barger, W.K. and Reza, Ernesto. Midwestern farmworkers and the farm labor movement. LA RED/THE NET, no. 78 (March 1984), p. 2-7. English. DESCR: *Farm Workers; Migrant Labor; Surveys.

4766 Barger, W.K. Public attitudes towards Mexican-American farmworkers in the Midwest. LA RED/THE NET, no. 63 (January 1983), p. 2-4. English. DESCR: Attitudes; *Farm Workers; *Public Opinion.

4767 Garcia, John R. Book reviews of: EL PUEBLO MEXICANO EN DETROIT Y MICHIGAN and MATERIALS ON THE HISTORY OF LATINOS IN MICHIGAN AND THE MIDWEST. LA RED/THE NET, no. 67 (April 1983), p. 13-14. English. DESCR: Book Reviews; *EL PUEBLO MEXICANO EN DETROIT Y MICHIGAN: A SOCIAL HISTORY; *MATERIALS ON THE HISTORY OF LATINOS IN MICHIGAN AND THE MIDWEST; Valdes, Dennis N.

4768 Report to the Network. LA RED/THE NET, No. 104 (January 1987), p. 1-2. English. DESCR: Computers; *Contreras, Reynaldo A.; *Higher Education; *Natural Support Systems; Research Methodology; Surveys.

4769 Wreford, Mary. Chicano Survey report #2: perceptions and experience of discrimination. LA RED/THE NET, no. 39 (February 1981), p. 7,16. English. DESCR: *Discrimination; Discrimination in Employment; *National Chicano Survey (NCS); Southwestern United States; *Surveys.

4770 Wreford, Mary. Reactions from the Chicano Survey respondents: no mas silencio. LA RED/THE NET, no. 33 (August 1980), p. 2-3. English. DESCR: Chicano Project of the University of Michigan; *National Chicano Survey (NCS); *Public Opinion; Social Science; Southwestern United States; *Surveys.

La Migra
USE: Immigration Regulation and Control

Migrant Children

4771 Chesser, Barbara and Inguanzo-Schleff, Dania. Loneliness among Mexican migrant children. LA RED/THE NET, no. 44 (July 1981), p. 3-4. English. DESCR: Depression (Psychological); Mental Health.

4772 Dewey, Kathryn G.; Strode, Margaret A.; and Fitch, Yolanda Ruiz. Dietary change among migrant and nonmigrant Mexican-American families in northern California. ECOLOGY OF FOOD AND NUTRITION, Vol. 14, no. 1 (1984), p. 11-24. English. DESCR: Culture; *Food Practices; Migrant Labor; Northern California; *Nutrition.

4773 Guzman, Ralph. Bi-national policy questions generated by Mexican school-age children who migrate between the United States and Mexico. LA RED/THE NET, no. 62 (December 1982), p. 2-4. English. DESCR: *Children; Immigrants; Public Policy; *Watsonville, CA.

Migrant Health Services

4774 Slesinger, Doris. Migrant workers in Wisconsin. LA RED/THE NET, no. 27 (February 1980), p. 2. English. DESCR: Migrant Labor; *Wisconsin.

4775 Smith, David M. Survey: hospitalization access for patients of migrant health centers and combined migrant and community health centers. MIGRATION WORLD MAGAZINE, Vol. 15, no. 3 (1987), p. 20-23. English. DESCR: *Surveys.

Migrant Labor

4776 Barger, W.K. and Reza, Ernesto. Midwestern farmworkers and the farm labor movement. LA RED/THE NET, no. 78 (March 1984), p. 2-7. English. **DESCR:** *Farm Workers; *Midwestern States; Surveys.

4777 Bennett, Jonathan A. At last, farmworkers are allowed clean water. GUARDIAN, Vol. 39, no. 20 (February 18, 1987), p. 9. English. **DESCR:** Farm Workers; *Occupational Hazards.

4778 Bustamante, Jorge A. International labor migration and external debt. MIGRATION WORLD MAGAZINE, Vol. 15, no. 3 (1987), p. 13-15. English. **DESCR:** Currency; *International Economic Relations; *Labor Supply and Market; *Undocumented Workers; United States-Mexico Relations.

4779 Dewey, Kathryn G.; Strode, Margaret A.; and Fitch, Yolanda Ruiz. Dietary change among migrant and nonmigrant Mexican-American families in northern California. ECOLOGY OF FOOD AND NUTRITION, Vol. 14, no. 1 (1984), p. 11-24. English. **DESCR:** Culture; *Food Practices; *Migrant Children; Northern California; *Nutrition.

4780 Gibson, Katherine and Graham, Julie. Situating migrants in theory. CAPITAL AND CLASS, no. 29 (Summer 1986), p. 130-149. English. **DESCR:** Philippines.

4781 O'Donnell, Patrick J. A preliminary report on the incidence of gestational diabetes in a Hispanic migrant population. MIGRATION WORLD MAGAZINE, Vol. 15, no. 1 (), p. 27-30. English. **DESCR:** *Diabetes; Farm Workers; *Public Health.

4782 Ramos, Hector. Latino caucuses in U.S. labor unions. RACE AND CLASS, Vol. 27, no. 4 (Spring 1986), p. 69. English. **DESCR:** Labor Unions; *Undocumented Workers.

4783 Slesinger, Doris. Migrant workers in Wisconsin. LA RED/THE NET, no. 27 (February 1980), p. 2. English. **DESCR:** *Migrant Health Services; *Wisconsin.

Migration Patterns

4784 Guendelman, Sylvia. The incorporation of Mexican women in seasonal migration: a study of gender differences. HISPANIC JOURNAL OF BEHAVIORAL SCIENCES, Vol. 9, no. 3 (September 1987), p. 245-264. English. **DESCR:** Chicanas; Immigrants; Marriage; Mexico; *Sex Roles; *Women; *Women Men Relations; Working Women.

4785 Hunsaker, Alan C. Mexican immigration patterns. LA RED/THE NET, no. 93 (January, February, 1986), p. 17-19. English. **DESCR:** Book Reviews; Immigration; *Jones, Richard C.; PATTERNS OF UNDOCUMENTED MIGRATION: MEXICO AND THE U.S.

4786 Massey, Douglas S. Do undocumented migrants earn lower wages than legal immigrants? New evidence from Mexico. INTERNATIONAL MIGRATION REVIEW, Vol. 21, no. 2 (Summer 1987), p. 236-274. English. **DESCR:** Employment; *Immigrants; *Income; *Mexico; *Undocumented Workers.

Migratory Labor
USE: Migrant Labor

THE MILAGRO BEANFIELD WAR [film]

4787 Beale, Stephen. A turning point in

Hollywood. HISPANIC BUSINESS, Vol. 9, no. 7 (July 1987), p. 20-24, 36. English. **DESCR:** *Films; LA BAMBA [film]; *Marketing; Spanish Language; Stereotypes.

4788 Rodriguez Flores, Juan. Robert Redford y THE MILAGRO BEANFIELD WAR. LA COMUNIDAD, No. 328 (November 2, 1986), p. 8-11+. Spanish. **DESCR:** Actors and Actresses; *Films; *Redford, Robert.

4789 Rodriguez Flores, Juan. Ruben Blades: siempre he apostado a la sensibilidad del publico. LA COMUNIDAD, No. 330 (November 16, 1986), p. 8-11. Spanish. **DESCR:** Actors and Actresses; *Biography; *Blades, Ruben; Films; Music.

EL MILAGRUCHO

4790 Hutter, Harriet S. EL MILAGRUCHO: a linguistic commentary on a pachuco text. HISPANIA, Vol. 67, no. 2 (May 1984), p. 256-261. English. **DESCR:** *Chicano Dialects.

Mile Hi Cablevision

4791 Abalos, J. Victor. Paul Sandoval. VISTA, Vol. 1, no. 4 (December 7, 1985), p. 10. English. **DESCR:** Business Enterprises; Denver, CO; *Financial Aid; *Sandoval, Paul.

Militancy

4792 Chicano activist "Kiko" Martinez convicted. GUARDIAN, Vol. 39, no. 7 (November 12, 1986), p. 4. English. **DESCR:** Criminal Justice System; Legal Cases; *Martinez, Francisco "Kiko".

4793 Garcia, Richard. The ordeal of "Kiko" Martinez. GUARDIAN, Vol. 39, no. 3 (October 15, 1986), p. 2. English. **DESCR:** Criminal Justice System; Legal Cases; *Martinez, Francisco "Kiko".

Military

4794 Banks, Marissa Elena. Army maneuvers. HISPANIC BUSINESS, Vol. 9, no. 12 (December 1987), p. 37-39. English. **DESCR:** Advertising Agencies; Government Contracts; *Sosa & Associates; U.S. Department of Defense (DOD).

4795 Beale, Stephen. Defense cuts on the horizon? HISPANIC BUSINESS, Vol. 9, no. 10 (October 1987), p. 18-21. English. **DESCR:** *Business Enterprises; *Government Contracts.

4796 Bradby, Marie. The naval research laboratory. HISPANIC ENGINEER, Vol. 3, no. 2 (Summer 1987), p. 34-38. English. **DESCR:** *Engineering as a Profession; *Naval Research Laboratory; Rojas, Richard Raimond; Urrutia, Jorge R.

4797 Brower, Monty. A proud street mourns its fallen sons. PEOPLE WEEKLY, Vol. 21, (May 28, 1984), p. 76-78+. English. **DESCR:** Sandoval, Frank; Sandoval, Joseph; Silvis, IL; *World War II.

4798 Callahan, Jaime M. LATINO: un nuevo concepto de cine. LA COMUNIDAD, No. 279 (November 24, 1985), p. 2-3. Spanish. **DESCR:** *Films; Identity; *LATINO [film]; Military Service; Wexler, Haskell.

Military (cont.)

4799 Perez, Renato E. Hispanics in uniform.
VISTA, Vol. 1, no. 3 (November 3, 1985), p.
12-15. English. **DESCR:** Military Education;
Statistics.

4800 Perez, Renato E. Skydiving daredevils.
VISTA, Vol. 1, no. 10 (June 8, 1986), p.
14-16. English. **DESCR:** Golden Knights
[skydiving team]; Minino, Virgilio; *U.S.
Army.

4801 Sellers, Jeff M. High tech directory.
HISPANIC BUSINESS, Vol. 9, no. 10 (October
1987), p. 7-9. English. **DESCR:** *Business
Enterprises; Computers; *Electronics
Industry; *Government Contracts.

4802 Sellers, Jeff M. Strategic defenses: new
niches for small firms. HISPANIC BUSINESS,
Vol. 9, no. 10 (October 1987), p. 13-17.
English. **DESCR:** *Advanced Sciences Inc.,
Albuquerque, NM; Business Enterprises;
Electronics Industry; *Government Contracts;
*Orion International Technologies, Inc.;
Rios, Miguel, Jr.; Romero, Ed.

4803 Wald, Karen. U.S. defector "didn't want to
fight in Central America". GUARDIAN, Vol.
38, no. 44 (September 10, 1986), p. 12.
English. **DESCR:** Central America; *Romeu
Almeida, Hugo.

4804 Zucca, Gary J. and Gorman, Benjamin.
Affirmative action: Blacks and Hispanics in
United States Navy occupational specialties.
ARMED FORCES AND SOCIETY, Vol. 12, no. 4
(Summer 1986), p. 513-524. English. **DESCR:**
*Affirmative Action; *Blacks;
*Discrimination in Employment.

Military Education

4805 Perez, Renato E. Hispanics in uniform.
VISTA, Vol. 1, no. 3 (November 3, 1985), p.
12-15. English. **DESCR:** *Military;
Statistics.

Military Service

4806 Callahan, Jaime M. LATINO: un nuevo concepto
de cine. LA COMUNIDAD, No. 279 (November 24,
1985), p. 2-3. Spanish. **DESCR:** *Films;
Identity; *LATINO [film]; Military; Wexler,
Haskell.

Miller, Beth

4807 Bieder, Maryellen. Book review of: WOMEN IN
HISPANIC LITERATURE. MODERN FICTION STUDIES,
Vol. 30, no. 4 (Winter 1984), p. 738-740.
English. **DESCR:** Book Reviews; Women; *WOMEN
IN HISPANIC LITERATURE: ICONS AND FALLEN
IDOLS.

4808 Scanlon, Geraldine M. Book review of: WOMEN
IN HISPANIC LITERATURE. MODERN LANGUAGE
REVIEW, Vol. 81, (October 1986), p. 1017.
English. **DESCR:** Book Reviews; *WOMEN IN
HISPANIC LITERATURE: ICONS AND FALLEN IDOLS.

Miller, C.L.

4809 Rips, Geoffrey. Civil rights and wrongs.
TEXAS OBSERVER, Vol. 76, (December 14,
1984), p. 49-55. English. **DESCR:** Briscoe,
Dolph, Jr., Governor of Texas; *Civil
Rights; Farm Workers; *Hidalgo County, TX;
La Raza Unida Party; Segregation and
Desegregation; Texas Farmworkers' Union;
Voting Rights.

Miller, Darlis A.

4810 Anderson, Karen. Book review of: NEW MEXICO
WOMEN: INTERCULTURAL PERSPECTIVES. NEW
MEXICO HISTORICAL REVIEW, Vol. 62, no. 4
(October 1987), p. 401-2. English. **DESCR:**
Book Reviews; *Jensen, Joan M.; *New Mexico;
*NEW MEXICO WOMEN: INTERCULTURAL
PERSPECTIVES; Women.

Miller-Soule, Danielle I.

4811 Jackson, James S. Book review of:
UNDERSTANDING MINORITY AGING: PERSPECTIVES
AND SOURCES. LA RED/THE NET, no. 68 (May
1983), p. 12-13. English. **DESCR:** Book
Reviews; Cuellar, Jose B.; Stanford, E.P.
Percil; *UNDERSTANDING MINORITY AGING:
PERSPECTIVES AND SOURCES.

Milwaukee, WI

4812 Haslanger, Phil. A rival to the gangs. THE
PROGRESSIVE, Vol. 50, (October 1986), p.
15. English. **DESCR:** Diaz, Ricardo; *Gangs.

Minino, Virgilio

4813 Perez, Renato E. Skydiving daredevils.
VISTA, Vol. 1, no. 10 (June 8, 1986), p.
14-16. English. **DESCR:** Golden Knights
[skydiving team]; *Military; *U.S. Army.

Minnesota Multiphasic Personality Inventory (MMPI)

4814 Bohn, Martin J. and Traub, Gary S.
Alienation of monolingual Hispanics in a
federal correctional institution.
PSYCHOLOGICAL REPORTS, Vol. 59, no. 2
(October 1986), p. 560-562. English. **DESCR:**
Bilingualism; *Prisoners; *Psychological
Testing.

Minorities
USE: Ethnic Groups

**MINORITIES IN AMERICAN HIGHER EDUCATION: RECENT
TRENDS, CURRENT PROSPECTS AND
RECOMMENDATIONS**

4815 Manning, Winston, et al. Book review of:
MINORITIES IN AMERICAN HIGHER EDUCATION:
RECENT TRENDS, CURRENT PROSPECTS AND
RECOMMENDATIONS. LA RED/THE NET, no. 60
(Fall 1982), p. 1-22. English. **DESCR:**
*Astin, Alexander W.; Book Reviews; Ethnic
Groups.

**Minority Engineering Program (California State
University at Los Angeles)**

4816 Minsky, Alyce. California State University
at Los Angeles. HISPANIC ENGINEER, Vol. 3,
(Summer, 1987), p. 30-33, 44. English.
DESCR: Colleges and Universities;
Educational Organizations; *Engineering as a
Profession; Mathematics, Engineering and
Science Achievement (MESA).

**Minority Enterprise Small Business Investment
Corporation (MESBIC)**

4817 Garcia, Art. Financing the corporate
take-off. HISPANIC BUSINESS, Vol. 9, no. 5
(May 1987), p. 22-27. English. **DESCR:**
Aguirre Architects, Dallas, TX; Aguirre,
Pedro; Banking Industry; *Business
Enterprises; Businesspeople; *Corporations;
*Investments; Morales, Ramon; Protocom
Devices, New York, NY; Villamil, Antonio.

Minority Literature
    USE: Third World Literature (U.S.)

Miracle, Andrew W.

4818 Lopez, David E. Book review of:
    BILINGUALISM: SOCIAL ISSUES AND POLICY
    IMPLICATIONS. CONTEMPORARY SOCIOLOGY: A
    JOURNAL OF REVIEWS, Vol. 15, no. 3 (May
    1986), p. 391-392. English. **DESCR:**
    *BILINGUALISM: SOCIAL ISSUES AND POLICY
    IMPLICATIONS; Book Reviews.

Miranda, Judy

4819 Rosas, Alejandro. Siete fotografos latinos
    en Los Angeles. LA COMUNIDAD, No. 241 (March
    3, 1985), p. 4-5. Spanish. **DESCR:** Aguilar,
    Laura; Art; Avila, Adam; Callwood, Dennis
    O.; Carlos, Jesus; Exhibits; *Photography;
    Self-Help Graphics, Los Angeles, CA; *SEVEN
    LATINO PHOTOGRAPHERS=SIETE FOTOGRAFOS
    LATINOS; Thewlis, Alan; Valverde, Richard.

Mirande, Alfredo

4820 Baca Zinn, Maxine. Book review of: LA
    CHICANA: MEXICAN AMERICAN WOMEN. LA RED/THE
    NET, no. 28 (March 1980), p. 10. English.
    DESCR: Book Reviews; Chicanas; Enriquez,
    Evangelina; LA CHICANA: THE MEXICAN AMERICAN
    WOMAN.

4821 Burns, Jeffrey M. Book review of: THE
    CHICANO EXPERIENCE. RELIGIOUS STUDIES
    REVIEW, Vol. 11, (October 1985), p. 418.
    English. **DESCR:** Book Reviews; *THE CHICANO
    EXPERIENCE: AN ALTERNATIVE PERSPECTIVE.

4822 Farley, J.E. Book review of: THE CHICANO
    EXPERIENCE. CHOICE, Vol. 23, no. 3 (November
    1985), p. [483]. English. **DESCR:** Book
    Reviews; *THE CHICANO EXPERIENCE: AN
    ALTERNATIVE PERSPECTIVE.

4823 Gutierrez, Ramon A. Book review of: THE
    CHICANO EXPERIENCE. AMERICAS, Vol. 43, no. 1
    (July 1986), p. 134-136. English. **DESCR:**
    Book Reviews; *THE CHICANO EXPERIENCE: AN
    ALTERNATIVE PERSPECTIVE.

4824 Tryon, Roy H. Book review of: THE CHICANO
    EXPERIENCE. LIBRARY JOURNAL, Vol. 110,
    (August 1985), p. 109. English. **DESCR:** Book
    Reviews; *THE CHICANO EXPERIENCE: AN
    ALTERNATIVE PERSPECTIVE.

4825 Valdez, Avelardo. Book review of: THE
    CHICANO EXPERIENCE. JOURNAL OF AMERICAN
    ETHNIC HISTORY, Vol. 6, no. 2 (Spring 1987),
    p. 98-101. English. **DESCR:** Book Reviews;
    Social History and Conditions; *THE CHICANO
    EXPERIENCE: AN ALTERNATIVE PERSPECTIVE.

MIRROR OF LANGUAGE: THE DEBATE ON BILINGUALISM

4826 Chavez, Gene T. Book review of: MIRROR OF
    LANGUAGE: THE DEBATE ON BILINGUALISM.
    JOURNAL OF THE ASSOCIATION OF MEXICAN
    AMERICAN EDUCATORS, (1986, 1987), p. 52-53.
    English. **DESCR:** Book Reviews; Hakuta, Kenji.

Miscegenation
    USE: Intermarriage

La Mision Dolores Iglesia Catolica

4827 Gonzales, Juan. San Francisco's Mission
    District: part I. LATIN QUARTER, Vol. 1, no.
    4 (July, August, 1975), p. 21-25. English.
    DESCR: *Local History; *Mission District,
    San Francisco, CA; Political Parties and
    Organizations; San Francisco, CA; *Urban
    Communities.

Mission District, San Francisco, CA

4828 Gonzales, Juan. San Francisco's Mission
    District: part I. LATIN QUARTER, Vol. 1, no.
    4 (July, August, 1975), p. 21-25. English.
    DESCR: La Mision Dolores Iglesia Catolica;
    *Local History; Political Parties and
    Organizations; San Francisco, CA; *Urban
    Communities.

4829 Kessel, Janet. Treasure hunt. SAN FRANCISCO,
    Vol. 25, no. 10 (October 1983), p. 103-110.
    English. **DESCR:** *Restaurants; San Francisco,
    CA.

Missions

4830 Diekemper, Barnabas C. The Catholic Church
    in the shadows: the southwestern United
    States during the Mexican period. JOURNAL OF
    THE WEST, Vol. 24, no. 2 (1985), p. 46-53.
    English. **DESCR:** *Catholic Church; Religion;
    *Southwestern United States.

4831 Holmes, John J. Sentinel of tradition.
    VISTA, Vol. 3, no. 3 (November 8, 1987), p.
    16. English. **DESCR:** New Mexico; *San
    Gregorio de Abo (Salinas National Monument,
    NM); Sisneros, Federico.

Mitos

4832 Barry, John M. Mito e ironia en LOS PASOS
    PERDIDOS. TINTA, Vol. 1, no. 4 (Summer
    1984), p. 3-9. Spanish. **DESCR:** Carpentier,
    Alejo; Latin American Literature; Literary
    Criticism; *LOS PASOS PERDIDOS; *Novel.

4833 Cerda, Gabriela. La serpiente. NOTEBOOK: A
    LITTLE MAGAZINE, Vol. 2, no. 2 (1986), p.
    14-26. English. **DESCR:** Cuentos; Leyendas;
    Mayas.

THE MIXQUIAHUALA LETTERS

4834 Paredes, Raymund A. Review essay: recent
    Chicano writing. ROCKY MOUNTAIN REVIEW OF
    LANGUAGE AND LITERATURE, Vol. 41, (1987),
    p. 124-129. English. **DESCR:** Castillo, Ana;
    Catholic Church; Chavez, Denise; Chicanas;
    Garcia, Lionel; GIVING UP THE GHOST; LEAVING
    HOME; *Literary Criticism; *Literature
    Reviews; Moraga, Cherrie; Poetry; Prose; Sex
    Roles; Silva, Beverly; SMALL FACES; Soto,
    Gary; THE CAT AND OTHER STORIES; THE LAST OF
    THE MENU GIRLS.

Mixtec Indians

4835 Cisneros, Henry. Mexico's poorest are
    heading North. AKWESASNE NOTES, Vol. 18, no.
    4 (Summer 1986), p. 7. English. **DESCR:**
    Alfaro, Victor Clark; Centro de Promocion
    Popular Urbana, Tijuana, Baja California,
    Mexico; Farm Workers; Kearney, Michael;
    Mexico; *Undocumented Workers.

Mohr, Nicolasa

4836 Mohr, Nicholasa. Puerto Rican writers in the
    United States, Puerto Rican writers in
    Puerto Rico: a separation beyond language.
    THE AMERICAS REVIEW, Vol. 15, no. 2 (Summer
    1987), p. 87-92. English. **DESCR:** Authors;
    Autobiography; Identity; Immigrants;
    *Language Usage; *Literature; *Puerto
    Ricans; Spanish Language.

Mohr, Nicolasa (cont.)

4837 Olivera, Mercedes. The new Hispanic women.
VISTA, Vol. 2, no. 11 (July 5, 1987), p.
6-8. English. **DESCR:** Alvarez, Linda;
*Chicanas; Esquiroz, Margarita; Garcia,
Juliet; *Hernandez, Antonia A.; Molina,
Gloria; Pabon, Maria; Working Women.

4838 Seeking more readers for Hispanic
literature. VISTA, Vol. 2, no. 3 (November
2, 1986), p. 25. English. **DESCR:**
Hinojosa-Smith, Rolando R.; *Literature;
*Miami Book Fair International; Munoz, Elias
Miguel; Rodriguez, Richard.

Mojados
USE: Undocumented Workers

Molina, Daniel

4839 NACME scholarships at Forum '87. HISPANIC
ENGINEER, Vol. 3, no. 3 (1987), p. 14.
English. **DESCR:** *Eastman Kodak Co.;
*Financial Aid; Fuentes, Theresa.

Molina [family name]

4840 Instituto Genealogico e Historico
Latino-Americano. Rootsearch: Robles:
Chacon: Molina. VISTA, Vol. 3, no. 1
(September 6, 1987), p. 30. English. **DESCR:**
*Chacon [family name]; Genealogy; History;
*Personal Names; *Robles [family name].

Molina, Gloria

4841 Mills, Kay. Gloria Molina. MS. MAGAZINE,
Vol. 13, (January 1985), p. 80-81+.
English. **DESCR:** Biography; Chicanas; Elected
Officials.

4842 Olivera, Mercedes. The new Hispanic women.
VISTA, Vol. 2, no. 11 (July 5, 1987), p.
6-8. English. **DESCR:** Alvarez, Linda;
*Chicanas; Esquiroz, Margarita; Garcia,
Juliet; *Hernandez, Antonia A.; Mohr,
Nicolasa; Pabon, Maria; Working Women.

Molina, Mario J.

4843 American Chemical Society honors Dr. Mario
J. Molina. HISPANIC ENGINEER, Vol. 3, no. 2
(Summer 1987), p. 12. English. **DESCR:**
American Chemical Society; *Awards.

Mondragon, Ricardo

4844 SHPE news. HISPANIC ENGINEER, Vol. 3, no. 3
(1987), p. 10-13. English. **DESCR:** *Awards;
Castillo, Hector; Colmenarez, Margarita;
Garcia, Raul; Herrera, Jess; Lopez-Martin,
Minnie; Reyes-Guerra, David; Silva, Juan;
Society of Hispanic Professional Engineers
(SHPE); Vargas, Jesus; Villanueva,
Bernadette.

Monroy, Douglas

4845 Garcia, Mario T. Chicano historiography: a
critique. LA RED/THE NET, no. 80 (May 1984),
p. 2-8. English. **DESCR:** "Anarquismo y
Comunismo: Mexican Radicalism and the
Communist Party in Los Angeles in the
1930s"; Historiography.

4846 Garcia, Mario T. [Letter to the editor about
Mexicans, radicals and communists in the
United States]. LABOR HISTORY, Vol. 25, no.
1 (Winter 1984), p. 152-154. English.
DESCR: *"Anarquismo y Comunismo: Mexican
Radicalism and the Communist Party in Los
Angeles in the 1930s"; *Communism; History;
*Labor Unions; Los Angeles, CA.

Montemayor [family name]

4847 Instituto Genealogico e Historico
Latino-Americano. Rootsearch: Olivares:
Yrigoyen: Montemayor. VISTA, Vol. 2, no. 12
(August 1, 1987), p. 30. English. **DESCR:**
Genealogy; History; *Olivares [family name];
*Personal Names; *Yrigoyen [family name].

Montes, Miguel

4848 Johnson, Richard. The California housewife
who succeeds as brave bullfighter. VISTA,
Vol. 1, no. 5 (January 5, 1986), p. 12-15.
English. **DESCR:** *Athletes; Chicanas;
*Martinez, Raquel; Munoz, Jesus.

Monteverde, Edwin

4849 SHPE holds first ever East coast conference
for Hispanic engineers. HISPANIC ENGINEER,
Vol. 3, no. 5 (Winter 1987), p. 12-14.
English. **DESCR:** Awards; Barrios, Eugene;
Chang-Diaz, Franklin; *Conferences and
Meetings; Cuevas, Brian L.; Garay, Charles
J.; Garcia, Ray; Marrero, Charles; Martinez,
Lisa; Plumey, Raymond; Reyes-Guerra, David;
Rivera, Angel; Society of Hispanic
Professional Engineers (SHPE); Soto,
Giovanni.

Montoya, Dennis

4850 Bi-centennial [editorial]. LATIN QUARTER,
Vol. 1, no. 3 (February 1975), p. 2.
English. **DESCR:** *American Bicentennial;
*Bicentennial Commission.

Montoya [family name]

4851 Instituto Genealogico e Historico
Latino-Americano. Rootsearch: Montoya:
Galvo. VISTA, Vol. 1, no. 4 (December 7,
1985), p. 22. English. **DESCR:** *Galvo [family
name]; Genealogy; History; *Personal Names.

Montoya, Jose E.

4852 Bruce-Novoa, Juan. Elegias a la frontera
hispanica. BILINGUAL REVIEW, Vol. 11, no. 3
(September, December, 1984), p. 37-44.
Spanish. **DESCR:** *"El Louie" [poem]; *LAS
COPLAS A LA MUERTE DE SU PADRE; Literary
Criticism; Manrique, Jorge; Poetry.

4853 Saldivar, Jose David. Towards a Chicano
poetics: the making of the Chicano subject.
CONFLUENCIA, Vol. 1, no. 2 (Spring 1986), p.
10-17. English. **DESCR:** Corridos; Feminism;
*Literary Criticism; "Los vatos" [poem];
*Poetry; RESTLESS SERPENTS; Rios, Alberto;
WHISPERING TO FOOL THE WIND; Zamora,
Bernice.

Moore, Joan W.

4854 Alexander, June Granatir. Book review of:
URBAN ETHNICITY IN THE UNITED STATES.
JOURNAL OF AMERICAN ETHNIC HISTORY, Vol. 7,
no. 1 (Fall 1987), p. 95-97. English.
DESCR: Book Reviews; Immigrants; Maldonado,
Lionel; *URBAN ETHNICITY IN THE UNITED
STATES: NEW IMMIGRANTS AND OLD MINORITIES.

Mora, Magdalena

4855 Soto, Shirlene. Book review of: MEXICAN
     WOMEN IN THE UNITED STATES: STRUGGLES PAST
     AND PRESENT. LA RED/THE NET, no. 35 (October
     1980), p. 4. English. **DESCR**: Book Reviews;
     *Chicanas; Del Castillo, Adelaida R.;
     *MEXICAN WOMEN IN THE UNITED STATES:
     STRUGGLES PAST AND PRESENT.

Mora, Pat

4856 Castillo-Speed, Lillian. Chicana/Latina
     literature and criticism: reviews of recent
     books. WLW JOURNAL, Vol. 11, no. 3
     (September 1987), p. 1-4. English. **DESCR**:
     Andrews, Lynn V.; *Book Reviews; BORDERS;
     Chavez, Denise; *Chicanas; CONTEMPORARY
     CHICANA POETRY: A CRITICAL APPROACH TO AN
     EMERGING LITERATURE; Flores, Angel; Flores,
     Kate; JAGUAR WOMAN; Sanchez, Marta Ester;
     Tafolla, Carmen; THE DEFIANT MUSE: HISPANIC
     FEMINIST POEMS FROM THE MIDDLE AGES TO THE
     PRESENT; THE LAST OF THE MENU GIRLS; TO
     SPLIT A HUMAN: MITOS, MACHOS Y LA MUJER
     CHICANA; Vigil-Pinon, Evangelina; WOMAN OF
     HER WORD: HISPANIC WOMEN WRITE.

4857 Mora, Pat and Alarcon, Norma. A poet
     analyzes her craft. NUESTRO, Vol. 11, no. 2
     (March 1987), p. 25-27. English. **DESCR**:
     *Authors; BORDERS; CHANTS; *Chicanas;
     *Poetry.

Moraga, Cherrie

4858 Aguilu de Murphy, Raquel. Book review of:
     GIVING UP THE GHOST. THE AMERICAS REVIEW,
     Vol. 15, no. 2 (Summer 1987), p. 105-107.
     Spanish. **DESCR**: Book Reviews; *GIVING UP THE
     GHOST; Teatro.

4859 Alarcon, Norma. Making "familia" from
     scratch: split subjectivities in the work of
     Helena Maria Viramontes and Cherrie Moraga.
     THE AMERICAS REVIEW, Vol. 15, no. 3-4 (Fall,
     Winter, 1987), p. 147-159. English. **DESCR**:
     Chicanas; GIVING UP THE GHOST; *Literary
     Criticism; *Sex Roles; "Snapshots" [short
     story]; THE MOTHS AND OTHER STORIES;
     *Viramontes, Helen.

4860 Cantu, Norma. Book review of: CUENTOS:
     STORIES BY LATINAS. LA RED/THE NET, no. 83
     (August 1984), p. 2-3. English. **DESCR**: Book
     Reviews; *CUENTOS: STORIES BY LATINAS;
     Gomez, Alma; Romo-Carmona, Mariana.

4861 Herrera-Sobek, Maria. The politics of rape:
     sexual transgression in Chicana fiction. THE
     AMERICAS REVIEW, Vol. 15, no. 3-4 (Fall,
     Winter, 1987), p. 171-181. English. **DESCR**:
     *Chicanas; Cisneros, Sandra; *Feminism;
     Fiction; GIVING UP THE GHOST; *Literary
     Criticism; Lizarraga, Sylvia; *Rape; "Red
     Clowns" [short story]; Sex Roles; "Silver
     Lake Road" [short story].

4862 Huerta, Jorge. Book review of: GIVING UP THE
     GHOST. THE AMERICAS REVIEW, Vol. 15, no. 2
     (Summer 1987), p. 104-105. English. **DESCR**:
     Book Reviews; *GIVING UP THE GHOST; Teatro.

4863 Paredes, Raymund A. Review essay: recent
     Chicano writing. ROCKY MOUNTAIN REVIEW OF
     LANGUAGE AND LITERATURE, Vol. 41, (1987),
     p. 124-129. English. **DESCR**: Castillo, Ana;
     Catholic Church; Chavez, Denise; Chicanas;
     Garcia, Lionel; GIVING UP THE GHOST; LEAVING
     HOME; *Literary Criticism; *Literature
     Reviews; Poetry; Prose; Sex Roles; Silva,
     Beverly; SMALL FACES; Soto, Gary; THE CAT
     AND OTHER STORIES; THE LAST OF THE MENU
     GIRLS; THE MIXQUIAHUALA LETTERS.

4864 Quintana, Alvina. Challenge and counter
     challenge: Chicana literary motifs. AGAINST
     THE CURRENT, Vol. 2, no. 2 (March, April,
     1987), p. 25,28-32. English. **DESCR**:
     Cervantes, Lorna Dee; *Chicanas; *Feminism;
     *Literature; THERE ARE NO MADMEN HERE;
     Valdes, Gina.

Moraga, Peter and family (Los Angeles, CA)

4865 Lit, Ed. Recognition for Hispanic families.
     VISTA, Vol. 1, no. 5 (January 5, 1986), p.
     18-20. English. **DESCR**: American Family
     Society; *Awards; *Hispanic Family of the
     Year Award; Pineda, Charles and family (Los
     Angeles, CA); Private Funding Sources.

Morales, Alejandro

4866 Bustamante, Nuria. Permanencia y cambio en
     CARAS VIEJAS Y VINO NUEVO. CONFLUENCIA, Vol.
     1, no. 2 (Spring 1986), p. 61-65. Spanish.
     DESCR: *CARAS VIEJAS Y VINO NUEVO; *Literary
     Criticism; Novel.

4867 Gonzalez, Maria. CARAS VIEJAS Y VINO NUEVO:
     analisis tematica y estructural. TINTA, Vol.
     1, no. 1 (May 1981), p. 15-18. Spanish.
     DESCR: *CARAS VIEJAS Y VINO NUEVO; *Literary
     Criticism; Novel.

4868 Mariscal, George. Alejandro Morales in
     utopia. CONFLUENCIA, Vol. 2, no. 1 (Fall
     1986), p. 78-83. English. **DESCR**: *Literary
     Criticism; Novel; *RETO EN EL PARAISO.

4869 Martin-Rodriguez, Manuel M. El sentimiento
     de culpa en RETO EN EL PARAISO de Alejandro
     Morales. THE AMERICAS REVIEW, Vol. 15, no. 1
     (Spring 1987), p. 89-97. Spanish. **DESCR**:
     Literary Criticism; Novel; *RETO EN EL
     PARAISO.

4870 Padilla, Genaro Miguel. The anti-romantic
     city in Chicano fiction. PUERTO DEL SOL,
     Vol. 23, no. 1 (1987), p. 159-169. English.
     DESCR: Acosta, Oscar Zeta; Anaya, Rudolfo
     A.; *Fiction; Lattin, Vernon E.; *Literary
     Criticism; *Urban Communities.

Morales, Esai

4871 Chavez, Lorenzo A. La Bamba. VISTA, Vol. 2,
     no. 11 (July 5, 1987), p. 12-13. English.
     DESCR: *Actors and Actresses; Biography; De
     Soto, Rosana; Films; LA BAMBA [film]; Pena,
     Elizabeth; Phillips, Lou Diamond.

4872 Lomeli, Maria Magdalena S. "LATC" un espacio
     para el teatro politico. LA COMUNIDAD, No.
     333 (December 7, 1986), p. 10-11. Spanish.
     DESCR: Actors and Actresses; *Los Angeles
     Theatre Center (LATC); *Teatro.

4873 Rodriguez Flores, Juan. Esai Morales: un
     joven de origen hispano con oficio de actor
     (1). LA COMUNIDAD, No. 335 (December 21,
     1986), p. 8-9. Spanish. **DESCR**: Actors and
     Actresses; *Biography.

4874 Rodriguez Flores, Juan. Esai Morales y la
     pasion por el arte escenico (II). LA
     COMUNIDAD, No. 336 (December 28, 1986), p.
     2-3. Spanish. **DESCR**: Actors and Actresses;
     *Biography; Films; LA BAMBA [film]; Valdez,
     Luis.

Morales, Ramon

4875 Garcia, Art. Financing the corporate
take-off. HISPANIC BUSINESS, Vol. 9, no. 5
(May 1987), p. 22-27. English. **DESCR:**
Aguirre Architects, Dallas, TX; Aguirre,
Pedro; Banking Industry; *Business
Enterprises; Businesspeople; *Corporations;
*Investments; Minority Enterprise Small
Business Investment Corporation (MESBIC);
Protocom Devices, New York, NY; Villamil,
Antonio.

Moreno, Mario "Cantinflas"

4876 Flores, Arturo C. El Teatro Campesino
(1965-1986): algunas orientaciones teoricas.
CONFLUENCIA, Vol. 2, no. 2 (Spring 1987), p.
116-121. Spanish. **DESCR:** Brecht, Bertolt;
*El Teatro Campesino; History; *Teatro;
Valdez, Luis.

Morgan, Gordon D.

4877 Garcia, John A. Book review of: AMERICA
WITHOUT ETHNICITY. LA RED/THE NET, no. 78
(March 1984), p. 8-9. English. **DESCR:**
*AMERICA WITHOUT ETHNICITY; Book Reviews.

Morones, Bob

4878 Jimenez, Luis. En busca del talento latino.
LA COMUNIDAD, No. 235 (January 20, 1985), p.
14-15. Spanish. **DESCR:** Actors and Actresses;
*Biography; Mass Media.

Mosqueda, Lawrence J.

4879 Garcia, Philip. Book review of: CHICANOS,
CATHOLICISM, AND POLITICAL IDEOLOGY.
AMERICAN POLITICAL SCIENCE REVIEW, Vol. 81,
(January 1987), p. 642-643. English.
DESCR: Book Reviews; Catholic Church;
*CHICANOS, CATHOLICISM, AND POLITICAL
IDEOLOGY.

4880 Herrick, R.L. Book review of: CHICANOS,
CATHOLICISM, AND POLITICAL IDEOLOGY. CHOICE,
Vol. 24, no. 3 (November 1986), p. 498.
English. **DESCR:** Book Reviews; *CHICANOS,
CATHOLICISM, AND POLITICAL IDEOLOGY.

Mosquera, Jaime "Jim"

4881 Winston, Bonnie. High tech jobs in the
Midwest. HISPANIC ENGINEER, Vol. 3, no. 1
(Spring 1987), p. 50-53. English. **DESCR:**
Chaves, Tony; *Engineering as a Profession;
Rodriguez Howell, Nilsa; Sanchez, Francisco
G.

Mother Theresa

4882 Search for Hispanic heroes informs,
surprises, confirms. VISTA, Vol. 1, no. 10
(June 8, 1986), p. 18-19. English. **DESCR:**
Pope John Paul II; *Public Opinion; Reagan,
Ronald.

THE MOTHS AND OTHER STORIES

4883 Alarcon, Norma. Making "familia" from
scratch: split subjectivities in the work of
Helena Maria Viramontes and Cherrie Moraga.
THE AMERICAS REVIEW, Vol. 15, no. 3-4 (Fall,
Winter, 1987), p. 147-159. English. **DESCR:**
Chicanas; GIVING UP THE GHOST; *Literary
Criticism; *Moraga, Cherrie; *Sex Roles;
"Snapshots" [short story]; *Viramontes,
Helen.

4884 Martinez, Beverly Ann. Book review of: THE
MOTHS AND OTHER STORIES. VISTA, Vol. 1, no.
11 (July 6, 1986), p. 16. English. **DESCR:**

Book Reviews; Viramontes, Helen.

Motion Picture Producers and Distributors of America (MPPDA)

4885 Delpar, Helen. Goodbye to the greaser:
Mexico, the MPPDA, and derogatory films,
1922-1926. JOURNAL OF POPULAR FILM AND
TELEVISION, no. 12 (Spring 1984), p. 34-41.
English. **DESCR:** *Films; Stereotypes.

Motion Pictures
USE: Films

LOS MOTIVOS DE CAIN

4886 Campbell, Federico. Paralelo 32: la frontera
como espacio literario. LA COMUNIDAD, No.
347 (March 15, 1987), p. 5. Spanish. **DESCR:**
Border Region; *Literary Criticism;
Revueltas, Jose; Tijuana, Baja California,
Mexico.

El Movimiento Chicano Conference, February 13-14, 1981

4887 East coast conference on "El Movimiento
Chicano". LA RED/THE NET, no. 40 (March
1981), p. 7. English. **DESCR:** Chicano
Movement; *Conferences and Meetings.

Movimiento Estudiantil Chicano de Aztlan (MEChA)

4888 MEChA - University of Texas at El Paso;
MAYO, University of Texas at Austin; and
PASO, Texas A and I University. Student
perspectives on Mexican/American studies.
EPOCA: NATIONAL CONCILIO FOR CHICANO STUDIES
JOURNAL, Vol. 1, no. 2 (Winter 1971), p.
87-96. English. **DESCR:** *Chicano Studies;
Curriculum; Mexican American Youth
Organization (MAYO); Student Organizations;
Students; Texas.

LA MUERTE DE ARTEMIO CRUZ

4889 Lower, Andrea. La unidad narrativa en LA
MUERTE DE ARTEMIO CRUZ. TINTA, Vol. 1, no. 3
(December 1983), p. 19-26. Spanish. **DESCR:**
Fuentes, Carlos; Literary Criticism; Mexican
Literature; *Novel.

Mujeres Activas en Letras y Cambio Social (MALCS)

4890 Perez, Emma. Networks. LA RED/THE NET, No.
103 (December 1986), p. 2-5. English.
DESCR: *Chicanas; *Educational
Organizations; *Higher Education.

LAS MUJERES: CONVERSATIONS FROM A HISPANIC COMMUNITY

4891 Ruiz, Ivette M. Resena testimonial. REVISTA
MUJERES, Vol. 1, no. 2 (June 1984), p. 7-10.
English. **DESCR:** Book Reviews; Chicanas;
Elsasser, Nan; MacKenzie, Kyle; Tixier y
Vigil, Yvonne.

4892 Ybarra, Lea. Book review of: LAS MUJERES:
CONVERSATIONS FROM A HISPANIC COMMUNITY. LA
RED/THE NET, no. 58 (September 1982), p.
5-6. English. **DESCR:** Book Reviews;
*Chicanas; *Elsasser, Nan; MacKenzie, Kyle;
New Mexico; Tixier y Vigil, Yvonne.

Las Mujeres, University of California, Santa Cruz

4893 Carrillo, Ana, et al. History of Las
Mujeres. REVISTA MUJERES, Vol. 1, no. 1
(January 1984), p. 4-5. English. **DESCR:**
Chicanas; *Organizations.

Multicultural Education
USE: Cultural Pluralism

Multinational Corporations

4894 Third world women in multinational corporations--the Mexican American border. LA RED/THE NET, no. 25 (December 1979), p. 2. English. DESCR: *Border Industries; Chicanas; *Ciudad Juarez, Chihuahua, Mexico; Labor Supply and Market; *Working Women.

Municipal Government
USE: Local Government

Munoz, Arthur

4895 Daydi-Tolson, Santiago. Book review of: FROM A COP'S JOURNAL & OTHER POEMS. THE AMERICAS REVIEW, Vol. 15, no. 1 (Spring 1987), p. 102-105. English. DESCR: Book Reviews; *FROM A COP'S JOURNAL & OTHER POEMS.

Munoz, Elias Miguel

4896 Seeking more readers for Hispanic literature. VISTA, Vol. 2, no. 3 (November 2, 1986), p. 25. English. DESCR: Hinojosa-Smith, Rolando R.; *Literature; *Miami Book Fair International; Mohr, Nicolasa; Rodriguez, Richard.

Munoz [family name]

4897 Instituto Genealogico e Historico Latino-Americano. Rootsearch: Ortega: Munoz. VISTA, Vol. 1, no. 3 (November 3, 1985), p. 22. English. DESCR: History; *Ortega [family name]; *Personal Names.

Munoz, Jesus

4898 Johnson, Richard. The California housewife who succeeds as brave bullfighter. VISTA, Vol. 1, no. 5 (January 5, 1986), p. 12-15. English. DESCR: *Athletes; Chicanas; *Martinez, Raquel; Montes, Miguel.

Mural Art

4899 Blanco, Gilbert M. A vehicle for positive change. LATIN QUARTER, Vol. 1, no. 2 (October 1974), p. 27-30. English. DESCR: Artists; East Los Angeles, CA; *Estrada Courts, Los Angeles, CA.

4900 Castano, Wilfredo Q. For the roses=Pa' las rosas. REVISTA MUJERES, Vol. 3, no. 2 (June 1986), p. 73. DESCR: *Alicia, Juana; *Photography.

4901 The institute, the artist, the art. NUESTRO, Vol. 11, no. 4 (May 1987), p. 15-17. English. DESCR: Artists; *Gonzales, Edward; *Technical-Vocational Institute (T-V), Albuquerque, NM.

4902 Jacobs, Carole. Bridging cultures. SOUTHWEST ART, Vol. 15, (April 1986), p. 86. English. DESCR: *Chicano Park, San Diego, CA; Ochoa, Victor.

4903 Malaspina, Ann. The city is my canvas. VISTA, Vol. 2, no. 3 (November 2, 1986), p. 14-15. English. DESCR: Artists; *Galvez, Daniel; Hispanic Murals Project (Cambridge, MA); Oakland, CA.

4904 Saul Solache: contemporary Chicano artist. LATIN QUARTER, Vol. 1, no. 3 (January, February, 1975), p. 24-26. English. DESCR: *Artists; Exhibits; Paintings; *Solache, Saul.

4905 Seal, Kathy. La pintura del barrio. LA COMUNIDAD, No. 266 (August 25, 1985), p. 13. Spanish. DESCR: Los Angeles, CA; Pule, Benny.

4906 Sykes, Maltby. Diego Rivera and the Hotel Reforma murals. ARCHIVES OF AMERICAN ART JOURNAL, Vol. 25, no. 1-2 (1985), p. 29-40. English. DESCR: Artists; Hotel Reforma, Mexico City; Marxism; Mexico City; *Rivera, Diego.

4907 Tineo, David. [Unidentified mural]. LLUEVE TLALOC, no. 12 (1985), p. Ft cover.

Murguia, Edward

4908 Abney, Armando. Chicano intermarriage: a theoretical and empirical study. LA RED/THE NET, no. 59 (October 1982), p. 4-6. English. DESCR: Book Reviews; *CHICANO INTERMARRIAGE: A THEORETICAL AND EMPIRICAL STUDY; *Intermarriage.

4909 Ramirez, Daniel Moriel. Book review of: CHICANO INTERMARRIAGE: A THEORETICAL AND EMPIRICAL STUDY. SOCIAL FORCES, Vol. 62, no. 3 (March 1984), p. 833-835. English. DESCR: Book Reviews; *CHICANO INTERMARRIAGE: A THEORETICAL AND EMPIRICAL STUDY; Intermarriage.

MURIERON A MITAD DEL RIO

4910 Lomeli, Francisco A. En torno a la literatura de la frontera (II). LA COMUNIDAD, No. 275 (October 27, 1985), p. 2-3. Spanish. DESCR: Border Region; Language Usage; *Literary Criticism; Spota, Luis.

Murrieta, Joaquin

4911 Rodriguez, Richard. The head of Joaquin Murrieta. CALIFORNIA MAGAZINE, Vol. 10, no. 7 (July 1985), p. 55-62, 89. English. DESCR: Bandidos; Leyendas.

Museum of New Mexico

4912 Ahlborn, Richard E. The Hispanic horseman: a sampling of horse gear from the Fred Harvey Collection. PALACIO, Vol. 89, no. 2 (1983), p. 12-21. English. DESCR: Fred Harvey Co.; *Vaqueros.

Museums

4913 The California Museum of Latino History=El Museo de California de la Historia de los Latinos. AMERICAS 2001, Premiere Issue, 1987, p. 18-19, 39. Bilingual. DESCR: Calderon, Charles M.; *California Museum of Latino History; History; Rios-Bustamante, Antonio; Social History and Conditions.

Music

4914 Alonso, Miguel Angel. El largo camino al estrellato. LA COMUNIDAD, No. 276 (November 3, 1985), p. 12-13+. Spanish. DESCR: *Los Blue Diamonds [musical group].

4915 Alonso, Miguel Angel. Los Lobos y la importancia de la continuidad musical. LA COMUNIDAD, No. 341 (February 1, 1987), p. 12-13. Spanish. DESCR: *Los Lobos del Este de Los Angeles (musical group); Rock Music.

4916 Alonso, Miguel Angel. El significado de cruzar la frontera. LA COMUNIDAD, No. 355 (May 10, 1987), p. 10-11. Spanish. DESCR: Biography; *Blades, Ruben.

Music (cont.)

4917 Arreola, Daniel D. The Mexican American cultural capital. GEOGRAPHICAL REVIEW, Vol. 77, (January 1987), p. 17-34. English. DESCR: Conjuntos; Food Industry; History; Immigration; LA PRENSA, San Antonio, TX; La Raza Unida Party; League of United Latin American Citizens (LULAC); Lozano, Ignacio; Mexican American Youth Organization, San Antonio, TX; Orden Hijos de America, San Antonio, TX; Railroads; *San Antonio, TX; *Social History and Conditions.

4918 Bensusan, Guy. A consideration of Nortena and Chicano music. STUDIES IN LATIN AMERICAN POPULAR CULTURE, Vol. 4, (1985), p. 158-169. English. DESCR: Corridos; *Nortenas.

4919 Douthat, Bill. Mariachi magic. VISTA, Vol. 2, no. 4 (December 7, 1986), p. 18. English. DESCR: Austin, TX; *Castro, Zeke; Mariachi Rebeldes del Sur; *Mariachis; Secondary School Education.

4920 Espinoza, Freddy. A proposito de la salsa y su historia. LA COMUNIDAD, No. 364 (July 12, 1987), p. 2-5. Spanish. DESCR: Salsa.

4921 Halley, Lindsey. Pachuco boggie [sic]. LA COMUNIDAD, No. 305 (May 25, 1986), p. 8-9. Spanish. DESCR: Cano, Eddie; Diaz, Raul; History; Ovalle, John; *PACHUCO BOOGIE; Smithsonian Institute; The Record Inn, East Los Angeles, CA; Tosti, Don.

4922 Holmes, John J. Zarzuela lives again. VISTA, Vol. 3, no. 3 (November 8, 1987), p. 10-12. English. DESCR: Directories; Festival de la Zarzuela; *La Zarzuela de Albuquerque; Musicals.

4923 Holscher, Louis M. Billboard charts and Chicanos, 1955-1974. LA RED/THE NET, no. 41 (April 1981), p. 10,12. English. DESCR: *Discography; *Musicians; *Recording Industry; Rock Music.

4924 Limon, Jose E. Texas-Mexican popular music and dancing: some notes on history and symbolic process. LATIN AMERICAN MUSIC REVIEW, Vol. 4, no. 2 (Fall, Winter, 1983), p. 229-246. English. DESCR: *Dance; Ethnomusicology; *Texas; *Texas Mexicans.

4925 Lliso, Joseph. Hispanic musicians. VISTA, Vol. 2, no. 5 (January 4, 1987), p. 22. English. DESCR: *Musicians.

4926 Machado, Melinda. Saying "no" to teenage sex. VISTA, Vol. 2, no. 11 (July 5, 1987), p. 14. English. DESCR: *CUANDO ESTEMOS JUNTOS [phonograph record]; DETENTE [phonograph record]; *Musical Lyrics; Planned Parenthood Federation of America; Sex Education; Tatiana and Johnny.

4927 Rodriguez Flores, Juan. Ruben Blades en busca de una nueva realidad musical (II). LA COMUNIDAD, no. 33 (November 23, 1986), p. 2-5. Spanish. DESCR: *Biography; *Blades, Ruben; Films.

4928 Rodriguez Flores, Juan. Ruben Blades: siempre he apostado a la sensibilidad del publico. LA COMUNIDAD, No. 330 (November 16, 1986), p. 8-11. Spanish. DESCR: Actors and Actresses; *Biography; *Blades, Ruben; Films; THE MILAGRO BEANFIELD WAR [film].

4929 Sellers, Jeff M. The sound of musica: moving into the mainstream. HISPANIC BUSINESS, Vol. 9, no. 7 (July 1987), p. 14-18. English.

DESCR: Los Lobos del Este de Los Angeles (musical group); *Marketing; Miami Sound Machine; *Musicians; The Cruzados [musical group]; Zerimar [musical group].

Musical Instruments

4930 Abalos, J. Victor. Whiz kids of the microchip melody. VISTA, Vol. 1, no. 5 (January 5, 1986), p. 9-10. English. DESCR: Computers; *Romero, Eddie, Jr.

4931 Murphy, Suzanne. The music makers. VISTA, Vol. 3, no. 4 (December 6, 1987), p. 28-29. English. DESCR: Candelas Guitar Shop, Los Angeles, CA; *Delgado, Porfirio.

4932 Pena, Manuel. From ranchero to jaiton: ethnicity and class in Texas-Mexican music (two styles in the form of a pair). ETHNOMUSICOLOGY, Vol. 29, no. 1 (Winter 1985), p. 29-55. English. DESCR: Conjuntos; *Ethnomusicology; Villa, Beto.

Musical Lyrics

4933 Machado, Melinda. Saying "no" to teenage sex. VISTA, Vol. 2, no. 11 (July 5, 1987), p. 14. English. DESCR: *CUANDO ESTEMOS JUNTOS [phonograph record]; DETENTE [phonograph record]; Music; Planned Parenthood Federation of America; Sex Education; Tatiana and Johnny.

Musicals

4934 Holmes, John J. Zarzuela lives again. VISTA, Vol. 3, no. 3 (November 8, 1987), p. 10-12. English. DESCR: Directories; Festival de la Zarzuela; *La Zarzuela de Albuquerque; *Music.

Musicians

4935 Aguirre, Antonio (Jake). Two little giants. LATIN QUARTER, Vol. 1, no. 2 (October 1974), p. 25. English. DESCR: Rock Music; *Ross, Gilbert (Gibby); *Salsa; San Francisco, CA; Vidales, Mark.

4936 Burciaga, Jose Antonio and Ronstadt, Linda. Linda Ronstadt: my Mexican soul. VISTA, Vol. 2, no. 10 (June 7, 1987), p. 6-8. English. DESCR: Biography; CORRIDOS [film]; *Ronstadt, Linda.

4937 Casteleiro, Gus. Hot salsa and other sounds. LATIN QUARTER, Vol. 1, no. 3 (January, February, 1975), p. 19-20. English. DESCR: *Los Angeles, CA; *Salsa; San Francisco, CA.

4938 Forte, Dan. Los Lobos: Tex-Mex rock from East L.A. GUITAR PLAYER, Vol. 21, no. 2 (February 1987), p. 68-94. English. DESCR: Biography; Discography; Hidalgo, David (Los Lobos); *Los Lobos del Este de Los Angeles (musical group); Lozano, Conrad (Los Lobos); Perez, Louie (Los Lobos); Recording Industry; *Rock Music; Rosas, Cesar (Los Lobos).

4939 Gordon, Polita C. Living the crossover dream. VISTA, Vol. 1, no. 8 (April 6, 1986), p. 6-9. English. DESCR: *Blades, Ruben; Colon, Willie; Los Lobos del Este de Los Angeles (musical group); Miami Sound Machine.

Musicians (cont.)

4940 Guevara, Ruben and Blades, Ruben. Ruben Blades: music, love and revolution=Ruben Blades: musica, amor y revolucion. AMERICAS 2001, Vol. 1, no. 2 (September, October, 1987), p. 26-29,31. Bilingual. **DESCR:** Biography; *Blades, Ruben; Films; Recording Industry.

4941 Holscher, Louis M. Billboard charts and Chicanos, 1955-1974. LA RED/THE NET, no. 41 (April 1981), p. 10,12. English. **DESCR:** *Discography; *Music; *Recording Industry; Rock Music.

4942 Lliso, Joseph. Hispanic musicians. VISTA, Vol. 2, no. 5 (January 4, 1987), p. 22. English. **DESCR:** *Music.

4943 La Mafia signs Pepsi contract. NUESTRO, Vol. 11, no. 4 (May 1987), p. 8-9. English. **DESCR:** Advertising; *La Mafia [musical group]; Pepsi-Cola Bottling Group; Rock Music.

4944 Muro, Rena. Tierra. AMERICAS 2001, Vol. 1, no. 3 (November, December, 1987), p. 15. Bilingual. **DESCR:** Salsa; *Tierra [musical group].

4945 Sellers, Jeff M. The sound of musica: moving into the mainstream. HISPANIC BUSINESS, Vol. 9, no. 7 (July 1987), p. 14-18. English. **DESCR:** Los Lobos del Este de Los Angeles (musical group); *Marketing; Miami Sound Machine; Music; The Cruzados [musical group]; Zerimar [musical group].

MUTUAL AID FOR SURVIVAL: THE CASE OF THE MEXICAN AMERICAN

4946 Garcia, Chris. Book review of: MUTUAL AID FOR SURVIVAL. HISPANIC AMERICAN HISTORICAL REVIEW, Vol. 64, no. 1 (February 1984), p. 205. English. **DESCR:** Book Reviews; Hernandez, Jose Amaro.

4947 Griswold del Castillo, Richard. Book review of: MUTUAL AID FOR SURVIVAL. SOUTHWESTERN HISTORICAL QUARTERLY, Vol. 88, no. 3 (1985), p. 330-332. English. **DESCR:** Book Reviews; Hernandez, Jose Amaro; Mutualistas.

4948 San Miguel, Guadalupe. Book review of: MUTUAL AID FOR SURVIVAL. LECTOR, Vol. 4, no. 4-6 (1987), p. 54-55. English. **DESCR:** Book Reviews; Hernandez, Jose Amaro; Mutualistas.

Mutual Aid Societies
USE: Mutualistas

Mutualistas

4949 Griswold del Castillo, Richard. Book review of: MUTUAL AID FOR SURVIVAL. SOUTHWESTERN HISTORICAL QUARTERLY, Vol. 88, no. 3 (1985), p. 330-332. English. **DESCR:** Book Reviews; Hernandez, Jose Amaro; *MUTUAL AID FOR SURVIVAL: THE CASE OF THE MEXICAN AMERICAN.

4950 San Miguel, Guadalupe. Book review of: MUTUAL AID FOR SURVIVAL. LECTOR, Vol. 4, no. 4-6 (1987), p. 54-55. English. **DESCR:** Book Reviews; Hernandez, Jose Amaro; *MUTUAL AID FOR SURVIVAL: THE CASE OF THE MEXICAN AMERICAN.

Myrna Salazar and Associates, Inc.

4951 Kwain, Constance. Searching for Hispanic talent. VISTA, Vol. 2, no. 6 (February 8, 1987), p. 6-7. English. **DESCR:** *Actors and Actresses; American Federation of Television & Radio Artists (AFTRA); *Business Enterprises; Films; Navas, Trina; Salazar, Myrna; Screen Actors Guild; Television.

Nahuatl Literature
USE: Precolumbian Literature

Naisbitt Group

4952 Morales, Cecilio. Upbeat future for Hispanics. VISTA, Vol. 1, no. 1 (September 8, 1985), p. 6-7. English. **DESCR:** *MEGATRENDS; Naisbitt, John; *Population.

Naisbitt, John

4953 Morales, Cecilio. Upbeat future for Hispanics. VISTA, Vol. 1, no. 1 (September 8, 1985), p. 6-7. English. **DESCR:** *MEGATRENDS; Naisbitt Group; *Population.

Nakasone, Yasuhiro [Prime Minister of Japan]

4954 Cruz, David V. Caucus & Co. orients the East. HISPANIC BUSINESS, Vol. 9, no. 11 (November 1987), p. 10-13, 71+. English. **DESCR:** Businesspeople; *Congressional Hispanic Caucus; Elected Officials; *International Relations; *Japan; Latin Business Foundation, Los Angeles, CA; *Taiwan.

Nalven, Joseph

4955 Maldonado, Lionel A. Book review of: BORDER PERSPECTIVES: ON THE US/MEXICO RELATIONSHIP. JOURNAL OF AMERICAN ETHNIC HISTORY, Vol. 7, no. 1 (Fall 1987), p. 106-107. English. **DESCR:** Book Reviews; *BORDER PERSPECTIVES: ON THE US/MEXICO RELATIONSHIP; Border Region.

Names
USE: Personal Names

Narcotic Addicts
USE: Drug Addicts

Narcotic Laws
USE: Drug Laws

Narcotic Traffic
USE: Drug Traffic

National Aeronautics and Space Administration (NASA)

4956 Mellado, Carmela. Adriana Ocampo. HISPANIC ENGINEER, Vol. 3, no. 4 (Fall 1987), p. 22-24. English. **DESCR:** *Ocampo, Adriana; *Science as a Profession; Stereotypes; Women.

National Assessment of Educational Progress

4957 Carpenter, Thomas P., et al. Achievement in mathematics: results from the National Assessment. THE ELEMENTARY SCHOOL JOURNAL, Vol. 84, no. 5 (May 1984), p. 485-495. English. **DESCR:** Academic Achievement; *Educational Tests and Measurements; *Mathematics.

4958 Latino reading and ed progress. LA RED/THE NET, No. 100 (September 1986), p. 11. English. **DESCR:** Education; *Literacy; National Institute of Education (NIE).

National Assessment of Educational Progress
(cont.)

4959 Magallan, Rafael J. 1983-84 NAEP data raises questions regarding the school experiences of language minority children. LA RED/THE NET, no. 92 (November, December, 1985), p. 9-11. English. **DESCR:** *Bilingual Bicultural Education; Bilingualism; Dropouts; English as a Second Language; Surveys.

National Association of Stock Car Automobile Racing (NASCAR)

4960 Corona, Al. Life in the fast lane. VISTA, Vol. 3, no. 3 (November 8, 1987), p. 30. English. **DESCR:** *Garcia, Ruben; *Sports.

National Association for Minority Automotive Dealers (NAMAD)

4961 Minority programs need tune-up. HISPANIC BUSINESS, Vol. 9, no. 6 (June 1987), p. 84-90. English. **DESCR:** *Automobile Industry; Business; Business Enterprises; *Organizations.

National Association of Hispanic Professors of Business Administration and Economics (Los Profesores)

4962 Academics and entrepreneurs talk trade. HISPANIC BUSINESS, Vol. 9, no. 6 (June 1987), p. 96. English. **DESCR:** *Business Enterprises; Conferences and Meetings; Fourth Symposium on Hispanic Business and Economy, San Juan, Puerto Rico, November 23-25, 1987; *International Economic Relations; Latin America; Organizations; Teaching Profession.

National Association for Chicano Studies (NACS)

4963 Martinez, Eliud. Book review of: HISTORY, CULTURE, AND SOCIETY. MODERN LANGUAGE JOURNAL, Vol. 69, no. 4 (Winter 1985), p. 436-437. English. **DESCR:** Book Reviews; Chicano Studies; Garcia, Mario T.; *HISTORY, CULTURE, AND SOCIETY: CHICANO STUDIES IN THE 1980s.

4964 Milo, Albert J. Book review of: HISTORY, CULTURE, AND SOCIETY. LECTOR, Vol. 4, no. 4-6 (1987), p. 55. English. **DESCR:** Book Reviews; *HISTORY, CULTURE, AND SOCIETY: CHICANO STUDIES IN THE 1980s; Social History and Conditions.

4965 Ramirez, Genevieve M. Book review of: CHICANA VOICES. THE AMERICAS REVIEW, Vol. 15, no. 1 (Spring 1987), p. 101-102. English. **DESCR:** Book Reviews; *CHICANA VOICES: INTERSECTIONS OF CLASS, RACE AND GENDER; Chicanas.

4966 Weas, Andrea T. Book review of: THE CHICANO STRUGGLE. LECTOR, Vol. 4, no. 4-6 (1987), p. 54. English. **DESCR:** Book Reviews; Social History and Conditions; *THE CHICANO STRUGGLE: ANALYSES OF PAST AND PRESENT EFFORTS.

National Association of Latino Elected Officials (NALEO)

4967 Morales, Cecilio. Budget cutting and Hispanics. VISTA, Vol. 1, no. 6 (February 2, 1986), p. 22. English. **DESCR:** *Federal Aid; *Gramm-Rudman Balanced Budget Amendment; National Council of La Raza (NCLR).

4968 Pachon, Harry. Allaying the fears of becoming a U.S. citizen. VISTA, Vol. 2, no. 7 (March 8, 1987), p. 26. English. **DESCR:** *Naturalization.

National Association for Chicano Studies (NACS) Annual Conference, El Paso, TX, April 9-12, 1986

4969 Solorzano, Daniel. Reflections on the 1986 National Association for Chicano Studies (NACS) held in El Paso, Texas, April 9-12. LA RED/THE NET, no. 96 (May 1986), p. 8-9. English. **DESCR:** *Conferences and Meetings.

National Center for Bilingual Research

4970 So, Alvin Yiu-cheong. The analysis of language minority issues in national data sets. LA RED/THE NET, no. 71 (August 1983), p. 3-5. English. **DESCR:** Bilingualism; Databases; *Language Usage; Surveys.

National Chicano Council on Higher Education (NCCHE)

4971 Madrid, Arturo. Letter to the Network. LA RED/THE NET, no. 56 (July 1982), p. 13. English. **DESCR:** Educational Organizations; *National Chicano Research Network (NCRN).

4972 Madrid, Arturo. Report to the Network. LA RED/THE NET, No. 103 (December 1986), p. 1-2. English. **DESCR:** Educational Organizations; *Higher Education.

4973 Report to the Network from NCCHE. LA RED/THE NET, no. 87 (July 1985), p. 1-2. English. **DESCR:** Chicano Studies; *Educational Organizations; LA RED/THE NET; National Chicano Research Network (NCRN); Tomas Rivera Center, Claremont, CA.

National Chicano Research Network (NCRN)

4974 Madrid, Arturo. Letter to the Network. LA RED/THE NET, no. 56 (July 1982), p. 13. English. **DESCR:** Educational Organizations; *National Chicano Council on Higher Education (NCCHE).

4975 Report to the Network from NCCHE. LA RED/THE NET, no. 87 (July 1985), p. 1-2. English. **DESCR:** Chicano Studies; *Educational Organizations; LA RED/THE NET; *National Chicano Council on Higher Education (NCCHE); Tomas Rivera Center, Claremont, CA.

National Chicano Survey (NCS)

4976 Arce, Carlos H. Chicano Survey report #4: characteristics of the survey sample. LA RED/THE NET, no. 41 (April 1981), p. 7-8. English. **DESCR:** *Surveys.

4977 Arce, Carlos H.; Murguia, Edward; and Frisbie, William Parker. Phenotype and life chances among Chicanos. HISPANIC JOURNAL OF BEHAVIORAL SCIENCES, Vol. 9, no. 1 (March 1987), p. 19-32. English. **DESCR:** *Discrimination; *Skin Color; Social Classes; *Socioeconomic Factors.

4978 Chicano Survey report #1: labor force experiences. LA RED/THE NET, no. 38 (January 1981), p. 1,12. English. **DESCR:** Labor; *Labor Supply and Market; Surveys.

4979 Garcia, John A. The political integration of Mexican immigrants: examining some political orientations. INTERNATIONAL MIGRATION REVIEW, Vol. 21, no. 2 (Summer 1987), p. 372-389. English. **DESCR:** Culture; *Immigrants; Political Ideology; *Political Socialization.

National Chicano Survey (NCS) (cont.)

4980 More findings based upon the NCS. LA RED/THE NET, No. 102 (November 1986), p. 9-11. English. DESCR: English Language; *Literacy.

4981 Nat'l Chicano Survey analyzed. LA RED/THE NET, No. 100 (September 1986), p. 10. English. DESCR: *Literacy; Surveys.

4982 Rodriguez-Scheel, Jaclyn and Beals, Janette. Chicano Survey report #5: group naming and cultural inclinations. LA RED/THE NET, no. 42 (May 1981), p. 3-4. English. DESCR: Cultural Characteristics; *Self-Referents.

4983 Snipp, C. Matthew and Tienda, Marta. Intergenerational occupational mobility of Chicanos. LA RED/THE NET, no. 42 (May 1981), p. 2. English. DESCR: Age Groups; *Income.

4984 Wreford, Mary. Chicano Survey report #2: perceptions and experience of discrimination. LA RED/THE NET, no. 39 (February 1981), p. 7,16. English. DESCR: *Discrimination; Discrimination in Employment; Midwestern States; Southwestern United States; *Surveys.

4985 Wreford, Mary. Chicano Survey report #3: political opinions. LA RED/THE NET, no. 40 (March 1981), p. 4-5. English. DESCR: Politics; *Voter Turnout.

4986 Wreford, Mary. Reactions from the Chicano Survey respondents: no mas silencio. LA RED/THE NET, no. 33 (August 1980), p. 2-3. English. DESCR: Chicano Project of the University of Michigan; Midwestern States; *Public Opinion; Social Science; Southwestern United States; *Surveys.

National City, CA

4987 Hernandez, Beatriz Johnston. A dogged attack on immigration. MOTHER JONES, Vol. 11, no. 6 (September 1986), p. 10,12. English. DESCR: *Immigration Regulation and Control.

National Coalition of Hispanic Mental Health and Human Services Organizations (COSSMHO)

4988 Morales, Cecilio. A question of health. VISTA, Vol. 3, no. 3 (November 8, 1987), p. 14, 19. English. DESCR: Delgado, Jane; *Health Education; Preventative Medicine.

National Council of La Raza (NCLR)

4989 Architects of America's future. VISTA, Vol. 1, no. 11 (July 6, 1986), p. 10. English. DESCR: *Conferences and Meetings; Social History and Conditions; *Yzaguirre, Raul.

4990 Beale, Stephen. Striking a deal with big business. HISPANIC BUSINESS, Vol. 9, no. 2 (February 1987), p. 26-33. English. DESCR: *Adolph Coors Co.; American G.I. Forum; Boycotts; Corporations; Cuban National Planning Council, Inc. Washington, D.C.; Employment; *Hispanic Association on Corporate Responsibility (HACER); League of United Latin American Citizens (LULAC); National IMAGE; National Puerto Rican Coalition; *Organizations; U.S. Hispanic Chamber of Commerce.

4991 Latino literacy update: NCLR reports on illiteracy among Latinos. LA RED/THE NET, No. 102 (November 1986), p. 8-9. English. DESCR: *English Language Proficiency Survey (ELPS); *Literacy.

4992 Morales, Cecilio. Budget cutting and

Hispanics. VISTA, Vol. 1, no. 6 (February 2, 1986), p. 22. English. DESCR: *Federal Aid; *Gramm-Rudman Balanced Budget Amendment; National Association of Latino Elected Officials (NALEO).

4993 National Council of La Raza (NCLR). Career information and Hispanic students. LA RED/THE NET, no. 75 (December 1983), p. 2-4. English. DESCR: *Careers; Educational Services; Secondary School Education; Survey of Career Information Systems in Secondary Schools; *Youth.

4994 Perez, Renato E. The business of Hispanics. VISTA, Vol. 2, no. 1 (September 7, 1986), p. 10. English. DESCR: Adolph Coors Co.; American G.I. Forum; Apodaca, Jerry [Gov. of New Mexico]; Business; *Collective Bargaining; Corporations; Cuban National Planning Council, Inc. Washington, D.C.; *Hispanic Association on Corporate Responsibility (HACER); League of United Latin American Citizens (LULAC); National IMAGE; U.S. Hispanic Chamber of Commerce.

4995 Yzaguirre critical of committee action. NUESTRO, Vol. 11, no. 4 (May 1987), p. 8. English. DESCR: *Bilingual Bicultural Education; English-Only Movement; Yzaguirre, Raul.

National Heritage Fellowship

4996 Middleman, Irene. Eppie Archuleta. VISTA, Vol. 1, no. 7 (March 2, 1986), p. 14. English. DESCR: *Archuleta, Eppie; *Artists; Arts and Crafts.

National Hispanic Book Fair and Writers Festival, Houston, TX, May 30-31, 1987

4997 National Hispanic Book Fair and Writers Festival [photographs]. THE AMERICAS REVIEW, Vol. 15, no. 2 (Summer 1987), p. 40-41. DESCR: Festivals; Publishing Industry.

National Hispanic Center for Advanced Studies and Policy Analysis (NHCAS)

4998 Chavaria, Elvira. Book review of: THE STATE OF HISPANIC AMERICA, VOL. II and LA CHICANA: BUILDING FOR THE FUTURE. LA RED/THE NET, no. 68 (May 1983), p. 10-12. English. DESCR: Book Reviews; *LA CHICANA: BUILDING FOR THE FUTURE; *THE STATE OF HISPANIC AMERICA.

National Hispanic Corporate Council (NHCC)

4999 Trager, Cara S. Manhattan executive forum. HISPANIC BUSINESS, Vol. 9, no. 4 (April 1987), p. 10-13. English. DESCR: Advertising; *Corporations; Marketing; *Organizations.

National Hispanic Family Against Drug Abuse (NHFADA)

5000 New Latino group to combat problem. NUESTRO, Vol. 11, no. 2 (March 1987), p. 8. English. DESCR: *Alcoholism; *Drug Use.

National Hispanic Pastoral Encounter

5001 Stevens-Arroyo, Antonio M. Cahensly revisited?: the National Pastoral Encounter of America's Hispanic Catholics. MIGRATION WORLD MAGAZINE, Vol. 15, no. 3 (1987), p. 16-19. English. DESCR: *Catholic Church; Clergy; The Lucerne Memorial.

National Hispanic Scholar Awards Program

5002 Chavez, Lorenzo A. A brief guide to
financial aid for college-bound students.
VISTA, Vol. 2, no. 1 (September 7, 1986), p.
7. English. DESCR: Directories; *Financial
Aid; LULAC National Scholarship Fund; MALDEF
Law School Fellowship; *National Hispano
Scholarship Fund.

National Hispano Scholarship Fund

5003 Chavez, Lorenzo A. A brief guide to
financial aid for college-bound students.
VISTA, Vol. 2, no. 1 (September 7, 1986), p.
7. English. DESCR: Directories; *Financial
Aid; LULAC National Scholarship Fund; MALDEF
Law School Fellowship; National Hispanic
Scholar Awards Program.

National IMAGE

5004 Beale, Stephen. Striking a deal with big
business. HISPANIC BUSINESS, Vol. 9, no. 2
(February 1987), p. 26-33. English. DESCR:
*Adolph Coors Co.; American G.I. Forum;
Boycotts; Corporations; Cuban National
Planning Council, Inc. Washington, D.C.;
Employment; *Hispanic Association on
Corporate Responsibility (HACER); League of
United Latin American Citizens (LULAC);
National Council of La Raza (NCLR); National
Puerto Rican Coalition; *Organizations; U.S.
Hispanic Chamber of Commerce.

5005 Perez, Renato E. The business of Hispanics.
VISTA, Vol. 2, no. 1 (September 7, 1986), p.
10. English. DESCR: Adolph Coors Co.;
American G.I. Forum; Apodaca, Jerry [Gov. of
New Mexico]; Business; *Collective
Bargaining; Corporations; Cuban National
Planning Council, Inc. Washington, D.C.;
*Hispanic Association on Corporate
Responsibility (HACER); League of United
Latin American Citizens (LULAC); National
Council of La Raza (NCLR); U.S. Hispanic
Chamber of Commerce.

National Institute of Education (NIE)

5006 Latino reading and ed progress. LA RED/THE
NET, No. 100 (September 1986), p. 11.
English. DESCR: Education; *Literacy;
National Assessment of Educational Progress.

National Institute of Mental Health

5007 Remas, Theodora A. Down and blue. VISTA,
Vol. 2, no. 5 (January 4, 1987), p. 16-18.
English. DESCR: Counseling (Psychological);
*Depression (Psychological); Social History
and Conditions; Spanish Family Guidance
Clinic, Miami, FL.

National Labor Relations Board (NLRB)

5008 Faxon, R. Paul. Employer sanctions for
hiring illegal aliens: a simplistic solution
to a complex problem. NORTHWESTERN JOURNAL
OF INTERNATIONAL LAW AND BUSINESS, Vol. 6,
(Spring 1984), p. 203-248. English. DESCR:
Agribusiness; Immigration Law and
Legislation; Simpson-Mazzoli Bill;
*Undocumented Workers.

National Latino Media Coalition (NLMC)

5009 Madrid, Vicente and Yepes, Maria Elena.
National Latino Media Coalition. LATIN
QUARTER, Vol. 1, no. 4 (July, August, 1975),
p. 4-7. English. DESCR: Affirmative Action
Programs; Bilingual/Bicultural Coalition on
Mass Media; *Broadcast Media; California

Association of Latins in Broadcasting;
Conferences and Meetings; Federal
Communications Commission (FCC); Puerto
Rican Media Action and Educational Council.

National Lawyer's Guild

5010 Zesch, Lindy. Visa issue heats up: PEN hopes
for "group waiver" of denials. AMERICAN
THEATRE, Vol. 2, no. 8 (November 1985), p.
24. English. DESCR: Artists; Authors; Book
Reviews; GETTING IN: A GUIDE TO OVERCOMING
THE POLITICAL DENIAL OF NON-IMMIGRANT VISAS;
Politics; *Visas.

National Merit Scholarships

5011 Alvarado, Raul. Against all odds. HISPANIC
ENGINEER, Vol. 3, no. 4 (Fall 1987), p.
10-11. English. DESCR: *Chicanas; Education;
Educational Statistics; Preliminary
Scholastic Aptitude Test (PSAT); *Scholastic
Aptitude Test (SAT); Stereotypes.

National Network of Hispanic Women

5012 Mellado, Carmela. Hispanic women as leaders:
expanding the stereotypes that bind us.
HISPANIC ENGINEER, Vol. 3, no. 4 (Fall
1987), p. 6. English. DESCR: *Chicanas;
Engineering as a Profession.

5013 A road fraught with challenge leads to view
from the top. HISPANIC TIMES, Vol. 8, no. 3
(May, June, 1987), p. 28. English. DESCR:
Authors; Biography; *Chicanas; Leadership;
Torres, Celia Gonzales.

5014 Sellers, Jeff M. Challenging the myth of the
traditional woman. HISPANIC BUSINESS, Vol.
9, no. 8 (August 1987), p. 15-16, 48.
English. DESCR: *Businesspeople; *Careers;
*Chicanas; *Management; Sex Roles; Torres,
Celia; Women; Zambrana, Ruth.

5015 Soto, Rose Marie. National Network of
Hispanic Women. HISPANIC ENGINEER, Vol. 3,
no. 4 (Fall 1987), p. 26-28. English.
DESCR: Castillo, Sylvia; Gonzales Torres,
Celia; Gutierrez, Nancy; *Professional
Organizations; Women; Zambrana, Ruth.

National Puerto Rican Coalition

5016 Beale, Stephen. Striking a deal with big
business. HISPANIC BUSINESS, Vol. 9, no. 2
(February 1987), p. 26-33. English. DESCR:
*Adolph Coors Co.; American G.I. Forum;
Boycotts; Corporations; Cuban National
Planning Council, Inc. Washington, D.C.;
Employment; *Hispanic Association on
Corporate Responsibility (HACER); League of
United Latin American Citizens (LULAC);
National Council of La Raza (NCLR); National
IMAGE; *Organizations; U.S. Hispanic Chamber
of Commerce.

National Science Foundation

5017 Paikoff, Mark. National Science Foundation
Programs for minority engineers, students,
and graduate students. HISPANIC ENGINEER,
Vol. 3, no. 5 (Winter 1987), p. 45. English.
DESCR: *Financial Aid.

National Study to Assess the Service Needs of the Hispanic Elderly

5018 Lacayo, Carmela G. Triple jeopardy among Hispanic elderly: results from first national needs assessment of older Hispanics. LA RED/THE NET, no. 56 (July 1982), p. 2-3. English. DESCR: *Ancianos; Asociacion Nacional Pro Personas Mayores; Research Methodology; *Social Services; Surveys.

National Systems & Research Co.

5019 The top 100--profiles. HISPANIC BUSINESS, Vol. 9, no. 11 (November 1987), p. 31-50. English. DESCR: Artco Contracting, Inc., Auburn Hills, MI; *Business Enterprises; Computer Trade Development Corp, Birmingham, MI; Corella Electric Inc., Phoenix, AZ; GSE Construction Co., Inc., Livermore, CA; Unique Construction Co., Hillside, IL.

Nationalism

5020 Allsup, Dan. The private war of Roy Benavidez. VISTA, Vol. 2, no. 5 (January 4, 1987), p. 19-20. English. DESCR: *Benavidez, Roy; Medal of Honor; *Veterans.

5021 Bueno, Patricia E. Los Chicanos y la politica II. LA COMUNIDAD, No. 268 (September 8, 1985), p. 2-3. Spanish. DESCR: American G.I. Forum; Chicano Movement; History; Leadership; Mexican American Political Association (MAPA); Political Association of Spanish-Speaking Organizations (PASO); *Political Parties and Organizations.

5022 Goldman, Shifra. Arte chicano: iconografia de la autodeterminacion. LA COMUNIDAD, No. 336 (December 28, 1986), p. 12-14+. Spanish. DESCR: *Art; Discrimination; EL PLAN ESPIRITUAL DE AZTLAN; History; Identity; Pachucos; Social Classes; *Symbolism.

Native Americans

5023 Dinwoodie, David H. Indians, Hispanos, and land reform: a new deal struggle in New Mexico. WESTERN HISTORICAL QUARTERLY, Vol. 17, no. 3 (July 1986), p. 291-323. English. DESCR: Bureau of Indian Affairs (BIA); History; Interdepartmental Rio Grande Board; Land Grants; Land Program of the Federal Emergency Relief Administration (FERA); *Land Reform; *New Mexico.

5024 Duncan, Marilyn H., et al. Childhood cancer epidemiology in New Mexico's American Indians, Hispanic whites, and non-Hispanic whites, 1970-82. JOURNAL OF THE NATIONAL CANCER INSTITUTE, Vol. 76, no. 6 (June 1986), p. 1013-1018. English. DESCR: Anglo Americans; *Cancer; *Children; Diseases.

5025 Powers, Stephen and Rossman, Mark H. Attributions for success and failure among Anglo, Black, Hispanic, and Native-American community-college students. JOURNAL OF PSYCHOLOGY, Vol. 117, no. 1 (May 1984), p. 27-31. English. DESCR: *Academic Achievement; Anglo Americans; Blacks; Community Colleges; *Locus of Control; Students.

Nativism
USE: Assimilation

Natural Support Systems

5026 Hardy-Fanta, Carol. Social action in Hispanic groups. SOCIAL WORK, Vol. 31, no. 2 (March, April, 1986), p. 119-123. English. DESCR: *Community Organizations; Psychotherapy; *Social Work.

5027 Report to the Network. LA RED/THE NET, No. 104 (January 1987), p. 1-2. English. DESCR: Computers; *Contreras, Reynaldo A.; *Higher Education; *Midwestern States; Research Methodology; Surveys.

5028 Rivera, Alvin D. Laying a foundation for learning: student peer workshop groups. NEW DIRECTIONS FOR TEACHING AND LEARNING, no. 16 (December 1983), p. 81-86. English. DESCR: *Careers; Counseling (Educational); *Engineering as a Profession; Organizations; Students.

5029 Sabogal, Fabio, et al. Hispanic familism and acculturation: what changes and what doesn't? HISPANIC JOURNAL OF BEHAVIORAL SCIENCES, Vol. 9, no. 4 (December 1987), p. 397-412. English. DESCR: *Acculturation; Attitudes; Cultural Characteristics; Ethnic Groups; Extended Family; *Family; Values.

5030 Wells, Miriam J. Power brokers and ethnicity: the rise of a Chicano movement. AZTLAN, Vol. 17, no. 1 (Spring 1986), p. 47-77. English. DESCR: *Chicano Movement; *Identity; *Patron System.

5031 Zavella, Patricia. "Abnormal intimacy": the varying work networks of Chicana cannery workers. FEMINIST STUDIES, Vol. 11, no. 3 (Fall 1985), p. 541-557. English. DESCR: Canneries; Chicanas; Discrimination in Employment; Labor Unions; *Working Women.

Naturalization

5032 Alvarez, Robert R. A profile of the citizenship process among Hispanics in the United States. INTERNATIONAL MIGRATION REVIEW, Vol. 21, no. 2 (Summer 1987), p. 327-351. English. DESCR: Chicanas; Identity; Immigration and Naturalization Service (INS).

5033 Baca, Reynaldo and Bryan, Dexter. Citizen aspirations and residency preferences: the Mexican undocumented worker in the binational community. LA RED/THE NET, no. 34 (September 1980), p. 2. English. DESCR: *Los Angeles, CA; *Undocumented Workers.

5034 DeSipio, Louis. Social science literature and the naturalization process. INTERNATIONAL MIGRATION REVIEW, Vol. 21, no. 2 (Summer 1987), p. 390-405. English. DESCR: Immigrants; *Research Methodology; *Social Science.

5035 Fernandez, Edward and Cresce, Arthur R. The Hispanic foreign-born and the assimilation experience. MIGRATION WORLD MAGAZINE, Vol. 14, no. 5 (1986), p. 7-11. English. DESCR: *Assimilation; *Immigrants; *Socioeconomic Factors; Undocumented Workers.

5036 Gill, Eric K. Notaries: clearing the air. HISPANIC BUSINESS, Vol. 9, no. 3 (March 1987), p. 14. English. DESCR: *Immigration Law and Legislation; *Legal Aid; Undocumented Workers.

5037 Pachon, Harry. Allaying the fears of becoming a U.S. citizen. VISTA, Vol. 2, no. 7 (March 8, 1987), p. 26. English. DESCR: *National Association of Latino Elected Officials (NALEO).

Naturalization (cont.)

5038 Pachon, Harry. An overview of citizenship in the Hispanic community. INTERNATIONAL MIGRATION REVIEW, Vol. 21, no. 2 (Summer 1987), p. 299-310. English. **DESCR:** *Immigrants.

5039 Portes, Alejandro and Curtis, John W. Changing flags: naturalization and its determinants among Mexican immigrants. INTERNATIONAL MIGRATION REVIEW, Vol. 21, no. 2 (Summer 1987), p. 352-371. English. **DESCR:** *Immigrants.

Nava, Greg

5040 Perez, Joel Oseas. EL NORTE: imagenes peyorativas de Mexico y los Chicanos. CHIRICU, Vol. 5, no. 1 (1987), p. 13-21. Spanish. **DESCR:** *EL NORTE [film]; Film Reviews; Thomas, Anna.

Naval Research Laboratory

5041 Bradby, Marie. The naval research laboratory. HISPANIC ENGINEER, Vol. 3, no. 2 (Summer 1987), p. 34-38. English. **DESCR:** *Engineering as a Profession; Military; Rojas, Richard Raimond; Urrutia, Jorge R.

Navarro [family name]

5042 Instituto Genealogico e Historico Latino-Americano. Rootsearch: Rivera: Navarro: Salazar. VISTA, Vol. 2, no. 3 (November 2, 1986), p. 24. English. **DESCR:** Genealogy; History; *Personal Names; *Rivera [family name]; *Salazar [family name].

Navas, Trina

5043 Kwain, Constance. Searching for Hispanic talent. VISTA, Vol. 2, no. 6 (February 8, 1987), p. 6-7. English. **DESCR:** *Actors and Actresses; American Federation of Television & Radio Artists (AFTRA); *Business Enterprises; Films; Myrna Salazar and Associates, Inc.; Salazar, Myrna; Screen Actors Guild; Television.

NCCHE

USE: National Chicano Council on Higher Education (NCCHE)

THE NEW BILINGUALISM: AN AMERICAN DILEMMA

5044 Macias, Reynaldo Flores. Book review of: THE NEW BILINGUALISM: AN AMERICAN DILEMMA. LA RED/THE NET, no. 61 (November 1982), p. 7-9. English. **DESCR:** *Bilingualism; Book Reviews; Public Policy; Ridge, Martin.

5045 Ornstein-Galicia, Jacob. Bilingualism, bilingual education, and language contact: the agony, the rewards--or how to unravel Babel. BILINGUAL REVIEW, Vol. 11, no. 3 (September, December, 1984), p. 72-82. English. **DESCR:** Bilingual Bicultural Education; Bilingualism; Book Reviews; *LANGUAGES IN CONFLICT: LINGUISTIC ACCULTURATION IN THE GREAT PLAINS; Ridge, Martin; Schach, Paul.

New Mexico

5046 Anderson, Karen. Book review of: NEW MEXICO WOMEN: INTERCULTURAL PERSPECTIVES. NEW MEXICO HISTORICAL REVIEW, Vol. 62, no. 4 (October 1987), p. 401-2. English. **DESCR:** Book Reviews; *Jensen, Joan M.; *Miller, Darlis A.; *NEW MEXICO WOMEN: INTERCULTURAL PERSPECTIVES; Women.

5047 Benson, Douglas K. Intuitions of a world in transition: the New Mexican poetry of Leroy V. Quintana. BILINGUAL REVIEW, Vol. 12, no. 1-2 (January, August, 1985), p. 62-80. English. **DESCR:** Authors; HIJO DEL PUEBLO; *Literary Criticism; Poetry; *Quintana, Leroy V.; SANGRE.

5048 Chavez, Denise. Words of wisdom. NEW MEXICO MAGAZINE, Vol. 65, no. 12 (December 1987), p. 72-78. English. **DESCR:** *Authors; *Literary History; Literature.

5049 Dinwoodie, David H. Indians, Hispanos, and land reform: a new deal struggle in New Mexico. WESTERN HISTORICAL QUARTERLY, Vol. 17, no. 3 (July 1986), p. 291-323. English. **DESCR:** Bureau of Indian Affairs (BIA); History; Interdepartmental Rio Grande Board; Land Grants; Land Program of the Federal Emergency Relief Administration (FERA); *Land Reform; Native Americans.

5050 Duda, Joan L. Goals and achievement orientations of Anglo and Mexican-American adolescents in sport and the classroom. INTERNATIONAL REVIEW OF SPORT SOCIOLOGY, Vol. 18, no. 4 (1983), p. 63-80. English. **DESCR:** Academic Achievement; Cultural Characteristics; Sports; *Youth.

5051 Foley, Patrick. Book review of: ALONG THE RIO GRANDE: PASTORAL VISIT TO SOUTHWEST NEW MEXICO IN 1902. NEW MEXICO HISTORICAL REVIEW, Vol. 62, no. 4 (October 1987), p. 405-6. English. **DESCR:** *ALONG THE RIO GRANDE: A PASTORAL VISIT TO SOUTHWEST NEW MEXICO IN 1902; Book Reviews; *Granjon, Henry.

5052 Gonzales-Berry, Erlinda. Enmienda de ingles en Nuevo Mexico. LA COMUNIDAD, No. 352 (April 19, 1987), p. 4-7. Spanish. **DESCR:** English Language; *English-Only Movement; History; Legislation; Spanish Language.

5053 Guerrero, Martha and Anaya, Toney. Toney Anaya: a man with convictions=Toney Anaya: un hombre de conviccion. AMERICAS 2001, Premiere Issue, 1987, p. 20-23, 44. Bilingual. **DESCR:** *Anaya, Toney, Governor of New Mexico; Biography; Elected Officials; Politics.

5054 Holmes, John J. Sentinel of tradition. VISTA, Vol. 3, no. 3 (November 8, 1987), p. 16. English. **DESCR:** *Missions; *San Gregorio de Abo (Salinas National Monument, NM); Sisneros, Federico.

5055 Jenkins, Myra Ellen. Land tenure history of New Mexico. EL CUADERNO, Vol. 4, no. 1 (Summer 1976), p. 33-46. English. **DESCR:** History; Land Grants; *Land Tenure; Pueblo Indians.

5056 Jensen, Joan M. Crossing ethnic barriers in the Southwest: women's agricultural extension education, 1914-1940. AGRICULTURAL HISTORY, Vol. 60, no. 2 (Spring 1986), p. 169-181. English. **DESCR:** *Agricultural Extension Service; Agriculture; Cabeza de Baca, Fabiola; Chicanas; History; *Rural Education.

5057 Meketa, Charles and Meketa, Jacqueline. Heroes or cowards? A new look at the role of native New Mexicans at the Battle of Valverde. NEW MEXICO HISTORICAL REVIEW, Vol. 62, no. 1 (January 1987), p. 33-46. English. **DESCR:** *Battle of Valverde; *Canby, Edward; History.

New Mexico (cont.)

5058 Miller, Darlis A. Los Pinos, New Mexico: civil war post on the Rio Grande. NEW MEXICO HISTORICAL REVIEW, Vol. 62, no. 1 (January 1987), p. 1-31. English. **DESCR:** History; *Los Pinos, NM; *Rio Grande; *Southwestern United States.

5059 Ortiz, Francisco. La cultura chicana, la cultura amenazada. LA COMUNIDAD, No. 305 (May 25, 1986), p. 10-11. Spanish. **DESCR:** Anaya, Rudolfo A.; *BLESS ME, ULTIMA; Bloomfield, NM; *Censorship; Literary Criticism; Textbooks.

5060 Sagel, Jim. A question of history. CONFLUENCIA, Vol. 1, no. 1 (Fall 1985), p. 94-101. English. **DESCR:** History; *Land Grants.

5061 Salmon, Roberto Mario. Book review of: MEXICANO RESISTANCE IN THE SOUTHWEST. LA RED/THE NET, no. 44 (July 1981), p. 6-7. English. **DESCR:** Book Reviews; *MEXICANO RESISTANCE IN THE SOUTHWEST: "THE SACRED RIGHT OF SELF-PRESERVATION"; Rosenbaum, Robert J.

5062 Valdez, Lorenzo. Labor history in the villages. EL CUADERNO, Vol. 3, no. 2 (Spring 1974), p. 54-63. English. **DESCR:** *Economic History and Conditions; *Labor; *Social History and Conditions.

5063 Wroth, William. New hope in hard times: Hispanic crafts are revived during troubled years. PALACIO, Vol. 89, no. 2 (1983), p. 22-31. English. **DESCR:** *Arts and Crafts; *Las Lunas Vocational Training School; Spanish Colonial Arts Society; Taos Vocational School; Works Progress Administration (WPA).

5064 Ybarra, Lea. Book review of: LAS MUJERES: CONVERSATIONS FROM A HISPANIC COMMUNITY. LA RED/THE NET, no. 58 (September 1982), p. 5-6. English. **DESCR:** Book Reviews; *Chicanas; *Elasser, Nan; *LAS MUJERES: CONVERSATIONS FROM A HISPANIC COMMUNITY; MacKenzie, Kyle; Tixier y Vigil, Yvonne.

NEW MEXICO WOMEN: INTERCULTURAL PERSPECTIVES

5065 Anderson, Karen. Book review of: NEW MEXICO WOMEN: INTERCULTURAL PERSPECTIVES. NEW MEXICO HISTORICAL REVIEW, Vol. 62, no. 4 (October 1987), p. 401-2. English. **DESCR:** Book Reviews; *Jensen, Joan M.; *Miller, Darlis A.; *New Mexico; Women.

THE NEW NOMADS: FROM IMMIGRANT LABOR TO TRANSNATIONAL WORKING CLASS

5066 Pena, Devon Gerardo. Book review of: THE NEW NOMADS: FROM IMMIGRANT LABOR TO TRANSNATIONAL WORKING CLASS. LA RED/THE NET, no. 67 (April 1983), p. 8-10. English. **DESCR:** Book Reviews; Dixon, Marlene; Jonas, Susanne; Labor.

New York, NY

5067 Olarte, Silvia W. and Masnik, Ruth. Benefits of long-term group therapy for disadvantaged Hispanic outpatients. HOSPITAL AND COMMUNITY PSYCHIATRY, Vol. 36, no. 10 (October 1985), p. 1093-1097. English. **DESCR:** Ethnic Groups; Metropolitan Hospital, New York, NY; Psychotherapy; Sex Roles; *Women.

5068 Perez, Renato E. Badge of Hispanic pride. VISTA, Vol. 1, no. 12 (August 2, 1986), p. 9-11. English. **DESCR:** Broward County, FL; Chicago, IL; Dallas, TX; Houston, TX; *Los Angeles, CA; *Police; San Antonio, TX; San Diego, CA; Tucson, AZ.

Newspapers

5069 Cecere, Linda. Newspapers attract attention in some categories. ADVERTISING AGE MAGAZINE, Vol. 57, no. 43 (August 11, 1986), p. S9-S10. English. **DESCR:** Advertising; DIARIO DE LAS AMERICAS; EL MIAMI HERALD; LA OPINION, Los Angeles, CA; NOTICIAS DEL MUNDO; Spanish Language.

5070 Fitch, Ed. Paving way for national ad sales. ADVERTISING AGE MAGAZINE, Vol. 57, no. 16 (February 27, 1986), p. 50-51. English. **DESCR:** *Advertising; Marketing.

5071 Greenberg, Bradley S., et al. Local newspaper coverage of Mexican Americans. JOURNALISM QUARTERLY, Vol. 60, no. 4 (Winter 1983), p. 671-676. English. **DESCR:** Journalism.

5072 Kane, Michael G. "Touching" minorities. EDITOR & PUBLISHER: THE FOURTH ESTATE, Vol. 119, no. 38 (September 20, 1986), p. 20-21. English. **DESCR:** Advertising; Consumers; Ethnic Groups; Marketing.

5073 Korzenny, Felipe, et al. Cultural identification as predictor of content preferences of Hispanics. JOURNALISM QUARTERLY, Vol. 60, no. 4 (Winter 1983), p. 677-685+. English. **DESCR:** Cultural Characteristics; English Language; Identity; Spanish Language.

5074 Shoemaker, Pamela J.; Reese, Stephen D.; and Danielson, Wayne A. Spanish-language print media use as an indicator of acculturation. JOURNALISM QUARTERLY, Vol. 62, no. 4 (Winter 1985), p. 734-740. English. **DESCR:** *Acculturation; Magazines; *Print Media; *Spanish Language.

Newton, Frank

5075 Arce, Carlos H. and Carlson, David. Book review of: HISPANIC MENTAL HEALTH RESEARCH: A REFERENCE GUIDE. LA RED/THE NET, no. 57 (August 1982), p. 5-7. English. **DESCR:** Book Reviews; *HISPANIC MENTAL HEALTH RESEARCH: A REFERENCE GUIDE; Mental Health; Olmedo, Esteban L.; Padilla, Amado M.; Reference Works.

5076 Castillo-Speed, Lillian. Annotated bibliography. LA RED/THE NET, no. 93 (January, February, 1986), p. 14-17. English. **DESCR:** A BIBLIOGRAPHY OF MEXICAN AMERICAN HISTORY; ARTE CHICANO; Book Reviews; Caballero, Cesar; CHICANO LITERATURE: A REFERENCE GUIDE; CHICANO ORGANIZATIONS DIRECTORY; CHICANO PERIODICAL INDEX; Goldman, Shifra M.; HISPANIC ALMANAC; HISPANIC MENTAL HEALTH RESEARCH: A REFERENCE GUIDE; Lomeli, Francisco A.; Martinez, Julio A.; Meier, Matt S.; *Reference Works; Ybarra-Frausto, Tomas.

Nicandro, Glugio J.L. (Gronk)
USE: Gronk (Pseud.)

Nicaragua

5077 Lopez-Flores, Beatriz. Testimonios de las campesinas de Pantasma. REVISTA MUJERES, Vol. 2, no. 2 (June 1985), p. 7-9. Spanish. **DESCR:** *Farm Workers; *Oral History.

Nicasio v. U.S. Immigration and Naturalization Service

5078 Schroeder, J. INS vehicle stops designed to discover illegal aliens ruled unconstitutional. CRIMINAL LAW REPORTER, Vol. 37, no. 23 (September 11, 1985), p. 2430-2431. English. **DESCR**: *Search and Seizure; U.S. v. Brignoni-Ponce.

Nineteenth century

5079 Griswold del Castillo, Richard. Familism, the extended family and Chicanos in the nineteenth century. LA RED/THE NET, no. 49 (December 1981), p. 2. English. **DESCR**: *Extended Family; *Family; Los Angeles, CA; San Antonio, TX; Santa Fe, NM; *Social History and Conditions; Tucson, AZ.

5080 Stewart, Kenneth L. and de Leon, Arnoldo. Age and sex composition among inmigrantes to Texas. LA RED/THE NET, no. 64 (February 1983), p. 2-3. English. **DESCR**: *Immigrants; *Texas.

Nochebuena
USE: Christmas

NorCal Frozen Foods

5081 Shapiro, Peter. Watsonville shows "it can be done". GUARDIAN, Vol. 39, no. 24 (March 25, 1987), p. 1,9. English. **DESCR**: Canneries; Chicanas; Labor Unions; *Strikes and Lockouts; *Watsonville Canning and Frozen Food Co.; Working Women.

EL NORTE [film]

5082 Perez, Joel Oseas. EL NORTE: imagenes peyorativas de Mexico y los Chicanos. CHIRICU, Vol. 5, no. 1 (1987), p. 13-21. Spanish. **DESCR**: Film Reviews; Nava, Greg; Thomas, Anna.

Nortenas

5083 Bensusan, Guy. A consideration of Nortena and Chicano music. STUDIES IN LATIN AMERICAN POPULAR CULTURE, Vol. 4, (1985), p. 158-169. English. **DESCR**: Corridos; Music.

Northern California

5084 Dewey, Kathryn G.; Strode, Margaret A.; and Fitch, Yolanda Ruiz. Dietary change among migrant and nonmigrant Mexican-American families in northern California. ECOLOGY OF FOOD AND NUTRITION, Vol. 14, no. 1 (1984), p. 11-24. English. **DESCR**: Culture; *Food Practices; *Migrant Children; Migrant Labor; *Nutrition.

5085 Rochin, Refugio I. Chicanos in rural labor markets. LA RED/THE NET, no. 31 (June 1980), p. 2. English. **DESCR**: *Labor Supply and Market; *Rural Population.

5086 Rochin, Refugio I. Chicanos in rural labor markets: part 2. LA RED/THE NET, no. 47 (October 1981), p. 2,10. English. **DESCR**: *Labor Supply and Market; *Rural Population; SURVEY OF INCOME AND EDUCATION, 1976; *Surveys.

NorthSun, Nila

5087 Avalos, Francisco. Book review of: SMALL BONES, LITTLE EYES. LECTOR, Vol. 4, no. 1-3 (1986), p. [60]. English. **DESCR**: Book Reviews; Sagel, Jim; *SMALL BONES, LITTLE EYES.

Northwestern United States

5088 Cook, Annabel Kirschner. Diversity among Northwest Hispanics. SOCIAL SCIENCE JOURNAL, Vol. 23, no. 2 (April 1986), p. 205-216. English. **DESCR**: Chicanas; *Population; *Socioeconomic Factors; Working Women.

Nosotros Golden Eagle Awards

5089 Kendall, Robert. Electric excitement at the 17th Annual Golden Eagle Awards ceremony sponsored by Nosotros at the Beverly Hilton Hotel. HISPANIC TIMES, Vol. 8, no. 5 (October, November, 1987), p. 32. English. **DESCR**: *Awards; Films; Television.

Nostrand, Richard L.

5090 Burnett, G. Wesley. Book review of: BORDERLANDS SOURCEBOOK. GEOGRAPHICAL REVIEW, Vol. 74, no. 1 (January 1984), p. 123-124. English. **DESCR**: Book Reviews; *BORDERLANDS SOURCEBOOK; Stoddard, Ellwyn R.; West, Jonathan P.

NOT BY THE SWORD

5091 Bruce-Novoa, Juan. Nash Candelaria: novelista (I). LA COMUNIDAD, No. 245 (March 31, 1985), p. 6-7. Spanish. **DESCR**: Biography; *Candelaria, Nash; *Literary Criticism; MEMORIES OF THE ALHAMBRA; Novel.

5092 Bruce-Novoa, Juan. Nash Candelaria: novelista (II). LA COMUNIDAD, No. 246 (April 7, 1985), p. 10-11. Spanish. **DESCR**: Biography; *Candelaria, Nash; *Literary Criticism; MEMORIES OF THE ALHAMBRA; Novel.

NOTICIAS DEL MUNDO

5093 Cecere, Linda. Newspapers attract attention in some categories. ADVERTISING AGE MAGAZINE, Vol. 57, no. 43 (August 11, 1986), p. S9-S10. English. **DESCR**: Advertising; DIARIO DE LAS AMERICAS; EL MIAMI HERALD; LA OPINION, Los Angeles, CA; *Newspapers; Spanish Language.

Noticiero SIN

5094 Beale, Stephen. More changes at SIN. HISPANIC BUSINESS, Vol. 9, no. 1 (January 1987), p. 10. English. **DESCR**: *Godoy, Gustavo; Journalism; *Spanish International Network (SIN); *Television.

Novel

5095 Anderson, Robert K. Marez y Luna and the masculine-feminine dialectic. CRITICA HISPANICA, Vol. 6, no. 2 (1984), p. 97-105. English. **DESCR**: Anaya, Rudolfo A.; *BLESS ME, ULTIMA; Literary Criticism; *Women Men Relations.

5096 Barry, John M. Mito e ironia en LOS PASOS PERDIDOS. TINTA, Vol. 1, no. 4 (Summer 1984), p. 3-9. Spanish. **DESCR**: Carpentier, Alejo; Latin American Literature; Literary Criticism; *LOS PASOS PERDIDOS; Mitos.

5097 Bernal, Alejandro. La estructura tematica en Y NO SE LO TRAGO LA TIERRA de Tomas Rivera. CHIRICU, Vol. 3, no. 1 (1982), p. 83-89. Spanish. **DESCR**: *Literary Criticism; Rivera, Tomas; *Y NO SE LO TRAGO LA TIERRA/AND THE EARTH DID NOT PART.

Novel (cont.)

5098 Bruce-Novoa, Juan. Ernest Brawley: un
escritor chicano desconocido. LA COMUNIDAD,
No. 277 (November 10, 1985), p. 6-7.
Spanish. **DESCR**: Authors; *Biography;
*Brawley, Ernest; Literary Criticism; SELENA
[novel]; THE ALAMO TREE [novel]; THE RAP
[novel].

5099 Bruce-Novoa, Juan. Homosexuality and the
Chicano novel. CONFLUENCIA, Vol. 2, no. 1
(Fall 1986), p. 69-77. English. **DESCR**:
Acosta, Oscar Zeta; CITY OF NIGHT; FAULTLINE
[novel]; *Homosexuality; Islas, Arturo;
*Literary Criticism; Machismo; Ortiz Taylor,
Sheila; POCHO; Rechy, John; Salas, Floyd;
SPRING FORWARD/FALL BACK; TATOO THE WICKED
CROSS; THE AUTOBIOGRAPHY OF A BROWN BUFFALO;
THE RAIN GOD: A DESERT TALE; THE REVOLT OF
THE COCKROACH PEOPLE; Villarreal, Jose
Antonio.

5100 Bruce-Novoa, Juan. Nash Candelaria:
novelista (I). LA COMUNIDAD, No. 245 (March
31, 1985), p. 6-7. Spanish. **DESCR**:
Biography; *Candelaria, Nash; *Literary
Criticism; MEMORIES OF THE ALHAMBRA; NOT BY
THE SWORD.

5101 Bruce-Novoa, Juan. Nash Candelaria:
novelista (II). LA COMUNIDAD, No. 246 (April
7, 1985), p. 10-11. Spanish. **DESCR**:
Biography; *Candelaria, Nash; *Literary
Criticism; MEMORIES OF THE ALHAMBRA; NOT BY
THE SWORD.

5102 Bruce-Novoa, Juan. Nuevo representantes de
la novela chicana. LA COMUNIDAD, No. 310
(June 29, 1986), p. 6-7+. Spanish. **DESCR**:
Brawley, Ernest; EL VAGO [novel]; FAULTLINE
[novel]; Gonzales, Laurence; *Literary
Criticism; Ortiz Taylor, Sheila; THE ALAMO
TREE [novel].

5103 Bustamante, Nuria. Permanencia y cambio en
CARAS VIEJAS Y VINO NUEVO. CONFLUENCIA, Vol.
1, no. 2 (Spring 1986), p. 61-65. Spanish.
DESCR: *CARAS VIEJAS Y VINO NUEVO; *Literary
Criticism; *Morales, Alejandro.

5104 Chavez, Noe M. Culminacion de una busqueda
de identidad. LA COMUNIDAD, No. 252 (May 19,
1985), p. 4-6. Spanish. **DESCR**: Anaya,
Rudolfo A.; *BLESS ME, ULTIMA; Identity;
*Literary Criticism.

5105 Cota-Cardenas, Margarita. La
creacion-protesta en CRISOL: (TRILOGIA).
CONFLUENCIA, Vol. 1, no. 2 (Spring 1986), p.
66-72. Spanish. **DESCR**: *Alarcon, Justo S.;
*CRISOL; *Literary Criticism.

5106 Ekstrom, Margaret V. Wanderers from an Aztec
land: Chicano naming devices used by Miguel
Mendez. LITERARY ONOMASTICS STUDIES, Vol.
12, (1985), p. 85-92. English. **DESCR**:
Literary Characters; *Literary Criticism;
Mendez M., Miguel; *PEREGRINOS DE AZTLAN.

5107 Galindo, Luis Alberto. El dios de la
lluvia=RAIN GOD. LA COMUNIDAD, No. 241
(March 3, 1985), p. 12-13. Spanish. **DESCR**:
Biography; Islas, Arturo; *Literary
Criticism; *THE RAIN GOD: A DESERT TALE.

5108 Gonzalez, Maria. CARAS VIEJAS Y VINO NUEVO:
analisis tematica y estructural. TINTA, Vol.
1, no. 1 (May 1981), p. 15-18. Spanish.
DESCR: *CARAS VIEJAS Y VINO NUEVO; *Literary
Criticism; Morales, Alejandro.

5109 Hinojosa-Smith, Rolando R. La realidad
chicana se forjo con dos culturas. LA

COMUNIDAD, No. 313 (July 20, 1986), p. 6-7.
Spanish. **DESCR**: *Biography; *Hinojosa-Smith,
Rolando R.; Literary Criticism.

5110 Lomeli, Francisco A. Entrevista con Rolando
Hinojosa (I). LA COMUNIDAD, No. 295 (March
16, 1986), p. 2-3+. Spanish. **DESCR**:
*Biography; *Hinojosa-Smith, Rolando R.;
Literary Criticism; Short Story.

5111 Lomeli, Francisco A. Novela chicana: sus
variantes y contradicciones (I). LA
COMUNIDAD, No. 292 (February 23, 1986), p.
12-13. Spanish. **DESCR**: *Literary Criticism;
Literature; Publishing Industry; Quinto Sol
Publishing, Inc..

5112 Lomeli, Francisco A. Novela chicana: sus
variantes y contradicciones (II). LA
COMUNIDAD, No. 293 (March 2, 1986), p.
14-15. Spanish. **DESCR**: *Literary Criticism;
Literature Reviews.

5113 Lower, Andrea. La unidad narrativa en LA
MUERTE DE ARTEMIO CRUZ. TINTA, Vol. 1, no. 3
(December 1983), p. 19-26. Spanish. **DESCR**:
Fuentes, Carlos; *LA MUERTE DE ARTEMIO CRUZ;
Literary Criticism; Mexican Literature.

5114 Mariscal, George. Alejandro Morales in
utopia. CONFLUENCIA, Vol. 2, no. 1 (Fall
1986), p. 78-83. English. **DESCR**: *Literary
Criticism; *Morales, Alejandro; *RETO EN EL
PARAISO.

5115 Martin-Rodriguez, Manuel M. El sentimiento
de culpa en RETO EN EL PARAISO de Alejandro
Morales. THE AMERICAS REVIEW, Vol. 15, no. 1
(Spring 1987), p. 89-97. Spanish. **DESCR**:
Literary Criticism; *Morales, Alejandro;
*RETO EN EL PARAISO.

5116 Randolph, Donald A. Death's aesthetic
proliferation in works of Hinojosa.
CONFLUENCIA, Vol. 1, no. 2 (Spring 1986), p.
38-47. English. **DESCR**: Death (Concept);
GENERACIONES Y SEMBLANZAS; *Hinojosa-Smith,
Rolando R.; KLAIL CITY Y SUS ALREDEDORES;
KOREAN LOVE SONGS; *Literary Criticism.

5117 Torres, Hector. Discourse and plot in
Rolando Hinojosa's THE VALLEY: narrativity
and the recovery of Chicano heritage.
CONFLUENCIA, Vol. 2, no. 1 (Fall 1986), p.
84-93. English. **DESCR**: *Hinojosa-Smith,
Rolando R.; *Literary Criticism; *THE
VALLEY.

5118 Toruno, Rhina. El protagonista verdadero de
EL SIGLO DE LAS LUCES de Alejo Carpentier.
CHIRICU, Vol. 4, no. 1 (1985), p. 19-39.
Spanish. **DESCR**: Carpentier, Alejo; *EL SIGLO
DE LAS LUCES; Literary Criticism.

LA NOVELA CHICANA ESCRITA EN ESPANOL

5119 Tatum, Charles. Book review of: LA NOVELA
CHICANA ESCRITA EN ESPANOL. WORLD LITERATURE
TODAY, Vol. 57, no. 4 (Fall 1983), p.
613-614. English. **DESCR**: Book Reviews;
Literary Criticism; Rodriguez del Pino,
Salvador.

5120 Tatum, Charles. Chicano literary criticism
comes of age. BILINGUAL REVIEW, Vol. 12, no.
1-2 (January, August, 1985), p. 144-149.
English. **DESCR**: Book Reviews; *CHICANO
THEATER: THEMES AND FORMS; Huerta, Jorge A.;
Literary Criticism; Rodriguez del Pino,
Salvador.

Novelists
USE: Authors

NUESTRO [magazine]

5121 Lopez, Daniel M. NUESTRO's 10th anniversary. NUESTRO, Vol. 11, no. 3 (April 1987), p. 11-21. English. **DESCR:** Periodicals.

NUEVE ARTISTAS CHICANOS [exhibit]

5122 Goldman, Shifra. Escena de San Diego: texto y contexto. LA COMUNIDAD, No. 239 (February 17, 1985), p. 6-7. Spanish. **DESCR:** *Art; Avalos, David; Chicano Park, San Diego, CA; Exhibits; San Diego, CA; Torres, Salvador Roberto; Ulloa, Domingo.

Nunez v. Boldin

5123 Protecting aliens from persecution without overloading the INS. VIRGINIA LAW REVIEW, Vol. 69, (June 1983), p. 901-930. English. **DESCR:** *Orantes, Hernandez v. Smith; Political Refugees; Refugee Act of 1980; *Undocumented Workers.

Nunez Wilson, Carmen

5124 Panas, Katia. The forgotten people. REVISTA MUJERES, Vol. 1, no. 2 (June 1984), p. 15. English. **DESCR:** Immigration; *"The Forgotten People" [senior thesis].

Nurseries (Children)
USE: Child Care Centers

Nursery School
USE: Child Care Centers

Nursing Homes

5125 Luevano, Richard. Attitudes of elderly Mexican Americans towards nursing homes in Stanislaus county. LA RED/THE NET, no. 45 (August 1981), p. 2. English. **DESCR:** *Ancianos; *Stanislaus County, CA.

Nutrition

5126 Dewey, Kathryn G.; Strode, Margaret A.; and Fitch, Yolanda Ruiz. Dietary change among migrant and nonmigrant Mexican-American families in northern California. ECOLOGY OF FOOD AND NUTRITION, Vol. 14, no. 1 (1984), p. 11-24. English. **DESCR:** Culture; *Food Practices; *Migrant Children; Migrant Labor; Northern California.

5127 Diet cited as cause of hypertension among Hispanics. HISPANIC TIMES, Vol. 8, no. 3 (May, June, 1987), p. 16. English. **DESCR:** *Heart Disease; *Hypertension.

5128 Plan and operation of the Hispanic Health and Nutrition Examination Survey 1982-84. VITAL AND HEALTH STATISTICS. SERIES 1, no. 19 (September 1985), p. 1-429. English. **DESCR:** *Hispanic Health and Nutrition Examination Survey (HHANES); Public Health.

5129 Remas, Theodora A. Can Latino cooking be tasty and healthy? VISTA, Vol. 2, no. 6 (February 8, 1987), p. 14-16. English.

5130 Remas, Theodora A. The threat of diabetes. VISTA, Vol. 1, no. 2 (October 5, 1985), p. 14-16. English. **DESCR:** *Diabetes; Health Education; *Mezitis, Nicholas; Public Health; Rico-Perez, Manuel.

Oakdale, LA

5131 Kahn, Robert. Oakdale prison: documenting the abuses. IN THESE TIMES, Vol. 10, no. 35 (September 17, 1986), p. 8, 22. English. **DESCR:** Allen Parish, LA; Legal Representation; Oakdale Legal Assistance (OLA); Political Refugees; Prisons; Undocumented Workers; U.S. Bureau of Prisons (BOP).

Oakdale Legal Assistance (OLA)

5132 Kahn, Robert. Oakdale prison: documenting the abuses. IN THESE TIMES, Vol. 10, no. 35 (September 17, 1986), p. 8, 22. English. **DESCR:** Allen Parish, LA; Legal Representation; *Oakdale, LA; Political Refugees; Prisons; Undocumented Workers; U.S. Bureau of Prisons (BOP).

Oakland, CA

5133 Malaspina, Ann. The city is my canvas. VISTA, Vol. 2, no. 3 (November 2, 1986), p. 14-15. English. **DESCR:** Artists; *Galvez, Daniel; Hispanic Murals Project (Cambridge, MA); *Mural Art.

Obesity

5134 Obese children focus of study. NUESTRO, Vol. 11, no. 3 (April 1987), p. 9. English. **DESCR:** *Children; Stanford University, Stanford, CA.

O'Brien, Jim

5135 Gutierrez, Silvio G. The odd couple. VISTA, Vol. 3, no. 1 (September 6, 1987), p. 12-13. English. **DESCR:** Actors and Actresses; *Humor; *Valdez, Alex.

Ocampo, Adriana

5136 Mellado, Carmela. Adriana Ocampo. HISPANIC ENGINEER, Vol. 3, no. 4 (Fall 1987), p. 22-24. English. **DESCR:** National Aeronautics and Space Administration (NASA); *Science as a Profession; Stereotypes; Women.

O'Campo Corporation, Walnut, CA

5137 Seven profiles of courage. HISPANIC BUSINESS, Vol. 9, no. 6 (June 1987), p. 57-70. English. **DESCR:** Alamo Technology Inc., San Antonio, TX; *Business Enterprises; *Businesspeople; Carrillo, Rosario C.; O'Campo, Peter; Rivas, Robert; TexPar Energy Inc., Milwaukee, WI; THE HISPANIC BUSINESS 500.

O'Campo, Peter

5138 Seven profiles of courage. HISPANIC BUSINESS, Vol. 9, no. 6 (June 1987), p. 57-70. English. **DESCR:** Alamo Technology Inc., San Antonio, TX; *Business Enterprises; *Businesspeople; Carrillo, Rosario C.; O'Campo Corporation, Walnut, CA; Rivas, Robert; TexPar Energy Inc., Milwaukee, WI; THE HISPANIC BUSINESS 500.

Occupational Aspirations
USE: Careers

Occupational Hazards

5139 Bennett, Jonathan A. At last, farmworkers are allowed clean water. GUARDIAN, Vol. 39, no. 20 (February 18, 1987), p. 9. English. **DESCR:** Farm Workers; Migrant Labor.

OCCUPIED AMERICA

5140 Romo, Ricardo. Book review of: OCCUPIED AMERICA. LA RED/THE NET, no. 39 (February 1981), p. 3. English. **DESCR:** *Acuna, Rudolfo; Book Reviews; History; *Social History and Conditions.

Ochoa, Victor

5141 Jacobs, Carole. Bridging cultures. SOUTHWEST ART, Vol. 15, (April 1986), p. 86. English. **DESCR:** *Chicano Park, San Diego, CA; *Mural Art.

DECADE OF HISPANIC LITERATURE: AN ANNIVERSARY ANTHOLOGY

5142 Elias, Edward F. Book review of: A DECADE OF HISPANIC LITERATURE. LA RED/THE NET, no. 68 (May 1983), p. 9-10. English. **DESCR:** Book Reviews; Literature; REVISTA CHICANO-RIQUENA.

OFF THE STREETS [exhibit]

5143 Haley, Lindsey. Gronk y su inquietante concepto del arte. LA COMUNIDAD, No. 252 (May 19, 1985), p. 2-3. Spanish. **DESCR:** *Artists; ASCO [art group], Los Angeles, CA; Biography; Exhibits; *Gronk (Pseud.)

Office of Bilingual Education, California State Department of Education

5144 Rodriguez, Ana Maria and Calderon, Margarita. Book review of: SCHOOLING AND LANGUAGE MINORITY STUDENTS: A THEORETICAL FRAMEWORK. LA RED/THE NET, no. 66 (March 1983), p. 8-10. English. **DESCR:** Book Reviews; *SCHOOLING AND LANGUAGE MINORITY STUDENTS: A THEORETICAL FRAMEWORK.

Office of Civil Rights, Labor Department, Washington, D.C.

5145 Labor department official challenges Hispanic program manager to maintain commitment, perseverance. HISPANIC TIMES, Vol. 8, no. 5 (October, November, 1987), p. 41. English. **DESCR:** *Affirmative Action; *Harris, William J.

Ohio

5146 Boycotts revisited: Campbell's concedes to farm worker campaign. DOLLARS AND SENSE, (July, August, 1986), p. 12-14, 18. English. **DESCR:** Boycotts; California; Campbell Soup Co.; Farm Labor Organizing Commmittee (FLOC); Farm Workers; *Labor Disputes; Labor Unions; Michigan; Strikes and Lockouts; United Farmworkers of America (UFW).

5147 Sanders, Bob. Boycott Campbell's: Ohio farmworkers take it to the top. DOLLARS AND SENSE, no. 92 (December 1983), p. 16-18. English. **DESCR:** Boycotts; Campbell Soup Co.; Chavez, Cesar E.; Farm Labor Organizing Commmittee (FLOC); Farm Workers; Guevas, Fernando; *Labor Disputes; Labor Unions; Strikes and Lockouts; United Farmworkers of America (UFW).

OJO DE LA CUEVA: CAVE SPRINGS

5148 Marin, Christine. Book review of: OJO DE LA CUEVA. LECTOR, Vol. 4, no. 4-6 (1987), p. 75. English. **DESCR:** Book Reviews; Candelaria, Cordelia.

Old Age
USE: Ancianos

OLDER MEXICAN AMERICANS: A STUDY IN AN URBAN BARRIO

5149 Cardenas, Gilbert. Book review of: OLDER MEXICAN AMERICANS: A STUDY IN AN URBAN BARRIO. CONTEMPORARY SOCIOLOGY: A JOURNAL OF REVIEWS, Vol. 14, no. 2 (March 1985), p. 243-244. English. **DESCR:** Ancianos; Book Reviews; Gomez, Ernesto; Markides, Kyriakos S.; Martin, Harry.

5150 Kastenbaum, Robert. Book review of: OLDER MEXICAN AMERICANS: A STUDY IN AN URBAN BARRIO. INTERNATIONAL JOURNAL OF AGING & HUMAN DEVELOPMENT, Vol. 19, no. 1 (1984), p. 75-76. English. **DESCR:** Ancianos; Book Reviews; Markides, Kyriakos S.; Martin, Harry.

5151 Manuel, Ron C. Book review of: OLDER MEXICAN AMERICANS: A STUDY IN AN URBAN BARRIO. JOURNAL OF GERONTOLOGY, Vol. 39, no. 4 (July 1984), p. 506-507. English. **DESCR:** Ancianos; Book Reviews; Markides, Kyriakos S.; Martin, Harry.

Olind, Rebecca Nieto

5152 Cornell, Nancy. Forging links between societies. VISTA, Vol. 3, no. 3 (November 8, 1987), p. 24. English. **DESCR:** 1984 Republican Convention (Dallas, TX); *Chicanas; Working Women.

Olivares [family name]

5153 Instituto Genealogico e Historico Latino-Americano. Rootsearch: Olivares: Yrigoyen: Montemayor. VISTA, Vol. 2, no. 12 (August 1, 1987), p. 30. English. **DESCR:** Genealogy; History; *Montemayor [family name]; *Personal Names; *Yrigoyen [family name].

Olivares, J.R.

5154 LeAna, Thomas. From dropout to role model: a VISTA postscript. VISTA, Vol. 2, no. 4 (December 7, 1986), p. 25. English. **DESCR:** Brownsville, TX; Gladys Porter High School; *Martinez, Dorella; *Rhetoric; Secondary School Education.

Oliver v. U.S.

5155 Search and seizure. CRIMINAL LAW REPORTER, Vol. 35, no. 3 (April 18, 1984), p. 3011-3027. English. **DESCR:** Hester v. U.S.; INS v. Delgado; Katz v. U.S.; Maine v. Thornton; *Search and Seizure; *U.S. Supreme Court.

Olivo, Joey

5156 Getting to the top against all odds. HISPANIC TIMES, Vol. 8, no. 5 (October, November, 1987), p. 26. English. **DESCR:** Biography; *Boxing.

Olmedo, Esteban L.

5157 Arce, Carlos H. and Carlson, David. Book review of: HISPANIC MENTAL HEALTH RESEARCH: A REFERENCE GUIDE. LA RED/THE NET, no. 57 (August 1982), p. 5-7. English. **DESCR:** Book Reviews; *HISPANIC MENTAL HEALTH RESEARCH: A REFERENCE GUIDE; Mental Health; Newton, Frank; Padilla, Amado M.; Reference Works.

Olmo [family name]

5158 Instituto Genealogico e Historico
Latino-Americano. Rootsearch: Jimenez
(Ximenez): Olmo. VISTA, Vol. 2, no. 4
(December 7, 1986), p. 25. English. DESCR:
Genealogy; History; *Jimenez [family name];
*Personal Names; *Ximenez [family name].

Olmos, Edward James

5159 Montane, Diane. Edward James Olmos: the man
behind the tough film facade. VISTA, Vol. 1,
no. 1 (September 8, 1985), p. 8-12. English.
DESCR: *Actors and Actresses; BALLAD OF
GREGORIO CORTEZ [film]; Biography; WOLFEN
[film]; ZOOT SUIT [film].

5160 Muro, Rena. Walking on water. AMERICAS 2001,
Vol. 1, no. 3 (November, December, 1987), p.
12-14. Bilingual. DESCR: Camhi, Morrie;
*Films; STAND AND DELIVER [film]; *WALKING
ON WATER [working title of film STAND AND
DELIVER].

ONCE A FAMILY [play]

5161 Rosas, Alejandro. Teatro chicano: un teatro
de la esperanza. LA COMUNIDAD, No. 247
(April 14, 1985), 2-3. Spanish. DESCR: El
Teatro de la Esperanza; Identity; *Teatro;
Teatro Reviews.

ONE HUNDRED YEARS OF SOLITUDE

5162 Bartlett, Catherine Vallejos. Magical
realism: the Latin American influence on
modern Chicano writers. CONFLUENCIA, Vol. 1,
no. 2 (Spring 1986), p. 27-37. English.
DESCR: Arias, Ron; Authors; Garcia Marquez,
Gabriel; Latin America; *Literary Criticism;
*Literary Influence; *Literature; Magical
realism; Rivera, Tomas; THE ROAD TO
TAMAZUNCHALE; Y NO SE LO TRAGO LA TIERRA/AND
THE EARTH DID NOT PART.

One-Day Paint & Auto Body Centers, Los Angeles, CA

5163 Kane, George D. Five blueprints for fueling
growth. HISPANIC BUSINESS, Vol. 9, no. 5
(May 1987), p. 18-21, 42+. English. DESCR:
*Business Enterprises; *Businesspeople;
Holguin Corporation, El Paso, TX;
Investments; Latin Industries, Ontario, CA;
Terrinvest, Miami, FL; TRU & Associates,
Orange County, CA.

OPERATION WETBACK: THE MASS DEPORTATION OF MEXICAN UNDOCUMENTED WORKERS IN 1954

5164 Lopez-Garza, Marta. Book review of:
OPERATION WETBACK. LA RED/THE NET, no. 50
(January 1982), p. 7-9. English. DESCR: Book
Reviews; *Deportation; *Garcia, Juan Ramon;
Immigration.

LA OPINION, Los Angeles, CA

5165 Cecere, Linda. Newspapers attract attention
in some categories. ADVERTISING AGE
MAGAZINE, Vol. 57, no. 43 (August 11, 1986),
p. S9-S10. English. DESCR: Advertising;
DIARIO DE LAS AMERICAS; EL MIAMI HERALD;
*Newspapers; NOTICIAS DEL MUNDO; Spanish
Language.

Oral History

5166 Alicia de Garcia's oral history=Historia
oral de Alicia de Garcia. REVISTA MUJERES,
Vol. 3, no. 2 (June 1986), p. 37-49.
Spanish. DESCR: *Committee of Mothers and
Relatives of Political Prisoners Disappeared
and Assassinated of El Salvador "Monsenor

Oscar Arnulfo Romero" (Comadres, El
Salvador); Community Organizations; de
Garcia, Alicia; *Federation of Latin
Americans for the Association of Relatives
of the Detained and Disappeared (FedeFam);
Terrorism; Violence; *Women.

5167 Foote, Cheryl. Book review of: IMAGES AND
CONVERSATIONS. JOURNAL OF THE WEST, Vol. 24,
no. 3 (July 1985), p. 121. English. DESCR:
Book Reviews; Chicanas; IMAGES AND
CONVERSATIONS: MEXICAN AMERICANS RECALL A
SOUTHWESTERN PAST; *Martin, Patricia
Preciado.

5168 Lopez-Flores, Beatriz. Testimonios de las
campesinas de Pantasma. REVISTA MUJERES,
Vol. 2, no. 2 (June 1985), p. 7-9. Spanish.
DESCR: *Farm Workers; *Nicaragua.

5169 Quintana, Alvina. Her story. REVISTA
MUJERES, Vol. 4, no. 1 (January 1987), p.
44-47. English. DESCR: Chicanas.

Orantes, Hernandez v. Smith

5170 Protecting aliens from persecution without
overloading the INS. VIRGINIA LAW REVIEW,
Vol. 69, (June 1983), p. 901-930. English.
DESCR: Nunez v. Boldin; Political Refugees;
Refugee Act of 1980; *Undocumented Workers.

Orden Hijos de America, San Antonio, TX

5171 Arreola, Daniel D. The Mexican American
cultural capital. GEOGRAPHICAL REVIEW, Vol.
77, (January 1987), p. 17-34. English.
DESCR: Conjuntos; Food Industry; History;
Immigration; LA PRENSA, San Antonio, TX; La
Raza Unida Party; League of United Latin
American Citizens (LULAC); Lozano, Ignacio;
Mexican American Youth Organization, San
Antonio, TX; Music; Railroads; *San Antonio,
TX; *Social History and Conditions.

5172 Bueno, Patricia E. Los Chicanos y la
politica. LA COMUNIDAD, No. 267 (September
1, 1985), p. 6-7. Spanish. DESCR: Community
Service Organization, Los Angeles, (CSO);
Discrimination; History; Leadership; League
of United Latin American Citizens (LULAC);
*Political Parties and Organizations.

Oregon

5173 Slatta, Richard W. and Atkinson, Maxine P.
The "Spanish origin" population of Oregon
and Washington: a demographic profile, 1980.
PACIFIC NORTHWEST QUARTERLY, Vol. 75, no. 3
(July 1984), p. 108-116. English. DESCR:
*Population; Self-Referents; Socioeconomic
Factors; Statistics; *Washington (state).

Organizations

5174 Academics and entrepreneurs talk trade.
HISPANIC BUSINESS, Vol. 9, no. 6 (June
1987), p. 96. English. DESCR: *Business
Enterprises; Conferences and Meetings;
Fourth Symposium on Hispanic Business and
Economy, San Juan, Puerto Rico, November
23-25, 1987; *International Economic
Relations; Latin America; *National
Association of Hispanic Professors of
Business Administration and Economics (Los
Profesores); Teaching Profession.

Organizations (cont.)

5175 Beale, Stephen. Friendly persuasion: pacts and covenants. HISPANIC BUSINESS, Vol. 9, no. 9 (September 1987), p. 20-26. English. **DESCR:** *Adolph Coors Co.; *Business; Community Organizations; Coors/HACER Agreement, 1984; *Corporations; *Hispanic Association on Corporate Responsibility (HACER); Pacific Bell; Southland Corporation.

5176 Beale, Stephen. MALDEF weathers a storm. HISPANIC BUSINESS, Vol. 9, no. 5 (May 1987), p. 10-11. English. **DESCR:** Anaya, Toney, Governor of New Mexico; Civil Rights; Hernandez, Antonia A.; *Mexican American Legal Defense and Educational Fund (MALDEF); Serna, Eric P.

5177 Beale, Stephen. Striking a deal with big business. HISPANIC BUSINESS, Vol. 9, no. 2 (February 1987), p. 26-33. English. **DESCR:** *Adolph Coors Co.; American G.I. Forum; Boycotts; Corporations; Cuban National Planning Council, Inc. Washington, D.C.; Employment; *Hispanic Association on Corporate Responsibility (HACER); League of United Latin American Citizens (LULAC); National Council of La Raza (NCLR); National IMAGE; National Puerto Rican Coalition; U.S. Hispanic Chamber of Commerce.

5178 Carrillo, Ana, et al. History of Las Mujeres. REVISTA MUJERES, Vol. 1, no. 1 (January 1984), p. 4-5. English. **DESCR:** Chicanas; *Las Mujeres, University of California, Santa Cruz.

5179 Frances Hesselbein. INTERCAMBIOS FEMENILES, Vol. 2, no. 6 (Spring 1987), p. 23. English. **DESCR:** *Chicanas; *Girl Scouts of the United States of America; Hesselbein, Frances; *Leadership; Women; Youth.

5180 Hernandez prevails in fight over job. NUESTRO, Vol. 11, no. 2 (March 1987), p. 6. English. **DESCR:** *Anaya, Toney, Governor of New Mexico; *Hernandez, Antonia A.; *Mexican American Legal Defense and Educational Fund (MALDEF).

5181 Information/Informacion. AMERICAS 2001, Premiere Issue, 1987, p. 11. Bilingual. **DESCR:** *Directories; *Immigration.

5182 Jimenez, Luis. Cambia la imagen del latino en Hollywood. LA COMUNIDAD, No. 255 (June 9, 1985), p. 14-15. Spanish. **DESCR:** Discrimination; Employment; Films; *Hispanic Academy of Media Arts and Sciences (HAMAS); *Mass Media; Reyna, Phil.

5183 Keep pace with MAES: Sociedad de Ingenieria de Mexicano Americanos (Mexican American Engineering Society). HISPANIC TIMES, Vol. 8, no. 1 (December, January, 1987), p. 28. Bilingual. **DESCR:** Engineering as a Profession; *Mexican American Engineering Society (MAES).

5184 MAES now has eleven professional chapters nationwide (and more to come). HISPANIC TIMES, Vol. 8, no. 5 (October, November, 1987), p. 42. English. **DESCR:** *Engineering as a Profession; *Mexican American Engineering Society (MAES).

5185 MAES sets the pace. HISPANIC TIMES, Vol. 8, no. 1 (December, January, 1987), p. 26. English. **DESCR:** Engineering as a Profession; *Mexican American Engineering Society (MAES).

5186 Marin, Christine. La Asociacion Hispano-Americana de Madres y Esposas: Tucson's Mexican American women in World War II. RENATO ROSALDO LECTURE SERIES MONOGRAPH, Vol. 1, (Summer 1985), p. [5]-18. English. **DESCR:** *Chicanas; Cultural Organizations; History; *La Asociacion Hispano-Americana de Madres y Esposas, Tucson, AZ; *Tucson, AZ; World War II.

5187 Minority programs need tune-up. HISPANIC BUSINESS, Vol. 9, no. 6 (June 1987), p. 84-90. English. **DESCR:** *Automobile Industry; Business; Business Enterprises; National Association for Minority Automotive Dealers (NAMAD).

5188 Rivera, Alvin D. Laying a foundation for learning: student peer workshop groups. NEW DIRECTIONS FOR TEACHING AND LEARNING, no. 16 (December 1983), p. 81-86. English. **DESCR:** *Careers; Counseling (Educational); *Engineering as a Profession; *Natural Support Systems; Students.

5189 Rivera, Yvette. Hispanic women's organizations and periodicals needed to communicate new options: Yvette Rivera report. MEDIA REPORT TO WOMEN, Vol. 12, no. 5 (September, October, 1984), p. 15. English. **DESCR:** *Chicanas; Periodicals.

5190 A salute to Hispanic excellence in America. HISPANIC BUSINESS, Vol. 9, no. 6 (June 1987), p. 7-9. English. **DESCR:** *Awards; *Businesspeople; *Latin Business Association (LBA), Los Angeles, CA.

5191 Sellers, Jeff M. Golden opportunity. HISPANIC BUSINESS, Vol. 9, no. 9 (September 1987), p. 14-18, 79. English. **DESCR:** *Adolph Coors Co.; Business Enterprises; *Coors/HACER Agreement, 1984; *Corporations; Employment; Hispanic Association on Corporate Responsibility (HACER).

5192 Trager, Cara S. Manhattan executive forum. HISPANIC BUSINESS, Vol. 9, no. 4 (April 1987), p. 10-13. English. **DESCR:** Advertising; *Corporations; Marketing; *National Hispanic Corporate Council (NHCC).

5193 Varela, Vivian. Hispanic women's resource guide. COMMONGROUND MAGAZINE, Vol. 1, no. 3 (May 1983), p. 14-15. English. **DESCR:** *Chicanas; *Directories.

Orion International Technologies, Inc.

5194 Sellers, Jeff M. Strategic defenses: new niches for small firms. HISPANIC BUSINESS, Vol. 9, no. 10 (October 1987), p. 13-17. English. **DESCR:** *Advanced Sciences Inc., Albuquerque, NM; Business Enterprises; Electronics Industry; *Government Contracts; *Military; Rios, Miguel, Jr.; Romero, Ed.

Ornstein-Galicia, Jacob

5195 Blanco, George M. Book review of: FORM AND FUNCTION IN CHICANO ENGLISH. MODERN LANGUAGE JOURNAL, Vol. 69, no. 3 (Fall 1985), p. 328. English. **DESCR:** Book Reviews; *FORM AND FUNCTION IN CHICANO ENGLISH.

5196 Dubois, Betty Lou. Book review of: CHICANO ENGLISH: AN ETHNIC CONTACT DIALECT. CHOICE, Vol. 24, no. 1 (September 1986), p. 114. English. **DESCR:** Book Reviews; *CHICANO ENGLISH: AN ETHNIC CONTACT DIALECT; Penfield, Joyce.

Ornstein-Galicia, Jacob (cont.)

5197 Penalosa, Fernando. Book review of:
BILINGUALISM AND LANGUAGE CONTACT: SPANISH,
ENGLISH AND NATIVE AMERICAN LANGUAGES. LA
RED/THE NET, no. 66 (March 1983), p. 5-8.
English. DESCR: Barkin, Florence;
*BILINGUALISM AND LANGUAGE CONTACT: SPANISH,
ENGLISH, AND NATIVE AMERICAN LANGUAGES; Book
Reviews; Brandt, Elizabeth H.

5198 Trueba, Henry T. Book review of: FORM AND
FUNCTION IN CHICANO ENGLISH. LANGUAGE IN
SOCIETY, Vol. 14, no. 2 (June 1985), p.
255-257. English. DESCR: Book Reviews; *FORM
AND FUNCTION IN CHICANO ENGLISH.

Oro del Barrio

5199 Atencio, Tomas. La Academia de la Nueva
Raza: su historia. EL CUADERNO, Vol. 1, no.
1 (1971), p. 4-9. English. DESCR:
Alternative Education; Chicano Studies;
Cultural Organizations; *Educational
Organizations; *La Academia de la Nueva
Raza, Dixon, NM.

5200 Atencio, Tomas. La Academia de la Nueva
Raza. EL CUADERNO, Vol. 2, no. 1 (1972), p.
6-13. English. DESCR: *Alternative
Education; Chicano Studies; Cultural
Characteristics; *Cultural Organizations;
Education; *Educational Organizations; *La
Academia de la Nueva Raza, Dixon, NM;
Philosophy; Values.

5201 Atencio, Tomas. La Academia de la Nueva
Raza: El Oro del Barrio. EL CUADERNO, Vol.
3, no. 1 (Winter 1973), p. 4-15. English.
DESCR: Alternative Education; Chicano
Studies; *Cultural Organizations;
*Educational Organizations; *La Academia de
la Nueva Raza, Dixon, NM.

Orozco, Cynthia

5202 Acuna, Rodolfo. Response to Cynthia Orozco.
LA RED/THE NET, no. 79 (April 1984), p.
13-15. English. DESCR: Chicanas; Sexism.

Ortega, Adolfo

5203 Duran, Richard P. Book review of: CALO
TAPESTRY. LA RED/THE NET, no. 32 (July
1980), p. 5. English. DESCR: CALO TAPESTRY;
*Chicano Dialects; Language Usage.

Ortega [family name]

5204 Instituto Genealogico e Historico
Latino-Americano. Rootsearch: Ortega: Munoz.
VISTA, Vol. 1, no. 3 (November 3, 1985), p.
22. English. DESCR: History; *Munoz [family
name]; *Personal Names.

Ortega, James

5205 Beale, Stephen. CEOs. HISPANIC BUSINESS,
Vol. 9, no. 4 (April 1987), p. 20-37, 52.
English. DESCR: Alvarez, Roberto; Batarse,
Anthony A.; Biography; Business Enterprises;
*Businesspeople; Carlo, Nelson; Estrada,
Anthony; Flores, Frank; Fullana, Jaime, Jr.;
Hernandez, George; *Management; Quirch,
Guillermo; Ruiz, Roberto; Santa Maria,
Yvonne Z.; Sugranes, Rosa; Tamaya, Carlos;
Young, Paul H., Jr.

Ortiz Taylor, Sheila

5206 Bruce-Novoa, Juan. Homosexuality and the
Chicano novel. CONFLUENCIA, Vol. 2, no. 1
(Fall 1986), p. 69-77. English. DESCR:
Acosta, Oscar Zeta; CITY OF NIGHT; FAULTLINE

[novel]; *Homosexuality; Islas, Arturo;
*Literary Criticism; Machismo; *Novel;
POCHO; Rechy, John; Salas, Floyd; SPRING
FORWARD/FALL BACK; TATOO THE WICKED CROSS;
THE AUTOBIOGRAPHY OF A BROWN BUFFALO; THE
RAIN GOD: A DESERT TALE; THE REVOLT OF THE
COCKROACH PEOPLE; Villarreal, Jose Antonio.

5207 Bruce-Novoa, Juan. Nuevo representantes de
la novela chicana. LA COMUNIDAD, No. 310
(June 29, 1986), p. 6-7+. Spanish. DESCR:
Brawley, Ernest; EL VAGO [novel]; FAULTLINE
[novel]; Gonzales, Laurence; *Literary
Criticism; Novel; THE ALAMO TREE [novel].

Osburne, Burl

5208 13-part series focuses on Hispanics in
America. EDITOR & PUBLISHER: THE FOURTH
ESTATE, Vol. 115, no. 14 (April 3, 1982), p.
37. English. DESCR: Books; Cultural
Characteristics; DALLAS MORNING NEWS;
Garcia, Juan; Gonzalez, John; Goodwin, Jay;
Grothe, Randy Eli; Hamilton, John; Hille,
Ed; LA VIDA AMERICANA; *LA VIDA
AMERICANA/HISPANICS IN AMERICA; Langer,
Ralph; McLemore, David; Parks, Scott; Pusey,
Allen; Sonnemair, Jan.

Osorio, Armando

5209 Gomez Pena, Guillermo. Dialogos fronterizos.
LA COMUNIDAD, No. 263 (August 4, 1985), p.
2-3. Spanish. DESCR: *Art; Avalos, David;
Border Region; DIALOGOS FRONTERIZOS [radio
program].

Osteopathy
USE: Curanderismo

Outlaws
USE: Bandidos

OUTLAWS IN THE PROMISED LAND: MEXICAN IMMIGRANT WORKERS AND AMERICA'S FUTURE

5210 Mosqueda, Lawrence Joseph. Mexican labor: a
most precious commodity on both sides of the
border. GUARDIAN, Vol. 39, no. 2 (October 8,
1986), p. 20. English. DESCR: Book Reviews;
Cockcroft, James D.

Ovalle, John

5211 Halley, Lindsey. Pachuco boggie [sic]. LA
COMUNIDAD, No. 305 (May 25, 1986), p. 8-9.
Spanish. DESCR: Cano, Eddie; Diaz, Raul;
History; *Music; *PACHUCO BOOGIE;
Smithsonian Institute; The Record Inn, East
Los Angeles, CA; Tosti, Don.

Ovando, Carlos J.

5212 Hopkins, Thomas. Book review of: BILINGUAL
AND ESL CLASSROOMS: TEACHING IN
MULTICULTURAL CONTEXTS. EDUCATIONAL
LEADERSHIP, Vol. 43, no. 6 (March 1986), p.
82. English. DESCR: *BILINGUAL AND ESL
CLASSROOMS: TEACHING IN MULTICULTURAL
CONTEXTS; Book Reviews; Collier, Virginia
P.

5213 Nieto, Sonia. Book review of: BILINGUAL AND
ESL CLASSROOMS: TEACHING IN MULTICULTURAL
CONTEXTS. INTERRACIAL BOOKS FOR CHILDREN,
Vol. 17, no. 3-4 (1986), p. 30. English.
DESCR: *BILINGUAL AND ESL CLASSROOMS:
TEACHING IN MULTICULTURAL CONTEXTS; Book
Reviews; Collier, Virginia P.

Overa, Agustin

5214 Heuer, Robert J. To save a neighborhood. VISTA, Vol. 3, no. 3 (November 8, 1987), p. 32-34. English. **DESCR**: *Eighteenth Street Development Corporation, Chicago, IL; *Housing; Pilsen, IL; Statistics.

Pabon, Maria

5215 Olivera, Mercedes. The new Hispanic women. VISTA, Vol. 2, no. 11 (July 5, 1987), p. 6-8. English. **DESCR**: Alvarez, Linda; *Chicanas; Esquiroz, Margarita; Garcia, Juliet; *Hernandez, Antonia A.; Mohr, Nicolasa; Molina, Gloria; Working Women.

Pacheco [family name]

5216 Instituto Genealogico e Historico Latino-Americano. Rootsearch: De La Garza: Pacheco. VISTA, Vol. 2, no. 6 (February 8, 1987), p. 21. English. **DESCR**: *de la Garza [family name]; Genealogy; History; *Personal Names.

PACHUCO BOOGIE

5217 Halley, Lindsey. Pachuco boggie [sic]. LA COMUNIDAD, No. 305 (May 25, 1986), p. 8-9. Spanish. **DESCR**: Cano, Eddie; Diaz, Raul; History; *Music; Ovalle, John; Smithsonian Institute; The Record Inn, East Los Angeles, CA; Tosti, Don.

Pachucos

5218 Campbell, Federico. Henry Reyna, pachuco. LA COMUNIDAD, No. 247 (April 14, 1985), p. 11. Spanish. **DESCR**: History; ZOOT SUIT [play]; *Zoot Suit Riots, Los Angeles, CA, 1943.

5219 Goldman, Shifra. Arte chicano: iconografia de la autodeterminacion. LA COMUNIDAD, No. 336 (December 28, 1986), p. 12-14+. Spanish. **DESCR**: *Art; Discrimination; EL PLAN ESPIRITUAL DE AZTLAN; History; Identity; Nationalism; Social Classes; *Symbolism.

5220 Monsivais, Carlos. Los cholos y la cultura de la frontera. LA COMUNIDAD, No. 242 (March 10, 1985), p. 14-15. Spanish. **DESCR**: Border Region; Culture; Identity; *Tijuana, Baja California, Mexico.

5221 Monsivais, Carlos. Este es el pachuco, un sujeto singular. LA COMUNIDAD, No. 243 (March 17, 1985), p. 4-5. Spanish. **DESCR**: Border Region; Culture; Identity.

5222 Ornstein-Galicia, Jacob. Chicano Calo: description and review of a border variety. HISPANIC JOURNAL OF BEHAVIORAL SCIENCES, Vol. 9, no. 4 (December 1987), p. 359-373. English. **DESCR**: Border Region; *Chicano Dialects; Sociolinguistics.

5223 Rodriguez, Salvador. El idioma de Aztlan: una lengua que surge. LA COMUNIDAD, No. 266 (August 25, 1985), p. 6-7. Spanish. **DESCR**: Bilingualism; *Chicano Dialects; Language Interference; Sociolinguistics; Spanish Language.

5224 Sanchez Tranquilino, Marcos. Un ensayo sobre la representacion del ZOOT SUIT en la obra de Octavio Paz. LA COMUNIDAD, No. 355 (May 10, 1987), p. 4-7+. Spanish. **DESCR**: Los Angeles, CA; *Paz, Octavio; Sleepy Lagoon Case; THE LABYRINTH OF SOLITUDE: LIFE AND THOUGHT IN MEXICO; Zoot Suit Riots, Los Angeles, CA, 1943.

Pachuquismos
USE: Chicano Dialects

Pacific Bell

5225 Beale, Stephen. Friendly persuasion: pacts and covenants. HISPANIC BUSINESS, Vol. 9, no. 9 (September 1987), p. 20-26. English. **DESCR**: *Adolph Coors Co.; *Business; Community Organizations; Coors/HACER Agreement, 1984; *Corporations; *Hispanic Association on Corporate Responsibility (HACER); Organizations; Southland Corporation.

Pacific Telesis

5226 Pacific Telesis senior fellows. HISPANIC ENGINEER, Vol. 3, no. 2 (Summer 1987), p. 10-11. English. **DESCR**: *Awards; Castaneda, Jesus; Cruz, Jacqueline; Education; Rodriguez, Jose; Sanchez, Alex.

5227 Smith, Chuck. Commitment to Hispanic education. HISPANIC ENGINEER, Vol. 3, no. 1 (Spring 1987), p. 16-20. English. **DESCR**: *Education; Engineering as a Profession.

Padilla, Amado M.

5228 Arce, Carlos H. and Carlson, David. Book review of: HISPANIC MENTAL HEALTH RESEARCH: A REFERENCE GUIDE. LA RED/THE NET, no. 57 (August 1982), p. 5-7. English. **DESCR**: Book Reviews; *HISPANIC MENTAL HEALTH RESEARCH: A REFERENCE GUIDE; Mental Health; Newton, Frank; Olmedo, Esteban L.; Reference Works.

5229 Dennedy-Frank, David P. Book review of: CROSSING CULTURES IN THERAPY. LA RED/THE NET, no. 41 (April 1981), p. 5-6. English. **DESCR**: Book Reviews; Counseling (Psychological); *CROSSING CULTURES IN THERAPY: PLURALISTIC COUNSELING FOR THE HISPANIC; Levine, Elaine S.; *Mental Health.

5230 Garcia, Philip. Book review of: ACCULTURATION: THEORY, MODELS, AND SOME NEW FINDINGS. LA RED/THE NET, no. 41 (April 1981), p. 4-5. English. **DESCR**: *Acculturation; *ACCULTURATION: THEORY, MODELS, AND SOME NEW FINDINGS; Book Reviews.

Padilla, Felix M.

5231 Raferty, Judith R. Book review of: LATINO ETHNIC CONSCIOUSNESS. WESTERN HISTORICAL QUARTERLY, Vol. 17, no. 4 (October 1986), p. 490. English. **DESCR**: Book Reviews; Identity; *LATINO ETHNIC CONSCIOUSNESS.

Padron [family name]

5232 Instituto Genealogico e Historico Latino-Americano. Rootsearch: Padron: Machado. VISTA, Vol. 2, no. 1 (September 7, 1986), p. 22. English. **DESCR**: Genealogy; History; *Machado [family name]; *Personal Names.

Painters
USE: Artists

Paintings

5233 Almaraz, Carlos. Greed [painting]. THE AMERICAS REVIEW, Vol. 15, no. 2 (Summer 1987), p. 11.

Paintings (cont.)

5234 Aparicio, Edgar. The virgin and child in the revolution [painting]. AMERICAS 2001, Vol. 1, no. 1 (June, July, 1987), p. [16-17]. DESCR: *El Salvador.

5235 Casarez Vasquez, Enedina. Maricela dreams. THE AMERICAS REVIEW, Vol. 15, no. 3-4 (Fall, Winter, 1987), p. 64.

5236 Casarez Vasquez, Enedina. My mother's altar. THE AMERICAS REVIEW, Vol. 15, no. 3-4 (Fall, Winter, 1987), p. [146].

5237 Cox, Charlene B. Motivos artisticos. AMERICAS, Vol. 37, no. 1 (January, February, 1985), p. 2-5, 64. Spanish. DESCR: *Arreguin, Alfredo; *Artists; Folk Art; *Mexican Art.

5238 Escamilla, Rafael. Claudia [painting]. AMERICAS 2001, Premiere Issue, 1987, Ft cover.

5239 Limon, Leo. Flecha de amor=Arrow of love. AMERICAS 2001, Vol. 1, no. 3 (November, December, 1987), p. [16-17].

5240 Lomas Garza, Carmen. Curandera barriendo el susto [painting]. THE AMERICAS REVIEW, Vol. 15, no. 3-4 (Fall, Winter, 1987), p. 40.

5241 Lomas Garza, Carmen. Tuna de nopal/pedacito de mi corazon [painting]. THE AMERICAS REVIEW, Vol. 15, no. 3-4 (Fall, Winter, 1987), p. 56.

5242 Malandrone, Gail. [Untitled painting]. LLUEVE TLALOC, no. 14 (1987), p. Ft cover.

5243 Orosco, Juan Ishi. Winter chant [painting]. AMERICAS 2001, Vol. 1, no. 2 (September, October, 1987), p. [24-25].

5244 Pazos, Antonio. [Untitled painting]. LLUEVE TLALOC, no. 10 (1983), p. Ft cover.

5245 Pena, Amado Maurilio, Jr. Acoma. CONFLUENCIA, Vol. 1, no. 2 (Spring 1986), p. 118.

5246 Pena, Amado Maurilio, Jr. Nacimiento. CONFLUENCIA, Vol. 1, no. 2 (Spring 1986), p. 124.

5247 Reyes Aponte, Cynthia. [Untitled collage]. LLUEVE TLALOC, no. 12 (1985), p. 32.

5248 Roche, Arnaldo. Burning the spirit of the flesh [painting]. THE AMERICAS REVIEW, Vol. 15, no. 2 (Summer 1987), p. 103.

5249 Saul Solache: contemporary Chicano artist. LATIN QUARTER, Vol. 1, no. 3 (January, February, 1975), p. 24-26. English. DESCR: *Artists; Exhibits; Mural Art; *Solache, Saul.

5250 Tineo, David. [Untitled painting]. LLUEVE TLALOC, no. 13 (1986), p. Ft cover.

5251 Tineo, David. [Untitled painting]. LLUEVE TLALOC, no. 13 (1986), p. 17.

5252 Tineo, David. [Untitled painting]. LLUEVE TLALOC, no. 13 (1986), p. 29.

5253 Yrigoyen, Edna A. [Untitled painting]. LLUEVE TLALOC, no. 13 (1986), p. 20.

5254 Yrigoyen, Edna A. [Untitled painting]. LLUEVE TLALOC, no. 13 (1986), p. 25.

PALABRA NUEVA: CUENTOS CHICANOS

5255 Garcia, Nasario. El cuento chicano visto por dentro y por fuera. BILINGUAL REVIEW, Vol. 12, no. 3 (September, December, 1985), p. 262-265. Spanish. DESCR: Aguilar, Ricardo; Armengol, Armando; Book Reviews; Somoza, Oscar U.

Pan American Games

5256 Miley, Scott L. Let the games begin. VISTA, Vol. 2, no. 12 (August 1, 1987), p. 13-14. English. DESCR: *Sports.

Pan American University, Edinburg, TX

5257 Chavez, Lorenzo A. The quest for Hispanic roots. VISTA, Vol. 2, no. 7 (March 8, 1987), p. 5-6, 24. English. DESCR: Church of Jesus Christ of Latter-Day Saints (Mormons); Directories; *Garcia, Clotilde; *Genealogy; Hispanic American Genealogical Associates, Washington, DC; Las Porciones Genealogical Society, Edinburg, TX; Los Bexarenos, San Antonio, TX; Los Californianos [genealogical society], San Jose, CA; Texas Southmost College.

Papa Maya's Restaurant, Paris, France

5258 Marambio, Gonzalo. From San Antonio to Paris: Tex-Mex food conquers the French. VISTA, Vol. 1, no. 6 (February 2, 1986), p. 18-20. English. DESCR: Business Enterprises; Cantu, Mario, Jr.; *Food Practices; Gonzales, Teresa; *Mario's Restaurant, San Antonio, TX.

Paredes, Americo

5259 Leal, Luis. Americo Paredes and modern Mexican American scholarship. ETHNIC AFFAIRS, no. 1 (Fall 1987), p. [1]-11. English. DESCR: Ethnology; Folklore; History; Literature Reviews.

5260 Rosaldo, Renato. When natives talk back: Chicano anthropology since the late 60s. RENATO ROSALDO LECTURE SERIES MONOGRAPH, Vol. 2, (Spring 1986), p. [3]-20. English. DESCR: *Anthropology; Culture; EL GRITO; *Identity; *Political Ideology; *Research Methodology; Romano-V., Octavio Ignacio; Valdez, Facundo.

Parent and Child Relationships

5261 Engle, Patricia L.; Scrimshaw, Susan C.M.; and Smidt, Robert. Sex differences in attitudes towards newborn infants among women of Mexican origin. MEDICAL ANTHROPOLOGY, Vol. 8, no. 2 (Spring 1984), p. 133-144. English. DESCR: *Attitudes; Chicanas; Cultural Characteristics; *Machismo; *Maternal and Child Welfare; Sex Roles.

5262 LeVine, Sarah Ethel; Correa, Clara Sunderland; and Uribe, F. Medardo Tapia. The marital morality of Mexican women--an urban study. JOURNAL OF ANTHROPOLOGICAL RESEARCH, Vol. 42, no. 2 (Summer 1986), p. 183-202. English. DESCR: Family; Los Robles, Cuernavaca, Morelos, Mexico; *Machismo; Marriage; *Sex Roles; *Women Men Relations.

Parent and Child Relationships (cont.)

5263 Nieto, Sonia. Who's afraid of bilingual
     parents? BILINGUAL REVIEW, Vol. 12, no. 3
     (September, December, 1985), p. 179-189.
     English. **DESCR**: *Bilingual Bicultural
     Education; *Community School Relationships;
     *Family; Teacher Training.

5264 Villalobos Galligan, Martha. The legacy of
     Mama. VISTA, Vol. 1, no. 9 (May 3, 1986), p.
     18-19. English. **DESCR**: *Essays; Parenting.

Parenting

5265 Miranda, Gloria E. Hispano-Mexican
     childrearing practices in pre-American Santa
     Barbara. SOUTHERN CALIFORNIA QUARTERLY, Vol.
     65, no. 4 (Winter 1983), p. 307-320.
     English. **DESCR**: *Children; Cultural
     Characteristics; *Family; History; *Santa
     Barbara, CA; Socialization.

5266 Villalobos Galligan, Martha. The legacy of
     Mama. VISTA, Vol. 1, no. 9 (May 3, 1986), p.
     18-19. English. **DESCR**: *Essays; Parent and
     Child Relationships.

PARENTING MODELS AND MEXICAN AMERICANS: A PROCESS ANALYSIS (2nd ed.)

5267 Luzod, Jimmy. Book review of: PARENTING
     MODELS AND MEXICAN AMERICANS: A PROCESS
     ANALYSIS. LA RED/THE NET, no. 71 (August
     1983), p. 8-11. English. **DESCR**: Arciniega,
     Miguel; Book Reviews; Casaus, Luis;
     Castillo, Max.

Parks, Scott

5268 13-part series focuses on Hispanics in
     America. EDITOR & PUBLISHER: THE FOURTH
     ESTATE, Vol. 115, no. 14 (April 3, 1982), p.
     37. English. **DESCR**: Books; Cultural
     Characteristics; DALLAS MORNING NEWS;
     Garcia, Juan; Gonzalez, John; Goodwin, Jay;
     Grothe, Randy Eli; Hamilton, John; Hille,
     Ed; LA VIDA AMERICANA; *LA VIDA
     AMERICANA/HISPANICS IN AMERICA; Langer,
     Ralph; McLemore, David; Osburne, Burl;
     Pusey, Allen; Sonnemair, Jan.

Partido Liberal Mexicano (PLM)

5269 Escobar, Edward J. Mexican revolutionaries
     and the Los Angeles police: harassment of
     the Partido Liberal Mexicano, 1907-1910.
     AZTLAN, Vol. 17, no. 1 (Spring 1986), p.
     1-46. English. **DESCR**: Civil Rights; *Flores
     Magon, Ricardo; Gutierrez de Lara, Lazaro;
     Los Angeles, CA; *Los Angeles Police
     Department; *Police; Police Brutality;
     Political Repression; Rico, Louis; Rico,
     Thomas; Talamantes, Felipe; United
     States-Mexico Relations.

5270 Parlee, Lorena M. The impact of United
     States railroad unions on organized labor
     and government policy in Mexico (1880-1911).
     HISPANIC AMERICAN HISTORICAL REVIEW, Vol.
     64, no. 3 (August 1984), p. 443-475.
     English. **DESCR**: Diaz, Porfirio;
     Discrimination in Employment; History;
     *Labor Unions; Mexico; Railroads; United
     States-Mexico Relations.

LOS PASOS PERDIDOS

5271 Barry, John M. Mito e ironia en LOS PASOS
     PERDIDOS. TINTA, Vol. 1, no. 4 (Summer
     1984), p. 3-9. Spanish. **DESCR**: Carpentier,
     Alejo; Latin American Literature; Literary
     Criticism; Mitos; *Novel.

P.A.S.S.O.
     USE: Political Association of
     Spanish-Speaking Organizations (PASO)

Passports
     USE: Visas

Pastoral Drama
     USE: Folk Drama

Los Pastores [folk drama]

5272 Igo, John N., Jr. Los Pastores: a
     triple-tradition. JOURNAL OF POPULAR
     CULTURE, Vol. 19, no. 3 (Winter 1985), p.
     131-138. English. **DESCR**: Christmas; Cultural
     Customs; *Folk Drama.

Patino [family name]

5273 Instituto Genealogico e Historico
     Latino-Americano. Rootsearch: Patino:
     Herrera: Escobar. VISTA, Vol. 2, no. 9 (May
     3, 1987), p. 22. English. **DESCR**: *Escobar
     [family name]; Genealogy; *Herrera [family
     name]; History; *Personal Names.

Patron System

5274 Wells, Miriam J. Power brokers and
     ethnicity: the rise of a Chicano movement.
     AZTLAN, Vol. 17, no. 1 (Spring 1986), p.
     47-77. English. **DESCR**: *Chicano Movement;
     *Identity; *Natural Support Systems.

Patssi
     USE: Valdez, Patssi

PATTERNS OF UNDOCUMENTED MIGRATION: MEXICO AND THE U.S.

5275 Hunsaker, Alan C. Mexican immigration
     patterns. LA RED/THE NET, no. 93 (January,
     February, 1986), p. 17-19. English. **DESCR**:
     Book Reviews; Immigration; *Jones, Richard
     C.; *Migration Patterns.

Paz, Octavio

5276 Sanchez Tranquilino, Marcos. Un ensayo sobre
     la representacion del ZOOT SUIT en la obra
     de Octavio Paz. LA COMUNIDAD, No. 355 (May
     10, 1987), p. 4-7+. Spanish. **DESCR**: Los
     Angeles, CA; *Pachucos; Sleepy Lagoon Case;
     THE LABYRINTH OF SOLITUDE: LIFE AND THOUGHT
     IN MEXICO; Zoot Suit Riots, Los Angeles, CA,
     1943.

Peace Corps

5277 Hispanic Peace Corps volunteers serve in
     Latin America. HISPANIC TIMES, Vol. 8, no. 5
     (October, November, 1987), p. 16. English.
     DESCR: Latin America.

Pearce, John K.

5278 Ramirez, Oscar. Book review of: ETHNICITY
     AND FAMILY THERAPY. LA RED/THE NET, no. 66
     (March 1983), p. 28-30. English. **DESCR**: Book
     Reviews; *ETHNICITY AND FAMILY THERAPY;
     Giordano, Joseph; McGoldrick, Monica.

Peckinpah, Sam

5279 Chavez, Andres. Film review of: BRING ME THE
     HEAD OF ALFREDO GARCIA. LATIN QUARTER, Vol.
     1, no. 2 (October 1974), p. 36. English.
     DESCR: *BRING ME THE HEAD OF ALFREDO GARCIA;
     *Film Reviews; Violence.

Pedraza-Bailey, Silvia

5280 Chiswick, Barry R. Book review of: POLITICAL AND ECONOMIC MIGRANTS IN AMERICA. JOURNAL OF AMERICAN ETHNIC HISTORY, Vol. 7, no. 1 (Fall 1987), p. 105-106. English. DESCR: Book Reviews; Immigrants; *POLITICAL AND ECONOMIC MIGRANTS IN AMERICA.

5281 Garcia, Mario T. Book review of: POLITICAL AND ECONOMIC MIGRANTS IN AMERICA. LA RED/THE NET, no. 96 (May 1986), p. 11-12. English. DESCR: Book Reviews; Immigration; *POLITICAL AND ECONOMIC MIGRANTS IN AMERICA.

5282 Garcia, Mario T. Book review of: POLITICAL AND ECONOMIC MIGRANTS IN AMERICA. AMERICAN HISTORICAL REVIEW, Vol. 91, no. 4 (October 1986), p. 1023-1024. English. DESCR: Book Reviews; Immigrants; Immigration; *POLITICAL AND ECONOMIC MIGRANTS IN AMERICA.

Pena, Amado Maurilio, Jr.

5283 Foto del artista chicano Amado Maurilio Pena. CONFLUENCIA, Vol. 1, no. 2 (Spring 1986), p. 116. DESCR: *Photography.

Pena, Elizabeth

5284 Chavez, Lorenzo A. La Bamba. VISTA, Vol. 2, no. 11 (July 5, 1987), p. 12-13. English. DESCR: *Actors and Actresses; Biography; De Soto, Rosana; Films; LA BAMBA [film]; *Morales, Esai; Phillips, Lou Diamond.

Pena, Federico

5285 Munoz, Carlos, Jr. and Henry, Charles. Rainbow coalitions in four big cities: San Antonio, Denver, Chicago and Philadelphia. P.S. [AMERICAN POLITICAL SCIENCE ASSOCIATION], Vol. 19, no. 3 (Summer 1986), p. 598-609. English. DESCR: Blacks; Chicago, IL; Cisneros, Henry, Mayor of San Antonio, TX; Denver, CO; Elected Officials; Ethnic Groups; Intergroup Relations; Philadelphia, PA; Political Parties and Organizations; Political Representation; *Politics; San Antonio, TX; Urban Communities.

Pena, Manuel

5286 Christian, Garna L. Book review of: THE TEXAS-MEXICAN CONJUNTO. JOURNAL OF SOUTHERN HISTORY, Vol. 52, (May 1986), p. 325. English. DESCR: Book Reviews; *THE TEXAS-MEXICAN CONJUNTO: HISTORY OF A WORKING-CLASS MUSIC.

5287 Griffith, James S. Book review of: THE TEXAS-MEXICAN CONJUNTO. AMERICAN ANTHROPOLOGIST, Vol. 88, no. 3 (September 1986), p. 733-734. English. DESCR: Book Reviews; *THE TEXAS-MEXICAN CONJUNTO: HISTORY OF A WORKING-CLASS MUSIC.

5288 Schmidt, Henry C. Book review of: THE TEXAS-MEXICAN CONJUNTO. AMERICAN HISTORICAL REVIEW, Vol. 91, no. 2 (April 1986), p. 488-489. English. DESCR: Book Reviews; *THE TEXAS-MEXICAN CONJUNTO: HISTORY OF A WORKING-CLASS MUSIC.

Penalosa, Fernando

5289 Aguirre, Adalberto, Jr. Book review of: CHICANO SOCIOLINGUISTICS. LA RED/THE NET, no. 51 (February 1982), p. 3-4. English. DESCR: Book Reviews; Chicano Dialects; *CHICANO SOCIOLINGUISTICS; *Language Usage; *Sociolinguistics.

5290 Duran, Richard P. Book review of: CHICANO SOCIOLINGUISTICS. LA RED/THE NET, no. 35 (October 1980), p. 3. English. DESCR: Book Reviews; Chicano Dialects; CHICANO SOCIOLINGUISTICS; *Language Usage; *Sociolinguistics.

Penfield, Joyce

5291 Dubois, Betty Lou. Book review of: CHICANO ENGLISH: AN ETHNIC CONTACT DIALECT. CHOICE, Vol. 24, no. 1 (September 1986), p. 114. English. DESCR: Book Reviews; *CHICANO ENGLISH: AN ETHNIC CONTACT DIALECT; Ornstein-Galicia, Jacob.

Peonage
USE: Patron System

People United to Serve Humanity (PUSH)

5292 Jesse Jackson makes appearance at CBS board meeting. BROADCASTING, Vol. 110, no. 16 (April 21, 1986), p. 100. English. DESCR: Broadcast Media; *Columbia Broadcasting Studios (CBS); Discrimination; Discrimination in Employment; *Jackson, Jesse; Stereotypes; Taylor, Hycel; Wyman, Thomas.

People v. Baez

5293 Interpreters--"borrowing" of defense interpreter by trial court. CRIMINAL LAW REPORTER, Vol. 38, no. 4 (October 23, 1985), p. 2077. English. DESCR: Courts of Law; *People v. Guillen; *Translations.

People v. Guillen

5294 Interpreters--"borrowing" of defense interpreter by trial court. CRIMINAL LAW REPORTER, Vol. 38, no. 4 (October 23, 1985), p. 2077. English. DESCR: Courts of Law; People v. Baez; *Translations.

People v. Harris

5295 Juries--peremptory challenges--Spanish surnames. CRIMINAL LAW REPORTER, Vol. 38, no. 1 (October 2, 1985), p. 2018. English. DESCR: *Juries; *People v. Trevino; People v. Wheeler.

People v. Trevino

5296 Juries--peremptory challenges--Spanish surnames. CRIMINAL LAW REPORTER, Vol. 38, no. 1 (October 2, 1985), p. 2018. English. DESCR: *Juries; People v. Harris; People v. Wheeler.

People v. Wheeler

5297 Juries--peremptory challenges--Spanish surnames. CRIMINAL LAW REPORTER, Vol. 38, no. 1 (October 2, 1985), p. 2018. English. DESCR: *Juries; People v. Harris; *People v. Trevino.

Pepsi-Cola Bottling Group

5298 Grant from L.A. Pepsi to benefit city program. BEVERAGE INDUSTRY, Vol. 74, no. 7 (April 8, 1983), p. 25. English. DESCR: Community Development; Los Angeles, CA; Private Funding Sources.

Pepsi-Cola Bottling Group (cont.)

5299 Hispanic marketing. ADVERTISING AGE MAGAZINE, Vol. 57, no. 16 (February 27, 1986), p. 11-51. English. DESCR: Adolph Coors Co.; Advertising; Allstate Insurance Co.; American Greetings; Anheuser-Busch, Inc.; Business Enterprises; Coca-Cola Company; Consumers; Ford Motor Company; Hallmark Cards; *Marketing; Mass Media; McDonald's Corporation; Metropolitan Life Insurance Corporation; Prudential; Spanish International Network (SIN); State Farm Mutual Insurance; Tylenol; United Insurance Co. of America.

5300 La Mafia signs Pepsi contract. NUESTRO, Vol. 11, no. 4 (May 1987), p. 8-9. English. DESCR: Advertising; *La Mafia [musical group]; Musicians; Rock Music.

5301 Marketing to Hispanics. ADVERTISING AGE MAGAZINE, Vol. 57, no. 43 (August 11, 1986), p. 51-528. English. DESCR: Advertising; Broadcast Media; De Armas Publications; Kinney Shoe Corp.; *Marketing; Print Media; Spanish International Network (SIN); U.S. Bureau of the Census.

Perales [family name]

5302 Instituto Genealogico e Historico Latino-Americano. Rootsearch: Cisneros: Perales: Zuniga. VISTA, Vol. 2, no. 10 (June 7, 1987), p. 26. English. DESCR: *Cisneros [family name]; Genealogy; History; *Personal Names; *Zuniga [family name].

Peraza [family name]

5303 Instituto Genealogico e Historico Latino-Americano. Rootsearch: Peraza: Yanez. VISTA, Vol. 1, no. 12 (August 2, 1986), p. 22. English. DESCR: Genealogy; History; *Personal Names; Yanez [family name].

PEREGRINOS DE AZTLAN

5304 Ekstrom, Margaret V. Wanderers from an Aztec land: Chicano naming devices used by Miguel Mendez. LITERARY ONOMASTICS STUDIES, Vol. 12, (1985), p. 85-92. English. DESCR: Literary Characters; *Literary Criticism; Mendez M., Miguel; Novel.

5305 Lomeli, Francisco A. En torno a la literatura...convergencia o divergencia? LA COMUNIDAD, No. 274 (October 20, 1985), p. 8-11. Spanish. DESCR: Anaya, Rudolfo A.; Aztlan; Border Region; HEART OF AZTLAN; *Literary Criticism; Mendez M., Miguel; *Primer Festival de Literatura Fronteriza Mexico-Estados Unidos.

Pereira, Eduardo

5306 Winston, Bonnie. INROADS: internships that work. HISPANIC ENGINEER, Vol. 3, no. 5 (Winter 1987), p. 38-42. English. DESCR: Almanza, John; Alvarez, Maria; Carr, Frank; *Educational Organizations; Educational Statistics; Garcia, Juan; Gonzales, Ana; *INROADS; Raimundo, Antonio; Reza, Priscilla.

Perenchio, A. Jerrold

5307 Gavin joins group pursuing SICC stations. BROADCASTING, Vol. 110, no. 22 (June 2, 1986), p. 68. English. DESCR: Gavin, John; KFTV, Fresno, CA [television station]; KMEX, Los Angeles, CA [television station]; KWEX, San Antonio, TX [television station]; Legal Cases; *Spanish International Communications Corp. (SICC); Spanish International Network (SIN); Spanish Language; Television; Thompson, William; WLTV, Miami, FL [television station]; WXTV, Paterson, NJ [television station].

Perez del Rio, Jose

5308 Breiter, Toni. Pepe del Rio. VISTA, Vol. 1, no. 6 (February 2, 1986), p. 20. English. DESCR: Broadcast Media; *BUENOS DIAS, AMERICA [radio news & features program]; del Rio, Pepe; *Radio; Voice of America.

Perez, Judith

5309 Ramirez, Arturo. SOLDIERBOY, una muestra de la eficacia del teatro chicano de hoy. LA COMUNIDAD, No. 357 (May 24, 1987), p. 12-13. Spanish. DESCR: Perez, Severo; *SOLDIERBOY [play]; *Teatro; Teatro Reviews; Vietnam War.

Perez, Louie (Los Lobos)

5310 Forte, Dan. Los Lobos: Tex-Mex rock from East L.A. GUITAR PLAYER, Vol. 21, no. 2 (February 1987), p. 68-94. English. DESCR: Biography; Discography; Hidalgo, David (Los Lobos); *Los Lobos del Este de Los Angeles (musical group); Lozano, Conrad (Los Lobos); *Musicians; Recording Industry; *Rock Music; Rosas, Cesar (Los Lobos).

Perez, Severo

5311 Ramirez, Arturo. SOLDIERBOY, una muestra de la eficacia del teatro chicano de hoy. LA COMUNIDAD, No. 357 (May 24, 1987), p. 12-13. Spanish. DESCR: Perez, Judith; *SOLDIERBOY [play]; *Teatro; Teatro Reviews; Vietnam War.

Perez, Steven

5312 Mejias-Rivera, Ann E. Steven Perez of Xerox. HISPANIC ENGINEER, Vol. 3, no. 1 (Spring 1987), p. 26-30. English. DESCR: *Engineering as a Profession; Language Arts; Xerox.

Periodical Indexes

5313 Woods, Richard D. Book review of: CHICANO PERIODICAL INDEX: A CUMULATIVE INDEX TO SELECTED CHICANO PERIODICALS BETWEEN 1967 AND 1978. LA RED/THE NET, no. 52 (March 1982), p. 5-6. English. DESCR: Book Reviews; *Chabran, Richard; *CHICANO PERIODICAL INDEX; *Garcia-Ayvens, Francisco.

Periodicals

5314 Index to volume 9. HISPANIC JOURNAL OF BEHAVIORAL SCIENCES, Vol. 9, no. 4 (December 1987), p. 469-473. English. DESCR: *HISPANIC JOURNAL OF BEHAVIORAL SCIENCES; *Indexes.

5315 Lopez, Daniel M. NUESTRO's 10th anniversary. NUESTRO, Vol. 11, no. 3 (April 1987), p. 11-21. English. DESCR: *NUESTRO [magazine].

5316 Rivera, Yvette. Hispanic women's organizations and periodicals needed to communicate new options: Yvette Rivera report. MEDIA REPORT TO WOMEN, Vol. 12, no. 5 (September, October, 1984), p. 15. English. DESCR: *Chicanas; Organizations.

Perot, Ross

5317 Rips, Geoffrey. Puritanism, pluralism, and Perot. TEXAS OBSERVOR, Vol. 75, no. 17 (September 2, 1983), p. 3-4. English. **DESCR:** Adler, Mortimer; *Bilingual Bicultural Education; Educational Theory and Practice.

Personal Names

5318 Briceno, Carlos. Defining the difference between Carlos and Chuck. VISTA, Vol. 2, no. 9 (May 3, 1987), p. 26. English. **DESCR:** *Identity.

5319 Instituto Genealogico e Historico Latino-Americano. Rootsearch: Aguilar: Echeverria. VISTA, Vol. 1, no. 11 (July 6, 1986), p. 22. English. **DESCR:** *Aguilar [family name]; Echeverria [family name]; Genealogy; History.

5320 Instituto Genealogico e Historico Latino-Americano. Rootsearch: Alarcon: Saavedra. VISTA, Vol. 1, no. 8 (April 6, 1986), p. 22. English. **DESCR:** *Alarcon [family name]; Genealogy; History; Saavedra [family name].

5321 Instituto Genealogico e Historico Latino-Americano. Rootsearch: Alvarez: Covarrubias. VISTA, Vol. 1, no. 6 (February 2, 1986), p. 22. English. **DESCR:** *Alvarez [family name]; *Covarrubias [family name]; Genealogy; History.

5322 Instituto Genealogico e Historico Latino-Americano. Rootsearch: Aragon: Trujillo: Ruelas. VISTA, Vol. 2, no. 8 (April 4, 1987), p. 24. English. **DESCR:** *Aragon [family name]; Genealogy; History; *Ruelas [family name]; *Trujillo [family name].

5323 Instituto Genealogico e Historico Latino-Americano. Rootsearch: Bello: Ramirez: Lopez. VISTA, Vol. 3, no. 2 (October 3, 1987), p. 37. English. **DESCR:** *Bello [family name]; Genealogy; History; *Lopez [family name]; *Ramirez [family name].

5324 Instituto Genealogico e Historico Latino-Americano. Rootsearch: Beltran: Flores: Gomez. VISTA, Vol. 2, no. 11 (May 7, 1987), p. 22. English. **DESCR:** *Beltran [family name]; *Flores [family name]; Genealogy; *Gomez [family name]; History.

5325 Instituto Genealogico e Historico Latino-Americano. Rootsearch: Castro: Velasco. VISTA, Vol. 2, no. 2 (October 4, 1986), p. 22. English. **DESCR:** *Castro [family name]; Genealogy; History; *Velasco [family name].

5326 Instituto Genealogico e Historico Latino-Americano. Rootsearch: Cisneros: Perales: Zuniga. VISTA, Vol. 2, no. 10 (June 7, 1987), p. 26. English. **DESCR:** *Cisneros [family name]; Genealogy; History; *Perales [family name]; *Zuniga [family name].

5327 Instituto Genealogico e Historico Latino-Americano. Rootsearch: Cortes: Ulibarri. VISTA, Vol. 1, no. 5 (January 5, 1986), p. 22. English. **DESCR:** *Cortes [family name]; Genealogy; History; Ulibarri [family name].

5328 Instituto Genealogico e Historico Latino-Americano. Rootsearch: De La Garza: Pacheco. VISTA, Vol. 2, no. 6 (February 8, 1987), p. 21. English. **DESCR:** *de la Garza [family name]; Genealogy; History; Pacheco [family name].

5329 Instituto Genealogico e Historico Latino-Americano. Rootsearch: Duarte: Sandoval. VISTA, Vol. 1, no. 9 (May 3, 1986), p. 22. English. **DESCR:** *Duarte [family name]; Genealogy; History; *Sandoval [family name].

5330 Instituto Genealogico e Historico Latino-Americano. Rootsearch: Garcia: Chaves. VISTA, Vol. 1, no. 10 (June 8, 1986), p. 26. English. **DESCR:** *Chaves [family name]; *Garcia [family name]; Genealogy; History.

5331 Instituto Genealogico e Historico Latino-Americano. Rootsearch: Gonzalez: Febres-Cordero. VISTA, Vol. 1, no. 7 (March 2, 1986), p. 22. English. **DESCR:** Febres-Cordero [family name]; Genealogy; *Gonzalez [family name]; History.

5332 Instituto Genealogico e Historico Latino-Americano. Rootsearch: Gutierrez. VISTA, Vol. 1, no. 2 (October 5, 1985), p. 22. English. **DESCR:** Genealogy; *Gutierrez [family name]; History.

5333 Instituto Genealogico e Historico Latino-Americano. Rootsearch: Guzman: Zamora. VISTA, Vol. 2, no. 7 (March 8, 1987), p. 25. English. **DESCR:** Genealogy; *Guzman [family name]; History; *Zamora [family name].

5334 Instituto Genealogico e Historico Latino-Americano. Rootsearch: Jimenez (Ximenez): Olmo. VISTA, Vol. 2, no. 4 (December 7, 1986), p. 25. English. **DESCR:** Genealogy; History; *Jimenez [family name]; *Olmo [family name]; *Ximenez [family name].

5335 Instituto Genealogico e Historico Latino-Americano. Rootsearch: Montoya: Galvo. VISTA, Vol. 1, no. 4 (December 7, 1985), p. 22. English. **DESCR:** *Galvo [family name]; Genealogy; History; *Montoya [family name].

5336 Instituto Genealogico e Historico Latino-Americano. Rootsearch: Olivares: Yrigoyen: Montemayor. VISTA, Vol. 2, no. 12 (August 1, 1987), p. 30. English. **DESCR:** Genealogy; History; *Montemayor [family name]; *Olivares [family name]; *Yrigoyen [family name].

5337 Instituto Genealogico e Historico Latino-Americano. Rootsearch: Ortega: Munoz. VISTA, Vol. 1, no. 3 (November 3, 1985), p. 22. English. **DESCR:** History; *Munoz [family name]; *Ortega [family name].

5338 Instituto Genealogico e Historico Latino-Americano. Rootsearch: Padron: Machado. VISTA, Vol. 2, no. 1 (September 7, 1986), p. 22. English. **DESCR:** Genealogy; History; *Machado [family name]; *Padron [family name].

5339 Instituto Genealogico e Historico Latino-Americano. Rootsearch: Patino: Herrera: Escobar. VISTA, Vol. 2, no. 9 (May 3, 1987), p. 22. English. **DESCR:** *Escobar [family name]; Genealogy; *Herrera [family name]; History; *Patino [family name].

Personal Names (cont.)

5340 Instituto Genealogico e Historico
Latino-Americano. Rootsearch: Peraza: Yanez.
VISTA, Vol. 1, no. 12 (August 2, 1986), p.
22. English. **DESCR:** Genealogy; History;
*Peraza [family name]; Yanez [family name].

5341 Instituto Genealogico e Historico
Latino-Americano. Rootsearch: Rivera:
Navarro: Salazar. VISTA, Vol. 2, no. 3
(November 2, 1986), p. 24. English. **DESCR:**
Genealogy; History; *Navarro [family name];
*Rivera [family name]; *Salazar [family
name].

5342 Instituto Genealogico e Historico
Latino-Americano. Rootsearch: Robles:
Chacon: Molina. VISTA, Vol. 3, no. 1
(September 6, 1987), p. 30. English. **DESCR:**
*Chacon [family name]; Genealogy; History;
*Molina [family name]; *Robles [family
name].

5343 Instituto Genealogico e Historico
Latino-Americano. Rootsearch: Rodriguez:
Garza (De La Garza). VISTA, Vol. 3, no. 3
(November 8, 1987), p. 37. English. **DESCR:**
*de la Garza [family name]; *Garza [family
name]; Genealogy; History; *Rodriguez,
[family name].

5344 Instituto Genealogico e Historico
Latino-Americano. Rootsearch: Villalobos:
Amador (Amado): Ibarra. VISTA, Vol. 3, no. 4
(December 6, 1987), p. 36. English. **DESCR:**
*Amado [family name]; *Amador [family name];
Genealogy; History; *Ibarra [family name];
*Villalobos [family name].

5345 Leonard, Karen. A note on given names and
Chicano intermarriage. LA RED/THE NET, no.
52 (March 1982), p. 4-5. English. **DESCR:**
*Intermarriage.

5346 Mujica, Barbara. What's in a name? VISTA,
Vol. 1, no. 1 (September 8, 1985), p. 18.
English. **DESCR:** Acculturation.

5347 Murguia, Edward. Given names and Chicano
intermarriage. LA RED/THE NET, no. 40 (March
1981), p. 2. English. **DESCR:** *Intermarriage.

5348 Vigelis, Adeline R. Book review of: HISPANIC
FIRST NAMES. LECTOR, Vol. 4, no. 4-6 (1987),
p. 55-56. English. **DESCR:** Book Reviews;
*HISPANIC FIRST NAMES: A COMPREHENSIVE
DICTIONARY OF 250 YEARS OF MEXICAN-AMERICAN
USAGE; Reference Works; Woods, Richard D.

Personal Narrative
USE: Oral History

PERSPECTIVES ON IMMIGRANT AND MINORITY EDUCATION

5349 Compean, Mario. Book review of: PERSPECTIVES
ON IMMIGRATION AND MINORITY EDUCATION. LA
RED/THE NET, no. 86 (November 1984), p. 3-7.
English. **DESCR:** Book Reviews; Samuda, Ronald
J.; Woods, Sandra L.

Philadelphia, PA

5350 Munoz, Carlos, Jr. and Henry, Charles.
Rainbow coalitions in four big cities: San
Antonio, Denver, Chicago and Philadelphia.
P.S. [AMERICAN POLITICAL SCIENCE
ASSOCIATION], Vol. 19, no. 3 (Summer 1986),
p. 598-609. English. **DESCR:** Blacks; Chicago,
IL; Cisneros, Henry, Mayor of San Antonio,
TX; Denver, CO; Elected Officials; Ethnic
Groups; Intergroup Relations; Pena,
Federico; Political Parties and
Organizations; Political Representation;

*Politics; San Antonio, TX; Urban
Communities.

Philip Morris, Inc.

5351 Beale, Stephen. The Maxwell House that
Marlboro bought. HISPANIC BUSINESS, Vol. 9,
no. 2 (February 1987), p. 20-21, 60.
English. **DESCR:** Advertising; Business
Enterprises; Corporations; *Marketing.

Philippines

5352 Gibson, Katherine and Graham, Julie.
Situating migrants in theory. CAPITAL AND
CLASS, no. 29 (Summer 1986), p. 130-149.
English. **DESCR:** *Migrant Labor.

Phillips, Lou Diamond

5353 Chavez, Lorenzo A. La Bamba. VISTA, Vol. 2,
no. 11 (July 5, 1987), p. 12-13. English.
DESCR: *Actors and Actresses; Biography; De
Soto, Rosana; Films; LA BAMBA [film];
*Morales, Esai; Pena, Elizabeth.

Philology
USE: Linguistics

Philosophy

5354 Anaya, Rudolfo A. A Chicano in China. VISTA,
Vol. 2, no. 1 (September 7, 1986), p. 19-21.
English. **DESCR:** *A CHICANO IN CHINA; Anaya,
Rudolfo A.; China; *Culture; *Tourism.

5355 Atencio, Tomas. La Academia de la Nueva
Raza. EL CUADERNO, Vol. 2, no. 1 (1972), p.
6-13. English. **DESCR:** *Alternative
Education; Chicano Studies; Cultural
Characteristics; *Cultural Organizations;
Education; *Educational Organizations; *La
Academia de la Nueva Raza, Dixon, NM; Oro
del Barrio; Values.

5356 Mares, E.A. The fiesta of life: impression
of Paulo Friere. EL CUADERNO, Vol. 3, no. 2
(Spring 1974), p. 5-16. English. **DESCR:**
*Aztlan; Cultural Characteristics; *Essays;
*Freire, Paulo.

Phoenix, AZ

5357 Luckingham, Bradford. The American
Southwest: an urban view. WESTERN HISTORICAL
QUARTERLY, Vol. 15, no. 3 (July 1984), p.
261-280. English. **DESCR:** Albuquerque, NM; El
Paso, TX; Social History and Conditions;
*Southwestern United States; Tucson, AZ;
*Urban Communities; Urban Economics.

Photography

5358 Bernal, Louis Carlos. Alma Rosa. LLUEVE
TLALOC, no. 8 (1981), p. 30.

5359 Bernal, Louis Carlos. Dia de los muertos.
LLUEVE TLALOC, no. 8 (1981), p. 7.

5360 Bernal, Louis Carlos. Marines. LLUEVE
TLALOC, no. 8 (1981), p. 37.

5361 Bernal, Louis Carlos. Miguel M. Mendez
[photograph]. LLUEVE TLALOC, no. 12 (1985),
p. iv. **DESCR:** *Mendez M., Miguel.

5362 Bernal, Louis Carlos. Panadero. LLUEVE
TLALOC, no. 8 (1981), p. 2.

5363 Bernal, Louis Carlos. La Raza. LLUEVE
TLALOC, no. 8 (1981), p. 21.

Photography (cont.)

5364 Bernal, Louis Carlos. Sin documentados.
LLUEVE TLALOC, no. 8 (1981), p. 14.

5365 Bernal, Louis Carlos. [Untitled
photographs]. LLUEVE TLALOC, no. 2 (1975),
p. 2-50.

5366 Betsky, Aaron. The Spanish influence:
architecture in America. HORIZON: A MAGAZINE
OF THE ARTS, Vol. 28, no. 10 (December
1985), p. 53-68. English. **DESCR:**
*Architecture; Spanish Influence.

5367 Castano, Wilfredo Q. For the roses=Pa' las
rosas. REVISTA MUJERES, Vol. 3, no. 2 (June
1986), p. 73. **DESCR:** *Alicia, Juana; *Mural
Art.

5368 Dia de los difuntos ofrenda. THE AMERICAS
REVIEW, Vol. 15, no. 3-4 (Fall, Winter,
1987), p. [84]. **DESCR:** *Altars.

5369 [Diosa de la fertilidad: San Agustin,
Colombia]. REVISTA MUJERES, Vol. 1, no. 1
(January 1984), p. 15.

5370 Foto del artista chicano Amado Maurilio
Pena. CONFLUENCIA, Vol. 1, no. 2 (Spring
1986), p. 116. **DESCR:** *Pena, Amado Maurilio,
Jr.

5371 Galeria 2001. AMERICAS 2001, Vol. 1, no. 3
(November, December, 1987), p. [8-9].
Bilingual. **DESCR:** Artists; Biographical
Notes; *Gamboa, Harry, Jr.

5372 Galvez, Jose. [Untitled photographs]. LLUEVE
TLALOC, no. 1 (1975), p. 4-42.

5373 [Julie Cabeza de Vaca, high school
graduation]. REVISTA MUJERES, Vol. 2, no. 1
(January 1985), p. 29.

5374 Lopez-Flores, Beatriz. [Woman holding UFW
flag (photograph)]. REVISTA MUJERES, Vol. 2,
no. 2 (June 1985), p. 52.

5375 Pazos, Antonio. [Untitled photograph of
mariachis]. LLUEVE TLALOC, no. 10 (1983), p.
11.

5376 Pazos, Antonio. [Untitled photograph of
laundered jeans]. LLUEVE TLALOC, no. 10
(1983), p. 18.

5377 Pazos, Antonio. [Untitled photograph of
agave plant]. LLUEVE TLALOC, no. 10 (1983),
p. 19.

5378 Pazos, Antonio. [Untitled photograph].
LLUEVE TLALOC, no. 10 (1983), p. 24.

5379 Pazos, Antonio. [Untitled photograph].
LLUEVE TLALOC, no. 10 (1983), p. 25.

5380 Pazos, Antonio. [Untitled photograph of
fisherman]. LLUEVE TLALOC, no. 10 (1983), p.
28.

5381 Pazos, Antonio. [Untitled photograph of
fisherman]. LLUEVE TLALOC, no. 10 (1983), p.
29.

5382 Pazos, Antonio. [Untitled photograph].
LLUEVE TLALOC, no. 10 (1983), p. 30.

5383 Pazos, Antonio. [Untitled photograph].
LLUEVE TLALOC, no. 10 (1983), p. 32.

5384 Pazos, Antonio. [Untitled photograph].
LLUEVE TLALOC, no. 10 (1983), p. 38.

5385 Pazos, Antonio. [Untitled photograph].
LLUEVE TLALOC, no. 10 (1983), p. 39.

5386 Rosas, Alejandro. Siete fotografos latinos
en Los Angeles. LA COMUNIDAD, No. 241 (March
3, 1985), p. 4-5. Spanish. **DESCR:** Aguilar,
Laura; Art; Avila, Adam; Callwood, Dennis
O.; Carlos, Jesus; Exhibits; Miranda, Judy;
Self-Help Graphics, Los Angeles, CA; *SEVEN
LATINO PHOTOGRAPHERS=SIETE FOTOGRAFOS
LATINOS; Thewlis, Alan; Valverde, Richard.

5387 Tineo, David. [Untitled portfolio]. LLUEVE
TLALOC, no. 13 (1986), p. 34-35. **DESCR:**
*Drawings.

5388 Toboada, John A. Irma Rangel [photograph].
AMERICAS 2001, Premiere Issue, 1987, In
BkCover. **DESCR:** *Rangel, Irma.

5389 Toboada, John A. [Untitled photograph].
AMERICAS 2001, Premiere Issue, 1987, In
FtCover.

5390 Torres, Ramon. Vision of the coming of the
new life. AMERICAS 2001, Premiere Issue,
1987, p. [24-25].

5391 Valva, Annie. [Pat Zavella (photograph)].
REVISTA MUJERES, Vol. 1, no. 1 (January
1984), p. 10. **DESCR:** Zavella, Pat.

5392 [Yvette Galindo]. REVISTA MUJERES, Vol. 2,
no. 1 (January 1985), p. 10.

Pilsen, IL

5393 Heuer, Robert J. To save a neighborhood.
VISTA, Vol. 3, no. 3 (November 8, 1987), p.
32-34. English. **DESCR:** *Eighteenth Street
Development Corporation, Chicago, IL;
*Housing; Overa, Agustin; Statistics.

Pima Community College, Tucson, AZ

5394 Mendez-M., Miguel. Introduccion. LLUEVE
TLALOC, no. 4 (1977), p. vii. Spanish.
DESCR: *Literature.

5395 Mendez-M., Miguel. Introduccion. LLUEVE
TLALOC, no. 10 (1983), p. iv. Spanish.
DESCR: Education; *Spanish Language.

5396 Mendez-M., Miguel. Introduccion. LLUEVE
TLALOC, no. 12 (1985), p. iv. Spanish.
DESCR: *Educational Theory and Practice;
Fiction; Poetry.

5397 Mendez-M., Miguel. Introduction. LLUEVE
TLALOC, no. 4 (1977), p. viii. English.
DESCR: *Literature.

5398 Mendez-M., Miguel. Introduction. LLUEVE
TLALOC, no. 10 (1983), p. iv. English.
DESCR: *Education; *Spanish Language.

5399 Mendez-M., Miguel. Introduction. LLUEVE
TLALOC, no. 12 (1985), p. iv. English.
DESCR: Educational Theory and Practice;
Fiction; Poetry.

Pineda, Cecile

5400 Bruce-Novoa, Juan. Book review of: FACE.
VISTA, Vol. 1, no. 11 (July 6, 1986), p. 16.
English. **DESCR:** Book Reviews; *FACE.

Pineda, Cecile (cont.)

5401 Bruce-Novoa, Juan. Meet the writers of the 80s. VISTA, Vol. 1, no. 11 (July 6, 1986), p. 15-16. English. **DESCR:** Anaya, Rudolfo A.; Arte Publico Press; *Authors; Bilingual Review Press; Cisneros, Sandra; Hinojosa-Smith, Rolando R.; Keller, Gary D.; *Literature; Quinto Sol Publishing, Inc.; Rivera, Tomas; Soto, Gary.

5402 Gonzales-Berry, Erlinda. Book review of: FACE. THE AMERICAS REVIEW, Vol. 15, no. 2 (Summer 1987), p. 107-109. English. **DESCR:** Book Reviews; *FACE.

Pineda, Charles and family (Los Angeles, CA)

5403 Lit, Ed. Recognition for Hispanic families. VISTA, Vol. 1, no. 5 (January 5, 1986), p. 18-20. English. **DESCR:** American Family Society; *Awards; *Hispanic Family of the Year Award; Moraga, Peter and family (Los Angeles, CA); Private Funding Sources.

Pinero, Miguel

5404 Ruiz, Ariel. Raza, sexo y politica en SHORT EYES by Miguel Pinero. THE AMERICAS REVIEW, Vol. 15, no. 2 (Summer 1987), p. 93-102. Spanish. **DESCR:** Homosexuality; Literary Criticism; Prisoners; Puerto Ricans; Sex Roles; *SHORT EYES; Teatro.

Pintos
   USE: Prisoners

Placas
   USE: Graffiti

EL PLAN ESPIRITUAL DE AZTLAN

5405 Goldman, Shifra. Arte chicano: iconografia de la autodeterminacion. LA COMUNIDAD, No. 336 (December 28, 1986), p. 12-14+. Spanish. **DESCR:** *Art; Discrimination; History; Identity; Nationalism; Pachucos; Social Classes; *Symbolism.

5406 Klor de Alva, J. Jorge. California Chicano literature and pre-Columbian motifs: foil and fetish. CONFLUENCIA, Vol. 1, no. 2 (Spring 1986), p. 18-26. English. **DESCR:** Alurista; Aztecs; Aztlan; *California; *Literature; *Precolumbian Images; *Precolumbian Philosophy; Symbolism.

Planned Parenthood Federation of America

5407 Machado, Melinda. Saying "no" to teenage sex. VISTA, Vol. 2, no. 11 (July 5, 1987), p. 14. English. **DESCR:** *CUANDO ESTEMOS JUNTOS [phonograph record]; DETENTE [phonograph record]; Music; *Musical Lyrics; Sex Education; Tatiana and Johnny.

Plays
   USE: Teatro

Plaza Vieja, Las Vegas, NM

5408 Sharpe, Maria Elena. Back to the future. VISTA, Vol. 3, no. 4 (December 6, 1987), p. 10-12, 32. English. **DESCR:** *Community Development; Las Vegas, NM; Santa Fe Trail.

PLEASE DON'T BURY ME ALIVE [film]

5409 Barrios, Greg. Efrain Gutierrez y el nuevo cine chicano. LA COMUNIDAD, No. 265 (August 18, 1985), p. 3. Spanish. **DESCR:** Biography; *Films; *Gutierrez, Efrain.

THE PLUM PLUM PICKERS

5410 Rodriguez, Ronald. Book review of: THE PLUM PLUM PICKERS. LECTOR, Vol. 4, no. 4-6 (1987), p. 70. English. **DESCR:** Barrio, Raymond; Book Reviews.

Plumey, Raymond

5411 SHPE holds first ever East coast conference for Hispanic engineers. HISPANIC ENGINEER, Vol. 3, no. 5 (Winter 1987), p. 12-14. English. **DESCR:** Awards; Barrios, Eugene; Chang-Diaz, Franklin; *Conferences and Meetings; Cuevas, Brian L.; Garay, Charles J.; Garcia, Ray; Marrero, Charles; Martinez, Lisa; Monteverde, Edwin; Reyes-Guerra, David; Rivera, Angel; Society of Hispanic Professional Engineers (SHPE); Soto, Giovanni.

Pluralism
   USE: Cultural Pluralism

Pocho
   USE: Chicano Dialects

POCHO

5412 Bruce-Novoa, Juan. Homosexuality and the Chicano novel. CONFLUENCIA, Vol. 2, no. 1 (Fall 1986), p. 69-77. English. **DESCR:** Acosta, Oscar Zeta; CITY OF NIGHT; FAULTLINE [novel]; *Homosexuality; Islas, Arturo; *Literary Criticism; Machismo; *Novel; Ortiz Taylor, Sheila; Rechy, John; Salas, Floyd; SPRING FORWARD/FALL BACK; TATOO THE WICKED CROSS; THE AUTOBIOGRAPHY OF A BROWN BUFFALO; THE RAIN GOD: A DESERT TALE; THE REVOLT OF THE COCKROACH PEOPLE; Villarreal, Jose Antonio.

Poems

5413 Acosta, Teresa Palomo. Balancing act. SAGUARO, Vol. 4, (1987), p. 15-17. English.

5414 Acosta, Teresa Palomo. Desaparecida. SAGUARO, Vol. 4, (1987), p. 47-49. English.

5415 Acosta, Teresa Palomo. Muralistas: poem one. SAGUARO, Vol. 3, (1986), p. 88-91. English.

5416 Agosin, Marjorie. Madre. CHIRICU, no. 2 (Spring 1977), p. 4. Spanish.

5417 Agosin, Marjorie. Norma Alarcon. CHIRICU, Vol. 2, no. 1 (Spring 1980), p. 9. Spanish. **DESCR:** *Alarcon, Norma.

5418 Agosin, Marjorie. (Sin titulo). CHIRICU, no. 2 (Spring 1977), p. 3. Spanish.

5419 Agosin, Marjorie. Tristezas. CHIRICU, no. 2 (Spring 1977), p. 4. Spanish.

5420 Agosin, Marjorie and Semones, Linda, trans. El vino=Wine. CHIRICU, no. 2 (Spring 1977), p. 21. Bilingual.

5421 Aguilar Gallardo, Hortensia. Cantar de un ayer. LLUEVE TLALOC, no. 7 (1980), p. 39. Spanish.

5422 Aguilar Gallardo, Hortensia. Mariposas negras. LLUEVE TLALOC, no. 7 (1980), p. 39. Spanish.

5423 Aguilar, Ricardo [Tepalcatero]. Tres veces la pua o nopaltzin. LLUEVE TLALOC, no. 7 (1980), p. 24. Spanish.

Poems (cont.)

5424 Alarcon, Francisco X. Banderas. CONFLUENCIA, Vol. 1, no. 2 (Spring 1986), p. 130. Spanish.

5425 Alarcon, Francisco X. Un beso is not a kiss. CONFLUENCIA, Vol. 1, no. 2 (Spring 1986), p. 138. Bilingual.

5426 Alarcon, Francisco X. Columna al amor. REVISTA MUJERES, Vol. 3, no. 1 (January 1986), p. 36. Spanish.

5427 Alarcon, Francisco X. Fugitive. CONFLUENCIA, Vol. 1, no. 2 (Spring 1986), p. 137. English.

5428 Alarcon, Francisco X. I used to be much much darker. CONFLUENCIA, Vol. 1, no. 2 (Spring 1986), p. 131. Bilingual.

5429 Alarcon, Francisco X. I'm really not crying. REVISTA MUJERES, Vol. 3, no. 1 (January 1986), p. 42. English.

5430 Alarcon, Francisco X. Palabras heridas. CONFLUENCIA, Vol. 1, no. 2 (Spring 1986), p. 132. Spanish.

5431 Alarcon, Francisco X. Patria. CONFLUENCIA, Vol. 1, no. 2 (Spring 1986), p. 139. Spanish.

5432 Alarcon, Francisco X. Profugo. CONFLUENCIA, Vol. 1, no. 2 (Spring 1986), p. 136. Spanish.

5433 Alarcon, Francisco X. Raices. CONFLUENCIA, Vol. 1, no. 2 (Spring 1986), p. 135. Spanish.

5434 Alarcon, Francisco X. Roots. CONFLUENCIA, Vol. 1, no. 2 (Spring 1986), p. 135. English.

5435 Alarcon, Francisco X. Triangulo gris. REVISTA MUJERES, Vol. 3, no. 1 (January 1986), p. 21. Spanish.

5436 Alarcon, Francisco X. Worded wounds. CONFLUENCIA, Vol. 1, no. 2 (Spring 1986), p. 133. English.

5437 Alarcon, Francisco X. The X in my name. REVISTA MUJERES, Vol. 3, no. 1 (January 1986), p. 19. English.

5438 Alarcon, Justo S. A la nanita, nana ...[y] epilogo. LLUEVE TLALOC, no. 10 (1983), p. 4. Spanish.

5439 Alarcon, Justo S. Las dos tortolas. LLUEVE TLALOC, no. 10 (1983), p. 25. Spanish.

5440 Alarcon, Justo S. Las mascaras. CONFLUENCIA, Vol. 1, no. 2 (Spring 1986), p. 120. Spanish.

5441 Alarcon, Norma. The American stage. CHIRICU, no. 2 (Spring 1977), p. 36. English.

5442 Alarcon, Norma. Chilean winter: a true story. CHIRICU, Vol. 2, no. 1 (Spring 1980), p. 7. English.

5443 Alarcon, Norma. Honey. CHIRICU, no. 2 (Spring 1977), p. 14. English.

5444 Alarcon, Norma. In pursuit of the white knight. CHIRICU, no. 1 (Spring 1976), p. 4-5. English.

5445 Alarcon, Norma. Jacking off. CHIRICU, no. 2 (Spring 1977), p. 13. English.

5446 Alarcon, Norma. Mexican twilight. CHIRICU, Vol. 2, no. 1 (Spring 1980), p. 6. English.

5447 Alarcon, Norma. Precision processing. CHIRICU, no. 2 (Spring 1977), p. 12. English.

5448 Alarcon, Norma. Undefined. CHIRICU, no. 1 (Spring 1976), p. 6. English.

5449 Alcocer, Daniel. La Raza. CHIRICU, no. 1 (Spring 1976), p. 1. English.

5450 Alire Saenz, Benjamin. Alejandro's funeral. SAGUARO, Vol. 4, (1987), p. 79-81. English.

5451 Alire Saenz, Benjamin. The ruins of Prieto's barrio. SAGUARO, Vol. 4, (1987), p. 83-85. English.

5452 Allen, David. La lluvia. LLUEVE TLALOC, no. 1 (1974), p. 23. Spanish.

5453 Allen, David. The rain. LLUEVE TLALOC, no. 1 (1974), p. 24. English.

5454 Allison, Martha. El amor que nunca se olvida: el de la madre. LLUEVE TLALOC, no. 14 (1987), p. 40. Spanish.

5455 Allison, Martha. Dejame pensar. LLUEVE TLALOC, no. 14 (1987), p. 39. Spanish.

5456 Allison, Martha. Madre querida. LLUEVE TLALOC, no. 14 (1987), p. 40. Spanish.

5457 Allison, Martha. Te quiero. LLUEVE TLALOC, no. 14 (1987), p. 40. Spanish.

5458 Almader Sandoval, Rigoberto. Mi muerte. LLUEVE TLALOC, no. 7 (1980), p. 40. Spanish.

5459 Almader Sandoval, Rigoberto. Triste mundo. LLUEVE TLALOC, no. 7 (1980), p. 40. Spanish.

5460 Alonso, Marisela. Me gusta. LLUEVE TLALOC, no. 11 (1984), p. 24. Spanish.

5461 Alonso, Marisela. Miedo. LLUEVE TLALOC, no. 11 (1984), p. 24. Spanish.

5462 Alonso, Marisela. Padre. LLUEVE TLALOC, no. 11 (1984), p. 31. Spanish.

5463 Alonso, Marisela. Por que me mentiste. LLUEVE TLALOC, no. 11 (1984), p. 14. Spanish.

5464 Alonso, Marisela. Porque te fuiste? LLUEVE TLALOC, no. 10 (1983), p. 37. Spanish.

5465 Alonso, Marisela. Triste realidad. LLUEVE TLALOC, no. 11 (1984), p. 26. Spanish.

5466 Alurista. Southwestern trek in four part harmony. SAGUARO, Vol. 4, (1987), p. 29-31. English.

5467 Andrews, Marta. Dolor materno. LLUEVE TLALOC, no. 10 (1983), p. 38. Spanish.

5468 Angel, Armando C. La Raza Chicana. LLUEVE TLALOC, no. 1 (1974), p. 29-30. Spanish.

5469 Angulo, Lourdes. Abuelito. LLUEVE TLALOC, no. 10 (1983), p. 35. Spanish.

5470 Angulo, Lourdes. Por fin. LLUEVE TLALOC, no. 10 (1983), p. 39. Spanish.

Poems (cont.)

5471 Annabelle. Enganame pues. LLUEVE TLALOC, no. 8 (1981), p. 35. Spanish.

5472 Arellano, Estevan. Azucenas. EL CUADERNO, Vol. 4, no. 1 (Summer 1976), p. 5. Spanish.

5473 Arellano, Estevan. Companero trabajador. EL CUADERNO, Vol. 4, no. 1 (Summer 1976), p. 63. Spanish.

5474 Arellano, Manuel. A Manuel Salazar. EL CUADERNO, Vol. 4, no. 1 (Summer 1976), p. 90-98. Spanish. DESCR: *Salazar, Manuel.

5475 Arenas, Andrea-Teresa. The circle weighs heavy with healing tears. REVISTA MUJERES, Vol. 2, no. 2 (June 1985), p. 43-44. English.

5476 Arenas, Andrea-Teresa. From a safe distance. REVISTA MUJERES, Vol. 4, no. 1 (January 1987), p. 61-62. English.

5477 Arenas, Andrea-Teresa. Greetings and salutations. TRABAJOS MONOGRAFICOS, Vol. 3, no. 1 (1987), p. [34]-35. English.

5478 Arenas, Andrea-Teresa. Queen of victory pray for us. REVISTA MUJERES, Vol. 4, no. 1 (January 1987), p. 63-64. English.

5479 Aros, Maria Teresa. Lo que pido. LLUEVE TLALOC, no. 4 (1977), p. 69. Spanish.

5480 Aros, Maria Teresa. El pensamiento de un nino. LLUEVE TLALOC, no. 4 (1977), p. 50. Spanish.

5481 Aros, Maria Teresa. El pequeno. LLUEVE TLALOC, no. 4 (1977), p. 46. Spanish.

5482 Aros, Maria Teresa. Tu olvido. LLUEVE TLALOC, no. 4 (1977), p. 99. Spanish.

5483 Astiazaron Aguilar, Guadalupe. Azul. LLUEVE TLALOC, no. 9 (1982), p. 32. Spanish.

5484 Astiazaron Aguilar, Guadalupe. El mundo y el hombre. LLUEVE TLALOC, no. 9 (1982), p. 32. Spanish.

5485 Astiazaron Aguilar, Guadalupe. El mundo y el hombre [long version]. LLUEVE TLALOC, no. 10 (1983), p. 13. Spanish.

5486 Astiazaron Aguilar, Guadalupe. Oracion. LLUEVE TLALOC, no. 9 (1982), p. 32. Spanish.

5487 Astiazaron Aguilar, Guadalupe. Senor, no llores mas. LLUEVE TLALOC, no. 9 (1982), p. 32. Spanish.

5488 Astiazaron Aguilar, Guadalupe. Sueno real. LLUEVE TLALOC, no. 10 (1983), p. 6-7. English.

5489 Badikian, Beatriz. Mapmaker. THE AMERICAS REVIEW, Vol. 15, no. 2 (Summer 1987), p. 73. English.

5490 Badikian, Beatriz. Rituals at Bennington: the elusive joy of writing. THE AMERICAS REVIEW, Vol. 15, no. 2 (Summer 1987), p. 71. English.

5491 Badikian, Beatriz. Words. THE AMERICAS REVIEW, Vol. 15, no. 2 (Summer 1987), p. 72. English.

5492 Barbara, Ana M. La despedida. LLUEVE TLALOC, no. 2 (1975), p. 31. Spanish.

5493 Bastidas, Laura E. A ti. LLUEVE TLALOC, no. 7 (1980), p. 38. Spanish.

5494 Bastidas, Laura E. No era de oro. LLUEVE TLALOC, no. 2 (1975), p. 22. Spanish.

5495 Bastidas, Laura E. Secretos. LLUEVE TLALOC, no. 2 (1975), p. 38. Spanish.

5496 Belli, Gioconda. Y Dios me hizo mujer. REVISTA MUJERES, Vol. 1, no. 1 (January 1984), p. 14-15. Spanish.

5497 Belli, Gioconda and Ellis, Miriam, trans. Y Dios me hizo mujer. REVISTA MUJERES, Vol. 1, no. 1 (January 1984), p. 16-17. English.

5498 Belloc Garcia, Jose. Que linda es la luz. LLUEVE TLALOC, no. 12 (1985), p. 34. Spanish.

5499 Beltran, Luis. Aun me duelen tus brazos empujandome. CHIRICU, Vol. 3, no. 1 (1982), p. 8. Spanish.

5500 Beltran, Luis. Travesura entre las ramas. CHIRICU, Vol. 3, no. 1 (1982), p. 7. Spanish.

5501 Bernal, Alejandro. Y jugamos a poetas. CHIRICU, Vol. 3, no. 1 (1982), p. 14-15. Spanish.

5502 Bernal, Esmeralda. Frida Kahlo. REVISTA MUJERES, Vol. 1, no. 2 (June 1984), p. 18. Bilingual. DESCR: *Kahlo, Frida.

5503 Bernal, Esmeralda. I wish. REVISTA MUJERES, Vol. 2, no. 1 (January 1985), p. 20. English.

5504 Bernal, Esmeralda. If I could. REVISTA MUJERES, Vol. 2, no. 2 (June 1985), p. 49-50. English.

5505 Bernal, Esmeralda. Sabes carino. REVISTA MUJERES, Vol. 2, no. 1 (January 1985), p. 43. Spanish.

5506 Bernal, Esmeralda. When my body longs for you... REVISTA MUJERES, Vol. 1, no. 2 (June 1984), p. 32. English.

5507 Bernal, Juan Manuel. Has atestiguado? SAGUARO, Vol. 3, (1986), p. 37-38. Spanish.

5508 Bernal, Juan Manuel. Poemas cortas [sic]. SAGUARO, Vol. 3, (1986), p. 39. Spanish.

5509 Biggs, Michelle. Adios. LLUEVE TLALOC, no. 3 (1976), p. 27. Spanish.

5510 Biggs, Michelle. Inescapable. LLUEVE TLALOC, no. 3 (1976), p. 48. Bilingual.

5511 Biggs, Michelle. Nina indigena=Indian maiden. LLUEVE TLALOC, no. 3 (1976), p. 32. Bilingual.

5512 Biggs, Michelle. On the lee shore. LLUEVE TLALOC, no. 3 (1976), p. 41. English.

5513 Biggs, Michelle. Tu. LLUEVE TLALOC, no. 4 (1977), p. 42. Spanish.

5514 Blanco, Pilar. Ayer. CHIRICU, Vol. 2, no. 2 (1981), p. 29. Spanish.

5515 Blanco, Pilar. Cuando te vea. CHIRICU, Vol. 2, no. 2 (1981), p. 28. Spanish.

Poems (cont.)

5516 Blea, Irene I. Damn, Sam. BILINGUAL REVIEW, Vol. 12, no. 3 (September, December, 1985), p. 245-246. English.

5517 Blea, Irene I. Female learning. BILINGUAL REVIEW, Vol. 12, no. 3 (September, December, 1985), p. 241-242. English.

5518 Blea, Irene I. Fire color. BILINGUAL REVIEW, Vol. 12, no. 3 (September, December, 1985), p. 243-244. English.

5519 Blea, Irene I. He never wrote. BILINGUAL REVIEW, Vol. 12, no. 3 (September, December, 1985), p. 244. English.

5520 Blea, Irene I. Inez. SAGUARO, Vol. 4, (1987), p. 41. Spanish.

5521 Blea, Irene I. Married. BILINGUAL REVIEW, Vol. 12, no. 3 (September, December, 1985), p. 242. English.

5522 Blea, Irene I. Mujeres contemporaneas. SAGUARO, Vol. 4, (1987), p. 39-40. Spanish.

5523 Blea, Irene I. An occasional baby. BILINGUAL REVIEW, Vol. 12, no. 3 (September, December, 1985), p. 242-243. English.

5524 Blea, Irene I. Once. NOTEBOOK: A LITTLE MAGAZINE, Vol. 2, no. 2 (1986), p. 34. English.

5525 Blea, Irene I. Singing women. NOTEBOOK: A LITTLE MAGAZINE, Vol. 2, no. 2 (1986), p. 28-29. English.

5526 Blea, Irene I. Singing women. REVISTA MUJERES, Vol. 2, no. 2 (June 1985), p. 4-5. English.

5527 Blea, Irene I. Why. BILINGUAL REVIEW, Vol. 12, no. 3 (September, December, 1985), p. 244-245. English.

5528 Bojorquez, Ricardo. El valenton. LLUEVE TLALOC, no. 3 (1976), p. 39. Spanish.

5529 Bolanos, Isabel. A donde va la nina. NOTEBOOK: A LITTLE MAGAZINE, Vol. 2, no. 2 (1986), p. 12. Spanish.

5530 Bolanos, Isabel. Los lirios y las violetas. NOTEBOOK: A LITTLE MAGAZINE, Vol. 2, no. 2 (1986), p. 32. Spanish.

5531 Bolanos, Isabel. Madre que tan cerca estas. NOTEBOOK: A LITTLE MAGAZINE, Vol. 2, no. 2 (1986), p. 35. Spanish.

5532 Bradley, Jacqueline. Circles of nostalgia. REVISTA MUJERES, Vol. 4, no. 1 (January 1987), p. 20-21. English.

5533 Brinson-Pineda, Barbara. Aqui venimos a pasar hambre y amarguras. REVISTA MUJERES, Vol. 3, no. 2 (June 1986), p. 64-65. Spanish.

5534 Brinson-Pineda, Barbara. Carta a L. SAGUARO, Vol. 1, no. 1 (1984), p. 50. Spanish.

5535 Brinson-Pineda, Barbara. Dolencias. REVISTA MUJERES, Vol. 3, no. 1 (January 1986), p. 4-6. English.

5536 Brinson-Pineda, Barbara. Ella. SAGUARO, Vol. 1, no. 1 (1984), p. 51. Spanish.

5537 Brinson-Pineda, Barbara. Maria yo. REVISTA MUJERES, Vol. 3, no. 2 (June 1986), p. 4-9. English.

5538 Brinson-Pineda, Barbara. Recipe: chorizo con huevo made in the microwave. REVISTA MUJERES, Vol. 3, no. 1 (January 1986), p. 8-10. English.

5539 Brinson-Pineda, Barbara. Sabado. SAGUARO, Vol. 1, no. 1 (1984), p. 49. Spanish.

5540 Brinson-Pineda, Barbara. The strawberry pickers. REVISTA MUJERES, Vol. 3, no. 2 (June 1986), p. 14. English.

5541 Brito, Aristeo. Insomnio. LLUEVE TLALOC, no. 4 (1977), p. 35-37. Spanish.

5542 Brito, Aristeo. Insomnio. LLUEVE TLALOC, no. 14 (1987), p. xiii-xiv. Spanish.

5543 Bruce-Novoa, Juan. Comunion. SAGUARO, Vol. 1, no. 1 (1984), p. 70. Spanish.

5544 Bruce-Novoa, Juan. La dama del libro. SAGUARO, Vol. 1, no. 1 (1984), p. 71. Spanish.

5545 Bruce-Novoa, Juan. Homenaje a Ricardo Sanchez. EL CUADERNO, Vol. 4, no. 1 (Summer 1976), p. 49. Spanish. **DESCR:** *Sanchez, Ricardo.

5546 Bruce-Novoa, Juan. Propiedad. SAGUARO, Vol. 1, no. 1 (1984), p. 69. Spanish.

5547 Canez, Luis P. De paso. LLUEVE TLALOC, no. 7 (1980), p. 39. Spanish.

5548 Canez, Luis P. El desierto. LLUEVE TLALOC, no. 6 (1979), p. 24. Spanish.

5549 Canez, Luis P. Falleciste. LLUEVE TLALOC, no. 6 (1979), p. 38. Spanish.

5550 Canez, Luis P. Pena. LLUEVE TLALOC, no. 7 (1980), p. 24. Spanish.

5551 Canez, Luis P. Preguntas. LLUEVE TLALOC, no. 7 (1980), p. 24. Spanish.

5552 Canez, Luis P. Vida libre. LLUEVE TLALOC, no. 7 (1980), p. 24. Spanish.

5553 Cartes, Rebeca. Me estas rechazando. SAGUARO, Vol. 1, no. 1 (1984), p. 65. Spanish.

5554 Cartes, Rebeca. Te sueno. LLUEVE TLALOC, no. 8 (1981), p. 26. Spanish.

5555 Casaus, Maria R. Mi pequeno. LLUEVE TLALOC, no. 11 (1984), p. 32. Spanish.

5556 Casaus, Maria R. Tengo miedo. LLUEVE TLALOC, no. 12 (1985), p. 19. Spanish.

5557 Castillo, Ana. Juego. REVISTA MUJERES, Vol. 4, no. 1 (January 1987), p. 36. Spanish.

5558 Castillo, Ana. No solo el ser chilena. REVISTA MUJERES, Vol. 4, no. 1 (January 1987), p. 37. English.

5559 Castillo, Ana. Paco and Rosa. REVISTA MUJERES, Vol. 3, no. 2 (June 1986), p. 52. English.

5560 Castillo, Ana. Querida Marina: I still love you. REVISTA MUJERES, Vol. 4, no. 1 (January 1987), p. 35. Bilingual.

5561 Castillo, Ana. Saturdays. REVISTA MUJERES, Vol. 3, no. 2 (June 1986), p. 54. English.

Poems (cont.)

5562 Castillo, Lupe. Para el ano nuevo. CHIRICU, Vol. 3, no. 1 (1982), p. 9. Spanish.

5563 Castillo, Lupe. Para la navidad. CHIRICU, Vol. 3, no. 1 (1982), p. 10. Spanish.

5564 Castillo, Victoria. Madre. LLUEVE TLALOC, no. 12 (1985), p. 19. Spanish.

5565 Castillo, Victoria. Por que, senor, por que. LLUEVE TLALOC, no. 12 (1985), p. 19. Spanish.

5566 Castro, E.M. El encaje. LLUEVE TLALOC, no. 4 (1977), p. 83. Spanish.

5567 Castro, E.M. Por que un poema? LLUEVE TLALOC, no. 4 (1977), p. 70. Spanish.

5568 Castro, E.M. Te veo. LLUEVE TLALOC, no. 4 (1977), p. 81. Spanish.

5569 Castro, E.M. La zorra. LLUEVE TLALOC, no. 4 (1977), p. 72. Spanish.

5570 Castro, E.M. El zorro. LLUEVE TLALOC, no. 4 (1977), p. 73. Spanish.

5571 Catalan E., Martina. Cuando tu ya no estes. LLUEVE TLALOC, no. 10 (1983), p. 9. Spanish.

5572 Catalan E., Martina. Un novio es... LLUEVE TLALOC, no. 10 (1983), p. 37. Spanish.

5573 Cerda, Gabriela. Sunset Boulevard. NOTEBOOK: A LITTLE MAGAZINE, Vol. 2, no. 2 (1986), p. 36-38. English.

5574 Cervantes, Lorna Dee and Carrillo, Victor, trans. Agosto en un pueblo canero. REVISTA MUJERES, Vol. 3, no. 2 (June 1986), p. 20. Spanish.

5575 Cervantes, Lorna Dee. Astro-no-mia. THE AMERICAS REVIEW, Vol. 15, no. 3-4 (Fall, Winter, 1987), p. 44. English.

5576 Cervantes, Lorna Dee. Bird Ave. THE AMERICAS REVIEW, Vol. 15, no. 3-4 (Fall, Winter, 1987), p. 41-43. English.

5577 Cervantes, Norma. Bendicion. LLUEVE TLALOC, no. 10 (1983), p. 35. Spanish.

5578 Cervantes, Norma. No importa el pasado. LLUEVE TLALOC, no. 11 (1984), p. 31. Spanish.

5579 Cervantes, Norma. Poema. LLUEVE TLALOC, no. 10 (1983), p. 40. Spanish.

5580 Cervantes, Norma. Te quiero con ternura. LLUEVE TLALOC, no. 11 (1984), p. 27. Spanish.

5581 Chabram, Angie. Colega... TRABAJOS MONOGRAFICOS, Vol. 3, no. 1 (1987), p. [36]-38. Spanish.

5582 Chavez, Denise. Artery of land. THE AMERICAS REVIEW, Vol. 15, no. 3-4 (Fall, Winter, 1987), p. 70. English.

5583 Chavez, Denise. Birth of me in my room at home. THE AMERICAS REVIEW, Vol. 15, no. 1 (Spring 1987), p. 56-58. English.

5584 Chavez, Denise. Chekov green love. THE AMERICAS REVIEW, Vol. 15, no. 3-4 (Fall, Winter, 1987), p. 79. English.

5585 Chavez, Denise. Cloud. THE AMERICAS REVIEW, Vol. 15, no. 3-4 (Fall, Winter, 1987), p. 69. English.

5586 Chavez, Denise. Cuckoo death crime. THE AMERICAS REVIEW, Vol. 15, no. 3-4 (Fall, Winter, 1987), p. 76-77. English.

5587 Chavez, Denise. Door. THE AMERICAS REVIEW, Vol. 15, no. 3-4 (Fall, Winter, 1987), p. 78. English.

5588 Chavez, Denise. Everything you are is teeth. THE AMERICAS REVIEW, Vol. 15, no. 3-4 (Fall, Winter, 1987), p. 75. English.

5589 Chavez, Denise. The feeling of going on. THE AMERICAS REVIEW, Vol. 15, no. 3-4 (Fall, Winter, 1987), p. 81. English.

5590 Chavez, Denise. For my sister in Paris. THE AMERICAS REVIEW, Vol. 15, no. 1 (Spring 1987), p. 59-61. English.

5591 Chavez, Denise. I am your Mary Magdalene. THE AMERICAS REVIEW, Vol. 15, no. 3-4 (Fall, Winter, 1987), p. 66. English.

5592 Chavez, Denise. Lagana of lace. THE AMERICAS REVIEW, Vol. 15, no. 1 (Spring 1987), p. 48-49. English.

5593 Chavez, Denise. Lagana of lace. JOURNAL OF ETHNIC STUDIES, Vol. 15, no. 1 (Spring 1987), p. 54-55. English.

5594 Chavez, Denise. Mercado day. THE AMERICAS REVIEW, Vol. 15, no. 1 (Spring 1987), p. 52-54. English.

5595 Chavez, Denise. Missss Rede. JOURNAL OF ETHNIC STUDIES, Vol. 15, no. 1 (Spring 1987), p. 64-67. English.

5596 Chavez, Denise. On mama Tona. JOURNAL OF ETHNIC STUDIES, Vol. 15, no. 1 (Spring 1987), p. 60-63. English.

5597 Chavez, Denise. [Our linkage...]. JOURNAL OF ETHNIC STUDIES, Vol. 15, no. 1 (Spring 1987), p. 51. English.

5598 Chavez, Denise. Progression from water to the absence. JOURNAL OF ETHNIC STUDIES, Vol. 15, no. 1 (Spring 1987), p. 52-53. English.

5599 Chavez, Denise. Purgatory is an ocean of flaming hearts. THE AMERICAS REVIEW, Vol. 15, no. 1 (Spring 1987), p. 55. English.

5600 Chavez, Denise. Saying "oh no". THE AMERICAS REVIEW, Vol. 15, no. 3-4 (Fall, Winter, 1987), p. 74. English.

5601 Chavez, Denise. Silver ingots of desire. THE AMERICAS REVIEW, Vol. 15, no. 3-4 (Fall, Winter, 1987), p. 71. English.

5602 Chavez, Denise. Sisters sisters sisters. JOURNAL OF ETHNIC STUDIES, Vol. 15, no. 1 (Spring 1987), p. 57-59. English.

5603 Chavez, Denise. The space between. JOURNAL OF ETHNIC STUDIES, Vol. 15, no. 1 (Spring 1987), p. 49. English.

5604 Chavez, Denise. Starflash. THE AMERICAS REVIEW, Vol. 15, no. 3-4 (Fall, Winter, 1987), p. 73. English.

5605 Chavez, Denise. The state of my inquietude. THE AMERICAS REVIEW, Vol. 15, no. 3-4 (Fall, Winter, 1987), p. 80. English.

Poems (cont.)

5606 Chavez, Denise. The study. THE AMERICAS REVIEW, Vol. 15, no. 3-4 (Fall, Winter, 1987), p. 72. English.

5607 Chavez, Denise. Tears. THE AMERICAS REVIEW, Vol. 15, no. 3-4 (Fall, Winter, 1987), p. 68. English.

5608 Chavez, Denise. [This river's praying place...]. JOURNAL OF ETHNIC STUDIES, Vol. 15, no. 1 (Spring 1987), p. 50. English.

5609 Chavez, Denise. This river's praying place. THE AMERICAS REVIEW, Vol. 15, no. 3-4 (Fall, Winter, 1987), p. 67. English.

5610 Chavez, Denise. This thin light. THE AMERICAS REVIEW, Vol. 15, no. 3-4 (Fall, Winter, 1987), p. 82. English.

5611 Chavez, Denise. [The train whistles...]. JOURNAL OF ETHNIC STUDIES, Vol. 15, no. 1 (Spring 1987), p. 48. English.

5612 Chavez, Denise. Two butterflies. THE AMERICAS REVIEW, Vol. 15, no. 3-4 (Fall, Winter, 1987), p. 83. English.

5613 Chavez, Denise. [Worm child...]. EL CUADERNO, Vol. 4, no. 1 (Summer 1976), p. 116. Spanish.

5614 Chavez, Denise. [Worm child...]. JOURNAL OF ETHNIC STUDIES, Vol. 15, no. 1 (Spring 1987), p. 56. English.

5615 Chavez, Denise. Ya. THE AMERICAS REVIEW, Vol. 15, no. 1 (Spring 1987), p. 50-51. Bilingual.

5616 Chavez, Eva. Perlas. REVISTA MUJERES, Vol. 2, no. 1 (January 1985), p. 36. English.

5617 Chavez, Maria Laura. El amor del creador. LLUEVE TLALOC, no. 6 (1979), p. 34. Spanish.

5618 Chema. Coraje-rabia. EL CUADERNO, Vol. 2, no. 1 (1972), p. 19. Spanish.

5619 Chema. No wall. EL CUADERNO, Vol. 2, no. 1 (1972), p. 26. English.

5620 Chema. Pajarito azul. EL CUADERNO, Vol. 2, no. 1 (1972), p. 26. Spanish.

5621 Chico, Elias. Orale pachuco! EL CUADERNO, Vol. 3, no. 2 (Spring 1974), p. 53. Spanish.

5622 Cirerol, Anna. Boxeador. LLUEVE TLALOC, no. 10 (1983), p. 35. Spanish.

5623 Cirerol, Anna. Primavera. LLUEVE TLALOC, no. 10 (1983), p. 39. Spanish.

5624 Cisek, Angela. Abajo la tierra. LLUEVE TLALOC, no. 13 (1986), p. 23. Spanish.

5625 Cisek, Angela. Un brindis al amor. LLUEVE TLALOC, no. 13 (1986), p. 16. Spanish.

5626 Cisek, Angela. Dias cuerdos. LLUEVE TLALOC, no. 13 (1986), p. 25. Spanish.

5627 Cisek, Angela. Una secuela de vida. LLUEVE TLALOC, no. 13 (1986), p. 30. Spanish.

5628 Cisneros, Sandra. Heartland. CHIRICU, Vol. 2, no. 1 (Spring 1980), p. 12-13. English.

5629 Cisneros, Sandra. The master. CHIRICU, Vol. 2, no. 1 (Spring 1980), p. 12. English.

5630 Cole, Maria Jose. The cage. LLUEVE TLALOC, no. 4 (1977), p. 30. English.

5631 Cole, Maria Jose. La jaula. LLUEVE TLALOC, no. 4 (1977), p. 29. Spanish.

5632 Cole, Maria Jose. Sangre espanola. LLUEVE TLALOC, no. 4 (1977), p. 40. Spanish.

5633 Cordova, Teresa. La mente. LLUEVE TLALOC, no. 4 (1977), p. 94. Spanish.

5634 Corpi, Lucha. Cancion de invierno. THE AMERICAS REVIEW, Vol. 15, no. 3-4 (Fall, Winter, 1987), p. 51. Spanish.

5635 Corpi, Lucha. Fuga. THE AMERICAS REVIEW, Vol. 15, no. 3-4 (Fall, Winter, 1987), p. 49-50. Spanish.

5636 Corpi, Lucha. Indocumentada angustia. THE AMERICAS REVIEW, Vol. 15, no. 3-4 (Fall, Winter, 1987), p. 52. Spanish.

5637 Corpi, Lucha. Invernario. THE AMERICAS REVIEW, Vol. 15, no. 3-4 (Fall, Winter, 1987), p. 47. Spanish.

5638 Corpi, Lucha. Llueve. THE AMERICAS REVIEW, Vol. 15, no. 3-4 (Fall, Winter, 1987), p. 55. Spanish.

5639 Corpi, Lucha. Recuerdo intimo. THE AMERICAS REVIEW, Vol. 15, no. 3-4 (Fall, Winter, 1987), p. 48. Spanish.

5640 Corpi, Lucha. Romance negro. THE AMERICAS REVIEW, Vol. 15, no. 3-4 (Fall, Winter, 1987), p. 45-46. Spanish.

5641 Corpi, Lucha. Sonata a dos voces. THE AMERICAS REVIEW, Vol. 15, no. 3-4 (Fall, Winter, 1987), p. 53-54. Spanish.

5642 Cota, Aide. Ahora y siempre. LLUEVE TLALOC, no. 5 (1978), p. 20. Spanish.

5643 Cota, Aide. El mar y tu. LLUEVE TLALOC, no. 5 (1978), p. 35. Spanish.

5644 Cota, Aide. Now and forever. LLUEVE TLALOC, no. 5 (1978), p. 20. English.

5645 Cota, Socorro. Confusion. LLUEVE TLALOC, no. 4 (1977), p. 96. Spanish.

5646 Cota-Cardenas, Margarita. A una madre de nuestros tiempos. REVISTA MUJERES, Vol. 1, no. 2 (June 1984), p. 6-7. Spanish.

5647 Cuando bese tu mano. LLUEVE TLALOC, no. 3 (1976), p. 42. Spanish.

5648 Dagnind, Dora. Grande. LLUEVE TLALOC, no. 10 (1983), p. 13. Spanish.

5649 Dagnind, Dora. El mar. LLUEVE TLALOC, no. 7 (1980), p. 27. Spanish.

5650 Dagnind, Dora. Mi flor azul. LLUEVE TLALOC, no. 10 (1983), p. 37. Spanish.

5651 Davila, Elisa. A una madre de mayo. REVISTA MUJERES, Vol. 1, no. 1 (January 1984), p. 21-22. Spanish.

5652 Davila, Elisa. Cuatro poemas del "nuevo ciclo del caballo". REVISTA MUJERES, Vol. 4, no. 1 (January 1987), p. 4-6. Spanish.

Poems (cont.)

5653 Davila, Elisa and Ellis, Miriam, trans. Four poems of the "new cycle of the horse". REVISTA MUJERES, Vol. 4, no. 1 (January 1987), p. 7-9. English.

5654 Davila, Elisa. A manera de introduccion: cuando las mujeres escribimos...=By way of introduction: when we women write... REVISTA MUJERES, Vol. 1, no. 2 (June 1984), p. 2-5. Bilingual. **DESCR:** *REVISTA MUJERES, University of California, Santa Cruz.

5655 Davila, Elisa. Operacion aguila/contras. REVISTA MUJERES, Vol. 1, no. 2 (June 1984), p. 24. Spanish.

5656 Davila, Elisa. Operation eagle/contras. REVISTA MUJERES, Vol. 1, no. 2 (June 1984), p. 29. English.

5657 Davila, Elisa. Palabra de mujer. REVISTA MUJERES, Vol. 2, no. 1 (January 1985), p. 4. Spanish.

5658 Davila, Elisa. Soledad USA. TINTA, Vol. 1, no. 3 (December 1983), p. 61-62. Spanish.

5659 Davila, Elisa and Ellis, Miriam, trans. To a mother of May. REVISTA MUJERES, Vol. 1, no. 1 (January 1984), p. 23-24. English.

5660 Davila, Elisa and Ellis, Miriam, trans. A woman's word. REVISTA MUJERES, Vol. 2, no. 1 (January 1985), p. 5. English.

5661 de Hoyos, Angela. Un llanto en seco. SAGUARO, Vol. 1, no. 1 (1984), p. 48. Spanish.

5662 de Hoyos, Angela. Poemanaya: 3 voces. CONFLUENCIA, Vol. 1, no. 2 (Spring 1986), p. 127. Spanish.

5663 de Hoyos, Angela. Tonantzin morena. SAGUARO, Vol. 1, no. 1 (1984), p. 47. Bilingual.

5664 de Martinez, Leonor E. Mi corazon te llora. LLUEVE TLALOC, no. 6 (1979), p. 30. Spanish.

5665 de Martinez, Leonor E. Mi madre. LLUEVE TLALOC, no. 6 (1979), p. 30. Spanish.

5666 de Martinez, Leonor E. Quien soy? LLUEVE TLALOC, no. 6 (1979), p. 38. Spanish.

5667 Delgado, Abelardo "Lalo". Los desraizados. EL CUADERNO, Vol. 3, no. 2 (Spring 1974), p. 17. Spanish.

5668 Delgado, Abelardo "Lalo". From Colorado Springs to Denver. SAGUARO, Vol. 4, (1987), p. 77-78. English.

5669 Di Ioli, Barbara. Al honorable. LLUEVE TLALOC, no. 14 (1987), p. 17. Spanish.

5670 Di Ioli, Barbara. Espiritu libre. LLUEVE TLALOC, no. 14 (1987), p. 15. Spanish.

5671 Di Ioli, Barbara. Just musing. LLUEVE TLALOC, no. 14 (1987), p. 18-19. English.

5672 Di Ioli, Barbara. La palabra amor. LLUEVE TLALOC, no. 14 (1987), p. 14. Spanish.

5673 Di Ioli, Barbara. Por la ventana del cielo. LLUEVE TLALOC, no. 14 (1987), p. 16. Spanish.

5674 Di Ioli, Barbara. Quiero ser. LLUEVE TLALOC, no. 14 (1987), p. 14. Spanish.

5675 Di Ioli, Barbara. El valor de una sonrisa. LLUEVE TLALOC, no. 14 (1987), p. 16. Spanish.

5676 Di Ioli, Barbara. What's in the hutch, Dutch? LLUEVE TLALOC, no. 14 (1987), p. 17-18. English.

5677 Diego M. Ser humano. LLUEVE TLALOC, no. 2 (1975), p. 45. Spanish.

5678 Dominguez, Alejo H. Miseria. LLUEVE TLALOC, no. 1 (1974), p. 13. Spanish.

5679 Dominguez, Alejo H. Misery. LLUEVE TLALOC, no. 1 (1974), p. 14. English.

5680 Dominguez, Jose M. A las dos semanas. TINTA, Vol. 1, no. 3 (December 1983), p. 63. Spanish.

5681 Draper, Bobsy. Rosita, born and buried in Montepeque, El Salvador. REVISTA MUJERES, Vol. 3, no. 2 (June 1986), p. 50-51. English.

5682 Duarte, Laurie. Para ser un nino otra vez. LLUEVE TLALOC, no. 12 (1985), p. 16. Spanish.

5683 Dunaca, Sandra Teresa. A nativitate. CHIRICU, Vol. 2, no. 2 (1981), p. 37. Spanish.

5684 Duran, Eddie. [Untitled poem]. EL CUADERNO, Vol. 1, no. 1 (1971), p. 9. English.

5685 Duran, Eddie. [Untitled poem]. EL CUADERNO, Vol. 1, no. 1 (1971), p. 10. English.

5686 Durand, Jose. El tiempo pasa. LLUEVE TLALOC, no. 13 (1986), p. 27. Spanish.

5687 Durand, Jose. La vida. LLUEVE TLALOC, no. 13 (1986), p. 27. Spanish.

5688 Edmonds, Gilberto. Los tiranos. EL CUADERNO, Vol. 3, no. 2 (Spring 1974), p. 27. Spanish.

5689 Eloisa. Que es un hijo? LLUEVE TLALOC, no. 12 (1985), p. 18. Spanish.

5690 Enguidanos, Miguel. Miles de veces canto el gallo. CHIRICU, no. 1 (Spring 1976), p. 3. Spanish.

5691 Enguidanos, Miguel. Tomas. CHIRICU, no. 1 (Spring 1976), p. 2. Spanish.

5692 Eroticus poetica. LLUEVE TLALOC, no. 9 (1982), p. 33. Spanish.

5693 Esperanza, Tino. Corazon, the subject is mujeres. REVISTA MUJERES, Vol. 1, no. 1 (January 1984), p. 18-19. English.

5694 Espinosa, Maria. Recuerdos. LLUEVE TLALOC, no. 3 (1976), p. 30. Spanish.

5695 Esquer, Frank E. Montana. LLUEVE TLALOC, no. 1 (1974), p. 37. English.

5696 Estrada, Javier. Todo es para todos. LLUEVE TLALOC, no. 13 (1986), p. 23. Spanish.

5697 Estrada, Larry. La pena que tengo. SAGUARO, Vol. 1, no. 1 (1984), p. 62-64. Spanish.

5698 Estrada, Rosalio S. Busco. LLUEVE TLALOC, no. 4 (1977), p. 59. Spanish.

5699 Estrada, Rosalio S. Desde al cabo al fin. LLUEVE TLALOC, no. 3 (1976), p. 34. Spanish.

Poems (cont.)

5700 Facto, Robert. Moment at sundown. TINTA, Vol. 1, no. 3 (December 1983), p. 65. English.

5701 Gallardo, Hortencia Aguilar. La cita. LLUEVE TLALOC, no. 5 (1978), p. 16. Spanish.

5702 Gallardo, Hortencia Aguilar. Conversacion por telefono. LLUEVE TLALOC, no. 5 (1978), p. 22. Spanish.

5703 Gallardo, Hortencia Aguilar. Eminente caminar. LLUEVE TLALOC, no. 5 (1978), p. 22. Spanish.

5704 Gallardo, Hortencia Aguilar. Para mi triste padre. LLUEVE TLALOC, no. 3 (1976), p. 36. Spanish.

5705 Gallardo, Hortencia Aguilar. Suspiro del alma. LLUEVE TLALOC, no. 5 (1978), p. 22. Spanish.

5706 Garcia R., Roberto. Oda a Cucamonga. BILINGUAL REVIEW, Vol. 11, no. 3 (September, December, 1984), p. 47-48. Spanish. **DESCR:** Braceros; Farm Workers.

5707 Garcia, Raquelle. Brisa. LLUEVE TLALOC, no. 11 (1984), p. 27. Spanish.

5708 Garcia, Raquelle. Creo. LLUEVE TLALOC, no. 11 (1984), p. 24. Spanish.

5709 Garcia, Raquelle. Esa tarde. LLUEVE TLALOC, no. 10 (1983), p. 31. Spanish.

5710 Garcia, Raquelle. Gracias. LLUEVE TLALOC, no. 10 (1983), p. 36. Spanish.

5711 Garcia, Raquelle. Mar. LLUEVE TLALOC, no. 11 (1984), p. 21. Spanish.

5712 Garcia, Raquelle. Sola. LLUEVE TLALOC, no. 11 (1984), p. 27. Spanish.

5713 Godoy, Irma. Cuanto te quiero. LLUEVE TLALOC, no. 11 (1984), p. 14. Spanish.

5714 Godoy, Irma. Gracias senor. LLUEVE TLALOC, no. 11 (1984), p. 14. Spanish.

5715 Gomez, Mercedes. Llanto y lluvia. LLUEVE TLALOC, no. 1 (1974), p. 43. Spanish.

5716 Gonzalez, Angel. Entreacto. EL CUADERNO, Vol. 4, no. 1 (Summer 1976), p. 26-27. Spanish.

5717 Gonzalez, Angel. Final conocido. EL CUADERNO, Vol. 4, no. 1 (Summer 1976), p. 29. Spanish.

5718 Gonzalez, Angel. Para que yo me llame Angel Gonzalez. EL CUADERNO, Vol. 4, no. 1 (Summer 1976), p. 25. Spanish.

5719 Gonzalez, Cristina. Aurora IX. CHIRICU, no. 2 (Spring 1977), p. 23. Spanish.

5720 Gonzalez, Cristina. Aurora X. CHIRICU, no. 2 (Spring 1977), p. 23. Spanish.

5721 Gonzalez, Cristina. [El destierro...]. CHIRICU, no. 2 (Spring 1977), p. 22. Spanish.

5722 Gonzalez, Cristina. [Rasgueos...]. CHIRICU, no. 2 (Spring 1977), p. 22. Spanish.

5723 Gonzalez, Gerson. Desierto de sonora. LLUEVE TLALOC, no. 1 (1974), p. 33. Spanish.

5724 Gonzalez, Gerson. Lluvia. LLUEVE TLALOC, no. 1 (1974), p. 31. Spanish.

5725 Gonzalez, Gerson. Rain. LLUEVE TLALOC, no. 1 (1974), p. 32. English.

5726 Gonzalez, Gerson. Sonora desert. LLUEVE TLALOC, no. 1 (1974), p. 34. English.

5727 Gonzalez, Maria. Cavando. TINTA, Vol. 1, no. 2 (May 1983), p. 44. Spanish.

5728 Gonzalez, Ray. After reading the death poems. THE AMERICAS REVIEW, Vol. 15, no. 1 (Spring 1987), p. 44. English.

5729 Gonzalez, Ray. Letter to Thomas McGrath. THE AMERICAS REVIEW, Vol. 15, no. 1 (Spring 1987), p. 47. English.

5730 Gonzalez, Ray. One day. THE AMERICAS REVIEW, Vol. 15, no. 1 (Spring 1987), p. 43. English.

5731 Gonzalez, Ray. A simple summer rain. THE AMERICAS REVIEW, Vol. 15, no. 1 (Spring 1987), p. 42. English.

5732 Gonzalez, Ray. Two wolf poems. THE AMERICAS REVIEW, Vol. 15, no. 1 (Spring 1987), p. 45-46. English.

5733 Gonzalez, Ray. Walk. THE AMERICAS REVIEW, Vol. 15, no. 1 (Spring 1987), p. 41. English.

5734 Gonzalez, Sylvia. Government grey. EL CUADERNO, Vol. 2, no. 1 (1972), p. 39. English.

5735 Gonzalez, Taurino. Poema a la memoria de Crista McAuliffe. JOURNAL OF THE ASSOCIATION OF MEXICAN AMERICAN EDUCATORS, (1986, 1987), p. 51. English.

5736 Granado, Virginia. [There's this man...]. EL CUADERNO, Vol. 3, no. 2 (Spring 1974), p. 68. English.

5737 Griffin, Mina. Amor. LLUEVE TLALOC, no. 12 (1985), p. 18. Spanish.

5738 Griffin, Mina. Amor. LLUEVE TLALOC, no. 12 (1985), p. 35. Spanish.

5739 Griffin, Mina and Griffin, Richard. Cuando pienso en ti. LLUEVE TLALOC, no. 12 (1985), p. 16. Spanish.

5740 Griffin, Mina. Dos locos de amor. LLUEVE TLALOC, no. 12 (1985), p. 15. Spanish.

5741 Griffin, Mina. Esta noche. LLUEVE TLALOC, no. 12 (1985), p. 19. Spanish.

5742 Griffin, Mina. Gracias. LLUEVE TLALOC, no. 12 (1985), p. 19. Spanish.

5743 Griffin, Mina. Mi viejo. LLUEVE TLALOC, no. 11 (1984), p. 30. Spanish.

5744 Griffin, Mina. No le escuches. LLUEVE TLALOC, no. 12 (1985), p. 18. Spanish.

5745 Griffin, Mina. No me digas adios. LLUEVE TLALOC, no. 12 (1985), p. 19. Spanish.

5746 Griffin, Mina. Significas tanto para mi. LLUEVE TLALOC, no. 12 (1985), p. 37. Spanish.

Poems (cont.)

5747 Griffin, Mina. Soledad. LLUEVE TLALOC, no. 11 (1984), p. 16. Spanish.

5748 Griffin, Mina. Te amo. LLUEVE TLALOC, no. 11 (1984), p. 26. Spanish.

5749 Griffin, Mina. Tu y yo. LLUEVE TLALOC, no. 12 (1985), p. 19. Spanish.

5750 Griffin, Mina. Wasting time. LLUEVE TLALOC, no. 12 (1985), p. 42. English.

5751 Griffin, Mina. You mean so much to me. LLUEVE TLALOC, no. 12 (1985), p. 35. English.

5752 Guerrero Bubala, Julie. A mi esposo. LLUEVE TLALOC, no. 13 (1986), p. 23. Spanish.

5753 Guerrero Bubala, Julie. El amor. LLUEVE TLALOC, no. 13 (1986), p. 23. Spanish.

5754 Guifarro, Josefa. Los dos gigantes. TINTA, Vol. 1, no. 2 (May 1983), p. 44. Spanish.

5755 Guifarro, Josefa. Noche negra. TINTA, Vol. 1, no. 2 (May 1983), p. 44. Spanish.

5756 H.-Aigla, Jorge. The maelstrom. THE AMERICAS REVIEW, Vol. 15, no. 2 (Summer 1987), p. 74. English.

5757 H.-Aigla, Jorge. Mi mama Cecilia. THE AMERICAS REVIEW, Vol. 15, no. 2 (Summer 1987), p. 76. Spanish.

5758 H.-Aigla, Jorge. The power of the word. THE AMERICAS REVIEW, Vol. 15, no. 2 (Summer 1987), p. 75. English.

5759 Haley, Carmen Emilia. El camino. LLUEVE TLALOC, no. 1 (1974), p. 38. Spanish.

5760 Hernandez, Alma. Amiga. LLUEVE TLALOC, no. 12 (1985), p. 42. Spanish.

5761 Hernandez, Alma. Amor mio. LLUEVE TLALOC, no. 12 (1985), p. 31. Spanish.

5762 Hernandez, Alma. Madre mia. LLUEVE TLALOC, no. 11 (1984), p. 36. Spanish.

5763 Hernandez, Alma. Un sueno nomas. LLUEVE TLALOC, no. 11 (1984), p. 26. Spanish.

5764 Hernandez, Angel. [Acaso estaras algun dia conmigo...]. LLUEVE TLALOC, no. 1 (1974), p. 44. English.

5765 Hernandez, Angel. Paredes de pima. LLUEVE TLALOC, no. 1 (1974), p. 3. Spanish.

5766 Hernandez, Jesus. Que es un hijo? LLUEVE TLALOC, no. 12 (1985), p. 18. Spanish.

5767 Hernandez, Robert G. Emerald eyes. NOTEBOOK: A LITTLE MAGAZINE, Vol. 2, no. 2 (1986), p. 42. English.

5768 Herrera, Frank. Infinito anhelo. LLUEVE TLALOC, no. 2 (1975), p. 8. Spanish.

5769 Hidalgo de la Riva, Teresa "Osa". Friday the thirteenth 1980. REVISTA MUJERES, Vol. 1, no. 2 (June 1984), p. 30. English.

5770 Hidalgo de la Riva, Teresa "Osa". Grandmother's will. REVISTA MUJERES, Vol. 1, no. 2 (June 1984), p. 30-31. English.

5771 Huez, Lupe. Se aleja. LLUEVE TLALOC, no. 4 (1977), p. 41. Spanish.

5772 Huez, Lupe. Soledad en compania. LLUEVE TLALOC, no. 4 (1977), p. 38. Spanish.

5773 Huici, Alvaro. Cantando a las cosas sin cauce. CHIRICU, no. 2 (Spring 1977), p. 33. Spanish.

5774 Huici, Alvaro. II [Y resulto que no eras un perro ingrato...]. CHIRICU, no. 2 (Spring 1977), p. 30. Spanish.

5775 Huici, Alvaro. III [Cuando las tardes en que la habitacion...]. CHIRICU, no. 2 (Spring 1977), p. 31. Spanish.

5776 Huici, Alvaro. V [Es aquel llanto que casi llega...]. CHIRICU, no. 2 (Spring 1977), p. 32. Spanish.

5777 Hurtado, Aida. Feb. 24, Denver Aztlan. REVISTA MUJERES, Vol. 3, no. 1 (January 1986), p. 41. English.

5778 Hurtado, Aida. Mi padre el filosofo. REVISTA MUJERES, Vol. 3, no. 1 (January 1986), p. 22. Spanish.

5779 Isabel, Maria. Podador de algas. LLUEVE TLALOC, no. 8 (1981), p. 31. Spanish.

5780 JRST. Nos mudamos al centro. REVISTA MUJERES, Vol. 1, no. 2 (June 1984), p. 16-17. Spanish.

5781 Kelzer, Pauline. La huerfana. LLUEVE TLALOC, no. 1 (1974), p. 35. Spanish.

5782 Lamadrid, Enrique R. El agua del aire. EL CUADERNO, Vol. 4, no. 1 (Summer 1976), p. 64-65. English.

5783 Lares Gaytan, Rosa Armida. Amistad (tu y yo). LLUEVE TLALOC, no. 6 (1979), p. 16. Spanish.

5784 Lares Gaytan, Rosa Armida. Amor. LLUEVE TLALOC, no. 6 (1979), p. 16. Spanish.

5785 Lares Gaytan, Rosa Armida. El dolor pensativo. LLUEVE TLALOC, no. 6 (1979), p. 26. Spanish.

5786 Lares Gaytan, Rosa Armida. Mi pensamiento. LLUEVE TLALOC, no. 6 (1979), p. 16. Spanish.

5787 Lau, Roger. Aurora. LLUEVE TLALOC, no. 11 (1984), p. 36. Spanish.

5788 Lau, Roger. En busca de un rey. LLUEVE TLALOC, no. 10 (1983), p. 30. Spanish.

5789 Lau, Roger. Estrella. LLUEVE TLALOC, no. 10 (1983), p. 8. Spanish.

5790 Lau, Roger. Indiferente. LLUEVE TLALOC, no. 10 (1983), p. 35. Spanish.

5791 Lau, Roger. Melinda. LLUEVE TLALOC, no. 10 (1983), p. 31. Spanish.

5792 Lau, Roger. Murmullo. LLUEVE TLALOC, no. 10 (1983), p. 9. Spanish.

5793 Lau, Roger. Valores. LLUEVE TLALOC, no. 10 (1983), p. 40. Spanish.

5794 Laviera, Tato. Bochinche bilingue. THE AMERICAS REVIEW, Vol. 15, no. 1 (Spring 1987), p. 67. Spanish.

Poems (cont.)

5795 Laviera, Tato. Latero story. THE AMERICAS
REVIEW, Vol. 15, no. 1 (Spring 1987), p.
62-63. English.

5796 Laviera, Tato. Melao. THE AMERICAS REVIEW,
Vol. 15, no. 1 (Spring 1987), p. 66.
English.

5797 Laviera, Tato. Viejo. THE AMERICAS REVIEW,
Vol. 15, no. 1 (Spring 1987), p. 64-65.
English.

5798 Lerma, Martin. Lluvia. LLUEVE TLALOC, no. 14
(1987), p. 59. Spanish.

5799 Lerma, Martin. Puro. LLUEVE TLALOC, no. 14
(1987), p. 59. Spanish.

5800 Lerma, Martin. La vida. LLUEVE TLALOC, no.
14 (1987), p. 59. Spanish.

5801 Lerma, Martin. Vive. LLUEVE TLALOC, no. 14
(1987), p. 59. Spanish.

5802 Leyva Corrales, Rosa. Boundless. LLUEVE
TLALOC, no. 11 (1984), p. 16. English.

5803 Leyva Corrales, Rosa. Conceptual. LLUEVE
TLALOC, no. 11 (1984), p. 16. English.

5804 Leyva Corrales, Rosa. Eros of four. LLUEVE
TLALOC, no. 11 (1984), p. 16. English.

5805 Limon, Mercedes. Llegas. CHIRICU, Vol. 3,
no. 2 (1983), p. 75. Spanish.

5806 Limon, Mercedes. Mentira. CHIRICU, Vol. 3,
no. 2 (1983), p. 76-77. Spanish.

5807 Lizarraga, Patricia. Dios. LLUEVE TLALOC,
no. 11 (1984), p. 24. Spanish.

5808 Lizarraga, Patricia. Mi triste nina. LLUEVE
TLALOC, no. 10 (1983), p. 9. Spanish.

5809 Lizarraga, Patricia. Primer beso de amor.
LLUEVE TLALOC, no. 11 (1984), p. 24.
Spanish.

5810 Lizarraga, Patricia. Sublime amor. LLUEVE
TLALOC, no. 11 (1984), p. 16. Spanish.

5811 Llamas, Genevieve. Mi querido amante. LLUEVE
TLALOC, no. 12 (1985), p. 15. Spanish.

5812 Logan, Roy. Un par. LLUEVE TLALOC, no. 2
(1975), p. 48-50. Spanish.

5813 Lomeli, Maria Magdalena S. Ever so
peacefully. LLUEVE TLALOC, no. 7 (1980), p.
32. English.

5814 Lopez, Alma. Amor. LLUEVE TLALOC, no. 6
(1979), p. 30. Spanish.

5815 Lopez, Alma. Carino. LLUEVE TLALOC, no. 7
(1980), p. 33. Spanish.

5816 Lopez, Alma. Tu. LLUEVE TLALOC, no. 7
(1980), p. 38. Spanish.

5817 Lopez Flores, Margarita. Untitled. CHIRICU,
Vol. 2, no. 1 (Spring 1980), p. 34. English.

5818 Lopez Flores, Margarita. Your light.
CHIRICU, Vol. 2, no. 1 (Spring 1980), p. 35.
English.

5819 Lopez, Maria. Debajo de una hoja. LLUEVE
TLALOC, no. 9 (1982), p. 19. Spanish.

5820 Lopez, Maria. Recuerdo... LLUEVE TLALOC, no.

8 (1981), p. 16. Spanish.

5821 Lopez, Raymundo. Por que le dicen la
marrana. LLUEVE TLALOC, no. 3 (1976), p.
44-45. Spanish.

5822 Lovato, Alberto. Agusa'o con la vida porque
no retona. EL CUADERNO, Vol. 3, no. 1
(Winter 1973), p. 50. Spanish.

5823 Lovato, Alberto. Ode to Wells Fargo. EL
CUADERNO, Vol. 2, no. 1 (1972), p. 13.
Bilingual.

5824 Loya, Elena. A ti. LLUEVE TLALOC, no. 11
(1984), p. 16. Spanish.

5825 Loya, Elena. Madre. LLUEVE TLALOC, no. 12
(1985), p. 34. Spanish.

5826 Loya, Elena. Por que te quiero. LLUEVE
TLALOC, no. 12 (1985), p. 19. Spanish.

5827 Loya, Elena. Ser. LLUEVE TLALOC, no. 11
(1984), p. 26. Spanish.

5828 Loya, Elena. Silencio. LLUEVE TLALOC, no. 12
(1985), p. 32. Spanish.

5829 Lucero, Rubel Jose. En memoria de un coyote.
EL CUADERNO, Vol. 3, no. 1 (Winter 1973), p.
3. Spanish.

5830 Luera, Yolanda. Las comadres. SAGUARO, Vol.
3, (1986), p. 57-58. Spanish.

5831 Luera, Yolanda. Martin. SAGUARO, Vol. 3,
(1986), p. 16. Spanish.

5832 Lujan, Frank. Aventuras de la seccion. EL
CUADERNO, Vol. 3, no. 1 (Winter 1973), p.
34. Spanish.

5833 Lujan, Frank. Plegaria: a Santa Maria Virgen
de Guadalupe. EL CUADERNO, Vol. 3, no. 1
(Winter 1973), p. 33. Spanish.

5834 Lynn, Donna. Of songs unsung. LLUEVE TLALOC,
no. 8 (1981), p. 22. English.

5835 Mancias, Ossie. The brown eyed son=El hijo
de ojos cafe. AMERICAS 2001, Vol. 1, no. 3
(November, December, 1987), p. In BkCover.
Bilingual.

5836 Mares, E.A. [Bajo la luna llena...]. EL
CUADERNO, Vol. 4, no. 1 (Summer 1976), p.
62. Spanish.

5837 Mares, E.A. Chasing the bogeyman in Tres
Pistolas Canyon. EL CUADERNO, Vol. 2, no. 1
(1972), p. 24. English.

5838 Mares, E.A. Homenaje a Antonio Machado. EL
CUADERNO, Vol. 4, no. 1 (Summer 1976), p.
30. Spanish. **DESCR:** *Machado, Antonio.

5839 Mares, E.A. A napkin poem. EL CUADERNO, Vol.
3, no. 2 (Spring 1974), p. 17. English.

5840 Mares, E.A. Question. EL CUADERNO, Vol. 2,
no. 1 (1972), p. 25. English.

5841 Mares, E.A. Sobre una foto de tres chicanas.
EL CUADERNO, Vol. 3, no. 2 (Spring 1974), p.
18. Spanish.

5842 Mares, E.A. Some reflections in the desert.
EL CUADERNO, Vol. 2, no. 1 (1972), p. 25.
English.

5843 Marquez Off, Maria. Vigil. EL CUADERNO, Vol.
3, no. 1 (Winter 1973), p. 61. English.

Poems (cont.)

5844 Marroquin de Hernandez, Celina. Resultates mujer. SAGUARO, Vol. 4, (1987), p. 37-38. Spanish.

5845 Martinez, Angelina S. For the memories. LLUEVE TLALOC, no. 8 (1981), p. 31. English.

5846 Martinez, Carmen. Madre. REVISTA MUJERES, Vol. 2, no. 2 (June 1985), p. 13-14. Spanish.

5847 Martinez, Carmen. Un mensaje de El Salvador. REVISTA MUJERES, Vol. 2, no. 2 (June 1985), p. 13. Spanish. **DESCR:** #El Salvador.

5848 Martinez, Carmen and Ellis, Miriam, trans. Mother. REVISTA MUJERES, Vol. 2, no. 2 (June 1985), p. 15-16. English.

5849 Martinez, Daniel C. Field gossip. BILINGUAL REVIEW, Vol. 11, no. 3 (September, December, 1984), p. 65. English.

5850 Martinez, Daniel C. La gran puta. BILINGUAL REVIEW, Vol. 11, no. 3 (September, December, 1984), p. 65-66. Spanish.

5851 Martinez, Daniel C. The lost dance. BILINGUAL REVIEW, Vol. 11, no. 3 (September, December, 1984), p. 61. English.

5852 Martinez, Daniel C. El menudero. BILINGUAL REVIEW, Vol. 11, no. 3 (September, December, 1984), p. 66. Spanish.

5853 Martinez, Daniel C. Mi perro agringado. BILINGUAL REVIEW, Vol. 11, no. 3 (September, December, 1984), p. 67-68. Spanish.

5854 Martinez, Daniel C. Polvos de Laredo. BILINGUAL REVIEW, Vol. 11, no. 3 (September, December, 1984), p. 61-64. Spanish.

5855 Martinez, Daniel C. Sentado pensando en la filosofia. BILINGUAL REVIEW, Vol. 11, no. 3 (September, December, 1984), p. 67. Spanish.

5856 Martinez, Daniel C. El viejo original. BILINGUAL REVIEW, Vol. 11, no. 3 (September, December, 1984), p. 64. Spanish.

5857 Martinez, Joe. La flor. LLUEVE TLALOC, no. 1 (1974), p. 36. Spanish.

5858 Martinez, Noemi. [Time will tell you when to start...]. REVISTA MUJERES, Vol. 3, no. 1 (January 1986), p. 56. English.

5859 Martinez, Ramon E. Cantinflas puppet. BILINGUAL REVIEW, Vol. 12, no. 1-2 (January, August, 1985), p. 119. English.

5860 Martinez, Ramon E. The emperor of helados. BILINGUAL REVIEW, Vol. 12, no. 1-2 (January, August, 1985), p. 118-119. English.

5861 Means-Ybarra, Ricardo. After the divorce. REVISTA MUJERES, Vol. 4, no. 1 (January 1987), p. 42. English.

5862 Means-Ybarra, Ricardo. East L.A. REVISTA MUJERES, Vol. 4, no. 1 (January 1987), p. 41. English.

5863 Means-Ybarra, Ricardo. A poem to be read before morning. REVISTA MUJERES, Vol. 4, no. 1 (January 1987), p. 43. English.

5864 Medina, Carlos. Que piensa el nino. LLUEVE TLALOC, no. 1 (1974), p. 8. Spanish.

5865 Medina Garcia, Jesus. Las montanas de Tucson. LLUEVE TLALOC, no. 5 (1978), p. 10. Spanish.

5866 Medrano, Lourdes. El amor. LLUEVE TLALOC, no. 10 (1983), p. 39. Spanish.

5867 Medrano, Lourdes. Recuerdos. LLUEVE TLALOC, no. 10 (1983), p. 8. Spanish.

5868 Melendez, Moises F. Amor sincero. LLUEVE TLALOC, no. 4 (1977), p. 65. Spanish.

5869 Mendez Aldecoa, Sarita. Caminante. LLUEVE TLALOC, no. 7 (1980), p. 17. Spanish.

5870 Mendez-M., Miguel. Anoranza. LLUEVE TLALOC, no. 3 (1976), p. 10-14. Spanish.

5871 Mendez-M., Miguel. Arizona. LLUEVE TLALOC, no. 2 (1975), p. 26-27. Spanish.

5872 Mendez-M., Miguel. Arizona. LLUEVE TLALOC, no. 2 (1975), p. 28-29. English.

5873 Mendez-M., Miguel. En torno a la poesia. LLUEVE TLALOC, no. 4 (1977), p. 1-17. Spanish.

5874 Mendez-M., Miguel. Genesis de la palabra. LLUEVE TLALOC, no. 5 (1978), p. 1-5. Spanish.

5875 Mendez-M., Miguel; Barrow, Leo (trans.); and Bolano, Luis (trans.). Genesis of the word. LLUEVE TLALOC, no. 5 (1978), p. 1-5. English.

5876 Mendez-M., Miguel and Price, Eva, trans. Imaginary workshop, enter. LLUEVE TLALOC, no. 6 (1979), p. 1-9. English.

5877 Mendez-M., Miguel and Bruce-Novoa, Juan. In search of poverty. LLUEVE TLALOC, no. 4 (1977), p. 2-18. English.

5878 Mendez-M., Miguel. Luna. LLUEVE TLALOC, no. 10 (1983), p. 18. Spanish.

5879 Mendez-M., Miguel and Price, Eva, trans. Moon. LLUEVE TLALOC, no. 10 (1983), p. 19. English.

5880 Mendez-M., Miguel and Nigro, Kristen, trans. Nostalgia. LLUEVE TLALOC, no. 3 (1976), p. 11-15. English.

5881 Mendez-M., Miguel. El rio y el poeta. LLUEVE TLALOC, no. 10 (1983), p. 12. Spanish.

5882 Mendez-M., Miguel. El rio y la vida. LLUEVE TLALOC, no. 8 (1981), p. 16. Spanish.

5883 Mendez-M., Miguel and Price, Eva, trans. The river and the poet. LLUEVE TLALOC, no. 10 (1983), p. 12. English.

5884 Mendez-M., Miguel and Price, Eva, trans. The river of life. LLUEVE TLALOC, no. 8 (1981), p. 16. English.

5885 Mendez-M., Miguel. Sahuaros. LLUEVE TLALOC, no. 7 (1980), p. 1-8. Bilingual.

5886 Mendez-M., Miguel. Sonora de mis amores. LLUEVE TLALOC, no. 13 (1986), p. 3-4. Spanish.

5887 Mendez-M., Miguel. Taller de imagenes pase. LLUEVE TLALOC, no. 6 (1979), p. 1-9. Spanish.

Poems (cont.)

5888 Mendez-Negrete, Josie. Daily struggle. REVISTA MUJERES, Vol. 2, no. 1 (January 1985), p. 6. English.

5889 Michel. Infinito. LLUEVE TLALOC, no. 9 (1982), p. 8. Spanish.

5890 Miguelez, Armando. En la plaza hay fiesta. SAGUARO, Vol. 1, no. 1 (1984), p. 54-57. Spanish.

5891 Miguelez, Armando. Nino muerto. SAGUARO, Vol. 1, no. 1 (1984), p. 53. Spanish.

5892 Miguelez, Armando. Viaje. SAGUARO, Vol. 1, no. 1 (1984), p. 58-59. Spanish.

5893 Miranda, Victoria. Sebastian del bio bio. REVISTA MUJERES, Vol. 4, no. 1 (January 1987), p. 57-59. Spanish.

5894 Mireles, Oscar. The family of doctors. REVISTA MUJERES, Vol. 3, no. 2 (June 1986), p. 67. English.

5895 Molina, Maria J. Dime. LLUEVE TLALOC, no. 14 (1987), p. 31-32. Spanish.

5896 Molina, Maria J. Madrecita linda. LLUEVE TLALOC, no. 14 (1987), p. 30. Spanish.

5897 Molina, Maria J. Pidiendo milagro. LLUEVE TLALOC, no. 14 (1987), p. 31. Spanish.

5898 Molina, Maria J. Vida. LLUEVE TLALOC, no. 14 (1987), p. 30-31. Spanish.

5899 Mondragon, Maria. On life. EL CUADERNO, Vol. 1, no. 1 (1971), p. 13. English.

5900 Mondragon, Maria. Psalm to the rib of man. EL CUADERNO, Vol. 1, no. 1 (1971), p. 22. English.

5901 Mondragon, Maria. Resurreccion. EL CUADERNO, Vol. 1, no. 1 (1971), p. 14. English.

5902 Mora, Pat. Diagnosis. NUESTRO, Vol. 11, no. 2 (March 1987), p. 27. English.

5903 Mora, Pat. Goblin. NUESTRO, Vol. 11, no. 2 (March 1987), p. 27. English.

5904 Mora, Pat. Home. NUESTRO, Vol. 11, no. 2 (March 1987), p. 27. English.

5905 Mora, Pat. Mothering me. NUESTRO, Vol. 11, no. 2 (March 1987), p. 27. English.

5906 Mora, Pat. My mask. NUESTRO, Vol. 11, no. 2 (March 1987), p. 27. English.

5907 Mora, Pat. Sonrisas. NUESTRO, Vol. 11, no. 2 (March 1987), p. 27. English.

5908 Mora, Pat. Tomas Rivera. NUESTRO, Vol. 11, no. 2 (March 1987), p. 27. English. **DESCR:** *Rivera, Tomas.

5909 Morones, Carmen. Periquita. REVISTA MUJERES, Vol. 4, no. 1 (January 1987), p. 50-52. English.

5910 Mungaray, Josefina C. Fruta prohibida. LLUEVE TLALOC, no. 5 (1978), p. 30. Spanish.

5911 Mungaray, Josefina C. Gracias. LLUEVE TLALOC, no. 11 (1984), p. 33. Spanish.

5912 Mungaray, Josefina C. Gracias...Senor. LLUEVE TLALOC, no. 5 (1978), p. 30. Spanish.

5913 Mungaray, Josefina C. Like a gypsy=Como un gitano. LLUEVE TLALOC, no. 3 (1976), p. 47. Bilingual.

5914 Mungaray, Josefina C. Mi amor...y tu. LLUEVE TLALOC, no. 3 (1976), p. 31. Spanish.

5915 Mungaray, Josefina C. Muy lejos de mi. LLUEVE TLALOC, no. 2 (1975), p. 30. Spanish.

5916 Mungaray, Josefina C. Otono. LLUEVE TLALOC, no. 6 (1979), p. 30. Spanish.

5917 Mungaray, Josefina C. La paloma del desierto. LLUEVE TLALOC, no. 7 (1980), p. 19. Spanish.

5918 Mungaray, Josefina C. Rosa...negra. LLUEVE TLALOC, no. 2 (1975), p. 47. Spanish.

5919 Mungaray, Josefina C. Seguire tus huellas. LLUEVE TLALOC, no. 3 (1976), p. 33. Spanish.

5920 Murrieta, Armando. Desde aqui. LLUEVE TLALOC, no. 1 (1974), p. 19-20. Bilingual.

5921 Murrieta, Maria del Socorro. Ella es una flor. LLUEVE TLALOC, no. 10 (1983), p. 11. Spanish.

5922 Murrieta, Maria del Socorro. La flor es una mujer. LLUEVE TLALOC, no. 10 (1983), p. 36. Spanish.

5923 Murrieta, Maria del Socorro. Hoy me pregunto. LLUEVE TLALOC, no. 8 (1981), p. 16. Spanish.

5924 Murrieta, Maria del Socorro. Manana. LLUEVE TLALOC, no. 10 (1983), p. 32. Spanish.

5925 Murrieta, Maria del Socorro. Miel de amor. LLUEVE TLALOC, no. 10 (1983), p. 8. Spanish.

5926 Murrieta, Maria del Socorro. La verdad. LLUEVE TLALOC, no. 10 (1983), p. 32. Spanish.

5927 Narvaez, Jeannette. Hoy lo vi, Andrea. LLUEVE TLALOC, no. 9 (1982), p. 23. Spanish.

5928 Narvaez, Jeannette. Mama no te vera crecer. LLUEVE TLALOC, no. 9 (1982), p. 26. Spanish.

5929 Narvaez, Jeannette. Por eso te quiero. LLUEVE TLALOC, no. 6 (1979), p. 39. Spanish.

5930 Narvaez, Jeannette. Un principe viene. LLUEVE TLALOC, no. 9 (1982), p. 19. Spanish.

5931 Narvaez, Jeannette. Tu y yo con el senor. LLUEVE TLALOC, no. 7 (1980), p. 38. Spanish.

5932 Narvaez, Jeannette. Vivir. LLUEVE TLALOC, no. 9 (1982), p. 21. Spanish.

5933 Navarro, Eleane. Un insecto anonimo. SAGUARO, Vol. 1, no. 1 (1984), p. 61. Spanish.

5934 Navarro, Patricia M. Believe. LLUEVE TLALOC, no. 8 (1981), p. 36. English.

5935 Navarro, Patricia M. Creer. LLUEVE TLALOC, no. 8 (1981), p. 36. Spanish.

5936 Navarro, Patricia M. I believe in=Creo en. LLUEVE TLALOC, no. 11 (1984), p. 17. Bilingual.

5937 Navarro, Patricia M. Jesu Cristo=Jesus Christ. LLUEVE TLALOC, no. 11 (1984), p. 17. Bilingual.

Poems (cont.)

5938 Navarro, Patricia M. The Lord nuestro padre.
LLUEVE TLALOC, no. 11 (1984), p. 17.
Bilingual.

5939 Navarro, Patricia M. Tu gran valor. LLUEVE
TLALOC, no. 11 (1984), p. 32. Spanish.

5940 Nervo, Gibian. Mi viejo hombre. SAGUARO,
Vol. 1, no. 1 (1984), p. 39. Spanish.

5941 Noches de octubre. LLUEVE TLALOC, no. 2
(1975), p. 37. Spanish.

5942 Noriega, Carlos Peralta. Alma. LLUEVE
TLALOC, no. 4 (1977), p. 88. Spanish.

5943 Noriega, Carlos Peralta. Cadenas
voluntarias. LLUEVE TLALOC, no. 4 (1977), p.
68. Spanish.

5944 Noriega, Carlos Peralta. Declaracion. LLUEVE
TLALOC, no. 4 (1977), p. 92. Spanish.

5945 Noriega, Carlos Peralta. El descuido. LLUEVE
TLALOC, no. 4 (1977), p. 68. Spanish.

5946 Noriega, Carlos Peralta. Fantasia. LLUEVE
TLALOC, no. 4 (1977), p. 88. Spanish.

5947 Noriega, Carlos Peralta. Inseguridad. LLUEVE
TLALOC, no. 4 (1977), p. 48. Spanish.

5948 Ohnesorgen, Jose. Con los gritos. LLUEVE
TLALOC, no. 9 (1982), p. 33. Spanish.

5949 Ohnesorgen, Jose. Con los tragos vive.
LLUEVE TLALOC, no. 9 (1982), p. 27. Spanish.

5950 Ohnesorgen, Jose. Cuando no te conocen.
LLUEVE TLALOC, no. 8 (1981), p. 20. Spanish.

5951 Ohnesorgen, Jose. El maton. LLUEVE TLALOC,
no. 9 (1982), p. 27. Spanish.

5952 Olivas, Eduardo. Lagrimas de verdad. LLUEVE
TLALOC, no. 2 (1975), p. 3-4. Spanish.

5953 Olivas, Eduardo. Tears of truth. LLUEVE
TLALOC, no. 2 (1975), p. 5-6. English.

5954 Olivas, Linda. Flor de rosa. REVISTA
MUJERES, Vol. 1, no. 2 (June 1984), p.
11-12. Spanish.

5955 Oropesa, Maria. I am thinking of you mother.
REVISTA MUJERES, Vol. 2, no. 1 (January
1985), p. 24. English.

5956 Orozco, Aurora E. El piscador. REVISTA
MUJERES, Vol. 2, no. 2 (June 1985), p. 34.
Spanish.

5957 Ortega, Koryne. 7 weeks mature. NOTEBOOK: A
LITTLE MAGAZINE, Vol. 2, no. 2 (1986), p. 9.
English.

5958 Ortega, Koryne. His mute mind. NOTEBOOK: A
LITTLE MAGAZINE, Vol. 1, no. 2 (1985), p. i.
English.

5959 Ortega, Koryne. In S.F. NOTEBOOK: A LITTLE
MAGAZINE, Vol. 1, no. 2 (1985), p. vi.
English.

5960 Ortega, Koryne. Inside her inside. NOTEBOOK:
A LITTLE MAGAZINE, Vol. 2, no. 2 (1986), p.
30. English.

5961 Ortega, Koryne. Jorje. NOTEBOOK: A LITTLE
MAGAZINE, Vol. 2, no. 2 (1986), p. 31.
English.

5962 Ortega, Koryne. Just one ear. NOTEBOOK: A
LITTLE MAGAZINE, Vol. 2, no. 2 (1986), p.
30. English.

5963 Ortega, Koryne. Just step outside. NOTEBOOK:
A LITTLE MAGAZINE, Vol. 1, no. 2 (1985), p.
iii. English.

5964 Ortega, Koryne. Keeping this in mind.
NOTEBOOK: A LITTLE MAGAZINE, Vol. 1, no. 2
(1985), p. viii. English.

5965 Ortega, Koryne. Leather. NOTEBOOK: A LITTLE
MAGAZINE, Vol. 1, no. 2 (1985), p. iv.
English.

5966 Ortega, Koryne. Martin. NOTEBOOK: A LITTLE
MAGAZINE, Vol. 2, no. 2 (1986), p. 31.
English.

5967 Ortega, Koryne. Minnie. NOTEBOOK: A LITTLE
MAGAZINE, Vol. 1, no. 2 (1985), p. vii.
English.

5968 Ortega, Koryne. Parting from cultivation.
NOTEBOOK: A LITTLE MAGAZINE, Vol. 2, no. 2
(1986), p. 33. English.

5969 Ortega, Koryne. Poor places. NOTEBOOK: A
LITTLE MAGAZINE, Vol. 2, no. 2 (1986), p.
13. English.

5970 Ortega, Koryne. Quake. Chance. Gift. Mexico.
NOTEBOOK: A LITTLE MAGAZINE, Vol. 1, no. 2
(1985), p. ix-x. English.

5971 Ortega, Koryne. Searching. NOTEBOOK: A
LITTLE MAGAZINE, Vol. 1, no. 2 (1985), p.
ii. English.

5972 Ortega, Koryne. To sistas alike. NOTEBOOK: A
LITTLE MAGAZINE, Vol. 1, no. 2 (1985), p. v.
English.

5973 Ortega-Butler, Norma. Una caminata en el
anochecer. LLUEVE TLALOC, no. 12 (1985), p.
42. Spanish.

5974 Ortega-Butler, Norma. Desde la ventana.
LLUEVE TLALOC, no. 12 (1985), p. 41.
Spanish.

5975 Ortiz Vasquez, Pedro. My father/my mother.
SAGUARO, Vol. 3, (1986), p. 28. English.

5976 Ortiz Vasquez, Pedro. Where have we America.
SAGUARO, Vol. 3, (1986), p. 27. English.

5977 Padilla, Ernesto. Premio dos reales.
SAGUARO, Vol. 3, (1986), p. 110-112.
Spanish.

5978 Padre, Chico. Lathe biosas. NOTEBOOK: A
LITTLE MAGAZINE, Vol. 2, no. 2 (1986), p.
32. English.

5979 Padre, Chico. Welcome to L.A. NOTEBOOK: A
LITTLE MAGAZINE, Vol. 2, no. 2 (1986), p.
33. English.

5980 Palacios, Arnoldo. Las ventanas parpadean.
LLUEVE TLALOC, no. 1 (1974), p. 4. Spanish.

5981 Paredes, Josefina. Descansa. LLUEVE TLALOC,
no. 7 (1980), p. 19. Spanish.

5982 Paredes, Josefina. En la primavera. LLUEVE
TLALOC, no. 8 (1981), p. 35. Spanish.

5983 Paredes, Josefina. Una flor y tus recuerdos.
LLUEVE TLALOC, no. 7 (1980), p. 33. Spanish.

Poems (cont.)

5984 Paredes, Josefina. Por un disimulo. LLUEVE
    TLALOC, no. 8 (1981), p. 35. Spanish.

5985 Parra, Elena. Esperanza de un sueno. LLUEVE
    TLALOC, no. 3 (1976), p. 23. Spanish.

5986 Parra, Elena. La huella del pueblo chicano.
    LLUEVE TLALOC, no. 3 (1976), p. 46. Spanish.

5987 Parra, Elena. El nino triste. LLUEVE TLALOC,
    no. 1 (1974), p. 5. Spanish.

5988 Parra, Elena. El nuevo dia. LLUEVE TLALOC,
    no. 3 (1976), p. 21. Spanish.

5989 Parra, Elena. Por que? LLUEVE TLALOC, no. 2
    (1975), p. 25. Spanish.

5990 Parra, Elena. La soledad. LLUEVE TLALOC, no.
    2 (1975), p. 11. Spanish.

5991 Parra, Elena. Suenos. LLUEVE TLALOC, no. 1
    (1974), p. 6. Spanish.

5992 Parra, Filiberto. A diario al caer el alba.
    LLUEVE TLALOC, no. 9 (1982), p. 40. Spanish.

5993 Parra, Filiberto. La soledad. LLUEVE TLALOC,
    (1982), p. 21. Spanish.

5994 Parra, Idolina. Me prometiste. LLUEVE
    TLALOC, no. 13 (1986), p. 27. Spanish.

5995 Parra, Idolina. Por eso te quiero. LLUEVE
    TLALOC, no. 13 (1986), p. 27. Spanish.

5996 Parra, Mauricio. [...de la savia mar
    universal sendero...]. TINTA, Vol. 1, no. 2
    (May 1983), p. 45. Spanish.

5997 Pastoriza, Benito. Cancion en no menor.
    TINTA, Vol. 1, no. 3 (December 1983), p. 66.
    Spanish.

5998 Pastoriza, Benito. Las cicatrices dulces.
    TINTA, Vol. 1, no. 2 (May 1983), p. 45.
    Spanish.

5999 Pastoriza, Benito. Danza de palabras. TINTA,
    Vol. 1, no. 2 (May 1983), p. 45. Spanish.

6000 Pazos, Hector Arenas. Aquel ayer. LLUEVE
    TLALOC, no. 6 (1979), p. 24. Spanish.

6001 Pensamiento de carino. LLUEVE TLALOC, no. 11
    (1984), p. 14. Spanish.

6002 Perez, Maria. Que es el amor. LLUEVE TLALOC,
    no. 13 (1986), p. 27. Spanish.

6003 Perez, Maria. Recuerdos. LLUEVE TLALOC, no.
    13 (1986), p. 27. Spanish.

6004 Perez, Maria. Rumores. LLUEVE TLALOC, no. 13
    (1986), p. 25. Spanish.

6005 La pesadez. THE AMERICAS REVIEW, Vol. 15,
    no. 3-4 (Fall, Winter, 1987), p. 65.
    Spanish.

6006 Pigno, Antonia Quintana. Annie. NOTEBOOK: A
    LITTLE MAGAZINE, Vol. 3, no. 1 (1987), p.
    71. English.

6007 Pigno, Antonia Quintana. La Llorona.
    NOTEBOOK: A LITTLE MAGAZINE, Vol. 3, no. 1
    (1987), p. 46. English.

6008 Pigno, Antonia Quintana. South Valley.
    NOTEBOOK: A LITTLE MAGAZINE, Vol. 3, no. 1
    (1987), p. 49-50. English.

6009 Pineda, Josefina. Chicana. LLUEVE TLALOC,
    no. 10 (1983), p. 10. Spanish.

6010 Pineda, Josefina. Crisis de identidad.
    LLUEVE TLALOC, no. 10 (1983), p. 31.
    Spanish.

6011 Pineda, Josefina. Diferentes culturas.
    LLUEVE TLALOC, no. 10 (1983), p. 10.
    Spanish.

6012 Pineda, Josefina. Donde estas mi dios?
    LLUEVE TLALOC, no. 10 (1983), p. 10.
    Spanish.

6013 Pineda, Josefina. El orgullo. LLUEVE TLALOC,
    no. 10 (1983), p. 10. Spanish.

6014 Pomalaza Padilla, Luciana. Untitled. REVISTA
    MUJERES, Vol. 4, no. 1 (January 1987), p.
    48. Spanish.

6015 Price, Eva. Cancion de cuna. LLUEVE TLALOC,
    no. 6 (1979), p. 26. Spanish.

6016 Price, Eva. Rubias y morenas. LLUEVE TLALOC,
    no. 6 (1979), p. 26. Spanish.

6017 Quinlan, Lisa. Aztlan. CHIRICU, Vol. 5, no.
    1 (1987), p. 24. English.

6018 Quintana, Alvina. Winter. REVISTA MUJERES,
    Vol. 3, no. 1 (January 1986), p. 12.
    English.

6019 Quintana, Graciela. Monday Monday. REVISTA
    MUJERES, Vol. 3, no. 2 (June 1986), p. 66.
    English.

6020 Quintana, Leroy V. Cotton candy for barrio
    midway. EL CUADERNO, Vol. 4, no. 1 (Summer
    1976), p. 88. English.

6021 Quintana, Leroy V. [Cuando l'abuelita
    murio...]. EL CUADERNO, Vol. 4, no. 1
    (Summer 1976), p. 20. Spanish. **DESCR:**
    Ancianos.

6022 Quintana, Leroy V. [In the barbershop...].
    EL CUADERNO, Vol. 3, no. 2 (Spring 1974), p.
    18. English.

6023 Quintanilla, Anita. Solitary confinement.
    REVISTA MUJERES, Vol. 4, no. 1 (January
    1987), p. 75-77. English.

6024 Quiroz, Francisco. Donde esta mi barrio?
    LLUEVE TLALOC, no. 2 (1975), p. 32. Spanish.

6025 Ramirez, Anna B. Te amo. LLUEVE TLALOC, no.
    7 (1980), p. 39. Spanish.

6026 Ramirez, Maria Theresa. Esta sera mi ultima
    carta. LLUEVE TLALOC, no. 3 (1976), p. 29.
    Spanish.

6027 Ramirez, Norma. El corrido de Jose Elisalde.
    LLUEVE TLALOC, no. 9 (1982), p. 1. Spanish.
    DESCR: Corridos; *Elisalde, Jose.

6028 Ramirez, Petra. Anoranza. LLUEVE TLALOC, no.
    14 (1987), p. 49. Spanish.

6029 Ramirez, Petra. Llamado infinito. LLUEVE
    TLALOC, no. 14 (1987), p. 50. Spanish.

6030 Ramirez, Petra. Mas alla del recuerdo.
    LLUEVE TLALOC, no. 14 (1987), p. 50-51.
    Spanish.

6031 Ramirez, Roberto. Agua. LLUEVE TLALOC, no.
    13 (1986), p. 27. Spanish.

Poems (cont.)

6032 Ramirez, Roberto. El amor. LLUEVE TLALOC, no. 13 (1986), p. 23. Spanish.

6033 Ramirez, Roberto. Nostalgia. LLUEVE TLALOC, no. 14 (1987), p. 56. Spanish.

6034 Ramirez, Roberto. Ojinaga querida. LLUEVE TLALOC, no. 13 (1986), p. 23. Spanish.

6035 Ramirez, Roberto. Pensamiento. LLUEVE TLALOC, no. 13 (1986), p. 27. Spanish.

6036 Ramirez, Roberto. La primavera. LLUEVE TLALOC, no. 13 (1986), p. 30. Spanish.

6037 Ramirez, Roberto. Tu recuerdo. LLUEVE TLALOC, no. 14 (1987), p. 56. Spanish.

6038 Ramirez, Steven Rey. Today's bigotry. NOTEBOOK: A LITTLE MAGAZINE, Vol. 3, no. 1 (1987), p. 14-15. English.

6039 Ramirez, Steven Rey. You look back. NOTEBOOK: A LITTLE MAGAZINE, Vol. 3, no. 1 (1987), p. 16-17. English.

6040 Rede Chavez, Delfina. El bano. JOURNAL OF ETHNIC STUDIES, Vol. 15, no. 1 (Spring 1987), p. 93-94. Spanish.

6041 Rede Chavez, Delfina. Rio Grande. JOURNAL OF ETHNIC STUDIES, Vol. 15, no. 1 (Spring 1987), p. 89-91. Spanish.

6042 Rede Chavez, Delfina. La vida. JOURNAL OF ETHNIC STUDIES, Vol. 15, no. 1 (Spring 1987), p. 92. Spanish.

6043 Retana, Nicolas. Abuela. CONFLUENCIA, Vol. 1, no. 2 (Spring 1986), p. 119. English.

6044 Retana, Nicolas. Para Amado Maurilio Pena. CONFLUENCIA, Vol. 1, no. 2 (Spring 1986), p. 117. Bilingual.

6045 Retes, Patricia. A Juan Pedro. LLUEVE TLALOC, no. 10 (1983), p. 31. Spanish.

6046 Retes, Patricia. Donde estas. LLUEVE TLALOC, no. 10 (1983), p. 31. Spanish.

6047 Retes, Patricia. Un hijo imaginario. LLUEVE TLALOC, no. 10 (1983), p. 13. Spanish.

6048 Retes, Patricia. Lo se. LLUEVE TLALOC, no. 10 (1983), p. 31. Spanish.

6049 Reyes, Sandra. Amigo mio. LLUEVE TLALOC, no. 13 (1986), p. 30. Spanish.

6050 Reyes, Sandra. Tenia duena. LLUEVE TLALOC, no. 13 (1986), p. 30. Spanish.

6051 Ricapito, Joseph. El cocinero afable. CHIRICU, no. 2 (Spring 1977), p. 28. Spanish.

6052 Ricapito, Joseph. (Sin titulo). CHIRICU, no. 2 (Spring 1977), p. 29. Spanish.

6053 Rich, Mary Alice. El nombre de la muerte. LLUEVE TLALOC, no. 14-6 (1987), p. 73. Spanish.

6054 Rincon, A. Cuatro pensamientos. LLUEVE TLALOC, no. 12 (1985), p. 24. Spanish.

6055 Rincon, A. Maria de los arcangeles. LLUEVE TLALOC, no. 12 (1985), p. 36. Spanish.

6056 Rincon, A. Tus imagenes, mis palabras. LLUEVE TLALOC, no. 12 (1985), p. 43. Spanish.

6057 Rincon, A. V.A. hospital. LLUEVE TLALOC, no. 12 (1985), p. 35. Spanish.

6058 Rivera, Armandina. A mi madre. LLUEVE TLALOC, no. 12 (1985), p. 18. Spanish.

6059 Rivera, Armandina. A mis hijos. LLUEVE TLALOC, no. 12 (1985), p. 43. Spanish.

6060 Rivera, Cecilia. A mi madre. LLUEVE TLALOC, no. 8 (1981), p. 35. Spanish.

6061 Rivera, Cecilia. Un corazon. LLUEVE TLALOC, no. 8 (1981), p. 32. Spanish.

6062 Rivera, Cecilia. Mi bella ilusion. LLUEVE TLALOC, no. 8 (1981), p. 28. Spanish.

6063 Rivera, Frances M. (Sin titulo). CHIRICU, no. 2 (Spring 1977), p. 5. Spanish.

6064 Rivera, Frances M. (Sin titulo). CHIRICU, no. 2 (Spring 1977), p. 6. Spanish.

6065 Rivera, Marcela. Mi tristeza. LLUEVE TLALOC, no. 8 (1981), p. 20. Spanish.

6066 Rivera, Rebecca. Vida. LLUEVE TLALOC, no. 8 (1981), p. 22. Spanish.

6067 Rivero, Eliana S. Esta bien. SAGUARO, Vol. 1, no. 1 (1984), p. 34. Spanish.

6068 Rivero, Eliana S. No es menos. SAGUARO, Vol. 1, no. 1 (1984), p. 35. Spanish.

6069 Rivero, Eliana S. Ocasionalmente proesia. SAGUARO, Vol. 1, no. 1 (1984), p. 38. Spanish.

6070 Rivero, Eliana S. Poetica de los ausentes. SAGUARO, Vol. 1, no. 1 (1984), p. 36. Spanish.

6071 Rivero, Eliana S. Tan lejos del azucar. SAGUARO, Vol. 1, no. 1 (1984), p. 37. Spanish.

6072 R.M. Plegaria a mi hija. LLUEVE TLALOC, no. 2 (1975), p. 21. Spanish.

6073 Robles, Maria J. La barranca. LLUEVE TLALOC, no. 4 (1977), p. 49. Spanish.

6074 Robles, Maria J. Caminemos. LLUEVE TLALOC, no. 6 (1979), p. 38. Spanish.

6075 Robles, Maria J. El cisne. LLUEVE TLALOC, no. 4 (1977), p. 91. Spanish.

6076 Robles, Maria J. La corriente. LLUEVE TLALOC, no. 6 (1979), p. 13. Spanish.

6077 Robles, Maria J. La espera. LLUEVE TLALOC, no. 4 (1977), p. 85. Spanish.

6078 Robles, Maria J. Las flores. LLUEVE TLALOC, no. 4 (1977), p. 100. Spanish.

6079 Robles, Maria J. Lamentos. LLUEVE TLALOC, no. 4 (1977), p. 56-57. Spanish.

6080 Robles, Maria J. Mensaje de amor. LLUEVE TLALOC, no. 4 (1977), p. 93. Spanish.

6081 Robles, Maria J. Morir! LLUEVE TLALOC, no. 5 (1978), p. 26. Spanish.

6082 Robles, Maria J. Reproche. LLUEVE TLALOC, no. 5 (1978), p. 26. Spanish.

Poems (cont.)

6083 Robles, Maria J. Senor, de que color son tus ojos? LLUEVE TLALOC, no. 4 (1977), p. 98. Spanish.

6084 Robles, Maria J. Timidez. LLUEVE TLALOC, no. 4 (1977), p. 104. Spanish.

6085 Rochin, Jose Ruben. De un amor broto mi vida. LLUEVE TLALOC, no. 8 (1981), p. 28. Spanish.

6086 Rochin, Jose Ruben. La mama de Sylvia. LLUEVE TLALOC, no. 8 (1981), p. 28. Spanish.

6087 Rodriguez, Alfonso. Afirmacion. CONFLUENCIA, Vol. 1, no. 2 (Spring 1986), p. 111. Spanish.

6088 Rodriguez, Alfonso. El gran buitre. SAGUARO, Vol. 4, (1987), p. 51-52. Spanish.

6089 Rodriguez, Alfonso. Himno de medianoche. CONFLUENCIA, Vol. 1, no. 2 (Spring 1986), p. 115. Spanish.

6090 Rodriguez, Alfonso. Manos. CONFLUENCIA, Vol. 1, no. 2 (Spring 1986), p. 114. Spanish.

6091 Rodriguez, Alfonso. Las palabras. CONFLUENCIA, Vol. 1, no. 2 (Spring 1986), p. 113. Spanish.

6092 Rodriguez Flores, Juan. Poesia chicana de hoy: una minima antologia. LA COMUNIDAD, No. 305 (May 25, 1986), p. 4-7. Spanish.

6093 Rodriguez, George Eagar. Hijos de Eva. LLUEVE TLALOC, no. 13 (1986), p. 14. Spanish.

6094 Rodriguez, George Eagar. La noche buena. LLUEVE TLALOC, no. 13 (1986), p. 9-10. Bilingual.

6095 Rodriguez, George Eagar. Nunca olvides. LLUEVE TLALOC, no. 13 (1986), p. 14. Spanish.

6096 Rodriguez, George Eagar. Tilmatli de ichtli mexitli. LLUEVE TLALOC, no. 13 (1986), p. 16. Spanish.

6097 Rodriguez, Luis. Operation jobs. REVISTA MUJERES, Vol. 1, no. 1 (January 1984), p. 25-27. English.

6098 Romero, Leo. For Denis Cowper. EL CUADERNO, Vol. 4, no. 1 (Summer 1976), p. 50. English.

6099 Romero, Leo. The inanimate had their night. EL CUADERNO, Vol. 4, no. 1 (Summer 1976), p. 48. English.

6100 Romero, Leo. Listening to the silence. EL CUADERNO, Vol. 3, no. 2 (Spring 1974), p. 53. English.

6101 Romero, Leo. The Llorona in Truchas, N. Mex. EL CUADERNO, Vol. 3, no. 2 (Spring 1974), p. 17. English.

6102 Romero, Leo. Silence exists here. EL CUADERNO, Vol. 4, no. 1 (Summer 1976), p. 48. English.

6103 Ruiz, Juliette. Ninita. LLUEVE TLALOC, no. 3 (1976), p. 28. Spanish.

6104 Ruiz, Raymundo. La muerte. LLUEVE TLALOC, no. 11 (1984), p. 30. Spanish.

6105 Ruiz, Raymundo. El ocotillo. LLUEVE TLALOC, no. 11 (1984), p. 21. Spanish.

6106 Ruiz, Raymundo. Perla negra. LLUEVE TLALOC, no. 10 (1983), p. 40. Spanish.

6107 Ruiz, Raymundo. Que bonito es... LLUEVE TLALOC, no. 10 (1983), p. 21. Spanish.

6108 Ruiz, Raymundo. El sahuaro. LLUEVE TLALOC, no. 11 (1984), p. 21. Spanish.

6109 Ruiz, Raymundo. Te amo. LLUEVE TLALOC, no. 11 (1984), p. 24. Spanish.

6110 Ruiz, Raymundo. La vida. LLUEVE TLALOC, no. 11 (1984), p. 14. Spanish.

6111 Saavedra, Carlos C. Solo su cuerpo dulce. LLUEVE TLALOC, no. 2 (1975), p. 7. Spanish.

6112 Sagel, Jim. El abuelo sabe. CHIRICU, Vol. 3, no. 1 (1982), p. 13. Bilingual.

6113 Sagel, Jim. Cuate Rafael y los lowriders. CHIRICU, Vol. 3, no. 1 (1982), p. 11-12. English.

6114 Sagel, Yuri and Van Olphen, Yone. Nuevo dia. LLUEVE TLALOC, no. 2 (1975), p. 51. Spanish.

6115 Saine, Ute Margarete. Mexico. SAGUARO, Vol. 3, (1986), p. 66. English.

6116 Saine, Ute Margarete. Milagro. SAGUARO, Vol. 4, (1987), p. 89. Spanish.

6117 Saine, Ute Margarete. The roofs of Puebla. SAGUARO, Vol. 4, (1987), p. 87. English.

6118 Salaz, Daniel. [El cielo esta negro y nublado...]. EL CUADERNO, Vol. 3, no. 2 (Spring 1974), p. 68. Spanish.

6119 Salaz, Daniel. Pregunta y contesta. EL CUADERNO, Vol. 3, no. 2 (Spring 1974), p. 18. Spanish.

6120 Salazar, Manuel. El camino. EL CUADERNO, Vol. 4, no. 1 (Summer 1976), p. 99. Spanish.

6121 Salcido, Rosanna L. El camino. LLUEVE TLALOC, no. 4 (1977), p. 27. Spanish.

6122 Salcido, Rosanna L. Un cuento a la vida. LLUEVE TLALOC, no. 4 (1977), p. 89-90. Spanish.

6123 Salcido, Rosanna L. The path. LLUEVE TLALOC, no. 4 (1977), p. 28. English.

6124 Salinas, Hermenegildo. A black tangent. CHIRICU, no. 1 (Spring 1976), p. 13. English.

6125 Salinas, Hermenegildo. The lone ranger. CHIRICU, no. 1 (Spring 1976), p. 18. English.

6126 Salinas, Hermenegildo. Los ninos del parque seco. CHIRICU, no. 2 (Spring 1977), p. 26. Spanish.

6127 Salinas, Hermenegildo. Saturday morning. CHIRICU, no. 1 (Spring 1976), p. 14. Spanish.

6128 Salinas, Hermenegildo. (Sin titulo). CHIRICU, no. 1 (Spring 1976), p. 16. Spanish.

6129 Salinas, Hermenegildo. A watermelon poem: el jardin. CHIRICU, no. 2 (Spring 1977), p. 25. Bilingual.

Poems (cont.)

6130 Sanchez, Elba R. Noche de octubre. REVISTA MUJERES, Vol. 4, no. 1 (January 1987), p. 18. Spanish.

6131 Sanchez, Elba R. Realizations. REVISTA MUJERES, Vol. 4, no. 1 (January 1987), p. 17. English.

6132 Sanchez, Lupita. Si no me quieres. LLUEVE TLALOC, no. 10 (1983), p. 31. Spanish.

6133 Sanchez, Ricardo. En lo en... THE AMERICAS REVIEW, Vol. 15, no. 2 (Summer 1987), p. 62-66. Spanish.

6134 Sanchez, Ricardo. Sentiments hacia Belen. THE AMERICAS REVIEW, Vol. 15, no. 2 (Summer 1987), p. 45-61. English.

6135 Sanchez, Ricardo and Parra, Antonio. El tercer caiman. EL CUADERNO, Vol. 3, no. 2 (Spring 1974), p. 45-52. English.

6136 Sanchez-Glazer, Rebeca. A rising star. REVISTA MUJERES, Vol. 3, no. 1 (January 1986), p. 48. English.

6137 Sancho. What goes around. NOTEBOOK: A LITTLE MAGAZINE, Vol. 1, no. 2 (1985), p. 14. English.

6138 Sancho, Anthony R. Who is my friend. NOTEBOOK: A LITTLE MAGAZINE, Vol. 1, no. 2 (1985), p. 15. English.

6139 Sandoval, Chela. For Maurice Bishop. REVISTA MUJERES, Vol. 1, no. 1 (January 1984), p. 20. English.

6140 Sandoval, Rigoberto Ahumada. Loco. LLUEVE TLALOC, no. 8 (1981), p. 20. Spanish.

6141 Sandoval, Sandra. Ayer. LLUEVE TLALOC, no. 6 (1979), p. 32. Spanish.

6142 Sandoval, Sandra. Dichos o refranes. LLUEVE TLALOC, no. 6 (1979), p. 32. Spanish.

6143 Santiago Baca, Jimmy. I have always compared the white man to snow. BILINGUAL REVIEW, Vol. 12, no. 1-2 (January, August, 1985), p. 116-117. English.

6144 Santiago Baca, Jimmy. Since you've come. BILINGUAL REVIEW, Vol. 12, no. 1-2 (January, August, 1985), p. 115. English.

6145 Santillan, Gladis. Ser estrano. LLUEVE TLALOC, no. 13 (1986), p. 21. Spanish.

6146 Santos, Christian. Delante de los ojos de sus madres. REVISTA MUJERES, Vol. 2, no. 2 (June 1985), p. 10. Spanish.

6147 Semones, Linda. At home. CHIRICU, no. 1 (Spring 1976), p. 7-11. English.

6148 Semones, Linda. Mercedes Buiza's song for a premature child. CHIRICU, no. 1 (Spring 1976), p. 12. English.

6149 Sepulveda, Concha. Father's prayer. NOTEBOOK: A LITTLE MAGAZINE, Vol. 3, no. 1 (1987), p. 22. English.

6150 Sepulveda, Concha. Sweetwater alchemy. NOTEBOOK: A LITTLE MAGAZINE, Vol. 3, no. 1 (1987), p. 72. English.

6151 Shannon, Lisa. Tamales. REVISTA MUJERES, Vol. 4, no. 1 (January 1987), p. 73. English.

6152 Sillik, Tony. Smiles. LLUEVE TLALOC, no. 1 (1974), p. 39. English.

6153 Sillik, Tony. Sonrisas. LLUEVE TLALOC, no. 1 (1974), p. 40. Spanish.

6154 Silva, Beverly. Genaro Rodriguez. NOTEBOOK: A LITTLE MAGAZINE, Vol. 1, no. 2 (1985), p. 17-18. English.

6155 Silva, Beverly. El halcon y el geranio. NOTEBOOK: A LITTLE MAGAZINE, Vol. 2, no. 2 (1986), p. 2. Spanish.

6156 Silva, Beverly. The hawk and the geranium. NOTEBOOK: A LITTLE MAGAZINE, Vol. 2, no. 2 (1986), p. 3. English.

6157 Silva, Beverly. Solamente Dios. NOTEBOOK: A LITTLE MAGAZINE, Vol. 2, no. 2 (1986), p. 10. English.

6158 Silva, Beverly. Stromboli. NOTEBOOK: A LITTLE MAGAZINE, Vol. 1, no. 2 (1985), p. 16. English.

6159 Silva, Beverly. Sundays at Zarape. NOTEBOOK: A LITTLE MAGAZINE, Vol. 2, no. 2 (1986), p. 40-41. English.

6160 Silvas, Lorenzo. Por ti. CHIRICU, no. 2 (Spring 1977), p. 35. Spanish.

6161 Solorio, Luis. Perdon. BILINGUAL REVIEW, Vol. 11, no. 3 (September, December, 1984), p. 46-47. Spanish.

6162 Solorio, Rosalva. Campesina, cafe como mi tierra. REVISTA MUJERES, Vol. 2, no. 2 (June 1985), p. 29-30. Spanish.

6163 Soraida. Canto a la vida. LLUEVE TLALOC, no. 13 (1986), p. 29. Spanish.

6164 Soraida. Costumbres de mi pueblo. LLUEVE TLALOC, no. 13 (1986), p. 4. Spanish.

6165 Soraida. Donde no hay abuelitas? LLUEVE TLALOC, no. 13 (1986), p. 14. Spanish.

6166 Soraida. En otro mundo. LLUEVE TLALOC, no. 13 (1986), p. 19. Spanish.

6167 Soraida. Hermosa cantar. LLUEVE TLALOC, no. 13 (1986), p. 29. Spanish.

6168 Soraida. Juan Comadres. LLUEVE TLALOC, no. 13 (1986), p. 16. Spanish.

6169 Soraida. Necio. LLUEVE TLALOC, no. 13 (1986), p. 14. Spanish.

6170 Soraida. Pasajes de mi ninez. LLUEVE TLALOC, no. 13 (1986), p. 11. Spanish.

6171 Soto, Rosario. Mi verso. LLUEVE TLALOC, no. 6 (1979), p. 24. Spanish.

6172 Sotomayor, Aurea. Itinerarios. CHIRICU, no. 1 (Spring 1976), p. 25. Spanish.

6173 Sotomayor, Aurea. (Sin titulo). CHIRICU, no. 1 (Spring 1976), p. 26. Spanish.

6174 Stevens, Kim Celeste. Sinceridad. LLUEVE TLALOC, no. 8 (1981), p. 36. Bilingual.

6175 Storni, Alfonsina. Tu me quieres blanca. REVISTA MUJERES, Vol. 3, no. 1 (January 1986), p. 30-31. Spanish.

Poems (cont.)

6176 Storni, Alfonsina and Ellis, Miriam, trans. You want me to be white. REVISTA MUJERES, Vol. 3, no. 1 (January 1986), p. 33-35. English.

6177 Stromei, Angelina. El rendimiento. LLUEVE TLALOC, no. 9 (1982), p. 8. Spanish.

6178 Tafolla, Carmen. Fighting paper. SAGUARO, Vol. 3, (1986), p. 75-76. English.

6179 Tafolla, Carmen. Los loquitos. SAGUARO, Vol. 3, (1986), p. 55-56. Spanish.

6180 Tafolla, Carmen. Of beer and sofa (or Frank's dilemma). SAGUARO, Vol. 3, (1986), p. 71-74. English.

6181 Tapia, Fernando. Detras de la furia. SAGUARO, Vol. 1, no. 1 (1984), p. 41. Spanish.

6182 Tapia, Fernando. La frente anuncia. SAGUARO, Vol. 1, no. 1 (1984), p. 42. Spanish.

6183 Tejeda, Alejandro. El canon circular de Branden. TINTA, Vol. 1, no. 3 (December 1983), p. 68-70. Spanish.

6184 Teran. Dime carnal. EL CUADERNO, Vol. 2, no. 1 (1972), p. 40. Spanish.

6185 Teran. Mi carnal-el pintor. EL CUADERNO, Vol. 2, no. 1 (1972), p. 23. Spanish.

6186 Teran. Second coming. EL CUADERNO, Vol. 2, no. 1 (1972), p. 44. English.

6187 Tieman, John Samuel. Bitter song for her. THE AMERICAS REVIEW, Vol. 15, no. 2 (Summer 1987), p. 70. English.

6188 Tieman, John Samuel. Dona Beatriz, una cancion a duo. THE AMERICAS REVIEW, Vol. 15, no. 2 (Summer 1987), p. 69. Bilingual.

6189 Tijerino, Eduardo. Te amo. LLUEVE TLALOC, no. 8 (1981), p. 32. Spanish.

6190 Toscano, Ignacio. Mi padre. LLUEVE TLALOC, no. 7 (1980), p. 19. Spanish.

6191 Trujillo, Lucy. Que pesadilla tan real. LLUEVE TLALOC, no. 2 (1975), p. 46. Spanish.

6192 Urguiaga, Manuel. Hermano de sangre. SAGUARO, Vol. 1, no. 1 (1984), p. 43-46. Spanish.

6193 Urrea, Maria Luisa. El pescador. SAGUARO, Vol. 1, no. 1 (1984), p. 60. Spanish.

6194 Valdes, Gina. After the reading. CONFLUENCIA, Vol. 1, no. 2 (Spring 1986), p. 121. English.

6195 Valdes, Gina. Eating fire. CONFLUENCIA, Vol. 1, no. 2 (Spring 1986), p. 122. English.

6196 Valdes, Gina. Sunday arrived. CONFLUENCIA, Vol. 1, no. 2 (Spring 1986), p. 123. English.

6197 Valdes, Gina. To Yoyontzin. CONFLUENCIA, Vol. 1, no. 2 (Spring 1986), p. 125. English.

6198 Valdes, Grisel. Etiopia. REVISTA MUJERES, Vol. 3, no. 1 (January 1986), p. 17-18. Spanish.

6199 Valdes, Grisel. Made of wax. REVISTA MUJERES, Vol. 3, no. 1 (January 1986), p. 46. English.

6200 Valdes, Grisel. Por nacer. REVISTA MUJERES, Vol. 3, no. 1 (January 1986), p. 50-51. Spanish.

6201 Valenzuela, Noemi. A night with the sea. LLUEVE TLALOC, no. 1 (1974), p. 42. English.

6202 Valenzuela, Noemi. Una noche con el mar. LLUEVE TLALOC, no. 1 (1974), p. 41. Spanish.

6203 Varela, Graciela. Si tu me quisieras. LLUEVE TLALOC, no. 9 (1982), p. 8. Spanish.

6204 Varela, Graciela. Si tu te vas. LLUEVE TLALOC, no. 9 (1982), p. 19. Spanish.

6205 Vasquez, Ruben. Donde jugaran los ninos? CHIRICU, Vol. 3, no. 2 (1983), p. 72-74. English.

6206 Vaughn, Artemisa. Tus hijos. LLUEVE TLALOC, no. 7 (1980), p. 37. Spanish.

6207 Velaquez [sic], Manuel. Gastronomical tidings. LLUEVE TLALOC, no. 5 (1978), p. 8. English.

6208 Velaquez [sic], Manuel. Puntada gastronomica. LLUEVE TLALOC, no. 5 (1978), p. 8. Spanish.

6209 Velasco, Magdalena. La luz. LLUEVE TLALOC, no. 10 (1983), p. 34. Spanish.

6210 Velasco, Magdalena. Movement. LLUEVE TLALOC, no. 9 (1982), p. 8. English.

6211 Velasco, Magdalena. Movimiento. LLUEVE TLALOC, no. 9 (1982), p. 8. Spanish.

6212 Vendrell, Luis. Ausencia. SAGUARO, Vol. 4, (1987), p. 53. Spanish.

6213 Vigil, Mary Helen. Setting sun. EL CUADERNO, Vol. 3, no. 2 (Spring 1974), p. 27. English.

6214 Vigil-Pinon, Evangelina. Equinox. THE AMERICAS REVIEW, Vol. 15, no. 3-4 (Fall, Winter, 1987), p. 61. English.

6215 Vigil-Pinon, Evangelina. The giving. THE AMERICAS REVIEW, Vol. 15, no. 3-4 (Fall, Winter, 1987), p. 59. English.

6216 Vigil-Pinon, Evangelina. Hacia un invierno. THE AMERICAS REVIEW, Vol. 15, no. 3-4 (Fall, Winter, 1987), p. 62-63. Spanish.

6217 Vigil-Pinon, Evangelina. In its absence. THE AMERICAS REVIEW, Vol. 15, no. 3-4 (Fall, Winter, 1987), p. 58. English.

6218 Vigil-Pinon, Evangelina. The parting. THE AMERICAS REVIEW, Vol. 15, no. 3-4 (Fall, Winter, 1987), p. 57. English.

6219 Vigil-Pinon, Evangelina. Spillage. THE AMERICAS REVIEW, Vol. 15, no. 3-4 (Fall, Winter, 1987), p. 60. English.

6220 Villa Leyva, Rosa. Conceptual. LLUEVE TLALOC, no. 13 (1986), p. 25. English.

6221 Villa Leyva, Rosa. Confusion. LLUEVE TLALOC, no. 13 (1986), p. 27. English.

6222 Villa Leyva, Rosa. Desire. LLUEVE TLALOC, no. 13 (1986), p. 25. English.

Poems (cont.)

6223 Villa Leyva, Rosa. Gleam of life. LLUEVE
TLALOC, no. 13 (1986), p. 29. English.

6224 Villa Leyva, Rosa. I feel. LLUEVE TLALOC,
no. 13 (1986), p. 27. English.

6225 Villa Leyva, Rosa. Omid (hope). LLUEVE
TLALOC, no. 13 (1986), p. 25. English.

6226 Villa Leyva, Rosa. Silence. LLUEVE TLALOC,
no. 13 (1986), p. 25. English.

6227 Villa Leyva, Rosa. Sometimes. LLUEVE TLALOC,
no. 13 (1986), p. 25. English.

6228 Villalobos, Romer A. Dos almas perdidas.
LLUEVE TLALOC, no. 9 (1982), p. 26. Spanish.

6229 Villalobos, Romer A. Madre. LLUEVE TLALOC,
no. 9 (1982), p. 26. Spanish.

6230 Villar, Ysis. A mis hijos. LLUEVE TLALOC,
no. 14 (1987), p. 77. Spanish.

6231 Villar, Ysis. Amistad. LLUEVE TLALOC, no. 14
(1987), p. 78. Spanish.

6232 Villar, Ysis. El amor. LLUEVE TLALOC, no. 14
(1987), p. 78. Spanish.

6233 Villareal, Maria Antonia. Espana. LLUEVE
TLALOC, no. 12 (1985), p. 18. Spanish.

6234 Villareal, Maria Antonia. Por favor. LLUEVE
TLALOC, no. 12 (1985), p. 16. Spanish.

6235 Villareal, Maria Antonia. Tu recuerdo.
LLUEVE TLALOC, no. 12 (1985), p. 15.
Spanish.

6236 Wilson, Maria. Mi vida, mi amor, mi
estrella. LLUEVE TLALOC, no. 6 (1979), p.
39. Spanish.

6237 Wilson, Patricia. Sor Juana (Juana de
Asbaje). CONFLUENCIA, Vol. 1, no. 2 (Spring
1986), p. 129. English. **DESCR:** *Juana Ines
de la Cruz, Sor.

6238 Yang, Eunice. El amor mas grande. LLUEVE
TLALOC, no. 9 (1982), p. 19. Spanish.

6239 Yang, Eunice. Madre. LLUEVE TLALOC, no. 9
(1982), p. 19. Spanish.

6240 Yang, Eunice. Madre mia. LLUEVE TLALOC, no.
9 (1982), p. 19. Spanish.

6241 Yarter, R. Alexandra. Belladona. LLUEVE
TLALOC, no. 13 (1986), p. 23. Spanish.

6242 Yarter, R. Alexandra. Cantame. LLUEVE
TLALOC, no. 13 (1986), p. 25. Spanish.

6243 Yarter, R. Alexandra. Contesta. LLUEVE
TLALOC, no. 13 (1986), p. 25. Spanish.

6244 Yarter, R. Alexandra. Venga conmigo. LLUEVE
TLALOC, no. 13 (1986), p. 23. Spanish.

6245 Ynclan, Maria Estela. Que son los padres.
LLUEVE TLALOC, no. 7 (1980), p. 41. Spanish.

6246 Yubeta, Alma. Querida amiga. LLUEVE TLALOC,
no. 13 (1986), p. 21. Spanish.

6247 Zepeda, Fabiola. Hasta cuando tata dios.
REVISTA MUJERES, Vol. 3, no. 2 (June 1986),
p. 31. Spanish.

Poetry

6248 Benson, Douglas K. and Quintana, Leroy V. A
conversation with Leroy V. Quintana.
BILINGUAL REVIEW, Vol. 12, no. 3 (September,
December, 1985), p. 218-229. English.
DESCR: Authors; Biography; HIJO DEL PUEBLO;
*Quintana, Leroy V.; SANGRE.

6249 Benson, Douglas K. Intuitions of a world in
transition: the New Mexican poetry of Leroy
V. Quintana. BILINGUAL REVIEW, Vol. 12, no.
1-2 (January, August, 1985), p. 62-80.
English. **DESCR:** Authors; HIJO DEL PUEBLO;
*Literary Criticism; New Mexico; *Quintana,
Leroy V.; SANGRE.

6250 Billings, Linda M. and Alurista. In verbal
murals: a study of Chicana herstory and
poetry. CONFLUENCIA, Vol. 2, no. 1 (Fall
1986), p. 60-68. English. **DESCR:** Candelaria,
Cordelia; Cervantes, Lorna Dee; *Chicanas;
Cisneros, Sandra; EMPLUMADA; *Feminism;
History; Literary Criticism; Xelina.

6251 Bruce-Novoa, Juan. Elegias a la frontera
hispanica. BILINGUAL REVIEW, Vol. 11, no. 3
(September, December, 1984), p. 37-44.
Spanish. **DESCR:** *"El Louie" [poem]; *LAS
COPLAS A LA MUERTE DE SU PADRE; Literary
Criticism; Manrique, Jorge; Montoya, Jose
E.

6252 Bruce-Novoa, Juan. Poesia de Gary Soto: una
autobiografia a plazos. LA COMUNIDAD, No.
270 (September 22, 1985), p. 8-10. Spanish.
DESCR: Authors; *Literary Criticism; *Soto,
Gary; TALE OF SUNLIGHT; THE ELEMENTS OF SAN
JOAQUIN; WHERE SPARROWS WORK HARD.

6253 Candelaria, Cordelia. Book review of: FIESTA
IN AZTLAN: ANTHOLOGY OF CHICANO POETRY and
FLOR Y CANTO IV AND V. LA RED/THE NET, no.
62 (December 1982), p. 6-9. English. **DESCR:**
Book Reviews; Empringham, Toni; *FIESTA IN
AZTLAN: AN ANTHOLOGY OF CHICANO POETRY;
*FLOR Y CANTO IV AND V: AN ANTHOLOGY OF
CHICANO LITERATURE FROM THE FESTIVALS HELD
IN ALBUQUERQUE, NEW MEXICO.

6254 Elias, Edward F. A meeting of poets from
east and west: Lorna Dee Cervantes, Gary
Soto, Tato Laviera. BILINGUAL REVIEW, Vol.
12, no. 1-2 (January, August, 1985), p.
150-155. English. **DESCR:** Authors; Cervantes,
Lorna Dee; *EMPLUMADA; *ENCLAVE; Laviera,
Tato; Literary Criticism; Literature
Reviews; Soto, Gary; *WHERE SPARROWS WORK
HARD.

6255 Espada, Martin and Perez-Erdelyi, Mireya.
With Martin Espada. THE AMERICAS REVIEW,
Vol. 15, no. 2 (Summer 1987), p. 77-85.
English. **DESCR:** Authors; *Espada, Martin;
Language Usage; Puerto Ricans.

6256 Garcia, Mario T. Bracero poetry of the
1940s: two samples. BILINGUAL REVIEW, Vol.
11, no. 3 (September, December, 1984), p.
45-48. English. **DESCR:** *Braceros; EL
ESPECTADOR, Pomona, CA.

6257 Grabo, Norman S. Book review of:
CONTEMPORARY CHICANA POETRY. AMERICAN
LITERATURE, Vol. 58, no. 3 (October 1986),
p. 473-475. English. **DESCR:** Book Reviews;
*CONTEMPORARY CHICANA POETRY: A CRITICAL
APPROACH TO AN EMERGING LITERATURE; Sanchez,
Marta Ester.

Poetry (cont.)

6258 Gurza, Esperanza. I AM JOAQUIN: speech act
theory applied. CONFLUENCIA, Vol. 1, no. 2
(Spring 1986), p. 85-97. English. **DESCR:**
Gonzales, Rodolfo (Corky); *I AM JOAQUIN
[book]; Rhetoric.

6259 Krauth, Leland. Book review of: CHICANO
POETRY: A CRITICAL INTRODUCTION. LIBRARY
JOURNAL, Vol. 111, (April 15, 1986), p. 82.
English. **DESCR:** Book Reviews; Candelaria,
Cordelia; *CHICANO POETRY: A CRITICAL
INTRODUCTION.

6260 Lewis, Tom J. Book review of: CONTEMPORARY
CHICANA POETRY. WORLD LITERATURE TODAY, Vol.
60, (Summer 1986), p. 453. English. **DESCR:**
Book Reviews; Chicanas; *CONTEMPORARY
CHICANA POETRY: A CRITICAL APPROACH TO AN
EMERGING LITERATURE; Sanchez, Marta Ester.

6261 Lomeli, Francisco A. El concepto del barrio
en tres poetas chicanos. LA COMUNIDAD, No.
316 (August 10, 1986), p. 4-5+. Spanish.
DESCR: Alurista; Barrios; Delgado, Abelardo
"Lalo"; *Literary Criticism; Sanchez,
Ricardo.

6262 Mendez-M., Miguel. Introduccion. LLUEVE
TLALOC, no. 12 (1985), p. iv. Spanish.
DESCR: *Educational Theory and Practice;
Fiction; *Pima Community College, Tucson,
AZ.

6263 Mendez-M., Miguel. Introduction. LLUEVE
TLALOC, no. 12 (1985), p. iv. English.
DESCR: Educational Theory and Practice;
Fiction; *Pima Community College, Tucson,
AZ.

6264 Mora, Pat and Alarcon, Norma. A poet
analyzes her craft. NUESTRO, Vol. 11, no. 2
(March 1987), p. 25-27. English. **DESCR:**
*Authors; BORDERS; CHANTS; *Chicanas; *Mora,
Pat.

6265 Olivares, Julian. Self and society in Tino
Villanueva's SHAKING OFF THE DARK.
CONFLUENCIA, Vol. 1, no. 2 (Spring 1986), p.
98-110. English. **DESCR:** Literary Criticism;
*SHAKING OFF THE DARK; Villanueva, Tino.

6266 Paredes, Raymund A. Review essay: recent
Chicano writing. ROCKY MOUNTAIN REVIEW OF
LANGUAGE AND LITERATURE, Vol. 41, (1987),
p. 124-129. English. **DESCR:** Castillo, Ana;
Catholic Church; Chavez, Denise; Chicanas;
Garcia, Lionel; GIVING UP THE GHOST; LEAVING
HOME; *Literary Criticism; *Literature
Reviews; Moraga, Cherrie; Prose; Sex Roles;
Silva, Beverly; SMALL FACES; Soto, Gary; THE
CAT AND OTHER STORIES; THE LAST OF THE MENU
GIRLS; THE MIXQUIAHUALA LETTERS.

6267 Quintana, Alvina. O mama, with what's inside
of me. REVISTA MUJERES, Vol. 3, no. 1
(January 1986), p. 38-40. English. **DESCR:**
*Alarcon, Norma; *Chicanas; Feminism;
*Literary Criticism; *"What Kind of Lover
Have You Made Me, Mother?: Towards a Theory
of Chicanas' Feminism and Cultural Identity
Through Poetry" [article].

6268 Saldivar, Jose David. Towards a Chicano
poetics: the making of the Chicano subject.
CONFLUENCIA, Vol. 1, no. 2 (Spring 1986), p.
10-17. English. **DESCR:** Corridos; Feminism;
*Literary Criticism; "Los vatos" [poem];
Montoya, Jose E.; RESTLESS SERPENTS; Rios,
Alberto; WHISPERING TO FOOL THE WIND;
Zamora, Bernice.

6269 Schmitt, Jack. Book review of: CONTEMPORARY

CHICANA POETRY. LOS ANGELES TIMES BOOK
REVIEW, (December 29, 1985), p. 8. English.
DESCR: Book Reviews; Chicanas; *CONTEMPORARY
CHICANA POETRY: A CRITICAL APPROACH TO AN
EMERGING LITERATURE; Sanchez, Marta Ester.

Poets
USE: Authors

Police

6270 Debro, Julius, et al. Workshop presentation:
stress and its control: a minority
perspective. POLICE CHIEF, Vol. 50, no. 3
(March 1983), p. 106-115. English. **DESCR:**
Stress.

6271 Escobar, Edward J. Mexican revolutionaries
and the Los Angeles police: harassment of
the Partido Liberal Mexicano, 1907-1910.
AZTLAN, Vol. 17, no. 1 (Spring 1986), p.
1-46. English. **DESCR:** Civil Rights; *Flores
Magon, Ricardo; Gutierrez de Lara, Lazaro;
Los Angeles, CA; *Los Angeles Police
Department; *Partido Liberal Mexicano (PLM);
Police Brutality; Political Repression;
Rico, Louis; Rico, Thomas; Talamantes,
Felipe; United States-Mexico Relations.

6272 Perez, Renato E. Badge of Hispanic pride.
VISTA, Vol. 1, no. 12 (August 2, 1986), p.
9-11. English. **DESCR:** Broward County, FL;
Chicago, IL; Dallas, TX; Houston, TX; *Los
Angeles, CA; New York, NY; San Antonio, TX;
San Diego, CA; Tucson, AZ.

6273 Rifkin, Jane M. Up from the barrio...to
fittest woman cop in the U.S.A. HISPANIC
TIMES, Vol. 8, no. 1 (December, January,
1987), p. 38. English. **DESCR:** Biography;
Careers; *Chicanas; *Lopez, Theresa (Terry).

Police Brutality

6274 Escobar, Edward J. Mexican revolutionaries
and the Los Angeles police: harassment of
the Partido Liberal Mexicano, 1907-1910.
AZTLAN, Vol. 17, no. 1 (Spring 1986), p.
1-46. English. **DESCR:** Civil Rights; *Flores
Magon, Ricardo; Gutierrez de Lara, Lazaro;
Los Angeles, CA; *Los Angeles Police
Department; *Partido Liberal Mexicano (PLM);
*Police; Political Repression; Rico, Louis;
Rico, Thomas; Talamantes, Felipe; United
States-Mexico Relations.

Policy
USE: Public Policy

POLITICAL AND ECONOMIC MIGRANTS IN AMERICA

6275 Chiswick, Barry R. Book review of: POLITICAL
AND ECONOMIC MIGRANTS IN AMERICA. JOURNAL OF
AMERICAN ETHNIC HISTORY, Vol. 7, no. 1 (Fall
1987), p. 105-106. English. **DESCR:** Book
Reviews; Immigrants; Pedraza-Bailey, Silvia.

6276 Garcia, Mario T. Book review of: POLITICAL
AND ECONOMIC MIGRANTS IN AMERICA. LA RED/THE
NET, no. 96 (May 1986), p. 11-12. English.
DESCR: Book Reviews; Immigration;
Pedraza-Bailey, Silvia.

6277 Garcia, Mario T. Book review of: POLITICAL
AND ECONOMIC MIGRANTS IN AMERICA. AMERICAN
HISTORICAL REVIEW, Vol. 91, no. 4 (October
1986), p. 1023-1024. English. **DESCR:** Book
Reviews; Immigrants; Immigration;
Pedraza-Bailey, Silvia.

Political Appointments
USE: Appointed Officials

Political Association of Spanish-Speaking Organizations (PASO)

6278 Bueno, Patricia E. Los Chicanos y la
     politica II. LA COMUNIDAD, No. 268
     (September 8, 1985), p. 2-3. Spanish.
     DESCR: American G.I. Forum; Chicano
     Movement; History; Leadership; Mexican
     American Political Association (MAPA);
     Nationalism; *Political Parties and
     Organizations.

Political History and Conditions

6279 Anaya, Toney and Lujan, Edward. Sanctuary:
     right or wrong? VISTA, Vol. 1, no. 11 (July
     6, 1986), p. 18-19, 21. English. **DESCR:**
     *Central America; Deportation; *Political
     Refugees.

6280 de Leon, Arnoldo. Tejano history
     scholarship: a review of the recent
     literature. WEST TEXAS HISTORICAL
     ASSOCIATION YEARBOOK, Vol. 61, (1985), p.
     116-133. English. **DESCR:** Historiography;
     *Literature Reviews; Social History and
     Conditions; *Texas.

6281 Falcon, Angelo. Puerto Rican politics in
     urban America: an introduction to the
     literature. LA RED/THE NET, no. 70 (July
     1983), p. 2-9. English. **DESCR:** Literature
     Reviews; Politics; *Puerto Ricans.

6282 Martinez, Walter. A deep cultural heritage
     enriches American society. VISTA, Vol. 1,
     no. 2 (October 5, 1985), p. 3. English.
     DESCR: *San Antonio, TX.

6283 Ruiz Garza, Pedro. Taking a fresh look at
     the decade of the Hispanic. VISTA, Vol. 1,
     no. 11 (July 6, 1986), p. 3. English.
     DESCR: Essays.

6284 Valenzuela-Crocker, Elvira. Small town
     Hispanic America. VISTA, Vol. 1, no. 11
     (July 6, 1986), p. 12-14. English. **DESCR:**
     Garcia, Frances [mayor of Hutchinson, KS];
     *Population; Spanish Speaking Affairs
     Council of St. Paul; *Trejo, Jose.

Political Ideology

6285 Bunge, Mario. Ciencia e ideologia en el
     mundo hispanico. INTERCIENCIA, Vol. 11, no.
     3 (May, June, 1986), p. 120-125. Spanish.
     DESCR: Political Repression; *Science.

6286 Communist Party, U.S.A. On
     Chicano/Mexican-American equality. POLITICAL
     AFFAIRS, Vol. 66, no. 4 (April 1987), p. 35.
     English. **DESCR:** Communist Party;
     *Discrimination; *Social History and
     Conditions.

6287 Garcia, John A. The political integration of
     Mexican immigrants: examining some political
     orientations. INTERNATIONAL MIGRATION
     REVIEW, Vol. 21, no. 2 (Summer 1987), p.
     372-389. English. **DESCR:** Culture;
     *Immigrants; *National Chicano Survey (NCS);
     *Political Socialization.

6288 Rosaldo, Renato. When natives talk back:
     Chicano anthropology since the late 60s.
     RENATO ROSALDO LECTURE SERIES MONOGRAPH,
     Vol. 2, (Spring 1986), p. [3]-20. English.
     DESCR: *Anthropology; Culture; EL GRITO;
     *Identity; Paredes, Americo; *Research
     Methodology; Romano-V., Octavio Ignacio;
     Valdez, Facundo.

6289 Sanchez, Rosaura. Ethnicity, ideology and
     academia. THE AMERICAS REVIEW, Vol. 15, no.

1 (Spring 1987), p. 80-88. English. **DESCR:**
Culture; *Ethnic Studies.

Political Participation
     USE: Voter Turnout

Political Parties and Organizations

6290 Bueno, Patricia E. Los Chicanos y la
     politica. LA COMUNIDAD, No. 267 (September
     1, 1985), p. 6-7. Spanish. **DESCR:** Community
     Service Organization, Los Angeles, (CSO);
     Discrimination; History; Leadership; League
     of United Latin American Citizens (LULAC);
     Orden Hijos de America, San Antonio, TX.

6291 Bueno, Patricia E. Los Chicanos y la
     politica II. LA COMUNIDAD, No. 268
     (September 8, 1985), p. 2-3. Spanish.
     DESCR: American G.I. Forum; Chicano
     Movement; History; Leadership; Mexican
     American Political Association (MAPA);
     Nationalism; Political Association of
     Spanish-Speaking Organizations (PASO).

6292 Cortes, Ernesto, Jr. Changing the locus of
     political decision making. CHRISTIANITY AND
     CRISIS, Vol. 47, no. 1 (February 2, 1987),
     p. 18-22. English. **DESCR:** Biography;
     *Communities Organized for Public Service
     (COPS); *Cortes, Ernesto, Jr.; San Antonio,
     TX.

6293 Gonzales, Juan. San Francisco's Mission
     District: part I. LATIN QUARTER, Vol. 1, no.
     4 (July, August, 1975), p. 21-25. English.
     DESCR: La Mision Dolores Iglesia Catolica;
     *Local History; *Mission District, San
     Francisco, CA; San Francisco, CA; *Urban
     Communities.

6294 Gutierrez, Jose Angel. Chicanos and
     Mexicans: under surveillance: 1940 to 1980.
     RENATO ROSALDO LECTURE SERIES MONOGRAPH,
     Vol. 2, (Spring 1986), p. [29]-58. English.
     DESCR: Acuna, Rudolfo; Border Coverage
     Program (BOCOV); *Civil Rights; COINTELPRO;
     *Federal Bureau of Investigation (FBI);
     *Federal Government; History; League of
     United Latin American Citizens (LULAC);
     Mexico; *Political Repression.

6295 Munoz, Carlos, Jr. Chicano politics: the
     current conjuncture. THE YEAR LEFT, Vol. 2,
     (1987), p. 35-52. English. **DESCR:** Chicano
     Movement; Identity; *Intergroup Relations;
     *Politics; Reagan Administration; Voter
     Turnout.

6296 Munoz, Carlos, Jr. and Henry, Charles.
     Rainbow coalitions in four big cities: San
     Antonio, Denver, Chicago and Philadelphia.
     P.S. [AMERICAN POLITICAL SCIENCE
     ASSOCIATION], Vol. 19, no. 3 (Summer 1986),
     p. 598-609. English. **DESCR:** Blacks; Chicago,
     IL; Cisneros, Henry, Mayor of San Antonio,
     TX; Denver, CO; Elected Officials; Ethnic
     Groups; Intergroup Relations; Pena,
     Federico; Philadelphia, PA; Political
     Representation; *Politics; San Antonio, TX;
     Urban Communities.

6297 Sonenshein, Raphe. Biracial coalition
     politics in Los Angeles. P.S. [AMERICAN
     POLITICAL SCIENCE ASSOCIATION], Vol. 19, no.
     3 (Summer 1986), p. 582-590. English.
     DESCR: Blacks; Bradley, Tom; Browning, Rufus
     P.; *Ethnic Groups; *Intergroup Relations;
     *Los Angeles, CA; Marshall, Dale Rogers;
     *Politics; PROTEST IS NOT ENOUGH: THE
     STRUGGLE OF BLACKS AND HISPANICS FOR
     EQUALITY IN URBAN POLITICS; Tabb, David H.

Political Parties and Organizations (cont.)

6298 Volsky, George. A new voting block making
its mark. HISPANIC BUSINESS, Vol. 9, no. 2
(February 1987), p. 9, 11. English. **DESCR:**
Cubanos; Democratic Party; Elections;
Republican Party; *Voter Turnout.

Political Prisoners

6299 Gordon, Charles. The rights of aliens: an
expanding role for trial lawyers. TRIAL,
Vol. 19, no. 12 (December 1983), p. 54-58.
English. **DESCR:** Deportation; Immigration Law
and Legislation; *Legal Profession;
*Undocumented Workers.

Political Refugees

6300 Anaya, Toney and Lujan, Edward. Sanctuary:
right or wrong? VISTA, Vol. 1, no. 11 (July
6, 1986), p. 18-19, 21. English. **DESCR:**
*Central America; Deportation; Political
History and Conditions.

6301 Kahn, Robert. Oakdale prison: documenting
the abuses. IN THESE TIMES, Vol. 10, no. 35
(September 17, 1986), p. 8, 22. English.
DESCR: Allen Parish, LA; Legal
Representation; *Oakdale, LA; Oakdale Legal
Assistance (OLA); Prisons; Undocumented
Workers; U.S. Bureau of Prisons (BOP).

6302 Protecting aliens from persecution without
overloading the INS. VIRGINIA LAW REVIEW,
Vol. 69, (June 1983), p. 901-930. English.
DESCR: Nunez v. Boldin; *Orantes, Hernandez
v. Smith; Refugee Act of 1980; *Undocumented
Workers.

6303 Rodriguez, Nestor. Undocumented Central
Americans in Houston: diverse populations.
INTERNATIONAL MIGRATION REVIEW, Vol. 21, no.
1 (Spring 1987), p. 4-26. English. **DESCR:**
*Central America; El Salvador; Ethnic
Groups; Guatemala; Honduras; *Houston, TX;
Immigrants; Intergroup Relations; Latin
Americans; *Undocumented Workers.

6304 Stacy, G. Palmer and Lutton, Wayne. The U.S.
immigration crisis. JOURNAL OF SOCIAL
POLITICAL AND ECONOMIC STUDIES, Vol. 10, no.
3 (Fall 1985), p. 333-350. English. **DESCR:**
*Immigration; Population.

Political Representation

6305 Avila, Joaquin; Arce, Carlos H.; and Mexican
American Legal Defense and Education Fund
(MALDEF). Task force on civic identity and
political participation. LA RED/THE NET, no.
88 (Winter 1984), p. 17-21. English. **DESCR:**
Elected Officials; *Public Policy.

6306 Browning, Rufus P.; Marshall, Dale Rogers;
and Tabb, David H. Protest is not enough: a
theory of political incorporation. P.S.
[AMERICAN POLITICAL SCIENCE ASSOCIATION],
Vol. 19, no. 3 (Summer 1986), p. 576-581.
English. **DESCR:** Blacks; Browning, Rufus P.;
Marshall, Dale Rogers; Politics; *PROTEST IS
NOT ENOUGH: THE STRUGGLE OF BLACKS AND
HISPANICS FOR EQUALITY IN URBAN POLITICS;
Tabb, David H.; Urban Communities.

6307 de la Garza, Rodolfo O. The Mexican American
electorate. LA RED/THE NET, no. 72
(September 1983), p. 2-6. English. **DESCR:**
*Southwest Voter Registration Education
Project (SVREP); *Voter Turnout.

6308 Garcia, John A. Chicano political
development: examining participation in the
"decade of Hispanics". LA RED/THE NET, no.

72 (September 1983), p. 8-18. English.
DESCR: Reapportionment; Voter Turnout.

6309 Hero, Rodney E. Mexican Americans and urban
politics: a consideration of governmental
structure and policy. AZTLAN, Vol. 17, no. 1
(Spring 1986), p. 131-147. English. **DESCR:**
Colorado; *Politics; Public Policy; *Urban
Communities.

6310 Los Angeles: arriba! ECONOMIST (London),
Vol. 297, no. 7424 (December 14, 1985), p.
26. English. **DESCR:** Bradley, Tom; *Los
Angeles, CA; Politics; Reapportionment;
Voter Turnout.

6311 Los Angeles: brown versus yellow. ECONOMIST
(London), Vol. 300, no. 7456 (July 26,
1986), p. 21-22. English. **DESCR:** Alatorre,
Richard; Bradley, Tom; Ethnic Groups; *Los
Angeles, CA; Politics; Reapportionment;
Voter Turnout; Woo, Michael.

6312 Munoz, Carlos, Jr. and Henry, Charles.
Rainbow coalitions in four big cities: San
Antonio, Denver, Chicago and Philadelphia.
P.S. [AMERICAN POLITICAL SCIENCE
ASSOCIATION], Vol. 19, no. 3 (Summer 1986),
p. 598-609. English. **DESCR:** Blacks; Chicago,
IL; Cisneros, Henry, Mayor of San Antonio,
TX; Denver, CO; Elected Officials; Ethnic
Groups; Intergroup Relations; Pena,
Federico; Philadelphia, PA; Political
Parties and Organizations; *Politics; San
Antonio, TX; Urban Communities.

6313 National Association of Latino Elected and
Appointed Officials. The Hispanic vote. LA
RED/THE NET, no. 72 (September 1983), p.
2-3. English. **DESCR:** *Voter Turnout.

Political Repression

6314 Bunge, Mario. Ciencia e ideologia en el
mundo hispanico. INTERCIENCIA, Vol. 11, no.
3 (May, June, 1986), p. 120-125. Spanish.
DESCR: Political Ideology; *Science.

6315 Escobar, Edward J. Mexican revolutionaries
and the Los Angeles police: harassment of
the Partido Liberal Mexicano, 1907-1910.
AZTLAN, Vol. 17, no. 1 (Spring 1986), p.
1-46. English. **DESCR:** Civil Rights; *Flores
Magon, Ricardo; Gutierrez de Lara, Lazaro;
Los Angeles, CA; *Los Angeles Police
Department; *Partido Liberal Mexicano (PLM);
*Police; Police Brutality; Rico, Louis;
Rico, Thomas; Talamantes, Felipe; United
States-Mexico Relations.

6316 Gutierrez, Jose Angel. Chicanos and
Mexicans: under surveillance: 1940 to 1980.
RENATO ROSALDO LECTURE SERIES MONOGRAPH,
Vol. 2, (Spring 1986), p. [29]-58. English.
DESCR: Acuna, Rudolfo; Border Coverage
Program (BOCOV); *Civil Rights; COINTELPRO;
*Federal Bureau of Investigation (FBI);
*Federal Government; History; League of
United Latin American Citizens (LULAC);
Mexico; Political Parties and Organizations.

6317 Martinez, David A. The nightmare of Kiko
Martinez. GUILD NOTES, Vol. 9, no. 2 (Spring
1985), p. 4. English. **DESCR:** Criminal
Justice System; Legal Cases; *Legal
Profession; *Martinez, Francisco "Kiko".

Political Repression (cont.)

6318 Martinez, Elizabeth. A decade of repression: update on the "Kiko" Martinez case. CRIME AND SOCIAL JUSTICE, no. 19 (Summer 1983), p. 100. English. **DESCR:** Chicano Movement; Civil Rights; Colorado; Criminal Justice System; Discrimination; Legal Cases; *Martinez, Francisco "Kiko".

Political Socialization

6319 Garcia, John A. The political integration of Mexican immigrants: examining some political orientations. INTERNATIONAL MIGRATION REVIEW, Vol. 21, no. 2 (Summer 1987), p. 372-389. English. **DESCR:** Culture; *Immigrants; *National Chicano Survey (NCS); Political Ideology.

6320 Howell-Martinez, Vicky. The influence of gender roles on political socialization: an experimental study of Mexican-American children. WOMEN & POLITICS, Vol. 2, (Fall 1982), p. 33-46. English. **DESCR:** Attitudes; Child Study; Children; Sex Roles; *Sex Stereotypes.

6321 Hurtado, Aida and Gurin, Patricia. Ethnic identity and bilingualism attitudes. HISPANIC JOURNAL OF BEHAVIORAL SCIENCES, Vol. 9, no. 1 (March 1987), p. 1-18. English. **DESCR:** *Attitudes; *Bilingualism; *Identity.

Political System

6322 Castro, Richard T. A role for Hispanic Americans in foreign policy formulation. VISTA, Vol. 1, no. 9 (May 3, 1986), p. 3. English. **DESCR:** *Essays; *Hispanic Caucus; International Relations.

6323 McNeely, Dave. Hispanic power at the polls. VISTA, Vol. 2, no. 3 (November 2, 1986), p. 8-12. English. **DESCR:** Austin, TX; *Barrera, Roy, Jr.; Chavez, Linda; Elected Officials; Gonzalez, Raul; Martinez, Bob; Maryland; San Antonio, TX; Statistics; Tampa, FL; *Voter Turnout.

Politicos
USE: Elected Officials

Politics

6324 Bethell, Tom. Senator Simpson's reward. AMERICAN SPECTATOR, Vol. 19, no. 2 (February 1986), p. 11-13. English. **DESCR:** Discrimination; Immigration Law and Legislation; *Simpson, Alan K.; Undocumented Workers.

6325 Bogart, Beth. Political power gives market vote of confidence. ADVERTISING AGE MAGAZINE, Vol. 58, no. 6 (February 9, 1987), p. S22. English. **DESCR:** Voter Turnout.

6326 Browning, Rufus P. and Marshall, Dale Rogers. Black and Hispanic power in city politics: a forum. P.S. [AMERICAN POLITICAL SCIENCE ASSOCIATION], Vol. 19, no. 3 (Summer 1986), p. 573-639. English. **DESCR:** Blacks; Browning, Rufus P.; Marshall, Dale Rogers; *PROTEST IS NOT ENOUGH: THE STRUGGLE OF BLACKS AND HISPANICS FOR EQUALITY IN URBAN POLITICS; Tabb, David H.; Urban Communities.

6327 Browning, Rufus P.; Marshall, Dale Rogers; and Tabb, David H. Protest is not enough: a theory of political incorporation. P.S. [AMERICAN POLITICAL SCIENCE ASSOCIATION], Vol. 19, no. 3 (Summer 1986), p. 576-581. English. **DESCR:** Blacks; Browning, Rufus P.;

Marshall, Dale Rogers; Political Representation; *PROTEST IS NOT ENOUGH: THE STRUGGLE OF BLACKS AND HISPANICS FOR EQUALITY IN URBAN POLITICS; Tabb, David H.; Urban Communities.

6328 Esman, Milton J. Two dimensions of ethnic politics: defense of homelands, immigrant rights. ETHNIC AND RACIAL STUDIES, Vol. 8, no. 3 (July 1985), p. 438-440. English. **DESCR:** Ethnic Groups; *Immigrants.

6329 Falcon, Angelo. Puerto Rican politics in urban America: an introduction to the literature. LA RED/THE NET, no. 70 (July 1983), p. 2-9. English. **DESCR:** Literature Reviews; Political History and Conditions; *Puerto Ricans.

6330 Garcia, John A. Book review of: AMERICA'S ETHNIC POLITICS. LA RED/THE NET, no. 67 (April 1983), p. 7-8. English. **DESCR:** *AMERICA'S ETHNIC POLITICS; Book Reviews; Eisenberg, Bernard; Roucek, Joseph S.

6331 Gonzales, Phillip B. Book review of: LATINOS IN THE UNITED STATES: THE SACRED AND THE POLITICAL. NEW MEXICO HISTORICAL REVIEW, Vol. 62, no. 4 (October 1987), p. 409-11. English. **DESCR:** *Abalos, David T.; Book Reviews; *LATINOS IN THE UNITED STATES: THE SACRED AND THE POLITICAL; Religion.

6332 Guerrero, Martha and Anaya, Toney. Toney Anaya: a man with convictions=Toney Anaya: un hombre de conviccion. AMERICAS 2001, Premiere Issue, 1987, p. 20-23, 44. Bilingual. **DESCR:** *Anaya, Toney, Governor of New Mexico; Biography; Elected Officials; New Mexico.

6333 Hero, Rodney E. Mexican Americans and urban politics: a consideration of governmental structure and policy. AZTLAN, Vol. 17, no. 1 (Spring 1986), p. 131-147. English. **DESCR:** Colorado; *Political Representation; Public Policy; *Urban Communities.

6334 Lena Guerrero. INTERCAMBIOS FEMENILES, Vol. 2, no. 6 (Spring 1987), p. 15,26. English. **DESCR:** Chicanas; *Guerrero, Lena; Leadership.

6335 Llorente, Elizabeth. Linda Chavez: thriving on controversy. VISTA, Vol. 3, no. 3 (November 8, 1987), p. 6-9. English. **DESCR:** *Chavez, Linda; *English Language; U.S. English.

6336 Los Angeles: arriba! ECONOMIST (London), Vol. 297, no. 7424 (December 14, 1985), p. 26. English. **DESCR:** Bradley, Tom; *Los Angeles, CA; Political Representation; Reapportionment; Voter Turnout.

6337 Los Angeles: brown versus yellow. ECONOMIST (London), Vol. 300, no. 7456 (July 26, 1986), p. 21-22. English. **DESCR:** Alatorre, Richard; Bradley, Tom; Ethnic Groups; *Los Angeles, CA; Political Representation; Reapportionment; Voter Turnout; Woo, Michael.

6338 Marketing to Hispanics. ADVERTISING AGE MAGAZINE, Vol. 58, no. 6 (February 9, 1987), p. S1-S23. English. **DESCR:** Advertising; Consumers; Immigrants; *Marketing; Mass Media; Undocumented Workers.

Politics (cont.)

6339 Munoz, Carlos, Jr. Chicano politics: the current conjuncture. THE YEAR LEFT, Vol. 2, (1987), p. 35-52. English. **DESCR:** Chicano Movement; Identity; *Intergroup Relations; *Political Parties and Organizations; Reagan Administration; Voter Turnout.

6340 Munoz, Carlos, Jr. and Henry, Charles. Rainbow coalitions in four big cities: San Antonio, Denver, Chicago and Philadelphia. P.S. [AMERICAN POLITICAL SCIENCE ASSOCIATION], Vol. 19, no. 3 (Summer 1986), p. 598-609. English. **DESCR:** Blacks; Chicago, IL; Cisneros, Henry, Mayor of San Antonio, TX; Denver, CO; Elected Officials; Ethnic Groups; Intergroup Relations; Pena, Federico; Philadelphia, PA; Political Parties and Organizations; Political Representation; San Antonio, TX; Urban Communities.

6341 Rodriguez, Roberto and Roybal, Edward R. Congressman Edward Roybal: elder statesman=El congresista Edward Roybal: un veterano estadista. AMERICAS 2001, Vol. 1, no. 1 (June, July, 1987), p. 23-25. Bilingual. **DESCR:** *Roybal, Edward R.

6342 Sonenshein, Raphe. Biracial coalition politics in Los Angeles. P.S. [AMERICAN POLITICAL SCIENCE ASSOCIATION], Vol. 19, no. 3 (Summer 1986), p. 582-590. English. **DESCR:** Blacks; Bradley, Tom; Browning, Rufus P.; *Ethnic Groups; *Intergroup Relations; *Los Angeles, CA; Marshall, Dale Rogers; Political Parties and Organizations; PROTEST IS NOT ENOUGH: THE STRUGGLE OF BLACKS AND HISPANICS FOR EQUALITY IN URBAN POLITICS; Tabb, David H.

6343 Wreford, Mary. Chicano Survey report #3: political opinions. LA RED/THE NET, no. 40 (March 1981), p. 4-5. English. **DESCR:** *National Chicano Survey (NCS); *Voter Turnout.

6344 Zesch, Lindy. Visa issue heats up: PEN hopes for "group waiver" of denials. AMERICAN THEATRE, Vol. 2, no. 8 (November 1985), p. 24. English. **DESCR:** Artists; Authors; Book Reviews; GETTING IN: A GUIDE TO OVERCOMING THE POLITICAL DENIAL OF NON-IMMIGRANT VISAS; National Lawyer's Guild; *Visas.

POLITICS & CHICANO CULTURE: A PERSPECTIVE ON EL TEATRO CAMPESINO

6345 Anderson de Barret, Judit. Book review of: POLITICS AND CHICANO CULTURE. LECTOR, Vol. 4, no. 4-6 (1987), p. 56. English. **DESCR:** Book Reviews; Teatro; Xavier, Roy Eric.

THE POLITICS OF SAN ANTONIO

6346 Hall, Linda B. The United States-Mexican borders: historical, political, and cultural perspectives. LATIN AMERICAN RESEARCH REVIEW, Vol. 20, no. 2 (1985), p. 223-229. English. **DESCR:** AMERICAN LABOR IN THE SOUTHWEST: THE FIRST ONE HUNDRED YEARS; *Book Reviews; *Border Region; BOSS RULE IN SOUTH TEXAS: THE PROGRESSIVE ERA; CHICANO INTERMARRIAGE: A THEORETICAL AND EMPIRICAL STUDY; HISPANIC CULTURE IN THE SOUTHWEST; IN DEFENSE OF LA RAZA: THE LOS ANGELES MEXICAN CONSULATE AND THE MEXICAN COMMUNITY; Literature Reviews; RACE AND CLASS IN THE SOUTHWEST: A THEORY OF RACIAL INEQUALITY; SOUTHWESTERN AGRICULTURE: PRE-COLUMBIAN TO MODERN; THE MEXICANS IN OKLAHOMA.

Ponce, Alice

6347 Rifkin, Jane M. New avenues for women in technology. HISPANIC TIMES, Vol. 8, no. 3 (May, June, 1987), p. 41. English. **DESCR:** Biographical Notes; *Chicanas; Engineering as a Profession.

Pope John Paul II

6348 Allsup, Dan. A Texas hello for John Paul II. VISTA, Vol. 3, no. 1 (September 6, 1987), p. 8-9. English. **DESCR:** Catholic Church; *Clergy; San Antonio, TX.

6349 Search for Hispanic heroes informs, surprises, confirms. VISTA, Vol. 1, no. 10 (June 8, 1986), p. 18-19. English. **DESCR:** Mother Theresa; *Public Opinion; Reagan, Ronald.

Population

6350 Alvirez, David. Book review of: THE CHANGING DEMOGRAPHY OF SPANISH AMERICANS. LA RED/THE NET, no. 48 (November 1981), p. 4. English. **DESCR:** Book Reviews; Boswell, Thomas D.; Cullen, Ruth M.; Jaffee, A.J.; *THE CHANGING DEMOGRAPHY OF SPANISH-AMERICANS.

6351 Balkan, D. Carlos. The Hispanic market's leading indicators. HISPANIC BUSINESS, Vol. 9, no. 12 (December 1987), p. 16-17. English. **DESCR:** Advertising; *Marketing; Statistics.

6352 Bos, Eduard. Estimates of the number of illegal aliens: an analysis of the sources of disagreement. POPULATION RESEARCH AND POLICY REVIEW, Vol. 3, (October 1984), p. 239-254. English. **DESCR:** *Undocumented Workers.

6353 Cook, Annabel Kirschner. Diversity among Northwest Hispanics. SOCIAL SCIENCE JOURNAL, Vol. 23, no. 2 (April 1986), p. 205-216. English. **DESCR:** Chicanas; *Northwestern United States; *Socioeconomic Factors; Working Women.

6354 Dunn, William. Chicago's Hispanics. AMERICAN DEMOGRAPHICS, Vol. 9, no. 2 (February 1987), p. 52-53. English. **DESCR:** *Chicago, IL; Statistics; U.S. Bureau of the Census.

6355 Estrada, Leobardo F. Demographic research on the Chicano population. LA RED/THE NET, no. 54 (May 1982), p. 4-7. English.

6356 Facing up to new occupational challenges. HISPANIC BUSINESS, Vol. 9, no. 6 (June 1987), p. 113. English. **DESCR:** *Employment; *Immigration; Rand Corporation.

6357 Garcia y Griego, Manuel. Estimating the undocumented population in the U.S. LA RED/THE NET, no. 58 (September 1982), p. 7-8,17. English. **DESCR:** *Undocumented Workers.

6358 Latino explosion continues for Latinos. HISPANIC TIMES, Vol. 8, no. 1 (December, January, 1987), p. 6. English.

6359 Macias, Reynaldo Flores and Cabello-Argandona, Roberto. Media research and the Chicano. LATIN QUARTER, Vol. 1, no. 2 (October 1974), p. 14-16,18. English. **DESCR:** Advertising; Consumers; Marketing; *Mass Media.

Population (cont.)

6360 Morales, Cecilio. Upbeat future for Hispanics. VISTA, Vol. 1, no. 1 (September 8, 1985), p. 6-7. English. **DESCR:** *MEGATRENDS; Naisbitt Group; Naisbitt, John.

6361 Perez, Renato E. Chicago: Hispanic melting pot. VISTA, Vol. 1, no. 3 (November 3, 1985), p. 20. English. **DESCR:** Camacho, Eduardo; Casuso, Jorge; *Chicago, IL; Cultural Pluralism; Ethnic Groups; HISPANICS IN CHICAGO.

6362 Slatta, Richard W. and Atkinson, Maxine P. The "Spanish origin" population of Oregon and Washington: a demographic profile, 1980. PACIFIC NORTHWEST QUARTERLY, Vol. 75, no. 3 (July 1984), p. 108-116. English. **DESCR:** *Oregon; Self-Referents; Socioeconomic Factors; Statistics; *Washington (state).

6363 Stacy, G. Palmer and Lutton, Wayne. The U.S. immigration crisis. JOURNAL OF SOCIAL POLITICAL AND ECONOMIC STUDIES, Vol. 10, no. 3 (Fall 1985), p. 333-350. English. **DESCR:** *Immigration; Political Refugees.

6364 Tienda, Marta. Task force on statistical policy and data needs. LA RED/THE NET, no. 88 (Winter, 1984), p. 2-6. English. **DESCR:** *Databases; Public Policy; Research Methodology; *Statistics; Vital Statistics.

6365 Torres-Gil, Fernando. The Latinization of a multigenerational population: Hispanics in an aging society. DAEDALUS, Vol. 115, no. 1 (Winter 1986), p. 325-348. English. **DESCR:** *Age Groups; Cultural Pluralism; *Public Policy; Social Classes; Socioeconomic Factors.

6366 U.S. Hispanic population: year 2080. HISPANIC BUSINESS, Vol. 9, no. 3 (March 1987), p. 50. English. **DESCR:** *Marketing.

6367 Valenzuela-Crocker, Elvira. Small town Hispanic America. VISTA, Vol. 1, no. 11 (July 6, 1986), p. 12-14. English. **DESCR:** Garcia, Frances [mayor of Hutchinson, KS]; Political History and Conditions; Spanish Speaking Affairs Council of St. Paul; *Trejo, Jose.

Population Distribution
USE: Population

Population Trends
USE: Population

Las Porciones Genealogical Society, Edinburg, TX

6368 Chavez, Lorenzo A. The quest for Hispanic roots. VISTA, Vol. 2, no. 7 (March 8, 1987), p. 5-6, 24. English. **DESCR:** Church of Jesus Christ of Latter-Day Saints (Mormons); Directories; *Garcia, Clotilde; *Genealogy; Hispanic American Genealogical Associates, Washington, DC; Los Bexarenos, San Antonio, TX; Los Californianos [genealogical society], San Jose, CA; Pan American University, Edinburg, TX; Texas Southmost College.

Portes, Alejandro

6369 Cobas, Jose A. Book review of: LATIN JOURNEY. INTERNATIONAL MIGRATION REVIEW, Vol. 21, no. 2 (Summer 1987), p. 434-435. English. **DESCR:** Bach, Robert L.; Book Reviews; *LATIN JOURNEY: CUBAN AND MEXICAN IMMIGRANTS IN THE UNITED STATES.

6370 Madrid, Arturo. Book reviews of: CLAMOR AT THE GATES and LATIN JOURNEY. LA RED/THE NET, no. 89 (August 1985), p. 7-10. English. **DESCR:** Bach, Robert L.; Book Reviews; *CLAMOR AT THE GATES: THE NEW AMERICAN IMMIGRATION; Glazer, Nathan; Immigration; *LATIN JOURNEY: CUBAN AND MEXICAN IMMIGRANTS IN THE UNITED STATES.

Las Posadas

6371 Hazen-Hammond, Susan and Fuss, Eduardo. Vivan las celebraciones. ARIZONA HIGHWAYS, Vol. 63, no. 8 (August 1987), p. 35-45. English. **DESCR:** Cinco de Mayo; Cultural Customs; Dia de los Muertos; Dieciseis de Septiembre; Fiestas Patrias; *Holidays; La Virgen de Guadalupe.

Post Secondary Education
USE: Higher Education

Poverty

6372 Jensen, Leif and Tienda, Marta. The new immigration: implications for poverty and public assistance utilization. MIGRATION WORLD MAGAZINE, Vol. 15, no. 5 (1987), p. 7-18. English. **DESCR:** History; Immigrants; *Immigration; *Immigration and Naturalization Act, 1965; Public Policy; *Welfare.

6373 Nieto, Sonia. Past accomplishments, current needs: la lucha continua. INTERRACIAL BOOKS FOR CHILDREN, Vol. 17, no. 2 (1986), p. 6-8. English. **DESCR:** Bilingual Bicultural Education; *Children's Literature; Council on Interracial Books for Children; Stereotypes.

6374 Schreiner, Tim. West: poor Hispanics. AMERICAN DEMOGRAPHICS, Vol. 9, no. 3 (March 1987), p. 54. English. **DESCR:** Low Income.

6375 Tienda, Marta. Rural poverty and Chicanos: have the seventies brought improvements? LA RED/THE NET, no. 26 (January 1980), p. 2. English. **DESCR:** *Rural Poor.

Poyesis Genetica [theater group]

6376 Gomez Pena, Guillermo. Declaracion de principios de un teatro bicultural. LA COMUNIDAD, No. 257 (June 23, 1985), p. 4-5. Spanish. **DESCR:** *Teatro.

Preciado Martin, Patricia

6377 Lopez, Steven. Book review of: IMAGES AND CONVERSATIONS. LA RED/THE NET, no. 77 (February 1984), p. 5-7. Magazine. **DESCR:** Book Reviews; *IMAGES AND CONVERSATIONS: MEXICAN AMERICANS RECALL A SOUTHWESTERN PAST.

Precolumbian Art
USE: Precolumbian Images

Precolumbian Images

6378 Braun, Barbara. The Aztecs: art and sacrifice. ART IN AMERICA, Vol. 72, no. 4 (April 1984), p. 126-139. English. **DESCR:** Anthropology; *Aztecs; Exhibits; Gods and Dieties; *Precolumbian Society; Templo Mayor, Tenochtitlan.

6379 Brito, Aristeo. [Note]. LLUEVE TLALOC, no. 14 (1987), p. xi. English. **DESCR:** *LLUEVE TLALOC.

Precolumbian Images (cont.)

6380 Klor de Alva, J. Jorge. California Chicano literature and pre-Columbian motifs: foil and fetish. CONFLUENCIA, Vol. 1, no. 2 (Spring 1986), p. 18-26. English. **DESCR:** Alurista; Aztecs; Aztlan; *California; EL PLAN ESPIRITUAL DE AZTLAN; *Literature; *Precolumbian Philosophy; Symbolism.

6381 Schon, Elizabeth. Introducing pre-Columbian and Hispanic art and artists to young adults through recent books. JOURNAL OF READING, Vol. 27, no. 3 (December 1983), p. 248-251. English. **DESCR:** Art; Artists; *Bibliography.

Precolumbian Literature

6382 Claymendez, Luis Felipe. La naturaleza en la literatura chicana y sus antecedentes prehispanicos. REVISTA DE ESTUDIOS HISPANICOS, Vol. 19, no. 2 (May 1985), p. 107-127. Spanish. **DESCR:** Literary Criticism; Literary History; *Literature.

Precolumbian Philosophy

6383 Klor de Alva, J. Jorge. California Chicano literature and pre-Columbian motifs: foil and fetish. CONFLUENCIA, Vol. 1, no. 2 (Spring 1986), p. 18-26. English. **DESCR:** Alurista; Aztecs; Aztlan; *California; EL PLAN ESPIRITUAL DE AZTLAN; *Literature; *Precolumbian Images; Symbolism.

6384 Segura, Andres. Continuidad de la tradicion filosofica Nahuatl en las danzas de concheros. EL CUADERNO, Vol. 3, no. 1 (Winter 1973), p. 16-33. Spanish. **DESCR:** Concheros Xinachtli; *Folklore.

Precolumbian Society

6385 Braun, Barbara. The Aztecs: art and sacrifice. ART IN AMERICA, Vol. 72, no. 4 (April 1984), p. 126-139. English. **DESCR:** Anthropology; *Aztecs; Exhibits; Gods and Dieties; *Precolumbian Images; Templo Mayor, Tenochtitlan.

6386 Bruce-Novoa, Juan. Mexico en la literatura chicana (I). LA COMUNIDAD, No. 267 (September 1, 1985), p. 12-13. Spanish. **DESCR:** History; *Literary Criticism; Mestizaje; Mexican Revolution - 1910-1920; *Mexico.

6387 Cordova, Gilbert Benito. Certain curious colonial Chicano cosmetological customs. EL CUADERNO, Vol. 3, no. 2 (Spring 1974), p. 19-27. English. **DESCR:** *Cosmetology; Women.

6388 Prehispanic America: a revelation. VISTA, Vol. 2, no. 6 (February 8, 1987), p. 18-20. English. **DESCR:** Art History; *Bowers Museum, Santa Ana, CA.

Pregnancy
USE: Fertility

Prejudice (Social)
USE: Discrimination

Preliminary Scholastic Aptitude Test (PSAT)

6389 Alvarado, Raul. Against all odds. HISPANIC ENGINEER, Vol. 3, no. 4 (Fall 1987), p. 10-11. English. **DESCR:** *Chicanas; Education; Educational Statistics; National Merit Scholarships; *Scholastic Aptitude Test (SAT); Stereotypes.

LA PRENSA, San Antonio, TX

6390 Arreola, Daniel D. The Mexican American cultural capital. GEOGRAPHICAL REVIEW, Vol. 77, (January 1987), p. 17-34. English. **DESCR:** Conjuntos; Food Industry; History; Immigration; La Raza Unida Party; League of United Latin American Citizens (LULAC); Lozano, Ignacio; Mexican American Youth Organization, San Antonio, TX; Music; Orden Hijos de America, San Antonio, TX; Railroads; *San Antonio, TX; *Social History and Conditions.

Preventative Medicine

6391 Morales, Cecilio. A question of health. VISTA, Vol. 3, no. 3 (November 8, 1987), p. 14, 19. English. **DESCR:** Delgado, Jane; *Health Education; *National Coalition of Hispanic Mental Health and Human Services Organizations (COSSMHO).

6392 Remas, Theodora A. Cancer: early detection can help prevent a deadly disease. VISTA, Vol. 1, no. 8 (April 6, 1986), p. 10-11. English. **DESCR:** *Diseases; Health Education.

6393 Remas, Theodora A. The threat of AIDS. VISTA, Vol. 2, no. 10 (June 7, 1987), p. 17-18, 25. English. **DESCR:** *Acquired Immune Deficiency Syndrome (AIDS); Directories; Health Education; *Medical Care.

Prietto, Carlos Alfredo

6394 Grayson, June. Sports medics. VISTA, Vol. 2, no. 9 (May 3, 1987), p. 17-18. English. **DESCR:** Bergin-Nader, Barbara; Cuadros, Hugo; Doctor Patient Relations; *Dominguez, Richard; *Medical Personnel; *Sports.

Primary School Education

6395 Gonzalez, Gilbert G. Segregation of Mexican children in a southern California city: the legacy of expansion and the American Southwest. WESTERN HISTORICAL QUARTERLY, Vol. 16, no. 1 (January 1985), p. 55-76. English. **DESCR:** *Discrimination in Education; Education; Educational Administration; *Santa Ana, CA; Segregation and Desegregation.

6396 Mortensen, Eileen. Reading achievement of native Spanish-speaking elementary students in bilingual vs. monolingual programs. BILINGUAL REVIEW, Vol. 11, no. 3 (September, December, 1984), p. 31-36. English. **DESCR:** *Academic Achievement; *Bilingual Bicultural Education; Language Usage; *Reading.

Primer Encuentro Nacional Hispano, Washington, DC, June 1972

6397 Gann, Lewis H. and Duignan, Peter J. Latinos & the Catholic Church in America. NUESTRO, Vol. 11, no. 4 (May 1987), p. 10-13. English. **DESCR:** *Catholic Church; Culture; Encuentro Movement [Catholic Church]; History.

Primer Festival de Literatura Fronteriza Mexico-Estados Unidos

6398 Lomeli, Francisco A. En torno a la literatura...convergencia o divergencia? LA COMUNIDAD, No. 274 (October 20, 1985), p. 8-11. Spanish. **DESCR:** Anaya, Rudolfo A.; Aztlan; Border Region; HEART OF AZTLAN; *Literary Criticism; Mendez M., Miguel; PEREGRINOS DE AZTLAN.

Primera Feria del Libro Latinoamericano

6399 Spanish/English. NEW YORKER, Vol. 61, (September 30, 1985), p. 26-27. English. **DESCR:** *Latin American Literature.

Print Media

6400 Ericksen, Charles. Wanted: Hispanics in the newsroom. CIVIL RIGHTS DIGEST/PERSPECTIVES, Vol. 14, no. 1 (Spring 1982), p. 40-44. English. **DESCR:** *Discrimination in Employment; Journalism; *Journalists; *Stereotypes.

6401 Marketing to Hispanics. ADVERTISING AGE MAGAZINE, Vol. 57, no. 43 (August 11, 1986), p. 51-528. English. **DESCR:** Advertising; Broadcast Media; De Armas Publications; Kinney Shoe Corp.; *Marketing; Pepsi-Cola Bottling Group; Spanish International Network (SIN); U.S. Bureau of the Census.

6402 Shoemaker, Pamela J.; Reese, Stephen D.; and Danielson, Wayne A. Spanish-language print media use as an indicator of acculturation. JOURNALISM QUARTERLY, Vol. 62, no. 4 (Winter 1985), p. 734-740. English. **DESCR:** *Acculturation; Magazines; Newspapers; *Spanish Language.

Prinze, Freddie

6403 Aceves Madrid, Vicente. Controversy surrounding NBC's CHICO AND THE MAN. LATIN QUARTER, Vol. 1, no. 2 (October 1974), p. 5-7. English. **DESCR:** Albertson, Jack; Artists; *CHICO AND THE MAN [television show]; Komack, James; Stereotypes; Teatros Unidos; *Television.

6404 Vasquez, Victor. More on CHICO AND THE MAN. LATIN QUARTER, Vol. 1, no. 3 (January, February, 1975), p. 13-15. English. **DESCR:** Albertson, Jack; Andrade, Ray; Artists; Boycotts; *CHICO AND THE MAN [television show]; Discrimination; Stereotypes; *Television.

Prisoners

6405 Aliens: detention in prisons. CRIMINAL LAW REPORTER, Vol. 35, no. 15 (July 18, 1984), p. 2265. English. **DESCR:** *Fernandez-Roque v. Smith; Undocumented Workers.

6406 Anson, Richard H. Inmate ethnicity and the suicide connection: a note on aggregate trends. THE PRISON JOURNAL, Vol. 63, no. 1 (March 1983), p. 91-99. English. **DESCR:** Suicide.

6407 Bohn, Martin J. and Traub, Gary S. Alienation of monolingual Hispanics in a federal correctional institution. PSYCHOLOGICAL REPORTS, Vol. 59, no. 2 (October 1986), p. 560-562. English. **DESCR:** Bilingualism; *Minnesota Multiphasic Personality Inventory (MMPI); *Psychological Testing.

6408 Castro, Agenor L. Hispanics in prison: reform...or riots. CIVIL RIGHTS DIGEST/PERSPECTIVES, Vol. 14, no. 1 (Spring 1982), p. 8-11. English. **DESCR:** *Prisons.

6409 Hoffman, Abraham. The controversial career of Martin Aguirre; the rise and fall of a Chicano lawman. CALIFORNIA HISTORY, Vol. 63, no. 4 (Fall 1984), p. 295-341. English. **DESCR:** *Aguirre, Martin; *Biography; History; Los Angeles County, CA; San Quentin Prison.

6410 McKanna, Clare V. The San Quentin prison pardon papers: a look at file no. 1808, the case of Francisco Javier Bonilla. SOUTHERN CALIFORNIA QUARTERLY, Vol. 67, no. 2 (Summer 1985), p. 187-196. English. **DESCR:** Administration of Justice; Archives; *Bonilla, Francisco Javier; *Criminal Justice System; History; *San Quentin Prison.

6411 Ruiz, Ariel. Raza, sexo y politica en SHORT EYES by Miguel Pinero. THE AMERICAS REVIEW, Vol. 15, no. 2 (Summer 1987), p. 93-102. Spanish. **DESCR:** Homosexuality; Literary Criticism; Pinero, Miguel; Puerto Ricans; Sex Roles; *SHORT EYES; Teatro.

Prisoners of War
USE: Political Prisoners

Prisons

6412 Castro, Agenor L. Hispanics in prison: reform...or riots. CIVIL RIGHTS DIGEST/PERSPECTIVES, Vol. 14, no. 1 (Spring 1982), p. 8-11. English. **DESCR:** Prisoners.

6413 Hamilton, Lawrence S. A profile of the Mexican migrant and his social and cultural adaptation to a federal prison. JOURNAL OF OFFENDER COUNSELING, SERVICES & REHABILITATION, Vol. 9, no. 3 (Spring 1985), p. 7-19. English. **DESCR:** *Undocumented Workers.

6414 Herrera Duran, Patricia and Mares, Renee. Ernest Duran: la ultima despedida. LATIN QUARTER, Vol. 1, no. 3 (January, February, 1975), p. 34-36. English. **DESCR:** Biography; Drug Abuse Programs; *Duran, Ernesto; Joint Efforts [prison organization].

6415 Kahn, Robert. Oakdale prison: documenting the abuses. IN THESE TIMES, Vol. 10, no. 35 (September 17, 1986), p. 8, 22. English. **DESCR:** Allen Parish, LA; Legal Representation; *Oakdale, LA; Oakdale Legal Assistance (OLA); Political Refugees; Undocumented Workers; U.S. Bureau of Prisons (BOP).

Private Education

6416 Estimating the demand for private school enrollment. AMERICAN JOURNAL OF EDUCATION, Vol. 92, no. 3 (May 1984), p. 262-279. English. **DESCR:** Enrollment.

Private Funding Sources

6417 Grant from L.A. Pepsi to benefit city program. BEVERAGE INDUSTRY, Vol. 74, no. 7 (April 8, 1983), p. 25. English. **DESCR:** Community Development; Los Angeles, CA; *Pepsi-Cola Bottling Group.

6418 Lit, Ed. Recognition for Hispanic families. VISTA, Vol. 1, no. 5 (January 5, 1986), p. 18-20. English. **DESCR:** American Family Society; *Awards; *Hispanic Family of the Year Award; Moraga, Peter and family (Los Angeles, CA); Pineda, Charles and family (Los Angeles, CA).

Proctor & Gamble, Cincinnati, OH

6419 Marsh, Betsa. Diversidad de valores en Proctor & Gamble. HISPANIC TIMES, Vol. 8, no. 3 (May, June, 1987), p. 32-3. Spanish. **DESCR:** Careers; *Engineering as a Profession.

Proctor & Gamble, Cincinnati, OH (cont.)

6420 Marsh, Betsa. Proctor & Gamble values diversity. HISPANIC TIMES, Vol. 8, no. 3 (May, June, 1987), p. 10-11. English. **DESCR:** Careers; *Engineering as a Profession.

Production
USE: Industries

Professional Organizations

6421 Ricardo Salazar. HISPANIC ENGINEER, Vol. 3, no. 2 (Summer), p. 14-18. English. **DESCR:** Biography; Magic of Science and Engineering Program; *Salazar, Ricardo; Society of Hispanic Professional Engineers Northern California Chapter.

6422 Soto, Rose Marie. National Network of Hispanic Women. HISPANIC ENGINEER, Vol. 3, no. 4 (Fall 1987), p. 26-28. English. **DESCR:** Castillo, Sylvia; Gonzales Torres, Celia; Gutierrez, Nancy; *National Network of Hispanic Women; Women; Zambrana, Ruth.

Pronunciation
USE: Accentedness

Proposition 63 (English as the Official Language of California)

6423 Acuna, Rodolfo and Hill, Frank. English as the official language?=El ingles como idioma oficial. AMERICAS 2001, Vol. 1, no. 1 (June, July, 1987), p. 6-11. Bilingual. **DESCR:** *English-Only Movement; Language Usage.

6424 What are your views on the new English-Only initiative?=Que piensas sobre la nueva ley, "English-Only". AMERICAS 2001, Vol. 1, no. 1 (June, July, 1987), p. 12-14. Bilingual. **DESCR:** Attitudes; *English-Only Movement; Public Opinion.

Prose

6425 Acuna, David. Memoria. LLUEVE TLALOC, no. 14 (1987), p. 64. Spanish.

6426 Acuna, David. Para vos. LLUEVE TLALOC, no. 14 (1987), p. 64-65. Spanish.

6427 Acuna, David. Realidad. LLUEVE TLALOC, no. 14 (1987), p. 65. Spanish.

6428 Aguilar Gallardo, Hortensia. Nostalgia. LLUEVE TLALOC, no. 3 (1976), p. 22. Spanish.

6429 Alonso, Humberto. Un brindis a Mexico. LLUEVE TLALOC, no. 11 (1984), p. 11. Spanish.

6430 Alonso, Humberto. Sin motivos. LLUEVE TLALOC, no. 12 (1985), p. 9. Spanish.

6431 Alonso, Marisela. Un sueno volvio mi tristeza en felicidad. LLUEVE TLALOC, no. 12 (1985), p. 28. Spanish.

6432 Amaya, Alma. Celos. LLUEVE TLALOC, no. 8 (1981), p. 15. Spanish.

6433 Amaya, Alma. La construccion. LLUEVE TLALOC, no. 8 (1981), p. 15. Spanish.

6434 Amaya, Alma. La espera de navidad. LLUEVE TLALOC, no. 8 (1981), p. 15. Spanish.

6435 Amaya, Alma. El trabajo de la mujer. LLUEVE TLALOC, no. 8 (1981), p. 15. Spanish.

6436 Angulo, Lourdes. Mi infancia. LLUEVE TLALOC, no. 11 (1984), p. 2. Spanish.

6437 Angulo, Lourdes. Mi primo Panchito. LLUEVE TLALOC, no. 10 (1983), p. 2. Spanish.

6438 Angulo, Lourdes. La muerte de mi abuelo. LLUEVE TLALOC, no. 11 (1984), p. 28. Spanish.

6439 Angulo, Lourdes. Quiero saber porque. LLUEVE TLALOC, no. 10 (1983), p. 16. Spanish.

6440 Angulo, Lourdes. La travesura que no se me olvida. LLUEVE TLALOC, no. 11 (1984), p. 20. Spanish.

6441 Angulo, Lourdes. La vida de hoy. LLUEVE TLALOC, no. 10 (1983), p. 17. Spanish.

6442 Aros, Maria Teresa. Por fin se cierran. LLUEVE TLALOC, no. 4 (1977), p. 60. Spanish.

6443 Arvizu, Delia. Una perspectiva de la muerte. LLUEVE TLALOC, no. 12 (1985), p. 35. Spanish.

6444 Astiazaron Aguilar, Guadalupe. Amistad. LLUEVE TLALOC, no. 11 (1984), p. 6. Spanish.

6445 Badilla M., Alejandro. De mi ninez. LLUEVE TLALOC, no. 8 (1981), p. 9. Spanish.

6446 Barbara, Ana M. Paloma. LLUEVE TLALOC, no. 2 (1975), p. 40-41. Spanish.

6447 Barbara, Ana M. Paloma. LLUEVE TLALOC, no. 2 (1975), p. 42-44. English.

6448 Bastidas, Laura E. Que contraste! LLUEVE TLALOC, no. 1 (1974), p. 11-12. Spanish.

6449 Bojorquez, Ricardo. El desierto. LLUEVE TLALOC, no. 3 (1976), p. 20. Spanish.

6450 Bubala, Julie. En la casa de mi abuelita. LLUEVE TLALOC, no. 13 (1986), p. 5. Spanish.

6451 Buczynski, Linda. Las montanas. LLUEVE TLALOC, no. 8 (1981), p. 34. Spanish.

6452 Burruel, Carlos J. Desilusion. LLUEVE TLALOC, no. 6 (1979), p. 19. Spanish.

6453 Byrd, W.W. Cocospora. LLUEVE TLALOC, no. 8 (1981), p. 18. Spanish.

6454 Campbell, T.C. Hasta nunca. LLUEVE TLALOC, no. 6 (1979), p. 42. Spanish.

6455 Cantu, Jesus "Chista". Se necesita un punto de vista para desarrollar una perspectiva. EL CUADERNO, Vol. 2, no. 1 (1972), p. 45-49. English.

6456 Carrizosa, Cecilia Rivera. Una carta a ti, con ternura infinita. LLUEVE TLALOC, no. 7 (1980), p. 14. Spanish.

6457 Casaus, Maria R. El cumpleanos. LLUEVE TLALOC, no. 11 (1984), p. 4. Spanish.

6458 Castillo, Victoria. A mis padres. LLUEVE TLALOC, no. 12 (1985), p. 16. Spanish.

6459 Castro, Anna. El buen juez por su casa empieza. LLUEVE TLALOC, no. 12 (1985), p. 20. Spanish.

6460 Castro, Anna. Curiosidades en variedad de fiestas para entierros. LLUEVE TLALOC, no. 12 (1985), p. 34. Spanish.

Prose (cont.)

6461 Chavez, Lulu. El 17 de diciembre. LLUEVE TLALOC, no. 11 (1984), p. 37. Spanish.

6462 Cirerol, Anna. Palomino. LLUEVE TLALOC, no. 9 (1982), p. 12. Spanish.

6463 Cisneros, Sandra. Do you know me?: I wrote THE HOUSE ON MANGO STREET. THE AMERICAS REVIEW, Vol. 15, no. 1 (Spring 1987), p. 77-79. English. **DESCR:** Authors; Autobiography; Chicanas; *Cisneros, Sandra; *THE HOUSE ON MANGO STREET.

6464 Cisneros, Sandra. Ghosts and voices: writing from obsession. THE AMERICAS REVIEW, Vol. 15, no. 1 (Spring 1987), p. 69-73. English. **DESCR:** *Authors; Autobiography; Chicanas; *Cisneros, Sandra.

6465 Cisneros, Sandra. Notes to a young(er) writer. THE AMERICAS REVIEW, Vol. 15, no. 1 (Spring 1987), p. 74-76. English. **DESCR:** *Authors; Autobiography; Chicanas; *Cisneros, Sandra.

6466 Colossio M., Marcela. Cucurpe. LLUEVE TLALOC, no. 6 (1979), p. 44. Spanish.

6467 Cruikshank, Lupita. El futuro. LLUEVE TLALOC, no. 12 (1985), p. 24. Spanish.

6468 Cruikshank, Lupita. Impresiones sobre las fiestas de octubre. LLUEVE TLALOC, no. 12 (1985), p. 10. Spanish.

6469 Cruikshank, Lupita. Una pequena nota en tus quince anos. LLUEVE TLALOC, no. 12 (1985), p. 25. Spanish.

6470 Dabdoub, Roberto. A don Juan. LLUEVE TLALOC, no. 7 (1980), p. 37. Spanish.

6471 Dagnind, Dora. La tradicion. LLUEVE TLALOC, no. 10 (1983), p. 3. Spanish.

6472 Davila, Elisa. Variacion 1-destierro. TINTA, Vol. 1, no. 2 (May 1983), p. 43. Spanish.

6473 Davila, Elisa. Variacion 2-ternura. TINTA, Vol. 1, no. 2 (May 1983), p. 43. Spanish.

6474 Davila, Elisa. Variacion 3. TINTA, Vol. 1, no. 2 (May 1983), p. 43. Spanish.

6475 de la Ossa, Maria Jesus. Con la vara que midas seras medido. LLUEVE TLALOC, no. 7 (1980), p. 10. Spanish.

6476 de la Ossa, Maria Jesus. Los mojarrines. LLUEVE TLALOC, no. 7 (1980), p. 10. Spanish.

6477 Dicochea, Luz Maria. Fernandon. LLUEVE TLALOC, no. 8 (1981), p. 15. Spanish.

6478 Durand, Jose. Lima, la ciudad de los reyes. LLUEVE TLALOC, no. 13 (1986), p. 5. Spanish.

6479 Durand, Jose. Los Pistachos. LLUEVE TLALOC, no. 13 (1986), p. 5. Spanish.

6480 Durazo, Marina. Jesus Garcia. LLUEVE TLALOC, no. 5 (1978), p. 14. Spanish.

6481 Escobar, Ricardo. Gente de Caracas. LLUEVE TLALOC, no. 10 (1983), p. 34. Spanish.

6482 Espinosa, Maria. Children. LLUEVE TLALOC, no. 3 (1976), p. 5-9. English. **DESCR:** Children; Lopez, Enrique Hank.

6483 Espinosa, Maria. Soledad. LLUEVE TLALOC, no. 3 (1976), p. 25-26. Spanish.

6484 Espinosa, Mary Lou. Cosas de ninos. LLUEVE TLALOC, no. 3 (1976), p. 4-8. Spanish. **DESCR:** Children; Lopez, Enrique Hank.

6485 Estrada, Javier. El amor. LLUEVE TLALOC, no. 13 (1986), p. 21. Spanish.

6486 Estrada, Javier. Jose. LLUEVE TLALOC, no. 13 (1986), p. 19. Spanish.

6487 Estrada, Javier. Nubes. LLUEVE TLALOC, no. 13 (1986), p. 19. Spanish.

6488 Estrada, Javier. El pescado y las aguilas. LLUEVE TLALOC, no. 13 (1986), p. 8. Spanish.

6489 Estrada, Javier. El rey bailarin. LLUEVE TLALOC, no. 13 (1986), p. 19. Journal. Spanish.

6490 Estrada, Javier. Los sacrificios de un buen atleta. LLUEVE TLALOC, no. 13 (1986), p. 30. Spanish.

6491 Estrada, Javier. El super Javier. LLUEVE TLALOC, no. 13 (1986), p. 19. Spanish.

6492 Fausto, Lupe. Anoranzas de mi ninez. LLUEVE TLALOC, no. 1 (1974), p. 15-16. Spanish.

6493 Fausto, Lupe. Reminiscences of my childhood. LLUEVE TLALOC, no. 1 (1974), p. 17-18. English.

6494 Fimbres, Guadalupe. El anima milagrosa de El Tiradito. LLUEVE TLALOC, no. 2 (1975), p. 33-34. Spanish.

6495 Fimbres, Guadalupe. The miraculous soul of el tiradito. LLUEVE TLALOC, no. 2 (1975), p. 35-36. English.

6496 Flores, Francisco. Cristeros. LLUEVE TLALOC, no. 8 (1981), p. 34. Spanish.

6497 Forget-me-not. LLUEVE TLALOC, no. 1 (1974), p. 10. English.

6498 Franco, Olga B. Danza fatal. LLUEVE TLALOC, no. 1 (1974), p. 7. Spanish.

6499 Gallardo, Hortencia Aguilar. Dulce sueno. LLUEVE TLALOC, no. 5 (1978), p. 16. Spanish.

6500 Gloria. Mi sabana. LLUEVE TLALOC, no. 12 (1985), p. 27. Spanish.

6501 Gonzales, Martin S. Libre al fin. LLUEVE TLALOC, no. 4 (1977), p. 101-103. Spanish.

6502 Gonzales, Martin S. Mi amigo Arturo. LLUEVE TLALOC, no. 4 (1977), p. 43-45. Spanish.

6503 Gonzalez, Beatriz. Canto al amor. LLUEVE TLALOC, no. 11 (1984), p. 9. Spanish.

6504 Gonzalez, Beatriz. Moraleja. LLUEVE TLALOC, no. 10 (1983), p. 28. Spanish.

6505 Gonzalez, Beatriz. Sentimientos. LLUEVE TLALOC, no. 11 (1984), p. 36. Spanish.

6506 Gonzalez, Humberto. Lo inhumano de llamarse humano. LLUEVE TLALOC, no. 7 (1980), p. 28. Spanish.

6507 Gonzalez, Jose. Cometa. LLUEVE TLALOC, no. 12 (1985), p. 25. Spanish.

6508 Griffin, Mina. El asilo. LLUEVE TLALOC, no. 11 (1984), p. 6. Spanish.

Prose (cont.)

6509 Griffin, Mina. Historia triste. LLUEVE
TLALOC, no. 12 (1985), p. 22. Spanish.

6510 Griffin, Mina. I dreamed. LLUEVE TLALOC, no.
12 (1985), p. 34. English.

6511 Griffin, Mina and Griffin, Richard. Juntos.
LLUEVE TLALOC, no. 12 (1985), p. 15.
Spanish.

6512 Griffin, Mina. Los ojos de mi madre. LLUEVE
TLALOC, no. 11 (1984), p. 4. Spanish.

6513 Griffin, Mina. Simon el viejo pescador.
LLUEVE TLALOC, no. 12 (1985), p. 29.
Spanish.

6514 Guerrero Bubala, Julie. Dios. LLUEVE TLALOC,
no. 13 (1986), p. 7. Spanish.

6515 Hanes, Cecilia. El sueno ciclico. LLUEVE
TLALOC, no. 7 (1980), p. 23. Spanish.

6516 Hanes, Cecilia. Sueno del pasado (otra
enigma). LLUEVE TLALOC, no. 7 (1980), p. 23.
Spanish.

6517 Hernandez, Ana Maria. Vivir para la
humanidad. LLUEVE TLALOC, no. 12 (1985), p.
27. Spanish.

6518 Huerta, Margarita A. La fe de nuestra gente.
LLUEVE TLALOC, no. 9 (1982), p. 10. Spanish.

6519 Huerta, Margarita A. Narraciones de dona
Mariquita. LLUEVE TLALOC, no. 9 (1982), p.
20. Spanish. **DESCR:** Cuentos.

6520 Lang, Carol. N.P.O. LLUEVE TLALOC, no. 11
(1984), p. 6. Spanish.

6521 Leal, Rose. El diablo dienton. LLUEVE
TLALOC, no. 6 (1979), p. 32. Spanish.

6522 Lizarraga, Patricia. Siempre te recordare.
LLUEVE TLALOC, no. 10 (1983), p. 32.
Spanish.

6523 Lopez, Maria. Los amigos de Jesus. LLUEVE
TLALOC, no. 8 (1981), p. 18. Spanish.

6524 Lopez, Raymundo. Dona Angelita. LLUEVE
TLALOC, no. 3 (1976), p. 16. Spanish.
DESCR: Curanderismo.

6525 Lopez, Raymundo. Maldito sueno. LLUEVE
TLALOC, no. 3 (1976), p. 50. Spanish.

6526 Loya, Elena. Mi dia conmemorable. LLUEVE
TLALOC, no. 12 (1985), p. 12. Spanish.

6527 Maldonado, Herlinda. Un paseo en el bosque.
LLUEVE TLALOC, no. 8 (1981), p. 10. Spanish.

6528 Maldonado, Herlinda. Pintura de la guerra.
LLUEVE TLALOC, no. 9 (1982), p. 14. Spanish.

6529 Mantiega, Victoria. Aureola de miseria.
LLUEVE TLALOC, no. 9 (1982), p. 23. Spanish.

6530 Marisabel. Es cosa de inspiracion. LLUEVE
TLALOC, no. 8 (1981), p. 1. Spanish.

6531 McCoy, Matilde. La sonrisa de Ivan. LLUEVE
TLALOC, no. 6 (1979), p. 28. Spanish.

6532 Meaney, Mark. El avaro y su oro. LLUEVE
TLALOC, no. 6 (1979), p. 13. Spanish.

6533 Medina, Beatriz. Mi hermanito Pablito.
LLUEVE TLALOC, no. 5 (1978), p. 32-33.
Spanish.

6534 Medina Garcia, Jesus. A una amazona. LLUEVE
TLALOC, no. 4 (1977), p. 39. Spanish.

6535 Medina Garcia, Jesus. Cronica. LLUEVE
TLALOC, no. 4 (1977), p. 31-34. Spanish.

6536 Medina Garcia, Jesus. Viendo llover en
Tucson. LLUEVE TLALOC, no. 11 (1984), p.
8-9. Spanish.

6537 Menard, Lupita. Los suenos. LLUEVE TLALOC,
no. 8 (1981), p. 9. Spanish.

6538 Menard, Lupita. Vio al diablo. LLUEVE
TLALOC, no. 8 (1981), p. 9. Spanish.

6539 Monroe, Michael. Un caso raro. LLUEVE
TLALOC, no. 6 (1979), p. 36. Spanish.

6540 Montano, Aurora. La ciguena. LLUEVE TLALOC,
no. 8 (1981), p. 18. Spanish.

6541 Montano, Aurora. El pueblo de Niera. LLUEVE
TLALOC, no. 8 (1981), p. 8-9. Spanish.

6542 Montano, Aurora. Ya en el ocaso de mi vida.
LLUEVE TLALOC, no. 9 (1982), p. 1. Spanish.

6543 Moran, Gris. Felicidad. LLUEVE TLALOC, no. 4
(1977), p. 67. Spanish.

6544 Moreno, Laura. Lolita la tortuguita. LLUEVE
TLALOC, no. 5 (1978), p. 18. Spanish.

6545 Mungaray, Josefina C. Historia real de un
nido. LLUEVE TLALOC, no. 2 (1975), p. 23-24.
Spanish.

6546 Murrieta, Maria del Socorro. El dia en que
las cebollas nadaron. LLUEVE TLALOC, no. 8
(1981), p. 4. Spanish.

6547 Narvaez, Soraya. Lola: la Salamera. LLUEVE
TLALOC, no. 7 (1980), p. 41. Spanish.

6548 Narvaez, Soraya. Recuerdos de una noche
inolvidable. LLUEVE TLALOC, no. 7 (1980), p.
22. Spanish.

6549 Navarro, Amada. Tardes de platicas. LLUEVE
TLALOC, no. 3 (1976), p. 38. Spanish.

6550 Navarro, Patricia M. Nuestro senor
Jesucristo. LLUEVE TLALOC, no. 8 (1981), p.
4. Spanish.

6551 Ohnesorgen, Jose. Como era Tucson. LLUEVE
TLALOC, no. 8 (1981), p. 4. Spanish.

6552 Orozco, Rafaela. Asi es. LLUEVE TLALOC, no.
8 (1981), p. 15. Spanish.

6553 Ortega-Butler, Norma. Carta a una hija
esperando su segundo bebe. LLUEVE TLALOC,
no. 12 (1985), p. 22. Spanish.

6554 Ortega-Butler, Norma. Dos pisapapeles en el
mar. LLUEVE TLALOC, no. 13 (1986), p. 7.
Spanish.

6555 Ortega-Butler, Norma. La sociedad perfecta:
restablecer la conciencia. LLUEVE TLALOC,
no. 12 (1985), p. 22. Spanish.

6556 Ortiz, Sara. La oida. LLUEVE TLALOC, no. 4
(1977), p. 62-64. Spanish.

Prose (cont.)

6557 Paredes, Raymund A. Review essay: recent Chicano writing. ROCKY MOUNTAIN REVIEW OF LANGUAGE AND LITERATURE, Vol. 41, (1987), p. 124-129. English. **DESCR:** Castillo, Ana; Catholic Church; Chavez, Denise; Chicanas; Garcia, Lionel; GIVING UP THE GHOST; LEAVING HOME; *Literary Criticism; *Literature Reviews; Moraga, Cherrie; Poetry; Sex Roles; Silva, Beverly; SMALL FACES; Soto, Gary; THE CAT AND OTHER STORIES; THE LAST OF THE MENU GIRLS; THE MIXQUIAHUALA LETTERS.

6558 Peralta, Gloria. Vamonos. LLUEVE TLALOC, no. 2 (1975), p. 52-53. Spanish.

6559 Peters, Jose. Los mojaditos regresan a Mexico. LLUEVE TLALOC, no. 6 (1979), p. 32. Spanish.

6560 Pineda, Josefina. Un carino. LLUEVE TLALOC, no. 10 (1983), p. 10. Spanish.

6561 Pineda, Josefina. Que amor es ese que no me traes? LLUEVE TLALOC, no. 10 (1983), p. 31 Spanish.

6562 Pineda, Josefina. Requiem. LLUEVE TLALOC, no. 10 (1983), p. 10. Spanish.

6563 Powell, Winona. Esta tarde. LLUEVE TLALOC, no. 1 (1974), p. 27. Spanish.

6564 Powell, Winona. This afternoon. LLUEVE TLALOC, no. 1 (1974), p. 28. English.

6565 Quiroz, Francisco. El cine plaza. LLUEVE TLALOC, no. 3 (1976), p. 43. Spanish.

6566 Quiroz, Francisco. Curaciones caseras. LLUEVE TLALOC, no. 3 (1976), p. 18. Spanish.

6567 Quiroz, Francisco. En la mananita. LLUEVE TLALOC, no. 3 (1976), p. 40. Spanish.

6568 Ramirez, Roberto. Pasos. LLUEVE TLALOC, no. 13 (1986), p. 21. Spanish.

6569 Ramirez, Roberto. El prisionero. LLUEVE TLALOC, no. 13 (1986), p. 12. Spanish.

6570 Reyes, J.E. Sin ganar. LLUEVE TLALOC, no. 12 (1985), p. 15. Spanish.

6571 Reyes, Sandra. Ya nos entenderemos. LLUEVE TLALOC, no. 13 (1986), p. 21. Spanish.

6572 Reyna, Hugo. Con razon. LLUEVE TLALOC, no. 7 (1980), p. 21. Spanish.

6573 Rivera, Armandina. La feria del cobre. LLUEVE TLALOC, no. 12 (1985), p. 10. Spanish.

6574 Roche, Sylvia. Amor inquieto. LLUEVE TLALOC, no. 7 (1980), p. 34. Spanish.

6575 Roche, Sylvia. Para nuestra madre. LLUEVE TLALOC, no. 7 (1980), p. 19. Spanish.

6576 Ruiz, Raymundo. Las piedras del rio. LLUEVE TLALOC, no. 11 (1984), p. 30. Spanish.

6577 Ruiz, Raymundo. El principe azul. LLUEVE TLALOC, no. 11 (1984), p. 11. Spanish.

6578 Ruiz, Raymundo. El senor Decker. LLUEVE TLALOC, no. 10 (1983), p. 16. Spanish.

6579 Ruiz, Ruben. El parque Balboa. LLUEVE TLALOC, no. 5 (1978), p. 28. Spanish. **DESCR:** *Balboa Park, San Diego, CA.

6580 Sainz, Olivia. Me mataron. LLUEVE TLALOC, no. 8 (1981), p. 10. Spanish.

6581 Sanchez, Lupita. Fosforito. LLUEVE TLALOC, no. 11 (1984), p. 1. Spanish.

6582 Sanchez, Lupita. La negra noche. LLUEVE TLALOC, no. 8 (1981), p. 10. Spanish.

6583 Sanchez, Lupita. La perla. LLUEVE TLALOC, no. 10 (1983), p. 2. Spanish.

6584 Sanchez, Lupita. El sueno. LLUEVE TLALOC, no. 11 (1984), p. 1. Spanish.

6585 Sanchez, Maria Isabel. El foro romano. LLUEVE TLALOC, no. 11 (1984), p. 13. Spanish.

6586 Sanchez, Maria Isabel. La suerte de los valenzuela. LLUEVE TLALOC, no. 12 (1985), p. 21. Spanish.

6587 Santillan, Gladis. Dos almas. LLUEVE TLALOC, no. 13 (1986), p. 21. Spanish.

6588 Una tarde de otono en Madrid. LLUEVE TLALOC, no. 9 (1982), p. 23. Spanish.

6589 Tovar, Graciela. Recuerdos de mi ninez. LLUEVE TLALOC, no. 9 (1982), p. 16-18. Spanish.

6590 Uribe, Ainoa. A mis amigos escritores. LLUEVE TLALOC, no. 12 (1985), p. 9. Spanish.

6591 Valenzuela, Nati. No-me-olvides. LLUEVE TLALOC, no. 1 (1974), p. 9. Spanish.

6592 Valenzuela, Oscar N. One of the many stories about la Llorona. LLUEVE TLALOC, no. 2 (1975), p. 10. English. **DESCR:** *La Llorona.

6593 Valenzuela, Oscar N. Uno de tantos cuentos de la Llorona. LLUEVE TLALOC, no. 2 (1975), p. 9. Spanish. **DESCR:** *La Llorona.

6594 Vaughn, Artemisa. Contradiccion y sueno. LLUEVE TLALOC, no. 7 (1980), p. 31. Spanish.

6595 Vaughn, Artemisa. Suma total. LLUEVE TLALOC, no. 7 (1980), p. 37. Spanish.

6596 Velasco, Magdalena. El apio. LLUEVE TLALOC, no. 10 (1983), p. 28. Spanish.

6597 Velasco, Magdalena. Dar a luz. LLUEVE TLALOC, no. 10 (1983), p. 34. Spanish.

6598 Velasco, Magdalena. La tortilla. LLUEVE TLALOC, no. 10 (1983), p. 2. Spanish.

6599 Velasco, Magdalena. Yo ante el mundo. LLUEVE TLALOC, no. 10 (1983), p. 11. Spanish.

6600 Velazquez, Manuel. Recuerdo: tendria yo unos siete u ocho anos. LLUEVE TLALOC, no. 6 (1979), p. 42. Spanish.

6601 Wilson, Maria. Mi madre. LLUEVE TLALOC, no. 6 (1979), p. 16. Spanish.

6602 Wilson, Maria. Viejecitos. LLUEVE TLALOC, no. 6 (1979), p. 28. Spanish.

6603 Ynclan, Maria Estela. Manana. LLUEVE TLALOC, no. 7 (1980), p. 12. Spanish.

6604 Yubeta, Alma. Amigas. LLUEVE TLALOC, no. 13 (1986), p. 11. Spanish.

6605 Yubeta, Alma. Te recuerdo. LLUEVE TLALOC, no. 13 (1986), p. 21. Spanish.

Prose (cont.)

6606 Zamorano, Christina. Vita. LLUEVE TLALOC, no. 11 (1984), p. 1. Spanish.

PROTEST IS NOT ENOUGH: THE STRUGGLE OF BLACKS AND HISPANICS FOR EQUALITY IN URBAN POLITICS

6607 Body-Gendrot, Sophie. Book review of: PROTEST IS NOT ENOUGH. INTERNATIONAL JOURNAL OF URBAN AND REGIONAL RESEARCH, Vol. 9, no. 4 (1985), p. 576-577. English. **DESCR**: Book Reviews; Browning, Rufus P.; Marshall, Dale Rogers; Tabb, David H.

6608 Browning, Rufus P. and Marshall, Dale Rogers. Black and Hispanic power in city politics: a forum. P.S. [AMERICAN POLITICAL SCIENCE ASSOCIATION], Vol. 19, no. 3 (Summer 1986), p. 573-639. English. **DESCR**: Blacks; Browning, Rufus P.; Marshall, Dale Rogers; *Politics; Tabb, David H.; Urban Communities.

6609 Browning, Rufus P.; Marshall, Dale Rogers; and Tabb, David H. Protest is not enough: a theory of political incorporation. P.S. [AMERICAN POLITICAL SCIENCE ASSOCIATION], Vol. 19, no. 3 (Summer 1986), p. 576-581. English. **DESCR**: Blacks; Browning, Rufus P.; Marshall, Dale Rogers; Political Representation; Politics; Tabb, David H.; Urban Communities.

6610 Sonenshein, Raphe. Biracial coalition politics in Los Angeles. P.S. [AMERICAN POLITICAL SCIENCE ASSOCIATION], Vol. 19, no. 3 (Summer 1986), p. 582-590. English. **DESCR**: Blacks; Bradley, Tom; Browning, Rufus P.; *Ethnic Groups; *Intergroup Relations; *Los Angeles, CA; Marshall, Dale Rogers; Political Parties and Organizations; *Politics; Tabb, David H.

Protestant Church

6611 Plowman, Edward E. Hispanic Christians in the United States. CHRISTIANITY TODAY, Vol. 30, no. 1 (January 17, 1986), p. 44-45. English. **DESCR**: *Hispanic Congress on Evangelization (HCE); Los Angeles, CA; Religion.

Protestant Work Ethic (PWE) Scale

6612 Isonio, Steven A. and Garza, Raymond T. Protestant work ethic endorsement among Anglo Americans, Chicanos and Mexicans: a comparison of factor structures. HISPANIC JOURNAL OF BEHAVIORAL SCIENCES, Vol. 9, no. 4 (December 1987), p. 413-425. English. **DESCR**: *Comparative Psychology; *Cultural Characteristics; Ethnic Groups; *Values.

Protocom Devices, New York, NY

6613 Garcia, Art. Financing the corporate take-off. HISPANIC BUSINESS, Vol. 9, no. 5 (May 1987), p. 22-27. English. **DESCR**: Aguirre Architects, Dallas, TX; Aguirre, Pedro; Banking Industry; *Business Enterprises; Businesspeople; *Corporations; *Investments; Minority Enterprise Small Business Investment Corporation (MESBIC); Morales, Ramon; Villamil, Antonio.

Proverbios
USE: Dichos

Proverbs
USE: Dichos

"Proverbs in Mexican-American Tradition"

6614 Duran, Richard P. Article review of: "Proverbs in Mexican-American Tradition". LA RED/THE NET, no. 56 (July 1982), p. 6-7. English. **DESCR**: Arora, Shirley L.; *Dichos.

Prudential

6615 Hispanic marketing. ADVERTISING AGE MAGAZINE, Vol. 57, no. 16 (February 27, 1986), p. 11-51. English. **DESCR**: Adolph Coors Co.; Advertising; Allstate Insurance Co.; American Greetings; Anheuser-Busch, Inc.; Business Enterprises; Coca-Cola Company; Consumers; Ford Motor Company; Hallmark Cards; *Marketing; Mass Media; McDonald's Corporation; Metropolitan Life Insurance Corporation; Pepsi-Cola Bottling Group; Spanish International Network (SIN); State Farm Mutual Insurance; Tylenol; United Insurance Co. of America.

Psychiatry

6616 Evans, Leonard A., et al. Orienting psychotherapists to better serve low income and minority patients. JOURNAL OF CLINICAL PSYCHOLOGY, Vol. 40, no. 1 (January 1984), p. 90-96. English. **DESCR**: Mental Health Personnel; *Psychotherapy.

6617 Zippin, David H. and Hough, Richard L. Perceived self-other differences in life events and mental health among Mexicans and Americans. JOURNAL OF PSYCHOLOGY, Vol. 119, no. 2 (March 1985), p. 143-155. English. **DESCR**: Anglo Americans; *Comparative Psychology; *Locus of Control; *Mental Health; Mexico; *Stress.

Psychological Testing

6618 Bohn, Martin J. and Traub, Gary S. Alienation of monolingual Hispanics in a federal correctional institution. PSYCHOLOGICAL REPORTS, Vol. 59, no. 2 (October 1986), p. 560-562. English. **DESCR**: Bilingualism; *Minnesota Multiphasic Personality Inventory (MMPI); *Prisoners.

6619 Marin, Gerardo, et al. Development of a short acculturation scale for Hispanics. HISPANIC JOURNAL OF BEHAVIORAL SCIENCES, Vol. 9, no. 2 (June 1987), p. 183-205. English. **DESCR**: *Acculturation.

6620 Powers, Stephen and Medina, Marcello, Jr. Factorial validity of the Cooperative Preschool Inventory for English- and Spanish-speaking Hispanic children. JOURNAL OF PSYCHOLOGY, Vol. 119, no. 3 (May 1985), p. 277-280. English. **DESCR**: *Cooperative Preschool Inventory (CPI); *Cooperative Preschool Inventory [Spanish edition]; *Educational Tests and Measurements.

Psychology

6621 Bernal, Martha E. Book review of: EXPLORATIONS IN CHICANO PSYCHOLOGY. LA RED/THE NET, no. 55 (June 1982), p. 5-6. English. **DESCR**: *Baron, Augustine Jr.; Book Reviews; *EXPLORATIONS IN CHICANO PSYCHOLOGY.

6622 Diaz-Guerrero, Rogelio. Psychology for the Mexican or the masses? PSYCHOLOGY: A QUARTERLY JOURNAL OF HUMAN BEHAVIOR, Vol. 21, no. 2 (1984), p. 1-7. English. **DESCR**: *Social Psychology.

Psychology (cont.)

6623 Hunsaker, Alan C. Contingency management with Chicano adolescents in a federal manpower program. CORRECTIVE AND SOCIAL PSYCHIATRY, Vol. 30, no. 1 (1984), p. 10-13. English. **DESCR**: *Employment; *Management; *Manpower Programs; *Youth.

Psychotherapy

6624 Acosta, Frank X., et al. Preparing low-income Hispanic, Black, and white patients for psychotherapy: evaluation of a new orientation program. JOURNAL OF CLINICAL PSYCHOLOGY, Vol. 39, no. 6 (November 1983), p. 872-877. English. **DESCR**: Anglo Americans; Blacks; *Comparative Psychology; Mental Health.

6625 Delgado, Melvin and Humm-Delgado, Denise. Hispanics and group work: a review of the literature. SOCIAL WORK WITH GROUPS, Vol. 7, no. 3 (Fall 1984), p. 85-96. English. **DESCR**: *Literature Reviews; *Social Work.

6626 Evans, Leonard A., et al. Orienting psychotherapists to better serve low income and minority patients. JOURNAL OF CLINICAL PSYCHOLOGY, Vol. 40, no. 1 (January 1984), p. 90-96. English. **DESCR**: Mental Health Personnel; Psychiatry.

6627 Hardy-Fanta, Carol. Social action in Hispanic groups. SOCIAL WORK, Vol. 31, no. 2 (March, April, 1986), p. 119-123. English. **DESCR**: *Community Organizations; Natural Support Systems; *Social Work.

6628 Olarte, Silvia W. and Masnik, Ruth. Benefits of long-term group therapy for disadvantaged Hispanic outpatients. HOSPITAL AND COMMUNITY PSYCHIATRY, Vol. 36, no. 10 (October 1985), p. 1093-1097. English. **DESCR**: Ethnic Groups; Metropolitan Hospital, New York, NY; New York, NY; Sex Roles; *Women.

6629 Valdez, William J. Impotence: a problem with a solution. NUESTRO, Vol. 11, no. 4 (May 1987), p. 18-20. English. **DESCR**: Centro de Impotencia, Coral Gables Hospital, Miami, FL; Diseases; *Impotence; Males; Medical Clinics.

6630 Vargas-Willis, Gloria and Cervantes, Richard C. Consideration of psychosocial stress in the treatment of the Latina immigrant. HISPANIC JOURNAL OF BEHAVIORAL SCIENCES, Vol. 9, no. 3 (September 1987), p. 315-329. English. **DESCR**: *Chicanas; Discrimination in Employment; *Immigrants; Mental Health; *Stress.

Public Administration

6631 Rosenfeld, Jose. Hispanic issues and challenges. PUBLIC MANAGEMENT, Vol. 67, (March 1985), p. 12-16. English. **DESCR**: Social History and Conditions; Social Services.

Public Broadcasting Act of 1967

6632 Ponce, Ramon. Does the public have access to public broadcasting? LATIN QUARTER, Vol. 1, no. 3 (January, February, 1975), p. 4-6. English. **DESCR**: *Public Television.

Public Education
USE: Education

Public Health

6633 Angel, Ronald. Problems in studying the impact of social structure and culture on the health and medical care utilization of Chicanos. LA RED/THE NET, no. 55 (June 1982), p. 2-3. English. **DESCR**: Medical Care.

6634 Angel, Ronald. The study of the health of Chicanos: some recent findings. LA RED/THE NET, no. 74 (November 1983), p. 2-7. English. **DESCR**: Medical Care; Research Methodology.

6635 Broderick, Stephanie H., et al. Ethnicity, acculturation, and health beliefs among diabetes patients. MIGRATION WORLD MAGAZINE, Vol. 15, no. 2 (1987), p. 30-32. English. **DESCR**: Acculturation; Attitudes; Culture; *Diabetes; *Identity.

6636 Gaviria, Moises; Gil, Ana A.; and Javaid, Javaid I. Nortriptyline kinetics in Hispanic and Anglo subjects. JOURNAL OF CLINICAL PSYCHOPHARMACOLOGY, Vol. 6, no. 4 (1986), p. 227-231. English. **DESCR**: Anglo Americans; *Comparative Psychology; *Drug Use; Genetics.

6637 Hayes-Bautista, David Emmett. Chicano health policy research. LA RED/THE NET, no. 41 (April 1981), p. 9-10. English. **DESCR**: *Public Policy; Research Methodology.

6638 Jorgensen, Stephen R. and Adams, Russell P. Family planning needs and behavior of Mexican American women: a study of health care professionals and their clientele. HISPANIC JOURNAL OF BEHAVIORAL SCIENCES, Vol. 9, no. 3 (September 1987), p. 265-286. English. **DESCR**: Acculturation; *Attitudes; Birth Control; *Chicanas; *Cultural Characteristics; *Family Planning; Fertility; Stereotypes; Sterilization.

6639 Levin, Jeffrey S. and Markides, Kyriakos S. Religious attendance and subjective health. JOURNAL FOR THE SCIENTIFIC STUDY OF RELIGION, Vol. 25, no. 1 (March 1986), p. 31-40. English. **DESCR**: *Religion.

6640 Marcus, Alfred C. and Crane, Lori A. Smoking behavior among Hispanics: a preliminary report. PROGRESS IN CLINICAL AND BIOLOGICAL RESEARCH, Vol. 156, (1984), p. 141-151. English. **DESCR**: *Smoking.

6641 Meyers, C.E.; Borthwick, S.A.; and Eyman, R.K. Place of residence by age, ethnicity, and level of retardation of the mentally retarded/developmentally disabled population of California. AMERICAN JOURNAL OF MENTAL DEFICIENCY, Vol. 90, no. 3 (November 1985), p. 266-270. English. **DESCR**: California; Identity; *Mentally Handicapped.

6642 Neibel, Barbara A. Health care utilization: the case of the Mexican-American. ANTHROPOLOGY UCLA, Vol. 14, (1985), p. 13-26. English. **DESCR**: Cultural Characteristics; *Medical Care; Vital Statistics.

6643 Newquist, Deborah. The health care barrier model: toward analyzing the underutilization of health care by older Mexican-Americans. ANTHROPOLOGY UCLA, Vol. 14, (1985), p. 1-12. English. **DESCR**: *Ancianos; *Cultural Characteristics; Discrimination; Folk Medicine; *Medical Care; Medical Clinics.

Public Health (cont.)

6644 O'Donnell, Patrick J. A preliminary report on the incidence of gestational diabetes in a Hispanic migrant population. MIGRATION WORLD MAGAZINE, Vol. 15, no. 1 (), p. 27-30. English. DESCR: *Diabetes; Farm Workers; *Migrant Labor.

6645 Olivares, Yvette. The sweatshop: the garment industry's reborn child. REVISTA MUJERES, Vol. 3, no. 2 (June 1986), p. 55-62. English. DESCR: Garment Industry; Labor; Third World; *Undocumented Workers; *Women; Working Women.

6646 Plan and operation of the Hispanic Health and Nutrition Examination Survey 1982-84. VITAL AND HEALTH STATISTICS. SERIES 1, no. 19 (September 1985), p. 1-429. English. DESCR: *Hispanic Health and Nutrition Examination Survey (HHANES); *Nutrition.

6647 Remas, Theodora A. The threat of diabetes. VISTA, Vol. 1, no. 2 (October 5, 1985), p. 14-16. English. DESCR: *Diabetes; Health Education; *Mezitis, Nicholas; *Nutrition; Rico-Perez, Manuel.

Public Hygiene
USE: Public Health

Public Libraries

6648 Chavez, Linda. Celebrate! The Chicano Resource Center's 10th anniversary. LECTOR, Vol. 4, no. 1-3 (1986), p. In FtCover. English. DESCR: *Chicano Resource Center, Los Angeles County Public Library; Library Collections.

Public Opinion

6649 Barger, W.K. California public endorses the United Farm Workers. LA RED/THE NET, No. 105 (February 1987), p. 4-6. English. DESCR: *Agricultural Labor Unions; California; *Farm Workers; *United Farmworkers of America (UFW).

6650 Barger, W.K. Public attitudes towards Mexican-American farmworkers in the Midwest. LA RED/THE NET, no. 63 (January 1983), p. 2-4. English. DESCR: Attitudes; *Farm Workers; *Midwestern States.

6651 Padilla, Steve. Lessons to be learned from a playful hoax. VISTA, Vol. 1, no. 7 (March 2, 1986), p. 3. English. DESCR: *Essays; Humor; Librarians; Sclar, Marta-Luisa; Stereotypes; *Valdez, Juan.

6652 Perez, Renato E. Who are the Hispanic heroes? VISTA, Vol. 1, no. 7 (March 2, 1986), p. 12-14. English. DESCR: Jaramillo, Mari-Luci; Leadership; University of New Mexico.

6653 Search for Hispanic heroes informs, surprises, confirms. VISTA, Vol. 1, no. 10 (June 8, 1986), p. 18-19. English. DESCR: Mother Theresa; Pope John Paul II; Reagan, Ronald.

6654 What are your views on the new English-Only initiative?=Que piensas sobre la nueva ley, "English-Only". AMERICAS 2001, Vol. 1, no. 1 (June, July, 1987), p. 12-14. Bilingual. DESCR: Attitudes; *English-Only Movement; *Proposition 63 (English as the Official Language of California).

6655 What is your opinion of U.S. policy towards Central America?=Cual es tu opinion sobre la politica norteamericana hacia Centro America? AMERICAS 2001, Vol. 1, no. 2 (September, October, 1987), p. 21. Bilingual. DESCR: *Central America; International Relations; Surveys.

6656 Wreford, Mary. Reactions from the Chicano Survey respondents: no mas silencio. LA RED/THE NET, no. 33 (August 1980), p. 2-3. English. DESCR: Chicano Project of the University of Michigan; Midwestern States; *National Chicano Survey (NCS); Social Science; Southwestern United States; *Surveys.

Public Policy

6657 Avila, Joaquin; Arce, Carlos H.; and Mexican American Legal Defense and Education Fund (MALDEF). Task force on civic identity and political participation. LA RED/THE NET, no. 88 (Winter 1984), p. 17-21. English. DESCR: Elected Officials; *Political Representation.

6658 Baker, George A. and Rocha, Pedro, Jr. Critical incident competencies of Mexican American and Anglo American administrators. COMMUNITY/JUNIOR COLLEGE QUARTERLY OF RESEARCH AND PRACTICE, Vol. 7, no. 4 (July, September, 1983), p. 319-332. English. DESCR: Anglo Americans; *Community Colleges; Comparative Psychology; Cultural Characteristics; Educational Administration; Management.

6659 Beale, Stephen. 100 influentials and their assessment of the critical issues. HISPANIC BUSINESS, Vol. 9, no. 8 (August 1987), p. 20-32. English. DESCR: Biographical Notes; *Leadership.

6660 Cohen, Gaynor. The politics of bilingual education. OXFORD REVIEW OF EDUCATION, Vol. 10, no. 2 (1984), p. 225-241. English. DESCR: *Bilingual Bicultural Education; Educational Law and Legislation.

6661 Dellinger, Robert W. Hispanic think tank. VISTA, Vol. 3, no. 3 (November 8, 1987), p. 28. English. DESCR: Madrid, Arturo; Research Centers; *Tomas Rivera Center, Claremont, CA.

6662 Estrada, Leobardo F. Task force on employment and economic well-being. LA RED/THE NET, no. 88 (Winter 1984), p. 6-10. English. DESCR: *Employment; Labor Supply and Market.

6663 Gillespie, Francis P., et al. Public policy, ethnic code, and Hispanic vital statistics. LA RED/THE NET, no. 70 (July 1983), p. 9-13. English. DESCR: *Texas; *Vital Statistics.

6664 Greenwood, Michael J. and McDowell, John H. U.S. immigration reform: policy issues and economic analysis. CONTEMPORARY POLICY ISSUES, Vol. 3, (Spring 1985), p. 59-75. English. DESCR: *Immigration; *Immigration Reform and Control Act of 1986.

6665 Guzman, Ralph. Bi-national policy questions generated by Mexican school-age children who migrate between the United States and Mexico. LA RED/THE NET, no. 62 (December 1982), p. 2-4. English. DESCR: *Children; Immigrants; Migrant Children; *Watsonville, CA.

Public Policy (cont.)

6666 Hayes-Bautista, David Emmett. Chicano health policy research. LA RED/THE NET, no. 41 (April 1981), p. 9-10. English. **DESCR**: *Public Health; Research Methodology.

6667 Hero, Rodney E. Mexican Americans and urban politics: a consideration of governmental structure and policy. AZTLAN, Vol. 17, no. 1 (Spring 1986), p. 131-147. English. **DESCR**: Colorado; *Political Representation; *Politics; *Urban Communities.

6668 Jensen, Leif and Tienda, Marta. The new immigration: implications for poverty and public assistance utilization. MIGRATION WORLD MAGAZINE, Vol. 15, no. 5 (1987), p. 7-18. English. **DESCR**: History; Immigrants; *Immigration; *Immigration and Naturalization Act, 1965; Poverty; *Welfare.

6669 Macias, Reynaldo Flores. Book review of: THE NEW BILINGUALISM: AN AMERICAN DILEMMA. LA RED/THE NET, no. 61 (November 1982), p. 7-9. English. **DESCR**: *Bilingualism; Book Reviews; Ridge, Martin; *THE NEW BILINGUALISM: AN AMERICAN DILEMMA.

6670 Olivas, Michael A. Task force on education. LA RED/THE NET, no. 88 (Winter 1984), p. 14-17. English. **DESCR**: *Education.

6671 Public policy research and the Hispanic community: recommendations from five task forces [special issue]. LA RED/THE NET, no. 88 (Winter 1984), p. 1-24. English. **DESCR**: Ford Foundation; *Ford Foundation's Hispanic Task Forces Policy Research Reports.

6672 Rotberg, Iris C. Bilingual education policy in the United States. PROSPECTS: QUARTERLY REVIEW OF EDUCATION, Vol. 14, no. 1 (1984), p. 133-147. English. **DESCR**: *Bilingual Bicultural Education; Federal Government.

6673 Texas' higher education "Adams" compliance report. LA RED/THE NET, No. 102 (November 1986), p. 2-5. English. **DESCR**: *Discrimination in Education; *Higher Education; Texas; *Texas Equal Education Opportunity Plan for Higher Education.

6674 Tienda, Marta. Task force on statistical policy and data needs. LA RED/THE NET, no. 88 (Winter, 1984), p. 2-6. English. **DESCR**: *Databases; *Population; Research Methodology; *Statistics; Vital Statistics.

6675 Torres-Gil, Fernando. The Latinization of a multigenerational population: Hispanics in an aging society. DAEDALUS, Vol. 115, no. 1 (Winter 1986), p. 325-348. English. **DESCR**: *Age Groups; Cultural Pluralism; Population; Social Classes; Socioeconomic Factors.

6676 Yzaguirre, Raul. Task force on social services and community development. LA RED/THE NET, no. 88 (Winter 1984), p. 10-14. English. **DESCR**: *Community Development; *Social Services.

Public Relations

6677 Moya, Steven. Foreign relations: implementing an Hispanic marketing program. S & MM [SALES & MARKETING MANAGEMENT], Vol. 135, no. 2 (July 22, 1985), p. A22+. English. **DESCR**: *Consumers; *Marketing.

Public Television

6678 Lopez, Jose Y. A visit to VILLA ALEGRE. LATIN QUARTER, Vol. 1, no. 3 (January, February, 1975), p. 8-12. English. **DESCR**: Bilingual Children's Television, Inc.; *Children's Television; Cultural Pluralism; *VILLA ALEGRE [television program].

6679 Ponce, Ramon. Does the public have access to public broadcasting? LATIN QUARTER, Vol. 1, no. 3 (January, February, 1975), p. 4-6. English. **DESCR**: *Public Broadcasting Act of 1967.

Public Welfare
USE: Welfare

Publications
USE: Books

Publicity
USE: Advertising

Publishing Industry

6680 Atencio, Tomas. La resolana [editorial]. EL CUADERNO, Vol. 4, no. 1 (Summer 1976), p. 2-4. English. **DESCR**: Academia Asociados, NM; Academia Educational Model; *Chicano Studies; Culture; EL CUADERNO; ENTRE VERDE Y SECO; *La Academia de la Nueva Raza, Dixon, NM; LA MADRUGADA.

6681 Caicedo, Harry. VISTA birthday review and renewal of goals. VISTA, Vol. 2, no. 1 (September 7, 1986), p. 3. English. **DESCR**: *VISTA [magazine].

6682 Frank, Jerome P. Problems of books en espanol. PUBLISHER'S WEEKLY, Vol. 226, (July 27, 1984), p. 89-92. English. **DESCR**: *Children's Literature.

6683 Lomeli, Francisco A. Novela chicana: sus variantes y contradicciones (I). LA COMUNIDAD, No. 292 (February 23, 1986), p. 12-13. Spanish. **DESCR**: *Literary Criticism; Literature; Novel; Quinto Sol Publishing, Inc.

6684 National Hispanic Book Fair and Writers Festival [photographs]. THE AMERICAS REVIEW, Vol. 15, no. 2 (Summer 1987), p. 40-41. **DESCR**: Festivals; *National Hispanic Book Fair and Writers Festival, Houston, TX, May 30-31, 1987.

6685 Tarin, Patricia and Josslin, Daniel. Books for the Spanish-speaking: si se puede. LIBRARY JOURNAL, (July 1987), p. 25-31. English. **DESCR**: *Library Collections; Library Services; *Spanish Language.

Pueblo Broadcasting Corp.

6686 Lawrence, Jennifer. TV signal expected to boost Houston market. ADVERTISING AGE MAGAZINE, Vol. 57, no. 43 (August 11, 1986), p. S24-S25. English. **DESCR**: Advertising; Houston, TX; *KXLN, Houston, TX [television station]; Marketing; Spanish Language; Television.

Pueblo Indians

6687 Jenkins, Myra Ellen. Land tenure history of New Mexico. EL CUADERNO, Vol. 4, no. 1 (Summer 1976), p. 33-46. English. **DESCR**: History; Land Grants; *Land Tenure; *New Mexico.

EL PUEBLO: THE GALLEGOS FAMILY'S AMERICAN JOURNEY 1503-1980

6688 Flores, Lauro. Book review of: EL PUEBLO: THE GALLEGOS FAMILY'S JOURNEY 1503-1980. MINNESOTA REVIEW, no. 22 (1984), p. 145-148. English. DESCR: Book Reviews; Bruce-Novoa, Juan; *CHICANO POETRY: A RESPONSE TO CHAOS; *FAMOUS ALL OVER TOWN; James, Dan; Johansen, Bruce; Maestas, Roberto.

Pueblos

USE: Barrios

Puerto Rican Council on Higher Education (PRCHE)

6689 Perez, Emma. Higher education organizations. LA RED/THE NET, No. 101 (October 1986), p. 6-10. English. DESCR: *Educational Organizations; Higher Education; *Hispanic Association of Higher Education (HAHE); *SUNY Hispanic Research and Information Network.

Puerto Rican Media Action and Educational Council

6690 Madrid, Vicente and Yepes, Maria Elena. National Latino Media Coalition. LATIN QUARTER, Vol. 1, no. 4 (July, August, 1975), p. 4-7. English. DESCR: Affirmative Action Programs; Bilingual/Bicultural Coalition on Mass Media; *Broadcast Media; California Association of Latins in Broadcasting; Conferences and Meetings; Federal Communications Commission (FCC); *National Latino Media Coalition (NLMC).

Puerto Ricans

6691 Espada, Martin and Perez-Erdelyi, Mireya. With Martin Espada. THE AMERICAS REVIEW, Vol. 15, no. 2 (Summer 1987), p. 77-85. English. DESCR: Authors; *Espada, Martin; Language Usage; Poetry.

6692 Falcon, Angelo. Puerto Rican politics in urban America: an introduction to the literature. LA RED/THE NET, no. 70 (July 1983), p. 2-9. English. DESCR: Literature Reviews; Political History and Conditions; Politics.

6693 Hidalgo, Margarita. On the question of "standard" versus "dialect": implications for teaching Hispanic college students. HISPANIC JOURNAL OF BEHAVIORAL SCIENCES, Vol. 9, no. 4 (December 1987), p. 375-395. English. DESCR: Bilingualism; Chicano Dialects; *Foreign Language Instruction; Language Usage; Sociolinguistics; Spanish for Native Speakers; *Spanish Language.

6694 Mohr, Nicholasa. Puerto Rican writers in the United States, Puerto Rican writers in Puerto Rico: a separation beyond language. THE AMERICAS REVIEW, Vol. 15, no. 2 (Summer 1987), p. 87-92. English. DESCR: Authors; Autobiography; Identity; Immigrants; *Language Usage; *Literature; *Mohr, Nicholasa; Spanish Language.

6695 Reyes, Felix Ojeda. Book review of: HISTORY OF THE PUERTO RICAN INDEPENDENCE MOVEMENT. LA RED/THE NET, no. 76 (January 1984), p. 4-7. Spanish. DESCR: Book Reviews; *HISTORY OF THE PUERTO RICAN INDEPENDENCE MOVEMENT; Lidin, Harold J.

6696 Ruiz, Ariel. Raza, sexo y politica en SHORT EYES by Miguel Pinero. THE AMERICAS REVIEW, Vol. 15, no. 2 (Summer 1987), p. 93-102. Spanish. DESCR: Homosexuality; Literary Criticism; Pinero, Miguel; Prisoners; Sex Roles; *SHORT EYES; Teatro.

Pule, Benny

6697 Seal, Kathy. La pintura del barrio. LA COMUNIDAD, No. 266 (August 25, 1985), p. 13. Spanish. DESCR: Los Angeles, CA; *Mural Art.

Pusey, Allen

6698 13-part series focuses on Hispanics in America. EDITOR & PUBLISHER: THE FOURTH ESTATE, Vol. 115, no. 14 (April 3, 1982), p. 37. English. DESCR: Books; Cultural Characteristics; DALLAS MORNING NEWS; Garcia, Juan; Gonzalez, John; Goodwin, Jay; Grothe, Randy Eli; Hamilton, John; Hille, Ed; LA VIDA AMERICANA; *LA VIDA AMERICANA/HISPANICS IN AMERICA; Langer, Ralph; McLemore, David; Osborne, Burl; Parks, Scott; Sonnemair, Jan.

Quinn, Anthony

6699 Gaspar, Tomas. Anthony Quinn Library receives collection=La Biblioteca Anthony Quinn recibe coleccion. AMERICAS 2001, Premiere Issue, 1987, p. 12-14. Bilingual. DESCR: *Anthony Quinn Library, East Los Angeles, CA; *Library Collections.

Quintana, Leroy V.

6700 Benson, Douglas K. and Quintana, Leroy V. A conversation with Leroy V. Quintana. BILINGUAL REVIEW, Vol. 12, no. 3 (September, December, 1985), p. 218-229. English. DESCR: Authors; Biography; HIJO DEL PUEBLO; Poetry; SANGRE.

6701 Benson, Douglas K. Intuitions of a world in transition: the New Mexican poetry of Leroy V. Quintana. BILINGUAL REVIEW, Vol. 12, no. 1-2 (January, August, 1985), p. 62-80. English. DESCR: Authors; HIJO DEL PUEBLO; *Literary Criticism; New Mexico; Poetry; SANGRE.

Quintanilla, Guadalupe

6702 From dropout to educator. VISTA, Vol. 2, no. 1 (September 7, 1986), p. 13. English. DESCR: *Academic Achievement; Discrimination in Education; Education; *Intelligence Tests.

Quintero, Carlos

6703 Barro, Mary Helen. 1973 Emmy Awards. LATIN QUARTER, Vol. 1, no. 1 (July 1974), p. 5-6. English. DESCR: Chavez, Andres; CINCO VIDAS; Emmy Awards; *Esparza, Moctezuma; Identity; *Recreation; REFLECCIONES; Rodriguez, Sandra; Rodriguez, Tony; Ruiz, Jose Luis; Stereotypes; Television.

Quinto Sol Publishing, Inc.

6704 Bruce-Novoa, Juan. Meet the writers of the 80s. VISTA, Vol. 1, no. 11 (July 6, 1986), p. 15-16. English. DESCR: Anaya, Rudolfo A.; Arte Publico Press; *Authors; Bilingual Review Press; Cisneros, Sandra; Hinojosa-Smith, Rolando R.; Keller, Gary D.; *Literature; Pineda, Cecile; Rivera, Tomas; Soto, Gary.

6705 Lomeli, Francisco A. Novela chicana: sus variantes y contradicciones (I). LA COMUNIDAD, No. 292 (February 23, 1986), p. 12-13. Spanish. DESCR: *Literary Criticism; Literature; Novel; Publishing Industry.

Quirch, Guillermo

6706 Beale, Stephen. CEOs. HISPANIC BUSINESS, Vol. 9, no. 4 (April 1987), p. 20-37, 52. English. **DESCR:** Alvarez, Roberto; Batarse, Anthony A.; Biography; Business Enterprises; *Businesspeople; Carlo, Nelson; Estrada, Anthony; Flores, Frank; Fullana, Jaime, Jr.; Hernandez, George; *Management; Ortega, James; Ruiz, Roberto; Santa Maria, Yvonne Z.; Sugranes, Rosa; Tamaya, Carlos; Young, Paul H., Jr.

Raat, W. Dirk

6707 de Baca, Vincent C. Book review of: INDEX TO SPANISH AMERICAN COLLECTIVE BIOGRAPHY, vol. 2: MEXICO and THE MEXICAN REVOLUTION: AN ANNOTATED GUIDE TO RECENT SCHOLARSHIP. LA RED/THE NET, no. 72 (September 1983), p. 19-21. English. **DESCR:** Book Reviews; de Mundo Lo, Sara; *INDEX TO SPANISH AMERICAN COLLECTIVE BIOGRAPHY, vol. 2: MEXICO; Reference Works; THE MEXICAN REVOLUTION: AN ANNOTATED GUIDE TO RECENT SCHOLARSHIP.

RACE AND CLASS IN THE SOUTHWEST: A THEORY OF RACIAL INEQUALITY

6708 Garcia, John A. Book review of: RACE AND CLASS IN THE SOUTHWEST: A THEORY OF INEQUALITY. LA RED/THE NET, no. 31 (June 1980), p. 4. English. **DESCR:** Barrera, Mario; Book Reviews; *Discrimination; *Economics; *Southwestern United States.

6709 Hall, Linda B. The United States-Mexican borders: historical, political, and cultural perspectives. LATIN AMERICAN RESEARCH REVIEW, Vol. 20, no. 2 (1985), p. 223-229. English. **DESCR:** AMERICAN LABOR IN THE SOUTHWEST: THE FIRST ONE HUNDRED YEARS; *Book Reviews; *Border Region; BOSS RULE IN SOUTH TEXAS: THE PROGRESSIVE ERA; CHICANO INTERMARRIAGE: A THEORETICAL AND EMPIRICAL STUDY; HISPANIC CULTURE IN THE SOUTHWEST; IN DEFENSE OF LA RAZA: THE LOS ANGELES MEXICAN CONSULATE AND THE MEXICAN COMMUNITY; Literature Reviews; SOUTHWESTERN AGRICULTURE: PRE-COLUMBIAN TO MODERN; THE MEXICANS IN OKLAHOMA; THE POLITICS OF SAN ANTONIO.

Race Awareness
USE: Identity

Race Identity
USE: Identity

Race Relations
USE: Intergroup Relations

Racism
USE: Discrimination

Radio

6710 Beale, Stephen. New blood, fresh money: Telemundo, Univision bullish on television market. HISPANIC BUSINESS, Vol. 9, no. 12 (December 1987), p. 30-36. English. **DESCR:** *Corporations; Hallmark Cards; LatCom; Spanish International Communications Corp. (SICC); *Spanish Language; *Telemundo Television Group; *Television; Univision.

6711 Berling-Manuel, Lynn. Expanding radio market battles research static. ADVERTISING AGE MAGAZINE, Vol. 57, no. 43 (August 11, 1986), p. S12-S16. English. **DESCR:** Arbitron; Marketing; Spanish Language; WADO-AM, New York, NY [radio station]; WAQI-AM, Miami, FL [radio station]; WOJO-FM, Chicago, IL [radio station].

6712 Breiter, Toni. Pepe del Rio. VISTA, Vol. 1, no. 6 (February 2, 1986), p. 20. English. **DESCR:** Broadcast Media; *BUENOS DIAS, AMERICA [radio news & features program]; del Rio, Pepe; Perez del Rio, Jose; Voice of America.

6713 Gomez Pena, Guillermo and Erana, Maria. Sobre el arte, la rebeldia y las fronteras. LA COMUNIDAD, No. 312 (July 13, 1986), p. 6-7+. Spanish. **DESCR:** Berkeley, CA; *BORDER-X-FRONTERA [radio program]; Gomez Pena, Guillermo; Schein, David; Teatro.

6714 Gonzalez, Marco Vinicio. En el pais de la frontera. LA COMUNIDAD, No. 291 (February 16, 1986), p. 6-7+. Spanish. **DESCR:** Border Region; Conde, Rosina; *DIALOGOS FRONTERIZOS [radio program]; Gomez Pena, Guillermo; Medina, Ruben; San Diego, CA; Tijuana, Baja California, Mexico.

6715 Gutierrez, Gloria. Chicano news-man wins award. LATIN QUARTER, Vol. 1, no. 4 (July, August, 1975), p. 17. English. **DESCR:** Golden Mike Award; Journalists; Southern California Radio and Television News Association; *Vasquez, Victor.

6716 Lopez, Jose Y. Chico Sesma: a man and his music. LATIN QUARTER, Vol. 1, no. 4 (July, August, 1975), p. 10-15. English. **DESCR:** Chico Sesma Radio Show; Los Angeles, CA; Salsa; *Sesma, Chico.

Railroads

6717 Arreola, Daniel D. The Mexican American cultural capital. GEOGRAPHICAL REVIEW, Vol. 77, (January 1987), p. 17-34. English. **DESCR:** Conjuntos; Food Industry; History; Immigration; LA PRENSA, San Antonio, TX; La Raza Unida Party; League of United Latin American Citizens (LULAC); Lozano, Ignacio; Mexican American Youth Organization, San Antonio, TX; Music; Orden Hijos de America, San Antonio, TX; *San Antonio, TX; *Social History and Conditions.

6718 Parlee, Lorena M. The impact of United States railroad unions on organized labor and government policy in Mexico (1880-1911). HISPANIC AMERICAN HISTORICAL REVIEW, Vol. 64, no. 3 (August 1984), p. 443-475. English. **DESCR:** Diaz, Porfirio; Discrimination in Employment; History; *Labor Unions; Mexico; Partido Liberal Mexicano (PLM); United States-Mexico Relations.

Raimundo, Antonio

6719 Winston, Bonnie. INROADS: internships that work. HISPANIC ENGINEER, Vol. 3, no. 5 (Winter 1987), p. 38-42. English. **DESCR:** Almanza, John; Alvarez, Maria; Carr, Frank; *Educational Organizations; Educational Statistics; Garcia, Juan; Gonzales, Ana; *INROADS; Pereira, Eduardo; Reza, Priscilla.

THE RAIN GOD: A DESERT TALE

6720 Bruce-Novoa, Juan. Homosexuality and the Chicano novel. CONFLUENCIA, Vol. 2, no. 1 (Fall 1986), p. 69-77. English. **DESCR:** Acosta, Oscar Zeta; CITY OF NIGHT; FAULTLINE [novel]; *Homosexuality; Islas, Arturo; *Literary Criticism; Machismo; *Novel; Ortiz Taylor, Sheila; POCHO; Rechy, John; Salas, Floyd; SPRING FORWARD/FALL BACK; TATOO THE WICKED CROSS; THE AUTOBIOGRAPHY OF A BROWN BUFFALO; THE REVOLT OF THE COCKROACH PEOPLE; Villarreal, Jose Antonio.

6721 Galindo, Luis Alberto. El dios de la lluvia=RAIN GOD. LA COMUNIDAD, No. 241 (March 3, 1985), p. 12-13. Spanish. **DESCR:** Biography; Islas, Arturo; *Literary Criticism; Novel.

6722 Gonzales-Berry, Erlinda. Sensuality, repression, and death in Arturo Isla's THE RAIN GOD. BILINGUAL REVIEW, Vol. 12, no. 3 (September, December, 1985), p. 258-261. English. **DESCR:** Book Reviews; Islas, Arturo.

Ramirez, Arnulfo G.

6723 La Salle, Robin Avelar. Book review of: BILINGUALISM THROUGH SCHOOLING. HISPANIC JOURNAL OF BEHAVIORAL SCIENCES, Vol. 9, no. 2 (June 1987), p. 237-240. English. **DESCR:** *BILINGUALISM THROUGH SCHOOLING: CROSS-CULTURAL EDUCATION FOR MINORITY AND MAJORITY STUDENTS; Book Reviews.

6724 Nieto, Sonia. Book review of: BILINGUALISM THROUGH SCHOOLING. INTERRACIAL BOOKS FOR CHILDREN, Vol. 17, no. 3-4 (1986), p. 30. English. **DESCR:** *BILINGUALISM THROUGH SCHOOLING: CROSS-CULTURAL EDUCATION FOR MINORITY AND MAJORITY STUDENTS; Book Reviews.

6725 Otheguy, Ricardo. Book review of: BILINGUALISM THROUGH SCHOOLING. MODERN LANGUAGE JOURNAL, Vol. 69, no. 3 (Fall 1985), p. 300-301. English. **DESCR:** Bilingualism; *BILINGUALISM THROUGH SCHOOLING: CROSS-CULTURAL EDUCATION FOR MINORITY AND MAJORITY STUDENTS; Book Reviews.

6726 Swing, E. S. Book review of: BILINGUALISM THROUGH SCHOOLING. CHOICE, Vol. 23, no. 2 (October 1985), p. 340. English. **DESCR:** *BILINGUALISM THROUGH SCHOOLING: CROSS-CULTURAL EDUCATION FOR MINORITY AND MAJORITY STUDENTS; Book Reviews.

6727 Trueba, Henry T. Book review of: BILINGUALISM THROUGH SCHOOLING. LA RED/THE NET, no. 92 (November, December, 1985), p. 18-20. English. **DESCR:** Bilingualism; *BILINGUALISM THROUGH SCHOOLING: CROSS-CULTURAL EDUCATION FOR MINORITY AND MAJORITY STUDENTS; Book Reviews.

Ramirez [family name]

6728 Instituto Genealogico e Historico Latino-Americano. Rootsearch: Bello: Ramirez: Lopez. VISTA, Vol. 3, no. 2 (October 3, 1987), p. 37. English. **DESCR:** *Bello [family name]; Genealogy; History; *Lopez [family name]; *Personal Names.

Ramirez, Martin (1885-1960)

6729 Cardinal, Roger. El mensaje de Martin Ramirez. LA COMUNIDAD, No. 361 (June 21, 1987), p. 2-3+. Spanish. **DESCR:** *Artists; Biography.

Ramirez v. Webb

6730 Enslen, J. INS enjoined from making vehicle stops on basis of alienage alone. CRIMINAL LAW REPORTER, Vol. 36, no. 16 (January 23, 1985), p. 2291-2293. English. **DESCR:** *Search and Seizure; Undocumented Workers; U.S. v. Brignoni-Ponce.

Ramos, Mario

6731 Latino culture making strides in film. HISPANIC TIMES, Vol. 8, no. 3 (May, June, 1987), p. 38. English. **DESCR:** *Films; Kansas.

6732 Ramos gives special enthusiasm to original Hispanic projects. HISPANIC TIMES, Vol. 8, no. 1 (December, January, 1987), p. 48. English. **DESCR:** *Businesspeople; Films.

Rand Corporation

6733 Facing up to new occupational challenges. HISPANIC BUSINESS, Vol. 9, no. 6 (June 1987), p. 113. English. **DESCR:** *Employment; *Immigration; *Population.

Rangel, Irma

6734 Toboada, John A. Irma Rangel [photograph]. AMERICAS 2001, Premiere Issue, 1987, In BkCover. **DESCR:** *Photography.

THE RAP [novel]

6735 Bruce-Novoa, Juan. Ernest Brawley: un escritor chicano desconocido. LA COMUNIDAD, No. 277 (November 10, 1985), p. 6-7. Spanish. **DESCR:** Authors; *Biography; *Brawley, Ernest; Literary Criticism; Novel; SELENA [novel]; THE ALAMO TREE [novel].

Rape

6736 Herrera-Sobek, Maria. The politics of rape: sexual transgression in Chicana fiction. THE AMERICAS REVIEW, Vol. 15, no. 3-4 (Fall, Winter, 1987), p. 171-181. English. **DESCR:** *Chicanas; Cisneros, Sandra; *Feminism; Fiction; GIVING UP THE GHOST; *Literary Criticism; Lizarraga, Sylvia; Moraga, Cherrie; "Red Clowns" [short story]; Sex Roles; "Silver Lake Road" [short story].

6737 LeBeau, James L. Rape and racial patterns. JOURNAL OF OFFENDER COUNSELING, SERVICES & REHABILITATION, Vol. 9, no. 1-2 (Winter, Fall, 1984), p. 125-148. English.

La Raza

6738 Lopez, Manuel I. The role of the Chicano student in the Chicano Studies Program. EPOCA: NATIONAL CONCILIO FOR CHICANO STUDIES JOURNAL, Vol. 1, no. 2 (Winter 1971), p. 13-17. English. **DESCR:** *Chicano Studies; Higher Education; *Student Movements; *Students.

6739 Sanchez, Lionel. La Raza community and Chicano Studies. EPOCA: NATIONAL CONCILIO FOR CHICANO STUDIES JOURNAL, Vol. 1, no. 2 (Winter 1971), p. 5-59. English. **DESCR:** *Chicano Studies; *Education.

Raza Advocates for California Higher Education (RACHE)

6740 Higher education organizations. LA RED/THE NET, no. 93 (January, February, 1986), p. 5-8. English. DESCR: Educational Organizations; *Higher Education.

La Raza Unida Party

6741 Arreola, Daniel D. The Mexican American cultural capital. GEOGRAPHICAL REVIEW, Vol. 77, (January 1987), p. 17-34. English. DESCR: Conjuntos; Food Industry; History; Immigration; LA PRENSA, San Antonio, TX; League of United Latin American Citizens (LULAC); Lozano, Ignacio; Mexican American Youth Organization, San Antonio, TX; Music; Orden Hijos de America, San Antonio, TX; Railroads; *San Antonio, TX; *Social History and Conditions.

6742 Rips, Geoffrey. Civil rights and wrongs. TEXAS OBSERVOR, Vol. 76, (December 14, 1984), p. 49-55. English. DESCR: Briscoe, Dolph, Jr., Governor of Texas; *Civil Rights; Farm Workers; *Hidalgo County, TX; Miller, C.L.; Segregation and Desegregation; Texas Farmworkers' Union; Voting Rights.

Reading

6743 Duran, Richard P. and Guerra, Elsa. Evidence for scripts governing bilingual children's oral reading behavior. LA RED/THE NET, no. 43 (June 1981), p. 6. English. DESCR: *Bilingualism; Children.

6744 Henkin, Alan B.; Singleton, Carole A.; and Nguyen, Liem T. Seeking goodness of fit: measuring the readability of bilingual learning materials. BILINGUAL REVIEW, Vol. 11, no. 3 (September, December, 1984), p. 9-24. English. DESCR: *Bilingual Bicultural Education; *Curriculum Materials.

6745 Lee, James F. The relationship between decoding accuracy and the reading achievement of monolingual Spanish-speaking children. BILINGUAL REVIEW, Vol. 12, no. 3 (September, December, 1985), p. 209-217. English. DESCR: Educational Tests and Measurements; *Language Development; *Spanish Language.

6746 Mortensen, Eileen. Reading achievement of native Spanish-speaking elementary students in bilingual vs. monolingual programs. BILINGUAL REVIEW, Vol. 11, no. 3 (September, December, 1984), p. 31-36. English. DESCR: *Academic Achievement; *Bilingual Bicultural Education; Language Usage; Primary School Education.

Reagan Administration

6747 High court upholds quotas. DUNS'S BUSINESS MONTH, Vol. 128, no. 2 (August 1986), p. 22. English. DESCR: *Affirmative Action; Discrimination in Employment; Sexism; U.S. Supreme Court.

6748 Munoz, Carlos, Jr. Chicano politics: the current conjuncture. THE YEAR LEFT, Vol. 2, (1987), p. 35-52. English. DESCR: Chicano Movement; Identity; *Intergroup Relations; *Political Parties and Organizations; *Politics; Voter Turnout.

6749 Report to the Network. LA RED/THE NET, no. 92 (January, February, 1986), p. 1-4. English. DESCR: Federal Aid; Finance; *Gramm-Rudman-Hollings Deficit Control Act (PL 99-177); *Higher Education; *School Finance.

Reagan, Ronald

6750 Search for Hispanic heroes informs, surprises, confirms. VISTA, Vol. 1, no. 10 (June 8, 1986), p. 18-19. English. DESCR: Mother Theresa; Pope John Paul II; *Public Opinion.

Reapportionment

6751 Garcia, John A. Chicano political development: examining participation in the "decade of Hispanics". LA RED/THE NET, no. 72 (September 1983), p. 8-18. English. DESCR: *Political Representation; Voter Turnout.

6752 Los Angeles: arriba! ECONOMIST (London), Vol. 297, no. 7424 (December 14, 1985), p. 26. English. DESCR: Bradley, Tom; *Los Angeles, CA; Political Representation; Politics; Voter Turnout.

6753 Los Angeles: brown versus yellow. ECONOMIST (London), Vol. 300, no. 7456 (July 26, 1986), p. 21-22. English. DESCR: Alatorre, Richard; Bradley, Tom; Ethnic Groups; *Los Angeles, CA; Political Representation; Politics; Voter Turnout; Woo, Michael.

Rechy, John

6754 Bruce-Novoa, Juan. Homosexuality and the Chicano novel. CONFLUENCIA, Vol. 2, no. 1 (Fall 1986), p. 69-77. English. DESCR: Acosta, Oscar Zeta; CITY OF NIGHT; FAULTLINE [novel]; *Homosexuality; Islas, Arturo; *Literary Criticism; Machismo; *Novel; Ortiz Taylor, Sheila; POCHO; Salas, Floyd; SPRING FORWARD/FALL BACK; TATOO THE WICKED CROSS; THE AUTOBIOGRAPHY OF A BROWN BUFFALO; THE RAIN GOD: A DESERT TALE; THE REVOLT OF THE COCKROACH PEOPLE; Villarreal, Jose Antonio.

Recipes

6755 Chile charm. VISTA, Vol. 2, no. 7 (March 8, 1987), p. 20-22. English. DESCR: *Crops; History.

The Record Inn, East Los Angeles, CA

6756 Halley, Lindsey. Pachuco boggie [sic]. LA COMUNIDAD, No. 305 (May 25, 1986), p. 8-9. Spanish. DESCR: Cano, Eddie; Diaz, Raul; History; *Music; Ovalle, John; *PACHUCO BOOGIE; Smithsonian Institute; Tosti, Don.

Recording Industry

6757 DeCurtis, Anthony. Los Lobos shake, rattle and worry. ROLLING STONE, (February 26, 1987), p. 51-53. English. DESCR: *BY THE LIGHT OF THE MOON; *Los Lobos del Este de Los Angeles (musical group); Rock Music.

6758 Forte, Dan. Los Lobos: Tex-Mex rock from East L.A. GUITAR PLAYER, Vol. 21, no. 2 (February 1987), p. 68-94. English. DESCR: Biography; Discography; Hidalgo, David (Los Lobos); *Los Lobos del Este de Los Angeles (musical group); Lozano, Conrad (Los Lobos); *Musicians; Perez, Louie (Los Lobos); *Rock Music; Rosas, Cesar (Los Lobos).

Recording Industry (cont.)

6759 Guevara, Ruben and Blades, Ruben. Ruben Blades: music, love and revolution=Ruben Blades: musica, amor y revolucion. AMERICAS 2001, Vol. 1, no. 2 (September, October, 1987), p. 26-29,31. Bilingual. **DESCR:** Biography; *Blades, Ruben; Films; *Musicians.

6760 Haley, Lindsey. Una premiacion controvertida. LA COMUNIDAD, No. 246 (April 7, 1985), p. 5-6. Spanish. **DESCR:** Awards; Discrimination; *Grammy Awards; Guevara, Ruben; Zanya Records Co., Los Angeles, CA.

6761 Holscher, Louis M. Billboard charts and Chicanos, 1955-1974. LA RED/THE NET, no. 41 (April 1981), p. 10,12. English. **DESCR:** *Discography; *Music; *Musicians; Rock Music.

Recreation

6762 Barro, Mary Helen. 1973 Emmy Awards. LATIN QUARTER, Vol. 1, no. 1 (July 1974), p. 5-6. English. **DESCR:** Chavez, Andres; CINCO VIDAS; Emmy Awards; *Esparza, Moctezuma; Identity; Quintero, Carlos; REFLECCIONES; Rodriguez, Sandra; Rodriguez, Tony; Ruiz, Jose Luis; Stereotypes; Television.

"Red Clowns" [short story]

6763 Herrera-Sobek, Maria. The politics of rape: sexual transgression in Chicana fiction. THE AMERICAS REVIEW, Vol. 15, no. 3-4 (Fall, Winter, 1987), p. 171-181. English. **DESCR:** *Chicanas; Cisneros, Sandra; *Feminism; Fiction; GIVING UP THE GHOST; *Literary Criticism; Lizarraga, Sylvia; Moraga, Cherrie; *Rape; Sex Roles; "Silver Lake Road" [short story].

Redford, Robert

6764 Rodriguez Flores, Juan. Robert Redford y THE MILAGRO BEANFIELD WAR. LA COMUNIDAD, No. 328 (November 2, 1986), p. 8-11+. Spanish. **DESCR:** Actors and Actresses; *Films; THE MILAGRO BEANFIELD WAR [film].

LA RED/THE NET

6765 Report to the Network from NCCHE. LA RED/THE NET, no. 87 (July 1985), p. 1-2. English. **DESCR:** Chicano Studies; *Educational Organizations; *National Chicano Council on Higher Education (NCCHE); National Chicano Research Network (NCRN); Tomas Rivera Center, Claremont, CA.

Reference Books
USE: Reference Works

Reference Works

6766 Andrachuk, Gregory Peter. Book review of: A SOURCEBOOK FOR HISPANIC LITERATURE AND LANGUAGE. CANADIAN MODERN LANGUAGE REVIEW, Vol. 43, no. 1 (October 1986), p. 168-169. English. **DESCR:** *A SOURCEBOOK FOR HISPANIC LITERATURE AND LANGUAGE; Bleznick, Donald W.; Book Reviews.

6767 Arce, Carlos H. and Carlson, David. Book review of: HISPANIC MENTAL HEALTH RESEARCH: A REFERENCE GUIDE. LA RED/THE NET, no. 57 (August 1982), p. 5-7. English. **DESCR:** Book Reviews; *HISPANIC MENTAL HEALTH RESEARCH: A REFERENCE GUIDE; Mental Health; Newton, Frank; Olmedo, Esteban L.; Padilla, Amado M.

6768 Book review of: BOOKS IN SPANISH FOR CHILDREN AND YOUNG ADULTS. BOOKLIST, Vol. 82, (July 1986), p. 1620. English. **DESCR:** Book Reviews; *BOOKS IN SPANISH FOR CHILDREN AND YOUNG ADULTS: AN ANNOTATED GUIDE; Children's Literature; Schon, Isabel.

6769 Book review of: CHICANO LITERATURE: A REFERENCE GUIDE. BOOKLIST, Vol. 82, no. 9 (January 1, 1986), p. 667-668. English. **DESCR:** Book Reviews; *CHICANO LITERATURE: A REFERENCE GUIDE; Lomeli, Francisco A.; Martinez, Julio A.

6770 Book review of: SPANISH-LANGUAGE BOOKS FOR PUBLIC LIBRARIES. BOOKLIST, Vol. 83, no. 9 (January 1, 1987), p. 700-701. English. **DESCR:** Book Reviews; Restrepo, Fabio; *SPANISH-LANGUAGE BOOKS FOR PUBLIC LIBRARIES.

6771 Book review of: THE IMMIGRANT WOMAN IN NORTH AMERICA. BOOKLIST, Vol. 82, no. 12 (February 15, 1986), p. 855-856. English. **DESCR:** Book Reviews; Cordasco, Francesco; *THE IMMIGRANT WOMAN IN NORTH AMERICA: AN ANNOTATED BIBLIOGRAPHY OF SELECTED REFERENCES.

6772 Brown, D.R. Book review of: CHICANO LITERATURE: A REFERENCE GUIDE. CHOICE, Vol. 23, no. 4 (December 1985), p. 578. English. **DESCR:** Book Reviews; *CHICANO LITERATURE: A REFERENCE GUIDE; Lomeli, Francisco A.; Martinez, Julio A.

6773 Castillo-Speed, Lillian. Annotated bibliography. LA RED/THE NET, no. 93 (January, February, 1986), p. 14-17. English. **DESCR:** A BIBLIOGRAPHY OF MEXICAN AMERICAN HISTORY; ARTE CHICANO; Book Reviews; Caballero, Cesar; CHICANO LITERATURE: A REFERENCE GUIDE; CHICANO ORGANIZATIONS DIRECTORY; CHICANO PERIODICAL INDEX; Goldman, Shifra M.; HISPANIC ALMANAC; HISPANIC MENTAL HEALTH RESEARCH: A REFERENCE GUIDE; Lomeli, Francisco A.; Martinez, Julio A.; Meier, Matt S.; Newton, Frank; Ybarra-Frausto, Tomas.

6774 Chabran, Richard and Garcia-Ayvens, Francisco. Book review of: THE MEXICAN AMERICAN: A CRITICAL GUIDE TO RESEARCH AIDS. LA RED/THE NET, no. 37 (December 1980), p. 4-5. English. **DESCR:** Bibliography; Book Reviews; *Robinson, Barbara J.; *Robinson, J. Cordell; *THE MEXICAN AMERICAN: A CRITICAL GUIDE TO RESEARCH AIDS.

6775 Chabran, Richard. Latino reference arrives. AMERICAN LIBRARIES, Vol. 18, no. 5 (May 1987), p. 384-388. English. **DESCR:** *Academic Libraries; *Bibliography; *Library Collections; Library Instruction.

6776 Chatham, James R. Book review of: A SOURCEBOOK FOR HISPANIC LITERATURE AND LANGUAGE. REVISTA DE ESTUDIOS HISPANICOS, Vol. 18, no. 3 (October 1984), p. 457-458. English. **DESCR:** *A SOURCEBOOK FOR HISPANIC LITERATURE AND LANGUAGE; Bleznick, Donald W.; Book Reviews.

6777 de Baca, Vincent C. Book review of: INDEX TO SPANISH AMERICAN COLLECTIVE BIOGRAPHY, vol. 2: MEXICO and THE MEXICAN REVOLUTION: AN ANNOTATED GUIDE TO RECENT SCHOLARSHIP. LA RED/THE NET, no. 72 (September 1983), p. 19-21. English. **DESCR:** Book Reviews; de Mundo Lo, Sara; *INDEX TO SPANISH AMERICAN COLLECTIVE BIOGRAPHY, vol. 2: MEXICO; Raat, W. Dirk; THE MEXICAN REVOLUTION: AN ANNOTATED GUIDE TO RECENT SCHOLARSHIP.

Reference Works (cont.)

6778 Hagle, C. Book review of: THE IMMIGRANT WOMAN IN NORTH AMERICA. CHOICE, Vol. 23, no. 8 (April 1986), p. 1191. English. **DESCR:** Book Reviews; Cordasco, Francesco; *THE IMMIGRANT WOMAN IN NORTH AMERICA: AN ANNOTATED BIBLIOGRAPHY OF SELECTED REFERENCES.

6779 Haro, Robert P. Book review of: CHICANO LITERATURE: A REFERENCE GUIDE. AMERICAN REFERENCE BOOKS ANNUAL, Vol. 17, (1986), p. 440. English. **DESCR:** Book Reviews; *CHICANO LITERATURE: A REFERENCE GUIDE; Lomeli, Francisco A.; Martinez, Julio A.

6780 Haro, Robert P. Book review of: CHICANO ORGANIZATIONS DIRECTORY. AMERICAN REFERENCE BOOKS ANNUAL, Vol. 17, (1986), p. 145. English. **DESCR:** Book Reviews; Caballero, Cesar; *CHICANO ORGANIZATIONS DIRECTORY.

6781 Haro, Robert P. Book review of: HISPANIC AMERICAN VOLUNTARY ORGANIZATIONS. AMERICAN REFERENCE BOOKS ANNUAL, Vol. 17, (1986), p. 146. English. **DESCR:** Book Reviews; Gonzales, Sylvia Alicia; *HISPANIC AMERICAN VOLUNTARY ORGANIZATIONS.

6782 Perry, Charles E. Book review of: CHICANO LITERATURE: A REFERENCE GUIDE. LIBRARY JOURNAL, Vol. 110, no. 5 (March 15, 1985), p. 53. English. **DESCR:** Book Reviews; *CHICANO LITERATURE: A REFERENCE GUIDE; Literature; Lomeli, Francisco A.; Martinez, Julio A.

6783 Vigelis, Adeline R. Book review of: HISPANIC FIRST NAMES. LECTOR, Vol. 4, no. 4-6 (1987), p. 55-56. English. **DESCR:** Book Reviews; *HISPANIC FIRST NAMES: A COMPREHENSIVE DICTIONARY OF 250 YEARS OF MEXICAN-AMERICAN USAGE; Personal Names; Woods, Richard D.

6784 Vigil, James Diego. Book review of: DICTIONARY OF MEXICAN AMERICAN HISTORY. PACIFIC HISTORICAL REVIEW, Vol. 53, no. 2 (1984), p. 241-242. English. **DESCR:** Book Reviews; *DICTIONARY OF MEXICAN AMERICAN HISTORY; Meier, Matt S.; Rivera, Feliciano.

6785 Woods, Richard D. Book review of: MEXICO-ESTADOS UNIDOS: BIBLIOGRAFIA GENERAL SOBRE ESTUDIOS FRONTERIZOS. LA RED/THE NET, no. 49 (December 1981), p. 4-5. English. **DESCR:** Book Reviews; Border Studies; *Bustamante, Jorge A.; Malagamba, Francisco; *MEXICO-ESTADOS UNIDOS: BIBLIOGRAFIA GENERAL SOBRE ESTUDIOS FRONTERIZOS.

REFLECCIONES

6786 Barro, Mary Helen. 1973 Emmy Awards. LATIN QUARTER, Vol. 1, no. 1 (July 1974), p. 5-6. English. **DESCR:** Chavez, Andres; CINCO VIDAS; Emmy Awards; *Esparza, Moctezuma; Identity; Quintero, Carlos; *Recreation; Rodriguez, Sandra; Rodriguez, Tony; Ruiz, Jose Luis; Stereotypes; Television.

Refranes
USE: Dichos

Refugee Act of 1980

6787 Protecting aliens from persecution without overloading the INS. VIRGINIA LAW REVIEW, Vol. 69, (June 1983), p. 901-930. English. **DESCR:** Nunez v. Boldin; *Orantes, Hernandez v. Smith; Political Refugees; *Undocumented Workers.

Refugees
USE: Political Refugees

Reina, Reuben

6788 Allsup, Dan. Run Reuben run. VISTA, Vol. 1, no. 12 (August 2, 1986), p. 18. English. **DESCR:** *Athletes; San Antonio, TX; Sports.

Religion

6789 Burciaga, Jose Antonio. In celebration of a man's ecumenism. VISTA, Vol. 2, no. 4 (December 7, 1986), p. 26. English. **DESCR:** *Catholic Church; Congregation B'nai Zion, El Paso, TX; Holidays; Jews.

6790 Cutter, Donald C. With a little help from their saints. PACIFIC HISTORICAL REVIEW, Vol. 53, no. 2 (1984), p. 123-140. English. **DESCR:** Catholic Church; *Santos.

6791 Diekemper, Barnabas C. The Catholic Church in the shadows: the southwestern United States during the Mexican period. JOURNAL OF THE WEST, Vol. 24, no. 2 (1985), p. 46-53. English. **DESCR:** *Catholic Church; Missions; *Southwestern United States.

6792 Gonzales, Phillip B. Book review of: LATINOS IN THE UNITED STATES: THE SACRED AND THE POLITICAL. NEW MEXICO HISTORICAL REVIEW, Vol. 62, no. 4 (October 1987), p. 409-11. English. **DESCR:** *Abalos, David T.; Book Reviews; *LATINOS IN THE UNITED STATES: THE SACRED AND THE POLITICAL; Politics.

6793 Levin, Jeffrey S. and Markides, Kyriakos S. Religious attendance and subjective health. JOURNAL FOR THE SCIENTIFIC STUDY OF RELIGION, Vol. 25, no. 1 (March 1986), p. 31-40. English. **DESCR:** *Public Health.

6794 Morales, Cecilio. Judaism's Hispanic thread. VISTA, Vol. 2, no. 3 (November 2, 1986), p. 20-23. English. **DESCR:** Cultural Customs; History; *Jews.

6795 Padilla, Eligio R. and O'Grady, Kevin E. Sexuality among Mexican Americans: a case of sexual stereotyping. JOURNAL OF PERSONALITY AND SOCIAL PSYCHOLOGY, Vol. 52, no. 1 (1987), p. 5-10. English. **DESCR:** Age Groups; Anglo Americans; Attitudes; *Sex Roles; *Stereotypes.

6796 Plowman, Edward E. Hispanic Christians in the United States. CHRISTIANITY TODAY, Vol. 30, no. 1 (January 17, 1986), p. 44-45. English. **DESCR:** *Hispanic Congress on Evangelization (HCE); Los Angeles, CA; Protestant Church.

Religious Art

6797 Griffith, James S. The Magdalena holy picture: religious folk art in two cultures. NEW YORK FOLKLORE QUARTERLY, Vol. 8, no. 3-4 (Winter 1982), p. 71-82. English. **DESCR:** Folk Art; *Magdalena de Kino, Mexico.

Religious Education

6798 Doyle, Janet. Escoja educacion catolica! MOMENTUM, Vol. 14, no. 1 (February 1983), p. 37-38. English. **DESCR:** *Catholic Church; Toledo, OH.

Religious Education (cont.)

6799 Elford, George. Catholic schools and bilingual education. MOMENTUM, Vol. 14, no. 1 (February 1983), p. 35-37. English. **DESCR:** Bilingual Bicultural Education; *Catholic Church.

6800 Jimenez, Ricardo. Understanding the culture and learning styles of Hispanic students. MOMENTUM, Vol. 14, no. 1 (February 1983), p. 15-18. English. **DESCR:** *Acculturation; Socialization; Students.

Rendon, Susana

6801 Susana Rendon. AMERICAS 2001, Vol. 1, no. 1 (June, July, 1987), p. [31]. Bilingual. **DESCR:** Biographical Notes; Businesspeople; Chicanas.

Repatriation
USE: Deportation

Reports and Reporting
USE: Journalism

Republican Party

6802 Volsky, George. A new voting block making its mark. HISPANIC BUSINESS, Vol. 9, no. 2 (February 1987), p. 9, 11. English. **DESCR:** Cubanos; Democratic Party; Elections; *Political Parties and Organizations; *Voter Turnout.

REQUISA TREINTA Y DOS

6803 Herrera-Sobek, Maria. Literatura y sociedad: la problematica del Chicano/Mexicano en los Estados Unidos a traves de la obra literaria. BILINGUAL REVIEW, Vol. 11, no. 3 (September, December, 1984), p. 83-87. Spanish. **DESCR:** Book Reviews; Literary Criticism; Literature; Sanchez, Rosaura.

Research Centers

6804 Dellinger, Robert W. Hispanic think tank. VISTA, Vol. 3, no. 3 (November 8, 1987), p. 28. English. **DESCR:** Madrid, Arturo; *Public Policy; *Tomas Rivera Center, Claremont, CA.

6805 Hunsaker, Alan C. Institutionally-based research centers: the Center for U.S.-Mexican Studies. LA RED/THE NET, no. 92 (November, December, 1985), p. 13-15. English. **DESCR:** *Center for U.S.-Mexican Studies, University of California at San Diego, La Jolla, CA; Del Castillo, Gustavo; Meyer, Lorenzo; United States-Mexico Relations.

6806 Perez, Emma. Higher education organizations. LA RED/THE NET, no. 94 (March 1986), p. 2-4. English. **DESCR:** Educational Organizations; Higher Education; *Mexican American Studies and Research Center, University of Arizona, Tucson, AZ.

6807 Perez, Emma. Institutionally-based research centers: the Stanford Center for Chicano Research. LA RED/THE NET, no. 93 (January, February, 1986), p. 9-11. English. **DESCR:** *Stanford Center for Chicano Research, Stanford, CA.

6808 Perez, Emma. Research centers. LA RED/THE NET, no. 95 (April 1986), p. 5-8. English. **DESCR:** *Chicano Studies Research Center, UCLA.

6809 Perez, Emma. Research centers. LA RED/THE NET, no. 96 (May 1986), p. 3-6.

DESCR: *Center for Mexican American Studies (CMAS), University of Texas, Austin, TX.

6810 Perez, Emma. Research centers. LA RED/THE NET, no. 97 (June 1986), p. 6-8. English. **DESCR:** *Centro de Estudios Puertorriquenos, Hunter College of the City University of New York.

6811 Perez, Emma. Research centers. LA RED/THE NET, no. 98 (July 1986), p. 6-9. English. **DESCR:** *Hispanic Research Center, Arizona State University, Tempe, AZ.

6812 Perez, Emma. Research centers. LA RED/THE NET, No. 100 (September 1986), p. 5-8. English. **DESCR:** *Spanish-Speaking Mental Health Research Center.

6813 Perez, Emma. Research centers. LA RED/THE NET, no. 10 (November 1986), p. 6-7. English. **DESCR:** *Bureau of Applied Research in Anthropology (BARA), University of Arizona.

Research Methodology

6814 Angel, Ronald. The study of the health of Chicanos: some recent findings. LA RED/THE NET, no. 74 (November 1983), p. 2-7. English. **DESCR:** Medical Care; *Public Health.

6815 Baker, Keith and de Kanter, Adriana. An answer from research on bilingual education. AMERICAN EDUCATION, Vol. 19, no. 6, p. 40-48. English. **DESCR:** *Bilingual Bicultural Education; Language Assessment; Language Development.

6816 Burnham, M. Audrey, et al. Measurement of acculturation in a community population of Mexican Americans. HISPANIC JOURNAL OF BEHAVIORAL SCIENCES, Vol. 9, no. 2 (June 1987), p. 105-130. English. **DESCR:** *Acculturation; Age Groups; Biculturalism; Sex Roles.

6817 Chacon, Maria A., et al. Chicanas in California postsecondary education. LA RED/THE NET, no. 65 (Winter 1983), p. 3-24. English. **DESCR:** *Chicanas; Higher Education.

6818 Comstock, Cathryn L. and Martin, Frederick N. A children's Spanish word discrimination test for non-Spanish-speaking children. EAR AND HEARING, Vol. 5, no. 3 (May, June, 1984), p. 166-170. English. **DESCR:** Child Study; English Language; *Language Assessment; Spanish Language.

6819 DeSipio, Louis. Social science literature and the naturalization process. INTERNATIONAL MIGRATION REVIEW, Vol. 21, no. 2 (Summer 1987), p. 390-405. English. **DESCR:** Immigrants; *Naturalization; *Social Science.

6820 Elizondo, Sergio D. Critical areas of need for research and scholastic study. EPOCA: NATIONAL CONCILIO FOR CHICANO STUDIES JOURNAL, Vol. 1, no. 2 (Winter 1971), p. 1-7. English. **DESCR:** *Chicano Studies; *Curriculum.

6821 Hayes-Bautista, David Emmett. Chicano health policy research. LA RED/THE NET, no. 41 (April 1981), p. 9-10. English. **DESCR:** *Public Health; *Public Policy.

Research Methodology (cont.)

6822 Lacayo, Carmela G. Triple jeopardy among Hispanic elderly: results from first national needs assessment of older Hispanics. LA RED/THE NET, no. 56 (July 1982), p. 2-3. English. **DESCR:** *Ancianos; Asociacion Nacional Pro Personas Mayores; *National Study to Assess the Service Needs of the Hispanic Elderly; *Social Services; Surveys.

6823 Report to the Network. LA RED/THE NET, No. 104 (January 1987), p. 1-2. English. **DESCR:** Computers; *Contreras, Reynaldo A.; *Higher Education; *Midwestern States; *Natural Support Systems; Surveys.

6824 Rosaldo, Renato. When natives talk back: Chicano anthropology since the late 60s. RENATO ROSALDO LECTURE SERIES MONOGRAPH, Vol. 2, (Spring 1986), p. [3]-20. English. **DESCR:** *Anthropology; Culture; EL GRITO; *Identity; Paredes, Americo; *Political Ideology; Romano-V., Octavio Ignacio; Valdez, Facundo.

6825 Samora, Julian and Galarza, Ernesto. Research and scholarly activity. EPOCA: NATIONAL CONCILIO FOR CHICANO STUDIES JOURNAL, Vol. 1, no. 2 (Winter 1971), p. 51-54. English. **DESCR:** *Chicano Studies; *Curriculum.

6826 Stern, Gwen. Research, action, and social betterment. AMERICAN BEHAVIOR SCIENTISTS, Vol. 29, no. 2 (November, December, 1985), p. 229-248. English. **DESCR:** Chicago, IL; *Chicanas; Medical Care; The Latina Mother-Infant Project, Chicago, IL.

6827 Sullivan, Teresa A. and Tienda, Marta. Integration of multiple data sources in immigrant studies. REVIEW OF PUBLIC DATA USE, Vol. 12, no. 4 (December 1984), p. 233-244. English. **DESCR:** *Immigrants; *Immigration; *Statistics.

6828 Tienda, Marta. Task force on statistical policy and data needs. LA RED/THE NET, no. 88 (Winter, 1984), p. 2-6. English. **DESCR:** *Databases; *Population; Public Policy; *Statistics; Vital Statistics.

6829 Wilde, Richard H. The establishment of a Chicano studies program and its relation to the total curriculum of a college or university. EPOCA: NATIONAL CONCILIO FOR CHICANO STUDIES JOURNAL, Vol. 1, no. 2 (Winter 1971), p. 70-78. English. **DESCR:** California State University, Long Beach; *Chicano Studies; *Curriculum.

Residential Segregation

6830 Krivo, Lauren J. and Mutchler, Jan E. Housing constraint and household complexity in metropolitan America: Black and Spanish-origin minorities. URBAN AFFAIRS QUARTERLY, Vol. 21, no. 3 (March 1986), p. 389-409. English. **DESCR:** Blacks; *Housing.

6831 Massey, Douglas S. and Mullan, Brendan P. Processes of Hispanic and Black spatial assimilation. AMERICAN JOURNAL OF SOCIOLOGY, Vol. 89, no. 4 (January 1984), p. 836-873. English. **DESCR:** Assimilation; Blacks; Census; *Ethnic Stratification; *Social Mobility.

Restaurants

6832 Arreola, Daniel D. Mexican restaurants in Tucson. JOURNAL OF CULTURAL GEOGRAPHY, Vol.

3, no. 2 (Spring, Summer, 1983), p. 108-114. English. **DESCR:** Architecture; Landscape Architecture; Tucson, AZ.

6833 Bain, Laurie. Alfonso's heats up San Antonio. RESTAURANT BUSINESS, Vol. 86, (January 20, 1987), p. 120-122. English. **DESCR:** *Alfonso's Restaurant, San Antonio, TX; Burke, John.

6834 Gindin, Rona L. Mexican. RESTAURANT BUSINESS, Vol. 83, (March 20, 1984), p. 144-146. English.

6835 Kessel, Janet. Treasure hunt. SAN FRANCISCO, Vol. 25, no. 10 (October 1983), p. 103-110. English. **DESCR:** *Mission District, San Francisco, CA; San Francisco, CA.

6836 Kochak, Jacque. Mexican menus invade American markets. RESTAURANT BUSINESS, Vol. 83, (April 10, 1984), p. 144-166. English. **DESCR:** *El Torito Restaurant.

6837 Lang, Joan M. Sizzler franchisee is going Cucos! RESTAURANT BUSINESS, Vol. 83, (June 10, 1984), p. 142-152. English. **DESCR:** *Cuco's Restaurant.

6838 Noeth, Louise Ann and Sellers, Jeff M. Fast food for thought. HISPANIC BUSINESS, Vol. 9, no. 3 (March 1987), p. 20-24. English. **DESCR:** *Business Enterprises; Food Industry.

6839 Raffel, Elaine. What makes Chilis hot? RESTAURANT BUSINESS, Vol. 82, (October 1, 1983), p. 147-153+. English. **DESCR:** *Chili's Restaurant; Larine, Larry.

6840 Raffio, Ralph. Del Taco targets adult audience. RESTAURANT BUSINESS, Vol. 84, (April 10, 1985), p. 260-264. English. **DESCR:** *Del Taco Restaurants; Marketing.

6841 Thomas, Marjorie. Taco Bell rings in new image. RESTAURANT BUSINESS, Vol. 83, (October 10, 1984), p. 210-218. English. **DESCR:** *Taco Bell.

RESTLESS SERPENTS

6842 Saldivar, Jose David. Towards a Chicano poetics: the making of the Chicano subject. CONFLUENCIA, Vol. 1, no. 2 (Spring 1986), p. 10-17. English. **DESCR:** Corridos; Feminism; *Literary Criticism; "Los vatos" [poem]; Montoya, Jose E.; *Poetry; Rios, Alberto; WHISPERING TO FOOL THE WIND; Zamora, Bernice.

Restrepo, Fabio

6843 Book review of: SPANISH-LANGUAGE BOOKS FOR PUBLIC LIBRARIES. BOOKLIST, Vol. 83, no. 9 (January 1, 1987), p. 700-701. English. **DESCR:** Book Reviews; Reference Works; *SPANISH-LANGUAGE BOOKS FOR PUBLIC LIBRARIES.

THE RETENTION OF MINORITY LANGUAGES IN THE UNITED STATES: A SEMINAR ON THE ANALYTIC WORK OF CALVIN VELTMAN

6844 Macias, Reynaldo Flores. Disambiguating the Veltman trilogy. BILINGUAL REVIEW, Vol. 12, no. 1-2 (January, August, 1985), p. 140-143. English. **DESCR:** Book Reviews; *CONTRACTOR REPORT: RELATIVE EDUCATIONAL ATTAINMENT OF MINORITY LANGUAGE CHILDREN, 1976: A COMPARISON TO BLACK AND WHITE ENGLISH LANGUAGE CHILDREN; *CONTRACTOR REPORT: THE ROLE OF LANGUAGE CHARACTERISTICS IN THE SOCIOECONOMIC PROCESS OF HISPANIC ORIGIN MEN AND WOMEN; Language Usage; Veltman, Calvin.

RETO EN EL PARAISO

6845 Mariscal, George. Alejandro Morales in utopia. CONFLUENCIA, Vol. 2, no. 1 (Fall 1986), p. 78-83. English. **DESCR:** *Literary Criticism; *Morales, Alejandro; Novel.

6846 Martin-Rodriguez, Manuel M. El sentimiento de culpa en RETO EN EL PARAISO de Alejandro Morales. THE AMERICAS REVIEW, Vol. 15, no. 1 (Spring 1987), p. 89-97. Spanish. **DESCR:** Literary Criticism; *Morales, Alejandro; Novel.

REVISTA CHICANO-RIQUENA

6847 Elias, Edward F. Book review of: A DECADE OF HISPANIC LITERATURE. LA RED/THE NET, no. 68 (May 1983), p. 9-10. English. **DESCR:** Book Reviews; *DECADE OF HISPANIC LITERATURE: AN ANNIVERSARY ANTHOLOGY; Literature.

REVISTA MUJERES, University of California, Santa Cruz

6848 Davila, Elisa. A manera de introduccion: cuando las mujeres escribimos...=By way of introduction: when we women write... REVISTA MUJERES, Vol. 1, no. 2 (June 1984), p. 2-5. Bilingual. **DESCR:** *Poems.

THE REVOLT OF THE COCKROACH PEOPLE

6849 Bruce-Novoa, Juan. Homosexuality and the Chicano novel. CONFLUENCIA, Vol. 2, no. 1 (Fall 1986), p. 69-77. English. **DESCR:** Acosta, Oscar Zeta; CITY OF NIGHT; FAULTLINE [novel]; *Homosexuality; Islas, Arturo; *Literary Criticism; Machismo; *Novel; Ortiz Taylor, Sheila; POCHO; Rechy, John; Salas, Floyd; SPRING FORWARD/FALL BACK; TATOO THE WICKED CROSS; THE AUTOBIOGRAPHY OF A BROWN BUFFALO; THE RAIN GOD: A DESERT TALE; Villarreal, Jose Antonio.

Revolutions

6850 Sandos, James A. Northern separatism during the Mexican revolution--an inquiry into the role of drug trafficking, 1910-1920. AMERICAS, Vol. 41, no. 2 (October 1984), p. 191-214. English. **DESCR:** Baja California, Mexico; Border Region; Cantu Jimenez, Esteban; Drug Addicts; Drug Laws; *Drug Traffic; *Drug Use; Medical Care; Mexican Revolution - 1910-1920.

Revueltas, Jose

6851 Campbell, Federico. Paralelo 32: la frontera como espacio literario. LA COMUNIDAD, No. 347 (March 15, 1987), p. 5. Spanish. **DESCR:** Border Region; *Literary Criticism; *LOS MOTIVOS DE CAIN; Tijuana, Baja California, Mexico.

Reyes Magos Tradition

6852 Cardenas, Antonio J. and Cardenas, Cecilia. Traditions of Christmas. VISTA, Vol. 2, no. 4 (December 7, 1986), p. 14-17. English. **DESCR:** El Paso, TX; Festivals; *Holidays; Miami, FL.

Reyes, Raul E. (Ernie)

6853 Reyes outstanding Hispanic at Kennedy Space Center. HISPANIC TIMES, Vol. 8, no. 5 (October, November, 1987), p. 60. English. **DESCR:** Biography; *Engineering as a Profession; John F. Kennedy Space Center, NASA, FL.

Reyes-Guerra, David

6854 SHPE holds first ever East coast conference for Hispanic engineers. HISPANIC ENGINEER, Vol. 3, no. 5 (Winter 1987), p. 12-14. English. **DESCR:** Awards; Barrios, Eugene; Chang-Diaz, Franklin; *Conferences and Meetings; Cuevas, Brian L.; Garay, Charles J.; Garcia, Ray; Marrero, Charles; Martinez, Lisa; Monteverde, Edwin; Plumey, Raymond; Rivera, Angel; Society of Hispanic Professional Engineers (SHPE); Soto, Giovanni.

6855 SHPE news. HISPANIC ENGINEER, Vol. 3, no. 3 (1987), p. 10-13. English. **DESCR:** *Awards; Castillo, Hector; Colmenarez, Margarita; Garcia, Raul; Herrera, Jess; Lopez-Martin, Minnie; Mondragon, Ricardo; Silva, Juan; Society of Hispanic Professional Engineers (SHPE); Vargas, Jesus; Villanueva, Bernadette.

Reyna, Phil

6856 Jimenez, Luis. Cambia la imagen del latino en Hollywood. LA COMUNIDAD, No. 255 (June 9, 1985), p. 14-15. Spanish. **DESCR:** Discrimination; Employment; Films; *Hispanic Academy of Media Arts and Sciences (HAMAS); *Mass Media; Organizations.

Reza, Priscilla

6857 Winston, Bonnie. INROADS: internships that work. HISPANIC ENGINEER, Vol. 3, no. 5 (Winter 1987), p. 38-42. English. **DESCR:** Almanza, John; Alvarez, Maria; Carr, Frank; *Educational Organizations; Educational Statistics; Garcia, Juan; Gonzales, Ana; *INROADS; Pereira, Eduardo; Raimundo, Antonio.

Rhetoric

6858 de la Garza, Rodolfo O. Book review of: A WAR OF WORDS. JOURNAL OF AMERICAN ETHNIC HISTORY, Vol. 6, no. 2 (Spring 1987), p. 97-98. English. **DESCR:** *A WAR OF WORDS: CHICANO PROTEST IN THE 1960S AND 1970S; Book Reviews; Gutierrez, Jose Angel; Hammerback, John C.; Jensen, Richard J.

6859 Gurza, Esperanza. I AM JOAQUIN: speech act theory applied. CONFLUENCIA, Vol. 1, no. 2 (Spring 1986), p. 85-97. English. **DESCR:** Gonzales, Rodolfo (Corky); *I AM JOAQUIN [book]; *Poetry.

6860 LeAna, Thomas. From dropout to role model: a VISTA postscript. VISTA, Vol. 2, no. 4 (December 7, 1986), p. 25. English. **DESCR:** Brownsville, TX; Gladys Porter High School; *Martinez, Dorella; Olivares, J.R.; Secondary School Education.

Ricardo-Campbell, Rita

6861 Interview: Rita Ricardo-Campbell.
INTERCAMBIOS FEMENILES, Vol. 2, no. 6
(Spring 1987), p. 10-11. English. DESCR:
*Appointed Officials; Chicanas; Economics;
Leadership.

Rico, Louis

6862 Escobar, Edward J. Mexican revolutionaries
and the Los Angeles police: harassment of
the Partido Liberal Mexicano, 1907-1910.
AZTLAN, Vol. 17, no. 1 (Spring 1986), p.
1-46. English. DESCR: Civil Rights; *Flores
Magon, Ricardo; Gutierrez de Lara, Lazaro;
Los Angeles, CA; *Los Angeles Police
Department; *Partido Liberal Mexicano (PLM);
*Police; Police Brutality; Political
Repression; Rico, Thomas; Talamantes,
Felipe; United States-Mexico Relations.

Rico, Thomas

6863 Escobar, Edward J. Mexican revolutionaries
and the Los Angeles police: harassment of
the Partido Liberal Mexicano, 1907-1910.
AZTLAN, Vol. 17, no. 1 (Spring 1986), p.
1-46. English. DESCR: Civil Rights; *Flores
Magon, Ricardo; Gutierrez de Lara, Lazaro;
Los Angeles, CA; *Los Angeles Police
Department; *Partido Liberal Mexicano (PLM);
*Police; Police Brutality; Political
Repression; Rico, Louis; Talamantes, Felipe;
United States-Mexico Relations.

Rico-Perez, Manuel

6864 Remas, Theodora A. The threat of diabetes.
VISTA, Vol. 1, no. 2 (October 5, 1985), p.
14-16. English. DESCR: *Diabetes; Health
Education; *Mezitis, Nicholas; *Nutrition;
Public Health.

Ridge, Martin

6865 Macias, Reynaldo Flores. Book review of: THE
NEW BILINGUALISM: AN AMERICAN DILEMMA. LA
RED/THE NET, no. 61 (November 1982), p. 7-9.
English. DESCR: *Bilingualism; Book Reviews;
Public Policy; *THE NEW BILINGUALISM: AN
AMERICAN DILEMMA.

6866 Ornstein-Galicia, Jacob. Bilingualism,
bilingual education, and language contact:
the agony, the rewards--or how to unravel
Babel. BILINGUAL REVIEW, Vol. 11, no. 3
(September, December, 1984), p. 72-82.
English. DESCR: Bilingual Bicultural
Education; Bilingualism; Book Reviews;
*LANGUAGES IN CONFLICT: LINGUISTIC
ACCULTURATION IN THE GREAT PLAINS; Schach,
Paul; *THE NEW BILINGUALISM: AN AMERICAN
DILEMMA.

Riding, Alan

6867 Loaeza, Soledad. Alan Riding: la fuerza del
prejuicio. LA COMUNIDAD, No. 255 (June 9,
1985), p. 2-5. Spanish. DESCR: Book Reviews;
*DISTANT NEIGHBORS: A PORTRAIT OF THE
MEXICANS; Mexico.

Rio Grande

6868 Baker, Ross K. Border follies. AMERICAN
DEMOGRAPHICS, Vol. 8, no. 8 (August 1986),
p. 60. English. DESCR: Guadalupe Hidalgo,
Treaty of 1848; Immigration; Texas;
*Undocumented Workers.

6869 Miller, Darlis A. Los Pinos, New Mexico:
civil war post on the Rio Grande. NEW MEXICO
HISTORICAL REVIEW, Vol. 62, no. 1 (January

1987), p. 1-31. English. DESCR: History;
*Los Pinos, NM; *New Mexico; *Southwestern
United States.

Rios, Alberto

6870 Saldivar, Jose David. Towards a Chicano
poetics: the making of the Chicano subject.
CONFLUENCIA, Vol. 1, no. 2 (Spring 1986), p.
10-17. English. DESCR: Corridos; Feminism;
*Literary Criticism; "Los vatos" [poem];
Montoya, Jose E.; *Poetry; RESTLESS
SERPENTS; WHISPERING TO FOOL THE WIND;
Zamora, Bernice.

Rios, Miguel, Jr.

6871 Sellers, Jeff M. Strategic defenses: new
niches for small firms. HISPANIC BUSINESS,
Vol. 9, no. 10 (October 1987), p. 13-17.
English. DESCR: *Advanced Sciences Inc.,
Albuquerque, NM; Business Enterprises;
Electronics Industry; *Government Contracts;
*Military; *Orion International
Technologies, Inc.; Romero, Ed.

Rios-Bustamante, Antonio

6872 Bracamonte, Jose A. Book review of: MEXICAN
IMMIGRANT WORKERS IN THE U.S. LA RED/THE
NET, no. 49 (December 1981), p. 3-4.
English. DESCR: Immigration; *MEXICAN
IMMIGRANT WORKERS IN THE U.S.

6873 The California Museum of Latino History=El
Museo de California de la Historia de los
Latinos. AMERICAS 2001, Premiere Issue,
1987, p. 18-19, 39. Bilingual. DESCR:
Calderon, Charles M.; *California Museum of
Latino History; History; *Museums; Social
History and Conditions.

6874 Hoffman, Abraham. Book review of: AN
ILLUSTRATED HISTORY OF MEXICAN LOS ANGELES:
1781-1985. NEW MEXICO HISTORICAL REVIEW,
Vol. 62, no. 4 (October 1987), p. 412-13.
English. DESCR: *AN ILLUSTRATED HISTORY OF
MEXICAN LOS ANGELES: 1781-1985; Book
Reviews; *Castillo, Pedro; *Los Angeles, CA.

Rivas, Robert

6875 Seven profiles of courage. HISPANIC
BUSINESS, Vol. 9, no. 6 (June 1987), p.
57-70. English. DESCR: Alamo Technology
Inc., San Antonio, TX; *Business
Enterprises; *Businesspeople; Carrillo,
Rosario C.; O'Campo Corporation, Walnut, CA;
O'Campo, Peter; TexPar Energy Inc.,
Milwaukee, WI; THE HISPANIC BUSINESS 500.

Rivera, Angel

6876 SHPE holds first ever East coast conference
for Hispanic engineers. HISPANIC ENGINEER,
Vol. 3, no. 5 (Winter 1987), p. 12-14.
English. DESCR: Awards; Barrios, Eugene;
Chang-Diaz, Franklin; *Conferences and
Meetings; Cuevas, Brian L.; Garay, Charles
J.; Garcia, Ray; Marrero, Charles; Martinez,
Lisa; Monteverde, Edwin; Plumey, Raymond;
Reyes-Guerra, David; Society of Hispanic
Professional Engineers (SHPE); Soto,
Giovanni.

Rivera, Betty

6877 Trager, Cara S. Women of the year. HISPANIC
BUSINESS, Vol. 9, no. 6 (June 1987), p.
78-82. English. DESCR: Biography;
*Businesspeople; *Chicanas.

Rivera, Diego

6878 Sykes, Maltby. Diego Rivera and the Hotel Reforma murals. ARCHIVES OF AMERICAN ART JOURNAL, Vol. 25, no. 1-2 (1985), p. 29-40. English. DESCR: Artists; Hotel Reforma, Mexico City; Marxism; Mexico City; Mural Art.

Rivera, Edward

6879 Ortiz, Vilma. Book review of: FAMILY INSTALLMENTS: MEMORIES OF GROWING UP HISPANIC. LA RED/THE NET, no. 76 (January 1984), p. 7-9. English. DESCR: Book Reviews; *FAMILY INSTALLMENTS: MEMORIES OF GROWING UP HISPANIC.

Rivera [family name]

6880 Instituto Genealogico e Historico Latino-Americano. Rootsearch: Rivera: Navarro: Salazar. VISTA, Vol. 2, no. 3 (November 2, 1986), p. 24. English. DESCR: Genealogy; History; *Navarro [family name]; *Personal Names; *Salazar [family name].

Rivera, Feliciano

6881 Acuna, Rodolfo. Book review of: DICTIONARY OF MEXICAN AMERICAN HISTORY. LA RED/THE NET, no. 57 (August 1982), p. 4-5. English. DESCR: Book Reviews; *DICTIONARY OF MEXICAN AMERICAN HISTORY; History; Meier, Matt S.

6882 Vigil, James Diego. Book review of: DICTIONARY OF MEXICAN AMERICAN HISTORY. PACIFIC HISTORICAL REVIEW, Vol. 53, no. 2 (1984), p. 241-242. English. DESCR: Book Reviews; *DICTIONARY OF MEXICAN AMERICAN HISTORY; Meier, Matt S.; Reference Works.

Rivera, Geraldo

6883 Hernandez, Roger E. Why is everyone picking on Geraldo Rivera? VISTA, Vol. 2, no. 8 (April 4, 1987), p. 8-10. English. DESCR: Biography; *Broadcast Media.

Rivera, Tomas

6884 Bartlett, Catherine Vallejos. Magical realism: the Latin American influence on modern Chicano writers. CONFLUENCIA, Vol. 1, no. 2 (Spring 1986), p. 27-37. English. DESCR: Arias, Ron; Authors; Garcia Marquez, Gabriel; Latin America; *Literary Criticism; *Literary Influence; *Literature; Magical realism; ONE HUNDRED YEARS OF SOLITUDE; THE ROAD TO TAMAZUNCHALE; Y NO SE LO TRAGO LA TIERRA/AND THE EARTH DID NOT PART.

6885 Bernal, Alejandro. La estructura tematica en Y NO SE LO TRAGO LA TIERRA de Tomas Rivera. CHIRICU, Vol. 3, no. 1 (1982), p. 83-89. Spanish. DESCR: *Literary Criticism; Novel; *Y NO SE LO TRAGO LA TIERRA/AND THE EARTH DID NOT PART.

6886 Bruce-Novoa, Juan. Meet the writers of the 80s. VISTA, Vol. 1, no. 11 (July 6, 1986), p. 15-16. English. DESCR: Anaya, Rudolfo A.; Arte Publico Press; *Authors; Bilingual Review Press; Cisneros, Sandra; Hinojosa-Smith, Rolando R.; Keller, Gary D.; *Literature; Pineda, Cecile; Quinto Sol Publishing, Inc.; Soto, Gary.

6887 Hinojosa-Smith, Rolando R. Tomas Rivera: remembrances of an educator and a poet. CONFLUENCIA, Vol. 1, no. 1 (Fall 1985), p. 90-93. English. DESCR: Authors; Biography.

6888 Mora, Pat. Tomas Rivera. NUESTRO, Vol. 11,

no. 2 (March 1987), p. 27. English. DESCR: *Poems.

THE ROAD TO TAMAZUNCHALE

6889 Bartlett, Catherine Vallejos. Magical realism: the Latin American influence on modern Chicano writers. CONFLUENCIA, Vol. 1, no. 2 (Spring 1986), p. 27-37. English. DESCR: Arias, Ron; Authors; Garcia Marquez, Gabriel; Latin America; *Literary Criticism; *Literary Influence; *Literature; Magical realism; ONE HUNDRED YEARS OF SOLITUDE; Rivera, Tomas; Y NO SE LO TRAGO LA TIERRA/AND THE EARTH DID NOT PART.

Robinson, Barbara J.

6890 Chabran, Richard and Garcia-Ayvens, Francisco. Book review of: THE MEXICAN AMERICAN: A CRITICAL GUIDE TO RESEARCH AIDS. LA RED/THE NET, no. 37 (December 1980), p. 4-5. English. DESCR: Bibliography; Book Reviews; *Reference Works; *Robinson, J. Cordell; *THE MEXICAN AMERICAN: A CRITICAL GUIDE TO RESEARCH AIDS.

Robinson, J. Cordell

6891 Chabran, Richard and Garcia-Ayvens, Francisco. Book review of: THE MEXICAN AMERICAN: A CRITICAL GUIDE TO RESEARCH AIDS. LA RED/THE NET, no. 37 (December 1980), p. 4-5. English. DESCR: Bibliography; Book Reviews; *Reference Works; *Robinson, Barbara J.; *THE MEXICAN AMERICAN: A CRITICAL GUIDE TO RESEARCH AIDS.

Robles [family name]

6892 Instituto Genealogico e Historico Latino-Americano. Rootsearch: Robles: Chacon: Molina. VISTA, Vol. 3, no. 1 (September 6, 1987), p. 30. English. DESCR: *Chacon [family name]; Genealogy; History; *Molina [family name]; *Personal Names.

Rock Music

6893 Aguirre, Antonio (Jake). Salsa Na Ma in San Francisco. LATIN QUARTER, Vol. 1, no. 2 (October 1974), p. 23. English. DESCR: KRVE, Los Gatos, CA [radio station]; *Salsa; San Francisco, CA; *Valentin, Ruben.

6894 Aguirre, Antonio (Jake). Two little giants. LATIN QUARTER, Vol. 1, no. 2 (October 1974), p. 25. English. DESCR: Musicians; *Ross, Gilbert (Gibby); *Salsa; San Francisco, CA; Vidales, Mark.

6895 Alonso, Miguel Angel. Los Lobos y la importancia de la continuidad musical. LA COMUNIDAD, No. 341 (February 1, 1987), p. 12-13. Spanish. DESCR: *Los Lobos del Este de Los Angeles (musical group); *Music.

6896 Bellinhausen, Hermann. El lobo estepario en Olvera Street. LA COMUNIDAD, No. 267 (September 1, 1985), p. 10-11. Spanish. DESCR: *Los Lobos del Este de Los Angeles (musical group); Valens, Ritchie [stage name for Richard Valenzuela].

6897 DeCurtis, Anthony. Los Lobos shake, rattle and worry. ROLLING STONE, (February 26, 1987), p. 51-53. English. DESCR: *BY THE LIGHT OF THE MOON; *Los Lobos del Este de Los Angeles (musical group); Recording Industry.

Rock Music (cont.)

6898 Duarte, Mario. El Chicano 5. LATIN QUARTER, Vol. 1, no. 1 (July 1974), p. 22. English. **DESCR**: *El Chicano Cinco.

6899 Forte, Dan. Los Lobos: Tex-Mex rock from East L.A. GUITAR PLAYER, Vol. 21, no. 2 (February 1987), p. 68-94. English. **DESCR**: Biography; Discography; Hidalgo, David (Los Lobos); *Los Lobos del Este de Los Angeles (musical group); Lozano, Conrad (Los Lobos); *Musicians; Perez, Louie (Los Lobos); Recording Industry; Rosas, Cesar (Los Lobos).

6900 Fricke, David. Los motivos del lobo. LA COMUNIDAD, No. 266 (August 25, 1985), p. 12. Spanish. **DESCR**: *Los Lobos del Este de Los Angeles (musical group).

6901 Holscher, Louis M. Billboard charts and Chicanos, 1955-1974. LA RED/THE NET, no. 41 (April 1981), p. 10,12. English. **DESCR**: *Discography; *Music; *Musicians; *Recording Industry.

6902 La Mafia signs Pepsi contract. NUESTRO, Vol. 11, no. 4 (May 1987), p. 8-9. English. **DESCR**: Advertising; *La Mafia [musical group]; Musicians; Pepsi-Cola Bottling Group.

Rockwell International, Thousand Oaks, CA

6903 Community and professional organizations honor Rockwell's Al Mejia at retirement dinner. HISPANIC ENGINEER, Vol. 3, no. 1 (Spring 1987), p. 22. English. **DESCR**: *Awards; *Mejia, Al.

Rodeo

USE: Charreada

Rodriguez del Pino, Salvador

6904 Tatum, Charles. Book review of: LA NOVELA CHICANA ESCRITA EN ESPANOL. WORLD LITERATURE TODAY, Vol. 57, no. 4 (Fall 1983), p. 613-614. English. **DESCR**: Book Reviews; *LA NOVELA CHICANA ESCRITA EN ESPANOL; Literary Criticism.

6905 Tatum, Charles. Chicano literary criticism comes of age. BILINGUAL REVIEW, Vol. 12, no. 1-2 (January, August, 1985), p. 144-149. English. **DESCR**: Book Reviews; *CHICANO THEATER: THEMES AND FORMS; Huerta, Jorge A.; *LA NOVELA CHICANA ESCRITA EN ESPANOL; Literary Criticism.

Rodriguez, [family name]

6906 Instituto Genealogico e Historico Latino-Americano. Rootsearch: Rodriguez: Garza (De La Garza). VISTA, Vol. 3, no. 3 (November 8, 1987), p. 37. English. **DESCR**: *de la Garza [family name]; *Garza [family name]; Genealogy; History; *Personal Names.

Rodriguez Howell, Nilsa

6907 Winston, Bonnie. High tech jobs in the Midwest. HISPANIC ENGINEER, Vol. 3, no. 1 (Spring 1987), p. 50-53. English. **DESCR**: Chaves, Tony; *Engineering as a Profession; Mosquera, Jaime "Jim"; Sanchez, Francisco G.

Rodriguez, Jose

6908 Pacific Telesis senior fellows. HISPANIC ENGINEER, Vol. 3, no. 2 (Summer 1987), p. 10-11. English. **DESCR**: *Awards; Castaneda, Jesus; Cruz, Jacqueline; Education; Pacific Telesis; Sanchez, Alex.

Rodriguez, Raul

6909 Krampner, John. Raul Rodriguez. VISTA, Vol. 2, no. 5 (January 4, 1987), p. 21. English. **DESCR**: Awards; *Design; Rose Parade (Pasadena, CA).

Rodriguez, Richard

6910 Holt, Patricia. Richard Rodriguez. PUBLISHER'S WEEKLY, Vol. 221, (March 26, 1982), p. 6-8. English. **DESCR**: *Bilingual Bicultural Education; *HUNGER OF MEMORY: THE EDUCATION OF RICHARD RODRIGUEZ.

6911 Madrid, Arturo. Book review of: HUNGER OF MEMORY. LA RED/THE NET, no. 53 (April 1982), p. 6-9. English. **DESCR**: Book Reviews; *HUNGER OF MEMORY: THE EDUCATION OF RICHARD RODRIGUEZ.

6912 Marquez, Antonio. Richard Rodriguez's HUNGER OF MEMORY and the poetics of experience. ARIZONA QUARTERLY, Vol. 40, no. 2 (Summer 1984), p. 130-141. English. **DESCR**: *Autobiography; Book Reviews; *HUNGER OF MEMORY: THE EDUCATION OF RICHARD RODRIGUEZ; Literary Criticism.

6913 Seeking more readers for Hispanic literature. VISTA, Vol. 2, no. 3 (November 2, 1986), p. 25. English. **DESCR**: Hinojosa-Smith, Rolando R.; *Literature; *Miami Book Fair International; Mohr, Nicolasa; Munoz, Elias Miguel.

6914 Taking bilingualism to task. TIME, Vol. 119, (April 19, 1982), p. 68. English. **DESCR**: *Bilingual Bicultural Education; *Bilingualism.

Rodriguez, Sandra

6915 Barro, Mary Helen. 1973 Emmy Awards. LATIN QUARTER, Vol. 1, no. 1 (July 1974), p. 5-6. English. **DESCR**: Chavez, Andres; CINCO VIDAS; Emmy Awards; *Esparza, Moctezuma; Identity; Quintero, Carlos; *Recreation; REFLECCIONES; Rodriguez, Tony; Ruiz, Jose Luis; Stereotypes; Television.

Rodriguez, Tony

6916 Barro, Mary Helen. 1973 Emmy Awards. LATIN QUARTER, Vol. 1, no. 1 (July 1974), p. 5-6. English. **DESCR**: Chavez, Andres; CINCO VIDAS; Emmy Awards; *Esparza, Moctezuma; Identity; Quintero, Carlos; *Recreation; REFLECCIONES; Rodriguez, Sandra; Ruiz, Jose Luis; Stereotypes; Television.

Rojas, Richard Raimond

6917 Bradby, Marie. The naval research laboratory. HISPANIC ENGINEER, Vol. 3, no. 2 (Summer 1987), p. 34-38. English. **DESCR**: *Engineering as a Profession; Military; *Naval Research Laboratory; Urrutia, Jorge R.

Rojas-Urista, Xelina

6918 Jacob, John. Book review of: SOUTHWEST TALES: A CONTEMPORY COLLECTION. BOOKLIST, Vol. 82, no. 17 (May 1, 1986), p. 1284. English. **DESCR**: Alurista; Book Reviews; *SOUTHWEST TALES: A CONTEMPORARY COLLECTION.

Rojas-Urista, Xelina (cont.)

6919 Vallejos, Tomas. Book review of: SOUTHWEST
TALES: A CONTEMPORY COLLECTION. THE AMERICAS
REVIEW, Vol. 15, no. 2 (Summer 1987), p.
111-113. English. **DESCR:** Alurista; Book
Reviews; *SOUTHWEST TALES: A CONTEMPORARY
COLLECTION.

Romano-V., Octavio Ignacio

6920 Bruce-Novoa, Juan. One more rosary for Dona
Marina. CONFLUENCIA, Vol. 1, no. 2 (Spring
1986), p. 73-84. English. **DESCR:** *A ROSARY
FOR DONA MARINA; *Literary Criticism; Sex
Roles; Short Story.

6921 Rosaldo, Renato. When natives talk back:
Chicano anthropology since the late 60s.
RENATO ROSALDO LECTURE SERIES MONOGRAPH,
Vol. 2, (Spring 1986), p. [3]-20. English.
DESCR: *Anthropology; Culture; EL GRITO;
*Identity; Paredes, Americo; *Political
Ideology; *Research Methodology; Valdez,
Facundo.

Romero, Cesar

6922 Guerrero, Dan. FALCON CREST: showcase for
Hispanic talent. VISTA, Vol. 2, no. 2
(October 4, 1986), p. 12-15. English.
DESCR: *Actors and Actresses; *Ana-Alicia;
FALCON CREST [television show]; Lamas,
Lorenzo; Television.

Romero, Ed

6923 Sellers, Jeff M. Strategic defenses: new
niches for small firms. HISPANIC BUSINESS,
Vol. 9, no. 10 (October 1987), p. 13-17.
English. **DESCR:** *Advanced Sciences Inc.,
Albuquerque, NM; Business Enterprises;
Electronics Industry; *Government Contracts;
*Military; *Orion International
Technologies, Inc.; Rios, Miguel, Jr.

Romero, Eddie, Jr.

6924 Abalos, J. Victor. Whiz kids of the
microchip melody. VISTA, Vol. 1, no. 5
(January 5, 1986), p. 9-10. English. **DESCR:**
Computers; *Musical Instruments.

Romero, Leo

6925 Challem, Jack. Pied piper of science. VISTA,
Vol. 3, no. 2 (October 3, 1987), p. 14.
English. **DESCR:** Education; *Science as a
Profession.

6926 Gardiol, Rita. Book review of: CELSO.
LECTOR, Vol. 4, no. 4-6 (1987), p. 76-77.
English. **DESCR:** Book Reviews; *CELSO.

Romeu Almeida, Hugo

6927 Wald, Karen. U.S. defector "didn't want to
fight in Central America". GUARDIAN, Vol.
38, no. 44 (September 10, 1986), p. 12.
English. **DESCR:** Central America; *Military.

Romo, Ricardo

6928 Garcia, Philip. Book review of: EAST LOS
ANGELES. LA RED/THE NET, no. 86 (November
1984), p. 2-3. English. **DESCR:** Book Reviews;
*EAST LOS ANGELES: HISTORY OF A BARRIO.

6929 Griswold del Castillo, Richard. Book review
of: EAST LOS ANGELES. PACIFIC HISTORICAL
REVIEW, Vol. 53, no. 4 (November 1984), p.
528-529. English. **DESCR:** Book Reviews; East
Los Angeles, CA; Los Angeles, CA.

6930 Meier, Matt S. Book review of: THE MEXICAN
AMERICAN EXPERIENCE: AN INTERDISCIPLINARY
ANTHOLOGY. HISPANIC AMERICAN HISTORICAL
REVIEW, Vol. 66, no. 3 (August 1986), p.
629-630. English. **DESCR:** Alvarez, Rodolfo;
Bean, Frank D.; Bonjean, Charles M.; Book
Reviews; de la Garza, Rodolfo O.; *THE
MEXICAN AMERICAN EXPERIENCE: AN
INTERDISCIPLINARY ANTHOLOGY.

6931 Monroy, Douglas. Book review of: EAST LOS
ANGELES. WESTERN HISTORICAL QUARTERLY, Vol.
15, no. 4 (October 1984), p. 453. English.
DESCR: Book Reviews; East Los Angeles, CA;
*EAST LOS ANGELES: HISTORY OF A BARRIO.

6932 Ruiz, Vicki Lynn. Book review of: THE
MEXICAN AMERICAN EXPERIENCE: AN
INTERDISCIPLINARY ANTHOLOGY. SOUTHWESTERN
HISTORICAL QUARTERLY, Vol. 90, no. 2 (1986),
p. 205-206. English. **DESCR:** Alvarez,
Rodolfo; Bean, Frank D.; Bonjean, Charles
M.; Book Reviews; de la Garza, Rodolfo O.;
*THE MEXICAN AMERICAN EXPERIENCE: AN
INTERDISCIPLINARY ANTHOLOGY.

6933 Salmon, Roberto Mario. Book review of: THE
MEXICAN AMERICAN EXPERIENCE: AN
INTERDISCIPLINARY ANTHOLOGY. LA RED/THE NET,
no. 93 (January, February, 1986), p. 12-14.
English. **DESCR:** Alvarez, Rodolfo; Bean,
Frank D.; Bonjean, Charles M.; Book Reviews;
de la Garza, Rodolfo O.; *THE MEXICAN
AMERICAN EXPERIENCE: AN INTERDISCIPLINARY
ANTHOLOGY.

Romo-Carmona, Mariana

6934 Cantu, Norma. Book review of: CUENTOS:
STORIES BY LATINAS. LA RED/THE NET, no. 83
(August 1984), p. 2-3. English. **DESCR:** Book
Reviews; *CUENTOS: STORIES BY LATINAS;
Gomez, Alma; Moraga, Cherrie.

Ronstadt, Linda

6935 Burciaga, Jose Antonio. Corridos. VISTA,
Vol. 3, no. 2 (October 3, 1987), p. 10.
English. **DESCR:** Corridos; *CORRIDOS [film];
*Teatro; Television; Valdez, Luis.

6936 Burciaga, Jose Antonio and Ronstadt, Linda.
Linda Ronstadt: my Mexican soul. VISTA, Vol.
2, no. 10 (June 7, 1987), p. 6-8. English.
DESCR: Biography; CORRIDOS [film];
*Musicians.

**ROOTS OF RESISTANCE: LAND TENURE IN NEW MEXICO,
1680-1980**

6937 Griswold del Castillo, Richard. Book review
of: ROOTS OF RESISTANCE: LAND TENURE IN NEW
MEXICO, 1680-1980. LA RED/THE NET, no. 42
(May 1981), p. 10. English. **DESCR:** Book
Reviews; Dunbar Ortiz, Roxanne; Land Tenure.

Rosaldo, Renato

6938 de Leon, Arnoldo. Book review of: CHICANO:
THE EVOLUTION OF A PEOPLE. SOUTHWESTERN
HISTORICAL QUARTERLY, Vol. 87, no. 3 (1984),
p. 343-344. English. **DESCR:** Book Reviews;
Calvert, Robert; *CHICANO: THE EVOLUTION OF
A PEOPLE; Seligmann, Gustav L.

A ROSARY FOR DONA MARINA

6939 Bruce-Novoa, Juan. One more rosary for Dona
Marina. CONFLUENCIA, Vol. 1, no. 2 (Spring
1986), p. 73-84. English. **DESCR:** *Literary
Criticism; *Romano-V., Octavio Ignacio; Sex
Roles; Short Story.

Rosas, Cesar (Los Lobos)

6940 Forte, Dan. Los Lobos: Tex-Mex rock from
East L.A. GUITAR PLAYER, Vol. 21, no. 2
(February 1987), p. 68-94. English. **DESCR:**
Biography; Discography; Hidalgo, David (Los
Lobos); *Los Lobos del Este de Los Angeles
(musical group); Lozano, Conrad (Los Lobos);
*Musicians; Perez, Louie (Los Lobos);
Recording Industry; *Rock Music.

Rose Parade (Pasadena, CA)

6941 Krampner, John. Raul Rodriguez. VISTA, Vol.
2, no. 5 (January 4, 1987), p. 21. English.
DESCR: Awards; *Design; *Rodriguez, Raul.

Rosenbaum, Robert J.

6942 Griswold del Castillo, Richard. New
perspectives on the Mexican and American
borderlands. LATIN AMERICAN RESEARCH REVIEW,
Vol. 19, no. 1 (1984), p. 199-209. English.
DESCR: AL NORTE DEL RIO BRAVO (PASADO
INMEDIATO, 1930-1981); AL NORTE DEL RIO
BRAVO (PASADO LEJANO, 1600-1930); *Book
Reviews; *Border Region; Gomez-Quinones,
Juan; Maciel, David; MEXICANO RESISTANCE IN
THE SOUTHWEST: "THE SACRED RIGHT OF
SELF-PRESERVATION"; THE MEXICAN FRONTIER,
1821-1846: THE AMERICAN SOUTHWEST UNDER
MEXICO; THE TEJANO COMMUNITY, 1836-1900;
Weber, David J.

6943 Salmon, Roberto Mario. Book review of:
MEXICANO RESISTANCE IN THE SOUTHWEST. LA
RED/THE NET, no. 44 (July 1981), p. 6-7.
English. **DESCR:** Book Reviews; *MEXICANO
RESISTANCE IN THE SOUTHWEST: "THE SACRED
RIGHT OF SELF-PRESERVATION"; New Mexico.

Ross, Gilbert (Gibby)

6944 Aguirre, Antonio (Jake). Two little giants.
LATIN QUARTER, Vol. 1, no. 2 (October 1974),
p. 25. English. **DESCR:** Musicians; Rock
Music; *Salsa; San Francisco, CA; Vidales,
Mark.

Ross, Stanley R.

6945 Cardenas, Gilbert. Book review of:
"TEMPORARY" ALIEN WORKERS IN THE UNITED
STATES. LA RED/THE NET, no. 63 (January
1983), p. 9-10. English. **DESCR:** Book
Reviews; *"TEMPORARY" ALIEN WORKERS IN THE
UNITED STATES: DESIGNING POLICY FROM FACT
AND OPINION; Undocumented Workers;
Weintraub, Sidney.

6946 Ganster, Paul. Book review of: ECOLOGY AND
DEVELOPMENT OF THE BORDER REGION. PACIFIC
HISTORICAL REVIEW, Vol. 55, no. 2 (1986), p.
318-320. English. **DESCR:** Book Reviews;
Border Region; *ECOLOGY AND DEVELOPMENT OF
THE BORDER REGION: SECOND SYMPOSIUM.

6947 Gutierrez, Armando. Book reviews of:
MEXICO-UNITED STATES RELATIONS and UNITED
STATES RELATIONS WITH MEXICO: CONTEXT AND
CONTENT. LA RED/THE NET, no. 62 (December
1982), p. 4-6. English. **DESCR:** Book Reviews;
Erb, Richard D.; Kaufman, Purcell;
*MEXICO-UNITED STATES RELATIONS; *UNITED
STATES RELATIONS WITH MEXICO: CONTEXT AND
CONTENT.

Roucek, Joseph S.

6948 Garcia, John A. Book review of: AMERICA'S
ETHNIC POLITICS. LA RED/THE NET, no. 67
(April 1983), p. 7-8. English. **DESCR:**
*AMERICA'S ETHNIC POLITICS; Book Reviews;
Eisenberg, Bernard; Politics.

Roybal, Edward R.

6949 Rodriguez, Roberto and Roybal, Edward R.
Congressman Edward Roybal: elder
statesman=El congresista Edward Roybal: un
veterano estadista. AMERICAS 2001, Vol. 1,
no. 1 (June, July, 1987), p. 23-25.
Bilingual. **DESCR:** Politics.

Roybal, Luis

6950 Atencio, Tomas. No estan todos los que son,
no son todos los que estan. EL CUADERNO,
Vol. 4, no. 1 (Summer 1976), p. 51-61.
Spanish. **DESCR:** Arellano, Estevan;
*Identity; *La Academia de la Nueva Raza,
Dixon, NM; Lovato, Alberto; Martinez,
Vicente.

Ruelas [family name]

6951 Instituto Genealogico e Historico
Latino-Americano. Rootsearch: Aragon:
Trujillo: Ruelas. VISTA, Vol. 2, no. 8
(April 4, 1987), p. 24. English. **DESCR:**
*Aragon [family name]; Genealogy; History;
*Personal Names; *Trujillo [family name].

Ruiz, Jose Luis

6952 Barro, Mary Helen. 1973 Emmy Awards. LATIN
QUARTER, Vol. 1, no. 1 (July 1974), p. 5-6.
English. **DESCR:** Chavez, Andres; CINCO VIDAS;
Emmy Awards; *Esparza, Moctezuma; Identity;
Quintero, Carlos; *Recreation; REFLECCIONES;
Rodriguez, Sandra; Rodriguez, Tony;
Stereotypes; Television.

Ruiz, Roberto

6953 Beale, Stephen. CEOs. HISPANIC BUSINESS,
Vol. 9, no. 4 (April 1987), p. 20-37, 52.
English. **DESCR:** Alvarez, Roberto; Batarse,
Anthony A.; Biography; Business Enterprises;
*Businesspeople; Carlo, Nelson; Estrada,
Anthony; Flores, Frank; Fullana, Jaime, Jr.;
Hernandez, George; *Management; Ortega,
James; Quirch, Guillermo; Santa Maria,
Yvonne Z.; Sugranes, Rosa; Tamaya, Carlos;
Young, Paul H., Jr.

Ruiz v. Blum

6954 Weinfield, J. Day care benefits ordered for
child born in U.S. to illegal alien. THE
FAMILY LAW REPORTER: COURT OPINIONS, Vol. 9,
no. 4 (November 23, 1982), p. 2054-2056.
English. **DESCR:** Child Care Centers;
*Undocumented Workers.

Ruiz, Vivian

6955 Montane, Diane. Learning survival Spanish.
VISTA, Vol. 1, no. 5 (January 5, 1986), p.
16. English. **DESCR:** Education; *Spanish
Language; *SURVIVAL SPANISH; Television.

Rural Education

6956 Jensen, Joan M. Crossing ethnic barriers in
the Southwest: women's agricultural
extension education, 1914-1940. AGRICULTURAL
HISTORY, Vol. 60, no. 2 (Spring 1986), p.
169-181. English. **DESCR:** *Agricultural
Extension Service; Agriculture; Cabeza de
Baca, Fabiola; Chicanas; History; New
Mexico.

Rural Poor

6957 Tienda, Marta. Rural poverty and Chicanos: have the seventies brought improvements? LA RED/THE NET, no. 26 (January 1980), p. 2. English. DESCR: Poverty.

Rural Population

6958 Rochin, Refugio I. Chicanos in rural labor markets. LA RED/THE NET, no. 31 (June 1980), p. 2. English. DESCR: *Labor Supply and Market; *Northern California.

6959 Rochin, Refugio I. Chicanos in rural labor markets: part 2. LA RED/THE NET, no. 47 (October 1981), p. 2,10. English. DESCR: *Labor Supply and Market; *Northern California; SURVEY OF INCOME AND EDUCATION, 1976; *Surveys.

Saavedra [family name]

6960 Instituto Genealogico e Historico Latino-Americano. Rootsearch: Alarcon: Saavedra. VISTA, Vol. 1, no. 8 (April 6, 1986), p. 22. English. DESCR: *Alarcon [family name]; Genealogy; History; *Personal Names.

Sabatini, Gabriela

6961 Chavez, Lorenzo A. Tennis superstars. VISTA, Vol. 1, no. 8 (April 6, 1986), p. 14-16. English. DESCR: *Athletes; Chicanas; Fernandez, Gigi; Fernandez, Mary Joe; Sports; Torres, Michele; Women.

Sagel, Jim

6962 Avalos, Francisco. Book review of: SMALL BONES, LITTLE EYES. LECTOR, Vol. 4, no. 1-3 (1986), p. [60]. English. DESCR: Book Reviews; NorthSun, Nila; *SMALL BONES, LITTLE EYES.

6963 Madrid, Arturo. Book reviews of: A DICTIONARY OF NEW MEXICO AND SOUTHERN COLORADO SPANISH and TUNOMAS HONEY. LA RED/THE NET, no. 77 (February 1984), p. 8-10. English. DESCR: *A DICTIONARY OF NEW MEXICO AND SOUTHERN COLORADO SPANISH; *Book Reviews; Cobos, Ruben; *TUNOMAS HONEY.

Saints

USE: Santos

SAL SOUL [record album]

6964 Duarte, Mario. SalSoul Joe Bataan. LATIN QUARTER, Vol. 1, no. 1 (July 1974), p. 23. English. DESCR: *Bataan, Joe; *Salsa.

Salas, Floyd

6965 Bruce-Novoa, Juan. Homosexuality and the Chicano novel. CONFLUENCIA, Vol. 2, no. 1 (Fall 1986), p. 69-77. English. DESCR: Acosta, Oscar Zeta; CITY OF NIGHT; FAULTLINE [novel]; *Homosexuality; Islas, Arturo; *Literary Criticism; Machismo; *Novel; Ortiz Taylor, Sheila; POCHO; Rechy, John; SPRING FORWARD/FALL BACK; TATOO THE WICKED CROSS; THE AUTOBIOGRAPHY OF A BROWN BUFFALO; THE RAIN GOD: A DESERT TALE; THE REVOLT OF THE COCKROACH PEOPLE; Villarreal, Jose Antonio.

Salazar, Diane

6966 Scenes from the February SHPE careers conference. HISPANIC ENGINEER, Vol. 3, no. 1 (Spring 1987), p. 14-15. English. DESCR: *Conferences and Meetings; Guerrero, Art; Society of Hispanic Professional Engineers (SHPE).

Salazar [family name]

6967 Instituto Genealogico e Historico Latino-Americano. Rootsearch: Rivera: Navarro: Salazar. VISTA, Vol. 2, no. 3 (November 2, 1986), p. 24. English. DESCR: Genealogy; History; *Navarro [family name]; *Personal Names; *Rivera [family name].

Salazar, Manuel

6968 Arellano, Manuel. A Manuel Salazar. EL CUADERNO, Vol. 4, no. 1 (Summer 1976), p. 90-98. Spanish. DESCR: *Poems.

Salazar, Myrna

6969 Kwain, Constance. Searching for Hispanic talent. VISTA, Vol. 2, no. 6 (February 8, 1987), p. 6-7. English. DESCR: *Actors and Actresses; American Federation of Television & Radio Artists (AFTRA); *Business Enterprises; Films; Myrna Salazar and Associates, Inc.; Navas, Trina; Screen Actors Guild; Television.

Salazar, Ricardo

6970 Ricardo Salazar. HISPANIC ENGINEER, Vol. 3, no. 2 (Summer), p. 14-18. English. DESCR: Biography; Magic of Science and Engineering Program; Professional Organizations; Society of Hispanic Professional Engineers Northern California Chapter.

Salgado de Snyder, Nelly

6971 Herrera, Irma D. Mixed marriages: will the happiness last? VISTA, Vol. 1, no. 10 (June 8, 1986), p. 8-10. English. DESCR: *Intermarriage; Spanish-Speaking Mental Health Research Center.

Salsa

6972 Aguirre, Antonio (Jake). Salsa Na Ma in San Francisco. LATIN QUARTER, Vol. 1, no. 2 (October 1974), p. 23. English. DESCR: KRVE, Los Gatos, CA [radio station]; *Rock Music; San Francisco, CA; *Valentin, Ruben.

6973 Aguirre, Antonio (Jake). Two little giants. LATIN QUARTER, Vol. 1, no. 2 (October 1974), p. 25. English. DESCR: Musicians; Rock Music; *Ross, Gilbert (Gibby); San Francisco, CA; Vidales, Mark.

6974 Ayala, Ernie. Richard Leon, L.A.'s leading Latin jazz D.J. LATIN QUARTER, Vol. 1, no. 1 (July 1974), p. 19-21. English. DESCR: *Leon, Richard; Los Angeles, CA.

6975 Casteleiro, Gus. Hot salsa and other sounds. LATIN QUARTER, Vol. 1, no. 3 (January, February, 1975), p. 19-20. English. DESCR: *Los Angeles, CA; Musicians; San Francisco, CA.

6976 Duarte, Mario. SalSoul Joe Bataan. LATIN QUARTER, Vol. 1, no. 1 (July 1974), p. 23. English. DESCR: *Bataan, Joe; SAL SOUL [record album].

6977 Espinoza, Freddy. A proposito de la salsa y su historia. LA COMUNIDAD, No. 364 (July 12, 1987), p. 2-5. Spanish. DESCR: *Music.

Salsa (cont.)

6978 Lopez, Jose Y. Chico Sesma: a man and his music. LATIN QUARTER, Vol. 1, no. 4 (July, August, 1975), p. 10-15. English. **DESCR:** Chico Sesma Radio Show; Los Angeles, CA; *Radio; *Sesma, Chico.

6979 Muro, Rena. Tierra. AMERICAS 2001, Vol. 1, no. 3 (November, December, 1987), p. 15. Bilingual. **DESCR:** *Musicians; *Tierra [musical group].

Samuda, Ronald J.

6980 Compean, Mario. Book review of: PERSPECTIVES ON IMMIGRATION AND MINORITY EDUCATION. LA RED/THE NET, no. 86 (November 1984), p. 3-7. English. **DESCR:** Book Reviews; *PERSPECTIVES ON IMMIGRANT AND MINORITY EDUCATION; Woods, Sandra L.

SAN ANGELENOS; MEXICAN AMERICANS IN SAN ANGELO, TEXAS

6981 Tijerina, Andres A. Book review of: SAN ANGELENOS: MEXICAN AMERICANS IN SAN ANGELO, TEXAS. SOUTHWESTERN HISTORICAL QUARTERLY, Vol. 89, no. 4 (1986), p. 569-570. English. **DESCR:** Book Reviews; de Leon, Arnoldo.

San Antonio, TX

6982 Allsup, Dan. Run Reuben run. VISTA, Vol. 1, no. 12 (August 2, 1986), p. 18. English. **DESCR:** *Athletes; *Reina, Reuben; Sports.

6983 Allsup, Dan. A Texas hello for John Paul II. VISTA, Vol. 3, no. 1 (September 6, 1987), p. 8-9. English. **DESCR:** Catholic Church; *Clergy; *Pope John Paul II.

6984 Arreola, Daniel D. The Mexican American cultural capital. GEOGRAPHICAL REVIEW, Vol. 77, (January 1987), p. 17-34. English. **DESCR:** Conjuntos; Food Industry; History; Immigration; LA PRENSA, San Antonio, TX; La Raza Unida Party; League of United Latin American Citizens (LULAC); Lozano, Ignacio; Mexican American Youth Organization, San Antonio, TX; Music; Orden Hijos de America, San Antonio, TX; Railroads; *Social History and Conditions.

6985 Cortes, Ernesto, Jr. Changing the locus of political decision making. CHRISTIANITY AND CRISIS, Vol. 47, no. 1 (February 2, 1987), p. 18-22. English. **DESCR:** Biography; *Communities Organized for Public Service (COPS); *Cortes, Ernesto, Jr.; *Political Parties and Organizations.

6986 de Leon, Arnoldo and Stewart, Kenneth L. A tale of 3 cities: a comparative analysis of the socio-economic conditions of Mexican-Americans in Los Angeles, Tucson, and San Antonio, 1850-1900. JOURNAL OF THE WEST, Vol. 24, no. 2 (1985), p. 64-74. English. **DESCR:** Economic History and Conditions; Employment; Griswold del Castillo, Richard; Labor; *Los Angeles, CA; *Social History and Conditions; Tucson, AZ; Urban Communities.

6987 Griswold del Castillo, Richard. Familism, the extended family and Chicanos in the nineteenth century. LA RED/THE NET, no. 49 (December 1981), p. 2. English. **DESCR:** *Extended Family; *Family; Los Angeles, CA; *Nineteenth century; Santa Fe, NM; *Social History and Conditions; Tucson, AZ.

6988 LeCompte, Mary Lou and Beezley, William H. Any Sunday in April: the rise of sport in San Antonio and the Hispanic borderlands. JOURNAL OF SPORT HISTORY, Vol. 13, no. 2 (Summer 1986), p. 128-146. English. **DESCR:** *Charreada; *Cultural Customs; History; *Sports.

6989 Martinez, Walter. A deep cultural heritage enriches American society. VISTA, Vol. 1, no. 2 (October 5, 1985), p. 3. English. **DESCR:** *Political History and Conditions.

6990 McNeely, Dave. Hispanic power at the polls. VISTA, Vol. 2, no. 3 (November 2, 1986), p. 8-12. English. **DESCR:** Austin, TX; *Barrera, Roy, Jr.; Chavez, Linda; Elected Officials; Gonzalez, Raul; Martinez, Bob; Maryland; Political System; Statistics; Tampa, FL; *Voter Turnout.

6991 Munoz, Carlos, Jr. and Henry, Charles. Rainbow coalitions in four big cities: San Antonio, Denver, Chicago and Philadelphia. P.S. [AMERICAN POLITICAL SCIENCE ASSOCIATION], Vol. 19, no. 3 (Summer 1986), p. 598-609. English. **DESCR:** Blacks; Chicago, IL; Cisneros, Henry, Mayor of San Antonio, TX; Denver, CO; Elected Officials; Ethnic Groups; Intergroup Relations; Pena, Federico; Philadelphia, PA; Political Parties and Organizations; Political Representation; *Politics; Urban Communities.

6992 Perez, Renato E. Badge of Hispanic pride. VISTA, Vol. 1, no. 12 (August 2, 1986), p. 9-11. English. **DESCR:** Broward County, FL; Chicago, IL; Dallas, TX; Houston, TX; *Los Angeles, CA; New York, NY; *Police; San Diego, CA; Tucson, AZ.

6993 Ross, I. Mayor Cisneros of San Antonio. READER'S DIGEST, Vol. 125, (December 1984), p. 193-194+. English. **DESCR:** Biography; *Cisneros, Henry, Mayor of San Antonio, TX; *Elected Officials; Local Government.

6994 Stern, Michael P. Epidemiology of diabetes and coronary heart disease among Mexican-Americans. TRANSACTIONS OF THE ASSOC. OF LIFE INSURANCE MEDICAL DIRECTORS, Vol. 67, (1983), p. 79-90. English. **DESCR:** Anglo Americans; *Diabetes; Heart Disease.

San Diego, CA

6995 Cuellar, Jose and Weeks, John R. Hispanic elders' needs, problems and access to public benefits and services. LA RED/THE NET, no. 36 (November 1980), p. 2,16. English. **DESCR:** *Ancianos; Social Services.

6996 Goldman, Shifra. Escena de San Diego: texto y contexto. LA COMUNIDAD, No. 239 (February 17, 1985), p. 6-7. Spanish. **DESCR:** *Art; Avalos, David; Chicano Park, San Diego, CA; Exhibits; *NUEVE ARTISTAS CHICANOS [exhibit]; Torres, Salvador Roberto; Ulloa, Domingo.

6997 Gonzalez, Marco Vinicio. En el pais de la frontera. LA COMUNIDAD, No. 291 (February 16, 1986), p. 6-7+. Spanish. **DESCR:** Border Region; Conde, Rosina; *DIALOGOS FRONTERIZOS [radio program]; Gomez Pena, Guillermo; Medina, Ruben; *Radio; Tijuana, Baja California, Mexico.

6998 Hawkins, Steve L. A cat-mouse game gets bloody. U.S. NEWS & WORLD REPORT, Vol. 100, (April 28, 1986), p. 30. English. **DESCR:** *Border Patrol; *Immigration Regulation and Control.

San Diego, CA (cont.)

6999 Perez, Renato E. Badge of Hispanic pride. VISTA, Vol. 1, no. 12 (August 2, 1986), p. 9-11. English. DESCR: Broward County, FL; Chicago, IL; Dallas, TX; Houston, TX; *Los Angeles, CA; New York, NY; *Police; San Antonio, TX; Tucson, AZ.

San Diego Chicano Federation, Inc.
USE: Chicano Federation of San Diego Co., Inc.

San Francisco, CA

7000 Aguirre, Antonio (Jake). Salsa Na Ma in San Francisco. LATIN QUARTER, Vol. 1, no. 2 (October 1974), p. 23. English. DESCR: KRVE, Los Gatos, CA [radio station]; *Rock Music; *Salsa; *Valentin, Ruben.

7001 Aguirre, Antonio (Jake). Two little giants. LATIN QUARTER, Vol. 1, no. 2 (October 1974), p. 25. English. DESCR: Musicians; Rock Music; *Ross, Gilbert (Gibby); *Salsa; Vidales, Mark.

7002 Avina, Jeffrey. The uninvited: immigration is a hot issue--but who's really getting burned? SAN FRANCISCO, Vol. 26, no. 8 (August 1984), p. 58+. English. DESCR: *Immigration Regulation and Control; *Undocumented Workers.

7003 Casteleiro, Gus. Hot salsa and other sounds. LATIN QUARTER, Vol. 1, no. 3 (January, February, 1975), p. 19-20. English. DESCR: *Los Angeles, CA; Musicians; *Salsa.

7004 Gonzales, Juan. San Francisco's Mission District: part I. LATIN QUARTER, Vol. 1, no. 4 (July, August, 1975), p. 21-25. English. DESCR: La Mision Dolores Iglesia Catolica; *Local History; *Mission District, San Francisco, CA; Political Parties and Organizations; *Urban Communities.

7005 Kessel, Janet. Treasure hunt. SAN FRANCISCO, Vol. 25, no. 10 (October 1983), p. 103-110. English. DESCR: *Mission District, San Francisco, CA; *Restaurants.

7006 Sommers, Laurie Kay. Symbol and style in Cinco de Mayo. JOURNAL OF AMERICAN FOLKLORE, Vol. 98, (October, December, 1985), p. 476-482. English. DESCR: *Cinco de Mayo; *Cultural Customs; History; *Holidays; Symbolism.

San Gregorio de Abo (Salinas National Monument, NM)

7007 Holmes, John J. Sentinel of tradition. VISTA, Vol. 3, no. 3 (November 8, 1987), p. 16. English. DESCR: *Missions; New Mexico; Sisneros, Federico.

San Juan Cafferty, Pastora

7008 Cordasco, Francesco. Book review of: HISPANICS IN THE UNITED STATES: A NEW SOCIAL AGENDA. CHOICE, Vol. 23, no. 6 (February 1986), p. 928. English. DESCR: Book Reviews; *HISPANICS IN THE UNITED STATES: A NEW SOCIAL AGENDA; McCready, William C.

7009 Griswold del Castillo, Richard. Book review of: HISPANICS IN THE UNITED STATES: A NEW SOCIAL AGENDA. JOURNAL OF AMERICAN ETHNIC HISTORY, Vol. 6, no. 1 (Fall 1986), p. 112-114. English. DESCR: Book Reviews; *HISPANICS IN THE UNITED STATES: A NEW SOCIAL AGENDA; McCready, William C.; Social History and Conditions.

7010 Griswold del Castillo, Richard. Book review of: HISPANICS IN THE UNITED STATES: A NEW SOCIAL AGENDA. HISPANIC AMERICAN HISTORICAL REVIEW, Vol. 66, no. 3 (August 1986), p. 627-629. English. DESCR: Book Reviews; *HISPANICS IN THE UNITED STATES: A NEW SOCIAL AGENDA; McCready, William C.

San Quentin Prison

7011 Hoffman, Abraham. The controversial career of Martin Aguirre; the rise and fall of a Chicano lawman. CALIFORNIA HISTORY, Vol. 63, no. 4 (Fall 1984), p. 295-341. English. DESCR: *Aguirre, Martin; *Biography; History; Los Angeles County, CA; Prisoners.

7012 McKanna, Clare V. The San Quentin prison pardon papers: a look at file no. 1808, the case of Francisco Javier Bonilla. SOUTHERN CALIFORNIA QUARTERLY, Vol. 67, no. 2 (Summer 1985), p. 187-196. English. DESCR: Administration of Justice; Archives; *Bonilla, Francisco Javier; *Criminal Justice System; History; *Prisoners.

Sanchez, Alex

7013 Pacific Telesis senior fellows. HISPANIC ENGINEER, Vol. 3, no. 2 (Summer 1987), p. 10-11. English. DESCR: *Awards; Castaneda, Jesus; Cruz, Jacqueline; Education; Pacific Telesis; Rodriguez, Jose.

Sanchez, Francisco G.

7014 Winston, Bonnie. High tech jobs in the Midwest. HISPANIC ENGINEER, Vol. 3, no. 1 (Spring 1987), p. 50-53. English. DESCR: Chaves, Tony; *Engineering as a Profession; Mosquera, Jaime "Jim"; Rodriguez Howell, Nilsa.

Sanchez, Marta Ester

7015 Castillo-Speed, Lillian. Chicana/Latina literature and criticism: reviews of recent books. WLW JOURNAL, Vol. 11, no. 3 (September 1987), p. 1-4. English. DESCR: Andrews, Lynn V.; *Book Reviews; BORDERS; Chavez, Denise; *Chicanas; CONTEMPORARY CHICANA POETRY: A CRITICAL APPROACH TO AN EMERGING LITERATURE; Flores, Angel; Flores, Kate; JAGUAR WOMAN; Mora, Pat; Tafolla, Carmen; THE DEFIANT MUSE: HISPANIC FEMINIST POEMS FROM THE MIDDLE AGES TO THE PRESENT; THE LAST OF THE MENU GIRLS; TO SPLIT A HUMAN: MITOS, MACHOS Y LA MUJER CHICANA; Vigil-Pinon, Evangelina; WOMAN OF HER WORD: HISPANIC WOMEN WRITE.

7016 Grabo, Norman S. Book review of: CONTEMPORARY CHICANA POETRY. AMERICAN LITERATURE, Vol. 58, no. 3 (October 1986), p. 473-475. English. DESCR: Book Reviews; *CONTEMPORARY CHICANA POETRY: A CRITICAL APPROACH TO AN EMERGING LITERATURE; Poetry.

7017 Isaacs, D.S. Book review of: CONTEMPORARY CHICANA POETRY. CHOICE, Vol. 23, no. 8 (April 1986), p. 1217. English. DESCR: Book Reviews; *CONTEMPORARY CHICANA POETRY: A CRITICAL APPROACH TO AN EMERGING LITERATURE.

7018 Lewis, Tom J. Book review of: CONTEMPORARY CHICANA POETRY. WORLD LITERATURE TODAY, Vol. 60, (Summer 1986), p. 453. English. DESCR: Book Reviews; Chicanas; *CONTEMPORARY CHICANA POETRY: A CRITICAL APPROACH TO AN EMERGING LITERATURE; Poetry.

Sanchez, Marta Ester (cont.)

7019 Schmitt, Jack. Book review of: CONTEMPORARY CHICANA POETRY. LOS ANGELES TIMES BOOK REVIEW, (December 29, 1985), p. 8. English. **DESCR:** Book Reviews; Chicanas; *CONTEMPORARY CHICANA POETRY: A CRITICAL APPROACH TO AN EMERGING LITERATURE; Poetry.

7020 Torres, Lourdes. Book review of: CONTEMPORARY CHICANA POETRY. WESTERN AMERICAN LITERATURE, Vol. 21, no. 4 (1987), p. 378-379. English. **DESCR:** Book Reviews; *CONTEMPORARY CHICANA POETRY: A CRITICAL APPROACH TO AN EMERGING LITERATURE.

Sanchez, Ricardo

7021 Bruce-Novoa, Juan. Homenaje a Ricardo Sanchez. EL CUADERNO, Vol. 4, no. 1 (Summer 1976), p. 49. Spanish. **DESCR:** *Poems.

7022 Lomeli, Francisco A. El concepto del barrio en tres poetas chicanos. LA COMUNIDAD, No. 316 (August 10, 1986), p. 4-5+. Spanish. **DESCR:** Alurista; Barrios; Delgado, Abelardo "Lalo"; *Literary Criticism; Poetry.

7023 Lovato, Alberto. La burra no era arisca, cabrones, los chingazos la hicieron asi... EL CUADERNO, Vol. 2, no. 1 (1972), p. 36-39. English. **DESCR:** Book Reviews; *CANTO Y GRITO MI LIBERACION.

Sanchez, Rosaura

7024 Herrera-Sobek, Maria. Literatura y sociedad: la problematica del Chicano/Mexicano en los Estados Unidos a traves de la obra literaria. BILINGUAL REVIEW, Vol. 11, no. 3 (September, December, 1984), p. 83-87. Spanish. **DESCR:** Book Reviews; Literary Criticism; Literature; *REQUISA TREINTA Y DOS.

7025 Jimenez, Francisco. Book review of: CHICANO DISCOURSE. LECTOR, Vol. 4, no. 4-6 (1987), p. 55. English. **DESCR:** Book Reviews; *CHICANO DISCOURSE: SOCIOHISTORIC PERSPECTIVE; Sociolinguistics.

7026 Trueba, Henry T. and Delgado-Gaitan, Concha. Book review of: CHICANO DISCOURSE. LANGUAGE IN SOCIETY, Vol. 14, no. 2 (June 1985), p. 257-259. English. **DESCR:** Book Reviews; *CHICANO DISCOURSE: SOCIOHISTORIC PERSPECTIVE.

Sanchez, Saul

7027 de Ortego y Gasca, Felipe. El crepusculo y la bandera. CHIRICU, Vol. 2, no. 2 (1981), p. 65-68. Spanish. **DESCR:** Book Reviews; *HAY PLESHA LICHENS TU DI FLAC.

Sandos, James

7028 de la Garza, Rodolfo O. Book review of: ACROSS THE BORDER: RURAL DEVELOPMENT IN MEXICO AND RECENT MIGRATION TO THE UNITED STATES. LA RED/THE NET, no. 69 (June 1983), p. 5-7. English. **DESCR:** *ACROSS THE BORDER: RURAL DEVELOPMENT IN MEXICO AND RECENT MIGRATION; Book Reviews; Border Industries; Cross, Harry E.

Sandoval [family name]

7029 Instituto Genealogico e Historico Latino-Americano. Rootsearch: Duarte: Sandoval. VISTA, Vol. 1, no. 9 (May 3, 1986), p. 22. English. **DESCR:** *Duarte [family name]; Genealogy; History; *Personal Names.

Sandoval, Frank

7030 Brower, Monty. A proud street mourns its fallen sons. PEOPLE WEEKLY, Vol. 21, (May 28, 1984), p. 76-78+. English. **DESCR:** *Military; Sandoval, Joseph; Silvis, IL; *World War II.

Sandoval, Joseph

7031 Brower, Monty. A proud street mourns its fallen sons. PEOPLE WEEKLY, Vol. 21, (May 28, 1984), p. 76-78+. English. **DESCR:** *Military; Sandoval, Frank; Silvis, IL; *World War II.

Sandoval, Paul

7032 Abalos, J. Victor. Paul Sandoval. VISTA, Vol. 1, no. 4 (December 7, 1985), p. 10. English. **DESCR:** Business Enterprises; Denver, CO; *Financial Aid; Mile Hi Cablevision.

Sandoval, Tanya

7033 Guerrero, Dan. Tanya Sandoval: death-defying stunts are all in her day's work. VISTA, Vol. 2, no. 6 (February 8, 1987), p. 21. English. **DESCR:** *Actors and Actresses; Films.

SANGRE

7034 Benson, Douglas K. and Quintana, Leroy V. A conversation with Leroy V. Quintana. BILINGUAL REVIEW, Vol. 12, no. 3 (September, December, 1985), p. 218-229. English. **DESCR:** Authors; Biography; HIJO DEL PUEBLO; Poetry; *Quintana, Leroy V.

7035 Benson, Douglas K. Intuitions of a world in transition: the New Mexican poetry of Leroy V. Quintana. BILINGUAL REVIEW, Vol. 12, no. 1-2 (January, August, 1985), p. 62-80. English. **DESCR:** Authors; HIJO DEL PUEBLO; *Literary Criticism; New Mexico; Poetry; *Quintana, Leroy V.

Santa Ana, CA

7036 Gonzalez, Gilbert G. Segregation of Mexican children in a southern California city: the legacy of expansion and the American Southwest. WESTERN HISTORICAL QUARTERLY, Vol. 16, no. 1 (January 1985), p. 55-76. English. **DESCR:** *Discrimination in Education; Education; Educational Administration; Primary School Education; Segregation and Desegregation.

Santa Barbara, CA

7037 Arce, Carlos H. Book review of: CHICANOS IN A CHANGING SOCIETY. LA RED/THE NET, no. 30 (May 1980), p. 8. English. **DESCR:** Book Reviews; Camarillo, Alberto; CHICANOS IN A CHANGING SOCIETY; History; *Social History and Conditions; *Southern California.

7038 de Uriarte, Mercedes Lynn. Santa Barbara: a touch of Spanish class. VISTA, Vol. 1, no. 12 (August 2, 1986), p. 6-8. English. **DESCR:** *Tourism.

7039 Miranda, Gloria E. Hispano-Mexican childrearing practices in pre-American Santa Barbara. SOUTHERN CALIFORNIA QUARTERLY, Vol. 65, no. 4 (Winter 1983), p. 307-320. English. **DESCR:** *Children; Cultural Characteristics; *Family; History; *Parenting; Socialization.

Santa Fe Festival of the Arts

7040 Bell, David. Report from Sante Fe:
figuration and fantasy. ART IN AMERICA, Vol.
72, no. 1 (January 1984), p. 31-35. English.
DESCR: Art; Exhibits.

Santa Fe, NM

7041 Griswold del Castillo, Richard. Familism,
the extended family and Chicanos in the
nineteenth century. LA RED/THE NET, no. 49
(December 1981), p. 2. English. DESCR:
*Extended Family; *Family; Los Angeles, CA;
*Nineteenth century; San Antonio, TX;
*Social History and Conditions; Tucson, AZ.

Santa Fe Trail

7042 Sharpe, Maria Elena. Back to the future.
VISTA, Vol. 3, no. 4 (December 6, 1987), p.
10-12, 32. English. DESCR: *Community
Development; Las Vegas, NM; *Plaza Vieja,
Las Vegas, NM.

Santa Maria, Yvonne Z.

7043 Beale, Stephen. CEOs. HISPANIC BUSINESS,
Vol. 9, no. 4 (April 1987), p. 20-37, 52.
English. DESCR: Alvarez, Roberto; Batarse,
Anthony A.; Biography; Business Enterprises;
*Businesspeople; Carlo, Nelson; Estrada,
Anthony; Flores, Frank; Fullana, Jaime, Jr.;
Hernandez, George; *Management; Ortega,
James; Quirch, Guillermo; Ruiz, Roberto;
Sugranes, Rosa; Tamaya, Carlos; Young, Paul
H., Jr.

Santiago, Danny
USE: James, Dan

Santos

7044 Cutter, Donald C. With a little help from
their saints. PACIFIC HISTORICAL REVIEW,
Vol. 53, no. 2 (1984), p. 123-140. English.
DESCR: Catholic Church; Religion.

7045 Lopez, Felix. San Jose. THE AMERICAS REVIEW,
Vol. 15, no. 2 (Summer 1987), p. 67.

Saragosa, TX

7046 Pena, Raymundo. Tornado disaster tests
mettle of Texas Latinos. VISTA, Vol. 3, no.
1 (September 6, 1987), p. 28. English.
DESCR: Emergency Services.

Scalabrini Center, Tijuana, Baja California, Mexico

7047 Rigoni, Florenzo. Tijuana: the borders on
the move. MIGRATION WORLD MAGAZINE, Vol. 15,
no. 2 (1987), p. [22]-29. English. DESCR:
*Border Region; Criminal Acts; Immigration;
*Tijuana, Baja California, Mexico;
*Undocumented Workers.

Schach, Paul

7048 Ornstein-Galicia, Jacob. Bilingualism,
bilingual education, and language contact:
the agony, the rewards--or how to unravel
Babel. BILINGUAL REVIEW, Vol. 11, no. 3
(September, December, 1984), p. 72-82.
English. DESCR: Bilingual Bicultural
Education; Bilingualism; Book Reviews;
*LANGUAGES IN CONFLICT: LINGUISTIC
ACCULTURATION IN THE GREAT PLAINS; Ridge,
Martin; *THE NEW BILINGUALISM: AN AMERICAN
DILEMMA.

Schein, David

7049 Gomez Pena, Guillermo and Erana, Maria.
Sobre el arte, la rebeldia y las fronteras.
LA COMUNIDAD, No. 312 (July 13, 1986), p.
6-7+. Spanish. DESCR: Berkeley, CA;
*BORDER-X-FRONTERA [radio program]; Gomez
Pena, Guillermo; *Radio; Teatro.

Schimmel, Julie

7050 Adams, Clinton. Book review of: ART IN NEW
MEXICO, 1900-1945: PATHS TO TAOS AND SANTA
FE. ARTSPACE, Vol. 10, (Fall 1986), p.
34-36. English. DESCR: *Art History; *ART IN
NEW MEXICO, 1900-1945: PATHS TO TAOS AND
SANTA FE; Book Reviews; Eldredge, Charles;
Exhibits; Truettner, William H.

Scholarship
USE: Financial Aid

Scholastic Aptitude Test (SAT)

7051 Alvarado, Raul. Against all odds. HISPANIC
ENGINEER, Vol. 3, no. 4 (Fall 1987), p.
10-11. English. DESCR: *Chicanas; Education;
Educational Statistics; National Merit
Scholarships; Preliminary Scholastic
Aptitude Test (PSAT); Stereotypes.

7052 Wainer, Howard. An exploratory analysis of
performance on the SAT. JOURNAL OF
EDUCATIONAL MEASUREMENT, Vol. 21, no. 2
(Summer 1984), p. 81-91. English. DESCR:
*Educational Tests and Measurements.

Schon, Isabel

7053 Book review of: BOOKS IN SPANISH FOR
CHILDREN AND YOUNG ADULTS. BOOKLIST, Vol.
82, (July 1986), p. 1620. English. DESCR:
Book Reviews; *BOOKS IN SPANISH FOR CHILDREN
AND YOUNG ADULTS: AN ANNOTATED GUIDE;
Children's Literature; Reference Works.

School Closures
USE: School Finance

School Finance

7054 Report to the Network. LA RED/THE NET, no.
92 (January, February, 1986), p. 1-4.
English. DESCR: Federal Aid; Finance;
*Gramm-Rudman-Hollings Deficit Control Act
(PL 99-177); *Higher Education; Reagan
Administration.

Schooling
USE: Education

SCHOOLING AND LANGUAGE MINORITY STUDENTS: A THEORETICAL FRAMEWORK

7055 Rodriguez, Ana Maria and Calderon,
Margarita. Book review of: SCHOOLING AND
LANGUAGE MINORITY STUDENTS: A THEORETICAL
FRAMEWORK. LA RED/THE NET, no. 66 (March
1983), p. 8-10. English. DESCR: Book
Reviews; Office of Bilingual Education,
California State Department of Education.

Science

7056 Bunge, Mario. Ciencia e ideologia en el
mundo hispanico. INTERCIENCIA, Vol. 11, no.
3 (May, June, 1986), p. 120-125. Spanish.
DESCR: Political Ideology; Political
Repression.

Science (cont.)

7057 Lopez-Knox wins fellowship award. HISPANIC TIMES, Vol. 8, no. 1 (December, January, 1987), p. 21. English. **DESCR**: Awards; Biographical Notes; Chicanas; *Lopez-Knox, Joanne.

7058 Luzod, Jimmy. Book review of: ASPECTS OF AMERICAN HISPANIC AND INDIAN INVOLVEMENT IN BIOMEDICAL RESEARCH. LA RED/THE NET, no. 79 (April 1984), p. 9-13. English. **DESCR**: *ASPECTS OF AMERICAN HISPANIC AND INDIAN INVOLVEMENT IN BIOMEDICAL RESEARCH; Book Reviews; Martinez, Diana I.; Martinez, J.V.

Science as a Profession

7059 Challem, Jack. Pied piper of science. VISTA, Vol. 3, no. 2 (October 3, 1987), p. 14. English. **DESCR**: Education; *Romero, Leo.

7060 Mellado, Carmela. Adriana Ocampo. HISPANIC ENGINEER, Vol. 3, no. 4 (Fall 1987), p. 22-24. English. **DESCR**: National Aeronautics and Space Administration (NASA); *Ocampo, Adriana; Stereotypes; Women.

7061 Taylor, Elena. Chicanas in science. REVISTA MUJERES, Vol. 1, no. 1 (January 1984), p. 6-7. English. **DESCR**: *Chicanas.

Sclar, Marta-Luisa

7062 Padilla, Steve. Lessons to be learned from a playful hoax. VISTA, Vol. 1, no. 7 (March 2, 1986), p. 3. English. **DESCR**: *Essays; Humor; Librarians; Public Opinion; Stereotypes; *Valdez, Juan.

Screen Actors Guild

7063 Kwain, Constance. Searching for Hispanic talent. VISTA, Vol. 2, no. 6 (February 8, 1987), p. 6-7. English. **DESCR**: *Actors and Actresses; American Federation of Television & Radio Artists (AFTRA); *Business Enterprises; Films; Myrna Salazar and Associates, Inc.; Navas, Trina; Salazar, Myrna; Television.

Sculptors
USE: Artists

Sculpture

7064 Archuleta, Felipe. Baboon [sculpture]. THE AMERICAS REVIEW, Vol. 15, no. 2 (Summer 1987), p. 86.

7065 Castaneda, Miriam. Creation [sculpture]. CHIRICU, Vol. 2, no. 2 (1981), p. [23].

7066 Castaneda, Miriam. The cry [sculpture]. CHIRICU, Vol. 2, no. 2 (1981), p. Ft cover.

7067 Goldman, Shifra. Zarco Guerrero: tradicion y transformacion. LA COMUNIDAD, No. 249 (April 28, 1985), p. 2-3. Spanish. **DESCR**: *Art; Biography; *Guerrero, Adolfo "El Zarco"; Masks.

7068 Moroles, Jesus Bautista. Artist's statement [and Texas shield, Texas stele, Georgia stele (sculptures)]. THE AMERICAS REVIEW, Vol. 15, no. 1 (Spring 1987), p. 20-21.

7069 Moroles, Jesus Bautista. Ellipse round, Spirit Las Mesas round, Lapstrake [sculptures]. THE AMERICAS REVIEW, Vol. 15, no. 1 (Spring 1987), p. 40.

7070 Moroles, Jesus Bautista. Las Mesas inner column #2 [sculpture]. THE AMERICAS REVIEW, Vol. 15, no. 1 (Spring 1987), p. 92.

7071 Moroles, Jesus Bautista. Zig zag Las Mesas [sculpture]. THE AMERICAS REVIEW, Vol. 15, no. 1 (Spring 1987), p. 68.

Search and Seizure

7072 Aguilar, J. Federal court halts workplace searches based on broad inspection warrants. CRIMINAL LAW REPORTER, Vol. 38, no. 8 (November 20, 1985), p. 2150-2151. English. **DESCR**: Blackie's House of Beef v. Castillo; *INS v. Delgado.

7073 Canby, J. Immigration board can't use evidence from stop based only on Hispanic appearance. CRIMINAL LAW REPORTER, Vol. 39, no. 5 (April 30, 1986), p. 2076. English. **DESCR**: *Arguelles-Vasquez v. INS; U.S. v. Brignoni-Ponce.

7074 Culp, Robert Alan. The Immigration and Naturalization Service and racially motivated questioning: does equal protection pick up where the Fourth Amendment left off? COLUMBIA LAW REVIEW, Vol. 86, no. 4 (May 1986), p. 800-822. English. **DESCR**: Border Patrol; *Constitutional Amendments - Fourth; *Discrimination; *Immigration and Naturalization Service (INS); Immigration Law and Legislation; Immigration Regulation and Control.

7075 District court sets guidelines for vehicle searches at border checkpoints. CRIMINAL LAW REPORTER, Vol. 35, no. 3 (April 18, 1984), p. 2043-2044. English. **DESCR**: *U.S. v. Oyarzun.

7076 Enslen, J. INS enjoined from making vehicle stops on basis of alienage alone. CRIMINAL LAW REPORTER, Vol. 36, no. 16 (January 23, 1985), p. 2291-2293. English. **DESCR**: *Ramirez v. Webb; Undocumented Workers; U.S. v. Brignoni-Ponce.

7077 Ferguson, J. Warrantless INS "farm checks" at migrant camps properly enjoined. CRIMINAL LAW REPORTER, Vol. 37, no. 14 (July 3, 1985), p. 2256. English. **DESCR**: INS v. Delgado; *La Duke v. Nelson.

7078 Schroeder, J. INS vehicle stops designed to discover illegal aliens ruled unconstitutional. CRIMINAL LAW REPORTER, Vol. 37, no. 23 (September 11, 1985), p. 2430-2431. English. **DESCR**: *Nicasio v. U.S. Immigration and Naturalization Service; U.S. v. Brignoni-Ponce.

7079 Search and seizure. CRIMINAL LAW REPORTER, Vol. 35, no. 3 (April 18, 1984), p. 3011-3027. English. **DESCR**: Hester v. U.S.; INS v. Delgado; Katz v. U.S.; Maine v. Thornton; Oliver v. U.S.; *U.S. Supreme Court.

Seasonal Labor
USE: Migrant Labor

THE SECOND ST. POEMS

7080 Tafolla, Carmen. Book review of: THE SECOND ST. POEMS. LA RED/THE NET, no. 83 (August 1984), p. 4-6. English. **DESCR**: Book Reviews; Silva, Beverly.

Secondary School Education

7081 Douthat, Bill. Mariachi magic. VISTA, Vol. 2, no. 4 (December 7, 1986), p. 18. English. DESCR: Austin, TX; *Castro, Zeke; Mariachi Rebeldes del Sur; *Mariachis; Music.

7082 Gottdiener, M. Group differentiation in a metropolitan high school: the influence of race, class, gender and culture. QUALITATIVE SOCIOLOGY, Vol. 8, no. 1 (Spring 1985), p. 29-41. English. DESCR: Anglo Americans; Blacks; Identity.

7083 LeAna, Thomas. From dropout to role model: a VISTA postscript. VISTA, Vol. 2, no. 4 (December 7, 1986), p. 25. English. DESCR: Brownsville, TX; Gladys Porter High School; *Martinez, Dorella; Olivares, J.R.; *Rhetoric.

7084 National Council of La Raza (NCLR). Career information and Hispanic students. LA RED/THE NET, no. 75 (December 1983), p. 2-4. English. DESCR: *Careers; Educational Services; *National Council of La Raza (NCLR); Survey of Career Information Systems in Secondary Schools; *Youth.

Segregation and Desegregation

7085 Gonzalez, Gilbert G. Segregation of Mexican children in a southern California city: the legacy of expansion and the American Southwest. WESTERN HISTORICAL QUARTERLY, Vol. 16, no. 1 (January 1985), p. 55-76. English. DESCR: *Discrimination in Education; Education; Educational Administration; Primary School Education; *Santa Ana, CA.

7086 Guppy, N. Positional centrality and racial segregation in professional baseball. INTERNATIONAL REVIEW OF SPORT SOCIOLOGY, Vol. 18, no. 4 (1983), p. 95-109. English. DESCR: *Baseball; Discrimination; Ethnic Groups.

7087 Olivas, Michael A. The condition of Hispanic education. LA RED/THE NET, no. 56 (July 1982), p. 3-6. English. DESCR: *Discrimination in Education; *Education.

7088 Rips, Geoffrey. Civil rights and wrongs. TEXAS OBSERVOR, Vol. 76, (December 14, 1984), p. 49-55. English. DESCR: Briscoe, Dolph, Jr., Governor of Texas; *Civil Rights; Farm Workers; *Hidalgo County, TX; La Raza Unida Party; Miller, C.L.; Texas Farmworkers' Union; Voting Rights.

SEGUIN [movie]

7089 Mindiola, Tatcho, Jr. Film review of: THE BALLAD OF GREGORIO CORTEZ. LA RED/THE NET, no. 80 (May 1984), p. 11-17. English. DESCR: *BALLAD OF GREGORIO CORTEZ [film]; *Film Reviews; ZOOT SUIT [film].

Segura, Roberto D.

7090 Garcia, Philip. Book review of: MEXICAN AMERICANS IN SCHOOL: A DECADE OF CHANGE. LA RED/THE NET, no. 33 (August 1980), p. 4. English. DESCR: Book Reviews; Carter, Thomas P.; *Education; *MEXICAN AMERICANS IN SCHOOL: A DECADE OF CHANGE.

Selective Service
USE: Military Service

SELENA [novel]

7091 Bruce-Novoa, Juan. Ernest Brawley: un

escritor chicano desconocido. LA COMUNIDAD, No. 277 (November 10, 1985), p. 6-7. Spanish. DESCR: Authors; *Biography; *Brawley, Ernest; Literary Criticism; Novel; THE ALAMO TREE [novel]; THE RAP [novel].

Self Concept
USE: Identity

Self Perception
USE: Identity

Self-Help Graphics, Los Angeles, CA

7092 Rosas, Alejandro. Siete fotografos latinos en Los Angeles. LA COMUNIDAD, No. 241 (March 3, 1985), p. 4-5. Spanish. DESCR: Aguilar, Laura; Art; Avila, Adam; Callwood, Dennis O.; Carlos, Jesus; Exhibits; Miranda, Judy; *Photography; *SEVEN LATINO PHOTOGRAPHERS=SIETE FOTOGRAFOS LATINOS; Thewlis, Alan; Valverde, Richard.

Self-Help Groups
USE: Mutualistas

Self-Referents

7093 Garcia, John A. Ethnic identity and background traits: explorations of Mexican-origin populations. LA RED/THE NET, no. 29 (April 1980), p. 2. English. DESCR: *Identity; *Southwestern United States; *SURVEY OF INCOME AND EDUCATION, 1976.

7094 Gutierrez, Ramon A. Unraveling America's Hispanic past: internal stratification and class boundaries. AZTLAN, Vol. 17, no. 1 (Spring 1986), p. 79-101. English. DESCR: *Chicano, Meaning of; Culture; *Ethnic Groups; *Identity; Intergroup Relations.

7095 Hayes-Bautista, David Emmett and Chapa, Jorge. Latino terminology: conceptual bases for standardized terminology. AMERICAN JOURNAL OF PUBLIC HEALTH, Vol. 77, no. 1 (January 1987), p. 61-68. English. DESCR: Ethnic Groups; *Identity.

7096 Hurtado, Aida and Arce, Carlos H. Mexicans, Chicanos, Mexican Americans, or pochos...Que somos? The impact of language and nativity on ethnic labeling. AZTLAN, Vol. 17, no. 1 (Spring 1986), p. 103-130. English. DESCR: *Ethnic Groups; *Identity; Language Usage.

7097 Lucero, Rubel Jose. The enemy within. EL CUADERNO, Vol. 1, no. 1 (1971), p. 10-13. English. DESCR: *Discrimination; *Identity.

7098 Rodriguez-Scheel, Jaclyn and Beals, Janette. Chicano Survey report #5: group naming and cultural inclinations. LA RED/THE NET, no. 42 (May 1981), p. 3-4. English. DESCR: Cultural Characteristics; *National Chicano Survey (NCS).

7099 Slatta, Richard W. and Atkinson, Maxine P. The "Spanish origin" population of Oregon and Washington: a demographic profile, 1980. PACIFIC NORTHWEST QUARTERLY, Vol. 75, no. 3 (July 1984), p. 108-116. English. DESCR: *Oregon; *Population; Socioeconomic Factors; Statistics; *Washington (state).

Seligmann, Gustav L.

7100 de Leon, Arnoldo. Book review of: CHICANO: THE EVOLUTION OF A PEOPLE. SOUTHWESTERN HISTORICAL QUARTERLY, Vol. 87, no. 3 (1984), p. 343-344. English. DESCR: Book Reviews; Calvert, Robert; *CHICANO: THE EVOLUTION OF A PEOPLE; Rosaldo, Renato.

Sephardic Jews
USE: Jews

September 16
USE: Dieciseis de Septiembre

Serna, Eric P.

7101 Beale, Stephen. MALDEF weathers a storm. HISPANIC BUSINESS, Vol. 9, no. 5 (May 1987), p. 10-11. English. **DESCR:** Anaya, Toney, Governor of New Mexico; Civil Rights; Hernandez, Antonia A.; *Mexican American Legal Defense and Educational Fund (MALDEF); Organizations.

Serna, Irene

7102 Soriano, Diane H. The struggle continues: an interview with Irene Serna. REVISTA MUJERES, Vol. 2, no. 1 (January 1985), p. 40-42. English. **DESCR:** *Biography.

Sesma, Chico

7103 Lopez, Jose Y. Chico Sesma: a man and his music. LATIN QUARTER, Vol. 1, no. 4 (July, August, 1975), p. 10-15. English. **DESCR:** Chico Sesma Radio Show; Los Angeles, CA; *Radio; Salsa.

SEVEN LATINO PHOTOGRAPHERS=SIETE FOTOGRAFOS LATINOS

7104 Rosas, Alejandro. Siete fotografos latinos en Los Angeles. LA COMUNIDAD, No. 241 (March 3, 1985), p. 4-5. Spanish. **DESCR:** Aguilar, Laura; Art; Avila, Adam; Callwood, Dennis O.; Carlos, Jesus; Exhibits; Miranda, Judy; *Photography; Self-Help Graphics, Los Angeles, CA; Thewlis, Alan; Valverde, Richard.

Sex Discrimination
USE: Sexism

Sex Education

7105 Machado, Melinda. Saying "no" to teenage sex. VISTA, Vol. 2, no. 11 (July 5, 1987), p. 14. English. **DESCR:** *CUANDO ESTEMOS JUNTOS [phonograph record]; DETENTE [phonograph record]; Music; *Musical Lyrics; Planned Parenthood Federation of America; Tatiana and Johnny.

Sex Roles

7106 Alarcon, Norma. Making "familia" from scratch: split subjectivities in the work of Helena Maria Viramontes and Cherrie Moraga. THE AMERICAS REVIEW, Vol. 15, no. 3-4 (Fall, Winter, 1987), p. 147-159. English. **DESCR:** Chicanas; GIVING UP THE GHOST; *Literary Criticism; *Moraga, Cherrie; "Snapshots" [short story]; THE MOTHS AND OTHER STORIES; *Viramontes, Helen.

7107 Attitudes are changing while women go to work. HISPANIC TIMES, Vol. 8, no. 3 (May, June, 1987), p. 14. English. **DESCR:** *Attitudes; *Working Women.

7108 Berger, Peggy S. Differences in importance of and satisfaction from job characteristics by sex and occupational type among Mexican-American employees. JOURNAL OF VOCATIONAL BEHAVIOR, Vol. 28, no. 3 (June 1986), p. 203-213. English. **DESCR:** *Attitudes; *Employment.

7109 Briody, Elizabeth K. Patterns of household immigration into South Texas. INTERNATIONAL MIGRATION REVIEW, Vol. 21, no. 1 (Spring 1987), p. 27-47. English. **DESCR:** Chicanas; *Family; *Immigrants; *Social Mobility; *South Texas.

7110 Bruce-Novoa, Juan. One more rosary for Dona Marina. CONFLUENCIA, Vol. 1, no. 2 (Spring 1986), p. 73-84. English. **DESCR:** *A ROSARY FOR DONA MARINA; *Literary Criticism; *Romano-V., Octavio Ignacio; Short Story.

7111 Burnham, M. Audrey, et al. Measurement of acculturation in a community population of Mexican Americans. HISPANIC JOURNAL OF BEHAVIORAL SCIENCES, Vol. 9, no. 2 (June 1987), p. 105-130. English. **DESCR:** *Acculturation; Age Groups; Biculturalism; Research Methodology.

7112 Curtis, Theodore T. and Baca Zinn, Maxine. Marital role orientation among Chicanos: an analysis of structural and cultural factors. LA RED/THE NET, no. 59 (October 1982), p. 2-4. English. **DESCR:** *Marriage.

7113 Engle, Patricia L.; Scrimshaw, Susan C.M.; and Smidt, Robert. Sex differences in attitudes towards newborn infants among women of Mexican origin. MEDICAL ANTHROPOLOGY, Vol. 8, no. 2 (Spring 1984), p. 133-144. English. **DESCR:** *Attitudes; Chicanas; Cultural Characteristics; *Machismo; *Maternal and Child Welfare; *Parent and Child Relationships.

7114 Guendelman, Sylvia. The incorporation of Mexican women in seasonal migration: a study of gender differences. HISPANIC JOURNAL OF BEHAVIORAL SCIENCES, Vol. 9, no. 3 (September 1987), p. 245-264. English. **DESCR:** Chicanas; Immigrants; Marriage; Mexico; *Migration Patterns; *Women; *Women Men Relations; Working Women.

7115 Gutierrez, Ramon A. Honor ideology, marriage negotiation, and class-gender domination in New Mexico, 1690-1846. LATIN AMERICAN PERSPECTIVES, Vol. 12, no. 1 (Winter 1985), p. 81-104. English. **DESCR:** Marriage; *Social Classes; Social History and Conditions; *Southwestern United States; Values; Women Men Relations.

7116 Herrera-Sobek, Maria. The politics of rape: sexual transgression in Chicana fiction. THE AMERICAS REVIEW, Vol. 15, no. 3-4 (Fall, Winter, 1987), p. 171-181. English. **DESCR:** *Chicanas; Cisneros, Sandra; *Feminism; Fiction; GIVING UP THE GHOST; *Literary Criticism; Lizarraga, Sylvia; Moraga, Cherrie; *Rape; "Red Clowns" [short story]; "Silver Lake Road" [short story].

7117 Howell-Martinez, Vicky. The influence of gender roles on political socialization: an experimental study of Mexican-American children. WOMEN & POLITICS, Vol. 2, (Fall 1982), p. 33-46. English. **DESCR:** Attitudes; Child Study; Children; Political Socialization; *Sex Stereotypes.

7118 Keremitsis, Dawn. Del metate al molino: la mujer mexicana de 1910 a 1940. HISTORIA MEXICANA, Vol. 33, no. 2 (1983), p. 285-302. Spanish. **DESCR:** Food Industry; Labor Unions; *Mexico; Strikes and Lockouts; Tortillas; *Working Women.

Sex Roles (cont.)

7119 LeVine, Sarah Ethel; Correa, Clara
     Sunderland; and Uribe, F. Medardo Tapia. The
     marital morality of Mexican women--an urban
     study. JOURNAL OF ANTHROPOLOGICAL RESEARCH,
     Vol. 42, no. 2 (Summer 1986), p. 183-202.
     English. **DESCR**: Family; Los Robles,
     Cuernavaca, Morelos, Mexico; *Machismo;
     Marriage; Parent and Child Relationships;
     *Women Men Relations.

7120 Martinez, Ruben and Dukes, Richard L. Race,
     gender and self-esteem among youth. HISPANIC
     JOURNAL OF BEHAVIORAL SCIENCES, Vol. 9, no.
     4 (December 1987), p. 427-443. English.
     DESCR: *Comparative Psychology; *Identity;
     *Youth.

7121 Olarte, Silvia W. and Masnik, Ruth. Benefits
     of long-term group therapy for disadvantaged
     Hispanic outpatients. HOSPITAL AND COMMUNITY
     PSYCHIATRY, Vol. 36, no. 10 (October 1985),
     p. 1093-1097. English. **DESCR**: Ethnic Groups;
     Metropolitan Hospital, New York, NY; New
     York, NY; Psychotherapy; *Women.

7122 Padilla, Eligio R. and O'Grady, Kevin E.
     Sexuality among Mexican Americans: a case of
     sexual stereotyping. JOURNAL OF PERSONALITY
     AND SOCIAL PSYCHOLOGY, Vol. 52, no. 1
     (1987), p. 5-10. English. **DESCR**: Age Groups;
     Anglo Americans; Attitudes; Religion;
     *Stereotypes.

7123 Paredes, Raymund A. Review essay: recent
     Chicano writing. ROCKY MOUNTAIN REVIEW OF
     LANGUAGE AND LITERATURE, Vol. 41, (1987),
     p. 124-129. English. **DESCR**: Castillo, Ana;
     Catholic Church; Chavez, Denise; Chicanas;
     Garcia, Lionel; GIVING UP THE GHOST; LEAVING
     HOME; *Literary Criticism; *Literature
     Reviews; Moraga, Cherrie; Poetry; Prose;
     Silva, Beverly; SMALL FACES; Soto, Gary; THE
     CAT AND OTHER STORIES; THE LAST OF THE MENU
     GIRLS; THE MIXQUIAHUALA LETTERS.

7124 Ruiz, Ariel. Raza, sexo y politica en SHORT
     EYES by Miguel Pinero. THE AMERICAS REVIEW,
     Vol. 15, no. 2 (Summer 1987), p. 93-102.
     Spanish. **DESCR**: Homosexuality; Literary
     Criticism; Pinero, Miguel; Prisoners; Puerto
     Ricans; *SHORT EYES; Teatro.

7125 Ruiz, Vicki Lynn. Obreras y madres: labor
     activism among Mexican women and its impact
     on the family. RENATO ROSALDO LECTURE SERIES
     MONOGRAPH, Vol. 1, (Summer 1985), p.
     [19]-38. English. **DESCR**: *Chicanas; Child
     Care Centers; Children; History; *Labor
     Unions; *Mexico; Women; *Working Women.

7126 Sellers, Jeff M. Challenging the myth of the
     traditional woman. HISPANIC BUSINESS, Vol.
     9, no. 8 (August 1987), p. 15-16, 48.
     English. **DESCR**: *Businesspeople; *Careers;
     *Chicanas; *Management; National Network of
     Hispanic Women; Torres, Celia; Women;
     Zambrana, Ruth.

7127 Tienda, Marta and Glass, Jennifer. Household
     structure and labor-force participation of
     Black, Hispanic, and white mothers.
     DEMOGRAPHY, Vol. 22, no. 3 (August 1985), p.
     381-394. English. **DESCR**: Anglo Americans;
     Blacks; Chicanas; *Extended Family; *Family;
     *Working Women.

7128 Yarbro-Bejarano, Yvonne. The female subject
     in Chicano theater: sexuality, race, and
     class. THEATRE JOURNAL, Vol. 38, no. 4
     (December 1986), p. 389-407. English.
     DESCR: *Chicanas; El Teatro Campesino; El
     Teatro de la Esperanza; Feminism; *Malinche;

*Teatro; Teatro Nacional de Aztlan (TENAZ);
WIT (Women in Teatro).

Sex Stereotypes

7129 Howell-Martinez, Vicky. The influence of
     gender roles on political socialization: an
     experimental study of Mexican-American
     children. WOMEN & POLITICS, Vol. 2, (Fall
     1982), p. 33-46. English. **DESCR**: Attitudes;
     Child Study; Children; Political
     Socialization; Sex Roles.

7130 Lomas, Clara. Libertad de no procrear: la
     voz de la mujer en "A una madre de nuestro
     tiempo" de Margarita Cota-Cardenas. REVISTA
     MUJERES, Vol. 2, no. 1 (January 1985), p.
     30-35. Spanish. **DESCR**: *Chicanas; Feminism;
     Literary Criticism.

7131 Rivera, Miquela. In battle of the sexes,
     time for a ceasefire. VISTA, Vol. 3, no. 2
     (October 3, 1987), p. 38. English. **DESCR**:
     *Hembrismo.

7132 Weller, David L. and Reyes, Laurie Hart.
     Stereotyping: impact on teachers and
     students. ACTION IN TEACHER EDUCATION, Vol.
     5, no. 3 (Fall 1983), p. 1-7. English.
     DESCR: Discrimination; Education;
     *Stereotypes.

Sexism

7133 Acuna, Rodolfo. Response to Cynthia Orozco.
     LA RED/THE NET, no. 79 (April 1984), p.
     13-15. English. **DESCR**: Chicanas; *Orozco,
     Cynthia.

7134 Barton, Amy E. Women farmworkers: their
     workplace and capitalist patriarchy. REVISTA
     MUJERES, Vol. 3, no. 2 (June 1986), p.
     11-13. English. **DESCR**: Capitalism;
     *Chicanas; Discrimination; *Farm Workers.

7135 High court upholds quotas. DUNS'S BUSINESS
     MONTH, Vol. 128, no. 2 (August 1986), p. 22.
     English. **DESCR**: *Affirmative Action;
     Discrimination in Employment; Reagan
     Administration; U.S. Supreme Court.

7136 Orozco, Cynthia. Chicana labor history: a
     critique of male consciousness in historical
     writing. LA RED/THE NET, no. 77 (January
     1984), p. 2-5. English. **DESCR**: *Chicanas;
     *Historiography; Working Women.

Sexual Harassment
     USE: Sexism

SHAKING OFF THE DARK

7137 Olivares, Julian. Self and society in Tino
     Villanueva's SHAKING OFF THE DARK.
     CONFLUENCIA, Vol. 1, no. 2 (Spring 1986), p.
     98-110. English. **DESCR**: Literary Criticism;
     *Poetry; Villanueva, Tino.

Shaw, David

7138 Bastida, Elena B. Book review of: THE
     HISPANIC ELDERLY. CONTEMPORARY SOCIOLOGY: A
     JOURNAL OF REVIEWS, Vol. 14, no. 1 (January
     1985), p. 41-42. English. **DESCR**: Ancianos;
     Becerra, Rosina; Book Reviews; *THE HISPANIC
     ELDERLY: A RESEARCH REFERENCE GUIDE.

7139 Delgado, Melvin. Book review of: THE
     HISPANIC ELDERLY. SOCIAL WORK, Vol. 31, no.
     2 (March, April, 1986), p. 153. English.
     DESCR: Ancianos; Becerra, Rosina; Book
     Reviews; *THE HISPANIC ELDERLY: A RESEARCH
     REFERENCE GUIDE.

Sheridan, Thomas E.

7140 Crisp, James E. Book review of: LOS TUCSONENSES: THE MEXICAN COMMUNITY IN TUCSON 1854-1941. JOURNAL OF ECONOMIC HISTORY, Vol. 47, (January 1987), p. 577-578. English. DESCR: Book Reviews; *LOS TUCSONENSES: THE MEXICAN COMMUNITY IN TUCSON, 1854-1941; Tucson, AZ.

7141 de Leon, Arnoldo. Book review of: LOS TUCSONENSES: THE MEXICAN COMMUNITY IN TUCSON 1854-1941. NEW MEXICO HISTORICAL REVIEW, Vol. 62, no. 4 (October 1987), p. 411-12. English. DESCR: Book Reviews; *LOS TUCSONENSES: THE MEXICAN COMMUNITY IN TUCSON, 1854-1941; *Tucson, AZ.

Shor, Ira

7142 Romero, Mary. Book review of: CRITICAL TEACHING AND EVERYDAY LIFE. LA RED/THE NET, no. 69 (June 1983), p. 3-5. English. DESCR: Book Reviews; *CRITICAL TEACHING AND EVERYDAY LIFE.

SHORT EYES

7143 Ruiz, Ariel. Raza, sexo y politica en SHORT EYES by Miguel Pinero. THE AMERICAS REVIEW, Vol. 15, no. 2 (Summer 1987), p. 93-102. Spanish. DESCR: Homosexuality; Literary Criticism; Pinero, Miguel; Prisoners; Puerto Ricans; Sex Roles; Teatro.

Short Story

7144 Acosta, Teresa Palomo. Catorce pedazos de una cosecha. SAGUARO, Vol. 3, (1986), p. 11-15. Spanish.

7145 Acuna, David. Cuento verdad. LLUEVE TLALOC, no. 14 (1987), p. 63-64. Spanish.

7146 Aguilar Melantzon, Ricardo. Cumplir mi justa condena. SAGUARO, Vol. 2, (1985), p. 94-111. Spanish.

7147 Aguilera-Hellwet, Max. An Aztec prince. SAGUARO, Vol. 3, (1986), p. 92-102. English.

7148 Alarcon, Justo S. Estructuras narrativas en TATA CASEHUA de Miguel Mendez. CONFLUENCIA, Vol. 1, no. 2 (Spring 1986), p. 48-54. Spanish. DESCR: *Literary Criticism; *Mendez M., Miguel; *"Tata Casehua" [short story].

7149 Alarcon, Justo S. Focos: el agonico visionario. CHIRICU, Vol. 2, no. 2 (1981), p. 40-44. Spanish.

7150 Alarcon, Norma. Once upon a time...the sculptor. CHIRICU, Vol. 2, no. 1 (Spring 1980), p. 4-5. English.

7151 Alarcon, Norma. Sunday afternoons. CHIRICU, no. 2 (Spring 1977), p. 9-11. English.

7152 Allison, Martha. Engano y traicion. LLUEVE TLALOC, no. 14 (1987), p. 35-39. Spanish.

7153 Allison, Martha. El pollito de la inocencia. LLUEVE TLALOC, no. 14 (1987), p. 39. Spanish.

7154 Alonso M. El huerfano. LLUEVE TLALOC, no. 12 (1985), p. 9. Spanish.

7155 Alonso, Marisela. Enamorado de un fantasma. LLUEVE TLALOC, no. 11 (1984), p. 19. Spanish.

7156 Alonso, Marisela. La nina. LLUEVE TLALOC, no. 11 (1984), p. 2. Spanish.

7157 Andrade, A. Roland. El zorro: un cuento. CHIRICU, Vol. 3, no. 1 (1982), p. 23-25. Spanish.

7158 Andres, Magda Albero. La capital. CHIRICU, Vol. 3, no. 1 (1982), p. 21-22. Spanish.

7159 Andrews, Zenia. Miseria y pobreza. LLUEVE TLALOC, no. 12 (1985), p. 1. Spanish.

7160 Angulo, Lourdes. La cruz. LLUEVE TLALOC, no. 10 (1983), p. 20. Spanish.

7161 Angulo, Lourdes. Mi castigo inolvidable. LLUEVE TLALOC, no. 10 (1983), p. 26. Spanish.

7162 Angulo, Lourdes. La noche en que crei en la Llorona. LLUEVE TLALOC, no. 11 (1984), p. 19. Spanish.

7163 Angulo, Lourdes. El viaje al gran canon. LLUEVE TLALOC, no. 11 (1984), p. 34. Spanish.

7164 Aragon, Maggie. Hombre o demonio. LLUEVE TLALOC, no. 10 (1983), p. 3. Spanish.

7165 Aragon, Maggie. La muerte. LLUEVE TLALOC, no. 10 (1983), p. 36. Spanish.

7166 Aragon, Maggie. La sirena del mar. LLUEVE TLALOC, no. 11 (1984), p. 28. Spanish.

7167 Arellano, Estevan. Chicanos nortenos. EL CUADERNO, Vol. 2, no. 1 (1972), p. 27-35. English. DESCR: *Cultural Characteristics; *Discrimination.

7168 Arellano, Estevan. Inocencio: ni siembra ni escarda y siempre se come el mejor elote. EL CUADERNO, Vol. 3, no. 1 (Winter 1973), p. 51-61. Spanish.

7169 Arellano, Estevan. Inocencio: tambien de gusto se llora como de dolor se canta. EL CUADERNO, Vol. 3, no. 2 (Spring 1974), p. 28-40. Spanish.

7170 Arvizu, Delia. El aborto. LLUEVE TLALOC, no. 12 (1985), p. 7. Spanish.

7171 Arvizu, Delia. El espejo. LLUEVE TLALOC, no. 12 (1985), p. 28. Spanish.

7172 Arvizu, Delia. El guerito de Teresita. LLUEVE TLALOC, no. 12 (1985), p. 12. Spanish.

7173 Avendano, Fausto. La enemistad. SAGUARO, Vol. 4, (1987), p. 9-14. Spanish.

7174 Avendano, Fausto. Juan Gonzalez, poeta. SAGUARO, Vol. 2, (1985), p. 43-46. Spanish.

7175 Berger, Andres. Cartas a mi amante. THE AMERICAS REVIEW, Vol. 15, no. 2 (Summer 1987), p. 12-27. Spanish.

7176 Bermudez-Gallegos, Marta. La sombra. SAGUARO, Vol. 1, no. 1 (1984), p. 31-32. Spanish.

7177 Bolivar, Maria Dolores. Silencios virgenes. SAGUARO, Vol. 4, (1987), p. 33-36. Spanish.

7178 Boyer, Jeanette. Gangue. CHIRICU, Vol. 5, no. 1 (1987), p. 44-48. English.

7179 Boyer, Jeanette. A vein is struck. CHIRICU, Vol. 4, no. 1 (1985), p. 153-158. English.

Short Story (cont.)

7180 Bruce-Novoa, Juan. One more rosary for Dona Marina. CONFLUENCIA, Vol. 1, no. 2 (Spring 1986), p. 73-84. English. **DESCR:** *A ROSARY FOR DONA MARINA; *Literary Criticism; *Romano-V., Octavio Ignacio; Sex Roles.

7181 Camach, Miguel. Idea atrazada. REVISTA MUJERES, Vol. 2, no. 2 (June 1985), p. 46-48. Spanish. **DESCR:** *Violence.

7182 Campos, Elba M. Un verano. LLUEVE TLALOC, no. 11 (1984), p. 20. Spanish.

7183 Canales, Michael James. Mala suerte. SAGUARO, Vol. 3, (1986), p. 77-87. English.

7184 Carrillo, Victor. Woman to woman. REVISTA MUJERES, Vol. 3, no. 1 (January 1986), p. 44-45. English.

7185 Cartes, Rebeca. Desnuda. SAGUARO, Vol. 1, no. 1 (1984), p. 67-68. Spanish.

7186 Cartes, Rebeca. El lobo. LLUEVE TLALOC, no. 8 (1981), p. 6. Spanish.

7187 Casaus, Maria R. Una apuesta. LLUEVE TLALOC, no. 11 (1984), p. 13. Spanish.

7188 Casaus, Maria R. Descansa pequeno. LLUEVE TLALOC, no. 11 (1984), p. 40. Spanish.

7189 Castillo, Jose Luis. Carta esperada. SAGUARO, Vol. 3, (1986), p. 20-26. Spanish.

7190 Castillo, Jose Luis. Sukaina. SAGUARO, Vol. 2, (1985), p. 8-17. English.

7191 Castillo, Rafael C. The goy from Aztlan. SAGUARO, Vol. 2, (1985), p. 88-93. English.

7192 Castillo, Rafael C. The poetry club. SAGUARO, Vol. 4, (1987), p. 23-28. English.

7193 Cerda, Gabriela. The call. NOTEBOOK: A LITTLE MAGAZINE, Vol. 3, no. 1 (1987), p. 25-36. English.

7194 Cervantes, Alma. Desarrollo. AMERICAS 2001, Premiere Issue, 1987, p. 30-33. Bilingual.

7195 Chavez, Lulu. El hombre del sahuaro. LLUEVE TLALOC, no. 11 (1984), p. 23. Spanish.

7196 Chumacero, Olivia. Recesses of my mind. REVISTA MUJERES, Vol. 3, no. 1 (January 1986), p. 13-15. English.

7197 Cirerol, Anna. La historia de Lina y la rana. LLUEVE TLALOC, no. 10 (1983), p. 1. Spanish.

7198 Cisek, Angela. Enamorados. LLUEVE TLALOC, no. 13 (1986), p. 11. Spanish.

7199 Cisek, Angela. Un marciano en mi bolsillo. LLUEVE TLALOC, no. 13 (1986), p. 9. Spanish.

7200 Cisneros, Sandra. Eleven. SAGUARO, Vol. 3, (1986), p. 17-19. English.

7201 Cruikshank, Lupita. La vista del diablo. LLUEVE TLALOC, no. 12 (1985), p. 7. Spanish.

7202 Davidson, Arnie. The Maria Capra. LLUEVE TLALOC, no. 9 (1982), p. 6. English.

7203 Davidson, Arnie. The newspaper boy. LLUEVE TLALOC, no. 7 (1980), p. 15. English.

7204 Davidson, Arnie. The officer. LLUEVE TLALOC, no. 8 (1981), p. 12-13. English.

7205 de Cervantes, Ma. Elena T. Un rey y sus tres hijos. LLUEVE TLALOC, no. 9 (1982), p. 28. Spanish.

7206 de Hoyos, Arturo. Davidas de Navidad. SAGUARO, Vol. 2, (1985), p. 32-37. Spanish.

7207 de Martinez, Leonor E. Dona Blanca. LLUEVE TLALOC, no. 6 (1979), p. 18. Spanish.

7208 Delgado, Abelardo "Lalo". Exit the frogs=Salida de las ranas. AMERICAS 2001, Vol. 1, no. 2 (September, October, 1987), p. 40-43+. Bilingual.

7209 Di Ioli, Barbara. Cuando yo este grande. LLUEVE TLALOC, no. 14 (1987), p. 3-6. Spanish.

7210 Di Ioli, Barbara. Fructouso. LLUEVE TLALOC, no. 14 (1987), p. 6-7. Spanish.

7211 Di Ioli, Barbara. Hooked on swapmeets. LLUEVE TLALOC, no. 14 (1987), p. 9-11. English.

7212 Di Ioli, Barbara. When I grow up. LLUEVE TLALOC, no. 14 (1987), p. 11-13. English.

7213 Di Ioli, Barbara. Witchcraft. LLUEVE TLALOC, no. 14 (1987), p. 7-9. English.

7214 Doval, Jose. El vino nuevo. CHIRICU, no. 2 (Spring 1977), p. 16-20. Spanish.

7215 Duarte, Laurie. De la calle. LLUEVE TLALOC, no. 11 (1984), p. 38. Spanish.

7216 Duarte, Laurie. Los hijos malagradecidos. LLUEVE TLALOC, no. 12 (1985), p. 16. Spanish.

7217 Duarte, Laurie. Por una noche. LLUEVE TLALOC, no. 12 (1985), p. 30. Spanish.

7218 Duarte, Laurie. Sola una vision. LLUEVE TLALOC, no. 11 (1984), p. 38. Spanish.

7219 Durango, Guadalupe. Manuel. LLUEVE TLALOC, no. 10 (1983), p. 34. Spanish.

7220 Duron, Manuel. Un lunes en febrero. SAGUARO, Vol. 2, (1985), p. 38-42. English.

7221 Elizondo, Sergio D. Tres ninas surumatas. SAGUARO, Vol. 4, (1987), p. 91-107. Spanish.

7222 Enguidanos, Miguel. Las mentiras que llegamos a creernos III. CHIRICU, no. 2 (Spring 1977), p. 40-41. Spanish.

7223 Espinoza, Sagrario. Un milagro. LLUEVE TLALOC, no. 8 (1981), p. 39. Spanish.

7224 Estrada, Javier. Coco y su amigo coco. LLUEVE TLALOC, no. 13 (1986), p. 30. Spanish.

7225 Estrada, Rosalio S. Sonar un sueno imposible: una pesadilla viva en tinta lavable. LLUEVE TLALOC, no. 3 (1976), p. 52-60. Spanish.

7226 Estrada, Rosalio S. To dream an impossible dream or a living nightmare in washable ink. LLUEVE TLALOC, no. 3 (1976), p. 53-61. English.

7227 Fernandez, Roberta. Andrea. THE AMERICAS REVIEW, Vol. 15, no. 3-4 (Fall, Winter, 1987), p. 106-128. English.

Short Story (cont.)

7228 Fernandez, Roberto G. Origenes. TINTA, Vol. 1, no. 4 (Summer 1984), p. 39-41. Spanish.

7229 Figueroa, Lupita S. Un chiste. LLUEVE TLALOC, no. 6 (1979), p. 14. Spanish.

7230 Flores, Francisco. Danzon. LLUEVE TLALOC, no. 8 (1981), p. 3. Spanish.

7231 Flores, Francisco. Malaria. LLUEVE TLALOC, no. 8 (1981), p. 6. Spanish.

7232 Flores, Lorenzo T. Your turn=Su turno. AMERICAS 2001, Vol. 1, no. 1 (June, July, 1987), p. 26-29. Bilingual. **DESCR:** English-Only Movement; Language Usage.

7233 Frontain, Michel. Edmundo. LLUEVE TLALOC, no. 10 (1983), p. 27-28. Spanish.

7234 Gallegos Douglas, Rosalie. Transition. SAGUARO, Vol. 2, (1985), p. 28-31. English.

7235 Garcia, Ignacio. Gracias a Dios por Christmas. SAGUARO, Vol. 2, (1985), p. 47-58. English.

7236 Garcia, Ignacio. The republic. SAGUARO, Vol. 4, (1987), p. 109-119. English.

7237 Garcia, Ignacio. Unfinished letter to Terry. SAGUARO, Vol. 3, (1986), p. 103-109. English.

7238 Garcia, Julian S. El viaje. SAGUARO, Vol. 3, (1986), p. 59-61. English.

7239 Garcia, Lionel G. The sergeant. THE AMERICAS REVIEW, Vol. 15, no. 1 (Spring 1987), p. 7-26. English.

7240 Garcia, Silvia. Ricardito. LLUEVE TLALOC, no. 12 (1985), p. 20. Spanish.

7241 Garcia, Valerie M. La egoista. LLUEVE TLALOC, no. 4 (1977), p. 74-80. Spanish.

7242 Garcia, Valerie M. A good woman. LLUEVE TLALOC, no. 4 (1977), p. 23-24. English.

7243 Garcia, Valerie M. Mediocridad. LLUEVE TLALOC, no. 4 (1977), p. 86-87. Spanish.

7244 Garcia, Valerie M. Una mujer buena. LLUEVE TLALOC, no. 4 (1977), p. 19-21. Spanish.

7245 Garza, Jose P. Carnaval de carcajadas. CHIRICU, Vol. 2, no. 1 (Spring 1980), p. 14-27. Spanish.

7246 Gilb, Dagoberto. Birthday. THE AMERICAS REVIEW, Vol. 15, no. 2 (Summer 1987), p. 42-44. English.

7247 Godoy, Irma. Tilin y las cucarachas. LLUEVE TLALOC, no. 11 (1984), p. 20. Spanish.

7248 Gomez, Rogelio R. Chente's American bar. SAGUARO, Vol. 2, (1985), p. 21-27. English.

7249 Gomez, Rogelio R. Functional man. SAGUARO, Vol. 4, (1987), p. 55-70. English.

7250 Gonzales, Martin S. Dona Alquimina. LLUEVE TLALOC, no. 5 (1978), p. 7. Spanish.

7251 Gonzales, Richard J. Dirty work. THE AMERICAS REVIEW, Vol. 15, no. 2 (Summer 1987), p. 28-39. English.

7252 Gonzalez, Humberto. Locuras. LLUEVE TLALOC, no. 7 (1980), p. 28. Spanish.

7253 Griffin, Mina. Bonito. LLUEVE TLALOC, no. 12 (1985), p. 22. Spanish.

7254 Gutierrez, Yolanda. Culture shock. CHIRICU, Vol. 4, no. 1 (1985), p. 149-152. English.

7255 Hanes, Cecilia. El metro. LLUEVE TLALOC, no. 8 (1981), p. 27. Spanish.

7256 Hanes, Cecilia. La sacerdotisa (artistas, dioses y filisteos). LLUEVE TLALOC, no. 9 (1982), p. 29. Spanish.

7257 Heyer, Sandra. El pequeno Martin. LLUEVE TLALOC, no. 10 (1983), p. 20. Spanish.

7258 Hinojosa-Smith, Rolando R. Coming home II. NUESTRO, Vol. 11, no. 3 (April 1987), p. 28-29. English.

7259 Hinojosa-Smith, Rolando R. Griegos y romanos. SAGUARO, Vol. 1, no. 1 (1984), p. 13-15. Spanish.

7260 Horta, Gerardo. Emigrante. LA COMUNIDAD, No. 347 (March 15, 1987), p. 2-3. Spanish. **DESCR:** Immigration.

7261 Huerta, Margarita A. No perdio el control. LLUEVE TLALOC, no. 8 (1981), p. 32. Spanish.

7262 Huerta, Margarita A. La zorra astuta y el coyote tonto. LLUEVE TLALOC, no. 8 (1981), p. 24. Spanish.

7263 Huez, Lupe. Miguel. LLUEVE TLALOC, no. 4 (1977), p. 26. Spanish.

7264 Hurtado, Aida. Lupe Laputa. REVISTA MUJERES, Vol. 3, no. 1 (January 1986), p. 23-24. Spanish.

7265 Jackson, Martha Elva. Inaudito destino. LLUEVE TLALOC, no. 7 (1980), p. 34. Spanish.

7266 Jackson, Martha Elva. Perdon y olvido. LLUEVE TLALOC, no. 7 (1980), p. 41-42. Spanish.

7267 Jerez, Marco A. Los olvidos. SAGUARO, Vol. 1, no. 1 (1984), p. 8-11. Spanish.

7268 Jordan-Linn, Cynthia. Esqueda. SAGUARO, Vol. 2, (1985), p. 75-77. English.

7269 Lamadrid, Enrique R. Enemy way. BILINGUAL REVIEW, Vol. 12, no. 1-2 (January, August, 1985), p. 92-96. English.

7270 Lamadrid, Enrique R. White woman's burden. BILINGUAL REVIEW, Vol. 12, no. 1-2 (January, August, 1985), p. 90-91. English.

7271 Lizarraga, Patricia. Dulce Maria. LLUEVE TLALOC, no. 10 (1983), p. 37. Spanish.

7272 Lizarraga, Patricia. Lindo encuentro. LLUEVE TLALOC, no. 11 (1984), p. 7. Spanish.

7273 Lizarraga, Patricia. Loco. LLUEVE TLALOC, no. 10 (1983), p. 33. Spanish.

7274 Lizarraga, Patricia. Manuel. LLUEVE TLALOC, no. 11 (1984), p. 38-39. Spanish.

7275 Lomeli, Francisco A. Entrevista con Rolando Hinojosa (I). LA COMUNIDAD, No. 295 (March 16, 1986), p. 2-3+. Spanish. **DESCR:** *Biography; *Hinojosa-Smith, Rolando R.; Literary Criticism; Novel.

Short Story (cont.)

7276 Lopez, Elena. Corte espeluznante. LLUEVE TLALOC, no. 11 (1984), p. 23. Spanish.

7277 Lopez, Maria Isabel. La tia Julia. REVISTA MUJERES, Vol. 2, no. 2 (June 1985), p. 11-12. Spanish. **DESCR:** Immigrants.

7278 Lovato, Alberto. Agusa'o con los velices. EL CUADERNO, Vol. 3, no. 2 (Spring 1974), p. 42-44. Spanish.

7279 Loya, Elena. Cascabel. LLUEVE TLALOC, no. 12 (1985), p. 39. Spanish.

7280 Loya, Elena. Destino cruel. LLUEVE TLALOC, no. 12 (1985), p. 33-34. Spanish.

7281 Loya, Elena. El pescador. LLUEVE TLALOC, no. 12 (1985), p. 37. Spanish.

7282 Luera, Yolanda. La chirrionera. SAGUARO, Vol. 4, (1987), p. 43-46. Spanish.

7283 Magana, Ester P. Down payments. CHIRICU, Vol. 4, no. 1 (1985), p. 141-144. English.

7284 Maldonado, Herlinda. El muchacho que no creia en Santo Claus. LLUEVE TLALOC, no. 9 (1982), p. 12. Spanish.

7285 Manjarre, Graciela. El viaje de Miguelito. LLUEVE TLALOC, no. 4 (1977), p. 47. Spanish.

7286 Marisabel. El padre y el joven mapuche. LLUEVE TLALOC, no. 8 (1981), p. 13. Spanish.

7287 Marroquin de Hernandez, Celina. No me llames maldito. SAGUARO, Vol. 4, (1987), p. 19-22. Spanish.

7288 Marroquin de Hernandez, Celina. Pepe. SAGUARO, Vol. 3, (1986), p. 62-65. Spanish.

7289 Martin, Patricia Preciado. Dias de mas, dias de menos (days of plenty, days of want). SAGUARO, Vol. 2, (1985), p. 65-71. English.

7290 Martin, Patricia Preciado. Tierra a tierra. SAGUARO, Vol. 3, (1986), p. 29-36. English.

7291 Martinez, Angelina S. La montana majestuosa. LLUEVE TLALOC, no. 8 (1981), p. 41. Spanish.

7292 Martinez, Margarita. Pagaron justos por pecadores. LLUEVE TLALOC, no. 9 (1982), p. 12. Spanish.

7293 Martinez, Raquel A. Un nino y un milagro. LLUEVE TLALOC, no. 10 (1983), p. 33. Spanish.

7294 Meaney, Mark. La gitana. LLUEVE TLALOC, no. 6 (1979), p. 40. Spanish.

7295 Meaney, Mark. La tienda de ropa vieja. LLUEVE TLALOC, no. 6 (1979), p. 40. Spanish.

7296 Medina, Beatriz. Clarisa's experience. LLUEVE TLALOC, no. 5 (1978), p. 36-37. English.

7297 Medina Garcia, Jesus. Lencho. LLUEVE TLALOC, no. 4 (1977), p. 107-109. Spanish.

7298 Medina Garcia, Jesus. El prieto. LLUEVE TLALOC, no. 10 (1983), p. 15-16. Spanish.

7299 Mendez-M., Miguel and Price, Eva, trans. The baby chicks. LLUEVE TLALOC, no. 13 (1986), p. 33. English.

7300 Mendez-M., Miguel. El bolerito bilingue.

7301 Mendez-M., Miguel. El bolerito bilingue. SAGUARO, Vol. 1, no. 1 (1984), p. 16-20. Spanish.

7302 Mendez-M., Miguel. Dona Emeteria. LLUEVE TLALOC, no. 13 (1986), p. iv. Spanish.

7303 Mendez-M., Miguel and Price, Eva, trans. Dona Emeteria. LLUEVE TLALOC, no. 13 (1986), p. 1. English.

7304 Mendez-M., Miguel. Huachusey. LLUEVE TLALOC, no. 9 (1982), p. 3-5. Bilingual. **DESCR:** Cuentos.

7305 Mendez-M., Miguel. El moro. LLUEVE TLALOC, no. 12 (1985), p. 2-4. Spanish.

7306 Mendez-M., Miguel and Price, Eva, trans. Moro. LLUEVE TLALOC, no. 12 (1985), p. 3-5. English.

7307 Mendez-M., Miguel. Los pollitos. LLUEVE TLALOC, no. 13 (1986), p. 32. Spanish.

7308 Mendez-M., Miguel. Que no mueran los suenos. SAGUARO, Vol. 2, (1985), p. 78-87. Spanish.

7309 Michel. Lienzo de alivio. LLUEVE TLALOC, no. 9 (1982), p. 31. Spanish.

7310 Molina, Maria J. Angelica. LLUEVE TLALOC, no. 14 (1987), p. 23-26. Spanish.

7311 Molina, Maria J. Remordimiento. LLUEVE TLALOC, no. 14 (1987), p. 28-30. Spanish.

7312 Molina, Maria J. Tu recuerdo. LLUEVE TLALOC, no. 14 (1987), p. 27. Spanish.

7313 Mondrus Engle, Margarita. A deeper shadow. THE AMERICAS REVIEW, Vol. 15, no. 1 (Spring 1987), p. 36-39. English.

7314 Mondrus Engle, Margarita. Nina. THE AMERICAS REVIEW, Vol. 15, no. 1 (Spring 1987), p. 32-35. English.

7315 Montano, Aurora. Ciega confianza. LLUEVE TLALOC, no. 8 (1981), p. 24. Spanish.

7316 Montano, Aurora. Don Jose Wing. LLUEVE TLALOC, no. 10 (1983), p. 22-24. Spanish.

7317 Montano, Aurora. El gato del caporal. LLUEVE TLALOC, no. 9 (1982), p. 34-39. Spanish.

7318 Montano, Salvador A. Epajoso. LLUEVE TLALOC, no. 11 (1984), p. 39-40. Spanish.

7319 Montano, Salvador A. Eso si que es. LLUEVE TLALOC, no. 11 (1984), p. 34. Bilingual.

7320 Morris, Blair. Tan venturoso caballero, Don Felipe Oseguera. LLUEVE TLALOC, no. 6 (1979), p. 36. Spanish.

7321 Murillo, Ramon. El hijo de roqueminas. LLUEVE TLALOC, no. 7 (1980), p. 25. Spanish.

7322 Narvaez, Soraya. La muerte. LLUEVE TLALOC, no. 7 (1980), p. 13. Spanish.

7323 Nava Monreal, David. Benito Garcia. BILINGUAL REVIEW, Vol. 12, no. 1-2 (January, August, 1985), p. 108-114. English.

7324 Nava Monreal, David. A matter of dignity. CHIRICU, Vol. 4, no. 1 (1985), p. 101-118. English.

Short Story (cont.)

7325 Olivas, Eduardo. Los machos no lloran. LLUEVE TLALOC, no. 6 (1979), p. 45-48. Bilingual.

7326 Opdahl, Martha Donovan. Esos malditos pafaros! CHIRICU, Vol. 3, no. 1 (1982), p. 45-55. Spanish.

7327 Orihuela, Rodolfo. Por unas plumas. LLUEVE TLALOC, no. 6 (1979), p. 20. Spanish.

7328 Orihuela, Rodolfo. El rio. LLUEVE TLALOC, no. 6 (1979), p. 41. Spanish.

7329 Ortega-Butler, Norma. Marcelina. LLUEVE TLALOC, no. 12 (1985), p. 6. Spanish.

7330 Ortega-Butler, Norma. Padre Anselmo. LLUEVE TLALOC, no. 12 (1985), p. 13. Spanish.

7331 Ortiz Vasquez, Pedro. Las cartas de Martin Flores. SAGUARO, Vol. 3, (1986), p. 1-10. English.

7332 Ospina, Sonia. El recibimiento. REVISTA MUJERES, Vol. 1, no. 2 (June 1984), p. 26-28. Spanish.

7333 Palma, Mauricio. Abuelita. REVISTA MUJERES, Vol. 3, no. 1 (January 1986), p. 25-29. English.

7334 Pavon, Juan Alberto. La historia de mis munequitos. LLUEVE TLALOC, no. 7 (1980), p. 29-30. Spanish.

7335 Pena, Martin. Bueno asi es la vida...la vida sigue. LLUEVE TLALOC, no. 12 (1985), p. 31. Spanish.

7336 Perches, Ana. Erase una tez... hez, bestia, un ajedrez. TINTA, Vol. 1, no. 4 (Summer 1984), p. 33-34. Spanish.

7337 Perches, Ana. Te amare hasta que las flores comiencen a marchitarse. TINTA, Vol. 1, no. 4 (Summer 1984), p. 35-37. Spanish.

7338 Perea, Robert L. Trip to Da Nang. BILINGUAL REVIEW, Vol. 12, no. 1-2 (January, August, 1985), p. 97-102. English.

7339 Perez, Maria. Cosas de la vida. LLUEVE TLALOC, no. 13 (1986), p. 13. Spanish.

7340 Perez, Maria. La momia. LLUEVE TLALOC, no. 13 (1986), p. 9. Spanish.

7341 Peters, Jose. Los antifaces y la cara verdadera. LLUEVE TLALOC, no. 6 (1979), p. 22. Spanish.

7342 Peters, Jose. Las tres bolitas de oro. LLUEVE TLALOC, no. 6 (1979), p. 18. Spanish.

7343 La polvareda. LLUEVE TLALOC, no. 4 (1977), p. 51-54. Spanish.

7344 Ponce, Mary Helen. Las animas. LA COMUNIDAD, No. 341 (February 1, 1987), p. 14. Spanish.

7345 Ponce, Mary Helen. Recuerdo: how I changed the war and won the game. TRABAJOS MONOGRAFICOS, Vol. 3, no. 1 (1987), p. [31]-33. English.

7346 Ponce, Mary Helen. La semana santa. LA COMUNIDAD, No. 305 (May 25, 1986), p. 12-13. Spanish.

7347 Preciado, Consuelo. El don precioso. LA COMUNIDAD, No. 283 (December 22, 1985), p.

10-12. Spanish.

7348 Quintana, Valeria. Almost grown. SAGUARO, Vol. 3, (1986), p. 67-70. English.

7349 Ramirez, Arthur. Book review of: CUENTOS CHICANOS: A SHORT STORY ANTHOLOGY. SAN FRANCISCO REVIEW OF BOOKS, Vol. 11, (1986), p. 11,23. English. **DESCR:** Anaya, Rudolfo A.; Book Reviews; *CUENTOS CHICANOS: A SHORT STORY ANTHOLOGY; Marquez, Antonio.

7350 Ramirez, Petra. Muerte inesperada. LLUEVE TLALOC, no. 14 (1987), p. 43-45. Spanish.

7351 Ramirez, Petra. La silampa. LLUEVE TLALOC, no. 14 (1987), p. 45-47. Spanish.

7352 Ramirez, Petra. El vendado fantasma. LLUEVE TLALOC, no. 14 (1987), p. 47-49. Spanish.

7353 Ramirez, Roberto. Juanito. LLUEVE TLALOC, no. 14 (1987), p. 55-56. Spanish.

7354 Reyes, Sabino. Me pregunto. EL CUADERNO, Vol. 4, no. 1 (Summer 1976), p. 20-23. Spanish.

7355 Reyna, Henry. No mueren los feos. LLUEVE TLALOC, no. 6 (1979), p. 14. Spanish.

7356 Reyna, Hugo. El deforme sin remedio. LLUEVE TLALOC, no. 6 (1979), p. 20. Spanish.

7357 Reyna, Hugo. Los que se hicieron ricos. LLUEVE TLALOC, no. 6 (1979), p. 34. Spanish.

7358 Reyna, Hugo. Quien cuida los animales? LLUEVE TLALOC, no. 7 (1980), p. 37. Spanish.

7359 Reyna, Hugo. Quien toca? LLUEVE TLALOC, no. 7 (1980), p. 21. Spanish.

7360 Rich, Mary Alice. El milagro del amor. LLUEVE TLALOC, no. 14 (1987), p. 69-70. Spanish.

7361 Rich, Mary Alice. Por los callejones. LLUEVE TLALOC, no. 14 (1987), p. 71-72. Spanish.

7362 Rich, Mary Alice. Quiza hoy. LLUEVE TLALOC, no. 14 (1987), p. 72-73. Spanish.

7363 Rivera, Alvaro. A que no me agarran! LLUEVE TLALOC, no. 2 (1975), p. 12-15. Spanish.

7364 Rivera, Alvaro. Bet you can't catch me! LLUEVE TLALOC, no. 2 (1975), p. 16-20. English.

7365 Rivera, Armandina. La vida de santa inocencia. LLUEVE TLALOC, no. 12 (1985), p. 25. Spanish.

7366 Robles, Terra. 1 centavo por cada vote. LLUEVE TLALOC, no. 5 (1978), p. 29. Spanish.

7367 Robles, Terra. 1 penny per can. LLUEVE TLALOC, no. 5 (1978), p. 29. English.

7368 Roche, Sylvia. La palomita y el nino. LLUEVE TLALOC, no. 7 (1980), p. 25. Spanish.

7369 Roche, Sylvia. Un pueblo raro. LLUEVE TLALOC, no. 8 (1981), p. 39. Spanish.

7370 Rodriguez, Alfonso. Manana sera otro dia. SAGUARO, Vol. 4, (1987), p. 71-75. Spanish.

7371 Rodriguez del Pino, Salvador. La Tia Pepita. BILINGUAL REVIEW, Vol. 11, no. 3 (September, December, 1984), p. 49-54. Spanish.

Short Story (cont.)

7372 Rodriguez, Natalia. Gente desperdiciada. LLUEVE TLALOC, no. 8 (1981), p. 20. Spanish.

7373 Rodriguez, Natalia. Los siete candados. LLUEVE TLALOC, no. 8 (1981), p. 1. Spanish.

7374 Rodriguez, Natalia. El viudo. LLUEVE TLALOC, no. 9 (1982), p. 14. Spanish.

7375 Romero, Rolando. Huida de Proteo. TINTA, Vol. 1, no. 2 (May 1983), p. 41-42. Spanish.

7376 Romero, Victor. The land of the lost. THE AMERICAS REVIEW, Vol. 15, no. 1 (Spring 1987), p. 27-31. English.

7377 Ruiz, Raymundo. La danza del venado. LLUEVE TLALOC, no. 11 (1984), p. 1. Spanish.

7378 Ruiz, Ruben. Como es la vida. LLUEVE TLALOC, no. 5 (1978), p. 39. Spanish.

7379 Ruiz, Ruben. Perico. LLUEVE TLALOC, no. 5 (1978), p. 24. Spanish.

7380 Sagel, Jim. El turco. CONFLUENCIA, Vol. 2, no. 1 (Fall 1986), p. 106-107. English.

7381 Salazar, Manuel. La historia de un caminante o sea Gervacio y Aurora. EL CUADERNO, Vol. 4, no. 1 (Summer 1976), p. 100-116. Spanish.

7382 Salinas, Hermenegildo. Recuerdos con una lagunita. CHIRICU, no. 1 (Spring 1976), p. 19-24. Spanish.

7383 Sampayo, Lupe. My father was macho. BILINGUAL REVIEW, Vol. 11, no. 3 (September, December, 1984), p. 55-58. English.

7384 Sanchez, Lupita. La cita. LLUEVE TLALOC, no. 11 (1984), p. 37. Spanish.

7385 Sanchez, Lupita. El relojero. LLUEVE TLALOC, no. 10 (1983), p. 33. Spanish.

7386 Sanchez, Marc. Two rivers. BILINGUAL REVIEW, Vol. 12, no. 1-2 (January, August, 1985), p. 103-107. English.

7387 Sanchez, Maria Isabel. Medianoche. LLUEVE TLALOC, no. 11 (1984), p. 22. Spanish.

7388 Sanchez, Rosaura. El Rudy. BILINGUAL REVIEW, Vol. 12, no. 1-2 (January, August, 1985), p. 81-89. Spanish.

7389 Sancho. Quetzalcoatl for governor. NOTEBOOK: A LITTLE MAGAZINE, Vol. 2, no. 2 (1986), p. 4-8. English.

7390 Sandoval, Maria. Por aqui pueden pasar. SAGUARO, Vol. 2, (1985), p. 59-64. Spanish.

7391 Sepulveda, Concha. A brother's pride. NOTEBOOK: A LITTLE MAGAZINE, Vol. 3, no. 1 (1987), p. 6-8. English.

7392 Sepulveda, Jose. Tragico accidente ocurre en un pueblito. LLUEVE TLALOC, no. 4 (1977), p. 105-106. Spanish.

7393 Shipley, Sydney. Animales contra maquinas. LLUEVE TLALOC, no. 13 (1986), p. 13. Spanish.

7394 Skinner, Jose. Color conspiracy in Honduras. CHIRICU, Vol. 4, no. 1 (1985), p. ,133-139. English.

7395 Soto, Gary. Dining in Fresno. PUERTO DEL SOL, Vol. 23, no. 1 (1987), p. 84-86.

English.

7396 Soto, Gary. How we stand. PUERTO DEL SOL, Vol. 23, no. 1 (1987), p. 81-83. English.

7397 Stromei, Angelina. Que habra pasado con la mujer de Chabolas? LLUEVE TLALOC, no. 9 (1982), p. 24-25. Bilingual.

7398 Tafolla, Carmen. Chencho's cow. SAGUARO, Vol. 4, (1987), p. 1-8. English.

7399 Tafoya, Edward. You can't drive to Aztlan. EL CUADERNO, Vol. 3, no. 1 (Winter 1973), p. 15. English.

7400 Talavera, Richard. Lost dogs, free puppies. SAGUARO, Vol. 3, (1986), p. 40-54. English.

7401 Tapia, Fernando. El suceso. SAGUARO, Vol. 2, (1985), p. 72-74. Spanish.

7402 Teheran, Jose. Ray Five Mendoza. SAGUARO, Vol. 2, (1985), p. 1-7. Spanish.

7403 Tijerino, Eduardo. El Manta Blanca. LLUEVE TLALOC, no. 8 (1981), p. 3. Spanish.

7404 Tobias, Margarita. No more corn tortillas. SAGUARO, Vol. 2, (1985), p. 18-20. English.

7405 Trevino, Mario. Sigues teniendo diecisiete anos para mi. LLUEVE TLALOC, no. 6 (1979), p. 11. Spanish.

7406 Valadez, I. Teodoro. LLUEVE TLALOC, no. 6 (1979), p. 11. Spanish.

7407 Varela, Graciela. La lecherita. LLUEVE TLALOC, no. 9 (1982), p. 14. Spanish.

7408 Vigil, Cleofes. El fletero y el ranchero. EL CUADERNO, Vol. 2, no. 1 (1972), p. 41-43. Spanish.

7409 Villar, Ysis. La esclava y los ninos. LLUEVE TLALOC, no. 14 (1987), p. 77. Spanish.

7410 Viramontes, Helen Maria. Miss Clairol. THE AMERICAS REVIEW, Vol. 15, no. 3-4 (Fall, Winter, 1987), p. 101-105. English.

7411 Vogt, Gregory M. Archetypal images of apocalypse in Miguel Mendez's TATA CASEHUA. CONFLUENCIA, Vol. 1, no. 2 (Spring 1986), p. 55-60. English. **DESCR:** *Literary Criticism; *Mendez M., Miguel; *"Tata Casehua" [short story].

7412 Wolfson, Mark. Caperucita Roja y yo. CHIRICU, no. 2 (Spring 1977), p. 27. Spanish.

7413 Wood, Silviana. Una canasta para los pobres. SAGUARO, Vol. 1, no. 1 (1984), p. 22-30. Spanish.

7414 Ynclan, Maria Estela. Olvidaba todo. LLUEVE TLALOC, no. 7 (1980), p. 12. Spanish.

7415 Zamorano, Christina. Celina. LLUEVE TLALOC, no. 11 (1984), p. 18-19. Spanish.

Shue, Henry

7416 Chernick, Marc W. Book review of: THE BORDER THAT JOINS: MEXICAN MIGRANTS AND U.S. RESPONSIBILITY. POLITICAL SCIENCE QUARTERLY, Vol. 99, (Spring 1984), p. 133. English. **DESCR:** Book Reviews; Brown, Peter G.; *THE BORDER THAT JOINS: MEXICAN MIGRANTS AND U.S. RESPONSIBILITY.

Shue, Henry (cont.)

7417 Zolberg, A.R. Book review of: THE BORDER
THAT JOINS: MEXICAN MIGRANTS AND U.S.
RESPONSIBILITY. ETHICS, Vol. 94, no. 3
(April 1984), p. 568. English. **DESCR:** Book
Reviews; Brown, Peter G.; *THE BORDER THAT
JOINS: MEXICAN MIGRANTS AND U.S.
RESPONSIBILITY.

EL SIGLO DE LAS LUCES

7418 Toruno, Rhina. El protagonista verdadero de
EL SIGLO DE LAS LUCES de Alejo Carpentier.
CHIRICU, Vol. 4, no. 1 (1985), p. 19-39.
Spanish. **DESCR:** Carpentier, Alejo; Literary
Criticism; Novel.

THE SILENCE OF THE LLANO

7419 Gonzalez, LaVerne. Book review of: THE
SILENCE OF THE LLANO. THE AMERICAS REVIEW,
Vol. 15, no. 2 (Summer 1987), p. 109-111.
English. **DESCR:** Anaya, Rudolfo A.; Book
Reviews.

Silva, Beverly

7420 Paredes, Raymund A. Review essay: recent
Chicano writing. ROCKY MOUNTAIN REVIEW OF
LANGUAGE AND LITERATURE, Vol. 41, (1987),
p. 124-129. English. **DESCR:** Castillo, Ana;
Catholic Church; Chavez, Denise; Chicanas;
Garcia, Lionel; GIVING UP THE GHOST; LEAVING
HOME; *Literary Criticism; *Literature
Reviews; Moraga, Cherrie; Poetry; Prose; Sex
Roles; SMALL FACES; Soto, Gary; THE CAT AND
OTHER STORIES; THE LAST OF THE MENU GIRLS;
THE MIXQUIAHUALA LETTERS.

7421 Tafolla, Carmen. Book review of: THE SECOND
ST. POEMS. LA RED/THE NET, no. 83 (August
1984), p. 4-6. English. **DESCR:** Book Reviews;
*THE SECOND ST. POEMS.

Silva, Juan

7422 SHPE news. HISPANIC ENGINEER, Vol. 3, no. 3
(1987), p. 10-13. English. **DESCR:** *Awards;
Castillo, Hector; Colmenarez, Margarita;
Garcia, Raul; Herrera, Jess; Lopez-Martin,
Minnie; Mondragon, Ricardo; Reyes-Guerra,
David; Society of Hispanic Professional
Engineers (SHPE); Vargas, Jesus; Villanueva,
Bernadette.

"Silver Lake Road" [short story]

7423 Herrera-Sobek, Maria. The politics of rape:
sexual transgression in Chicana fiction. THE
AMERICAS REVIEW, Vol. 15, no. 3-4 (Fall,
Winter, 1987), p. 171-181. English. **DESCR:**
*Chicanas; Cisneros, Sandra; *Feminism;
Fiction; GIVING UP THE GHOST; *Literary
Criticism; Lizarraga, Sylvia; Moraga,
Cherrie; *Rape; "Red Clowns" [short story];
Sex Roles.

Silvis, IL

7424 Brower, Monty. A proud street mourns its
fallen sons. PEOPLE WEEKLY, Vol. 21, (May
28, 1984), p. 76-78+. English. **DESCR:**
*Military; Sandoval, Frank; Sandoval,
Joseph; *World War II.

Simoni-Abbat, Mireille

7425 Book review of: LE MEXIQUE, DES ORIGINES AUX
AZTEQUES. OEIL-REVUE D'ART MENSUELLE,
(December 1986), p. 75. Other. **DESCR:**
Aztecs; Bernal y Garcia Pimentel, Ignacio;
Book Reviews; *LE MEXIQUE, DES ORIGENES AUX
AZTEQUES.

Simpson, Alan K.

7426 Bethell, Tom. Senator Simpson's reward.
AMERICAN SPECTATOR, Vol. 19, no. 2 (February
1986), p. 11-13. English. **DESCR:**
Discrimination; Immigration Law and
Legislation; Politics; Undocumented Workers.

Simpson-Mazzoli Bill

7427 Faxon, R. Paul. Employer sanctions for
hiring illegal aliens: a simplistic solution
to a complex problem. NORTHWESTERN JOURNAL
OF INTERNATIONAL LAW AND BUSINESS, Vol. 6,
(Spring 1984), p. 203-248. English. **DESCR:**
Agribusiness; Immigration Law and
Legislation; National Labor Relations Board
(NLRB); *Undocumented Workers.

7428 Flores, Estevan T. 1982 Simpson-Mazzoli
immigration reform and the Hispanic
community. LA RED/THE NET, no. 64 (February
1983), p. 14-16. English. **DESCR:**
*Immigration Law and Legislation.

7429 Gunderson, Kay. White does about-face on
Simpson-Mazzoli. TEXAS OBSERVOR, Vol. 75,
(March 25, 1983), p. 4. English. **DESCR:**
*Immigration Law and Legislation; League of
United Latin American Citizens (LULAC);
Texas; White, Mark.

Simpson-Rodino Bill

7430 Mosqueda, Lawrence Joseph. How to keep a bad
bill from getting worse. GUARDIAN, Vol. 38,
no. 46 (September 24, 1986), p. 5. English.
DESCR: Immigration and Naturalization
Service (INS); *Immigration Law and
Legislation; Immigration Regulation and
Control; Undocumented Workers.

7431 Novick, Michael. INS makes a bad
Simpson-Rodino law worse. GUARDIAN, Vol. 39,
no. 16 (January 21, 1987), p. 5. English.
DESCR: *Immigration Law and Legislation;
*Immigration Reform and Control Act of 1986;
Undocumented Workers.

7432 Roth, Michael. Panic and fear in Latino
communities. GUARDIAN, Vol. 39, no. 8
(November 19, 1986), p. 10-11. English.
DESCR: *Immigration Law and Legislation;
Undocumented Workers.

7433 Vanderpool, Tim. Immigration reform crosses
an uncertain border into law. IN THESE
TIMES, Vol. 11, no. 6 (December 17, 1986),
p. 5, 7. English. **DESCR:** Immigration and
Naturalization Service (INS); Immigration
Law and Legislation; *Immigration Reform and
Control Act of 1986; Undocumented Workers.

Sisneros, Federico

7434 Holmes, John J. Sentinel of tradition.
VISTA, Vol. 3, no. 3 (November 8, 1987), p.
16. English. **DESCR:** *Missions; New Mexico;
*San Gregorio de Abo (Salinas National
Monument, NM).

Skin Color

7435 Arce, Carlos H.; Murguia, Edward; and
Frisbie, William Parker. Phenotype and life
chances among Chicanos. HISPANIC JOURNAL OF
BEHAVIORAL SCIENCES, Vol. 9, no. 1 (March
1987), p. 19-32. English. **DESCR:**
*Discrimination; National Chicano Survey
(NCS); Social Classes; *Socioeconomic
Factors.

Skin Color (cont.)

7436 Herrera, Irma D. The color barrier to full
     equality. VISTA, Vol. 1, no. 6 (February 2,
     1986), p. 3. English. **DESCR:** Discrimination.

7437 Korzenny, Felipe and Schiff, Elizabeth.
     Hispanic perceptions of communication
     discrimination. HISPANIC JOURNAL OF
     BEHAVIORAL SCIENCES, Vol. 9, no. 1 (March,
     1987), p. 33-48. English. **DESCR:** Accentedness;
     *Discrimination; *Intercultural
     Communication.

7438 Lawlor, William T. Ethnic identification:
     shades of gray in living color. VISTA, Vol.
     2, no. 11 (May 7, 1987), p. 21. English.
     DESCR: *Identity.

Slang

7439 Hopper, Richard H. The road from Mexico's
     Jalapa to jalopies. VISTA, Vol. 2, no. 11
     (July 5, 1987), p. 16. English. **DESCR:**
     *Jalapa, Veracruz, Mexico.

7440 Mendoza, Agapito. Barrio slang has value as
     communications tool. VISTA, Vol. 2, no. 12
     (August 1, 1987), p. 29. English. **DESCR:**
     *Chicano Dialects.

Sleepy Lagoon Case

7441 Sanchez Tranquilino, Marcos. Un ensayo sobre
     la representacion del ZOOT SUIT en la obra
     de Octavio Paz. LA COMUNIDAD, No. 355 (May
     10, 1987), p. 4-7+. Spanish. **DESCR:** Los
     Angeles, CA; *Pachucos; *Paz, Octavio; THE
     LABYRINTH OF SOLITUDE: LIFE AND THOUGHT IN
     MEXICO; Zoot Suit Riots, Los Angeles, CA,
     1943.

SMALL BONES, LITTLE EYES

7442 Avalos, Francisco. Book review of: SMALL
     BONES, LITTLE EYES. LECTOR, Vol. 4, no. 1-3
     (1986), p. [60]. English. **DESCR:** Book
     Reviews; NorthSun, Nila; Sagel, Jim.

Small Business Administration 8(a) Program

7443 SBA procurements dropping off. HISPANIC
     BUSINESS, Vol. 9, no. 5 (May 1987), p. 41.
     English. **DESCR:** *Business Enterprises;
     *Government Contracts.

7444 Sellers, Jeff M. Wedtech fallout hits 8(a)
     program. HISPANIC BUSINESS, Vol. 9, no. 6
     (June 1987), p. 12-13, 17. English. **DESCR:**
     *Business Enterprises; Government Contracts;
     *Wedtech Corporation, Bronx, NY.

SMALL FACES

7445 Fields, Alicia. Small but telling moments.
     THE BLOOMSBURY REVIEW, no. 1-2 (1987), p.
     10. English. **DESCR:** Book Reviews; Soto,
     Gary.

7446 Laguna Diaz, Elpidio. Book review of: SMALL
     FACES. VISTA, Vol. 1, no. 11 (July 6, 1986),
     p. 16. English. **DESCR:** Book Reviews; Soto,
     Gary.

7447 Molina, Ida. Book review of: SMALL FACES.
     CHOICE, Vol. 24, no. 2 (October 1986), p.
     310-311. English. **DESCR:** Book Reviews; Soto,
     Gary.

7448 Paredes, Raymund A. Review essay: recent
     Chicano writing. ROCKY MOUNTAIN REVIEW OF
     LANGUAGE AND LITERATURE, Vol. 41, (1987),
     p. 124-129. English. **DESCR:** Castillo, Ana;
     Catholic Church; Chavez, Denise; Chicanas;
     Garcia, Lionel; GIVING UP THE GHOST; LEAVING
     HOME; *Literary Criticism; *Literature
     Reviews; Moraga, Cherrie; Poetry; Prose; Sex
     Roles; Silva, Beverly; Soto, Gary; THE CAT
     AND OTHER STORIES; THE LAST OF THE MENU
     GIRLS; THE MIXQUIAHUALA LETTERS.

7449 Quinn, Mary Ellen. Book review of: SMALL
     FACES. BOOKLIST, Vol. 82, no. 21 (July
     1986), p. 1582. English. **DESCR:** Book
     Reviews; Soto, Gary.

Smithsonian Institution Traveling Exhibition Service

7450 Mexico as seen by her children. VISTA, Vol.
     1, no. 8 (April 6, 1986), p. 12-13. English.
     DESCR: *Children's Art.

Smithsonian Institute

7451 Halley, Lindsey. Pachuco boggie [sic]. LA
     COMUNIDAD, No. 305 (May 25, 1986), p. 8-9.
     Spanish. **DESCR:** Cano, Eddie; Diaz, R ul;
     History; *Music; Ovalle, John; *PACHUCO
     BOOGIE; The Record Inn, East Los Angeles,
     CA; Tosti, Don.

Smoking

7452 Marcus, Alfred C. and Crane, Lori A. Smoking
     behavior among Hispanics: a preliminary
     report. PROGRESS IN CLINICAL AND BIOLOGICAL
     RESEARCH, Vol. 156, (1984), p. 141-151.
     English. **DESCR:** *Public Health.

"Snapshots" [short story]

7453 Alarcon, Norma. Making "familia" from
     scratch: split subjectivities in the work of
     Helena Maria Viramontes and Cherrie Moraga.
     THE AMERICAS REVIEW, Vol. 15. no. 3-4 (Fall,
     Winter, 1987), p. 147-159. English. **DESCR:**
     Chicanas; GIVING UP THE GHOST; *Literary
     Criticism; *Moraga, Cherrie; *Sex Roles; THE
     MOTHS AND OTHER STORIES; *Viramontes, Helen.

Social Bandits
     USE: Bandidos

Social Classes

7454 Anderson, John W. The effects of culture and
     social class on client preference for
     counseling methods. JOURNAL OF NON-WHITE
     CONCERNS IN PERSONNEL AND GUIDANCE, Vol. 11.
     no. 3 (April 1983), p. 84-88. English.
     DESCR: *Counseling (Psychological); Cultural
     Characteristics; Ethnic Groups.

7455 Arce, Carlos H.; Murguia, Edward; and
     Frisbie, William Parker. Phenotype and life
     chances among Chicanos. HISPANIC JOURNAL OF
     BEHAVIORAL SCIENCES, Vol. 9, no. 1 (March
     1987), p. 19-32. English. **DESCR:**
     *Discrimination; National Chicano Survey
     (NCS); *Skin Color; *Socioeconomic Factors.

7456 Goldman, Shifra. Arte chicano: iconografia
     de la autodeterminacion. LA COMUNIDAD, No.
     336 (December 28, 1986), p. 12-14+. Spanish.
     DESCR: *Art; Discrimination; EL PLAN
     ESPIRITUAL DE AZTLAN; History; Identity;
     Nationalism; Pachucos; *Symbolism.

Social Classes (cont.)

7457 Gutierrez, Ramon A. Honor ideology, marriage negotiation, and class-gender domination in New Mexico, 1690-1846. LATIN AMERICAN PERSPECTIVES, Vol. 12, no. 1 (Winter 1985), p. 81-104. English. **DESCR**: Marriage; Sex Roles; Social History and Conditions; *Southwestern United States; Values; Women Men Relations.

7458 Torres-Gil, Fernando. The Latinization of a multigenerational population: Hispanics in an aging society. DAEDALUS, Vol. 115, no. 1 (Winter 1986), p. 325-348. English. **DESCR**: *Age Groups; Cultural Pluralism; Population; *Public Policy; Socioeconomic Factors.

Social History and Conditions

7459 Alvarado, Raul. Another "decade of the Hispanic"? HISPANIC ENGINEER, Vol. 3, no. 1 (Spring 1987), p. 10-11. English. **DESCR**: *Engineering as a Profession; *Society of Hispanic Professional Engineers (SHPE).

7460 Arce, Carlos H. Book review of: CHICANOS IN A CHANGING SOCIETY. LA RED/THE NET, no. 30 (May 1980), p. 8. English. **DESCR**: Book Reviews; Camarillo, Alberto; CHICANOS IN A CHANGING SOCIETY; History; *Santa Barbara, CA; *Southern California.

7461 Architects of America's future. VISTA, Vol. 1, no. 11 (July 6, 1986), p. 10. English. **DESCR**: *Conferences and Meetings; National Council of La Raza (NCLR); *Yzaguirre, Raul.

7462 Arreola, Daniel D. The Mexican American cultural capital. GEOGRAPHICAL REVIEW, Vol. 77, (January 1987), p. 17-34. English. **DESCR**: Conjuntos; Food Industry; History; Immigration; LA PRENSA, San Antonio, TX; La Raza Unida Party; League of United Latin American Citizens (LULAC); Lozano, Ignacio; Mexican American Youth Organization, San Antonio, TX; Music; Orden Hijos de America, San Antonio, TX; Railroads; *San Antonio, TX.

7463 The California Museum of Latino History=El Museo de California de la Historia de los Latinos. AMERICAS 2001, Premiere Issue, 1987, p. 18-19, 39. Bilingual. **DESCR**: Calderon, Charles M.; *California Museum of Latino History; History; *Museums; Rios-Bustamante, Antonio.

7464 Communist Party, U.S.A. On Chicano/Mexican-American equality. POLITICAL AFFAIRS, Vol. 66, no. 4 (April 1987), p. 35. English. **DESCR**: Communist Party; *Discrimination; Political Ideology.

7465 de Leon, Arnoldo and Stewart, Kenneth L. A tale of 3 cities: a comparative analysis of the socio-economic conditions of Mexican-Americans in Los Angeles, Tucson, and San Antonio, 1850-1900. JOURNAL OF THE WEST, Vol. 24, no. 2 (1985), p. 64-74. English. **DESCR**: Economic History and Conditions; Employment; Griswold del Castillo, Richard; Labor; *Los Angeles, CA; San Antonio, TX; Tucson, AZ; Urban Communities.

7466 de Leon, Arnoldo. Tejano history scholarship: a review of the recent literature. WEST TEXAS HISTORICAL ASSOCIATION YEARBOOK, Vol. 61, (1985), p. 116-133. English. **DESCR**: Historiography; *Literature Reviews; Political History and Conditions; *Texas.

7467 Garibay, Ricardo. Una frontera de lujo y hambre [excerpt]. LA COMUNIDAD, No. 318 (August 24, 1986), p. 6-7. Spanish. **DESCR**: *Border Region; *Tijuana, Baja California. Mexico.

7468 Griswold del Castillo, Richard. Book review of: HISPANICS IN THE UNITED STATES: A NEW SOCIAL AGENDA. JOURNAL OF AMERICAN ETHNIC HISTORY, Vol. 6, no. 1 (Fall 1986), p. 112-114. English. **DESCR**: Book Reviews; *HISPANICS IN THE UNITED STATES: A NEW SOCIAL AGENDA; McCready, William C.; San Juan Cafferty, Pastora.

7469 Griswold del Castillo, Richard. Familism, the extended family and Chicanos in the nineteenth century. LA RED/THE NET, no. 49 (December 1981), p. 2. English. **DESCR**: *Extended Family; *Family; Los Angeles, CA; *Nineteenth century; San Antonio, TX; Santa Fe, NM; Tucson, AZ.

7470 Griswold del Castillo, Richard. Quantitative history in the American Southwest: a survey and critique. WESTERN HISTORICAL QUARTERLY, Vol. 15, no. 4 (October 1984), p. 407-426. English. **DESCR**: Economic History and Conditions; Historiography; History; *Southwestern United States.

7471 Gutierrez, Ramon A. Honor ideology, marriage negotiation, and class-gender domination in New Mexico, 1690-1846. LATIN AMERICAN PERSPECTIVES, Vol. 12. no. 1 (Winter 1985), p. 81-104. English. **DESCR**: Marriage; Sex Roles; *Social Classes; *Southwestern United States; Values; Women Men Relations.

7472 Hurtado, Aida. Book review of: WORK, FAMILY, SEX ROLES, LANGUAGE. LA RED/THE NET, no. 40 (March 1981), p. 3. English. **DESCR**: Barrera, Mario; Book Reviews; Camarillo, Alberto; Hernandez, Francisco; *WORK, FAMILY, SEX ROLES, LANGUAGE: SELECTED PAPERS OF THE NATIONAL ASSOCIATION FOR CHICANO STUDIES CONFERENCE, 1979.

7473 Luckingham, Bradford. The American Southwest: an urban view. WESTERN HISTORICAL QUARTERLY, Vol. 15, no. 3 (July 1984), p. 261-280. English. **DESCR**: Albuquerque, NM; El Paso, TX; Phoenix, AZ; *Southwestern United States; Tucson, AZ; *Urban Communities; Urban Economics.

7474 Melville, Margarita B. Book review of: FROM INDIANS TO CHICANOS. LA RED/THE NET, no. 45 (August 1981), p. 3. English. **DESCR**: Book Reviews; *FROM INDIANS TO CHICANOS: A SOCIOCULTURAL HISTORY; Vigil, James Diego.

7475 Milo, Albert J. Book review of: HISTORY, CULTURE, AND SOCIETY. LECTOR, Vol. 4, no. 4-6 (1987), p. 55. English. **DESCR**: Book Reviews; *HISTORY, CULTURE, AND SOCIETY: CHICANO STUDIES IN THE 1980s; National Association for Chicano Studies (NACS).

7476 Miranda, Gloria E. Book review of: CHICANOS IN CALIFORNIA. SOUTHERN CALIFORNIA QUARTERLY, Vol. 67, no. 4 (Winter 1985), p. 474-476. English. **DESCR**: Book Reviews; Camarillo, Alberto; *CHICANOS IN CALIFORNIA.

7477 Quintanilla, Guadalupe. Dropping out of school. VISTA, Vol. 2, no. 1 (September 7, 1986), p. 12-14. English. **DESCR**: *Dropouts; Educational Statistics; Language Interference.

Social History and Conditions (cont.)

7478 Remas, Theodora A. Down and blue. VISTA, Vol. 2, no. 5 (January 4, 1987), p. 16-18. English. **DESCR:** Counseling (Psychological); *Depression (Psychological); *National Institute of Mental Health; Spanish Family Guidance Clinic, Miami, FL.

7479 Romo, Ricardo. Book review of: OCCUPIED AMERICA. LA RED/THE NET, no. 39 (February 1981), p. 3. English. **DESCR:** *Acuna, Rudolfo; Book Reviews; History; *OCCUPIED AMERICA.

7480 Rosenfeld, Jose. Hispanic issues and challenges. PUBLIC MANAGEMENT, Vol. 67, (March 1985), p. 12-16. English. **DESCR:** *Public Administration; Social Services.

7481 Tryon, Roy H. Book review of: THE HISPANICS IN THE UNITED STATES: A HISTORY. LIBRARY JOURNAL, Vol. 111, no. 18 (November 1, 1986), p. 107. English. **DESCR:** Book Reviews; Duignan, Peter J.; Gann, L.H.; *HISPANICS IN THE UNITED STATES: A HISTORY.

7482 Valdes, Dennis. Book review of: THE LOS ANGELES BARRIO 1850-1890: A SOCIAL HISTORY. LA RED/THE NET, no. 36 (November 1980), p. 5. English. **DESCR:** Book Reviews; Griswold del Castillo, Richard; History; *Los Angeles, CA; *THE LOS ANGELES BARRIO 1850-1890: A SOCIAL HISTORY.

7483 Valdez, Avelardo. Book review of: THE CHICANO EXPERIENCE. JOURNAL OF AMERICAN ETHNIC HISTORY, Vol. 6, no. 2 (Spring 1987), p. 98-101. English. **DESCR:** Book Reviews; Mirande, Alfredo; *THE CHICANO EXPERIENCE: AN ALTERNATIVE PERSPECTIVE.

7484 Valdez, Lorenzo. Labor history in the villages. EL CUADERNO, Vol. 3, no. 2 (Spring 1974), p. 54-63. English. **DESCR:** *Economic History and Conditions; *Labor; *New Mexico.

7485 Weas, Andrea T. Book review of: THE CHICANO STRUGGLE. LECTOR, Vol. 4, no. 4-6 (1987), p. 54. English. **DESCR:** Book Reviews; National Association for Chicano Studies (NACS); *THE CHICANO STRUGGLE: ANALYSES OF PAST AND PRESENT EFFORTS.

Social Mobility

7486 Briody, Elizabeth K. Patterns of household immigration into South Texas. INTERNATIONAL MIGRATION REVIEW, Vol. 21, no. 1 (Spring 1987), p. 27-47. English. **DESCR:** Chicanas; *Family; *Immigrants; Sex Roles; *South Texas.

7487 Massey, Douglas S. and Mullan, Brendan P. Processes of Hispanic and Black spatial assimilation. AMERICAN JOURNAL OF SOCIOLOGY, Vol. 89, no. 4 (January 1984), p. 836-873. English. **DESCR:** Assimilation; Blacks; Census; *Ethnic Stratification; *Residential Segregation.

Social Organizations
USE: Cultural Organizations

Social Psychology

7488 Diaz-Guerrero, Rogelio. Psychology for the Mexican or the masses? PSYCHOLOGY: A QUARTERLY JOURNAL OF HUMAN BEHAVIOR, Vol. 21, no. 2 (1984), p. 1-7. English. **DESCR:** Psychology.

Social Science

7489 Campbell, Duane. How the grinch stole the social sciences: moving teaching to the right in California. JOURNAL OF THE ASSOCIATION OF MEXICAN AMERICAN EDUCATORS, (1986, 1987), p. 43-50. English. **DESCR:** Education.

7490 DeSipio, Louis. Social science literature and the naturalization process. INTERNATIONAL MIGRATION REVIEW, Vol. 21, no. 2 (Summer 1987), p. 390-405. English. **DESCR:** Immigrants; *Naturalization; *Research Methodology.

7491 Wreford, Mary. Reactions from the Chicano Survey respondents: no mas silencio. LA RED/THE NET, no. 33 (August 1980), p. 2-3. English. **DESCR:** Chicano Project of the University of Michigan; Midwestern States; *National Chicano Survey (NCS); *Public Opinion; Southwestern United States; *Surveys.

Social Science Research Council

7492 Hispanic inter-university program grants awarded to 17 projects. LA RED/THE NET, no. 92 (November, December, 1985), p. 7-9. English. **DESCR:** Committee on Public Policy Research on Contemporary Hispanic Issues; *Ford Foundation; Funding Sources; Inter-University Program for Latino Research.

Social Services

7493 Cuellar, Jose and Weeks, John R. Hispanic elders' needs, problems and access to public benefits and services. LA RED/THE NET, no. 36 (November 1980), p. 2,16. English. **DESCR:** *Ancianos; *San Diego, CA.

7494 Lacayo, Carmela G. Triple jeopardy among Hispanic elderly: results from first national needs assessment of older Hispanics. LA RED/THE NET, no. 56 (July 1982), p. 2-3. English. **DESCR:** *Ancianos; Asociacion Nacional Pro Personas Mayores; *National Study to Assess the Service Needs of the Hispanic Elderly; Research Methodology; Surveys.

7495 Ramirez, Oscar. Book review of: HUMAN SERVICES FOR MEXICAN-AMERICAN CHILDREN. LA RED/THE NET, no. 55 (June 1982), p. 7-8. English. **DESCR:** Book Reviews; *Children; *Tijerina, Andres A.

7496 Rosenfeld, Jose. Hispanic issues and challenges. PUBLIC MANAGEMENT, Vol. 67, (March 1985), p. 12-16. English. **DESCR:** *Public Administration; Social History and Conditions.

7497 Yzaguirre, Raul. Task force on social services and community development. LA RED/THE NET, no. 88 (Winter 1984), p. 10-14. English. **DESCR:** *Community Development; *Public Policy.

Social Stratification
USE: Social Classes

Social Studies
USE: Social Science

Social Work

7498 Delgado, Melvin and Humm-Delgado, Denise. Hispanics and group work: a review of the literature. SOCIAL WORK WITH GROUPS, Vol. 7, no. 3 (Fall 1984), p. 85-96. English. DESCR: *Literature Reviews; *Psychotherapy.

7499 Hardy-Fanta, Carol. Social action in Hispanic groups. SOCIAL WORK, Vol. 31, no. 2 (March, April, 1986), p. 119-123. English. DESCR: *Community Organizations; Natural Support Systems; Psychotherapy.

Socialization

7500 Jimenez, Ricardo. Understanding the culture and learning styles of Hispanic students. MOMENTUM, Vol. 14, no. 1 (February 1983), p. 15-18. English. DESCR: *Acculturation; Religious Education; Students.

7501 Miranda, Gloria E. Hispano-Mexican childrearing practices in pre-American Santa Barbara. SOUTHERN CALIFORNIA QUARTERLY, Vol. 65, no. 4 (Winter 1983), p. 307-320. English. DESCR: *Children; Cultural Characteristics; *Family; History; *Parenting; *Santa Barbara, CA.

Society of Hispanic Professional Engineers (SHPE)

7502 Alvarado, Raul. Another "decade of the Hispanic"? HISPANIC ENGINEER, Vol. 3, no. 1 (Spring 1987), p. 10-11. English. DESCR: *Engineering as a Profession; Social History and Conditions.

7503 Gonzalez, Lawrence F. The University of Illinois, Chicago. HISPANIC ENGINEER, Vol. 3, no. 3 (1987), p. 34-36. English. DESCR: Association of Minority Engineers (AME); Colleges and Universities; *University of Illinois, Chicago, IL.

7504 Scenes from the February SHPE careers conference. HISPANIC ENGINEER, Vol. 3, no. 1 (Spring 1987), p. 14-15. English. DESCR: *Conferences and Meetings; Guerrero, Art; *Salazar, Diane.

7505 SHPE holds first ever East coast conference for Hispanic engineers. HISPANIC ENGINEER, Vol. 3, no. 5 (Winter 1987), p. 12-14. English. DESCR: Awards; Barrios, Eugene; Chang-Diaz, Franklin; *Conferences and Meetings; Cuevas, Brian L.; Garay, Charles J.; Garcia, Ray; Marrero, Charles; Martinez, Lisa; Monteverde, Edwin; Plumey, Raymond; Reyes-Guerra, David; Rivera, Angel; Soto, Giovanni.

7506 SHPE news. HISPANIC ENGINEER, Vol. 3, no. 3 (1987), p. 10-13. English. DESCR: *Awards; Castillo, Hector; Colmenarez, Margarita; Garcia, Raul; Herrera, Jess; Lopez-Martin, Minnie; Mondragon, Ricardo; Reyes-Guerra, David; Silva, Juan; Vargas, Jesus; Villanueva, Bernadette.

Society of Hispanic Professional Engineers Northern California Chapter

7507 Ricardo Salazar. HISPANIC ENGINEER, Vol. 3, no. 2 (Summer), p. 14-18. English. DESCR: Biography; Magic of Science and Engineering Program; Professional Organizations; *Salazar, Ricardo.

Socioeconomic Factors

7508 Arce, Carlos H.; Murguia, Edward; and Frisbie, William Parker. Phenotype and life chances among Chicanos. HISPANIC JOURNAL OF BEHAVIORAL SCIENCES, Vol. 9, no. 1 (March 1987), p. 19-32. English. DESCR: *Discrimination; National Chicano Survey (NCS); *Skin Color; Social Classes.

7509 Cook, Annabel Kirschner. Diversity among Northwest Hispanics. SOCIAL SCIENCE JOURNAL, Vol. 23, no. 2 (April 1986), p. 205-216. English. DESCR: Chicanas; *Northwestern United States; *Population; Working Women.

7510 Fernandez, Edward and Cresce, Arthur R. The Hispanic foreign-born and the assimilation experience. MIGRATION WORLD MAGAZINE, Vol. 14, no. 5 (1986), p. 7-11. English. DESCR: *Assimilation; *Immigrants; Naturalization; Undocumented Workers.

7511 Garcia, Steve. Language usage and status attainment of Chicanos. LA RED/THE NET, no. 30 (May 1980), p. 2-3. English. DESCR: *Language Usage; *SURVEY OF INCOME AND EDUCATION, 1976.

7512 Slatta, Richard W. and Atkinson, Maxine P. The "Spanish origin" population of Oregon and Washington: a demographic profile, 1980. PACIFIC NORTHWEST QUARTERLY, Vol. 75, no. 3 (July 1984), p. 108-116. English. DESCR: *Oregon; *Population; Self-Referents; Statistics; *Washington (state).

7513 Torres-Gil, Fernando. The Latinization of a multigenerational population: Hispanics in an aging society. DAEDALUS, Vol. 115, no. 1 (Winter 1986), p. 325-348. English. DESCR: *Age Groups; Cultural Pluralism; Population; *Public Policy; Social Classes.

Sociolinguistics

7514 Aguirre, Adalberto, Jr. Book review of: CHICANO SOCIOLINGUISTICS. LA RED/THE NET, no. 51 (February 1982), p. 3-4. English. DESCR: Book Reviews; Chicano Dialects; *CHICANO SOCIOLINGUISTICS; *Language Usage; *Penalosa, Fernando.

7515 Duran, Richard P. Book review of: CHICANO SOCIOLINGUISTICS. LA RED/THE NET, no. 35 (October 1980), p. 3. English. DESCR: Book Reviews; Chicano Dialects; CHICANO SOCIOLINGUISTICS; *Language Usage; *Penalosa, Fernando.

7516 Fishman, Joshua A. What is happening to Spanish on the U.S. mainland? ETHNIC AFFAIRS, no. 1 (Fall 1987), p. [12]-23. English. DESCR: *Language Usage; *Spanish Language.

7517 Hidalgo, Margarita. On the question of "standard" versus "dialect": implications for teaching Hispanic college students. HISPANIC JOURNAL OF BEHAVIORAL SCIENCES. Vol. 9, no. 4 (December 1987), p. 375-395. English. DESCR: Bilingualism; Chicano Dialects; *Foreign Language Instruction; Language Usage; Puerto Ricans; Spanish for Native Speakers; *Spanish Language.

7518 Jimenez, Francisco. Book review of: CHICANO DISCOURSE. LECTOR, Vol. 4, no. 4-6 (1987), p. 55. English. DESCR: Book Reviews; *CHICANO DISCOURSE: SOCIOHISTORIC PERSPECTIVE; Sanchez, Rosaura.

7519 Koike, Dale April. Theoretical linguistics: code-switching in the bilingual Chicano narrative. THE AMERICAN MERCURY, Vol. 70, no. 1 (March 1987), p. 148-154. English. DESCR: Bilingualism; Language Usage; *Linguistic Theory.

Sociolinguistics (cont.)

7520 Nuessel, Frank H., Jr. Book review of: SPANISH IN THE UNITED STATES: SOCIOLINGUISTIC ASPECTS. LINGUA, Vol. 62, no. 3 (1984), p. 247-255. English. DESCR: Amastae, Jon; Book Reviews; Elias-Olivares, Lucia; *SPANISH IN THE UNITED STATES: SOCIOLINGUISTIC ASPECTS.

7521 Ornstein-Galicia, Jacob. Chicano Calo: description and review of a border variety. HISPANIC JOURNAL OF BEHAVIORAL SCIENCES, Vol. 9, no. 4 (December 1987), p. 359-373. English. DESCR: Border Region; *Chicano Dialects; Pachucos.

7522 Penalosa, Fernando. Book review of: SPANISH IN THE UNITED STATES: SOCIOLINGUISTIC ASPECTS. LANGUAGE, Vol. 60, no. 1 (March 1984), p. 152-159. English. DESCR: Amastae, Jon; Book Reviews; Elias-Olivares, Lucia; *SPANISH IN THE UNITED STATES: SOCIOLINGUISTIC ASPECTS.

7523 Rodriguez, Salvador. El idioma de Aztlan: una lengua que surge. LA COMUNIDAD, No. 266 (August 25, 1985), p. 6-7. Spanish. DESCR: Bilingualism; *Chicano Dialects; Language Interference; Pachucos; Spanish Language.

Sociology

7524 Mirande, Alfredo. Chicano sociology: a critique and evaluation of prevailing theoretical perspectives. HUMBOLDT JOURNAL OF SOCIAL RELATIONS, Vol. 10. no. 1 (Winter, Fall, 1982), p. 204-223. English.

Solache, Saul

7525 Saul Solache: contemporary Chicano artist. LATIN QUARTER, Vol. 1, no. 3 (January, February, 1975), p. 24-26. English. DESCR: *Artists; Exhibits; Mural Art; Paintings.

SOLDIERBOY [play]

7526 Ramirez, Arturo. SOLDIERBOY, una muestra de la eficacia del teatro chicano de hoy. LA COMUNIDAD, No. 357 (May 24, 1987), p. 12-13. Spanish. DESCR: Perez, Judith; Perez, Severo; *Teatro; Teatro Reviews; Vietnam War.

Solinas, Lisa

7527 Taylor, Elena. Conversations with a Chicana physician. REVISTA MUJERES, Vol. 1, no. 2 (June 1984), p. 44-46. English. DESCR: *Chicanas; Medical Education; Medical Personnel.

Somoza, Oscar U.

7528 Garcia, Nasario. El cuento chicano visto por dentro y por fuera. BILINGUAL REVIEW, Vol. 12, no. 3 (September, December, 1985), p. 262-265. Spanish. DESCR: Aguilar, Ricardo; Armengol, Armando; Book Reviews; *PALABRA NUEVA: CUENTOS CHICANOS.

Sonnemair, Jan

7529 13-part series focuses on Hispanics in America. EDITOR & PUBLISHER: THE FOURTH ESTATE, Vol. 115, no. 14 (April 3, 1982), p. 37. English. DESCR: Books; Cultural Characteristics; DALLAS MORNING NEWS; Garcia, Juan; Gonzalez, John; Goodwin, Jay; Grothe, Randy Eli; Hamilton, John; Hille, Ed; LA VIDA AMERICANA; *LA VIDA AMERICANA/HISPANICS IN AMERICA; Langer, Ralph; McLemore, David; Osburne, Burl; Parks, Scott; Pusey, Allen.

Sonora, Mexico

7530 Coerver, Don and Hall, Linda B. The Arizona-Sonora border and the Mexican revolution, 1910-1920. JOURNAL OF THE WEST, Vol. 24, no. 2 (1985), p. 75-87. English. DESCR: Arizona; Arizona Rangers; *History; *Villa, Pancho.

Sosa & Associates

7531 Banks, Marissa Elena. Army maneuvers. HISPANIC BUSINESS, Vol. 9, no. 12 (December 1987), p. 37-39. English. DESCR: Advertising Agencies; Government Contracts; *Military; U.S. Department of Defense (DOD).

Soto, Gary

7532 Bruce-Novoa, Juan. Meet the writers of the 80s. VISTA, Vol. 1, no. 11 (July 6, 1986), p. 15-16. English. DESCR: Anaya, Rudolfo A.; Arte Publico Press; *Authors; Bilingual Review Press; Cisneros, Sandra; Hinojosa-Smith, Rolando R.; Keller, Gary D.; *Literature; Pineda, Cecile; Quinto Sol Publishing, Inc.; Rivera, Tomas.

7533 Bruce-Novoa, Juan. Poesia de Gary Soto: una autobiografia a plazos. LA COMUNIDAD, No. 270 (September 22, 1985), p. 8-10. Spanish. DESCR: Authors; *Literary Criticism; Poetry; TALE OF SUNLIGHT; THE ELEMENTS OF SAN JOAQUIN; WHERE SPARROWS WORK HARD.

7534 Dunn, Geoffrey. Book review of: LIVING UP THE STREET. SAN FRANCISCO REVIEW OF BOOKS, Vol. 11, (Summer 1986), p. 11. English. DESCR: Book Reviews; *LIVING UP THE STREET.

7535 Elias, Edward F. A meeting of poets from east and west: Lorna Dee Cervantes, Gary Soto, Tato Laviera. BILINGUAL REVIEW, Vol. 12, no. 1-2 (January, August, 1985), p. 150-155. English. DESCR: Authors; Cervantes, Lorna Dee; *EMPLUMADA; *ENCLAVE; Laviera, Tato; Literary Criticism; Literature Reviews; Poetry; *WHERE SPARROWS WORK HARD.

7536 Espada, Martin. Book review of: BLACK HAIR. LECTOR, Vol. 4, no. 4-6 (1987), p. 77. English. DESCR: *BLACK HAIR; Book Reviews.

7537 Fields, Alicia. Small but telling moments. THE BLOOMSBURY REVIEW, no. 1-2 (1987), p. 10. English. DESCR: Book Reviews; *SMALL FACES.

7538 Laguna Diaz, Elpidio. Book review of: SMALL FACES. VISTA, Vol. 1, no. 11 (July 6, 1986), p. 16. English. DESCR: Book Reviews; *SMALL FACES.

7539 Marin, Christine. Book review of: WHERE SPARROWS WORK HARD. LECTOR, Vol. 4, no. 4-6 (1987), p. 77. English. DESCR: Book Reviews; *WHERE SPARROWS WORK HARD.

7540 Molina, Ida. Book review of: SMALL FACES. CHOICE, Vol. 24, no. 2 (October 1986), p. 310-311. English. DESCR: Book Reviews; *SMALL FACES.

Soto, Gary (cont.)

7541 Paredes, Raymund A. Review essay: recent Chicano writing. ROCKY MOUNTAIN REVIEW OF LANGUAGE AND LITERATURE, Vol. 41, (1987), p. 124-129. English. **DESCR**: Castillo, Ana; Catholic Church; Chavez, Denise; Chicanas; Garcia, Lionel; GIVING UP THE GHOST; LEAVING HOME; *Literary Criticism; *Literature Reviews; Moraga, Cherrie; Poetry; Prose; Sex Roles; Silva, Beverly; SMALL FACES; THE CAT AND OTHER STORIES; THE LAST OF THE MENU GIRLS; THE MIXQUIAHUALA LETTERS.

7542 Quinn, Mary Ellen. Book review of: SMALL FACES. BOOKLIST, Vol. 82, no. 21 (July 1986), p. 1582. English. **DESCR**: Book Reviews; *SMALL FACES.

Soto, Giovanni

7543 SHPE holds first ever East coast conference for Hispanic engineers. HISPANIC ENGINEER, Vol. 3, no. 5 (Winter 1987), p. 12-14. English. **DESCR**: Awards; Barrios, Eugene; Chang-Diaz, Franklin; *Conferences and Meetings; Cuevas, Brian L.; Garay, Charles J.; Garcia, Ray; Marrero, Charles; Martinez, Lisa; Monteverde, Edwin; Plumey, Raymond; Reyes-Guerra, David; Rivera, Angel; Society of Hispanic Professional Engineers (SHPE).

Soto, Grace

7544 Norris, Eileen. Print suffers in tale of two languages. ADVERTISING AGE MAGAZINE, Vol. 57, no. 16 (February 27, 1986), p. 49-51. English. **DESCR**: Advertising; Chavarria, Jesus; English Language; HISPANIC BUSINESS; LATINA [magazine]; *Magazines; Spanish Language; Villar, Arturo; VISTA [magazine].

Soto, Talisa

7545 Reyes, Sonia. Hispanic models pursue high stakes fashion. VISTA, Vol. 1, no. 2 (October 5, 1985), p. 6-9. English. **DESCR**: Apodaca, Roseanne; Careers; Dominguez, Peter; *Fashion; Jerez, Alicia.

A SOURCEBOOK FOR HISPANIC LITERATURE AND LANGUAGE

7546 Andrachuk, Gregory Peter. Book review of: A SOURCEBOOK FOR HISPANIC LITERATURE AND LANGUAGE. CANADIAN MODERN LANGUAGE REVIEW, Vol. 43, no. 1 (October 1986), p. 168-169. English. **DESCR**: Bleznick, Donald W.; Book Reviews; Reference Works.

7547 Chatham, James R. Book review of: A SOURCEBOOK FOR HISPANIC LITERATURE AND LANGUAGE. REVISTA DE ESTUDIOS HISPANICOS, Vol. 18, no. 3 (October 1984), p. 457-458. English. **DESCR**: Bleznick, Donald W.; Book Reviews; Reference Works.

SOUTH BY SOUTHWEST: THE MEXICAN-AMERICAN AND HIS HERITAGE

7548 Cooke, John Byrne. Book review of: SOUTH BY SOUTHWEST: 24 STORIES FROM MODERN TEXAS. NEW MEXICO HISTORICAL REVIEW, Vol. 62, no. 2 (April 1987), p. 217-218. English. **DESCR**: Book Reviews; *Graham, Don.

South Texas

7549 Briody, Elizabeth K. Patterns of household immigration into South Texas. INTERNATIONAL MIGRATION REVIEW, Vol. 21, no. 1 (Spring 1987), p. 27-47. English. **DESCR**: Chicanas; *Family; *Immigrants; Sex Roles; *Social Mobility.

7550 Catalano, Julia. Fajitas madness. VISTA, Vol. 2, no. 4 (December 7, 1986), p. 23-24. English. **DESCR**: Food Industry; *Food Practices.

7551 Rendon, Laura Ignacia. Chicano student and institution related determinants of educational outcomes in south Texas community colleges. LA RED/THE NET, no. 73 (October 1983), p. 2-6. English. **DESCR**: *Academic Achievement; Community Colleges; Surveys.

Southern California

7552 Arce, Carlos H. Book review of: CHICANOS IN A CHANGING SOCIETY. LA RED/THE NET, no. 30 (May 1980), p. 8. English. **DESCR**: Book Reviews; Camarillo, Alberto; CHICANOS IN A CHANGING SOCIETY; History; *Santa Barbara, CA; *Social History and Conditions.

Southern California Radio and Television News Association

7553 Gutierrez, Gloria. Chicano news-man wins award. LATIN QUARTER, Vol. 1, no. 4 (July, August, 1975), p. 17. English. **DESCR**: Golden Mike Award; Journalists; *Radio; *Vasquez, Victor.

Southern California Edison Co.

7554 Rifkin, Jane M. Ralph de la Parra travels the MAES "bridge to the future". HISPANIC TIMES, Vol. 8, no. 1 (December, January, 1987), p. 30. English. **DESCR**: Biography; *De la Parra, Ralph; *Engineering as a Profession; Mexican American Engineering Society (MAES).

Southland Corporation

7555 Beale, Stephen. Friendly persuasion: pacts and covenants. HISPANIC BUSINESS, Vol. 9, no. 9 (September 1987), p. 20-26. English. **DESCR**: *Adolph Coors Co.; *Business; Community Organizations; Coors/HACER Agreement, 1984; *Corporations; *Hispanic Association on Corporate Responsibility (HACER); Organizations; Pacific Bell.

SOUTHWEST TALES: A CONTEMPORARY COLLECTION

7556 Jacob, John. Book review of: SOUTHWEST TALES: A CONTEMPORY COLLECTION. BOOKLIST, Vol. 82, no. 17 (May 1, 1986), p. 1284. English. **DESCR**: Alurista; Book Reviews; Rojas-Urista, Xelina.

7557 Vallejos, Tomas. Book review of: SOUTHWEST TALES: A CONTEMPORY COLLECTION. THE AMERICAS REVIEW, Vol. 15. no. 2 (Summer 1987), p. 111-113. English. **DESCR**: Alurista; Book Reviews; Rojas-Urista, Xelina.

Southwest Voter Registration Education Project (SVREP)

7558 de la Garza, Rodolfo O. The Mexican American electorate. LA RED/THE NET, no. 72 (September 1983), p. 2-6. English. **DESCR**: Political Representation; *Voter Turnout.

SOUTHWESTERN AGRICULTURE: PRE-COLUMBIAN TO MODERN

7559 Hall, Linda B. The United States-Mexican borders: historical, political, and cultural perspectives. LATIN AMERICAN RESEARCH REVIEW, Vol. 20, no. 2 (1985), p. 223-229. English. DESCR: AMERICAN LABOR IN THE SOUTHWEST: THE FIRST ONE HUNDRED YEARS; *Book Reviews; *Border Region; BOSS RULE IN SOUTH TEXAS: THE PROGRESSIVE ERA; CHICANO INTERMARRIAGE: A THEORETICAL AND EMPIRICAL STUDY; HISPANIC CULTURE IN THE SOUTHWEST; IN DEFENSE OF LA RAZA: THE LOS ANGELES MEXICAN CONSULATE AND THE MEXICAN COMMUNITY; Literature Reviews; RACE AND CLASS IN THE SOUTHWEST: A THEORY OF RACIAL INEQUALITY; THE MEXICANS IN OKLAHOMA; THE POLITICS OF SAN ANTONIO.

Southwestern United States

7560 Andrade, Sally J. Chicana adolescents and contraception issues. LA RED/THE NET, no. 35 (October 1980), p. 2,14. English. DESCR: *Birth Control; *Chicanas; *Youth.

7561 Arce, Carlos H. Chicano voting. LA RED/THE NET, no. 53 (April 1982), p. 2-4. English. DESCR: Chicago, IL; *Voter Turnout.

7562 Diekemper, Barnabas C. The Catholic Church in the shadows: the southwestern United States during the Mexican period. JOURNAL OF THE WEST, Vol. 24, no. 2 (1985), p. 46-53. English. DESCR: *Catholic Church; Missions; Religion.

7563 Educational hierarchies and social differentiation. LA RED/THE NET, no. 37 (December 1980), p. 2-3. English. DESCR: Discrimination in Education; Enrollment; *Higher Education.

7564 Garcia, John A. Book review of: RACE AND CLASS IN THE SOUTHWEST: A THEORY OF INEQUALITY. LA RED/THE NET, no. 31 (June 1980), p. 4. English. DESCR: Barrera, Mario; Book Reviews; *Discrimination; *Economics; RACE AND CLASS IN THE SOUTHWEST: A THEORY OF RACIAL INEQUALITY.

7565 Garcia, John A. Ethnic identity and background traits: explorations of Mexican-origin populations. LA RED/THE NET, no. 29 (April 1980), p. 2. English. DESCR: *Identity; *Self-Referents; *SURVEY OF INCOME AND EDUCATION, 1976.

7566 Griswold del Castillo, Richard. Quantitative history in the American Southwest: a survey and critique. WESTERN HISTORICAL QUARTERLY, Vol. 15, no. 4 (October 1984), p. 407-426. English. DESCR: Economic History and Conditions; Historiography; History; *Social History and Conditions.

7567 Gutierrez, Ramon A. Honor ideology, marriage negotiation, and class-gender domination in New Mexico, 1690-1846. LATIN AMERICAN PERSPECTIVES, Vol. 12, no. 1 (Winter 1985), p. 81-104. English. DESCR: Marriage; Sex Roles; *Social Classes; Social History and Conditions; Values; Women Men Relations.

7568 Karnig, Albert K.; Welch, Susan; and Eribes, Richard A. Employment of women by cities in the Southwest. SOCIAL SCIENCE JOURNAL, Vol. 21, no. 4 (October 1984), p. 41-48. English. DESCR: Chicanas; *Employment; Local Government; Women.

7569 Luckingham, Bradford. The American Southwest: an urban view. WESTERN HISTORICAL QUARTERLY, Vol. 15, no. 3 (July 1984), p.

261-280. English. DESCR: Albuquerque, NM; El Paso, TX; Phoenix, AZ; Social History and Conditions; Tucson, AZ; *Urban Communities; Urban Economics.

7570 Miller, Darlis A. Los Pinos, New Mexico: civil war post on the Rio Grande. NEW MEXICO HISTORICAL REVIEW, Vol. 62, no. 1 (January 1987), p. 1-31. English. DESCR: History; *Los Pinos, NM; *New Mexico; *Rio Grande.

7571 Wreford, Mary. Chicano Survey report #2: perceptions and experience of discrimination. LA RED/THE NET, no. 39 (February 1981), p. 7,16. English. DESCR: *Discrimination; Discrimination in Employment; Midwestern States; *National Chicano Survey (NCS); *Surveys.

7572 Wreford, Mary. Reactions from the Chicano Survey respondents: no mas silencio. LA RED/THE NET, no. 33 (August 1980), p. 2-3. English. DESCR: Chicano Project of the University of Michigan; Midwestern States; *National Chicano Survey (NCS); *Public Opinion; Social Science; *Surveys.

Spanish Colonial Arts Society

7573 Wroth, William. New hope in hard times: Hispanic crafts are revived during troubled years. PALACIO, Vol. 89, no. 2 (1983), p. 22-31. English. DESCR: *Arts and Crafts; *Las Lunas Vocational Training School; New Mexico; Taos Vocational School; Works Progress Administration (WPA).

Spanish Family Guidance Clinic, Miami, FL

7574 Remas, Theodora A. Down and blue. VISTA, Vol. 2, no. 5 (January 4, 1987), p. 16-18. English. DESCR: Counseling (Psychological); *Depression (Psychological); *National Institute of Mental Health; Social History and Conditions.

Spanish for Native Speakers

7575 Hidalgo, Margarita. On the question of "standard" versus "dialect": implications for teaching Hispanic college students. HISPANIC JOURNAL OF BEHAVIORAL SCIENCES, Vol. 9, no. 4 (December 1987), p. 375-395. English. DESCR: Bilingualism; Chicano Dialects; *Foreign Language Instruction; Language Usage; Puerto Ricans; Sociolinguistics; *Spanish Language.

SPANISH IN THE UNITED STATES: SOCIOLINGUISTIC ASPECTS

7576 Nuessel, Frank H., Jr. Book review of: SPANISH IN THE UNITED STATES: SOCIOLINGUISTIC ASPECTS. LINGUA, Vol. 62, no. 3 (1984), p. 247-255. English. DESCR: Amastae, Jon; Book Reviews; Elias-Olivares, Lucia; Sociolinguistics.

7577 Penalosa, Fernando. Book review of: SPANISH IN THE UNITED STATES: SOCIOLINGUISTIC ASPECTS. LANGUAGE, Vol. 60, no. 1 (March 1984), p. 152-159. English. DESCR: Amastae, Jon; Book Reviews; Elias-Olivares, Lucia; Sociolinguistics.

SPANISH IN THE UNITED STATES: SOCIOLINGUISTIC ASPECTS (cont.)

7578 Powers, Michael D. Spanish in contact with other languages: lexical or profound structural influence? BILINGUAL REVIEW, Vol. 12, no. 3 (September, December, 1985), p. 254-257. English. DESCR: Amastae, Jon; Elias-Olivares, Lucia; Language Usage; Literature Reviews; *SPANISH IN THE WESTERN HEMISPHERE IN CONTACT WITH ENGLISH, PORTUGUESE, AND THE AMERINDIAN LANGUAGES; *Spanish Language; Zaragoza, Jorge.

SPANISH IN THE WESTERN HEMISPHERE IN CONTACT WITH ENGLISH, PORTUGUESE, AND THE AMERINDIAN LANGUAGES

7579 Powers, Michael D. Spanish in contact with other languages: lexical or profound structural influence? BILINGUAL REVIEW, Vol. 12, no. 3 (September, December, 1985), p. 254-257. English. DESCR: Amastae, Jon; Elias-Olivares, Lucia; Language Usage; Literature Reviews; *SPANISH IN THE UNITED STATES: SOCIOLINGUISTIC ASPECTS; *Spanish Language; Zaragoza, Jorge.

Spanish Influence

7580 Betsky, Aaron. The Spanish influence: architecture in America. HORIZON: A MAGAZINE OF THE ARTS, Vol. 28, no. 10 (December 1985), p. 53-68. English. DESCR: *Architecture; Photography.

7581 Engstrand, Iris H.W. California ranchos: their Hispanic heritage. SOUTHERN CALIFORNIA QUARTERLY, Vol. 67, no. 3 (Fall 1985), p. 281-290. English. DESCR: *California; *Californios; History; *Land Grants.

7582 Machado, Melinda. Happy 500th, America. VISTA, Vol. 3, no. 2 (October 3, 1987), p. 8, 34, 35. English. DESCR: Festivals.

Spanish International Communications Corp. (SICC)

7583 Beale, Stephen. New blood, fresh money: Telemundo, Univision bullish on television market. HISPANIC BUSINESS, Vol. 9, no. 12 (December 1987), p. 30-36. English. DESCR: *Corporations; Hallmark Cards; LatCom; Radio; *Spanish Language; *Telemundo Television Group; *Television; Univision.

7584 Fever, Jack. Hispanic marketplace: the SICC sale: it is indeed a Hallmark. ADWEEK, Vol. 36, (July 28, 1986), p. 18. English. DESCR: *Hallmark Cards; KMEX, Los Angeles, CA [television station]; *Television.

7585 Gavin joins group pursuing SICC stations. BROADCASTING, Vol. 110, no. 22 (June 2, 1986), p. 68. English. DESCR: Gavin, John; KFTV, Fresno, CA [television station]; KMEX, Los Angeles, CA [television station]; KWEX, San Antonio, TX [television station]; Legal Cases; Perenchio, A. Jerrold; Spanish International Network (SIN); Spanish Language; Television; Thompson, William; WLTV, Miami, FL [television station]; WXTV, Paterson, NJ [television station].

7586 Mass media bureau settlement would allow SICC to sell its stations. BROADCASTING, Vol. 110, no. 26 (June 30, 1986), p. 45. English. DESCR: Anselmo, Rene; Azcarraga Family; Federal Communications Commission (FCC); KDTV, San Francisco, CA [television station]; KFTV, Fresno, CA [television station]; KMEX, Los Angeles, CA [television station]; KTVW, Phoenix, AZ [television station]; KWEX, San Antonio, TX [television

station]; Legal Cases; Spanish International Network (SIN); Spanish Language; Television; WLTV, Miami, FL [television station]; WXTV, Paterson, NJ [television station].

7587 SICC sale opposed. BROADCASTING, Vol. 111, no. 7 (August 18, 1986), p. 46-52. English. DESCR: Azcarraga, Emilio; Federal Communications Commission (FCC); First Chicago Venture Capital; Hallmark Cards; KFTV, Fresno, CA [television station]; KMEX, Los Angeles, CA [television station]; KWEX, San Antonio, TX [television station]; Legal Cases; Spanish Language; Tapia, Raul R.; Television; TVL Corp.; WLTV, Miami, FL [television station]; WXTV, Paterson, NJ [television station].

7588 SICC sells TVs for $301.5 million. BROADCASTING, Vol. 111, no. 4 (July 28, 1986), p. 91-92. English. DESCR: Azcarraga, Emilio; First Chicago Venture Capital; Hallmark Cards; KFTV, Fresno, CA [television station]; KMEX, Los Angeles, CA [television station]; KWEX, San Antonio, TX [television station]; Legal Cases; Spanish International Network (SIN); Spanish Language; Television; Villanueva, Daniel; WLTV, Miami, FL [television station]; WXTV, Paterson, NJ [television station].

7589 SICC to sell off stations. BROADCASTING, Vol. 110, no. 20 (May 19, 1986), p. 79-80. English. DESCR: Anselmo, Rene; Federal Communications Commission (FCC); Fouce, Frank; KFTV, Fresno, CA [television station]; KMEX, Los Angeles, CA [television station]; KWEX, San Antonio, TX [television station]; Legal Cases; Spanish International Network (SIN); Spanish Language; Television; WLTV, Miami, FL [television station]; WXTV, Paterson, NJ [television station].

Spanish International Network (SIN)

7590 Beale, Stephen. More changes at SIN. HISPANIC BUSINESS, Vol. 9, no. 1 (January 1987), p. 10. English. DESCR: *Godoy, Gustavo; Journalism; *Noticiero SIN; *Television.

7591 Gavin joins group pursuing SICC stations. BROADCASTING, Vol. 110, no. 22 (June 2, 1986), p. 68. English. DESCR: Gavin, John; KFTV, Fresno, CA [television station]; KMEX, Los Angeles, CA [television station]; KWEX, San Antonio, TX [television station]; Legal Cases; Perenchio, A. Jerrold; *Spanish International Communications Corp. (SICC); Spanish Language; Television; Thompson, William; WLTV, Miami, FL [television station]; WXTV, Paterson, NJ [television station].

7592 Hispanic marketing. ADVERTISING AGE MAGAZINE, Vol. 57, no. 16 (February 27, 1986), p. 11-51. English. DESCR: Adolph Coors Co.; Advertising; Allstate Insurance Co.; American Greetings; Anheuser-Busch, Inc.; Business Enterprises; Coca-Cola Company; Consumers; Ford Motor Company; Hallmark Cards; *Marketing; Mass Media; McDonald's Corporation; Metropolitan Life Insurance Corporation; Pepsi-Cola Bottling Group; Prudential; State Farm Mutual Insurance; Tylenol; United Insurance Co. of America.

Spanish International Network (SIN) (cont.)

7593 Marketing to Hispanics. ADVERTISING AGE MAGAZINE, Vol. 57, no. 43 (August 11, 1986), p. 51-528. English. **DESCR:** Advertising; Broadcast Media; De Armas Publications; Kinney Shoe Corp.; *Marketing; Pepsi-Cola Bottling Group; Print Media; U.S. Bureau of the Census.

7594 Mass media bureau settlement would allow SICC to sell its stations. BROADCASTING, Vol. 110, no. 26 (June 30, 1986), p. 45. English. **DESCR:** Anselmo, Rene; Azcarraga Family; Federal Communications Commission (FCC); KDTV, San Francisco, CA [television station]; KFTV, Fresno, CA [television station]; KMEX, Los Angeles, CA [television station]; KTVW, Phoeniz, AZ [television station]; KWEX, San Antonio, TX [television station]; Legal Cases; *Spanish International Communications Corp. (SICC); Spanish Language; Television; WLTV, Miami, FL [television station]; WXTV, Paterson, NJ [television station].

7595 Rubin, Marcy Gray. Advertiser apathy hampers TV growth. ADVERTISING AGE MAGAZINE, Vol. 57, no. 43 (August 11, 1986), p. S22-S23. English. **DESCR:** *Advertising; Arbitron; Spanish Language; Strategy Research Corp.; Television.

7596 SICC sells TVs for $301.5 million. BROADCASTING, Vol. 111, no. 4 (July 28, 1986), p. 91-92. English. **DESCR:** Azcarraga, Emilio; First Chicago Venture Capital; Hallmark Cards; KFTV, Fresno, CA [television station]; KMEX, Los Angeles, CA [television station]; KWEX, San Antonio, TX [television station]; Legal Cases; *Spanish International Communications Corp. (SICC); Spanish Language; Television; Villanueva, Daniel; WLTV, Miami, FL [television station]; WXTV, Paterson, NJ [television station].

7597 SICC to sell off stations. BROADCASTING, Vol. 110, no. 20 (May 19, 1986), p. 79-80. English. **DESCR:** Anselmo, Rene; Federal Communications Commission (FCC); Fouce, Frank; KFTV, Fresno, CA [television station]; KMEX, Los Angeles, CA [television station]; KWEX, San Antonio, TX [television station]; Legal Cases; *Spanish International Communications Corp. (SICC); Spanish Language; Television; WLTV, Miami, FL [television station]; WXTV, Paterson, NJ [television station].

Spanish Language

7598 Beale, Stephen. New blood, fresh money: Telemundo, Univision bullish on television market. HISPANIC BUSINESS, Vol. 9, no. 12 (December 1987), p. 30-36. English. **DESCR:** *Corporations; Hallmark Cards; LatCom; Radio; Spanish International Communications Corp. (SICC); *Telemundo Television Group; *Television; Univision.

7599 Beale, Stephen. A turning point in Hollywood. HISPANIC BUSINESS, Vol. 9, no. 7 (July 1987), p. 20-24, 36. English. **DESCR:** *Films; LA BAMBA [film]; *Marketing; Stereotypes; THE MILAGRO BEANFIELD WAR [film].

7600 Berling-Manuel, Lynn. Expanding radio market battles research static. ADVERTISING AGE MAGAZINE, Vol. 57, no. 43 (August 11, 1986), p. S12-S16. English. **DESCR:** Arbitron; Marketing; *Radio; WADO-AM, New York, NY [radio station]; WAQI-AM, Miami, FL [radio station]; WOJO-FM, Chicago, IL [radio station].

7601 Cecere, Linda. Newspapers attract attention in some categories. ADVERTISING AGE MAGAZINE, Vol. 57, no. 43 (August 11, 1986), p. S9-S10. English. **DESCR:** Advertising; DIARIO DE LAS AMERICAS; EL MIAMI HERALD; LA OPINION, Los Angeles, CA; *Newspapers; NOTICIAS DEL MUNDO.

7602 Comstock, Cathryn L. and Martin, Frederick N. A children's Spanish word discrimination test for non-Spanish-speaking children. EAR AND HEARING, Vol. 5, no. 3 (May, June, 1984), p. 166-170. English. **DESCR:** Child Study; English Language; *Language Assessment; Research Methodology.

7603 Fishman, Joshua A. What is happening to Spanish on the U.S. mainland? ETHNIC AFFAIRS, no. 1 (Fall 1987), p. [12]-23. English. **DESCR:** *Language Usage; Sociolinguistics.

7604 Gavin joins group pursuing SICC stations. BROADCASTING, Vol. 110, no. 22 (June 2, 1986), p. 68. English. **DESCR:** Gavin, John; KFTV, Fresno, CA [television station]; KMEX, Los Angeles, CA [television station]; KWEX, San Antonio, TX [television station]; Legal Cases; Perenchio, A. Jerrold; *Spanish International Communications Corp. (SICC); Spanish International Network (SIN); Television; Thompson, William; WLTV, Miami, FL [television station]; WXTV, Paterson, NJ [television station].

7605 Gonzales-Berry, Erlinda. Enmienda de ingles en Nuevo Mexico. LA COMUNIDAD, No. 352 (April 19, 1987), p. 4-7. Spanish. **DESCR:** English Language; *English-Only Movement; History; Legislation; *New Mexico.

7606 Gynan, Shaw Nicholas. The influence of language background on attitudes toward native and nonnative Spanish. BILINGUAL REVIEW, Vol. 12, no. 1-2 (January, August, 1985), p. 33-42. English. **DESCR:** Anglo Americans; *Attitudes; *Foreign Language Instruction; Language Proficiency; *Language Usage.

7607 Hidalgo, Margarita. On the question of "standard" versus "dialect": implications for teaching Hispanic college students. HISPANIC JOURNAL OF BEHAVIORAL SCIENCES, Vol. 9, no. 4 (December 1987), p. 375-395. English. **DESCR:** Bilingualism; Chicano Dialects; *Foreign Language Instruction; Language Usage; Puerto Ricans; Sociolinguistics; Spanish for Native Speakers.

7608 Joe, Barbara E. Safeguarding Spanish. NUESTRO, Vol. 11, no. 2 (March 1987), p. 32. English. **DESCR:** *Academia Norteamericana de la Lengua.

7609 Korzenny, Felipe, et al. Cultural identification as predictor of content preferences of Hispanics. JOURNALISM QUARTERLY, Vol. 60, no. 4 (Winter 1983), p. 677-685+. English. **DESCR:** Cultural Characteristics; English Language; Identity; *Newspapers.

Spanish Language (cont.)

7610 Lawrence, Jennifer. TV signal expected to boost Houston market. ADVERTISING AGE MAGAZINE, Vol. 57, no. 43 (August 11, 1986), p. S24-S25. English. **DESCR**: Advertising; Houston, TX; *KXLN, Houston, TX [television station]; Marketing; Pueblo Broadcasting Corp.; Television.

7611 Lee, James F. The relationship between decoding accuracy and the reading achievement of monolingual Spanish-speaking children. BILINGUAL REVIEW, Vol. 12, no. 3 (September, December, 1985), p. 209-217. English. **DESCR**: Educational Tests and Measurements; *Language Development; *Reading.

7612 Levin, Gary. Publisher seeks to improve "image". ADVERTISING AGE MAGAZINE, Vol. 57, no. 43 (August 11, 1986), p. S25-S27. English. **DESCR**: Advertising; Asencio, John; English Language; *HISPANIC IMAGE; Magazines.

7613 Martin, Laura. Language form and language function in ZOOT SUIT and THE BORDER: a contribution to the analysis of the role of foreign language in film. STUDIES IN LATIN AMERICAN POPULAR CULTURE, Vol. 3, (1984), p. 57-69. English. **DESCR**: *Films; Language Usage; THE BORDER [film]; *ZOOT SUIT [film].

7614 Martinez, Jose. Please disregard this notice if full payment has been made. CHIRICU, Vol. 3, no. 2 (1983), p. 47-54. Spanish. **DESCR**: *Actos.

7615 Mass media bureau settlement would allow SICC to sell its stations. BROADCASTING, Vol. 110, no. 26 (June 30, 1986), p. 45. English. **DESCR**: Anselmo, Rene; Azcarraga Family; Federal Communications Commission (FCC); KDTV, San Francisco, CA [television station]; KFTV, Fresno, CA [television station]; KMEX, Los Angeles, CA [television station]; KTVW, Phoenix, AZ [television station]; KWEX, San Antonio, TX [television station]; Legal Cases; *Spanish International Communications Corp. (SICC); Spanish International Network (SIN); Television; WLTV, Miami, FL [television station]; WXTV, Paterson, NJ [television station].

7616 Mendez-M., Miguel. Introduccion. LLUEVE TLALOC, no. 10 (1983), p. iv. Spanish. **DESCR**: Education; Pima Community College, Tucson, AZ.

7617 Mendez-M., Miguel. Introduction. LLUEVE TLALOC, no. 10 (1983), p. iv. English. **DESCR**: *Education; *Pima Community College, Tucson, AZ.

7618 Mohr, Nicholasa. Puerto Rican writers in the United States, Puerto Rican writers in Puerto Rico: a separation beyond language. THE AMERICAS REVIEW, Vol. 15, no. 2 (Summer 1987), p. 87-92. English. **DESCR**: Authors; Autobiography; Identity; Immigrants; *Language Usage; *Literature; *Mohr, Nicholasa; *Puerto Ricans.

7619 Montane, Diane. Learning survival Spanish. VISTA, Vol. 1, no. 5 (January 5, 1986), p. 16. English. **DESCR**: Education; Ruiz, Vivian; *SURVIVAL SPANISH; Television.

7620 Norris, Eileen. Print suffers in tale of two languages. ADVERTISING AGE MAGAZINE, Vol. 57, no. 16 (February 27, 1986), p. 49-51. English. **DESCR**: Advertising; Chavarria, Jesus; English Language; HISPANIC BUSINESS; LATINA [magazine]; *Magazines; Soto, Grace; Villar, Arturo; VISTA [magazine].

7621 Powers, Michael D. Spanish in contact with other languages: lexical or profound structural influence? BILINGUAL REVIEW, Vol. 12, no. 3 (September, December, 1985), p. 254-257. English. **DESCR**: Amastae, Jon; Elias-Olivares, Lucia; Language Usage; Literature Reviews; *SPANISH IN THE UNITED STATES: SOCIOLINGUISTIC ASPECTS; *SPANISH IN THE WESTERN HEMISPHERE IN CONTACT WITH ENGLISH, PORTUGUESE, AND THE AMERINDIAN LANGUAGES; Zaragoza, Jorge.

7622 Rios-Bustamante, Antonio. California's bilingual constitution=La constitucion bilingue de California. AMERICAS 2001, Vol. 1, no. 1 (June, July, 1987), p. 15. Bilingual. **DESCR**: *California State Constitution; History.

7623 Rodriguez, Salvador. El idioma de Aztlan: una lengua que surge. LA COMUNIDAD, No. 266 (August 25, 1985), p. 6-7. Spanish. **DESCR**: Bilingualism; *Chicano Dialects; Language Interference; Pachucos; Sociolinguistics.

7624 Rubin, Marcy Gray. Advertiser apathy hampers TV growth. ADVERTISING AGE MAGAZINE, Vol. 57, no. 43 (August 11, 1986), p. S22-S23. English. **DESCR**: *Advertising; Arbitron; Spanish International Network (SIN); Strategy Research Corp.; Television.

7625 Sellers, Jeff M. Market growth boosts ad rates. HISPANIC BUSINESS, Vol. 9, no. 12 (December 1987), p. 41-42, 63+. English. **DESCR**: *Advertising; *Marketing; *Television.

7626 Shoemaker, Pamela J.; Reese, Stephen D.; and Danielson, Wayne A. Spanish-language print media use as an indicator of acculturation. JOURNALISM QUARTERLY, Vol. 62, no. 4 (Winter 1985), p. 734-740. English. **DESCR**: *Acculturation; Magazines; Newspapers; *Print Media.

7627 SICC sale opposed. BROADCASTING, Vol. 111, no. 7 (August 18, 1986), p. 46-52. English. **DESCR**: Azcarraga, Emilio; Federal Communications Commission (FCC); First Chicago Venture Capital; Hallmark Cards; KFTV, Fresno, CA [television station]; KMEX, Los Angeles, CA [television station]; KWEX, San Antonio, TX [television station]; Legal Cases; *Spanish International Communications Corp. (SICC); Tapia, Raul R.; Television; TVL Corp.; WLTV, Miami, FL [television station]; WXTV, Paterson, NJ [television station].

7628 SICC sells TVs for $301.5 million. BROADCASTING, Vol. 111, no. 4 (July 28, 1986), p. 91-92. English. **DESCR**: Azcarraga, Emilio; First Chicago Venture Capital; Hallmark Cards; KFTV, Fresno, CA [television station]; KMEX, Los Angeles, CA [television station]; KWEX, San Antonio, TX [television station]; Legal Cases; *Spanish International Communications Corp. (SICC); Spanish International Network (SIN); Television; Villanueva, Daniel; WLTV, Miami, FL [television station]; WXTV, Paterson, NJ [television station].

Spanish Language (cont.)

7629 SICC to sell off stations. BROADCASTING, Vol. 110, no. 20 (May 19, 1986), p. 79-80. English. **DESCR:** Anselmo, Rene; Federal Communications Commission (FCC); Fouce, Frank; KFTV, Fresno, CA [television station]; KMEX, Los Angeles, CA [television station]; KWEX, San Antonio, TX [television station]; Legal Cases; *Spanish International Communications Corp. (SICC); Spanish International Network (SIN); Television; WLTV, Miami, FL [television station]; WXTV, Paterson, NJ [television station].

7630 Tarin, Patricia and Josslin, Daniel. Books for the Spanish-speaking: si se puede. LIBRARY JOURNAL, (July 1987), p. 25-31. English. **DESCR:** *Library Collections; Library Services; Publishing Industry.

Spanish Speaking Affairs Council of St. Paul

7631 Valenzuela-Crocker, Elvira. Small town Hispanic America. VISTA, Vol. 1, no. 11 (July 6, 1986), p. 12-14. English. **DESCR:** Garcia, Frances [mayor of Hutchinson, KS]; Political History and Conditions; *Population; *Trejo, Jose.

SPANISH-LANGUAGE BOOKS FOR PUBLIC LIBRARIES

7632 Book review of: SPANISH-LANGUAGE BOOKS FOR PUBLIC LIBRARIES. BOOKLIST, Vol. 83, no. 9 (January 1, 1987), p. 700-701. English. **DESCR:** Book Reviews; Reference Works; Restrepo, Fabio.

7633 Whatley, Patricia L. Book review of: SPANISH-LANGUAGE BOOKS FOR PUBLIC LIBRARIES. AMERICAN REFERENCE BOOKS ANNUAL, Vol. 18, (1987), p. 241. English. **DESCR:** Bibliography; Book Reviews; Lestrepo, Fabio.

Spanish-Speaking Mental Health Research Center

7634 Herrera, Irma D. Mixed marriages: will the happiness last? VISTA, Vol. 1, no. 10 (June 8, 1986), p. 8-10. English. **DESCR:** *Intermarriage; *Salgado de Snyder, Nelly.

7635 Perez, Emma. Research centers. LA RED/THE NET, No. 100 (September 1986), p. 5-8. English. **DESCR:** *Research Centers.

Special Education

7636 Argulewicz, Ed N. Effects of ethnic membership, socioeconomic status, and home language on LD, EMR, and EH placements. LEARNING DISABILITY QUARTERLY, Vol. 6, no. 2 (Spring 1983), p. 195-200. English. **DESCR:** Educable Mentally Retarded (EMR); Ethnic Groups.

7637 Wolfe, David E. Book review of: BILINGUALISM AND SPECIAL EDUCATION: ISSUES IN ASSESSMENT AND PEDAGOGY. MODERN LANGUAGE JOURNAL, Vol. 71, (Spring 1987), p. 81. English. **DESCR:** Bilingualism; *BILINGUALISM AND SPECIAL EDUCATION; Book Reviews; Cummins, Jim.

Speech Patterns
USE: Accentedness

Speeches
USE: Rhetoric

Sports

7638 Allsup, Dan. Run Reuben run. VISTA, Vol. 1, no. 12 (August 2, 1986), p. 18. English.

DESCR: *Athletes; *Reina, Reuben; San Antonio, TX.

7639 Chavez, Lorenzo A. Tennis superstars. VISTA, Vol. 1, no. 8 (April 6, 1986), p. 14-16. English. **DESCR:** *Athletes; Chicanas; Fernandez, Gigi; Fernandez, Mary Joe; *Sabatini, Gabriela; Torres, Michele; Women.

7640 Corona, Al. Life in the fast lane. VISTA, Vol. 3, no. 3 (November 8, 1987), p. 30. English. **DESCR:** *Garcia, Ruben; National Association of Stock Car Automobile Racing (NASCAR).

7641 Duda, Joan L. Goals and achievement orientations of Anglo and Mexican-American adolescents in sport and the classroom. INTERNATIONAL REVIEW OF SPORT SOCIOLOGY, Vol. 18, no. 4 (1983), p. 63-80. English. **DESCR:** Academic Achievement; Cultural Characteristics; New Mexico; *Youth.

7642 Grayson, June. Sports medics. VISTA, Vol. 2, no. 9 (May 3, 1987), p. 17-18. English. **DESCR:** Bergin-Nader, Barbara; Cuadros, Hugo; Doctor Patient Relations; *Dominguez, Richard; *Medical Personnel; Prietto, Carlos Alfredo.

7643 Holmes, John J. Up and away: ballooning fever grips America and Latinos have caught the bug. VISTA, Vol. 3, no. 2 (October 3, 1987), p. 16-18. English. **DESCR:** *Albuquerque International Balloon Fiesta; *Festivals.

7644 LeCompte, Mary Lou and Beezley, William H. Any Sunday in April: the rise of sport in San Antonio and the Hispanic borderlands. JOURNAL OF SPORT HISTORY, Vol. 13, no. 2 (Summer 1986), p. 128-146. English. **DESCR:** *Charreada; *Cultural Customs; History; *San Antonio, TX.

7645 Miley, Scott L. Let the games begin. VISTA, Vol. 2, no. 12 (August 1, 1987), p. 13-14. English. **DESCR:** *Pan American Games.

7646 Quintana, Al. Gaining yardage in football. VISTA, Vol. 1, no. 2 (October 5, 1985), p. 10-11. English. **DESCR:** *Athletes; Casillas, Tony; *Flores, Tom.

7647 Sanchez, Tom. Jeff Apodaca. VISTA, Vol. 1, no. 8 (April 6, 1986), p. 21. English. **DESCR:** *Apodaca, Jeff; *Athletes; Diseases.

Spota, Luis

7648 Lomeli, Francisco A. En torno a la literatura de la frontera (II). LA COMUNIDAD. No. 275 (October 27, 1985), p. 2-3. Spanish. **DESCR:** Border Region; Language Usage; *Literary Criticism; MURIERON A MITAD DEL RIO.

SPRING FORWARD/FALL BACK

7649 Bruce-Novoa, Juan. Homosexuality and the Chicano novel. CONFLUENCIA, Vol. 2, no. 1 (Fall 1986), p. 69-77. English. **DESCR:** Acosta, Oscar Zeta; CITY OF NIGHT; FAULTLINE [novel]; *Homosexuality; Islas, Arturo; *Literary Criticism; Machismo; *Novel; Ortiz Taylor, Sheila; POCHO; Rechy, John; Salas, Floyd; TATOO THE WICKED CROSS; THE AUTOBIOGRAPHY OF A BROWN BUFFALO; THE RAIN GOD: A DESERT TALE; THE REVOLT OF THE COCKROACH PEOPLE; Villarreal, Jose Antonio.

St. Luke's Catholic Church, San Antonio, TX

7650 Pinon, Fernando. A dance of worship. VISTA, Vol. 1, no. 3 (November 3, 1985), p. 16. English. DESCR: *Aztecs; *Dance.

STAND AND DELIVER [film]

7651 Muro, Rena. Walking on water. AMERICAS 2001, Vol. 1, no. 3 (November, December, 1987), p. 12-14. Bilingual. DESCR: Camhi, Morrie; *Films; Olmos, Edward James; *WALKING ON WATER [working title of film STAND AND DELIVER].

Standard of Living
USE: Economic History and Conditions

Stanford Center for Chicano Research, Stanford, CA

7652 Perez, Emma. Institutionally-based research centers: the Stanford Center for Chicano Research. LA RED/THE NET, no. 93 (January, February, 1986), p. 9-11. English. DESCR: *Research Centers.

Stanford, E.P. Percil

7653 Jackson, James S. Book review of: UNDERSTANDING MINORITY AGING: PERSPECTIVES AND SOURCES. LA RED/THE NET, no. 68 (May 1983), p. 12-13. English. DESCR: Book Reviews; Cuellar, Jose B.; Miller-Soule, Danielle I.; *UNDERSTANDING MINORITY AGING: PERSPECTIVES AND SOURCES.

Stanford University, Stanford, CA

7654 Obese children focus of study. NUESTRO, Vol. 11, no. 3 (April 1987), p. 9. English. DESCR: *Children; *Obesity.

Stanislaus County, CA

7655 Luevano, Richard. Attitudes of elderly Mexican Americans towards nursing homes in Stanislaus county. LA RED/THE NET, no. 45 (August 1981), p. 2. English. DESCR: *Ancianos; Nursing Homes.

State Farm Mutual Insurance

7656 Hispanic marketing. ADVERTISING AGE MAGAZINE, Vol. 57, no. 16 (February 27, 1986), p. 11-51. English. DESCR: Adolph Coors Co.; Advertising; Allstate Insurance Co.; American Greetings; Anheuser-Busch, Inc.; Business Enterprises; Coca-Cola Company; Consumers; Ford Motor Company; Hallmark Cards; *Marketing; Mass Media; McDonald's Corporation; Metropolitan Life Insurance Corporation; Pepsi-Cola Bottling Group; Prudential; Spanish International Network (SIN); Tylenol; United Insurance Co. of America.

THE STATE OF CHICANO RESEARCH IN FAMILY, LABOR AND MIGRATION STUDIES

7657 Garcia, Mario T. Book review of: THE STATE OF CHICANO RESEARCH ON FAMILY, LABOR, AND MIGRATION: PROCEEDINGS OF THE FIRST STANFORD SYMPOSIUM ON CHICANO RESEARCH AND PUBLIC POLICY. CALIFORNIA HISTORY, Vol. 63, no. 3 (Summer 1984), p. 261-262. English. DESCR: Almaguer, Tomas; Book Reviews; Camarillo, Alberto; Chicano Studies; Valdez, Armando.

7658 Griswold del Castillo, Richard. Book review of: THE STATE OF CHICANO RESEARCH ON FAMILY, LABOR, AND MIGRATION: PROCEEDINGS OF THE FIRST STANFORD SYMPOSIUM ON CHICANO RESEARCH AND PUBLIC POLICY. PACIFIC HISTORICAL REVIEW, Vol. 54, no. 3 (August 1985), p.

381-382. English. DESCR: Almaguer, Tomas; Book Reviews; Camarillo, Alberto; Chicano Studies; Valdez, Armando.

THE STATE OF HISPANIC AMERICA

7659 Chavaria, Elvira. Book review of: THE STATE OF HISPANIC AMERICA, VOL. II and LA CHICANA: BUILDING FOR THE FUTURE. LA RED/THE NET, no. 68 (May 1983), p. 10-12. English. DESCR: Book Reviews; *LA CHICANA: BUILDING FOR THE FUTURE; National Hispanic Center for Advanced Studies and Policy Analysis (NHCAS).

State v. Castonguay

7660 Grand juries: underrepresentation of Hispanics. CRIMINAL LAW REPORTER, Vol. 36, no. 2 (October 10, 1984), p. 2033-2034. English. DESCR: *Juries.

Statistics

7661 The 500 largest Hispanic-owned companies in sales. HISPANIC BUSINESS, Vol. 9, no. 6 (June 1987), p. 30-47. English. DESCR: *Business Enterprises; *THE HISPANIC BUSINESS 500.

7662 Balkan, D. Carlos. The Hispanic market's leading indicators. HISPANIC BUSINESS, Vol. 9, no. 12 (December 1987), p. 16-17. English. DESCR: Advertising; *Marketing; Population.

7663 Business and population maintain high growth rates. HISPANIC BUSINESS, Vol. 9, no. 2 (February 1987), p. 55. English. DESCR: *Business Enterprises; *Income.

7664 Dunn, William. Chicago's Hispanics. AMERICAN DEMOGRAPHICS, Vol. 9, no. 2 (February 1987), p. 52-53. English. DESCR: *Chicago, IL; Population; U.S. Bureau of the Census.

7665 Guedella, Juan. A new benchmark. HISPANIC BUSINESS, Vol. 9, no. 1 (January 1987), p. 12,16. English. DESCR: *Business Enterprises.

7666 Heuer, Robert J. To save a neighborhood. VISTA, Vol. 3, no. 3 (November 8, 1987), p. 32-34. English. DESCR: *Eighteenth Street Development Corporation, Chicago, IL; *Housing; Overa, Agustin; Pilsen, IL.

7667 McNeely, Dave. Hispanic power at the polls. VISTA, Vol. 2, no. 3 (November 2, 1986), p. 8-12. English. DESCR: Austin, TX; *Barrera, Roy, Jr.; Chavez, Linda; Elected Officials; Gonzalez, Raul; Martinez, Bob; Maryland; Political System; San Antonio, TX; Tampa, FL; *Voter Turnout.

7668 Perez, Renato E. Hispanics in uniform. VISTA, Vol. 1, no. 3 (November 3, 1985), p. 12-15. English. DESCR: *Military; Military Education.

7669 Perkins, Claranne. We the minorities of CASE: a special survey of minorities working in institutional advancement. CURRENTS, Vol. 10, no. 5 (May 1984), p. 34-40. English. DESCR: *Careers; Higher Education.

7670 Report to the Network. LA RED/THE NET, no. 98 (July 1986), p. 1-2. English. DESCR: *Enrollment; *Higher Education.

Statistics (cont.)

7671 Rodriguez, Eloy. Chicanos/Hispanics in higher education: now and beyond. HISPANIC TIMES, Vol. 8, no. 3 (May, June, 1987), p. 44-45. English. DESCR: Dropouts; *Higher Education.

7672 Sellers, Jeff M. Out in front: the 100 fastest-growing companies. HISPANIC BUSINESS, Vol. 9, no. 11 (November 1987), p. 20-26. English. DESCR: *Business Enterprises.

7673 Slatta, Richard W. and Atkinson, Maxine P. The "Spanish origin" population of Oregon and Washington: a demographic profile, 1980. PACIFIC NORTHWEST QUARTERLY, Vol. 75, no. 3 (July 1984), p. 108-116. English. DESCR: *Oregon; *Population; Self-Referents; Socioeconomic Factors; *Washington (state).

7674 Sullivan, Teresa A. and Tienda, Marta. Integration of multiple data sources in immigrant studies. REVIEW OF PUBLIC DATA USE, Vol. 12, no. 4 (December 1984), p. 233-244. English. DESCR: *Immigrants; *Immigration; *Research Methodology.

7675 Tienda, Marta. Task force on statistical policy and data needs. LA RED/THE NET, no. 88 (Winter, 1984), p. 2-6. English. DESCR: *Databases; *Population; Public Policy; Research Methodology; Vital Statistics.

7676 Trevino, Fernando M. Health indicators for Hispanic, Black and white Americans. VITAL AND HEALTH STATISTICS. SERIES 10, (September 1984), p. 1-88. English. DESCR: Anglo Americans; Blacks; *Medical Care.

7677 Valencia, Bert. Purchasing power rises 10 percent. HISPANIC BUSINESS, Vol. 9, no. 12 (December 1987), p. 15. English. DESCR: *Consumers; *Income.

Stereotypes

7678 Aceves Madrid, Vicente. Controversy surrounding NBC's CHICO AND THE MAN. LATIN QUARTER, Vol. 1, no. 2 (October 1974), p. 5-7. English. DESCR: Albertson, Jack; Artists; *CHICO AND THE MAN [television show]; Komack, James; Prinze, Freddie; Teatros Unidos; *Television.

7679 Aceves Madrid, Vicente. Film review of: FREEBIE AND THE BEAN. LATIN QUARTER, Vol. 1, no. 3 (January, February, 1975), p. 22-23. English. DESCR: *Film Reviews; FREEBIE AND THE BEAN; Violence.

7680 Alvarado, Raul. Against all odds. HISPANIC ENGINEER, Vol. 3, no. 4 (Fall 1987), p. 10-11. English. DESCR: *Chicanas; Education; Educational Statistics; National Merit Scholarships; Preliminary Scholastic Aptitude Test (PSAT); *Scholastic Aptitude Test (SAT).

7681 Barro, Mary Helen. 1973 Emmy Awards. LATIN QUARTER, Vol. 1, no. 1 (July 1974), p. 5-6. English. DESCR: Chavez, Andres; CINCO VIDAS; Emmy Awards; *Esparza, Moctezuma; Identity; Quintero, Carlos; *Recreation; REFLECCIONES; Rodriguez, Sandra; Rodriguez, Tony; Ruiz, Jose Luis; Television.

7682 Beale, Stephen and Valdez, Luis. Connecting with the American experience: an interview with Luis Valdez. HISPANIC BUSINESS, Vol. 9, no. 7 (July 1987), p. 10-13. English. DESCR: Biography; Films; LA BAMBA [film]; Teatro; *Valdez, Luis.

7683 Beale, Stephen. A turning point in Hollywood. HISPANIC BUSINESS, Vol. 9, no. 7 (July 1987), p. 20-24, 36. English. DESCR: *Films; LA BAMBA [film]; *Marketing; Spanish Language; THE MILAGRO BEANFIELD WAR [film].

7684 Delpar, Helen. Goodbye to the greaser: Mexico, the MPPDA, and derogatory films, 1922-1926. JOURNAL OF POPULAR FILM AND TELEVISION, no. 12 (Spring 1984), p. 34-41. English. DESCR: *Films; *Motion Picture Producers and Distributors of America (MPPDA).

7685 Ericksen, Charles. Wanted: Hispanics in the newsroom. CIVIL RIGHTS DIGEST/PERSPECTIVES, Vol. 14, no. 1 (Spring 1982), p. 40-44. English. DESCR: *Discrimination in Employment; Journalism; *Journalists; *Print Media.

7686 Garcia, Ed. On red-haired girls and the greaser in me. TEXAS OBSERVOR, Vol. 75, (October 28, 1983), p. 24-25. English. DESCR: Book Reviews; de Leon, Arnoldo; Essays; Identity; Texas; *THEY CALLED THEM GREASERS: ANGLO ATTITUDES TOWARD MEXICANS IN TEXAS, 1821-1900.

7687 Jesse Jackson makes appearance at CBS board meeting. BROADCASTING, Vol. 110, no. 16 (April 21, 1986), p. 100. English. DESCR: Broadcast Media; *Columbia Broadcasting Studios (CBS); Discrimination; Discrimination in Employment; *Jackson, Jesse; People United to Serve Humanity (PUSH); Taylor, Hycel; Wyman, Thomas.

7688 Jorgensen, Stephen R. and Adams, Russell P. Family planning needs and behavior of Mexican American women: a study of health care professionals and their clientele. HISPANIC JOURNAL OF BEHAVIORAL SCIENCES, Vol. 9, no. 3 (September 1987), p. 265-286. English. DESCR: Acculturation; *Attitudes; Birth Control; *Chicanas; *Cultural Characteristics; *Family Planning; Fertility; Public Health; Sterilization.

7689 Mares, E.A. Myth and reality: observations on American myths and the myth of Aztlan. EL CUADERNO, Vol. 3, no. 1 (Winter 1973), p. 35-50. English. DESCR: *Aztlan.

7690 Mellado, Carmela. Adriana Ocampo. HISPANIC ENGINEER, Vol. 3, no. 4 (Fall 1987), p. 22-24. English. DESCR: National Aeronautics and Space Administration (NASA); *Ocampo, Adriana; *Science as a Profession; Women.

7691 Nieto, Sonia. Past accomplishments, current needs: la lucha continua. INTERRACIAL BOOKS FOR CHILDREN, Vol. 17, no. 2 (1986), p. 6-8. English. DESCR: Bilingual Bicultural Education; *Children's Literature; Council on Interracial Books for Children; Poverty.

7692 Padilla, Eligio R. and O'Grady, Kevin E. Sexuality among Mexican Americans: a case of sexual stereotyping. JOURNAL OF PERSONALITY AND SOCIAL PSYCHOLOGY, Vol. 52. no. 1 (1987), p. 5-10. English. DESCR: Age Groups; Anglo Americans; Attitudes; Religion; *Sex Roles.

7693 Padilla, Steve. Lessons to be learned from a playful hoax. VISTA, Vol. 1, no. 7 (March 2, 1986), p. 3. English. DESCR: *Essays; Humor; Librarians; Public Opinion; Sclar, Marta-Luisa; *Valdez, Juan.

Stereotypes (cont.)

7694 Thomson, David. The Texas that got away. FILM COMMENT, Vol. 21, no. 3 (June 1985), p. 32-35. English. **DESCR:** Actors and Actresses; *Films.

7695 Trevino, Jesus Salvador. Latino portrayals in film and television. JUMP CUT, no. 30 (March 1985), p. 14. English. **DESCR:** Discrimination; *Films.

7696 Vasquez, Victor. More on CHICO AND THE MAN. LATIN QUARTER, Vol. 1, no. 3 (January, February, 1975), p. 13-15. English. **DESCR:** Albertson, Jack; Andrade, Ray; Artists; Boycotts; *CHICO AND THE MAN [television show]; Discrimination; Prinze, Freddie; *Television.

7697 Weller, David L. and Reyes, Laurie Hart. Stereotyping: impact on teachers and students. ACTION IN TEACHER EDUCATION, Vol. 5, no. 3 (Fall 1983), p. 1-7. English. **DESCR:** Discrimination; Education; Sex Stereotypes.

Sterilization

7698 Jorgensen, Stephen R. and Adams, Russell P. Family planning needs and behavior of Mexican American women: a study of health care professionals and their clientele. HISPANIC JOURNAL OF BEHAVIORAL SCIENCES, Vol. 9, no. 3 (September 1987), p. 265-286. English. **DESCR:** Acculturation; *Attitudes; Birth Control; *Chicanas; *Cultural Characteristics; *Family Planning; Fertility; Public Health; Stereotypes.

Stoddard, Ellwyn R.

7699 Burnett, G. Wesley. Book review of: BORDERLANDS SOURCEBOOK. GEOGRAPHICAL REVIEW, Vol. 74, no. 1 (January 1984), p. 123-124. English. **DESCR:** Book Reviews; *BORDERLANDS SOURCEBOOK; Nostrand, Richard L.; West, Jonathan P.

Strategy Research Corp.

7700 Rubin, Marcy Gray. Advertiser apathy hampers TV growth. ADVERTISING AGE MAGAZINE, Vol. 57, no. 43 (August 11, 1986), p. S22-S23. English. **DESCR:** *Advertising; Arbitron; Spanish International Network (SIN); Spanish Language; Television.

Street Theater
USE: Teatro

Stress

7701 Debro, Julius, et al. Workshop presentation: stress and its control: a minority perspective. POLICE CHIEF, Vol. 50, no. 3 (March 1983), p. 106-115. English. **DESCR:** *Police.

7702 Mena, Francisco; Padilla, Amado M.; and Maldonado, Margarita. Acculturative stress and specific coping statgies among immigrant and later generation college students. HISPANIC JOURNAL OF BEHAVIORAL SCIENCES, Vol. 9, no. 2 (June 1987), p. 207-225. English. **DESCR:** *Acculturation; Age Groups; Colleges and Universities; Identity; Immigrants; Students.

7703 Neff, James Alan; Hoppe, Sue K.; and Perea, Patricia. Acculturation and alcohol use: drinking patterns and problems among Anglo and Mexican American male drinkers. HISPANIC JOURNAL OF BEHAVIORAL SCIENCES, Vol. 9, no. 2 (June 1987), p. 151-181. English. **DESCR:** *Acculturation; Age Groups; *Alcoholism; Anglo Americans; *Males.

7704 Vargas-Willis, Gloria and Cervantes, Richard C. Consideration of psychosocial stress in the treatment of the Latina immigrant. HISPANIC JOURNAL OF BEHAVIORAL SCIENCES, Vol. 9, no. 3 (September 1987), p. 315-329. English. **DESCR:** *Chicanas; Discrimination in Employment; *Immigrants; Mental Health; *Psychotherapy.

7705 Zippin, David H. and Hough, Richard L. Perceived self-other differences in life events and mental health among Mexicans and Americans. JOURNAL OF PSYCHOLOGY, Vol. 119, no. 2 (March 1985), p. 143-155. English. **DESCR:** Anglo Americans; *Comparative Psychology; *Locus of Control; *Mental Health; Mexico; Psychiatry.

Strikes and Lockouts

7706 Boycotts revisited: Campbell's concedes to farm worker campaign. DOLLARS AND SENSE, (July, August, 1986), p. 12-14, 18. English. **DESCR:** Boycotts; California; Campbell Soup Co.; Farm Labor Organizing Commmittee (FLOC); Farm Workers; *Labor Disputes; Labor Unions; Michigan; Ohio; United Farmworkers of America (UFW).

7707 Castellanos, Teresa and Lopez, Margarita. La huelga nos ha ensenado a hablar. REVISTA MUJERES, Vol. 3, no. 2 (June 1986), p. 22-28. Spanish. **DESCR:** Biography; Canneries; *Chicanas.

7708 Keremitsis, Dawn. Del metate al molino: la mujer mexicana de 1910 a 1940. HISTORIA MEXICANA, Vol. 33, no. 2 (1983), p. 285-302. Spanish. **DESCR:** Food Industry; Labor Unions; *Mexico; Sex Roles; Tortillas; *Working Women.

7709 Romero, Bertha. The exploitation of Mexican women in the canning industry and the effects of capital accumulation on striking workers. REVISTA MUJERES, Vol. 3, no. 2 (June 1986), p. 16-20. English. **DESCR:** Canneries; Capitalism; *Chicanas; Labor Unions; *Watsonville Canning and Frozen Food Co.

7710 Sanders, Bob. Boycott Campbell's: Ohio farmworkers take it to the top. DOLLARS AND SENSE, no. 92 (December 1983), p. 16-18. English. **DESCR:** Boycotts; Campbell Soup Co.; Chavez, Cesar E.; Farm Labor Organizing Commmittee (FLOC); Farm Workers; Guevas, Fernando; *Labor Disputes; Labor Unions; Ohio; United Farmworkers of America (UFW).

7711 Segal, William. New alliances in Watsonville strike. IN THESE TIMES, Vol. 10, no. 29 (July 9, 1986), p. 5. English. **DESCR:** Collective Bargaining; Jackson, Jesse; Labor Unions; Teamsters Union; *Watsonville, CA; Watsonville Canning and Frozen Food Co.

7712 Shapiro, Peter. Watsonville shows "it can be done". GUARDIAN, Vol. 39, no. 24 (March 25, 1987), p. 1,9. English. **DESCR:** Canneries; Chicanas; Labor Unions; NorCal Frozen Foods; *Watsonville Canning and Frozen Food Co.; Working Women.

THE STRUGGLE FOR RURAL MEXICO

7713 de la Torre, Adela. Book review of: THE
STRUGGLE FOR RURAL MEXICO. LA RED/THE NET,
no. 85 (October 1984), p. 5-6. English.
DESCR: Book Reviews; Esteva, Gustavo.

Student Movements

7714 Lopez, Manuel I. The role of the Chicano
student in the Chicano Studies Program.
EPOCA: NATIONAL CONCILIO FOR CHICANO STUDIES
JOURNAL, Vol. 1, no. 2 (Winter 1971), p.
13-17. English. **DESCR**: *Chicano Studies;
Higher Education; La Raza; *Students.

7715 MEChA, Cal State Long Beach. The role of the
Chicano student. EPOCA: NATIONAL CONCILIO
FOR CHICANO STUDIES JOURNAL, Vol. 1, no. 2
(Winter 1971), p. 18-22. English. **DESCR**:
*Chicano Studies; Higher Education;
*Students.

Student Organizations

7716 MEChA - University of Texas at El Paso;
MAYO, University of Texas at Austin; and
PASO, Texas A and I University. Student
perspectives on Mexican/American studies.
EPOCA: NATIONAL CONCILIO FOR CHICANO STUDIES
JOURNAL, Vol. 1, no. 2 (Winter 1971), p.
87-96. English. **DESCR**: *Chicano Studies;
Curriculum; Mexican American Youth
Organization (MAYO); Movimiento Estudiantil
Chicano de Aztlan (MEChA); Students; Texas.

7717 Ramirez, Salvador. The establishment and
administration of a master's program in
Chicano Studies at the University of
Colorado. EPOCA: NATIONAL CONCILIO FOR
CHICANO STUDIES JOURNAL, Vol. 1, no. 2
(Winter 1971), p. 39-50. English. **DESCR**:
*Chicano Studies; *Curriculum;
Discrimination in Education; Educational
Theory and Practice; *Students; United
Mexican American Students (UMAS);
*University of Colorado, Boulder; Youth.

Student Teachers
USE: Teacher Training

Students

7718 Jimenez, Ricardo. Understanding the culture
and learning styles of Hispanic students.
MOMENTUM, Vol. 14, no. 1 (February 1983), p.
15-18. English. **DESCR**: *Acculturation;
Religious Education; Socialization.

7719 Kuner, Charles. Peer group counseling:
applied psychology in the high school.
CURRICULUM REVIEW, Vol. 23, no. 1 (February
1984), p. 89-92. English. **DESCR**: Chicago,
IL; Counseling (Educational); *Counseling
(Psychological); Education; Farragut High
School, Chicago, IL.

7720 Leon, David Jess and McNeill, Daniel. The
fifth class: a 19th century forerunner of
affirmative action. CALIFORNIA HISTORY, Vol.
64, no. 1 (Winter 1985), p. 52-57. English.
DESCR: *Affirmative Action; Colleges and
Universities; Discrimination in Education;
*Enrollment; *Higher Education; History;
*University of California.

7721 Loo, Chalsa M. and Rolison, Garry.
Alienation of ethnic minority students at a
predominantly white university. JOURNAL OF
HIGHER EDUCATION, Vol. 57, no. 1 (January,
February, 1986), p. 58-77. English. **DESCR**:
*Alienation; Attitudes; Discrimination in
Education; Surveys; Teacher-pupil
Interaction.

7722 Looking for a few good MDs. HISPANIC
BUSINESS, Vol. 9, no. 4 (April 1987), p. 16.
English. **DESCR**: *Medical Education; *Texas
Association of Mexican-American Medical
Students (TAMAMS).

7723 Lopez, Manuel I. The role of the Chicano
student in the Chicano Studies Program.
EPOCA: NATIONAL CONCILIO FOR CHICANO STUDIES
JOURNAL, Vol. 1, no. 2 (Winter 1971), p.
13-17. English. **DESCR**: *Chicano Studies;
Higher Education; La Raza; *Student
Movements.

7724 MEChA - University of Texas at El Paso;
MAYO, University of Texas at Austin; and
PASO, Texas A and I University. Student
perspectives on Mexican/American studies.
EPOCA: NATIONAL CONCILIO FOR CHICANO STUDIES
JOURNAL, Vol. 1, no. 2 (Winter 1971), p.
87-96. English. **DESCR**: *Chicano Studies;
Curriculum; Mexican American Youth
Organization (MAYO); Movimiento Estudiantil
Chicano de Aztlan (MEChA); Student
Organizations; Texas.

7725 MEChA, Cal State Long Beach. The role of the
Chicano student. EPOCA: NATIONAL CONCILIO
FOR CHICANO STUDIES JOURNAL, Vol. 1, no. 2
(Winter 1971), p. 18-22. English. **DESCR**:
*Chicano Studies; Higher Education; *Student
Movements.

7726 Mena, Francisco; Padilla, Amado M.; and
Maldonado, Margarita. Acculturative stress
and specific coping stategies among
immigrant and later generation college
students. HISPANIC JOURNAL OF BEHAVIORAL
SCIENCES, Vol. 9, no. 2 (June 1987), p.
207-225. English. **DESCR**: *Acculturation; Age
Groups; Colleges and Universities; Identity;
Immigrants; Stress.

7727 Nunez, Rene. Criteria for employment of
Chicano studies staff. EPOCA: NATIONAL
CONCILIO FOR CHICANO STUDIES JOURNAL, Vol.
1, no. 2 (Winter 1971), p. 23-30. English.
DESCR: *Chicano Studies; Higher Education;
*Teaching Profession.

7728 Powers, Stephen and Rossman, Mark H.
Attributions for success and failure among
Anglo, Black, Hispanic, and Native-American
community-college students. JOURNAL OF
PSYCHOLOGY, Vol. 117, no. 1 (May 1984), p.
27-31. English. **DESCR**: *Academic
Achievement; Anglo Americans; Blacks;
Community Colleges; *Locus of Control;
Native Americans.

7729 Ramirez, Salvador. The establishment and
administration of a master's program in
Chicano Studies at the University of
Colorado. EPOCA: NATIONAL CONCILIO FOR
CHICANO STUDIES JOURNAL, Vol. 1, no. 2
(Winter 1971), p. 39-50. English. **DESCR**:
*Chicano Studies; *Curriculum;
Discrimination in Education; Educational
Theory and Practice; Student Organizations;
United Mexican American Students (UMAS);
*University of Colorado, Boulder; Youth.

7730 Rendon, Laura Ignacia. Mathematics education
for Hispanic students in community colleges.
LA RED/THE NET, no. 76 (January 1984), p.
2-4. English. **DESCR**: Community Colleges;
*Mathematics; Surveys.

Students (cont.)

7731 Rivera, Alvin D. Laying a foundation for learning: student peer workshop groups. NEW DIRECTIONS FOR TEACHING AND LEARNING, no. 16 (December 1983), p. 81-86. English. **DESCR:** *Careers; Counseling (Educational); *Engineering as a Profession; *Natural Support Systems; Organizations.

Subject Headings

7732 Chabran, Richard. Book review of: BILINDEX. LA RED/THE NET, no. 87 (July 1985), p. 6-8. English. **DESCR:** *BILINDEX: A BILINGUAL SPANISH-ENGLISH SUBJECT HEADING LIST; Book Reviews; HISPANEX (Oakland, CA).

Suffrage
USE: Voting Rights

Sugranes, Rosa

7733 Beale, Stephen. CEOs. HISPANIC BUSINESS, Vol. 9, no. 4 (April 1987), p. 20-37, 52. English. **DESCR:** Alvarez, Roberto; Batarse, Anthony A.; Biography; Business Enterprises; *Businesspeople; Carlo, Nelson; Estrada, Anthony; Flores, Frank; Fullana, Jaime, Jr.; Hernandez, George; *Management; Ortega, James; Quirch, Guillermo; Ruiz, Roberto; Santa Maria, Yvonne Z.; Tamaya, Carlos; Young, Paul H., Jr.

Suicide

7734 Anson, Richard H. Inmate ethnicity and the suicide connection: a note on aggregate trends. THE PRISON JOURNAL, Vol. 63, no. 1 (March 1983), p. 91-99. English. **DESCR:** *Prisoners.

SUNY Hispanic Research and Information Network

7735 Perez, Emma. Higher education organizations. LA RED/THE NET, No. 101 (October 1986), p. 6-10. English. **DESCR:** *Educational Organizations; Higher Education; *Hispanic Association of Higher Education (HAHE); *Puerto Rican Council on Higher Education (PRCHE).

Support Groups
USE: Natural Support Systems

Survey of Career Information Systems in Secondary Schools

7736 National Council of La Raza (NCLR). Career information and Hispanic students. LA RED/THE NET, no. 75 (December 1983), p. 2-4. English. **DESCR:** *Careers; Educational Services; *National Council of La Raza (NCLR); Secondary School Education; *Youth.

SURVEY OF INCOME AND EDUCATION, 1976

7737 Garcia, John A. Ethnic identity and background traits: explorations of Mexican-origin populations. LA RED/THE NET, no. 29 (April 1980), p. 2. English. **DESCR:** *Identity; *Self-Referents; *Southwestern United States.

7738 Garcia, Steve. Language usage and status attainment of Chicanos. LA RED/THE NET, no. 30 (May 1980), p. 2-3. English. **DESCR:** *Language Usage; *Socioeconomic Factors.

7739 Rochin, Refugio I. Chicanos in rural labor markets: part 2. LA RED/THE NET, no. 47 (October 1981), p. 2,10. English. **DESCR:** *Labor Supply and Market; *Northern California; *Rural Population; *Surveys.

Surveys

7740 Arce, Carlos H. Chicano Survey report #4: characteristics of the survey sample. LA RED/THE NET, no. 41 (April 1981), p. 7-8. English. **DESCR:** *National Chicano Survey (NCS).

7741 Barger, W.K. and Reza, Ernesto. Midwestern farmworkers and the farm labor movement. LA RED/THE NET, no. 78 (March 1984), p. 2-7. English. **DESCR:** *Farm Workers; *Midwestern States; Migrant Labor.

7742 Chicano Survey report #1: labor force experiences. LA RED/THE NET, no. 38 (January 1981), p. 1,12. English. **DESCR:** Labor; *Labor Supply and Market; *National Chicano Survey (NCS).

7743 Lacayo, Carmela G. Triple jeopardy among Hispanic elderly: results from first national needs assessment of older Hispanics. LA RED/THE NET, no. 56 (July 1982), p. 2-3. English. **DESCR:** *Ancianos; Asociacion Nacional Pro Personas Mayores; *National Study to Assess the Service Needs of the Hispanic Elderly; Research Methodology; *Social Services.

7744 Latino literacy update: ELPS/survey updates illiteracy profile. LA RED/THE NET, no. 98 (July 1986), p. 10-12. English. **DESCR:** *English Language Proficiency Survey (ELPS); *Literacy.

7745 Loo, Chalsa M. and Rolison, Garry. Alienation of ethnic minority students at a predominantly white university. JOURNAL OF HIGHER EDUCATION, Vol. 57, no. 1 (January, February, 1986), p. 58-77. English. **DESCR:** *Alienation; Attitudes; Discrimination in Education; *Students; Teacher-pupil Interaction.

7746 Magallan, Rafael J. 1983-84 NAEP data raises questions regarding the school experiences of language minority children. LA RED/THE NET, no. 92 (November, December, 1985), p. 9-11. English. **DESCR:** *Bilingual Bicultural Education; Bilingualism; Dropouts; English as a Second Language; *National Assessment of Educational Progress.

7747 Nat'l Chicano Survey analyzed. LA RED/THE NET, No. 100 (September 1986), p. 10. English. **DESCR:** *Literacy; *National Chicano Survey (NCS).

7748 Rendon, Laura Ignacia. Chicano student and institution related determinants of educational outcomes in south Texas community colleges. LA RED/THE NET, no. 73 (October 1983), p. 2-6. English. **DESCR:** *Academic Achievement; Community Colleges; *South Texas.

7749 Rendon, Laura Ignacia. Mathematics education for Hispanic students in community colleges. LA RED/THE NET, no. 76 (January 1984), p. 2-4. English. **DESCR:** Community Colleges; *Mathematics; Students.

7750 Report to the Network. LA RED/THE NET, No. 104 (January 1987), p. 1-2. English. **DESCR:** Computers; *Contreras, Reynaldo A.; *Higher Education; *Midwestern States; *Natural Support Systems; Research Methodology.

Surveys (cont.)

7751 Rochin, Refugio I. Chicanos in rural labor markets: part 2. LA RED/THE NET, no. 47 (October 1981), p. 2,10. English. **DESCR:** *Labor Supply and Market; *Northern California; *Rural Population; SURVEY OF INCOME AND EDUCATION, 1976.

7752 Smith, David M. Survey: hospitalization access for patients of migrant health centers and combined migrant and community health centers. MIGRATION WORLD MAGAZINE, Vol. 15, no. 3 (1987), p. 20-23. English. **DESCR:** *Migrant Health Services.

7753 So, Alvin Yiu-cheong. The analysis of language minority issues in national data sets. LA RED/THE NET, no. 71 (August 1983), p. 3-5. English. **DESCR:** Bilingualism; Databases; *Language Usage; *National Center for Bilingual Research.

7754 Survey report #5: language of Chicanos. LA RED/THE NET, no. 43 (June 1981), p. 7. English. **DESCR:** Language Proficiency; *Language Usage.

7755 What is your opinion of U.S. policy towards Central America?=Cual es tu opinion sobre la politica norteamericana hacia Centro America? AMERICAS 2001, Vol. 1, no. 2 (September, October, 1987), p. 21. Bilingual. **DESCR:** *Central America; International Relations; *Public Opinion.

7756 Wreford, Mary. Chicano Survey report #2: perceptions and experience of discrimination. LA RED/THE NET, no. 39 (February 1981), p. 7,16. English. **DESCR:** *Discrimination; Discrimination in Employment; Midwestern States; *National Chicano Survey (NCS); Southwestern United States.

7757 Wreford, Mary. Reactions from the Chicano Survey respondents: no mas silencio. LA RED/THE NET, no. 33 (August 1980), p. 2-3. English. **DESCR:** Chicano Project of the University of Michigan; Midwestern States; *National Chicano Survey (NCS); *Public Opinion; Social Science; Southwestern United States.

SURVIVAL SPANISH

7758 Montane, Diane. Learning survival Spanish. VISTA, Vol. 1, no. 5 (January 5, 1986), p. 16. English. **DESCR:** Education; Ruiz, Vivian; *Spanish Language; Television.

Swicegood, Gray

7759 Hastings, D.W. Book review of: MEXICAN AMERICAN FERTILITY PATTERNS. CHOICE, Vol. 23, no. 11-12 (July, August, 1986), p. 1738. English. **DESCR:** Bean, Frank D.; Book Reviews; *MEXICAN AMERICAN FERTILITY PATTERNS.

Symbolism

7760 Goldman, Shifra. Arte chicano: iconografia de la autodeterminacion. LA COMUNIDAD, No. 336 (December 28, 1986), p. 12-14+. Spanish. **DESCR:** *Art; Discrimination; EL PLAN ESPIRITUAL DE AZTLAN; History; Identity; Nationalism; Pachucos; Social Classes.

7761 Klor de Alva, J. Jorge. California Chicano literature and pre-Columbian motifs: foil and fetish. CONFLUENCIA, Vol. 1, no. 2 (Spring 1986), p. 18-26. English. **DESCR:** Alurista; Aztecs; Aztlan; *California; EL PLAN ESPIRITUAL DE AZTLAN; *Literature; *Precolumbian Images; *Precolumbian Philosophy.

7762 Limon, Jose E. La Llorona, the third legend of greater Mexico: cultural symbols, women, and the political unconscious. RENATO ROSALDO LECTURE SERIES MONOGRAPH, Vol. 2, (Spring 1986), p. [59]-93. English. **DESCR:** *Feminism; Folklore; *La Llorona; La Virgen de Guadalupe; *Leyendas; Malinche; Mexico; Women.

7763 Sommers, Laurie Kay. Symbol and style in Cinco de Mayo. JOURNAL OF AMERICAN FOLKLORE, Vol. 98, (October, December, 1985), p. 476-482. English. **DESCR:** *Cinco de Mayo; *Cultural Customs; History; *Holidays; *San Francisco, CA.

Tabb, David H.

7764 Body-Gendrot, Sophie. Book review of: PROTEST IS NOT ENOUGH. INTERNATIONAL JOURNAL OF URBAN AND REGIONAL RESEARCH, Vol. 9, no. 4 (1985), p. 576-577. English. **DESCR:** Book Reviews; Browning, Rufus P.; Marshall, Dale Rogers; *PROTEST IS NOT ENOUGH: THE STRUGGLE OF BLACKS AND HISPANICS FOR EQUALITY IN URBAN POLITICS.

7765 Browning, Rufus P. and Marshall, Dale Rogers. Black and Hispanic power in city politics: a forum. P.S. [AMERICAN POLITICAL SCIENCE ASSOCIATION], Vol. 19, no. 3 (Summer 1986), p. 573-639. English. **DESCR:** Blacks; Browning, Rufus P.; Marshall, Dale Rogers; *Politics; *PROTEST IS NOT ENOUGH: THE STRUGGLE OF BLACKS AND HISPANICS FOR EQUALITY IN URBAN POLITICS; Urban Communities.

7766 Browning, Rufus P.; Marshall, Dale Rogers; and Tabb, David H. Protest is not enough: a theory of political incorporation. P.S. [AMERICAN POLITICAL SCIENCE ASSOCIATION], Vol. 19, no. 3 (Summer 1986), p. 576-581. English. **DESCR:** Blacks; Browning, Rufus P.; Marshall, Dale Rogers; Political Representation; Politics; *PROTEST IS NOT ENOUGH: THE STRUGGLE OF BLACKS AND HISPANICS FOR EQUALITY IN URBAN POLITICS; Urban Communities.

7767 Sonenshein, Raphe. Biracial coalition politics in Los Angeles. P.S. [AMERICAN POLITICAL SCIENCE ASSOCIATION], Vol. 19, no. 3 (Summer 1986), p. 582-590. English. **DESCR:** Blacks; Bradley, Tom; Browning, Rufus P.; *Ethnic Groups; *Intergroup Relations; *Los Angeles, CA; Marshall, Dale Rogers; Political Parties and Organizations; *Politics; PROTEST IS NOT ENOUGH: THE STRUGGLE OF BLACKS AND HISPANICS FOR EQUALITY IN URBAN POLITICS.

Taco Bell

7768 Thomas, Marjorie. Taco Bell rings in new image. RESTAURANT BUSINESS, Vol. 83, (October 10, 1984), p. 210-218. English. **DESCR:** *Restaurants.

Tafolla, Carmen

7769 Castillo-Speed, Lillian. Chicana/Latina
     literature and criticism: reviews of recent
     books. WLW JOURNAL, Vol. 11, no. 3
     (September 1987), p. 1-4. English. DESCR:
     Andrews, Lynn V.; *Book Reviews; BORDERS;
     Chavez, Denise; *Chicanas; CONTEMPORARY
     CHICANA POETRY: A CRITICAL APPROACH TO AN
     EMERGING LITERATURE; Flores, Angel; Flores,
     Kate; JAGUAR WOMAN; Mora, Pat; Sanchez,
     Marta Ester; THE DEFIANT MUSE: HISPANIC
     FEMINIST POEMS FROM THE MIDDLE AGES TO THE
     PRESENT; THE LAST OF THE MENU GIRLS; TO
     SPLIT A HUMAN: MITOS, MACHOS Y LA MUJER
     CHICANA; Vigil-Pinon, Evangelina; WOMAN OF
     HER WORD: HISPANIC WOMEN WRITE.

Taiwan

7770 Cruz, David V. Caucus & Co. orients the
     East. HISPANIC BUSINESS, Vol. 9, no. 11
     (November 1987), p. 10-13, 71+. English.
     DESCR: Businesspeople; *Congressional
     Hispanic Caucus; Elected Officials;
     *International Relations; *Japan; Latin
     Business Foundation, Los Angeles, CA;
     Nakasone, Yasuhiro [Prime Minister of
     Japan].

Talamantes, Felipe

7771 Escobar, Edward J. Mexican revolutionaries
     and the Los Angeles police: harassment of
     the Partido Liberal Mexicano, 1907-1910.
     AZTLAN, Vol. 17, no. 1 (Spring 1986), p.
     1-46. English. DESCR: Civil Rights; *Flores
     Magon, Ricardo; Gutierrez de Lara, Lazaro;
     Los Angeles, CA; *Los Angeles Police
     Department; *Partido Liberal Mexicano (PLM);
     *Police; Police Brutality; Political
     Repression; Rico, Louis; Rico, Thomas;
     United States-Mexico Relations.

TALE OF SUNLIGHT

7772 Bruce-Novoa, Juan. Poesia de Gary Soto: una
     autobiografia a plazos. LA COMUNIDAD, No.
     270 (September 22, 1985), p. 8-10. Spanish.
     DESCR: Authors; *Literary Criticism; Poetry;
     *Soto, Gary; THE ELEMENTS OF SAN JOAQUIN;
     WHERE SPARROWS WORK HARD.

Tamaya, Carlos

7773 Beale, Stephen. CEOs. HISPANIC BUSINESS,
     Vol. 9, no. 4 (April 1987), p. 20-37, 52.
     English. DESCR: Alvarez, Roberto; Batarse,
     Anthony A.; Biography; Business Enterprises;
     *Businesspeople; Carlo, Nelson; Estrada,
     Anthony; Flores, Frank; Fullana, Jaime, Jr.;
     Hernandez, George; *Management; Ortega,
     James; Quirch, Guillermo; Ruiz, Roberto;
     Santa Maria, Yvonne Z.; Sugranes, Rosa;
     Young, Paul H., Jr.

Tampa, FL

7774 McNeely, Dave. Hispanic power at the polls.
     VISTA, Vol. 2, no. 3 (November 2, 1986), p.
     8-12. English. DESCR: Austin, TX; *Barrera,
     Roy, Jr.; Chavez, Linda; Elected Officials;
     Gonzalez, Raul; Martinez, Bob; Maryland;
     Political System; San Antonio, TX;
     Statistics; *Voter Turnout.

Taos Vocational School

7775 Wroth, William. New hope in hard times:
     Hispanic crafts are revived during troubled
     years. PALACIO, Vol. 89, no. 2 (1983), p.
     22-31. English. DESCR: *Arts and Crafts;
     *Las Lunas Vocational Training School; New
     Mexico; Spanish Colonial Arts Society; Works

Progress Administration (WPA).

Tapia, Raul R.

7776 SICC sale opposed. BROADCASTING, Vol. 111,
     no. 7 (August 18, 1986), p. 46-52. English.
     DESCR: Azcarraga, Emilio; Federal
     Communications Commission (FCC); First
     Chicago Venture Capital; Hallmark Cards;
     KFTV, Fresno, CA [television station]; KMEX,
     Los Angeles, CA [television station]; KWEX,
     San Antonio, TX [television station]; Legal
     Cases; *Spanish International Communications
     Corp. (SICC); Spanish Language; Television;
     TVL Corp.; WLTV, Miami, FL [television
     station]; WXTV, Paterson, NJ [television
     station].

THE TARNISHED DOOR

7777 Cardenas, Gilbert. Book review of: IN
     DEFENSE OF LA RAZA. LA RED/THE NET, no. 85
     (October 1984), p. 2-5. English. DESCR:
     Balderrama, Francisco E.; Book Reviews;
     Crewdson, John; *IN DEFENSE OF LA RAZA: THE
     LOS ANGELES MEXICAN CONSULATE AND THE
     MEXICAN COMMUNITY.

"Tata Casehua" [short story]

7778 Alarcon, Justo S. Estructuras narrativas en
     TATA CASEHUA de Miguel Mendez. CONFLUENCIA,
     Vol. 1, no. 2 (Spring 1986), p. 48-54.
     Spanish. DESCR: *Literary Criticism; *Mendez
     M., Miguel; Short Story.

7779 Vogt, Gregory M. Archetypal images of
     apocalypse in Miguel Mendez's TATA CASEHUA.
     CONFLUENCIA, Vol. 1, no. 2 (Spring 1986), p.
     55-60. English. DESCR: *Literary Criticism;
     *Mendez M., Miguel; Short Story.

Tatiana and Johnny

7780 Machado, Melinda. Saying "no" to teenage
     sex. VISTA, Vol. 2, no. 11 (July 5, 1987),
     p. 14. English. DESCR: *CUANDO ESTEMOS
     JUNTOS [phonograph record]; DETENTE
     [phonograph record]; Music; *Musical Lyrics;
     Planned Parenthood Federation of America;
     Sex Education.

TATOO THE WICKED CROSS

7781 Bruce-Novoa, Juan. Homosexuality and the
     Chicano novel. CONFLUENCIA, Vol. 2, no. 1
     (Fall 1986), p. 69-77. English. DESCR:
     Acosta, Oscar Zeta; CITY OF NIGHT; FAULTLINE
     [novel]; *Homosexuality; Islas, Arturo;
     *Literary Criticism; Machismo; *Novel; Ortiz
     Taylor, Sheila; POCHO; Rechy, John; Salas,
     Floyd; SPRING FORWARD/FALL BACK; THE
     AUTOBIOGRAPHY OF A BROWN BUFFALO; THE RAIN
     GOD: A DESERT TALE; THE REVOLT OF THE
     COCKROACH PEOPLE; Villarreal, Jose Antonio.

Taylor, Hycel

7782 Jesse Jackson makes appearance at CBS board
     meeting. BROADCASTING, Vol. 110, no. 16
     (April 21, 1986), p. 100. English. DESCR:
     Broadcast Media; *Columbia Broadcasting
     Studios (CBS); Discrimination;
     Discrimination in Employment; *Jackson,
     Jesse; People United to Serve Humanity
     (PUSH); Stereotypes; Wyman, Thomas.

Taylor, Pat Ellis

7783 Milner, Clyde A. Book review of: BORDER
     HEALING WOMAN: THE STORY OF JEWEL BABB.
     JOURNAL OF THE WEST, Vol. 22, (January
     1983), p. 95. English. DESCR: Book Reviews;
     *BORDER HEALING WOMAN: THE STORY OF JEWEL
     BABB.

Teacher Attitudes

7784 Licon, Lena. Socioeconomic and ethnic biases
     of pre-service teachers. LA RED/THE NET, no.
     46 (September 1981), p. 2. English. DESCR:
     *Teacher Training; Teaching Profession.

Teacher Training

7785 Eddy, John P. and Martin, William.
     Application of competency-based criteria to
     bilingual-bicultural education. FOCUS ON
     LEARNING, Vol. 11, no. 1 (Spring 1985), p.
     13-16. English. DESCR: *Bilingual Bicultural
     Education.

7786 Licon, Lena. Socioeconomic and ethnic biases
     of pre-service teachers. LA RED/THE NET, no.
     46 (September 1981), p. 2. English. DESCR:
     *Teacher Attitudes; Teaching Profession.

7787 Nieto, Sonia. Who's afraid of bilingual
     parents? BILINGUAL REVIEW, Vol. 12, no. 3
     (September, December, 1985), p. 179-189.
     English. DESCR: *Bilingual Bicultural
     Education; *Community School Relationships;
     *Family; *Parent and Child Relationships.

7788 Smith, G. Pritchy. The critical issue of
     excellence and equity in competency testing.
     JOURNAL OF TEACHER EDUCATION, Vol. 35, no. 2
     (March, April, 1984), p. 6-9. English.

Teacher-pupil Interaction

7789 Chesterfield, Ray A. and Chesterfield,
     Kathleen Barrows. "Hojas with the H":
     spontaneous peer teaching in bilingual
     classrooms. BILINGUAL REVIEW, Vol. 12, no. 3
     (September, December, 1985), p. 198-208.
     English. DESCR: *Bilingual Bicultural
     Education; Bilingualism; Education.

7790 Loo, Chalsa M. and Rolison, Garry.
     Alienation of ethnic minority students at a
     predominantly white university. JOURNAL OF
     HIGHER EDUCATION, Vol. 57, no. 1 (January,
     February, 1986), p. 58-77. English. DESCR:
     *Alienation; Attitudes; Discrimination in
     Education; *Students; Surveys.

Teaching
     USE: Education

Teaching Profession

7791 Academics and entrepreneurs talk trade.
     HISPANIC BUSINESS, Vol. 9, no. 6 (June
     1987), p. 96. English. DESCR: *Business
     Enterprises; Conferences and Meetings;
     Fourth Symposium on Hispanic Business and
     Economy, San Juan, Puerto Rico, November
     23-25, 1987; *International Economic
     Relations; Latin America; *National
     Association of Hispanic Professors of
     Business Administration and Economics (Los
     Profesores); Organizations.

7792 Garza, Hisauro A. The "barrioization" of
     Hispanic faculty. EDUCATIONAL RECORD,
     (Fall, Winter, 1987, 1988), p. 122-124.
     English. DESCR: *Colleges and Universities;
     *Discrimination in Education;
     *Discrimination in Employment; *Higher
     Education.

7793 Gutierrez, Felix. Ralph Guzman remembered.
     LA RED/THE NET, no. 91 (October 1985), p.
     1-2. English. DESCR: Biography; *Guzman,
     Ralph.

7794 Licon, Lena. Socioeconomic and ethnic biases
     of pre-service teachers. LA RED/THE NET, no.
     46 (September 1981), p. 2. English. DESCR:
     *Teacher Attitudes; *Teacher Training.

7795 Nunez, Rene. Criteria for employment of
     Chicano studies staff. EPOCA: NATIONAL
     CONCILIO FOR CHICANO STUDIES JOURNAL, Vol.
     1, no. 2 (Winter 1971), p. 23-30. English.
     DESCR: *Chicano Studies; Higher Education;
     Students.

7796 Texas update. LA RED/THE NET, no. 97 (June
     1986), p. 3. English. DESCR: *Educational
     Tests and Measurements; *Texas Examination
     of Current Administrators and Teachers
     (TECAT).

7797 Trujillo, Marcela L. Guidelines for
     employment in Chicano studies. EPOCA:
     NATIONAL CONCILIO FOR CHICANO STUDIES
     JOURNAL, Vol. 1, no. 2 (Winter 1971), p.
     60-65. English. DESCR: *Chicano Studies.

Teamsters Union

7798 Segal, William. New alliances in Watsonville
     strike. IN THESE TIMES, Vol. 10, no. 29
     (July 9, 1986), p. 5. English. DESCR:
     Collective Bargaining; Jackson, Jesse; Labor
     Unions; Strikes and Lockouts; *Watsonville,
     CA; Watsonville Canning and Frozen Food Co.

Teatro

7799 Aguilu de Murphy, Raquel. Book review of:
     GIVING UP THE GHOST. THE AMERICAS REVIEW,
     Vol. 15, no. 2 (Summer 1987), p. 105-107.
     Spanish. DESCR: Book Reviews; *GIVING UP THE
     GHOST; Moraga, Cherrie.

7800 Anderson de Barret, Judit. Book review of:
     POLITICS AND CHICANO CULTURE. LECTOR, Vol.
     4, no. 4-6 (1987), p. 56. English. DESCR:
     Book Reviews; *POLITICS & CHICANO CULTURE: A
     PERSPECTIVE ON EL TEATRO CAMPESINO; Xavier,
     Roy Eric.

7801 Beale, Stephen and Valdez, Luis. Connecting
     with the American experience: an interview
     with Luis Valdez. HISPANIC BUSINESS, Vol. 9,
     no. 7 (July 1987), p. 10-13. English.
     DESCR: Biography; Films; LA BAMBA [film];
     Stereotypes; *Valdez, Luis.

7802 Burciaga, Jose Antonio. Corridos. VISTA,
     Vol. 3, no. 2 (October 3, 1987), p. 10.
     English. DESCR: Corridos; *CORRIDOS [film];
     Ronstadt, Linda; Television; Valdez, Luis.

7803 Burciaga, Jose Antonio. A man with his
     teatro. VISTA, Vol. 1, no. 3 (November 3,
     1985), p. 8-10. English. DESCR: CORRIDOS
     [play]; El Teatro Campesino; *Valdez, Luis;
     ZOOT SUIT [play].

7804 Chavez, Denise. NOVENA NARRATIVAS y OFRENDAS
     NUEVOMEXICANAS. THE AMERICAS REVIEW, Vol.
     15, no. 3-4 (Fall, Winter, 1987), p. 85-100.
     English. DESCR: Altars.

Teatro (cont.)

7805 Flores, Arturo C. El Teatro Campesino (1965-1986): algunas orientaciones teoricas. CONFLUENCIA, Vol. 2, no. 2 (Spring 1987), p. 116-121. Spanish. **DESCR:** Brecht, Bertolt; *El Teatro Campesino; History; Moreno, Mario "Cantinflas"; Valdez, Luis.

7806 Gomez Pena, Guillermo. Declaracion de principios de un teatro bicultural. LA COMUNIDAD, No. 257 (June 23, 1985), p. 4-5. Spanish. **DESCR:** *Poyesis Genetica [theater group].

7807 Gomez Pena, Guillermo and Erana, Maria. Sobre el arte, la rebeldia y las fronteras. LA COMUNIDAD, No. 312 (July 13, 1986), p. 6-7+. Spanish. **DESCR:** Berkeley, CA; *BORDER-X-FRONTERA [radio program]; Gomez Pena, Guillermo; *Radio; Schein, David.

7808 Gonzales, Juan. Quinto Festival de los Teatros Chicanos - Primer Encuentro Latinoamericano. LATIN QUARTER, Vol. 1, no. 2 (October 1974), p. 31-33,35. English. **DESCR:** *Festivals; *Mexico.

7809 Huerta, Jorge. Book review of: GIVING UP THE GHOST. THE AMERICAS REVIEW, Vol. 15, no. 2 (Summer 1987), p. 104-105. English. **DESCR:** Book Reviews; *GIVING UP THE GHOST; Moraga, Cherrie.

7810 Lomeli, Maria Magdalena S. "LATC" un espacio para el teatro politico. LA COMUNIDAD, No. 333 (December 7, 1986), p. 10-11. Spanish. **DESCR:** Actors and Actresses; *Los Angeles Theatre Center (LATC); Morales, Esai.

7811 Lowe, Virginia A.P. Presentation of ethnic identity in Chicano theater. CHIRICU, Vol. 2, no. 1 (Spring 1980), p. 52-58. English. **DESCR:** Ethnic Groups; Folklore Institute at Indiana University; Gary, IN; Identity; *Teatro Desangano del Pueblo, Washington Park, East Chicago, IN.

7812 Medina, David. America's Hispanic Theater Olympics. VISTA, Vol. 1, no. 12 (August 2, 1986), p. 12-14. English. **DESCR:** Actors and Actresses; Dance; *Festival Latino.

7813 Mejias Rentas, Antonio. Luis Valdez y su Teatro Campesino de nuevo en L.A. LA COMUNIDAD, No. 294 (March 9, 1986), p. 8-9. Spanish. **DESCR:** *I DON'T HAVE TO SHOW YOU NO STINKING BADGES; Teatro Reviews; *Valdez, Luis.

7814 Pena, Luis H. Praxis dramatica, praxis politica: los actos de Luis Valdez. REVISTA DE CRITICA LITERARIA LATINOAMERICANA, Vol. 10, no. 19 (1984), p. 161-166. Spanish. **DESCR:** Actos; ACTOS; El Teatro Campesino; *Valdez, Luis.

7815 Preciado, Consuelo. CORRIDOS: the movie=CORRIDOS: la pelicula. AMERICAS 2001, Vol. 1, no. 2 (September, October, 1987), p. 5-6. Bilingual. **DESCR:** Corridos; *CORRIDOS [film]; El Teatro Campesino; *Films; Valdez, Luis.

7816 Ramirez, Arturo. SOLDIERBOY, una muestra de la eficacia del teatro chicano de hoy. LA COMUNIDAD, No. 357 (May 24, 1987), p. 12-13. Spanish. **DESCR:** Perez, Judith; Perez, Severo; *SOLDIERBOY [play]; Teatro Reviews; Vietnam War.

7817 Rosas, Alejandro. Teatro chicano: un teatro de la esperanza. LA COMUNIDAD, No. 247 (April 14, 1985), 2-3. Spanish. **DESCR:** El

Teatro de la Esperanza; Identity; *ONCE A FAMILY [play]; Teatro Reviews.

7818 Ruiz, Ariel. Raza, sexo y politica en SHORT EYES by Miguel Pinero. THE AMERICAS REVIEW, Vol. 15, no. 2 (Summer 1987), p. 93-102. Spanish. **DESCR:** Homosexuality; Literary Criticism; Pinero, Miguel; Prisoners; Puerto Ricans; Sex Roles; *SHORT EYES.

7819 Yarbro-Bejarano, Yvonne. The female subject in Chicano theater: sexuality, race, and class. THEATRE JOURNAL, Vol. 38, no. 4 (December 1986), p. 389-407. English. **DESCR:** *Chicanas; El Teatro Campesino; El Teatro de la Esperanza; Feminism; *Malinche; *Sex Roles; Teatro Nacional de Aztlan (TENAZ); WIT (Women in Teatro).

El Teatro Campesino

7820 Burciaga, Jose Antonio. A man with his teatro. VISTA, Vol. 1, no. 3 (November 3, 1985), p. 8-10. English. **DESCR:** CORRIDOS [play]; *Teatro; *Valdez, Luis; ZOOT SUIT [play].

7821 Flores, Arturo C. El Teatro Campesino (1965-1986): algunas orientaciones teoricas. CONFLUENCIA, Vol. 2, no. 2 (Spring 1987), p. 116-121. Spanish. **DESCR:** Brecht, Bertolt; History; Moreno, Mario "Cantinflas"; *Teatro; Valdez, Luis.

7822 Pena, Luis H. Praxis dramatica, praxis politica: los actos de Luis Valdez. REVISTA DE CRITICA LITERARIA LATINOAMERICANA, Vol. 10, no. 19 (1984), p. 161-166. Spanish. **DESCR:** Actos; ACTOS; *Teatro; *Valdez, Luis.

7823 Preciado, Consuelo. CORRIDOS: the movie=CORRIDOS: la pelicula. AMERICAS 2001, Vol. 1, no. 2 (September, October, 1987), p. 5-6. Bilingual. **DESCR:** Corridos; *CORRIDOS [film]; *Films; Teatro; Valdez, Luis.

7824 Yarbro-Bejarano, Yvonne. The female subject in Chicano theater: sexuality, race, and class. THEATRE JOURNAL, Vol. 38, no. 4 (December 1986), p. 389-407. English. **DESCR:** *Chicanas; El Teatro de la Esperanza; Feminism; *Malinche; *Sex Roles; *Teatro; Teatro Nacional de Aztlan (TENAZ); WIT (Women in Teatro).

El Teatro de la Esperanza

7825 Rosas, Alejandro. Teatro chicano: un teatro de la esperanza. LA COMUNIDAD, No. 247 (April 14, 1985), 2-3. Spanish. **DESCR:** Identity; *ONCE A FAMILY [play]; *Teatro; Teatro Reviews.

7826 Yarbro-Bejarano, Yvonne. The female subject in Chicano theater: sexuality, race, and class. THEATRE JOURNAL, Vol. 38, no. 4 (December 1986), p. 389-407. English. **DESCR:** *Chicanas; El Teatro Campesino; Feminism; *Malinche; *Sex Roles; *Teatro; Teatro Nacional de Aztlan (TENAZ); WIT (Women in Teatro).

Teatro Desangano del Pueblo, Washington Park, East Chicago, IN

7827 Lowe, Virginia A.P. Presentation of ethnic identity in Chicano theater. CHIRICU, Vol. 2, no. 1 (Spring 1980), p. 52-58. English. **DESCR:** Ethnic Groups; Folklore Institute at Indiana University; Gary, IN; Identity; *Teatro.

Teatro Nacional de Aztlan (TENAZ)

7828 Yarbro-Bejarano, Yvonne. The female subject
in Chicano theater: sexuality, race, and
class. THEATRE JOURNAL, Vol. 38, no. 4
(December 1986), p. 389-407. English.
DESCR: *Chicanas; El Teatro Campesino; El
Teatro de la Esperanza; Feminism; *Malinche;
*Sex Roles; *Teatro; WIT (Women in Teatro).

Teatro Reviews

7829 Mejias Rentas, Antonio. Luis Valdez y su
Teatro Campesino de nuevo en L.A. LA
COMUNIDAD, No. 294 (March 9, 1986), p. 8-9.
Spanish. DESCR: *I DON'T HAVE TO SHOW YOU NO
STINKING BADGES; *Teatro; *Valdez, Luis.

7830 Ramirez, Arturo. SOLDIERBOY, una muestra de
la eficacia del teatro chicano de hoy. LA
COMUNIDAD, No. 357 (May 24, 1987), p. 12-13.
Spanish. DESCR: Perez, Judith; Perez,
Severo; *SOLDIERBOY [play]; *Teatro; Vietnam
War.

7831 Rosas, Alejandro. Teatro chicano: un teatro
de la esperanza. LA COMUNIDAD, No. 247
(April 14, 1985), 2-3. Spanish. DESCR: El
Teatro de la Esperanza; Identity; *ONCE A
FAMILY [play]; *Teatro.

Teatros Unidos

7832 Aceves Madrid, Vicente. Controversy
surrounding NBC's CHICO AND THE MAN. LATIN
QUARTER, Vol. 1, no. 2 (October 1974), p.
5-7. English. DESCR: Albertson, Jack;
Artists; *CHICO AND THE MAN [television
show]; Komack, James; Prinze, Freddie;
Stereotypes; *Television.

Tecatos
USE: Drug Addicts

Technical-Vocational Institute (T-V), Albuquerque, NM

7833 The institute, the artist, the art. NUESTRO,
Vol. 11, no. 4 (May 1987), p. 15-17.
English. DESCR: Artists; *Gonzales, Edward;
Mural Art.

THE TEJANO COMMUNITY, 1836-1900

7834 Griswold del Castillo, Richard. New
perspectives on the Mexican and American
borderlands. LATIN AMERICAN RESEARCH REVIEW,
Vol. 19, no. 1 (1984), p. 199-209. English.
DESCR: AL NORTE DEL RIO BRAVO (PASADO
INMEDIATO, 1930-1981); AL NORTE DEL RIO
BRAVO (PASADO LEJANO, 1600-1930); *Book
Reviews; *Border Region; Gomez-Quinones,
Juan; Maciel, David; MEXICANO RESISTANCE IN
THE SOUTHWEST: "THE SACRED RIGHT OF
SELF-PRESERVATION"; Rosenbaum, Robert J.;
THE MEXICAN FRONTIER, 1821-1846: THE
AMERICAN SOUTHWEST UNDER MEXICO; Weber,
David J.

7835 Montejano, David. Book review of: THE TEJANO
COMMUNITY, 1836-1900. LA RED/THE NET, no. 64
(February 1983), p. 5-6. English. DESCR:
Book Reviews; de Leon, Arnoldo.

Telemundo Television Group

7836 Beale, Stephen. New blood, fresh money:
Telemundo, Univision bullish on television
market. HISPANIC BUSINESS, Vol. 9, no. 12
(December 1987), p. 30-36. English. DESCR:
*Corporations; Hallmark Cards; LatCom;
Radio; Spanish International Communications
Corp. (SICC); *Spanish Language;
*Television; Univision.

7837 Poole, Claire. Viewers looking for the U.S.
look. HISPANIC BUSINESS, Vol. 9, no. 12
(December 1987), p. 26-28. English. DESCR:
*Advertising; Advertising Agencies;
Marketing; *Television.

Television

7838 Aceves Madrid, Vicente. Controversy
surrounding NBC's CHICO AND THE MAN. LATIN
QUARTER, Vol. 1, no. 2 (October 1974), p.
5-7. English. DESCR: Albertson, Jack;
Artists; *CHICO AND THE MAN [television
show]; Komack, James; Prinze, Freddie;
Stereotypes; Teatros Unidos.

7839 Ayala, Ernie. Henry Alfaro, ABC's Eyewitness
News reporter. LATIN QUARTER, Vol. 1, no. 1
(July 1974), p. 13-15. English. DESCR:
*Alfaro, Henry; California Chicano News
Media Association (CCNMA); Golden Mike
Award; Journalists.

7840 Barro, Mary Helen. 1973 Emmy Awards. LATIN
QUARTER, Vol. 1, no. 1 (July 1974), p. 5-6.
English. DESCR: Chavez, Andres; CINCO VIDAS;
Emmy Awards; *Esparza, Moctezuma; Identity;
Quintero, Carlos; *Recreation; REFLECCIONES;
Rodriguez, Sandra; Rodriguez, Tony; Ruiz,
Jose Luis; Stereotypes.

7841 Beale, Stephen. More changes at SIN.
HISPANIC BUSINESS, Vol. 9, no. 1 (January
1987), p. 10. English. DESCR: *Godoy,
Gustavo; Journalism; *Noticiero SIN;
*Spanish International Network (SIN).

7842 Beale, Stephen. New blood, fresh money:
Telemundo, Univision bullish on television
market. HISPANIC BUSINESS, Vol. 9, no. 12
(December 1987), p. 30-36. English. DESCR:
*Corporations; Hallmark Cards; LatCom;
Radio; Spanish International Communications
Corp. (SICC); *Spanish Language; *Telemundo
Television Group; Univision.

7843 Burciaga, Jose Antonio. Corridos. VISTA,
Vol. 3, no. 2 (October 3, 1987), p. 10.
English. DESCR: Corridos; *CORRIDOS [film];
Ronstadt, Linda; *Teatro; Valdez, Luis.

7844 Fever, Jack. Hispanic marketplace: the SICC
sale: it is indeed a Hallmark. ADWEEK, Vol.
36, (July 28, 1986), p. 18. English.
DESCR: *Hallmark Cards; KMEX, Los Angeles,
CA [television station]; *Spanish
International Communications Corp. (SICC).

7845 Gavin joins group pursuing SICC stations.
BROADCASTING, Vol. 110, no. 22 (June 2,
1986), p. 68. English. DESCR: Gavin, John;
KFTV, Fresno, CA [television station]; KMEX,
Los Angeles, CA [television station]; KWEX,
San Antonio, TX [television station]; Legal
Cases; Perenchio, A. Jerrold; *Spanish
International Communications Corp. (SICC);
Spanish International Network (SIN); Spanish
Language; Thompson, William; WLTV, Miami, FL
[television station]; WXTV, Paterson, NJ
[television station].

7846 Guerrero, Dan. FALCON CREST: showcase for
Hispanic talent. VISTA, Vol. 2, no. 2
(October 4, 1986), p. 12-15. English.
DESCR: *Actors and Actresses; *Ana-Alicia;
FALCON CREST [television show]; Lamas,
Lorenzo; Romero, Cesar.

Television (cont.)

7847 Kendall, Robert. Electric excitement at the
17th Annual Golden Eagle Awards ceremony
sponsored by Nosotros at the Beverly Hilton
Hotel. HISPANIC TIMES, Vol. 8, no. 5
(October, November, 1987), p. 32. English.
DESCR: *Awards; Films; *Nosotros Golden
Eagle Awards.

7848 Kwain, Constance. Searching for Hispanic
talent. VISTA, Vol. 2, no. 6 (February 8,
1987), p. 6-7. English. **DESCR**: *Actors and
Actresses; American Federation of Television
& Radio Artists (AFTRA); *Business
Enterprises; Films; Myrna Salazar and
Associates, Inc.; Navas, Trina; Salazar,
Myrna; Screen Actors Guild.

7849 Lawrence, Jennifer. TV signal expected to
boost Houston market. ADVERTISING AGE
MAGAZINE, Vol. 57, no. 43 (August 11, 1986),
p. S24-S25. English. **DESCR**: Advertising;
Houston, TX; *KXLN, Houston, TX [television
station]; Marketing; Pueblo Broadcasting
Corp.; Spanish Language.

7850 Mass media bureau settlement would allow
SICC to sell its stations. BROADCASTING,
Vol. 110, no. 26 (June 30, 1986), p. 45.
English. **DESCR**: Anselmo, Rene; Azcarraga
Family; Federal Communications Commission
(FCC); KDTV, San Francisco, CA [television
station]; KFTV, Fresno, CA [television
station]; KMEX, Los Angeles, CA [television
station]; KTVW, Phoeniz, AZ [television
station]; KWEX, San Antonio, TX [television
station]; Legal Cases; *Spanish
International Communications Corp. (SICC);
Spanish International Network (SIN); Spanish
Language; WLTV, Miami, FL [television
station]; WXTV, Paterson, NJ [television
station].

7851 Montane, Diane. Learning survival Spanish.
VISTA, Vol. 1, no. 5 (January 5, 1986), p.
16. English. **DESCR**: Education; Ruiz, Vivian;
*Spanish Language; *SURVIVAL SPANISH.

7852 Perez, Renato E. As American as babalu.
VISTA, Vol. 2, no. 6 (February 8, 1987), p.
22. English. **DESCR**: *Acculturation; *Arnaz,
Desi; Essays; I LOVE LUCY.

7853 Poole, Claire. Viewers looking for the U.S.
look. HISPANIC BUSINESS, Vol. 9, no. 12
(December 1987), p. 26-28. English. **DESCR**:
*Advertising; Advertising Agencies;
Marketing; Telemundo Television Group.

7854 Rubin, Marcy Gray. Advertiser apathy hampers
TV growth. ADVERTISING AGE MAGAZINE, Vol.
57, no. 43 (August 11, 1986), p. S22-S23.
English. **DESCR**: *Advertising; Arbitron;
Spanish International Network (SIN); Spanish
Language; Strategy Research Corp..

7855 Sellers, Jeff M. Market growth boosts ad
rates. HISPANIC BUSINESS, Vol. 9, no. 12
(December 1987), p. 41-42, 63+. English.
DESCR: *Advertising; *Marketing; *Spanish
Language.

7856 SICC sale opposed. BROADCASTING, Vol. 111,
no. 7 (August 18, 1986), p. 46-52. English.
DESCR: Azcarraga, Emilio; Federal
Communications Commission (FCC); First
Chicago Venture Capital; Hallmark Cards;
KFTV, Fresno, CA [television station]; KMEX,
Los Angeles, CA [television station]; KWEX,
San Antonio, TX [television station]; Legal
Cases; *Spanish International Communications
Corp. (SICC); Spanish Language; Tapia, Raul
R.; TVL Corp.; WLTV, Miami, FL [television

station]; WXTV, Paterson, NJ [television
station].

7857 SICC sells TVs for $301.5 million.
BROADCASTING, Vol. 111, no. 4 (July 28,
1986), p. 91-92. English. **DESCR**: Azcarraga,
Emilio; First Chicago Venture Capital;
Hallmark Cards; KFTV, Fresno, CA [television
station]; KMEX, Los Angeles, CA [television
station]; KWEX, San Antonio, TX [television
station]; Legal Cases; *Spanish
International Communications Corp. (SICC);
Spanish International Network (SIN); Spanish
Language; Villanueva, Daniel; WLTV, Miami,
FL [television station]; WXTV, Paterson, NJ
[television station].

7858 SICC to sell off stations. BROADCASTING,
Vol. 110, no. 20 (May 19, 1986), p. 79-80.
English. **DESCR**: Anselmo, Rene; Federal
Communications Commission (FCC); Fouce,
Frank; KFTV, Fresno, CA [television
station]; KMEX, Los Angeles, CA [television
station]; KWEX, San Antonio, TX [television
station]; Legal Cases; *Spanish
International Communications Corp. (SICC);
Spanish International Network (SIN); Spanish
Language; WLTV, Miami, FL [television
station]; WXTV, Paterson, NJ [television
station].

7859 Trevino, Jesus Salvador. Chicano cinema
overview. AREITO, Vol. 10, no. 37 (1984), p.
40-43. English. **DESCR**: BALLAD OF GREGORIO
CORTEZ [film]; Discrimination in Employment;
*Films.

7860 Vasquez, Victor. More on CHICO AND THE MAN.
LATIN QUARTER, Vol. 1, no. 3 (January,
February, 1975), p. 13-15. English. **DESCR**:
Albertson, Jack; Andrade, Ray; Artists;
Boycotts; *CHICO AND THE MAN [television
show]; Discrimination; Prinze, Freddie;
Stereotypes.

7861 Zwiebach, Elliot. An important and growing
consumer segment. SUPERMARKET NEWS, Vol. 34,
(May 7, 1984), p. 8,10,120. English.
DESCR: *Marketing; Mexican American Grocers
Association (MAGA).

Templo Mayor, Tenochtitlan

7862 Braun, Barbara. The Aztecs: art and
sacrifice. ART IN AMERICA, Vol. 72, no. 4
(April 1984), p. 126-139. English. **DESCR**:
Anthropology; *Aztecs; Exhibits; Gods and
Dieties; *Precolumbian Images; *Precolumbian
Society.

**"TEMPORARY" ALIEN WORKERS IN THE UNITED STATES:
DESIGNING POLICY FROM FACT AND OPINION**

7863 Cardenas, Gilbert. Book review of:
"TEMPORARY" ALIEN WORKERS IN THE UNITED
STATES. LA RED/THE NET, no. 63 (January
1983), p. 9-10. English. **DESCR**: Book
Reviews; Ross, Stanley R.; Undocumented
Workers; Weintraub, Sidney.

Tenepal, Malintzin
USE: Malinche

Terrinvest, Miami, FL

7864 Kane, George D. Five blueprints for fueling growth. HISPANIC BUSINESS, Vol. 9, no. 5 (May 1987), p. 18-21, 42+. English. DESCR: *Business Enterprises; *Businesspeople; Holguin Corporation, El Paso, TX; Investments; Latin Industries, Ontario, CA; One-Day Paint & Auto Body Centers, Los Angeles, CA; TRU & Associates, Orange County, CA.

Terrorism

7865 Alicia de Garcia's oral history=Historia oral de Alicia de Garcia. REVISTA MUJERES, Vol. 3, no. 2 (June 1986), p. 37-49. Spanish. DESCR: *Committee of Mothers and Relatives of Political Prisoners Disappeared and Assassinated of El Salvador "Monsenor Oscar Arnulfo Romero" (Comadres, El Salvador); Community Organizations; de Garcia, Alicia; *Federation of Latin Americans for the Association of Relatives of the Detained and Disappeared (FedeFam); *Oral History; Violence; *Women.

7866 Peace with justice. REVISTA MUJERES, Vol. 3, no. 2 (June 1986), p. 32-35. English. DESCR: *Committee of Mothers and Relatives of Political Prisoners Disappeared and Assassinated of El Salvador "Monsenor Oscar Arnulfo Romero" (Comadres, El Salvador); Community Organizations; *Federation of Latin Americans for the Association of Relatives of the Detained and Disappeared (FedeFam); Violence; *Women.

TESTING LANGUAGE ABILITY IN THE CLASSROOM

7867 Duran, Richard P. Book review of: TESTING LANGUAGE ABILITY IN THE CLASSROOM. LA RED/THE NET, no. 45 (August 1981), p. 5. English. DESCR: Book Reviews; Cohen, Andrew D.; Language Proficiency.

Texas

7868 Almaraz, Felix D., Jr. Texas as a Mexican borderland: a review and appraisal of salient events. JOURNAL OF THE WEST, Vol. 24, no. 2 (1985), p. 108-112. English. DESCR: *Border Region; History.

7869 Baker, Ross K. Border follies. AMERICAN DEMOGRAPHICS, Vol. 8, no. 8 (August 1986), p. 60. English. DESCR: Guadalupe Hidalgo, Treaty of 1848; Immigration; Rio Grande; *Undocumented Workers.

7870 Cardoso, Lawrence A. Book review of: THEY CALLED THEM GREASERS. WESTERN HISTORICAL QUARTERLY, Vol. 15, no. 4 (October 1984), p. 452-453. English. DESCR: Book Reviews; *de Leon, Arnoldo; THEY CALLED THEM GREASERS: ANGLO ATTITUDES TOWARD MEXICANS IN TEXAS, 1821-1900.

7871 de Leon, Arnoldo. Tejano history scholarship: a review of the recent literature. WEST TEXAS HISTORICAL ASSOCIATION YEARBOOK, Vol. 61, (1985), p. 116-133. English. DESCR: Historiography; *Literature Reviews; Political History and Conditions; Social History and Conditions.

7872 de los Santos, Alfredo G., Jr.; Montemayor, Joaquin; and Solis, Enrique, Jr. Chicano students in higher education: access, attrition and achievement. LA RED/THE NET, no. 41 (April 1981), p. 2-3. English. DESCR: Academic Achievement; *California; Enrollment; *Higher Education.

7873 Galindo, Letticia. Perceptions of pachuquismo and use of Calo/pachuco Spanish by various Chicana women. LA RED/THE NET, no. 48 (November 1981), p. 2,10. English. DESCR: *Chicanas; Chicano Dialects.

7874 Gambrell, Jamey. Texas: state of the art. ART IN AMERICA, Vol. 75, no. 3 (March 1987), p. 114-131+. English. DESCR: *Art; Art Galleries; Art Organizations and Groups; *Artists; Dia de los Muertos; Folk Art; Mexican Art.

7875 Garcia, Ed. On red-haired girls and the greaser in me. TEXAS OBSERVOR, Vol. 75, (October 28, 1983), p. 24-25. English. DESCR: Book Reviews; de Leon, Arnoldo; Essays; Identity; *Stereotypes; *THEY CALLED THEM GREASERS: ANGLO ATTITUDES TOWARD MEXICANS IN TEXAS, 1821-1900.

7876 Gillespie, Francis P., et al. Public policy, ethnic code, and Hispanic vital statistics. LA RED/THE NET, no. 70 (July 1983), p. 9-13. English. DESCR: Public Policy; *Vital Statistics.

7877 Gomez, Linda. Borderland: between Texas and Mexico, a river and a troublesome future. LIFE, Vol. 9, (August 1986), p. 40-50. English. DESCR: *Border Region.

7878 Gunderson, Kay. White does about-face on Simpson-Mazzoli. TEXAS OBSERVOR, Vol. 75, (March 25, 1983), p. 4. English. DESCR: *Immigration Law and Legislation; League of United Latin American Citizens (LULAC); *Simpson-Mazzoli Bill; White, Mark.

7879 Herrera-Sobek, Maria. Book review of: AND OTHER NEIGHBORLY NAMES: SOCIAL PROCESS AND CULTURAL IMAGE IN TEXAS FOLKLORE. LA RED/THE NET, no. 47 (October 1981), p. 3-4. English. DESCR: Abrahams, Roger D.; Bauman, Richard; Book Reviews; *Folklore.

7880 Limon, Jose E. Texas-Mexican popular music and dancing: some notes on history and symbolic process. LATIN AMERICAN MUSIC REVIEW, Vol. 4, no. 2 (Fall, Winter, 1983), p. 229-246. English. DESCR: *Dance; Ethnomusicology; *Music; *Texas Mexicans.

7881 Martin, Jeanne and Suarez, Lucina. Cancer mortality among Mexican Americans and other whites in Texas, 1969-80. AMERICAN JOURNAL OF PUBLIC HEALTH, Vol. 77, no. 7 (July 1987), p. 851-853. English. DESCR: *Cancer; Generally Useful Ethnic Search System (GUESS); Vital Statistics.

7882 MEChA - University of Texas at El Paso; MAYO, University of Texas at Austin; and PASO, Texas A and I University. Student perspectives on Mexican/American studies. EPOCA: NATIONAL CONCILIO FOR CHICANO STUDIES JOURNAL, Vol. 1, no. 2 (Winter 1971), p. 87-96. English. DESCR: *Chicano Studies; Curriculum; Mexican American Youth Organization (MAYO); Movimiento Estudiantil Chicano de Aztlan (MEChA); Student Organizations; Students.

7883 Pearce, James E. and Gunther, Jeffery W. Illegal immigration from Mexico: effects on the Texas economy. ECONOMIC REVIEW (FEDERAL RESERVE BANK OF DALLAS), no. 9 (1985), p. 1-14. English. DESCR: Economics; *Mexico; *Undocumented Workers.

Texas (cont.)

7884 Rivera, Julius. The implementation of Mexican-American Studies in Texas colleges and universities. EPOCA: NATIONAL CONCILIO FOR CHICANO STUDIES JOURNAL, Vol. 1, no. 2 (Winter 1971), p. 79-86. English. **DESCR:** *Chicano Studies; Colleges and Universities; *Curriculum; *Textbooks.

7885 Stewart, Kenneth L. and de Leon, Arnoldo. Age and sex composition among inmigrantes to Texas. LA RED/THE NET, no. 64 (February 1983), p. 2-3. English. **DESCR:** *Immigrants; Nineteenth century.

7886 Stewart, Kenneth L. and de Leon, Arnoldo. Education, literacy, and occupational structure in West Texas, 1860-1900. WEST TEXAS HISTORICAL ASSOCIATION YEARBOOK, Vol. 60, (1984), p. 127-143. English. **DESCR:** Discrimination in Education; Economic Development; Education; Employment; *Labor; Literacy.

7887 Texas' higher education "Adams" compliance report. LA RED/THE NET, No. 102 (November 1986), p. 2-5. English. **DESCR:** *Discrimination in Education; *Higher Education; Public Policy; *Texas Equal Education Opportunity Plan for Higher Education.

7888 Trager, Cara S. Carving out a niche in politics. HISPANIC BUSINESS, Vol. 9, no. 10 (October 1987), p. 29-31. English. **DESCR:** Biography; *Chicanas; *Elected Officials; *Guerrero, Lena.

TEXAS AND THE MEXICAN REVOLUTION: A STUDY IN STATE AND NATIONAL BORDER POLICY

7889 Hart, John M. Book review of: TEXAS AND THE MEXICAN REVOLUTION. PACIFIC HISTORICAL REVIEW, Vol. 55, no. 2 (1986), p. 324-325. English. **DESCR:** Book Reviews; Coerver, Don M.; Hall, Linda B.

7890 Hill, Larry D. Book review of: TEXAS AND THE MEXICAN REVOLUTION. JOURNAL OF SOUTHERN HISTORY, Vol. 52, no. 4 (November 1986), p. 651-652. English. **DESCR:** Book Reviews; Coerver, Don M.; Hall, Linda B.

7891 Raat, W. Dirk. Book review of: TEXAS AND THE MEXICAN REVOLUTION. WESTERN HISTORICAL QUARTERLY, Vol. 17, no. 1 (January 1986), p. 91-92. English. **DESCR:** Book Reviews; Border Region; Coerver, Don M.; Hall, Linda B.

Texas Association of Mexican-American Medical Students (TAMAMS)

7892 Looking for a few good MDs. HISPANIC BUSINESS, Vol. 9, no. 4 (April 1987), p. 16. English. **DESCR:** *Medical Education; Students.

Texas Association of Chicanos in Higher Education (TACHE)

7893 Higher education organizations. LA RED/THE NET, no. 92 (November, December, 1985), p. 11-13. English. **DESCR:** Educational Organizations; *Higher Education.

7894 Texas Association of Chicanos in Higher Education (TACHE) holds annual conference. LA RED/THE NET, No. 100 (September 1986), p. 2-5. English. **DESCR:** *Conferences and Meetings; *Educational Organizations; *Higher Education.

Texas Equal Education Opportunity Plan for Higher Education

7895 Texas' higher education "Adams" compliance report. LA RED/THE NET, No. 102 (November 1986), p. 2-5. English. **DESCR:** *Discrimination in Education; *Higher Education; Public Policy; Texas.

Texas Examination of Current Administrators and Teachers (TECAT)

7896 Texas update. LA RED/THE NET, no. 97 (June 1986), p. 3. English. **DESCR:** *Educational Tests and Measurements; Teaching Profession.

Texas Farmworkers' Union

7897 Rips, Geoffrey. Civil rights and wrongs. TEXAS OBSERVOR, Vol. 76, (December 14, 1984), p. 49-55. English. **DESCR:** Briscoe, Dolph, Jr., Governor of Texas; *Civil Rights; Farm Workers; *Hidalgo County, TX; La Raza Unida Party; Miller, C.L.; Segregation and Desegregation; Voting Rights.

Texas Mexicans

7898 Limon, Jose E. Texas-Mexican popular music and dancing: some notes on history and symbolic process. LATIN AMERICAN MUSIC REVIEW, Vol. 4, no. 2 (Fall, Winter, 1983), p. 229-246. English. **DESCR:** *Dance; Ethnomusicology; *Music; *Texas.

Texas Southmost College

7899 Chavez, Lorenzo A. The quest for Hispanic roots. VISTA, Vol. 2, no. 7 (March 8, 1987), p. 5-6, 24. English. **DESCR:** Church of Jesus Christ of Latter-Day Saints (Mormons); Directories; *Garcia, Clotilde; *Genealogy; Hispanic American Genealogical Associates, Washington, DC; Las Porciones Genealogical Society, Edinburg, TX; Los Bexarenos, San Antonio, TX; Los Californianos [genealogical society], San Jose, CA; Pan American University, Edinburg, TX.

THE TEXAS-MEXICAN CONJUNTO: HISTORY OF A WORKING-CLASS MUSIC

7900 Christian, Garna L. Book review of: THE TEXAS-MEXICAN CONJUNTO. JOURNAL OF SOUTHERN HISTORY, Vol. 52, (May 1986), p. 325. English. **DESCR:** Book Reviews; Pena, Manuel.

7901 Griffith, James S. Book review of: THE TEXAS-MEXICAN CONJUNTO. AMERICAN ANTHROPOLOGIST, Vol. 88, no. 3 (September 1986), p. 733-734. English. **DESCR:** Book Reviews; Pena, Manuel.

7902 Schmidt, Henry C. Book review of: THE TEXAS-MEXICAN CONJUNTO. AMERICAN HISTORICAL REVIEW, Vol. 91, no. 2 (April 1986), p. 488-489. English. **DESCR:** Book Reviews; Pena, Manuel.

TexPar Energy Inc., Milwaukee, WI

7903 Seven profiles of courage. HISPANIC BUSINESS, Vol. 9, no. 6 (June 1987), p. 57-70. English. **DESCR:** Alamo Technology Inc., San Antonio, TX; *Business Enterprises; *Businesspeople; Carrillo, Rosario C.; O'Campo Corporation, Walnut, CA; O'Campo, Peter; Rivas, Robert; THE HISPANIC BUSINESS 500.

Textbooks

7904 Ortiz, Francisco. La cultura chicana, la cultura amenazada. LA COMUNIDAD, No. 305 (May 25, 1986), p. 10-11. Spanish. **DESCR:** Anaya, Rudolfo A.; *BLESS ME, ULTIMA; Bloomfield, NM; *Censorship; Literary Criticism; New Mexico.

7905 Rivera, Julius. The implementation of Mexican-American Studies in Texas colleges and universities. EPOCA: NATIONAL CONCILIO FOR CHICANO STUDIES JOURNAL, Vol. 1, no. 2 (Winter 1971), p. 79-86. English. **DESCR:** *Chicano Studies; Colleges and Universities; *Curriculum; Texas.

"The Second Language Learner in the Context of the Study of Language Acquisition"

7906 Duran, Richard P. Article review of: "The Second Language Learner in the Context of the Study of Language Acquisition". LA RED/THE NET, no. 57 (August 1982), p. 8. English. **DESCR:** Hakuta, Kenji; Language Development.

Theater
USE: Teatro

THERE ARE NO MADMEN HERE

7907 Quintana, Alvina. Challenge and counter challenge: Chicana literary motifs. AGAINST THE CURRENT, Vol. 2, no. 2 (March, April, 1987), p. 25,28-32. English. **DESCR:** Cervantes, Lorna Dee; *Chicanas; *Feminism; *Literature; Moraga, Cherrie; Valdes, Gina.

Thewlis, Alan

7908 Rosas, Alejandro. Siete fotografos latinos en Los Angeles. LA COMUNIDAD, No. 241 (March 3, 1985), p. 4-5. Spanish. **DESCR:** Aguilar, Laura; Art; Avila, Adam; Callwood, Dennis O.; Carlos, Jesus; Exhibits; Miranda, Judy; *Photography; Self-Help Graphics, Los Angeles, CA; *SEVEN LATINO PHOTOGRAPHERS=SIETE FOTOGRAFOS LATINOS; Valverde, Richard.

THEY CALLED THEM GREASERS: ANGLO ATTITUDES TOWARD MEXICANS IN TEXAS, 1821-1900

7909 Butler, Anne M. Book review of: THEY CALLED THEM GREASERS. MARYLAND HISTORIAN, Vol. 15, no. 2 (Fall, Winter, 1984), p. 50-51. English. **DESCR:** Book Reviews; de Leon, Arnoldo; History.

7910 Cardoso, Lawrence A. Book review of: THEY CALLED THEM GREASERS. WESTERN HISTORICAL QUARTERLY, Vol. 15, no. 4 (October 1984), p. 452-453. English. **DESCR:** Book Reviews; *de Leon, Arnoldo; Texas.

7911 Crisp, James E. Book review of: THEY CALLED THEM GREASERS. JOURNAL OF SOUTHERN HISTORY, Vol. 50, no. 2 (1984), p. 313-314. English. **DESCR:** Book Reviews; de Leon, Arnoldo.

7912 Garcia, Ed. On red-haired girls and the greaser in me. TEXAS OBSERVOR, Vol. 75, (October 28, 1983), p. 24-25. English. **DESCR:** Book Reviews; de Leon, Arnoldo; Essays; Identity; *Stereotypes; Texas.

7913 Garcia, Mario T. Book review of: THEY CALLED THEM GREASERS. HISPANIC AMERICAN HISTORICAL REVIEW, Vol. 64, no. 2 (May 1984), p. 405-406. English. **DESCR:** Book Reviews; de Leon, Arnoldo.

7914 Harrington, James C. GREASERS chronicles

Texas racism, past and present. TEXAS OBSERVOR, Vol. 75, (October 28, 1983), p. 23-25. English. **DESCR:** Book Reviews; de Leon, Arnoldo.

7915 Paredes, Raymund A. Book review of: THEY CALLED THEM GREASERS. PACIFIC HISTORICAL REVIEW, Vol. 53, no. 3 (1984), p. 390-391. English. **DESCR:** Book Reviews; de Leon, Arnoldo.

7916 Salmon, Roberto Mario. Book review of: THEY CALLED THEM GREASERS. LA RED/THE NET, no. 75 (December 1983), p. 8-9. English. **DESCR:** Book Reviews; de Leon, Arnoldo.

7917 Saragoza, Alex M. Book review of: THEY CALLED THEM GREASERS. SOUTHWESTERN HISTORICAL QUARTERLY, Vol. 88, (1985), p. 334-336. English. **DESCR:** Book Reviews; de Leon, Arnoldo.

Third World

7918 Olivares, Yvette. The sweatshop: the garment industry's reborn child. REVISTA MUJERES, Vol. 3, no. 2 (June 1986), p. 55-62. English. **DESCR:** Garment Industry; Labor; Public Health; *Undocumented Workers; *Women; Working Women.

Third World Literature (U.S.)

7919 Leal, Luis. Literary criticism and minority literatures: the case of the Chicano writer. CONFLUENCIA, Vol. 1, no. 2 (Spring 1986), p. 4-9. English. **DESCR:** Authors; Ethnic Groups; *Literary Criticism; Literary Influence; *Literature.

Thomas, Anna

7920 Perez, Joel Oseas. EL NORTE: imagenes peyorativas de Mexico y los Chicanos. CHIRICU, Vol. 5, no. 1 (1987), p. 13-21. Spanish. **DESCR:** *EL NORTE [film]; Film Reviews; Nava, Greg.

Thompson, William

7921 Gavin joins group pursuing SICC stations. BROADCASTING, Vol. 110, no. 22 (June 2, 1986), p. 68. English. **DESCR:** Gavin, John; KFTV, Fresno, CA [television station]; KMEX, Los Angeles, CA [television station]; KWEX, San Antonio, TX [television station]; Legal Cases; Perenchio, A. Jerrold; *Spanish International Communications Corp. (SICC); Spanish International Network (SIN); Spanish Language; Television; WLTV, Miami, FL [television station]; WXTV, Paterson, NJ [television station].

Thonis, Elenor

7922 Hewlett-Gomez, Michele. Book review of: THE ENGLISH-SPANISH CONNECTION. LA RED/THE NET, no. 84 (September 1984), p. 2. English. **DESCR:** Book Reviews; *THE ENGLISH-SPANISH CONNECTION.

THREE AMERICAN LITERATURES: ESSAYS IN CHICANO, NATIVE AMERICAN, AND ASIAN-AMERICAN LITERATURE FOR TEACHERS OF AMERICAN LITERATURE

7923 Belkind, A. Book review of: THREE AMERICAN LITERATURES. WORLD LITERATURE TODAY, Vol. 57, no. 4 (Fall 1983), p. 643. English. **DESCR:** Baker, Houston A., Jr.; Book Reviews.

THE THREE WARS OF ROY BENAVIDEZ

7924 Benavidez, Roy. An embattled Chicano. VISTA, Vol. 2, no. 5 (January 4, 1987), p. 20. English. DESCR: Benavidez, Roy; *Books; Green Berets; Griffin, Oscar; Vietnam War.

Tienda, Marta

7925 Matta, Benjamin. Book review of: HISPANICS IN THE U.S. ECONOMY. INDUSTRIAL AND LABOR RELATIONS REVIEW, Vol. 40, no. 2 (January 1987), p. 299-300. English. DESCR: Book Reviews; Borjas, George J.; *HISPANICS IN THE U.S. ECONOMY.

Tierra [musical group]

7926 Muro, Rena. Tierra. AMERICAS 2001, Vol. 1, no. 3 (November, December, 1987), p. 15. Bilingual. DESCR: *Musicians; Salsa.

Tijerina, Andres A.

7927 Ramirez, Oscar. Book review of: HUMAN SERVICES FOR MEXICAN-AMERICAN CHILDREN. LA RED/THE NET, no. 55 (June 1982), p. 7-8. English. DESCR: Book Reviews; *Children; Social Services.

Tijuana, Baja California, Mexico

7928 Campbell, Federico. Paralelo 32: la frontera como espacio literario. LA COMUNIDAD, No. 347 (March 15, 1987), p. 5. Spanish. DESCR: Border Region; *Literary Criticism; *LOS MOTIVOS DE CAIN; Revueltas, Jose.

7929 Garibay, Ricardo. Una frontera de lujo y hambre [excerpt]. LA COMUNIDAD, No. 318 (August 24, 1986), p. 6-7. Spanish. DESCR: *Border Region; Social History and Conditions.

7930 Gonzalez, Marco Vinicio. En el pais de la frontera. LA COMUNIDAD, No. 291 (February 16, 1986), p. 6-7+. Spanish. DESCR: Border Region; Conde, Rosina; *DIALOGOS FRONTERIZOS [radio program]; Gomez Pena, Guillermo; Medina, Ruben; *Radio; San Diego, CA.

7931 Monsivais, Carlos. Los cholos y la cultura de la frontera. LA COMUNIDAD, No. 242 (March 10, 1985), p. 14-15. Spanish. DESCR: Border Region; Culture; Identity; *Pachucos.

7932 Nuestra casa es su casa. HISPANIC TIMES, Vol. 8, no. 3 (May, June, 1987), p. 39. English. DESCR: *Border Region; University of California, Irvine.

7933 Rigoni, Florenzo. Tijuana: the borders on the move. MIGRATION WORLD MAGAZINE, Vol. 15, no. 2 (1987), p. [22]-29. English. DESCR: *Border Region; Criminal Acts; Immigration; Scalabrini Center, Tijuana, Baja California, Mexico; *Undocumented Workers.

Tixier y Vigil, Yvonne

7934 Ruiz, Ivette M. Resena testimonial. REVISTA MUJERES, Vol. 1, no. 2 (June 1984), p. 7-10. English. DESCR: Book Reviews; Chicanas; Elsasser, Nan; *LAS MUJERES: CONVERSATIONS FROM A HISPANIC COMMUNITY; MacKenzie, Kyle.

7935 Ybarra, Lea. Book review of: LAS MUJERES: CONVERSATIONS FROM A HISPANIC COMMUNITY. LA RED/THE NET, no. 58 (September 1982), p. 5-6. English. DESCR: Book Reviews; *Chicanas; *Elasser, Nan; *LAS MUJERES: CONVERSATIONS FROM A HISPANIC COMMUNITY; MacKenzie, Kyle; New Mexico.

TO SPLIT A HUMAN: MITOS, MACHOS Y LA MUJER CHICANA

7936 Castillo-Speed, Lillian. Chicana/Latina literature and criticism: reviews of recent books. WLW JOURNAL, Vol. 11, no. 3 (September 1987), p. 1-4. English. DESCR: Andrews, Lynn V.; *Book Reviews; BORDERS; Chavez, Denise; *Chicanas; CONTEMPORARY CHICANA POETRY: A CRITICAL APPROACH TO AN EMERGING LITERATURE; Flores, Angel; Flores, Kate; JAGUAR WOMAN; Mora, Pat; Sanchez, Marta Ester; Tafolla, Carmen; THE DEFIANT MUSE: HISPANIC FEMINIST POEMS FROM THE MIDDLE AGES TO THE PRESENT; THE LAST OF THE MENU GIRLS; Vigil-Pinon, Evangelina; WOMAN OF HER WORD: HISPANIC WOMEN WRITE.

TO THE HALLS OF THE MONTEZUMAS: THE MEXICAN WAR IN THE AMERICAN IMAGINATION

7937 Paredes, Raymund A. Book review of: TO THE HALLS OF THE MONTEZUMAS. PACIFIC HISTORICAL REVIEW, Vol. 56, no. 1 (February 1987), p. 123-124. English. DESCR: Book Reviews; Johannsen, Robert W.; Mexican American War, 1846-1848.

Toledo, OH

7938 Doyle, Janet. Escoja educacion catolica! MOMENTUM, Vol. 14, no. 1 (February 1983), p. 37-38. English. DESCR: *Catholic Church; Religious Education.

Tomas Rivera Center, Claremont, CA

7939 Dellinger, Robert W. Hispanic think tank. VISTA, Vol. 3, no. 3 (November 8, 1987), p. 28. English. DESCR: Madrid, Arturo; *Public Policy; Research Centers.

7940 Latino literacy update: Tomas Rivera Center focuses on illiteracy. LA RED/THE NET, no. 95 (April 1986), p. 10-12. English. DESCR: Latino Literacy Project, Tomas Rivera Center, Claremont, CA; *Literacy; Macias, Reynaldo F.

7941 Report to the Network from NCCHE. LA RED/THE NET, no. 87 (July 1985), p. 1-2. English. DESCR: Chicano Studies; *Educational Organizations; LA RED/THE NET; *National Chicano Council on Higher Education (NCCHE); National Chicano Research Network (NCRN).

El Torito Restaurant

7942 Kochak, Jacque. Mexican menus invade American markets. RESTAURANT BUSINESS, Vol. 83, (April 10, 1984), p. 144-166. English. DESCR: *Restaurants.

Torres, Averi

7943 Gutierrez, Silvio G. On wings of mercy. VISTA, Vol. 2, no. 3 (November 2, 1986), p. 17-18. English. DESCR: Angel Flight; *Emergency Services; Malibu, CA; Medical Care; Torres, Dennis; Transportation.

Torres, Celia

7944 Sellers, Jeff M. Challenging the myth of the traditional woman. HISPANIC BUSINESS, Vol. 9, no. 8 (August 1987), p. 15-16, 48. English. DESCR: *Businesspeople; *Careers; *Chicanas; *Management; National Network of Hispanic Women; Sex Roles; Women; Zambrana, Ruth.

Torres, Celia Gonzales

7945 A road fraught with challenge leads to view from the top. HISPANIC TIMES, Vol. 8, no. 3 (May, June, 1987), p. 28. English. **DESCR:** Authors; Biography; *Chicanas; Leadership; National Network of Hispanic Women.

Torres, Dennis

7946 Gutierrez, Silvio G. On wings of mercy. VISTA, Vol. 2, no. 3 (November 2, 1986), p. 17-18. English. **DESCR:** Angel Flight; *Emergency Services; Malibu, CA; Medical Care; *Torres, Averi; Transportation.

Torres, Eliseo

7947 de la Cancela, Victor. Book review of: GREEN MEDICINE. LECTOR, Vol. 4, no. 1-3 (1986), p. [64]. English. **DESCR:** Book Reviews; *GREEN MEDICINE: TRADITIONAL MEXICAN-AMERICAN HERBAL REMEDIES.

7948 Watts, Jake. Book review of: THE FOLK HEALER. LECTOR, Vol. 4, no. 1-3 (1986), p. [63-64]. English. **DESCR:** Book Reviews; *THE FOLK HEALER: THE MEXICAN-AMERICAN TRADITION OF CURANDERISMO.

Torres, Michele

7949 Chavez, Lorenzo A. Tennis superstars. VISTA, Vol. 1, no. 8 (April 6, 1986), p. 14-16. English. **DESCR:** *Athletes; Chicanas; Fernandez, Gigi; Fernandez, Mary Joe; *Sabatini, Gabriela; Sports; Women.

Torres, Salvador Roberto

7950 Goldman, Shifra. Escena de San Diego: texto y contexto. LA COMUNIDAD, No. 239 (February 17, 1985), p. 6-7. Spanish. **DESCR:** *Art; Avalos, David; Chicano Park, San Diego, CA; Exhibits; *NUEVE ARTISTAS CHICANOS [exhibit]; San Diego, CA; Ulloa, Domingo.

Torrez, Esther A.

7951 Banks, Marissa Elena. Doing it right. HISPANIC BUSINESS, Vol. 9, no. 11 (November 1987), p. 56-61. English. **DESCR:** *Businesspeople; *Chicanas; Torrez, Garnett & Associates, Los Angeles, CA.

Torrez, Garnett & Associates, Los Angeles, CA

7952 Banks, Marissa Elena. Doing it right. HISPANIC BUSINESS, Vol. 9, no. 11 (November 1987), p. 56-61. English. **DESCR:** *Businesspeople; *Chicanas; *Torrez, Esther A.

Tortillas

7953 Keremitsis, Dawn. Del metate al molino: la mujer mexicana de 1910 a 1940. HISTORIA MEXICANA, Vol. 33, no. 2 (1983), p. 285-302. Spanish. **DESCR:** Food Industry; Labor Unions; *Mexico; Sex Roles; Strikes and Lockouts; *Working Women.

Tosti, Don

7954 Halley, Lindsey. Pachuco boggie [sic]. LA COMUNIDAD, No. 305 (May 25, 1986), p. 8-9. Spanish. **DESCR:** Cano, Eddie; Diaz, Raul; History; *Music; Ovalle, John; *PACHUCO BOOGIE; Smithsonian Institute; The Record Inn, East Los Angeles, CA.

Tourism

7955 Anaya, Rudolfo A. A Chicano in China. VISTA, Vol. 2, no. 1 (September 7, 1986), p. 19-21. English. **DESCR:** *A CHICANO IN CHINA; Anaya, Rudolfo A.; China; *Culture; Philosophy.

7956 de Uriarte, Mercedes Lynn. Santa Barbara: a touch of Spanish class. VISTA, Vol. 1, no. 12 (August 2, 1986), p. 6-8. English. **DESCR:** *Santa Barbara, CA.

Translations

7957 Evans, James. The voice in between. VISTA, Vol. 2, no. 6 (February 8, 1987), p. 9-10. English. **DESCR:** *Courts of Law.

7958 Interpreters--"borrowing" of defense interpreter by trial court. CRIMINAL LAW REPORTER, Vol. 38, no. 4 (October 23, 1985), p. 2077. English. **DESCR:** Courts of Law; People v. Baez; *People v. Guillen.

THE TRANSPLANTED: A HISTORY OF IMMIGRANTS IN URBAN AMERICA

7959 Engerman, Stanley L. Book review of: THE TRANSPLANTED. JOURNAL OF ECONOMIC HISTORY, Vol. 46, no. 2 (June 1986), p. 552-553. English. **DESCR:** *Bodnar, John; Book Reviews; Immigrants.

7960 Stolarik, M. Mark. Book review of: THE TRANSPLANTED. JOURNAL OF AMERICAN ETHNIC HISTORY, Vol. 6, no. 2 (Spring 1987), p. 66-68. English. **DESCR:** Bodnar, John; Book Reviews; Immigrants.

Transportation

7961 Gutierrez, Silvio G. On wings of mercy. VISTA, Vol. 2, no. 3 (November 2, 1986), p. 17-18. English. **DESCR:** Angel Flight; *Emergency Services; Malibu, CA; Medical Care; *Torres, Averi; Torres, Dennis.

Trejo, Jose

7962 Valenzuela-Crocker, Elvira. Small town Hispanic America. VISTA, Vol. 1, no. 11 (July 6, 1986), p. 12-14. English. **DESCR:** Garcia, Frances [mayor of Hutchinson, KS]; Political History and Conditions; *Population; Spanish Speaking Affairs Council of St. Paul.

Trevino, Jesus (Jesse)

7963 Shaw, Katherine. Mira! a look at America's Hispanic artists. VISTA, Vol. 1, no. 5 (January 5, 1986), p. 6-8. English. **DESCR:** *Art; Artists; Canadian Club Hispanic Art Tour; Delgadillo, Ramon; Gamboa, Diane; Gonzalez, Nivia.

Trotter, Robert

7964 Blea, Irene I. Book review of: CURANDERISMO. LA RED/THE NET, no. 55 (June 1982), p. 3-4. English. **DESCR:** Book Reviews; Chavira, Juan Antonio; Curanderismo.

7965 Thiederman, Sondra Barrett. Book review of: CURANDERISMO. WESTERN FOLKLORE, Vol. 42, no. 4 (October 1983), p. 317-318. English. **DESCR:** Book Reviews; Chavira, Juan Antonio; *CURANDERISMO, MEXICAN-AMERICAN FOLK HEALING.

TRU & Associates, Orange County, CA

7966 Kane, George D. Five blueprints for fueling growth. HISPANIC BUSINESS, Vol. 9, no. 5 (May 1987), p. 18-21, 42+. English. **DESCR:** *Business Enterprises; *Businesspeople; Holguin Corporation, El Paso, TX; Investments; Latin Industries, Ontario, CA; One-Day Paint & Auto Body Centers, Los Angeles, CA; Terrinvest, Miami, FL.

Trueba, Henry T.

7967 Duran, Richard P. Book review of: CULTURE AND THE BILINGUAL CLASSROOM. LA RED/THE NET, no. 44 (July 1981), p. 4-5. English. **DESCR:** Bilingualism; Book Reviews; *CULTURE AND THE BILINGUAL CLASSROOM: STUDIES IN CLASSROOM ETHNOLOGY; Guthrie, Grace Pung; Hu-Pei Au, Kathryn.

7968 Nieto, Sonia. Book review of: BILINGUAL MULTICULTURAL EDUCATION AND THE PROFESSIONAL: FROM THEORY TO PRACTICE. INTERRACIAL BOOKS FOR CHILDREN, Vol. 17, no. 3-4 (1986), p. 30. English. **DESCR:** Barnett-Mizrahi, Carol; *BILINGUAL MULTICULTURAL EDUCATION AND THE PROFESSIONAL; Book Reviews.

Truettner, William H.

7969 Adams, Clinton. Book review of: ART IN NEW MEXICO, 1900-1945: PATHS TO TAOS AND SANTA FE. ARTSPACE, Vol. 10, (Fall 1986), p. 34-36. English. **DESCR:** *Art History; *ART IN NEW MEXICO, 1900-1945: PATHS TO TAOS AND SANTA FE; Book Reviews; Eldredge, Charles; Exhibits; Schimmel, Julie.

Trujillo [family name]

7970 Instituto Genealogico e Historico Latino-Americano. Rootsearch: Aragon: Trujillo: Ruelas. VISTA, Vol. 2, no. 8 (April 4, 1987), p. 24. English. **DESCR:** *Aragon [family name]; Genealogy; History; *Personal Names; *Ruelas [family name].

Trujillo, Solomon

7971 Bradby, Marie. Solomon Trujillo of US West. HISPANIC ENGINEER, Vol. 3, no. 5 (Winter 1987), p. 26-30. English. **DESCR:** *Biography; Engineering as a Profession; US West [telecommunications company].

TRW Defense Systems Group

7972 Taylor, Wendy. Una asociacion que trabaja. HISPANIC TIMES, Vol. 8, no. 5 (October, November, 1987), p. 36-38. Spanish. **DESCR:** *Engineering as a Profession; Mexican American Engineering Society (MAES).

7973 Taylor, Wendy. A working partnership. HISPANIC TIMES, Vol. 8, no. 5 (October, November, 1987), p. 12-13. English. **DESCR:** *Engineering as a Profession; *Mexican American Engineering Society (MAES).

Tucson, AZ

7974 Arreola, Daniel D. Mexican restaurants in Tucson. JOURNAL OF CULTURAL GEOGRAPHY, Vol. 3, no. 2 (Spring, Summer, 1983), p. 108-114. English. **DESCR:** Architecture; Landscape Architecture; *Restaurants.

7975 Crisp, James E. Book review of: LOS TUCSONENSES: THE MEXICAN COMMUNITY IN TUCSON 1854-1941. JOURNAL OF ECONOMIC HISTORY, Vol. 47, (January 1987), p. 577-578. English. **DESCR:** Book Reviews; *LOS TUCSONENSES: THE MEXICAN COMMUNITY IN TUCSON, 1854-1941; Sheridan, Thomas E.

7976 de Leon, Arnoldo. Book review of: LOS TUCSONENSES: THE MEXICAN COMMUNITY IN TUCSON 1854-1941. NEW MEXICO HISTORICAL REVIEW, Vol. 62, no. 4 (October 1987), p. 411-12. English. **DESCR:** Book Reviews; *LOS TUCSONENSES: THE MEXICAN COMMUNITY IN TUCSON, 1854-1941; *Sheridan, Thomas E.

7977 de Leon, Arnoldo and Stewart, Kenneth L. A tale of 3 cities: a comparative analysis of the socio-economic conditions of Mexican-Americans in Los Angeles, Tucson, and San Antonio, 1850-1900. JOURNAL OF THE WEST, Vol. 24, no. 2 (1985), p. 64-74. English. **DESCR:** Economic History and Conditions; Employment; Griswold del Castillo, Richard; Labor; *Los Angeles, CA; San Antonio, TX; *Social History and Conditions; Urban Communities.

7978 Griswold del Castillo, Richard. Familism, the extended family and Chicanos in the nineteenth century. LA RED/THE NET, no. 49 (December 1981), p. 2. English. **DESCR:** *Extended Family; *Family; Los Angeles, CA; *Nineteenth century; San Antonio, TX; Santa Fe, NM; *Social History and Conditions.

7979 Luckingham, Bradford. The American Southwest: an urban view. WESTERN HISTORICAL QUARTERLY, Vol. 15, no. 3 (July 1984), p. 261-280. English. **DESCR:** Albuquerque, NM; El Paso, TX; Phoenix, AZ; Social History and Conditions; *Southwestern United States; *Urban Communities; Urban Economics.

7980 Marin, Christine. La Asociacion Hispano-Americana de Madres y Esposas: Tucson's Mexican American women in World War II. RENATO ROSALDO LECTURE SERIES MONOGRAPH, Vol. 1, (Summer 1985), p. [5]-18. English. **DESCR:** *Chicanas; Cultural Organizations; History; *La Asociacion Hispano-Americana de Madres y Esposas, Tucson, AZ; Organizations; World War II.

7981 Perez, Renato E. Badge of Hispanic pride. VISTA, Vol. 1, no. 12 (August 2, 1986), p. 9-11. English. **DESCR:** Broward County, FL; Chicago, IL; Dallas, TX; Houston, TX; *Los Angeles, CA; New York, NY; *Police; San Antonio, TX; San Diego, CA.

7982 Zanger, Maggy. Trial of an activist lawyer. THE PROGRESSIVE, Vol. 50, no. 12 (December 1986), p. 16-17. English. **DESCR:** Criminal Justice System; Legal Cases; *Martinez, Francisco "Kiko".

LOS TUCSONENSES: THE MEXICAN COMMUNITY IN TUCSON, 1854-1941

7983 Crisp, James E. Book review of: LOS TUCSONENSES: THE MEXICAN COMMUNITY IN TUCSON 1854-1941. JOURNAL OF ECONOMIC HISTORY, Vol. 47, (January 1987), p. 577-578. English. **DESCR:** Book Reviews; Sheridan, Thomas E.; Tucson, AZ.

7984 de Leon, Arnoldo. Book review of: LOS TUCSONENSES: THE MEXICAN COMMUNITY IN TUCSON 1854-1941. NEW MEXICO HISTORICAL REVIEW, Vol. 62, no. 4 (October 1987), p. 411-12. English. **DESCR:** Book Reviews; *Sheridan, Thomas E.; *Tucson, AZ.

TUNOMAS HONEY

7985 Madrid, Arturo. Book reviews of: A DICTIONARY OF NEW MEXICO AND SOUTHERN COLORADO SPANISH and TUNOMAS HONEY. LA RED/THE NET, no. 77 (February 1984), p. 8-10. English. **DESCR:** *A DICTIONARY OF NEW MEXICO AND SOUTHERN COLORADO SPANISH; *Book Reviews; Cobos, Ruben; Sagel, Jim.

TVL Corp.

7986 SICC sale opposed. BROADCASTING, Vol. 111, no. 7 (August 18, 1986), p. 46-52. English. **DESCR:** Azcarraga, Emilio; Federal Communications Commission (FCC); First Chicago Venture Capital; Hallmark Cards; KFTV, Fresno, CA [television station]; KMEX, Los Angeles, CA [television station]; KWEX, San Antonio, TX [television station]; Legal Cases; *Spanish International Communications Corp. (SICC); Spanish Language; Tapia, Raul R.; Television; WLTV, Miami, FL [television station]; WXTV, Paterson, NJ [television station].

TWICE A MINORITY: MEXICAN-AMERICAN WOMEN

7987 Baca Zinn, Maxine. Book review of: TWICE A MINORITY: MEXICAN-AMERICAN WOMEN. LA RED/THE NET, no. 32 (July 1980), p. 3-4. English. **DESCR:** Book Reviews; *Chicanas; Melville, Margarita B.

Tylenol

7988 Hispanic marketing. ADVERTISING AGE MAGAZINE, Vol. 57, no. 16 (February 27, 1986), p. 11-51. English. **DESCR:** Adolph Coors Co.; Advertising; Allstate Insurance Co.; American Greetings; Anheuser-Busch, Inc.; Business Enterprises; Coca-Cola Company; Consumers; Ford Motor Company; Hallmark Cards; *Marketing; Mass Media; McDonald's Corporation; Metropolitan Life Insurance Corporation; Pepsi-Cola Bottling Group; Prudential; Spanish International Network (SIN); State Farm Mutual Insurance; United Insurance Co. of America.

Ulibarri [family name]

7989 Instituto Genealogico e Historico Latino-Americano. Rootsearch: Cortes: Ulibarri. VISTA, Vol. 1, no. 5 (January 5, 1986), p. 22. English. **DESCR:** *Cortes [family name]; Genealogy; History; *Personal Names.

Ulloa, Domingo

7990 Goldman, Shifra. El arte social de Domingo Ulloa. LA COMUNIDAD, No. 277 (November 10, 1985), p. 8-9. Spanish. **DESCR:** *Artists; Biography.

7991 Goldman, Shifra. Escena de San Diego: texto y contexto. LA COMUNIDAD, No. 239 (February 17, 1985), p. 6-7. Spanish. **DESCR:** *Art; Avalos, David; Chicano Park, San Diego, CA; Exhibits; *NUEVE ARTISTAS CHICANOS [exhibit]; San Diego, CA; Torres, Salvador Roberto.

UNDERSTANDING MINORITY AGING: PERSPECTIVES AND SOURCES

7992 Jackson, James S. Book review of: UNDERSTANDING MINORITY AGING: PERSPECTIVES AND SOURCES. LA RED/THE NET, no. 68 (May 1983), p. 12-13. English. **DESCR:** Book Reviews; Cuellar, Jose B.; Miller-Soule, Danielle I.; Stanford, E.P. Percil.

Undocumented Children

7993 Torres, Isaias D. The U.S. Supreme Court and public education for undocumented immigrants. LA RED/THE NET, no. 58 (September 1982), p. 2-4. English. **DESCR:** Education; Educational Law and Legislation; *U.S. Supreme Court.

Undocumented Workers

7994 Aliens: detention in prisons. CRIMINAL LAW REPORTER, Vol. 35, no. 15 (July 18, 1984), p. 2265. English. **DESCR:** *Fernandez-Roque v. Smith; *Prisoners.

7995 Avina, Jeffrey. The uninvited: immigration is a hot issue--but who's really getting burned? SAN FRANCISCO, Vol. 26, no. 8 (August 1984), p. 58+. English. **DESCR:** *Immigration Regulation and Control; San Francisco, CA.

7996 Baca, Reynaldo and Bryan, Dexter. Citizen aspirations and residency preferences: the Mexican undocumented worker in the binational community. LA RED/THE NET, no. 34 (September 1980), p. 2. English. **DESCR:** *Los Angeles, CA; Naturalization.

7997 Baker, Ross K. Border follies. AMERICAN DEMOGRAPHICS, Vol. 8, no. 8 (August 1986), p. 60. English. **DESCR:** Guadalupe Hidalgo, Treaty of 1848; Immigration; Rio Grande; Texas.

7998 Bethell, Tom. Senator Simpson's reward. AMERICAN SPECTATOR, Vol. 19, no. 2 (February 1986), p. 11-13. English. **DESCR:** Discrimination; Immigration Law and Legislation; Politics; *Simpson, Alan K.

7999 Bos, Eduard. Estimates of the number of illegal aliens: an analysis of the sources of disagreement. POPULATION RESEARCH AND POLICY REVIEW, Vol. 3, (October 1984), p. 239-254. English. **DESCR:** Population.

8000 Bustamante, Jorge A. International labor migration and external debt. MIGRATION WORLD MAGAZINE, Vol. 15, no. 3 (1987), p. 13-15. English. **DESCR:** Currency; *International Economic Relations; *Labor Supply and Market; *Migrant Labor; United States-Mexico Relations.

8001 Cabeza de Vaca, Darlene. Can a person be illegal? REVISTA MUJERES, Vol. 2, no. 2 (June 1985), p. 31-33. English. **DESCR:** *Immigration Regulation and Control.

8002 Cardenas, Gilbert. Book review of: "TEMPORARY" ALIEN WORKERS IN THE UNITED STATES. LA RED/THE NET, no. 63 (January 1983), p. 9-10. English. **DESCR:** Book Reviews; Ross, Stanley R.; *"TEMPORARY" ALIEN WORKERS IN THE UNITED STATES: DESIGNING POLICY FROM FACT AND OPINION; Weintraub, Sidney.

8003 Chiswick, Barry R. The labor market status of Hispanic men. JOURNAL OF AMERICAN ETHNIC HISTORY, Vol. 7, no. 1 (Fall 1987), p. 30-58. English. **DESCR:** Census; Discrimination in Employment; *Employment; Ethnic Groups; Income; *Labor Supply and Market; Language Usage; *Males.

Undocumented Workers (cont.)

8004 Cisneros, Henry. Mexico's poorest are heading North. AKWESASNE NOTES, Vol. 18, no. 4 (Summer 1986), p. 7. English. **DESCR:** Alfaro, Victor Clark; Centro de Promocion Popular Urbana, Tijuana, Baja California, Mexico; Farm Workers; Kearney, Michael; Mexico; Mixtec Indians.

8005 Enslen, J. INS enjoined from making vehicle stops on basis of alienage alone. CRIMINAL LAW REPORTER, Vol. 36, no. 16 (January 23, 1985), p. 2291-2293. English. **DESCR:** *Ramirez v. Webb; *Search and Seizure; U.S. v. Brignoni-Ponce.

8006 Ezell, Howard. Why immigration reform passed=Porque fue aprobada la reforma de inmigracion. AMERICAS 2001, Premiere Issue, 1987, p. 7, 9, 40-41. Bilingual. **DESCR:** *Immigration Law and Legislation; *Immigration Reform and Control Act of 1986.

8007 Faxon, R. Paul. Employer sanctions for hiring illegal aliens: a simplistic solution to a complex problem. NORTHWESTERN JOURNAL OF INTERNATIONAL LAW AND BUSINESS, Vol. 6, (Spring 1984), p. 203-248. English. **DESCR:** Agribusiness; Immigration Law and Legislation; National Labor Relations Board (NLRB); Simpson-Mazzoli Bill.

8008 Fernandez, Edward and Cresce, Arthur R. The Hispanic foreign-born and the assimilation experience. MIGRATION WORLD MAGAZINE, Vol. 14, no. 5 (1986), p. 7-11. English. **DESCR:** *Assimilation; *Immigrants; Naturalization; *Socioeconomic Factors.

8009 Flores, Estevan T. Book review of: ILLEGAL ALIENS IN THE WESTERN HEMISPHERE. LA RED/THE NET, no. 56 (July 1982), p. 7-9. English. **DESCR:** Book Reviews; *ILLEGAL ALIENS IN THE WESTERN HEMISPHERE: POLITICAL AND ECONOMIC FACTORS; Johnson, Kenneth F.; Williams, Miles W.

8010 Ford, Theresa Y. United States v. Hannigan: federal statute used to prosecute torturers. CRIMINAL JUSTICE JOURNAL, Vol. 6, no. 1 (Fall 1982), p. 79-97. English. **DESCR:** Civil Rights; Hobbs Act; *U.S. v. Hanigan.

8011 Garcia y Griego, Manuel. Estimating the undocumented population in the U.S. LA RED/THE NET, no. 58 (September 1982), p. 7-8,17. English. **DESCR:** *Population.

8012 Gill, Eric K. Notaries: clearing the air. HISPANIC BUSINESS, Vol. 9, no. 3 (March 1987), p. 14. English. **DESCR:** *Immigration Law and Legislation; *Legal Aid; *Naturalization.

8013 Gollobin, Ira. No pasaran. NATION, Vol. 243, no. 14 (November 1, 1986), p. 429. English. **DESCR:** *Immigration Law and Legislation; *Immigration Reform and Control Act of 1986.

8014 Gordon, Charles. The rights of aliens: an expanding role for trial lawyers. TRIAL, Vol. 19, no. 12 (December 1983), p. 54-58. English. **DESCR:** Deportation; Immigration Law and Legislation; *Legal Profession; *Political Prisoners.

8015 Guevara, Ruben. Richard "Cheech" Marin. AMERICAS 2001, Vol. 1, no. 1 (June, July, 1987), p. 18-21. Bilingual. **DESCR:** *Actors and Actresses; *BORN IN EAST L.A. [film]; Films; Immigration; *Marin, Richard "Cheech".

8016 Hamilton, Lawrence S. A profile of the Mexican migrant and his social and cultural adaptation to a federal prison. JOURNAL OF OFFENDER COUNSELING, SERVICES & REHABILITATION, Vol. 9, no. 3 (Spring 1985), p. 7-19. English. **DESCR:** Prisons.

8017 Kahn, Robert. Oakdale prison: documenting the abuses. IN THESE TIMES, Vol. 10, no. 35 (September 17, 1986), p. 8, 22. English. **DESCR:** Allen Parish, LA; Legal Representation; *Oakdale, LA; Oakdale Legal Assistance (OLA); Political Refugees; Prisons; U.S. Bureau of Prisons (BOP).

8018 Kelly, Peter. American bosses have jobs; Mexicans need work. GUARDIAN, Vol. 39, no. 8 (November 19, 1986), p. 11. English. **DESCR:** Immigration; Labor Supply and Market.

8019 Kramer, Mark. U.S.-Mexican border: life on the line. THE AMERICAN MERCURY, Vol. 167, (June 1985), p. 720-749. English. **DESCR:** Border Industries; Border Patrol; *Border Region; Border Studies; Drug Traffic.

8020 Magiera, Marcy. New arrivals find warm welcome as consumers. ADVERTISING AGE MAGAZINE, Vol. 58, no. 6 (February 9, 1987), p. S14. English. **DESCR:** Consumers; Immigrants; *Marketing.

8021 Marketing to Hispanics. ADVERTISING AGE MAGAZINE, Vol. 58, no. 6 (February 9, 1987), p. S1-S23. English. **DESCR:** Advertising; Consumers; Immigrants; *Marketing; Mass Media; Politics.

8022 Massey, Douglas S. Do undocumented migrants earn lower wages than legal immigrants? New evidence from Mexico. INTERNATIONAL MIGRATION REVIEW, Vol. 21, no. 2 (Summer 1987), p. 236-274. English. **DESCR:** Employment; *Immigrants; *Income; *Mexico; Migration Patterns.

8023 Morales, Patricia. Indocumentados y chicanos: un intento de aproximacion. LA COMUNIDAD, No. 318 (August 24, 1986), p. 2-5. Spanish. **DESCR:** History; *Immigration; Labor.

8024 Mosqueda, Lawrence Joseph. How to keep a bad bill from getting worse. GUARDIAN, Vol. 38, no. 46 (September 24, 1986), p. 5. English. **DESCR:** Immigration and Naturalization Service (INS); *Immigration Law and Legislation; Immigration Regulation and Control; Simpson-Rodino Bill.

8025 Munoz, Rosalio. The Simpson-Rodino immigration law: an assault on the working class. POLITICAL AFFAIRS, Vol. 66, no. 6 (June 1987), p. 12-18. English. **DESCR:** Civil Rights; *Immigration Law and Legislation; *Immigration Reform and Control Act of 1986.

8026 Novick, Michael. INS makes a bad Simpson-Rodino law worse. GUARDIAN, Vol. 39, no. 16 (January 21, 1987), p. 5. English. **DESCR:** *Immigration Law and Legislation; *Immigration Reform and Control Act of 1986; *Simpson-Rodino Bill.

8027 Olivares, Yvette. The sweatshop: the garment industry's reborn child. REVISTA MUJERES, Vol. 3, no. 2 (June 1986), p. 55-62. English. **DESCR:** Garment Industry; Labor; Public Health; Third World; *Women; Working Women.

Undocumented Workers (cont.)

8028 Passel, Jeffrey S. Estimating the number of undocumented aliens. MONTHLY LABOR REVIEW, Vol. 109, no. 9 (September 1986), p. 33. English. DESCR: *Census.

8029 Pearce, James E. and Gunther, Jeffery W. Illegal immigration from Mexico: effects on the Texas economy. ECONOMIC REVIEW (FEDERAL RESERVE BANK OF DALLAS), no. 9 (1985), p. 1-14. English. DESCR: Economics; *Mexico; Texas.

8030 Protecting aliens from persecution without overloading the INS. VIRGINIA LAW REVIEW, Vol. 69, (June 1983), p. 901-930. English. DESCR: Nunez v. Boldin; *Orantes, Hernandez v. Smith; Political Refugees; Refugee Act of 1980.

8031 Ramos, Hector. Latino caucuses in U.S. labor unions. RACE AND CLASS, Vol. 27, no. 4 (Spring 1986), p. 69. English. DESCR: Labor Unions; *Migrant Labor.

8032 Rigoni, Florenzo. Tijuana: the borders on the move. MIGRATION WORLD MAGAZINE, Vol. 15, no. 2 (1987), p. [22]-29. English. DESCR: *Border Region; Criminal Acts; Immigration; Scalabrini Center, Tijuana, Baja California, Mexico; *Tijuana, Baja California, Mexico.

8033 Rodriguez Flores, Juan. Una historia de todos los dias. LA COMUNIDAD, No. 321 (September 14, 1986), p. 12-13. Spanish. DESCR: *Immigration.

8034 Rodriguez, Nestor. Undocumented Central Americans in Houston: diverse populations. INTERNATIONAL MIGRATION REVIEW, Vol. 21, no. 1 (Spring 1987), p. 4-26. English. DESCR: *Central America; El Salvador; Ethnic Groups; Guatemala; Honduras; *Houston, TX; Immigrants; Intergroup Relations; Latin Americans; *Political Refugees.

8035 Roth, Michael. Panic and fear in Latino communities. GUARDIAN, Vol. 39, no. 8 (November 19, 1986), p. 10-11. English. DESCR: *Immigration Law and Legislation; *Simpson-Rodino Bill.

8036 Sellers, Jeff M. Opportunity no, regulations yes. HISPANIC BUSINESS, Vol. 9, no. 2 (February 1987), p. 12-[14]. English. DESCR: Discrimination; Employment; *Immigration Law and Legislation; *Immigration Reform and Control Act of 1986.

8037 Toney, Bill. Employment is the key. U.S. NEWS & WORLD REPORT, Vol. 101, (August 4, 1986), p. 65. English. DESCR: *Immigration Law and Legislation.

8038 Totality of circumstances justified stop of vehicle carrying Hispanics. CRIMINAL LAW REPORTER, Vol. 35, no. 11 (June 13, 1984), p. 2186-2187. English. DESCR: Border Patrol; U.S. v. Brignoni-Ponce; *U.S. v. Garcia.

8039 Vanderpool, Tim. Immigration reform crosses an uncertain border into law. IN THESE TIMES, Vol. 11, no. 6 (December 17, 1986), p. 5, 7. English. DESCR: Immigration and Naturalization Service (INS); Immigration Law and Legislation; *Immigration Reform and Control Act of 1986; Simpson-Rodino Bill.

8040 Weinfield, J. Day care benefits ordered for child born in U.S. to illegal alien. THE FAMILY LAW REPORTER: COURT OPINIONS, Vol. 9, no. 4 (November 23, 1982), p. 2054-2056. English. DESCR: Child Care Centers; *Ruiz v.

Blum.

Unemployment

USE: Employment

Unemployment Insurance

USE: Employment

Unique Construction Co., Hillside, IL

8041 The top 100--profiles. HISPANIC BUSINESS, Vol. 9, no. 11 (November 1987), p. 31-50. English. DESCR: Artco Contracting, Inc., Auburn Hills, MI; *Business Enterprises; Computer Trade Development Corp, Birmingham, MI; Corella Electric Inc., Phoenix, AZ; GSE Construction Co., Inc., Livermore, CA; National Systems & Research Co.

United Farmworkers of America (UFW)

8042 Barger, W.K. California public endorses the United Farm Workers. LA RED/THE NET, No. 105 (February 1987), p. 4-6. English. DESCR: *Agricultural Labor Unions; California; *Farm Workers; *Public Opinion.

8043 Barger, W.K. Views of California farmworkers regarding the farm labor movement. LA RED/THE NET, no. 91 (October 1985), p. 3-5. English. DESCR: Agricultural Labor Unions; Attitudes; California; *Farm Workers.

8044 Boycotts revisited: Campbell's concedes to farm worker campaign. DOLLARS AND SENSE, (July, August, 1986), p. 12-14, 18. English. DESCR: Boycotts; California; Campbell Soup Co.; Farm Labor Organizing Commmittee (FLOC); Farm Workers; *Labor Disputes; Labor Unions; Michigan; Ohio; Strikes and Lockouts.

8045 Echaveste, Beatrice and Huerta, Dolores. In the shadow of the eagle: Huerta=A la sombra del aguila: Huerta. AMERICAS 2001, Vol. 1, no. 3 (November, December, 1987), p. 26-30. Bilingual. DESCR: Agricultural Labor Unions; Boycotts; Chicanas; *Farm Workers; *Huerta, Dolores.

8046 Fraser, Laura. Old boycott, new battle. THE PROGRESSIVE, Vol. 49, (October 1985), p. 16. English. DESCR: *Boycotts; Labor Disputes.

8047 Sanders, Bob. Boycott Campbell's: Ohio farmworkers take it to the top. DOLLARS AND SENSE, no. 92 (December 1983), p. 16-18. English. DESCR: Boycotts; Campbell Soup Co.; Chavez, Cesar E.; Farm Labor Organizing Commmittee (FLOC); Farm Workers; Guevas, Fernando; *Labor Disputes; Labor Unions; Ohio; Strikes and Lockouts.

United Insurance Co. of America

8048 Hispanic marketing. ADVERTISING AGE MAGAZINE, Vol. 57, no. 16 (February 27, 1986), p. 11-51. English. DESCR: Adolph Coors Co.; Advertising; Allstate Insurance Co.; American Greetings; Anheuser-Busch, Inc.; Business Enterprises; Coca-Cola Company; Consumers; Ford Motor Company; Hallmark Cards; *Marketing; Mass Media; McDonald's Corporation; Metropolitan Life Insurance Corporation; Pepsi-Cola Bottling Group; Prudential; Spanish International Network (SIN); State Farm Mutual Insurance; Tylenol.

United Mexican American Students (UMAS)

8049 Ramirez, Salvador. The establishment and administration of a master's program in Chicano Studies at the University of Colorado. EPOCA: NATIONAL CONCILIO FOR CHICANO STUDIES JOURNAL, Vol. 1, no. 2 (Winter 1971), p. 39-50. English. DESCR: *Chicano Studies; *Curriculum; Discrimination in Education; Educational Theory and Practice; Student Organizations; *Students; *University of Colorado, Boulder; Youth.

UNITED STATES RELATIONS WITH MEXICO: CONTEXT AND CONTENT

8050 Gutierrez, Armando. Book reviews of: MEXICO-UNITED STATES RELATIONS and UNITED STATES RELATIONS WITH MEXICO: CONTEXT AND CONTENT. LA RED/THE NET, no. 62 (December 1982), p. 4-6. English. DESCR: Book Reviews; Erb, Richard D.; Kaufman, Purcell; *MEXICO-UNITED STATES RELATIONS; Ross, Stanley R.

United States-Mexico Relations

8051 Bustamante, Jorge A. International labor migration and external debt. MIGRATION WORLD MAGAZINE, Vol. 15, no. 3 (1987), p. 13-15. English. DESCR: Currency; *International Economic Relations; *Labor Supply and Market; *Migrant Labor; *Undocumented Workers.

8052 de la Garza, Rodolfo O. On the question of Chicano ambassadors. LA RED/THE NET, no. 66 (March 1983), p. 15-16. English. DESCR: Appointed Officials.

8053 Escobar, Edward J. Mexican revolutionaries and the Los Angeles police: harassment of the Partido Liberal Mexicano, 1907-1910. AZTLAN, Vol. 17, no. 1 (Spring 1986), p. 1-46. English. DESCR: Civil Rights; *Flores Magon, Ricardo; Gutierrez de Lara, Lazaro; Los Angeles, CA; *Los Angeles Police Department; *Partido Liberal Mexicano (PLM); *Police; Police Brutality; Political Repression; Rico, Louis; Rico, Thomas; Talamantes, Felipe.

8054 Gettman, Dawn and Pena, Devon Gerardo. Women, mental health, and the workplace in a transnational setting. SOCIAL WORK, Vol. 31, no. 1 (January, February, 1986), p. 5-11. English. DESCR: *Border Industries; *Chicanas; Employment; *Mental Health; Mexico; Women; *Working Women.

8055 Gomez Pena, Guillermo. Nuevo continente artistico. LA COMUNIDAD, No. 275 (October 27, 1985), p. 8-10. Spanish. DESCR: *Art; Artists; Border Region; Chicano Movement; DIALOGOS DE LAS AMERICAS; Indigenismo; International Relations; Mexico.

8056 Hunsaker, Alan C. Institutionally-based research centers: the Center for U.S.-Mexican Studies. LA RED/THE NET, no. 92 (November, December, 1985), p. 13-15. English. DESCR: *Center for U.S.-Mexican Studies, University of California at San Diego, La Jolla, CA; Del Castillo, Gustavo; Meyer, Lorenzo; *Research Centers.

8057 Parlee, Lorena M. The impact of United States railroad unions on organized labor and government policy in Mexico (1880-1911). HISPANIC AMERICAN HISTORICAL REVIEW, Vol. 64, no. 3 (August 1984), p. 443-475. English. DESCR: Diaz, Porfirio; Discrimination in Employment; History; *Labor Unions; Mexico; Partido Liberal Mexicano (PLM); Railroads.

United States-Mexico War

USE: Mexican American War, 1846-1848

Universities

USE: Colleges and Universities

University of California, Irvine

8058 Nuestra casa es su casa. HISPANIC TIMES, Vol. 8, no. 3 (May, June, 1987), p. 39. English. DESCR: *Border Region; *Tijuana, Baja California, Mexico.

University of California

8059 Leon, David Jess and McNeill, Daniel. The fifth class: a 19th century forerunner of affirmative action. CALIFORNIA HISTORY, Vol. 64, no. 1 (Winter 1985), p. 52-57. English. DESCR: *Affirmative Action; Colleges and Universities; Discrimination in Education; *Enrollment; *Higher Education; History; Students.

8060 Leon, David Jess and McNeill, Daniel. Hispanics, the fifth class, and the University of California, 1870-72. LA RED/THE NET, no. 67 (April 1983), p. 5-6. English. DESCR: College Preparation; *Colleges and Universities; Enrollment; Local History.

University of California, Berkeley

8061 Smith, Mary Perry. Early identification and support: the University of California-Berkeley's MESA program. NEW DIRECTIONS FOR TEACHING AND LEARNING, no. 24 (December 1985), p. 19-25. English. DESCR: *Counseling (Educational); *Engineering as a Profession; Enrollment; Higher Education; *Mathematics, Engineering and Science Achievement (MESA).

8062 Vitelmo V. Bertero wins ASCE's Moisseiff Award. HISPANIC ENGINEER, Vol. 3, no. 5 (Winter 1987), p. 14. English. DESCR: American Society of Civil Engineers (ASCE) Moisseif Award; *Awards; *Bertero, Vitelmo V.

University of Colorado, Boulder

8063 Ramirez, Salvador. The establishment and administration of a master's program in Chicano Studies at the University of Colorado. EPOCA: NATIONAL CONCILIO FOR CHICANO STUDIES JOURNAL, Vol. 1, no. 2 (Winter 1971), p. 39-50. English. DESCR: *Chicano Studies; *Curriculum; Discrimination in Education; Educational Theory and Practice; Student Organizations; *Students; United Mexican American Students (UMAS); Youth.

University of Illinois, Chicago, IL

8064 Gonzalez, Lawrence F. The University of Illinois, Chicago. HISPANIC ENGINEER, Vol. 3, no. 3 (1987), p. 34-36. English. DESCR: Association of Minority Engineers (AME); Colleges and Universities; Society of Hispanic Professional Engineers (SHPE).

University of New Mexico

8065 Perez, Renato E. Who are the Hispanic heroes? VISTA, Vol. 1, no. 7 (March 2, 1986), p. 12-14. English. DESCR: Jaramillo, Mari-Luci; Leadership; *Public Opinion.

Univision

8066 Beale, Stephen. New blood, fresh money: Telemundo, Univision bullish on television market. HISPANIC BUSINESS, Vol. 9, no. 12 (December 1987), p. 30-36. English. **DESCR:** *Corporations; Hallmark Cards; LatCom; Radio; Spanish International Communications Corp. (SICC); *Spanish Language; *Telemundo Television Group; *Television.

Upper Class
USE: Social Classes

Urban Communities

8067 Browning, Rufus P. and Marshall, Dale Rogers. Black and Hispanic power in city politics: a forum. P.S. [AMERICAN POLITICAL SCIENCE ASSOCIATION], Vol. 19, no. 3 (Summer 1986), p. 573-639. English. **DESCR:** Blacks; Browning, Rufus P.; Marshall, Dale Rogers; *Politics; *PROTEST IS NOT ENOUGH: THE STRUGGLE OF BLACKS AND HISPANICS FOR EQUALITY IN URBAN POLITICS; Tabb, David H.

8068 Browning, Rufus P.; Marshall, Dale Rogers; and Tabb, David H. Protest is not enough: a theory of political incorporation. P.S. [AMERICAN POLITICAL SCIENCE ASSOCIATION], Vol. 19, no. 3 (Summer 1986), p. 576-581. English. **DESCR:** Blacks; Browning, Rufus P.; Marshall, Dale Rogers; Political Representation; Politics; *PROTEST IS NOT ENOUGH: THE STRUGGLE OF BLACKS AND HISPANICS FOR EQUALITY IN URBAN POLITICS; Tabb, David H.

8069 de Leon, Arnoldo and Stewart, Kenneth L. A tale of 3 cities: a comparative analysis of the socio-economic conditions of Mexican-Americans in Los Angeles, Tucson, and San Antonio, 1850-1900. JOURNAL OF THE WEST, Vol. 24, no. 2 (1985), p. 64-74. English. **DESCR:** Economic History and Conditions; Employment; Griswold del Castillo, Richard; Labor; *Los Angeles, CA; San Antonio, TX; *Social History and Conditions; Tucson, AZ.

8070 Gonzales, Juan. San Francisco's Mission District: part I. LATIN QUARTER, Vol. 1, no. 4 (July, August, 1975), p. 21-25. English. **DESCR:** La Mision Dolores Iglesia Catolica; *Local History; *Mission District, San Francisco, CA; Political Parties and Organizations; San Francisco, CA.

8071 Hero, Rodney E. Mexican Americans and urban politics: a consideration of governmental structure and policy. AZTLAN, Vol. 17, no. 1 (Spring 1986), p. 131-147. English. **DESCR:** Colorado; *Political Representation; *Politics; Public Policy.

8072 Luckingham, Bradford. The American Southwest: an urban view. WESTERN HISTORICAL QUARTERLY, Vol. 15, no. 3 (July 1984), p. 261-280. English. **DESCR:** Albuquerque, NM; El Paso, TX; Phoenix, AZ; Social History and Conditions; *Southwestern United States; Tucson, AZ; Urban Economics.

8073 Munoz, Carlos, Jr. and Henry, Charles. Rainbow coalitions in four big cities: San Antonio, Denver, Chicago and Philadelphia. P.S. [AMERICAN POLITICAL SCIENCE ASSOCIATION], Vol. 19, no. 3 (Summer 1986), p. 598-609. English. **DESCR:** Blacks; Chicago, IL; Cisneros, Henry, Mayor of San Antonio, TX; Denver, CO; Elected Officials; Ethnic Groups; Intergroup Relations; Pena, Federico; Philadelphia, PA; Political Parties and Organizations; Political Representation; *Politics; San Antonio, TX.

8074 Padilla, Genaro Miguel. The anti-romantic city in Chicano fiction. PUERTO DEL SOL, Vol. 23, no. 1 (1987), p. 159-169. English. **DESCR:** Acosta, Oscar Zeta; Anaya, Rudolfo A.; *Fiction; Lattin, Vernon E.; *Literary Criticism; Morales, Alejandro.

8075 Sifuentes, Frank. Huntington Park: city on the upswing=Huntington Park: una ciudad ascendiente. AMERICAS 2001, Premiere Issue, 1987, p. 36-39. Bilingual. **DESCR:** History; *Huntington Park, CA.

Urban Economics

8076 Luckingham, Bradford. The American Southwest: an urban view. WESTERN HISTORICAL QUARTERLY, Vol. 15, no. 3 (July 1984), p. 261-280. English. **DESCR:** Albuquerque, NM; El Paso, TX; Phoenix, AZ; Social History and Conditions; *Southwestern United States; Tucson, AZ; *Urban Communities.

URBAN ETHNICITY IN THE UNITED STATES: NEW IMMIGRANTS AND OLD MINORITIES

8077 Alexander, June Granatir. Book review of: URBAN ETHNICITY IN THE UNITED STATES. JOURNAL OF AMERICAN ETHNIC HISTORY, Vol. 7, no. 1 (Fall 1987), p. 95-97. English. **DESCR:** Book Reviews; Immigrants; Maldonado, Lionel; Moore, Joan W.

Urban Poverty
USE: Urban Economics

Urbanization
USE: Urban Communities

Urrutia, Jorge R.

8078 Bradby, Marie. The naval research laboratory. HISPANIC ENGINEER, Vol. 3, no. 2 (Summer 1987), p. 34-38. English. **DESCR:** *Engineering as a Profession; Military; *Naval Research Laboratory; Rojas, Richard Raimond.

U.S. Air Force

8079 Allsup, Dan. The story of Stella. VISTA, Vol. 2, no. 1 (September 7, 1986), p. 16. English. **DESCR:** Business Enterprises; *Cosmetology; *Guerra, Stella; U.S. Department of Defense (DOD).

U.S. Army

8080 Perez, Renato E. Skydiving daredevils. VISTA, Vol. 1, no. 10 (June 8, 1986), p. 14-16. English. **DESCR:** Golden Knights [skydiving team]; *Military; Minino, Virgilio.

U.S. Bureau of Prisons (BOP)

8081 Kahn, Robert. Oakdale prison: documenting the abuses. IN THESE TIMES, Vol. 10, no. 35 (September 17, 1986), p. 8, 22. English. **DESCR:** Allen Parish, LA; Legal Representation; *Oakdale, LA; Oakdale Legal Assistance (OLA); Political Refugees; Prisons; Undocumented Workers.

U.S. Bureau of the Census

8082 Dunn, William. Chicago's Hispanics. AMERICAN DEMOGRAPHICS, Vol. 9, no. 2 (February 1987), p. 52-53. English. **DESCR:** *Chicago, IL; Population; Statistics.

U.S. Bureau of the Census (cont.)

8083 Fitch, Ed. Census bureau tries to clean up its act. ADVERTISING AGE MAGAZINE, Vol. 57, no. 43 (August 11, 1986), p. S18-S20. English. **DESCR:** Census; Marketing.

8084 Marketing to Hispanics. ADVERTISING AGE MAGAZINE, Vol. 57, no. 43 (August 11, 1986), p. 51-528. English. **DESCR:** Advertising; Broadcast Media; De Armas Publications; Kinney Shoe Corp.; *Marketing; Pepsi-Cola Bottling Group; Print Media; Spanish International Network (SIN).

U.S. Constitution
      USE: Constitution of the United States

U.S. Department of Defense (DOD)

8085 Allsup, Dan. The story of Stella. VISTA, Vol. 2, no. 1 (September 7, 1986), p. 16. English. **DESCR:** Business Enterprises; *Cosmetology; *Guerra, Stella; U.S. Air Force.

8086 Banks, Marissa Elena. Army maneuvers. HISPANIC BUSINESS, Vol. 9, no. 12 (December 1987), p. 37-39. English. **DESCR:** Advertising Agencies; Government Contracts; *Military; *Sosa & Associates.

U.S. English

8087 Llorente, Elizabeth. Linda Chavez: thriving on controversy. VISTA, Vol. 3, no. 3 (November 8, 1987), p. 6-9. English. **DESCR:** *Chavez, Linda; *English Language; Politics.

U.S. Health Examination Survey (HES)

8088 Molina, Robert M.; Brown, Kathryn H.; and Zavaleta, Antonio N. Relative lower extremity length in Mexican American and in American Black and white youth. AMERICAN JOURNAL OF PHYSICAL ANTHROPOLOGY, Vol. 72, (1987), p. 89-94. English. **DESCR:** Anglo Americans; *Anthropometry; Blacks; *Body Mass Index (BMI); Youth.

U.S. Hispanic Chamber of Commerce

8089 Beale, Stephen. Networking the networks. HISPANIC BUSINESS, Vol. 9, no. 9 (September 1987), p. 38-43. English. **DESCR:** Business; Conferences and Meetings.

8090 Beale, Stephen. Striking a deal with big business. HISPANIC BUSINESS, Vol. 9, no. 2 (February 1987), p. 26-33. English. **DESCR:** *Adolph Coors Co.; American G.I. Forum; Boycotts; Corporations; Cuban National Planning Council, Inc. Washington, D.C.; Employment; *Hispanic Association on Corporate Responsibility (HACER); League of United Latin American Citizens (LULAC); National Council of La Raza (NCLR); National IMAGE; National Puerto Rican Coalition; *Organizations.

8091 Hispanic chamber endorses insurance marketing plan. HISPANIC TIMES, Vol. 8, no. 3 (May, June, 1987), p. 26. English. **DESCR:** Business Enterprises; Insurance; Lopez, Ruben; *Metropolitan Life Insurance Corporation.

8092 Perez, Renato E. The business of Hispanics. VISTA, Vol. 2, no. 1 (September 7, 1986), p. 10. English. **DESCR:** Adolph Coors Co.; American G.I. Forum; Apodaca, Jerry [Gov. of New Mexico]; Business; *Collective Bargaining; Corporations; Cuban National

Planning Council, Inc. Washington, D.C.; *Hispanic Association on Corporate Responsibility (HACER); League of United Latin American Citizens (LULAC); National Council of La Raza (NCLR); National IMAGE.

8093 Sellers, Jeff M. Metropolitan Life continues to lead. HISPANIC BUSINESS, Vol. 9, no. 5 (May 1987), p. 12-14. English. **DESCR:** Advertising; Corporations; *Insurance; *Marketing; *Metropolitan Life Insurance Corporation.

8094 USHCC to host 8th annual convention in Los Angeles. HISPANIC ENGINEER, Vol. 3, no. 3 (1987), p. 16. English. **DESCR:** *Conferences and Meetings.

U.S. Supreme Court

8095 High court upholds quotas. DUNS'S BUSINESS MONTH, Vol. 128, no. 2 (August 1986), p. 22. English. **DESCR:** *Affirmative Action; Discrimination in Employment; Reagan Administration; Sexism.

8096 Search and seizure. CRIMINAL LAW REPORTER, Vol. 35, no. 3 (April 18, 1984), p. 3011-3027. English. **DESCR:** Hester v. U.S.; INS v. Delgado; Katz v. U.S.; Maine v. Thornton; Oliver v. U.S.; *Search and Seizure.

8097 Torres, Isaias D. The U.S. Supreme Court and public education for undocumented immigrants. LA RED/THE NET, no. 58 (September 1982), p. 2-4. English. **DESCR:** Education; Educational Law and Legislation; *Undocumented Children.

U.S. Task Force on Women, Minorities & the Handicapped in Science and Technology

8098 Herb Fernandez to serve on presidential task force. HISPANIC ENGINEER, Vol. 3, no. 5 (Winter 1987), p. 15. English. **DESCR:** *Appointed Officials; *Fernandez, Herb.

U.S. v. Brignoni-Ponce

8099 Canby, J. Immigration board can't use evidence from stop based only on Hispanic appearance. CRIMINAL LAW REPORTER, Vol. 39, no. 5 (April 30, 1986), p. 2076. English. **DESCR:** *Arguelles-Vasquez v. INS; *Search and Seizure.

8100 Enslen, J. INS enjoined from making vehicle stops on basis of alienage alone. CRIMINAL LAW REPORTER, Vol. 36, no. 16 (January 23, 1985), p. 2291-2293. English. **DESCR:** *Ramirez v. Webb; *Search and Seizure; Undocumented Workers.

8101 Schroeder, J. INS vehicle stops designed to discover illegal aliens ruled unconstitutional. CRIMINAL LAW REPORTER, Vol. 37, no. 23 (September 11, 1985), p. 2430-2431. English. **DESCR:** *Nicasio v. U.S. Immigration and Naturalization Service; *Search and Seizure.

8102 Totality of circumstances justified stop of vehicle carrying Hispanics. CRIMINAL LAW REPORTER, Vol. 35, no. 11 (June 13, 1984), p. 2186-2187. English. **DESCR:** Border Patrol; *Undocumented Workers; *U.S. v. Garcia.

U.S. v. Garcia

8103 Totality of circumstances justified stop of vehicle carrying Hispanics. CRIMINAL LAW REPORTER, Vol. 35, no. 11 (June 13, 1984), p. 2186-2187. English. DESCR: Border Patrol; *Undocumented Workers; U.S. v. Brignoni-Ponce.

U.S. v. Hanigan

8104 Ford, Theresa Y. United States v. Hannigan: federal statute used to prosecute torturers. CRIMINAL JUSTICE JOURNAL, Vol. 6, no. 1 (Fall 1982), p. 79-97. English. DESCR: Civil Rights; Hobbs Act; *Undocumented Workers.

U.S. v. Mendoza-Lopez

8105 Immigration violations--collateral attack on deportation order. CRIMINAL LAW REPORTER, Vol. 38, no. 16 (January 22, 1986), p. 2311-2312. English. DESCR: *Deportation.

U.S. v. Oyarzun

8106 District court sets guidelines for vehicle searches at border checkpoints. CRIMINAL LAW REPORTER, Vol. 35, no. 3 (April 18, 1984), p. 2043-2044. English. DESCR: *Search and Seizure.

U.S. v. Ritter

8107 Statutes and ordinances--aliens failure to carry immigration documents. CRIMINAL LAW REPORTER, Vol. 36, no. 21 (February 27, 1985), p. 2405. English. DESCR: *Civil Rights.

US West [telecommunications company]

8108 Bradby, Marie. Solomon Trujillo of US West. HISPANIC ENGINEER, Vol. 3, no. 5 (Winter 1987), p. 26-30. English. DESCR: *Biography; Engineering as a Profession; *Trujillo, Solomon.

EL VAGO [novel]

8109 Bruce-Novoa, Juan. Nuevo representantes de la novela chicana. LA COMUNIDAD, No. 310 (June 29, 1986), p. 6-7+. Spanish. DESCR: Brawley, Ernest; FAULTLINE [novel]; Gonzales, Laurence; *Literary Criticism; Novel; Ortiz Taylor, Sheila; THE ALAMO TREE [novel].

Valadez, John

8110 Gamboa, Harry, Jr. El artista chicano dentro y fuera de la "corriente" artistica. LA COMUNIDAD, No. 351 (April 12, 1987), 2-5+. Spanish. DESCR: *Art; Artists; Carrasco, Barbara; Gamboa, Diane; Gronk (Pseud.); Martinez, Daniel J.; Valdez, Patssi.

Valdes, Dennis N.

8111 Garcia, John R. Book reviews of: EL PUEBLO MEXICANO EN DETROIT Y MICHIGAN and MATERIALS ON THE HISTORY OF LATINOS IN MICHIGAN AND THE MIDWEST. LA RED/THE NET, no. 67 (April 1983), p. 13-14. English. DESCR: Book Reviews; *EL PUEBLO MEXICANO EN DETROIT Y MICHIGAN: A SOCIAL HISTORY; *MATERIALS ON THE HISTORY OF LATINOS IN MICHIGAN AND THE MIDWEST; Midwestern States.

Valdes, Gina

8112 Quintana, Alvina. Challenge and counter challenge: Chicana literary motifs. AGAINST THE CURRENT, Vol. 2, no. 2 (March, April, 1987), p. 25,28-32. English. DESCR: Cervantes, Lorna Dee; *Chicanas; *Feminism; *Literature; Moraga, Cherrie; THERE ARE NO MADMEN HERE.

Valdez, Alex

8113 Gutierrez, Silvio G. The odd couple. VISTA, Vol. 3, no. 1 (September 6, 1987), p. 12-13. English. DESCR: Actors and Actresses; *Humor; O'Brien, Jim.

Valdez, Armando

8114 Garcia, Mario T. Book review of: THE STATE OF CHICANO RESEARCH ON FAMILY, LABOR, AND MIGRATION: PROCEEDINGS OF THE FIRST STANFORD SYMPOSIUM ON CHICANO RESEARCH AND PUBLIC POLICY. CALIFORNIA HISTORY, Vol. 63, no. 3 (Summer 1984), p. 261-262. English. DESCR: Almaguer, Tomas; Book Reviews; Camarillo, Alberto; Chicano Studies; *THE STATE OF CHICANO RESEARCH IN FAMILY, LABOR AND MIGRATION STUDIES.

8115 Griswold del Castillo, Richard. Book review of: THE STATE OF CHICANO RESEARCH ON FAMILY, LABOR, AND MIGRATION: PROCEEDINGS OF THE FIRST STANFORD SYMPOSIUM ON CHICANO RESEARCH AND PUBLIC POLICY. PACIFIC HISTORICAL REVIEW, Vol. 54, no. 3 (August 1985), p. 381-382. English. DESCR: Almaguer, Tomas; Book Reviews; Camarillo, Alberto; Chicano Studies; *THE STATE OF CHICANO RESEARCH IN FAMILY, LABOR AND MIGRATION STUDIES.

Valdez, Facundo

8116 Rosaldo, Renato. When natives talk back: Chicano anthropology since the late 60s. RENATO ROSALDO LECTURE SERIES MONOGRAPH, Vol. 2, (Spring 1986), p. [3]-20. English. DESCR: *Anthropology; Culture; EL GRITO; *Identity; Paredes, Americo; *Political Ideology; *Research Methodology; Romano-V., Octavio Ignacio.

Valdez, Juan

8117 Padilla, Steve. Lessons to be learned from a playful hoax. VISTA, Vol. 1, no. 7 (March 2, 1986), p. 3. English. DESCR: *Essays; Humor; Librarians; Public Opinion; Sclar, Marta-Luisa; Stereotypes.

Valdez, Luis

8118 Beale, Stephen and Valdez, Luis. Connecting with the American experience: an interview with Luis Valdez. HISPANIC BUSINESS, Vol. 9, no. 7 (July 1987), p. 10-13. English. DESCR: Biography; Films; LA BAMBA [film]; Stereotypes; Teatro.

8119 Burciaga, Jose Antonio. Corridos. VISTA, Vol. 3, no. 2 (October 3, 1987), p. 10. English. DESCR: Corridos; *CORRIDOS [film]; Ronstadt, Linda; *Teatro; Television.

8120 Burciaga, Jose Antonio. A man with his teatro. VISTA, Vol. 1, no. 3 (November 3, 1985), p. 8-10. English. DESCR: CORRIDOS [play]; El Teatro Campesino; *Teatro; ZOOT SUIT [play].

8121 Flores, Arturo C. El Teatro Campesino (1965-1986): algunas orientaciones teoricas. CONFLUENCIA, Vol. 2, no. 2 (Spring 1987), p. 116-121. Spanish. DESCR: Brecht, Bertolt; *El Teatro Campesino; History; Moreno, Mario "Cantinflas"; *Teatro.

Valdez, Luis (cont.)

8122 Mejias Rentas, Antonio. Luis Valdez y su Teatro Campesino de nuevo en L.A. LA COMUNIDAD, No. 294 (March 9, 1986), p. 8-9. Spanish. DESCR: *I DON'T HAVE TO SHOW YOU NO STINKING BADGES; *Teatro; Teatro Reviews.

8123 Pena, Luis H. Praxis dramatica, praxis politica: los actos de Luis Valdez. REVISTA DE CRITICA LITERARIA LATINOAMERICANA, Vol. 10, no. 19 (1984), p. 161-166. Spanish. DESCR: Actos; ACTOS; El Teatro Campesino; *Teatro.

8124 Preciado, Consuelo. LA BAMBA triumphs=LA BAMBA triunfa. AMERICAS 2001, Vol. 1, no. 2 (September, October, 1987), p. 7. Bilingual. DESCR: *Films; *LA BAMBA [film]; Valens, Ritchie [stage name for Richard Valenzuela].

8125 Preciado, Consuelo. CORRIDOS: the movie=CORRIDOS: la pelicula. AMERICAS 2001, Vol. 1, no. 2 (September, October, 1987), p. 5-6. Bilingual. DESCR: Corridos; *CORRIDOS [film]; El Teatro Campesino; *Films; Teatro.

8126 Rodriguez Flores, Juan. Esai Morales y la pasion por el arte escenico (II). LA COMUNIDAD, No. 336 (December 28, 1986), p. 2-3. Spanish. DESCR: Actors and Actresses; *Biography; Films; LA BAMBA [film]; *Morales, Esai.

Valdez, Patssi

8127 Gamboa, Harry, Jr. El artista chicano dentro y fuera de la "corriente" artistica. LA COMUNIDAD, No. 351 (April 12, 1987), 2-5+. Spanish. DESCR: *Art; Artists; Carrasco, Barbara; Gamboa, Diane; Gronk (Pseud.); Martinez, Daniel J.; Valadez, John.

Valencia, Elena

8128 Stone, Eric. The daring designs of Elena Valencia. VISTA, Vol. 1, no. 9 (May 3, 1986), p. 6-8. English. DESCR: Biography; Chicanas; *Fashion; La Blanca [fashion label].

Valens, Ritchie [stage name for Richard Valenzuela]

8129 Bellinhausen, Hermann. El lobo estepario en Olvera Street. LA COMUNIDAD, No. 267 (September 1, 1985), p. 10-11. Spanish. DESCR: *Los Lobos del Este de Los Angeles (musical group); *Rock Music.

8130 Kael, Pauline. The current cinema: siblings and cyborgs. NEW YORKER, (August 10, 1987), p. 70-73. English. DESCR: Film Reviews; *LA BAMBA [film].

8131 Preciado, Consuelo. LA BAMBA triumphs=LA BAMBA triunfa. AMERICAS 2001, Vol. 1, no. 2 (September, October, 1987), p. 7. Bilingual. DESCR: *Films; *LA BAMBA [film]; Valdez, Luis.

Valentin, Ruben

8132 Aguirre, Antonio (Jake). Salsa Na Ma in San Francisco. LATIN QUARTER, Vol. 1, no. 2 (October 1974), p. 23. English. DESCR: KRVE, Los Gatos, CA [radio station]; *Rock Music; *Salsa; San Francisco, CA.

Valenzuela, Ralph

8133 Cano, Oscar. Profiles in engineering. HISPANIC TIMES, Vol. 8, no. 3 (May, June, 1987), p. 43. English. DESCR: Biography; *Engineering as a Profession.

Valle, Ramon

8134 Martinez, Alejandro M. Book review of: HISPANIC NATURAL SUPPORT SYSTEMS: MENTAL HEALTH PROMOTIONS PERSPECTIVES. LA RED/THE NET, no. 73 (October 1983), p. 7-12. English. DESCR: Book Reviews; *HISPANIC NATIONAL SUPPORT SYSTEMS: MENTAL HEALTH PROMOTIONS PERSPECTIVES; Vega, William A.

THE VALLEY

8135 Sanchez, Saul. Book review of: THE VALLEY. LA RED/THE NET, no. 81 (June 1984), p. 7. Spanish. DESCR: Book Reviews; Hinojosa-Smith, Rolando R.

8136 Torres, Hector. Discourse and plot in Rolando Hinojosa's THE VALLEY: narrativity and the recovery of Chicano heritage. CONFLUENCIA, Vol. 2, no. 1 (Fall 1986), p. 84-93. English. DESCR: *Hinojosa-Smith, Rolando R.; *Literary Criticism; Novel.

Values

8137 Atencio, Tomas. La Academia de la Nueva Raza. EL CUADERNO, Vol. 2, no. 1 (1972), p. 6-13. English. DESCR: *Alternative Education; Chicano Studies; Cultural Characteristics; *Cultural Organizations; Education; *Educational Organizations; *La Academia de la Nueva Raza, Dixon, NM; Oro del Barrio; Philosophy.

8138 Cortese, Anthony J. Ethnic ethics: subjective choice and interference in Chicano, white and Black children. LA RED/THE NET, no. 38 (January 1981), p. 2-3. English. DESCR: *Ethnic Groups.

8139 Domino, George and Acosta, Alexandria. The relation of acculturation and values in Mexican Americans. HISPANIC JOURNAL OF BEHAVIORAL SCIENCES, Vol. 9, no. 2 (June 1987), p. 131-150. English. DESCR: *Acculturation.

8140 Gutierrez, Ramon A. Honor ideology, marriage negotiation, and class-gender domination in New Mexico, 1690-1846. LATIN AMERICAN PERSPECTIVES, Vol. 12, no. 1 (Winter 1985), p. 81-104. English. DESCR: Marriage; Sex Roles; *Social Classes; Social History and Conditions; *Southwestern United States; Women Men Relations.

8141 Isonio, Steven A. and Garza, Raymond T. Protestant work ethic endorsement among Anglo Americans, Chicanos and Mexicans: a comparison of factor structures. HISPANIC JOURNAL OF BEHAVIORAL SCIENCES, Vol. 9, no. 4 (December 1987), p. 413-425. English. DESCR: *Comparative Psychology; *Cultural Characteristics; Ethnic Groups; *Protestant Work Ethic (PWE) Scale.

8142 Martinez, Thomas M. Chicanismo. EPOCA: NATIONAL CONCILIO FOR CHICANO STUDIES JOURNAL, Vol. 1, no. 2 (Winter 1971), p. 35-39. English. DESCR: *Chicanismo; *Chicano Studies.

8143 Sabogal, Fabio, et al. Hispanic familism and acculturation: what changes and what doesn't? HISPANIC JOURNAL OF BEHAVIORAL SCIENCES, Vol. 9, no. 4 (December 1987), p. 397-412. English. DESCR: *Acculturation; Attitudes; Cultural Characteristics; Ethnic Groups; Extended Family; *Family; Natural Support Systems.

Valverde, Richard

8144 Rosas, Alejandro. Siete fotografos latinos en Los Angeles. LA COMUNIDAD, No. 241 (March 3, 1985), p. 4-5. Spanish. **DESCR**: Aguilar, Laura; Art; Avila, Adam; Callwood, Dennis O.; Carlos, Jesus; Exhibits; Miranda, Judy; *Photography; Self-Help Graphics, Los Angeles, CA; *SEVEN LATINO PHOTOGRAPHERS=SIETE FOTOGRAFOS LATINOS; Thewlis, Alan.

Van Horne, Winston A.

8145 Kivisto, Peter. Book review of: ETHNICITY AND THE WORK FORCE. JOURNAL OF AMERICAN ETHNIC HISTORY, Vol. 6, no. 2 (Spring 1987), p. 68-69. English. **DESCR**: Book Reviews; *ETHNICITY AND THE WORK FORCE; Laboring Classes.

Vaqueros

8146 Ahlborn, Richard E. The Hispanic horseman: a sampling of horse gear from the Fred Harvey Collection. PALACIO, Vol. 89, no. 2 (1983), p. 12-21. English. **DESCR**: Fred Harvey Co.; Museum of New Mexico.

Vargas, Jesus

8147 SHPE news. HISPANIC ENGINEER, Vol. 3, no. 3 (1987), p. 10-13. English. **DESCR**: *Awards; Castillo, Hector; Colmenarez, Margarita; Garcia, Raul; Herrera, Jess; Lopez-Martin, Minnie; Mondragon, Ricardo; Reyes-Guerra, David; Silva, Juan; Society of Hispanic Professional Engineers (SHPE); Villanueva, Bernadette.

Vasquez, Victor

8148 Gutierrez, Gloria. Chicano news-man wins award. LATIN QUARTER, Vol. 1, no. 4 (July, August, 1975), p. 17. English. **DESCR**: Golden Mike Award; Journalists; *Radio; Southern California Radio and Television News Association.

"Los vatos" [poem]

8149 Saldivar, Jose David. Towards a Chicano poetics: the making of the Chicano subject. CONFLUENCIA, Vol. 1, no. 2 (Spring 1986), p. 10-17. English. **DESCR**: Corridos; Feminism; *Literary Criticism; Montoya, Jose E.; *Poetry; RESTLESS SERPENTS; Rios, Alberto; WHISPERING TO FOOL THE WIND; Zamora, Bernice.

Vega, Jose E.

8150 Cardenas, Jose A. Book review of: EDUCATION, POLITICS, AND BILINGUAL EDUCATION IN TEXAS. LA RED/THE NET, no. 75 (December 1983), p. 5-8. English. **DESCR**: Book Reviews; *EDUCATION, POLITICS, AND BILINGUAL EDUCATION IN TEXAS.

Vega, William A.

8151 Martinez, Alejandro M. Book review of: HISPANIC NATURAL SUPPORT SYSTEMS: MENTAL HEALTH PROMOTIONS PERSPECTIVES. LA RED/THE NET, no. 73 (October 1983), p. 7-12. English. **DESCR**: Book Reviews; *HISPANIC NATIONAL SUPPORT SYSTEMS: MENTAL HEALTH PROMOTIONS PERSPECTIVES; Valle, Ramon.

Velasco [family name]

8152 Instituto Genealogico e Historico Latino-Americano. Rootsearch: Castro: Velasco. VISTA, Vol. 2, no. 2 (October 4, 1986), p. 22. English. **DESCR**: *Castro [family name]; Genealogy; History; *Personal Names.

Veltman, Calvin

8153 Macias, Reynaldo Flores. Disambiguating the Veltman trilogy. BILINGUAL REVIEW, Vol. 12, no. 1-2 (January, August, 1985), p. 140-143. English. **DESCR**: Book Reviews; *CONTRACTOR REPORT: RELATIVE EDUCATIONAL ATTAINMENT OF MINORITY LANGUAGE CHILDREN, 1976: A COMPARISON TO BLACK AND WHITE ENGLISH LANGUAGE CHILDREN; *CONTRACTOR REPORT: THE ROLE OF LANGUAGE CHARACTERISTICS IN THE SOCIOECONOMIC PROCESS OF HISPANIC ORIGIN MEN AND WOMEN; Language Usage; *THE RETENTION OF MINORITY LANGUAGES IN THE UNITED STATES: A SEMINAR ON THE ANALYTIC WORK OF CALVIN VELTMAN.

Vera, Ron

8154 Magallan, Rafael J. Community college update. LA RED/THE NET, no. 98 (July 1986), p. 3-6. English. **DESCR**: *California Master Plan for Higher Education; *Community College Reassessment Study; Community Colleges; Enrollment.

Veterans

8155 Allsup, Dan. The private war of Roy Benavidez. VISTA, Vol. 2, no. 5 (January 4, 1987), p. 19-20. English. **DESCR**: *Benavidez, Roy; Medal of Honor; Nationalism.

8156 Jimenez, Angel. Twenty years later: a Latino remembers 'Nam. VISTA, Vol. 3, no. 4 (December 6, 1987), p. 38. English. **DESCR**: *Vietnam War.

Vice

USE: Criminal Acts

LA VIDA AMERICANA

8157 13-part series focuses on Hispanics in America. EDITOR & PUBLISHER: THE FOURTH ESTATE, Vol. 115, no. 14 (April 3, 1982), p. 37. English. **DESCR**: Books; Cultural Characteristics; DALLAS MORNING NEWS; Garcia, Juan; Gonzalez, John; Goodwin, Jay; Grothe, Randy Eli; Hamilton, John; Hille, Ed; *LA VIDA AMERICANA/HISPANICS IN AMERICA; Langer, Ralph; McLemore, David; Osburne, Burl; Parks, Scott; Pusey, Allen; Sonnemair, Jan.

LA VIDA AMERICANA/HISPANICS IN AMERICA

8158 13-part series focuses on Hispanics in America. EDITOR & PUBLISHER: THE FOURTH ESTATE, Vol. 115, no. 14 (April 3, 1982), p. 37. English. **DESCR**: Books; Cultural Characteristics; DALLAS MORNING NEWS; Garcia, Juan; Gonzalez, John; Goodwin, Jay; Grothe, Randy Eli; Hamilton, John; Hille, Ed; LA VIDA AMERICANA; Langer, Ralph; McLemore, David; Osburne, Burl; Parks, Scott; Pusey, Allen; Sonnemair, Jan.

Vidales, Mark

8159 Aguirre, Antonio (Jake). Two little giants. LATIN QUARTER, Vol. 1, no. 2 (October 1974), p. 25. English. **DESCR**: Musicians; Rock Music; *Ross, Gilbert (Gibby); *Salsa; San Francisco, CA.

Vietnam War

Sonora, Mexico.

8160 Benavidez, Roy. An embattled Chicano. VISTA, Vol. 2, no. 5 (January 4, 1987), p. 20. English. DESCR: Benavidez, Roy; *Books; Green Berets; Griffin, Oscar; *THE THREE WARS OF ROY BENAVIDEZ.

8161 Jimenez, Angel. Twenty years later: a Latino remembers 'Nam. VISTA, Vol. 3, no. 4 (December 6, 1987), p. 38. English. DESCR: *Veterans.

8162 Ramirez, Arturo. SOLDIERBOY, una muestra de la eficacia del teatro chicano de hoy. LA COMUNIDAD, No. 357 (May 24, 1987), p. 12-13. Spanish. DESCR: Perez, Judith; Perez, Severo; *SOLDIERBOY [play]; *Teatro; Teatro Reviews.

Vigil, James Diego

8163 Melville, Margarita B. Book review of: FROM INDIANS TO CHICANOS. LA RED/THE NET, no. 45 (August 1981), p. 3. English. DESCR: Book Reviews; *FROM INDIANS TO CHICANOS: A SOCIOCULTURAL HISTORY; Social History and Conditions.

Vigil-Pinon, Evangelina

8164 Cantu, Norma. Book review of: WOMAN OF HER WORD: HISPANIC WOMEN WRITE. LA RED/THE NET, no. 83 (August 1984), p. 4. English. DESCR: Book Reviews; *WOMAN OF HER WORD: HISPANIC WOMEN WRITE.

8165 Castillo-Speed, Lillian. Chicana/Latina literature and criticism: reviews of recent books. WLW JOURNAL, Vol. 11, no. 3 (September 1987), p. 1-4. English. DESCR: Andrews, Lynn V.; *Book Reviews; BORDERS; Chavez, Denise; *Chicanas; CONTEMPORARY CHICANA POETRY: A CRITICAL APPROACH TO AN EMERGING LITERATURE; Flores, Angel; Flores, Kate; JAGUAR WOMAN; Mora, Pat; Sanchez, Marta Ester; Tafolla, Carmen; THE DEFIANT MUSE: HISPANIC FEMINIST POEMS FROM THE MIDDLE AGES TO THE PRESENT; THE LAST OF THE MENU GIRLS; TO SPLIT A HUMAN: MITOS, MACHOS Y LA MUJER CHICANA; WOMAN OF HER WORD: HISPANIC WOMEN WRITE.

8166 Miller, Beth. Book review of: WOMAN OF HER WORD: HISPANIC WOMEN WRITE. HISPANIA, Vol. 68, no. 2 (May 1985), p. 326-327. English. DESCR: Book Reviews; *WOMAN OF HER WORD: HISPANIC WOMEN WRITE.

VILLA ALEGRE [television program]

8167 Lopez, Jose Y. A visit to VILLA ALEGRE. LATIN QUARTER, Vol. 1, no. 3 (January, February, 1975), p. 8-12. English. DESCR: Bilingual Children's Television, Inc.; *Children's Television; Cultural Pluralism; Public Television.

Villa, Beto

8168 Pena, Manuel. From ranchero to jaiton: ethnicity and class in Texas-Mexican music (two styles in the form of a pair). ETHNOMUSICOLOGY, Vol. 29, no. 1 (Winter 1985), p. 29-55. English. DESCR: Conjuntos; *Ethnomusicology; Musical Instruments.

Villa, Pancho

8169 Coerver, Don and Hall, Linda B. The Arizona-Sonora border and the Mexican revolution, 1910-1920. JOURNAL OF THE WEST, Vol. 24, no. 2 (1985), p. 75-87. English. DESCR: Arizona; Arizona Rangers; *History;

Villalobos [family name]

8170 Instituto Genealogico e Historico Latino-Americano. Rootsearch: Villalobos: Amador (Amado): Ibarra. VISTA, Vol. 3, no. 4 (December 6, 1987), p. 36. English. DESCR: *Amado [family name]; *Amador [family name]; Genealogy; History; *Ibarra [family name]; Personal Names.

Villamil, Antonio

8171 Garcia, Art. Financing the corporate take-off. HISPANIC BUSINESS, Vol. 9, no. 5 (May 1987), p. 22-27. English. DESCR: Aguirre Architects, Dallas, TX; Aguirre, Pedro; Banking Industry; *Business Enterprises; Businesspeople; *Corporations; *Investments; Minority Enterprise Small Business Investment Corporation (MESBIC); Morales, Ramon; Protocom Devices, New York, NY.

Villanueva, Alma

8172 Conde, Hilda Rosina. Book review of: LIFE SPAN. LECTOR, Vol. 4, no. 4-6 (1987), p. 77-78. English. DESCR: Book Reviews; *LIFE SPAN.

Villanueva, Bernadette

8173 SHPE news. HISPANIC ENGINEER, Vol. 3, no. 3 (1987), p. 10-13. English. DESCR: *Awards; Castillo, Hector; Colmenarez, Margarita; Garcia, Raul; Herrera, Jess; Lopez-Martin, Minnie; Mondragon, Ricardo; Reyes-Guerra, David; Silva, Juan; Society of Hispanic Professional Engineers (SHPE); Vargas, Jesus.

Villanueva, Daniel

8174 SICC sells TVs for $301.5 million. BROADCASTING, Vol. 111, no. 4 (July 28, 1986), p. 91-92. English. DESCR: Azcarraga, Emilio; First Chicago Venture Capital; Hallmark Cards; KFTV, Fresno, CA [television station]; KMEX, Los Angeles, CA [television station]; KWEX, San Antonio, TX [television station]; Legal Cases; *Spanish International Communications Corp. (SICC); Spanish International Network (SIN); Spanish Language; Television; WLTV, Miami, FL [television station]; WXTV, Paterson, NJ [television station].

Villanueva, Tino

8175 Olivares, Julian. Self and society in Tino Villanueva's SHAKING OFF THE DARK. CONFLUENCIA, Vol. 1, no. 2 (Spring 1986), p. 98-110. English. DESCR: Literary Criticism; *Poetry; *SHAKING OFF THE DARK.

Villar, Arturo

8176 Norris, Eileen. Print suffers in tale of two languages. ADVERTISING AGE MAGAZINE, Vol. 57, no. 16 (February 27, 1986), p. 49-51. English. DESCR: Advertising; Chavarria, Jesus; English Language; HISPANIC BUSINESS; LATINA [magazine]; *Magazines; Soto, Grace; Spanish Language; VISTA [magazine].

Villarreal, Jose Antonio

8177 Bruce-Novoa, Juan. Homosexuality and the
Chicano novel. CONFLUENCIA, Vol. 2, no. 1
(Fall 1986), p. 69-77. English. **DESCR:**
Acosta, Oscar Zeta; CITY OF NIGHT; FAULTLINE
[novel]; *Homosexuality; Islas, Arturo;
*Literary Criticism; Machismo; *Novel; Ortiz
Taylor, Sheila; POCHO; Rechy, John; Salas,
Floyd; SPRING FORWARD/FALL BACK; TATOO THE
WICKED CROSS; THE AUTOBIOGRAPHY OF A BROWN
BUFFALO; THE RAIN GOD: A DESERT TALE; THE
REVOLT OF THE COCKROACH PEOPLE.

8178 Lomeli, Francisco A. En la voragine del
destino [book review of: THE FIFTH
HORSEMAN]. LA COMUNIDAD, No. 258 (June 30,
1985), p. 12-13. Spanish. **DESCR:** Book
Reviews; *Literary Criticism; *THE FIFTH
HORSEMAN.

Violence

8179 Aceves Madrid, Vicente. Film review of:
FREEBIE AND THE BEAN. LATIN QUARTER, Vol. 1,
no. 3 (January, February, 1975), p. 22-23.
English. **DESCR:** *Film Reviews; FREEBIE AND
THE BEAN; Stereotypes.

8180 Alicia de Garcia's oral history=Historia
oral de Alicia de Garcia. REVISTA MUJERES,
Vol. 3, no. 2 (June 1986), p. 37-49.
Spanish. **DESCR:** *Committee of Mothers and
Relatives of Political Prisoners Disappeared
and Assassinated of El Salvador "Monsenor
Oscar Arnulfo Romero" (Comadres, El
Salvador); Community Organizations; de
Garcia, Alicia; *Federation of Latin
Americans for the Association of Relatives
of the Detained and Disappeared (FedeFam);
*Oral History; Terrorism; *Women.

8181 Camach, Miguel. Idea atrazada. REVISTA
MUJERES, Vol. 2, no. 2 (June 1985), p.
46-48. Spanish. **DESCR:** *Short Story.

8182 Chavez, Andres. Film review of: BRING ME THE
HEAD OF ALFREDO GARCIA. LATIN QUARTER, Vol.
1, no. 2 (October 1974), p. 36. English.
DESCR: *BRING ME THE HEAD OF ALFREDO GARCIA;
*Film Reviews; Peckinpah, Sam.

8183 Peace with justice. REVISTA MUJERES, Vol. 3,
no. 2 (June 1986), p. 32-35. English.
DESCR: *Committee of Mothers and Relatives
of Political Prisoners Disappeared and
Assassinated of El Salvador "Monsenor Oscar
Arnulfo Romero" (Comadres, El Salvador);
Community Organizations; *Federation of
Latin Americans for the Association of
Relatives of the Detained and Disappeared
(FedeFam); Terrorism; *Women.

Viramontes, Helen

8184 Alarcon, Norma. Making "familia" from
scratch: split subjectivities in the work of
Helena Maria Viramontes and Cherrie Moraga.
THE AMERICAS REVIEW, Vol. 15, no. 3-4 (Fall,
Winter, 1987), p. 147-159. English. **DESCR:**
Chicanas; GIVING UP THE GHOST; *Literary
Criticism; *Moraga, Cherrie; *Sex Roles;
"Snapshots" [short story]; THE MOTHS AND
OTHER STORIES.

8185 Martinez, Beverly Ann. Book review of: THE
MOTHS AND OTHER STORIES. VISTA, Vol. 1, no.
11 (July 6, 1986), p. 16. English. **DESCR:**
Book Reviews; *THE MOTHS AND OTHER STORIES.

La Virgen de Guadalupe

8186 Hazen-Hammond, Susan and Fuss, Eduardo.
Vivan las celebraciones. ARIZONA HIGHWAYS,
Vol. 63, no. 8 (August 1987), p. 35-45.
English. **DESCR:** Cinco de Mayo; Cultural
Customs; Dia de los Muertos; Dieciseis de
Septiembre; Fiestas Patrias; *Holidays; Las
Posadas.

8187 Limon, Jose E. La Llorona, the third legend
of greater Mexico: cultural symbols, women,
and the political unconscious. RENATO
ROSALDO LECTURE SERIES MONOGRAPH, Vol. 2,
(Spring 1986), p. [59]-93. English. **DESCR:**
*Feminism; Folklore; *La Llorona; *Leyendas;
Malinche; Mexico; *Symbolism; Women.

Visas

8188 Zesch, Lindy. Visa issue heats up: PEN hopes
for "group waiver" of denials. AMERICAN
THEATRE, Vol. 2, no. 8 (November 1985), p.
24. English. **DESCR:** Artists; Authors; Book
Reviews; GETTING IN: A GUIDE TO OVERCOMING
THE POLITICAL DENIAL OF NON-IMMIGRANT VISAS;
National Lawyer's Guild; Politics.

VISTA [magazine]

8189 Caicedo, Harry. VISTA birthday review and
renewal of goals. VISTA, Vol. 2, no. 1
(September 7, 1986), p. 3. English. **DESCR:**
*Publishing Industry.

8190 Norris, Eileen. Print suffers in tale of two
languages. ADVERTISING AGE MAGAZINE, Vol.
57, no. 16 (February 27, 1986), p. 49-51.
English. **DESCR:** Advertising; Chavarria,
Jesus; English Language; HISPANIC BUSINESS;
LATINA [magazine]; *Magazines; Soto, Grace;
Spanish Language; Villar, Arturo.

Vital Statistics

8191 Gillespie, Francis P., et al. Public policy,
ethnic code, and Hispanic vital statistics.
LA RED/THE NET, no. 70 (July 1983), p. 9-13.
English. **DESCR:** Public Policy; *Texas.

8192 Martin, Jeanne and Suarez, Lucina. Cancer
mortality among Mexican Americans and other
whites in Texas, 1969-80. AMERICAN JOURNAL
OF PUBLIC HEALTH, Vol. 77, no. 7 (July
1987), p. 851-853. English. **DESCR:** *Cancer;
Generally Useful Ethnic Search System
(GUESS); Texas.

8193 Neibel, Barbara A. Health care utilization:
the case of the Mexican-American.
ANTHROPOLOGY UCLA, Vol. 14, (1985), p.
13-26. English. **DESCR:** Cultural
Characteristics; *Medical Care; *Public
Health.

8194 Tienda, Marta. Task force on statistical
policy and data needs. LA RED/THE NET, no.
88 (Winter, 1984), p. 2-6. English. **DESCR:**
*Databases; *Population; Public Policy;
Research Methodology; *Statistics.

Voice of America

8195 Breiter, Toni. Pepe del Rio. VISTA, Vol. 1,
no. 6 (February 2, 1986), p. 20. English.
DESCR: Broadcast Media; *BUENOS DIAS,
AMERICA [radio news & features program]; del
Rio, Pepe; Perez del Rio, Jose; *Radio.

Volunteer Associations
USE: Mutualistas

Voter Turnout

8196 Arce, Carlos H. Chicano voting. LA RED/THE NET, no. 53 (April 1982), p. 2-4. English. **DESCR:** Chicago, IL; *Southwestern United States.

8197 Bogart, Beth. Political power gives market vote of confidence. ADVERTISING AGE MAGAZINE, Vol. 58, no. 6 (February 9, 1987), p. S22. English. **DESCR:** *Politics.

8198 de la Garza, Rodolfo O. The Mexican American electorate. LA RED/THE NET, no. 72 (September 1983), p. 2-6. English. **DESCR:** Political Representation; *Southwest Voter Registration Education Project (SVREP).

8199 Garcia, John A. Chicano political development: examining participation in the "decade of Hispanics". LA RED/THE NET, no. 72 (September 1983), p. 8-18. English. **DESCR:** *Political Representation; Reapportionment.

8200 Los Angeles: arriba! ECONOMIST (London), Vol. 297, no. 7424 (December 14, 1985), p. 26. English. **DESCR:** Bradley, Tom; *Los Angeles, CA; Political Representation; Politics; Reapportionment.

8201 Los Angeles: brown versus yellow. ECONOMIST (London), Vol. 300, no. 7456 (July 26, 1986), p. 21-22. English. **DESCR:** Alatorre, Richard; Bradley, Tom; Ethnic Groups; *Los Angeles, CA; Political Representation; Politics; Reapportionment; Woo, Michael.

8202 McNeely, Dave. Hispanic power at the polls. VISTA, Vol. 2, no. 3 (November 2, 1986), p. 8-12. English. **DESCR:** Austin, TX; *Barrera, Roy, Jr.; Chavez, Linda; Elected Officials; Gonzalez, Raul; Martinez, Bob; Maryland; Political System; San Antonio, TX; Statistics; Tampa, FL.

8203 Munoz, Carlos, Jr. Chicano politics: the current conjuncture. THE YEAR LEFT, Vol. 2, (1987), p. 35-52. English. **DESCR:** Chicano Movement; Identity; *Intergroup Relations; *Political Parties and Organizations; *Politics; Reagan Administration.

8204 National Association of Latino Elected and Appointed Officials. The Hispanic vote. LA RED/THE NET, no. 72 (September 1983), p. 2-3. English. **DESCR:** Political Representation.

8205 Volsky, George. A new voting block making its mark. HISPANIC BUSINESS, Vol. 9, no. 2 (February 1987), p. 9, 11. English. **DESCR:** Cubanos; Democratic Party; Elections; *Political Parties and Organizations; Republican Party.

8206 Wreford, Mary. Chicano Survey report #3: political opinions. LA RED/THE NET, no. 40 (March 1981), p. 4-5. English. **DESCR:** *National Chicano Survey (NCS); Politics.

Voting Rights

8207 Rips, Geoffrey. Civil rights and wrongs. TEXAS OBSERVOR, Vol. 76, (December 14, 1984), p. 49-55. English. **DESCR:** Briscoe, Dolph, Jr., Governor of Texas; *Civil Rights; Farm Workers; *Hidalgo County, TX; La Raza Unida Party; Miller, C.L.; Segregation and Desegregation; Texas Farmworkers' Union.

WADO-AM, New York, NY [radio station]

8208 Berling-Manuel, Lynn. Expanding radio market battles research static. ADVERTISING AGE MAGAZINE, Vol. 57, no. 43 (August 11, 1986), p. S12-S16. English. **DESCR:** Arbitron; Marketing; *Radio; Spanish Language; WAQI-AM, Miami, FL [radio station]; WOJO-FM, Chicago, IL [radio station].

Wages

USE: Income

WALKING ON WATER [working title of film STAND AND DELIVER]

8209 Muro, Rena. Walking on water. AMERICAS 2001, Vol. 1, no. 3 (November, December, 1987), p. 12-14. Bilingual. **DESCR:** Camhi, Morrie; *Films; Olmos, Edward James; STAND AND DELIVER [film].

WAQI-AM, Miami, FL [radio station]

8210 Berling-Manuel, Lynn. Expanding radio market battles research static. ADVERTISING AGE MAGAZINE, Vol. 57, no. 43 (August 11, 1986), p. S12-S16. English. **DESCR:** Arbitron; Marketing; *Radio; Spanish Language; WADO-AM, New York, NY [radio station]; WOJO-FM, Chicago, IL [radio station].

A WAR OF WORDS: CHICANO PROTEST IN THE 1960S AND 1970S

8211 de la Garza, Rodolfo O. Book review of: A WAR OF WORDS. JOURNAL OF AMERICAN ETHNIC HISTORY, Vol. 6, no. 2 (Spring 1987), p. 97-98. English. **DESCR:** Book Reviews; Gutierrez, Jose Angel; Hammerback, John C.; Jensen, Richard J.; Rhetoric.

WAR, REVOLUTION, AND THE KU KLUX KLAN: A STUDY OF INTOLERANCE IN A BORDER CITY

8212 Alexander, Charles C. Book review of: WAR, REVOLUTION, AND THE KU KLUX KLAN: A STUDY OF INTOLERANCE IN A BORDER CITY. NEW MEXICO HISTORICAL REVIEW, Vol. 62, no. 1 (January 1987), p. 110-111. English. **DESCR:** Book Reviews; *Lay, Shawn.

Washington (state)

8213 Slatta, Richard W. and Atkinson, Maxine P. The "Spanish origin" population of Oregon and Washington: a demographic profile, 1980. PACIFIC NORTHWEST QUARTERLY, Vol. 75, no. 3 (July 1984), p. 108-116. English. **DESCR:** *Oregon; *Population; Self-Referents; Socioeconomic Factors; Statistics.

WATER IN THE HISPANIC SOUTHWEST: A SOCIAL AND LEGAL HISTORY, 1550-1850

8214 Fireman, Janet R. Book review of: WATER IN THE HISPANIC SOUTHWEST. SOUTHWESTERN HISTORICAL QUARTERLY, Vol. 88, no. 4 (1985), p. 430-431. English. **DESCR:** Book Reviews; Meyer, Michael C..

8215 Langum, David J. Book review of: WATER IN THE HISPANIC SOUTHWEST. AMERICAN JOURNAL OF LEGAL HISTORY, Vol. 30, no. 3 (July 1986), p. 273-276. English. **DESCR:** Book Reviews; Meyer, Michael C..

WATER IN THE HISPANIC SOUTHWEST: A SOCIAL AND LEGAL HISTORY, 1550-1850 (cont.)

8216 Tutino, John. Book review of: WATER IN THE HISPANIC SOUTHWEST. AMERICAS, Vol. 42, no. 3 (January 1986), p. 355-356. English. DESCR: Book Reviews; Meyer, Michael C.

Watsonville, CA

8217 Guzman, Ralph. Bi-national policy questions generated by Mexican school-age children who migrate between the United States and Mexico. LA RED/THE NET, no. 62 (December 1982), p. 2-4. English. DESCR: *Children; Immigrants; Migrant Children; Public Policy.

8218 Segal, William. New alliances in Watsonville strike. IN THESE TIMES, Vol. 10, no. 29 (July 9, 1986), p. 5. English. DESCR: Collective Bargaining; Jackson, Jesse; Labor Unions; Strikes and Lockouts; Teamsters Union; Watsonville Canning and Frozen Food Co.

Watsonville Canning and Frozen Food Co.

8219 Romero, Bertha. The exploitation of Mexican women in the canning industry and the effects of capital accumulation on striking workers. REVISTA MUJERES, Vol. 3, no. 2 (June 1986), p. 16-20. English. DESCR: Canneries; Capitalism; *Chicanas; Labor Unions; Strikes and Lockouts.

8220 Segal, William. New alliances in Watsonville strike. IN THESE TIMES, Vol. 10, no. 29 (July 9, 1986), p. 5. English. DESCR: Collective Bargaining; Jackson, Jesse; Labor Unions; Strikes and Lockouts; Teamsters Union; *Watsonville, CA.

8221 Shapiro, Peter. Watsonville shows "it can be done". GUARDIAN, Vol. 39, no. 24 (March 25, 1987), p. 1,9. English. DESCR: Canneries; Chicanas; Labor Unions; NorCal Frozen Foods; *Strikes and Lockouts; Working Women.

Weber, David J.

8222 Griswold del Castillo, Richard. New perspectives on the Mexican and American borderlands. LATIN AMERICAN RESEARCH REVIEW, Vol. 19, no. 1 (1984), p. 199-209. English. DESCR: AL NORTE DEL RIO BRAVO (PASADO INMEDIATO, 1930-1981); AL NORTE DEL RIO BRAVO (PASADO LEJANO, 1600-1930); *Book Reviews; *Border Region; Gomez-Quinones, Juan; Maciel, David; MEXICANO RESISTANCE IN THE SOUTHWEST: "THE SACRED RIGHT OF SELF-PRESERVATION"; Rosenbaum, Robert J.; THE MEXICAN FRONTIER, 1821-1846: THE AMERICAN SOUTHWEST UNDER MEXICO; THE TEJANO COMMUNITY, 1836-1900.

8223 Miller, Robert Ryal. Book review of: THE MEXICAN FRONTIER 1821-1846. CALIFORNIA HISTORY, Vol. 63, no. 3 (Summer 1984), p. 260-261. English. DESCR: Book Reviews; *THE MEXICAN FRONTIER, 1821-1846: THE AMERICAN SOUTHWEST UNDER MEXICO.

8224 Riley, James D. Book review of: THE MEXICAN FRONTIER 1821-1846. AMERICAS, Vol. 40, no. 4 (April 1984), p. 592-593. English. DESCR: Book Reviews; *THE MEXICAN FRONTIER, 1821-1846: THE AMERICAN SOUTHWEST UNDER MEXICO.

Wedtech Corporation, Bronx, NY

8225 Sellers, Jeff M. Wedtech fallout hits 8(a) program. HISPANIC BUSINESS, Vol. 9, no. 6 (June 1987), p. 12-13, 17. English. DESCR: *Business Enterprises; Government Contracts; *Small Business Administration 8(a) Program.

Weigle, Marta

8226 Griffith, James S. Book review of: HISPANIC ARTS AND ETHNOHISTORY IN THE SOUTHWEST: NEW PAPERS INSPIRED BY THE WORKS OF E. BOYD. ARIZONA AND THE WEST, Vol. 26, no. 2 (Summer 1984), p. 188-189. English. DESCR: Book Reviews; *HISPANIC ARTS AND ETHNOHISTORY IN THE SOUTHWEST: NEW PAPERS INSPIRED BY THE WORKS OF E. BOYD.

Weinberg, Meyer

8227 Burnham-Kidwell, Debbie. Book review of: THE EDUCATION OF POOR AND MINORITY CHILDREN: A WORLD BIBLIOGRAPHY: SUPPLEMENT, 1979-1985. AMERICAN REFERENCE BOOKS ANNUAL, Vol. 18, (1987), p. 134. English. DESCR: Book Reviews; *THE EDUCATION OF POOR AND MINORITY CHILDREN: A WORLD BIBLIOGRAPHY: SUPPLEMENT 1979-01985.

Weintraub, Sidney

8228 Book review of: FREE TRADE BETWEEN MEXICO AND THE UNITED STATES? FOREIGN AFFAIRS, Vol. 63, no. 1 (Fall 1984), p. 196. English. DESCR: Book Reviews; *FREE TRADE BETWEEN MEXICO AND THE UNITED STATES?

8229 Cardenas, Gilbert. Book review of: "TEMPORARY" ALIEN WORKERS IN THE UNITED STATES. LA RED/THE NET, no. 63 (January 1983), p. 9-10. English. DESCR: Book Reviews; Ross, Stanley R.; *"TEMPORARY" ALIEN WORKERS IN THE UNITED STATES: DESIGNING POLICY FROM FACT AND OPINION; Undocumented Workers.

Weisman, Alan

8230 Perez, Renato E. Book review of: LA FRONTERA: THE U.S. BORDER WITH MEXICO. VISTA, Vol. 2, no. 10 (June 7, 1987), p. 24. English. DESCR: *Book Reviews; Dusard, Jay; *LA FRONTERA: THE U.S. BORDER WITH MEXICO.

Welfare

8231 Jensen, Leif and Tienda, Marta. The new immigration: implications for poverty and public assistance utilization. MIGRATION WORLD MAGAZINE, Vol. 15, no. 5 (1987), p. 7-18. English. DESCR: History; Immigrants; *Immigration; *Immigration and Naturalization Act, 1965; Poverty; Public Policy.

8232 Out of marriage, onto welfare and into poverty. REVISTA MUJERES, Vol. 4, no. 1 (January 1987), p. 39-40. English. DESCR: *Chicanas; Divorce; Education.

West, Jonathan P.

8233 Burnett, G. Wesley. Book review of: BORDERLANDS SOURCEBOOK. GEOGRAPHICAL REVIEW, Vol. 74, no. 1 (January 1984), p. 123-124. English. DESCR: Book Reviews; *BORDERLANDS SOURCEBOOK; Nostrand, Richard L.; Stoddard, Ellwyn R.

West Texas

8234 Graham, Joe S. Folk medicine and intra-cultural diversity among West Texas Americans. WESTERN FOLKLORE, Vol. 44, no. 3 (July 1985), p. 168-193. English. DESCR: Attitudes; *Folk Medicine.

Westphall, Victor

8235 Weber, David J. Book review of: MERCEDES
      REALES: HISPANIC LAND GRANTS OF THE UPPER
      RIO GRANDE REGION. AMERICAN HISTORICAL
      REVIEW, Vol. 89, no. 4 (October 1984), p.
      1156-1157. English. DESCR: Book Reviews;
      *MERCEDES REALES: HISPANIC LAND GRANTS OF
      THE UPPER RIO GRANDE REGION.

Wexler, Haskell

8236 Callahan, Jaime M. LATINO: un nuevo concepto
      de cine. LA COMUNIDAD, No. 279 (November 24,
      1985), p. 2-3. Spanish. DESCR: *Films;
      Identity; *LATINO [film]; Military; Military
      Service.

**"What Kind of Lover Have You Made Me, Mother?:
Towards a Theory of Chicanas' Feminism and
Cultural Identity Through Poetry" [article]**

8237 Quintana, Alvina. O mama, with what's inside
      of me. REVISTA MUJERES, Vol. 3, no. 1
      (January 1986), p. 38-40. English. DESCR:
      *Alarcon, Norma; *Chicanas; Feminism;
      *Literary Criticism; Poetry.

WHERE SPARROWS WORK HARD

8238 Bruce-Novoa, Juan. Poesia de Gary Soto: una
      autobiografia a plazos. LA COMUNIDAD, No.
      270 (September 22, 1985), p. 8-10. Spanish.
      DESCR: Authors; *Literary Criticism; Poetry;
      *Soto, Gary; TALE OF SUNLIGHT; THE ELEMENTS
      OF SAN JOAQUIN.

8239 Elias, Edward F. A meeting of poets from
      east and west: Lorna Dee Cervantes, Gary
      Soto, Tato Laviera. BILINGUAL REVIEW, Vol.
      12, no. 1-2 (January, August, 1985), p.
      150-155. English. DESCR: Authors; Cervantes,
      Lorna Dee; *EMPLUMADA; *ENCLAVE; Laviera,
      Tato; Literary Criticism; Literature
      Reviews; Poetry; Soto, Gary.

8240 Marin, Christine. Book review of: WHERE
      SPARROWS WORK HARD. LECTOR, Vol. 4, no. 4-6
      (1987), p. 77. English. DESCR: Book Reviews;
      Soto, Gary.

WHERE THE AIR IS CLEAR

8241 Eberstadt, Fernanda. Montezuma's literary
      revenge. COMMENTARY, Vol. 81, no. 5 (May
      1986), p. 35-40. English. DESCR: *Fuentes,
      Carlos; GRINGO VIEJO; *Literary Criticism;
      Mexican Literature; THE DEATH OF ARTEMIO
      CRUZ; THE GOOD CONSCIENCE.

WHISPERING TO FOOL THE WIND

8242 Saldivar, Jose David. Towards a Chicano
      poetics: the making of the Chicano subject.
      CONFLUENCIA, Vol. 1, no. 2 (Spring 1986), p.
      10-17. English. DESCR: Corridos; Feminism;
      *Literary Criticism; "Los vatos" [poem];
      Montoya, Jose E.; *Poetry; RESTLESS
      SERPENTS; Rios, Alberto; Zamora, Bernice.

White, Mark

8243 Gunderson, Kay. White does about-face on
      Simpson-Mazzoli. TEXAS OBSERVOR, Vol. 75,
      (March 25, 1983), p. 4. English. DESCR:
      *Immigration Law and Legislation; League of
      United Latin American Citizens (LULAC);
      *Simpson-Mazzoli Bill; Texas.

Whittier Blvd., Los Angeles, CA

8244 Muro, Rena. Hispanic walk of fame=Camino
      hispano de la fama. AMERICAS 2001, Vol. 1,
      no. 2 (September, October, 1987), p. 33.

Bilingual. DESCR: Community Development;
*Hispanic Walk of Fame.

**Wight Art Gallery, University of California, Los
Angeles**

8245 Major exhibition planned by UCLA. NUESTRO,
      Vol. 11, no. 1-2 (1987), p. 6-7. English.
      DESCR: *Art; *Exhibits.

Williams, Miles W.

8246 Flores, Estevan T. Book review of: ILLEGAL
      ALIENS IN THE WESTERN HEMISPHERE. LA RED/THE
      NET, no. 56 (July 1982), p. 7-9. English.
      DESCR: Book Reviews; *ILLEGAL ALIENS IN THE
      WESTERN HEMISPHERE: POLITICAL AND ECONOMIC
      FACTORS; Johnson, Kenneth F.; Undocumented
      Workers.

Wisconsin

8247 Slesinger, Doris. Migrant workers in
      Wisconsin. LA RED/THE NET, no. 27 (February
      1980), p. 2. English. DESCR: *Migrant Health
      Services; Migrant Labor.

**Wisconsin Hispanic Council on Higher Education
(WHCHE)**

8248 Perez, Emma. Higher education organizations.
      LA RED/THE NET, no. 96 (May 1986), p. 6-8.
      English. DESCR: Educational Organizations;
      *Higher Education.

WISDOM [film]

8249 WISDOM: a showcase for the many talents of
      Emilio Estevez. NUESTRO, Vol. 11, no. 3
      (April 1987), p. 25. English. DESCR: *Actors
      and Actresses; *Estevez, Emilio.

WIT (Women in Teatro)

8250 Yarbro-Bejarano, Yvonne. The female subject
      in Chicano theater: sexuality, race, and
      class. THEATRE JOURNAL, Vol. 38, no. 4
      (December 1986), p. 389-407. English.
      DESCR: *Chicanas; El Teatro Campesino; El
      Teatro de la Esperanza; Feminism; *Malinche;
      *Sex Roles; *Teatro; Teatro Nacional de
      Aztlan (TENAZ).

WLTV, Miami, FL [television station]

8251 Gavin joins group pursuing SICC stations.
      BROADCASTING, Vol. 110, no. 22 (June 2,
      1986), p. 68. English. DESCR: Gavin, John;
      KFTV, Fresno, CA [television station]; KMEX,
      Los Angeles, CA [television station]; KWEX,
      San Antonio, TX [television station]; Legal
      Cases; Perenchio, A. Jerrold; *Spanish
      International Communications Corp. (SICC);
      Spanish International Network (SIN); Spanish
      Language; Television; Thompson, William;
      WXTV, Paterson, NJ [television station].

8252 Mass media bureau settlement would allow
      SICC to sell its stations. BROADCASTING,
      Vol. 110, no. 26 (June 30, 1986), p. 45.
      English. DESCR: Anselmo, Rene; Azcarraga
      Family; Federal Communications Commission
      (FCC); KDTV, San Francisco, CA [television
      station]; KFTV, Fresno, CA [television
      station]; KMEX, Los Angeles, CA [television
      station]; KTVW, Phoenix, AZ [television
      station]; KWEX, San Antonio, TX [television
      station]; Legal Cases; *Spanish
      International Communications Corp. (SICC);
      Spanish International Network (SIN); Spanish
      Language; Television; WXTV, Paterson, NJ
      [television station].

WLTV, Miami, FL [television station] (cont.)

8253 SICC sale opposed. BROADCASTING, Vol. 111, no. 7 (August 18, 1986), p. 46-52. English. **DESCR:** Azcarraga, Emilio; Federal Communications Commission (FCC); First Chicago Venture Capital; Hallmark Cards; KFTV, Fresno, CA [television station]; KMEX, Los Angeles, CA [television station]; KWEX, San Antonio, TX [television station]; Legal Cases; *Spanish International Communications Corp. (SICC); Spanish Language; Tapia, Raul R.; Television; TVL Corp.; WXTV, Paterson, NJ [television station].

8254 SICC sells TVs for $301.5 million. BROADCASTING, Vol. 111, no. 4 (July 28, 1986), p. 91-92. English. **DESCR:** Azcarraga, Emilio; First Chicago Venture Capital; Hallmark Cards; KFTV, Fresno, CA [television station]; KMEX, Los Angeles, CA [television station]; KWEX, San Antonio, TX [television station]; Legal Cases; *Spanish International Communications Corp. (SICC); Spanish International Network (SIN); Spanish Language; Television; Villanueva, Daniel; WXTV, Paterson, NJ [television station].

8255 SICC to sell off stations. BROADCASTING, Vol. 110, no. 20 (May 19, 1986), p. 79-80. English. **DESCR:** Anselmo, Rene; Federal Communications Commission (FCC); Fouce, Frank; KFTV, Fresno, CA [television station]; KMEX, Los Angeles, CA [television station]; KWEX, San Antonio, TX [television station]; Legal Cases; *Spanish International Communications Corp. (SICC); Spanish International Network (SIN); Spanish Language; Television; WXTV, Paterson, NJ [television station].

WOJO-FM, Chicago, IL [radio station]

8256 Berling-Manuel, Lynn. Expanding radio market battles research static. ADVERTISING AGE MAGAZINE, Vol. 57, no. 43 (August 11, 1986), p. S12-S16. English. **DESCR:** Arbitron; Marketing; *Radio; Spanish Language; WADO-AM, New York, NY [radio station]; WAQI-AM, Miami, FL [radio station].

WOLFEN [film]

8257 Montane, Diane. Edward James Olmos: the man behind the tough film facade. VISTA, Vol. 1, no. 1 (September 8, 1985), p. 8-12. English. **DESCR:** *Actors and Actresses; BALLAD OF GREGORIO CORTEZ [film]; Biography; *Olmos, Edward James; ZOOT SUIT [film].

Woll, Allen L.

8258 Garcia, Philip. Book review of: THE LATIN IMAGE IN AMERICAN FILM. LA RED/THE NET, no. 50 (January 1982), p. 11-12. English. **DESCR:** Films; *THE LATIN IMAGE IN AMERICAN FILM.

WOMAN OF HER WORD: HISPANIC WOMEN WRITE

8259 Cantu, Norma. Book review of: WOMAN OF HER WORD: HISPANIC WOMEN WRITE. LA RED/THE NET, no. 83 (August 1984), p. 4. English. **DESCR:** Book Reviews; Vigil-Pinon, Evangelina.

8260 Castillo-Speed, Lillian. Chicana/Latina literature and criticism: reviews of recent books. WLW JOURNAL, Vol. 11, no. 3 (September 1987), p. 1-4. English. **DESCR:** Andrews, Lynn V.; *Book Reviews; BORDERS; Chavez, Denise; *Chicanas; CONTEMPORARY CHICANA POETRY: A CRITICAL APPROACH TO AN EMERGING LITERATURE; Flores, Angel; Flores, Kate; JAGUAR WOMAN; Mora, Pat; Sanchez, Marta Ester; Tafolla, Carmen; THE DEFIANT MUSE: HISPANIC FEMINIST POEMS FROM THE MIDDLE AGES TO THE PRESENT; THE LAST OF THE MENU GIRLS; TO SPLIT A HUMAN: MITOS, MACHOS Y LA MUJER CHICANA; Vigil-Pinon, Evangelina.

8261 Miller, Beth. Book review of: WOMAN OF HER WORD: HISPANIC WOMEN WRITE. HISPANIA, Vol. 68, no. 2 (May 1985), p. 326-327. English. **DESCR:** Book Reviews; Vigil-Pinon, Evangelina.

Women Here are entered works about non-Chicanas. For Mexican-American women USE Chicanas

8262 Alicia de Garcia's oral history=Historia oral de Alicia de Garcia. REVISTA MUJERES, Vol. 3, no. 2 (June 1986), p. 37-49. Spanish. **DESCR:** *Committee of Mothers and Relatives of Political Prisoners Disappeared and Assassinated of El Salvador "Monsenor Oscar Arnulfo Romero" (Comadres, El Salvador); Community Organizations; de Garcia, Alicia; *Federation of Latin Americans for the Association of Relatives of the Detained and Disappeared (FedeFam); *Oral History; Terrorism; Violence.

8263 Anderson, Karen. Book review of: NEW MEXICO WOMEN: INTERCULTURAL PERSPECTIVES. NEW MEXICO HISTORICAL REVIEW, Vol. 62, no. 4 (October 1987), p. 401-2. English. **DESCR:** Book Reviews; *Jensen, Joan M.; *Miller, Darlis A.; *New Mexico; *NEW MEXICO WOMEN: INTERCULTURAL PERSPECTIVES.

8264 Baezconde-Garbanati, Lourdes and Salgado de Snyder, Nelly. Mexican immigrant women: a selected bibliography. HISPANIC JOURNAL OF BEHAVIORAL SCIENCES, Vol. 9, no. 3 (September 1987), p. 331-358. English. **DESCR:** *Bibliography; *Chicanas; *Immigrants.

8265 Bieder, Maryellen. Book review of: WOMEN IN HISPANIC LITERATURE. MODERN FICTION STUDIES, Vol. 30, no. 4 (Winter 1984), p. 738-740. English. **DESCR:** Book Reviews; Miller, Beth; *WOMEN IN HISPANIC LITERATURE: ICONS AND FALLEN IDOLS.

8266 Chavez, Lorenzo A. Tennis superstars. VISTA, Vol. 1, no. 8 (April 6, 1986), p. 14-16. English. **DESCR:** *Athletes; Chicanas; Fernandez, Gigi; Fernandez, Mary Joe; *Sabatini, Gabriela; Sports; Torres, Michele.

8267 Cordova, Gilbert Benito. Certain curious colonial Chicano cosmetological customs. EL CUADERNO, Vol. 3, no. 2 (Spring 1974), p. 19-27. English. **DESCR:** *Cosmetology; *Precolumbian Society.

8268 Frances Hesselbein. INTERCAMBIOS FEMENILES, Vol. 2, no. 6 (Spring 1987), p. 23. English. **DESCR:** *Chicanas; *Girl Scouts of the United States of America; Hesselbein, Frances; *Leadership; Organizations; Youth.

8269 Gettman, Dawn and Pena, Devon Gerardo. Women, mental health, and the workplace in a transnational setting. SOCIAL WORK, Vol. 31, no. 1 (January, February, 1986), p. 5-11. English. **DESCR:** *Border Industries; *Chicanas; Employment; *Mental Health; Mexico; United States-Mexico Relations; *Working Women.

Women (cont.)

8270 Guendelman, Sylvia. The incorporation of Mexican women in seasonal migration: a study of gender differences. HISPANIC JOURNAL OF BEHAVIORAL SCIENCES, Vol. 9, no. 3 (September 1987), p. 245-264. English. DESCR: Chicanas; Immigrants; Marriage; Mexico; *Migration Patterns; *Sex Roles; *Women Men Relations; Working Women.

8271 Hayghe, Howard. Working mothers reach record number in 1984. MONTHLY LABOR REVIEW, Vol. 107, no. 12 (1984), p. 31-34. English. DESCR: Laborers; *Working Women.

8272 Herrera, Yvonne R. Professional development. INTERCAMBIOS FEMENILES, Vol. 2, no. 6 (Spring 1987), p. 21. English. DESCR: *Chicanas; *Leadership.

8273 Karnig, Albert K.; Welch, Susan; and Eribes, Richard A. Employment of women by cities in the Southwest. SOCIAL SCIENCE JOURNAL, Vol. 21, no. 4 (October 1984), p. 41-48. English. DESCR: Chicanas; *Employment; Local Government; *Southwestern United States.

8274 Limon, Jose E. La Llorona, the third legend of greater Mexico: cultural symbols, women, and the political unconscious. RENATO ROSALDO LECTURE SERIES MONOGRAPH, Vol. 2, (Spring 1986), p. [59]-93. English. DESCR: *Feminism; Folklore; *La Llorona; La Virgen de Guadalupe; *Leyendas; Malinche; Mexico; *Symbolism.

8275 Mellado, Carmela. Adriana Ocampo. HISPANIC ENGINEER, Vol. 3, no. 4 (Fall 1987), p. 22-24. English. DESCR: National Aeronautics and Space Administration (NASA); *Ocampo, Adriana; *Science as a Profession; Stereotypes.

8276 Olarte, Silvia W. and Masnik, Ruth. Benefits of long-term group therapy for disadvantaged Hispanic outpatients. HOSPITAL AND COMMUNITY PSYCHIATRY, Vol. 36, no. 10 (October 1985), p. 1093-1097. English. DESCR: Ethnic Groups; Metropolitan Hospital, New York, NY; New York, NY; Psychotherapy; Sex Roles.

8277 Olivares, Yvette. The sweatshop: the garment industry's reborn child. REVISTA MUJERES, Vol. 3, no. 2 (June 1986), p. 55-62. English. DESCR: Garment Industry; Labor; Public Health; Third World; *Undocumented Workers; Working Women.

8278 Peace with justice. REVISTA MUJERES, Vol. 3, no. 2 (June 1986), p. 32-35. English. DESCR: *Committee of Mothers and Relatives of Political Prisoners Disappeared and Assassinated of El Salvador "Monsenor Oscar Arnulfo Romero" (Comadres, El Salvador); Community Organizations; *Federation of Latin Americans for the Association of Relatives of the Detained and Disappeared (FedeFam); Terrorism; Violence.

8279 Reyes, Sonia. America's Hispanic sweethearts. VISTA, Vol. 1, no. 6 (February 2, 1986), p. 6-7. English. DESCR: Awards; Carthy-Deu, Deborah [Miss Universe]; *Martinez-Herring, Laura [Miss USA].

8280 Ruiz, Vicki Lynn. Obreras y madres: labor activism among Mexican women and its impact on the family. RENATO ROSALDO LECTURE SERIES MONOGRAPH, Vol. 1, (Summer 1985), p. [19]-38. English. DESCR: *Chicanas; Child Care Centers; Children; History; *Labor Unions; *Mexico; Sex Roles; *Working Women.

8281 Salgado de Snyder, Nelly. The role of ethnic loyalty among Mexican immigrant women. HISPANIC JOURNAL OF BEHAVIORAL SCIENCES, Vol. 9, no. 3 (September 1987), p. 287-298. English. DESCR: Acculturation; Chicanas; *Culture; *Identity; Immigrants; Mental Health; *Mexico.

8282 Sellers, Jeff M. Challenging the myth of the traditional woman. HISPANIC BUSINESS, Vol. 9, no. 8 (August 1987), p. 15-16, 48. English. DESCR: *Businesspeople; *Careers; *Chicanas; *Management; National Network of Hispanic Women; Sex Roles; Torres, Celia; Zambrana, Ruth.

8283 Soto, Rose Marie. National Network of Hispanic Women. HISPANIC ENGINEER, Vol. 3, no. 4 (Fall 1987), p. 26-28. English. DESCR: Castillo, Sylvia; Gonzales Torres, Celia; Gutierrez, Nancy; *National Network of Hispanic Women; *Professional Organizations; Zambrana, Ruth.

8284 Tienda, Marta and Guhlman, Pat. The occupational position of employed Hispanic females. LA RED/THE NET, no. 69 (June 1983), p. 2-3. English. DESCR: *Chicanas; Employment; Ethnic Stratification.

WOMEN IN HISPANIC LITERATURE: ICONS AND FALLEN IDOLS

8285 Bieder, Maryellen. Book review of: WOMEN IN HISPANIC LITERATURE. MODERN FICTION STUDIES, Vol. 30, no. 4 (Winter 1984), p. 738-740. English. DESCR: Book Reviews; Miller, Beth; Women.

8286 Scanlon, Geraldine M. Book review of: WOMEN IN HISPANIC LITERATURE. MODERN LANGUAGE REVIEW, Vol. 81, (October 1986), p. 1017. English. DESCR: Book Reviews; Miller, Beth.

Women Men Relations

8287 Anderson, Robert K. Marez y Luna and the masculine-feminine dialectic. CRITICA HISPANICA, Vol. 6, no. 2 (1984), p. 97-105. English. DESCR: Anaya, Rudolfo A.; *BLESS ME, ULTIMA; Literary Criticism; Novel.

8288 Anonymous UCSC Community Member. An extinct relationship. REVISTA MUJERES, Vol. 2, no. 1 (January 1985), p. 21-22. English. DESCR: Divorce; *Marriage.

8289 Guendelman, Sylvia. The incorporation of Mexican women in seasonal migration: a study of gender differences. HISPANIC JOURNAL OF BEHAVIORAL SCIENCES, Vol. 9, no. 3 (September 1987), p. 245-264. English. DESCR: Chicanas; Immigrants; Marriage; Mexico; *Migration Patterns; *Sex Roles; *Women; Working Women.

8290 Gutierrez, Ramon A. Honor ideology, marriage negotiation, and class-gender domination in New Mexico, 1690-1846. LATIN AMERICAN PERSPECTIVES, Vol. 12, no. 1 (Winter 1985), p. 81-104. English. DESCR: Marriage; Sex Roles; *Social Classes; Social History and Conditions; *Southwestern United States; Values.

8291 Hayghe, Howard. Married couples: work and income patterns. MONTHLY LABOR REVIEW, Vol. 106, no. 12 (December 1983), p. 26-29. English. DESCR: Income; *Laborers; Marriage; Working Women.

Women Men Relations (cont.)

8292 LeVine, Sarah Ethel; Correa, Clara Sunderland; and Uribe, F. Medardo Tapia. The marital morality of Mexican women--an urban study. JOURNAL OF ANTHROPOLOGICAL RESEARCH, Vol. 42, no. 2 (Summer 1986), p. 183-202. English. **DESCR:** Family; Los Robles, Cuernavaca, Morelos, Mexico; *Machismo; Marriage; Parent and Child Relationships; *Sex Roles.

WOMEN OF THE DEPRESSION: CASTE AND CULTURE IN SAN ANTONIO, 1929-1939

8293 Ruiz, Vicki Lynn. Book review of: WOMEN OF THE DEPRESSION. SOUTHWESTERN HISTORICAL QUARTERLY, Vol. 88, no. 3 (1985), p. 337-338. English. **DESCR:** Blackwelder, Julia Kirk; Book Reviews.

Women's Rights
USE: Feminism

Woo, Michael

8294 Los Angeles: brown versus yellow. ECONOMIST (London), Vol. 300, no. 7456 (July 26, 1986), p. 21-22. English. **DESCR:** Alatorre, Richard; Bradley, Tom; Ethnic Groups; *Los Angeles, CA; Political Representation; Politics; Reapportionment; Voter Turnout.

Woodcuts

8295 Hernandez, Nicolas, Jr. Olmeca. CONFLUENCIA, Vol. 1, no. 2 (Spring 1986), p. 134.

Woods, Richard D.

8296 Vigelis, Adeline R. Book review of: HISPANIC FIRST NAMES. LECTOR, Vol. 4, no. 4-6 (1987), p. 55-56. English. **DESCR:** Book Reviews; *HISPANIC FIRST NAMES: A COMPREHENSIVE DICTIONARY OF 250 YEARS OF MEXICAN-AMERICAN USAGE; Personal Names; Reference Works.

Woods, Sandra L.

8297 Compean, Mario. Book review of: PERSPECTIVES ON IMMIGRATION AND MINORITY EDUCATION. LA RED/THE NET, no. 86 (November 1984), p. 3-7. English. **DESCR:** Book Reviews; *PERSPECTIVES ON IMMIGRANT AND MINORITY EDUCATION; Samuda, Ronald J.

WORK, FAMILY, SEX ROLES, LANGUAGE: SELECTED PAPERS OF THE NATIONAL ASSOCIATION FOR CHICANO STUDIES CONFERENCE, 1979

8298 Hurtado, Aida. Book review of: WORK, FAMILY, SEX ROLES, LANGUAGE. LA RED/THE NET, no. 40 (March 1981), p. 3. English. **DESCR:** Barrera, Mario; Book Reviews; Camarillo, Alberto; Hernandez, Francisco; Social History and Conditions.

Workers
USE: Laborers

Working Force
USE: Laborers

Working Women

8299 Almaguer, Tomas. Urban Chicano workers in historical perspective: a review of recent literature. LA RED/THE NET, no. 68 (May 1983), p. 2-6. English. **DESCR:** *Labor; Laborers; *Literature Reviews.

8300 Attitudes are changing while women go to work. HISPANIC TIMES, Vol. 8, no. 3 (May, June, 1987), p. 14. English. **DESCR:**

*Attitudes; *Sex Roles.

8301 Cook, Annabel Kirschner. Diversity among Northwest Hispanics. SOCIAL SCIENCE JOURNAL, Vol. 23, no. 2 (April 1986), p. 205-216. English. **DESCR:** Chicanas; *Northwestern United States; *Population; *Socioeconomic Factors.

8302 Cornell, Nancy. Forging links between societies. VISTA, Vol. 3, no. 3 (November 8, 1987), p. 24. English. **DESCR:** 1984 Republican Convention (Dallas, TX); *Chicanas; *Olind, Rebecca Nieto.

8303 Gettman, Dawn and Pena, Devon Gerardo. Women, mental health, and the workplace in a transnational setting. SOCIAL WORK, Vol. 31, no. 1 (January, February, 1986), p. 5-11. English. **DESCR:** *Border Industries; *Chicanas; Employment; *Mental Health; Mexico; United States-Mexico Relations; Women.

8304 Guendelman, Sylvia. The incorporation of Mexican women in seasonal migration: a study of gender differences. HISPANIC JOURNAL OF BEHAVIORAL SCIENCES, Vol. 9, no. 3 (September 1987), p. 245-264. English. **DESCR:** Chicanas; Immigrants; Marriage; Mexico; *Migration Patterns; *Sex Roles; *Women; *Women Men Relations.

8305 Hayghe, Howard. Married couples: work and income patterns. MONTHLY LABOR REVIEW, Vol. 106, no. 12 (December 1983), p. 26-29. English. **DESCR:** Income; *Laborers; Marriage; Women Men Relations.

8306 Hayghe, Howard. Working mothers reach record number in 1984. MONTHLY LABOR REVIEW, Vol. 107, no. 12 (1984), p. 31-34. English. **DESCR:** Laborers; Women.

8307 Keremitsis, Dawn. Del metate al molino: la mujer mexicana de 1910 a 1940. HISTORIA MEXICANA, Vol. 33, no. 2 (1983), p. 285-302. Spanish. **DESCR:** Food Industry; Labor Unions; *Mexico; Sex Roles; Strikes and Lockouts; Tortillas.

8308 Olivares, Yvette. The sweatshop: the garment industry's reborn child. REVISTA MUJERES, Vol. 3, no. 2 (June 1986), p. 55-62. English. **DESCR:** Garment Industry; Labor; Public Health; Third World; *Undocumented Workers; *Women.

8309 Olivera, Mercedes. The new Hispanic women. VISTA, Vol. 2, no. 11 (July 5, 1987), p. 6-8. English. **DESCR:** Alvarez, Linda; *Chicanas; Esquiroz, Margarita; Garcia, Juliet; *Hernandez, Antonia A.; Mohr, Nicolasa; Molina, Gloria; Pabon, Maria.

8310 Orozco, Cynthia. Chicana labor history: a critique of male consciousness in historical writing. LA RED/THE NET, no. 77 (January 1984), p. 2-5. English. **DESCR:** *Chicanas; *Historiography; *Sexism.

8311 Romero, Mary. Domestic service in the transition from rural to urban life: the case of la Chicana. WOMEN'S STUDIES QUARTERLY, Vol. 13, no. 3 (1987), p. 199-222. English. **DESCR:** *Chicanas.

Working Women (cont.)

8312 Ruiz, Vicki Lynn. Obreras y madres: labor activism among Mexican women and its impact on the family. RENATO ROSALDO LECTURE SERIES MONOGRAPH, Vol. 1, (Summer 1985), p. [19]-38. English. DESCR: *Chicanas; Child Care Centers; Children; History; *Labor Unions; *Mexico; Sex Roles; Women.

8313 Salazar-Nobles, Mary. Latinas must chart own course in workplace. VISTA, Vol. 2, no. 3 (November 2, 1986), p. 26. English. DESCR: Chicanas; Essays; *Feminism.

8314 Shapiro, Peter. Watsonville shows "it can be done". GUARDIAN, Vol. 39, no. 24 (March 25, 1987), p. 1,9. English. DESCR: Canneries; Chicanas; Labor Unions; NorCal Frozen Foods; *Strikes and Lockouts; *Watsonville Canning and Frozen Food Co.

8315 Third world women in multinational corporations--the Mexican American border. LA RED/THE NET, no. 25 (December 1979), p. 2. English. DESCR: *Border Industries; Chicanas; *Ciudad Juarez, Chihuahua, Mexico; Labor Supply and Market; *Multinational Corporations.

8316 Tienda, Marta. Hispanics in the U.S. labor market: an overview of recent evidence. LA RED/THE NET, no. 50 (January 1982), p. 4-7. English. DESCR: *Labor Supply and Market; Laborers.

8317 Tienda, Marta and Glass, Jennifer. Household structure and labor-force participation of Black, Hispanic, and white mothers. DEMOGRAPHY, Vol. 22, no. 3 (August 1985), p. 381-394. English. DESCR: Anglo Americans; Blacks; Chicanas; *Extended Family; *Family; *Sex Roles.

8318 Zavella, Patricia. "Abnormal intimacy": the varying work networks of Chicana cannery workers. FEMINIST STUDIES, Vol. 11, no. 3 (Fall 1985), p. 541-557. English. DESCR: Canneries; Chicanas; Discrimination in Employment; Labor Unions; *Natural Support Systems.

Works Progress Administration (WPA)

8319 Wroth, William. New hope in hard times: Hispanic crafts are revived during troubled years. PALACIO, Vol. 89, no. 2 (1983), p. 22-31. English. DESCR: *Arts and Crafts; *Las Lunas Vocational Training School; New Mexico; Spanish Colonial Arts Society; Taos Vocational School.

World War II

8320 Brower, Monty. A proud street mourns its fallen sons. PEOPLE WEEKLY, Vol. 21, (May 28, 1984), p. 76-78+. English. DESCR: *Military; Sandoval, Frank; Sandoval, Joseph; Silvis, IL.

8321 Marin, Christine. La Asociacion Hispano-Americana de Madres y Esposas: Tucson's Mexican American women in World War II. RENATO ROSALDO LECTURE SERIES MONOGRAPH, Vol. 1, (Summer 1985), p. [5]-18. English. DESCR: *Chicanas; Cultural Organizations; History; *La Asociacion Hispano-Americana de Madres y Esposas, Tucson, AZ; Organizations; *Tucson, AZ.

Writers

USE: Authors

Wroth, William

8322 Turner, Kay F. Book review of: CHRISTIAN IMAGES IN HISPANIC NEW MEXICO. JOURNAL OF AMERICAN FOLKLORE, Vol. 97, no. 385 (1984), p. 361-363. English. DESCR: Book Reviews; *CHRISTIAN IMAGES IN HISPANIC NEW MEXICO.

WXTV, Paterson, NJ [television station]

8323 Gavin joins group pursuing SICC stations. BROADCASTING, Vol. 110, no. 22 (June 2, 1986), p. 68. English. DESCR: Gavin, John; KFTV, Fresno, CA [television station]; KMEX, Los Angeles, CA [television station]; KWEX, San Antonio, TX [television station]; Legal Cases; Perenchio, A. Jerrold; *Spanish International Communications Corp. (SICC); Spanish International Network (SIN); Spanish Language; Television; Thompson, William; WLTV, Miami, FL [television station].

8324 Mass media bureau settlement would allow SICC to sell its stations. BROADCASTING, Vol. 110, no. 26 (June 30, 1986), p. 45. English. DESCR: Anselmo, Rene; Azcarraga Family; Federal Communications Commission (FCC); KDTV, San Francisco, CA [television station]; KFTV, Fresno, CA [television station]; KMEX, Los Angeles, CA [television station]; KTVW, Phoeniz, AZ [television station]; KWEX, San Antonio, TX [television station]; Legal Cases; *Spanish International Communications Corp. (SICC); Spanish International Network (SIN); Spanish Language; Television; WLTV, Miami, FL [television station].

8325 SICC sale opposed. BROADCASTING, Vol. 111, no. 7 (August 18, 1986), p. 46-52. English. DESCR: Azcarraga, Emilio; Federal Communications Commission (FCC); First Chicago Venture Capital; Hallmark Cards; KFTV, Fresno, CA [television station]; KMEX, Los Angeles, CA [television station]; KWEX, San Antonio, TX [television station]; Legal Cases; *Spanish International Communications Corp. (SICC); Spanish Language; Tapia, Raul R.; Television; TVL Corp.; WLTV, Miami, FL [television station].

8326 SICC sells TVs for $301.5 million. BROADCASTING, Vol. 111, no. 4 (July 28, 1986), p. 91-92. English. DESCR: Azcarraga, Emilio; First Chicago Venture Capital; Hallmark Cards; KFTV, Fresno, CA [television station]; KMEX, Los Angeles, CA [television station]; KWEX, San Antonio, TX [television station]; Legal Cases; *Spanish International Communications Corp. (SICC); Spanish International Network (SIN); Spanish Language; Television; Villanueva, Daniel; WLTV, Miami, FL [television station].

8327 SICC to sell off stations. BROADCASTING, Vol. 110, no. 20 (May 19, 1986), p. 79-80. English. DESCR: Anselmo, Rene; Federal Communications Commission (FCC); Fouce, Frank; KFTV, Fresno, CA [television station]; KMEX, Los Angeles, CA [television station]; KWEX, San Antonio, TX [television station]; Legal Cases; *Spanish International Communications Corp. (SICC); Spanish International Network (SIN); Spanish Language; Television; WLTV, Miami, FL [television station].

Wyman, Thomas

8328 Jesse Jackson makes appearance at CBS board meeting. BROADCASTING, Vol. 110, no. 16 (April 21, 1986), p. 100. English. **DESCR:** Broadcast Media; *Columbia Broadcasting Studios (CBS); Discrimination; Discrimination in Employment; *Jackson, Jesse; People United to Serve Humanity (PUSH); Stereotypes; Taylor, Hycel.

Xavier, Roy Eric

8329 Anderson de Barret, Judit. Book review of: POLITICS AND CHICANO CULTURE. LECTOR, Vol. 4, no. 4-6 (1987), p. 56. English. **DESCR:** Book Reviews; *POLITICS & CHICANO CULTURE: A PERSPECTIVE ON EL TEATRO CAMPESINO; Teatro.

Xelina

8330 Billings, Linda M. and Alurista. In verbal murals: a study of Chicana herstory and poetry. CONFLUENCIA, Vol. 2, no. 1 (Fall 1986), p. 60-68. English. **DESCR:** Candelaria, Cordelia; Cervantes, Lorna Dee; *Chicanas; Cisneros, Sandra; EMPLUMADA; *Feminism; History; Literary Criticism; *Poetry.

Xerox

8331 Mejias-Rivera, Ann E. Steven Perez of Xerox. HISPANIC ENGINEER, Vol. 3, no. 1 (Spring 1987), p. 26-30. English. **DESCR:** *Engineering as a Profession; Language Arts; *Perez, Steven.

Ximenez [family name]

8332 Instituto Genealogico e Historico Latino-Americano. Rootsearch: Jimenez (Ximenez): Olmo. VISTA, Vol. 2, no. 4 (December 7, 1986), p. 25. English. **DESCR:** Genealogy; History; *Jimenez [family name]; *Olmo [family name]; *Personal Names.

Y NO SE LO TRAGO LA TIERRA/AND THE EARTH DID NOT PART

8333 Bartlett, Catherine Vallejos. Magical realism: the Latin American influence on modern Chicano writers. CONFLUENCIA, Vol. 1, no. 2 (Spring 1986), p. 27-37. English. **DESCR:** Arias, Ron; Authors; Garcia Marquez, Gabriel; Latin America; *Literary Criticism; *Literary Influence; *Literature; Magical realism; ONE HUNDRED YEARS OF SOLITUDE; Rivera, Tomas; THE ROAD TO TAMAZUNCHALE.

8334 Bernal, Alejandro. La estructura tematica en Y NO SE LO TRAGO LA TIERRA de Tomas Rivera. CHIRICU, Vol. 3, no. 1 (1982), p. 83-89. Spanish. **DESCR:** *Literary Criticism; Novel; Rivera, Tomas.

THE YALE MURDER: THE FATAL ROMANCE OF BONNIE GARLAND AND RICHARD HERRIN

8335 Aguirre, Adalberto, Jr. Book review of: THE YALE MURDER: THE FATAL ROMANCE OF BONNIE GARLAND AND RICHARD HERRIN. LA RED/THE NET, no. 71 (August 1983), p. 5-7. English. **DESCR:** Book Reviews; Meyer, Peter.

Yanez [family name]

8336 Instituto Genealogico e Historico Latino-Americano. Rootsearch: Peraza: Yanez. VISTA, Vol. 1, no. 12 (August 2, 1986), p. 22. English. **DESCR:** Genealogy; History; *Peraza [family name]; *Personal Names.

Ybarra-Frausto, Tomas

8337 Castillo-Speed, Lillian. Annotated bibliography. LA RED/THE NET, no. 93 (January, February, 1986), p. 14-17. English. **DESCR:** A BIBLIOGRAPHY OF MEXICAN AMERICAN HISTORY; ARTE CHICANO; Book Reviews; Caballero, Cesar; CHICANO LITERATURE: A REFERENCE GUIDE; CHICANO ORGANIZATIONS DIRECTORY; CHICANO PERIODICAL INDEX; Goldman, Shifra M.; HISPANIC ALMANAC; HISPANIC MENTAL HEALTH RESEARCH: A REFERENCE GUIDE; Lomeli, Francisco A.; Martinez, Julio A.; Meier, Matt S.; Newton, Frank; *Reference Works.

Young, Paul H., Jr.

8338 Beale, Stephen. CEOs. HISPANIC BUSINESS, Vol. 9, no. 4 (April 1987), p. 20-37, 52. English. **DESCR:** Alvarez, Roberto; Batarse, Anthony A.; Biography; Business Enterprises; *Businesspeople; Carlo, Nelson; Estrada, Anthony; Flores, Frank; Fullana, Jaime, Jr.; Hernandez, George; *Management; Ortega, James; Quirch, Guillermo; Ruiz, Roberto; Santa Maria, Yvonne Z.; Sugranes, Rosa; Tamaya, Carlos.

Youth

8339 Andrade, Sally J. Chicana adolescents and contraception issues. LA RED/THE NET, no. 35 (October 1980), p. 2,14. English. **DESCR:** *Birth Control; *Chicanas; *Southwestern United States.

8340 Blanco, Gilbert M. Las Adelitas del Barrio. LATIN QUARTER, Vol. 1, no. 3 (January, February, 1975), p. 30-32. English. **DESCR:** *Chicanas; City Terrace, CA; Community Development; Gangs; *Latin Empresses.

8341 Duda, Joan L. Goals and achievement orientations of Anglo and Mexican-American adolescents in sport and the classroom. INTERNATIONAL REVIEW OF SPORT SOCIOLOGY, Vol. 18, no. 4 (1983), p. 63-80. English. **DESCR:** Academic Achievement; Cultural Characteristics; New Mexico; Sports.

8342 Fitzpatrick, Sherahe B., et al. Do health care needs of Mexican-American and Caucasian teens differ? PEDIATRIC RESEARCH, Vol. 20, no. 4 (1986), p. A153. English. **DESCR:** Medical Care.

8343 Frances Hesselbein. INTERCAMBIOS FEMENILES, Vol. 2, no. 6 (Spring 1987), p. 23. English. **DESCR:** *Chicanas; *Girl Scouts of the United States of America; Hesselbein, Frances; *Leadership; Organizations; Women.

8344 Humm-Delgado, Denise and Delgado, Melvin. Hispanic adolescents and substance abuse: issues for the 1980s. CHILDREN AND YOUTH SERVICES REVIEW, Vol. 6, no. 1-2 (Spring, Summer, 1983), p. 71-87. English. **DESCR:** Drug Use.

8345 Hunsaker, Alan C. and Vicario, Tony D. A behavioral/ecological model of intervention alternatives with Chicano gang delinquents. LA RED/THE NET, no. 43 (June 1981), p. 2-3. English. **DESCR:** *Behavior Modification; *Delinquency; *Gangs.

Youth (cont.)

8346 Hunsaker, Alan C. Contingency management with Chicano adolescents in a federal manpower program. CORRECTIVE AND SOCIAL PSYCHIATRY, Vol. 30, no. 1 (1984), p. 10-13. English. **DESCR:** *Employment; *Management; *Manpower Programs; Psychology.

8347 Ismail, Amid L.; Burt, Brian A.; and Brunelle, Janet A. Prevalence of dental caries and periodontal disease in Mexican American children aged 5 to 17 years: results from Southwestern HHANES, 1982-83. AMERICAN JOURNAL OF PUBLIC HEALTH, Vol. 77, no. 8 (August 1987), p. 967-970. English. **DESCR:** Decays, Missing, Filed Surfaces (DMFS) [dental scale]; *Dentistry; *Hispanic Health and Nutrition Examination Survey (HHANES).

8348 Martinez, Ruben and Dukes, Richard L. Race, gender and self-esteem among youth. HISPANIC JOURNAL OF BEHAVIORAL SCIENCES, Vol. 9, no. 4 (December 1987), p. 427-443. English. **DESCR:** *Comparative Psychology; *Identity; *Sex Roles.

8349 Melendez, Pablo. Happy Thanksgiving. CALIFORNIA MAGAZINE, Vol. 11, no. 11 (November 1986), p. 136. English. **DESCR:** *Biography; *Essays; *Immigrants; *Melendez, Pablo.

8350 Molina, Robert M.; Brown, Kathryn H.; and Zavaleta, Antonio N. Relative lower extremity length in Mexican American and in American Black and white youth. AMERICAN JOURNAL OF PHYSICAL ANTHROPOLOGY, Vol. 72, (1987), p. 89-94. English. **DESCR:** Anglo Americans; *Anthropometry; Blacks; *Body Mass Index (BMI); U.S. Health Examination Survey (HES).

8351 National Council of La Raza (NCLR). Career information and Hispanic students. LA RED/THE NET, no. 75 (December 1983), p. 2-4. English. **DESCR:** *Careers; Educational Services; *National Council of La Raza (NCLR); Secondary School Education; Survey of Career Information Systems in Secondary Schools.

8352 Ortiz, Vilma. Educational attainment among Hispanic youth and non-Hispanic white youth. LA RED/THE NET, no. 67 (April 1983), p. 2-4. English. **DESCR:** Academic Achievement; Educational Statistics.

8353 Ramirez, Salvador. The establishment and administration of a master's program in Chicano Studies at the University of Colorado. EPOCA: NATIONAL CONCILIO FOR CHICANO STUDIES JOURNAL, Vol. 1, no. 2 (Winter 1971), p. 39-50. English. **DESCR:** *Chicano Studies; *Curriculum; Discrimination in Education; Educational Theory and Practice; Student Organizations; *Students; United Mexican American Students (UMAS); *University of Colorado, Boulder.

8354 Santos, Richard. A profile of Hispanic youth. LA RED/THE NET, no. 54 (May 1982), p. 2-4. English.

Yrigoyen [family name]

8355 Instituto Genealogico e Historico Latino-Americano. Rootsearch: Olivares: Yrigoyen: Montemayor. VISTA, Vol. 2, no. 12 (August 1, 1987), p. 30. English. **DESCR:** Genealogy; History; *Montemayor [family name]; *Olivares [family name]; *Personal Names.

Yzaguirre, Raul

8356 Architects of America's future. VISTA, Vol. 1, no. 11 (July 6, 1986), p. 10. English. **DESCR:** *Conferences and Meetings; National Council of La Raza (NCLR); Social History and Conditions.

8357 Yzaguirre critical of committee action. NUESTRO, Vol. 11, no. 4 (May 1987), p. 8. English. **DESCR:** *Bilingual Bicultural Education; English-Only Movement; National Council of La Raza (NCLR).

Zacky, Dolores Valdes

8358 Fever, Jack. ADWEEK's honor roll: women to watch: Dolores Valdes Zacky. ADWEEK, Vol. 36, (July 7, 1986), p. W16. English. **DESCR:** *Advertising; Advertising Agencies.

Zambrana, Ruth

8359 Sellers, Jeff M. Challenging the myth of the traditional woman. HISPANIC BUSINESS, Vol. 9, no. 8 (August 1987), p. 15-16, 48. English. **DESCR:** *Businesspeople; *Careers; *Chicanas; *Management; National Network of Hispanic Women; Sex Roles; Torres, Celia; Women.

8360 Soto, Rose Marie. National Network of Hispanic Women. HISPANIC ENGINEER, Vol. 3, no. 4 (Fall 1987), p. 26-28. English. **DESCR:** Castillo, Sylvia; Gonzales Torres, Celia; Gutierrez, Nancy; *National Network of Hispanic Women; *Professional Organizations; Women.

Zamora, Bernice

8361 Saldivar, Jose David. Towards a Chicano poetics: the making of the Chicano subject. CONFLUENCIA, Vol. 1, no. 2 (Spring 1986), p. 10-17. English. **DESCR:** Corridos; Feminism; *Literary Criticism; "Los vatos" [poem]; Montoya, Jose E.; *Poetry; RESTLESS SERPENTS; Rios, Alberto; WHISPERING TO FOOL THE WIND.

Zamora [family name]

8362 Instituto Genealogico e Historico Latino-Americano. Rootsearch: Guzman: Zamora. VISTA, Vol. 2, no. 7 (March 8, 1987), p. 25. English. **DESCR:** Genealogy; *Guzman [family name]; History; *Personal Names.

Zanya Records Co., Los Angeles, CA

8363 Haley, Lindsey. Una premiacion controvertida. LA COMUNIDAD, No. 246 (April 7, 1985), p. 5-6. Spanish. **DESCR:** Awards; Discrimination; *Grammy Awards; Guevara, Ruben; *Recording Industry.

Zaragoza, Jorge

8364 Powers, Michael D. Spanish in contact with other languages: lexical or profound structural influence? BILINGUAL REVIEW, Vol. 12, no. 3 (September, December, 1985), p. 254-257. English. **DESCR:** Amastae, Jon; Elias-Olivares, Lucia; Language Usage; Literature Reviews; *SPANISH IN THE UNITED STATES: SOCIOLINGUISTIC ASPECTS; *SPANISH IN THE WESTERN HEMISPHERE IN CONTACT WITH ENGLISH, PORTUGUESE, AND THE AMERINDIAN LANGUAGES; *Spanish Language.

El Zarco
      USE: Guerrero, Adolfo "El Zarco"

La Zarzuela de Albuquerque

8365 Holmes, John J. Zarzuela lives again. VISTA,
      Vol. 3, no. 3 (November 8, 1987), p. 10-12.
      English. **DESCR**: Directories; Festival de la
      Zarzuela; *Music; Musicals.

Zavella, Pat

8366 Davila, Elisa. Conozcamos: de charla con Pat
      Zavella. REVISTA MUJERES, Vol. 1, no. 1
      (January 1984), p. 10-11. Spanish. **DESCR**:
      *Biography.

8367 Valva, Annie. [Pat Zavella (photograph)].
      REVISTA MUJERES, Vol. 1, no. 1 (January
      1984), p. 10. **DESCR**: *Photography.

Zentella, Ana Celia

8368 Mujica, Barbara. Creative code switching.
      VISTA, Vol. 1, no. 5 (January 5, 1986), p.
      22. English. **DESCR**: Bilingualism;
      *Cognition; Language Usage.

Zerimar [musical group]

8369 Sellers, Jeff M. The sound of musica: moving
      into the mainstream. HISPANIC BUSINESS, Vol.
      9, no. 7 (July 1987), p. 14-18. English.
      DESCR: Los Lobos del Este de Los Angeles
      (musical group); *Marketing; Miami Sound
      Machine; Music; *Musicians; The Cruzados
      [musical group].

Zeta Acosta, Oscar
      USE: Acosta, Oscar Zeta

ZOOT SUIT [film]

8370 Martin, Laura. Language form and language
      function in ZOOT SUIT and THE BORDER: a
      contribution to the analysis of the role of
      foreign language in film. STUDIES IN LATIN
      AMERICAN POPULAR CULTURE, Vol. 3, (1984),
      p. 57-69. English. **DESCR**: *Films; Language
      Usage; Spanish Language; THE BORDER [film].

8371 Mindiola, Tatcho, Jr. Film review of: THE
      BALLAD OF GREGORIO CORTEZ. LA RED/THE NET,
      no. 80 (May 1984), p. 11-17. English.
      DESCR: *BALLAD OF GREGORIO CORTEZ [film];
      *Film Reviews; SEGUIN [movie].

8372 Montane, Diane. Edward James Olmos: the man
      behind the tough film facade. VISTA, Vol. 1,
      no. 1 (September 8, 1985), p. 8-12. English.
      DESCR: *Actors and Actresses; BALLAD OF
      GREGORIO CORTEZ [film]; Biography; *Olmos,
      Edward James; WOLFEN [film].

ZOOT SUIT [play]

8373 Burciaga, Jose Antonio. A man with his
      teatro. VISTA, Vol. 1, no. 3 (November 3,
      1985), p. 8-10. English. **DESCR**: CORRIDOS
      [play]; El Teatro Campesino; *Teatro;
      *Valdez, Luis.

8374 Campbell, Federico. Henry Reyna, pachuco. LA
      COMUNIDAD, No. 247 (April 14, 1985), p. 11.
      Spanish. **DESCR**: History; *Pachucos; *Zoot
      Suit Riots, Los Angeles, CA, 1943.

Zoot Suit Riots, Los Angeles, CA, 1943

8375 Campbell, Federico. Henry Reyna, pachuco. LA
      COMUNIDAD, No. 247 (April 14, 1985), p. 11.
      Spanish. **DESCR**: History; *Pachucos; ZOOT
      SUIT [play].

8376 Cortes, Carlos E. Book review of: THE
      ZOOT-SUIT RIOTS. PACIFIC HISTORICAL REVIEW,
      Vol. 55, no. 3 (1986), p. 498-499. English.
      DESCR: Book Reviews; Mazon, Mauricio; *THE
      ZOOT-SUIT RIOTS: THE PSYCHOLOGY OF SYMBOLIC
      ANNIHILATION.

8377 Sanchez Tranquilino, Marcos. Un ensayo sobre
      la representacion del ZOOT SUIT en la obra
      de Octavio Paz. LA COMUNIDAD, No. 355 (May
      10, 1987), p. 4-7+. Spanish. **DESCR**: Los
      Angeles, CA; *Pachucos; *Paz, Octavio;
      Sleepy Lagoon Case; THE LABYRINTH OF
      SOLITUDE: LIFE AND THOUGHT IN MEXICO.

Zoot Suiter
      USE: Pachucos

**THE ZOOT-SUIT RIOTS: THE PSYCHOLOGY OF SYMBOLIC
      ANNIHILATION**

8378 Cortes, Carlos E. Book review of: THE
      ZOOT-SUIT RIOTS. PACIFIC HISTORICAL REVIEW,
      Vol. 55, no. 3 (1986), p. 498-499. English.
      DESCR: Book Reviews; Mazon, Mauricio; Zoot
      Suit Riots, Los Angeles, CA, 1943.

8379 Cosgrove, Stuart. Book review of: THE
      ZOOT-SUIT RIOTS. THE TIMES LITERARY
      SUPPLEMENT, (July 12, 1985), p. 782.
      English. **DESCR**: Book Reviews; Mazon,
      Mauricio.

8380 Farley, J.E. Book review of: THE ZOOT-SUIT
      RIOTS. CHOICE, Vol. 22, no. 11-12 (July,
      August, 1985), p. 1691-1692. English.
      DESCR: Book Reviews; Mazon, Mauricio.

Zuniga [family name]

8381 Instituto Genealogico e Historico
      Latino-Americano. Rootsearch: Cisneros:
      Perales: Zuniga. VISTA, Vol. 2, no. 10 (June
      7, 1987), p. 26. English. **DESCR**: *Cisneros
      [family name]; Genealogy; History; *Perales
      [family name]; *Personal Names.

AUTHOR INDEX

Abalos, David
    Book review of: GALILEAN JOURNEY, 811.
Abalos, J. Victor
    Paul Sandoval, 1319.
    Whiz kids of the microchip melody, 1924.
Abelardo
    USE: Delgado, Abelardo "Lalo"
Abney, Armando
    Chicano intermarriage: a theoretical and
        empirical study, 812.
    Regional differences in Chicano intermarriage,
        3870.
Aboud, Frances E.
    The development of ethnic attitudes: a
        critical review, 414.
Aceves Madrid, Vicente
    Controversy surrounding NBC's CHICO AND THE
        MAN, 164.
    Film review of: FREEBIE AND THE BEAN, 3056.
Acosta, Alexandria
    The relation of acculturation and values in
        Mexican Americans, 30.
Acosta, Frank X., et al.
    Preparing low-income Hispanic, Black, and
        white patients for psychotherapy: evaluation
        of a new orientation program, 270.
Acosta, Teresa Palomo
    Balancing act, 5413.
    Catorce pedazos de una cosecha, 7144.
    Desaparecida, 5414.
    Muralistas: poem one, 5415.
Acuna, David
    Cuento verdad, 7145.
    Memoria, 6425.
    Para vos, 6426.
    Realidad, 6427.
Acuna, Rodolfo
    Book review of: DICTIONARY OF MEXICAN AMERICAN
        HISTORY, 813.
    English as the official language?=El ingles
        como idioma oficial, 2829.
    Response to Cynthia Orozco, 1565.
Adams, Clinton
    Book review of: ART IN NEW MEXICO, 1900-1945:
        PATHS TO TAOS AND SANTA FE, 353.
Adams, Russell P.
    Family planning needs and behavior of Mexican
        American women: a study of health care
        professionals and their clientele, 34.
Agosin, Marjorie
    Madre, 5416.
    Norma Alarcon, 160.
    (Sin titulo), 5418.
    Tristezas, 5419.
    El vino=Wine, 5420.
Aguero Rojas, Pilar
    [Untitled drawing], 2342.
    [Untitled drawing], 2343.
    [Untitled drawing], 2344.
    [Untitled drawing], 2345.
    [Untitled drawing], 2346.
    [Woman and broom (drawing)], 2347.
    [Woman and iron (drawing)], 2348.
Aguiar, Antonia
    [Arms], 2349.
    [Bodies], 2350.
    [Untitled drawing], 2351.
    [Untitled drawing], 2352.
    [Untitled drawing], 2353.
Aguilar, Andy
    Mexico's children, 1713.
Aguilar Gallardo, Hortensia
    Cantar de un ayer, 5421.
    Mariposas negras, 5422.
    Nostalgia, 6428.
Aguilar, J.
    Federal court halts workplace searches based
        on broad inspection warrants, 773.
Aguilar Melantzon, Ricardo
    Cumplir mi justa condena, 7146.
Aguilar, Ricardo
    La frontera, 27.
    Hacia un tercer lenguaje, 148.
Aguilar, Ricardo [Tepalcatero]

    Tres veces la pua o nopaltzin, 5423.
Aguilera-Hellwet, Max
    An Aztec prince, 7147.
Aguilu de Murphy, Raquel
    Book review of: GIVING UP THE GHOST, 815.
Aguirre, Adalberto, Jr.
    Book review of: CHICANO SOCIOLINGUISTICS, 816.
    Book review of: THE YALE MURDER: THE FATAL
        ROMANCE OF BONNIE GARLAND AND RICHARD
        HERRIN, 817.
Aguirre, Antonio (Jake)
    Salsa Na Ma in San Francisco, 3976.
    Two little giants, 4935.
Ahlborn, Richard E.
    The Hispanic horseman: a sampling of horse
        gear from the Fred Harvey Collection, 3163.
Aitchison, Jean
    Book review of: BILINGUAL EDUCATION:
        EVALUATION, ASSESSMENT AND METHODOLOGY, 626.
Alarcon, Francisco X.
    Banderas, 5424.
    Un beso is not a kiss, 5425.
    Columna al amor, 5426.
    Fugitive, 5427.
    I used to be much much darker, 5428.
    I'm really not crying, 5429.
    Palabras heridas, 5430.
    Patria, 5431.
    Profugo, 5432.
    Raices, 5433.
    Roots, 5434.
    Triangulo gris, 5435.
    Worded wounds, 5436.
    The X in my name, 5437.
Alarcon, Justo S.
    A la nanita, nana ...[y] epilogo, 5438.
    Book review of: CHULIFEAS FRONTERAS, 158.
    Las dos tortolas, 5439.
    Estructuras narrativas en TATA CASEHUA de
        Miguel Mendez, 4215.
    Focos: el agonico visionario, 7149.
    Las mascaras, 5440.
Alarcon, Norma
    The American stage, 5441.
    Book Review of: BRUJAS Y ALGO MAS/WITCHES AND
        OTHER THINGS, 136.
    Chilean winter: a true story, 5442.
    Honey, 5443.
    Honey [drawing], 2354.
    In pursuit of the white knight, 5444.
    Jacking off, 5445.
    Making "familia" from scratch: split
        subjectivities in the work of Helena Maria
        Viramontes and Cherrie Moraga, 1566.
    Mexican twilight, 5446.
    Once upon a time...the sculptor, 7150.
    A poet analyzes her craft, 455.
    Precision processing, 5447.
    Sunday afternoons, 7151.
    Undefined, 5448.
Albert, Bill
    Book review of: MAN, LAND, AND WATER: MEXICO'S
        FARMLAND IRRIGATION POLICIES, 1885-1911,
        821.
Alberts, Don E.
    Book review of: LEGACY OF HONOR: THE LIFE OF
        RAFAEL CHACON, A NINETEENTH-CENTURY NEW
        MEXICAN, 822.
Alcocer, Daniel
    La Raza, 5449.
Alexander, Charles C.
    Book review of: WAR, REVOLUTION, AND THE KU
        KLUX KLAN: A STUDY OF INTOLERANCE IN A
        BORDER CITY, 823.
Alexander, June Granatir
    Book review of: URBAN ETHNICITY IN THE UNITED
        STATES, 824.
Alire Saenz, Benjamin
    Alejandro's funeral, 5450.
    The ruins of Prieto's barrio, 5451.
Allen, David
    Bilingual education: door to the society of
        the future, 589.
    Educacion bilingue: puerta a la sociedad del

Inocencio: ni siembra ni escarda y siempre se
   come el mejor elote, 7168.
Inocencio: tambien de gusto se llora como de
   dolor se canta, 7169.
Arellano, Manuel
   A Manuel Salazar, 5474.
Arenas, Andrea-Teresa
   The circle weighs heavy with healing tears,
      5475.
   From a safe distance, 5476.
   Greetings and salutations, 5477.
   Queen of victory pray for us, 5478.
Arenas, Soledad
   The evaluation of four Head Start bilingual
      multicultural curriculum models, 591.
Argulewicz, Ed N.
   Effects of ethnic membership, socioeconomic
      status, and home language on LD, EMR, and EH
      placements, 2628.
Armstrong, Ruth W.
   Christmas in Albuquerque, 167.
Aros, Maria Teresa
   Lo que pido, 5479.
   El pensamiento de un nino, 5480.
   El pequeno, 5481.
   Por fin se cierran, 6442.
   Tu olvido, 5482.
Arreola, Daniel D.
   Book review of: CITY BOUND, 834.
   The Mexican American cultural capital, 1946.
   Mexican restaurants in Tucson, 311.
Arroyo, Luis Leobardo
   Book review of: DESERT IMMIGRANTS, 835.
Arvizu, Delia
   El aborto, 7170.
   El espejo, 7171.
   El guerito de Teresita, 7172.
   Una perspectiva de la muerte, 6443.
Astiazaron Aguilar, Guadalupe
   Amistad, 6444.
   Azul, 5483.
   El mundo y el hombre, 5484.
   El mundo y el hombre [long version], 5485.
   Oracion, 5486.
   Senor, no llores mas, 5487.
   Sueno real, 5488.
Atencio, Tomas
   La Academia de la Nueva Raza: su historia, 7.
   La Academia de la Nueva Raza, 8.
   La Academia de la Nueva Raza: El Oro del
      Barrio, 9.
   No estan todos los que son, no son todos los
      que estan, 10.
   La resolana, 2250.
   La resolana [editorial], 6.
   La resolana: entre el dicho y el hecho, 2251.
Atkinson, Maxine P.
   The "Spanish origin" population of Oregon and
      Washington: a demographic profile, 1980,
      5173.
Autry, Brick
   Book review of: LATINO FAMILIES IN THE UNITED
      STATES, 836.
Avalos, Francisco
   Book review of: SMALL BONES, LITTLE EYES, 837.
Avendano, Fausto
   La enemistad, 7173.
   Fragmento dramatico, 69.
   Juan Gonzalez, poeta, 7174.
Avila, Joaquin
   Task force on civic identity and political
      participation, 2736.
Avina, Jeffrey
   The uninvited: immigration is a hot issue--but
      who's really getting burned?, 3822.
Ayala, Ernie
   Henry Alfaro, ABC's Eyewitness News reporter,
      174.
   Richard Leon, L.A.'s leading Latin jazz D.J.,
      4182.
Baca, Reynaldo
   Citizen aspirations and residency preferences:
      the Mexican undocumented worker in the
      binational community, 4372.

Baca Zinn, Maxine
   Book review of: LA CHICANA: MEXICAN AMERICAN
      WOMEN, 838.
   Book review of: TWICE A MINORITY:
      MEXICAN-AMERICAN WOMEN, 839.
   Marital role orientation among Chicanos: an
      analysis of structural and cultural factors,
      4517.
Badikian, Beatriz
   Mapmaker, 5489.
   Rituals at Bennington: the elusive joy of
      writing, 5490.
   Words, 5491.
Badilla M., Alejandro
   De mi ninez, 6445.
Baezconde-Garbanati, Lourdes
   Mexican immigrant women: a selected
      bibliography, 572.
Bain, Laurie
   Alfonso's heats up San Antonio, 176.
Baker, George A.
   Critical incident competencies of Mexican
      American and Anglo American administrators,
      271.
Baker, Keith
   An answer from research on bilingual
      education, 592.
Baker, Ross K.
   Border follies, 3346.
Balderrama, Francisco E.
   Book review of: A BIBLIOGRAPHY OF
      MEXICAN-AMERICAN HISTORY, 580.
Balkan, D. Carlos
   The Hispanic market's leading indicators, 94.
Banker, Cynthia A., et al.
   Primary dental arch characteristics of
      Mexican-American children, 1784.
Banks, Leo W.
   The Latinization of U.S. baseball, 546.
Banks, Marissa Elena
   Army maneuvers, 122.
   Doing it right, 1349.
Barbara, Ana M.
   La despedida, 5492.
   Paloma, 6446.
   Paloma, 6447.
Barger, W.K.
   California public endorses the United Farm
      Workers, 139.
   Midwestern farmworkers and the farm labor
      movement, 2976.
   Public attitudes towards Mexican-American
      farmworkers in the Midwest, 416.
   Views of California farmworkers regarding the
      farm labor movement, 140.
Barnes, Jill
   The Latin pitch, 405.
   The winning formula of Nancy Lopez, 406.
Barona, Andres
   Chicano psychology: a new field?, 841.
Barr, Evan T.
   Borderline hypocrisy, 3782.
Barragan, Ma. Antonieta
   Carlos Almaraz: "El arte contemporaneo no
      tiene mucha emocion, es estatico...", 189.
Barrera, Nancy
   Mi sueno, 459.
Barrios, Greg
   Efrain Gutierrez y el nuevo cine chicano, 682.
Barro, Mary Helen
   1973 Emmy Awards, 1541.
Barrow, Leo (trans.)
   Genesis of the word, 5875.
Barry, John M.
   Mito e ironia en LOS PASOS PERDIDOS, 1464.
Bartlett, Catherine Vallejos
   Magical realism: the Latin American influence
      on modern Chicano writers, 319.
Barton, Amy E.
   Women farmworkers: their workplace and
      capitalist patriarchy, 1436.
Bastida, Elena B.
   Book review of: THE HISPANIC ELDERLY, 251.
Bastidas, Laura E.

A ti, 5493.
No era de oro, 5494.
Que contraste!, 6448.
Secretos, 5495.
Bayard, C.J.
Book review of: LABOR IN NEW MEXICO: UNIONS,
STRIKES AND SOCIAL HISTORY SINCE 1881, 843.
Beale, Stephen
100 influentials and their assessment of the
critical issues, 672.
CEOs, 203.
Connecting with the American experience: an
interview with Luis Valdez, 527.
Defense cuts on the horizon?, 1323.
Friendly persuasion: pacts and covenants, 86.
Inertia in the corporate boardroom, 1351.
MALDEF weathers a storm, 248.
The Maxwell House that Marlboro bought, 95.
More changes at SIN, 3268.
Moving trucks in New Mexico, 470.
Networking the networks, 1314.
New blood, fresh money: Telemundo, Univision
bullish on television market, 1991.
A piece of the big picture, 1325.
Striking a deal with big business, 87.
A turning point in Hollywood, 528.
Beals, Janette
Chicano Survey report #5: group naming and
cultural inclinations, 2102.
Beauford, Olivia
A tiempo, 70.
Beezley, William H.
Any Sunday in April: the rise of sport in San
Antonio and the Hispanic borderlands, 1536.
Belkind, A.
Book review of: THREE AMERICAN LITERATURES,
514.
Bell, David
Report from Sante Fe: figuration and fantasy,
330.
Belli, Gioconda
Y Dios me hizo mujer, 5496.
Y Dios me hizo mujer, 5497.
Bellinhausen, Hermann
El lobo estepario en Olvera Street, 4343.
Belloc Garcia, Jose
Que linda es la luz, 5498.
Beltran, Christina
Minority access into higher education, 2294.
Beltran, Luis
Aun me duelen tus brazos empujandome, 5499.
Travesura entre las ramas, 5500.
Benavidez, Roy
An embattled Chicano, 566.
Bennett, Jonathan A.
At last, farmworkers are allowed clean water,
2980.
Bennett, Priscilla
Book review of: BILINGUAL BOOKS IN SPANISH AND
ENGLISH FOR CHILDREN, 619.
Bennett, Ruth
A bilingual perspective on teaching history,
2631.
Benson, Douglas K.
A conversation with Leroy V. Quintana, 437.
Intuitions of a world in transition: the New
Mexican poetry of Leroy V. Quintana, 438.
Bensusan, Guy
A consideration of Nortena and Chicano music,
2001.
Berger, Andres
Cartas a mi amante, 7175.
Berger, Peggy S.
Differences in importance of and satisfaction
from job characteristics by sex and
occupational type among Mexican-American
employees, 418.
Berling-Manuel, Lynn
Expanding radio market battles research
static, 309.
Bermudez-Gallegos, Marta
La sombra, 7176.
Bernal, Alejandro
La estructura tematica en Y NO SE LO TRAGO LA

TIERRA de Tomas Rivera, 4221.
Y jugamos a poetas, 5501.
Bernal, Ernesto
The fate of bilingual education during an era
of school reform, 593.
Bernal, Esmeralda
...And she became a proletarian, 687.
Frida Kahlo, 3930.
I wish, 5503.
If I could, 5504.
Sabes carino, 5505.
When my body longs for you..., 5506.
Bernal, Juan Manuel
Has atestiguado?, 5507.
Poemas cortas [sic], 5508.
Bernal, Louis Carlos
Alma Rosa, 5358.
Dia de los muertos, 5359.
Marines, 5360.
Miguel M. Mendez [photograph], 4629.
Panadero, 5362.
La Raza, 5363.
Sin documentados, 5364.
[Untitled photographs], 5365.
Bernal, Martha E.
Book review of: EXPLORATIONS IN CHICANO
PSYCHOLOGY, 539.
Bethell, Tom
Senator Simpson's reward, 2272.
Betsky, Aaron
The Spanish influence: architecture in
America, 312.
Bieder, Maryellen
Book review of: WOMEN IN HISPANIC LITERATURE,
847.
Biggs, Michelle
Adios, 5509.
Inescapable, 5510.
Nina indigena=Indian maiden, 5511.
On the lee shore, 5512.
Tu, 5513.
Billings, Linda M.
In verbal murals: a study of Chicana herstory
and poetry, 1418.
Bixler-Marquez, Dennis J.
The introduction of bilingual education
programs--a collaborative approach, 594.
Blades, Ruben
Ruben Blades: music, love and revolution=Ruben
Blades: musica, amor y revolucion, 718.
Blanco, George M.
Book review of: FORM AND FUNCTION IN CHICANO
ENGLISH, 848.
Blanco, Gilbert M.
Las Adelitas del Barrio, 1577.
A vehicle for positive change, 362.
Blanco, Pilar
Ayer, 5514.
Cuando te vea, 5515.
Blea, Irene I.
Book review of: CURANDERISMO, 849.
Damn, Sam, 5516.
Female learning, 5517.
Fire color, 5518.
He never wrote, 5519.
Inez, 5520.
Married, 5521.
Mujeres contemporaneas, 5522.
An occasional baby, 5523.
Once, 5524.
Singing women, 5525.
Singing women, 5526.
Why, 5527.
Body-Gendrot, Sophie
Book review of: PROTEST IS NOT ENOUGH, 850.
Bogart, Beth
Political power gives market vote of
confidence, 6325.
Bohn, Martin J.
Alienation of monolingual Hispanics in a
federal correctional institution, 635.
Bojorquez, Ricardo
El desierto, 6449.
El valenton, 5528.

Bolano, Luis (trans.)
  Genesis of the word, 5875.
Bolanos, Isabel
  A donde va la nina, 5529.
  Los lirios y las violetas, 5530.
  Madre que tan cerca estas, 5531.
Bolivar, Maria Dolores
  Silencios virgenes, 7177.
Borboa, Roberto
  [Untitled drawing], 2355.
  [Untitled drawing], 2356.
  [Untitled drawing], 2357.
  [Untitled drawing], 2358.
  [Untitled drawing], 2359.
  [Untitled drawing], 2360.
  [Untitled drawing], 2361.
  [Untitled drawing], 2362.
Borthwick, S.A.
  Place of residence by age, ethnicity, and
    level of retardation of the mentally
    retarded/developmentally disabled population
    of California, 1385.
Bos, Eduard
  Estimates of the number of illegal aliens: an
    analysis of the sources of disagreement,
    6352.
Boyer, Jeanette
  Gangue, 7178.
  A vein is struck, 7179.
Bracamonte, Jose A.
  Book review of: MEXICAN IMMIGRANT WORKERS IN
    THE U.S., 3752.
Bradby, Marie
  The naval research laboratory, 2786.
  Solomon Trujillo of US West, 688.
Bradley, Jacqueline
  Circles of nostalgia, 5532.
Bransford, Luis A.
  The Chicano as surplus population, 2890.
Braun, Barbara
  The Aztecs: art and sacrifice, 292.
Breiter, Toni
  Pepe del Rio, 1287.
  Speaker for Uncle Sam, 2258.
Briceno, Carlos
  Defining the difference between Carlos and
    Chuck, 3672.
Brinson-Pineda, Barbara
  Aqui venimos a pasar hambre y amarguras, 5533.
  Carta a L., 5534.
  Dolencias, 5535.
  Ella, 5536.
  Maria yo, 5537.
  Recipe: chorizo con huevo made in the
    microwave, 5538.
  Sabado, 5539.
  The strawberry pickers, 5540.
Briody, Elizabeth K.
  Patterns of household immigration into South
    Texas, 1578.
Brito, Aristeo
  Insomnio, 5541.
  Insomnio, 5542.
  [Note], 4341.
Broderick, Stephanie H., et al.
  Ethnicity, acculturation, and health beliefs
    among diabetes patients, 28.
Brower, Monty
  A proud street mourns its fallen sons, 4797.
Brown, D.R.
  Book review of: CHICANO LITERATURE: A
    REFERENCE GUIDE, 863.
Brown, Kathryn H.
  Relative lower extremity length in Mexican
    American and in American Black and white
    youth, 277.
Browning, Rufus P.
  Black and Hispanic power in city politics: a
    forum, 775.
  Protest is not enough: a theory of political
    incorporation, 776.
Bruce-Novoa, Juan
  Book review of: FACE, 864.
  Comunion, 5543.

La critica chicana de Luis Leal (I), 439.
La critica chicana de Luis Leal (II), 440.
La dama del libro, 5544.
Elegias a la frontera hispanica, 1983.
Ernest Brawley: un escritor chicano
  desconocido, 155.
Homenaje a Ricardo Sanchez, 5545.
Homosexuality and the Chicano novel, 44.
In search of poverty, 5877.
Meet the writers of the 80s, 237.
Mexico en la literatura chicana (I), 3541.
Mexico en la literatura chicana (II), 45.
Nash Candelaria: novelista (I), 692.
Nash Candelaria: novelista (II), 693.
Nuevo representantes de la novela chicana,
  156.
One more rosary for Dona Marina, 4234.
Poesia de Gary Soto: una autobiografia a
  plazos, 443.
Propiedad, 5546.
Brunelle, Janet A.
  Prevalence of dental caries and periodontal
    disease in Mexican American children aged 5
    to 17 years: results from Southwestern
    HHANES, 1982-83, 2202.
Bryan, Dexter
  Citizen aspirations and residency preferences:
    the Mexican undocumented worker in the
    binational community, 4372.
Bubala, Julie
  En la casa de mi abuelita, 6450.
Buczynski, Linda
  Las montanas, 6451.
Bueno, Patricia E.
  Los Chicanos y la politica, 1912.
  Los Chicanos y la politica II, 223.
Bunge, Mario
  Ciencia e ideologia en el mundo hispanico,
    6285.
Burciaga, Jose Antonio
  Corridos, 2002.
  In celebration of a man's ecumenism, 1491.
  Linda Ronstadt: my Mexican soul, 694.
  A man with his teatro, 2010.
Burnett, G. Wesley
  Book review of: BORDERLANDS SOURCEBOOK, 865.
Burnham, M. Audrey, et al.
  Measurement of acculturation in a community
    population of Mexican Americans, 29.
Burnham-Kidwell, Debbie
  Book review of: THE EDUCATION OF POOR AND
    MINORITY CHILDREN: A WORLD BIBLIOGRAPHY:
    SUPPLEMENT, 1979-1985, 866.
Burns, Jeffrey M.
  Book review of: THE CHICANO EXPERIENCE, 867.
Burruel, Carlos J.
  Desilusion, 6452.
Burt, Brian A.
  Prevalence of dental caries and periodontal
    disease in Mexican American children aged 5
    to 17 years: results from Southwestern
    HHANES, 1982-83, 2202.
Bustamante, Jorge A.
  International labor migration and external
    debt, 2150.
Bustamante, Nuria
  Permanencia y cambio en CARAS VIEJAS Y VINO
    NUEVO, 1441.
Butler, Anne M.
  Book review of: THE GENTLEMEN'S CLUB: THE
    STORY OF PROSTITUTION IN EL PASO, TEXAS,
    868.
  Book review of: THEY CALLED THEM GREASERS,
    869.
Byrd, W.W.
  Cocospora, 6453.
Cabello-Argandona, Roberto
  Hispanex is here to stay, 2171.
  Media research and the Chicano, 110.
Cabeza de Vaca, Darlene
  [Campesina], 2363.
  Can a person be illegal?, 3823.
  Home, 2364.
  Knowing the value God places on me..., 1579.

Nursing mother, 2365.
[Untitled drawing], 2366.
[Woman (drawing)], 2367.
[Woman's torso (drawing)], 2368.
Caicedo, Harry
  VISTA birthday review and renewal of goals,
    6681.
Calderon, Margarita
  Book review of: SCHOOLING AND LANGUAGE
    MINORITY STUDENTS: A THEORETICAL FRAMEWORK,
    1130.
Callahan, Jaime M.
  LATINO: un nuevo concepto de cine, 3066.
Camach, Miguel
  Idea atrazada, 7181.
Campbell, Duane
  How the grinch stole the social sciences:
    moving teaching to the right in California,
    2632.
Campbell, Federico
  Carlos Castaneda: escribo como brujo, no como
    escritor, 1474.
  Henry Reyna, pachuco, 3546.
  Paralelo 32: la frontera como espacio
    literario, 1219.
Campbell, T.C.
  Hasta nunca, 6454.
Campos, Elba M.
  Un verano, 7182.
Campos, Jorge
  Noticia de la literatura chicana, 4239.
Canales, Michael James
  Mala suerte, 7183.
Canby, J.
  Immigration board can't use evidence from stop
    based only on Hispanic appearance, 318.
Candelaria, Cordelia
  Book review of: FIESTA IN AZTLAN: ANTHOLOGY OF
    CHICANO POETRY and FLOR Y CANTO IV AND V,
    870.
Canez, Luis P.
  De paso, 5547.
  El desierto, 5548.
  Falleciste, 5549.
  Pena, 5550.
  Preguntas, 5551.
  Vida libre, 5552.
Canive, Jose
  Book review of: MENTAL HEALTH AND HISPANIC
    AMERICANS: CLINICAL PERSPECTIVES, 252.
Cano, Oscar
  MAES technical brief, 2606.
  Profiles in engineering, 695.
Cantu, Jesus "Chista"
  Se necesita un punto de vista para desarrollar
    una perspectiva, 6455.
Cantu, Norma
  Book review of: CUENTOS: STORIES BY LATINAS,
    872.
  Book review of: WOMAN OF HER WORD: HISPANIC
    WOMEN WRITE, 873.
Cardenas, Antonio J.
  Asado: churrasco: piquete: barbacoa: barbecue,
    3143.
  Traditions of Christmas, 2726.
Cardenas, Cecilia
  Asado: churrasco: piquete: barbacoa: barbecue,
    3143.
  Traditions of Christmas, 2726.
Cardenas, Gilbert
  Book review of: IN DEFENSE OF LA RAZA, 516.
  Book review of: OLDER MEXICAN AMERICANS: A
    STUDY IN AN URBAN BARRIO, 253.
  Book review of: "TEMPORARY" ALIEN WORKERS IN
    THE UNITED STATES, 876.
Cardenas, Jose A.
  Book review of: EDUCATION, POLITICS, AND
    BILINGUAL EDUCATION IN TEXAS, 877.
Cardinal, Roger
  El mensaje de Martin Ramirez, 363.
Cardoso, Lawrence A.
  Book review of: THEY CALLED THEM GREASERS,
    878.
Carillo, Fred M.

Ethnic minority students, admissions policies,
    and academic support programs in
    institutions of higher education, 18.
Carlson, David
  Book review of: HISPANIC MENTAL HEALTH
    RESEARCH: A REFERENCE GUIDE, 833.
Carpenter, Thomas P., et al.
  Achievement in mathematics: results from the
    National Assessment, 14.
Carranza, Miguel A.
  Book review of: LATINO LANGUAGE AND
    COMMUNICATIVE BEHAVIOR, 879.
Carrillo, Ana, et al.
  History of Las Mujeres, 1580.
Carrillo, Victor
  Woman to woman, 7184.
Carrillo, Victor, trans.
  Agosto en un pueblo canero, 5574.
Carrizosa, Cecilia Rivera
  Una carta a ti, con ternura infinita, 6456.
Carter, David L.
  Hispanic interaction with the criminal justice
    system in Texas: experiences, attitudes, and
    perceptions, 2035.
Cartes, Rebeca
  Desnuda, 7185.
  El lobo, 7186.
  Me estas rechazando, 5553.
  Te sueno, 5554.
Casarez Vasquez, Enedina
  Maricela dreams, 5235.
  My mother's altar, 5236.
Casaus, Maria R.
  Una apuesta, 7187.
  El cumpleanos, 6457.
  Descansa pequeno, 7188.
  Mi pequeno, 5555.
  Tengo miedo, 5556.
Castaneda, Miriam
  Creation [sculpture], 7065.
  The cry [sculpture], 7066.
Castano, Wilfredo Q.
  For the roses=Pa' las rosas, 177.
Casteleiro, Gus
  Hot salsa and other sounds, 4373.
Castellanos, Teresa
  La huelga nos ha ensenado a hablar, 697.
  I never lose a dream: an interview with Yvette
    Galindo, 698.
Castillo, Ana
  Juego, 5557.
  No solo el ser chilena, 5558.
  Paco and Rosa, 5559.
  Querida Marina: I still love you, 5560.
  Saturdays, 5561.
Castillo, Jose Luis
  Carta esperada, 7189.
  Sukaina, 7190.
Castillo, Lupe
  Para el ano nuevo, 5562.
  Para la navidad, 5563.
Castillo, Rafael C.
  The goy from Aztlan, 7191.
  The poetry club, 7192.
Castillo, Victoria
  A mis padres, 6458.
  Madre, 5564.
  Por que, senor, por que, 5565.
  Las tres naranjas, 2064.
Castillo-Speed, Lillian
  Annotated bibliography, 358.
  Chicana/Latina literature and criticism:
    reviews of recent books, 268.
Castro, Agenor L.
  Hispanics in prison: reform...or riots, 6408.
Castro, Anna
  El buen juez por su casa empieza, 6459.
  Curiosidades en variedad de fiestas para
    entierros, 6460.
  La leyenda de la siquanaba y el zipitillo,
    2065.
  El zipitillo, 2066.
Castro, E.M.
  El encaje, 5566.

Por que un poema?, 5567.
Te veo, 5568.
La zorra, 5569.
El zorro, 5570.
Castro Feinberg, Rosa
The English-only debate, 1383.
Castro, Raymond
Objectives of Chicano studies, 1751.
Castro, Richard T.
A role for Hispanic Americans in foreign
policy formulation, 2870.
Catalan E., Martina
Cuando tu ya no estes, 5571.
Un novio es..., 5572.
Catalano, Julia
Fajitas madness, 3139.
Pinata, 2.
Raul Jimenez, 254.
Cecere, Linda
Newspapers attract attention in some
categories, 96.
Cejas, Paul
The English-only debate, 1383.
Cerda, Gabriela
The call, 7193.
Hidden jewel: the Frida Kahlo house of
Coyoacan, 364.
La serpiente, 2067.
Sunset Boulevard, 5573.
Cervantes, Alma
Desarrollo, 7194.
Cervantes, Lorna Dee
Agosto en un pueblo canero, 5574.
Astro-no-mia, 5575.
Bird Ave, 5576.
Cervantes, Norma
Bendicion, 5577.
No importa el pasado, 5578.
Poema, 5579.
Te quiero con ternura, 5580.
Cervantes, Richard C.
Consideration of psychosocial stress in the
treatment of the Latina immigrant, 1671.
Cervantes, Robert A.
Ethnocentric pedagogy and minority student
growth: implications for the common school,
595.
Cespedes, Marisa
"Que viva la vida" biografia de Frida Kahlo,
365.
Chabram, Angie
Colega..., 5581.
Chabran, Richard
Book review of: BILINDEX, 586.
Book review of: MEXICAN AMERICAN ARCHIVES AT
THE BENSON COLLECTION: A GUIDE FOR USERS,
313.
Book review of: THE MEXICAN AMERICAN: A
CRITICAL GUIDE TO RESEARCH AIDS, 574.
Latino reference arrives, 24.
Chacon, Maria A., et al.
Chicanas in California postsecondary
education, 1583.
Challem, Jack
Pied piper of science. 2634.
Chapa, Jorge
Latino terminology: conceptual bases for
standardized terminology, 2900.
Chatham, James R.
Book review of: A SOURCEBOOK FOR HISPANIC
LITERATURE AND LANGUAGE, 800.
Chavanell, Joe
Folk art's gift of Christmas joy, 388.
Chavaria, Elvira
Book review of: THE STATE OF HISPANIC AMERICA,
VOL. II and LA CHICANA: BUILDING FOR THE
FUTURE, 886.
Chavez, Andres
Film review of: BRING ME THE HEAD OF ALFREDO
GARCIA, 1284.
Film review of: LENNY, 1304.
Chavez, Denise
Artery of land, 5582.
Birth of me in my room at home, 5583.

Chekov green love, 5584.
Cloud, 5585.
Cuckoo death crime, 5586.
Door, 5587.
Everything you are is teeth, 5588.
The feeling of going on, 5589.
For my sister in Paris, 5590.
I am your Mary Magdalene, 5591.
Lagana of lace, 5592.
Lagana of lace, 5593.
Mercado day, 5594.
Missss Rede, 5595.
NOVENA NARRATIVAS y OFRENDAS NUEVOMEXICANAS,
191.
On mama Tona, 5596.
[Our linkage...], 5597.
Progression from water to the absence, 5598.
Purgatory is an ocean of flaming hearts, 5599.
Saying "oh no", 5600.
Silver ingots of desire, 5601.
Sisters sisters sisters, 5602.
The space between, 5603.
Starflash, 5604.
The state of my inquietude, 5605.
The study, 5606.
Tears, 5607.
[This river's praying place...], 5608.
This river's praying place, 5609.
This thin light, 5610.
[The train whistles...], 5611.
Two butterflies, 5612.
Words of wisdom, 444.
[Worm child...], 5613.
[Worm child...], 5614.
Ya, 5615.
Chavez, Eva
Perlas, 5616.
Chavez, Gene T.
Book review of: MIRROR OF LANGUAGE: THE DEBATE
ON BILINGUALISM, 887.
Chavez, Linda
Celebrate! The Chicano Resource Center's 10th
anniversary, 1738.
Trivia, 2127.
Trivia, 2128.
Chavez, Lorenzo A.
La Bamba, 51.
A brief guide to financial aid for
college-bound students, 2259.
The eyes of Texas are upon them, 331.
Images of ethnic pride, 332.
Pancho Gonzales: pioneering champion, 407.
Passport to success, 1868.
The quest for Hispanic roots, 571.
Ramon Duarte, 702.
Tennis superstars, 408.
Chavez, Lulu
El 17 de diciembre, 6461.
El hombre del sahuaro, 7195.
Chavez, Maria Laura
El amor del creador, 5617.
Chavez, Noe M.
Culminacion de una busqueda de identidad, 238.
Chema
Coraje-rabia, 5618.
No wall, 5619.
Pajarito azul, 5620.
Chernick, Marc W.
Book review of: THE BORDER THAT JOINS: MEXICAN
MIGRANTS AND U.S. RESPONSIBILITY, 888.
Chesser, Barbara
Loneliness among Mexican migrant children,
2225.
Chesterfield, Kathleen Barrows
"Hojas with the H": spontaneous peer teaching
in bilingual classrooms, 596.
Chesterfield, Ray A.
"Hojas with the H": spontaneous peer teaching
in bilingual classrooms, 596.
Chico, Elias
Orale pachuco!, 5621.
Chista
USE: Cantu, Jesus "Chista"
Chiswick, Barry R.

Book review of: POLITICAL AND ECONOMIC
   MIGRANTS IN AMERICA, 889.
The labor market status of Hispanic men, 1505.
Christian, Garna L.
   Book review of: THE TEXAS-MEXICAN CONJUNTO,
   890.
Chumacero, Olivia
   Recesses of my mind, 7196.
Cirerol, Anna
   Boxeador, 5622.
   La historia de Lina y la rana, 7197.
   Palomino, 6462.
   Primavera, 5623.
Cisek, Angela
   Abajo la tierra, 5624.
   Un brindis al amor, 5625.
   Dias cuerdos, 5626.
   Enamorados, 7198.
   Un marciano en mi bolsillo, 7199.
   Una secuela de vida, 5627.
Cisneros, Henry
   The meaning for Hispanics of 5 de Mayo, 1813.
   Mexico's poorest are heading North, 175.
Cisneros, Sandra
   Do you know me?: I wrote THE HOUSE ON MANGO
   STREET, 445.
   Eleven, 7200.
   Ghosts and voices: writing from obsession,
   446.
   Heartland, 5628.
   Living as a writer: choice and circumstance,
   447.
   The master, 5629.
   Notes to a young(er) writer, 448.
Clair, Denise
   [Working woman], 2369.
Clair, Robert T.
   A comparative analysis of mature
   Hispanic-owned banks, 535.
Claymendez, Luis Felipe
   La naturaleza en la literatura chicana y sus
   antecedentes prehispanicos, 4241.
Cobas, Jose A.
   Book review of: LATIN JOURNEY, 511.
Cobos, Ruben
   Cantares nuevomexicanos, 2003.
Coerver, Don
   The Arizona-Sonora border and the Mexican
   revolution, 1910-1920, 320.
Cohen, Albert K.
   Book review of: HONOR AND THE AMERICAN DREAM,
   892.
Cohen, Gaynor
   The politics of bilingual education, 597.
Cole, Maria Jose
   The cage, 5630.
   La jaula, 5631.
   Sangre espanola, 5632.
Colecchia, F.
   Book review of: THE DEFIANT MUSE: HISPANIC
   FEMINIST POEMS FROM THE MIDDLE AGES TO THE
   PRESENT, 893.
Colossio M., Marcela
   Cucurpe, 6466.
Communist Party, U.S.A.
   On Chicano/Mexican-American equality, 1893.
Compean, Mario
   Book review of: PERSPECTIVES ON IMMIGRATION
   AND MINORITY EDUCATION, 894.
Comstock, Cathryn L.
   A children's Spanish word discrimination test
   for non-Spanish-speaking children, 1782.
Conde, Hilda Rosina
   Book review of: LIFE SPAN, 895.
Conner, Roger
   The Immigration Reform Law: how fair to
   Hispanics?, 3017.
Cook, Annabel Kirschner
   Diversity among Northwest Hispanics, 1589.
Cooke, John Byrne
   Book review of: SOUTH BY SOUTHWEST: 24 STORIES
   FROM MODERN TEXAS, 896.
Cordasco, Francesco
   Book review of: HISPANICS IN THE UNITED

STATES: A NEW SOCIAL AGENDA, 897.
Cordova, Gilbert Benito
   Certain curious colonial Chicano
   cosmetological customs, 2015.
Cordova, Teresa
   La mente, 5633.
Cornell, Nancy
   Forging links between societies, 1.
Corona, Al
   Life in the fast lane, 3216.
Corpi, Lucha
   Cancion de invierno, 5634.
   Fuga, 5635.
   Indocumentada angustia, 5636.
   Invernario, 5637.
   Llueve, 5638.
   Recuerdo intimo, 5639.
   Romance negro, 5640.
   Sonata a dos voces, 5641.
Corpus, Alfonso
   [Untitled drawing], 2370.
   [Untitled drawing], 2371.
Correa, Clara Sunderland
   The marital morality of Mexican women--an
   urban study, 2962.
Cortes, Carlos E.
   Book review of: THE ZOOT-SUIT RIOTS, 898.
Cortes, Ernesto, Jr.
   Changing the locus of political decision
   making, 703.
Cortese, Anthony J.
   Ethnic ethics: subjective choice and
   interference in Chicano, white and Black
   children, 2892.
Cortina, Rodolfo J.
   Book review of: KLAIL CITY, 899.
Cosgrove, Stuart
   Book review of: THE ZOOT-SUIT RIOTS, 900.
Costello, Raymond M.
   Hispanic alcoholic treatment considerations,
   169.
Cota, Aide
   Ahora y siempre, 5642.
   El mar y tu, 5643.
   Now and forever, 5644.
Cota, Socorro
   Confusion, 5645.
Cota-Cardenas, Margarita
   A una madre de nuestros tiempos, 5646.
   La creacion-protesta en CRISOL: (TRILOGIA),
   159.
Cox, Charlene B.
   Motivos artisticos, 328.
Crane, Lori A.
   Smoking behavior among Hispanics: a
   preliminary report, 6640.
Cresce, Arthur R.
   The Hispanic foreign-born and the assimilation
   experience, 397.
Crisp, James E.
   Book review of: LOS TUCSONENSES: THE MEXICAN
   COMMUNITY IN TUCSON 1854-1941, 901.
   Book review of: THE LOST LAND, 902.
   Book review of: THEY CALLED THEM GREASERS,
   903.
Crocker, Elvira Valenzuela
   USE: Valenzuela-Crocker, Elvira
Cruikshank, Lupita
   El futuro, 6467.
   Impresiones sobre las fiestas de octubre,
   6468.
   Una pequena nota en tus quince anos, 6469.
   La vista del diablo, 7201.
Cruz, David V.
   Caucus & Co. orients the East, 1354.
Cruz, Frank
   [Untitled drawing], 2372.
Cuellar, Jose
   Hispanic elders' needs, problems and access to
   public benefits and services, 255.
Culp, Robert Alan
   The Immigration and Naturalization Service and
   racially motivated questioning: does equal
   protection pick up where the Fourth

California ranchos: their Hispanic heritage,
1381.

Enguidanos, Miguel
Las mentiras que llegamos a creernos III,
7222.
Miles de veces canto el gallo, 5690.
Tomas, 5691.

Enslen, J.
INS enjoined from making vehicle stops on
basis of alienage alone, 6730.

Erana, Maria
Sobre el arte, la rebeldia y las fronteras,
568.

Eribes, Richard A.
Employment of women by cities in the
Southwest, 1613.

Ericksen, Charles
Wanted: Hispanics in the newsroom, 2312.

Escamilla, Rafael
Claudia [painting], 5238.

Escobar, Edward J.
Mexican revolutionaries and the Los Angeles
police: harassment of the Partido Liberal
Mexicano, 1907-1910, 1836.

Escobar, Ricardo
Gente de Caracas, 6481.

Esman, Milton J.
Two dimensions of ethnic politics: defense of
homelands, immigrant rights, 2895.

Espada, Martin
Book review of: BLACK HAIR, 772.
With Martin Espada, 450.

Esperanza, Tino
Corazon, the subject is mujeres, 5693.

Espinosa, Maria
Children, 1787.
Recuerdos, 5694.
Soledad, 6483.

Espinosa, Mary Lou
Cosas de ninos, 1788.

Espinoza, Freddy
A proposito de la salsa y su historia, 4920.

Espinoza, Sagrario
Un milagro, 7223.

Esquer, Frank E.
Montana, 5695.

Estrada, Javier
El amor, 6485.
Coco y su amigo coco, 7224.
Jose, 6486.
Nubes, 6487.
El pescado y las aguilas, 6488.
El pez espada y la langosta, 2068.
El rey bailarin, 6489.
Los sacrificios de un buen atleta, 6490.
El super Javier, 6491.
Todo es para todos, 5696.

Estrada, Larry
La pena que tengo, 5697.

Estrada, Leobardo F.
Demographic research on the Chicano
population, 6355.
Task force on employment and economic
well-being, 2765.

Estrada, Rosalio S.
Busco, 5698.
Desde al cabo al fin, 5699.
Sonar un sueno imposible: una pesadilla viva
en tinta lavable, 7225.
To dream an impossible dream or a living
nightmare in washable ink, 7226.

Estrada, William
The life and legend of Ernesto Galarza=La vida
y legado de Ernesto Galarza, 673.

Evans, James
From chaos to quality education. 480.
The voice in between, 2027.

Evans, Leonard A., et al.
Orienting psychotherapists to better serve low
income and minority patients, 4651.

Everett, D.E.
Book review of: LA FAMILIA, 935.

Eyman, R.K.
Place of residence by age, ethnicity, and

level of retardation of the mentally
retarded/developmentally disabled population
of California, 1385.

Eysturoy, Annie O.
EL DIABLO EN TEXAS: una historia popular a
traves de arquetipos y simbolos, 936.

Ezell, Howard
Why immigration reform passed=Porque fue
aprobada la reforma de inmigracion, 3785.

Facto, Robert
Moment at sundown, 5700.

Falcon, Angelo
Puerto Rican politics in urban America: an
introduction to the literature, 4325.

Farley, J.E.
Book review of: THE CHICANO EXPERIENCE, 937.
Book review of: THE ZOOT-SUIT RIOTS, 938.

Fausto, Lupe
Anoranzas de mi ninez, 6492.
Reminiscences of my childhood, 6493.

Faxon, R. Paul
Employer sanctions for hiring illegal aliens:
a simplistic solution to a complex problem,
137.

Ferguson, J.
Warrantless INS "farm checks" at migrant camps
properly enjoined, 3853.

Fernandez, Castor A.
Differences within the Hispanic market, 4479.

Fernandez, Celestino
Book review of: LA CLASE OBRERA EN LA HISTORIA
DE MEXICO: AL NORTE DEL RIO BRAVO (PASADO
INMEDIATO, 1930-1981), 939.

Fernandez, Celia
The biggest Hispanic fiesta in the USA, 1463.

Fernandez, Edward
The Hispanic foreign-born and the assimilation
experience, 397.

Fernandez, Roberta
Andrea, 7227.

Fernandez, Roberto G.
Origenes, 7228.

Fever, Jack
ADWEEK's honor roll: women to watch: Dolores
Valdes Zacky, 98.
Hispanic marketplace: the SICC sale: it is
indeed a Hallmark, 3374.

Fields, Alicia
Small but telling moments, 940.

Figoli, Haydee
Dos textos a proposito de la frontera, 1714.

Figueroa, Lupita S.
Un chiste, 7229.

Fimbres, Guadalupe
El anima milagrosa de El Tiradito, 6494.
The miraculous soul of el tiradito, 6495.

Finch, Mark S.
Book review of: CHICANO AUTHORS: INQUIRY BY
INTERVIEW, 941.

Fireman, Janet R.
Book review of: WATER IN THE HISPANIC
SOUTHWEST, 942.

Fischer, Dale
The 1982 Mexican peso devaluation and border
area employment, 1207.

Fishman, Joshua A.
Minority mother tongues in education, 600.
What is happening to Spanish on the U.S.
mainland?, 4074.

Fitch, Ed
Buying power bursts poverty-stricken image,
99.
Census bureau tries to clean up its act, 1506.
Paving way for national ad sales, 100.
Prime space available at low rates, 101.

Fitch, Yolanda Ruiz
Dietary change among migrant and nonmigrant
Mexican-American families in northern
California, 2130.

Fitzpatrick, Sherahe B., et al.
Do health care needs of Mexican-American and
Caucasian teens differ?, 4594.

Flores, Arturo C.
La literatura de Aztlan y su reconocimiento,

504.

El Teatro Campesino (1965-1986): algunas
orientaciones teoricas, 1278.

Flores, Estevan T.
1982 Simpson-Mazzoli immigration reform and
the Hispanic community, 3787.
Book review of: ILLEGAL ALIENS IN THE WESTERN
HEMISPHERE, 943.

Flores, Francisco
Cristeros, 6496.
Danzon, 7230.
Malaria, 7231.

Flores, Juan
Chicanos and the computer age: the best of
times, the worst of times, 1925.

Flores, Lauro
Book review of: EL PUEBLO: THE GALLEGOS
FAMILY'S JOURNEY 1503-1980, 944.

Flores, Lorenzo T.
Your turn=Su turno, 2831.

Floyd, Mary Beth
Language use and communicative behavior:
Hispanic bilinguals in the United States,
945.

Flynn, Ken
A triumph of diplomacy, 1221.

Foley, Patrick
Book review of: ALONG THE RIO GRANDE: PASTORAL
VISIT TO SOUTHWEST NEW MEXICO IN 1902, 190.

Foote, Cheryl
Book review of: IMAGES AND CONVERSATIONS, 947.

Ford, Theresa Y.
United States v. Hannigan: federal statute
used to prosecute torturers, 1837.

Forte, Dan
Los Lobos: Tex-Mex rock from East L.A., 706.

Foster, James C.
Book review of: LABOR IN NEW MEXICO: UNIONS,
STRIKES AND SOCIAL HISTORY SINCE 1881, 948.

Fradd, Sandra
Latin Americans at the university level:
implications for instruction, 3454.

Franco, Olga B.
Danza fatal, 6498.

Frank, Jerome P.
Problems of books en espanol, 1801.

Fraser, Laura
Old boycott, new battle, 1264.

Freiband, Susan J.
Book review of: THE IMMIGRANT WOMAN IN NORTH
AMERICA, 949.

Frias, Armando
[Graffiti], 3314.

Fricke, David
Los motivos del lobo, 4346.

Frisbie, William Parker
Marital instability trends among Mexican
Americans as compared to Blacks and Anglos:
new evidence, 1598.
Phenotype and life chances among Chicanos,
2269.

Frontain, Michel
Edmundo, 7233.

Fuss, Eduardo
Vivan las celebraciones, 1814.

Galarza, Ernesto
Platica con Galarza [interview], 1437.
Research and scholarly activity, 1760.

Galindo, Letticia
Perceptions of pachuquismo and use of
Calo/pachuco Spanish by various Chicana
women, 1599.

Galindo, Luis Alberto
El dios de la lluvia=RAIN GOD, 707.

Galindo, P.
USE: Hinojosa-Smith, Rolando R.

Galindo-Ramirez, Tina
Educacion monolingue: opresion o liberacion?,
178.

Gallardo, Hortencia Aguilar
La cita, 5701.
Conversacion por telefono, 5702.
Dulce sueno, 6499.
Eminente caminar, 5703.

Para mi triste padre, 5704.
Suspiro del alma, 5705.

Gallegos Douglas, Rosalie
Transition, 7234.

Galvez, Jose
[Untitled photographs], 5372.

Gamboa, Harry, Jr.
El artista chicano dentro y fuera de la
"corriente" artistica, 333.

Gambrell, Jamey
Texas: state of the art, 334.

Gann, Lewis H.
Latinos & the Catholic Church in America,
1496.

Ganster, Paul
Book review of: ECOLOGY AND DEVELOPMENT OF THE
BORDER REGION, 950.

Garcia, Alma
Journal review of: CRITICA: A JOURNAL OF
CRITICAL ESSAYS, 951.

Garcia, Art
Financing the corporate take-off, 149.

Garcia, Chris
Book review of: MUTUAL AID FOR SURVIVAL, 952.

Garcia, Ed
On red-haired girls and the greaser in me,
953.

Garcia, Herman S.
Ethnic minority students, admissions policies,
and academic support programs in
institutions of higher education, 18.

Garcia, Ignacio
Gracias a Dios por Christmas, 7235.
The republic, 7236.
Unfinished letter to Terry, 7237.

Garcia, Jesus
Multiethnic education: past, present, and
future, 2117.

Garcia, John A.
Book review of: AMERICA'S ETHNIC POLITICS,
231.
Book review of: AMERICA WITHOUT ETHNICITY,
215.
Book review of: RACE AND CLASS IN THE
SOUTHWEST: A THEORY OF INEQUALITY, 540.
Chicano political development: examining
participation in the "decade of Hispanics",
6308.
Chicano unemployment in the seventies, 2767.
Ethnic identity and background traits:
explorations of Mexican-origin populations,
3680.
The political integration of Mexican
immigrants: examining some political
orientations, 2132.

Garcia, John R.
Book reviews of: EL PUEBLO MEXICANO EN DETROIT
Y MICHIGAN and MATERIALS ON THE HISTORY OF
LATINOS IN MICHIGAN AND THE MIDWEST, 957.

Garcia, Julian S.
El viaje, 7238.

Garcia, Lionel G.
The sergeant, 7239.

Garcia, Mario T.
Book review of: A COMMUNITY UNDER SIEGE, 79.
Book review of: A COMMUNITY UNDER SIEGE, 80.
Book review of: DEVELOPMENT OF THE MEXICAN
WORKING CLASS NORTH OF THE RIO BRAVO: WORK
AND CULTURE AMONG LABORERS AND ARTISANS,
1600-1900, 960.
Book review of: FRAGMENTS OF THE MEXICAN
REVOLUTION, 961.
Book review of: LA FAMILIA, 962.
Book review of: POLITICAL AND ECONOMIC
MIGRANTS IN AMERICA, 963.
Book review of: POLITICAL AND ECONOMIC
MIGRANTS IN AMERICA, 964.
Book review of: THE STATE OF CHICANO RESEARCH
ON FAMILY, LABOR, AND MIGRATION: PROCEEDINGS
OF THE FIRST STANFORD SYMPOSIUM ON CHICANO
RESEARCH AND PUBLIC POLICY, 185.
Book review of: THEY CALLED THEM GREASERS,
966.
Bracero poetry of the 1940s: two samples,

1268.
Chicano historiography: a critique, 233.
[Letter to the editor about Mexicans, radicals
and communists in the United States], 234.
Garcia, Nasario
El cuento chicano visto por dentro y por
fuera, 147.
Garcia, Philip
Book review of: ACCULTURATION: THEORY, MODELS,
AND SOME NEW FINDINGS, 31.
Book review of: CHICANO CINEMA, 969.
Book review of: CHICANOS, CATHOLICISM, AND
POLITICAL IDEOLOGY, 970.
Book review of: EAST LOS ANGELES, 971.
Book review of: MEXICAN AMERICANS IN SCHOOL: A
DECADE OF CHANGE, 972.
Book review of: THE LATIN IMAGE IN AMERICAN
FILM, 3070.
Robert Davila, 2174.
Garcia, Philip J.
Ready to go on board?, 1356.
Garcia R., Roberto
Oda a Cucamonga, 1269.
Garcia, Raquelle
Brisa, 5707.
Creo, 5708.
Esa tarde, 5709.
Gracias, 5710.
Mar, 5711.
Sola, 5712.
Garcia, Richard
The ordeal of "Kiko" Martinez, 2037.
Garcia, Silvia
Ricardito, 7240.
Garcia, Steve
Language usage and status attainment of
Chicanos, 4077.
Garcia, Valerie M.
La egoista, 7241.
A good woman, 7242.
Mediocridad, 7243.
Una mujer buena, 7244.
Garcia y Griego, Manuel
Estimating the undocumented population in the
U.S., 6357.
Garcia-Ayvens, Francisco
Book review of: THE MEXICAN AMERICAN: A
CRITICAL GUIDE TO RESEARCH AIDS, 574.
Gardiol, Rita
Book review of: CELSO, 973.
Garibay, Ricardo
Una frontera de lujo y hambre [excerpt], 1223.
Garza, Hisauro A.
The "barrioization" of Hispanic faculty, 1870.
Garza, Jose P.
Carnaval de carcajadas, 7245.
Garza, Raymond T.
Protestant work ethic endorsement among Anglo
Americans, Chicanos and Mexicans: a
comparison of factor structures, 1920.
Gaspar, Tomas
Anthony Quinn Library receives collection=La
Biblioteca Anthony Quinn recibe coleccion,
291.
Gaviria, Moises
Nortriptyline kinetics in Hispanic and Anglo
subjects, 274.
Gaxiola, Blanca
Vamonos a ver al padre Antonio, 71.
Gettman, Dawn
Women, mental health, and the workplace in a
transnational setting, 1206.
Gibson, Guadalupe
Book review of: MENTAL HEALTH AND HISPANIC
AMERICANS: CLINICAL PERSPECTIVES, 561.
Gibson, Katherine
Situating migrants in theory, 4780.
Gil, Ana A.
Nortriptyline kinetics in Hispanic and Anglo
subjects, 274.
Gilb, Dagoberto
Birthday, 7246.
Gilbert, M. Jean
Alcohol consumption patterns in immigrant and

later generation Mexican American women, 32.
Gill, Eric K.
Notaries: clearing the air, 3788.
Gillespie, Francis P., et al.
Public policy, ethnic code, and Hispanic vital
statistics, 6663.
Gindin, Rona L.
Mexican, 6834.
Ginghofer, R.
[Mary Corralejo], 2376.
Glass. Jennifer
Household structure and labor-force
participation of Black, Hispanic, and white
mothers, 283.
Glazer, Mark
Traditionalization of the contemporary
legend--the Mexican-American example, 4186.
Gloria
Mi sabana, 6500.
Godoy, Irma
Cuanto te quiero, 5713.
Gracias senor, 5714.
Tilin y las cucarachas, 7247.
Goldman, Shifra
Arte chicano: iconografia de la
autodeterminacion, 335.
El arte hispano en Houston, 336.
El arte social de Domingo Ulloa, 370.
En medio de la tormenta de "Gronk", 337.
Escena de San Diego: texto y contexto, 338.
Hecho en Aztlan, 339.
Zarco Guerrero: tradicion y transformacion,
340.
Gollobin, Ira
No pasaran, 3789.
Gomez, Efrain A.
Folk healing among Hispanic Americans, 2146.
Gomez, Gerda E.
Folk healing among Hispanic Americans, 2146.
Gomez, Linda
Borderland: between Texas and Mexico, a river
and a troublesome future, 1224.
Gomez, Mercedes
Llanto y lluvia, 5715.
Gomez Pena, Guillermo
La cultura fronteriza: un proceso de
negociacion hacia la utopia, 1225.
Declaracion de principios de un teatro
bicultural, 6376.
Dialogos fronterizos, 341.
Nuevo continente artistico, 342.
Sobre el arte, la rebeldia y las fronteras,
568.
Gomez, Rogelio R.
Chente's American bar, 7248.
Functional man, 7249.
Gomez-Quinones, Juan
Objectives of Chicano studies, 1751.
September 16th: a historical perspective,
2256.
Gonzales, Juan
Quinto Festival de los Teatros Chicanos -
Primer Encuentro Latinoamericano, 3042.
San Francisco's Mission District: part I,
4351.
Gonzales, Juan L., Jr.
Book review of: FARM WORKERS, AGRIBUSINESS,
AND THE STATE, 975.
Gonzales, Martin S.
Dona Alquimina, 7250.
Libre al fin, 6501.
Mi amigo Arturo, 6502.
Gonzales, Phillip B.
Book review of: LATINOS IN THE UNITED STATES:
THE SACRED AND THE POLITICAL, 3.
Gonzales, Richard J.
Dirty work, 7251.
Gonzales-Berry, Erlinda
Book review of: BILINGUAL EDUCATION: A
SOURCEBOOK, 212.
Book review of: FACE, 978.
Enmienda de ingles en Nuevo Mexico, 2814.
Sensuality, repression, and death in Arturo
Isla's THE RAIN GOD, 979.

What are the objectives of Chicano studies?,
1749.

Guerrero Bubala, Julie
A mi esposo, 5752.
El amor, 5753.
Dios, 6514.

Guerrero, Dan
FALCON CREST: showcase for Hispanic talent,
52.
Tanya Sandoval: death-defying stunts are all
in her day's work, 53.

Guerrero, Martha
Toney Anaya: a man with convictions=Toney
Anaya: un hombre de conviccion, 249.

Guevara, Ruben
Richard "Cheech" Marin, 54.
Ruben Blades: music, love and revolution=Ruben
Blades: musica, amor y revolucion, 718.

Guhlman, Pat
The occupational position of employed Hispanic
females, 1667.

Guifarro, Josefa
Los dos gigantes, 5754.
Noche negra, 5755.

Gunderson, Kay
White does about-face on Simpson-Mazzoli,
3791.

Gunther, Jeffery W.
Illegal immigration from Mexico: effects on
the Texas economy, 2627.

Guppy, N.
Positional centrality and racial segregation
in professional baseball, 548.

Gurin, Patricia
Ethnic identity and bilingualism attitudes,
425.

Gurza, Esperanza
I AM JOAQUIN: speech act theory applied, 3292.

Gutierrez, Armando
Book reviews of: MEXICO-UNITED STATES
RELATIONS and UNITED STATES RELATIONS WITH
MEXICO: CONTEXT AND CONTENT, 996.

Gutierrez, Daniel M.
MAES Houston chapter sponsors 3rd annual
scholarship banquet, 482.

Gutierrez, Felix
House approves Higher Education Act
amendments, 2673.
Ralph Guzman remembered, 719.

Gutierrez, Gloria
Chicano news-man wins award, 3273.

Gutierrez, Jose Angel
Chicanos and Mexicans: under surveillance:
1940 to 1980, 81.

Gutierrez, Ramon A.
Book review of: THE CHICANO EXPERIENCE, 997.
Book review of: THE FOLKLORE OF SPAIN IN THE
AMERICAN SOUTHWEST, 998.
Honor ideology, marriage negotiation, and
class-gender domination in New Mexico,
1690-1846, 4520.
Unraveling America's Hispanic past: internal
stratification and class boundaries, 1715.

Gutierrez, Silvio G.
The odd couple, 55.
On wings of mercy, 269.

Gutierrez, Yolanda
Culture shock, 7254.

Guzman, Ralph
Bi-national policy questions generated by
Mexican school-age children who migrate
between the United States and Mexico, 1789.

Gynan, Shaw Nicholas
The influence of language background on
attitudes toward native and nonnative
Spanish, 276.

Hagle, C.
Book review of: THE IMMIGRANT WOMAN IN NORTH
AMERICA, 999.

H.-Aigla, Jorge
The maelstrom, 5756.
Mi mama Cecilia, 5757.
The power of the word, 5758.

Haines, Michael R.

Book review of: IMMIGRATION POLICY AND THE
AMERICAN LABOR FORCE, 1000.

Haley, Carmen Emilia
El camino, 5759.

Haley, Lindsey
Gronk y su inquietante concepto del arte, 374.
Una premiacion controvertida, 483.

Hall, Linda B.
The Arizona-Sonora border and the Mexican
revolution, 1910-1920, 320.
The United States-Mexican borders: historical,
political, and cultural perspectives, 227.

Halley, Lindsey
Pachuco boggie [sic], 1431.

Hamilton, Lawrence S.
A profile of the Mexican migrant and his
social and cultural adaptation to a federal
prison, 6413.

Hanes, Cecilia
El metro, 7255.
La sacerdotisa (artistas, dioses y filisteos),
7256.
El sueno ciclico, 6515.
Sueno del pasado (otra enigma), 6516.

Hardy-Fanta, Carol
Social action in Hispanic groups, 1908.

Haro, Robert P.
Book review of: CHICANO LITERATURE: A
REFERENCE GUIDE, 1002.
Book review of: CHICANO ORGANIZATIONS
DIRECTORY, 1003.
Book review of: HISPANIC AMERICAN VOLUNTARY
ORGANIZATIONS, 1004.

Harrell, Louis
The 1982 Mexican peso devaluation and border
area employment, 1207.

Harrington, James C.
GREASERS chronicles Texas racism, past and
present, 1005.

Hart, John M.
Book review of: TEXAS AND THE MEXICAN
REVOLUTION, 1006.

Haslanger, Phil
A rival to the gangs, 2248.

Hastings, D.W.
Book review of: MEXICAN AMERICAN FERTILITY
PATTERNS, 553.
Book review of: MEXICAN IMMIGRANTS AND MEXICAN
AMERICANS: AN EVOLVING RELATION, 1008.

Hawkins, Steve L.
A cat-mouse game gets bloody, 1212.

Hayakawa, S.I.
The English-only debate, 1383.

Hayes-Bautista, David Emmett
Book review of: THE HEALTH REVOLUTION IN CUBA,
1009.
Chicano health policy research, 6637.
Latino terminology: conceptual bases for
standardized terminology, 2900.

Hayghe, Howard
Married couples: work and income patterns,
3841.
Working mothers reach record number in 1984,
4028.

Hazen-Hammond, Susan
Vivan las celebraciones, 1814.

Heaney, Thomas W.
"Hanging on" or "gaining ground": educating
marginal adults, 91.

Hendershott, C.
Book review of: IMMIGRANTS AND THEIR CHILDREN
IN THE UNITED STATES: A BIBLIOGRAPHY OF
DOCTORAL DISSERTATIONS, 1885-1982, 1010.

Henkin, Alan B.
Seeking goodness of fit: measuring the
readability of bilingual learning materials,
602.

Henry, Charles
Rainbow coalitions in four big cities: San
Antonio, Denver, Chicago and Philadelphia,
781.

Hernandez, Alma
Amiga, 5760.
Amor mio, 5761.

Madre mia, 5762.

Un sueno nomas, 5763.

Hernandez, Ana Maria

Vivir para la humanidad, 6517.

Hernandez, Angel

[Acaso estaras algun dia conmigo...], 5764.

Paredes de pima, 5765.

[Untitled drawing], 2377.

[Untitled drawing], 1790.

[Untitled drawing], 2379.

Hernandez, Antonia A.

The politics of the new immigration law=La
politica de la nueva ley de inmigracion,
3793.

Hernandez, Beatriz Johnston

A dogged attack on immigration, 3826.

Hernandez, Jesus

Que es un hijo?, 5766.

Hernandez, Lucha Corpi

USE: Corpi, Lucha

Hernandez, Nicolas, Jr.

Olmeca, 8295.

Hernandez, Robert G.

Emerald eyes, 5767.

Hernandez, Roger E.

Why is everyone picking on Geraldo Rivera?,
721.

Hero, Rodney E.

Mexican Americans and urban politics: a
consideration of governmental structure and
policy, 1884.

Herrera, Alexandra

Desde Los Angeles con amor, 1604.

Herrera Duran, Patricia

Ernest Duran: la ultima despedida, 722.

Herrera, Frank

Infinito anhelo, 5768.

Herrera, Irma D.

The color barrier to full equality, 2282.

Mixed marriages: will the happiness last?,
3872.

Herrera, Yvonne R.

Professional development, 1605.

Herrera-Sobek, Maria

Book review of: AND OTHER NEIGHBORLY NAMES:
SOCIAL PROCESS AND CULTURAL IMAGE IN TEXAS
FOLKLORE, 5.

Book review of: CUBAN AMERICANS: MASTERS OF
SURVIVAL, 1012.

Introduction, 1606.

Literatura y sociedad: la problematica del
Chicano/Mexicano en los Estados Unidos a
traves de la obra literaria, 1013.

The politics of rape: sexual transgression in
Chicana fiction, 1607.

Herrick, R.L.

Book review of: CHICANOS, CATHOLICISM, AND
POLITICAL IDEOLOGY, 1014.

Heuer, Robert J.

To save a neighborhood, 2721.

Hewlett-Gomez, Michele

Book review of: THE ENGLISH-SPANISH
CONNECTION, 1015.

Heyer, Sandra

El pequeno Martin, 7257.

Hidalgo de la Riva, Teresa "Osa"

Friday the thirteenth 1980, 5769.

Grandmother's will, 5770.

Hidalgo, Margarita

On the question of "standard" versus
"dialect": implications for teaching
Hispanic college students, 642.

Hill, Frank

English as the official language?=El ingles
como idioma oficial, 2829.

Hill, Larry D.

Book review of: TEXAS AND THE MEXICAN
REVOLUTION, 1016.

Hinojosa-Smith, Rolando R.

Coming home II, 7258.

Griegos y romanos, 7259.

La realidad chicana se forjo con dos culturas,
723.

Tomas Rivera: remembrances of an educator and

a poet, 451.

Hiura, Barbara L.

Chicano ethnicity and aging [and critiques],
241.

Hoffman, Abraham

Book review of: A COMMUNITY UNDER SIEGE, 82.

Book review of: AN ILLUSTRATED HISTORY OF
MEXICAN LOS ANGELES: 1781-1985, 1018.

The controversial career of Martin Aguirre;
the rise and fall of a Chicano lawman, 150.

Holmes, John J.

Sentinel of tradition, 4831.

Up and away: ballooning fever grips America
and Latinos have caught the bug, 166.

Zarzuela lives again, 2261.

Holscher, Louis M.

Billboard charts and Chicanos, 1955-1974,
2267.

Holt, Patricia

Richard Rodriguez, 603.

Hopkins, Thomas

Book review of: BILINGUAL AND ESL CLASSROOMS:
TEACHING IN MULTICULTURAL CONTEXTS, 587.

Hoppe, Sue K.

Acculturation and alcohol use: drinking
patterns and problems among Anglo and
Mexican American male drinkers, 38.

Hopper, Richard H.

The road from Mexico's Jalapa to jalopies,
3896.

Horta, Gerardo

Emigrante, 3759.

Hough, Richard L.

Perceived self-other differences in life
events and mental health among Mexicans and
Americans, 286.

Howell-Martinez, Vicky

The influence of gender roles on political
socialization: an experimental study of
Mexican-American children, 424.

Huaco-Nuzum, Carmen J.

Half-moon bay, 2380.

Kachina #2, 2381.

Kachina #3, 2382.

Light my bulb, 2383.

Lollipop #1, 2384.

[Untitled drawing], 2385.

[Untitled drawing], 2386.

[Untitled drawing], 2387.

[Untitled drawing], 2388.

Huerta, Dolores

In the shadow of the eagle: Huerta=A la sombra
del aguila: Huerta, 141.

Huerta, Jorge

Book review of: GIVING UP THE GHOST, 1020.

Huerta, Margarita A.

La fe de nuestra gente, 6518.

Narraciones de dona Mariquita, 2069.

No perdio el control, 7261.

La zorra astuta y el coyote tonto, 7262.

Huez, Lupe

Miguel, 7263.

Se aleja, 5771.

Soledad en compania, 5772.

Huici, Alvaro

Cantando a las cosas sin cauce, 5773.

II [Y resulto que no eras un perro
ingrato...], 5774.

III [Cuando las tardes en que la
habitacion...], 5775.

V [Es aquel llanto que casi llega...], 5776.

Humm-Delgado, Denise

Hispanic adolescents and substance abuse:
issues for the 1980s, 2594.

Hispanics and group work: a review of the
literature, 4323.

Hunsaker, Alan C.

A behavioral/ecological model of intervention
alternatives with Chicano gang delinquents,
562.

Contingency management with Chicano
adolescents in a federal manpower program,
2769.

Institutionally-based research centers: the

Center for U.S.-Mexican Studies, 1510.
Mexican immigration patterns, 1021.
Hurtado, Aida
Book review of: WORK, FAMILY, SEX ROLES,
LANGUAGE, 541.
Ethnic identity and bilingualism attitudes,
425.
Feb. 24, Denver Aztlan, 5777.
Lupe Laputa, 7264.
Mexicans, Chicanos, Mexican Americans, or
pochos...Que somos? The impact of language
and nativity on ethnic labeling, 2901.
Mi padre el filosofo, 5778.
Midwife practices in Hildago County, Texas,
1608.
Hutter, Harriet S.
EL MILAGRUCHO: a linguistic commentary on a
pachuco text, 1689.
Igo, John N., Jr.
Los Pastores: a triple-tradition, 1809.
Inguanzo-Schleff, Dania
Loneliness among Mexican migrant children,
2225.
Instituto Genealogico e Historico Latino-Americano
Rootsearch: Aguilar: Echeverria, 143.
Rootsearch: Alarcon: Saavedra, 157.
Rootsearch: Alvarez: Covarrubias, 200.
Rootsearch: Aragon: Trujillo: Ruelas, 305.
Rootsearch: Bello: Ramirez: Lopez, 563.
Rootsearch: Beltran: Flores: Gomez, 564.
Rootsearch: Castro: Velasco, 1483.
Rootsearch: Cisneros: Perales: Zuniga, 1817.
Rootsearch: Cortes: Ulibarri, 2012.
Rootsearch: De La Garza: Pacheco, 2178.
Rootsearch: Duarte: Sandoval, 2597.
Rootsearch: Garcia: Chaves, 1539.
Rootsearch: Gonzalez: Febres-Cordero, 3001.
Rootsearch: Gutierrez, 3240.
Rootsearch: Guzman: Zamora, 3241.
Rootsearch: Jimenez (Ximenez): Olmo, 3242.
Rootsearch: Montoya: Galvo, 3186.
Rootsearch: Olivares: Yrigoyen: Montemayor,
3244.
Rootsearch: Ortega: Munoz, 3582.
Rootsearch: Padron: Machado, 3245.
Rootsearch: Patino: Herrera: Escobar, 2854.
Rootsearch: Peraza: Yanez, 3247.
Rootsearch: Rivera: Navarro: Salazar, 3248.
Rootsearch: Robles: Chacon: Molina, 1527.
Rootsearch: Rodriguez: Garza (De La Garza),
2177.
Rootsearch: Villalobos: Amador (Amado):
Ibarra, 207.
Isaacs, D.S.
Book review of: CONTEMPORARY CHICANA POETRY,
1023.
Isabel, Maria
Podador de algas, 5779.
Isgro, Francesco
Implementation of the legalization provisions
under the Immigration Reform and Control Act
of 1986, 3795.
Ismail, Amid L.
Prevalence of dental caries and periodontal
disease in Mexican American children aged 5
to 17 years: results from Southwestern
HHANES, 1982-83, 2202.
Isonio, Steven A.
Protestant work ethic endorsement among Anglo
Americans, Chicanos and Mexicans: a
comparison of factor structures, 1920.
Jackson, James S.
Book review of: UNDERSTANDING MINORITY AGING:
PERSPECTIVES AND SOURCES, 1024.
Jackson, Martha Elva
Inaudito destino, 7265.
Perdon y olvido, 7266.
Jacob, John
Book review of: SOUTHWEST TALES: A CONTEMPORY
COLLECTION, 196.
Jacobs, Carole
Bridging cultures, 1728.
Jacobson, Harold
Upward trend in expenditures continues, 105.

Jaramillo, Luis
A Modern Parable; Too Late Your Tears!!, 1498.
Javaid, Javaid I.
Nortriptyline kinetics in Hispanic and Anglo
subjects, 274.
Jenkins, Myra Ellen
Land tenure history of New Mexico, 3590.
Jensen, Joan M.
Crossing ethnic barriers in the Southwest:
women's agricultural extension education,
1914-1940, 138.
Jensen, Leif
The new immigration: implications for poverty
and public assistance utilization, 3592.
Jerez, Marco A.
Los olvidos, 7267.
Jimenez, Angel
Twenty years later: a Latino remembers 'Nam,
8156.
Jimenez, Francisco
Book review of: CHICANO DISCOURSE, 1026.
Jimenez, Luis
Cambia la imagen del latino en Hollywood,
2284.
En busca del talento latino, 56.
Jimenez, Ricardo
Understanding the culture and learning styles
of Hispanic students, 33.
Joe, Barbara E.
Safeguarding Spanish, 13.
Johnson, Richard
The California housewife who succeeds as brave
bullfighter, 409.
Jones, Maria
Las comadres, 72.
Jordan-Linn, Cynthia
Esqueda, 7268.
Jorgensen, Stephen R.
Family planning needs and behavior of Mexican
American women: a study of health care
professionals and their clientele, 34.
Josslin, Daniel
Books for the Spanish-speaking: si se puede,
4194.
JRST
Nos mudamos al centro, 5780.
Juana Alicia
La mujer del Rio Sumpul, 2389.
Kael, Pauline
The current cinema: siblings and cyborgs, 530.
Kahn, Robert
Oakdale prison: documenting the abuses, 181.
Kane, George D.
The entrepreneurial professional, 727.
Five blueprints for fueling growth, 1334.
Kane, Michael G.
"Touching" minorities, 106.
Kanellos, Nicolas
Book review of: HISPANICS IN THE UNITED
STATES: AN ANTHOLOGY OF CREATIVE WRITING,
1027.
Karnig, Albert K.
Employment of women by cities in the
Southwest, 1613.
Kastenbaum, Robert
Book review of: OLDER MEXICAN AMERICANS: A
STUDY IN AN URBAN BARRIO, 258.
Kelly, Peter
American bosses have jobs; Mexicans need work,
3763.
Kelly, William R.
Marital instability trends among Mexican
Americans as compared to Blacks and Anglos:
new evidence, 1598.
Kelzer, Pauline
La huerfana, 5781.
Kendall, Robert
Electric excitement at the 17th Annual Golden
Eagle Awards ceremony sponsored by Nosotros
at the Beverly Hilton Hotel, 485.
Keremitsis, Dawn
Del metate al molino: la mujer mexicana de
1910 a 1940, 3140.
Kerr, Louise A.

Book review of: THE LOS ANGELES BARRIO
1850-1890: A SOCIAL HISTORY, 1029.
Kesler, Lori
A-B benefits from regional approach, 107.
Kessel, Janet
Treasure hunt, 4829.
Kilgore, Julia
A risk taker, 301.
Kivisto, Peter
Book review of: ETHNICITY AND THE WORK FORCE,
1030.
Klor de Alva, J. Jorge
California Chicano literature and
pre-Columbian motifs: foil and fetish, 197.
Kochak, Jacque
Mexican menus invade American markets, 6836.
Koike, Dale April
Theoretical linguistics: code-switching in the
bilingual Chicano narrative, 644.
Koop, C. Everett
Plain talk on AIDS for Hispanic Americans, 47.
Korzenny, Felipe
Hispanic perceptions of communication
discrimination, 25.
Korzenny, Felipe, et al.
Cultural identification as predictor of
content preferences of Hispanics, 2093.
Kraly, Ellen Percy
Book review of: CLAMOR AT THE GATES, 1031.
Kramer, Mark
U.S.-Mexican border: life on the line, 1208.
Krampner, John
Raul Rodriguez, 486.
Krauth, Leland
Book review of: CHICANO POETRY: A CRITICAL
INTRODUCTION, 1032.
Kreisberg, Polly
[Untitled drawing], 2390.
Krivo, Lauren J.
Housing constraint and household complexity in
metropolitan America: Black and
Spanish-origin minorities, 778.
Kuner, Charles
Peer group counseling: applied psychology in
the high school, 1557.
Kwain, Constance
Searching for Hispanic talent, 57.
La Salle, Robin Avelar
Book review of: BILINGUALISM THROUGH
SCHOOLING, 667.
Lacayo, Carmela G.
Triple jeopardy among Hispanic elderly:
results from first national needs assessment
of older Hispanics, 259.
Laguna Diaz, Elpidio
Book review of: SMALL FACES, 1034.
Lamadrid, Enrique R.
El agua del aire, 5782.
Enemy way, 7269.
White woman's burden, 7270.
Lang, Carol
N.P.O., 6520.
Lang, Joan M.
Sizzler franchisee is going Cucos!, 2061.
Langum, David J.
Book review of: WATER IN THE HISPANIC
SOUTHWEST, 1035.
Lares Gaytan, Rosa Armida
Amistad (tu y yo), 5783.
Amor, 5784.
El dolor pensativo, 5785.
Mi pensamiento, 5786.
Larrazabal, John
Captain Zoom and his canine wonder, 1460.
Lau, Roger
Aurora, 5787.
En busca de un rey, 5788.
Estrella, 5789.
Indiferente, 5790.
Melinda, 5791.
Murmullo, 5792.
Valores, 5793.
Laviera, Tato
Bochinche bilingue, 5794.

Latero story, 5795.
Melao, 5796.
Viejo, 5797.
Lawhn, Juanita
USE: Luna-Lawhn, Juanita
Lawlor, William T.
Ethnic identification: shades of gray in
living color, 3688.
Lawrence, Gene
Grampa's car: a reminiscence, 2872.
Lawrence, Jennifer
TV signal expected to boost Houston market,
108.
Leal, Luis
Americo Paredes and modern Mexican American
scholarship, 2923.
Book review of: THE LEGEND OF LA LLORONA, 240.
Literary criticism and minority literatures:
the case of the Chicano writer, 452.
Leal, Rose
El diablo dienton, 6521.
LeAna, Thomas
Dorella Martinez, 19.
From dropout to role model: a VISTA
postscript, 1303.
LeBeau, James L.
Rape and racial patterns, 6737.
Lecca, Pedro J.
Cultural factors affecting the compliance of
older Mexican-Americans with hypertension
regimens, 260.
LeCompte, Mary Lou
Any Sunday in April: the rise of sport in San
Antonio and the Hispanic borderlands, 1536.
The Hispanic influence on the history of
rodeo, 1823-1922, 1537.
Lee, James F.
The relationship between decoding accuracy and
the reading achievement of monolingual
Spanish-speaking children, 2705.
Lefton, Doug
Culture a factor in treating Latino patients,
2094.
Some Latinos place trust in cures of folk
healers, 2147.
Leon, David Jess
The fifth class: a 19th century forerunner of
affirmative action, 127.
Hispanics, the fifth class, and the University
of California, 1870-72, 1867.
Leonard, Karen
A note on given names and Chicano
intermarriage, 3873.
Lerma, Martin
Lluvia, 5798.
Puro, 5799.
La vida, 5800.
Vive, 5801.
Levin, Gary
Publisher seeks to improve "image", 109.
Levin, Jeffrey S.
Religious attendance and subjective health,
6639.
LeVine, Sarah Ethel
The marital morality of Mexican women--an
urban study, 2962.
Levy, Deborah M.
By invitation only, 3796.
Lewis, Marvin A.
Chicano ethnicity and aging [and critiques],
241.
Lewis, Tom J.
Book review of: CONTEMPORARY CHICANA POETRY,
1037.
Leyva Corrales, Rosa
Boundless, 5802.
Conceptual, 5803.
Eros of four, 5804.
Licon, Lena
Socioeconomic and ethnic biases of pre-service
teachers, 7784.
Limon, Jose E.
La Llorona, the third legend of greater
Mexico: cultural symbols, women, and the

RESEARCH, 395.
Book review of: PARENTING MODELS AND MEXICAN
AMERICANS: A PROCESS ANALYSIS, 316.

Lynn, Donna
Of songs unsung, 5834.

Lyons, Joseph
The problem of exit criteria in second
language learners: California as a case
study, 2706.

Machado, Manuel A., Jr.
Book review of: A BIBLIOGRAPHY OF
MEXICAN-AMERICAN HISTORY, 582.

Machado, Melinda
Happy 500th, America, 3044.
Saying "no" to teenage sex, 2054.

Macias, Reynaldo Flores
Book review of: THE NEW BILINGUALISM: AN
AMERICAN DILEMMA, 645.
Disambiguating the Veltman trilogy, 1050.
Language studies and Chicanos, 4085.
Media research and the Chicano, 110.
Objectives of Chicano studies, 1751.

Maciel, David R.
Book review of: MEXICO AND THE UNITED STATES,
1051.

Madrid, Arturo
Book review of: HUNGER OF MEMORY, 1052.
Book review of: THE IMMIGRATION TIME BOMB,
1053.
Book reviews of: A DICTIONARY OF NEW MEXICO
AND SOUTHERN COLORADO SPANISH and TUNOMAS
HONEY, 1054.
Book reviews of: CLAMOR AT THE GATES and LATIN
JOURNEY, 512.
Letter to the Network, 2683.
Report to the Network, 2304.
Report to the Network, 3432.
Report to the Network, 2684.

Madrid, Vicente
National Latino Media Coalition, 129.

Madson, J. Diego
Demonio en el matrimonio, 73.

Maes, Jim
Latinos in high technology=Latinos en alta
tecnologia, 2791.

Magallan, Rafael J.
1983-84 NAEP data raises questions regarding
the school experiences of language minority
children, 604.
Community college update, 1389.
Hispanic organizations concerned with higher
education, 216.

Magana, Ester P.
Down payments, 7283.

Magiera, Marcy
New arrivals find warm welcome as consumers,
1963.

Malandrone, Gail
[Untitled painting], 5242.

Malaspina, Ann
The city is my canvas, 376.

MALDEF
USE: Mexican American Legal Defense and
Education Fund (MALDEF)

Maldonado, Herlinda
El muchacho que no creia en Santo Claus, 7284.
Un paseo en el bosque, 6527.
Pintura de la guerra, 6528.

Maldonado, Lionel A.
Book review of: BORDER PERSPECTIVES: ON THE
US/MEXICO RELATIONSHIP, 1056.

Maldonado, Margarita
Acculturative stress and specific coping
stategies among immigrant and later
generation college students, 36.

Mancias, Ossie
The brown eyed son=El hijo de ojos cafe, 5835.

Manjarre, Graciela
El viaje de Miguelito, 7285.

Manning, Winston, et al.
Book review of: MINORITIES IN AMERICAN HIGHER
EDUCATION: RECENT TRENDS, CURRENT PROSPECTS
AND RECOMMENDATIONS, 402.

Mantiega, Victoria

Aureola de miseria, 6529.

Manuel, Ron C.
Book review of: OLDER MEXICAN AMERICANS: A
STUDY IN AN URBAN BARRIO, 263.

Marambio, Gonzalo
From San Antonio to Paris: Tex-Mex food
conquers the French, 1336.

Marcos, Luis R.
Book review of: MENTAL HEALTH AND HISPANIC
AMERICANS: CLINICAL PERSPECTIVES, 1059.

Marcus, Alfred C.
Smoking behavior among Hispanics: a
preliminary report, 6640.

Mares, Antonio
El coyote: between two cultures, 585.

Mares, E.A.
[Bajo la luna llena...], 5836.
Chasing the bogeyman in Tres Pistolas Canyon,
5837.
The fiesta of life: impression of Paulo
Friere, 507.
Homenaje a Antonio Machado, 4414.
Myth and reality: observations on American
myths and the myth of Aztlan, 508.
A napkin poem, 5839.
Question, 5840.
Sobre una foto de tres chicanas, 5841.
Some reflections in the desert, 5842.

Mares, Renee
Ernest Duran: la ultima despedida, 722.

Margolis, Eric
Tending the beets: campesinas and the Great
Western Sugar Company, 1645.

Marin, Christine
La Asociacion Hispano-Americana de Madres y
Esposas: Tucson's Mexican American women in
World War II, 393.
Book review of: OJO DE LA CUEVA, 1060.
Book review of: WHERE SPARROWS WORK HARD,
1061.

Marin, Gerardo, et al.
Development of a short acculturation scale for
Hispanics, 35.

Marisabel
Es cosa de inspiracion, 6530.
El padre y el joven mapuche, 7286.

Mariscal, George
Alejandro Morales in utopia, 4266.

Mark, Samuel
Dia de la Raza deserves wide-scoped
celebration, 2232.

Markides, Kyriakos S.
Religious attendance and subjective health,
6639.

Marquez, Antonio
Richard Rodriguez's HUNGER OF MEMORY and the
poetics of experience, 464.

Marquez Off, Maria
Vigil, 5843.

Marroquin de Hernandez, Celina
No me llames maldito, 7287.
Pepe, 7288.
Resultates mujer, 5844.

Marsh, Betsa
Diversidad de valores en Proctor & Gamble,
1449.
Proctor & Gamble values diversity, 1450.

Marshall, Dale Rogers
Black and Hispanic power in city politics: a
forum, 775.
Protest is not enough: a theory of political
incorporation, 776.

Martin, Frederick N.
A children's Spanish word discrimination test
for non-Spanish-speaking children, 1782.

Martin, Jeanne
Cancer mortality among Mexican Americans and
other whites in Texas, 1969-80, 1415.

Martin, Laura
Language form and language function in ZOOT
SUIT and THE BORDER: a contribution to the
analysis of the role of foreign language in
film, 1203.

Martin, Patricia Preciado

Dias de mas, dias de menos (days of plenty, days of want), 7289.
Tierra a tierra, 7290.

Martin, William
Application of competency-based criteria to bilingual-bicultural education, 598.

Martinez, Alejandro M.
Book review of: HISPANIC NATURAL SUPPORT SYSTEMS: MENTAL HEALTH PROMOTIONS PERSPECTIVES. 1063.

Martinez, Angelina S.
For the memories, 5845.
La montana majestuosa, 7291.

Martinez, Beverly Ann
Book review of: THE MOTHS AND OTHER STORIES, 1064.

Martinez, Carmen
Madre, 5846.
Un mensaje de El Salvador, 2732.
Mother, 5848.

Martinez, Daniel C.
Field gossip, 5849.
La gran puta, 5850.
The lost dance, 5851.
El menudero, 5852.
Mi perro agringado, 5853.
Polvos de Laredo, 5854.
Sentado pensando en la filosofia, 5855.
El viejo original, 5856.

Martinez, David A.
The nightmare of Kiko Martinez, 2038.

Martinez, Eliud
Book review of: HISTORY, CULTURE, AND SOCIETY, 1065.

Martinez, Elizabeth
A decade of repression: update on the "Kiko" Martinez case, 1721.

Martinez, Ferdinand
[This is Debra...(drawing)], 2392.

Martinez, Joe
La flor, 5857.

Martinez, Jose
Juan Ladron, 2070.
Please disregard this notice if full payment has been made, 74.

Martinez, Julio A.
Book review of: BILINGUAL BOOKS IN SPANISH AND ENGLISH FOR CHILDREN, 620.

Martinez, Margarita
Pagaron justos por pecadores, 7292.

Martinez, Noemi
[Time will tell you when to start...], 5858.

Martinez, Ramon E.
Cantinflas puppet, 5859.
The emperor of helados, 5860.

Martinez, Raquel A.
Un nino y un milagro, 7293.

Martinez, Ruben
Race, gender and self-esteem among youth, 1921.

Martinez, Sue
[Woman (drawing)], 2393.

Martinez, Thomas M.
Chicanismo, 1677.

Martinez, Walter
A deep cultural heritage enriches American society, 6282.

Martin-Rodriguez, Manuel M.
El sentimiento de culpa en RETO EN EL PARAISO de Alejandro Morales, 4268.

Masnik, Ruth
Benefits of long-term group therapy for disadvantaged Hispanic outpatients, 2910.

Massey, Douglas S.
Do undocumented migrants earn lower wages than legal immigrants? New evidence from Mexico, 2773.
Processes of Hispanic and Black spatial assimilation, 398.

Matta, Benjamin
Book review of: HISPANICS IN THE U.S. ECONOMY, 1067.

MAYO, University of Texas at Austin
Student perspectives on Mexican/American studies, 1754.

Mazon, Mauricio
Report to the Network, 732.

McBride, P.W.
Book review of: IMMIGRANT WOMEN IN THE LAND OF DOLLARS, 1068.

McCoy, Matilde
La sonrisa de Ivan, 6531.

McCoy, Michelle
[Untitled drawing], 2394.
[Woman and man (drawing)], 2395.
[Woman (drawing)], 2396.

McCracken, Ellen
Book review of: CHICANO THEATER: THEMES AND FORMS. 1069.

McDermott, Douglas
Book review of: CHICANO THEATER: THEMES AND FORMS, 1070.

McDowell, John H.
U.S. immigration reform: policy issues and economic analysis, 3757.

McIlroy, Christopher
Book review of: IN DEFENSE OF LA RAZA, 518.

McKanna, Clare V.
The San Quentin prison pardon papers: a look at file no. 1808, the case of Francisco Javier Bonilla, 85.

McKesson, Jon
El jardin [drawing], 2397.
Sunday afternoons [drawing], 2398.
[Untitled drawing], 2399.

McMenamin, Jerry
Language deficits in a bilingual child with cerebral cysticercosis, 647.

McNeely, Dave
Hispanic power at the polls, 435.

McNeil, John S.
Cultural factors affecting the compliance of older Mexican-Americans with hypertension regimens, 260.

McNeill, Daniel
The fifth class: a 19th century forerunner of affirmative action, 127.
Hispanics, the fifth class, and the University of California, 1870-72, 1867.

Meaney, Mark
El avaro y su oro, 6532.
La gitana, 7294.
La tienda de ropa vieja, 7295.

Means-Ybarra, Ricardo
After the divorce, 5861.
East L.A., 5862.
A poem to be read before morning, 5863.

MEChA - University of Texas at El Paso
Student perspectives on Mexican/American studies, 1754.

MEChA, Cal State Long Beach
The role of the Chicano student, 1755.

Medina, Beatriz
Clarisa's experience, 7296.
Mi hermanito Pablito, 6533.

Medina, Carlos
Que piensa el nino, 5864.

Medina, David
America's Hispanic Theater Olympics, 59.

Medina Garcia, Jesus
A una amazona, 6534.
Cronica, 6535.
Lencho, 7297.
Las montanas de Tucson, 5865.
El prieto, 7298.
Viendo llover en Tucson, 6536.

Medina, Jesus G.
USE: Medina Garcia, Jesus

Medina, Marcello, Jr.
Factorial validity of the Cooperative Preschool Inventory for English- and Spanish-speaking Hispanic children, 1979.

Medrano, Lourdes
El amor, 5866.
Recuerdos, 5867.

Meier, Matt S.
Book review of: IN DEFENSE OF LA RAZA, 519.
Book review of: THE MEXICAN AMERICAN

EXPERIENCE: AN INTERDISCIPLINARY ANTHOLOGY, 204.

Mejia, Gabriella S.
    "Ni he tenido tiempo para mi:" entrevista con Gabriella S. Mejia, 467.

Mejias Rentas, Antonio
    Luis Valdez y su Teatro Campesino de nuevo en L.A., 3665.

Mejias-Rivera, Ann E.
    Steven Perez of Xerox, 2796.

Meketa, Charles
    Heroes or cowards? A new look at the role of native New Mexicans at the Battle of Valverde, 551.

Meketa, Jacqueline
    Heroes or cowards? A new look at the role of native New Mexicans at the Battle of Valverde, 551.

Melendez, Moises F.
    Amor sincero, 5868.

Melendez, Pablo
    Happy Thanksgiving, 733.

Mellado, Carmela
    Adriana Ocampo, 4956.
    Dr. George Castro: research scientist with IBM, San Jose, 734.
    Hispanic women as leaders: expanding the stereotypes that bind us, 1621.
    Mitch Maidique, 735.
    SHPE co-founder Rodrigo T. Garcia, 736.

Melson, Robert
    Book review of: ETHNIC GROUPS AND THE STATE, 1074.

Melville, Margarita B.
    Book review of: FROM INDIANS TO CHICANOS, 1075.

Mena, Francisco
    Acculturative stress and specific coping stategies among immigrant and later generation college students, 36.

Menard, Lupita
    Los suenos, 6537.
    Vio al diablo, 6538.

Mendes de Leon, Carlos F., et al.
    Alcohol consumption and physical symptoms in a Mexican American population, 171.

Mendez Aldecoa, Sarita
    Caminante, 5869.

Mendez-M., Miguel
    Anoranza, 5870.
    Arizona, 5871.
    Arizona, 5872.
    The baby chicks, 7299.
    El bolerito bilingue, 7300.
    El bolerito bilingue, 7301.
    Dona Emeteria, 7302.
    Dona Emeteria, 7303.
    En torno a la poesia, 5873.
    Genesis de la palabra, 5874.
    Genesis of the word, 5875.
    Huachusey, 2071.
    Imaginary workshop, enter, 5876.
    In search of poverty, 5877.
    Introduccion, 4312.
    Introduccion, 2649.
    Introduccion, 2716.
    Introduction, 4313.
    Introduction, 2650.
    Introduction, 2717.
    Luna, 5878.
    Moon, 5879.
    El moro, 7305.
    Moro, 7306.
    Nostalgia, 5880.
    Observaciones sobre la literatura fronteriza, 1236.
    Los pollitos, 7307.
    Que no mueran los suenos, 7308.
    El rio y el poeta, 5881.
    El rio y la vida, 5882.
    The river and the poet, 5883.
    The river of life, 5884.
    Sahuaros, 5885.
    Sonora de mis amores, 5886.

Taller de imagenes pase, 5887.

Mendez-Negrete, Josie
    Daily struggle, 5888.

Mendoza, Agapito
    Barrio slang has value as communications tool, 1690.

Mendoza, Lupe
    Porque lo podemos hacer--a poco no?, 465.

Merino, Barbara J.
    The problem of exit criteria in second language learners: California as a case study, 2706.

Mexican American Legal Defense and Education Fund (MALDEF)
    Task force on civic identity and political participation, 2736.

Meyers, C.E.
    Place of residence by age, ethnicity, and level of retardation of the mentally retarded/developmentally disabled population of California, 1385.

Michel
    Infinito, 5889.
    Lienzo de alivio, 7309.

Middleman, Irene
    Eppie Archuleta, 315.

Miguelez, Armando
    En la plaza hay fiesta, 5890.
    Nino muerto, 5891.
    Viaje, 5892.

Miley, Scott L.
    Let the games begin, 5256.

Miller, Beth
    Book review of: WOMAN OF HER WORD: HISPANIC WOMEN WRITE, 1076.

Miller, Darlis A.
    Los Pinos, New Mexico: civil war post on the Rio Grande, 3600.

Miller, Robert Ryal
    Book review of: THE MEXICAN FRONTIER 1821-1846, 1077.

Mills, Kay
    Gloria Molina, 737.

Milner, Clyde A.
    Book review of: BORDER HEALING WOMAN: THE STORY OF JEWEL BABB, 1078.

Milo, Albert J.
    Book review of: HISTORY, CULTURE, AND SOCIETY, 1079.

Mindiola, Tatcho, Jr.
    Film review of: THE BALLAD OF GREGORIO CORTEZ, 522.

Minsky, Alyce
    California State University at Los Angeles, 1875.

Miranda, Gloria E.
    Book review of: CHICANOS IN CALIFORNIA, 1080.
    Hispano-Mexican childrearing practices in pre-American Santa Barbara, 1792.

Miranda, Victoria
    Sebastian del bio bio, 5893.

Mirande, Alfredo
    Chicano sociology: a critique and evaluation of prevailing theoretical perspectives, 7524.

Mireles, Oscar
    The family of doctors, 5894.

Mohr, Nicholasa
    Puerto Rican writers in the United States, Puerto Rican writers in Puerto Rico: a separation beyond language, 454.

Molina, Ida
    Book review of: SMALL FACES, 1081.

Molina, Maria J.
    Angelica, 7310.
    Dime, 5895.
    Madrecita linda, 5896.
    Pidiendo milagro, 5897.
    Remordimiento, 7311.
    Tu recuerdo, 7312.
    Vida, 5898.

Molina, Robert M.
    Relative lower extremity length in Mexican American and in American Black and white

Recuerdos de una noche inolvidable, 6548.
National Association of Latino Elected and
    Appointed Officials
    The Hispanic vote, 6313.
National Commission for Employment Policy
    Hispanics and jobs: barriers to progress,
    2774.
National Council of La Raza (NCLR)
    Career information and Hispanic students,
    1452.
Nava Monreal, David
    Benito Garcia, 7323.
    A matter of dignity, 7324.
Navarro, Amada
    Tardes de platicas, 6549.
Navarro, Eleane
    Un insecto anonimo, 5933.
Navarro, Patricia M.
    Believe, 5934.
    Creer, 5935.
    I believe in=Creo en, 5936.
    Jesu Cristo=Jesus Christ, 5937.
    The Lord nuestro padre, 5938.
    Nuestro senor Jesucristo, 6550.
    Tu gran valor, 5939.
Neff, James Alan
    Acculturation and alcohol use: drinking
    patterns and problems among Anglo and
    Mexican American male drinkers, 38.
Neibel, Barbara A.
    Health care utilization: the case of the
    Mexican-American, 2097.
Nelson, Candace
    The structuring of Hispanic ethnicity:
    historical and contemporary perspectives,
    2098.
Nelson, F. Howard
    Issues in state funding for bilingual
    education, 607.
Nervo, Gibian
    Mi viejo hombre, 5940.
Newquist, Deborah
    The health care barrier model: toward
    analyzing the underutilization of health
    care by older Mexican-Americans, 264.
Nguyen, Liem T.
    Seeking goodness of fit: measuring the
    readability of bilingual learning materials,
    602.
Nieto, Margarita
    Fronteras en la obra de Carlos Castaneda,
    1475.
Nieto, Sonia
    Book review of: BILINGUAL EDUCATION: A
    SOURCEBOOK, 213.
    Book review of: BILINGUAL-BICULTURAL
    EDUCATION: AN ANNOTATED BIBLIOGRAPHY,
    1936-1982, 526.
    Book review of: BILINGUALISM AND
    MINORITY-LANGUAGE CHILDREN, 664.
    Book review of: BILINGUAL EDUCATION FOR
    HISPANIC STUDENTS IN THE UNITED STATES, 625.
    Book review of: BILINGUAL AND ESL CLASSROOMS:
    TEACHING IN MULTICULTURAL CONTEXTS, 588.
    Book review of: BILINGUALISM THROUGH
    SCHOOLING, 668.
    Book review of: BILINGUAL MULTICULTURAL
    EDUCATION AND THE PROFESSIONAL: FROM THEORY
    TO PRACTICE, 538.
    Past accomplishments, current needs: la lucha
    continua, 608.
    Who's afraid of bilingual parents?, 609.
Nigro, Kristen, trans.
    Nostalgia, 5880.
Noeth, Louise Ann
    Fast food for thought, 1338.
Noriega, Carlos Peralta
    Alma, 5942.
    Cadenas voluntarias, 5943.
    Declaracion, 5944.
    El descuido, 5945.
    Fantasia, 5946.
    Inseguridad, 5947.
Norris, Eileen

Print suffers in tale of two languages, 114.
Novick, Michael
    "English only" gets go-ahead in California,
    2823.
    English-only crusade threatens bilingual
    program, 2824.
    INS makes a bad Simpson-Rodino law worse,
    3799.
Novoa, Juan Bruce
    USE: Bruce-Novoa, Juan
Nuessel, Frank H., Jr.
    Book review of: SPANISH IN THE UNITED STATES:
    SOCIOLINGUISTIC ASPECTS, 209.
Nunez, Rene
    Criteria for employment of Chicano studies
    staff, 1756.
Ockerman, Janet D.
    Book review of: MEXICAN-AMERICANS AND THE
    MASS-MEDIA, 1095.
O'Donnell, Patrick J.
    A preliminary report on the incidence of
    gestational diabetes in a Hispanic migrant
    population, 2236.
O'Grady, Kevin E.
    Sexuality among Mexican Americans: a case of
    sexual stereotyping, 133.
O'Hagen, Linda
    [Woman], 2400.
Ohnesorgen, Jose
    Como era Tucson, 6551.
    Con los gritos, 5948.
    Con los tragos vive, 5949.
    Cuando no te conocen, 5950.
    El maton, 5951.
Olarte, Silvia W.
    Benefits of long-term group therapy for
    disadvantaged Hispanic outpatients, 2910.
Olivares, Julian
    Hispanic art in the United States: thirty
    contemporary painters & sculptors, 345.
    Sandra Cisneros' THE HOUSE ON MANGO STREET and
    the poetics of space, 1828.
    Self and society in Tino Villanueva's SHAKING
    OFF THE DARK, 4271.
Olivares, Yvette
    The sweatshop: the garment industry's reborn
    child, 3218.
Olivas, Eduardo
    Lagrimas de verdad, 5952.
    Los machos no lloran, 7325.
    Tears of truth, 5953.
Olivas, Linda
    Flor de rosa, 5954.
Olivas, Michael A.
    The condition of Hispanic education, 2305.
    Task force on education, 2653.
Olivera, Mercedes
    The new Hispanic women, 201.
Olmedo Williams, Irma
    Functions of code-switching as a communicative
    strategy in a Spanish-English bilingual
    classroom, 610.
Opdahl, Martha Donovan
    Esos malditos pafaros!, 7326.
Opitz, Wolfgang
    Marital instability trends among Mexican
    Americans as compared to Blacks and Anglos:
    new evidence, 1598.
Ordaz, Carmel
    [Untitled drawing], 2401.
    [Untitled drawing], 2402.
    [Untitled drawing], 2403.
    [Untitled drawing], 2404.
Orihuela, Rodolfo
    Por unas plumas, 7327.
    El rio, 7328.
Ornelas, Yolanda
    Determined to be acknowledged, 428.
Ornstein-Galicia, Jacob
    Bilingualism, bilingual education, and
    language contact: the agony, the rewards--or
    how to unravel Babel, 611.
    Chicano Calo: description and review of a
    border variety, 1240.

Oropesa, Maria
    I am thinking of you mother, 5955.
Orosco, Juan Ishi
    Winter chant [painting], 5243.
Orozco, Aurora E.
    Un dia en la pisca de algodon, 740.
    El piscador, 5956.
Orozco, Cynthia
    Chicana labor history: a critique of male
        consciousness in historical writing, 1628.
Orozco, Rafaela
    Asi es, 6552.
Ortega, Koryne
    7 weeks mature, 5957.
    His mute mind, 5958.
    In S.F., 5959.
    Inside her inside, 5960.
    Jorje, 5961.
    Just one ear, 5962.
    Just step outside, 5963.
    Keeping this in mind, 5964.
    Leather, 5965.
    Martin, 5966.
    Minnie, 5967.
    Parting from cultivation, 5968.
    Poor places, 5969.
    Quake. Chance. Gift. Mexico, 5970.
    Searching, 5971.
    To sistas alike, 5972.
Ortega-Butler, Norma
    Una caminata en el anochecer, 5973.
    Carta a una hija esperando su segundo bebe,
        6553.
    Desde la ventana, 5974.
    Dos pisapapeles en el mar, 6554.
    Marcelina, 7329.
    Padre Anselmo, 7330.
    La sociedad perfecta: restablecer la
        conciencia, 6555.
Ortiz, Francisco
    La cultura chicana, la cultura amenazada, 243.
Ortiz, Sara
    La oida, 6556.
Ortiz Vasquez, Pedro
    Las cartas de Martin Flores, 7331.
    My father/my mother, 5975.
    Where have we America, 5976.
Ortiz, Vilma
    Book review of: FAMILY INSTALLMENTS: MEMORIES
        OF GROWING UP HISPANIC, 1097.
    Educational attainment among Hispanic youth
        and non-Hispanic white youth, 21.
Ortiz-Muraida, Thelma
    [Untitled drawing], 2405.
Ospina, Sonia
    El recibimiento, 7332.
Otheguy, Ricardo
    Book review of: BILINGUALISM THROUGH
        SCHOOLING, 652.
Oxford-Carpenter, R., et al.
    Projections of number of limited English
        proficient (LEP) persons to the year 2000,
        612.
Pachon, Harry
    Allaying the fears of becoming a U.S. citizen,
        4968.
    An overview of citizenship in the Hispanic
        community, 3739.
Padilla, Amado M.
    Acculturative stress and specific coping
        stategies among immigrant and later
        generation college students, 36.
Padilla, Eligio R.
    Sexuality among Mexican Americans: a case of
        sexual stereotyping, 133.
Padilla, Ernesto
    Premio dos reales, 5977.
Padilla, Genaro Miguel
    The anti-romantic city in Chicano fiction, 46.
Padilla, Raymond V.
    A general framework for action in Chicano
        higher education, 321.
Padilla, Steve
    Lessons to be learned from a playful hoax,

2875.
    The mad mad world of Sergio Aragones, 306.
Padre, Chico
    Lathe biosas, 5978.
    Welcome to L.A., 5979.
Paikoff, Mark
    National Science Foundation Programs for
        minority engineers, students, and graduate
        students, 3098.
Palacios, Arnoldo
    Las ventanas parpadean, 5980.
Palma, Mauricio
    Abuelita, 7333.
Palomo, Juan R.
    Ernest Garcia, 303.
Panas, Katia
    The forgotten people, 3156.
    Postsecondary retention and graduation:
        strategies for change, 399.
Papademetriou, Demetrios G.
    Book review of: IMMIGRATION POLICY AND THE
        AMERICAN LABOR FORCE, 1099.
Paredes, Josefina
    Descansa, 5981.
    En la primavera, 5982.
    Una flor y tus recuerdos, 5983.
    Por un disimulo, 5984.
Paredes, Raymund A.
    Book review of: CUENTOS CHICANOS: A SHORT
        STORY ANTHOLOGY, 245.
    Book review of: THE LOST LAND, 1101.
    Book review of: THEY CALLED THEM GREASERS,
        1102.
    Book review of: TO THE HALLS OF THE
        MONTEZUMAS, 1103.
    Review essay: recent Chicano writing, 1477.
Parlee, Lorena M.
    The impact of United States railroad unions on
        organized labor and government policy in
        Mexico (1880-1911), 2246.
Parra, Antonio
    El tercer caiman, 6135.
Parra, Elena
    Esperanza de un sueno, 5985.
    La huella del pueblo chicano, 5986.
    El nino triste, 5987.
    El nuevo dia, 5988.
    Por que?, 5989.
    La soledad, 5990.
    Suenos, 5991.
Parra, Filiberto
    A diario al caer el alba, 5992.
    La soledad, 5993.
Parra, Idolina
    Me prometiste, 5994.
    Por eso te quiero, 5995.
Parra, Mauricio
    [...de la savia mar universal sendero...],
        5996.
Pasas
    Reflexiones, 2407.
    [Untitled drawing], 2408.
Pascual, Jose Elias
    A hope for Micheal [sic]=Una esperanza para
        Miguel, 1416.
PASO, Texas A and I University
    Student perspectives on Mexican/American
        studies, 1754.
Passel, Jeffrey S.
    Estimating the number of undocumented aliens,
        1508.
Pastoriza, Benito
    Cancion en no menor, 5997.
    Las cicatrices dulces, 5998.
    Danza de palabras, 5999.
Pavon, Juan Alberto
    La historia de mis munequitos, 7334.
Paynter, Earlene Tash
    Articulation skills of Spanish-speaking
        Mexican-American children: normative data,
        26.
Pazos, Antonio
    [340 W. Simpson drawing], 2409.
    El cholo, 2410.

form of a pair), 1947.

Pena, Margarita
    Apuntes para un retrato chicano (I), 379.
    Apuntes para un retrato chicano (II), 380.
Pena, Martin
    Bueno asi es la vida...la vida sigue, 7335.
Pena, Raymundo
    Tornado disaster tests mettle of Texas
        Latinos, 2758.
Penalosa, Fernando
    Book review of: BILINGUALISM AND LANGUAGE
        CONTACT: SPANISH, ENGLISH AND NATIVE
        AMERICAN LANGUAGES, 537.
    Book review of: SPANISH IN THE UNITED STATES:
        SOCIOLINGUISTIC ASPECTS, 210.
Peralta, Gloria
    Vamonos, 6558.
Perches, Ana
    Erase una tez... hez, bestia, un ajedrez,
        7336.
    Te amare hasta que las flores comiencen a
        marchitarse, 7337.
Perea, Patricia
    Acculturation and alcohol use: drinking
        patterns and problems among Anglo and
        Mexican American male drinkers, 38.
Perea, Robert L.
    Trip to Da Nang, 7338.
Perez, Emma
    Higher education organizations, 2687.
    Higher education organizations, 2688.
    Higher education organizations, 322.
    Higher education organizations, 1886.
    Higher education organizations, 2691.
    Institutionally-based research centers: the
        Stanford Center for Chicano Research, 6807.
    Networks, 1632.
    Report to the Network, 2693.
    Research centers, 1765.
    Research centers, 1509.
    Research centers, 1517.
    Research centers, 3516.
    Research centers, 6812.
    Research centers, 1310.
Perez, Joel Oseas
    EL NORTE: imagenes peyorativas de Mexico y los
        Chicanos, 3061.
Perez, Maria
    Cosas de la vida, 7339.
    La momia, 7340.
    Que es el amor, 6002.
    Recuerdos, 6003.
    Rumores, 6004.
Perez, Renato E.
    As American as babalu, 39.
    Badge of Hispanic pride, 1295.
    Book review of: GENEALOGICAL RECORDS IN TEXAS,
        1107.
    Book review of: LA FRONTERA: THE U.S. BORDER
        WITH MEXICO, 1108.
    The business of Hispanics, 89.
    Chicago: Hispanic melting pot, 1400.
    A governor named Martinez, 743.
    Hispanics in uniform, 4799.
    Skydiving daredevils, 3271.
    The United States Constitution: an inspiration
        to Latin America, 1949.
    Who are the Hispanic heroes?, 3901.
Perez-Erdelyi, Mireya
    With Martin Espada, 450.
Perkins, Claranne
    We the minorities of CASE: a special survey of
        minorities working in institutional
        advancement, 1453.
Perry, Charles E.
    Book review of: CHICANO LITERATURE: A
        REFERENCE GUIDE, 1109.
Peters, Jose
    Los antifaces y la cara verdadera, 7341.
    Los mojaditos regresan a Mexico, 6559.
    Las tres bolitas de oro, 7342.
Pigno, Antonia Quintana
    Annie, 6006.
    La Llorona, 6007.

South Valley, 6008.

Pineda, Josefina
    Un carino, 6560.
    Chicana, 6009.
    Crisis de identidad, 6010.
    Diferentes culturas, 6011.
    Donde estas mi dios?, 6012.
    El orgullo, 6013.
    Que amor es ese que no me traes?, 6561.
    Requiem, 6562.
Pinkney, James W.
    Career-planning myths of Chicano students,
        1454.
Pinon, Fernando
    Conquistadors of space, 403.
    A dance of worship, 503.
Plowman, Edward E.
    Hispanic Christians in the United States,
        3499.
Pochio
    Death, 2546.
Poma, Pedro A.
    A dangerous folk therapy, 1794.
Pomalaza Padilla, Luciana
    Untitled, 6014.
Ponce, Mary Helen
    Las animas, 7344.
    Recuerdo: how I changed the war and won the
        game, 7345.
    La semana santa, 7346.
Ponce, Ramon
    Does the public have access to public
        broadcasting?, 6632.
Poole, Claire
    Viewers looking for the U.S. look, 115.
Portes, Alejandro
    Changing flags: naturalization and its
        determinants among Mexican immigrants, 3740.
Powell, Carolyn L.
    Book review of: CHICANO ORGANIZATIONS
        DIRECTORY, 1110.
Powell, Winona
    Esta tarde, 6563.
    This afternoon, 6564.
Powers, Michael D.
    Spanish in contact with other languages:
        lexical or profound structural influence?,
        211.
Powers, Stephen
    Attributions for success and failure among
        Anglo, Black, Hispanic, and Native-American
        community-college students, 22.
    Factorial validity of the Cooperative
        Preschool Inventory for English- and
        Spanish-speaking Hispanic children, 1979.
Preciado, Consuelo
    LA BAMBA triumphs=LA BAMBA triunfa, 531.
    CORRIDOS: the movie=CORRIDOS: la pelicula,
        2004.
    El don precioso, 7347.
Price, Eva
    Cancion de cuna, 6015.
    Rubias y morenas, 6016.
Price, Eva, trans.
    The baby chicks, 7299.
    Dona Emeteria, 7303.
    Imaginary workshop, enter, 5876.
    Moon, 5879.
    Moro, 7306.
    The river and the poet, 5883.
    The river of life, 5884.
Proefriedt, William A.
    Equality of opportunity and bilingual
        education, 613.
Quinlan, Lisa
    Aztlan, 6017.
Quinn, Mary Ellen
    Book review of: SMALL FACES, 1111.
Quintana, Al
    Gaining yardage in football, 411.
Quintana, Alvina
    Challenge and counter challenge: Chicana
        literary motifs, 1524.
    Expanding a feminist view: challenge and

--   --

Reyes, Felix Ojeda
    Book review of: HISTORY OF THE PUERTO RICAN
        INDEPENDENCE MOVEMENT, 1125.
Reyes, J.E.
    Sin ganar, 6570.
Reyes, Laurie Hart
    Stereotyping: impact on teachers and students,
        2292.
Reyes, Sabino
    Me pregunto, 7354.
Reyes, Sandra
    Amigo mio, 6049.
    Tenia duena, 6050.
    Ya nos entenderemos, 6571.
Reyes, Sonia
    America's Hispanic sweethearts, 492.
    Hispanic models pursue high stakes fashion,
        297.
Reyna, Henry
    No mueren los feos, 7355.
Reyna, Hugo
    Con razon, 6572.
    El deforme sin remedio, 7356.
    Los que se hicieron ricos, 7357.
    Quien cuida los animales?, 7358.
    Quien toca?, 7359.
Reyna, Jose R.
    Book review of: MERIENDA TEJANA, 1126.
Reza, Ernesto
    Midwestern farmworkers and the farm labor
        movement, 2976.
Ricapito, Joseph
    El cocinero afable, 6051.
    (Sin titulo), 6052.
Rich, Mary Alice
    El milagro del amor, 7360.
    El nombre de la muerte, 6053.
    Por los callejones, 7361.
    Quiza hoy, 7362.
Rifkin, Jane M.
    Courting the Latino market, 1967.
    The Lil' Scholars: responding to a tragedy in
        the noblest way!, 1439.
    Manuel Castro--founder of MAES: a
        compassionate commitment, 749.
    New avenues for women in technology, 677.
    Ralph de la Parra travels the MAES "bridge to
        the future", 750.
    Up from the barrio...to fittest woman cop in
        the U.S.A., 751.
Rigoni, Florenzo
    Tijuana: the borders on the move, 1242.
Riley, James D.
    Book review of: THE MEXICAN FRONTIER
        1821-1846, 1127.
Rincon, A.
    Cuatro pensamientos, 6054.
    Maria de los arcangeles, 6055.
    Tus imagenes, mis palabras, 6056.
    V.A. hospital, 6057.
Rios-Bustamante, Antonio
    California's bilingual constitution=La
        constitucion bilingue de California, 1392.
Rips, Geoffrey
    Civil rights and wrongs, 1285.
    Puritanism, pluralism, and Perot, 84.
Rivera, Alvaro
    A que no me agarran!, 7363.
    Bet you can't catch me!, 7364.
Rivera, Alvin D.
    Laying a foundation for learning: student peer
        workshop groups, 1457.
Rivera, Armandina
    A mi madre, 6058.
    A mis hijos, 6059.
    La feria del cobre, 6573.
    La vida de santa inocencia, 7365.
Rivera, Cecilia
    A mi madre, 6060.
    Un corazon, 6061.
    Mi bella ilusion, 6062.
Rivera, Diego
    Frida Kahlo y el arte mexicano, 381.
Rivera, Frances M.

(Sin titulo), 6063.
(Sin titulo), 6064.
Rivera, Julius
    The implementation of Mexican-American Studies
        in Texas colleges and universities, 1759.
Rivera, Marcela
    Mi tristeza, 6065.
Rivera, Miquela
    In battle of the sexes, time for a ceasefire,
        3396.
Rivera, Rebecca
    Vida, 6066.
Rivera, Yvette
    Hispanic women's organizations and periodicals
        needed to communicate new options: Yvette
        Rivera report, 1641.
Rivero, Eliana S.
    Esta bien, 6067.
    No es menos, 6068.
    Ocasionalmente proesia, 6069.
    Poetica de los ausentes, 6070.
    Tan lejos del azucar, 6071.
Rizo-Patron, Jenny
    Cycad, 2559.
    [Dinosaurs], 2560.
    Magnolia bud, 2561.
R.M.
    Plegaria a mi hija, 6072.
Roberts, Robert E.
    Minority status and psychological distress
        reexamined: the case of Mexican Americans,
        281.
Robles, Maria J.
    La barranca, 6073.
    Caminemos, 6074.
    El cisne, 6075.
    La corriente, 6076.
    La espera, 6077.
    Las flores, 6078.
    Lamentos, 6079.
    Mensaje de amor, 6080.
    Morir!, 6081.
    Reproche, 6082.
    Senor, de que color son tus ojos?, 6083.
    Timidez, 6084.
Robles, Terra
    1 centavo por cada vote, 7366.
    1 penny per can, 7367.
Rocha, Pedro, Jr.
    Critical incident competencies of Mexican
        American and Anglo American administrators,
        271.
Roche, Arnaldo
    Burning the spirit of the flesh [painting],
        5248.
Roche, Sylvia
    Amor inquieto, 6574.
    La palomita y el nino, 7368.
    Para nuestra madre, 6575.
    Un pueblo raro, 7369.
Rochin, Jose Ruben
    De un amor broto mi vida, 6085.
    La mama de Sylvia, 6086.
Rochin, Refugio I.
    Chicanos in rural labor markets, 4009.
    Chicanos in rural labor markets: part 2, 4010.
Rockman, Ilene F.
    Book review of: BILINGUAL BOOKS IN SPANISH AND
        ENGLISH FOR CHILDREN, 621.
    Book review of: HISPANIC AMERICAN VOLUNTARY
        ORGANIZATIONS, 1129.
Rodriguez, Alfonso
    Afirmacion, 6087.
    El gran buitre, 6088.
    Himno de medianoche, 6089.
    Manana sera otro dia, 7370.
    Manos, 6090.
    Las palabras, 6091.
Rodriguez, Ana Maria
    Book review of: SCHOOLING AND LANGUAGE
        MINORITY STUDENTS: A THEORETICAL FRAMEWORK,
        1130.
Rodriguez del Pino, Salvador
    Book review of: CHICANO THEATER: THEMES AND

mothers, 283.
Integration of multiple data sources in
immigrant studies, 3745.
Intergenerational occupational mobility of
Chicanos, 134.
The new immigration: implications for poverty
and public assistance utilization, 3592.
The occupational position of employed Hispanic
females, 1667.
Rural poverty and Chicanos: have the seventies
brought improvements?, 6375.
The structuring of Hispanic ethnicity:
historical and contemporary perspectives,
2098.
Task force on statistical policy and data
needs, 2173.
Tijerina, Andres A.
Book review of: SAN ANGELENOS: MEXICAN
AMERICANS IN SAN ANGELO, TEXAS, 1166.
Tijerino, Eduardo
El Manta Blanca, 7403.
Te amo, 6189.
Tineo, David
[Unidentified mural], 4907.
[Untitled drawing], 2567.
[Untitled drawing], 2568.
[Untitled drawing], 2569.
[Untitled drawing], 2570.
[Untitled painting], 5250.
[Untitled painting], 5251.
[Untitled painting], 5252.
[Untitled portfolio], 2571.
Tobias, Margarita
No more corn tortillas, 7404.
Toboada, John A.
Irma Rangel [photograph], 5388.
[Untitled photograph], 5389.
Toney, Bill
Employment is the key, 3803.
Torres, Hector
Discourse and plot in Rolando Hinojosa's THE
VALLEY: narrativity and the recovery of
Chicano heritage, 3473.
Torres, Isaias D.
The U.S. Supreme Court and public education
for undocumented immigrants, 2662.
Torres, Lourdes
Book review of: A CHICANO IN CHINA, 247.
Book review of: CONTEMPORARY CHICANA POETRY,
1168.
Torres, Ramon
Vision of the coming of the new life, 5390.
Torres-Gil, Fernando
The Latinization of a multigenerational
population: Hispanics in an aging society,
135.
Toruno, Rhina
El protagonista verdadero de EL SIGLO DE LAS
LUCES de Alejo Carpentier, 1465.
Toscano, Ignacio
Mi padre, 6190.
Tovar, Graciela
Recuerdos de mi ninez, 6589.
Trager, Cara S.
Carving out a niche in politics, 768.
Manhattan executive forum, 120.
Women of the year, 769.
Traub, Gary S.
Alienation of monolingual Hispanics in a
federal correctional institution, 635.
Trevino, Fernando M.
Health indicators for Hispanic, Black and
white Americans, 284.
Trevino, Jesus Salvador
Chicano cinema overview, 524.
Latino portrayals in film and television,
2290.
Trevino, Mario
Sigues teniendo diecisiete anos para mi, 7405.
Trueba, Henry T.
Book review of: BILINGUALISM THROUGH
SCHOOLING, 660.
Book review of: CHICANO DISCOURSE, 1170.
Book review of: FORM AND FUNCTION IN CHICANO

ENGLISH, 1171.
Trujillo, Lorenzo A.
The evaluation of four Head Start bilingual
multicultural curriculum models, 591.
Trujillo, Lucy
Que pesadilla tan real, 6191.
Trujillo, Marcela L.
Guidelines for employment in Chicano studies,
1762.
Tryon, Roy H.
Book review of: THE CHICANO EXPERIENCE, 1172.
Book review of: THE HISPANICS IN THE UNITED
STATES: A HISTORY, 1173.
Turner, Kay F.
Book review of: CHRISTIAN IMAGES IN HISPANIC
NEW MEXICO, 1174.
Tutino, John
Book review of: WATER IN THE HISPANIC
SOUTHWEST, 1175.
Ugalde, Sharon E.
Two visions of cultural domination: Carrero's
EL HOMBRE QUE NO SUDABA and Hinojosa's MI
QUERIDO RAFA, 1468.
Urdaneta, Maria Luisa
Book review of: LATINO FAMILIES IN THE UNITED
STATES, 267.
Urguiaga, Manuel
Hermano de sangre, 6192.
Uribe, Ainoa
A mis amigos escritores, 6590.
Rumbo hacia el Salto Angel (Canaima), 2072.
Uribe, F. Medardo Tapia
The marital morality of Mexican women--an
urban study, 2962.
Urrea, Maria Luisa
El pescador, 6193.
Valadez, I.
Teodoro, 7406.
Valdes, Dennis
Book review of: THE LOS ANGELES BARRIO
1850-1890: A SOCIAL HISTORY, 1177.
Valdes, Gina
After the reading, 6194.
Eating fire, 6195.
Sunday arrived, 6196.
To Yoyontzin, 6197.
Valdes, Grisel
Etiopia, 6198.
Made of wax, 6199.
Por nacer, 6200.
Valdes Medellin, Gonzalo
Hacia un tercer lenguaje, 148.
Valdez, Avelardo
Book review of: THE CHICANO EXPERIENCE, 1178.
Valdez, Lorenzo
Labor history in the villages, 2623.
Valdez, Luis
Connecting with the American experience: an
interview with Luis Valdez, 527.
Valdez, William J.
Impotence: a problem with a solution, 1518.
Valencia, Bert
Purchasing power rises 10 percent, 1969.
Valencia, Humberto
Sales pitch to Hispanics must strike right
chord, 121.
Valenzuela, Nati
No-me-olvides, 6591.
Valenzuela, Noemi
A night with the sea, 6201.
Una noche con el mar, 6202.
Valenzuela, Oscar N.
One of the many stories about la Llorona,
4339.
Uno de tantos cuentos de la Llorona, 4340.
Valenzuela-Crocker, Elvira
Small town Hispanic America, 3201.
Vallejos, Tomas
Book review of: SOUTHWEST TALES: A CONTEMPORY
COLLECTION, 199.
Valva, Annie
[Pat Zavella (photograph)], 5391.
Van Olphen, Yone
Llanto de lluvia, 77.

Nuevo dia, 6114.

Vanderpool, Tim
   Immigration reform crosses an uncertain border
      into law, 3781.

Varela, Graciela
   La lecherita, 7407.
   Si tu me quisieras, 6203.
   Si tu te vas, 6204.

Varela, Vivian
   Hispanic women's resource guide, 1670.

Vargas-Willis, Gloria
   Consideration of psychosocial stress in the
      treatment of the Latina immigrant, 1671.

Vasquez, Enedina Casarez
   USE: Casarez Vasquez, Enedina

Vasquez, Ruben
   Donde jugaran los ninos?, 6205.
   Welcome back vato, 78.

Vasquez, Victor
   More on CHICO AND THE MAN, 165.

Vaughn, Artemisa
   Contradiccion y sueno, 6594.
   Suma total, 6595.
   Tus hijos, 6206.

Vela, Esther
   Estrellas, 2577.

Velaquez [sic], Manuel
   Gastronomical tidings, 6207.
   Puntada gastronomica, 6208.

Velasco, Magdalena
   El apio, 6596.
   Dar a luz, 6597.
   La luz, 6209.
   Movement, 6210.
   Movimiento, 6211.
   La tortilla, 6598.
   Yo ante el mundo, 6599.

Velazquez, Manuel
   Recuerdo: tendria yo unos siete u ocho anos,
      6600.

Vendrell, Luis
   Ausencia, 6212.

Verdugo, Naomi
   Income differentials between Chicano and white
      male workers, 285.

Verdugo, Richard
   Income differentials between Chicano and white
      male workers, 285.

Vernon, Sally W.
   Minority status and psychological distress
      reexamined: the case of Mexican Americans,
      281.

Vicario, Tony D.
   A behavioral/ecological model of intervention
      alternatives with Chicano gang delinquents,
      562.

Vigelis, Adeline R.
   Book review of: HISPANIC FIRST NAMES, 1180.

Vigil, Cleofes
   El carbonero, 2073.
   El fletero y el ranchero, 7408.

Vigil, Evangelina
   USE: Vigil-Pinon, Evangelina

Vigil, James Diego
   Book review of: DICTIONARY OF MEXICAN AMERICAN
      HISTORY, 1181.

Vigil, Mary Helen
   Setting sun, 6213.

Vigil-Pinon, Evangelina
   Equinox, 6214.
   The giving, 6215.
   Hacia un invierno, 6216.
   In its absence, 6217.
   The parting, 6218.
   Spillage, 6219.

Villa Leyva, Rosa
   Conceptual, 6220.
   Confusion, 6221.
   Desire, 6222.
   Gleam of life, 6223.
   I feel, 6224.
   Omid (hope), 6225.
   Silence, 6226.
   Sometimes, 6227.

Villalobos Galligan, Martha
   The legacy of Mama, 2881.

Villalobos, Romer A.
   Dos almas perdidas, 6228.
   Madre, 6229.

Villar, Ysis
   A mis hijos, 6230.
   Amistad, 6231.
   El amor, 6232.
   La esclava y los ninos, 7409.

Villareal, Maria Antonia
   El cuento del gallo pipirripin, 2074.
   Espana, 6233.
   Por favor, 6234.
   Tu recuerdo, 6235.

Viramontes, Helen Maria
   Miss Clairol, 7410.

Viuker, Steve
   Man with the golden toe, 180.

Vogt, Gregory M.
   Archetypal images of apocalypse in Miguel
      Mendez's TATA CASEHUA, 4286.

Volsky, George
   A new voting block making its mark, 2060.

Wainer, Howard
   An exploratory analysis of performance on the
      SAT, 2711.

Wald, Karen
   U.S. defector "didn't want to fight in Central
      America", 1514.

Walker, Constance L.
   Book review of: HISPANIC AMERICA: FREEING THE
      FREE, HONORING HEROES, 1182.

Wallendorf, Melanie
   A longitudinal study of Mexican-American
      assimilation, 400.

Watts, Jake
   Book review of: THE FOLK HEALER, 1183.

Weas, Andrea T.
   Book review of: THE CHICANO STRUGGLE, 1184.

Weber, David J.
   Book review of: MERCEDES REALES: HISPANIC LAND
      GRANTS OF THE UPPER RIO GRANDE REGION, 1185.

Weeks, John R.
   Hispanic elders' needs, problems and access to
      public benefits and services, 255.

Weinfield, J.
   Day care benefits ordered for child born in
      U.S. to illegal alien, 1781.

Weiss, K.M.
   Phenotype amplification, as illustrated by
      cancer of the gallbladder in New World
      peoples, 1417.

Welch, Susan
   Employment of women by cities in the
      Southwest, 1613.

Weller, David L.
   Stereotyping: impact on teachers and students,
      2292.

Wells, Miriam J.
   Power brokers and ethnicity: the rise of a
      Chicano movement, 1723.

West, Dennis
   Book review of: CHICANO CINEMA, 1186.

Whatley, Patricia L.
   Book review of: BILINGUAL BOOKS IN SPANISH AND
      ENGLISH FOR CHILDREN, 622.
   Book review of: SPANISH-LANGUAGE BOOKS FOR
      PUBLIC LIBRARIES, 579.

Wilde, Richard H.
   The establishment of a Chicano studies program
      and its relation to the total curriculum of
      a college or university, 1393.

Williams, Dennis A.
   Spanish as a learning tongue, 617.

Wilson, Maria
   Mi madre, 6601.
   Mi vida, mi amor, mi estrella, 6236.
   Viejecitos, 6602.

Wilson, Patricia
   Sor Juana (Juana de Asbaje), 3927.

Winston, Bonnie
   High tech jobs in the Midwest, 1540.
   INROADS: internships that work, 188.

Wolfe, David E.
    Book review of: BILINGUALISM AND SPECIAL
        EDUCATION: ISSUES IN ASSESSMENT AND
        PEDAGOGY, 662.
Wolfson, Mark
    Caperucita Roja y yo, 7412.
Wood, Silviana
    Una canasta para los pobres, 7413.
Woods, Richard D.
    Book review of: CHICANO PERIODICAL INDEX: A
        CUMULATIVE INDEX TO SELECTED CHICANO
        PERIODICALS BETWEEN 1967 AND 1978, 1190.
    Book review of: MEXICO-ESTADOS UNIDOS:
        BIBLIOGRAFIA GENERAL SOBRE ESTUDIOS
        FRONTERIZOS, 1191.
Wreford, Mary
    Book review of: CHICANO AUTHORS: INQUIRY BY
        INTERVIEW, 457.
    Book review of: THE BRACERO EXPERIENCE:
        ELITELORE VERSUS FOLKLORE., 1193.
    Chicano Survey report #2: perceptions and
        experience of discrimination, 2293.
    Chicano Survey report #3: political opinions,
        4985.
    Reactions from the Chicano Survey respondents:
        no mas silencio, 1736.
Wroth, William
    New hope in hard times: Hispanic crafts are
        revived during troubled years, 390.
Yang, Eunice
    El amor mas grande, 6238.
    Madre, 6239.
    Madre mia, 6240.
Yarbro-Bejarano, Yvonne
    Chicana literature from a Chicana feminist
        perspective, 1672.
    The female subject in Chicano theater:
        sexuality, race, and class, 1673.
Yarter, R. Alexandra
    Belladona, 6241.
    Cantame, 6242.
    Contesta, 6243.
    Venga conmigo, 6244.
Ybarra, Lea
    Book review of: LAS MUJERES: CONVERSATIONS
        FROM A HISPANIC COMMUNITY, 1194.
    Empirical and theoretical developments in the
        study of Chicano families, 2968.
Yepes, Maria Elena
    Lady bugs, 1440.
    National Latino Media Coalition, 129.
Ynclan, Maria Estela
    Manana, 6603.
    Olvidaba todo, 7414.
    Que son los padres, 6245.
Yrigoyen, Edna A.
    [Untitled drawing], 2578.
    [Untitled drawing], 2579.
    [Untitled drawing], 2580.
    [Untitled drawing], 2581.
    [Untitled drawing], 2582.
    [Untitled drawing], 2583.
    [Untitled painting], 5253.
    [Untitled painting], 5254.
Yubeta, Alma
    Amigas, 6604.
    La Llorona, 2075.
    Querida amiga, 6246.
    Te recuerdo, 6605.
Yzaguirre, Raul
    Task force on social services and community
        development, 1905.
Zamora, Alfredo
    The Mexican American community and Mexican
        American studies, 1764.
Zamora, Emilio
    Book review of: LA CLASE OBRERA EN LA HISTORIA
        DE MEXICO: AL NORTE DEL RIO BRAVO (PASADO
        INMEDIATO, 1930-1981), 1195.
Zamorano, Christina
    Celina, 7415.
    Vita, 6606.
Zanger, Maggy
    Trial of an activist lawyer, 2041.

Zatz, Marjorie S.
    Race, ethnicity, and determinate sentencing: a
        new dimension to an old controversy, 1386.
Zavaleta, Antonio N.
    Relative lower extremity length in Mexican
        American and in American Black and white
        youth, 277.
Zavella, Patricia
    "Abnormal intimacy": the varying work networks
        of Chicana cannery workers, 1430.
Zepeda, Fabiola
    Hasta cuando tata dios, 6247.
Zesch, Lindy
    Visa issue heats up: PEN hopes for "group
        waiver" of denials, 387.
Zippin, David H.
    Perceived self-other differences in life
        events and mental health among Mexicans and
        Americans, 286.
Zolberg, A.R.
    Book review of: THE BORDER THAT JOINS: MEXICAN
        MIGRANTS AND U.S. RESPONSIBILITY, 1197.
Zucca, Gary J.
    Affirmative action: Blacks and Hispanics in
        United States Navy occupational specialties,
        128.
Zwiebach, Elliot
    An important and growing consumer segment,
        4509.

TITLE INDEX

1 centavo por cada vote, 7366.
1 penny per can, 7367.
100 influentials and their assessment of the
     critical issues, 672.
13-part series focuses on Hispanics in America,
     1198.
El 17 de diciembre, 6461.
1973 Emmy Awards, 1541.
The 1982 Mexican peso devaluation and border area
     employment, 1207.
1982 Simpson-Mazzoli immigration reform and the
     Hispanic community, 3787.
1983-84 NAEP data raises questions regarding the
     school experiences of language minority
     children, 604.
[340 W. Simpson drawing], 2409.
The 500 largest Hispanic-owned companies in sales,
     1318.
7 weeks mature, 5957.
99th Congress fails to act on literacy
     legislation, 2671.
A diario al caer el alba, 5992.
A don Juan, 6470.
A donde va la nina, 5529.
A Juan Pedro, 6045.
A la nanita, nana ...[y] epilogo, 5438.
A las dos semanas, 5680.
A Manuel Salazar, 5474.
A mi esposo, 5752.
A mi madre, 6058, 6060.
A mis amigos escritores, 6590.
A mis hijos, 6059, 6230.
A mis padres, 6458.
A nativitate, 5683.
A proposito de la salsa y su historia, 4920.
A que no me agarran!, 7363.
A ti, 5493, 5824.
A tiempo, 70.
A una amazona, 6534.
A una madre de mayo, 5651.
A una madre de nuestros tiempos, 5646.
A-B benefits from regional approach, 107.
Abajo la tierra, 5624.
"Abnormal intimacy": the varying work networks of
     Chicana cannery workers, 1430.
El aborto, 7170.
Abuela, 6043.
Abuelita, 7333.
Abuelito, 5469.
El abuelo sabe, 6112.
La Academia de la Nueva Raza: su historia, 7.
La Academia de la Nueva Raza, 8.
La Academia de la Nueva Raza: El Oro del Barrio,
     9.
Academics and entrepreneurs talk trade, 1320.
[Acaso estaras algun dia conmigo...], 5764.
Acculturation and alcohol use: drinking patterns
     and problems among Anglo and Mexican
     American male drinkers, 38.
Acculturative stress and specific coping stategies
     among immigrant and later generation college
     students, 36.
Achievement in mathematics: results from the
     National Assessment, 14.
Acoma, 5245.
Las Adelitas del Barrio, 1577.
Adios, 5509.
Adriana Ocampo, 4956.
Advertiser apathy hampers TV growth, 116.
ADWEEK's honor roll: women to watch: Dolores
     Valdes Zacky, 98.
Affirmative action: Blacks and Hispanics in United
     States Navy occupational specialties, 128.
Afirmacion, 6087.
After reading the death poems, 5728.
After the divorce, 5861.
After the reading, 6194.
Against all odds, 1567.
Age and sex composition among inmigrantes to
     Texas, 3743.
Agosto en un pueblo canero, 5574.
Agua, 6031.
El agua del aire, 5782.
Agusa'o con la vida porque no retona, 5822.

Agusa'o con los velices, 7278.
Ahora y siempre, 5642.
Al honorable, 5669.
Alan Riding: la fuerza del prejuicio, 1039.
Alcohol consumption patterns in immigrant and
     later generation Mexican American women, 32.
Alcohol consumption and physical symptoms in a
     Mexican American population, 171.
Alejandro Morales in utopia, 4266.
Alejandro's funeral, 5450.
Alfonso's heats up San Antonio, 176.
Alicia de Garcia's oral history=Historia oral de
     Alicia de Garcia, 1888.
Alienation of ethnic minority students at a
     predominantly white university, 179.
Alienation of monolingual Hispanics in a federal
     correctional institution, 635.
Aliens: detention in prisons, 3035.
Allaying the fears of becoming a U.S. citizen,
     4968.
Alma, 5942.
Alma Rosa, 5358.
Almost grown, 7348.
America needs to face world in many languages,
     2821.
American bosses have jobs; Mexicans need work,
     3763.
American Chemical Society honors Dr. Mario J.
     Molina, 218.
The American Southwest: an urban view, 168.
The American stage, 5441.
America's Hispanic sweethearts, 492.
America's Hispanic Theater Olympics, 59.
Americo Paredes and modern Mexican American
     scholarship, 2923.
Amiga, 5760.
Amigas, 6604.
Amigo mio, 6049.
Los amigos de Jesus, 6523.
Amistad, 6231, 6444.
Amistad (tu y yo), 5783.
Amor, 5737, 5738, 5784, 5814.
El amor, 5753, 5866, 6032, 6232, 6485.
El amor del creador, 5617.
Amor inquieto, 6574.
El amor mas grande, 6238.
Amor mio, 5761.
El amor que nunca se olvida: el de la madre, 5454.
Amor sincero, 5868.
The analysis of language minority issues in
     national data sets, 657.
...And she became a proletarian, 687.
Andrea, 7227.
Andy Garcia: un "Intocable" orgulloso de ser
     latino, 61.
El anima milagrosa de El Tiradito, 6494.
Animales contra maquinas, 7393.
Las animas, 7344.
Annie, 6006.
Annotated bibliography, 358.
Anoranza, 5870, 6028.
Anoranzas de mi ninez, 6492.
Another "decade of the Hispanic"?, 2785.
An answer from research on bilingual education,
     592.
Anthony Quinn Library receives collection=La
     Biblioteca Anthony Quinn recibe coleccion,
     291.
Los antifaces y la cara verdadera, 7341.
The anti-romantic city in Chicano fiction, 46.
Antonia Hernandez, 762.
Any Sunday in April: the rise of sport in San
     Antonio and the Hispanic borderlands, 1536.
El apio, 6596.
Application of competency-based criteria to
     bilingual-bicultural education, 598.
Una apuesta, 7187.
Apuntes para un retrato chicano (I), 379.
Apuntes para un retrato chicano (II), 380.
Aquel ayer, 6000.
Aqui venimos a pasar hambre y amarguras, 5533.
Archetypal images of apocalypse in Miguel Mendez's
     TATA CASEHUA, 4286.

Architects of America's future, 1932.
Arizona, 5871, 5872.
Arizona Bank targets Hispanic market, 323.
The Arizona-Sonora border and the Mexican
    revolution, 1910-1920, 320.
[Arms], 2349.
Army maneuvers, 122.
Arte chicano: iconografia de la autodeterminacion,
    335.
El arte hispano en Houston, 336.
El arte social de Domingo Ulloa, 370.
Artery of land, 5582.
Article review of: "Proverbs in Mexican-American
    Tradition", 327.
Article review of: "The Second Language Learner in
    the Context of the Study of Language
    Acquisition", 3369.
Articulation skills of Spanish-speaking
    Mexican-American children: normative data,
    26.
El artista chicano dentro y fuera de la
    "corriente" artistica, 333.
Artist's statement [and Texas shield, Texas stele,
    Georgia stele (sculptures)], 7068.
As American as babalu, 39.
Asado: churrasco: piquete: barbacoa: barbecue,
    3143.
Asi es, 6552.
El asilo, 6508.
La Asociacion Hispano-Americana de Madres y
    Esposas: Tucson's Mexican American women in
    World War II, 393.
Una asociacion que trabaja, 2807.
Astro-no-mia, 5575.
At home, 6147.
At last, farmworkers are allowed clean water,
    2980.
Attitudes are changing while women go to work,
    415.
Attitudes of elderly Mexican Americans towards
    nursing homes in Stanislaus county, 262.
Attributions for success and failure among Anglo,
    Black, Hispanic, and Native-American
    community-college students, 22.
Aun me duelen tus brazos empujandome, 5499.
Aureola de miseria, 6529.
Aurora, 5787.
Aurora IX, 5719.
Aurora X, 5720.
Ausencia, 6212.
Austin: growing fast, start-ups tough, 433.
Autochthonous church and liberation, 1500.
El avaro y su oro, 6532.
Aventuras de la seccion, 5832.
Ayer, 5514, 6141.
An Aztec prince, 7147.
The Aztecs: art and sacrifice, 292.
Aztlan, 6017.
Azucenas, 5472.
Azul, 5483.
Baboon [sculpture], 7064.
The baby chicks, 7299.
Back to the future, 1904.
Badge of Hispanic pride, 1295.
[Bajo la luna llena...], 5836.
Balancing act, 5413.
La Bamba, 51.
LA BAMBA triumphs=LA BAMBA triunfa, 531.
Banderas, 5424.
El bano, 6040.
La barranca, 6073.
Barrio slang has value as communications tool,
    1690.
The "barrioization" of Hispanic faculty, 1870.
The beauty in cosmetics, 2016.
A behavioral/ecological model of intervention
    alternatives with Chicano gang delinquents,
    562.
Believe, 5934.
Belladona, 6241.
Bendicion, 5577.
Benefits of long-term group therapy for
    disadvantaged Hispanic outpatients, 2910.
Benito Garcia, 7323.

Un beso is not a kiss, 5425.
Bet you can't catch me!, 7364.
Bibliography, 573.
Bi-centennial [editorial], 217.
The biggest Hispanic fiesta in the USA, 1463.
Bilingual education: door to the society of the
    future, 589.
Bilingual education policy in the United States,
    615.
A bilingual perspective on teaching history, 2631.
A bilingual printwheel, 1928.
Bilingualism and language change: the extension of
    estar in Los Angeles Spanish, 656.
Bilingualism, bilingual education, and language
    contact: the agony, the rewards--or how to
    unravel Babel, 611.
Bilingualism creates more problems than solutions,
    655.
Billboard charts and Chicanos, 1955-1974, 2267.
Bi-national policy questions generated by Mexican
    school-age children who migrate between the
    United States and Mexico, 1789.
La biografa se espanto de una vida abierta, 767.
Biracial coalition politics in Los Angeles, 784.
Bird Ave, 5576.
Birth of me in my room at home, 5583.
Birthday, 7246.
Bitter song for her, 6187.
Black and Hispanic power in city politics: a
    forum, 775.
A black tangent, 6124.
Bochinche bilingue, 5794.
[Bodies], 2350.
El bolerito bilingue, 7300, 7301.
Bonito, 7253.
Book review of: A BIBLIOGRAPHY OF MEXICAN-AMERICAN
    HISTORY, 580, 582.
Book review of: A BORDERLANDS TOWN IN TRANSITION:
    LAREDO, 1755-1870, 986.
Book review of: A CHICANO IN CHINA, 247.
Book review of: A COMMUNITY UNDER SIEGE, 79, 80,
    82.
Book review of: A DECADE OF HISPANIC LITERATURE,
    932.
Book review of: A SOURCEBOOK FOR HISPANIC
    LITERATURE AND LANGUAGE, 799, 800.
Book review of: A WAR OF WORDS, 908.
Book review of: ACCULTURATION: THEORY, MODELS, AND
    SOME NEW FINDINGS, 31.
Book review of: ACROSS THE BORDER: RURAL
    DEVELOPMENT IN MEXICO AND RECENT MIGRATION
    TO THE UNITED STATES, 50.
Book review of: ALONG THE RIO GRANDE: PASTORAL
    VISIT TO SOUTHWEST NEW MEXICO IN 1902, 190.
Book review of: AMERICA'S ETHNIC POLITICS, 231.
Book review of: AMERICA WITHOUT ETHNICITY, 215.
Book review of: AMERICAN LABOR IN THE SOUTHWEST:
    THE 1ST 100 YEARS, 228.
Book review of: AN ILLUSTRATED HISTORY OF MEXICAN
    LOS ANGELES: 1781-1985, 1018.
Book review of: AND OTHER NEIGHBORLY NAMES: SOCIAL
    PROCESS AND CULTURAL IMAGE IN TEXAS
    FOLKLORE, 5.
Book review of: ART IN NEW MEXICO, 1900-1945:
    PATHS TO TAOS AND SANTA FE, 353.
Book review of: ASPECTS OF AMERICAN HISPANIC AND
    INDIAN INVOLVEMENT IN BIOMEDICAL RESEARCH,
    395.
Book review of: BEARING WITNESS/SOBREVIVIENDO,
    557.
Book review of: BILINGUAL MULTICULTURAL EDUCATION
    AND THE PROFESSIONAL: FROM THEORY TO
    PRACTICE, 538.
Book review of: BILINDEX, 586.
Book review of: BILINGUAL EDUCATION: A SOURCEBOOK,
    212, 213, 214.
Book review of: BILINGUAL-BICULTURAL EDUCATION: AN
    ANNOTATED BIBLIOGRAPHY, 1936-1982, 525, 526.
Book review of: BILINGUALISM THROUGH SCHOOLING,
    652, 660, 667, 668, 670.
Book review of: BILINGUALISM AND LANGUAGE CONTACT:
    SPANISH, ENGLISH AND NATIVE AMERICAN
    LANGUAGES, 537.
Book review of: BILINGUAL BOOKS IN SPANISH AND

COLLECTIVE BIOGRAPHY, vol. 2: MEXICO and THE MEXICAN REVOLUTION: AN ANNOTATED GUIDE TO RECENT SCHOLARSHIP, 906.
Book review of: KLAIL CITY, 899.
Book review of: LA CHICANA: MEXICAN AMERICAN WOMEN, 838.
Book review of: LA CLASE OBRERA EN LA HISTORIA DE MEXICO: AL NORTE DEL RIO BRAVO (PASADO INMEDIATO, 1930-1981), 939, 1195.
Book review of: LA FAMILIA, 913, 922, 935, 962, 981, 1114.
Book review of: LA FRONTERA: THE U.S. BORDER WITH MEXICO, 1108.
Book review of: LA NOVELA CHICANA ESCRITA EN ESPANOL, 1161.
Book review of: LABOR IN NEW MEXICO: UNIONS, STRIKES AND SOCIAL HISTORY SINCE 1881, 843, 948, 1158.
Book review of: LAS MUJERES: CONVERSATIONS FROM A HISPANIC COMMUNITY, 1194.
Book review of: LATINO LANGUAGE AND COMMUNICATIVE BEHAVIOR, 879.
Book review of: LATINO ETHNIC CONSCIOUSNESS, 1113.
Book review of: LATIN JOURNEY, 511.
Book review of: LATINO FAMILIES IN THE UNITED STATES, 267, 836.
Book review of: LATINOS IN THE UNITED STATES: THE SACRED AND THE POLITICAL, 3.
Book review of: LE MEXIQUE, DES ORIGINES AUX AZTEQUES, 500.
Book review of: LEGACY OF HONOR: THE LIFE OF RAFAEL CHACON, A NINETEENTH-CENTURY NEW MEXICAN, 822.
Book review of: LIFE SPAN, 895.
Book review of: LIVING UP THE STREET, 925.
Book review of: LOS TUCSONENSES: THE MEXICAN COMMUNITY IN TUCSON 1854-1941, 901, 914.
Book review of: MAN, LAND, AND WATER: MEXICO'S FARMLAND IRRIGATION POLICIES, 1885-1911, 821.
Book review of: MENTAL HEALTH AND HISPANIC AMERICANS: CLINICAL PERSPECTIVES, 252, 561, 1059.
Book review of: MERCEDES REALES: HISPANIC LAND GRANTS OF THE UPPER RIO GRANDE REGION, 1185.
Book review of: MERIENDA TEJANA, 1126.
Book review of: MEXICAN WOMEN IN THE UNITED STATES: STRUGGLES PAST AND PRESENT, 1154.
Book review of: MEXICAN AMERICAN THEATRE: THEN AND NOW, 1153.
Book review of: MEXICO AND THE UNITED STATES, 1051.
Book review of: MEXICAN AMERICANS IN SCHOOL: A DECADE OF CHANGE, 972.
Book review of: MEXICANO RESISTANCE IN THE SOUTHWEST, 1142.
Book review of: MEXICAN IMMIGRANT WORKERS IN THE U.S., 3752.
Book review of: MEXICO-ESTADOS UNIDOS: BIBLIOGRAFIA GENERAL SOBRE ESTUDIOS FRONTERIZOS, 1191.
Book review of: MEXICAN AMERICAN ARCHIVES AT THE BENSON COLLECTION: A GUIDE FOR USERS, 313.
Book review of: MEXICO'S POLITICAL ECONOMY: CHALLENGES AT HOME AND ABROAD, 910.
Book review of: MEXICAN AMERICAN FERTILITY PATTERNS, 553.
Book review of: MEXICAN IMMIGRANTS AND MEXICAN AMERICANS: AN EVOLVING RELATION, 1008.
Book review of: MEXICAN AND MEXICAN AMERICAN FARM WORKERS, 1124, 1164.
Book review of: MEXICAN-AMERICANS IN COMPARATIVE PERSPECTIVES, 921.
Book review of: MEXICAN-AMERICANS AND THE MASS-MEDIA, 918, 1095, 1121, 1157.
Book review of: MINORITIES IN AMERICAN HIGHER EDUCATION: RECENT TRENDS, CURRENT PROSPECTS AND RECOMMENDATIONS, 402.
Book review of: MIRROR OF LANGUAGE: THE DEBATE ON BILINGUALISM, 887.
Book review of: MUTUAL AID FOR SURVIVAL, 952, 992, 1145.
Book review of: NEW MEXICO WOMEN: INTERCULTURAL PERSPECTIVES, 830.

Book review of: OCCUPIED AMERICA, 83.
Book review of: OJO DE LA CUEVA, 1060.
Book review of: OLDER MEXICAN AMERICANS: A STUDY IN AN URBAN BARRIO, 253, 258, 263.
Book review of: OPERATION WETBACK, 1043.
Book review of: PARENTING MODELS AND MEXICAN AMERICANS: A PROCESS ANALYSIS, 316.
Book review of: PERSPECTIVES ON IMMIGRATION AND MINORITY EDUCATION, 894.
Book review of: POLITICAL AND ECONOMIC MIGRANTS IN AMERICA, 889, 963, 964.
Book review of: POLITICS AND CHICANO CULTURE, 829.
Book review of: PROTEST IS NOT ENOUGH, 850.
Book review of: RACE AND CLASS IN THE SOUTHWEST: A THEORY OF INEQUALITY, 540.
Book review of: ROOTS OF RESISTANCE: LAND TENURE IN NEW MEXICO, 1680-1980, 993.
Book review of: SAN ANGELENOS: MEXICAN AMERICANS IN SAN ANGELO, TEXAS, 1166.
Book review of: SCHOOLING AND LANGUAGE MINORITY STUDENTS: A THEORETICAL FRAMEWORK, 1130.
Book review of: SMALL BONES, LITTLE EYES, 837.
Book review of: SMALL FACES, 1034, 1081, 1111.
Book review of: SOUTHWEST TALES: A CONTEMPORY COLLECTION, 196, 199.
Book review of: SOUTH BY SOUTHWEST: 24 STORIES FROM MODERN TEXAS, 896.
Book review of: SPANISH IN THE UNITED STATES: SOCIOLINGUISTIC ASPECTS, 209, 210.
Book review of: SPANISH-LANGUAGE BOOKS FOR PUBLIC LIBRARIES, 579, 859.
Book review of: "TEMPORARY" ALIEN WORKERS IN THE UNITED STATES, 876.
Book review of: TESTING LANGUAGE ABILITY IN THE CLASSROOM, 928.
Book review of: TEXAS AND THE MEXICAN REVOLUTION, 1006, 1016, 1112.
Book review of: THE BORDER THAT JOINS: MEXICAN MIGRANTS AND U.S. RESPONSIBILITY, 888, 1197.
Book review of: THE BRACERO EXPERIENCE: ELITELORE VERSUS FOLKLORE., 1193.
Book review of: THE BORDER ECONOMY: REGIONAL DEVELOPMENT IN THE SOUTHWEST, 924.
Book review of: THE CHICANO EXPERIENCE, 867, 937, 997, 1172, 1178.
Book review of: THE CHICANO STRUGGLE, 1184.
Book review of: THE CHANGING DEMOGRAPHY OF SPANISH AMERICANS, 826.
Book review of: THE CHICANO WAR, 860.
Book review of: THE DEFIANT MUSE: HISPANIC FEMINIST POEMS FROM THE MIDDLE AGES TO THE PRESENT, 893.
Book review of: THE ENGLISH-SPANISH CONNECTION, 1015.
Book review of: THE EDUCATION OF POOR AND MINORITY CHILDREN: A WORLD BIBLIOGRAPHY: SUPPLEMENT, 1979-1985, 866.
Book review of: THE FOLK HEALER, 1183.
Book review of: THE FOLKLORE OF SPAIN IN THE AMERICAN SOUTHWEST, 827, 998.
Book review of: THE G.I. FORUM: ORIGINS AND EVOLUTION, 184.
Book review of: THE GENTLEMEN'S CLUB: THE STORY OF PROSTITUTION IN EL PASO, TEXAS, 868.
Book review of: THE HEALTH REVOLUTION IN CUBA, 1009.
Book review of: THE HISPANIC ELDERLY, 251, 256.
Book review of: THE HISPANICS IN THE UNITED STATES: A HISTORY, 1173.
Book review of: THE HISPANIC ALMANAC, 187.
Book review of: THE IMPACT OF INTIMACY: MEXICAN-ANGLO INTERMARRIAGE IN NEW MEXICO, 1821-1846, 930.
Book review of: THE IMMIGRATION TIME BOMB, 1053.
Book review of: THE IMMIGRANT WOMAN IN NORTH AMERICA, 862, 949, 999.
Book review of: THE LOS ANGELES BARRIO 1850-1890: A SOCIAL HISTORY, 915, 1029, 1177.
Book review of: THE LEGEND OF LA LLORONA, 240.
Book review of: THE LOST LAND, 825, 902, 916, 1101.
Book review of: THE LAST OF THE MENU GIRLS, 828.
Book review of: THE LATIN IMAGE IN AMERICAN FILM, 3070.

The implementation of Mexican-American Studies in
    Texas colleges and universities, 1759.
Implementation of the legalization provisions
    under the Immigration Reform and Control Act
    of 1986, 3795.
An important and growing consumer segment, 4509.
Impotence: a problem with a solution, 1518.
Impresiones sobre las fiestas de octubre, 6468.
Impressions from the 1986 American Education
    Research Association (AERA), held in San
    Francisco, April 16-20, 219.
In battle of the sexes, time for a ceasefire,
    3396.
In celebration of a man's ecumenism, 1491.
In its absence, 6217.
In pursuit of the white knight, 5444.
In search of poverty, 5877.
In S.F., 5959.
In support of lapses into radicalism: a response
    to Mario Garcia, 3210.
[In the barbershop...], 6022.
In the shadow of the eagle: Huerta=A la sombra del
    aguila: Huerta, 141.
In verbal murals: a study of Chicana herstory and
    poetry, 1418.
The inanimate had their night, 6099.
Inaudito destino, 7265.
Income differentials between Chicano and white
    male workers, 285.
The incorporation of Mexican women in seasonal
    migration: a study of gender differences,
    1603.
Index to volume 9, 3510.
Indians, Hispanos, and land reform: a new deal
    struggle in New Mexico, 1311.
Indiferente, 5790.
Indocumentada angustia, 5636.
Indocumentados y chicanos: un intento de
    aproximacion, 3604.
Inertia in the corporate boardroom, 1351.
Inescapable, 5510.
Inez, 5520.
Infinito, 5889.
Infinito anhelo, 5768.
The influence of gender roles on political
    socialization: an experimental study of
    Mexican-American children, 424.
The influence of language background on attitudes
    toward native and nonnative Spanish, 276.
Information/Informacion, 2262.
Inmate ethnicity and the suicide connection: a
    note on aggregate trends, 6406.
Inocencio: ni siembra ni escarda y siempre se come
    el mejor elote, 7168.
Inocencio: tambien de gusto se llora como de dolor
    se canta, 7169.
INROADS: internships that work, 188.
INS enjoined from making vehicle stops on basis of
    alienage alone, 6730.
INS makes a bad Simpson-Rodino law worse, 3799.
INS vehicle stops designed to discover illegal
    aliens ruled unconstitutional, 5078.
Un insecto anonimo, 5933.
Inseguridad, 5947.
Inside her inside, 5960.
Insomnio, 5541, 5542.
The institute, the artist, the art, 375.
Institutionally-based research centers: the Center
    for U.S.-Mexican Studies, 1510.
Institutionally-based research centers: the
    Stanford Center for Chicano Research, 6807.
Integration of multiple data sources in immigrant
    studies, 3745.
An interdisciplinary perspective on the bilingual
    experience, 654.
Intergenerational occupational mobility of
    Chicanos, 134.
International labor migration and external debt,
    2150.
Interpersonal tactics and communicative strategies
    of Anglo-American and Mexican-American
    mildly mentally retarded and nonretarded
    students, 1796.
Interpreters--"borrowing" of defense interpreter

by trial court, 2028.
Interview: Rita Ricardo-Campbell, 300.
Introduccion. 2649, 2716, 4312.
Introducing pre-Columbian and Hispanic art and
    artists to young adults through recent
    books, 348.
Introduction, 1606, 2650, 2717, 4313.
The introduction of bilingual education
    programs--a collaborative approach, 594.
Introduction: the Mexican borderlands. 1217.
Intuitions of a world in transition: the New
    Mexican poetry of Leroy V. Quintana, 438.
Invernario, 5637.
Irma Castro, 715.
Irma Rangel [photograph], 5388.
Issues in state funding for bilingual education,
    607.
Itinerarios, 6172.
Jacking off, 5445.
El jardin [drawing], 2397.
La jaula, 5631.
Jeff Apodaca, 295.
Jesse Jackson makes appearance at CBS board
    meeting, 1290.
Jesu Cristo=Jesus Christ, 5937.
Jesus Garcia, 6480.
Job security? It could be a myth!, 1995.
John Roy Castillo, 705.
Jorje, 5961.
Jose, 6486.
Journal review of: CRITICA: A JOURNAL OF CRITICAL
    ESSAYS, 951.
Juan Comadres, 6168.
Juan Gonzalez, poeta, 7174.
Juan Ladron, 2070.
Juanito, 7353.
Judaism's Hispanic thread, 2110.
Juego, 5557.
[Julie Cabeza de Vaca, high school graduation],
    5373.
Juntos, 6511.
Juries--peremptory challenges--Spanish surnames,
    3929.
Just musing, 5671.
Just one ear, 5962.
Just step outside, 5963.
Kachina #2, 2381.
Kachina #3, 2382.
Keep pace with MAES: Sociedad de Ingenieria de
    Mexicano Americanos (Mexican American
    Engineering Society), 2790.
Keep the kids in school, 2587.
Keeping this in mind, 5964.
Knowing the value God places on me..., 1579.
La Tia Pepita, 7371.
Labor department official challenges Hispanic
    program manager to maintain commitment,
    perseverance, 126.
Labor history in the villages, 2623.
The labor market status of Hispanic men, 1505.
Lady bugs, 1440.
Lagana of lace, 5592, 5593.
Lagrimas de verdad, 5952.
Lamentos, 6079.
The land of the lost, 7376.
Land tenure history of New Mexico, 3590.
Language deficits in a bilingual child with
    cerebral cysticercosis, 647.
Language form and language function in ZOOT SUIT
    and THE BORDER: a contribution to the
    analysis of the role of foreign language in
    film, 1203.
Language studies and Chicanos, 4085.
Language usage and status attainment of Chicanos,
    4077.
Language use and communicative behavior: Hispanic
    bilinguals in the United States, 945.
El largo camino al estrellato, 802.
Las Mesas inner column #2 [sculpture], 7070.
"LATC" un espacio para el teatro politico, 58.
Latero story, 5795.
Lathe biosas, 5978.
Latin Americans at the university level:
    implications for instruction, 3454.

The quest for Hispanic roots, 571.
Question, 5840.
A question of health, 2211.
A question of history, 3612.
Quetzalcoatl for governor, 7389.
Quien cuida los animales?, 7358.
Quien soy?, 5666.
Quien toca?, 7359.
Quiero saber porque, 6439.
Quiero ser, 5674.
Quinto Festival de los Teatros Chicanos - Primer
    Encuentro Latinoamericano, 3042.
Quiza hoy, 7362.
Race, ethnicity, and determinate sentencing: a new
    dimension to an old controversy, 1386.
Race, gender and self-esteem among youth, 1921.
Raices, 5433.
Rain, 5725.
The rain, 5453.
Rainbow coalitions in four big cities: San
    Antonio, Denver, Chicago and Philadelphia,
    781.
Ralph de la Parra travels the MAES "bridge to the
    future", 750.
Ralph Guzman remembered, 719.
Ramon Duarte, 702.
Ramos gives special enthusiasm to original
    Hispanic projects, 1359.
Rape and racial patterns, 6737.
[Rasgueos...], 5722.
Raul Jimenez, 254.
Raul Rodriguez, 486.
Ray Five Mendoza, 7402.
La Raza, 5363, 5449.
La Raza Chicana, 5468.
La Raza community and Chicano Studies, 1761.
Raza, sexo y politica en SHORT EYES by Miguel
    Pinero, 3632.
Reactions from the Chicano Survey respondents: no
    mas silencio, 1736.
Reading achievement of native Spanish-speaking
    elementary students in bilingual vs.
    monolingual programs, 20.
Ready to go on board?, 1356.
Realidad, 6427.
La realidad chicana se forjo con dos culturas,
    723.
Realizations, 6131.
Recesses of my mind, 7196.
El recibimiento, 7332.
Recipe: chorizo con huevo made in the microwave,
    5538.
Recipients of Ford Foundation postdoctoral
    fellowships for minorities have been
    announced, 491.
Recognition for Hispanic families, 220.
Recuerdo..., 5820.
Recuerdo: how I changed the war and won the game,
    7345.
Recuerdo intimo, 5639.
Recuerdo: tendria yo unos siete u ocho anos, 6600.
Recuerdos, 5694, 5867, 6003.
Recuerdos con una lagunita, 7382.
Recuerdos de mi ninez, 6589.
Recuerdos de una noche inolvidable, 6548.
Reflections on the 1986 National Association for
    Chicano Studies (NACS) held in El Paso,
    Texas, April 9-12, 1941.
Reflexiones, 2407.
Regional differences in Chicano intermarriage,
    3870.
The relation of acculturation and values in
    Mexican Americans, 30.
The relationship between decoding accuracy and the
    reading achievement of monolingual
    Spanish-speaking children, 2705.
Relative lower extremity length in Mexican
    American and in American Black and white
    youth, 277.
Religious attendance and subjective health, 6639.
El relojero, 7385.
Reminiscences of my childhood, 6493.
Remordimiento, 7311.
El rendimiento, 6177.

Report from Sante Fe: figuration and fantasy, 330.
Report to the Network from NCCHE, 1758.
Report to the Network, 732, 1279, 1390, 1926,
    2304, 2684, 2693, 2709, 2836, 2849, 3004,
    3432.
Reproche, 6082.
The republic, 7236.
Requiem, 6562.
Research, action, and social betterment, 1561.
Research and scholarly activity, 1760.
Research centers, 1310, 1509, 1517, 1765, 3516,
    6812.
Resena testimonial, 1136.
La resolana, 2250.
La resolana [editorial], 6.
La resolana: entre el dicho y el hecho, 2251.
Response to a quake: hands across the border,
    1293.
Response to Cynthia Orozco, 1565.
Resultates mujer, 5844.
Resurreccion, 5901.
Review essay: recent Chicano writing, 1477.
El rey bailarin, 6489.
Un rey y sus tres hijos, 7205.
Reyes outstanding Hispanic at Kennedy Space
    Center, 746.
Ricardito, 7240.
Ricardo Salazar, 747.
Richard "Cheech" Marin, 54.
Richard Leon, L.A.'s leading Latin jazz D.J.,
    4182.
Richard Rodriguez, 603.
Richard Rodriguez's HUNGER OF MEMORY and the
    poetics of experience, 464.
Riding the range at Golden West. 748.
The rights of aliens: an expanding role for trial
    lawyers, 2222.
El rio, 7328.
Rio Grande. 6041.
El rio y el poeta, 5881.
El rio y la vida, 5882.
A rising star, 6136.
A risk taker, 301.
Rituals at Bennington: the elusive joy of writing,
    5490.
A rival to the gangs, 2248.
The river and the poet, 5883.
The river of life, 5884.
A road fraught with challenge leads to view from
    the top, 456.
The road from Mexico's Jalapa to jalopies, 3896.
Robert Davila, 2174.
Robert Redford y THE MILAGRO BEANFIELD WAR, 64.
A role for Hispanic Americans in foreign policy
    formulation, 2870.
The role of ethnic loyalty among Mexican immigrant
    women, 41.
The role of the Chicano student in the Chicano
    Studies Program, 1750.
The role of the Chicano student, 1755.
Romance negro, 5640.
The roofs of Puebla, 6117.
Roots, 5434.
Rootsearch: Aguilar: Echeverria, 143.
Rootsearch: Alarcon: Saavedra, 157.
Rootsearch: Alvarez: Covarrubias, 200.
Rootsearch: Aragon: Trujillo: Ruelas, 305.
Rootsearch: Bello: Ramirez: Lopez, 563.
Rootsearch: Beltran: Flores: Gomez, 564.
Rootsearch: Castro: Velasco, 1483.
Rootsearch: Cisneros: Perales: Zuniga, 1817.
Rootsearch: Cortes: Ulibarri, 2012.
Rootsearch: De La Garza: Pacheco, 2178.
Rootsearch: Duarte: Sandoval, 2597.
Rootsearch: Garcia: Chaves, 1539.
Rootsearch: Gonzalez: Febres-Cordero, 3001.
Rootsearch: Gutierrez, 3240.
Rootsearch: Guzman: Zamora, 3241.
Rootsearch: Jimenez (Ximenez): Olmo, 3242.
Rootsearch: Montoya: Galvo, 3186.
Rootsearch: Olivares: Yrigoyen: Montemayor, 3244.
Rootsearch: Ortega: Munoz, 3582.
Rootsearch: Padron: Machado, 3245.
Rootsearch: Patino: Herrera: Escobar, 2854.

---   ---